MW01040264

Configuring SAP S/4HANA® Finance

Stoil Jotev

Configuring SAP S/4HANA® Finance

Editor Meagan White
Acquisitions Editor Emily Nicholls
Copyeditor Yvette Chin
Cover Design Graham Geary
Photo Credit Shutterstock.com: 546064642/© StudioDin
Layout Design Vera Brauner
Production Hannah Lane
Typesetting SatzPro, Krefeld (Germany)
Printed and bound in the United States of America, on paper from sustainable sources

ISBN 978-1-4932-2159-2

2nd edition 2021

Library of Congress Cataloging-in-Publication Data
Names: Jotev, Stoil, author.
Title: Configuring SAP S/4HANA finance / by Stoil Jotev.
Description: 2nd edition. | Bonn ; Boston : Rheinwerk Publishing, [2021] | Includes index.
Identifiers: LCCN 2021029402 | ISBN 9781493221592 (hardcover) | ISBN 9781493221608 (ebook)
Subjects: LCSH: SAP HANA (Electronic resource) | Accounting--Data processing. | Financial statements--Data processing.
Classification: LCC HF5679 .J6358 2021 | DDC 657.0285/53--dc23
LC record available at https://lccn.loc.gov/2021029402

Contents at a Glance

Dear Reader,

This is my third book with finance guru Stoil Jotev, and I dearly hope for more in the future. His work continues to be a delight to read and edit—I always walk away with the impression that I, too, could configure an SAP S/4HANA Finance system. After all, it's all laid out so clearly between these pages! Whether you need me to set up a business partner record or run reports in SAP Fiori apps, I'm sure I'm up to the task!

We've made some improvements to this second edition, starting with an all-new chapter on predictive accounting and another chapter on the newly redesigned margin analysis. Stoil has also carefully recreated each screenshot in the book in the latest UI; we wanted to make sure that the images in the book match the system you're working in.

As we maintain this key finance resource, it's important that we hear from you, the reader. What did you think about the second edition of *Configuring SAP S/4HANA Finance*? Your comments and suggestions are the most useful tools to help us make our books the best they can be. Please feel free to contact me and share any praise or criticism you may have.

Thank you for purchasing a book from SAP PRESS!

Meagan White
Editor, SAP PRESS

meaganw@rheinwerk-publishing.com
www.sap-press.com
Rheinwerk Publishing · Boston, MA

I would like to thank my lovely wife, Mina, and my wonderful children, Petar and Dimitar, for their support and for enduring all the long nights and weekends without me, which made possible the completion of this book.

Contents

Appendices 721

Preface

SAP S/4HANA is the biggest innovation in the world of business software applications in more than a quarter of a century. With SAP S/4HANA, SAP introduced a fundamentally improved cloud-based solution that takes full advantage of the revolutionary in-memory database SAP HANA. SAP S/4HANA is a game changer and will set trends in business software computing for many years to come.

The number of companies using SAP S/4HANA has grown quickly, and many SAP customers are still planning to move to SAP S/4HANA. In addition, many companies that currently do not run SAP are planning SAP implementations to take advantage of the new in-memory cloud solution. The interest in SAP S/4HANA is enormous and dwarfs all previous major release upgrade plans. The projection for the next few years is that so many companies will start or continue major SAP S/4HANA projects that the shortage of SAP consultants with experience in SAP S/4HANA will be enormous. A real fight for talent will be waged among companies because an experienced consulting team is the number one factor for the success of an SAP implementation.

Objective of This Book

The objective of this book is to provide a comprehensive guide to customizing SAP S/4HANA Finance. The goal is to cover all main financial and controlling functionalities so that this book can serve as a single source of truth for anyone who is looking to configure SAP S/4HANA Finance—much like the new Universal Journal, which will be discussed in detail later and which is referred to as the single source of truth for financial accounting in SAP S/4HANA. We'll cover both the financial accounting and controlling areas of the system. The motivation for this book is to be equally helpful for new greenfield implementations and for system conversions from older SAP systems.

This book aims not only to cover all main system functionalities from a finance point of view, but also to provide deep insight into the whole implementation process, drawing on the author's 20 years of practical experience overcoming numerous challenging SAP projects. This book will discuss in detail not only the technicalities and the configuration options available, but also methods to gather business requirements and to create system solutions that can fully meet those requirements. The objective of this book will be fulfilled if after reading it you've been transformed into a real SAP S/4HANA financial solution architect, capable of creating real state-of-the-art system solutions.

Target Audience

The target audience of this book includes FI/CO consultants, SAP S/4HANA project managers, finance managers, and business process owners. This book is not for beginners. We won't cover SAP basics such as how to log on or post a financial document. Some SAP experience is required, but this book should be useful not only for senior consultants, but also for junior consultants and financial users alike who want to gain more technical experience under the hood of SAP S/4HANA Finance.

This book will cover the whole configuration process in SAP S/4HANA Finance, so some information will not be new for experienced FI/CO consultants coming from an SAP ERP background. However, we'll emphasize the changes between SAP ERP and SAP S/4HANA and explain the fundamental improvements of SAP S/4HANA.

This book is not only technical. You'll learn the methods to delivering successful projects and solutions using the latest techniques from SAP, so this book should be also quite beneficial for project managers and team leads who need to learn best practices for leading their projects and at the same time to become more familiar with the underlying technical architecture.

Last but not least, this book should also benefit FI/CO experts who already have SAP S/4HANA experience because its scope is vast and covers all the main financial and controlling areas. Usually, SAP consultants tend to focus on specific areas, and this book can be a useful guide to expand into other areas or just to check your current level of knowledge.

Organization of This Book

This book teaches you how to implement SAP S/4HANA Finance, covering all the phases of the project. We'll explain in detail not only how to configure all financial accounting and controlling functional areas, but also how to organize a project, perform fit/gap analysis, test the system, perform migration, and support the productive system.

The book is organized to follow the phases of the project, starting with project preparation and finishing with production support, as described in the following chapters:

- **Chapter 1: Project Preparation**
  In this chapter, we discuss how to effectively prepare for an SAP S/4HANA Finance implementation. You'll learn how to choose a greenfield or brownfield implementation approach, how to define the project scope and objectives, and how to assemble the project team.

- **Chapter 2: Requirements Analysis**
  This chapter explains how to analyze the business requirements for a new SAP S/4HANA system, how to identify gaps with the standard functionalities provided by SAP, and how to manage localization requirements.
- **Chapter 3: Financial Accounting Global Settings**
  In this chapter, we'll cover global settings for financial accounting, which must be configured first and which are the basis for all the other financial functional areas.
- **Chapter 4: General Ledger**
  In this chapter, you'll learn how to configure the general ledger in the new SAP S/4HANA environment, placing special emphasis on the new Universal Journal and the real-time integration with controlling and other functional areas.
- **Chapter 5: Accounts Payable**
  In this chapter, we'll configure accounts payable and discuss the new integrated business partner concept. You'll also learn how to set up various business transactions with vendors.
- **Chapter 6: Accounts Receivable**
  In this chapter, we'll configure accounts receivable, configure business partners as customers, and explore various business transactions involving customers.
- **Chapter 7: Fixed Assets**
  This chapter provides an extensive configuration guide for the fixed assets functional area, which has been completely redesigned to take advantage of the new SAP HANA database and has tremendously improved, providing real-time integration in all processes with the general ledger.
- **Chapter 8: Bank Accounting**
  In this chapter, you'll learn how to set up house banks and bank accounts, using the new SAP Fiori app, as well as learn how to configure the payment program, payment file formats, and the electronic bank statements.
- **Chapter 9: General Controlling and Cost Element Accounting**
  In this chapter, we'll start configuring controlling with the general controlling settings and start configuring cost elements, which are now completely integrated as general ledger accounts. We'll pay special attention to the new integration between financial accounting and controlling.
- **Chapter 10: Cost Center Accounting**
  In this chapter, we'll start configuring overhead costing with the settings for cost center accounting. You'll learn how to set up the required master data, actual postings, periodic allocations, and planning.
- **Chapter 11: Internal Orders**
  This chapter provides a detailed guide to customizing internal orders in SAP S/4HANA. Topics covered include the required master data, the settings for internal order budgeting and planning, and actual postings.

- **Chapter 12: Profit Center Accounting**
  In this chapter, we'll configure profit centers, which in SAP S/4HANA are tightly integrated with the general ledger. You'll learn how to set up the relevant master data and how to configure profit center derivation and substitution.
- **Chapter 13: Margin Analysis**
  This chapter provides a guide to configuring profitability analysis. Special emphasis is placed on account-based profitability analysis (now called margin analysis), which is the recommended type of profitability analysis in SAP S/4HANA, fully benefiting from the revolutionary SAP HANA database. We'll also cover the required configuration for costing-based profitability analysis, which is especially important for brownfield SAP S/4HANA implementations, in which often both forms of profitability analysis are used.
- **Chapter 14: Predictive Accounting**
  This chapter provides a guide to configuring predictive accounting. Predictive accounting had been introduced with SAP S/4HANA and enables you to predict future financial postings and flows based on incoming sales order data. In this chapter, you'll learn how to configure and use predictive accounting to enable powerful financial reporting based on predictive data.
- **Chapter 15: Product Costing**
  This chapter explains how to configure product costing. As with profitability analysis, this functional area has undergone major redesign and improvement in SAP S/4HANA, and special emphasis is placed on new and changed features such as in the material ledger and actual costing.
- **Chapter 16: Group Reporting**
  This chapter provides an overview configuration guide to SAP S/4HANA Finance for group reporting, which is the SAP solution for consolidation introduced with SAP S/4HANA 1809. In this chapter, we'll walk you through the settings required to use group reporting.
- **Chapter 17: Data Migration**
  After configuring the various financial functional areas in the previous chapters, in this chapter, we'll focus on the data migration process in the area of finance. Separately, we'll discuss the migration tools and processes for brownfield and greenfield implementations. You'll also learn best practices and find advice for various financial migration objects.
- **Chapter 18: Testing**
  This chapter teaches you how to perform various testing cycles during the implementation projects. Specially emphasized are the SAP S/4HANA financial processes and objects, but the best practices and tools discussed should benefit testing efforts in other application areas and systems as well.

- **Chapter 19: Go-Live and Support**
  This chapter finally takes you to the most exciting phase of the project: go-live and ensuing support. We'll first discuss how to prepare for and execute go-live. Then, you'll learn how to perform and manage the initial hypercare support of the new SAP S/4HANA system and how to hand over long-term support to assigned resources.

How to Read This Book

This book is a guide to configuring SAP S/4HANA Finance, both during new implementations and system conversions from SAP ERP. New SAP S/4HANA implementations are referred to as *greenfield implementations*, whereas an upgrade from a previous SAP release is referred to as a *brownfield implementation*.

New (Greenfield) Implementations

Greenfield implementations fall into two categories: implementations for completely new SAP customers and implementations for customers who already run SAP ERP or an older SAP release but have decided not to upgrade the current system and instead to implement SAP S/4HANA from scratch. Many reasons exist for such an approach. Conversion from an existing SAP system to SAP S/4HANA isn't merely an upgrade. SAP S/4HANA is the biggest SAP release and most fundamental change in almost 25 years. Many challenges arise when migrating existing SAP systems, especially heavily customized systems with a lot of custom developments. In addition, many SAP systems are already quite old, with obsolete business processes, which are often cumbersome to change—thus, often the choice of a greenfield implementation, even when SAP ERP may be already in place, is quite logical.

So how should readers interested in a greenfield implementation read this book? After the Preface and Introduction, we'll begin at the start of the implementation project with project strategy definition and requirements analysis. These chapters should be quite important for both greenfield and brownfield implementations, but especially for greenfield ones, which may very well be your first SAP project. In these chapters, you'll learn the main concepts behind properly setting up your project and how to go about gathering the important business requirements.

Chapter 3 through **Chapter 16** are the most technical chapters, teaching you in detail how to configure all the different financial and controlling areas of SAP S/4HANA Finance, including the newly redesigned SAP S/4HANA Finance for group reporting, included in release 1809, and the redesigned account-based profitability analysis, now rebranded as margin analysis in release 2020. These chapters will include all the settings required for new implementations, pointing out the required steps for system conversion, which can be skipped for new implementations.

Chapter 17 focuses on migration and on brownfield implementations: Some specific migration activities are generally performed in the system to be upgraded. However, greenfield readers also will find this chapter useful because we'll discuss the various migration objects needed from legacy systems and the best practices for obtaining and preparing the data and executing the migration.

Chapter 18 is equally important for greenfield and brownfield readers: Profound and extensive testing is of crucial importance for the success of every SAP S/4HANA project. Greenfield readers will find this chapter especially interesting because they may not have much experience in testing in SAP projects. These readers in particular will learn the important concepts that form the backbone of successful testing.

Chapter 19 will teach you how to organize and execute a successful go-live and hypercare support, which again will benefit both greenfield and brownfield users. However, important and fundamental concepts will be discussed for readers that are new to implementation projects. In brownfield implementations, some specific steps must be executed post go-live, which will also be explained in this chapter.

System Conversion (Brownfield) Implementations

For existing SAP customers, this approach is the most desired. Building and maintaining an SAP ERP system is a huge effort and expense, and most companies want to keep this investment while still benefiting from the new revolutionary technology brought by SAP S/4HANA. Each existing SAP customer normally will perform extensive and deep analysis, which involves all IT and business counterparts relevant to the SAP ERP system to assess whether it makes sense to upgrade the existing system. Normally, with a newer system that serves the business well without obsolete and hard-to-change processes, the prudent choice is to go with a brownfield approach, even if this approach will involve a lot of technical effort. These users will benefit tremendously from this book, which will provide them with all the technical and project management knowledge needed to execute the system upgrade.

Chapter 1 and **Chapter 2** teach you how to set up your project definition and perform the requirements analysis. Normally, less effort will be required in these stages of the project during a system conversion than in a new implementation, but establishing a high-performing project structure and gathering detailed, correct business requirements are important. A system upgrade to SAP S/4HANA is the perfect time to revisit your core business processes and make improvements as necessary. In **Chapter 2**, we'll point out specific areas where SAP S/4HANA offers improvements and cover how to discuss these areas with the business to define the best possible solution.

The functional chapters, **Chapters 3** through **Chapter 15**, will cover a lot of settings that are already set up in an existing SAP ERP system and may not need to change. Specific areas that are required to change and others that are optional to change in SAP S/4HANA will be pointed out and emphasized. Pay specific attention to **Chapter 3** and

Chapter 4, in which we discuss the general ledger architecture. Important in **Chapter 5** and **Chapter 6** is the business partner concept, which is new to SAP S/4HANA. **Chapter 7** is essential because SAP S/4HANA offers what's called the new asset accounting, which is fundamentally improved when compared with the classic asset accounting in SAP ERP and previous releases. From a controlling point of view, especially important are **Chapter 14**, which details the redesigned in SAP S/4HANA 2020 of margin analysis, and **Chapter 15** because now the material ledger is required and actual costing is completely redesigned. **Chapter 16** will also offer a lot of value for any brownfield reader because group reporting was redesigned and improved in SAP S/4HANA 2020.

Chapter 17 focuses on the data migration process during a brownfield system conversion, so reading this chapter carefully is crucial. **Chapter 18** and **Chapter 19**, as discussed earlier, will prove equally important for brownfield and greenfield readers alike because comprehensive testing is key to any successful SAP project, as is a well-organized and executed go-live and continuing production support.

Introduction

In this Introduction, we'll discuss the core functional and technical components of an SAP S/4HANA implementation and explain how SAP S/4HANA offers process- and user-oriented improvements for financial departments.

Congratulations on starting your journey with the most fascinating and revolutionary new technology in the ERP world—SAP S/4HANA! SAP S/4HANA is the latest enterprise resource planning (ERP) solution from SAP. SAP calls SAP S/4HANA its biggest innovation in the last 25 years. We'll examine in detail why SAP S/4HANA is so different and improved when compared with previous SAP ERP systems.

This Introduction will start by showing you what's new with your SAP S/4HANA system, then dive more deeply into what's new specifically in SAP S/4HANA Finance. We'll also introduce the configuration interface you'll be using throughout this book.

Your New SAP S/4HANA System

Let's now look under the hood of the SAP S/4HANA system. We'll discuss in detail the new SAP HANA database, which empowers SAP S/4HANA with its great performance and data simplification.

SAP HANA Database

Let's first start with some history. It all started with the development of a new database by SAP called SAP HANA in 2011. *SAP HANA*—SAP's *h*igh-performance *an*alytic *a*ppliance—is a fundamentally new type of database that uses in-memory database technology, which enables the processing of vast amounts of data in real time.

The SAP ERP software runs on a relational database management system (RDMS). Before SAP S/4HANA, SAP didn't offer these database systems itself; instead, SAP customers would have to buy databases from other vendors such as Oracle, IBM, or Microsoft. This model proved to be extremely successful, with SAP becoming the de facto standard for financial, sales, purchasing, and manufacturing applications across the globe. These applications formed the SAP ERP system, which is an online transaction processing (OLTP) system, because its main function is to process transactions. Analytical and reporting systems that use data for performing complex and resource-intensive analysis are known as online analytical processing (OLAP) systems. SAP's goal had always been to provide a single system that covers both needs, but the core SAP ERP solution focused on OLTP applications; OLAP applications were provided as separate data warehouse systems. To solve this problem, SAP developed the SAP HANA database, which takes advantage of advancements in processing power and the lower cost of memory and unites the two types of systems.

SAP HANA is fundamentally different than the previous databases first used to run SAP ERP because SAP HANA is an in-memory database. An in-memory database stores its data online in its memory. Thus, the data is not stored in hard disk storage devices like in traditional databases but instead in random access memory (RAM). RAM access is much faster, which enables SAP HANA to achieve tremendous speed compared to other databases.

The other key difference between SAP HANA and older databases is the column store. Traditionally, databases store their data in rows. As a result, each data record is presented as a row, with each field from this record in a separate column. The data is stored in a table form. To access these records, the database searches by specific fields, but all the rows must be checked to obtain the relevant data. In the column store, each column in the table performs as a separate table and is stored individually. Thus, the database can index and compress each of these columns separately, containing only unique records, without duplicate values, enabling the efficient processing of data.

Let's see how this looks schematically. Figure 1 shows some sample data related to vendors.

ID	Vendor Number	Last Name	First Name	Payabl e
1	1001	Jones	Joe	1000
2	1002	Smith	Mary	2000
3	1003	Connor	Cathy	5000
4	1004	Peterson	Bob	8000
5	1005	Connor	Steve	1400
6	1006	Reagan	Anton	750
7	1007	Bishop	Tom	800
8	1008	Jameson	Stewart	25000
9	1009	Smith	Harry	1300

Figure 1 Vendor Data

A classic row-based representation of this data is shown in Figure 2. Notice how each data record is represented as a row consisting of multiple fields.

But how is this data represented in a new column-store database like SAP HANA? In this case, all the values of a field are serialized into one column, then followed by the values of the next column, and so on, as shown in Figure 3.

```
1,1001,Jones,Joe,1000
2,1002,Smith,Mary,2000
3,1003,Connor,Cathy,5000
4,1004,Peterson,Bob,8000
5,1005,Connor,Steve,1400
6,1006,Reagan,Anton,750
7,1007,Bishop,Tom,800
8,1008,Jameson,Stewart,25000
9,1009,Smith,Harry,1300
```

Figure 2 Classic Row-Oriented Database

Vendor Number	ID	Last Name	ID	First Name	ID	Payable	ID
1001	1	Jones	1	Joe	1	1000	1
1002	2	Smith	2	Mary	2	2000	2
1003	3	Connor	3	Cathy	3	5000	3
1004	4	Peterson	4	Bob	4	8000	4
1005	5	Connor	5	Steve	5	1400	5
1006	6	Reagan	6	Anton	6	750	6
1007	7	Bishop	7	Tom	7	800	7
1008	8	Jameson	8	Stewart	8	25000	8
1009	9	Smith	9	Harry	9	1300	9

Figure 3 Column Store

Now, when the system needs to find all records pertaining to, for example, vendor number 1002, only the vendor number column will be searched. The system will identify the ID for that vendor (1002) and then retrieve the rest of the data from the other columns. Therefore, the system avoids going over all the data records as in a traditional row-based database.

As you can see, the new in-memory, column-based SAP HANA database offers significant advantages and, not surprisingly, is much faster than the traditional database systems of the past. Combine this speed with the fact that now you can have both ERP software and a database system from the same vendor, SAP, and it's not surprising that SAP S/4HANA is the biggest improvement in the SAP world in the last 25 years.

Note

Anyone interested in learning more about how SAP HANA evolved from an idea to the revolutionary product of today and how SAP HANA can benefit companies looking to combine the power of OLTP and OLAP systems can read the excellent article "A Common Database Approach for OLTP and OLAP Using an In-Memory Column Database" from the inventor of SAP HANA, SAP founder Hasso Plattner himself, which is available at *http://s-prs.co/v485708*.

SAP S/4HANA

SAP S/4HANA has had a long journey. Starting in 2011, SAP transitioned more and more SAP ERP transactions to work on the SAP HANA database. This development led to SAP Business Suite powered by SAP HANA, which became available in 2013. This solution allowed a traditional SAP ERP system to work entirely on the SAP HANA database, instead of on another database provided by a third-party provider. SAP customers could now take advantage of the faster in-memory, column-based database. However, from a functionality point of view, not much change was visible to end users.

Then, in 2014, SAP released the first completely rewritten application for the SAP HANA database: SAP Simple Finance. Finance had always been the backbone of the SAP ERP solution, so not surprisingly SAP chose finance to be the first area to be completely redesigned to benefit fully from the new SAP HANA database. SAP Simple Finance was an add-on that could be installed on an existing SAP ERP system, which provided a redesigned table structure and integration at the general ledger level of the various financial components.

Logically, this trend continued: In 2015 SAP, released SAP S/4HANA, a fully functional, fully integrated product entirely based on the SAP HANA database. SAP S/4HANA is the replacement for SAP ERP. With SAP S/4HANA, the use of the SAP HANA database is mandatory. All components are redesigned and rewritten to take full advantage of the enormous capabilities of SAP HANA.

Another tremendous improvement in the SAP S/4HANA system is the new SAP Fiori user experience (UX). SAP Fiori provides a web-based interface that makes working with SAP transactions and reports more approachable for users.

SAP S/4HANA comes with two product offerings: SAP S/4HANA (by default, this name refers to the on-premise version) and SAP S/4HANA Cloud. SAP S/4HANA is the main product, which covers all functionalities provided previously by SAP Business Suite/ SAP ERP. SAP S/4HANA Cloud is a software as a service (SaaS) offering, which has somewhat limited functionalities and is suitable for customers looking for a solution that is easier, quicker, and cheaper to deploy, benefiting from standardized provided processes. Note, however, that SAP S/4HANA also can be hosted in the cloud by another provider. So, companies can benefit fully from the on-premise version and develop the complex business processes they need without having to physically host the system themselves.

The release strategy for SAP S/4HANA involves annual updates, which originally used a naming convention that includes the name and year of the release. Starting in 2020, the naming convention switched to just include the full year. As of the writing of this book, the following SAP S/4HANA releases had been released:

- SAP S/4HANA Finance 1503: March 2015
- SAP S/4HANA 1511: November 2015
- SAP S/4HANA Finance 1605: May 2016
- SAP S/4HANA 1610: October 2016
- SAP S/4HANA 1709: September 2017
- SAP S/4HANA 1809: September 2018
- SAP S/4HANA 1909: September 2019
- SAP S/4HANA 2020: October 2020

This book is based on the SAP S/4HANA 2020 release. As we proceed, we'll point out functionalities that become available only with certain releases and that aren't available in prior releases.

Your New Finance Solution

SAP S/4HANA Finance is the most mature solution in SAP S/4HANA. Originally, this solution was released as the SAP Simple Finance add-on back in 2014, which means that 7 years of continuous improvements have been made, along with a solid customer base that continues to grow quickly. Every new SAP S/4HANA release brings new fundamental improvements.

In this section, we'll discuss the most important advancements in SAP S/4HANA in the finance area, including the new SAP Fiori user interface (UI), which provides a beautiful and streamlined UX.

Advances in Finance

Let's look at the key advancements in the finance area in SAP S/4HANA. So many advancements have been achieved, but the most fundamental include the following:

- Universal Journal
- Material ledger
- Margin analysis
- New asset accounting
- Group reporting

Universal Journal

The Universal Journal, the most fundamental advancement in SAP S/4HANA Finance, combines all finance relevant data into a single table, table ACDOCA, which is often referred to as the *single source of truth*. People working for a long time with finance applications can fully appreciate what an amazing, revolutionary improvement table ACDOCA is. Now, all financial and controlling fields, such fixed assets, cost centers, or internal orders, are available together in the same table with pure general ledger information such as the general ledger account, company code, and amount.

SAP's financial solutions traveled a long way to get to this point. Another major improvement in the past was the new general ledger, available from 2005. Previously, in the classic general ledger, you could have only one general ledger, but from accounting point of view, companies often had to generate reports based on different accounting frameworks. An early solution for this need involved the so-called *account approach*, in which all accounts were duplicated in another range (often starting with the letter *Z* followed by the same account number) to portray another accounting principle's postings. This approach, however, was cumbersome, both to maintain the additional master data and for users to make all these redundant postings. A more advanced solution for the time was to use a component called the *special purpose ledger* to provide additional ledgers, which could be used to make postings for additional accounting frameworks using the same general ledger accounts. However, these ledgers were not integrated with the general ledger, and the solution involved a lot of reconciliation and custom developments.

Based on the fundamentals of special purpose ledgers, SAP delivered the new general ledger, which provides multiple ledgers integrated into the general ledger component. This step was a huge leap forward, but still not perfect; more often than not, postings to the nonleading ledgers did not occur in real time. Also, additional reconciliation between financial accounting and controlling often was required, using the so-called *reconciliation ledger*.

With the Universal Journal in SAP S/4HANA Finance, SAP delivered the perfect solution, fully integrated across all the modules and fully in real time. Now, every ledger can post in real time in the Universal Journal, and all controlling, fixed asset, and other financial fields are available in the same table ACDOCA. Let's look at the structure of table ACDOCA, as shown in Figure 4.

This screenshot shows the structure of table ACDOCA, the Universal Journal entry line items table, as seen in the data dictionary. This table contains all finance-related line-item data, which makes many index and summarization tables obsolete. These obsolete tables have not been removed altogether, however, for compatibility reasons, but continue to exist as core data services (CDS) views.

The Universal Journal includes several includes, which contain the fields from controlling, fixed assets, and so on. For example, include ACDOC_SI_GL_ACCAS contains additional account assignments, as shown in Figure 5.

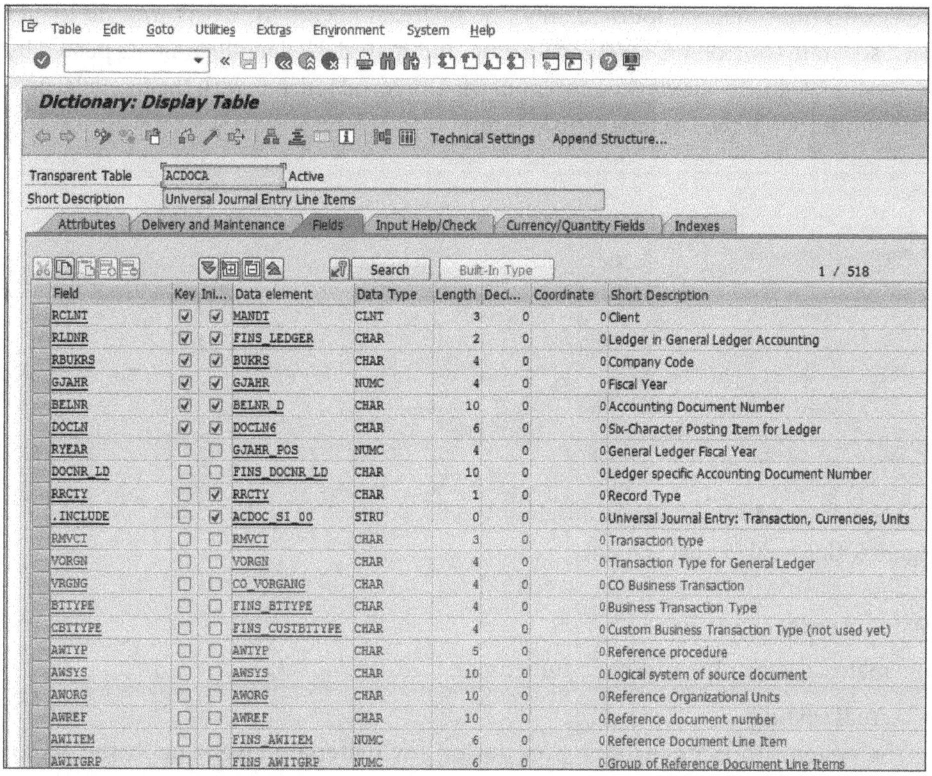

Dictionary: Display Table

Transparent Table: ACDOCA Active
Short Description: Universal Journal Entry Line Items

Attributes | Delivery and Maintenance | Fields | Input Help/Check | Currency/Quantity Fields | Indexes

1 / 518

Field	Key	Ini...	Data element	Data Type	Length	Deci...	Coordinate	Short Description
RCLNT	☑	☑	MANDT	CLNT	3	0	0	Client
RLDNR	☑	☑	FINS_LEDGER	CHAR	2	0	0	Ledger in General Ledger Accounting
RBUKRS	☑	☑	BUKRS	CHAR	4	0	0	Company Code
GJAHR	☑	☑	GJAHR	NUMC	4	0	0	Fiscal Year
BELNR	☑	☑	BELNR_D	CHAR	10	0	0	Accounting Document Number
DOCLN	☑	☑	DOCLN6	CHAR	6	0	0	Six-Character Posting Item for Ledger
RYEAR	☐	☐	GJAHR_POS	NUMC	4	0	0	General Ledger Fiscal Year
DOCNR_LD	☐	☐	FINS_DOCNR_LD	CHAR	10	0	0	Ledger specific Accounting Document Number
RRCTY	☐	☑	RRCTY	CHAR	1	0	0	Record Type
.INCLUDE	☐	☑	ACDOC_SI_00	STRU	0	0	0	Universal Journal Entry: Transaction, Currencies, Units
RMVCT	☐	☐	RMVCT	CHAR	3	0	0	Transaction type
VORGN	☐	☐	VORGN	CHAR	4	0	0	Transaction Type for General Ledger
VRGNG	☐	☐	CO_VORGANG	CHAR	4	0	0	CO Business Transaction
BTTYPE	☐	☐	FINS_BTTYPE	CHAR	4	0	0	Business Transaction Type
CBTTYPE	☐	☐	FINS_CUSTBTTYPE	CHAR	4	0	0	Custom Business Transaction Type (not used yet)
AWTYP	☐	☐	AWTYP	CHAR	5	0	0	Reference procedure
AWSYS	☐	☐	AWSYS	CHAR	10	0	0	Logical system of source document
AWORG	☐	☐	AWORG	CHAR	10	0	0	Reference Organizational Units
AWREF	☐	☐	AWREF	CHAR	10	0	0	Reference document number
AWITEM	☐	☐	FINS_AWITEM	NUMC	6	0	0	Reference Document Line Item
AWITGRP	☐	☐	FINS_AWITGRP	NUMC	6	0	0	Group of Reference Document Line Items

Figure 4 Table ACDOCA Universal Journal Entry Line Items

Dictionary: Display Structure

Structure: ACDOC_SI_GL_ACCAS Active
Short Description: Universal Journal Entry: G/L additional account assignments

Attributes | Components | Input Help/Check | Currency/quantity fields

1 / 12

Component	Typing Method	Component Type	Data Type	Length	Deci...	Coordinate	Short Description
RCNTR	1 Types	KOSTL	CHAR	10	0	0	Cost Center
PRCTR	1 Types	PRCTR	CHAR	10	0	0	Profit Center
RFAREA	1 Types	FKBER	CHAR	16	0	0	Functional Area
RBUSA	1 Types	GSBER	CHAR	4	0	0	Business Area
KOKRS	1 Types	KOKRS	CHAR	4	0	0	Controlling Area
SEGMENT	1 Types	FB_SEGMENT	CHAR	10	0	0	Segment for Segmental Reporting
SCNTR	1 Types	SKOST	CHAR	10	0	0	Sender cost center
PPRCTR	1 Types	PPRCTR	CHAR	10	0	0	Partner Profit Center
SFAREA	1 Types	SFKBER	CHAR	16	0	0	Partner Functional Area
SBUSA	1 Types	PARGB	CHAR	4	0	0	Trading partner's business area
RASSC	1 Types	RASSC	CHAR	6	0	0	Company ID of Trading Partner
PSEGMENT	1 Types	FB_PSEGMENT	CHAR	10	0	0	Partner Segment for Segmental Reporting

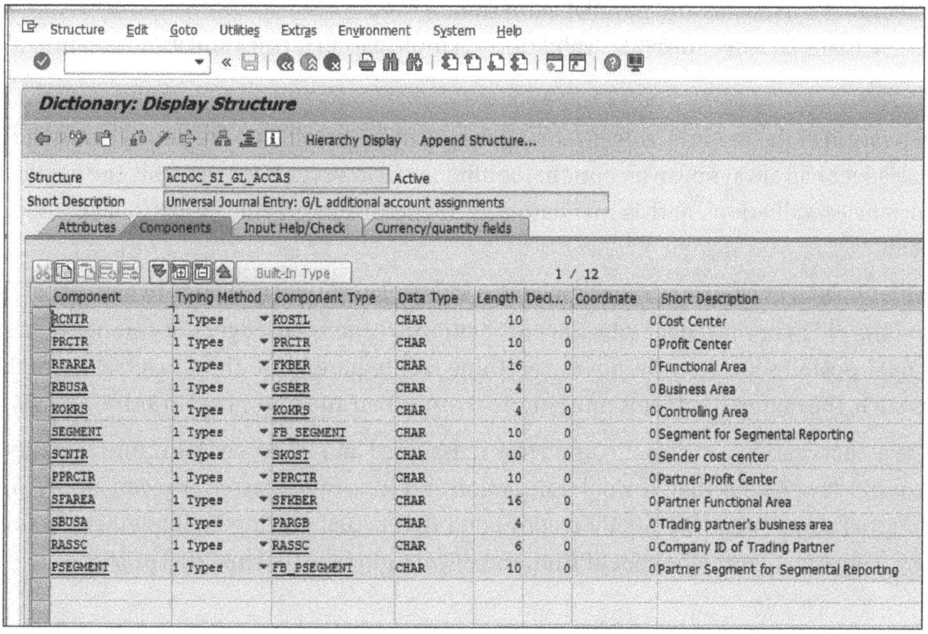

Figure 5 Additional Account Assignments in Universal Journal

Now, with the Universal Journal, only one financial document exists. You no longer need separate controlling, asset accounting, and material ledger documents posted by the system. Figure 6 shows the content of the Universal Journal, with the financial document number in the **DocumentNo** column.

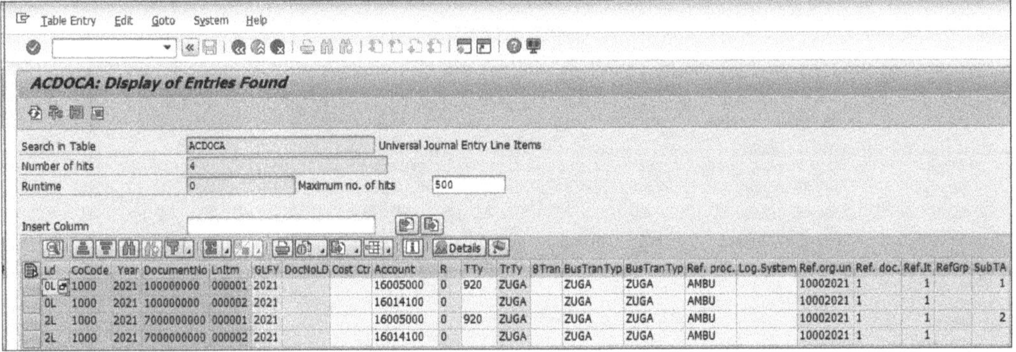

Ld	CoCode	Year	DocumentNo	LnItm	GLFY	DocNoLD	Cost Ctr	Account	R	TTy	TrTy	BTran	BusTranTyp	BusTranTyp	Ref. proc.	Log.System	Ref.org.un	Ref. doc.	Ref.It	RefGrp	SubTA
0L	1000	2021	100000000	000001	2021			16005000	0	920	ZUGA		ZUGA	ZUGA	AMBU		10002021	1	1		1
0L	1000	2021	100000000	000002	2021			16014100	0		ZUGA		ZUGA	ZUGA	AMBU		10002021	1	1		
2L	1000	2021	7000000000	000001	2021			16005000	0	920	ZUGA		ZUGA	ZUGA	AMBU		10002021	1	1		2
2L	1000	2021	7000000000	000002	2021			16014100	0		ZUGA		ZUGA	ZUGA	AMBU		10002021	1	1		

Figure 6 Universal Journal Content

Material Ledger

The material ledger has two main functions:

- **Actual costing**
  The system stores price differences during any material movement. At the end of the month, the actual costing run calculates the actual prices for inventory in stock and for inventory for consumption.
- **Parallel currencies and parallel valuations**
  The material ledger provides valuations in multiple currencies and valuation principles.

Activation of the material ledger is mandatory, unlike in SAP ERP. Previously, the material ledger had always been an optional component. However, note that only the parallel currencies/valuations part is mandatory; actual costing remains an optional component.

With SAP S/4HANA, the tables of the material ledger are also aggregated to table ACDOCA, and the old material ledger tables are obsolete. Also, material ledger documents are no longer posted separately because everything is integrated into the Universal Journal. As such, the material ledger is much more streamlined and optimized in SAP S/4HANA.

The actual costing run also is completely redesigned and improved. This functionality requires fewer steps than the old transaction and runs much faster. So, even if only an optional component, we highly recommend that actual costing be implemented for any company that might benefit from the calculation of actual material prices.

Margin Analysis (Account-Based Profitability Analysis)

Profitability analysis had been for a long time one of the most powerful tools in finance. This capability provides a deep, sophisticated analysis of the profitability of a company, which naturally is one of the most important analyses for any business. However, some confusion always existed between the two types of profitability analysis: account-based and costing-based. Account-based profitability analysis was easy to reconcile with the general ledger because it was based on cost elements, but lacked the flexibility to analyze vital sales data in every possible way needed. Therefore, SAP provided the costing-based option, which was based on value fields that grouped together various postings based on complex configuration rules. The costing-based profitability analysis capability didn't please accountants, though, because this analysis was virtually impossible to reconcile with financial accounting. Many companies chose to implement both, which added complexity to implementation, support, and data volumes—and profitability analysis reports were always some of the slowest-running SAP transactions due to the underlying data architecture.

Then, SAP S/4HANA came along. Profitability analysis is one of the areas that benefits the most from the SAP HANA database and the new integrated data architecture of the financial modules. In SAP S/4HANA, account-based profitability analysis is mandatory, whereas costing-based version is optional. The account-based option is fully integrated with the Universal Journal so it should be able to fulfill both profitability analysis needs and accounting reconciliation needs. One of the main reasons that account-based profitability analysis now should fulfill all needs is that it provides cost of goods sold (COGS) split functionality. Now, with SAP S/4HANA 2020, account-based profitability analysis had been rebranded as *margin analysis*. With margin analysis, cost and revenue information is always current and fully reconciled with the income statement.

New Asset Accounting

Asset accounting (commonly referred to as fixed assets) is another finance area that has been completely redesigned to take full advantage of the SAP HANA database. Available as an add-on in SAP ERP, now in SAP S/4HANA, the new asset accounting is mandatory. This capability offers real-time integration with the Universal Journal, as shown in Figure 7.

Include `ACDOC_SI_FAA` provides the fields for fixed assets. Every asset posting is fully integrated with the Universal Journal, and no separate asset documents are generated.

A key benefit of the new asset accounting is that now valuations according to different valuation frameworks, such as International Financial Reporting Standards (IFRS) and US Generally Accepted Accounting Principles (US GAAP), for example, are fully integrated and can post in real time to the general ledger. In classic asset accounting, this integration was performed using periodic programs and delta postings with the leading ledger, but now separate documents can be posted in real time to both leading and nonleading ledgers.

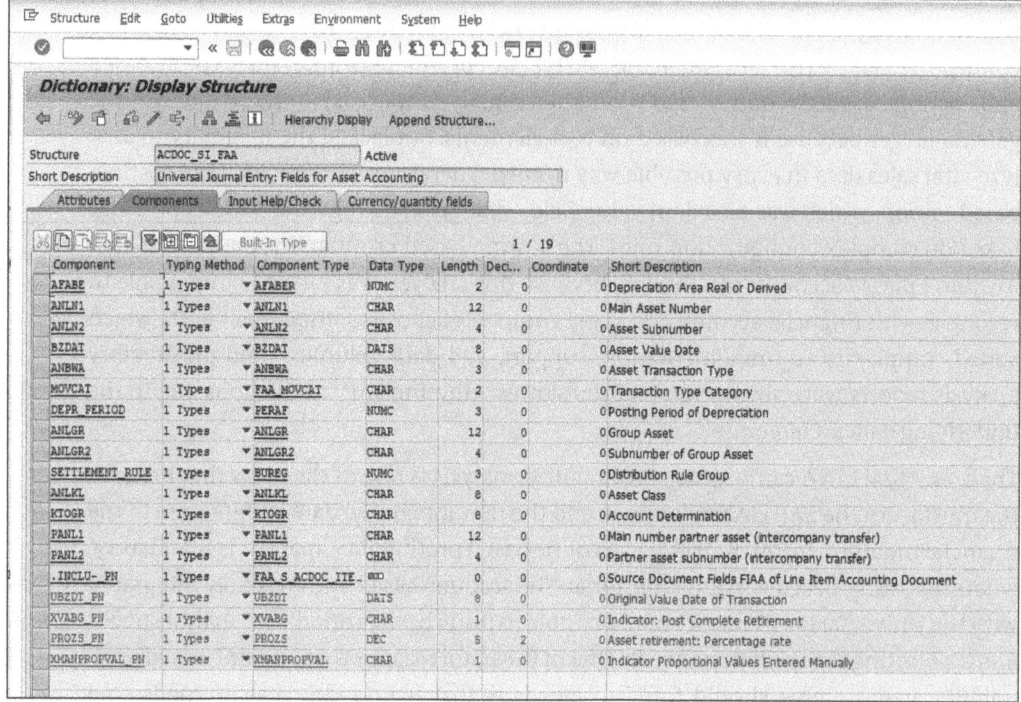

Figure 7 Universal Journal Asset Fields

Group Reporting

Group reporting is an area in which SAP changed its solution a few times in the past. Among the more recent solutions were SAP Business Planning and Consolidation (SAP BPC) and SAP Strategic Enterprise Management Business Consolidation (SEMC-BCS). Starting with SAP S/4HANA 1809, SAP provided SAP S/4HANA Finance for group reporting, which is fully based on SAP HANA and provides the following benefits:

- Complete package of consolidation functions, such as interunit eliminations and intercompany profit eliminations
- Integrated planning, budgeting, and data analysis in the cloud
- SAP Fiori UX
- Full integration with Microsoft Excel through an Excel add-in
- Open architecture for cloud-based and on-premise systems
- Single application for local closing and group closing procedures

Thus, with SAP S/4HANA, group reporting in SAP also is fundamentally redesigned and offers many key benefits. Now, with the SAP S/4HANA Finance for group reporting

2020 release, many new innovations support multiple fiscal year variants and parallel data entries from multiple users.

SAP Fiori User Experience

From a user's point of view, one of the main benefits of SAP S/4HANA is the SAP Fiori UX. In a world of connected devices in which users expect access to their ERP systems increasingly on mobile devices such as tablets and mobile phones, SAP provides the new SAP Fiori UX, which can be used in addition to the classic SAP GUI.

SAP Fiori is entirely web-based and quite intuitive and easy to use. It continues to evolve as more and more SAP transactions become available as SAP Fiori apps. The focus is now on user transactions since user reports especially are quite convenient with SAP Fiori. However, many configuration transactions also are becoming available on SAP Fiori, and some transactions are now only possible via SAP Fiori apps, as the old SAP GUI transaction codes are made obsolete. For example, Figure 8 shows the Maintain Banks app, which has completely replaced Transaction FI12.

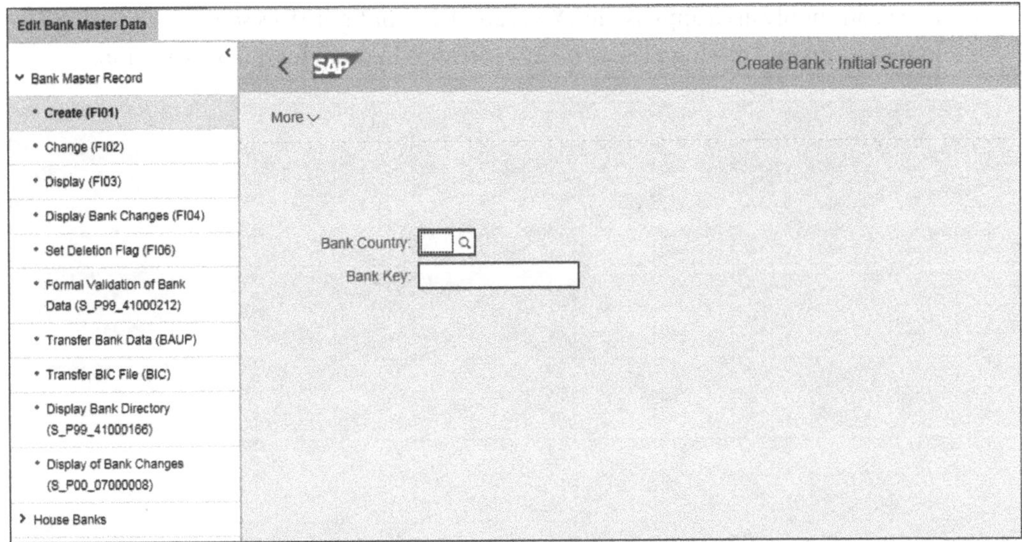

Figure 8 SAP Fiori App Maintain Banks

You can access SAP Fiori apps via the SAP Fiori launchpad. You can start the launchpad from SAP GUI by entering Transaction /UI2/FLP from your SAP S/4HANA system. (Normally, a dedicated system in your SAP GUI has SAP Fiori enabled because it needs the SAP Fiori server.) You can also use a web link provided by your system administrator, which you can enter into a web browser.

If you enter the link directly in a web browser, you'll see a beautiful logon screen, as shown in Figure 9. Fill out the **User** and **Password** fields with your SAP S/4HANA system credentials and click the **Log On** button.

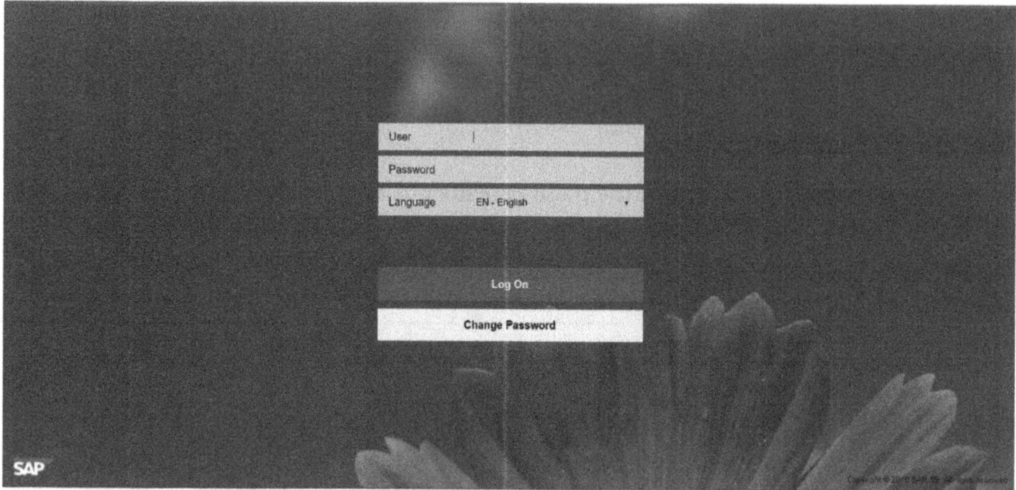

Figure 9 SAP Fiori Logon Screen

Figure 10 shows the home screen of the SAP Fiori launchpad, where you can set up your most commonly used apps as tiles. You can easily configure this screen by creating various sections and placing tiles with SAP Fiori apps in them for quick execution.

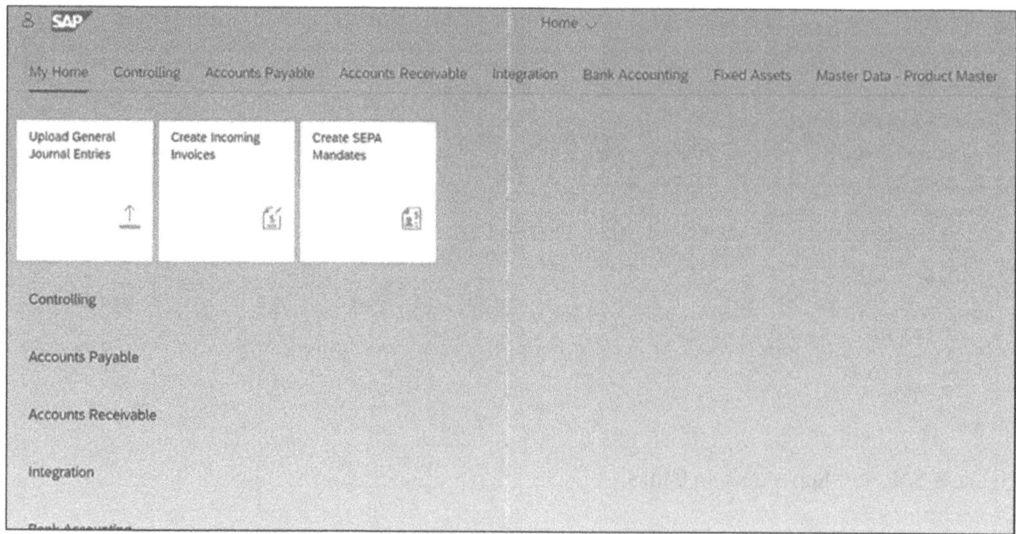

Figure 10 SAP Fiori Home Screen

If you click the (<your name>) button in the top-left corner, you can modify the settings of the SAP Fiori launchpad, as shown in Figure 11. With the **(Edit Home Page)** button, you can add and remove apps as tiles on the homepage. The **(Settings)** button allows you to modify general settings, such as appearance, language, and region.

You can also click the **(App Finder)** button to search for SAP Fiori apps.

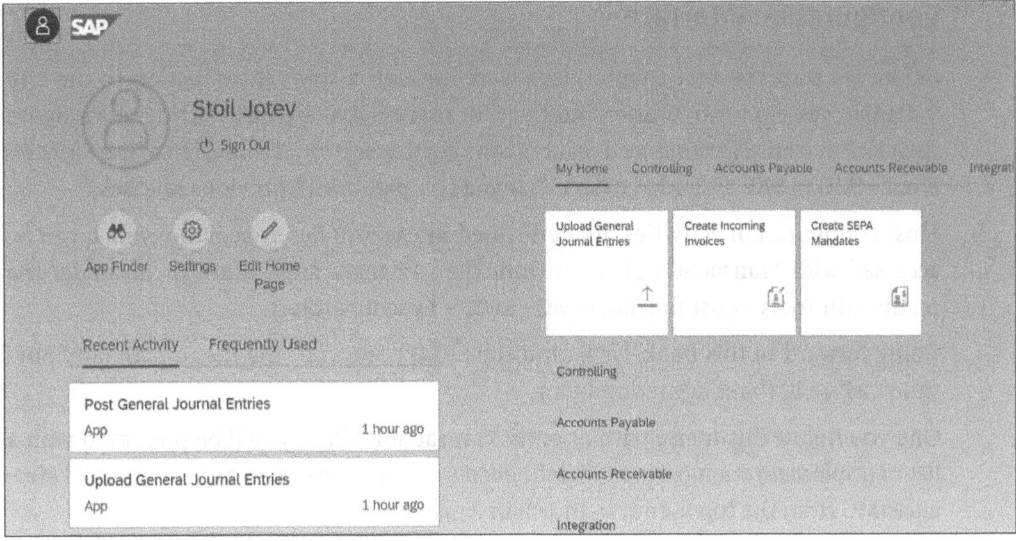

Figure 11 SAP Fiori Settings

As shown in Figure 12, in the App Finder, you can search for apps by process area.

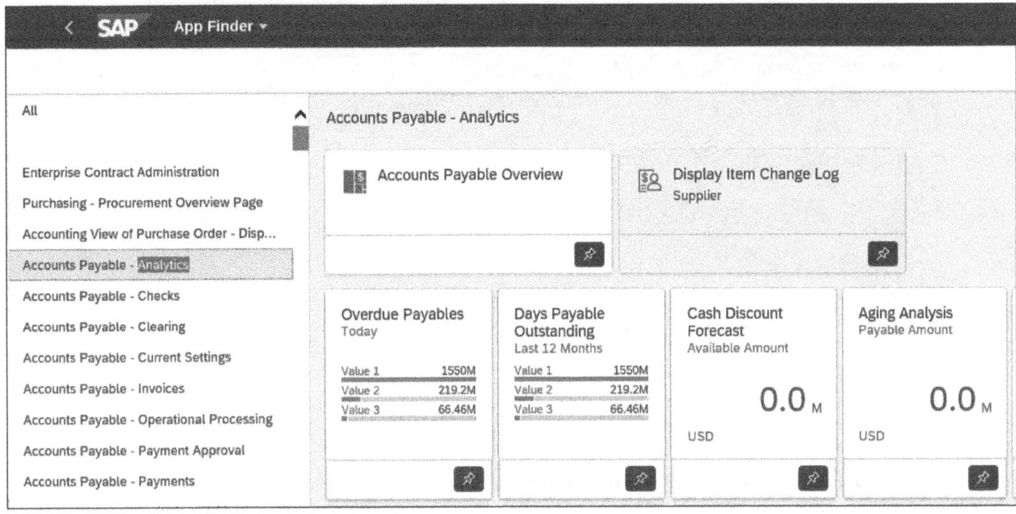

Figure 12 Finding SAP Fiori Apps

Many SAP Fiori apps are available, but your Basis team will need to configure them for use in your system. Normally, finance consultants on the project together with the client users will discuss which apps will be beneficial to use and prepare an inventory of them, and the Basis team then will configure those apps.

A list of all available SAP Fiori apps can be found in the SAP Fiori apps reference library, available at *https://s-prs.co/v485709*.

Configuration Interface

Before we start the first chapter, let's walk through a short introduction to the SAP S/4HANA system configuration interface for readers that are just starting to configure their SAP systems. Experienced readers can skip this section: The design of the SAP Reference IMG in SAP S/4HANA hasn't changed compared with previous releases.

Most configuration activities are performed in the SAP Reference IMG, which can be accessed with Transaction SPRO or from the SAP main application menu under the menu path **Tools • Customizing • IMG • SPRO • Execute Project**.

Going forward in this book, we'll omit the SPRO portion of the menu path (and anything before it) to reduce redundancy.

One you follow this menu path or enter Transaction SPRO, you'll be presented with a list of implementation projects, if defined. If no projects exist, simply select **SAP Reference IMG** from the top menu, as shown in Figure 13.

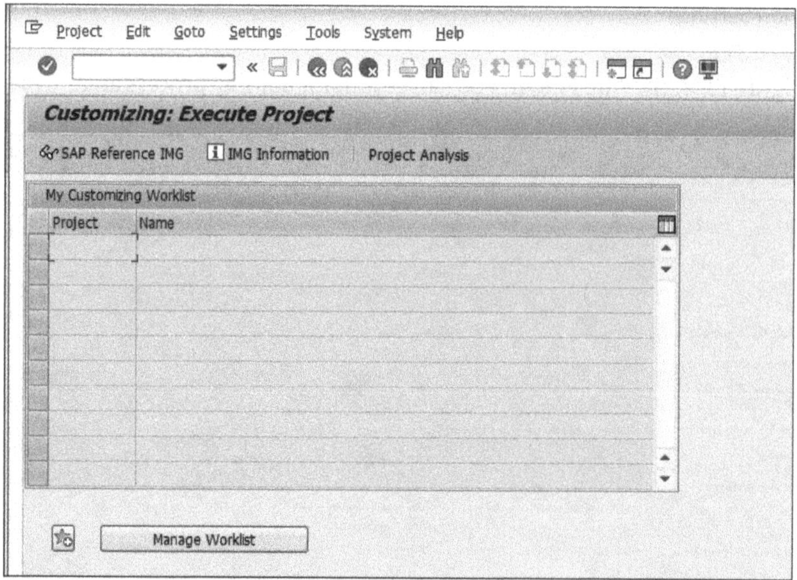

Figure 13 SAP Reference IMG Initial Screen

Then, you'll see the whole tree-like configuration menu, shown in Figure 14, which is separated into sections such as **Enterprise Structure**, where we'll define objects; **Financial Accounting**; **Controlling**; and so on.

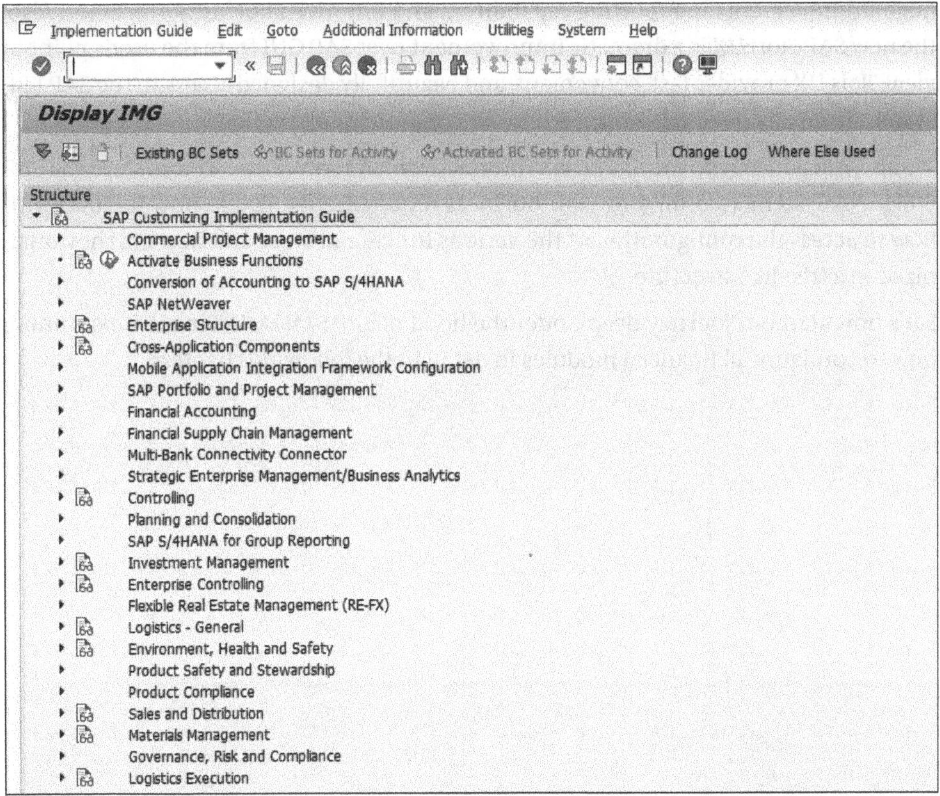

Figure 14 SAP Configuration Menu

Summary

In this Introduction, we discussed how the SAP HANA database came into existence and its evolution from an idea to best-selling SAP product. Now, you should know about the key benefits that the SAP HANA database offers compared to traditional row-based database systems. We outlined how the SAP HANA-based ERP solution has evolved to become today's mature, highly sought after, state-of-the-art solution that virtually all SAP customers are looking to implement, if they haven't already started or completed such a project.

We discussed the key benefits in the finance area that SAP S/4HANA brings and touched on the most important ones in this chapter. In coming chapters, we'll go into deep detail about these and other key advancements in SAP S/4HANA Finance.

The biggest benefit of SAP S/4HANA from a finance point of view is the simplicity it provides, both in terms of processes and in terms of database design. Unsurprisingly, the solution initially was called SAP Simple Finance because that name highlights exactly what it provides: simplification. This solution enables faster data processing, huge improvements in reporting capabilities, and improved business processes. Also, the new SAP Fiori UX is a dramatic improvement over SAP GUI from the user's point of view. This UX provides fast, convenient, and beautifully designed access to the SAP ERP system from any device, from anywhere with a mobile connection.

We also introduced the configuration interface, which enables you to configure the SAP S/4HANA system according to your business requirements. You're now familiar with how to access the configuration of the various functional areas and how are they organized in a tree-like structure.

Let's now start our journey deep under the hood of SAP S/4HANA Finance, examining how to configure all financial modules in detail in the following chapters.

Chapter 1
Project Preparation

This chapter discusses how to choose the right implementation approach for your SAP S/4HANA project (greenfield or brownfield) and outlines best practices for setting up the project scope, timeline, and implementation team.

Careful and well thought-out project preparation is required to ensure a successful enterprise resource planning (ERP) project, especially in such an important and challenging project as an SAP S/4HANA implementation. Even if your company is already running SAP ERP, you should consider SAP S/4HANA not just as the next technical upgrade, but as a great opportunity to rethink and improve business processes, taking advantage of the breakthroughs in simplification offered by SAP S/4HANA's technology.

Many key elements of project preparation, which we'll now explain in detail, can enable a successful implementation project.

We'll start with the definition of project objectives because every successful implementation is based on clearly defined and realistic objectives. We'll then discuss the differences between greenfield and brownfield SAP S/4HANA implementations and the benefits and drawbacks of each approach. This decision is critical for existing SAP customers, so we'll provide a solid basis on which to make this key decision. We'll guide you through how to define the project scope, which must be carefully thought out so that the project will add maximum value for the company, but at the same time must be realistic and within the agreed-upon budget. We'll also discuss the project timeline, which is dependent mainly on the project scope. Setting a project timeline that's agreed upon by project management and customer management, and then adhering strictly to this timeline, is vitally important.

Finally, we'll show you how to assemble a project team that can perform effectively and deliver SAP S/4HANA projects successfully, adding value to the business.

1.1 Defining Your Project Objectives

First, clearly defining your project objectives is one of the most important steps. Carefully established project objectives that are accepted by all levels of your organization ensure that the project will be successful.

For new SAP customers, clearly, the objective is to implement the leading and most advanced ERP system in the world: SAP S/4HANA. However, different options exist. Companies that have a well-defined budget at their disposal and with diverse regional and product footprints should look at SAP S/4HANA (the on-premise version) to maximize the value and the benefits they can get from the new software system. Stakeholders must be fully aware that such an implementation takes time and effort, and you must assemble a project team that's prepared for challenging tasks, both technically and from a business process point of view.

New SAP customers looking for a quicker, lower-cost implementation could consider SAP S/4HANA Cloud. This solution comes delivered with predefined business scenarios and content and is more suitable for companies with less complicated business requirements that can benefit from predefined template processes.

Most SAP S/4HANA implementations are performed by existing SAP customers because SAP already has an enormous customer base. SAP is by far the world market leader in ERP systems, and most big international companies already run one of its ERP business suites, most commonly SAP ERP. You need to set up your project objectives and expectations carefully. SAP S/4HANA is the perfect opportunity to rethink your business processes and be rid of old, obsolete processes while implementing new, streamlined ones that can fully benefit from the simplified data architecture of SAP S/4HANA. Especially for customers that implemented SAP 10 years ago or more, their current ERP systems probably aren't in line with the latest business global trends and requirements, and project objectives should include not only moving to SAP S/4HANA but also redesigning core processes.

However, many companies that have implemented SAP ERP relatively recently. Their systems likely are functioning well, and management and business users are satisfied. Still, those companies should not postpone a migration to SAP S/4HANA because the benefits are enormous, especially with the Universal Journal, the new asset accounting, and account-based profitability analysis (now called margin analysis), to name just a few improvements in the finance area. For these companies, the main project objectives will be not so much involve the redesign of processes, but adopting the latest functionalities SAP HANA technology can bring.

Defining the project scope is vital because this task determines how much value the implementation of SAP S/4HANA can bring to your business. SAP S/4HANA delivers cutting-edge technology, but it's how you employ the technology to streamline your business and enhance its processes that could make your implementation a tremendous success. A well-defined project scope will help you utilize SAP S/4HANA to the best benefit to your company.

To define the scope properly, answering the following questions may be helpful:

- How will the new system help optimize business processes?
- How will it increase the efficiency of operations?

- How will it decrease operational costs?
- How will it increase the return on investment (ROI)?
- How will it motivate our business users?

If you can't find reasonable answers to some of these questions, perhaps you should rethink the scope and what the system will be used for. The implementation should not be a goal in itself. The business case for implementing SAP S/4HANA should answer these questions, and then you can more easily define the project scope because you'll select functionalities that will increase ROI, decrease operational costs, optimize your business processes, and add overall value to your business.

Regardless of when the current ERP system was implemented, any existing SAP customer will inevitably need to have a deep discussion and go through a decision-making process to determine whether to undertake a greenfield or brownfield approach for your SAP S/4HANA implementation.

1.2 Comparing Greenfield versus Brownfield Implementations

A greenfield SAP S/4HANA implementation is implementing a completely new system from scratch, similar to implementation at a new SAP customer. In this case, the existing SAP system is treated as a legacy system and used as a source for legacy data migration.

A brownfield SAP S/4HANA implementation, on the other hand, is the conversion of an existing SAP system to SAP S/4HANA without reimplementation. This approach does require checking and modifying some of the existing customizing and existing custom programs.

Companies that are already running SAP Business Suite face a difficult dilemma. As mentioned earlier, migrating to SAP S/4HANA can't be compared with previous SAP upgrades from one SAP ERP Enhancement Package (EHP) to another, or even from the old SAP R/3 system to SAP ERP. SAP S/4HANA is fundamentally different and comes with a new database and a much enhanced and simplified data model. Therefore, upgrading an existing SAP ERP system to SAP S/4HANA is a huge effort, especially for heavily customized systems with a lot of custom developments. A lot of custom programs must be changed. All the obsolete tables still exist as core data services (CDS) views, and in general, programs that only read from these tables should work without modification because the `SELECT` statement shouldn't be impacted. However, programs that write to those tables will need to be modified.

Therefore, choosing the greenfield approach can be compelling: In this case, companies don't have to worry about modifying their old custom code programs and can benefit from a system designed for the new SAP HANA simplified data architecture. But another element to consider is the cost factor. Companies have already invested a huge amount of money, time, and effort into their existing SAP systems, and implementing a new system may seem too much, especially if the current system is relatively new.

No clear recommendations exist for deciding which option in better. You must assess both approaches carefully on a case-by-case basis, comparing the costs and benefits of both the greenfield and brownfield approaches. Some key factors to consider include the following:

- **Data volume**
  SAP S/4HANA enormously increases speed and performance. Therefore, companies with huge data volumes can benefit dramatically by converting an existing system to SAP S/4HANA.
- **Business processes**
  If your company is satisfied with how business processes are portrayed in the current system, you should consider the brownfield approach. If, on the contrary, a lot of room for improvement exists or if a lot of business processes in the current system are obsolete, the greenfield approach should be considered.
- **Custom code**
  A system with fewer modifications and custom enhancements is a better candidate for brownfield system conversion. If you're running a highly customized SAP system, in the end, implementing SAP S/4HANA as a greenfield implementation may turn out to be more cost-effective.
- **Technical readiness**
  For an existing system to be converted to SAP S/4HANA, it needs to fulfill several technical prerequisites. SAP S/4HANA only supports Unicode. If your existing system is on multiple code pages, your data must be converted to Unicode first. Also, the existing system should be running a minimum of SAP ERP 6.0 EHP 7, so older systems will need to be upgraded first. All these factors will add time, effort, and cost to the conversion and may be a good reason to go for a greenfield approach.

To summarize, Table 1.1 shows the pros and cons of the greenfield and brownfield approaches.

	Brownfield Approach	Greenfield Approach
Pros	■ Lower cost ■ Shorter implementation time ■ Keeping current custom developments and modifications ■ Keeping existing system processes	■ Opportunity to implement new processes and improve current processes ■ New configuration designed for SAP S/4HANA ■ Opportunity for data cleaning and harmonization ■ Limiting number of custom developments

Table 1.1 Pros and Cons of Brownfield and Greenfield Approaches

	Brownfield Approach	Greenfield Approach
Cons	■ Higher system complexity ■ Existing custom developments need to be checked and modified ■ Using older processes	■ Higher implementation cost ■ Longer implementation time ■ Need to develop custom developments from scratch

Table 1.1 Pros and Cons of Brownfield and Greenfield Approaches (Cont.)

1.3 Defining the Project Scope

The project scope is the key element of the project preparation phase. It involves clearly defining which modules, components, and functionalities will need to be delivered as part of an SAP S/4HANA implementation project.

This topic usually causes a lot of discussions at all levels of the organization. SAP provides myriad modules and functionalities, and no SAP implementations use all of them. Some functionalities require additional licensing fees, but most are included in the standard SAP S/4HANA license. However, even these included functionalities come with high implementation and support costs for consulting services and subject matter expert know-how. Therefore, carefully analyzing and selecting the most needed and beneficial functionalities is important.

You should analyze functionalities and designate them as *mandatory* or *nice to have*. Mandatory functionalities consist of processes that are needed to run the business and local legal requirements. These functionalities must be implemented. Typical examples include value-added (VAT) tax reporting and whatever other reports are mandatory according to local tax authorities.

Many functionalities might benefit the business but can be classified as only nice to have. For these functionalities, you should perform a cost-benefit analysis and assess potential manual workarounds. Usually, many requirements are competing, and a task for the project management team, usually represented by the steering committee of the project, is to assess all options and decide which to include in the project scope. Some functionalities may be left for the next project phase; others may be deemed too expensive or too complex relative to their presumed benefit.

More specifically, in terms of the financial areas in SAP S/4HANA, typically core areas such as the general ledger, accounts payable, accounts receivable, and fixed assets will be included in the project scope. On the controlling side, overhead costing is almost always included, as well as profitability analysis. Product costing should be included at least for production companies. Other finance-related functional areas, such as project system and financial supply chain management solutions, are more often optional and included in the project scope only with good reason; some companies in specific industries will benefit from these functionalities more than others.

Numerous functionalities are needed for specific countries or business processes, which are not included in the project scope by default and are often delivered as add-ons for SAP systems. For example, one functionality is the SAP Revenue Accounting and Reporting tool, which is an SAP solution for the requirements of International Financial Reporting Standard (IFRS) 15 (Revenue from Contracts with Customers). This tool obviously provides an important solution for companies that have a lot of customer contracts, but manual workarounds are also possible to satisfy reporting requirements, so you'll need to conduct a cost-benefit assessment to decide whether to include this tool in the project scope or not. Also consider the Suministro Inmediato de Información del IVA (SII) tax requirement in Spain, which stipulates that all invoices should be reported to tax authorities in a specific electronic format. For this requirement, SAP provides a solution based on the eDocument add-on, which involves additional licensing. Still, because this format is required by law, all companies that implement SAP S/4HANA in Spain must include this add-on in the project scope.

The project scope is defined not only by the functionalities implemented, but also geographically. SAP is used by many global companies that have diverse footprints across the globe. These companies need to decide which regions and countries will be included in which implementation waves. Many companies take the cluster wave approach, in which countries that are similar in terms of geographical location and local requirements go live together in the same wave, for example, Spain together with Portugal or Belgium with the Netherlands and Luxembourg. Big countries such as the United States usually will be in implementation waves by themselves.

Clearly defining the functional and geographical scope of the project is an important prerequisite for a successful SAP S/4HANA implementation. Of course, as the project goes along, small changes to the scope are possible, but having a well-defined scope from the beginning is crucial for keeping the budget under control and having a well-motivated project team.

1.4 Defining the Project Timeline

The project timeline is the next key element in your project planning. You must realistically plan how much time it will take to implement the project scope. This planning directly impacts the project budget and expectations of high-level management and other interested parties.

Sometimes, SAP projects don't meet the established timeline, perhaps due to unrealistic goals or due to deficiencies in the project execution. SAP S/4HANA projects are not immune to such problems. The fact that a cutting-edge technology solution is being implemented doesn't guarantee that it will be delivered on time and in line with the planned budget. The human factor is as important in an SAP S/4HANA implementation, as has been the case in traditional SAP implementations. Therefore, setting timeline expectations ambitiously, but also realistically, is imperative. Some time ago, we were involved in an implementation in which the implementation partner promised to implement SAP in 70 countries within 4 years. For anyone experienced in SAP implementations, this selling point is far from reality. And in fact, in 4 years, only one country went live. You can imagine the disappointment at all levels of the organization.

In general, the project timeline should be planned aggressively since SAP implementation projects take a lot of expensive resources from both technical side and the business. However, significant delays and postponements in the project plan should be avoided; not only are they bad for the high-level management and the project sponsors, but also demotivate the whole project team. Therefore, a cushion should be planned to counter some unforeseen obstacles.

A good idea is to choose some of the countries and companies with less complex requirements to go live first and prove the system template is working fine, and then to add complexity into the system landscape. The project timeline should take into account the complexity of the business processes and the local legal requirements in the project scope. This project timeline should be developed and communicated as soon as possible to all interested parties of the project and be discussed in detail before the project officially announced to the outside world. Every project is different, and the timeline will vary from project to project, but Figure 1.1 shows a sample project plan timeline with the major phases that are typically part of an SAP S/4HANA implementation project.

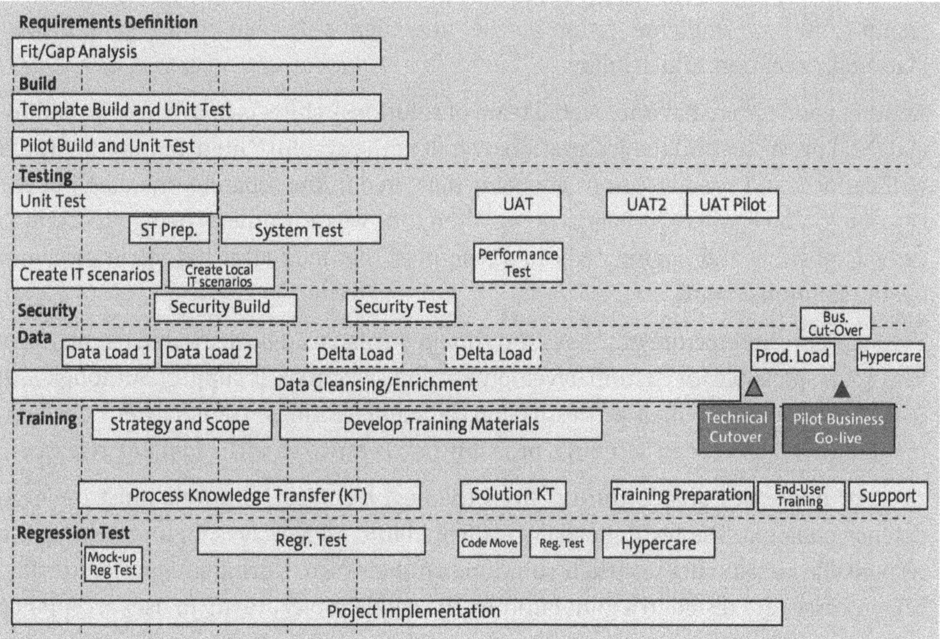

Figure 1.1 Sample Project Timeline

1.5 Assembling the Project Team

The human factor is perhaps the most important element of a successful SAP S/4HANA implementation. You need a well-motivated and technically competent team of project managers, SAP consultants, subject matter experts, and business process owners to navigate through such a complex implementation.

Most companies should engage an implementation partner to provide most of the consulting services and to manage an SAP S/4HANA project. Some companies opt out and assemble an entirely internal team. However, this approach requires a lot of effort and energy, and currently, attracting and retaining SAP talent, especially with strong SAP S/4HANA experience, is quite difficult. Therefore, the default choice is to contract with an experienced IT solution provider that has strong experience in SAP S/4HANA implementations.

A key factor for the success of the implementation project is the commitment of senior management to the success of the project and the engagement of key client resources early on. Even the best consultants will fail if the client side lacks motivation and engagement. Knowledgeable subject matter experts from the client side should be gathered as part of the project team. These experts should be familiar with business specifics and the key requirements that the system should fulfill.

The project team should be structured by process area—for example, record-to-report (which corresponds to financial accounting and controlling in SAP S/4HANA), purchase-to-pay, order-to-cash, and so on. Each process team should have workstream leads both from the consulting side and from the customer side. Only strong joint leadership from both implementation partner and client sides can ensure good project planning, execution, and delivery.

Another good idea to have an overall team of solution architects to oversee the end-to-end (E2E) processes and the integration overall in the system. Often, requirements are well defined, and good solutions are being delivered in the separate modules, but the E2E integration is where problems occur. Therefore, we recommend being proactive as early as possible and having dedicated resources that look after the integration and overall solution architecture.

The technical architecture of the system should be managed by dedicated team(s) also, who are responsible for custom development and system basis support. Although SAP S/4HANA offers simplified processes and data architectures, some custom development may still be needed, although probably not as much as with older SAP releases.

Another important area is testing. Even the best technical solutions must undergo extensive testing. The testing usually is divided into a few waves. In unit testing, the responsible consultants test their solutions on their own. During integration testing, E2E processes are tested in a joint effort by the whole project team. In user acceptance testing, users test the processes and functionalities and sign off after successful testing.

The testing effort should be managed by a dedicated test lead/manager, and a team of testers should be available to help with test execution and documentation.

Once an SAP S/4HANA template is implemented and the project goes into the country rollout implementation phase, for each country/cluster wave, a similar, albeit smaller team should be responsible for the country-level implementation, including the specific local requirements. A good idea is to engage some local experts in the finance area. Local tax requirements vary greatly from country to country, and taxation is an important topic in most countries.

Finally, a dedicated team for the organization should be in charge of go-live and hypercare production support. The initial support after go-live—usually 1 month, but sometimes more—is called *hypercare* and should be provided by a team formed from the original implementation team. This team should perform knowledge transfers to the team that will be responsible for ongoing support and maintenance, which often are more or less offshore based.

The project team should be well structured, with clear areas of responsibility, as shown in Figure 1.2.

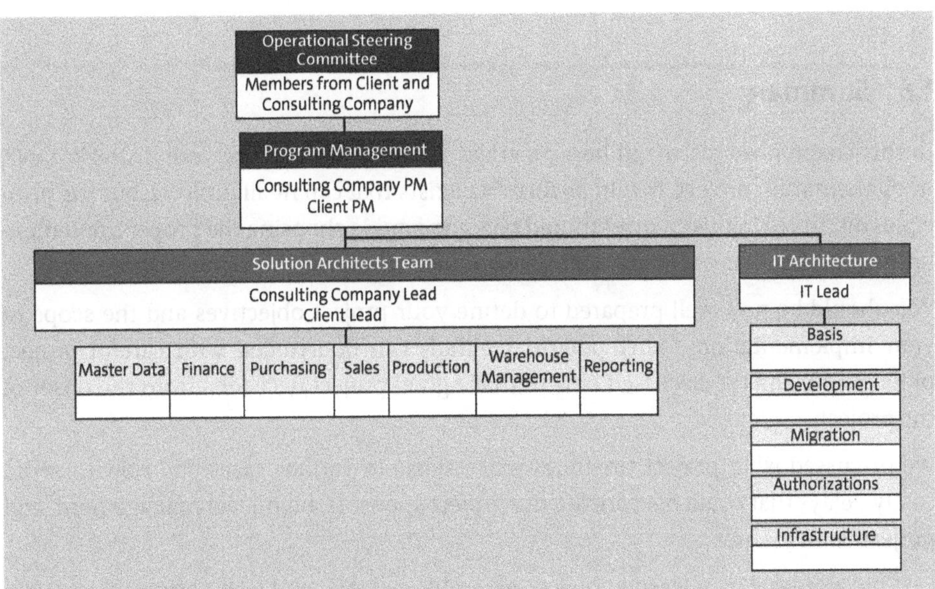

Figure 1.2 Project Organizational Structure

In terms of size, the teams we've experienced really vary a lot from project to project. Some projects are huge, multiyear implementations, which require project teams consisting of hundreds of experts. But SAP S/4HANA is also implemented in much smaller companies, with much smaller budgets and project teams. Whatever the size of the business and the size of the budget, the principles for successful project preparation remain the same. Teams should be clearly defined (smaller or bigger), with clearly defined responsibilities and strong leadership from both the consulting side and the client side.

Another consideration to take into account is that the demand for SAP S/4HANA implementation services is strong and in constantly increasing. At the time of this writing (early 2021), we're seeing very strong customer demand for SAP S/4HANA implementations. The slowdown of the economy in 2020 due to COVID-19 only temporarily impacted SAP S/4HANA projects, and in the later half of 2020 and beginning of 2021, we're seeing that the competition for highly skilled SAP consultants is fierce. You need to take this demand into consideration when planning your project since finding good resources for your project may take time and effort. Resources with experience with the latest releases, which is important, are even harder to find, as SAP is constantly adding new functionalities and improving the SAP S/4HANA system. For example, with SAP S/4HANA 2020, the redesigned profitability analysis solution is now called margin analysis. New functions are in place in bank accounting and in predictive accounting, as well as new SAP Fiori applications. You must have resources that are knowledgeable in the latest SAP S/4HANA technologies; therefore, assembling the proper project team is of utmost importance.

1.6 Summary

In this chapter, we discussed best practices for how to structure your SAP S/4HANA implementation project. No single formula exists that can fit all projects, but the principles discussed in this chapter should be a good guide choosing the proper implementation type for your company: greenfield or brownfield.

You should be now well prepared to define your project objectives and the scope of your implementation. Many potential pitfalls can be avoided with careful project preparation, and we discussed how to make good project decisions from the onset of the project.

We discussed what project timelines make sense in various cases and how to avoid costly delays that could demotivate the project sponsors, high-level management, and project team members.

Last but not least, you learned how to assemble a strong and well-performing project team and what types of managers and experts are needed at the various stages of the project. As discussed, acquiring and retaining smart and knowledgeable talent for your project is the most important factor for the success of the implementation. Arguably one of the biggest challenges currently is the lack of strong, senior SAP consultants with SAP S/4HANA experience because the market is booming and many companies are implementing SAP S/4HANA or planning to start an SAP S/4HANA implementation soon. Hopefully, this book will help resolve this situation to some extent, by helping more and more SAP FI/CO consultants learn the secrets of SAP S/4HANA.

2

Chapter 2
Requirements Analysis

This chapter explains how to conduct and document the business requirement analysis process that provides the foundation for an SAP S/4HANA implementation. We'll discuss the best practices for collecting vital information from the business, both on the template level and the localization-specific level, and how to manage multiple requirements from various countries within budget.

After project preparation is complete, the official kickoff of the project follows, and it starts with the requirements analysis phase. This extremely important phase lays down in document form what business processes the system should perform, how they should be executed, and what legal and business requirements should be met. The backbone for an SAP S/4HANA implementation, requirements analysis consists of multiple meetings, workshops, and requirements-gathering sessions, performed at various levels of the organization. At the end, this analysis should produce a full set of documents that clearly define the business requirements for the new SAP S/4HANA system.

The form and naming of these documents vary from project to project. Sometimes, a single, very big document with all the requirements should be produced, which often is called a *business blueprint*. Sometimes, you'll instead create a set of documents per process area, or even per process, which could be called *business requirement specifications*, *fit/gap analysis*, *business process definition*, or some other name used exclusively by a particular implementation partner. Whatever the name, these documents should contain well-defined business processes and their expected design in the system and are the result of months of hard work by both project team members and the relevant business resources.

The requirements analysis is performed at the template level and at the localization level. In the beginning of the project, requirements for the system template are defined, and after its successful build and testing, the country implementation phase continues with the localization requirements definition for the pilot countries. We'll examine these phases separately, starting with the template requirements analysis.

2.1 Template Requirements Analysis

In the old days of SAP implementations, many companies were implementing separate SAP systems in their major markets, sometimes even in countries with smaller market representation. Now, in the current highly globalized business environment, this approach is long gone, and companies want to have one central system, either globally or at least per major region, such as Americas, Europe and Middle East (EMEA), Asia Pacific (APAC), and so on.

The implementation of such a centralized system starts with defining and building what's called the *system template*. The template is a system that fulfills all the global requirements of the business and is the foundation for future country implementations. After the build is complete, rollout starts to the various markets where your company operates. Clearly, the template is the foundation for a successful SAP S/4HANA system that meets your business requirements.

We'll discuss in detail how the template requirements analysis should be performed and what to expect from it in the financials area, starting with financial accounting.

2.1.1 Financial Accounting

Financial accounting is the foundation of all SAP ERP systems: All other areas post into financial accounting. The only area that isn't optional; financial accounting must be implanted in every SAP system. Sometimes, early on in implementations, its importance may be underestimated by some non-finance managers or users ("Finance? It's just numbers" or "Sales is what matters most," you may even hear), but the proper implementation and the careful definition of business requirements in the area of financial accounting is of paramount importance for every project. This statement is especially true for SAP S/4HANA, in which finance completely integrates all information into one table, the single source of truth: the Universal Journal. To fully benefit from the great simplification in finance that comes with SAP S/4HANA, you must define its requirements in great detail.

Several ways exist for structuring a requirements document as well as different methods for how to proceed with discussions with the business and perform the review and approval process. The following section describes an example structure and process based on our 20 years of experience, both in SAP S/4HANA and older SAP implementations. This information can be used as best practices guidelines, but of course, each company and project team should implement its own specific activities to enhance the process.

The following is a sample list of process areas for financial accounting, under which the content of business requirements documents may be divided:

- Manage financial organizational structures
- Manage financial global setting

- Manage general ledger accounting
- Manage accounting subledgers
- Manage bank accounting

Within each of these areas, several documents will be defined, all of which correspond to particular process areas. From our point of view, this approach is better than having a single business blueprint document for financial accounting. In this way, the requirements are better structured and easier to read and approve. Also, this approach is in line with the latest SAP project methodology, which involves using an SAP-specific project implementation tool called *SAP Solution Manager* to manage the requirements definition process.

Each of these documents should be well structured and should include administrative information such as who created the document, when, and which versions have been created with what major changes to the document. These details will give the reviewer important information about how the requirements-gathering process evolved. Documents should also include information about who verified and approved the document and when. An overview section should describe the process in general business terms. Then, all the different process steps should be covered by the requirements document. A convenient approach is to assign each of these process steps an identifier for better tracking. For each of these process steps, what requirements the system should perform should be clearly written.

Where relevant, the documents should note for which process areas you need to develop reports, interfaces, conversions, enhancements, forms, and workflows (RICEFW) objects. These objects are custom developed for each project, rather than delivered as standard by SAP. *Reports* are executable programs that retrieve data from the database and meet specific customer reporting requirements. *Interfaces* provide a link between an SAP S/4HANA system and other SAP or non-SAP systems. *Conversions* are programs that convert data to meet specific requirements. *Enhancements* provide custom code to be triggered in specific areas of the system, such as using user exits and BAdIs. *Forms* provide custom layouts for printed or electronically sent documents from the system. *Workflows* provide custom workflow functionality to trigger some approval processes within the system, for instance, the purchase order (PO) approval process.

The requirements definition document also should contain information about dependencies with other configuration documents and test case information.

Each requirements definition document should be uploaded as a separate business requirement definition item in SAP Solution Manager, in which the whole review and approval process is organized, as shown in Figure 2.1.

Figure 2.1 shows a **Manage fixed assets accounting** requirements document, which is part of the process to manage accounting subledgers as defined in SAP Solution Manager. In this section of SAP Solution Manager, you can track testing requirements, the approval process, changes to the document, and the configuration performed in the system related to these requirements.

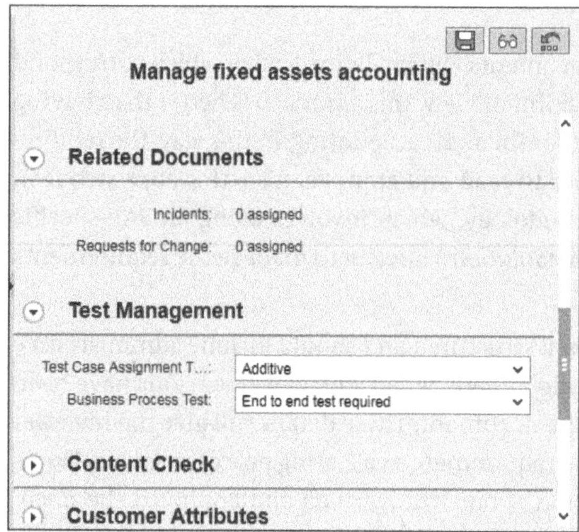

Figure 2.1 Manage Fixed Assets Requirements Document in SAP Solution Manager

SAP Solution Manager is a convenient repository for everything related to the configuration of the system, and as an SAP-delivered tool, SAP Solution Manager is fully integrated with SAP S/4HANA systems. You can assign a configuration unit to each configuration document, which contains the various configuration activities to be performed. This configuration unit in turn contains several configuration transactions. From within SAP Solution Manager, if properly configured, you can double-click a configuration element to go to the relevant configuration transaction in the linked SAP S/4HANA system. Figure 2.2 shows a list of configuration elements for defining financial global settings.

Elements of 'Define accounting global settings'

Name	Type	Group	F
Define Field Status Variants	IMG Object <Conf.>	Configuration	/S
Assign Company Code to Field Status Vari...	IMG Object <Conf.>	Configuration	/S
Define Accounting Principles	IMG Object <Conf.>	Configuration	/S
Define Settings for Ledgers and Currency ...	IMG Object <Conf.>	Configuration	/S
Deactivate a Ledger for a Company Code	IMG Object <Conf.>	Configuration	/S
Define Ledger Group	IMG Object <Conf.>	Configuration	/S
Assign Accounting Principle to Ledger Groups	IMG Object <Conf.>	Configuration	/S
Maintain Fiscal Year Variant	IMG Object <Conf.>	Configuration	/S
Assign Company Code to a Fiscal Year Var...	IMG Object <Conf.>	Configuration	/S
Define Variants for Open Posting Periods	IMG Object <Conf.>	Configuration	/S
Assign Variants to Company Code	IMG Object <Conf.>	Configuration	/S
Open and Close Posting Periods	IMG Object <Conf.>	Configuration	/S

Figure 2.2 Configuration Elements in SAP Solution Manager

Double-clicking any of these elements would take you directly to the relevant configuration path in the SAP Reference IMG. For example, double-clicking **Define Accounting Principles** would open a new SAP GUI window within the linked SAP S/4HANA system and take you to the configuration transaction, as shown in Figure 2.3.

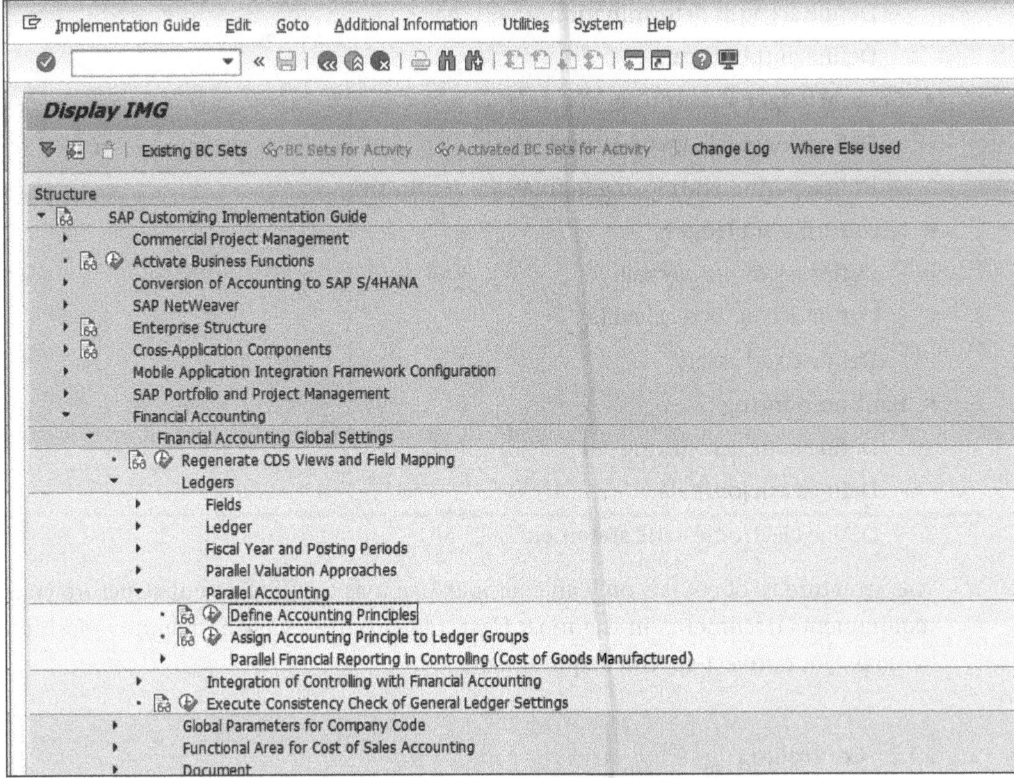

Figure 2.3 Direct Link to Define Accounting Principles from SAP Solution Manager

This function is convenient for anyone reviewing, approving, or checking the requirements gathered and how they are fulfilled in the system.

The structuring of specific financial accounting configuration documents should be logical, so in one configuration document the complete configuration elements for a particular function are included. These documents should enable a business reviewer to check and approve all the steps within his realm of knowledge. The following is an example structure for financial accounting requirement documents:

- **Financial organizational structures**
  - Define accounting structures
  - Define fixed asset structures
  - Define controlling structures

- **Financial global settings**
  - Define currencies
  - Define ledgers
  - Define tax codes and tax determination
  - Define account determination
  - Define output forms
- **General ledger accounting**
  - Define general ledger postings
  - Define period-end closing in financial accounting
- **Accounting subledgers**
  - Define accounts payable
  - Define accounts receivable
  - Define fixed assets
- **Bank accounting**
  - Define bank accounting
  - Define cash journals
  - Define electronic bank statement

This structure is, of course, only an example. Use it as a guideline but structure your requirements documents in the most clear and easy-to-review and approve fashion based on your project-specific requirements.

2.1.2 Controlling

Similarly, in controlling, the requirements definition documents should be organized in logical, coherent process areas. This organization also varies from project to project, especially given that only certain subareas of controlling are used in some projects.

The following list is an example of a possible structuring for the controlling requirements definition documents for a company using all the main controlling functionalities, including product costing:

- **Overhead costing**
  - Define general controlling settings
  - Define master data for overhead costing
  - Manage actual costs in overhead costing
  - Define planning in overhead costing

- **Profitability**
  - Manage profit center accounting
  - Manage profitability analysis
  - Manage period-end closing in controlling
- **Inventory valuation and product costing**
  - Define inventory valuation
  - Perform actual costing
  - Define material ledger
  - Perform inventory controlling and reporting

As with financial accounting, this structure is just a guideline; most companies and industries have some specifics that must be taken into account.

In terms of the content of the controlling documents, they should have the same structure that we already outlined for the financial accounting documents. In general, all requirements definition documents for all areas should follow the same structure and be consistent, even if they're being prepared by different consultants and reviewed by different business users.

2.1.3 Integration with Logistics

Many functions are integration points between finance and logistics. The requirements definition in these areas should be a joint effort of both the financial and logistic teams. SAP is a highly integrated system, which is where its main strength lies. To define efficient processes that meet the business requirements of all departments, you must have many integration meetings in which both the financial and logistic teams discuss the end-to-end (E2E) processes, not only separate processes within a process area.

Typical requirements definition areas that should be a joint effort between finance and logistics are inventory valuation, account determination, and tax code determination. Indeed, the configuration transactions for those areas can be found in both the finance and logistics areas of the SAP Reference IMG.

For example, tax codes are defined by the finance department. But the automatic determination of the proper tax code in the different purchase and sales processes comes from what are called *condition records* and *condition tables*, which are typically maintained by the sales and purchasing consultants. The discussion of these logistic processes should involve users from both finance and logistics to determine the proper tax treatment for each process.

Account determination is typically a finance task, but many logistic processes post automatically in financial accounting and thus must have correct the accounts assigned to work properly. Normally, the requirements definition document for this topic should be owned by finance, but the document should be worked on in conjunction with the logistics team. Similarly, inventory valuation usually is owned by finance, but its nature requires development in close integration with logistics.

Also, many requirements definition documents are typically owned by logistics but may also require consultation with finance. Just to name a few, these areas include material master data, credit management, and pricing.

As you can see, requirements analysis is a complex stage of the project that must be conducted in a highly integrated manner between financial and logistic consultants and subject matter experts.

2.2 Localization Fit/Gap Analysis

The system template is the foundation of the SAP S/4HANA implementation, but the real deployments are done at a country level. Typically, once the template is configured, tested, and signed off on, country-level deployments start in earnest. Most companies opt for a wave approach, in which one or a few similar countries are selected as pilot countries, and then over the next couple of years, all the other countries are deployed in carefully selected waves. In large companies operating in many markets, these deployments can last for 5 or 10 years, or even longer (in rare cases).

In the following sections, we'll discuss in detail how to localize your SAP S/4HANA system. We'll start with an overview of the localization process, then we'll deep-dive into the implementation of local accounting standards, tax requirements, and other localization topics for the various countries in scope.

2.2.1 Localization Overview

The method to roll out the template to different countries is the same, whether for the pilot country or a few years down the implementation, and whether rollout is for one of the major markets for the company or for some small market with limited presence. The template must be localized, which essentially means performing a fit/gap analysis for the local business and legal requirements.

Fit/gap analysis is a process in which the baseline solution (the template solution) is analyzed in all its process areas and discussed with the local business and consulting resources. Any identified gaps should be recorded—either in the original requirements definition documents, which are being "localized" and enhanced, or in a new set of localized requirements definition documents on the country level.

Then, all the gaps should be assessed in terms of their importance. Obviously, fulfilling each gap comes at a certain cost and should be compared with the benefit it provides. This assessment is called a *cost-benefit analysis*. The gaps should be classified as mandatory to fulfill, essential, and nice to have. Accordingly, project management will decide which gaps should be addressed based on the available budget and timing.

Because each country has its own specifics—and some country-specific uses of SAP solutions can be sciences of their own due to the high complexity of local tax and statutory requirements (notably, Russia)—enlisting the help of local consultants makes sense. Of course, no SAP implementation team is knowledgeable about all the specifics of all the countries. Therefore, a good approach is to have lead consultants from the template project team manage the rollout effort, but also hire one or more local SAP financial consultants that know about the local taxation, value-added tax (VAT), and other relevant topics. Of course, another key factor to properly gather the local requirements is to engage deeply with local subject matter experts and discuss all local topics with them.

Still, the core implementation team should educate itself about local specifics as much as possible prior to starting the requirements analysis. A good source for this information is the SAP Globalization Services website, which provides detailed information about country and language versions for various countries, available at *https://support.sap.com/en/product/globalization.html*. At this site, you can browse by region and by country and find important country-specific localization information. Another good source for country-specific localization information is found in SAP Notes, available at *https://support.sap.com*.

An SAP ID, usually provided by your project manager, is required to access SAP Notes. SAP Notes provide up-to-date information as SAP constantly monitors changes in the legal requirements in various countries and provides updates in these SAP Notes, which can be implemented before the change becomes part of the standard system. Be sure you gather all the relevant SAP Notes for the countries for which you're performing requirements analysis.

In the areas of financial accounting and controlling, you may find localization gaps in few key areas: local accounting standards requirements, local tax requirements, and other business-related local requirements, which we'll analyze next.

2.2.2 Local Accounting Standards

In the current globalized world, a huge movement exists toward international harmonization in the area of accounting. International Financial Reporting Standards (IFRS) have gone a long way toward defining common accounting rules for most business transactions and situations. This standard is being adopted in many regions and countries in the world, including the European Union, Russia, many Asian countries—such as South Korea, India, Singapore, and Hong Kong—Australia, South Africa, Turkey, and many others. However, IFRS not universally accepted everywhere, and notably is still not adopted in the United States, where US Generally Accepted Accounting Principles (US GAAP) is the main accounting standard.

Managing different accounting standards is a major requirement for most SAP S/4HANA systems. In fact, the new general ledger architecture, powered by the simplified SAP HANA database is perfect for managing these requirements, which we'll discuss detail in Chapter 3 and Chapter 7. For now, however, let's just say that using the leading ledger to portray the leading accounting principle from a group point of view, while using nonleading ledgers for the other accounting principles, is the perfect technical solution.

From a requirements definition point of view, with each country consultants must discuss which accounting standards must be represented in the system. Even in some countries in which IFRS is adopted, some companies may need to follow another local accounting standard in parallel. Fortunately, with the new SAP S/4HANA Finance solution, this parallel accounting is much easier than before. In the past, sometimes a complete set of duplicated general ledger accounts was deployed for this task.

After confirming the required accounting standard framework, the necessary requirements definition documents should be enhanced and signed off on to reflect the desired setup. Typically, this setup will include setting up nonleading ledgers for each accounting framework to be reported on. For example, let's say, from the template point of view, we need to set up a leading ledger for US GAAP and one nonleading ledger for IFRS. Then, as part of the localization fit/gap phase, you could set up an additional nonleading ledger to be activated to cover the requirements of local accounting principles.

2.2.3 Local Tax Requirements

In many countries, specific tax rules differ both from IFRS and from locally accepted accounting principles. As a result, from an accounting point of view, companies can follow certain rules and guidelines, but then when preparing their tax declarations and calculating their taxes due, they'll need to follow rules specifically postulated by the local tax authorities. Therefore, in such countries, requirements analysis to include these tax rules and define how the system should meet them is key. These requirements are mandatory, and not meeting them in your SAP S/4HANA system could result in severe penalties.

Some countries have more stringent tax requirements than others. In most countries, these local tax requirements revolve around VAT, which is a tax added on most sales and purchases. As the main source of taxes for tax administrations, VAT is difficult to track, with a lot of fraud, and many countries have tough reporting requirements related to VAT. For example, in Spain, Suministro Inmediato de Información del IVA

(SII) reporting is mandatory and requires that all incoming and outgoing invoices should be reported to the tax office no later than 4 days after their issue. This type of requirement is quite important to capture during the fit/gap localization phase. Also, many other countries have a specific form required for VAT reporting to be produced by the accounting system.

SAP aims to cover all these legally required specifics in different countries. It constantly monitors tax requirements around the world (which often change and create greater demands on information systems) and provides updates and new functionalities to meet those requirements. For most countries and most requirements, these functionalities are part of the standard system. But for some requirements, you may need to install additional add-ons to your system, which may require additional licensing costs. For example, for the SII requirement in Spain, as well as for similar real-time reporting requirements to tax offices in other countries, you'll need the eDocument processing add-on from SAP. In some countries, third-party add-ons have been developed by other companies with locality-specific experience. Choosing the right solution is part of the requirements analysis phase and is a joint effort of the consulting and business teams on the project.

In countries with sophisticated local tax requirements, usually a local tax ledger also is activated. This ledger is another nonleading ledger, similar to the nonleading ledger for local accounting standards, and is activated only in countries with extremely unique tax needs. Using this tax ledger, you can make ledger-specific postings that allow different tax treatments for some transactions. For example, in fixed assets, often local tax authorities stipulate different depreciation rules from a tax point of view. These complex depreciation requirements are easy to accomplish using the tax ledger. Local tax depreciation areas are set up that reflect those rules, and these areas are mapped to the tax nonleading ledger. Now, in SAP S/4HANA, this process has been greatly enhanced compared to older SAP systems because these postings occur in real time. In the past, these differences were tracked in delta depreciation areas and posted to the nonleading ledgers offline. The nonleading ledger concept is quite advanced in SAP S/4HANA, as we'll discuss in detail in Chapter 3 and Chapter 7.

As with local accounting standards, local tax requirements must be written down in deep detail in the relevant requirements definition documents, which should include how the solution should work to meet these requirements—a key deliverable of the requirements analysis phase.

2.2.4 Other Local Requirements

Other local requirements may not fall neatly into the category of local accounting standards or local tax codes. These requirements stem from local business practices or local ways of accounting for certain transactions, even though they may not be written explicitly in accounting laws. Depending on their significance, these requirements range from nice to have to mandatory.

These requirements also must be discussed in detail with the local subject matter experts, and then you'll need to carefully analyze the costs and benefits of each requirement. It's easy to get carried away and promise to fulfill countless local requirements, but remember that the template is what is being rolled out. Normally, this template should be able to function properly in each country with only limited local changes, so most of the nice-to-have elements should be scrutinized carefully to decide whether implementing them makes sense.

Let's look at a few examples for local business requirements. Inventory valuation is a topic that deserves a lot of attention on the local level. Some countries have specific requirements for inventory valuation, which are indeed required to be implemented. Countries such as Brazil, Russia, and Turkey require that inventory be valued at actual cost. Therefore, in these countries, you must implement actual costing. Understanding local requirements properly is vital. In this case, the requirement isn't to use parallel currencies and valuation, but to use actual costing. This point sometimes raises confusion regarding SAP S/4HANA. Indeed, in SAP S/4HANA, the material ledger is required, but this solution doesn't provide actual costing by default. Actual costing is a different functionality, activated separately from the material ledger. Therefore, the material ledger is always a template requirement in SAP S/4HANA, whereas actual costing could be a local requirement activated only for specific countries. (The material ledger will be discussed in detail in Chapter 15.)

Other key local requirements that usually should be implemented include a local chart of accounts, translation into the local language of various forms and reports, and any required interfaces with tax and other government offices.

Other requirements may arise when a country expects particular business processes be executed in a specific way—which may not explicitly be required by local law and which may not be in line with group policies and template settings—and are prime targets for optimization. In this situation, the SAP S/4HANA implementation could be viewed as an opportunity to help improve obsolete processes and optimize the business at a local level.

2.3 Summary

In this chapter, we covered requirements gathering: a vital, yet sometimes underestimated phase of the project. We cannot emphasize strongly enough that the proper definition of the business requirements, both on the template level and the localization level, is crucial for delivering a good SAP S/4HANA solution that meets all key requirements.

In this chapter, you learned a method for how to approach requirements analysis, what the key elements are that need to be discussed in detail with the business, and how to document them. You learned one possible way to structure your requirements definition documents in financial accounting and controlling. This approach can serve as a guideline and adapted to meet your project- and business-specific requirements.

The key to success for the requirements analysis project phase is to cover all the business requirements and discuss these requirements with the business as well as to assess properly the costs and benefits of them. In most projects, one of the main challenges is the infinite desire of various business users to include more and more requirements. The success of the project depends on the ability of the senior project management, subject matter experts, and consultants to select only the key, important requirements and deliver key functionalities within the agreed-upon budget and timeframe.

Hopefully, with the methods and guidelines discussed in this chapter, you'll play an important role in your SAP S/4HANA implementation and deliver good, clear, and successful requirements analysis.

Chapter 3
Financial Accounting Global Settings

This chapter introduces the new data model in SAP S/4HANA and describes how it improves financial processes and reporting. We'll describe configuring global finance settings in SAP S/4HANA, such as organizational structure, ledgers, document types, and other settings in this chapter.

After completing the requirements gathering phase of the project, which produces signed-off business requirements definition documents, it's time to start configuring SAP S/4HANA Finance. The configuration process starts with configuring the global settings for financial accounting, which define the organizational structure and basic configuration elements such as ledgers, document types, currencies, and tax codes.

As briefly discussed in the Introduction, SAP S/4HANA offers a new simplified data model, which greatly increases the speed and performance of the finance processes. Understanding this new data model is of paramount importance as is understanding the real-time integration of financial accounting and controlling and how the new Universal Journal functions. So, we'll start with detailed explanations of the new data model in SAP S/4HANA Finance.

3.1 The New Finance Data Model in SAP S/4HANA

SAP is a highly integrated system that manages data from various areas of the business, such as accounting, sales, purchasing, production, and so on. This integration comes with a certain degree of complexity, which results in the data being stored in many different tables. Thus, sometimes, even for experienced consultants, finding the best way to find and retrieve the relevant data can be a challenge.

In the area of finance, traditionally, financial accounting and controlling (management accounting) were separate applications in SAP, which was a design mainly driven from traditions in the German-language world. However, in today's globalized world, a strong case exists for the integration of processes and applications and the simplification of systems. SAP's answer to this need is the excellent SAP S/4HANA Finance solution, which provides full integration of the financial accounting and controlling applications, both from a process point of view and a database point of view.

We'll discuss in detail the two key elements of the new finance data model in SAP S/4HANA: the Universal Journal and real-time integration between financial accounting and controlling.

3.1.1 Universal Journal

The Universal Journal provides a solution for a seemingly simple but, until SAP S/4HANA, elusive goal: bringing together and fully integrating all financial information in one single line-item table that has all financial accounting, controlling, and material valuation information. Previously, for many reasons, multiple financial accounting and controlling tables stored data that now, with SAP S/4HANA, are stored in the Universal Journal. Some tables were business process-based on the presumption that financial accounting and controlling should be separate applications, which is not the case in the current business world. Some reasons were technical: Only now with the amazing speed and columnar design of SAP S/4HANA is having such a vast amount of data in a single table technically feasible.

The Universal Journal is a new table in SAP S/4HANA, called table ACDOCA. This line-item table brings together information from the general ledger, controlling, asset accounting, and the material ledger, as shown in Figure 3.1.

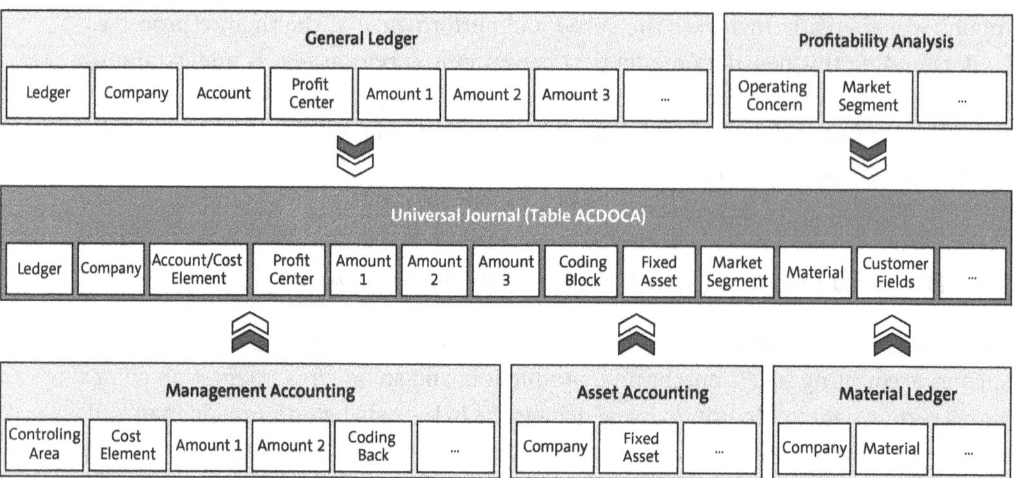

Figure 3.1 Universal Journal

As shown in Figure 3.1, table ACDOCA, the Universal Journal table, combines fields that previously were stored in the tables of various financial accounting and controlling modules. Once a financial document is posted in table ACDOCA, fields such as cost center, asset number, profitability segment fields, and so on are also recorded. Thus, a whole lot of tables from controlling, fixed assets, and the material ledger have been made redundant because the information is now integrated in the Universal Journal. For compatibility reasons, these tables still exist as core data services (CDS) views so that they can still be referenced in custom programs, important for companies pursuing brownfield implementations of SAP S/4HANA.

Table 3.1 shows the main financial accounting tables that are now obsolete in SAP S/4HANA because their data is part of table ACDOCA.

Table	Description
BSIS	Accounting: Secondary Index for G/L Accounts
BSAS	Accounting: Secondary Index for G/L Accounts (Clearing Postings)
BSID	Accounting: Secondary Index for Customers
BSAD	Accounting: Secondary Index for Customers (Clearing Postings)
BSIK	Accounting: Secondary Index for Vendors
BSAK	Accounting: Secondary Index for Vendors (Clearing Postings)
GLTO	G/L Account Master Record Transaction Figures (Totals Table)
FAGLFLEXT	General Ledger: Totals (New GL Totals Table)

Table 3.1 Obsolete Tables in Financial Accounting

Tables BSIS, BSAS, BSID, BSAD, BSIK, and BSAK are index tables containing open and cleared items for general ledger accounts, customers, and vendors, which are now all in table ACDOCA. Tables GLTO and FAGLFLEXT are totals tables (FAGLFLEXT was introduced with the new general ledger), which are now also obsolete because SAP S/4HANA calculates totals on the fly. Table 3.2 shows other important controlling, fixed assets, and material ledger tables which are now obsolete due to the Universal Journal.

Table	Description
COEP	CO Object: Line Items (by Period)
COBK	CO Object: Document Header
ANEP	Asset Line Items
ANEA	Asset Line Items for Proportional Values
ANLP	Asset Line Items
MLHD	Material Ledger Document: Header
MLIT	Material Ledger Document: Items

Table 3.2 Obsolete Tables in Controlling, Fixed Assets, and Material Ledger

As you can see, now in SAP S/4HANA, the Universal Journal combines the key tables of all the financial applications into a single table, which is commonly referred to as the *single source of truth*. Now, you have all the information you need to present the financials of your company in one place—an enormous advantage compared to previous SAP releases and to other enterprise resource planning (ERP) systems.

3.1.2 Real-Time Integration with Controlling

The real-time integration of financial accounting with controlling follows logically from the integration design of the Universal Journal as discussed earlier. Indeed, because controlling-relevant data now is brought together with financial accounting data in the Universal Journal, no technical obstacles prevent the system from providing real-time integration between any financial accounting and controlling documents.

In the past, the reconciliation ledger had to be configured to ensure that financial accounting and controlling were always in sync. This configuration is no longer required because, with the real-time integration with financial accounting, such reconciliation is obsolete. Also, secondary cost elements are created as general ledger accounts to ensure this integration.

In SAP S/4HANA, controlling documents are still generated along with financial accounting document numbers. However, even internal controlling movements, such as the reallocation of costs from one controlling object to another, also generate financial accounting document numbers, thus ensuring real-time integration, which wasn't the case in SAP ERP. In terms of configuration, document types that are used for posting in controlling are defined to post to general ledger accounts as well. These document types are linked to the controlling internal business transactions and generate financial accounting postings as well as controlling postings.

3.2 Organizational Structure

We'll start configuring an SAP S/4HANA Finance system by defining an organizational structure. The organizational structure in SAP represents the business organizational structure of your enterprise and consists of various configuration objects in finance, controlling, sales, purchasing, production, and so on. So, as the foundation of any further system setup, the organizational structure is extremely important and must be designed and defined in a proper, flexible way.

We'll examine in detail how to configure organizational structures in finance and controlling in SAP S/4HANA, such as company, company code, controlling area, and operating concern.

3.2.1 Company

A *company* in SAP is an organizational unit that represents a business from a commercial point of view. This organizational unit can consist of multiple legal entities and is used to perform consolidation in SAP.

If no consolidation process is needed, you can avoid setting up companies in SAP. As an optional organizational object, you can also set up companies later. However, doing so would require significant effort, so we recommend setting up a company in the beginning even if consolidation won't be performed until later.

To create a company, follow the menu path **Enterprise Structure • Definition • Financial Accounting • Define Company.** As you'll recall from the Introduction, this menu path and all other menu paths are accessed via Transaction SPRO.

Now, you can create a new company using the **New Entries** option from the top menu. As shown in Figure 3.2, let's create a new company for the United States and give it code 1000. The naming conventions of companies, company codes, controlling areas, and so on vary greatly from project to project. A good idea is to use simple, easy-to-remember numbering. You should make a well-defined proposal for numbering conventions and confirm it with the business.

In this configuration transaction, enter the name and address of the company, the country, the language key, and the currency and then save by clicking the **Save** button in the lower-right corner. If you're configuring in a development system, you'll be prompted with a customizing request that stores the changed configuration settings, which will need to be transported to other systems, for instance, test and productive systems.

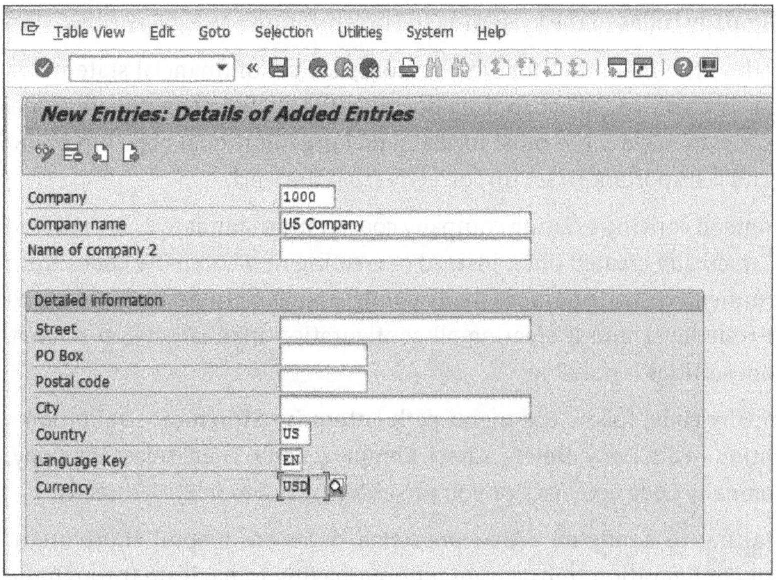

Table View Edit Goto Selection Utilities System Help

New Entries: Details of Added Entries

Company	1000
Company name	US Company
Name of company 2	

Detailed information

Street	
PO Box	
Postal code	
City	
Country	US
Language Key	EN
Currency	USD

Figure 3.2 Creating a Company

Configuration changes in SAP S/4HANA, as in previous SAP releases, are essentially changes to configuration tables. Normally, you would do a first round of configuration in a so-called *sandbox system*, which doesn't record the changes in customizing transports. After initial testing in the sandbox system, you would make the configuration settings in the development "golden" client, which should have the settings to be transported to other clients and no data. Then, these transports are transported to test systems for unit testing, integration testing, and user-acceptance testing, and finally to the production system. This concept will be discussed in detail in Chapter 18.

Now, you've created your first company. Your enterprise may decide to set up one company for each country in which it operates and then assign the various legal entities in this country to that company. Then, in the consolidation process, users can view financial statements from the group point of view on the level of the company, eliminating intercompany profit and transactions between the different legal entities. We'll come back to this point after you create your first company codes.

3.2.2 Company Code

A *company code* is the main organizational unit in financial accounting. Usually, a company code represents a separate legal entity. For example, a global pharmaceutical company may have a few different legal entities in the United States, each registered as legally independent companies: Perhaps one manufactures generic drugs, one develops biotechnology medications, and one performs testing for the pharmaceutical industry. Setting up each of these companies as separate company codes in SAP S/4HANA makes sense. Then, if those companies have a common parent company, that parent company can also be set up as a company in SAP. Thus, normally, you will have as many company codes in the system as the organization has legal entities.

The company code is the main unit for which a complete set of financial statements can be generated. Every financial accounting document is posted per company code. Therefore, the company code is the most fundamental organizational object in financial accounting and is important to set up correctly from the start.

We highly recommend copying existing company codes, either standard SAP-provided company codes or already created ones, instead of creating new company codes from scratch. We recommend copying because many configuration settings are maintained at the company code level, and if creating all configuration manually from scratch, missing important settings is possible.

To create a company code, follow the menu path **Enterprise Structure • Definition • Financial Accounting • Edit, Copy, Delete, Check Company Code**. Then, select the **Copy, Delete, Check Company Code** activity—or you can enter Transaction EC01 directly.

If you're just starting to configure SAP, *transaction codes* are helpful shortcuts to enter into user or configuration transactions without having to navigate through the application or configuration menu. Transaction codes are entered in the command field in the top-left section of the main SAP application screen, as shown in Figure 3.3.

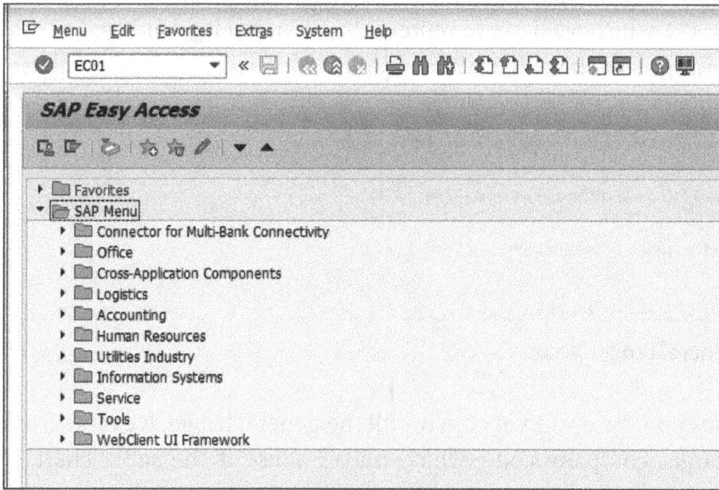

Figure 3.3 Command Field in SAP

You can enter also "/N" before a transaction code from within any transaction, which will end the current transaction and start the new transaction. Alternatively, you can enter "/O" before the transaction, which will open the transaction in a new SAP GUI window.

Back to our example, select **Copy Org. Object** (copy organizational object) from the top menu and select the source and target company codes to be copied, as shown in Figure 3.4.

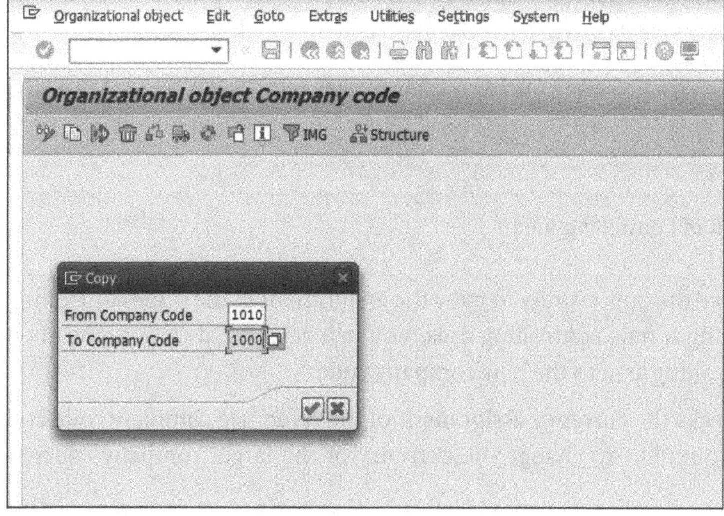

Figure 3.4 Copying a Company Code

In the **From Company Code** field, enter the source company code to copy from. You can use one of the SAP-provided sample company codes for the country you want to create new company code. In the **To Company Code** field, enter "1000" to copy the settings to new company code 1000, which we'll use to represent a US-based legal entity. The system will issue the message shown in Figure 3.5.

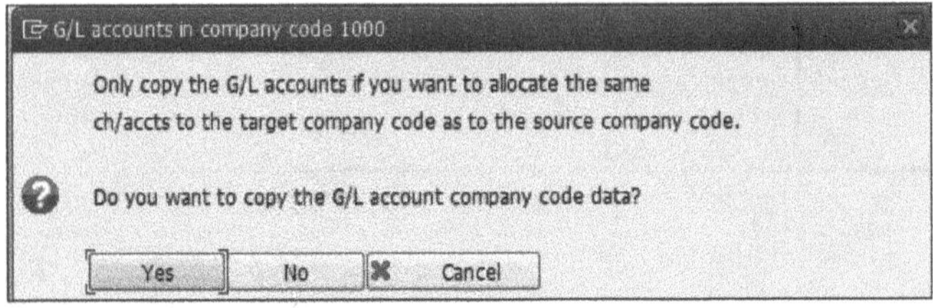

Figure 3.5 Copying General Ledger Accounts

This message provides you the option of copying all the general ledger accounts from the source to the target company code, which makes sense if the same chart of accounts is used. General ledger accounts are maintained at the chart of accounts level and at the company code level, and confirming this option allows you to automatically extend all the relevant accounts also to the new company code.

Now, the system issues another message regarding the assignment of the controlling area to the company code, as shown in Figure 3.6.

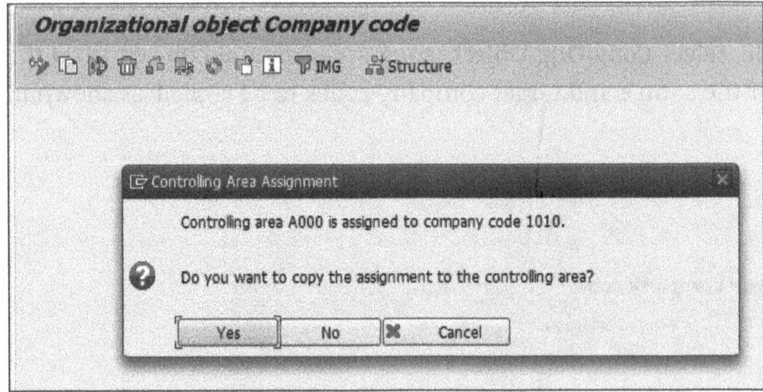

Figure 3.6 Assignment of Controlling Area

At this point, you have the opportunity to copy the assignment of the same controlling area. If you're creating a new controlling area, you can reject that option and then assign the new controlling area to the new company code.

Next, the system checks the currency assignment of the reference company code and asks whether you would like to change the currency of the target company code, as shown in Figure 3.7.

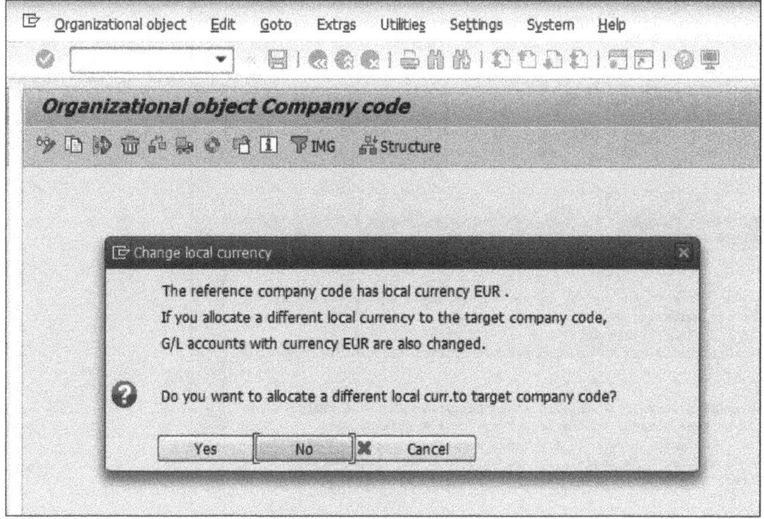

Figure 3.7 Currency Assignment

Enter "USD" in the **Currency** field, as shown in Figure 3.8.

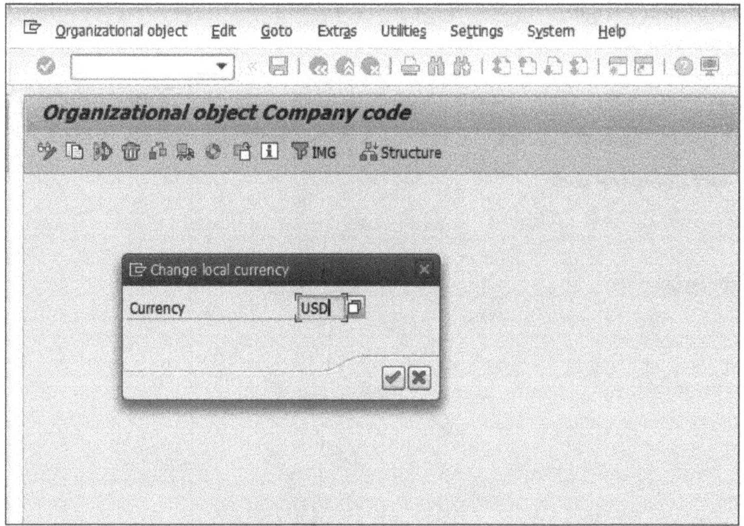

Figure 3.8 Entering a Currency

Next, the system asks if you want to copy the number ranges of the source company code, as shown in Figure 3.9. However, we don't recommend copying number ranges, which could cause inconsistencies.

The system confirms the copying of the company code, as shown in Figure 3.10.

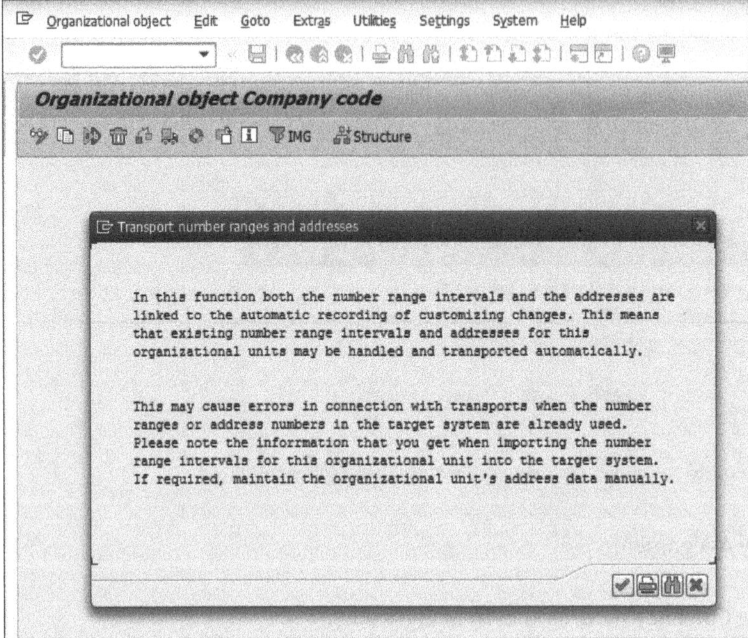

Figure 3.9 Copying a Number Range

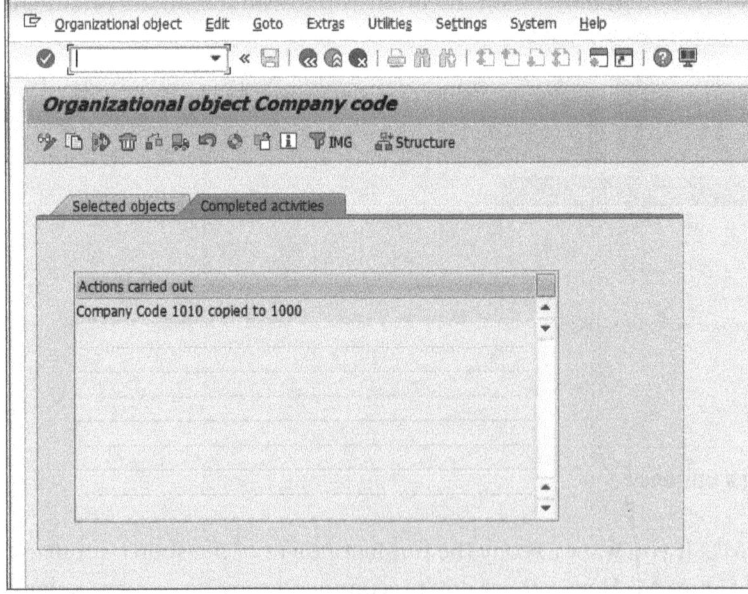

Figure 3.10 Copy Company Code Confirmation Screen

Now, go back and select the **Edit Company Code Data** activity to display the list of company codes that exist in the system. Double-click the new company code **1000** from the list shown in Figure 3.11, to change its basic data.

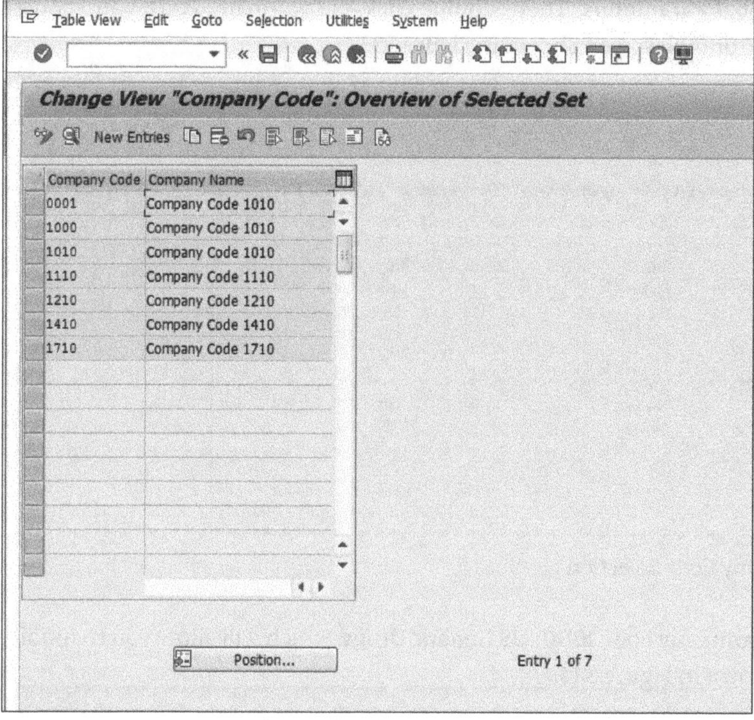

Figure 3.11 Selecting a Company Code

Enter the required details for this company code by maintaining the **Company Name**, **City**, **Country**, **Currency**, and **Language** fields, as shown in Figure 3.12.

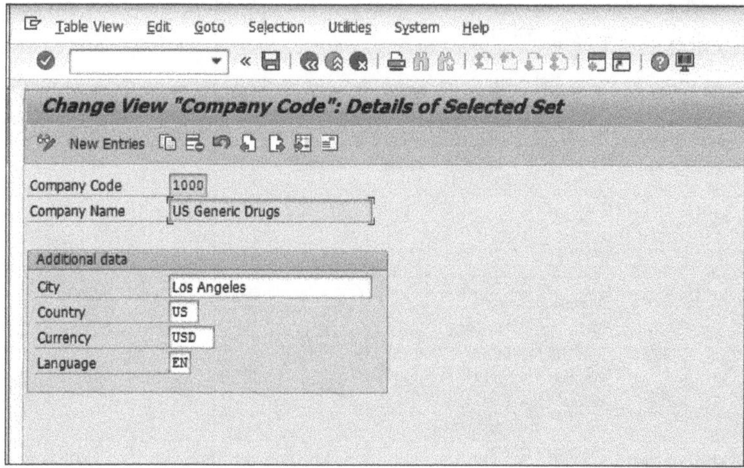

Figure 3.12 Company Code Details

Next, maintain the global company code settings by following the menu path **Financial Accounting • Financial Accounting Global Settings • Global Parameters for Company**

Code • Enter Global Parameters. Then, double-click the company code you want to check or modify from the screen shown in Figure 3.13.

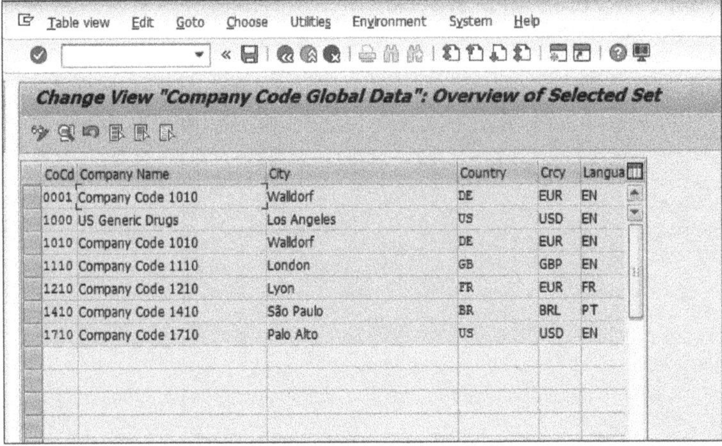

CoCd	Company Name	City	Country	Crcy	Langua
0001	Company Code 1010	Walldorf	DE	EUR	EN
1000	US Generic Drugs	Los Angeles	US	USD	EN
1010	Company Code 1010	Walldorf	DE	EUR	EN
1110	Company Code 1110	London	GB	GBP	EN
1210	Company Code 1210	Lyon	FR	EUR	FR
1410	Company Code 1410	São Paulo	BR	BRL	PT
1710	Company Code 1710	Palo Alto	US	USD	EN

Figure 3.13 Company Code Selection

Double-click on company code **1000: US Generic Drugs**, which will allow you to modify its settings, as shown in Figure 3.14.

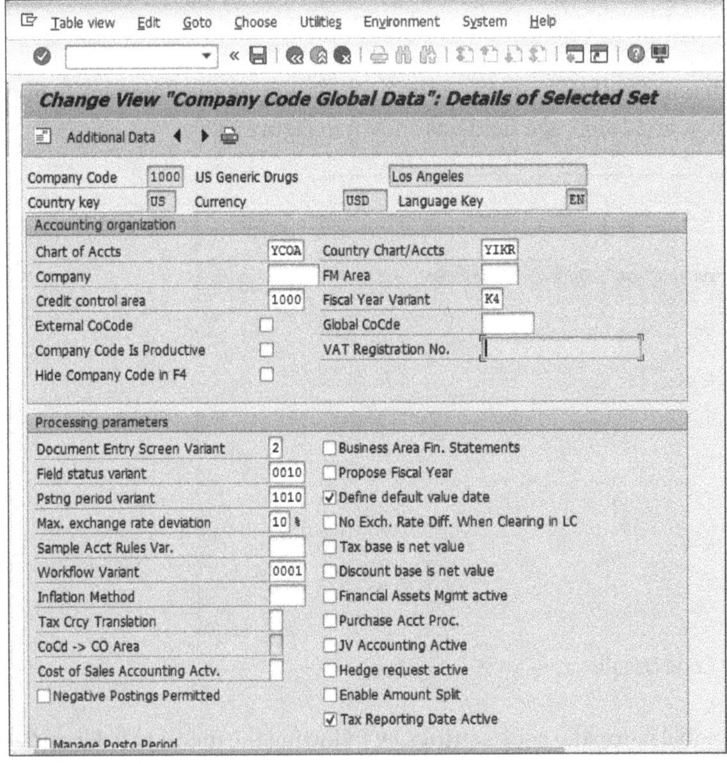

Figure 3.14 Company Code Global Settings

On this screen, some of the important fields that must be configured include the following:

- **Chart of Accts**
  The chart of accounts defines the general ledger accounts used and is maintained at a central level (valid for all company codes) and a company code level. We'll examine the chart of accounts in detail in Chapter 4. In this field, you can configure the chart of accounts to be used by the company code.
- **Company**
  In this field, you can enter the company to which the company code is assigned. The company represents the parent legal entity for the company code.
- **Credit Control Area**
  This field is used to perform credit management for the company code. With this control area, the available credit limits for customers of the company code are managed.
- **Fiscal Year Variant**
  This field is the fiscal year variant used for this company code. The fiscal year variant determines the periods and calendar assignments used to post documents in financial accounting. For example, standard SAP fiscal year variant K4 matches the calendar periods: Period 01 corresponds to January, period 02 to February, and so on. However, you can use other fiscal year variants, such as the 4-4-5 calendar popular in the United States, in which each quarter consists of three periods, consisting of 4 weeks, 4 weeks, and 5 weeks.
- **Pstng period Variant (posting period variant)**
  The posting period variant in SAP determines which periods are open and closed for postings. This variant provides separate options to open and close periods for various types of accounts (general ledger, customer, vendor, assets, and so on). In this field, specify the posting variant used for the company code.
- **Field Status Variant**
  The field status variant determines which fields are required, optional, and suppressed when posting financial documents.

3.2.3 Controlling Area

A *controlling area* is the main organizational unit in the controlling area and structures the organization from a cost point of view. A controlling area can include one or more company codes and defines which components of controlling are active. In SAP S/4HANA, financial accounting and controlling are integrated, but the controlling area is still the core configuration object, which determines the global controlling settings.

To create a controlling area, follow the menu path **Enterprise Structure • Definition • Controlling • Maintain Controlling Area**. Then, select the **Copy, Delete, Check Controlling Area** activity. As with company codes, we highly recommend copying an existing controlling area to copy all the important settings that are linked to it. Copying a controlling area is similar to copying a company code. The configuration settings that go along with the controlling area are copied, and then you can adapt these setting in subsequent steps.

First, select the **Maintain Controlling Area** activity from the list of activities shown in Figure 3.15.

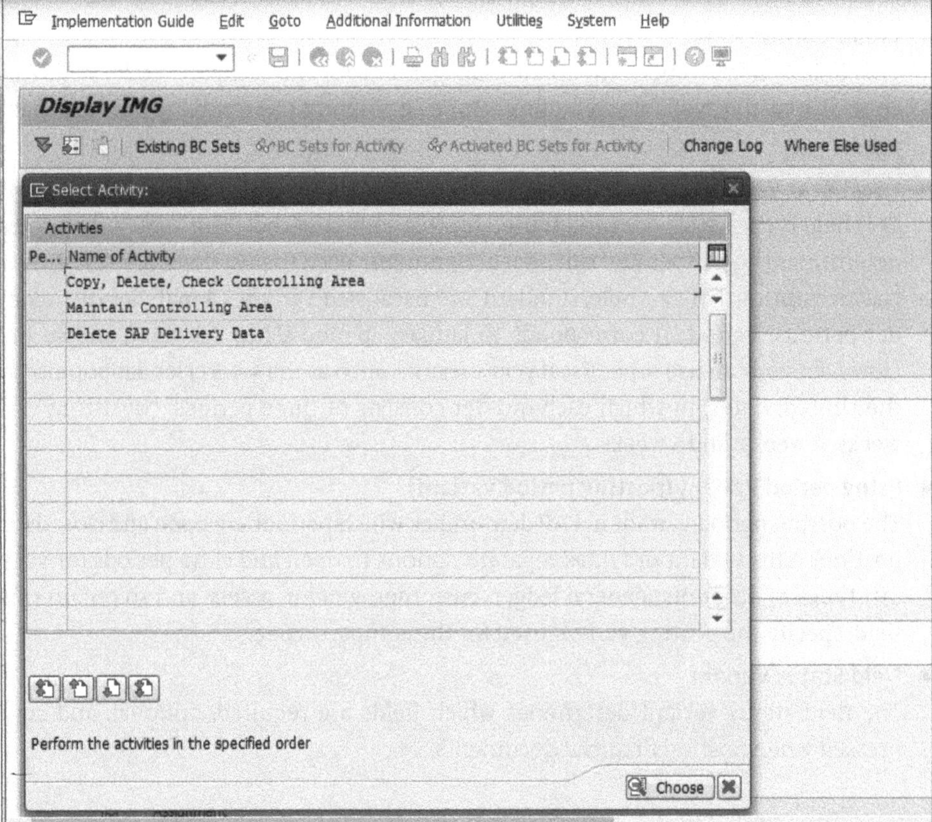

Figure 3.15 Controlling Area Activities

From the list shown in Figure 3.16, we'll use controlling area **US01** to explore the relevant settings. Double-click on **US01** to open the screen shown in Figure 3.17.

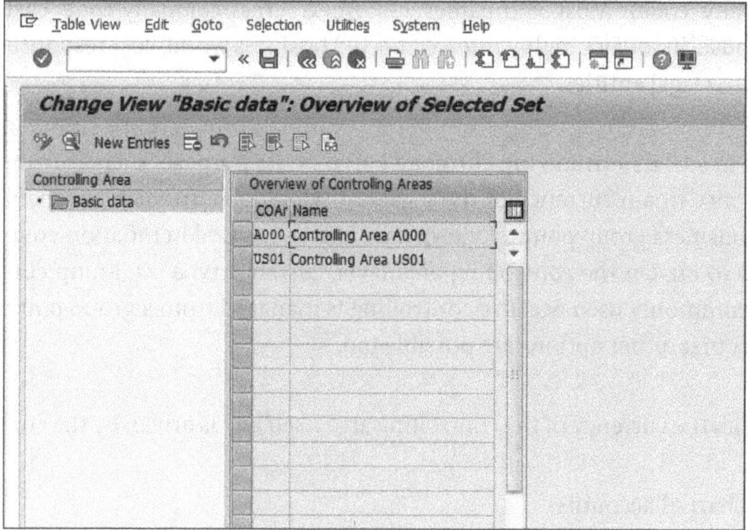

Figure 3.16 Selecting a Controlling Area

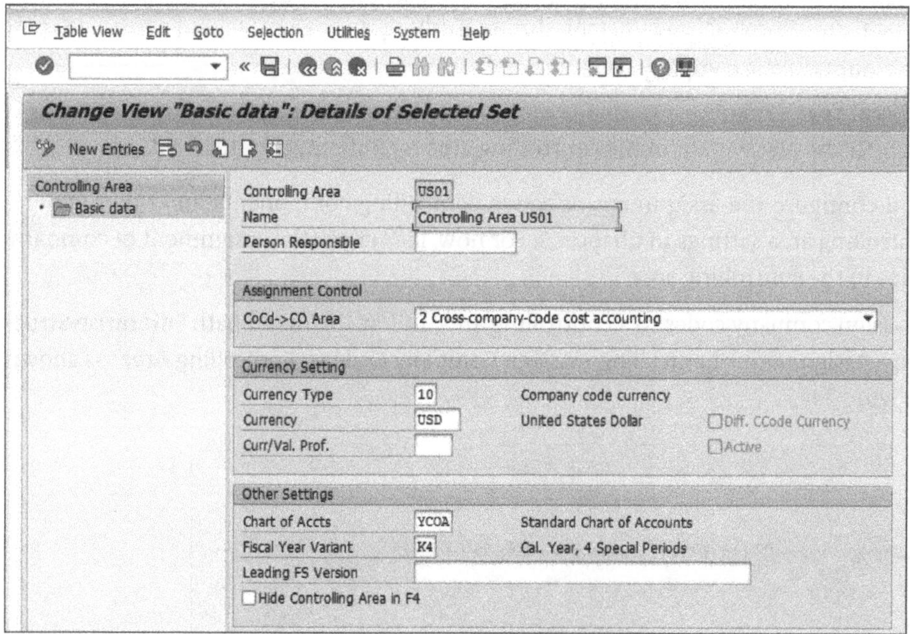

Figure 3.17 Controlling Area Settings

On this screen, some of the important fields that must configured include the following:

- **CoCd->Co Area (company code to controlling area)**
  This field controls whether multiple company codes are managed for this controlling area (cross-company-code cost accounting) or just one (controlling area

same as company code). Most companies choose **2: Cross-company-code cost accounting** because, in today's highly interconnected business world, cost responsibilities span across legal entities.

- **Currency Type**
  Currency types in SAP determine the currency based on its purpose, such as company code currency (main currency of the legal entity), group currency (the main currency from business group point of view), hard currency (used in inflation environments), and so on. On the controlling area level, currency type 30 (group currency) is most commonly used because controlling is managed from a group point of view, but of course, other options are possible too.
- **Currency**
  This field specifies the currency of the controlling area itself and is driven by the currency type.
- **Chart of Accts (chart of accounts)**
  The chart of accounts defines the general ledger accounts used by this controlling area and is maintained at a central level (valid for all company codes) and at a company code level. We'll examine the chart of accounts in detail in Chapter 4. In this field, the chart of accounts of the controlling area should match the chart of accounts of the company code.
- **Fiscal Year Variant**
  The fiscal year variant of the controlling area is configured in this field.

We'll configure the assignment of active controlling components and other general controlling area settings in Chapter 9. For now, let's check the assignment of company codes to the controlling area.

To assign company codes to a controlling area, follow the menu path **Enterprise Structure • Assignment • Controlling • Assign Company Code to Controlling Area**, as shown in Figure 3.18.

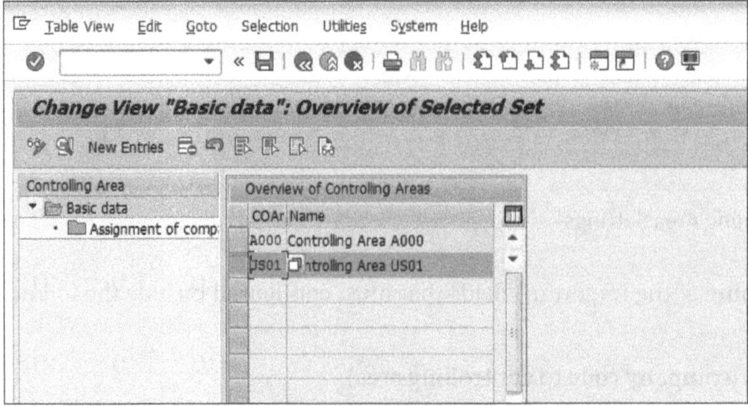

Figure 3.18 Assignment of Controlling Area and Company Codes

On this screen, select the controlling area and then click **Assignment of company code(s)** in the left pane of the configuration screen, which shows the company codes assigned to the controlling area, as shown in Figure 3.19.

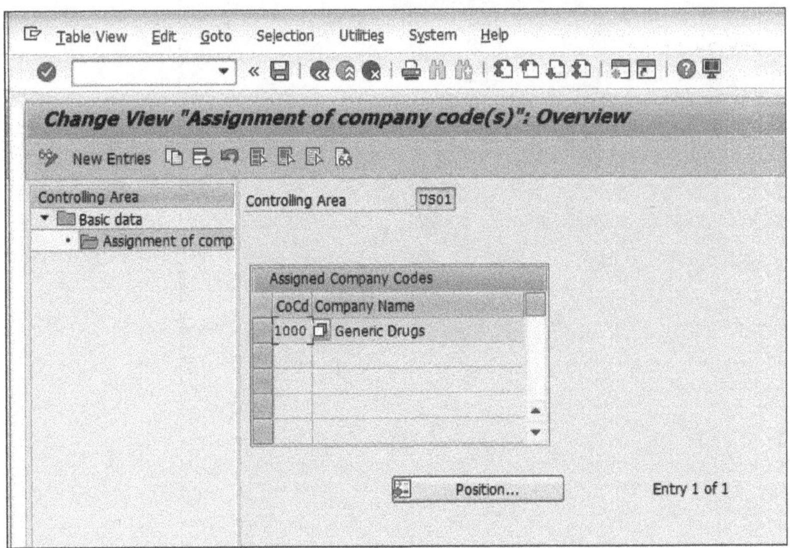

Figure 3.19 Assigning the Company Code to Controlling Area 1000

3.2.4 Operating Concern

An *operating concern* is the main organizational unit from a profitability analysis point of view. Profitability analysis is part of controlling, which analyzes the costs against the revenues per various market characteristics and therefore provides invaluable profitability analysis on various levels of the organization.

In the organizational structure, you can simply define the operating concern as an organizational object and assign it to controlling area. Follow the menu path **Enterprise Structure • Definition • Controlling • Create Operating Concern**, which takes you to a table listing existing operating concerns, as shown in Figure 3.20.

As with company codes and operating concerns, SAP has provided sample organizational objects that you can use as references. Select one of these objects by selecting the checkbox to its left and then selecting **Copy As...** from the top menu. Create a new operating concern (US01) in this way and call it "US Operating Concern," as shown in Figure 3.21.

The next step for the operating concern is to define its data structure before the operating concern can be assigned to a controlling area, which we'll cover in Chapter 13.

Now that you've defined the main organizational structures, let's discuss the main general settings that must be configured in the system, starting with ledgers.

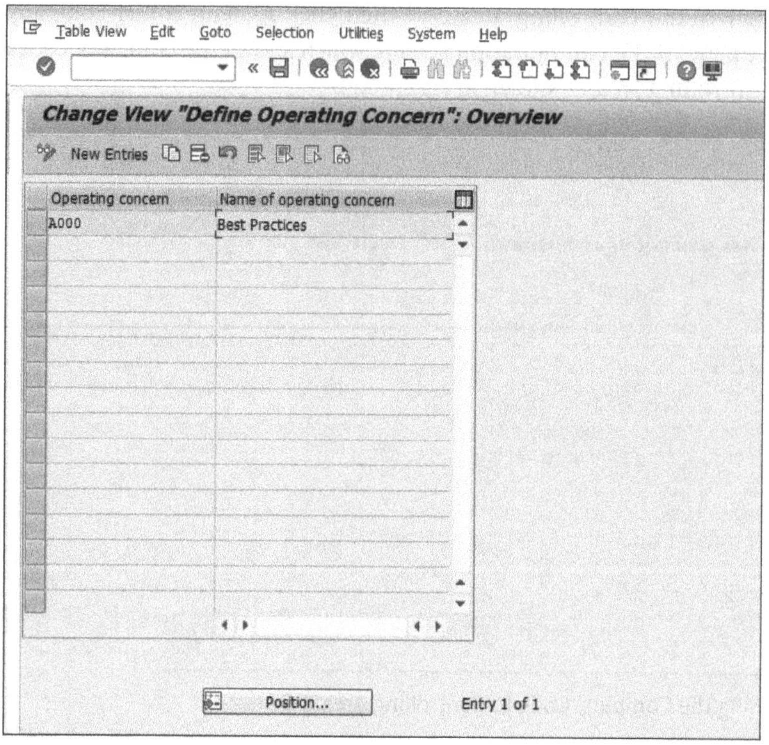

Change View "Define Operating Concern": Overview

New Entries

Operating concern	Name of operating concern
A000	Best Practices

Position... Entry 1 of 1

Figure 3.20 Defining the Operating Concern

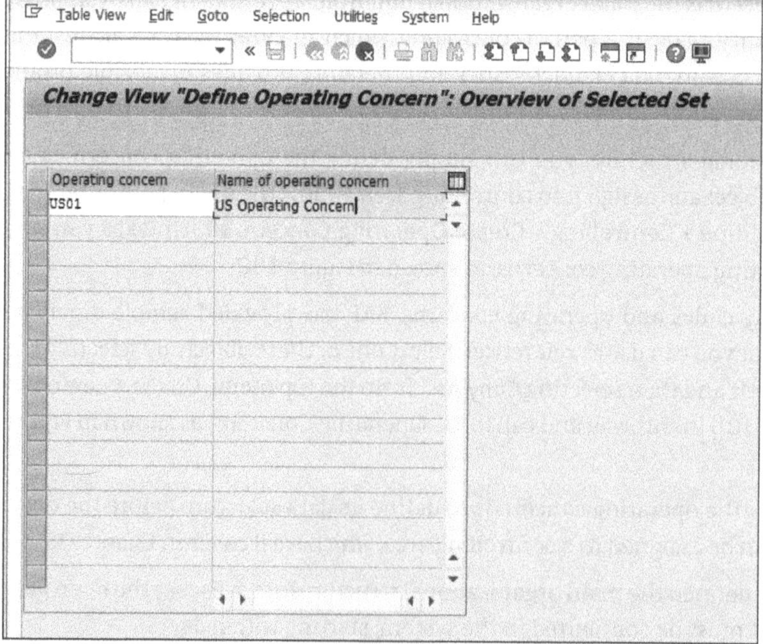

Figure 3.21 Copied Operating Concern

3

3.3 Ledgers

Ledgers are an area in the general ledger application that stores accounting documents based on different accounting principles. At a minimum, you're required to have a leading ledger, which always is called 0L and which represents the main accounting principle from a group point of view. Then, you can set up as many nonleading ledgers as required, to represent, for example, local accounting principles, local taxation rules, and so on.

In the old days, you would use a separate financial module called Special Purpose Ledger, which followed this concept of separate ledgers to store postings and data related to different accounting principles or purposes. For example, different special purpose ledgers were used to handle profit center accounting, consolidation, and funds management.

With SAP S/4HANA, nonleading ledgers are fully integrated and post in real time across all applications. So, let's examine how you can configure ledgers in SAP S/4HANA.

Most importantly, you must define which ledgers are required in your organization from the beginning; subsequent introductions of ledgers can be complicated and will require additional effort. The accounting and taxation reporting requirements must be discussed in detail with the business. The leading ledger should represent the main accounting framework used by the group.

For most companies in Europe and other regions, that main accounting framework would be International Financial Reporting Standards (IFRS)—but in the United States, the main accounting rules are based on US Generally Accepted Accounting Principles (US GAAP). So, most big US companies opt for US GAAP for the leading ledger, then many of them have IFRS in a nonleading ledger. In addition, a wise approach is to set up nonleading ledgers that represent local US GAAP and local tax rules for companies with significant international footprints. Companies that will roll out to various markets would undoubtedly find that, at least in some countries, these ledgers will be required, so we recommend setting them up from the beginning and activating them only for the countries where they're needed. Some countries are known to have complex local tax requirements, such as Russia and Brazil, among others, and for them, local tax ledgers are a must.

Now, let's delve into the configuration for ledgers. Follow the menu path **Financial Accounting • Financial Accounting Global Settings • Ledgers • Ledger • Define Settings for Ledgers and Currency Types**, which shows a list of ledgers already in the system, as shown in Figure 3.22.

On this screen, you can define new ledgers by selecting either **New Entries** or **Copy As...** from the top menu. In our example, we've set up our leading ledger, which is always called 0L, to represent US GAAP valuation, and we've created two nonleading ledgers: Z1 to represent local GAAP and Z2 to represent local tax. The checkmark in the **Leading** column indicates that 0L is the leading ledger; only one ledger can be marked as leading. The **Ldgr Type** (ledger type) column determines whether the ledger is standard or an extension. Most ledgers are defined as standard. An *extension ledger* extends a standard ledger and contains the postings of its linked standard ledger. This kind of ledger is used to make additional manual entries, such as adjustments needed for a specific accounting principle.

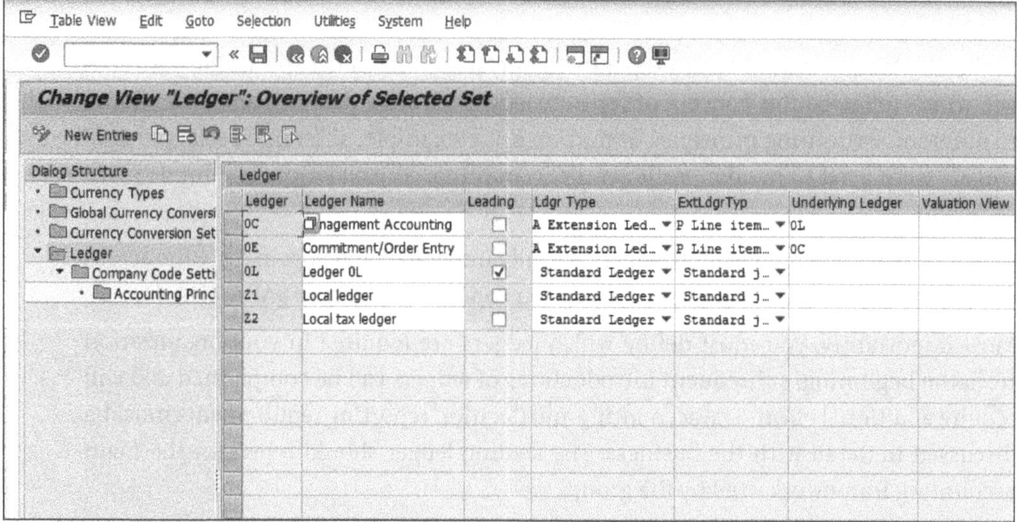

Figure 3.22 Defining Ledgers

Now, you should make the company code and currency settings for each ledger. Select each ledger individually and click the **Company Code Settings for the Ledger** option on the left side of the screen. Then, using the **New Entries** command from the top menu, you can add the required company codes. Figure 3.23 shows the following important settings:

- **Fiscal Year Variant**
  This setting specifies the fiscal year variant used for this ledger. Different ledgers can have different fiscal year variants, which is normal; different valuation principles may require different fiscal years. For example, the 4-4-5 calendar variant used often in the United States doesn't correspond with the calendar year, which is used most often throughout the world.
- **Pstng. period Variant (posting period variant)**
  The posting period variant in SAP determines which periods are open and closed for postings. This variant provides separate options to open and close periods for various types of accounts (general ledger, customer, vendor, assets, and so on). Here on the ledger level, you can specify a variant.

- **Accounting Principle**
  The accounting principle assigned to the ledger.
- **Parallel Accounting Using Additional G/L Accounts**
  This checkbox indicates that, for this ledger, parallel general ledger accounts will be used instead of different ledgers to portray parallel accounting principles. This option is rarely used, generally when one ledger needs to portray parallel accounting principles.
- **Local Currency**
  In this field, you'll specify the currency type of the local currency of the ledger. The local currency is the main currency of the company, is stored in each posting, and is maintained at the company code level. However, you can also have different local currencies for each ledger.
- **Global Currency**
  In this field, you'll specify the currency type of the global currency of the ledger. The global currency is the group currency of the company and is stored in parallel to the local currency for each posting.
- **CO Object Currency (controlling object currency)**
  In this field, you'll specify the currency type of the controlling object currency of the ledger. This currency is used in the controlling objects master and may differ from the transaction currency.

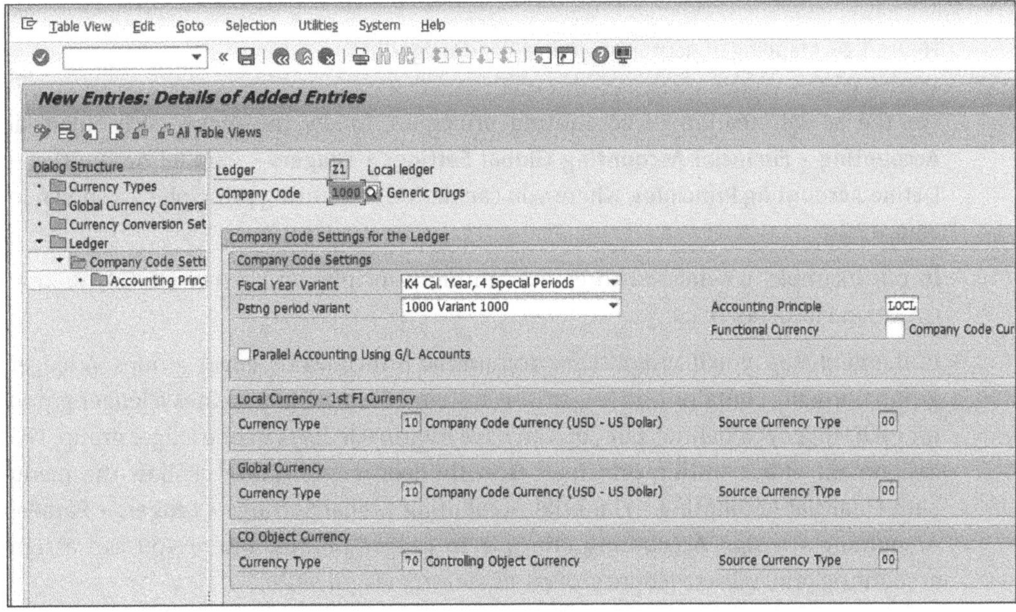

Figure 3.23 Ledger Company Code and Currency Settings

The next step is to define the accounting principles for the ledgers. The accounting principle is a new configuration object in SAP S/4HANA (the ACC_PRINCIPLE field). This object maps the ledger with the relevant accounting framework that it needs to portray. To view the accounting principle for the ledger, click the **Accounting Principles for Ledger and Company Code** activity on the left side of the same configuration screen.

As shown in Figure 3.24, accounting principle LOCL, which represents local accounting standards, has been mapped to ledger Z1.

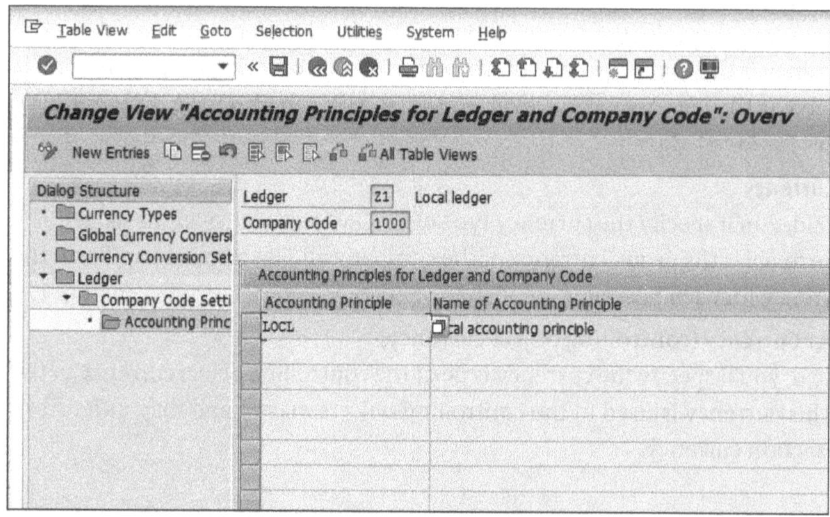

Figure 3.24 Mapping of Accounting Principle to Ledger

For the actual creation of accounting principles, follow the menu path **Financial Accounting • Financial Accounting Global Settings • Ledgers • Parallel Accounting • Define Accounting Principles**, where you can define accounting principles, as shown in Figure 3.25.

In our example, we defined three accounting principles to portray US GAAP, local GAAP, and local tax rules.

In the next step, you'll assign these accounting principles to ledger groups. A ledger group normally contains one ledger (the system automatically creates a ledger group for each ledger you define), but you can have multiple ledgers in one ledger group. The assignment of accounting principles is at the ledger group level. Follow the menu path **Financial Accounting • Financial Accounting Global Settings • Ledgers • Parallel Accounting • Assign Accounting Principle to Ledger Groups**, where you can assign accounting principles to ledger groups, as shown in Figure 3.26.

This step is where the link between the ledger and the accounting principle, shown earlier in Figure 3.24, comes from.

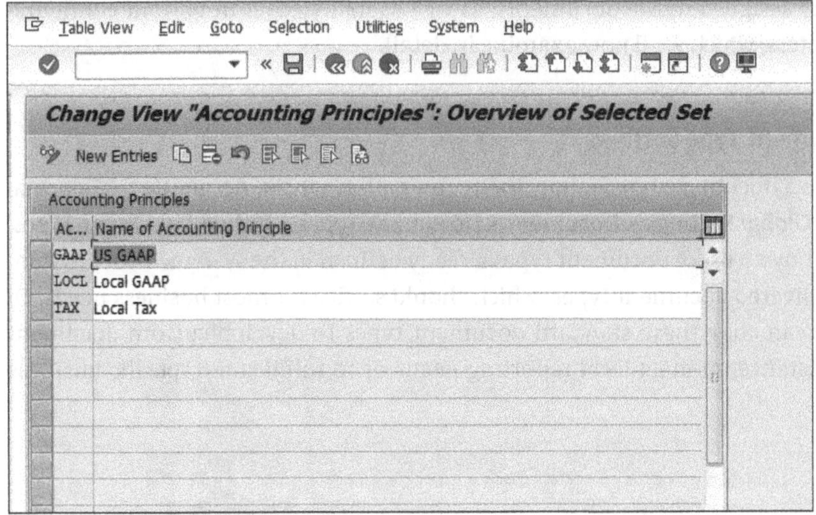

Figure 3.25 Defining Accounting Principles

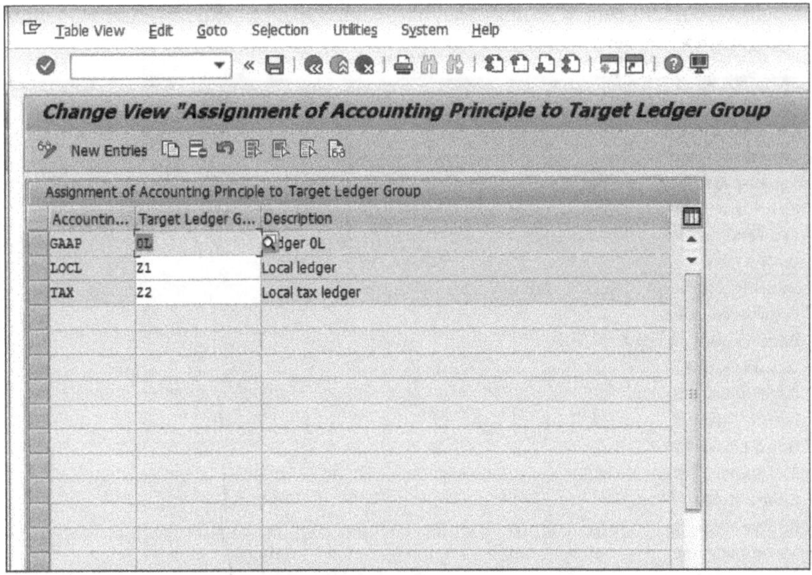

Figure 3.26 Assigning Accounting Principles to Ledger Groups

3.4 Document Types

Document types in SAP serve to classify the various transactions posted in financial accounting. Each financial accounting document is assigned a document type, such as vendor invoice, customer invoice, asset posting, and so on. Document types determine the numbers assigned to the documents, as well as many other important configuration parameters, which we'll now examine in detail.

3.4.1 Document Type Settings

To configure a document type, follow the menu path **Financial Accounting • Financial Accounting Global Settings • Document • Document Types • Define Document Types.** Figure 3.27 shows a list of document types already defined in the system. Most are standard SAP-delivered document types, which should suffice for most business needs. Of course, you can copy these standard document types to develop custom document types, for instance, to meet local reporting needs or to fulfill some specific business process.

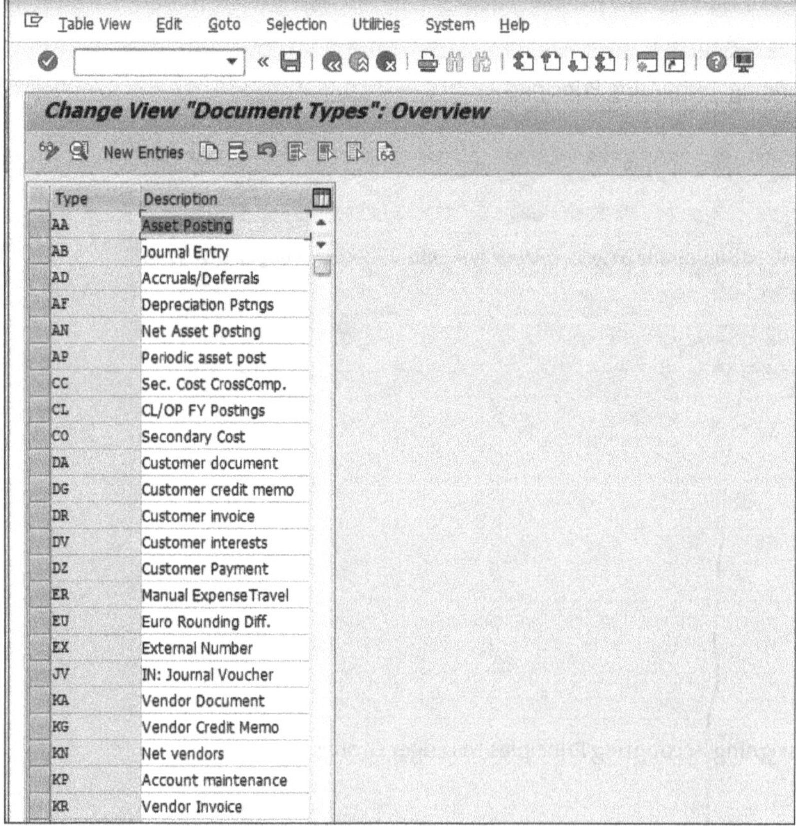

Figure 3.27 Defining Document Types

Double-click document type **KR: Vendor Invoice** to examine the relevant settings, as shown in Figure 3.28.

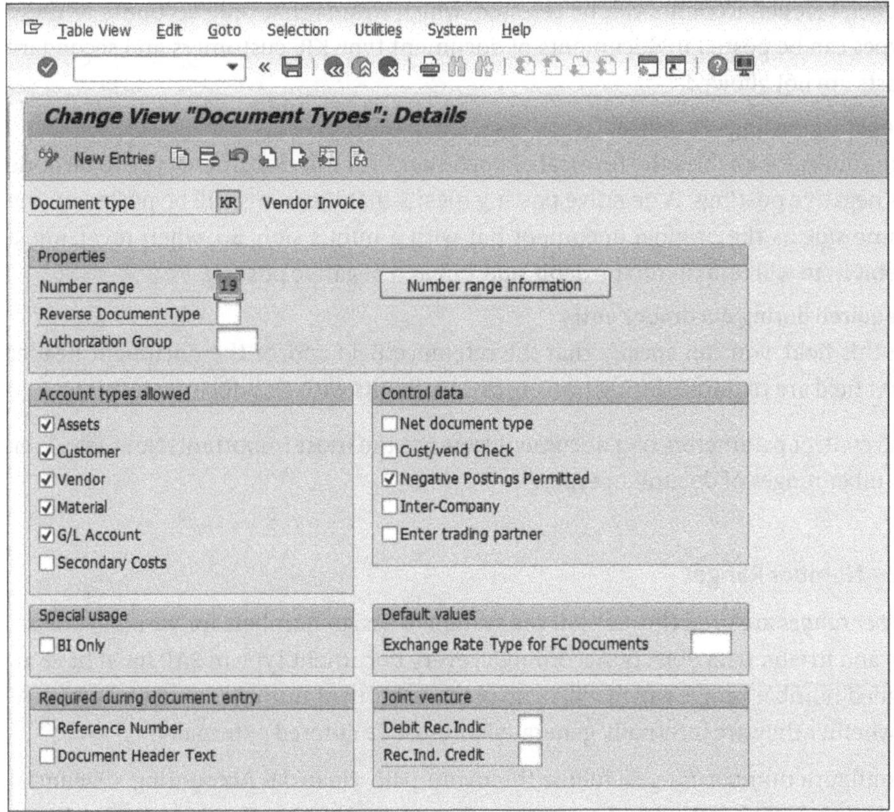

Figure 3.28 Document Type Settings

As shown in Figure 3.28, on this screen, some of the important fields that must configured include the following:

- **Number range**
  The number range determines the document numbers assigned when posting documents for this document type. You'll create the actual number range in the following section; in this field, you'll assign the number range object to the document type.
- **Reverse DocumentType**
  This field specifies the document type that will be used when making reversals of postings with the selected document type. If a value isn't maintained in this field, the reversal will be done with the same document type as the original document.
- **Authorization Group**
  This field allows you to set up an authorization check on this document type level.
- **Account types allowed**
  In this field, you can select what types of accounts are allowed to be posted using this document type. For example, for document type KR, assets, vendors, materials, and

general ledger accounts can be selected, which means that only accounts of these types can be posted in documents of document type KR; customers and secondary costs are not allowed.

- **Negative Postings Permitted**
  This indicator enables the reversal of documents for this document type to be done as negative postings. A negative posting means that the items will be posted on the same side as the original document but with a minus sign. So, when reversing, a debit item will remain on the debit side, but as a negative posting.
- **Required during document entry**
  In this field, you can specify that the reference field and/or the document header text field are required during posting of documents with this document type.

These control parameters of a document type are the most important. Now, let's look at number ranges of document types.

3.4.2 Number Ranges

Number ranges are used throughout the system to assign numbers for various transactions and master data objects. Accordingly, every document type in SAP must have an assigned number range, which will control the document numbers assigned and control whether they are internally generated or must be entered externally.

To configure number ranges, follow the menu path **Financial Accounting • Financial Accounting Global Settings • Document • Document Number Ranges • Define Document Number Ranges.** Enter "1000" in the **Company Code** field and click the Intervals button to modify the number ranges for the company code, as shown in Figure 3.29.

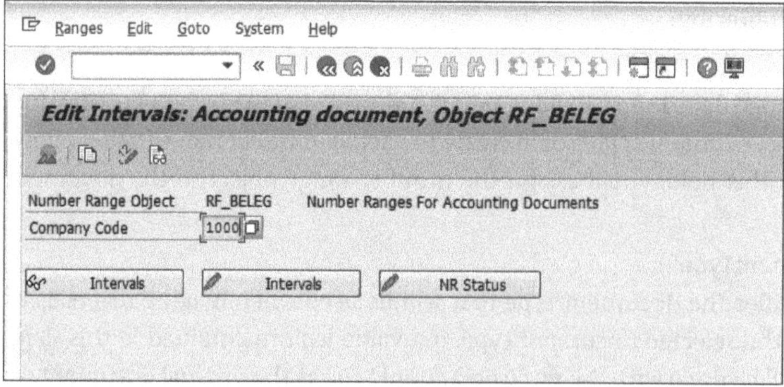

Figure 3.29 Defining Number Ranges

The number ranges for your new company code 1000 were copied along with other parameters when you created the company code. The ranges are shown in Figure 3.30.

Interval Edit Goto System Help

Edit Intervals: Accounting document, Object RF_BELEG, Subobject 1000

Number Range No.	Year	From No.	To Number	NR Status	External
00	9999	0090000000	0099999999	0	☑
01	9999	0100000000	0199999999	0	☐
02	9999	0200000000	0299999999	0	☐
03	9999	0300000000	0399999999	0	☑
04	9999	0400000000	0499999999	0	☐
05	9999	0500000000	0599999999	0	☐
12	9999	1200000000	1299999999	0	☐
13	9999	1300000000	1399999999	0	☐
14	9999	1400000000	1499999999	0	☐
15	9999	1500000000	1599999999	0	☐
16	9999	1600000000	1699999999	0	☐
17	9999	1700000000	1799999999	0	☐
18	9999	1800000000	1899999999	0	☐
19	9999	1900000000	1999999999	0	☐
20	9999	2000000000	2099999999	0	☐
47	9999	4700000000	4799999999	0	☐

Figure 3.30 Number Range Intervals

Each interval is identified with its number in the first column from the left (01, 02, 03, and so on), and this number is the number to be assigned in the document type. Then, you'll see the validity year; a good practice is to set this value to 9999, which means no limitation exists. Next, you'll enter values into the **From No.** and **To Number** fields to define the interval, within which the system will assign the document numbers consecutively (if numbers are to be internally assigned). In the **NR Status** column, you can see the current number (which is 0 in a development system without data). In the last column, **Ext**, a checkmark means that numbers in this interval must be entered manually by the user when entering a document.

Changes to number ranges are not automatically transported because doing so could lead to inconsistencies in the target clients. A good practice is to set the number ranges manually in each client, which should be part of cutover activities during production start.

3.4.3 Document Types for Entry View in a Ledger

Document types that should be posted to nonleading ledgers only should be configured separately. By default, when you post to the leading ledger, the system also posts the same document to all the nonleading ledgers. However, you can make ledger-specific postings, but you must configure the document types for them with their number ranges by following the menu path **Financial Accounting • Financial Accounting Global Settings • Document • Document Types • Define Document Types in a Ledger**.

Enter the nonleading ledger for which you want to maintain document types, as shown in Figure 3.31. The system will not allow you to enter the leading ledger in this popup window.

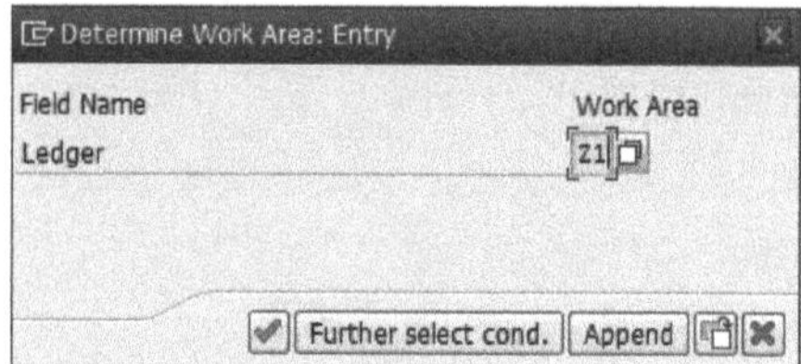

Figure 3.31 Selecting a Ledger

Next, you're presented with the configuration screen shown in Figure 3.32.

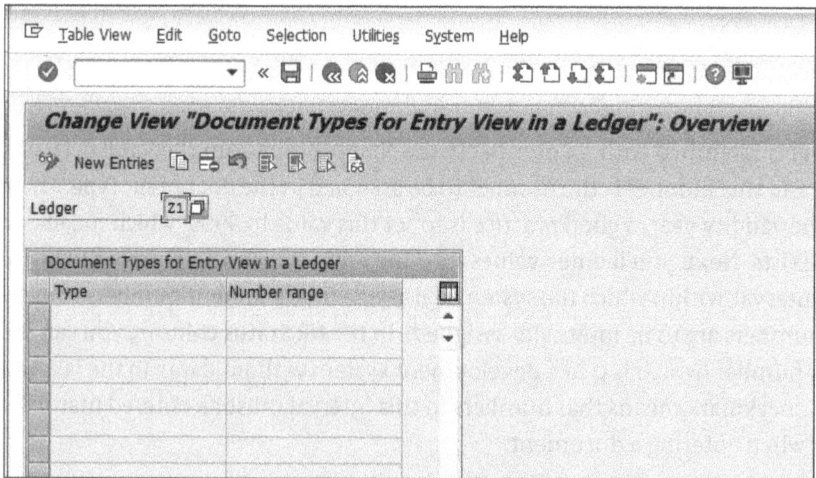

Figure 3.32 Document Types for Entry View in Ledger

On this screen, select **New Entries** from the top menu, then enter the document type in the **Type** field and maintain the **Number range** field, as shown in Figure 3.33, which can be then posted to this nonleading ledger. Save your entries.

Similarly, you can add document types for the entry view in other nonleading ledgers.

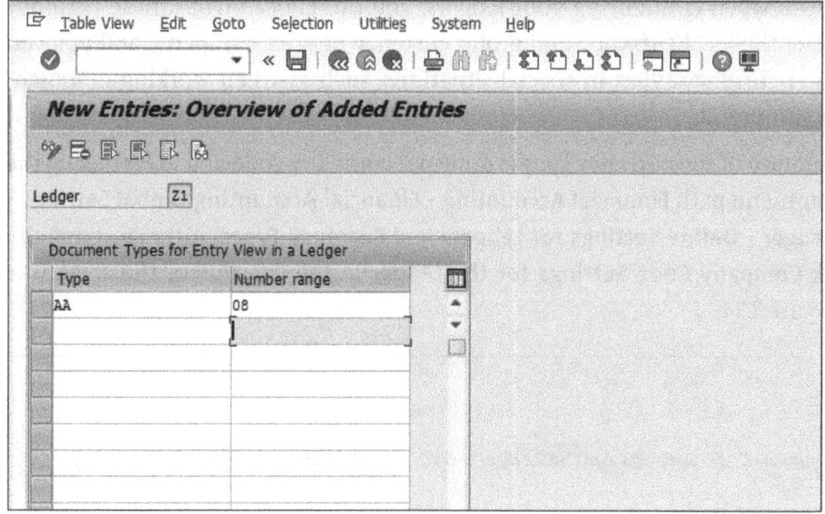

Figure 3.33 Document Type AA for Ledger Z1

3.5 Currencies

SAP provides all the currency codes you'll need. In the system, you must configure which currencies should be used for which purposes. The currency type in SAP defines the purpose of the use for a particular currency, such as local currency or group currency. Then, as transaction currency, you can have any currency for which exchange rates are maintained. This capability enables parallel currency valuation, which is quite important in today's globalized business world. A significant improvement in SAP is that you can have up to 10 parallel currencies per ledger, enabling you to easily monitor balances and line items in all these currencies.

In this section, we'll first discuss currency types before moving on to an exploration of exchange rates.

3.5.1 Currency Types

A *currency type* defines what the purpose of a currency is. The following standard currency types are defined:

- 10: Company code currency
- 30: Group currency
- 40: Hard currency
- 50: Index-based currency
- 60: Global company currency

As you've seen when configuring your ledgers, you can choose from these currency types to select the local currency and group currency of your company, and you can also use other currency types in special situations, such as when working in a high-inflation environment.

The configuration of the currency type is done per company code and ledger using the now-familiar menu path **Financial Accounting • Financial Accounting Global Settings • Ledgers • Ledger • Define Settings for Ledgers and Currency Types**. After selecting the ledger, click **Company Code Settings for the Ledger** in the left side of the screen, as shown in Figure 3.34.

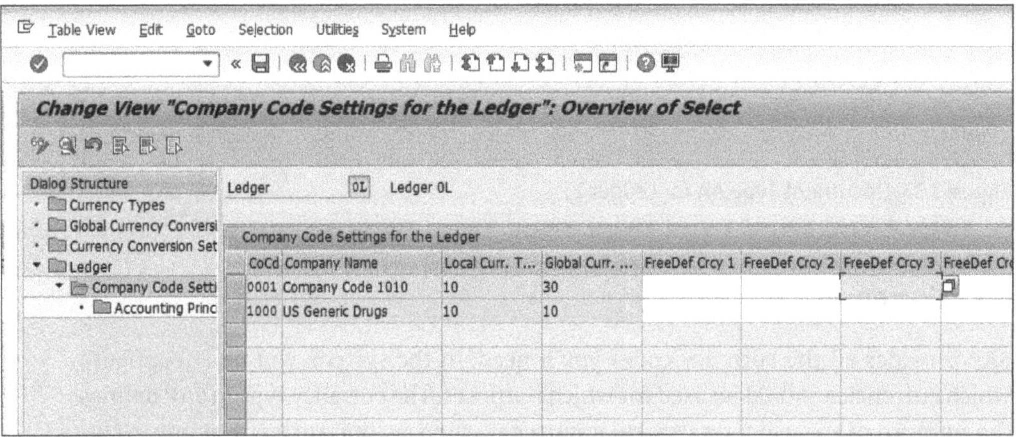

Figure 3.34 Currency Types per Ledger and Company Code

Now, you'll see the settings for the company code for the selected ledger. You can maintain the local and global currency types as well as other free definition currencies. Then, in this ledger and company code, each transaction will be stored also in these currencies.

3.5.2 Exchange Rate Type

Exchange rates in the system must be maintained for the currencies you use. These exchange rates are always maintained for each exchange rate type, which are keys that store exchange rates of particular types. For example, you can enter specific buy, sell, and average exchange rates under different exchange rate types.

As with other important general settings, SAP provides a list of standard exchange rate types, which usually meet most requirements. To review the available exchange rate types, follow the menu path **SAP NetWeaver • General Settings • Currencies • Check Exchange Rate Types**, as shown in Figure 3.35.

You'll see a list of defined exchange rate types for various purposes. In accounting, the most commonly used standard exchange rate is type **M**: **Standard translation at average rate.**

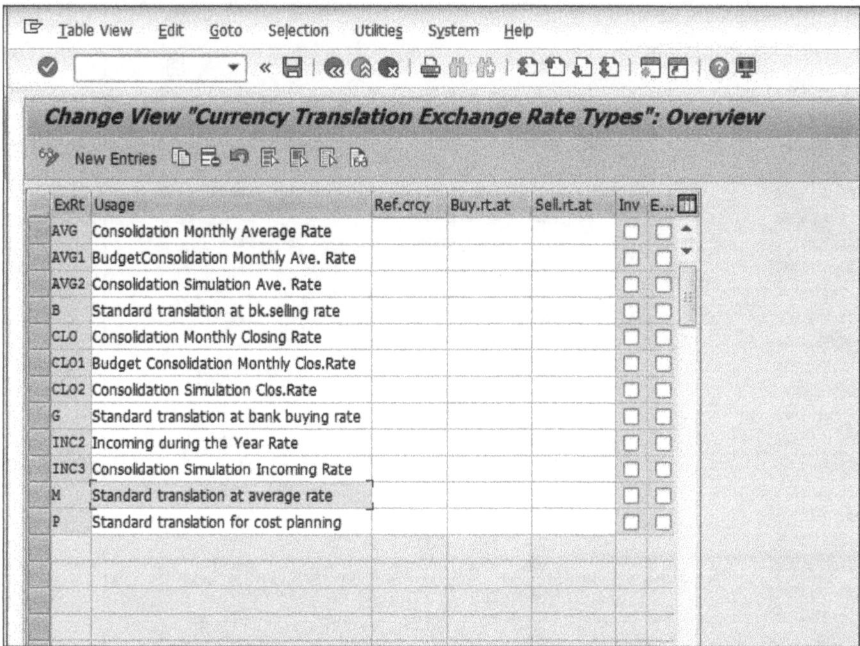

Figure 3.35 Exchange Rate Types

3.5.3 Exchange Rates

Now, let's maintain exchange rates between the currencies we're using. Maintaining exchange rates during when the system is in production use is normally a user task, and many companies also establish an interface to automatically upload exchange rates from a feed from a central bank or other financial institution.

To enter exchange rates, follow the menu path **SAP NetWeaver • General Settings • Currencies • Enter Exchange Rates**, as shown in Figure 3.36.

On this screen, for each exchange rate type (in our example, M), you'll maintain the exchange rates between the currencies specified in the **From** and **To** fields, using either direct or indirect quotation. In the direct quotation method, the exchange rate provides the price in the **To** currency that you must pay for a unit of the **From** currency. In the indirect method, the rate is reversed. The **Valid From** date determines the date from which the entered exchange rate is valid, and exchange rates remain valid until a rate with a subsequent date is maintained.

You can maintain as many exchange rates as required and then save your entries.

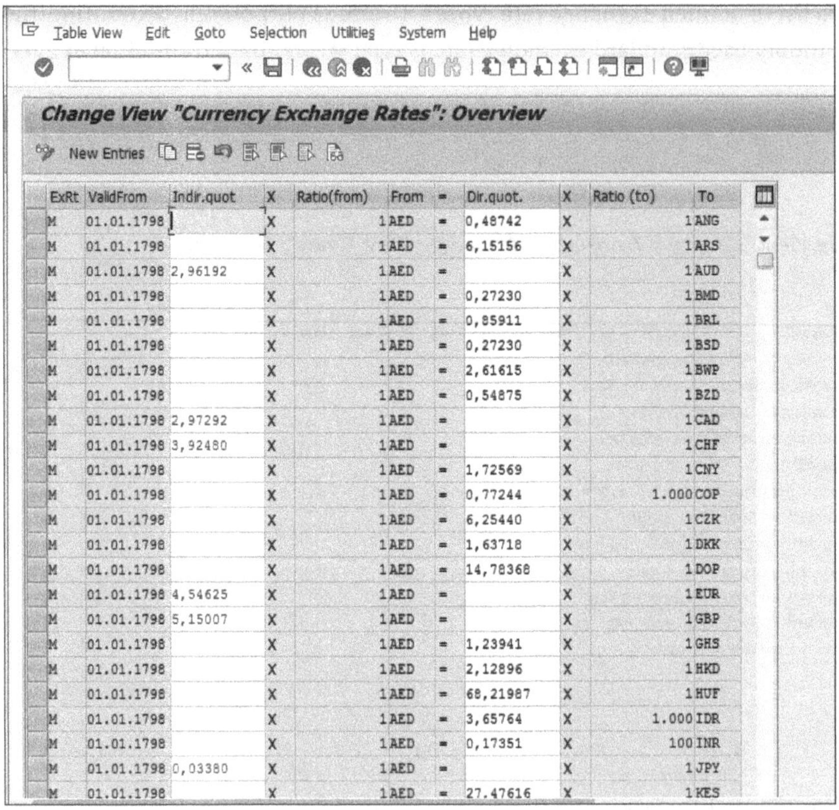

Table View Edit Goto Selection Utilities System Help

Change View "Currency Exchange Rates": Overview

New Entries

ExRt	ValidFrom	Indir.quot	X	Ratio(from)	From	=	Dir.quot.	X	Ratio (to)	To
M	01.01.1798		X	1	AED	=	0,48742	X	1	ANG
M	01.01.1798		X	1	AED	=	6,15156	X	1	ARS
M	01.01.1798	2,96192	X	1	AED	=		X	1	AUD
M	01.01.1798		X	1	AED	=	0,27230	X	1	BMD
M	01.01.1798		X	1	AED	=	0,85911	X	1	BRL
M	01.01.1798		X	1	AED	=	0,27230	X	1	BSD
M	01.01.1798		X	1	AED	=	2,61615	X	1	BWP
M	01.01.1798		X	1	AED	=	0,54875	X	1	BZD
M	01.01.1798	2,97292	X	1	AED	=		X	1	CAD
M	01.01.1798	3,92480	X	1	AED	=		X	1	CHF
M	01.01.1798		X	1	AED	=	1,72569	X	1	CNY
M	01.01.1798		X	1	AED	=	0,77244	X	1.000	COP
M	01.01.1798		X	1	AED	=	6,25440	X	1	CZK
M	01.01.1798		X	1	AED	=	1,63718	X	1	DKK
M	01.01.1798		X	1	AED	=	14,78368	X	1	DOP
M	01.01.1798	4,54625	X	1	AED	=		X	1	EUR
M	01.01.1798	5,15007	X	1	AED	=		X	1	GBP
M	01.01.1798		X	1	AED	=	1,23941	X	1	GHS
M	01.01.1798		X	1	AED	=	2,12896	X	1	HKD
M	01.01.1798		X	1	AED	=	68,21987	X	1	HUF
M	01.01.1798		X	1	AED	=	3,65764	X	1.000	IDR
M	01.01.1798		X	1	AED	=	0,17351	X	100	INR
M	01.01.1798	0,03380	X	1	AED	=		X	1	JPY
M	01.01.1798		X	1	AED	=	27.47616	X	1	KES

Figure 3.36 Maintaining Exchange Rates

3.6 Taxes

Taxes are a major topic in SAP. Most selling and purchasing transactions are affected by taxes, and quite stringent requirements for tax reporting exist around the world. Therefore, the tax setup in your SAP S/4HANA system thus must reflect the tax requirements from both process and reporting points of view.

As part of financial accounting global settings, you must set up the tax procedure and assign tax procedures to your company codes. Then, you must set up the relevant tax codes that this procedure uses. The tax determination process will be discussed in detail in Chapter 5 for purchasing processes and also in Chapter 6 for sales processes.

3.6.1 Tax Procedure

A *tax procedure* contains the settings for performing tax calculations in SAP S/4HANA. This complex configuration object uses access sequences and condition techniques to determine the proper tax codes, which in turn determine the tax rates, general ledger accounts to be posted to, and other relevant settings.

The tax procedure is maintained at the country level, which makes the tax procedure valid for all company codes for a given country. SAP supplies sample tax procedures for each country. You should copy these samples to create new tax procedures by modifying them or, if no changes are envisioned, you can use the standard procedures.

Check the settings for standard tax procedures for the United States by following the menu path **Financial Accounting • Financial Accounting Global Settings • Tax on Sales/Purchases • Basic Settings • Check Calculation Procedure.** You'll find the following three activities related to setting up the calculation procedure, as shown in Figure 3.37:

- **Access Sequences**
- **Define Condition Types**
- **Define Procedures**

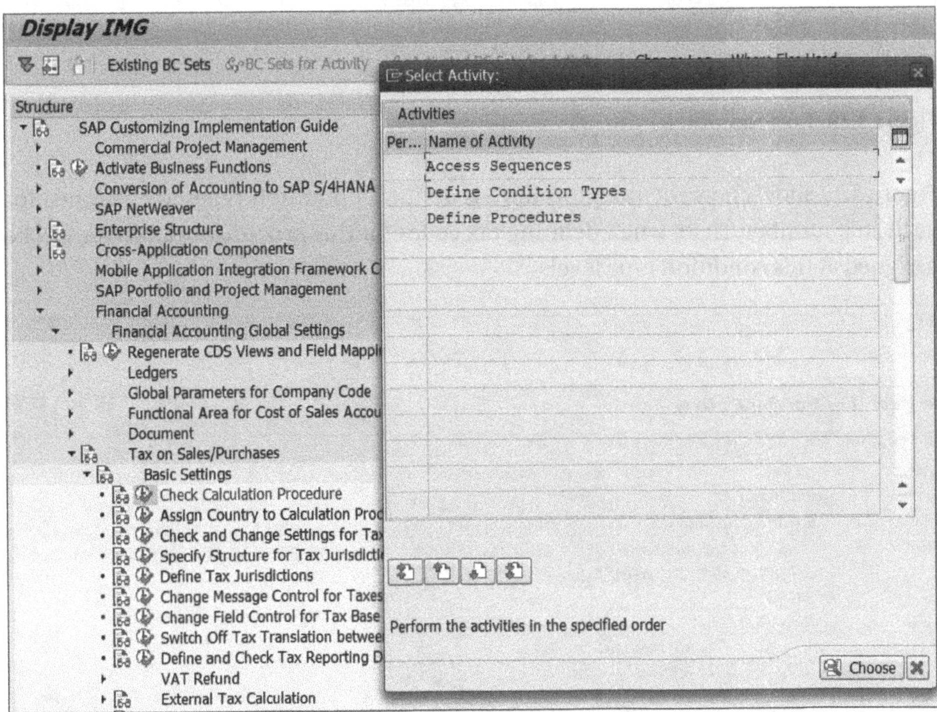

Figure 3.37 Tax Procedure Configuration Activities

A tax procedure is a collection of condition types, which in turn use access sequences to determine tax records based on specific fields, as defined in those access sequences.

Double-click the **Define Procedures** activity to examine the tax procedure for the United States. Figure 3.38 shows a list of the tax procedures. Notice tax procedures for the United States **OTXUSX** and **TAXUSJ**, which are based on jurisdiction codes (the tax rates differ by jurisdiction, which are determined with these jurisdiction codes). Procedure **OTXUSX** is designed to use an external calculation of the rates for each jurisdiction from third-party software. Select procedure **TAXUSJ** and click **Control Data** on the left side of the screen.

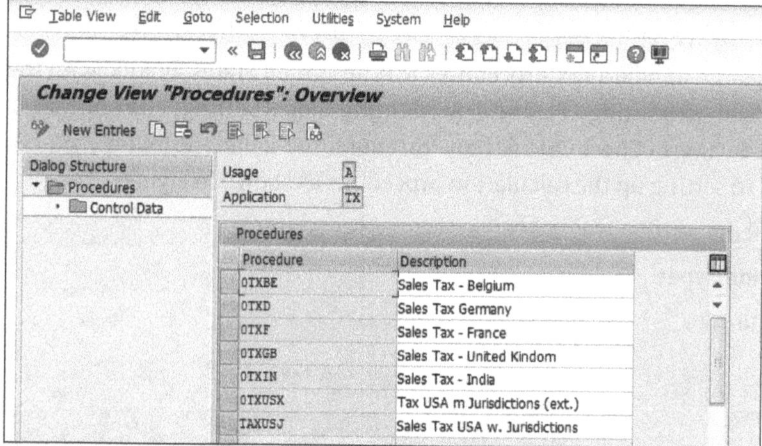

Procedure	Description
OTXBE	Sales Tax - Belgium
OTXD	Sales Tax Germany
OTXF	Sales Tax - France
OTXGB	Sales Tax - United Kindom
OTXIN	Sales Tax - India
OTXUSX	Tax USA m Jurisdictions (ext.)
TAXUSJ	Sales Tax USA w. Jurisdictions

Figure 3.38 Tax Procedures

Figure 3.39 shows how the tax procedure is defined. Condition types are assigned for each step number. Then, when defining tax codes for this procedure, tax codes will be assigned at this condition type level.

Table View Edit Goto Selection Utilities System Help

Change View "Control Data": Overview

New Entries

Dialog Structure
- Procedures
  - Control Data

Procedure TAXUSJ Sales Tax USA w. Jurisdictions

Control Data

Reference Step Overview

Step	Co...	Co...	Description	Fro...	To ...	Ma...	R...	St...	Print T...	Subtotal	Requir...	Alt. Ca...	Alt. Cn...	Accou...
100	0	BASB	Base Amount_babu			☐	☐	☐						
120	0					☐	☐	☑						
200	0			100	110	☐	☐	☑						
210	0	JP1I	A/P Sales Tax 1 Inv.	120		☐	☐	☐						NVV
220	0	JP2I	A/P Sales Tax 2 Inv.	120		☐	☐	☐						NVV
230	0	JP3I	A/P Sales Tax 3 Inv.	120		☐	☐	☐						NVV
240	0	JP4I	A/P Sales Tax 4 Inv.	120		☐	☐	☐						NVV
300	0					☐	☐	☑						
310	0	JP1E	A/P Sales Tax 1 Exp.	120		☐	☐	☐						VS1
320	0	JP2E	A/P Sales Tax 2 Exp.	120		☐	☐	☐						VS2
330	0	JP3E	A/P Sales Tax 3 Exp.	120		☐	☐	☐						VS3
340	0	JP4E	A/P Sales Tax 4 Exp.	120		☐	☐	☐						VS4
400	0					☐	☐	☑						
410	0	JP1U	A/P Sales Tax 1 Use	210		☐	☐	☐						MW1
420	0	JP2U	A/P Sales Tax 2 Use	220		☐	☐	☐						MW2
430	0	JP3U	A/P Sales Tax 3 Use	230		☐	☐	☐						MW3
440	0	JP4U	A/P Sales Tax 4 Use	240		☐	☐	☐						MW4
500	0					☐	☐	☑						
510	0	JR1	A/R Sales Tax 1	120		☐	☐	☐						MW1
520	0	JR2	A/R Sales Tax 2	120		☐	☐	☐						MW2

Figure 3.39 Tax Procedure TAXUSJ Definition

Now, go back and select the **Define Condition Types** activity. Figure 3.40 shows a list of condition types, which can be assigned to steps in the tax procedures.

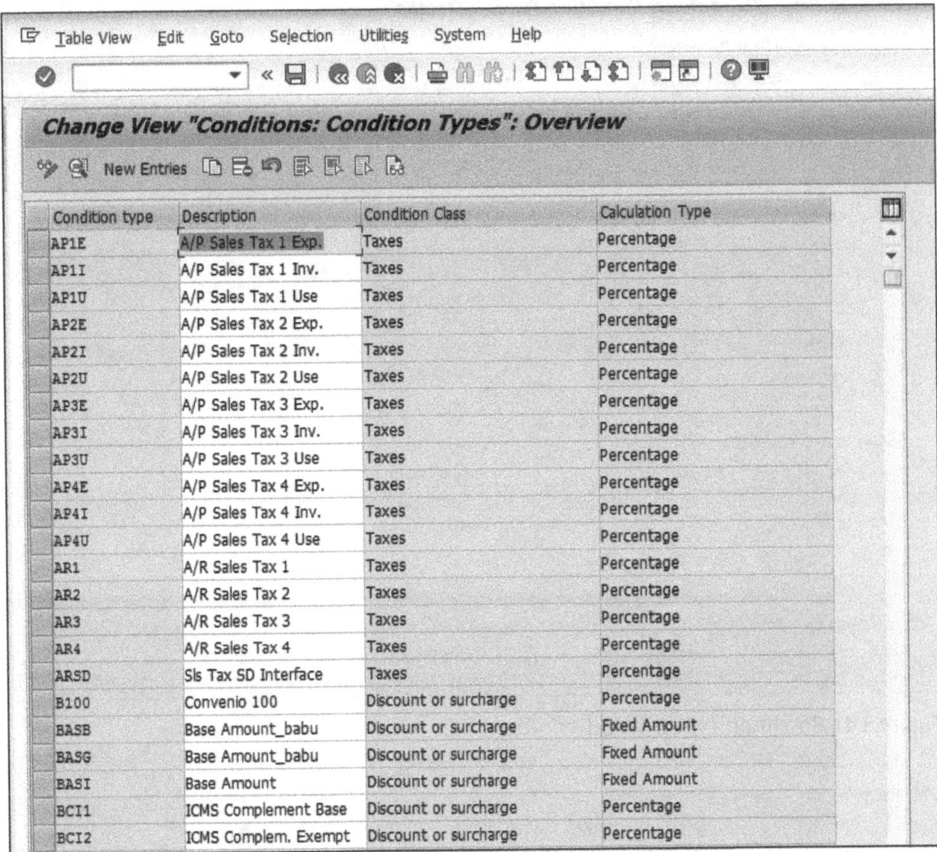

Condition type	Description	Condition Class	Calculation Type
AP1E	A/P Sales Tax 1 Exp.	Taxes	Percentage
AP1I	A/P Sales Tax 1 Inv.	Taxes	Percentage
AP1U	A/P Sales Tax 1 Use	Taxes	Percentage
AP2E	A/P Sales Tax 2 Exp.	Taxes	Percentage
AP2I	A/P Sales Tax 2 Inv.	Taxes	Percentage
AP2U	A/P Sales Tax 2 Use	Taxes	Percentage
AP3E	A/P Sales Tax 3 Exp.	Taxes	Percentage
AP3I	A/P Sales Tax 3 Inv.	Taxes	Percentage
AP3U	A/P Sales Tax 3 Use	Taxes	Percentage
AP4E	A/P Sales Tax 4 Exp.	Taxes	Percentage
AP4I	A/P Sales Tax 4 Inv.	Taxes	Percentage
AP4U	A/P Sales Tax 4 Use	Taxes	Percentage
AR1	A/R Sales Tax 1	Taxes	Percentage
AR2	A/R Sales Tax 2	Taxes	Percentage
AR3	A/R Sales Tax 3	Taxes	Percentage
AR4	A/R Sales Tax 4	Taxes	Percentage
ARSD	Sls Tax SD Interface	Taxes	Percentage
B100	Convenio 100	Discount or surcharge	Percentage
BASB	Base Amount_babu	Discount or surcharge	Fixed Amount
BASG	Base Amount_babu	Discount or surcharge	Fixed Amount
BASI	Base Amount	Discount or surcharge	Fixed Amount
BCI1	ICMS Complement Base	Discount or surcharge	Percentage
BCI2	ICMS Complem. Exempt	Discount or surcharge	Percentage

Figure 3.40 Condition Types

Select and double-click on **MWAS**, which is the output tax condition, to see its settings, as shown in Figure 3.41.

Now, if you click the **Records for Access** button, you can see the condition records, based on the fields defined in access sequence MWST. As shown in Figure 3.42, **Country** and **Tax Code** are the fields that would determine the taxes in this case.

Click the **Execute** button to see the existing records, as shown in Figure 3.43.

Finally, let's check the definition of this access sequence. Go back to the screen shown earlier in Figure 3.33 and select **Access Sequences**. The system issues a message that this table is a cross-client table. In other words, the configuration in this table is fundamental and affects all clients of the SAP system. Such configuration should be maintained only in the golden configuration client, and you must proceed with caution.

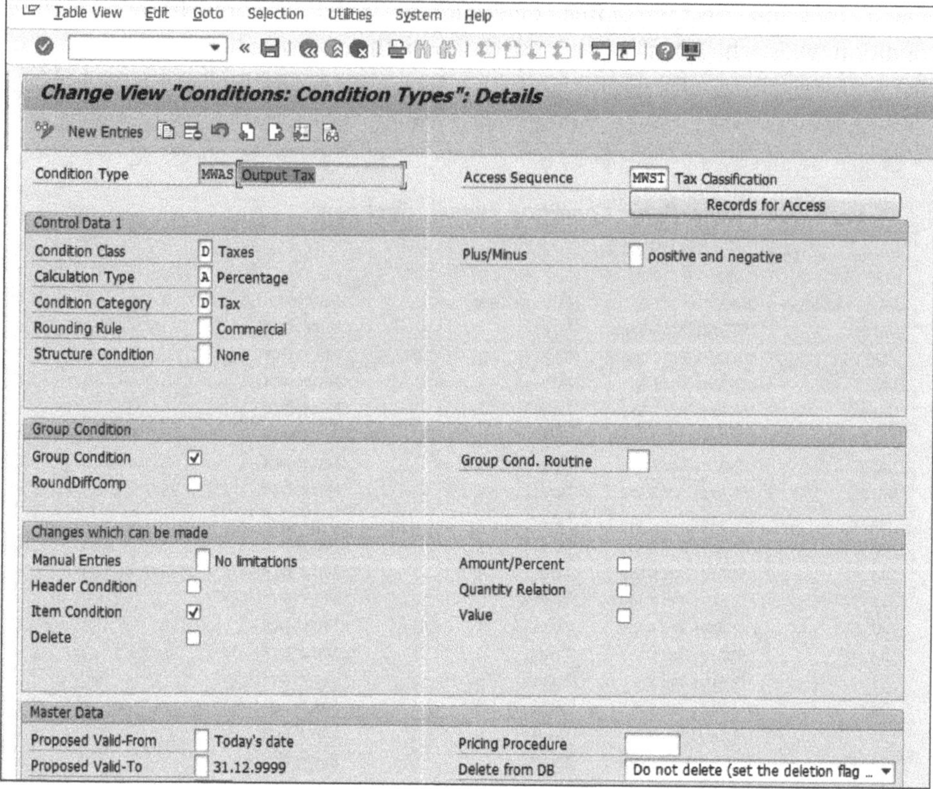

Figure 3.41 Condition Type MWAS Definition

Figure 3.42 Condition Record Fields

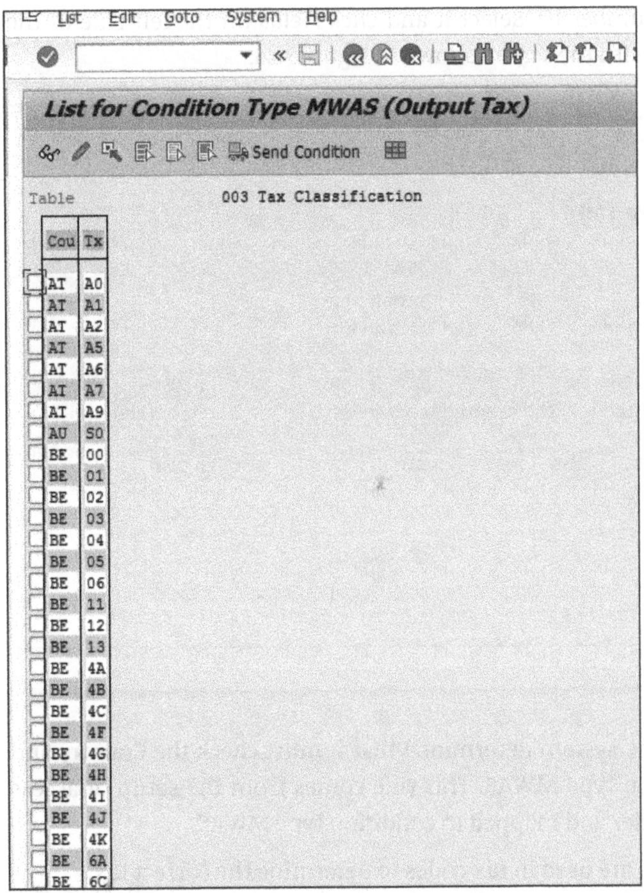

Figure 3.43 Condition Record Values for MWAS

Figure 3.44 shows a list of defined access sequences. Select **MWST** and then click **Accesses** in the left side of the screen. You can have one or more access sequences.

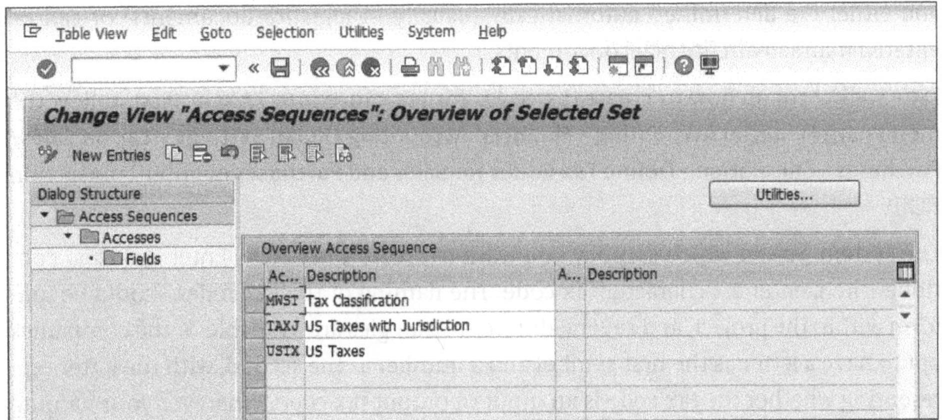

Figure 3.44 Access Sequences

In this case, it's just one, number 10. Select it and click **Fields** on the left side of the screen; you'll be presented with the screen shown in Figure 3.45.

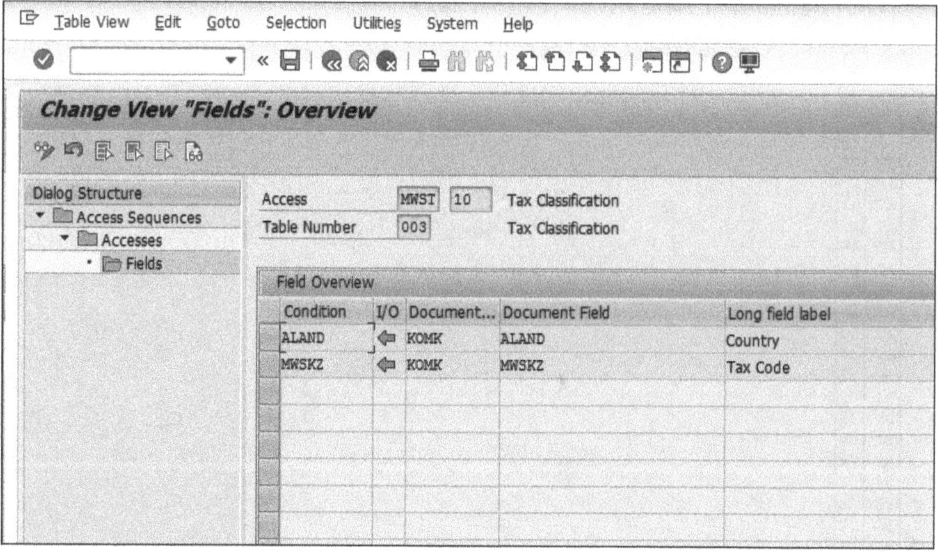

Figure 3.45 Access Fields

The tax procedure is how the system determined that it must check the **Country** and **Tax Code** fields for condition type MWAS. This rule comes from the setup of access sequence MWST, shown earlier and mapped to condition type MWAS.

Let's see how tax procedures are used in tax codes to determine the correct tax.

3.6.2 Tax Codes

Tax codes in SAP determine the tax percentage and tax account posted and are assigned at the line-item level in documents. Tax codes are created per tax procedure, and either are determined automatically (usually in logistics documents) or can be entered manually in financial documents.

Let's walk through how to create tax codes for tax procedure TAXUS. First, follow the menu path **Financial Accounting • Financial Accounting Global Settings • Tax on Sales/ Purchases • Calculation • Define Tax Codes for Sales and Purchases** or enter Transaction FTXP.

The system asks in which country you want to create a tax code. Enter "US" and continue. Then, enter a 2-character tax code. The naming of the tax codes should be uniform within the project, and several different strategies are available. Some companies opt to have a letter as the first symbol and a number as the second, with the letter representing whether the tax code is an input or output tax code. Whatever your naming convention is, you must ensure that enough space exists in the naming ranges to accommodate all the tax codes needed. A country normally uses 30 to 40 tax codes, and sometimes, even more tax codes are required.

In this case, let's name the new tax code "O2" to represent a 10% sales tax, as shown in Figure 3.46. The "O" indicates that this tax code is an output tax code, whereas one of our input tax codes would start with "I." The various tax codes, O1, O2, O3, and so on, will represent output tax codes with different rates or purposes.

Once you enter a tax code number, the system opens the properties screen for the new tax code. On this screen, you must select whether the tax code is an input (for purchasing transactions) or an output (for sales transactions) tax code. Add a description for the tax code and define other optional settings. For example, the **CheckID** indicator ensures that an error message is displayed if the tax amount entered is incorrect. The **EU Code/Code** setting is used for European Union reporting.

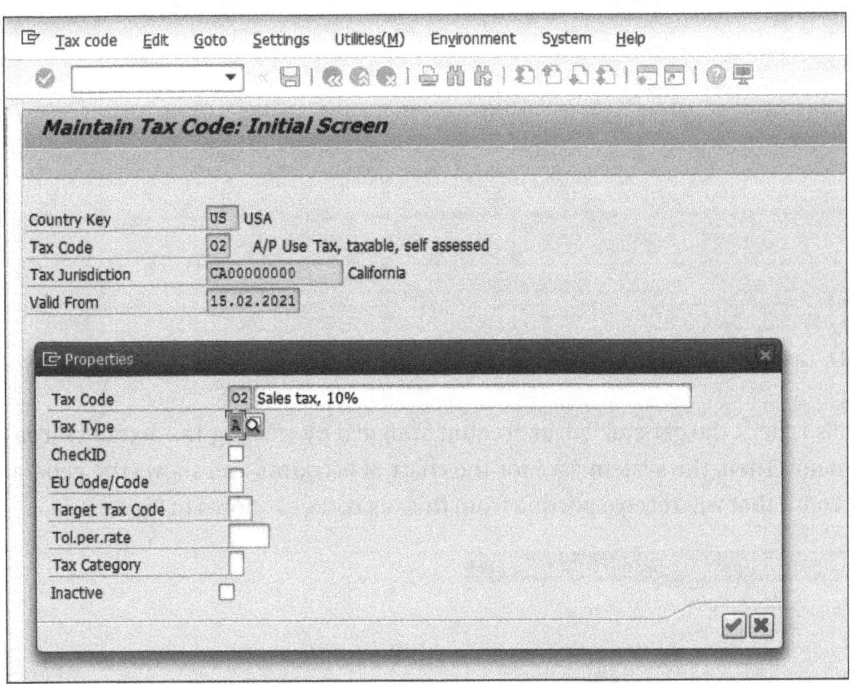

Figure 3.46 Creating a Tax Code

After you click **Continue**, you'll see the main configuration screen for your new tax code. Figure 3.47 shows the condition types available from the tax procedure for which you created the tax code. For the US, we'll use a calculation procedure with jurisdiction codes: Rates are entered for each jurisdiction, in this case, California. The condition types are mapped with account keys (in our example, account key NVV), which determine the general ledger accounts to be posted to. You can enter tax rates in one or more condition type levels. The system will go through all the levels of the tax code when determining the proper taxes.

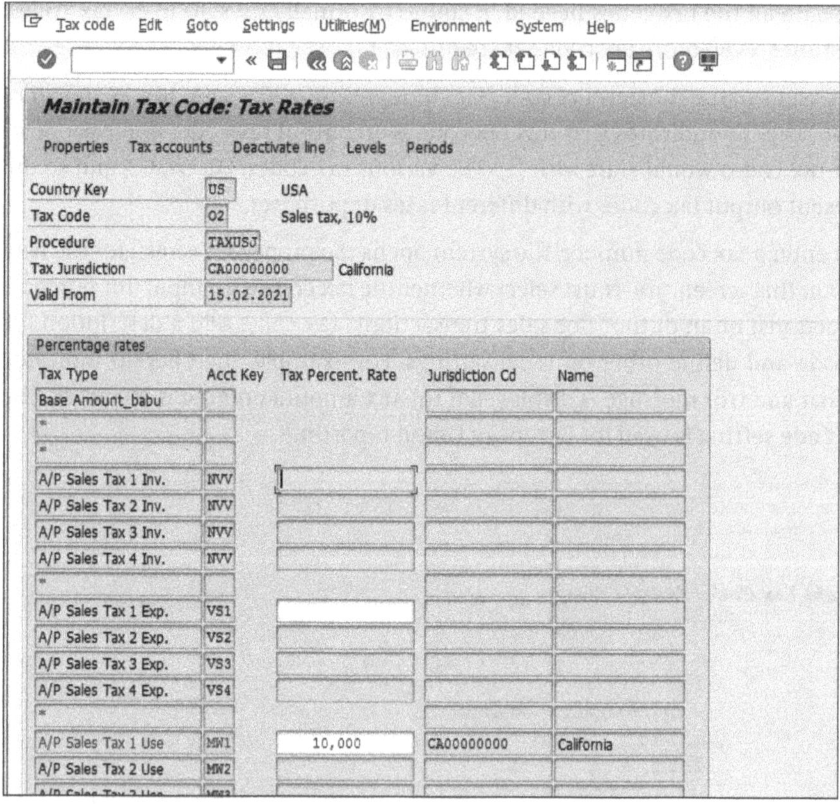

Figure 3.47 Tax Code Configuration

You can also check the general ledger account assigned by clicking **Tax accounts** from the top menu. Then, the system asks for the chart of accounts and shows the general ledger account that will receive posting from this tax code, as shown in Figure 3.48.

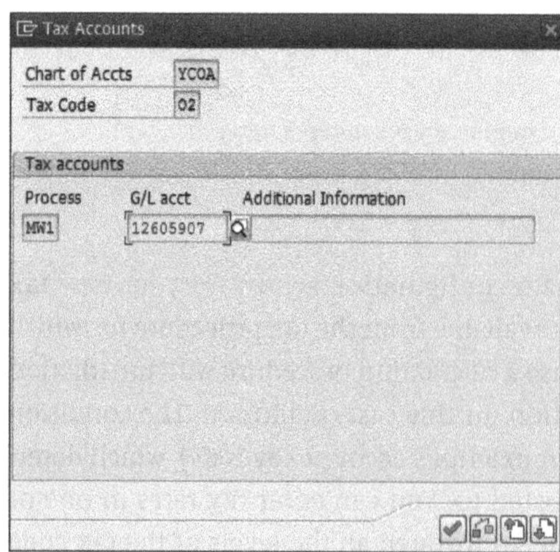

Figure 3.48 Tax Code General Ledger Account Definition

We'll examine tax code determination in various purchasing and sales flows in detail in Chapter 5 and Chapter 6.

3.7 Summary

In this chapter, we examined the global settings that must be maintained in SAP S/4HANA Finance in detail. We started by explaining the concept of the new finance data model in SAP S/4HANA so that you're in a position to properly define your organizational setup and global settings, taking into consideration the advancements SAP S/4HANA offers in the finance area.

We then explained how to configure the organizational structure of your enterprise, including the company, company code, controlling area, and operating concern. The proper decisions about how to structure your organization in the system provide a good foundation on which the system can be built and meet your business requirements. With the guidelines and practical advice from this chapter, you should be in a position to design your organizational structure accurately and with ease.

Then, we covered the main configuration objects that are part of the global settings of the system, such as ledgers, document types, currencies, and taxes. These settings are used throughout the system and by all modules, so their proper configuration is of paramount importance. We examined the various important settings that you can adjust for these objects to ensure the proper functioning of your SAP S/4HANA system.

With that done, now let's start configuring the various financial accounting and controlling areas of the system, starting with the general ledger.

Chapter 4
General Ledger

This chapter provides step-by-step instructions for configuring the general ledger in SAP S/4HANA. We'll explain how the general ledger integrates with the rest of the system and how account determination works.

So far, you've configured the financial global settings required for SAP S/4HANA, and now, you'll learn how to configure the backbone of all financial processes: the general ledger. The general ledger contains all financial and controlling postings in SAP S/4HANA and provides the full accounting picture of your organization. In SAP S/4HANA, previously separate components, such as controlling and fixed assets, are fully integrated in the general ledger. Therefore, its proper configuration is of paramount importance.

In the following sections, we'll cover the following general ledger topics in detail:

- Master data
- Document splitting
- Automatic postings and account determination
- Periodic processing and financial closing
- Information system

We'll also look at a few SAP Fiori apps available for the general ledger that should be useful to you.

4.1 Master Data

The master data for the general ledger consists of general ledger accounts. These accounts are used to record accounting transactions and are organized in a chart of accounts, which structures them into main accounting categories such as asset accounts, liabilities, profit and loss (P&L) accounts, and so on.

At the general ledger accounts level, you can clearly see a main benefit of SAP S/4HANA. In SAP S/4HANA, financial accounting and controlling are fully integrated, so now cost elements are a type of general ledger accounts. Cost elements previously were separate master data objects in controlling used to record controlling transactions.

Now, cost elements are just a type of general ledger account in the SAP S/4HANA's simplified data model.

Let's look at how charts of accounts are configured.

4.1.1 Chart of Accounts

A *chart of accounts* is a classification structure for the general ledger accounts you're using. Three types of charts of accounts exist:

- **Operational chart of accounts**
  The operational chart of accounts is your main chart of accounts and is assigned to the company code. This chart of accounts is used to make postings in financial accounting.
- **Group chart of accounts**
  The group chart of accounts links one or more operational general ledger account numbers to a group account number. This chart of accounts is used in the consolidation process.
- **Country chart of accounts**
  This chart of accounts can be used on the country level to portray local requirements. This chart of accounts is optional and can be used for only some countries. When the country chart of accounts is assigned to the company code, you can assign an alternative account number in the master record of the operational general ledger account.

Now, let's examine the settings for charts of accounts. Follow the menu path **Financial Accounting • General Ledger Accounting • Master Data • G/L Accounts • Preparations • Edit Chart of Accounts List** or enter Transaction OB13.

Figure 4.1 shows a list of defined charts of accounts in the system. SAP delivers sample charts of accounts as best practices content for some countries.

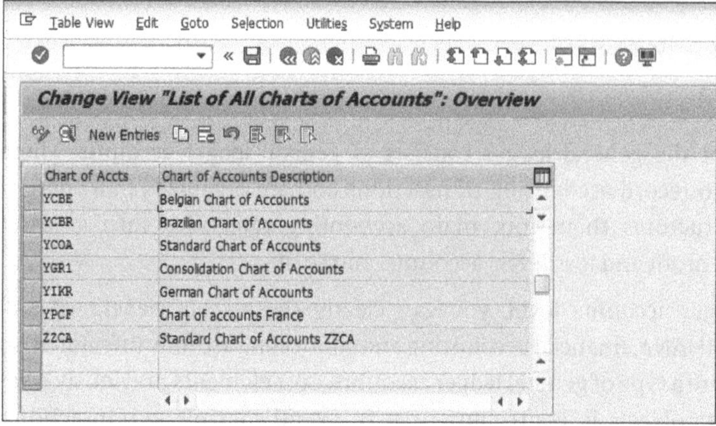

Figure 4.1 Chart of Accounts List

Double-click the **YCOA** chart of accounts (**Standard Chart of Accounts**), which will open the screen shown in Figure 4.2.

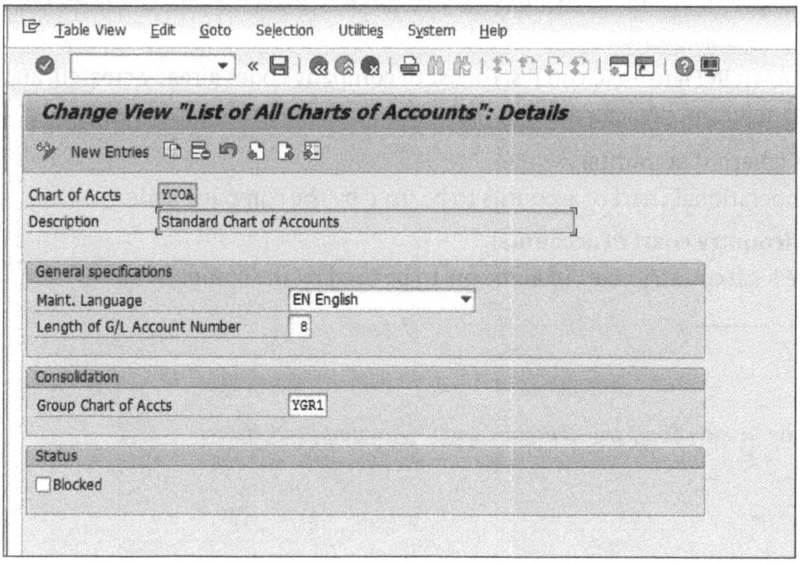

Figure 4.2 Chart of Accounts Settings

On this screen, the following fields can be configured:

- **Description**
  The description of the chart of accounts, which should indicate its use.
- **Maint. Language (maintenance language)**
  The main language under which the general ledger accounts for the chart of accounts will be maintained. General ledger accounts can have descriptions in other languages, but in this field, you'll specify the main language used in the country.
- **Length of G/L Account Number**
  The length of the general ledger account number. For example, a length of 8 would mean that account numbers will be 10000001, 10000002, 10000003, and so on. Commonly used lengths include 6 or 8 digits. Just make sure you have enough digits to structure your accounts in logical account number ranges.
- **Group Chart of Accts**
  In this field, the operational chart of accounts is linked with the group chart of accounts. Then, in each account from the operational chart of accounts, an account from the group chart of accounts will be entered.
- **Blocked**
  If this checkbox is selected, no accounts can be created for this chart of accounts.

After you finish reviewing or changing these settings, save and proceed to the next configuration transaction to assign a chart of accounts to a company code. Follow the menu path **Financial Accounting • General Ledger Accounting • Master Data • G/L Accounts • Preparations • Assign Company Code to Chart of Accounts** or enter Transaction OB62. On the screen shown in Figure 4.3, assign a chart of accounts to your company code.

In the table shown in Figure 4.3, you'll see a list of company codes already created, and in the last two columns, you can make assignments in the following columns:

- **Chrt/Accts (chart of accounts)**
  The main operational chart of accounts to be used by the company code.
- **Cty ch/act (country chart of accounts)**
  Alternative local country chart of accounts to be used by the company code.

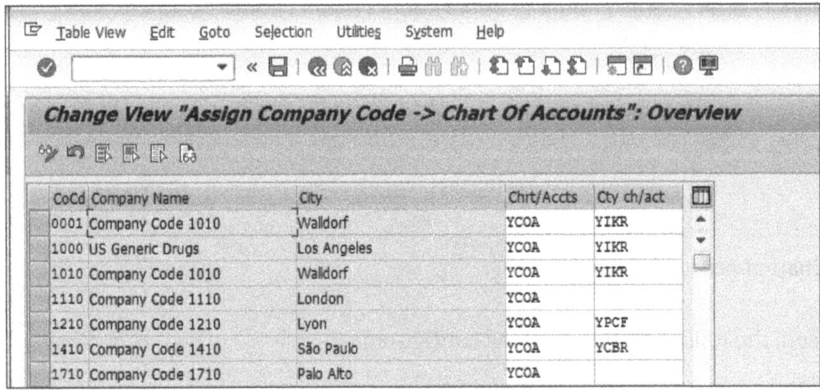

CoCd	Company Name	City	Chrt/Accts	Cty ch/act
0001	Company Code 1010	Walldorf	YCOA	YIKR
1000	US Generic Drugs	Los Angeles	YCOA	YIKR
1010	Company Code 1010	Walldorf	YCOA	YIKR
1110	Company Code 1110	London	YCOA	
1210	Company Code 1210	Lyon	YCOA	YPCF
1410	Company Code 1410	São Paulo	YCOA	YCBR
1710	Company Code 1710	Palo Alto	YCOA	

Figure 4.3 Assignment of Chart of Accounts to Company Code

The next step is to define the account groups used for your chart of accounts.

4.1.2 Account Groups

Account groups classify general ledger accounts based on common accounting purposes. Typically, separate account groups are created for fixed asset accounts, material accounts, P&L accounts, and so on.

Follow the menu path **Financial Accounting • General Ledger Accounting • Master Data • G/L Accounts • Preparations • Define Account Group** or enter Transaction OBD4. As shown in Figure 4.4, multiple account groups can be defined for each chart of accounts.

For example, for chart of accounts YCOA, the following account groups are defined:

- **Recon.account AP/AR**
- **Fixed assets accounts**
- **Income statement accounts**
- **Liquid funds accounts**
- **Materials management accounts**

- **ReconAcct ARAP Ready for Input**
- **G/L accounts (general)**
- **G/L accounts (ledger-spec. OI)**
- **Secondary costs / revenues**

Table view Edit Goto Choose Utilities System Help

Change View "G/L Account Groups": Overview of Selected Set

Field status New entries Print field status

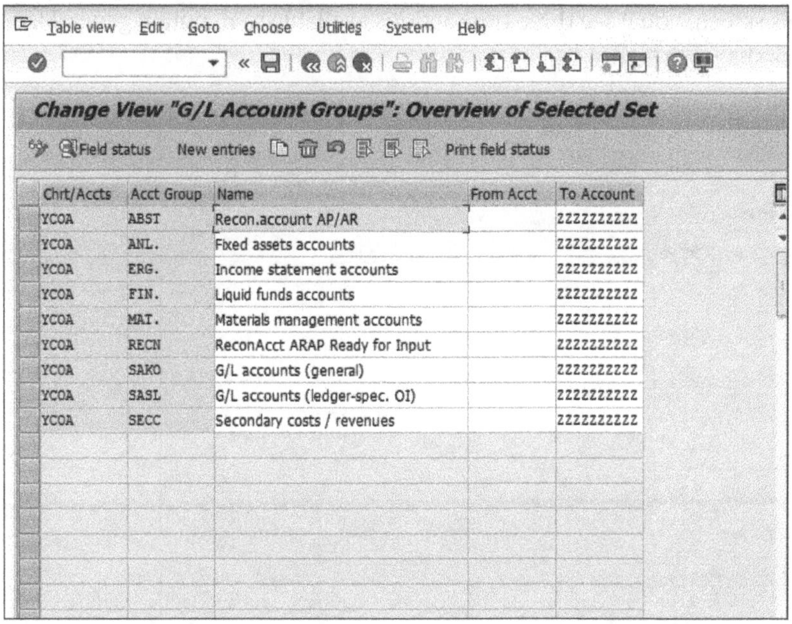

Chrt/Accts	Acct Group	Name	From Acct	To Account
YCOA	ABST	Recon.account AP/AR		ZZZZZZZZZZ
YCOA	ANL.	Fixed assets accounts		ZZZZZZZZZZ
YCOA	ERG.	Income statement accounts		ZZZZZZZZZZ
YCOA	FIN.	Liquid funds accounts		ZZZZZZZZZZ
YCOA	MAT.	Materials management accounts		ZZZZZZZZZZ
YCOA	RECN	ReconAcct ARAP Ready for Input		ZZZZZZZZZZ
YCOA	SAKO	G/L accounts (general)		ZZZZZZZZZZ
YCOA	SASL	G/L accounts (ledger-spec. OI)		ZZZZZZZZZZ
YCOA	SECC	Secondary costs / revenues		ZZZZZZZZZZ

Figure 4.4 Defining Account Groups

Each account group is defined with an identifier entered in the **Acct Group** (account group) column. In the **From Acct** (from account) and **To Account** columns, the possible numbers of the accounts are defined. From an empty value to 999999 means that accounts must consist of numbers up to 999999. You can also define more precise ranges, such as 100000 to 199999 for one group, 200000 to 299999 for another, and so on. You can also have accounts consisting of letters, defined as ZZZZZZZZZZ.

4.1.3 General Ledger Accounts

General ledger accounts are master data and are maintained from the SAP S/4HANA application menu. These accounts can be maintained in each client individually, but the more common and recommended approach is to maintain them centrally in a single master data client and distribute them to all other systems and clients via Application Link Enabling (ALE).

General ledger accounts are maintained at the chart of accounts level and company code level. At the chart of accounts level, settings valid for all company codes that use this chart of accounts are maintained, such as the long and short descriptions and the group account number. Then, at the company code level, most of the control settings of the accounts are maintained, such as the currency, open item management, line-item display, and so on.

To maintain general ledger accounts, follow the application menu path **Accounting • Financial Accounting • General Ledger • Master Records • G/L Accounts • Individual Processing**. On this screen, you'll see three transactions available to maintain general ledger accounts, as shown in Figure 4.5.

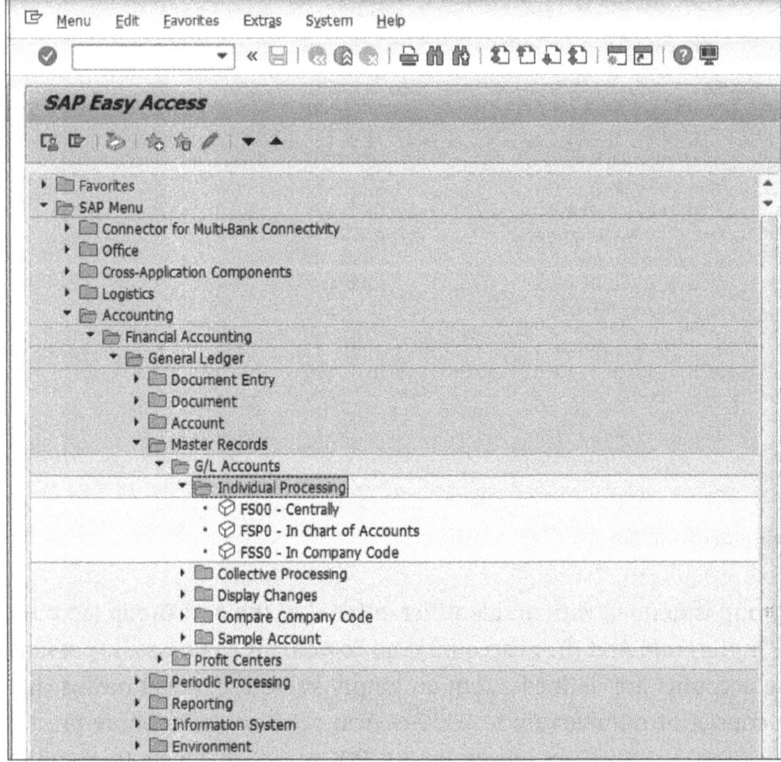

Figure 4.5 Maintaining General Ledger Account Transactions

These three transactions are as follows:

- **FS00 – Centrally**
- **FSP0 – In Chart of Accounts**
- **FSS0 – In Company Code**

Enter transaction **FS00 – Centrally**, which gives you access to both the chart of accounts and company codes settings. On the screen shown in Figure 4.6, enter "94202000" in the **G/L Account** field and "1000" in the **Company Code** field for your new company code. Then, click the (**Change**) button, which allows you to change the fields of the general ledger account.

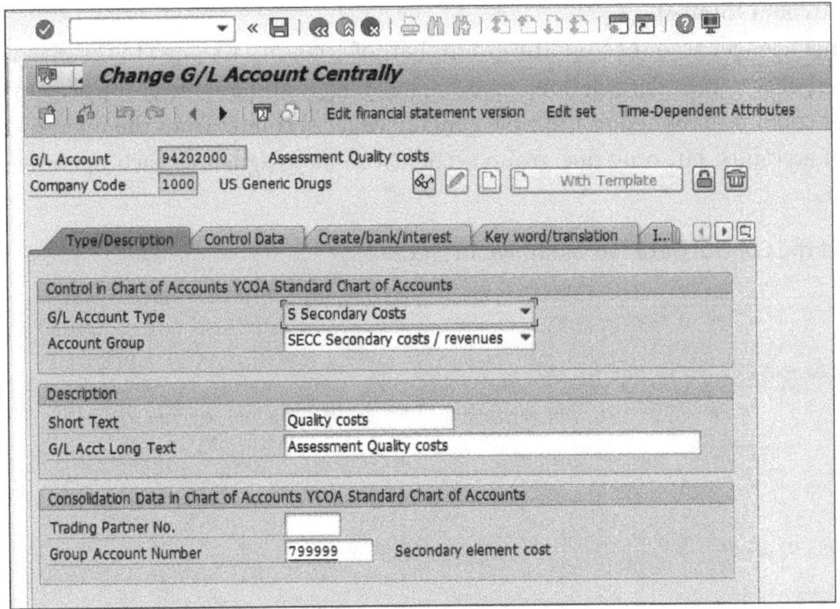

Figure 4.6 Displaying the General Ledger Account Centrally

These fields are organized under different tabs. Which fields are optional or required or hidden is controlled by the field status group of the account. Let's examine the most commonly used fields.

Under the **Type/Description** tab, which is maintained at the chart of accounts level, the following fields are available:

- **G/L Account Type (general ledger account type)**
  Determines the type of account, such as balance sheet account or P&L account.
- **Account Group**
  In this field, select one of the account groups we discussed in Section 4.1.2.
- **P&L Statement Acct Type (P&L statement account type)**
  This field is relevant for P&L accounts and determines the target retained earnings account to which the result of year-end closing will be transferred so you can calculate profits or losses.
- **Short Text**
  The short description of the general ledger account.
- **G/L Acct Long Text (general ledger account long text)**
  The long description of the general ledger account.

If you scroll down, you'll see more fields, which are related to consolidation:

- **Trading Partner No.**
  Used to determine the intercompany partner related to this account.

- **Group Account Number**
  The general ledger account from the group chart of accounts assigned to the operative chart of accounts. The relationship is *1:n*, meaning that the same group account number could be assigned to multiple general ledger accounts from the operative chart of accounts, but only one group account can be assigned to each operative account.

Now, select the **Control Data** tab, as shown in Figure 4.7.

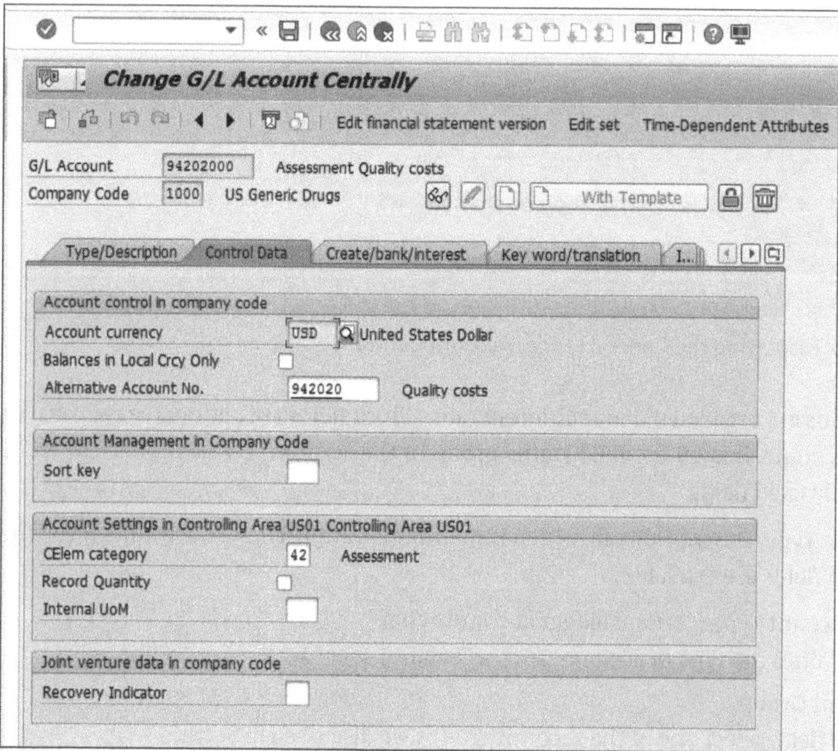

Figure 4.7 General Ledger Account Control Data

Different fields are available, based on the account. The most commonly used fields include the following:

- **Account currency**
  The currency of the account, which is stored in every posting.
- **Balances in Local Crcy Only (balances in local currency only)**
  If selected, balances will be updated only in local currency when posting to this account.
- **Tax Category**
  Determines what type of taxes are allowed to be posted to this account.

- **Posting without Tax Allowed**
  If selected, entering a tax code when posting to the account is optional.
- **Recon Account for Acct Type (reconciliation account for account type)**
  This field is used for general ledger accounts, which are reconciliation accounts for assets, customers, or vendor accounts. Each posting to the relevant asset, customer, or vendor also updates the reconciliation general ledger account.
- **Alternative Account No (alternative account number)**
  This field is the local account number from the country chart of accounts assigned to the operative chart of accounts. Its use is optional in countries where a country chart of accounts is needed and is used to depict local accounting rules.
- **Sort Key**
  Defines a rule for the default sorting of the line items in line-item reports.
- **CElem. Category (cost element category)**
  As discussed previously, in SAP S/4HANA, financial accounting and controlling are fully integrated, which means that now cost elements are general ledger accounts. With this field, you determine their category and use; previously, this field was available in the cost element master.
- **Record Quantity**
  Indicates that the system will also record quantity for postings to this cost element.
- **Internal UoM (internal unit of measure)**
  Default unit of measure (UoM) used for postings to this cost element.

Now, click on the **Create/bank/interest** tab, where the most commonly used fields include the following:

- **Field status group**
  This field controls which fields are optional, required, and hidden in the general ledger account master record.
- **Post Automatically Only**
  If this field is selected, then manual postings are not allowed. Typically, this option is used for accounts posted by automatic processes from logistics, such as sales revenue accounts or material accounts.

Next, under the **Create/bank/interest** tab, you can maintain other fields related to the account field status, automatic postings, and bank transactions if applicable, as shown in Figure 4.8.

Under this tab, the available fields depend on the account group selected earlier in Figure 4.6. In our example, we'll maintain the following fields:

- **Field status group**
  This field controls the fields that will be required, optional, or suppressed when posting to this account.

- **Post Automatically Only**
  If selected, no manual postings are allowed in financial accounting to the account. Only automatic postings, for instance, from sales or purchasing, are allowed. Typical examples include inventory accounts, which normally are posted in financial accounting from stock movements arising from goods receipts (GRs) and goods issues.
- **Supplement Auto. Postings**
  Indicates that line items that have been generated automatically can be supplemented manually. This capability is used for general ledger accounts for bank charges. When an incoming payment is posted that contains bank charges, the system automatically would generate a line item for these charges. Then, you can supplement this line item with an account assignment such as cost center.

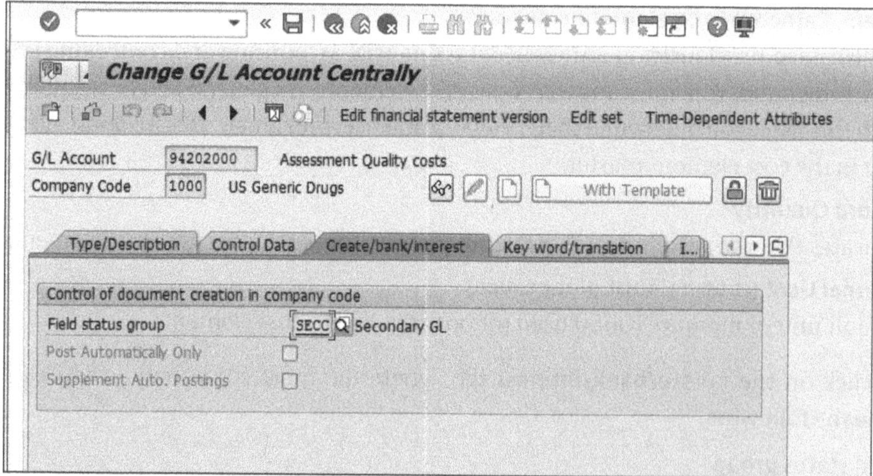

Figure 4.8 General Ledger Account Create/Bank/Interest Data

Next, under the **Key word/translation** tab, you can maintain keywords related to the account in different languages, and you can maintain the account description in multiple languages, as shown in Figure 4.9.

Go to the **Information (C/A)** tab to find administrative information about who created the account on the chart of accounts level and when, as well as relevant change documents for its changes.

Finally, visit the **Information (CoCd)** tab to find administrative information about who created the account on the company code level and when, as well as relevant change documents for its changes.

After you've finished making changes to the general ledger account, you can save your settings.

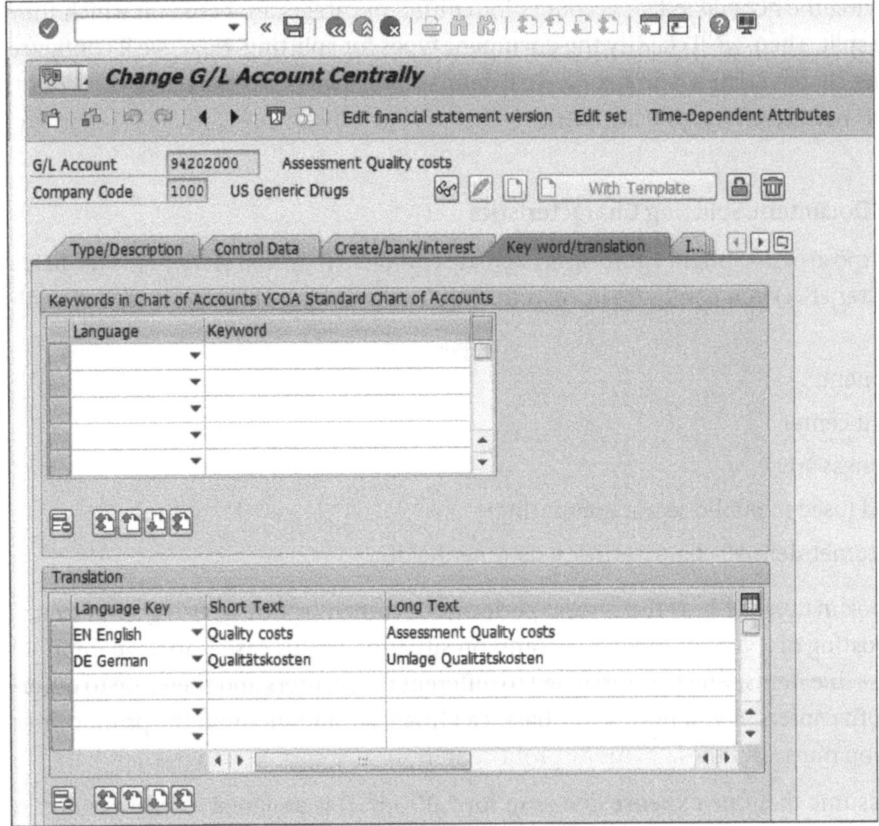

Figure 4.9 General Ledger AccountDifferent Language Descriptions

4.2 Document Splitting

Document splitting is an extremely powerful concept that was first introduced as a special feature in the special purpose ledger, then was included as standard functionality with the new general ledger, and now in SAP S/4HANA is commonly used to provide a full set of balanced financial statements on various types of characteristic levels, such as profit center or segment.

Essentially, *document splitting* enables you to automatically split financial line items for selected dimensions (such as receivable line items by profit center or payable line items by segment) and therefore to have zero balance in the document per those dimensions. During document splitting, the system creates additional clearing lines to balance these dimensions.

We'll now examine the various configuration elements that you need to configure for the document splitting functionality. We'll start by discussing the various splitting characteristics that can be used to split the documents. We'll start the configuration by classifying the general ledger accounts into different categories, based on which they will be split. Then, we'll classify the document types for splitting. Next, we'll configure splitting characteristics, and finally, we'll define a zero-balance general ledger account, which is used to offset splitting entries.

4.2.1 Document Splitting Characteristics

The purpose of document splitting is to create complete financial statements for fields (characteristics) you configure in customizing. The following characteristics are available:

- Segment
- Profit center
- Business area
- Fund (used in public-sector accounting)
- Customer-defined characteristic (customer field)

Let's look in detail at how the system performs document splitting, using as an example a posting of a vendor invoice. A common situation in this case is to have multiple expense line items, which are assigned to different cost centers and therefore to different profit centers. If you need a full, balanced financial statement on the profit center level, you must split these items by profit center.

Let's assume that one expense line item for 5,000 USD is assigned to profit center A and another one for 10,000 USD is assigned to profit center B. Then, the system will perform the splitting as shown in Figure 4.10.

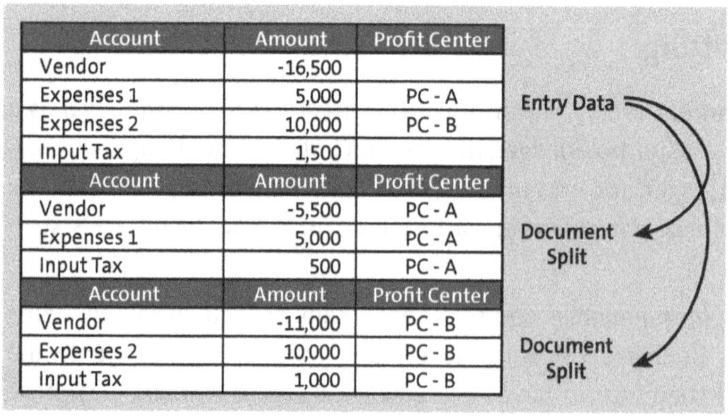

Account	Amount	Profit Center	
Vendor	-16,500		
Expenses 1	5,000	PC - A	Entry Data
Expenses 2	10,000	PC - B	
Input Tax	1,500		
Account	**Amount**	**Profit Center**	
Vendor	-5,500	PC - A	
Expenses 1	5,000	PC - A	Document Split
Input Tax	500	PC - A	
Account	**Amount**	**Profit Center**	
Vendor	-11,000	PC - B	
Expenses 2	10,000	PC - B	Document Split
Input Tax	1,000	PC - B	

Figure 4.10 Document Splitting Example

Notice how the system uses the ratio between the expense line items (1:2 in this case, as the first line item is 5,000 and the second is 10,000) to determine the amounts that must be allocated to each of the profit centers. In this process, the system posts additional line items at the general ledger level for each of the profit centers. Then, it splits the input tax line item into two line items based on this 1:2 ratio. Thus, the system enhances this input tax item for which originally no profit center could be determined with profit center information based on the expense line items. These line items are available only in the general ledger view, which is different from the entry view in which the document is posted in financial accounting.

Now, let's examine how to configure document splitting in SAP S/4HANA.

4.2.2 Classification of General Ledger Accounts for Document Splitting

First, you must tell the system how your general ledger accounts should be split by assigning general ledger accounts to item categories. *Item categories* are predefined objects that contain the logic for splitting based on the type of account.

To classify general ledger accounts for splitting, follow the menu path **Financial Accounting • General Ledger Accounting • Business Transactions • Document Splitting • Classify G/L Accounts for Document Splitting**. As shown in Figure 4.11, on this screen, you can define ranges of general ledger accounts and assign them to item categories.

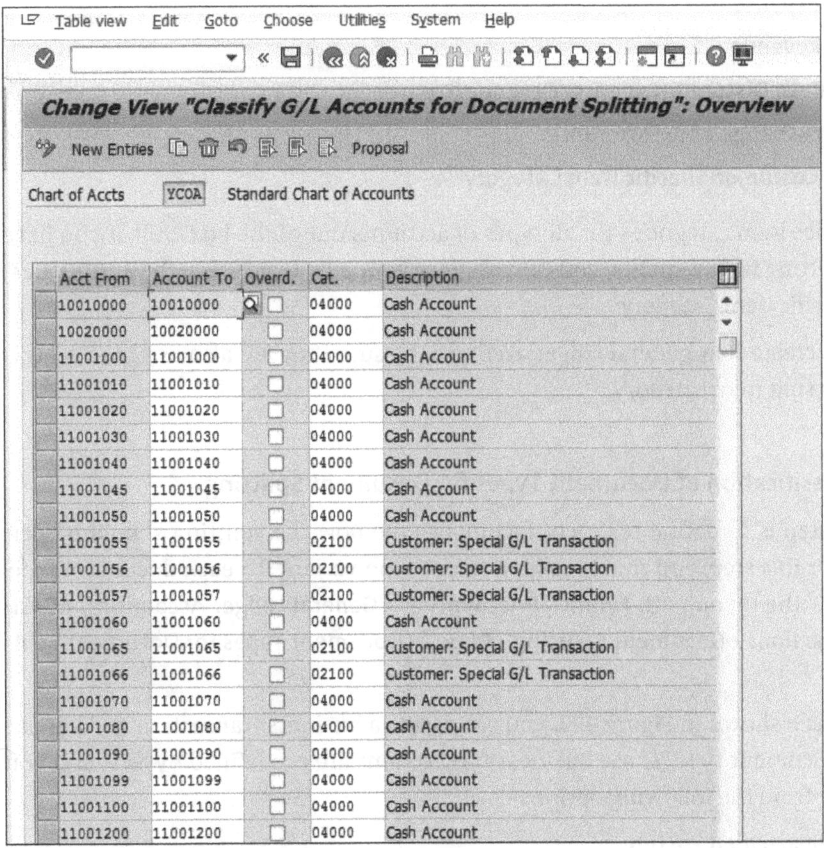

Acct From	Account To	Overrd.	Cat.	Description
10010000	10010000		04000	Cash Account
10020000	10020000		04000	Cash Account
11001000	11001000		04000	Cash Account
11001010	11001010		04000	Cash Account
11001020	11001020		04000	Cash Account
11001030	11001030		04000	Cash Account
11001040	11001040		04000	Cash Account
11001045	11001045		04000	Cash Account
11001050	11001050		04000	Cash Account
11001055	11001055		02100	Customer: Special G/L Transaction
11001056	11001056		02100	Customer: Special G/L Transaction
11001057	11001057		02100	Customer: Special G/L Transaction
11001060	11001060		04000	Cash Account
11001065	11001065		02100	Customer: Special G/L Transaction
11001066	11001066		02100	Customer: Special G/L Transaction
11001070	11001070		04000	Cash Account
11001080	11001080		04000	Cash Account
11001090	11001090		04000	Cash Account
11001099	11001099		04000	Cash Account
11001100	11001100		04000	Cash Account
11001200	11001200		04000	Cash Account

Figure 4.11 Classifying General Ledger Accounts for Splitting

The following standard item categories are available:

- **01000: Balance Sheet Account**
- **01001: Zero Balance Posting (Free Balancing Units)**
- **01100: Company Code Clearing**
- **01300: Cash Discount Clearing**
- **02000: Customer**
- **02100: Customer: Special G/L Transaction**
- **03000: Vendor**
- **03100: Vendor: Special G/L Transaction**
- **04000: Cash Account**
- **05100: Taxes on Sales/Purchases**
- **05200: Withholding Tax**
- **06000: Material**
- **07000: Fixed Assets**
- **20000: Expense**
- **30000: Revenue**
- **40100: Cash Discount (Expense/Revenue/Loss)**
- **40200: Exchange Rate Difference**
- **80000: Customer-Specific Item Category**

SAP provides item categories for all types of accounts out of the box. Still, if you have special splitting requirements, you can program your own logic using the **80000: Customer-Specific Item Category**.

When you create new general ledger accounts, be sure they are also assigned on this screen to a split item category.

4.2.3 Classification of Document Types for Document Splitting

The next step is to define for each document type how the splitting should be performed. For this step, you must assign a transaction variant for each document type. First, follow the menu path **Financial Accounting • General Ledger Accounting • Business Transactions • Document Splitting • Classify Document Types for Document Splitting**.

On the screen shown in Figure 4.12, you can assign a business transaction and variant for each document type. These business transactions are predefined by SAP, and you can choose from the following options:

- **0000: Unspecified Posting**
- **0100: Transfer Posting from P&L to B/S Account**

- **0200: Customer Invoice**
- **0300: Vendor Invoice**
- **0400: Bank Account Statement**
- **0500: Advance Tax Return (Regular Tax Burden)**
- **0600: Goods Receipt for Purchase Order**
- **1000: Payments**
- **1010: Clearing Transactions (Account Maint.)**
- **1020: Reset Cleared Items**
- **2000: CO Posting**

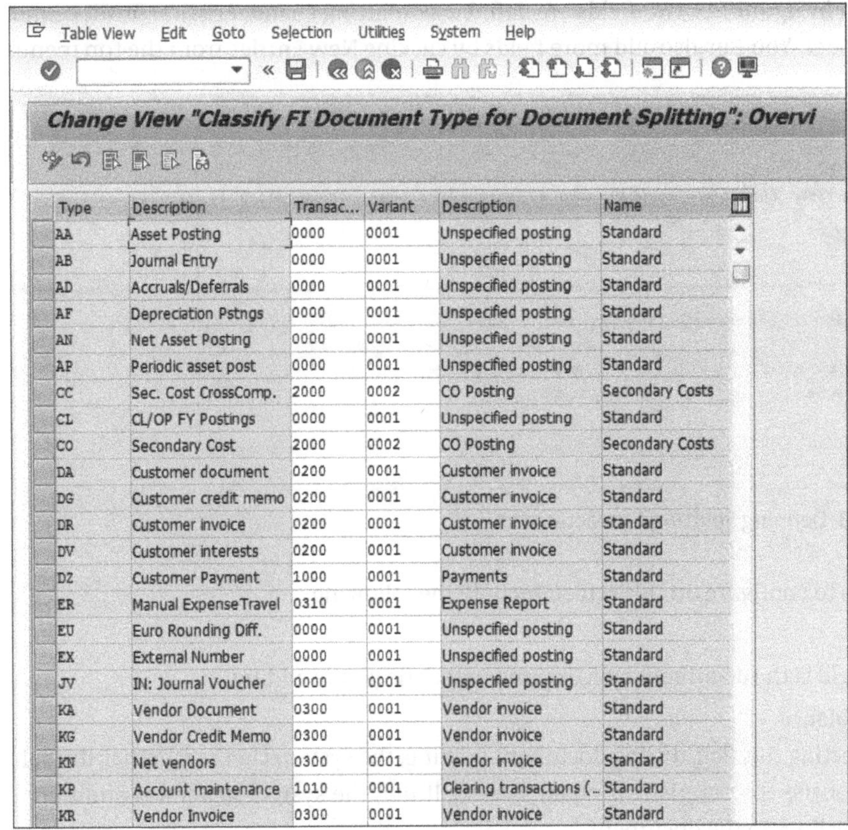

Type	Description	Transac...	Variant	Description	Name
AA	Asset Posting	0000	0001	Unspecified posting	Standard
AB	Journal Entry	0000	0001	Unspecified posting	Standard
AD	Accruals/Deferrals	0000	0001	Unspecified posting	Standard
AF	Depreciation Pstngs	0000	0001	Unspecified posting	Standard
AN	Net Asset Posting	0000	0001	Unspecified posting	Standard
AP	Periodic asset post	0000	0001	Unspecified posting	Standard
CC	Sec. Cost CrossComp.	2000	0002	CO Posting	Secondary Costs
CL	CL/OP FY Postings	0000	0001	Unspecified posting	Standard
CO	Secondary Cost	2000	0002	CO Posting	Secondary Costs
DA	Customer document	0200	0001	Customer invoice	Standard
DG	Customer credit memo	0200	0001	Customer invoice	Standard
DR	Customer invoice	0200	0001	Customer invoice	Standard
DV	Customer interests	0200	0001	Customer invoice	Standard
DZ	Customer Payment	1000	0001	Payments	Standard
ER	Manual ExpenseTravel	0310	0001	Expense Report	Standard
EU	Euro Rounding Diff.	0000	0001	Unspecified posting	Standard
EX	External Number	0000	0001	Unspecified posting	Standard
JV	IN: Journal Voucher	0000	0001	Unspecified posting	Standard
KA	Vendor Document	0300	0001	Vendor invoice	Standard
KG	Vendor Credit Memo	0300	0001	Vendor invoice	Standard
KN	Net vendors	0300	0001	Vendor invoice	Standard
KP	Account maintenance	1010	0001	Clearing transactions (...	Standard
KR	Vendor Invoice	0300	0001	Vendor invoice	Standard

Figure 4.12 Classifying Document Types for Splitting

The business transaction variant further enhances the business transaction, which is necessary to have different splitting rules.

When you create a new document type, be sure you also configure it in this transaction to assign a business transaction and variant to it.

4.2.4 Defining Document Splitting Characteristics for General Ledger Accounting

You must also define which document splitting characteristics you'll use. These characteristics tell the system on which fields the document line items should be split and if you require zero balances to be achieved on these fields. This option means that the system will always balance the document to achieve zero-balance characteristics by creating additional line items.

To define document splitting characteristics, follow the menu path **Financial Accounting • General Ledger Accounting • Business Transactions • Document Splitting • Define Document Splitting Characteristics for General Ledger Accounting.**

As shown in Figure 4.13, two fields are defined as splitting characteristics: profit center and segment. You can also add more fields by clicking **New Entries** from the top menu.

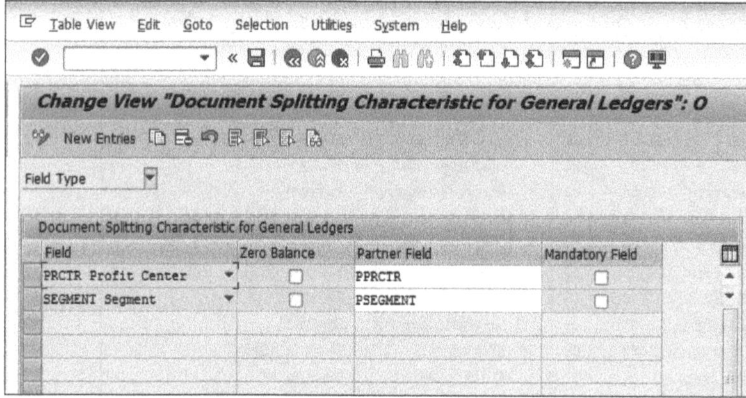

Figure 4.13 Defining Splitting Characteristics

The fields to configure on this screen include the following:

- **Field**
  This field is the document splitting characteristic you're adding.
- **Zero Balance**
  By selecting this flag, during document posting, the system checks whether the balance for the characteristic is equal to zero. If not, the system generates additional clearing lines in the document.
- **Partner Field**
  A sender/receiver relationship is established in the additionally created clearing lines for this field.
- **Mandatory Field**
  Specifies that this field must be filled with a value after the document splitting.

4.2.5 Defining Zero-Balance Clearing Account

You also must configure a zero-balance clearing account if you require balanced financial statements on a certain field's level. For fields for which you want the zero-balance setting, the system checks whether the balance for those objects is zero after document splitting. If not, the system generates additional clearing items, which are posted to this clearing account.

To define a zero-balance clearing account, follow the menu path **Financial Accounting • General Ledger Accounting • Business Transactions • Document Splitting • Define Zero-Balance Clearing Account.**

Figure 4.14 shows three account keys: one for postings originating from financial accounting, one from controlling, and one for cash pooling. Select **000** and click **Accounts** on the left side of the screen.

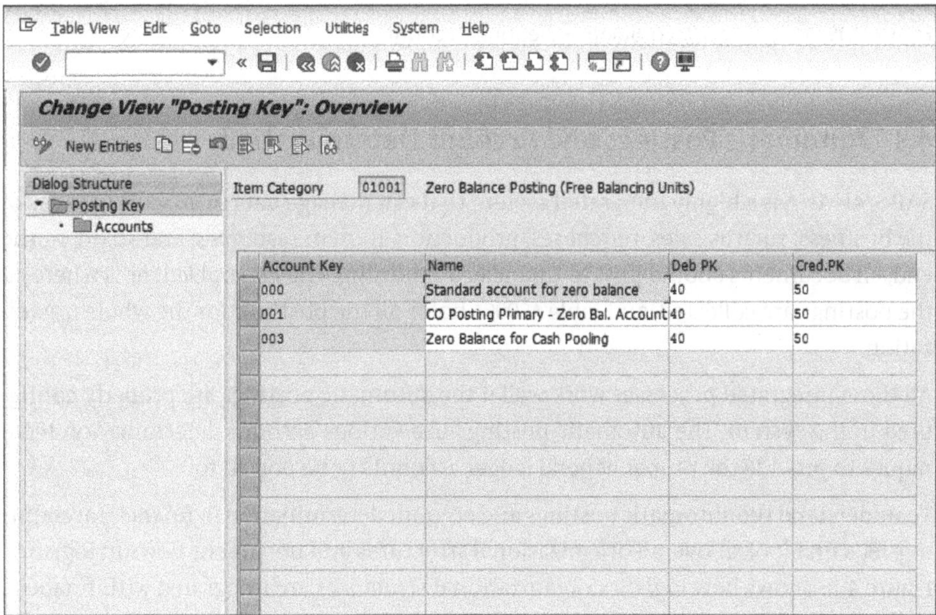

Figure 4.14 Zero Balance Keys

After entering your chart of accounts, you have the opportunity to enter the account used as the zero-balance clearing account, as shown in Figure 4.15.

Then, save your entry by clicking the **Save** button.

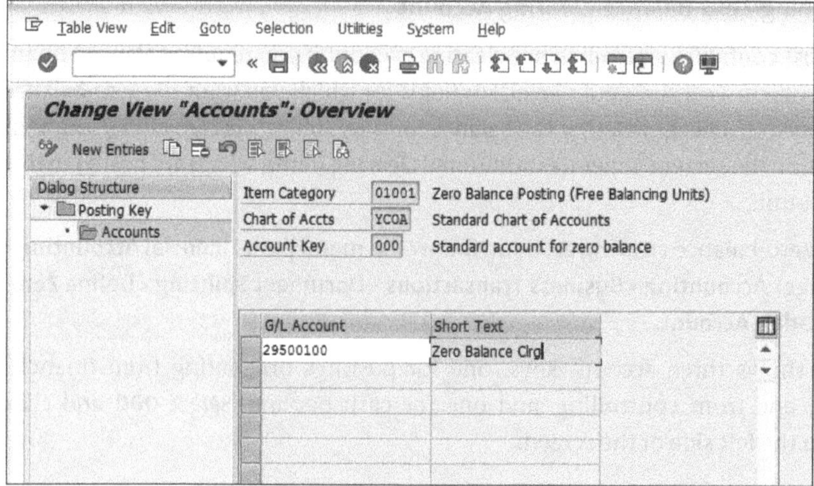

Figure 4.15 Assigning a Zero-Balance Clearing Account

4.3 Automatic Postings and Account Determination

SAP S/4HANA is a highly integrated system that can manage data from various areas of the business, such as sales, purchases, production, human resources, and so on. At the end, all documents should post to financial accounting. The general ledger is where all the postings are collected, and table ACDOCA holds all the postings for the whole organization.

All these integrated processes work well if the automatic postings are properly configured in the system. The automatic postings use various account determination techniques to provide the proper general ledger accounts to be posted to.

To understand the automatic postings and account determination in financial accounting, let's first look at overall organizational structures and document flows in logistics. Figure 4.16 shows how logistics organizational structures are integrated with financial organizational structures.

The company code, controlling area, and operating concern are financial organization structures that sit on top of the integration flow and receive postings from the logistics processes. Not all logistics transactions result in finance documents; for example, a purchase order (PO) doesn't generate a finance document. However, ultimately, every logistics flow ends up in finance. For example, after a PO is fulfilled, the goods received and invoice received are posted in materials management, which generates financial documents. Similar logic results from the sales flows. Therefore, logistical organizational objects, such as purchasing organization and sales organization, fall under financial organizational objects.

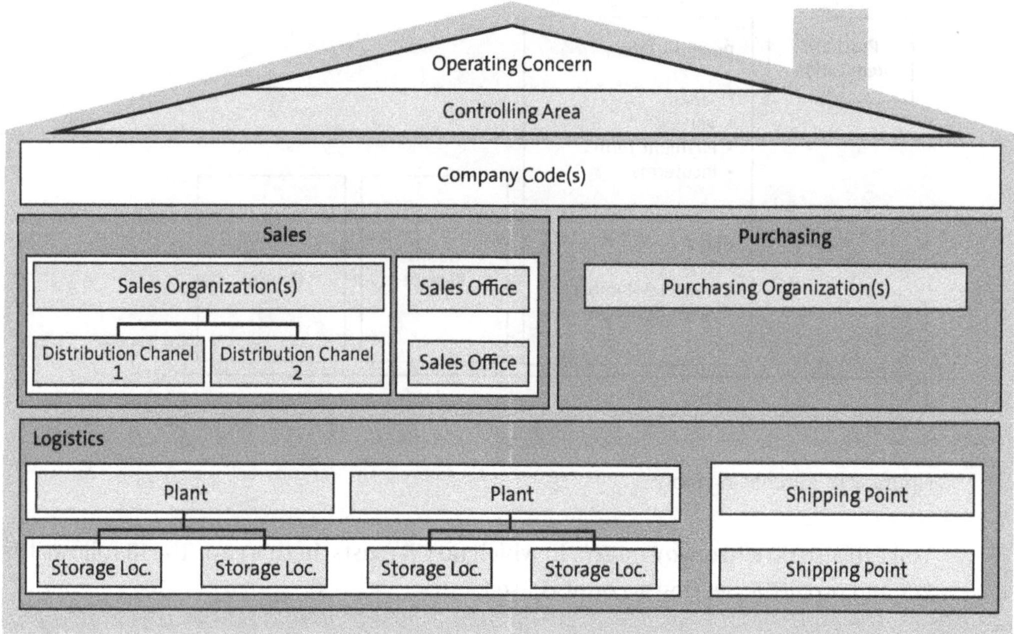

Figure 4.16 Organizational Structures

Let's examine now in detail the relevant logistics flows, starting with purchasing.

4.3.1 Purchasing Flows

From a purchasing point of view, the purchasing organization is the main organizational unit in which purchasing is planned and executed. Goods are supplied to storage locations, which belong to plants. These plants are mapped to company codes.

Figure 4.17 shows the basic purchasing flow in SAP S/4HANA. Most commonly, the process starts with a purchase requisition, which establishes the requirement for certain goods or services and is sent to a vendor. Then, a PO is created, which among other elements has the account assignment, which determines how the resulting GR and invoice receipt (IR) will be posted in accounting. Note that, at the time of the purchase requisition and PO, no accounting documents are created; these documents are purely logistics documents.

Next, in a typical process with GRs and IRs—which is commonly referred to as a *three-way match* because the system matches the PO, GR, and IR—accounting documents are generated, which usually debit an expense account and credit a vendor account. In between the GR/IR, the clearing account is posted to, which is credited during GR and debited during IR; therefore, its balance should be zero at the end of the complete process.

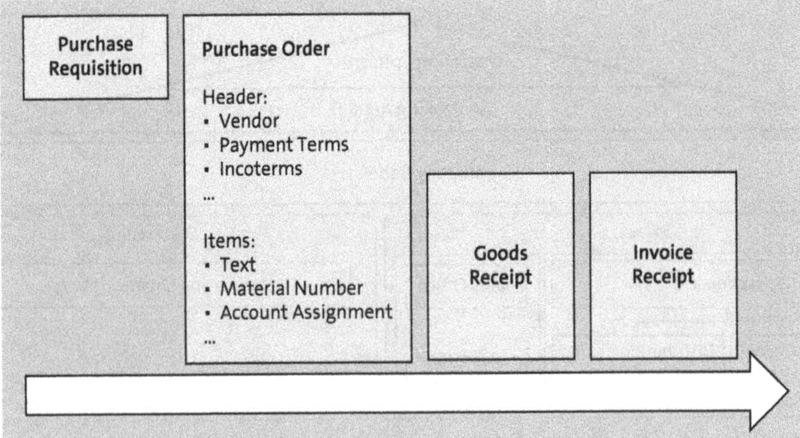

Figure 4.17 Purchasing Flow

You can also do a *two-way match*, in which no GR exists. In this case, the IR follows the PO, and no GR/IR clearing account is used.

4.3.2 Sales Flows

As shown earlier in Figure 4.16, notice that the sales organization is the main organizational unit in the sales processes. At lower levels, sales are performed at the distribution channel, division, and sales office levels. Figure 4.18 shows the main sales flow in the system.

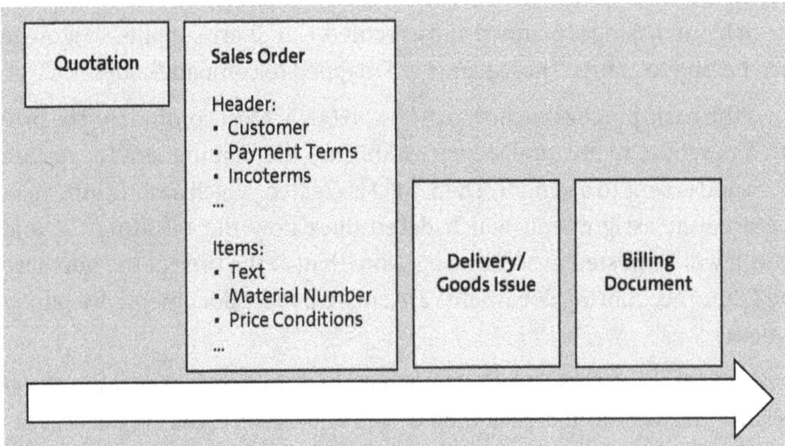

Figure 4.18 Sales Flow

The sales process usually starts with a quotation that is sent to the customer. Then, if he decides to proceed, a sales order is created, which contains elements that later determine the automatic account determination during the delivery of the goods, when goods issue is posted, and when creating the billing document, which generates the financial document for the customer invoice. SAP uses sophisticated techniques involving condition tables and access sequences to determine the correct revenue accounts, in which the material and customer master play key roles, along with other characteristics. We'll examine these techniques in detail in Chapter 6.

Now, let's examine how the automatic postings are configured.

4.3.3 Automatic Postings in Financial Accounting

Because SAP S/4HANA is such an integrated system that can manage virtually every area of an organization, numerous automatic postings can be configured. These postings come from different process areas and modules, so no single configuration path in Transaction SPRO can set up all automatic posting configurations. However, you can use a convenient configuration code that SAP financial experts should know by heart: Transaction FBKP. This transaction provides most account determinations for automatic postings in one place. A notable exception is the automatic sales postings process, which we'll examine in Chapter 6, along with the pricing procedure.

So now, let's enter Transaction FBKP. You're taken to the screen shown in Figure 4.19. Notice the link to many financial configuration tasks, such as automatic postings, but also posting keys, document types, fiscal year variants, and so on.

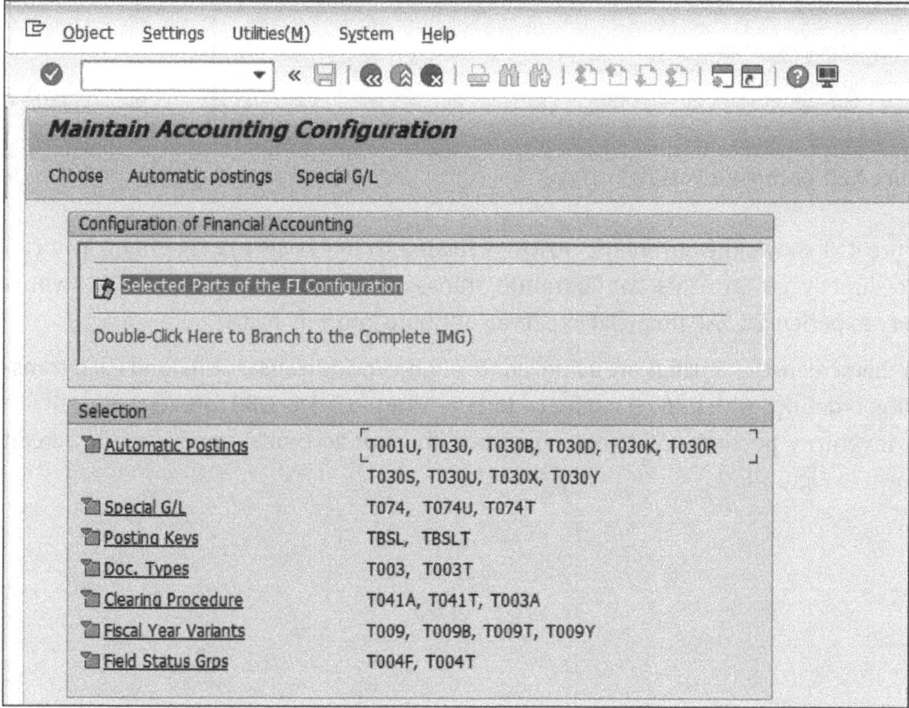

Figure 4.19 Automatic Postings Configuration

Expand the automatic postings section by clicking it. As shown in Figure 4.20, you'll see the various automatic posting settings, organized by group. Select the **Materials Management postings (MM)** group.

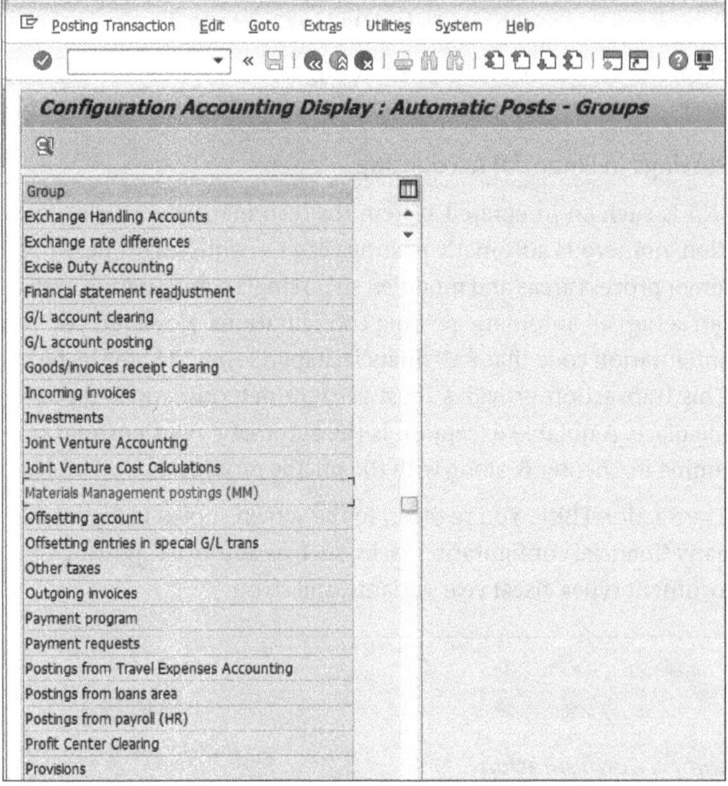

Figure 4.20 Automatic Postings Groups

Figure 4.21 shows the automatic postings related to materials management. You can also directly go into this configuration transaction with Transaction OBYC (which every experienced SAP financial expert also should know by heart).

On this screen, the settings are achieved through various transactions, and each transaction is defined with its 3-character code. For example, select **GBB** for offsetting entries for inventory postings. After entering your chart of accounts, you'll see the screen shown in Figure 4.22.

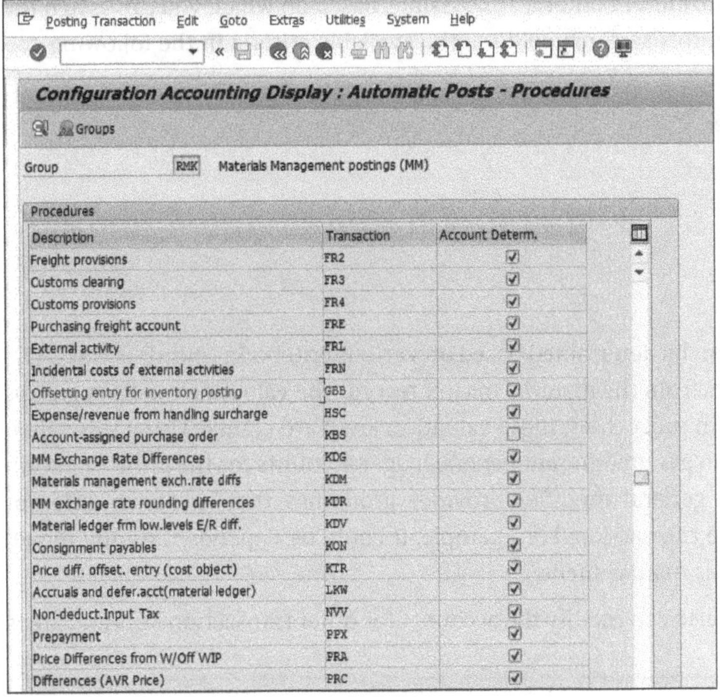

Figure 4.21 Materials Management Automatic Postings

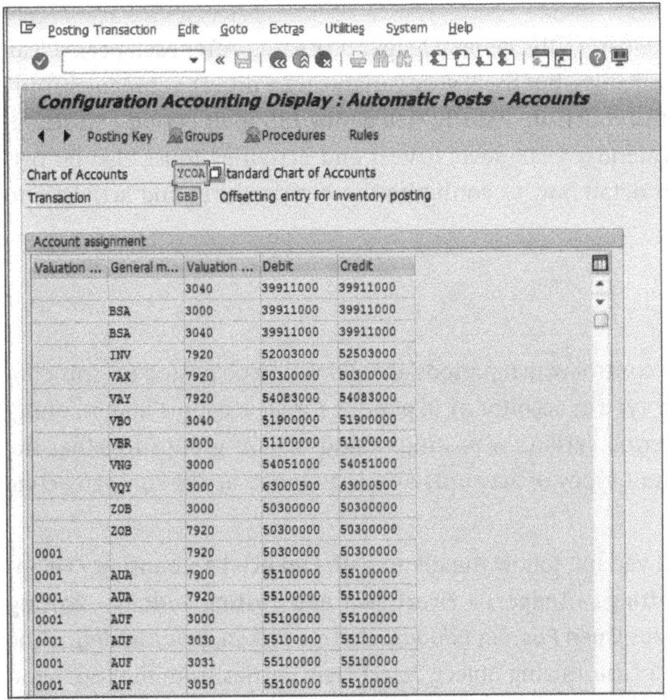

Figure 4.22 Automatic Postings for Offsetting Entry for Inventory Postings

For each transaction, different criteria are possible, based on which you can assign the desired accounts. On this screen, you'll see the available criteria in the following columns:

- **Valuation modifier**
- **General modifier**
- **Valuation class**
- **Debit**
- **Credit**

Different accounts can be determined based on various criteria in countless ways. The valuation class comes from the material master record. The valuation modifier groups the valuation areas (in most cases, these valuation areas are plants). Using this valuation modifier, you can assign different general ledger accounts for the same valuation class materials. The general modifier provides groupings that can have different options based on the transaction. For example, it could be dependent on the movement type in materials management.

Using this logic, you also can modify the accounts for other transaction keys and areas in SAP S/4HANA.

4.4 Periodic Processing and Financial Closing

Period-end closing is a vital part of the general ledger processes. After each period (calendar month for most companies, but fiscal year variants may differ), companies must perform several procedures, which are usually well defined in their period-end schedules. At the end of the calendar year, several year-end activities must also be performed. We'll examine in detail how to configure these procedures and activities in SAP S/4HANA.

4.4.1 Posting Periods

In SAP S/4HANA, you can control which periods are allowed to be posted to. This control can be determined by type of account or in general for all accounts and is configured using the posting period variant. A posting period variant groups together the posting periods for different types of accounts and is assigned at the company code level.

To define a posting period variant, follow the menu path **Financial Accounting • Financial Accounting Global Settings • Ledgers • Fiscal Year and Posting Periods • Posting Periods • Define Variants for Open Posting Periods**. On this screen, you can define the posting period variant as a customizing object. Select **New Entries** from the top menu and create a new variant, 1000, for company code 1000, as shown in Figure 4.23.

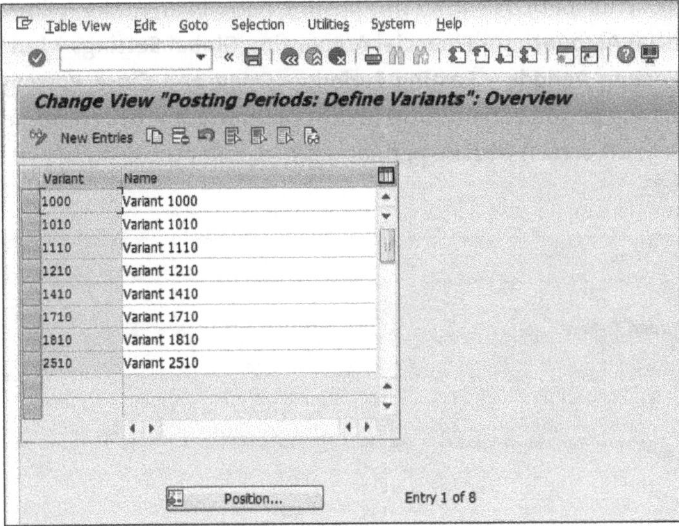

Figure 4.23 Defining a Posting Period Variant

The next step is to assign the posting period variant to the company code. Follow the menu path **Financial Accounting • Financial Accounting Global Settings • Ledgers • Fiscal Year and Posting Periods • Posting Periods • Assign Variants to Company Code.**

Assign the variant you just created (1000) to company code 1000 and save your entry by clicking the **Save** button, as shown in Figure 4.24.

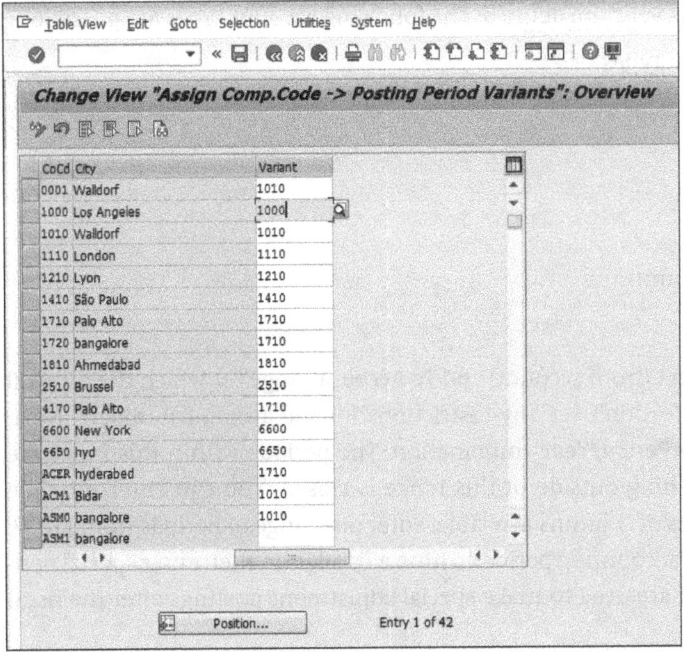

Figure 4.24 Assigning a Posting Period Variant

Now, you must define the actual periods within this posting period variant by following the menu path **Financial Accounting • Financial Accounting Global Settings • Ledgers • Fiscal Year and Posting Periods • Posting Periods • Open and Close Posting Periods.** After entering posting period variant 1000 in the popup window to determine the work area, you'll see a blank screen with no periods defined. Enter the posting periods, as shown in Figure 4.25.

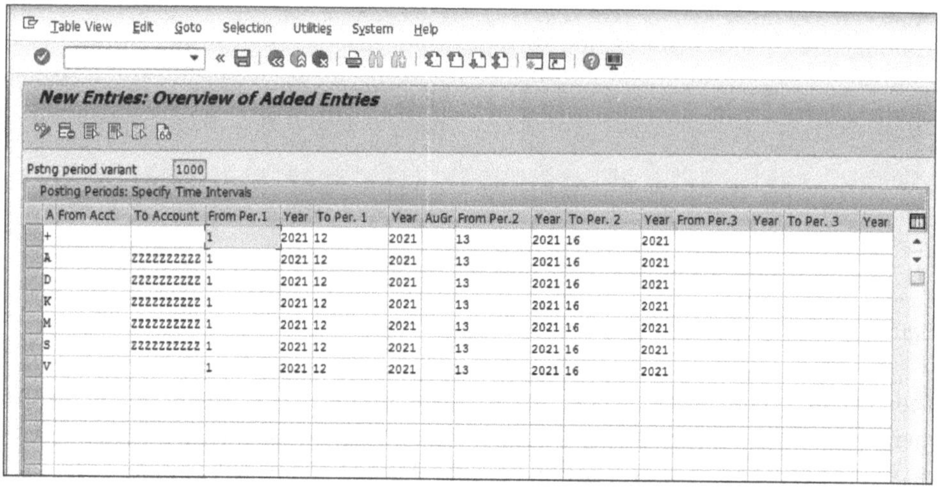

Table View Edit Goto Selection Utilities System Help

New Entries: Overview of Added Entries

Pstng period variant 1000

Posting Periods: Specify Time Intervals

A	From Acct	To Account	From Per.1	Year	To Per. 1	Year	AuGr	From Per.2	Year	To Per. 2	Year	From Per.3	Year	To Per. 3	Year
+			1	2021	12	2021		13	2021	16	2021				
A		ZZZZZZZZZZ	1	2021	12	2021		13	2021	16	2021				
D		ZZZZZZZZZZ	1	2021	12	2021		13	2021	16	2021				
K		ZZZZZZZZZZ	1	2021	12	2021		13	2021	16	2021				
M		ZZZZZZZZZZ	1	2021	12	2021		13	2021	16	2021				
S		ZZZZZZZZZZ	1	2021	12	2021		13	2021	16	2021				
V			1	2021	12	2021		13	2021	16	2021				

Figure 4.25 Defining Posting Periods

In the first column, **Account Type**, the different account types for which the posting periods rule in the row is valid are defined. The following account types are possible:

- **+**: Valid for all account types
- **A**: Assets
- **D**: Customers
- **K**: Vendors
- **M**: Materials
- **S**: General ledger accounts
- **V**: Contract accounts

Now, define the **From Acct** (from account) and **To Account** range for which the rule will be valid. In this example, don't set any restrictions for the account numbers. Next, define the **From** and **To Period/Year** combination. The periods within this range are open for postings; anything outside of this range is closed. You can enter multiple intervals in the three sets of columns available. Enter one range of periods from 1 to 12, which are the normal 12 accounting periods within a fiscal year, then enter special periods from 13 to 16, which are used to make special adjustment postings after the fiscal year is closed.

When you implement SAP S/4HANA, you must configure these periods initially. Normally, you leave the older periods open, but after the system is productive, configuring periods to maintain the posting periods is a user task, also available in the application menu. Accounting policy will determine whether only the current period will be open, which is the most common case, or if perhaps two or more periods will be kept open.

4.4.2 Intercompany Reconciliation

Intercompany reconciliation (ICR) provides for the periodic reconciliation of documents between legal entities within a group. Its purpose is to ensure that intercompany documents from different legal entities within the group match each another. This capability checks that documents have been correctly assigned and allows you to find corresponding intercompany documents and to assign them if needed.

To configure ICR, you must configure the intercompany relations between the company codes. For all company codes that post in intercompany documents, you need to assign general ledger accounts that are debited and credited when posting between them.

To assign general ledger accounts, follow the menu path **Financial Accounting • General Ledger Accounting • Business Transactions • Prepare Cross-Company Code Transactions.**

The system prompts you to enter the two company codes for which you're configuring the relationship. Enter the two company codes, as shown in Figure 4.26.

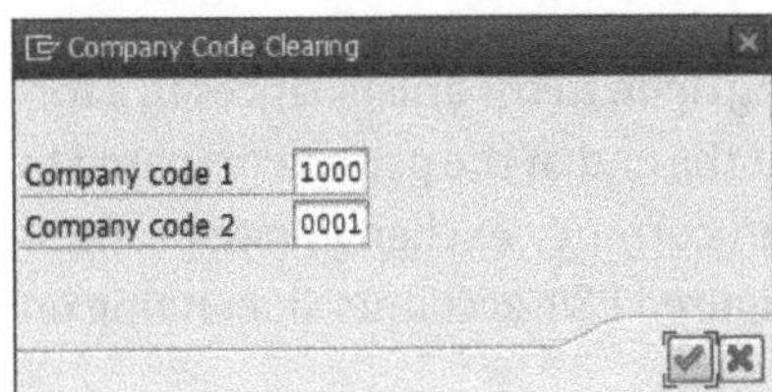

Figure 4.26 Cross-Company Code Relations

On the next screen, enter the accounts receivable and accounts payable accounts posted in each company code when posting the intercompany code with the other company code. As shown in Figure 4.27, enter the accounts receivable and accounts payable accounts posted in company code 1000 and cleared against 0001, and vice versa.

Update these accounts for your company codes and save your entries.

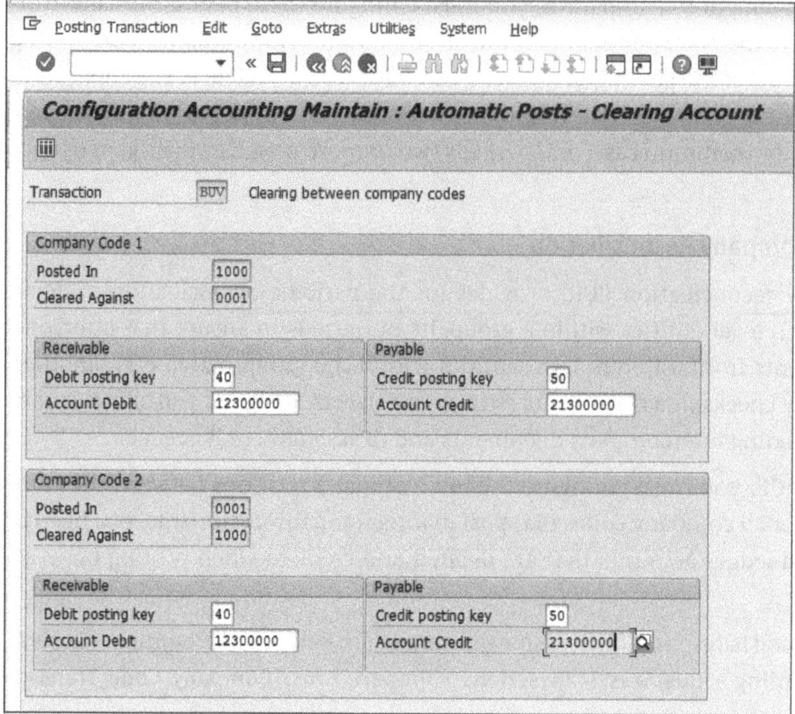

Figure 4.27 Intercompany Code Accounts

4.4.3 Foreign Currency Valuation

Foreign currency valuation is the process of revaluing open items and balances in a foreign currency to reflect changes in exchange rates at the end of the period compared to the time the transactions were posted. Thus, foreign currency exchange rate profit or loss can be recognized, which can be posted to configured P&L accounts, depending on your requirements.

You must configure the accounts to be automatically posted in the process. Follow the menu path **Financial Accounting • General Ledger Accounting • Periodic Processing • Valuate • Foreign Currency Valuation • Prepare Automatic Postings for Foreign Currency Valuation** or enter Transaction OBA1.

As shown in Figure 4.28, you can configure various exchange rate difference processes. The most commonly used are transactions **KDB: Exch. Rate Diff. using Exch. Rate Key** (exchange rate difference using exchange rate key), which is used for revaluation of general ledger account balances, and **KDF: Exchange Rate Dif.: Open Items/GL Acct** (exchange rate difference: open items/general ledger account), which is used to revalue open items in foreign currency.

Double-click **KDF** and enter your chart of accounts, and you'll see the screen shown in Figure 4.29.

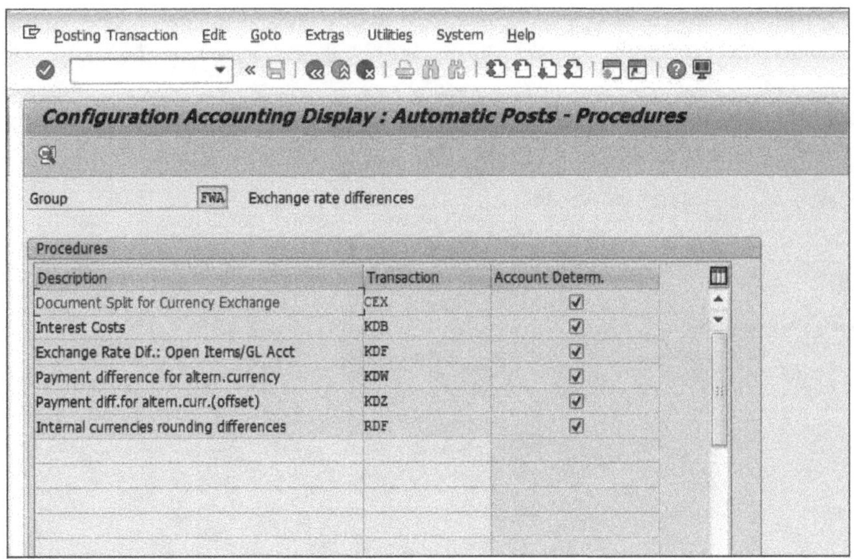

Figure 4.28 Foreign Currency Exchange Rate Differences Automatic Postings

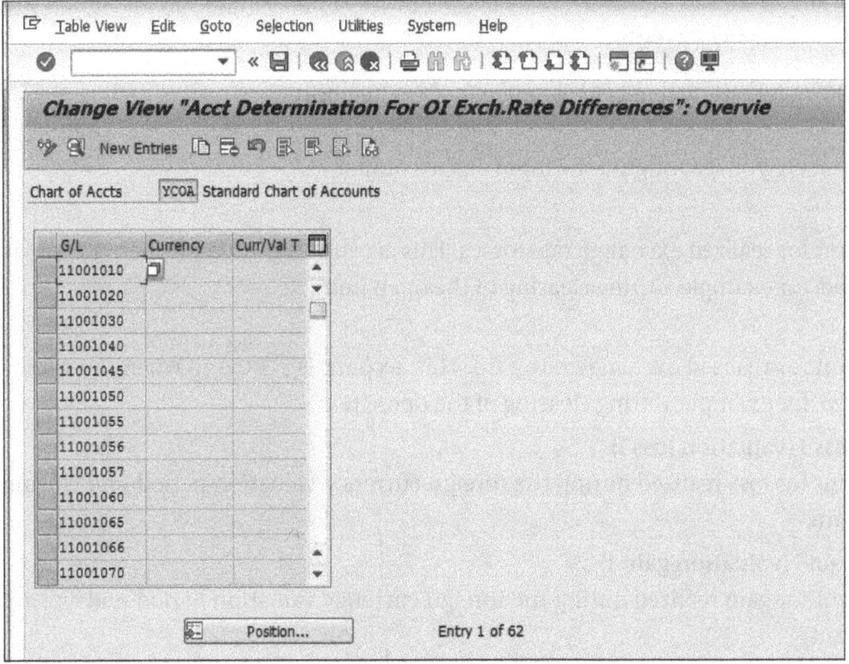

Figure 4.29 Open Item Automatic Postings

Figure 4.29 shows a list of general ledger open item accounts, which are configured to be revalued for foreign exchange rate differences. Double-click the first line to see the screen shown in Figure 4.30.

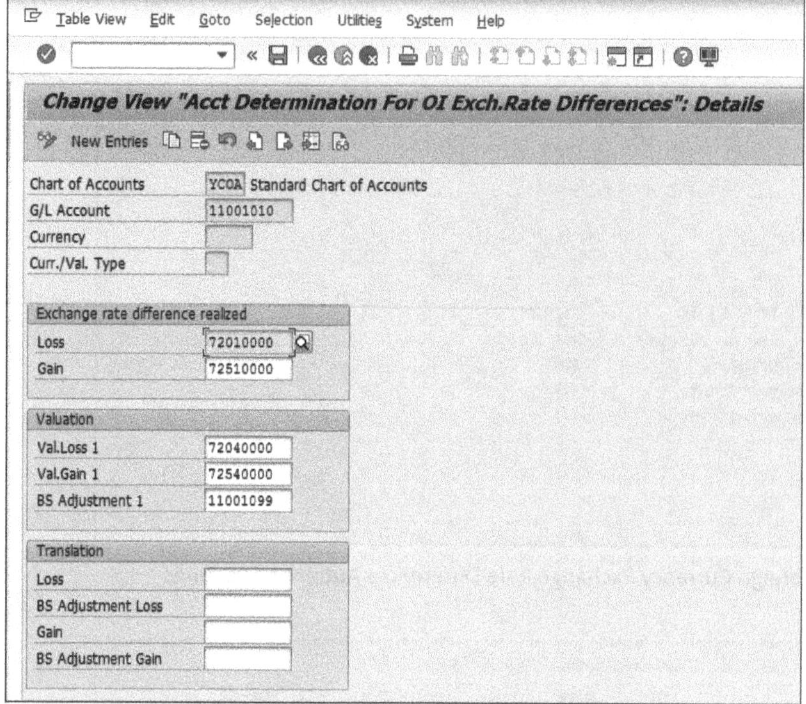

Figure 4.30 Automatic Accounts Assignment for FX Differences

On this screen, you'll configure the following accounts:

- **Loss**
  Account for realized exchange rate losses. This account is posted to when the loss is realized, for example, during clearing of the open item.
- **Gain**
  Account for realized exchange rate gain. This account is posted to when the gain is realized, for example, during clearing of the open item.
- **Val. Loss 1 (valuation loss 1)**
  Account for loss realized during the foreign currency valuation period-end closing program.
- **Val. Gain 1 (valuation gain 1)**
  Account for gain realized during the foreign currency valuation period-end closing program.
- **BS Adjustment 1**
  Account used to post the receivables and payables adjustment during the foreign currency valuation of open items.

In the **Translation** section, you can configure the following accounts:

- **Loss**
  After the foreign currency valuation program posts a loss and after the item is cleared, the loss is posted to this account.
- **BS Adjustment Loss**
  This account is used as a clearing account for translation based on a gain.
- **Gain**
  After the foreign currency valuation program posts a gain and after the item is cleared, the gain is posted to this account.
- **BS Adjustment Gain**
  This account is used as a clearing account for translation based on a loss.

In a similar fashion, you also can configure the other automatic exchange rate transactions.

4.4.4 Account Clearing

General ledger accounts can be managed on an open item basis, and in such cases, running the account clearing program also as part of the period-end closing, which automatically clears open items that correspond to specific criteria, makes sense. However, you must configure these criteria.

To configure automatic clearing criteria, follow the menu path **Financial Accounting • General Ledger Accounting • Business Transactions • Open Item Clearing • Open Item Processing • Prepare Automatic Clearing.**

As shown in Figure 4.31, you can configure the following fields:

- **ChAcct (chart of accounts)**
  In this field, which is optional, you can specify that the criteria are valid only for a particular chart of accounts.
- **AccTy (account type)**
  The account type, which could be a customer, vendor, or general ledger account. In this example, we're interested in the account type S for general ledger accounts, but the same configuration transaction can be used when you configure the rules for automatic clearing of customers and vendors.
- **From...To Account**
  You can specify a range of accounts for which the criteria are valid.
- **Criterion 1...5**
  You can specify up to five criteria in these columns. The automatic clearing program will clear only open items that match in terms of all criteria specified in this fields for the selected type and range of accounts. The criteria are entered with the technical

names of the fields, such as ZUONR, which is the assignment field, or GSBER, which is the business area.

Usually, at a minimum, you should use the assignment field because often items that should be cleared contain the same information in this field.

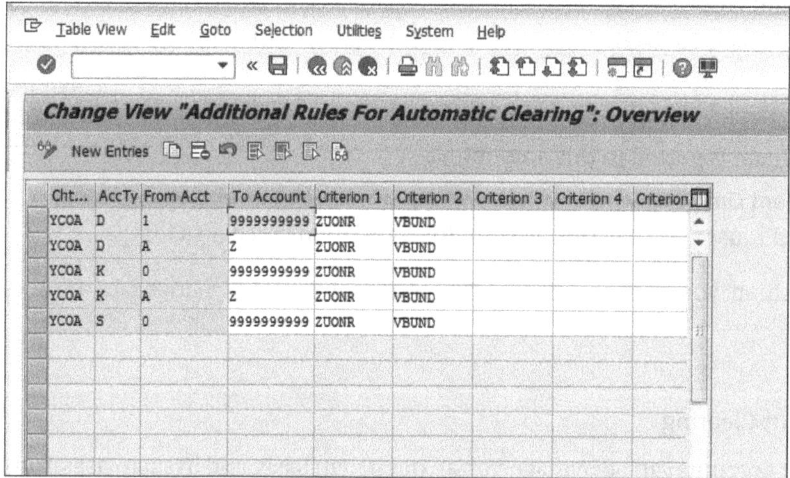

Figure 4.31 Automatic Clearing Configuration

Update the criteria based on your requirements for clearing, then save your entries.

4.4.5 Balance Carry-Forward

Balance carry-forward is a technical step in the year-end closing process that transfers the closing balances of accounts as starting balances in the new year and calculates the retained earnings for the P&L accounts.

SAP S/4HANA features a new transaction for balance carry-forward: Transaction FAGLVTR. In fact, the balance carry-forward procedure in SAP S/4HANA works differently because now the totals tables (table GLT0 in the classic general ledger and table FAGLFLEXT in the new general ledger) are obsolete, and the totals are calculated from table ACDOCA, which is a line-item table. However, table ACDOCA also contains general ledger carry-forward balances, but these balances posted in the table as period 0 documents. The balance carry-forward program creates documents in period 0 of the newly opened fiscal year, which represents the cumulative balances as of the beginning of the fiscal year.

For the balance carry-forward program, you must configure the retained earnings accounts to be posted to by following the menu path **Financial Accounting • General Ledger Accounting • Periodic Processing • Carry Forward • Define Retained Earnings Account**. After entering your chart of accounts in the popup window, you'll see the screen shown in Figure 4.32.

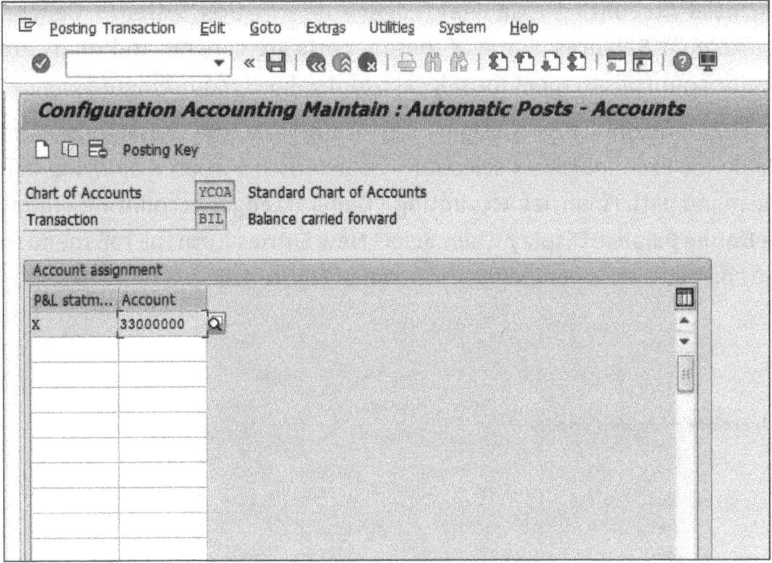

Figure 4.32 Configuring Retained Earnings Accounts

On this screen, you'll assign a retained earnings account to be posted to per P&L statement account type, which is part of the general ledger account master record (**Type/Description** tab). When executing the balance carry-forward program, the system will check the P&L type from the general ledger account master record and will transfer the result from that account to the retained earnings account specified here. At the beginning of the new year, the P&L accounts will start with a zero balance.

Thus completes our review of the settings related to period-end closing procedures. Next, we'll look at some of the reports provided by the general ledger information system.

4.5 Information System

The general ledger is the main area for providing accounting and taxation reports and, not surprisingly, provides a robust and extensive information system that can suit even the most complicated reporting requirements.

From the myriad of reports provided, we'll look at the most important: balance reports, financial statements, tax reports, and drilldown reporting.

4.5.1 Balance Reports

Several standard reports are available that provide various balance information on the general ledger account level. These reports are located in the application menu under

Accounting • Financial Accounting • General Ledger • Information System • General Ledger Reports • Account Balances. Some of these reports are general, and many are provided for specific countries to meet most local country-level requirements.

Still, you also have the flexibility to configure balance reports, the characteristics of which are available for each ledger as selection characteristics when displaying balances. Follow the menu path **Financial Accounting • General Ledger Accounting • Information System • Define Balance Display.** Then, select **New Entries** from the top menu to specify up to five characteristics per ledger, as shown in Figure 4.33.

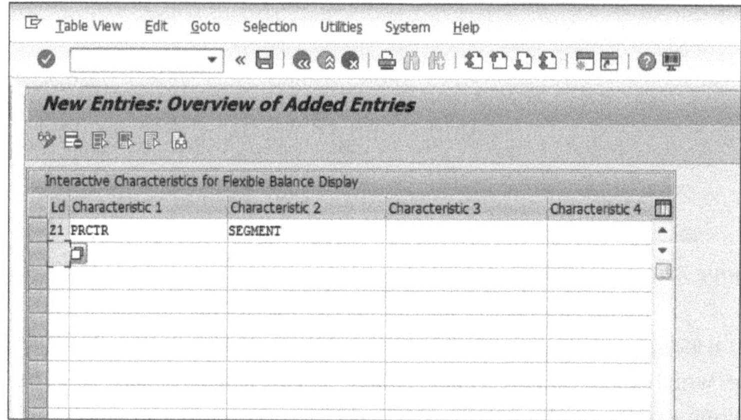

Figure 4.33 Configuring Balance Reports

On this screen, you can specify which characteristics are available for the ledgers as selection characteristics when displaying balances. You can specify up to five characteristics per ledger. Configuring the main reporting dimensions you would use, such as profit center and segment, for example, makes sense now. Configure the desired characteristics for each ledger and save your entries.

4.5.2 Financial Statements

Financial statements are legally required financial reports, such as balance sheets and P&L statements. They're configured in SAP S/4HANA as a collection of accounts, organized in sections and rows.

These settings are maintained in financial statement versions. To configure financial statement versions, follow the menu path **Financial Accounting • General Ledger Accounting • Master Data • G/L Accounts • Financial Statement Structures • Define Financial Statement Versions.** The system displays the available financial statement versions, as shown in Figure 4.34.

Normally, each country requires a separate financial statement version. Select **$US2: Financial Statement Version US** and copy it to create your new financial statement version by selecting **Copy As...** from the top menu.

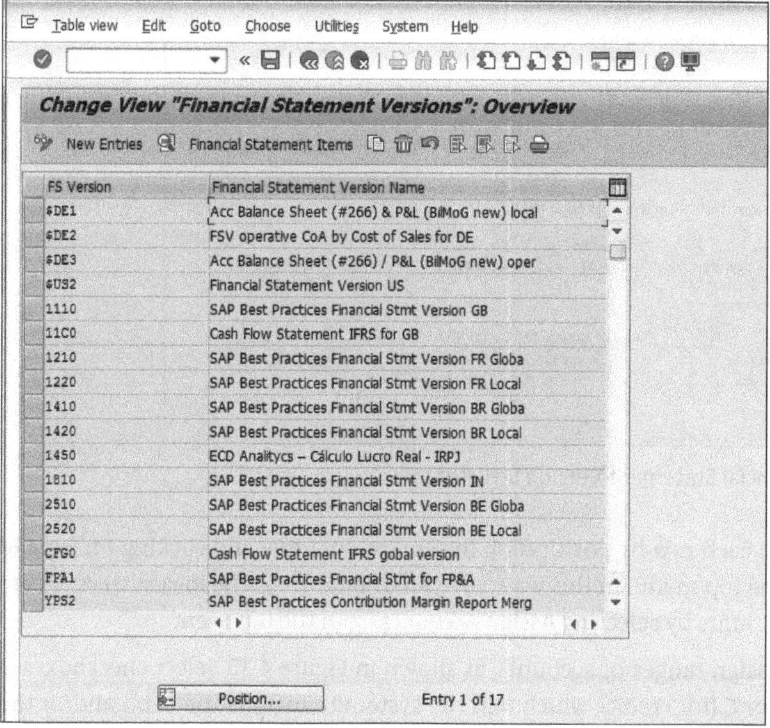

Figure 4.34 Financial Statement Versions

Next, give the new financial statement version a name and a description and map this version to your chart of accounts, as shown in Figure 4.35.

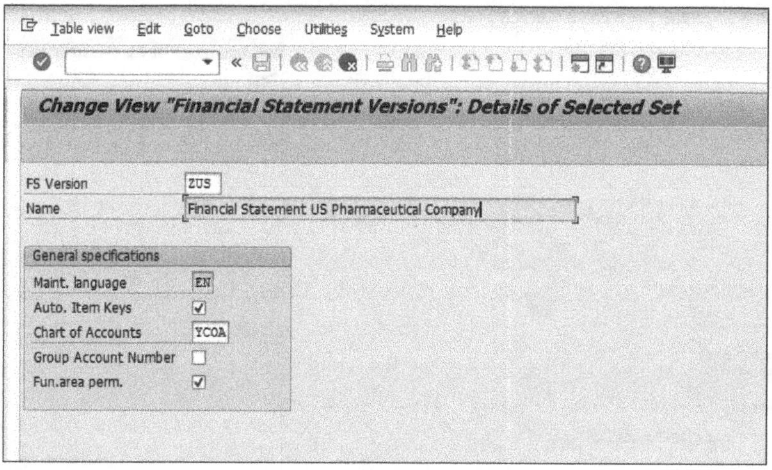

Figure 4.35 Copying a Financial Statement Version

Now, select **Financial Statement Items** from the top menu, which shows the structure of the financial statement, as shown in Figure 4.36.

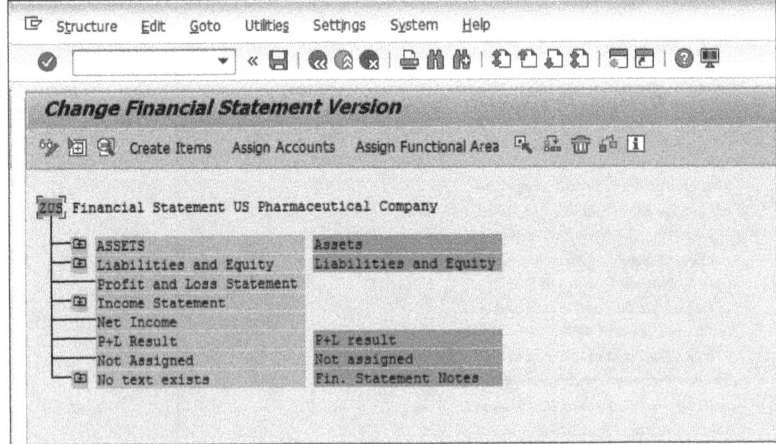

Figure 4.36 Financial Statement Version Structure

You can expand each row by positioning the cursor on a row and clicking on **Expand Subtree** from the top menu. In this way, you can drill down to the lowest rows, where you'll assign accounts by selecting **Assign Accounts** from the top menu.

Now, you can assign ranges of accounts, as shown in Figure 4.37. Select checkboxes **D** (for debit) and/or **C** (for credit), which tells the system to include the debit and/or the credit balances.

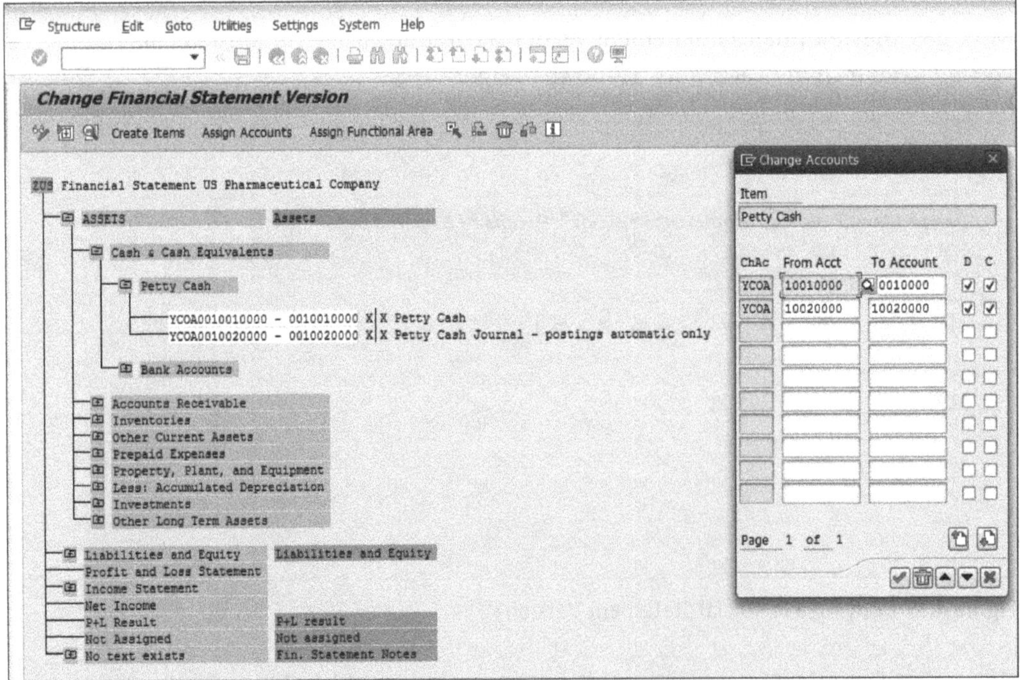

Figure 4.37 Assigning Accounts in Financial Statement Version

In this fashion, you can assign accounts to all the lines of the financial statement version.

4.5.3 Tax Reports

Tax reports are some of the most important reports provided by the general ledger in SAP S/4HANA because tax requirements are some of the most important legal requirements. These reports are located in the application menu under **Accounting • Financial Accounting • General Ledger • Reporting • Tax Reports**. Some of these reports are in the **General** folder, which means they're designed for use in most countries. Numerous country-specific reports are also available.

Most of these reports revolve around requirements for sales/use taxes on transactions, which are known as value-added tax (VAT) in most countries but as sales or use tax in the United States. Because these taxes are main sources of revenue for tax authorities and are difficult to track, stringent requirements exist for enterprise resource planning (ERP) systems for reporting on them.

The main report for sales tax in the United States is located in the application menu under **Accounting • Financial Accounting • General Ledger • Reporting • Tax Reports • USA • S_ALR_87012394 - Record of Use and Sales Taxes (USA)**, as shown in Figure 4.38.

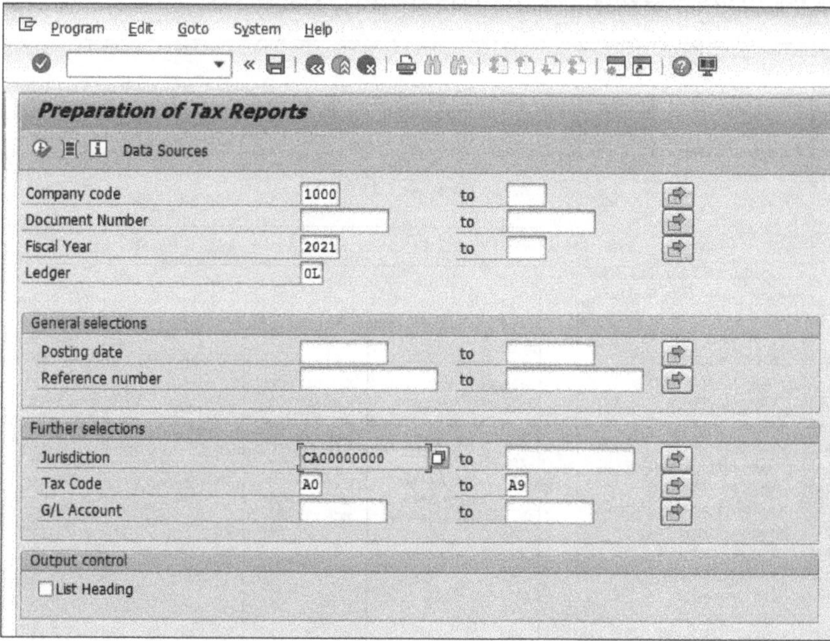

Figure 4.38 Sales and Use Tax Report

This report is based on jurisdiction codes and tax codes. Jurisdiction codes play the important role of determining the local tax rates for each jurisdiction (state, county, city) in the United States, and their configuration will be covered in detail in the next chapter.

4.5.4 Drilldown Reporting

Drilldown reporting is a flexible and convenient reporting technique in SAP in which a user can interactively navigate through a report by clicking certain characteristics to see additional details for any combination of these characteristics. Originally developed mostly for the Controlling module in SAP ERP, in SAP S/4HANA, drilldown reports are widely available and useful in the general ledger.

Several standard drilldown reports are available for the general ledger, and you can easily configure additional reports. The necessary configuration activities are located under the menu path **Financial Accounting • General Ledger Accounting • Information System • Drilldown Reports (G/L Accounts)**. First, you must define a *form*, which defines the structure of available characteristics and their values. Then, you'll define reports based on this form, specifying the report layout, selection criteria, and output settings.

Let's see how a form is defined. Follow the menu path **Financial Accounting • General Ledger Accounting • Information System • Drilldown Reports (G/L Accounts) • Form • Specify Form**. Then, select the **Change Form** activity. In the resulting screen, navigate to the **0SAPBLNCE-01 G/L Accounts—Bal.** form, as shown in Figure 4.39.

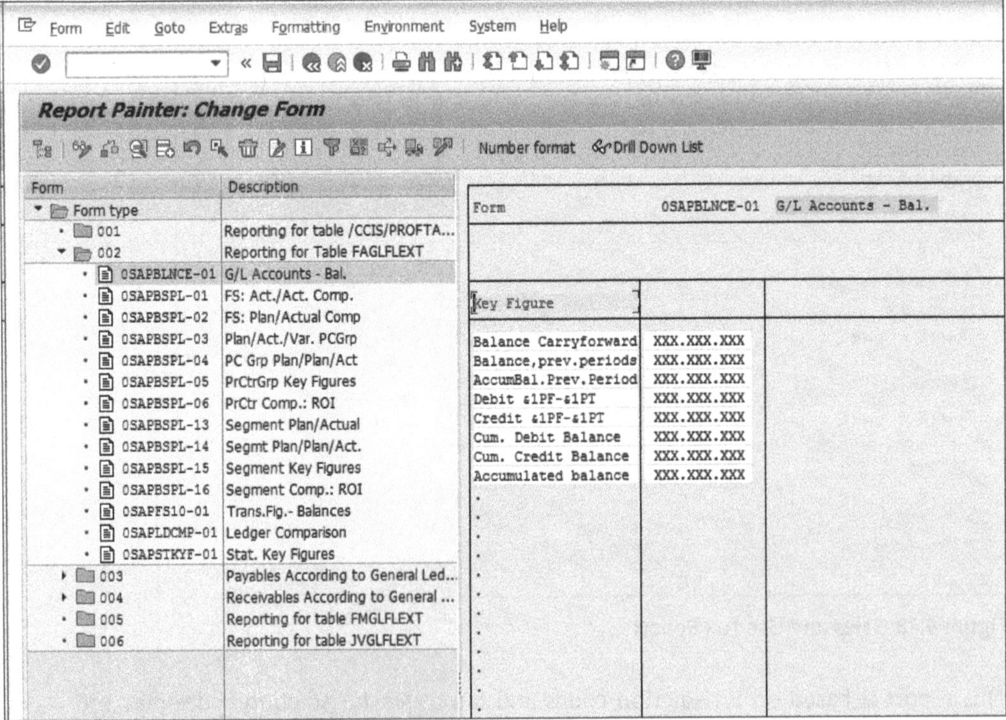

Figure 4.39 Drilldown Reporting Form

This standard form can be used for reporting general ledger account balances. You can copy it to your form and change it as needed. Each line in the form is defined with its characteristics and values. Double-click on the **Balance Carryforward** line, for example, to open the screen shown in Figure 4.40.

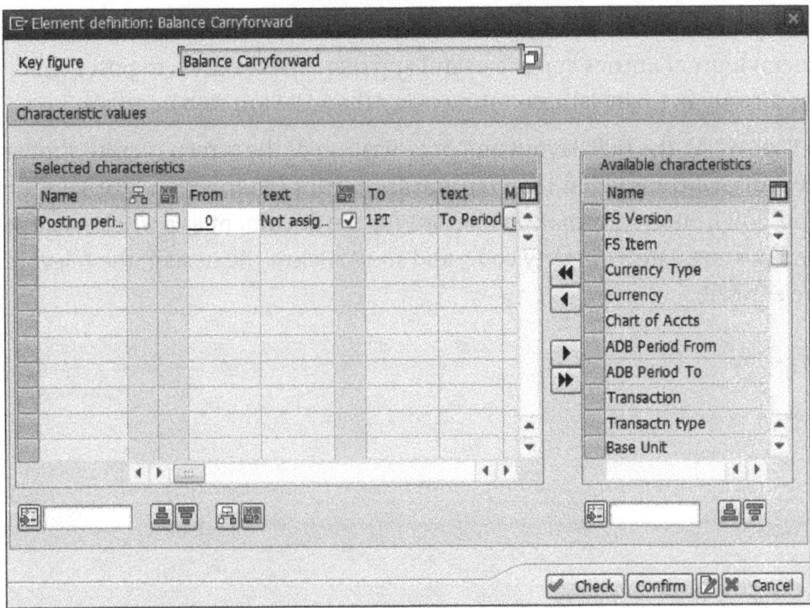

Figure 4.40 Drilldown Report Line Definition

On the right side, you'll see a list of available characteristics and, on the left side, the posting period is selected. The **From** and **To** columns contain the values to be included in the report. These values can be entered directly in the columns. Alternatively, you can use sets (predefined group of values), if you select the checkbox in the column, or variables (parameters to be entered during program executing in the selection screen), if you select the checkbox in the column. As shown in Figure 4.39, a variable called **1PT** is selected. In this case, the posting period will be entered in the selection screen of the drilldown reports based on this form.

In this fashion, you also can define the other lines and columns of the report form and then create your own reports based on the form.

4.6 SAP Fiori Applications

As you now know, SAP Fiori is user interface (UI) especially designed and optimized for SAP S/4HANA. Although adoption may take some time because SAP keeps adding functions as SAP Fiori apps and because existing SAP users are quite used to using the classic SAP GUI, SAP Fiori is the future and will become even more important as it matures.

SAP Fiori by itself could be a topic for another large volume, but for our purposes, we'll just look at a few useful SAP Fiori apps available for the general ledger, such as the Post General Journal Entries app and the Upload Journal Entries app.

4.6.1 Post General Journal Entries App

The Post General Journal Entries app is a useful app that enables users to post general ledger entries directly in financial accounting using the SAP Fiori web interface.

As shown in Figure 4.41, the field layout and organization of the screen is quite similar to the classic SAP GUI transaction to enter journal entries (Transaction FB50). In the header section, you'll enter information relevant for the document as a whole, such as document and posting date, company code, and so on. Below the header, the relevant line items are entered.

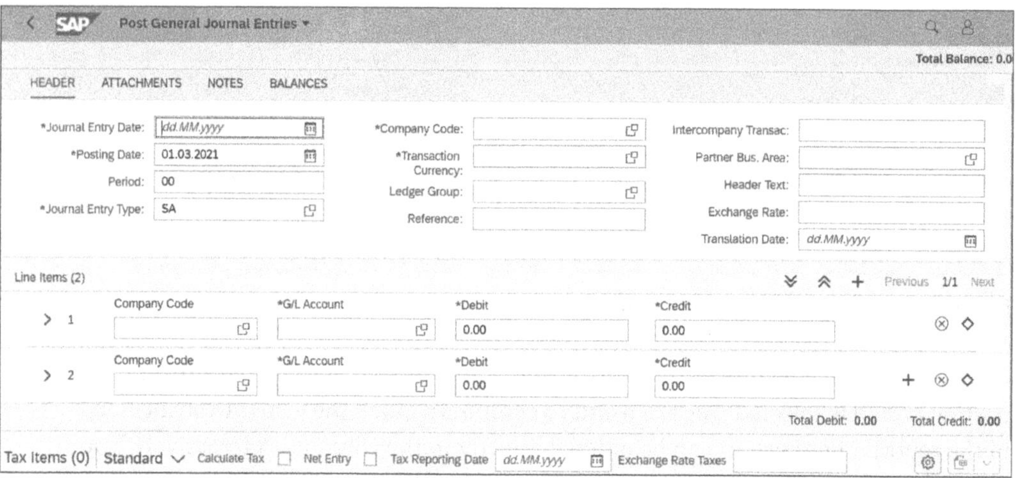

Figure 4.41 Post Journal Entries App

Users of the classic SAP GUI transaction should be quite comfortable with this app, but using the SAP Fiori web-based interface will be easier because the SAP Fiori app offers an intuitive web interface with a responsive design that automatically adapts to the type of device being used.

4.6.2 Upload General Journal Entries App

The Upload General Journal Entries app is a particularly useful SAP Fiori app. People who've worked with previous SAP ERP systems are well aware that SAP didn't have a convenient out of the box transaction for the mass upload of general ledger journals via an Excel file. Because this capability is an important and commonly used function in most companies, SAP customers often would buy additional third-party tools to integrate with their SAP systems or would develop their own custom programs in SAP.

Starting with SAP S/4HANA 1709, an SAP Fiori app is available for uploading journal entries, as shown in Figure 4.42.

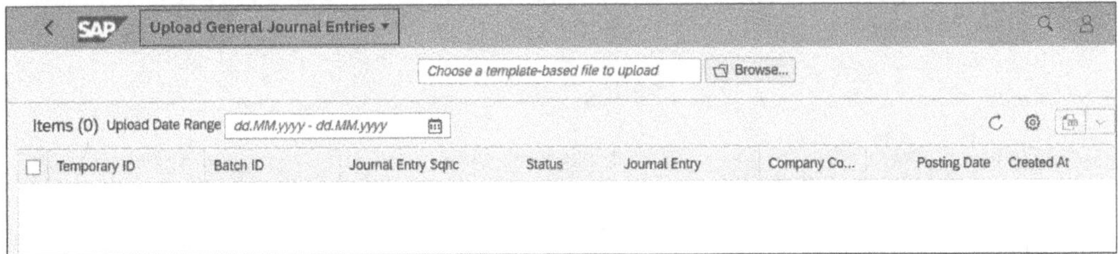

Figure 4.42 Upload Journal Entries App

With this app, you can select a template-based file by clicking the **Browse** button, which can then be uploaded easily as journal entries in the system. No additional programming is required now for this important task!

4.7 Summary

In this chapter, we covered the configuration of the general ledger in SAP S/4HANA in depth. The general ledger is the most fundamental functionality in SAP S/4HANA, and ultimately, all postings flow into and are recorded in the Universal Journal. As such, the general ledger is an area where you can most clearly see the great improvements that SAP S/4HANA brings to finance through its simplification and streamlining of processes.

After finishing this chapter, you should understand the master data in the general ledger. You're now in a position to properly organize your chart of accounts and create efficient general ledger accounts that enable your organization to accurately depict its financial processes.

We also covered document splitting, which is a fundamental feature of SAP S/4HANA that enables full reporting on various levels of characteristics.

We discussed account determination and automatic postings, which allow all financial data to be posted in the general ledger. We also discussed the main logistic processes in the system so that you can better understand the flow of values to the general ledger.

We then configured the main periodic processes and financial closing processes, such as managing posting periods, ICR, foreign currency revaluation, account clearing, and balance carry-forward. Month-end and year-end closing are some of the most important activities in the general ledger area because they provide financial results for the company.

Then, we explained the various important reports available from the general ledger information system and described the configuration needed for them. Last but not least, we provided an overview of some useful general ledger SAP Fiori apps. With that topic, we've finished with general ledger configuration, and we can now move on to configuring the subledgers in accounting, starting with accounts payable.

Chapter 5
Accounts Payable

This chapter provides step-by-step instructions for configuring accounts payable in SAP S/4HANA and explains the integration with materials management processes. We'll also introduce you to the new business partner concept in SAP S/4HANA, payment processing, and available reporting for accounts payable.

The next area we'll configure is accounts payable, which is used to manage the financial processes related to purchasing, including posting vendor invoices, payment processing, and the clearing and reconciliation of open items. We'll provide a detailed explanation of how to configure the master data, business transactions, and information system for accounts payable.

5.1 Business Partner

In SAP S/4HANA, the master data for accounts payable is managed via the business partner master data object. Business partners are not an entirely new concept in SAP S/4HANA. In an SAP ERP system, business partners were used to manage certain partner master data objects, mostly in financial supply chain management. However, now in SAP S/4HANA, the use of business partners is mandatory in financial accounting, and both vendor master records (used in accounts payable) and customer master records (used in accounts receivable) are managed via the business partner concept.

This new business partner concept enables many benefits, including the following:

- Now, a fully integrated relationship exists between vendors and customers when the same company/person serves as both a supplier and a customer of the organization.
- General data is shared between different business partner roles.
- Application-specific business partner roles can be created that extend already defined business partners, such as for credit management or collections management.
- A harmonized architecture now exists between SAP functional areas.

A single transaction, Transaction BP, is available for managing all business partner master data processes, which makes obsolete the previous create/change/display transaction codes for vendors, such as Transaction FK01/02/03, Transaction XK01/02/03, and so on. In fact, if you execute one of these transaction codes to maintain a business partner, you'll be redirected to Transaction BP.

As you'll learn in the following sections, the finance data for vendors in the business partner record is divided into general data and company code data. Once we've covered the finance data, we'll quickly walk you through the underlying configuration for business partners.

5.1.1 General Data

Let's see how you can navigate through the business partner master record. Enter Transaction BP to see the screen shown in Figure 5.1.

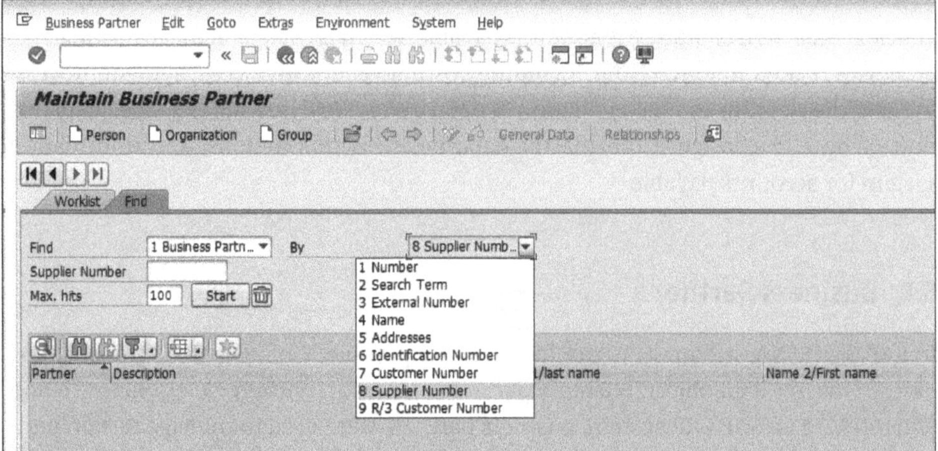

Figure 5.1 Business Partner Search

On this screen, using the dropdown option on the right side, you can search business partners by various roles. From the **By** dropdown list, select **8: By Supplier Number** to view the business partners maintained as vendors. Delete the value **100** in the **MaxHit** (max hits) field so that the search has no limitation, then click the **Start** button. In the resulting list, double-click any vendor number, which takes you to the general data for that business partner, as shown in Figure 5.2.

This data is valid for all partner functions of the business partner. It's organized into tabs, which group together similar fields, such as address data, control, payment transactions, and so on. When you click the **Display in BP Role** (display in business partner role) dropdown list, you'll see the roles maintained for the business partner. The **FI Supplier Role** (financial accounting supplier role) contains the vendor's financial data, and **Supplier** holds the purchasing data for the vendor. Now, in the **Display in BP Role** dropdown list, select the **FI Supplier Role** to see financial accounting-related tabs, such as **Tax Data**.

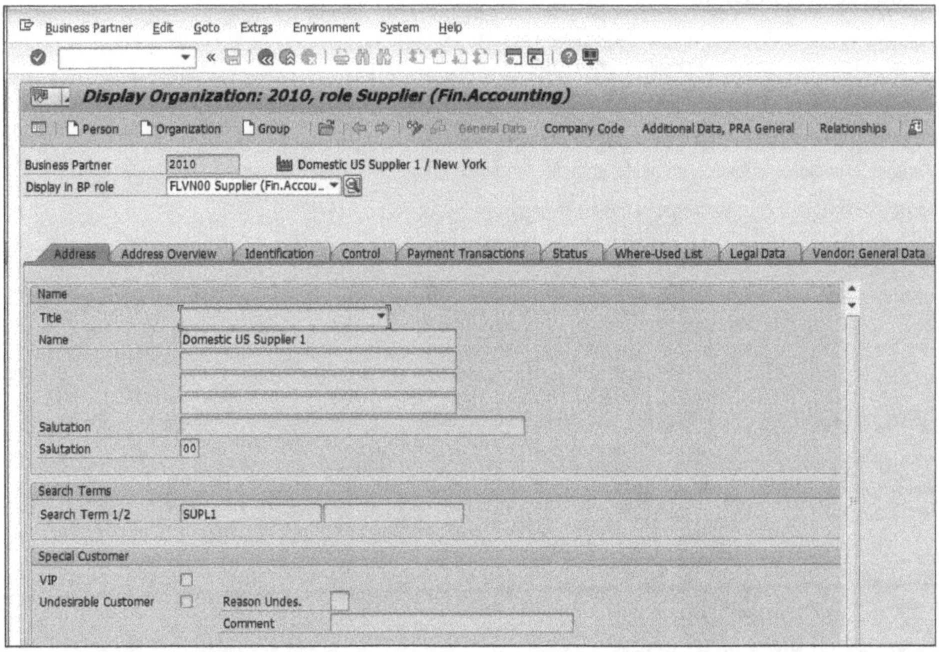

Figure 5.2 Business Partner General Data

You can update fields by selecting **Switch Between Display and Change** in the top menu.

5.1.2 Company Code Data

To view the company code-level data for the vendor, first, select the **Supplier (Fin. Accounting)** business partner role in the dropdown list. Then, select **Company Code** from the top menu. Figure 5.3 shows the company code data of the financial accounting vendor account. You can change the company code and maintain the vendor for another company code by clicking the **Switch Company Code** button.

All these fields are maintained on the company code level and can be different from company code to company code. In the **Reconciliation acct.** (reconciliation account) field, you'll maintain the reconciliation account, which is the general ledger account posted to each time something is posted to this vendor. This reconciliation account is the account that's normally credited for vendor invoices and debited for payments, credit memos, or when otherwise clearing open vendor items.

Notice how the business partner and vendor have the same account numbers. This best practice is controlled with the configuration of the number ranges assigned to vendor account groups and to business partner account groups. These groups are separate objects and can have different number ranges, but using different number ranges could cause confusion.

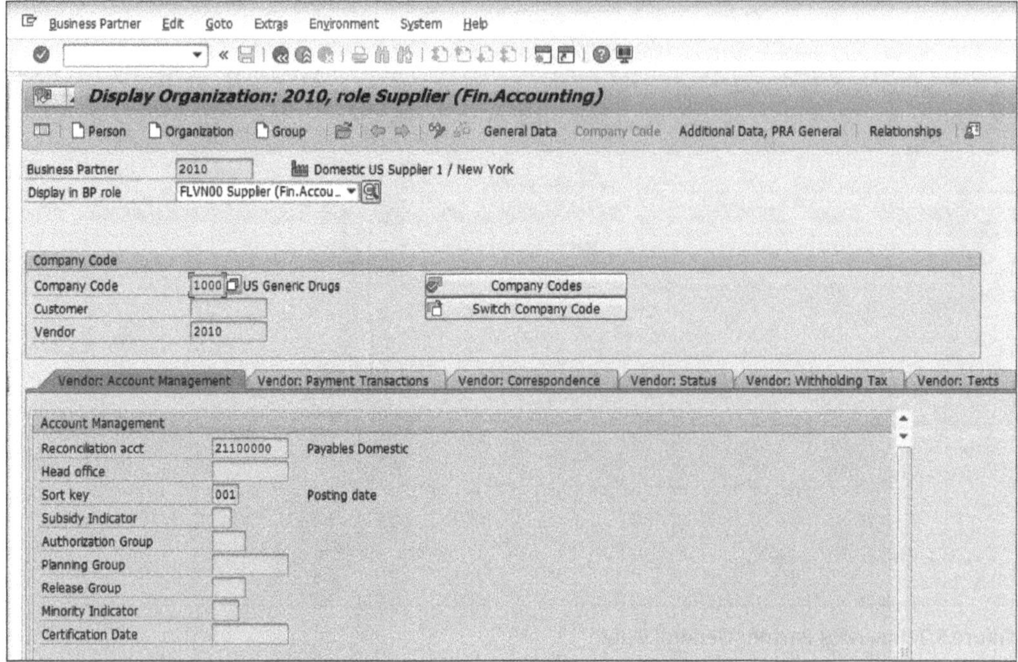

Figure 5.3 Business Partner Company Code Data

5.1.3 Business Partner Configuration

Now, let's look at the underlying configuration for business partners. To define business partner groups and number ranges, follow the menu path **Cross-Application Components • SAP Business Partner • Business Partner • Basic Settings • Number Ranges and Groupings • Define Groupings and Assign Number Ranges.**

Figure 5.4 shows a list of business partner groups and their number ranges. When creating a business partner from a specific group, a number will be assigned from the corresponding number range. Note that the system creates separate account numbers for the business partner and the vendor. When posting to the vendor, the vendor account number is used, but you should have the same numbers assigned on the business partner and vendor levels.

The actual number ranges for business partners are maintained by following the menu path **Cross-Application Components • SAP Business Partner • Business Partner • Basic Settings • Number Ranges and Groupings • Define Number Ranges.** As shown in Figure 5.5, the number range object is **BU_PARTNER**.

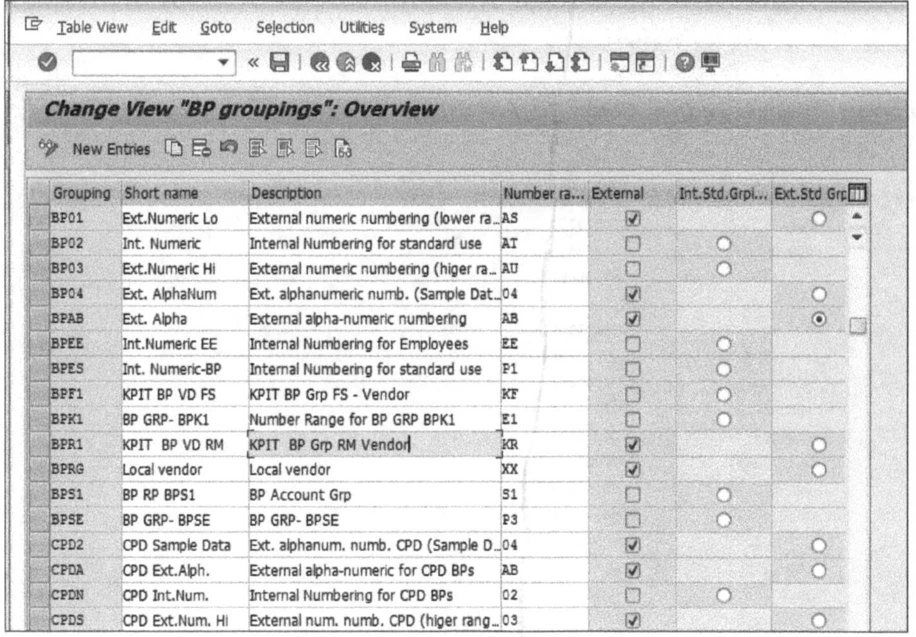

Figure 5.4 Business Partner Groups and Number Ranges

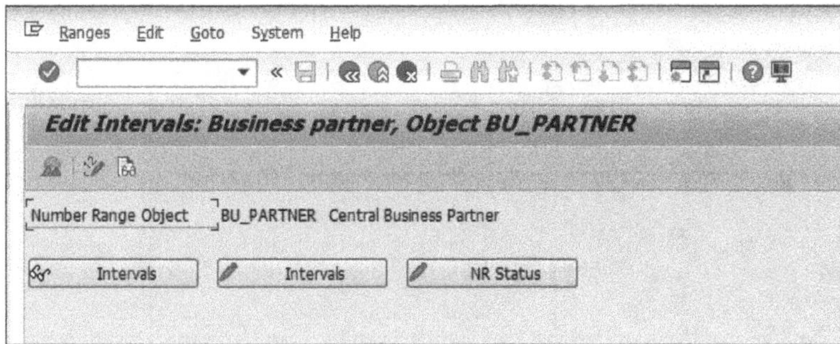

Figure 5.5 Business Partner Number Ranges

Click the Intervals button to modify the number ranges. On the screen shown in Figure 5.6, you can modify number ranges or create new ones for use in business partner groups.

The next step is to define the vendor groups with their number ranges. Follow the menu path **Financial Accounting • Accounts Receivable and Accounts Payable • Vendor Accounts • Master Data • Preparations for Creating Vendor Master Data • Assign Number Ranges to Vendor Account Groups.** Figure 5.7 shows how number ranges can be assigned to various vendor groups.

Edit Intervals: Business partner, Object BU_PARTNER

Number Range No.	From No.	To Number	NR Status	External
01	0000001000	0000001999	1009	☐
02	0001000000	0001999999	1000049	☐
03	0010000000	0999999999	0	☑
04	0A	8Z	0	☑
AB	A	ZZZZZZZZZZ	0	☑
AS	0000000700	0000000799	0	☑
AT	0000000800	0000000899	809	☐
AU	0000000900	0000000999	0	☐
BF	0000000501	0000000600	530	☐
BR	0000000601	0000000650	0	☑
E1	0000500300	0000500399	500309	☐
EE	9980000000	9999999999	9980000009	☐
K1	0000002000	0000002999	2019	☐
K2	0000003000	0000003999	3019	☐
KF	0000000401	0000000450	410	☐
KR	0000000451	0000000500	0	☑

Figure 5.6 Changing Business Partner Number Ranges

Change View "Assign Vendor Account Groups->Number Range": Overview

Group	Name	Number range
EMPL	Employee as Supplier	BP
KPFV	Financial Services for KPIT	KF
KPRM	Raw Material for KPIT	KR
KRED		MM
LIEF		
SUPL	Supplier	MM

Figure 5.7 Vendor Account Groups and Number Ranges

The actual number ranges are defined by following the menu path **Financial Accounting • Accounts Receivable and Accounts Payable • Vendor Accounts • Master Data • Preparations for Creating Vendor Master Data • Create Number Ranges for Vendor Accounts**. As shown in Figure 5.8, the number range object is **KREDITOR**. Click the **Intervals** button to change the number ranges.

On the screen shown in Figure 5.9, you can change the numbers behind the vendor number ranges by changing the numbers in the **From** and **To** columns of the range.

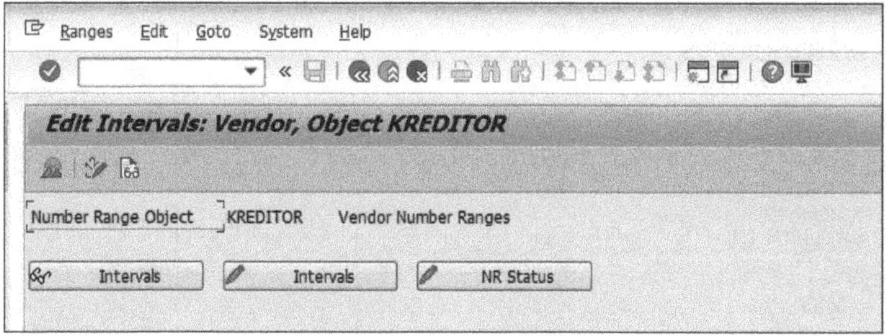

Figure 5.8 Vendor Number Ranges

Interval Edit Goto System Help

Edit Intervals: Vendor, Object KREDITOR

Number Range No.	From No.	To Number	NR Status	External
01	0000000300	0000000400	309	☐
AS	0000000700	0000000799	0	☑
AT	0000000800	0000000899	0	☑
AU	0000000900	0000000999	0	☑
BP	0000000001	0000000101	0	☑
E2	0000500700	0000500799	0	☐
K1	0000002000	0000002999	0	☑
KF	0000000401	0000000450	405	☐
KR	0000000451	0000000500	0	☑

Figure 5.9 Defining Vendor Number Ranges

The next step is to configure the customer-vendor integration (CVI). CVI is the link between the business partner from one side and the vendor and customer from on the other.

First, you must configure the synchronization control for business partners by following the menu path **Cross-Application Components • Master Data Synchronization • Synchronization Control • Synchronization Control • Activate PPO Requests for Platform Objects in the Dialog**. As shown in Figure 5.10, make sure that synchronization object **BP** is active for postprocessing by selecting the **PPO Active** (postprocessing active) checkbox.

Now, you'll need to configure the link between the business partner and the vendor by following the menu path **Cross-Application Components • Master Data Synchronization • Customer/Vendor Integration • Business Partner Settings • Settings for Vendor Integration • Set BP Role Category for Direction BP to Vendor**. Figure 5.11 shows a list of business partner roles related to vendors. Double-click **FLVN00**, which is the business partner role for financial accounting vendors.

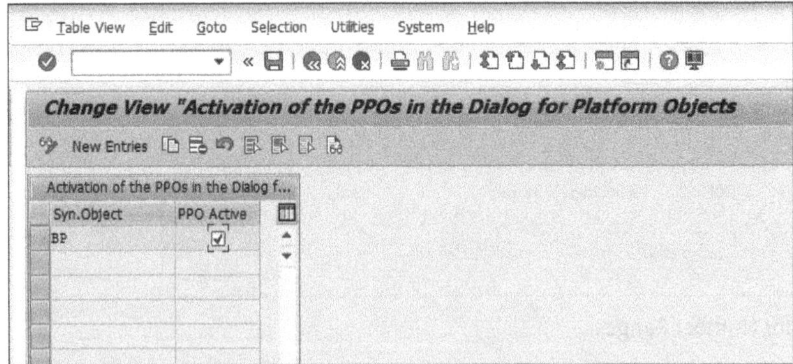

Figure 5.10 Activation of Postprocessing in the Business Partner

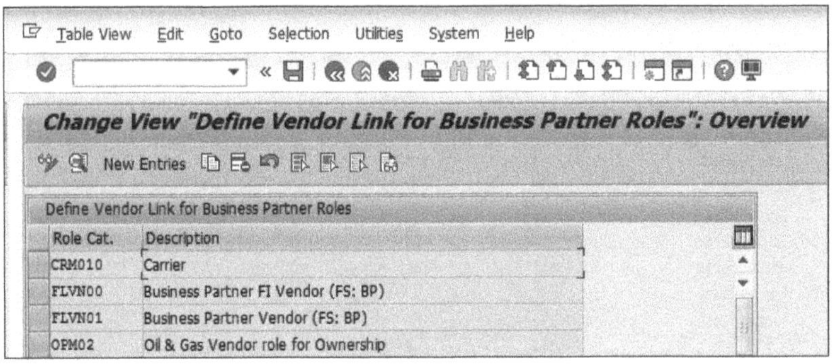

Figure 5.11 Link Business Partner to Vendors

Now, on the screen shown in Figure 5.12, make sure that **Vendor-Based** is selected. This selection ensures having a vendor for this business partner role is mandatory. Then, when you process a business partner in this role, the system automatically creates or updates the vendor with the relevant data in financial accounting.

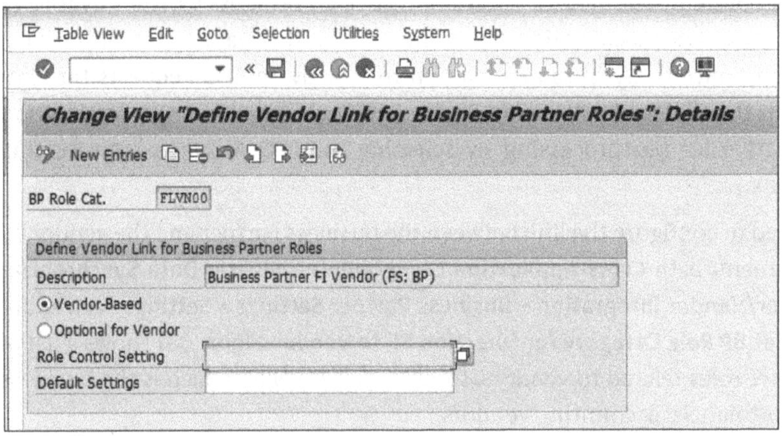

Figure 5.12 Business Partner to Vendor Settings for Finance Vendors

The next step is to configure the integration from vendor to business partner by following the menu path **Cross-Application Components • Master Data Synchronization • Customer/Vendor Integration • Business Partner Settings • Settings for Vendor Integration • Define BP Role for Direction Vendor to BP**.

On the screen shown in Figure 5.13, you can map vendor groups with business partner roles. Select **New Entries** from the top menu and link the relevant vendor groups with the desired business partner roles. This step ensures that, when you process a vendor with the relevant account group, the system will create or update a business partner in the business partner roles that are assigned to the vendor group.

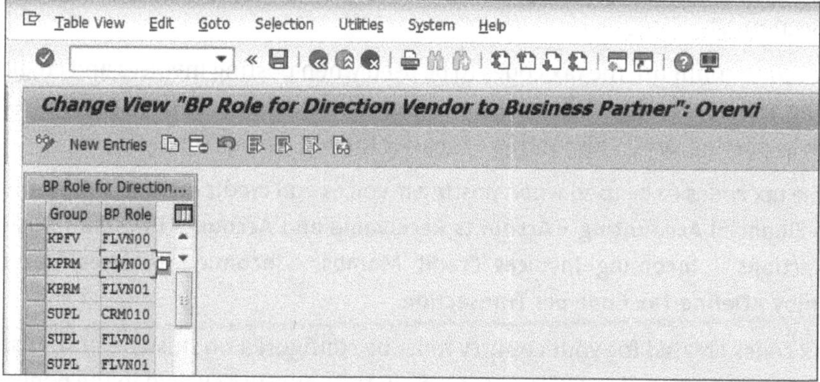

Figure 5.13 Linking Vendor Groups to Business Partner Roles

Now that we've established the settings for business partners, let's examine the configuration of various related business transactions.

5.2 Business Transactions

The main business transactions that are managed in accounts payable are incoming invoices and credit memos from vendors, as well as outgoing payments for these invoices and supporting processes such as goods receipt/invoice receipt (GR/IR) clearing. In this section, we'll explain not only those processes, but also the integration with vendor invoice management, which scans for vendor invoices and provides automatic postings in SAP S/4HANA, as well as enables tax determination in purchasing processes.

5.2.1 Incoming Invoices/Credit Memos in Financial Accounting

In SAP S/4HANA, two ways exist for posting vendor invoices and credit memos. The most common way is to post these items through materials management, where they will reference a purchase order (PO) and are integrated with the purchasing process.

However, in some cases, you may also need to post invoices and credit memos directly into financial accounting, without reference to a PO. This scenario arises usually for smaller purchases that don't require specific approvals, such as stationery supplies. These costs are posted in financial accounting, usually debiting an expense account and cost center or another cost object and crediting a vendor account.

Not much specific customizing is needed to enable the processing of these transactions in financial accounting. Your vendor accounts must be set up as business partners, as described in the previous section. The document types you're going to use must also be defined—typically the standard SAP document type KR for vendor invoices and document type KG for vendor credit memos. We covered document type configuration in Chapter 3, Section 3.4.

You'll also need to configure the tax codes to be used when posting invoices and credit memos using Transaction FB60, in which you won't have to specify overly technical objects such as posting keys. This interface is easier for end users to use.

To enable the tax codes to be used when posting invoices and credit memos, follow the menu path **Financial Accounting • Accounts Receivable and Accounts Payable • Business Transactions • Incoming Invoices/Credit Memos • Incoming Invoices/Credit Memos—Enjoy • Define Tax Code per Transaction**.

Any new tax codes created for your country must be configured on this screen so that they can be used in Transaction FB60. Enter "US" in the **Country Key** field in the popup window, as shown in Figure 5.14.

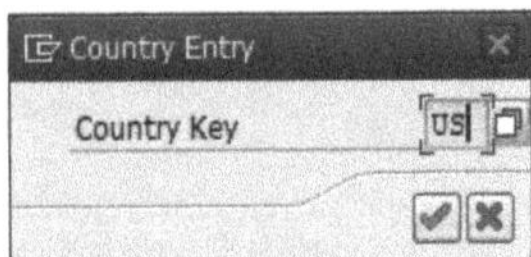

Figure 5.14 Selecting a Country

Initially, the following screen is blank, as shown in Figure 5.15. Select **New Entries** from the top menu to configure new tax codes.

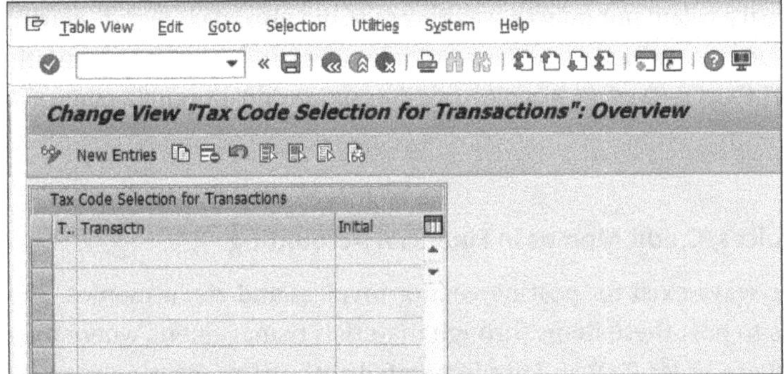

Figure 5.15 Defining Tax Codes for Invoices and Credit Memos: Initial Screen

As shown in Figure 5.16, you'll now enter the input tax codes. In the **Transaction** column, you can select **Relevant for All Transactions** or select **Financial Accounting Invoice Receipt** if you want to limit the tax code to financial accounting document posting only. If you check the **Initial** flag, the tax code will be the default for the transaction.

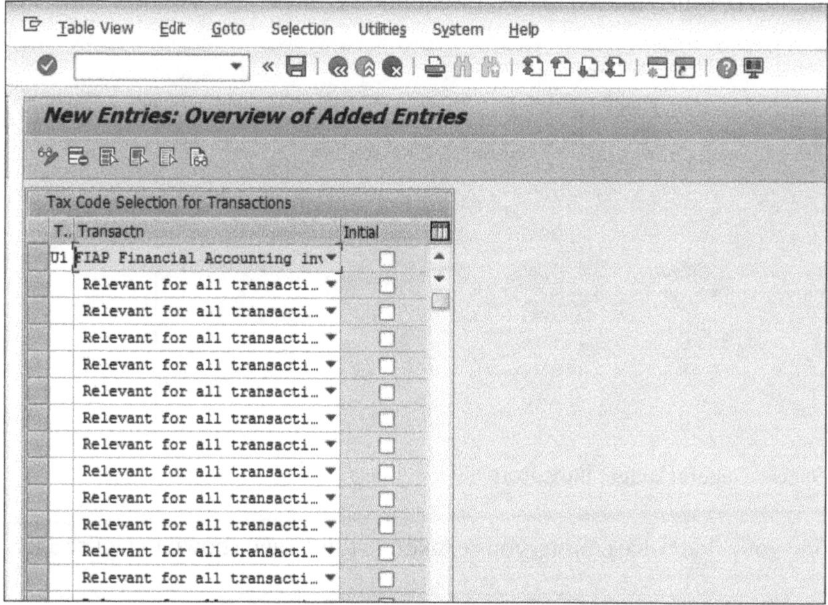

Figure 5.16 Defining Tax Codes for Enjoy Invoices/Credit Memos

5.2.2 Posting with Alternative Reconciliation Account

We've seen that, in the business partner master record, when maintaining the financial accounting vendor data on the company code, you'll specify a reconciliation account, which is the general ledger account automatically posted with each posting to the vendor account. This is only one account, which you can specify in the master record—but sometimes, for various business cases, you may need to post to another account. This flexibility is necessary because, from an accounting point of view, certain transactions—such as the posting of discounts, guarantees, or payment requests—must be posted to specific accounts. Therefore, SAP provides functionality to post to alternative reconciliation accounts.

In this process, the special general ledger indicator is used. This indicator can be entered in documents and will swap the general ledger reconciliation account from the vendor master record with another alternative general ledger account configured for this special general ledger indicator. Let's walk through setting up and configuring special general ledger indicators.

To define alternative reconciliation accounts, follow the menu path **Financial Accounting • Accounts Receivable and Accounts Payable • Business Transactions • Postings with**

Alternative Reconciliation Accounts • Other Special G/L Transactions • Define Alternative Reconciliation Account for Vendors.

As shown in Figure 5.17, you'll see a list of predefined special general ledger indicators provided by SAP. You can also create new indicators to meet your specific needs. Double-click indicator **D**, which is used to post discounts.

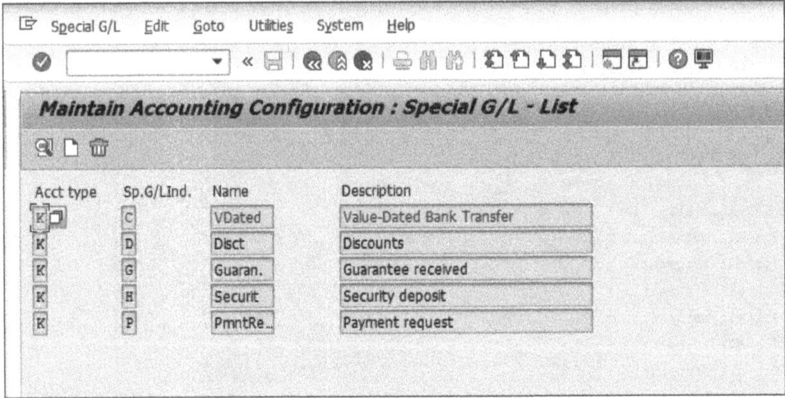

Figure 5.17 Special General Ledger Indicators

After entering your chart of accounts, you're taken to the screen shown in Figure 5.18.

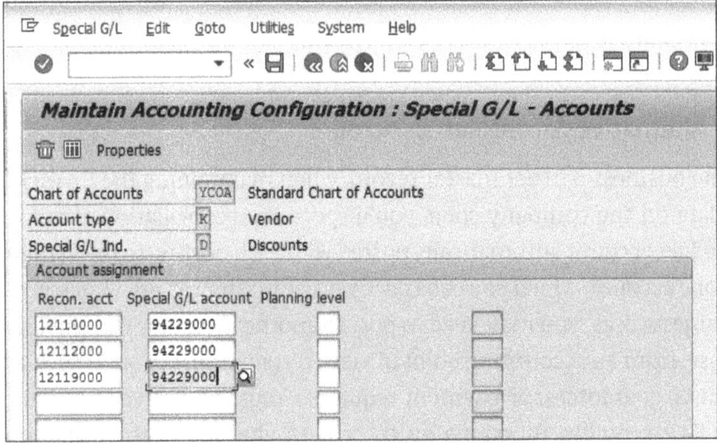

Figure 5.18 Accounts for Special General Ledger Indicators

On this screen, for each account defined in the **Recon. Acct** (reconciliation account) column, which are used in vendor master records, you can define an alternative account in the **Special G/L Account** column. Then, when posting with the special general ledger indicator for a vendor linked with this reconciliation account, the system will automatically reroute the posting to the alternative reconciliation account.

5.2.3 Incoming Invoices/Credit Memos from Materials Management

Most incoming vendor invoices and credit memos will be posted through integration with materials management. The resulting documents in financial accounting will be posted automatically based on the account determination we covered in Chapter 4, Section 4.3.3.

Most of the configuration for materials management vendor invoices and credit memos (which are commonly referred to as logistics invoice verification) lies within the materials management area of responsibility and thus are configured there. However, as a finance expert, you must be aware of this capability and, in some projects, will have to configure it.

One important aspect that affects financial accounting is the automatic invoice block for payment. SAP S/4HANA is a system designed to provide excellent business controls, and one part of this control is its ability to automatically block vendor invoices that match certain criteria. Let's see what options are available.

To configure tolerance limits, follow the menu path **Materials Management • Logistics Invoice Verification • Invoice Block • Set Tolerance Limits.** Figure 5.19 shows the tolerance limits set by company code (which were copied from the original company code used as a source company code in Chapter 3).

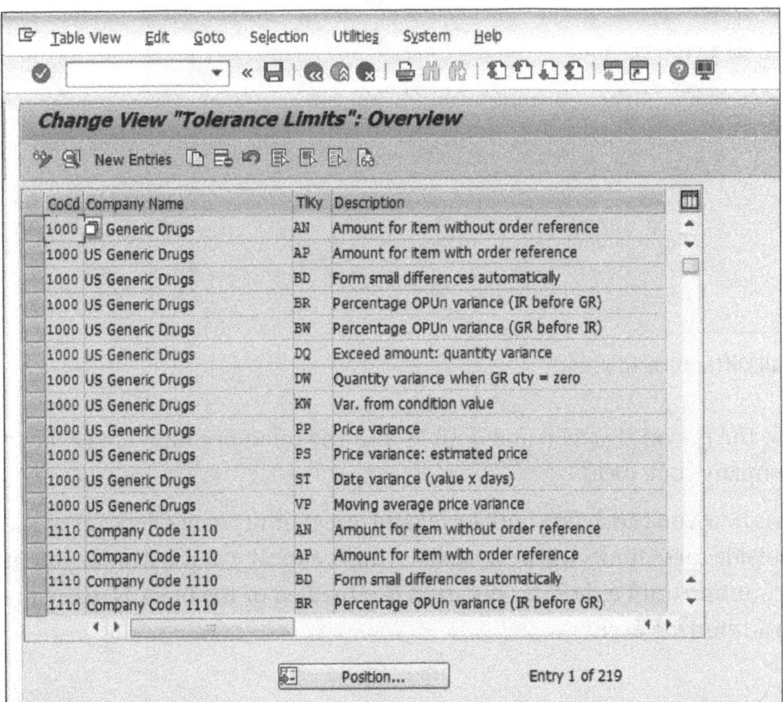

CoCd	Company Name	TIKy	Description
1000	Generic Drugs	AN	Amount for item without order reference
1000	US Generic Drugs	AP	Amount for item with order reference
1000	US Generic Drugs	BD	Form small differences automatically
1000	US Generic Drugs	BR	Percentage OPUn variance (IR before GR)
1000	US Generic Drugs	BW	Percentage OPUn variance (GR before IR)
1000	US Generic Drugs	DQ	Exceed amount: quantity variance
1000	US Generic Drugs	DW	Quantity variance when GR qty = zero
1000	US Generic Drugs	KW	Var. from condition value
1000	US Generic Drugs	PP	Price variance
1000	US Generic Drugs	PS	Price variance: estimated price
1000	US Generic Drugs	ST	Date variance (value x days)
1000	US Generic Drugs	VP	Moving average price variance
1110	Company Code 1110	AN	Amount for item without order reference
1110	Company Code 1110	AP	Amount for item with order reference
1110	Company Code 1110	BD	Form small differences automatically
1110	Company Code 1110	BR	Percentage OPUn variance (IR before GR)

Figure 5.19 Tolerance Limits in Logistics Invoice Verification

Many different tolerance keys are available, each applying to different business cases, and you can also define new rules. Double-click tolerance key **BD: Form Small Differences Automatically** for company code 1000. This tolerance key is used to enable posting of invoices that don't match on the debit and credit side if the difference isn't significant and will also post that difference automatically to a small differences account.

As shown in Figure 5.20, you'll set the upper limit of the tolerance amount. In this case, we'll enter "2.00" USD in the **Value** field under the **Check Limit** radio button. With these settings, all invoices that have mismatches between debits and credits of up to $2 will be posted.

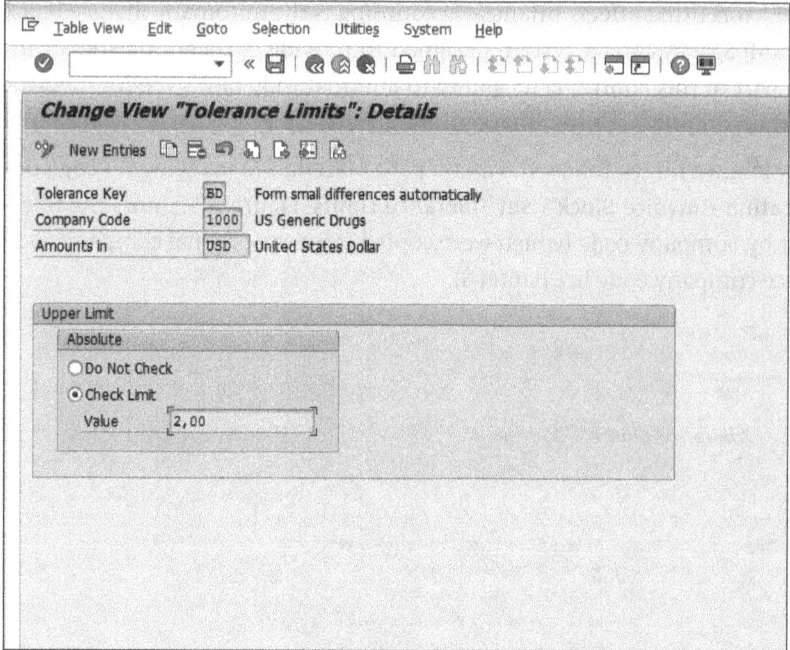

Figure 5.20 Small Difference Tolerance

Now, go back to the previous screen and double-click the tolerance limit for **PP: Price variance** for company code 1000.

Figure 5.21 shows how you can define both lower and upper limits for a tolerance check. Any invoices outside these limits will be posted but automatically blocked for payment in financial accounting until either the situation is remedied or the block is manually removed by an authorized user.

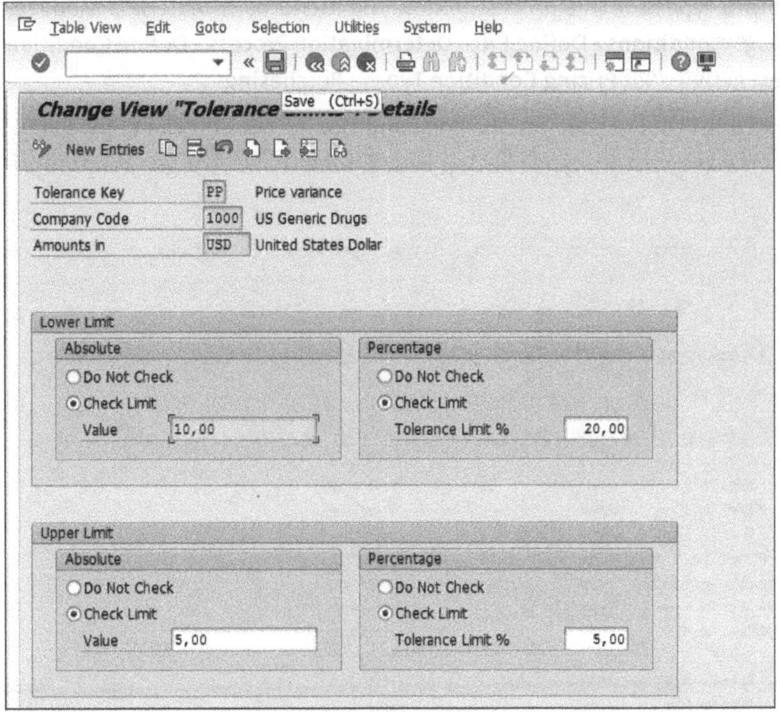

Figure 5.21 Tolerance Limit Price Variance

5.2.4 Tax Determination in the Purchasing Process

We discussed how tax procedures and tax codes are configured in Chapter 3, Section 3.6. You'll also need to configure how tax codes are determined automatically in purchasing processes so that financial documents can receive their proper tax treatment.

A tax code can be entered manually, which would overwrite the system's tax code determination. Tax codes are determined from POs using what's called the *condition technique*. Condition records are created based on configured condition tables, which are based on certain parameters (coming mostly from the vendor master record), and the material master record determines the proper tax code for the different business cases. Also, the system could derive the tax code from another related document (in the following sequence): reference item, contract, request for quotation, and info record.

A PO may have a pricing procedure that includes a tax condition, which accesses the relevant condition records and determines the tax code and the tax rate. (The standard SAP condition is MWST input tax.) The configuration of this procedure is a cross-topic between finance and purchasing, but usually, the finance consultant should ultimately be responsible for the tax setup. Let's see how these tax condition records are configured.

To define condition types for this process, follow the menu path **Materials Management • Purchasing • Conditions • Define Price Determination Process • Define Condition Types**, then select activity **Set Pricing Condition Types - Purchasing**.

Figure 5.22 shows a list of available purchasing condition types. You can copy a standard condition type as a custom type starting with Z, then make changes as appropriate.

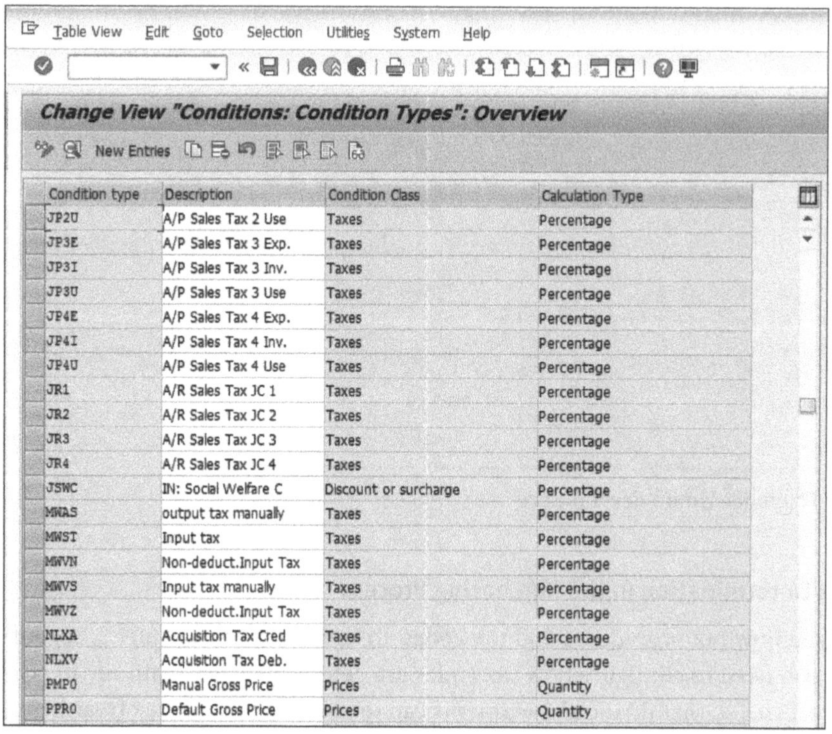

Table View Edit Goto Selection Utilities System Help

Change View "Conditions: Condition Types": Overview

New Entries

Condition type	Description	Condition Class	Calculation Type
JP2U	A/P Sales Tax 2 Use	Taxes	Percentage
JP3E	A/P Sales Tax 3 Exp.	Taxes	Percentage
JP3I	A/P Sales Tax 3 Inv.	Taxes	Percentage
JP3U	A/P Sales Tax 3 Use	Taxes	Percentage
JP4E	A/P Sales Tax 4 Exp.	Taxes	Percentage
JP4I	A/P Sales Tax 4 Inv.	Taxes	Percentage
JP4U	A/P Sales Tax 4 Use	Taxes	Percentage
JR1	A/R Sales Tax JC 1	Taxes	Percentage
JR2	A/R Sales Tax JC 2	Taxes	Percentage
JR3	A/R Sales Tax JC 3	Taxes	Percentage
JR4	A/R Sales Tax JC 4	Taxes	Percentage
JSWC	IN: Social Welfare C	Discount or surcharge	Percentage
MWAS	output tax manually	Taxes	Percentage
MWST	Input tax	Taxes	Percentage
MWVN	Non-deduct.Input Tax	Taxes	Percentage
MWVS	Input tax manually	Taxes	Percentage
MWVZ	Non-deduct.Input Tax	Taxes	Percentage
NLXA	Acquisition Tax Cred	Taxes	Percentage
NLXV	Acquisition Tax Deb.	Taxes	Percentage
PMP0	Manual Gross Price	Prices	Quantity
PPR0	Default Gross Price	Prices	Quantity

Figure 5.22 Purchasing Condition Types

Double-click condition type **MWST: Input Tax** to see its settings, as shown in Figure 5.23.

The following fields are important:

- **Condition Class**
  Determines the usage of the condition type; for tax conditions, this value is always **D: Taxes**.
- **Calculation Type**
  Specifies the type of calculation and, for taxes, is normally **A: Percentage**.
- **Condition Category**
  Classifies the conditions and, for tax conditions, should be **D: Tax**.
- **Item Condition**
  Should be selected for taxes to ensure that the calculation happens at the item level, which is required for taxes.

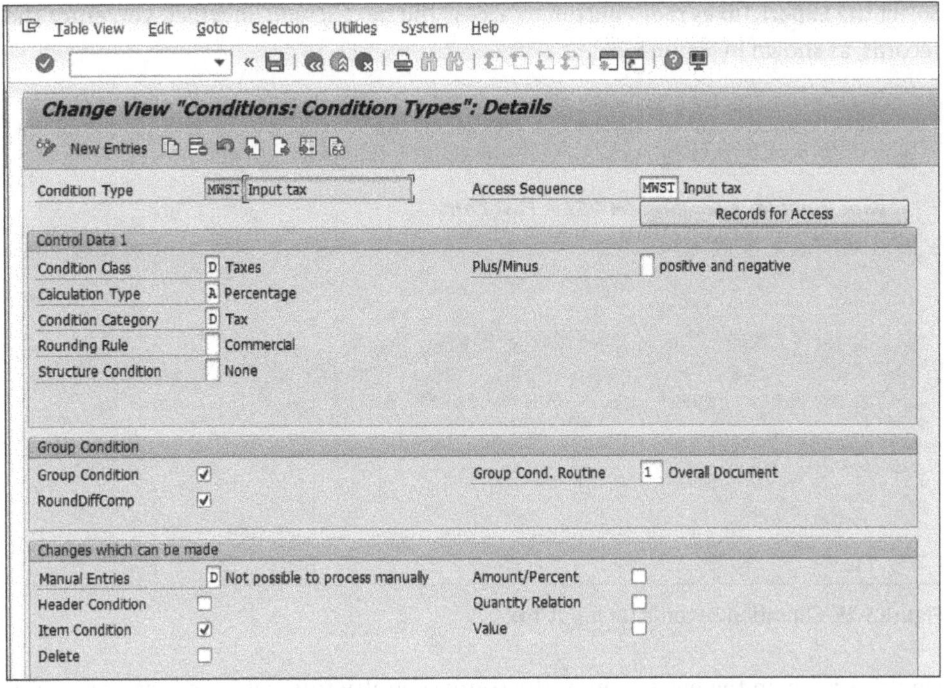

Figure 5.23 Input Tax Condition Type

By clicking the **Records for Access** button, you can see what records for access are maintained for the condition types, which determine the tax codes.

You can maintain these records using Transaction MEK1. These records are considered application data, and you can also navigate to them through the application menu path **Materials Management • Purchasing • Master Data • Conditions • Other • MEK1—Create.** Then, enter "MWST" for the **Condition Type** to open a popup window asking for the combination of characteristics for which you want to create records, as shown in Figure 5.24. The available characteristics depend on the configuration of the condition record.

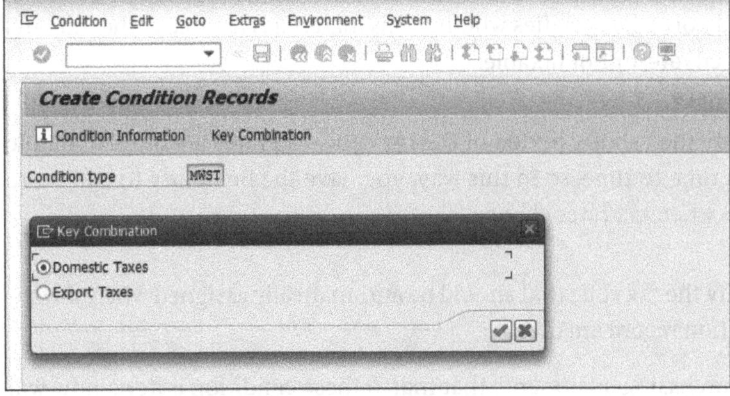

Figure 5.24 Key Combination for Condition Records

Select the **Export Taxes** radio button to access the next screen, in which you enter the records, as shown in Figure 5.25.

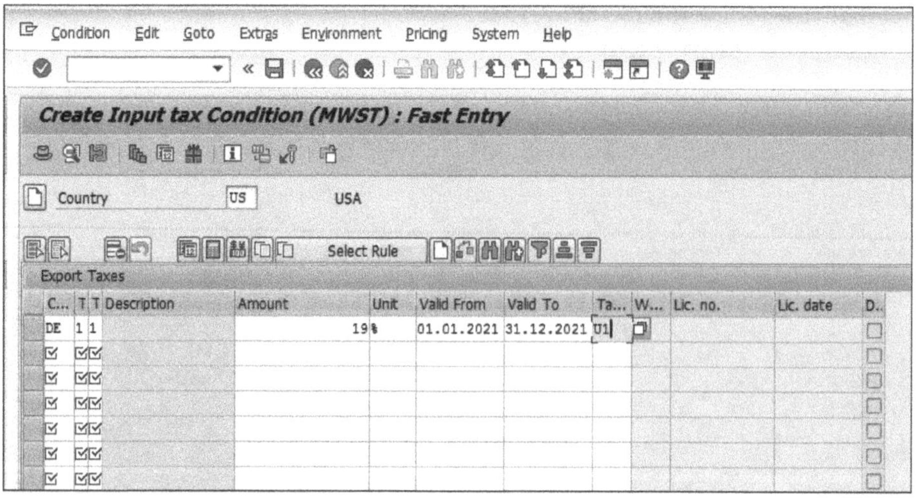

Figure 5.25 Condition Records for Input Tax

On this screen, in the header, enter the source country from which goods or services are sent. In the lines below, you can have multiple records for each destination country.

The following fields must be configured:

- **Destination Country**
  This field is the country to which the goods/services are supplied.
- **Tax Classification 1**
  In this field, select a tax classification indicator, which is maintained in the business partner master record and normally specifies whether this business partner is liable for taxes or exempt from taxes.
- **Tax Classification Material**
  In this field, select a tax classification indicator, which is maintained in the material master record and normally specifies whether this material is taxable at the full rate, taxable at a reduced rate, or not taxable.
- **Valid From and Valid To**
  In this field, specify the validity period of the tax code. Tax rates are often dynamic and change from time to time, so in this way, you have the flexibility to add more condition records when tax rates change.
- **Tax Code**
  In this field, specify the tax code that should be automatically assigned when the criteria in the condition record are met.

Save your entries. Purchasing documents that match these condition criteria now will receive the assigned tax codes automatically, which will then flow into the financial documents and post automatically to tax general ledger accounts, configured in the tax codes (see Chapter 3, Section 3.6.2).

5.2.5 Goods Receipt/Invoice Receipt Clearing

When posting materials management-based vendor invoices, the GR/IR clearing account is often used, which in a perfect world should be balanced out if invoices and their corresponding GR match. In reality, differences between GRs and IRs almost always exist.

The GR/IR clearing process is executed with Transaction MR11, which is designed to show the GRs that are not yet fully invoiced and the IRs that are yet fully received.

In the normal course of business, sometimes, invoices may not have been received yet, and some GRs may not have been invoiced yet. But the GR/IR clearing process is designed to clear old items that probably won't be completed. Not much configuration is required in Transaction MR11, which uses the tolerances we configured in Section 5.2.3.

You must also set up document types and number ranges for the GR/IR clearing process by following the menu path **Materials Management • Logistics Invoice Verification • Clearing Account Maintenance • Maintain Number Assignments for Accounting Documents.** On the screen shown in Figure 5.26, click the **Document Types in Invoice Verification** button.

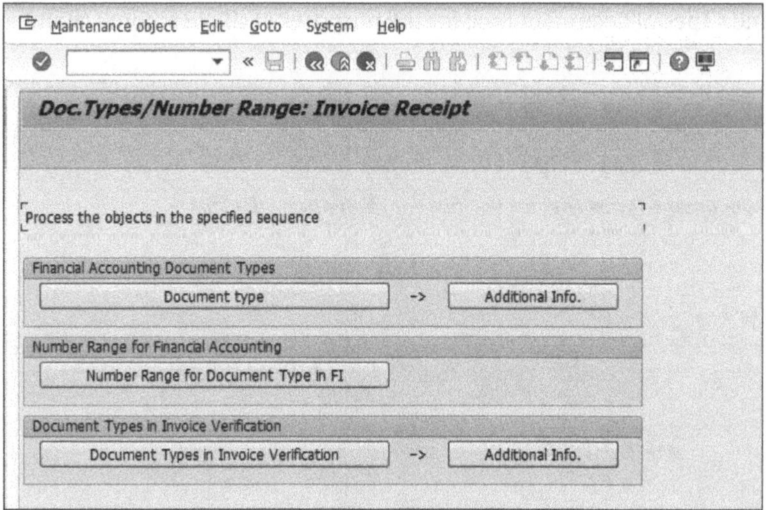

Figure 5.26 Document Types Assignment

Then, you'll see the screen shown in Figure 5.27, listing the various transactions used in the invoice verification process. Double-click **MR11: GR/IR account maintenance.**

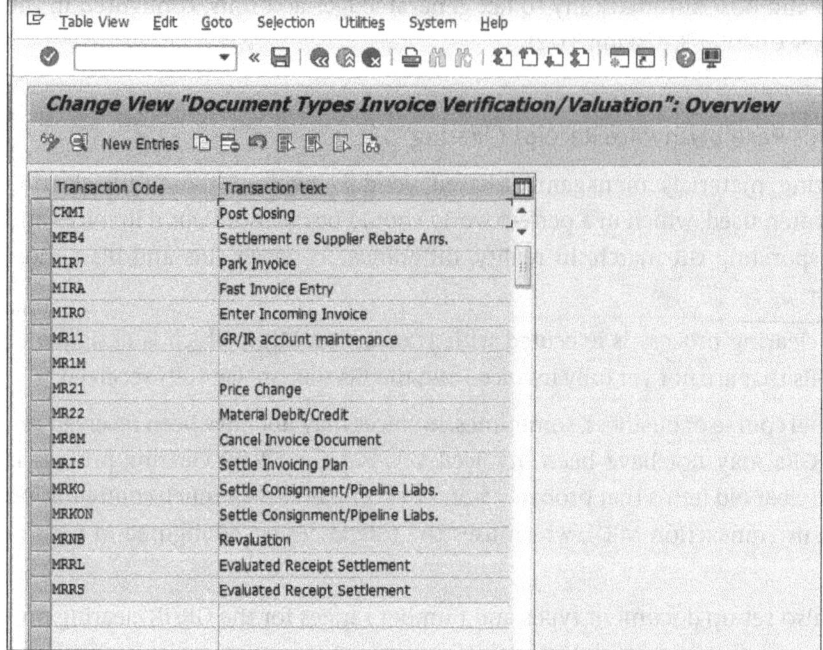

Figure 5.27 Invoice Verification Transactions

As shown in Figure 5.28, specify the document type to be used in the GR/IR clearing process. The default is **KP: Account maintenance**. You can change this document type if you need to define a special document type for the purposes of GR/IR account maintenance.

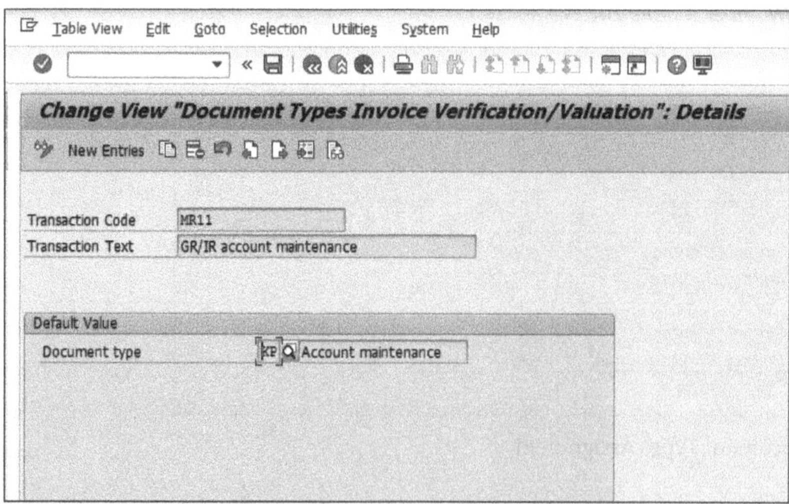

Figure 5.28 GR/IR Clearing Document Type Configuration

In the next step, select the number range to be used for this document type by following the menu path **Materials Management • Logistics Invoice Verification • Clearing Account Maintenance • Maintain Number Assignment for Account Maintenance Documents • Maintain Number Range for Account Maintenance Document.** On this screen, you can assign the number range to be used with the document type configured for the GR/IR process. Specify **No. range** "04" for document type **KP**, as shown in Figure 5.29.

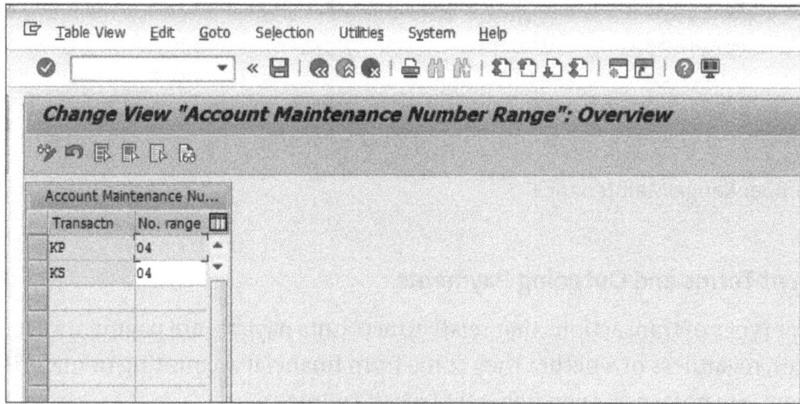

Figure 5.29 GR/IR Clearing Number Range Assignment

The last step is to define the numbers for this number range by following the menu path **Materials Management • Logistics Invoice Verification • Clearing Account Maintenance • Maintain Number Assignment for Account Maintenance Documents • Maintain Number Range Interval for Account Maintenance Document.** The name of the number range object is **RE_BELEG**, as shown in Figure 5.30.

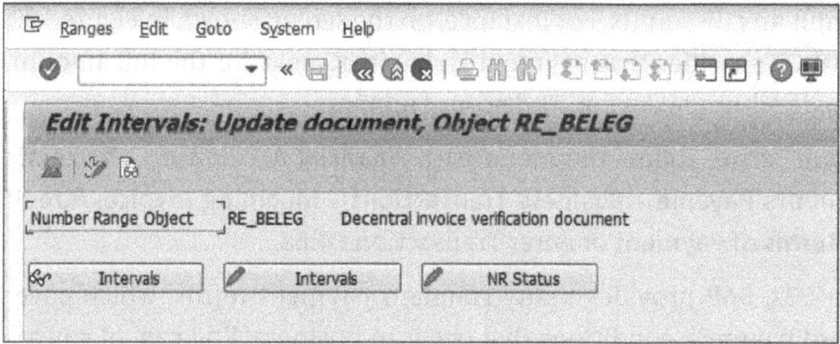

Figure 5.30 Number Ranges for IR Documents

Click the Intervals button to maintain the ranges, as shown in Figure 5.31.

Maintain the **From No.** and **To Number** fields of range 04, valid indefinitely (represented by entering a year of 9999). Then, save your entries. As with other number ranges, no automatic transport is assigned because number ranges should be maintained in each individual client.

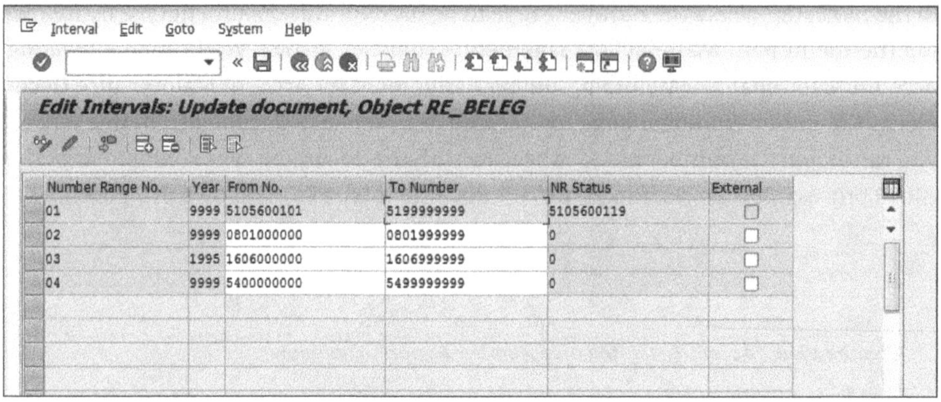

Interval Edit Goto System Help

Edit Intervals: Update document, Object RE_BELEG

Number Range No.	Year	From No.	To Number	NR Status	External
01	9999	5105600101	5199999999	5105600119	☐
02	9999	0801000000	0801999999	0	☐
03	1995	1606000000	1606999999	0	☐
04	9999	5400000000	5499999999	0	☐

Figure 5.31 Number Range Maintenance

5.2.6 Payment Terms and Outgoing Payments

The next major types of transactions that relate to accounts payable are payments. The posted invoices, regardless of whether they come from financial accounting or materials management, are posted as open items that await payments.

We'll examine the configuration of payment methods, the automatic payment program, and the electronic bank statement in Chapter 8 in detail; for now, we'll configure the terms of payment and the payment block.

The conditions of payments depend on the payment terms. A *payment term* is a configuration object, which is part of the vendor line item. Payment terms determine when payments are due and if discounts are applicable. For example, payment terms can be payable immediately due net, when no grace period exists and the whole amount should be paid without any discounts. For instance, on the screen shown in Figure 5.32, the payment term 0002 specifies that payment is due in 30 days for the full amount, but if payment is made within 14 days, a 2% discount applies.

To configure payment terms, follow the menu path **Financial Accounting • Accounts Receivable and Accounts Payable • Business Transactions • Incoming Invoices/Credit Memos • Maintain Terms of Payment** or enter Transaction OBB8.

As shown in Figure 5.32, SAP provides many standard payment terms, which cover many of the standard payment conditions that occur in business. You can, of course, create new ones, and as with other configuration objects, a good practice is to name them in a custom number range starting with Z or Y.

Let's create a new payment term for a payment to a vendor within 14 days for a 4% cash discount, or within 45 days due net. First, find a similar standard payment term, such as 0002. Select the checkbox to the left of 0002, then select **Copy As...** from the top menu, which will result in the screen shown in Figure 5.33.

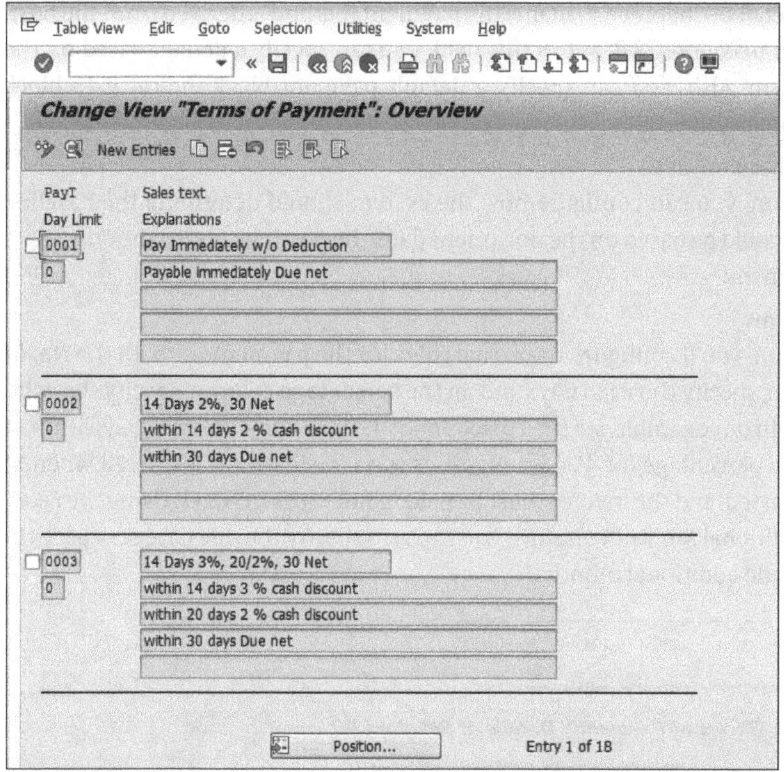

Figure 5.32 Payment Terms

As shown in Figure 5.33, the following fields must be configured:

- **Payment terms**
  Specify the new payment term code—in this case, Z001.
- **Sales text**
  Enter a meaningful description for the payment term.
- **Account type**
  Determines for which types of accounts the payment term is valid: customers, vendors, or both. Payment terms are objects used both in accounts payable and accounts receivable, but in this field, you can restrict its use if not needed in the other application.
- **Baseline date calculation**
  The baseline date is the date from which the calculation of the payment term starts. Normally, the baseline date determined from the open item itself. However, in this field, you can specify a different determination to start from a fixed date and/or to add additional months to the baseline date.
- **Pmnt block/pmnt method default (payment block/payment method default)**
  The payment of each open item also depends on the payment method, which we'll

discuss in detail in Chapter 8. Usually, the payment method is derived from the business partner master record, but in this field, you can specify a default based on the payment term. Also, you can specify a default payment block indicator to block invoices from payment.

- **Default for baseline date**
  In this section, you can configure how the system should determine the baseline date, which could be based on the document date, the posting date, or the entry date of the document.
- **Payment terms**
  In this section, you'll configure the actual rules for the payment term. In the **No. of Days** column, specify the valid days and, in the **Percentage** column, specify the valid percentage. In our example, we set a discount of 4% for payments received within 14 days, and no percentage for 45 days. In other ways, no discount is offered when 14 days have passed, and the invoice must be paid in full within 45 days. Using the **Fixed Day** and **Additional Months** columns, you can also specify the due date on a particular day and add additional months.

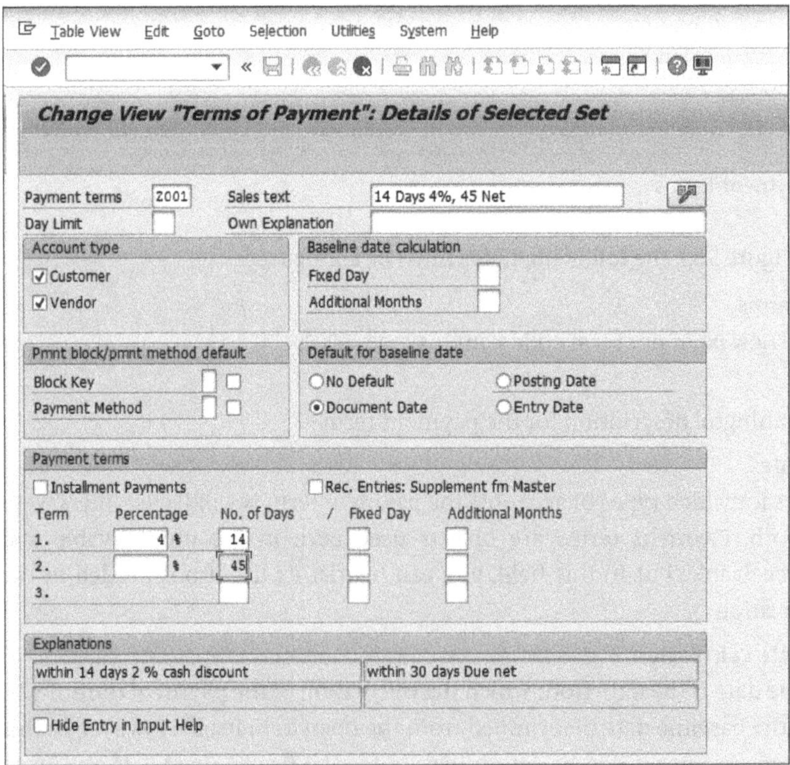

Figure 5.33 New Payment Term Creation

After maintaining these fields, save your entries, and you're ready to start using your new custom payment term.

Now, let's configure the payment blocks. By default, when invoices are posted, they are open for payment. However, you may want to block them for various reasons until further review or a further event—for example, when a mismatch exists between a GR and an IR or when you have reason to believe you've received duplicate invoices.

Because different reasons may exist for various payment blocks, you must configure payment block reason codes. Follow the menu path **Financial Accounting • Accounts Receivable and Accounts Payable • Business Transactions • Outgoing Payments • Outgoing Payments Global Settings • Payment Block Reasons • Define Payment Block Reasons** or enter Transaction OB27.

A list of available payment block reasons is shown in Figure 5.34.

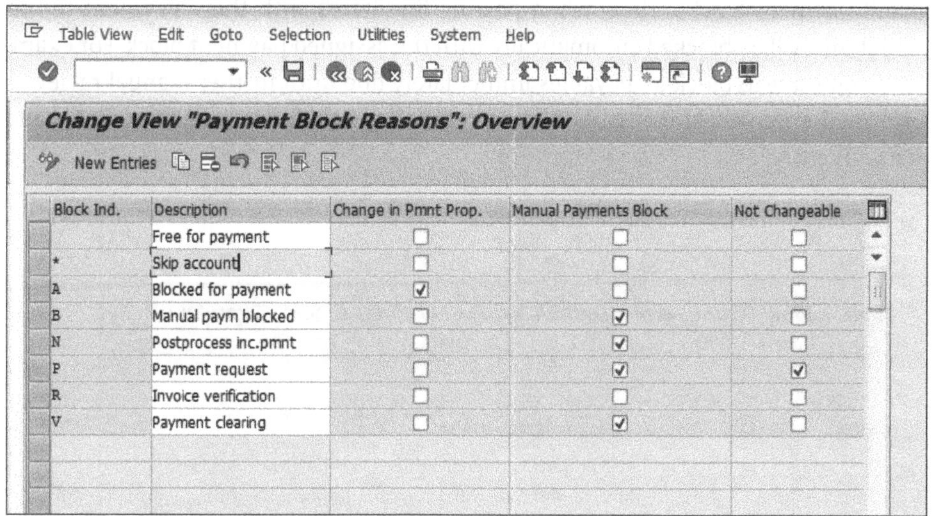

Block Ind.	Description	Change in Pmnt Prop.	Manual Payments Block	Not Changeable
	Free for payment	☐	☐	☐
*	Skip account	☐	☐	☐
A	Blocked for payment	☑	☐	☐
B	Manual paym blocked	☐	☑	☐
N	Postprocess inc.pmnt	☐	☑	☐
P	Payment request	☐	☑	☑
R	Invoice verification	☐	☐	☐
V	Payment clearing	☐	☑	☐

Figure 5.34 Payment Block Reasons

On this screen, you'll configure the following fields:

- **Block Ind. (block indicator)**
  This field is the block code, which is entered in the document line item. This code could be entered manually or automatically. For example, block A is commonly used manually in financial accounting invoices, whereas block R is the automatic block set up to address mismatches between GRs and IRs.
- **Description**
  In this field, enter a meaningful description for the blocking reason.
- **Change in Pmnt Prop. (change in payment proposal)**
  Selecting this checkbox allows the block to be manually removed in the payment proposal. The payment proposal is the first step in running the automatic payment program, which we'll discuss in detail in Chapter 8. Enabling this option gives you the flexibility to make payments during the payment program process, albeit manually.

- **Manual Payment Block**
  Selecting this option prevents the clearing of items with manual payments.
- **Not Changeable**
  Selecting this option prevents the manual removal of the blocking reason. In other words, this block can only be removed as part of a workflow approval process.

In the next step, you'll define default block reasons for each payment term by following the menu path **Financial Accounting • Accounts Receivable and Accounts Payable • Business Transactions • Outgoing Payments • Outgoing Payments Global Settings • Payment Block Reasons • Define Default Values for Payment Block.**

As shown in Figure 5.35, from the list of available payment terms, and you can assign default payment blocks. Then, when posting line items with these payment terms, these items will be blocked automatically with the assigned payment block. For example, if you want to block all payables immediately due until further manual review is performed, enter blocking reason "A" in the **Block Key** field for payment term 0001 and save your entry.

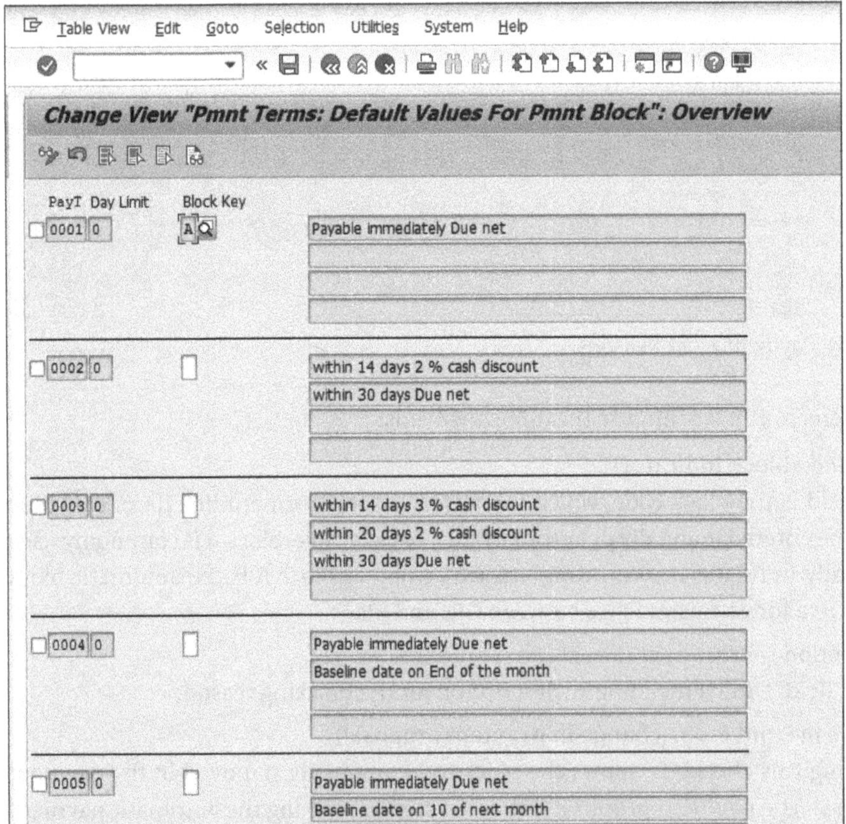

Figure 5.35 Default Payment Block per Payment Term

5.2.7 Integration with Vendor Invoice Management

With vendor invoice management, paper invoices can be scanned and automatically posted in SAP S/4HANA. This capability uses optical character recognition (OCR) to transfer written information into digital form in the system. Also, a workflow approval process is usually part of the functionality offered in the integration between SAP S/4HANA and such a system, which invoices undergoing an approval process through various chains until the document is posted and ready for payment. Thus, vendor invoice management applications reduce manual work and costs and improve control processes within accounts payable. Usually, when a vendor invoice management solution is implemented, most vendor invoices are posted through that system.

Hardly a new idea, many different applications exist on the market that have good track records in integration with SAP ERP systems. Commonly used are vendor invoice management systems from vendors such as OpenText, ReadSoft, IXOS, and others. SAP Invoice Management by OpenText is the most integrated with SAP solutions.

The configuration of an SAP S/4HANA system with the selected vendor invoice management system lies outside the scope of this book, but when selecting such system and designing the process, keep in mind the following common integration points generally apply:

1. The invoice is received through email, fax, or paper.
2. The invoice is scanned.
3. The invoice transferred to an archive server and archived.
4. The document is sent to the SAP S/4HANA vendor invoice management application, where it's stored and identified by a designated document processing number.
5. The vendor invoice management application extracts data such as vendor number, currency, document date, amount, and so on from the document.
6. The extracted data is validated and allocated to posting fields in SAP S/4HANA.
7. The approval process is performed through a workflow.
8. If an exception exists, the invoice is posted automatically through regular invoice posting transaction.

With this list of integration points, we've finished our guide to accounts payable business transactions. Let's move on to the various reports available in the accounts payable information system.

5.3 Information System

Accounts payable in SAP S/4HANA offers a robust and extensive information system, which should meet even the most demanding reporting requirements. Reports can be grouped into the following categories:

- Master data reports
- Balance reports
- Line-item reports

These reports do not require specific configuration and should function out of the box.

Let's start by examining the master data reports available for accounts payable.

5.3.1 Master Data Reports

As mentioned earlier, vendor master data in SAP S/4HANA is managed using the business partner concept, which is a major improvement compared with previous releases since now vendor master records are fully integrated within all modules.

Master data reports for vendors are available at the application menu path **Accounting • Financial Accounting • Accounts Payable • Information System • Reports for Accounts Payable • Master Data**.

Report S_ALR_87012086 (Vendor List) provides a simple list of all vendor master data, whereas report S_ALR_87012087 (Address List) is useful for a snapshot of only the vendor addresses. Report S_ALR_87012089 (Display Changes to Vendors) can show you the creation and change history of vendors, as shown in Figure 5.36.

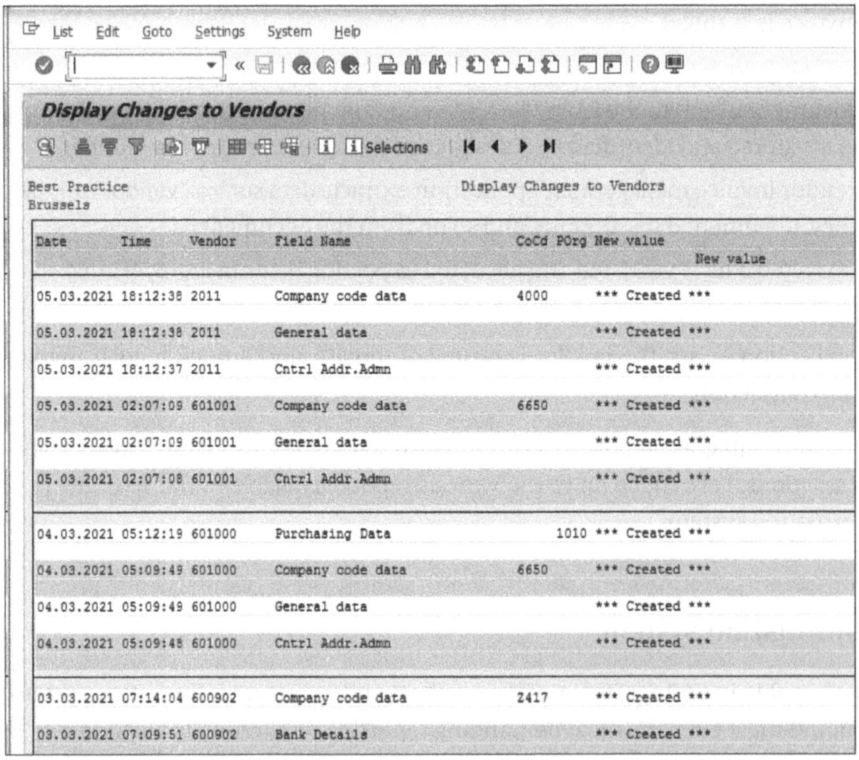

List Edit Goto Settings System Help

Display Changes to Vendors

Selections

Best Practice Display Changes to Vendors
Brussels

Date	Time	Vendor	Field Name	CoCd	POrg	New value
05.03.2021	18:12:38	2011	Company code data	4000		*** Created ***
05.03.2021	18:12:38	2011	General data			*** Created ***
05.03.2021	18:12:37	2011	Cntrl Addr.Admn			*** Created ***
05.03.2021	02:07:09	601001	Company code data	6650		*** Created ***
05.03.2021	02:07:09	601001	General data			*** Created ***
05.03.2021	02:07:08	601001	Cntrl Addr.Admn			*** Created ***
04.03.2021	05:12:19	601000	Purchasing Data		1010	*** Created ***
04.03.2021	05:09:49	601000	Company code data	6650		*** Created ***
04.03.2021	05:09:49	601000	General data			*** Created ***
04.03.2021	05:09:48	601000	Cntrl Addr.Admn			*** Created ***
03.03.2021	07:14:04	600902	Company code data	2417		*** Created ***
03.03.2021	07:09:51	600902	Bank Details			*** Created ***

Figure 5.36 Changes to Vendors Report

This report is quite useful for monitoring master data. Especially important are changes to sensitive fields, such as bank information, which you can monitor using report S_ALR_87012090 (Display/Confirm Critical Vendor Changes). You can configure that certain fields require confirmation from an additional user when changed, and this report can show you changes that are pending, as shown in Figure 5.37.

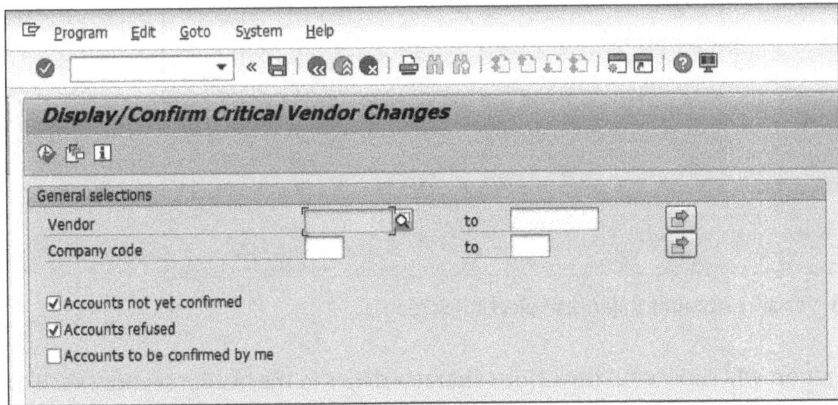

Figure 5.37 Display Vendors to Confirm Report

In addition to the range of vendor accounts and company codes, you can select the following checkboxes for this report:

- **Accounts Not Yet Confirmed**
  By selecting this checkbox, the report will show you vendor accounts that are pending confirmation.
- **Accounts Refused**
  By selecting this checkbox, the report will show you vendor accounts for which confirmations were rejected.
- **Accounts to Be Confirmed by Me**
  By selecting this checkbox, the report will show you vendor accounts that your user has authorization to confirm.

5.3.2 Balance Reports

Balance reports are important because they provide summarized information about your payables. These reports are available at the application menu path **Accounting • Financial Accounting • Accounts Payable • Information System • Reports for Accounts Payable • Vendor Balances.**

Report S_ALR_87012079 (Transaction Figures: Account Balance) is quite user friendly. You can execute this report as a drilldown report to navigate through the different characteristics of interest. For this capability, however, you must select the **Classic drilldown report** option, as shown in Figure 5.38.

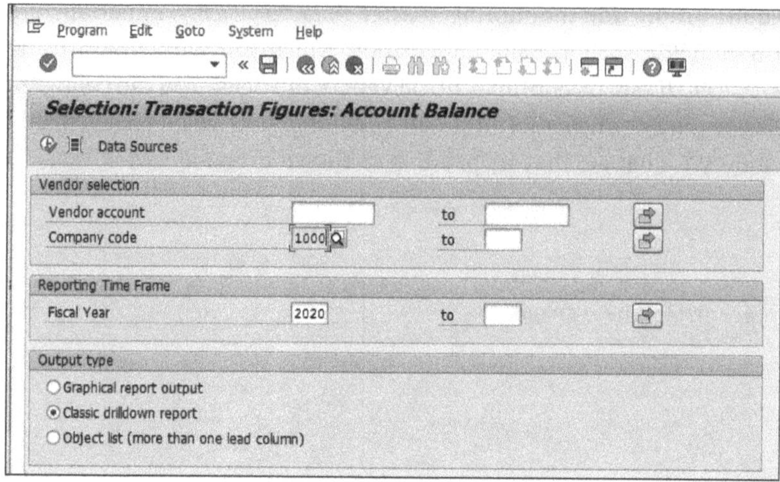

Figure 5.38 Vendors Account Balances Selection Screen

Then, the report will show you the various characteristics in the header section, such as vendor, fiscal year, company code, and period, that you can drill down into. If you don't make any selections, as shown in Figure 5.39, the result section contains the values for all characteristics.

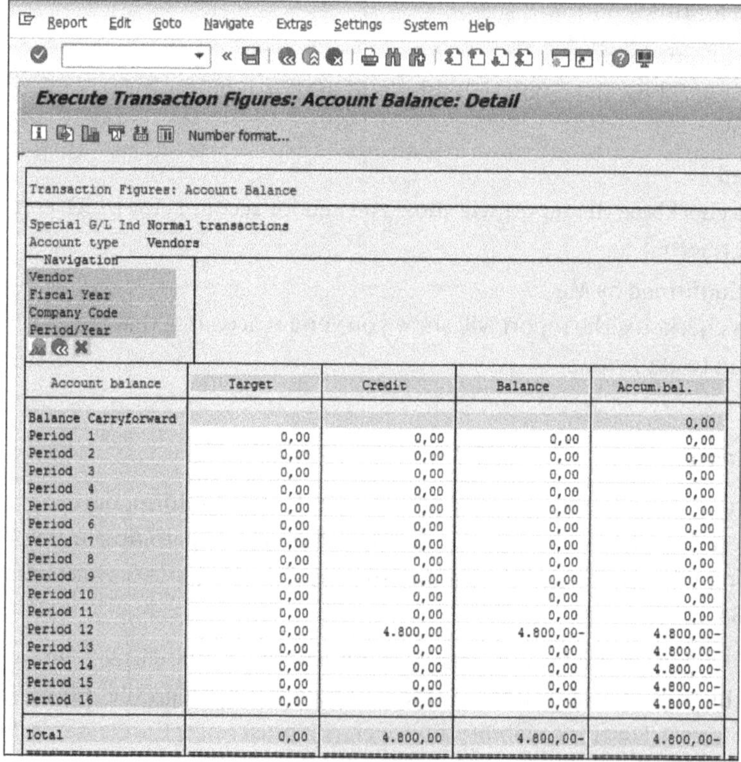

Account balance	Target	Credit	Balance	Accum.bal.
Balance Carryforward				0,00
Period 1	0,00	0,00	0,00	0,00
Period 2	0,00	0,00	0,00	0,00
Period 3	0,00	0,00	0,00	0,00
Period 4	0,00	0,00	0,00	0,00
Period 5	0,00	0,00	0,00	0,00
Period 6	0,00	0,00	0,00	0,00
Period 7	0,00	0,00	0,00	0,00
Period 8	0,00	0,00	0,00	0,00
Period 9	0,00	0,00	0,00	0,00
Period 10	0,00	0,00	0,00	0,00
Period 11	0,00	0,00	0,00	0,00
Period 12	0,00	4.800,00	4.800,00-	4.800,00-
Period 13	0,00	0,00	0,00	4.800,00-
Period 14	0,00	0,00	0,00	4.800,00-
Period 15	0,00	0,00	0,00	4.800,00-
Period 16	0,00	0,00	0,00	4.800,00-
Total	0,00	4.800,00	4.800,00-	4.800,00-

Figure 5.39 Vendor Balances Drilldown Screen

When you click on a characteristic, you can display the result only for the selected values. In this way, you can make combinations of their values, such as interactively displaying the report for period 01 for a specific vendor.

5.3.3 Line-Item Reports

Finally, line-item reports can provide the most detailed analysis on the document level. These reports are located at the application menu path **Accounting • Financial Accounting • Accounts Payable • Information System • Reports for Accounts Payable • Vendors: Items.**

Report S_ALR_87012078 (Due Date Analysis for Open Items) also can run as a drilldown report, which then breaks down your payables by due date, as shown in Figure 5.40.

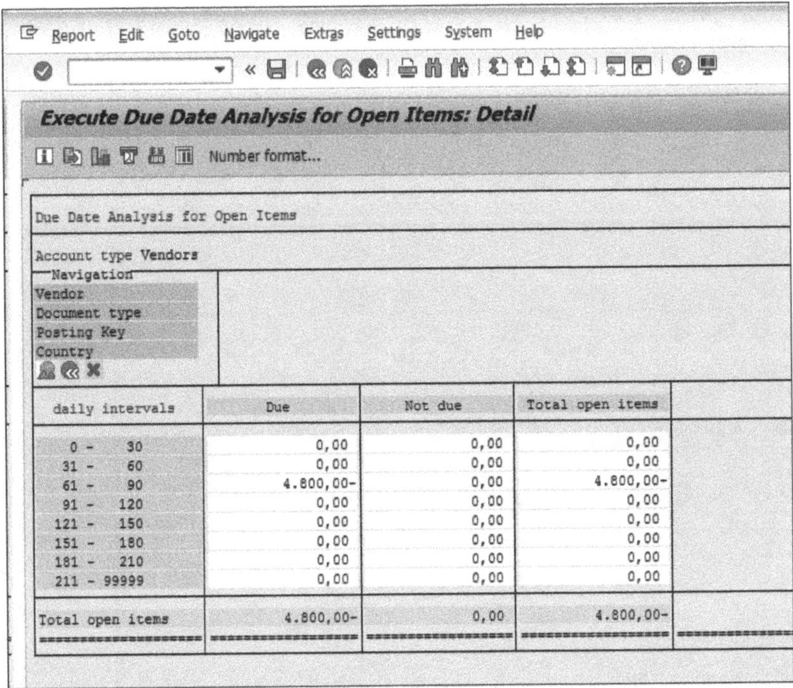

daily intervals	Due	Not due	Total open items
0 - 30	0,00	0,00	0,00
31 - 60	0,00	0,00	0,00
61 - 90	4.800,00-	0,00	4.800,00-
91 - 120	0,00	0,00	0,00
121 - 150	0,00	0,00	0,00
151 - 180	0,00	0,00	0,00
181 - 210	0,00	0,00	0,00
211 - 99999	0,00	0,00	0,00
Total open items	4.800,00-	0,00	4.800,00-

Figure 5.40 Due Date Analysis for Vendors

Notice how the report breaks down the payables by periods, such as 0–30 days, 31–60 days, 61–90 days, and so on. Again, by selecting characteristics such as vendor, country, and the like, you can see the specific values for which the report is run based on your selections.

Another rather useful report is report S_ALR_87012103 (List of Vendor Line Items), which gives you information about all accounts payable line items.

As shown in Figure 5.41, you can select from the following options:

- **Open items**
  Shows only the open items as of the key date you enter in this field.
- **Cleared items**
  Shows only the cleared items (paid or otherwise cleared, e.g., manually) from within the date range specified.
- **All items**
  Shows all items that are open and cleared within the date range specified.

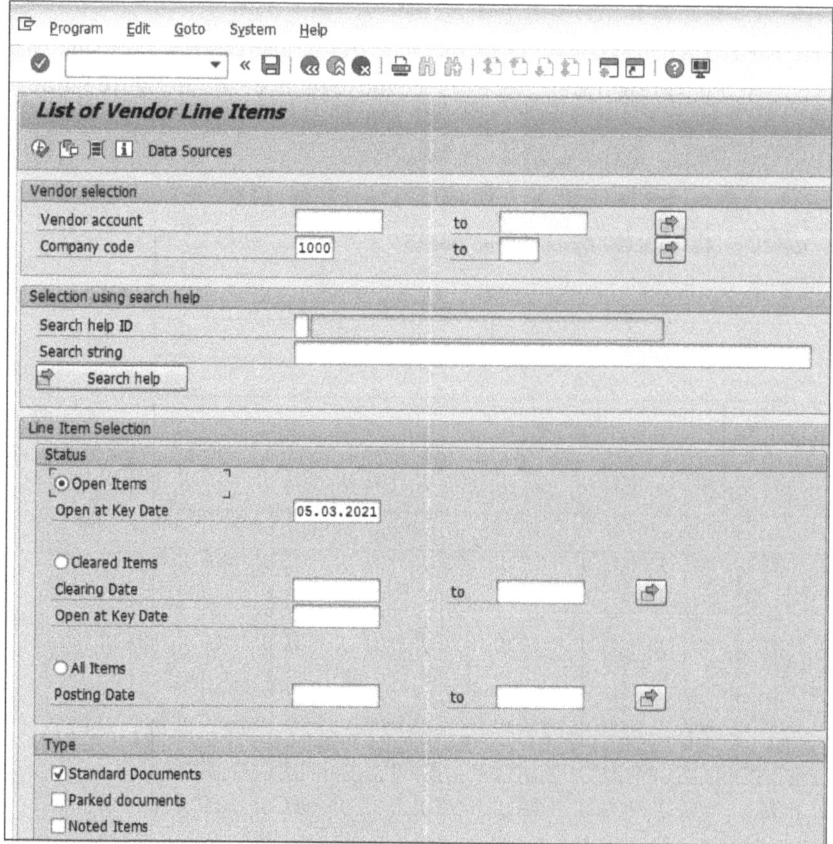

Figure 5.41 Vendor Line Items Report Selections

The report then shows the output list, as shown in Figure 5.42. On this screen, as with other standard SAP reports, you have various options for displaying, summarizing, filtering, or otherwise changing the output. For example, by clicking the **Change layout** button from the top menu, you can select the displayed fields in the report from all the available fields, as shown in Figure 5.43.

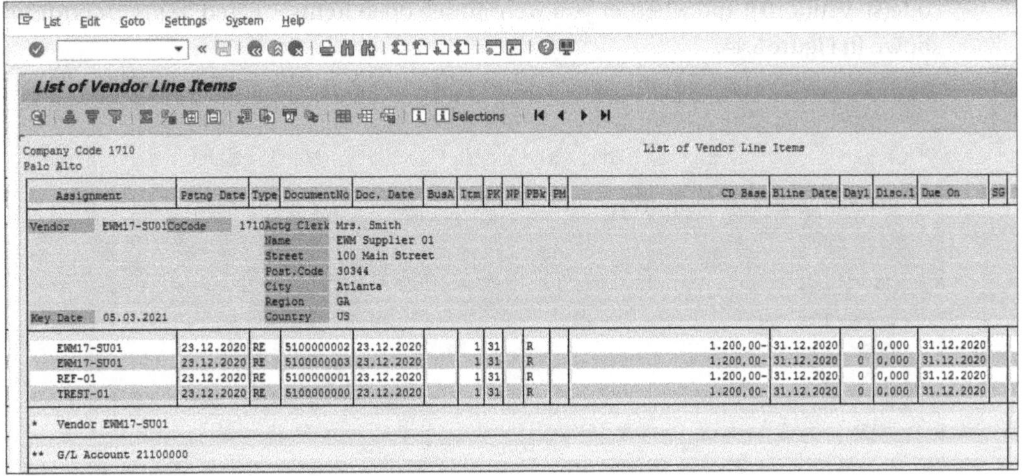

Figure 5.42 Vendor Line Items Output Screen

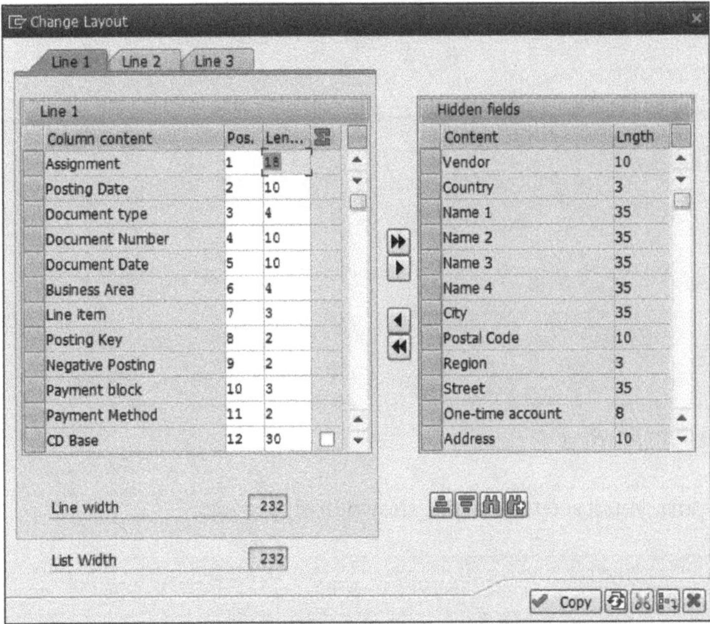

Figure 5.43 Change Layout in Vendor Line Item Report

You can show hidden fields by clicking the **Show Sel. Fields** (show selected fields) button [<], and you can hide displayed fields by clicking the **Hide Sel. Fields** (hide selected fields) button [>]. Then, you can confirm the selections by clicking the **Copy** button.

Another useful line-item report, new with SAP S/4HANA, is the line-item browser, located at the application menu path **Accounting • Financial Accounting • Accounts Payable • Account • FBL1H—Line Item Browser**. As in earlier reports, select the company code(s); vendor(s); and whether you want to see open items, cleared items, or both, as shown in Figure 5.44.

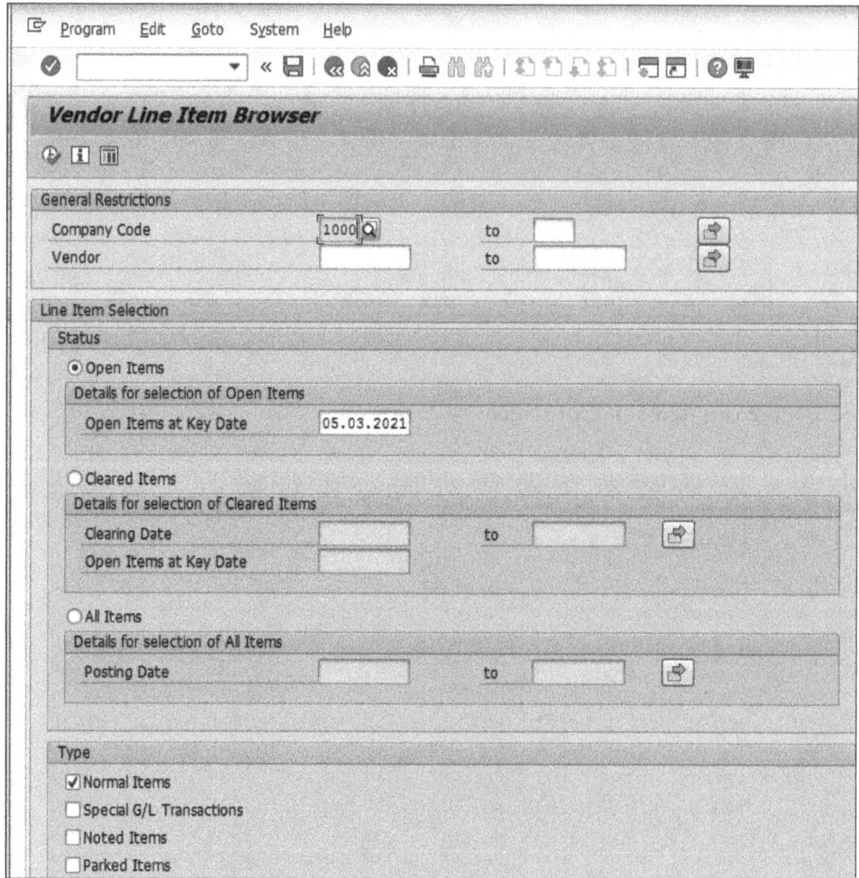

Figure 5.44 Vendor Line Item Browser

After executing the report, you'll see the output shown in Figure 5.45.

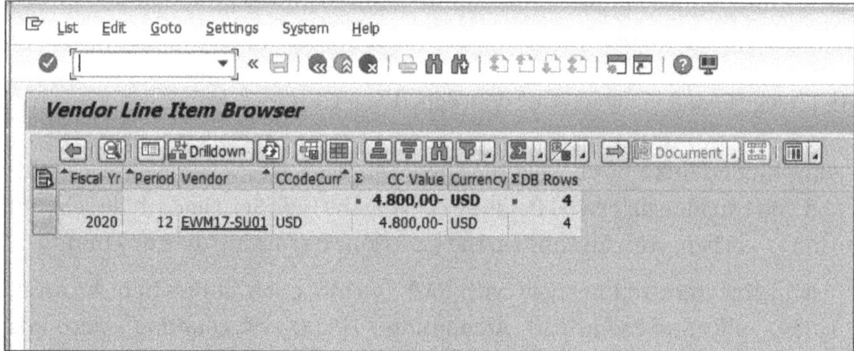

Figure 5.45 Vendor Line Item Browser Output

You can change the layout of displayed columns by clicking the **Change layout** button on the top menu. You can also drill down into further levels of detail. For example, if you double-click a document number, a new window will open with this document displayed. Similarly, if you double-click a vendor account, you'll be taken to the vendor master record in a new window.

Finally, let's look at the classic report FBL1N (Display/Change Line Items), which was widely used in SAP ERP and is also available and useful in SAP S/4HANA. Follow the application menu path **Accounting • Financial Accounting • Accounts Payable • Account • FBL1N—Display/Change Line Items**. Again, select company code(s); vendor(s); and whether you want to see open items, cleared items, or both, as shown in Figure 5.46.

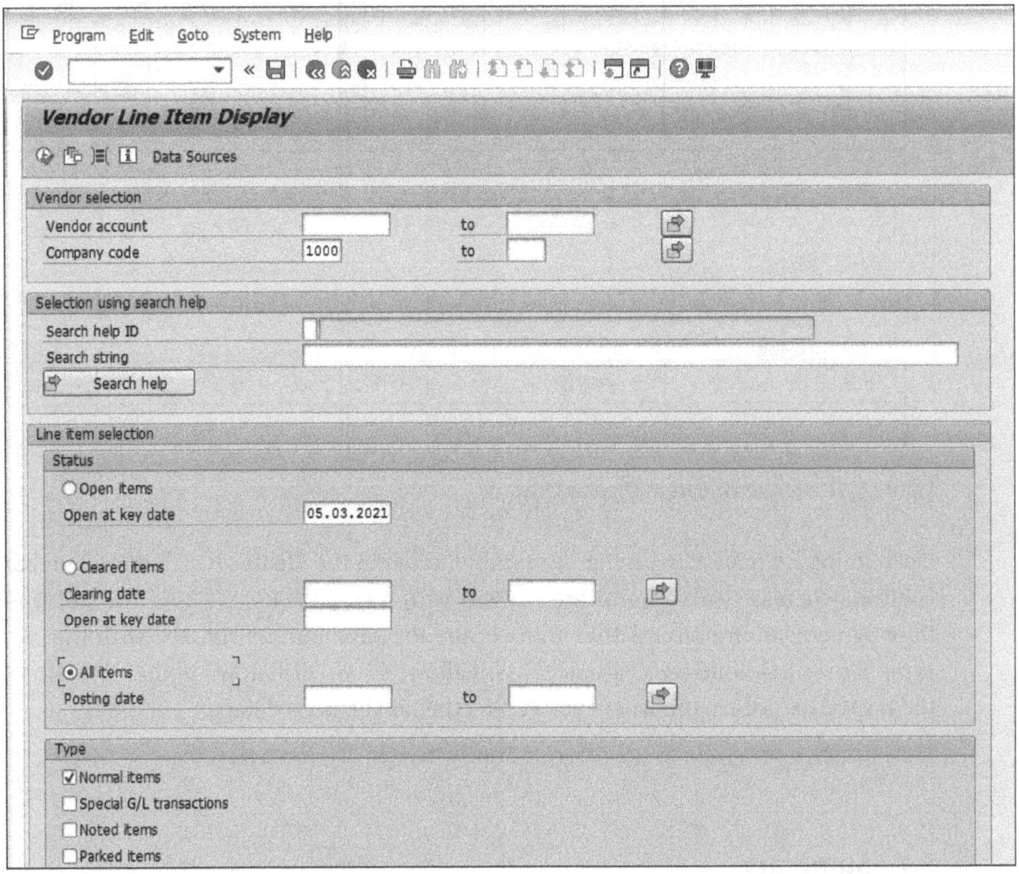

Program Edit Goto System Help

Vendor Line Item Display

Data Sources

Vendor selection

Vendor account		to	
Company code	1000	to	

Selection using search help

Search help ID

Search string

Search help

Line item selection

Status

○ Open items

Open at key date 05.03.2021

○ Cleared items

Clearing date ___ to ___

Open at key date

◉ All items

Posting date ___ to ___

Type

☑ Normal items

☐ Special G/L transactions

☐ Noted items

☐ Parked items

Figure 5.46 Vendor Line Item Display

Then, after executing, you'll see the screen shown in Figure 5.47, which should be familiar if you're coming from an SAP ERP background.

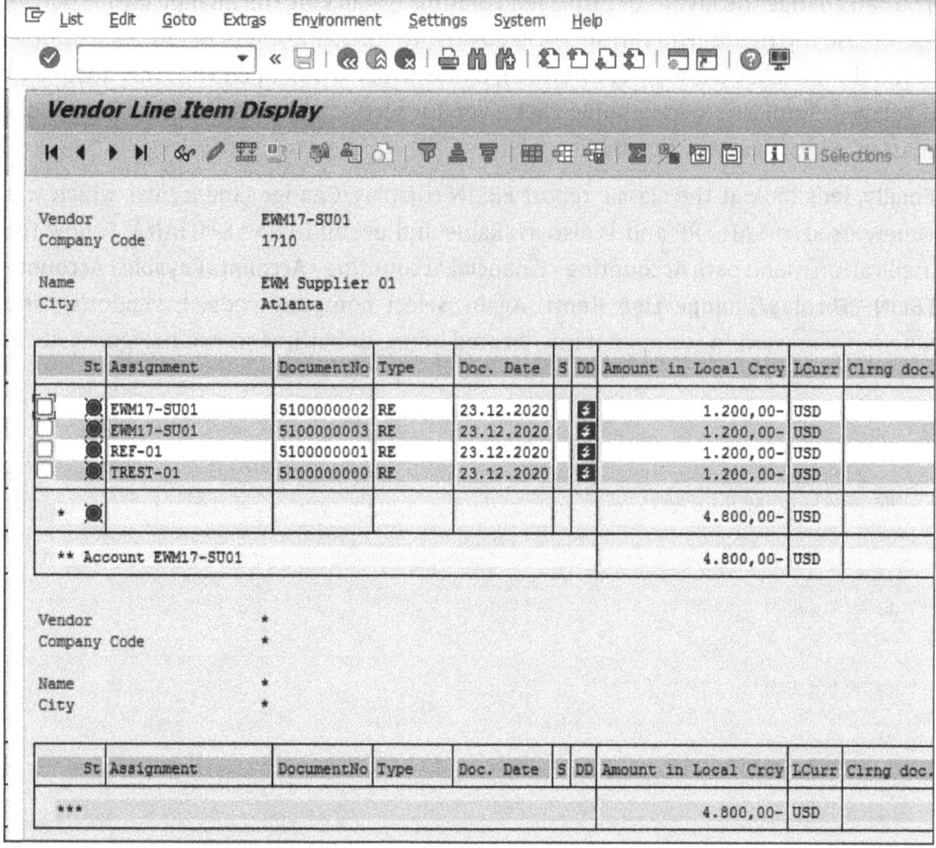

Figure 5.47 Vendor Line Item Display Output

Open items are marked with the symbol in red in the **Cleared/Open Items Symbol** column, whereas cleared items are marked with a green square. In the **Net Due Date Symbol** column, items that are overdue for payment are marked with the symbol in red. Double-clicking a document allows you to drill down to the line item of the respective document, where you can further analyze the details.

Thus finishes our guide to the information system in accounts payable.

5.4 Summary

In this chapter, we provided an extensive guide on configuring accounts payable in SAP S/4HANA and using its information system. We covered the following main topics:

- Vendor master data, maintained as business partners
- Business transactions
- Information system

One key benefit of SAP S/4HANA in the finance area is its full integration of vendors and customers with the business partner concept. We explained how you can set up your vendors as business partners and how to fully integrate their financial views and postings.

We also covered the main business transactions posted through accounts payable. We made settings for the processing of invoices both in financial accounting and integrated with materials management. On this topic, we also covered important integration aspects, such as the tax code determination in the purchasing process, the GR/IR clearing process, and integration with vendor invoice management systems. We also covered in detail the configuration required for payment terms and payment blocks. We'll further expand on the payments for outgoing invoices in Chapter 8, in which you'll learn how to set up payment methods and the automatic payment program and create payment file formats.

Finally, we examined in detail the information system of accounts payable, which provides invaluable reports for managing the liabilities of your organization. You learned how to execute and navigate through the main reports for vendor master data, balances, and line items.

Thus ends our guide to accounts payable. Next, we'll move to accounts receivable in SAP S/4HANA.

Chapter 6
Accounts Receivable

This chapter provides step-by-step instructions for configuring accounts receivable in SAP S/4HANA and explains its integration with sales and distribution processes. You'll learn how to set up business partners as customers, as we explain the sales flow in SAP S/4HANA and introduce you to the reporting capabilities of the receivables subledger.

Now, we'll explain in detail how to configure accounts receivable in your SAP S/4HANA system. Accounts receivable is used to manage financial processes related to sales, including posting customer invoices and incoming payments and clearing and reconciling open items. We'll teach you how to set up the required master data, business transactions, and information system for accounts receivable.

In a sense, accounts receivable is a mirror of accounts payable. Even in the configuration menu, they share the following common path: **Financial Accounting • Accounts Receivable and Accounts Payable**.

6.1 Business Partners

Accounts receivable uses the business partner as a central object to manage customer master data, much like accounts payable manages vendor master data. Separate business partner roles exist to maintain the business partner master as a customer in financial accounting and as customer in sales. In this way, the full integration of the customer with its other potential roles, like vendor, credit management, and so on, is enabled.

The customer is maintained on a general level, which is valid for all company codes and sales areas and provides general data, such as name and address, and, on a company code level, provides some more specific settings such as the reconciliation account in the general ledger.

Let's start by examining the setup for general data.

6.1.1 General Data

As with vendors, to create, change, or display a customer, enter Transaction BP. As shown in Figure 6.1, select the **7: Customer Number** option in the **By** field.

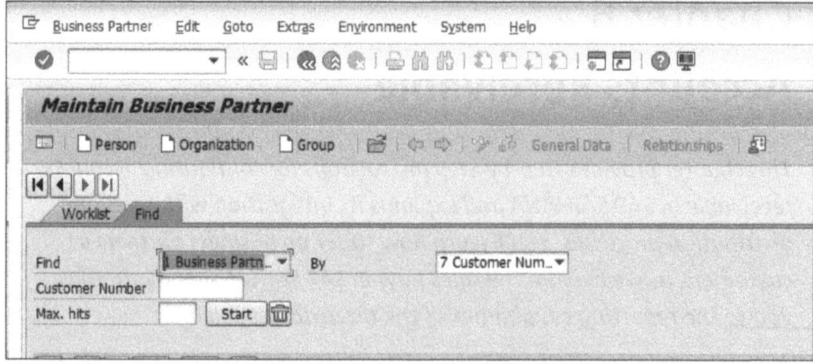

Figure 6.1 Business Partner Search by Customer Number

Then, after you click the **Start** button, you'll see a list of business partners created in the customer role. Double-click any customer number to examine its master record.

Figure 6.2 shows the general data of the selected customer in its address tab. You're already familiar with the tab structure of business partner master record from previous chapters. In the **Change in BP role** (change in business partner role) field, you'll see the role you're currently maintaining—in this case, general data. Below that field, you'll see tabs such as **Address, Control, Payment Transactions,** and so on. All these fields are valid for all company codes for that business partner. You can update fields by selecting **Switch Between Display and Change** in the top menu.

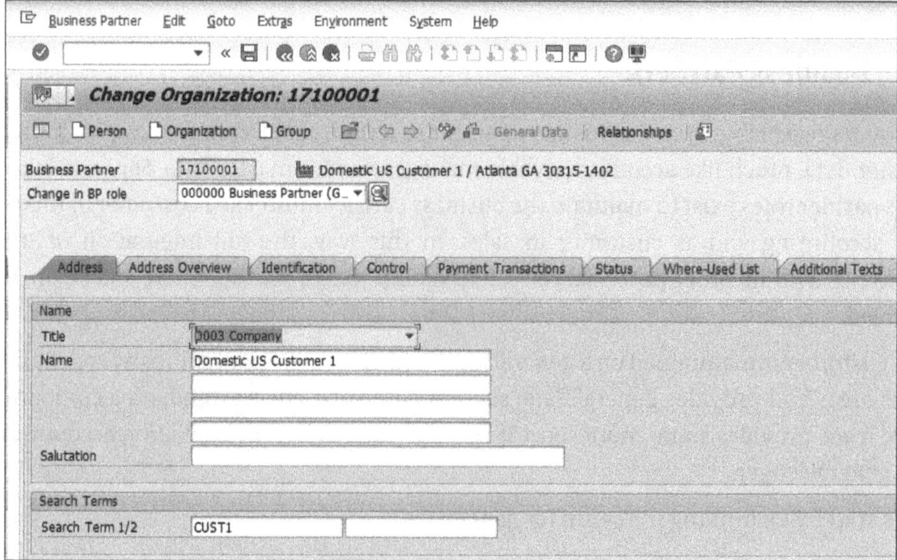

Figure 6.2 Customer Address Data

Now, select the **Customer (Financial Accounting)** role in the **Change in BP role** field, and you'll see additional tabs that are relevant for the financial accounting customer role.

As shown in Figure 6.3, you can now maintain customer-specific fields such as tax data, which determines the proper tax treatment when posting integrated transactions for this customer.

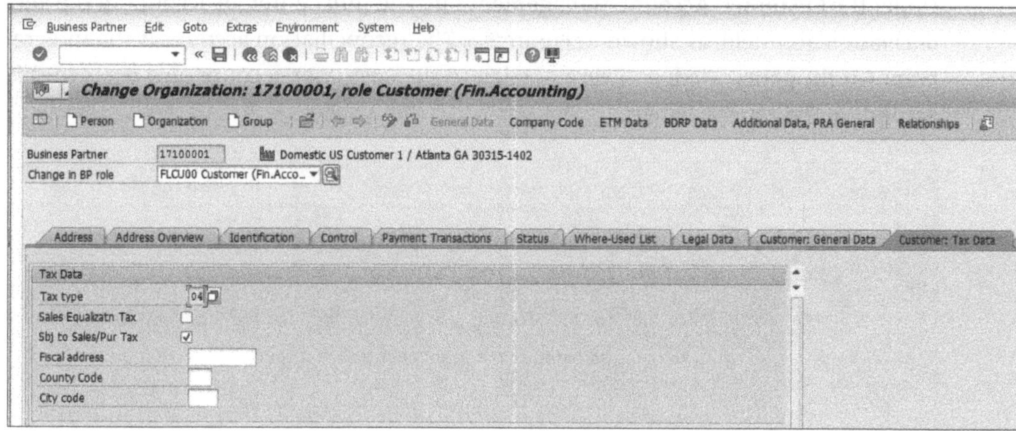

Figure 6.3 Customer (Financial Accounting) Role General Data

6.1.2 Company Code Data

To view the company code-level data for the customer, select **Company Code** from the top menu, which will bring you to the screen shown in Figure 6.4.

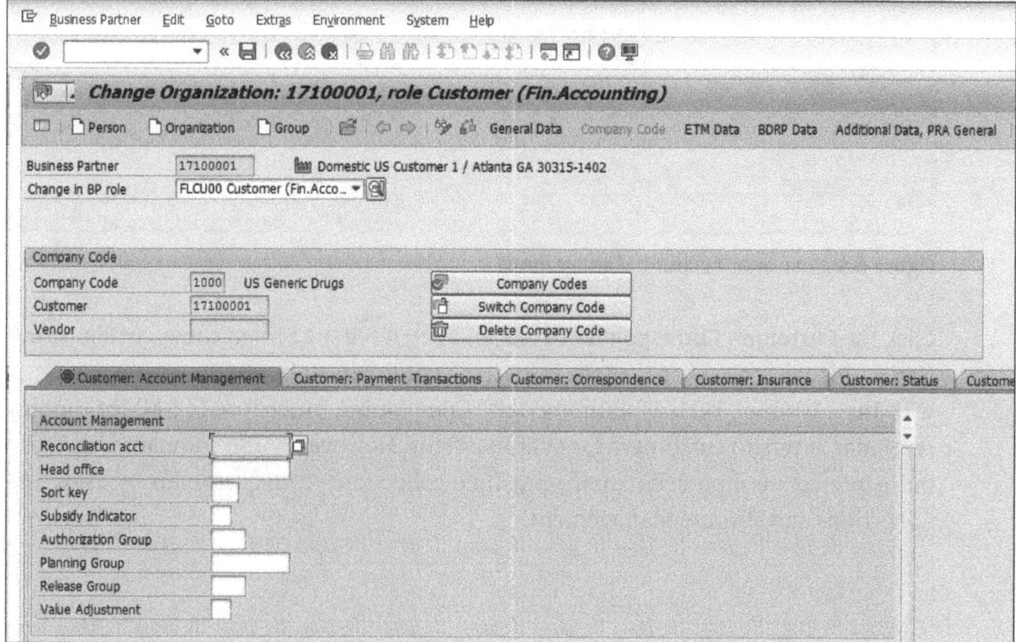

Figure 6.4 Customer Company Code Level

Select the company code by clicking on the **Company Codes** button, shown in Figure 6.4. You can also switch between the different company codes for which the customer is maintained via the **Switch Company Code** button.

Under the **Customer: Account Management** tab, you must enter an account in the **Reconciliation acct** field, as shown in Figure 6.5. The reconciliation account is the integral point for the general ledger. Every posting to the customer account also posts to this account in the general ledger.

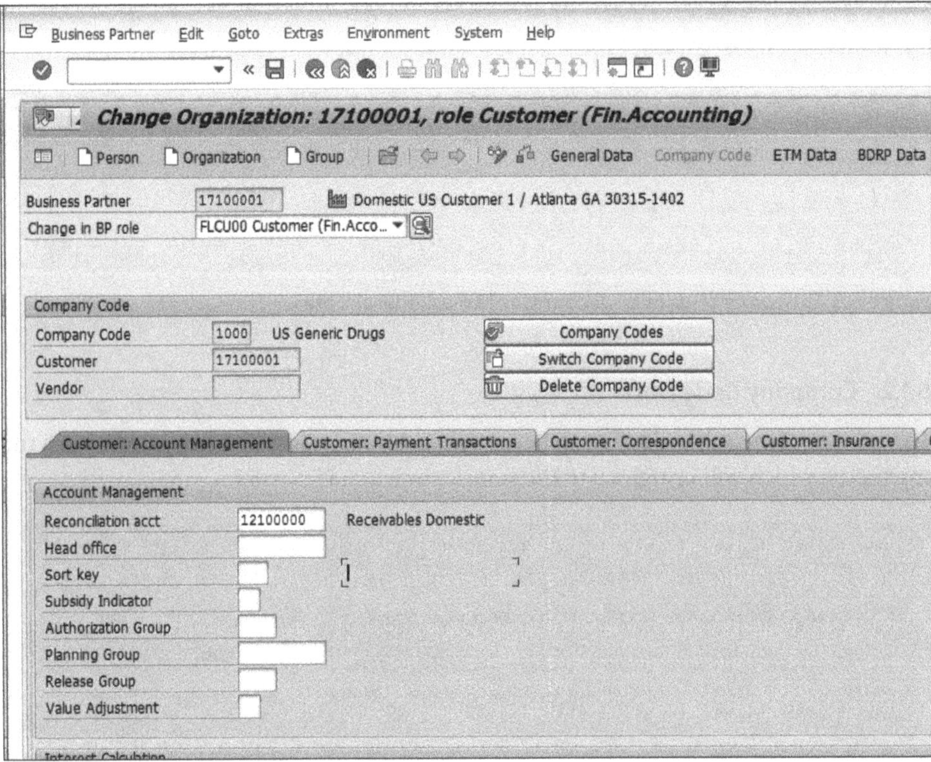

Figure 6.5 Customer Account Management

Click the **Customer: Correspondence** tab, and you'll see the screen shown in Figure 6.6. Under this tab, you can maintain important parameters about your correspondence with the customer, such as dunning data. *Dunning* is a procedure in SAP for sending reminder letters to customers for overdue items. However, some companies opt for a more interactive approach to managing their collections from customers by using SAP Collections and Dispute Management.

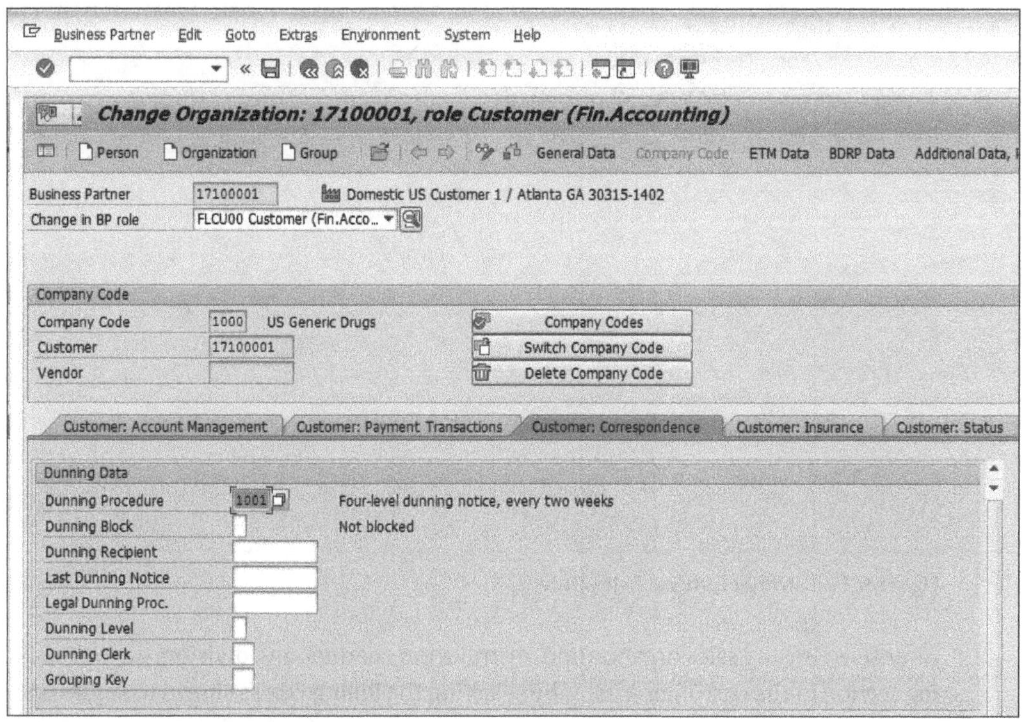

Figure 6.6 Customer Correspondence

6.1.3 Sales Data

You'll also need to maintain the sales data for the customer, which is used by sales and distribution. Most customer invoices are processed through the integrated sales and distribution process, based on the parameters maintained in the sales data for the business partner.

Select the **FLCU01 Customer** role in the **Change in BP role** field, and you'll see additional tabs that are relevant for sales processes, as shown in Figure 6.7.

Notice that the business partner and customer have the same account numbers. This correspondence isn't the only option; you can also have different number ranges. But a best practice is for these numbers to be the same, which is controlled with the configuration of the number ranges assigned to customer account groups and to business partner account groups, which we'll examine in the next section.

The **Account group** field shows the account group used for the customer. This account group was also used in the old customer creation process in SAP ERP.

To define the sales area level-settings, click the **Sales and Distribution** option in the top menu of Figure 6.7. Similar to how you can have different settings on the company code level in financial accounting, the different settings on the sales area level enable different processing for the same customer in various sales areas.

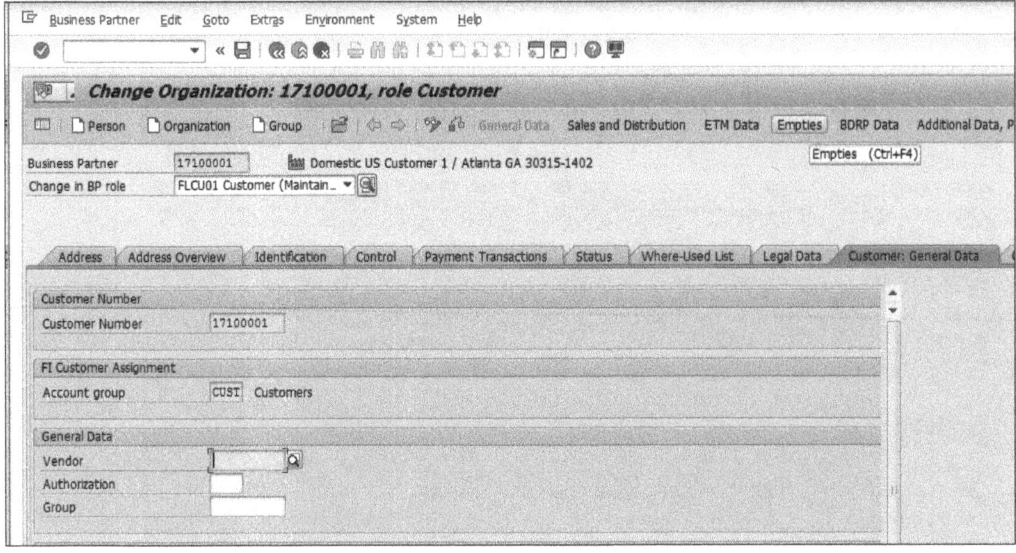

Figure 6.7 Customer General Sales Data

After selecting the sales organization, distribution channel, and division, go to the billing section of the customer master by selecting the **Billing** tab, as shown in Figure 6.8.

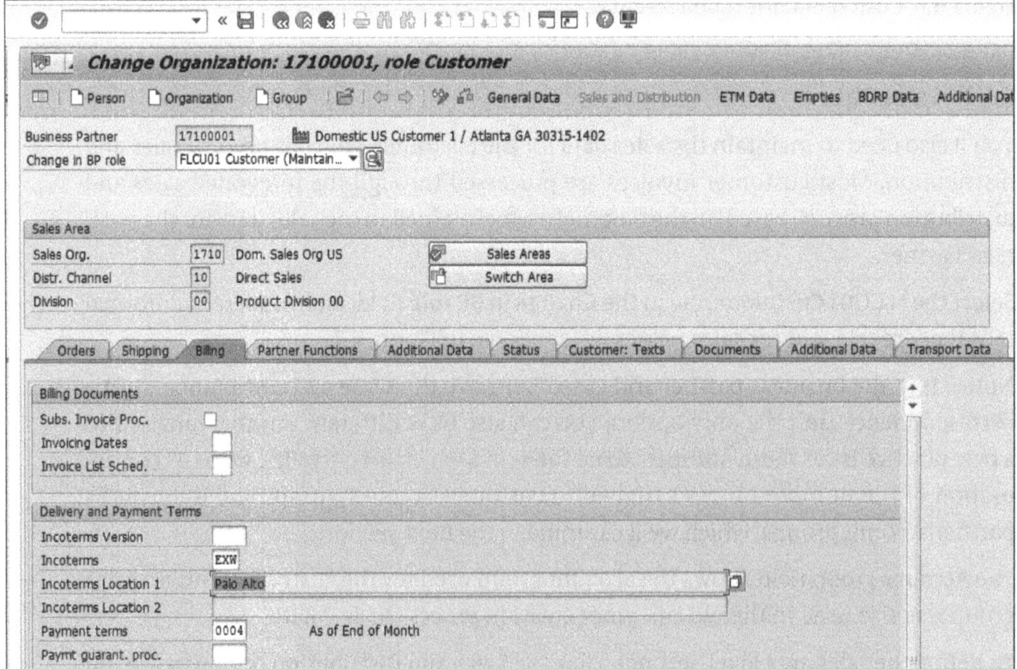

Figure 6.8 Customer Billing Data

Under this tab, you can enter various settings related to billing. For example, as shown in Figure 6.8 we've entered "EXW" in the **Incoterms** field for *Ex Works* and "0004" in the **Payment terms** field, which specifies that payment is due at the end of the month.

Now, click on the **Partner Functions** tab to maintain the partner functions of the customer, as shown in Figure 6.9.

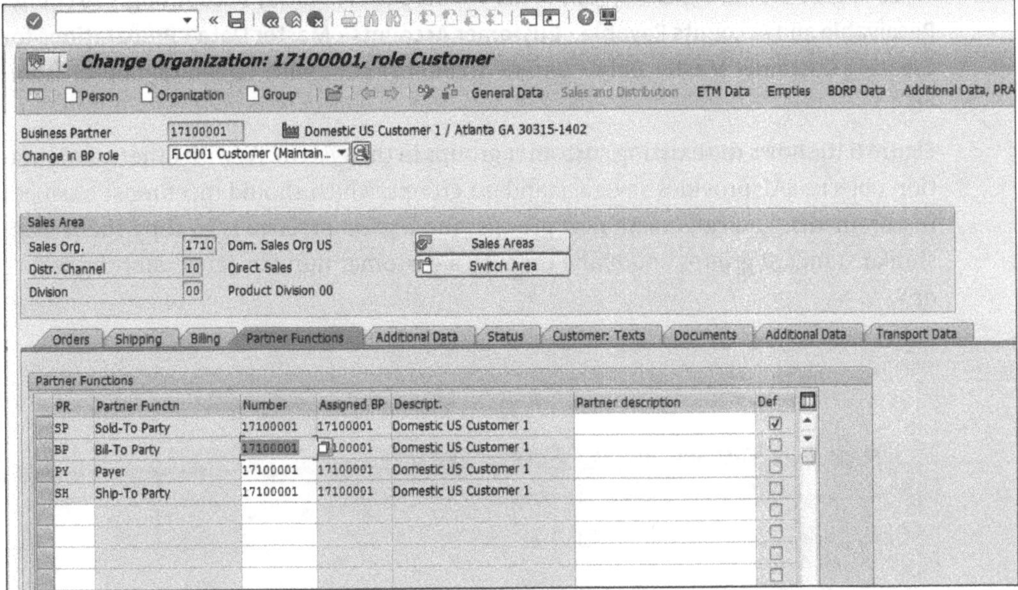

Figure 6.9 Customer Partner Functions

By default, the same customer is used for all partner functions, such as sold-to party, bill-to party, payer, and ship-to party. However, you can also enter a different customer if, for example, one customer receives the goods (ship-to party) but another customer pays for them (payer). This scenario is commonly used in drop-shipping.

After saving the business partner master record on the general level, the company code level, and the sales level, you're ready to use the business partner in both financial and the sales transactions.

Now, let's examine the elements that must be configured for the business partner as a customer.

6.1.4 Business Partner Configuration

We'll now configure a business partner so it can be used in accounts receivable. We'll configure account groups, number ranges, and the customer-vendor integration (CVI), which we introduced in Chapter 5.

Account Groups

You must set up financial accounting customer groups to be used when creating customers. Figure 6.7 showed how this group is mapped in the business partner master record. This group determines the number range for the customer account and the screen layout of the fields in the master record.

To configure account groups, follow the menu path **Financial Accounting • Accounts Receivable and Accounts Payable • Customer Accounts • Master Data • Preparations for Creating Customer Master Data • Define Account Groups with Screen Layout (Customers).**

Figure 6.10 shows the existing customer groups in the system. As with other configuration objects, SAP provides several standard groups, which should meet most business requirements. You can create new groups, and a good practice is to copy them from similar standard groups and name them in a customer number range, starting with Z or Y.

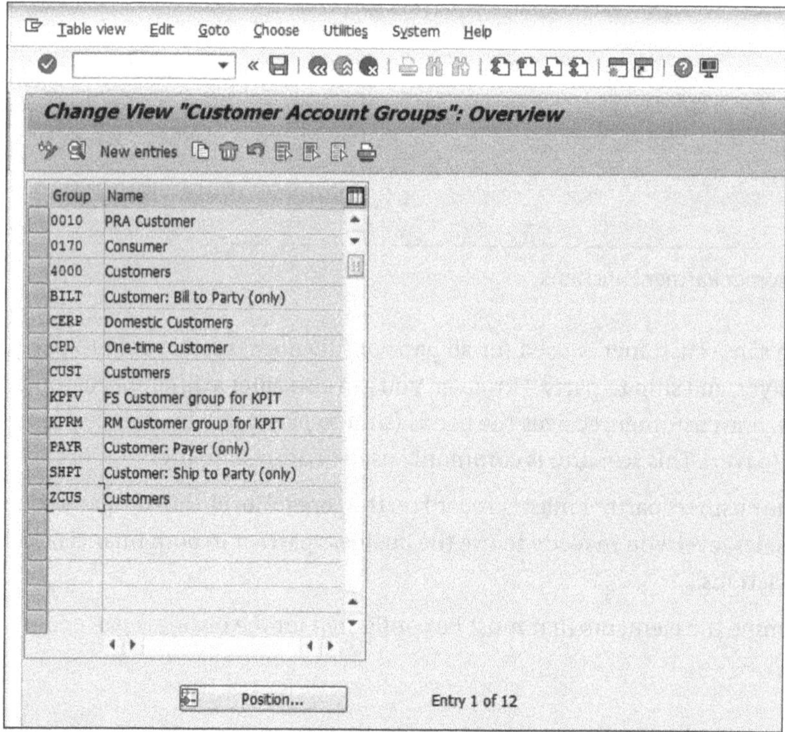

Figure 6.10 Financial Accounting Account Groups

Let's copy the standard group **CUST: Customers** to our own group. Select the group and select **Copy As...** from the top menu. Then, enter the name "Z001" to the **Account group** field and enter a meaningful description in the **Meaning** field, as shown in Figure 6.11.

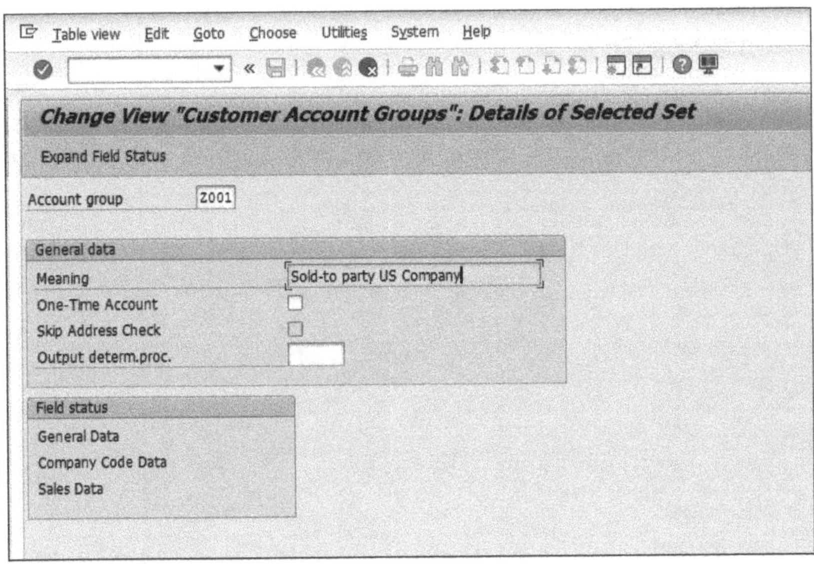

Figure 6.11 Copying an Account Group

You can then check and change the related field status by clicking the options in the **Field status** section:

- **General Data**
- **Company Code Data**
- **Sales Data**

First, select **General Data**. You'll see the relevant field status groups for the general data, as shown in Figure 6.12.

These field status groups correspond to the tabs you've seen in the business partner master record. The text for the groups is blue because at least one field is optional. If all fields are hidden within a group, the text of the group will be displayed in black.

Double-click one of the groups, for example, **Payment transactions**, which will bring you to the screen shown in Figure 6.13.

On this screen, you can set fields as optional, required, or hidden. In our example, the **Bank details, Alternative payer account**, and **Alternative payer in document** fields are set as optional, which means that these fields are available for input in the master record but are not required; you can save the record while leaving these fields empty. The **DME details** field (DME stands for data medium exchange in this context) is suppressed, which means that you would not see this field in the master record.

In this fashion, modify the fields based on your business requirements. Proceed through the company code data and sales data fields for all the customer groups you need.

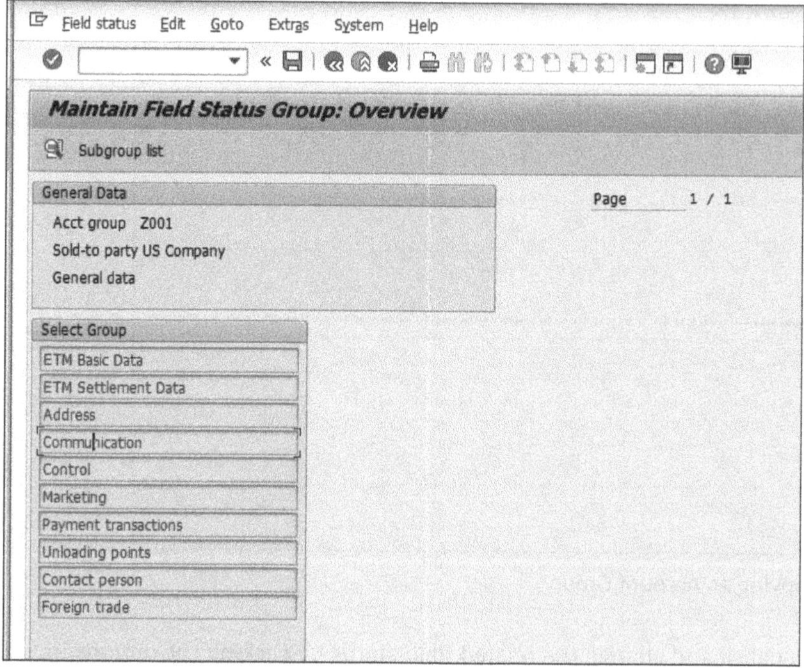

Figure 6.12 Field Status Groups

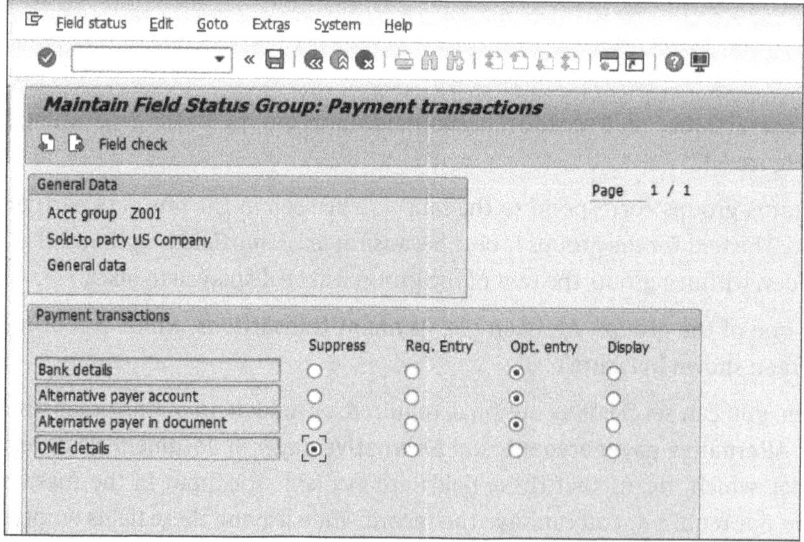

Figure 6.13 Payment Transactions Field Status

In general, a good practice is to not leave too many fields in the master record that won't be used, which could cause confusion. We recommend having a clear strategy for which fields are needed and which fields should be required and to hide fields that you know will never be used.

Number Ranges

The next step is to create and assign number ranges for the customer groups by following the menu path **Financial Accounting • Accounts Receivable and Accounts Payable • Customer Accounts • Master Data • Preparations for Creating Customer Master Data • Assign Number Ranges to Customer Account Groups.** As shown in Figure 6.14, number ranges are assigned to customer groups.

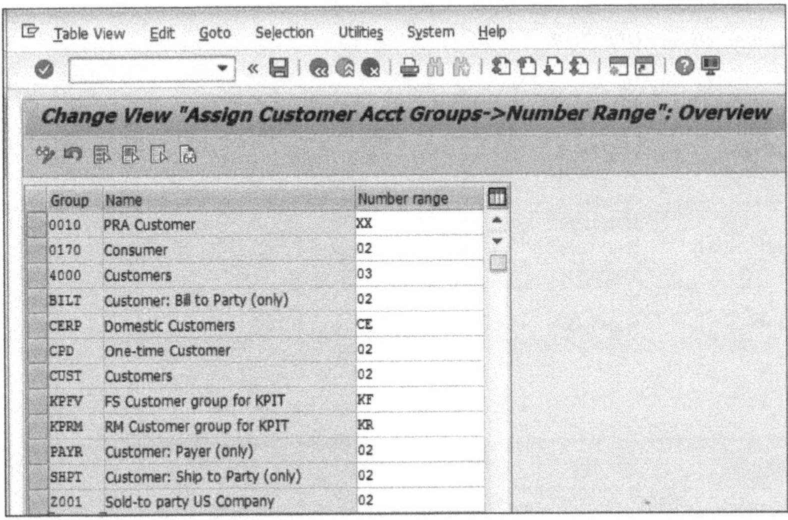

Figure 6.14 Customer Groups with Number Ranges

To define number ranges, follow the menu path **Financial Accounting • Accounts Receivable and Accounts Payable • Customer Accounts • Master Data • Preparations for Creating Customer Master Data • Create Number Ranges for Customer Accounts.** As shown in Figure 6.15, the **Number Range Object** for customers is **DEBITOR**. Click the Intervals button to change the number ranges.

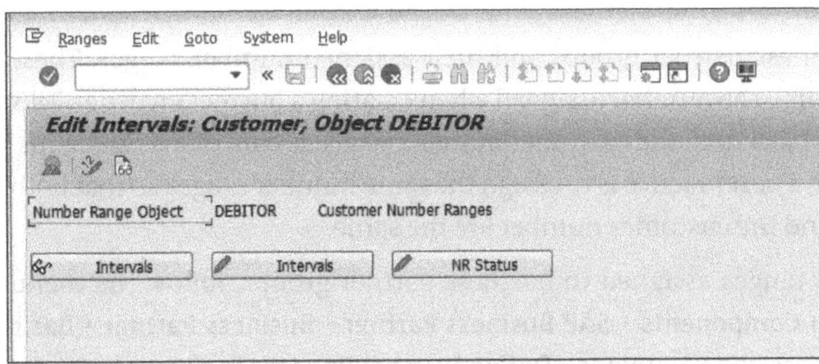

Figure 6.15 Number Range Object for Customers

As shown in Figure 6.16, you can maintain values in the **From** and **To** fields for the number range assigned to customer groups. For range **02**, which we assigned previously, the numbers start from 0001000000, which is how our customer accounts will be numbered.

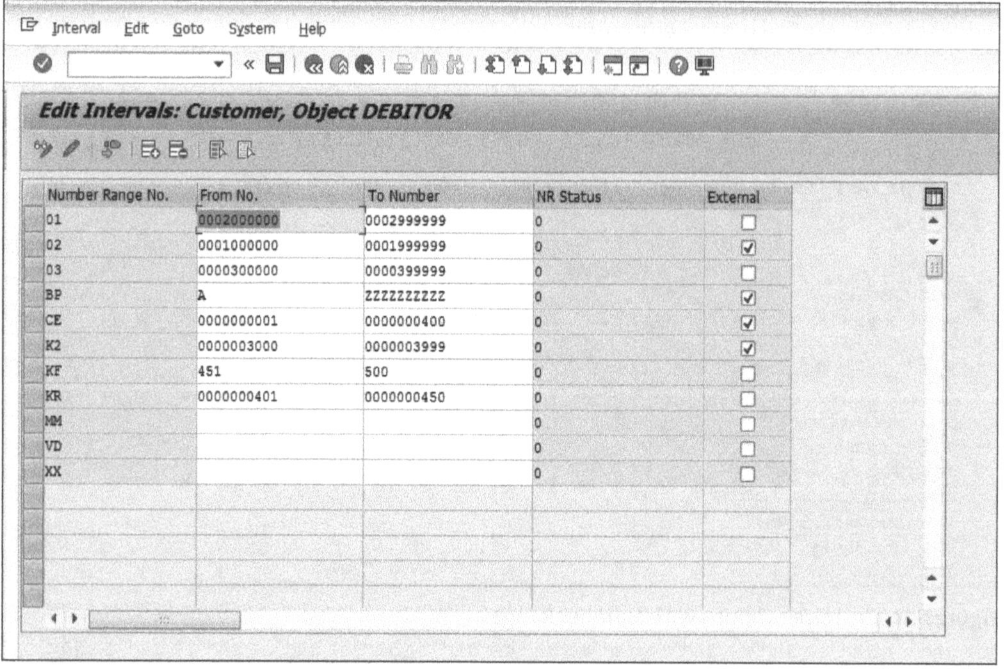

Number Range No.	From No.	To Number	NR Status	External
01	0002000000	0002999999	0	☐
02	0001000000	0001999999	0	☑
03	0000300000	0000399999	0	☐
BP	A	ZZZZZZZZZZ	0	☑
CE	0000000001	0000000400	0	☑
K2	0000003000	0000003999	0	☑
KF	451	500	0	☐
KR	0000000401	0000000450	0	☐
MM			0	☐
VD			0	☐
XX			0	☐

Figure 6.16 Number Range Maintenance for Customers

The next step is to define the business partner groups and their number ranges by following the menu path **Cross-Application Components • SAP Business Partner • Business Partner • Basic Settings • Number Ranges and Groupings • Define Groupings and Assign Number Ranges.**

Figure 6.17 shows business partner groups and their assigned number ranges. These number ranges determine the number assigned when creating a business partner. This number is a different object than the customer number, which is controlled by the customer group. However, a best practice is to assign the same number ranges so that both the business partner and the customer number are the same.

To create the number ranges assigned to business partner groups, follow the menu path **Cross-Application Components • SAP Business Partner • Business Partner • Basic Settings • Number Ranges and Groupings • Define Number Ranges.** As shown in Figure 6.18, define the number ranges to be assigned to business partner groups.

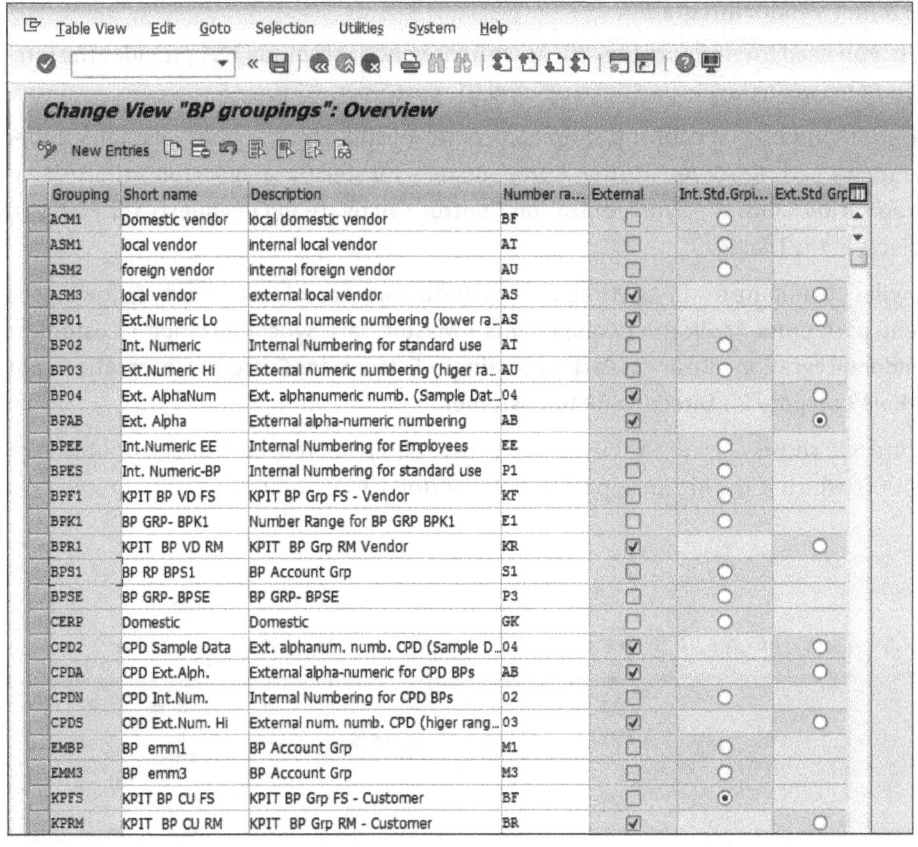

Table View Edit Goto Selection Utilities System Help

Change View "BP groupings": Overview

New Entries

Grouping	Short name	Description	Number ra...	External	Int.Std.Grpi...	Ext.Std Grp
ACM1	Domestic vendor	local domestic vendor	BF	☐	○	
ASM1	local vendor	internal local vendor	AT	☐	○	
ASM2	foreign vendor	internal foreign vendor	AU	☐	○	
ASM3	local vendor	external local vendor	AS	☑		○
BP01	Ext.Numeric Lo	External numeric numbering (lower ra...	AS	☑		○
BP02	Int. Numeric	Internal Numbering for standard use	AT	☐	○	
BP03	Ext.Numeric Hi	External numeric numbering (higer ra...	AU	☐	○	
BP04	Ext. AlphaNum	Ext. alphanumeric numb. (Sample Dat...	04	☑		○
BPAB	Ext. Alpha	External alpha-numeric numbering	AB	☑		◉
BPEE	Int.Numeric EE	Internal Numbering for Employees	EE	☐	○	
BPES	Int. Numeric-BP	Internal Numbering for standard use	P1	☐	○	
BPF1	KPIT BP VD FS	KPIT BP Grp FS - Vendor	KF	☐	○	
BPK1	BP GRP- BPK1	Number Range for BP GRP BPK1	E1	☐	○	
BPR1	KPIT BP VD RM	KPIT BP Grp RM Vendor	KR	☑		○
BPS1	BP RP BPS1	BP Account Grp	S1	☐	○	
BPSE	BP GRP- BPSE	BP GRP- BPSE	P3	☐	○	
CERP	Domestic	Domestic	GK	☐	○	
CPD2	CPD Sample Data	Ext. alphanum. numb. CPD (Sample D...	04	☑		○
CPDA	CPD Ext.Alph.	External alpha-numeric for CPD BPs	AB	☑		○
CPDN	CPD Int.Num.	Internal Numbering for CPD BPs	02	☐	○	
CPDS	CPD Ext.Num. Hi	External num. numb. CPD (higer rang...	03	☑		○
EMBP	BP emm1	BP Account Grp	M1	☐	○	
EMM3	BP emm3	BP Account Grp	M3	☐	○	
KPFS	KPIT BP CU FS	KPIT BP Grp FS - Customer	BF	☐	◉	
KPRM	KPIT BP CU RM	KPIT BP Grp RM - Customer	BR	☑		○

Figure 6.17 Business Partner Groups

Interval Edit Goto System Help

Edit Intervals: Business partner, Object BU_PARTNER

Number Range No.	From No.	To Number	NR Status	External
01	0000001000	0000001999	1009	☐
02	0001000000	0001999999	1000049	☐
03	0010000000	0999999999	0	☑
04	0A	8Z	0	☑
AB	A	ZZZZZZZZZZ	0	☑
AS	0000000700	0000000799	0	☑
AT	0000000800	0000000899	809	☐
AU	0000000900	0000000999	0	☐
BF	0000000501	0000000600	0	☐
BR	0000000601	0000000650	0	☑

Figure 6.18 Business Partner Number Ranges

Customer Vendor Integration

Now, you need to configure the CVI. As with the vendor accounts, CVI provides the integration between the business partner and the customer.

We configured the synchronization control for business partners in Chapter 5 under the menu path **Cross-Application Components • Master Data Synchronization • Synchronization Control • Synchronization Control • Activate PPO Requests for Platform Objects in the Dialog.**

Now, let's configure the link between the business partner and customer by following the menu path **Cross-Application Components • Master Data Synchronization • Customer/ Vendor Integration • Business Partner Settings • Settings for Customer Integration • Set BP Role Category for Direction BP to Customer.**

Figure 6.19 shows a list of the business partner roles related to customers. Double-click **FLCU00**, which is the business partner role for finance customers.

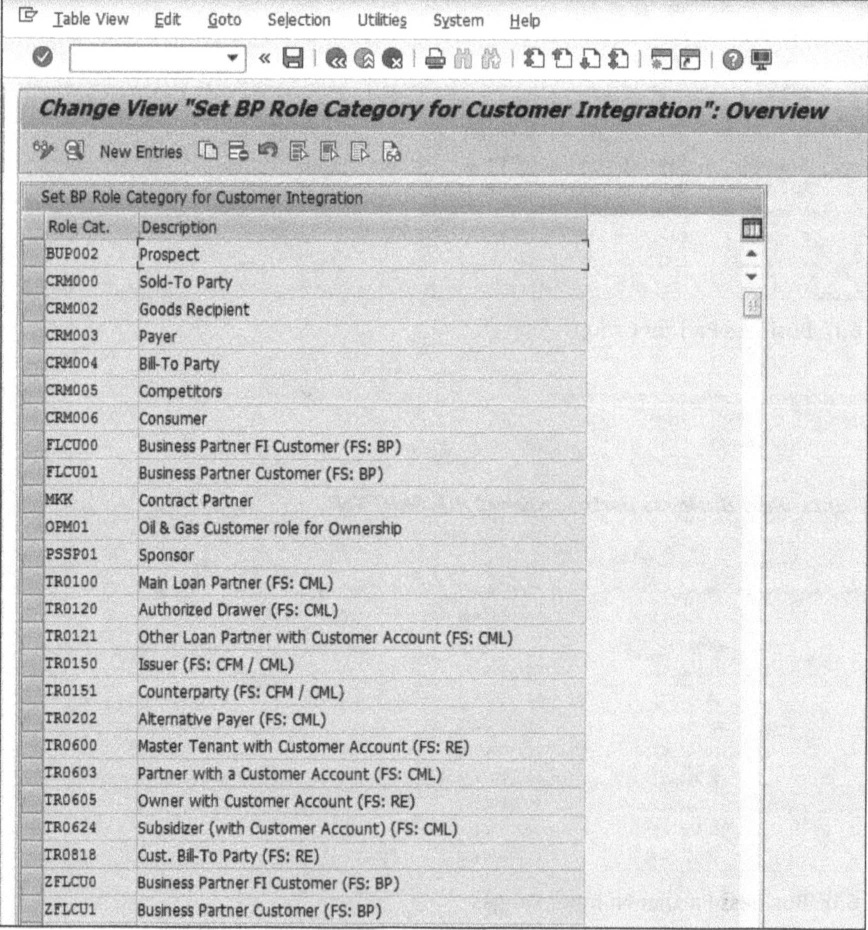

Figure 6.19 Linking a Business Partner to a Customer

As shown in Figure 6.20, select the **Custmr-Based** (customer-based) checkbox. This step indicates that, for this business partner role, having a customer is mandatory. Then, when you create or change a business partner in this role, the system automatically creates or changes a customer with the relevant data in financial accounting.

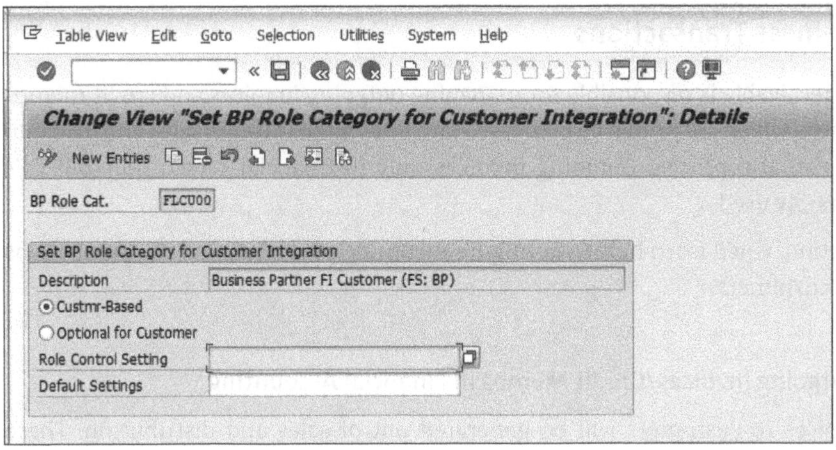

Table View Edit Goto Selection Utilities System Help

Change View "Set BP Role Category for Customer Integration": Details

New Entries

BP Role Cat. FLCU00

Set BP Role Category for Customer Integration

Description: Business Partner FI Customer (FS: BP)

Custmr-Based

Optional for Customer

Role Control Setting

Default Settings

Figure 6.20 Business Partner to Customer Settings for Financial Accounting Customer

Then, you must configure the opposite integration, from customer to business partner, by following the menu path **Cross-Application Components • Master Data Synchronization • Customer/Vendor Integration • Business Partner Settings • Settings for Customer Integration • Define BP Role for Direction Customer to BP.**

Select **New Entries** from the top menu and link the relevant customer groups with the business partner roles, as shown in Figure 6.21.

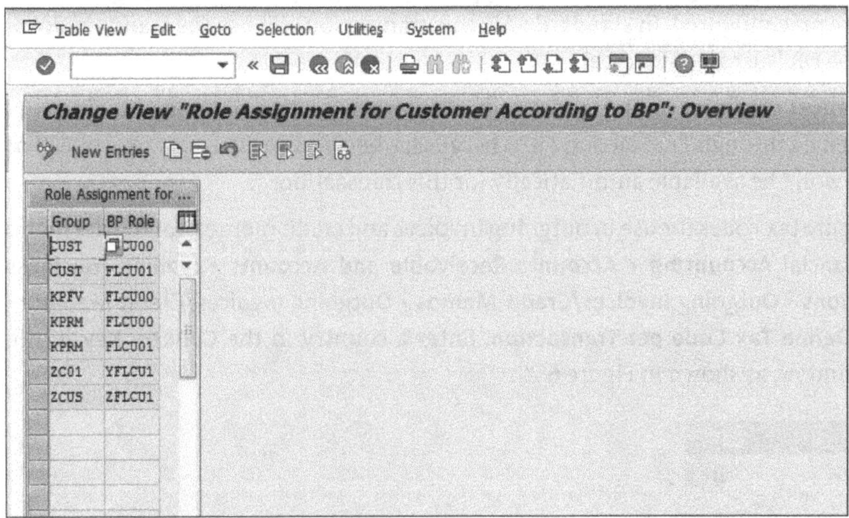

Figure 6.21 Linking Customer Groups to Business Partner Roles

Then, when you process a customer with the relevant account group, the system also will update the business partner in the business partner roles that are assigned to the customer groups.

6.2 Business Transactions

Accounts receivable is responsible for managing outgoing invoices and credit memos to customers, which are primarily processed and integrated through sales and distribution. You can also process outgoing invoices only in financial accounting, but this option is rarely used.

In this section, you'll learn how to configure incoming payments and payment terms related to customers.

6.2.1 Outgoing Invoices/Credit Memos in Financial Accounting

Most invoices to customers will be generated out of sales and distribution. These invoices reference the sales order, will include materials, and will affect inventory; we'll discuss these topics in detail in the next section. However, you can also enter a customer invoice directly in financial accounting. As such, many companies also require posting the customer invoice to financial accounting to generate an actual invoice that can be sent to customers, either printed or sent electronically as a PDF or in some other format.

Similar to posting vendor invoices, for customer invoices, SAP S/4HANA offers Transaction FB70, which provides an easier user interface (UI) to post customer invoices without knowing the specific document types or posting keys to use since all these elements are preconfigured. In standard SAP, this transaction will use the standard document type DR (customer invoice).

You still must configure the tax codes to be used when posting outgoing invoices and credit memos through Transaction FB70 because, when you create a new tax code, that tax code won't be available automatically for this transaction.

To configure tax codes for use in outgoing invoices and credit memos, follow the menu path **Financial Accounting • Accounts Receivable and Accounts Payable • Business Transactions • Outgoing Invoices/Credit Memos • Outgoing Invoices/Credit Memos—Enjoy • Define Tax Code per Transaction**. Enter a country in the **Country Key** in the popup window, as shown in Figure 6.22.

Figure 6.22 Selecting a Country

Select **New Entries** from the top menu, as shown in Figure 6.23.

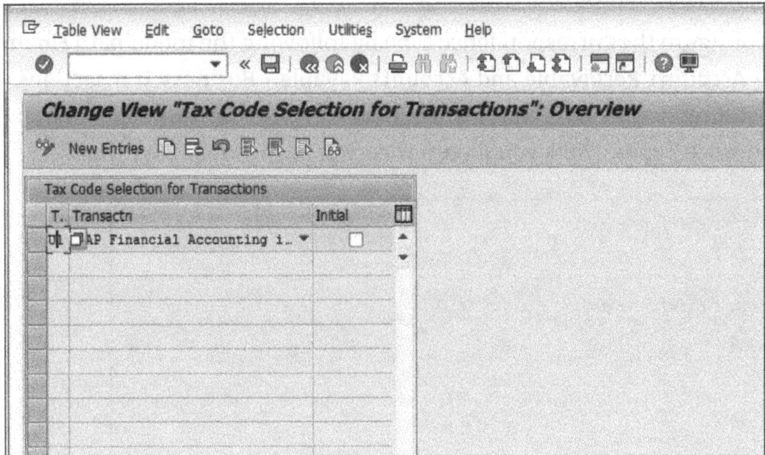

Figure 6.23 Initial Screen Defining Tax Codes for Outgoing Invoices and Credit Memos

Next, as shown in Figure 6.24, enter the output sales tax codes that you'll use with customer invoices. In the **Transaction** column, if you select **Relevant for All Transactions**, then the code can be used for all types of transactions. If you select the **Initial** flag, this tax code will be the default for the transaction.

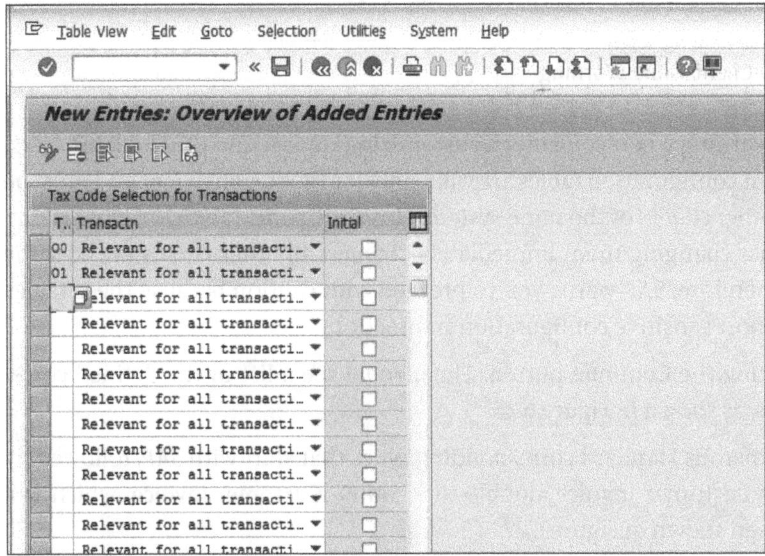

Figure 6.24 Defining Tax Codes for Outgoing Invoices

You can also customize the settings to generate printed invoices from within financial accounting customer invoices. You must configure the correspondence for the customer invoice. SAP provides several predefined forms and print programs to generate various documents from financial accounting, such as customer invoices, balance confirmations, open item lists, and so on.

First, you must configure the correspondence type by following the menu path **Financial Accounting • Accounts Receivable and Accounts Payable • Business Transactions • Outgoing Invoices/Credit Memos • Make and Check Settings for Correspondence • Define Correspondence Types**. Then, you'll see a warning, as shown in Figure 6.25.

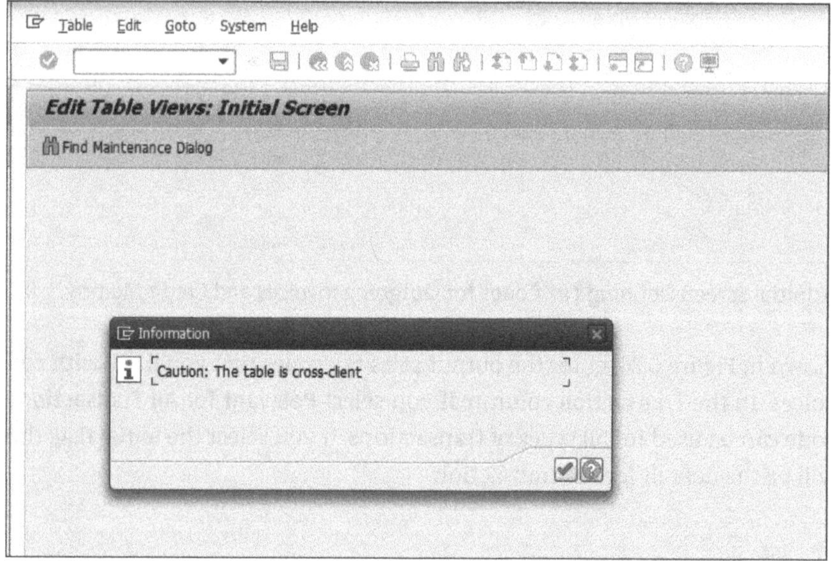

Figure 6.25 Cross-Client Table Warning

SAP issues this warning when you enter a customizing transaction that updates cross-client tables. Most configuration tables are valid only for the current client and must be transported to other clients of the same system. However, some tables are cross-client, which means that changing them immediately changes all other clients of the same SAP instance. Therefore, SAP warns you to proceed with caution because these tables usually are the most sensitive configuration transactions.

Proceed by clicking the **Continue** button. Then, you'll see a list of the defined correspondence types, as shown in Figure 6.26.

SAP delivers numerous standard corresponding types that start with *SAP*, followed by two digits. For a customer invoice, double-click **SAP19: Customer Invoice**, which will result in the screen shown in Figure 6.27.

The **Doc. Necessary** checkbox ensures that correspondence—in this case, a customer invoice—is always generated for the given document number for which it's requested.

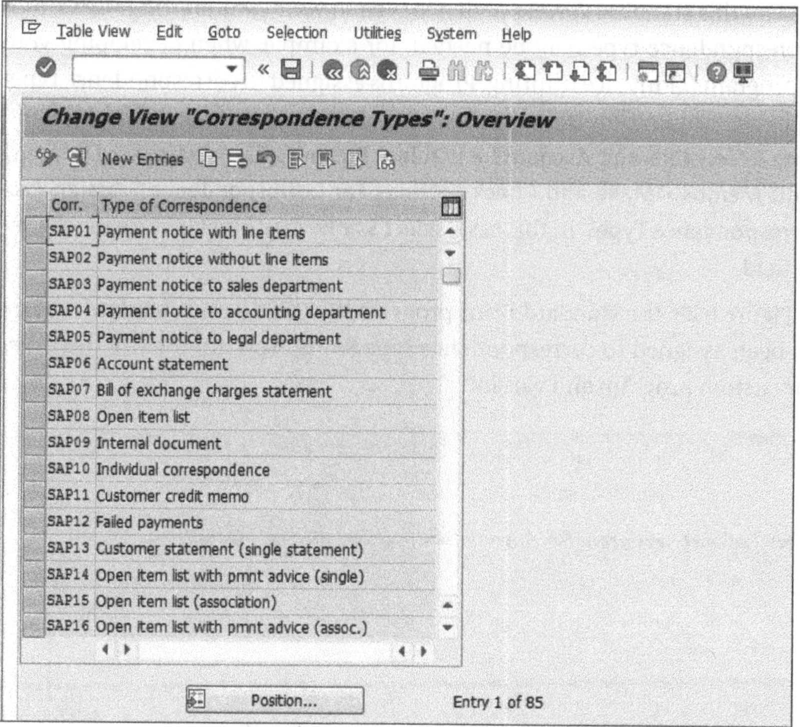

Figure 6.26 Correspondence Types

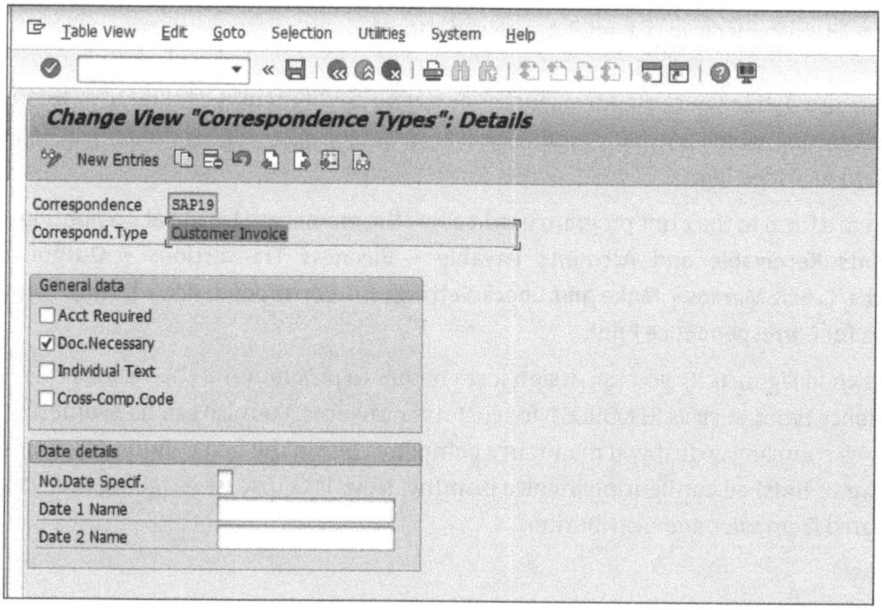

Table View Edit Goto Selection Utilities System Help

Change View "Correspondence Types": Details

New Entries

Correspondence SAP19

Correspond.Type Customer Invoice

General data

- [ ] Acct Required
- [x] Doc.Necessary
- [ ] Individual Text
- [ ] Cross-Comp.Code

Date details

No.Date Specif.

Date 1 Name

Date 2 Name

Figure 6.27 Correspondence Type Customer Invoice

You can also copy this standard correspondence type to your own, starting with Z or Y. A custom correspondence type may be needed, for example, when developing your own custom program for invoice printing. Programs assigned to correspondence types are assigned in a configuration transaction under the menu path **Financial Accounting • Accounts Receivable and Accounts Payable • Business Transactions • Outgoing Invoices/Credit Memos • Make and Check Settings for Correspondence • Assign Programs for Correspondence Types**. In this case, select **SAP19: Customer Invoice** in the **Correspondence** field.

As shown in Figure 6.28, the standard print program **RFKORD50** and standard variant **SAP&19** have been assigned to correspondence type **SAP19**. You can modify these settings for your custom program and variant.

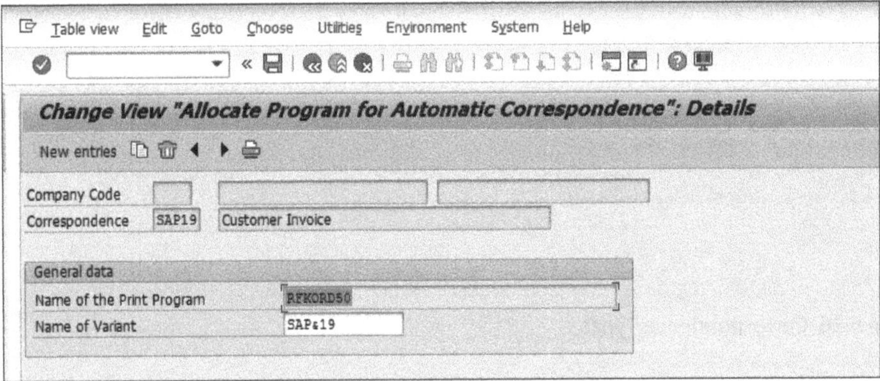

Figure 6.28 Customer Invoice Print Program and Variant

You can also define your own forms for invoices and credit memos generated in financial accounting, which is usually required because the company logo should replace the standard provided logo.

To assign a form to the print program used, follow the menu path **Financial Accounting • Accounts Receivable and Accounts Payable • Business Transactions • Outgoing Invoices/Credit Memos • Make and Check Settings for Correspondence • Define Form Names for Correspondence Print**.

As shown in Figure 6.29, you can assign form names to programs for the various correspondence types, such as RFKORD50 for customer invoices. You also can have different forms by company code if you maintain a company code in the first column. With this step, we've finished configuring invoice printing. Now, let's discuss outgoing invoices generated from sales and distribution.

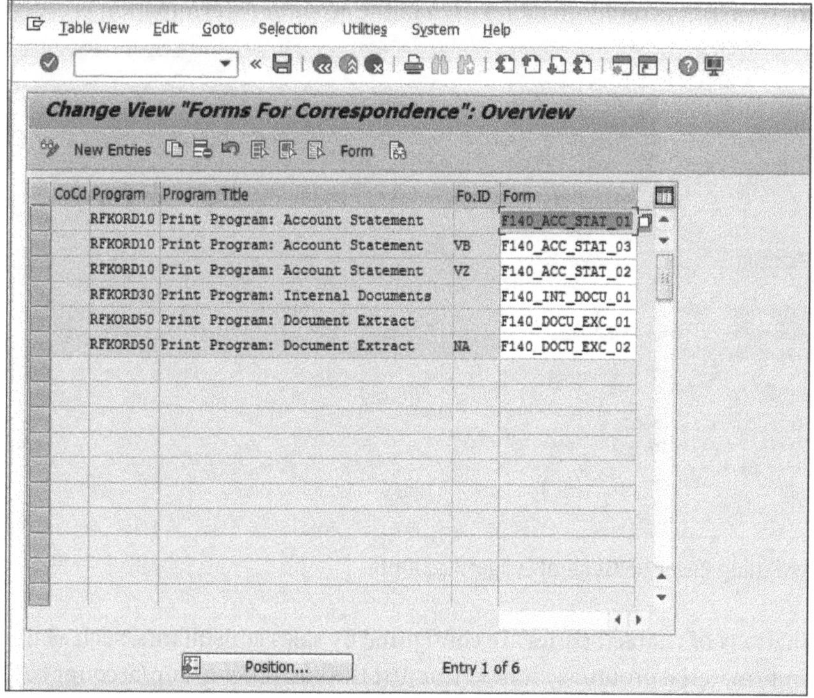

Figure 6.29 Correspondence Form Names

6.2.2 Outgoing Invoices/Credit Memos in Sales and Distribution

As discussed earlier, the vast majority of the outgoing customer invoices and credit memos will be posted through the integration with SAP S/4HANA Sales. This is common because customer invoices normally follow sales orders and reference at least one material in the system. Financial documents for customer invoices will be posted automatically in financial accounting, as well as goods issues to customers based on the account determination, set up via condition techniques, similar to what we discussed regarding tax code determination in Chapter 5.

Most of the configuration for SAP S/4HANA Sales billing documents, which generate the customer invoice posting in financial accounting and the relevant postings to controlling objects, lies within the configuration of sales and distribution. Most important is the pricing procedure, which determines the values posted. The account determination, which is determined based on the relevant condition records, also is part of the configuration of SAP S/4HANA Sales in the system. However, typically, this configuration is the joint responsibility of sales and financial consultants because finance should specify which accounts should be posted in which cases.

To assign revenue general ledger accounts for integral sales invoices, follow the menu path **Sales and Distribution • Basic Functions • Account Assignment/Costing • Revenue Account Determination • Assign G/L Accounts.**

Figure 6.30 shows a list of condition tables used in the account determination process.

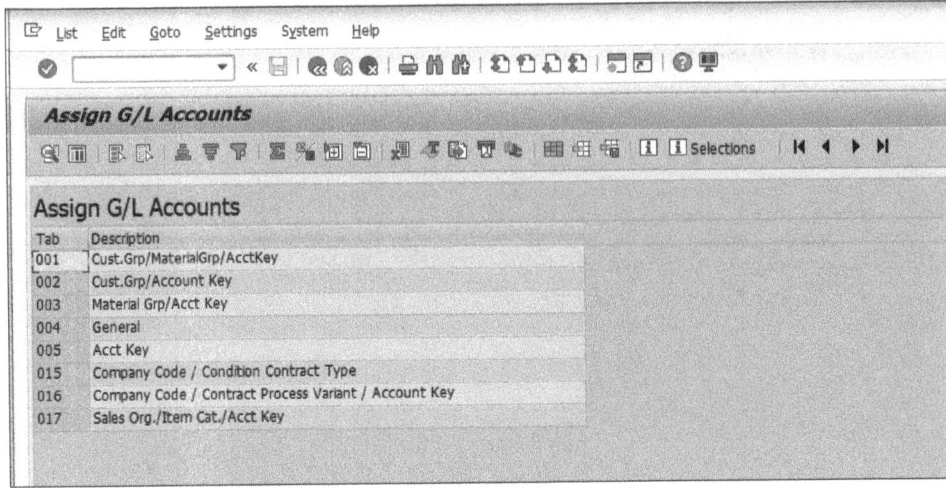

Figure 6.30 Assigning Revenue General Ledger Accounts

These combinations of characteristics are configured by sales consultants, such as the customer group/material group/account key or just the customer group/account key, as shown by the text descriptions in the table. The system first checks the most detailed condition table, and if an assigned account is found based on all its elements, the system stops and uses that account as its determination. If not, the system goes to the next table until it reaches the most generic condition table. If no account can be determined, the billing document in SAP S/4HANA Sales is still posted, but not released to accounting. This scenario typically occurs when master data, such as customer or material data, isn't properly maintained or if something is entered incorrectly on the sales order. When the issue is resolved, the document can be released to accounting.

6.2.3 Pricing Procedure in Sales

We mentioned earlier that the values of the customer invoices that are generated by sales and distribution are determined by the sales pricing procedure, which is a combination of condition types that represent various items such as price, discounts, and taxes. The pricing procedure derives from complex configuration in SAP S/4HANA Sales and is part of the sales order. From the sales order, the pricing procedure flows into the billing document and determines the values in the financial document. Figure 6.31 shows a pricing procedure in a sales order.

In our example, the sales price is determined by condition **PR00**: **Price**. The tax is determined by condition **UTXJ**: **Tax Jurisdict. Code**, which determines the tax based on jurisdiction codes.

Sales A | Sales B | Shipping | Billing Document | Tax Exemption License | Excise duty | Conditions | Account Assignment | Schedule lines | Partner

View: 1 Pricing Elements: Table | Quantity: 2 EA | Net: 19,00 USD | Tax: 0,00

CumltvConfdQty: 2,000

Condition Record | Analysis | Update | Update Commodity Prices

Pricing Elements

I... CnTy	Description	Amount	Crcy	per		B/N	Condition Value	Curr.	Status	Num...	ATO/MTS Component	OUn	CCon...	Un
PPR0	Price	10,00	USD	1	EA		20,00	USD		1		EA	1	EA
	Gross Amount	10,00	USD	1	EA		20,00	USD		1		EA	1	EA
DPG2	Customer Price Group	5,000-	%				1,00-	USD		0			0	
	Sum Surcharges/Disco	0,50-	USD	1	EA		1,00-	USD		1		EA	1	EA
	Net Amount 1	9,50	USD	1	EA		19,00	USD		1		EA	1	EA
UTXJ	Tax Jurisdict.Code	1,000	%				0,19	USD		0			0	
	Total Amount	9,50	USD	1	EA		19,00	USD		1		EA	1	EA

Figure 6.31 Pricing Procedure in a Sales Order

To see how these values were determined, click the **Analysis** button above the conditions. The system will show a tree-like structure of the various conditions, as shown in Figure 6.32. You can expand each condition and see how its value was determined. When the system finds a condition value based on the access sequences performed, the log on the right side shows **Condition Record Has Been Found**.

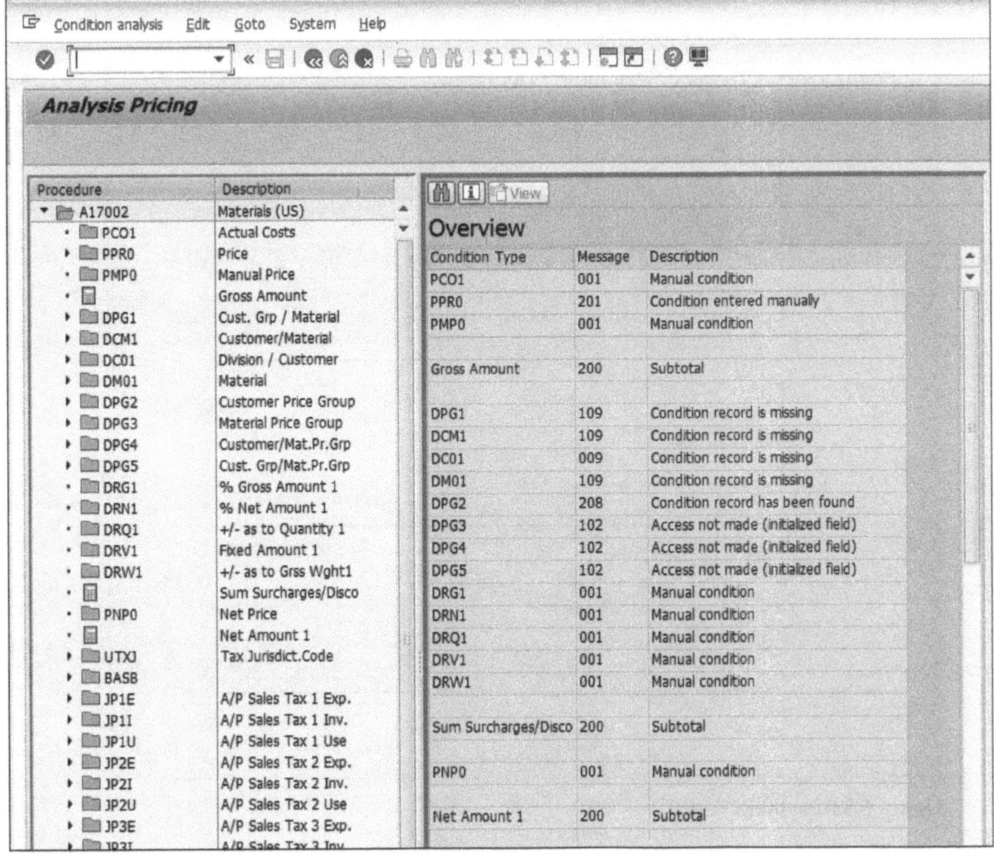

Figure 6.32 Analysis Pricing in a Sales Order

6.2.4 Incoming Payments and Payment Terms

The next major type of transactions related to accounts receivable are incoming payments from customers. All outgoing invoices, posted from sales and distribution or directly in financial accounting, are posted as open items and are awaiting incoming payments. The configuration of payment methods, the automatic payment program, and electronic bank statement are covered in detail in Chapter 8 for both incoming and outgoing payments.

For now, let's examine the configuration of the payment terms. Payment terms are used both in accounts receivable and accounts payable. The configuration of the payment term itself determines whether it can be used for customer accounts. To configure payment terms, follow the menu path **Financial Accounting • Accounts Receivable and Accounts Payable • Business Transactions • Outgoing Invoices/Credit Memos • Maintain Terms of Payment.**

Figure 6.33 shows the **Change View "Terms of Payment" Overview** screen, familiar from Chapter 5; in fact, the configuration transaction is the same.

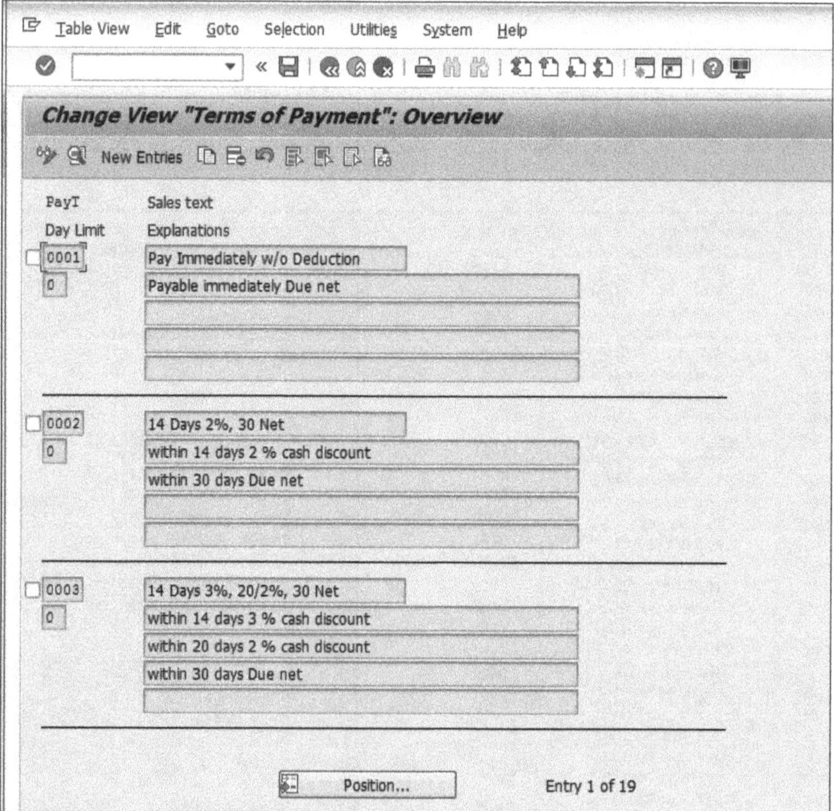

Figure 6.33 Payment Terms

Let's examine the configuration for the payment term SEPA, which is specifically designed for customer payments, according to Single Euro Payments Area (SEPA) direct debit. SEPA direct debit is a payment system that allows companies to collect payments from customer accounts. In this procedure, customers agree that the money for their invoices will be automatically deducted from their bank accounts, for which they sign an agreement (SEPA mandate). We'll examine the configuration of SEPA direct debit payments in detail in Chapter 8.

For now, select payment term **SEPA** to review its configuration, as shown in Figure 6.34.

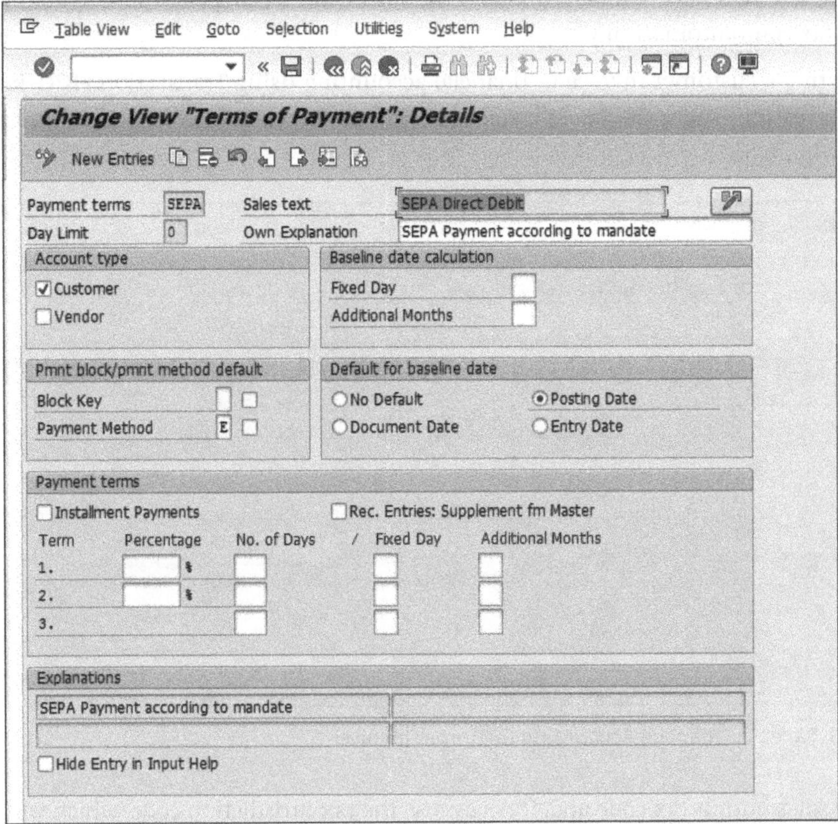

Figure 6.34 SEPA Direct Debit Payment Term

Selecting the **Customer** checkbox in the **Account type** section specifies that this payment term can be used only for customers. A specific payment method is assigned that is used for SEPA direct debit. The default for the baseline date calculation is set to the posting date.

6.3 Taxes

Now, let's examine taxes in accounts receivable processes. Sales (output) tax codes are used, which usually are entered manually in financial accounting invoices and automatically determined in integrated sales and distribution billing documents.

6.3.1 Taxes in Financial Accounting Invoices

When you enter an outgoing invoice directly in financial accounting, normally, you would enter the tax code manually, unless some substitution is in place that can determine the tax code automatically.

When posting a customer invoice in financial accounting using Transaction FB70, in the header section, under the **Tax** tab, you can enter the necessary tax information, as shown in Figure 6.35.

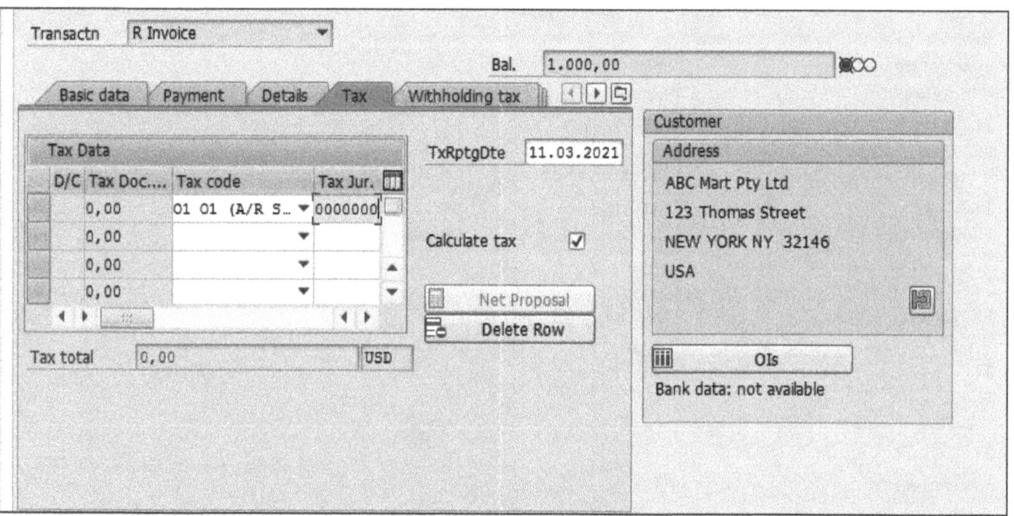

Figure 6.35 Taxes in Financial Accounting Customer Invoice

Select the sales output tax code and, if necessary, the tax jurisdiction code, which will use a tax rate based on a specific US jurisdiction. If you select the **Calculate tax** checkbox, taxes will be calculated automatically by the system.

No additional configuration is required to make this work other than properly setting up your tax codes, as described in Chapter 3, and enabling the relevant tax codes in the outgoing financial accounting invoice **Enjoy** screen, as described in Section 6.2.1.

6.3.2 Tax Determination in the Sales Process

Tax codes can be automatically determined in the sales process using the same condition technique used by other elements of the pricing procedure we discussed. In fact, the tax is a separate condition type in the pricing procedure, which is on the sales order level.

Let's revisit the screen shown earlier in Figure 6.30. Double-click on condition type **UTXJ: Tax Jurisdict.Code.** As shown in Figure 6.36, the system determines tax codes O0 based on the condition record found.

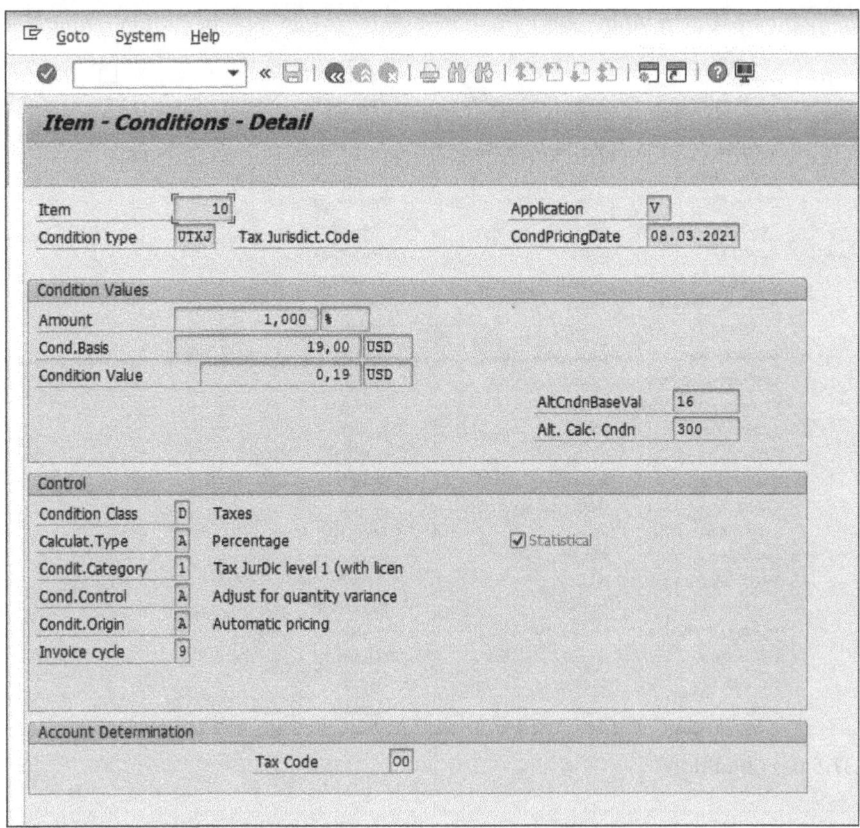

Figure 6.36 Tax Condition Record

Tax determination in sales uses a similar condition technique as purchasing (condition, access sequences, condition tables) to automatically determine the taxes. Special pricing conditions for taxes can be used to determine the proper tax code based on fields configured for use in condition tables.

To define a condition type, follow the menu path **Sales and Distribution • Basic Functions • Pricing • Pricing Control • Define Condition Types**. Then, select the **Set Condition Types for Pricing** activity. The system shows the sales condition defined, as shown in Figure 6.37. The standard SAP condition for output tax is MWAS, which you can copy as your own condition starting with Z or Y if needed.

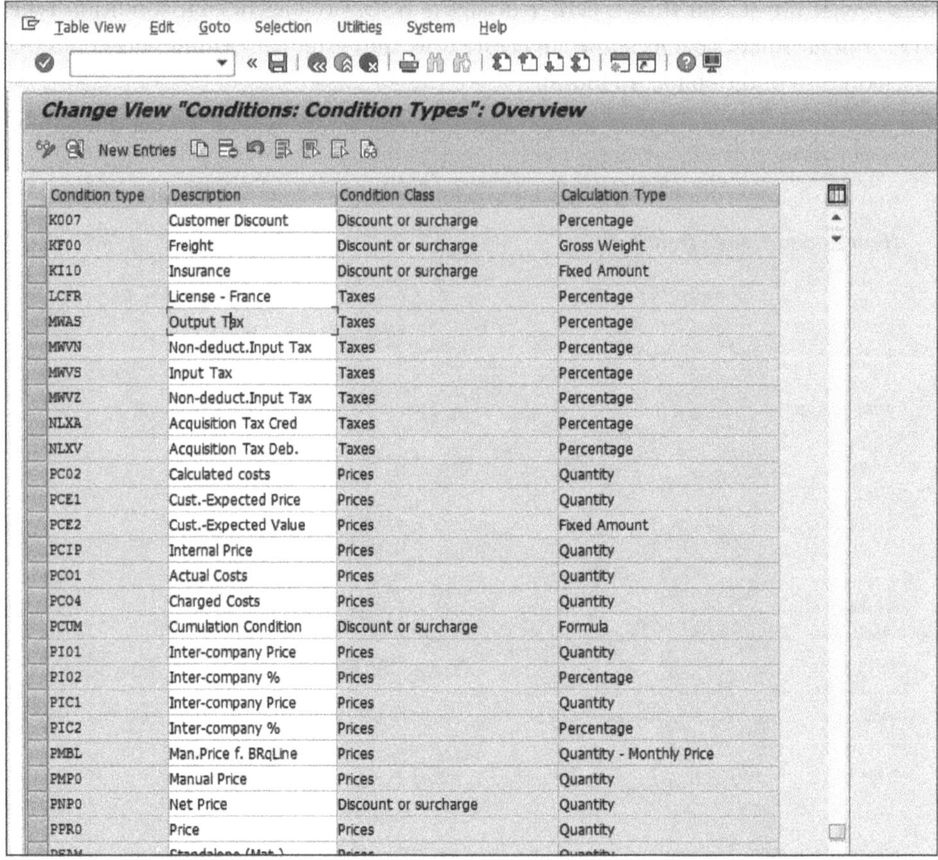

Condition type	Description	Condition Class	Calculation Type
K007	Customer Discount	Discount or surcharge	Percentage
KF00	Freight	Discount or surcharge	Gross Weight
KI10	Insurance	Discount or surcharge	Fixed Amount
LCFR	License - France	Taxes	Percentage
MWAS	Output Tax	Taxes	Percentage
MWVN	Non-deduct.Input Tax	Taxes	Percentage
MWVS	Input Tax	Taxes	Percentage
MWVZ	Non-deduct.Input Tax	Taxes	Percentage
NLXA	Acquisition Tax Cred	Taxes	Percentage
NLXV	Acquisition Tax Deb.	Taxes	Percentage
PC02	Calculated costs	Prices	Quantity
PCE1	Cust.-Expected Price	Prices	Quantity
PCE2	Cust.-Expected Value	Prices	Fixed Amount
PCIP	Internal Price	Prices	Quantity
PC01	Actual Costs	Prices	Quantity
PC04	Charged Costs	Prices	Quantity
PCUM	Cumulation Condition	Discount or surcharge	Formula
PI01	Inter-company Price	Prices	Quantity
PI02	Inter-company %	Prices	Percentage
PIC1	Inter-company Price	Prices	Quantity
PIC2	Inter-company %	Prices	Percentage
PMBL	Man.Price f. BRqLine	Prices	Quantity - Monthly Price
PMP0	Manual Price	Prices	Quantity
PNP0	Net Price	Discount or surcharge	Quantity
PPR0	Price	Prices	Quantity

Figure 6.37 Sales Conditions

Double-click **MWAS** to see its configuration, as shown in Figure 6.38.

The following fields are important:

- **Condition Class**
  This field determines the usage of the condition type. In our case, the condition class is set to **D: Taxes**, which defines this condition as a tax condition.
- **Calculation Type**
  Specifies the type of calculation and is set to **A: Percentage** because the output sales tax should be calculated as a percentage.

- **Condition Category**
  Classifies the conditions and for tax conditions should be **D: Tax**.
- **Item Condition**
  Should be selected for taxes because this checkbox ensures that the calculation occurs at the item level, which is required for taxes.

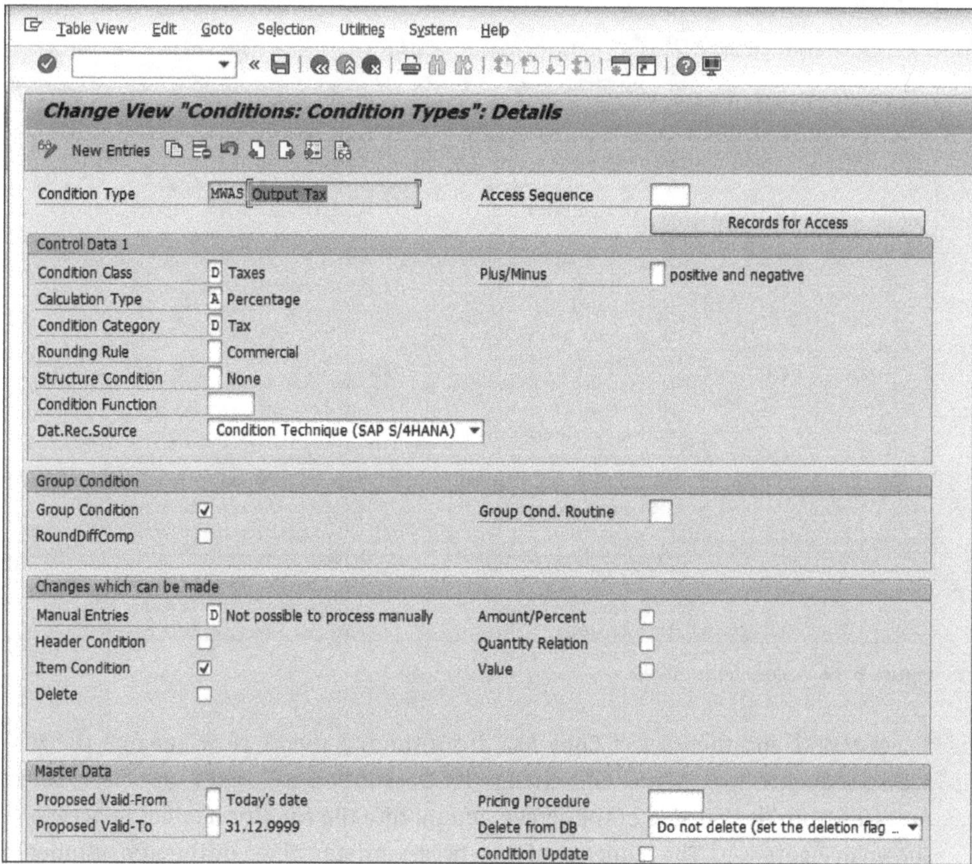

Figure 6.38 Output Tax Sales Condition

By clicking the **Records for Access** button, you which records for access are maintained for the condition types, which determine the tax codes.

Now, let`s define our own custom access sequence ZMWS, which is a copy of the standard MWST but accesses different tables. To set up this access sequence, follow the menu path **Sales and Distribution • Basic Functions • Pricing • Pricing Control • Access Sequences • Set Access Sequences.** This table is a cross-client table, and after confirming the warning message, you'll see a list of defined access sequences, as shown in Figure 6.39.

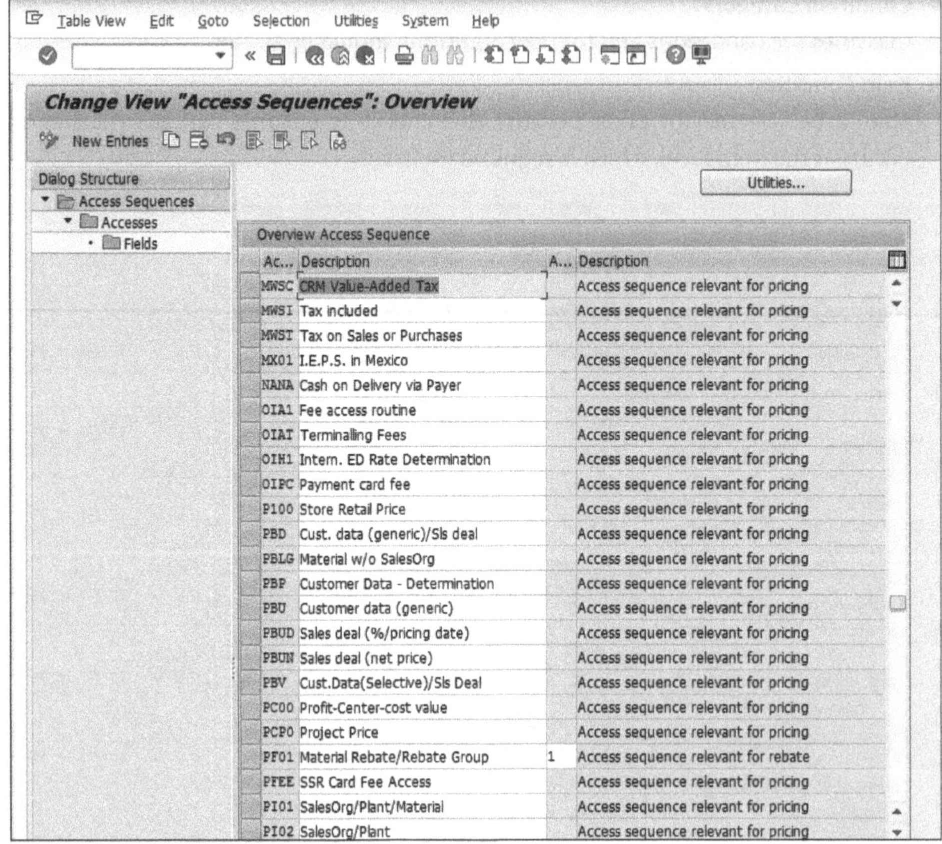

Figure 6.39 Access Sequences

Select **MWST** and then select **Copy As...** from the top menu. Now, rename the new access sequence to "ZMWS" and change its **Description** to "Taxes on Sales." Select **Accesses** from the left side of the screen and modify the condition tables to access, as shown in Figure 6.40. The sequence of their access is determined by the step number in the first **Access** column. The **Exclusive** checkbox controls whether the system will stop searching for a record after the first successful access finds a value.

Select the first step and click **Fields** from the left side of the screen to see the fields that are being used by the condition table access sequence.

As shown in Figure 6.41, the **Country** (**ALAND**) and **Destination Country** (**LAND1**) fields are used in our access sequence. Therefore, when searching using this step, the system will look for matches in both the sending and destination countries of the goods. If a match exists, the tax code maintained for the combination will be determined.

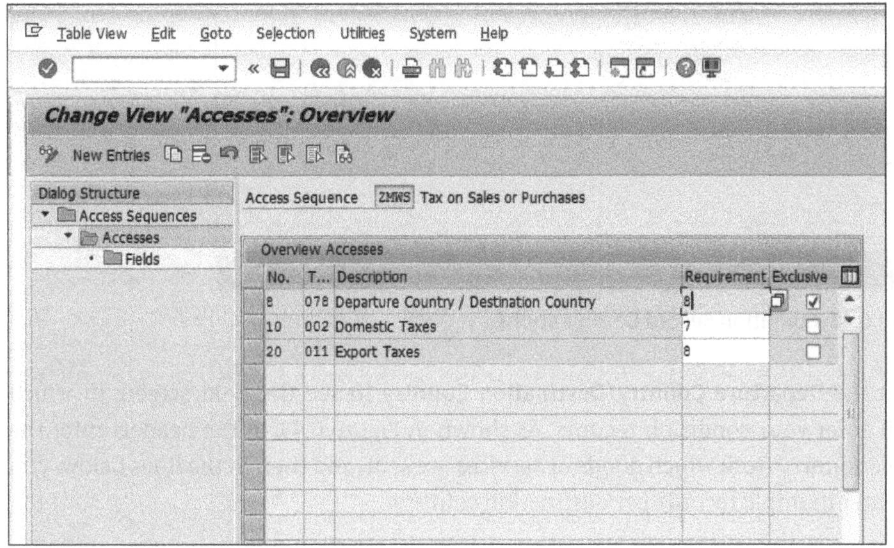

Figure 6.40 Access Sequence ZMWS

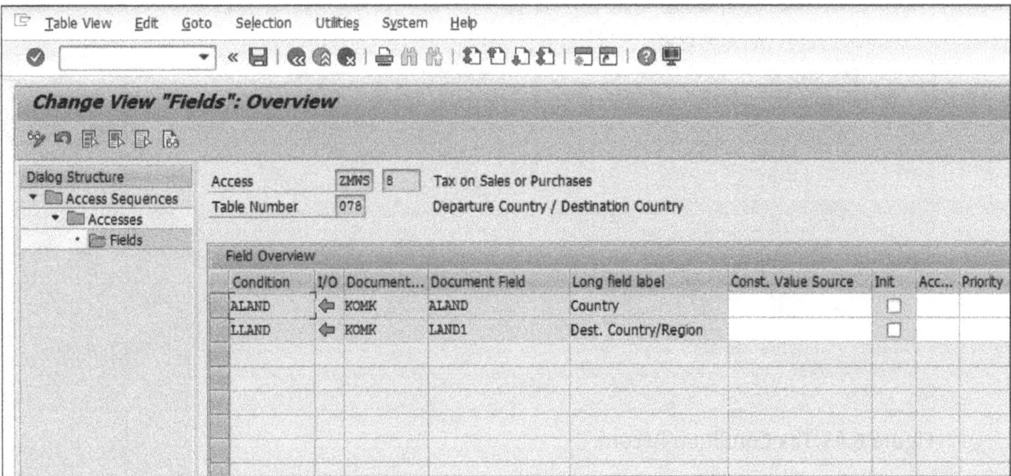

Figure 6.41 Condition Table Access Fields

You can maintain these condition records using Transaction VK11. Condition records are considered application data, and you can also navigate to these settings through the application menu path **Logistics • Sales and Distribution • Master Data • Conditions • Select Using Condition Type • VK11—Create**. Now, enter condition type "MWST" to see a popup window asking for the combination of characteristics for which you want to create records, as shown in Figure 6.42. These characteristics are dependent on the configuration of the condition record.

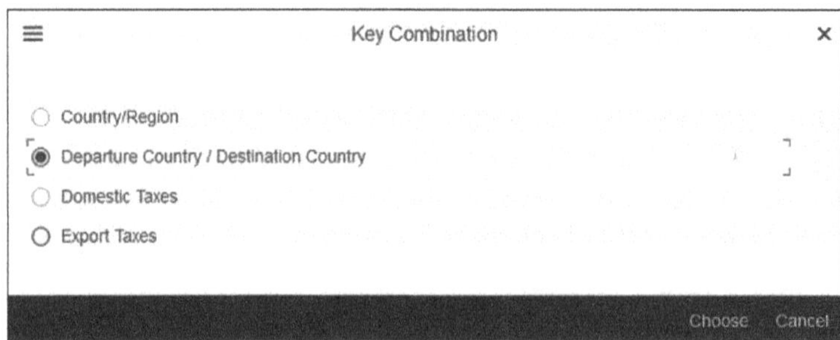

Figure 6.42 Condition Record Combinations

Select the **Departure Country/Destination Country** to see the next screen, in which you'll enter your condition records. As shown in Figure 6.43, in the header, enter the source country from which goods or services are sent, and then in the lines below, you can enter multiple records per destination country.

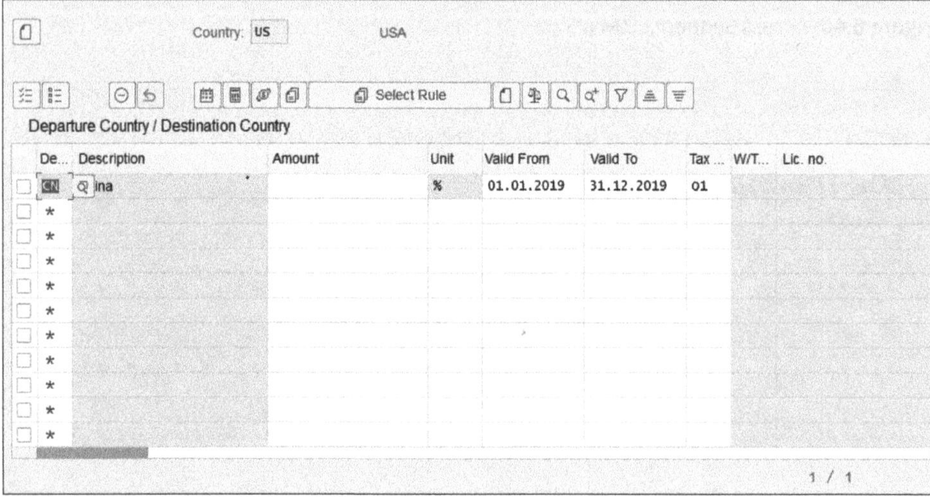

Figure 6.43 Tax Condition Record

The following fields are considered:

- **Destination Country**
  This field is the country to which the goods/services are supplied.
- **Tax Classification 1**
  The tax classification indicator, which is maintained in the customer master records, normally specifies whether this business partner is liable for or exempt from taxes.
- **Tax Classification Material**
  The tax classification indicator, which is maintained in the material master records, normally specifies whether this material is taxable at the full rate, taxable at a reduced rate, or not taxable.

- **Valid From and Valid To**
  In this field, you'll specify the validity period of the tax code. Tax rates change from time to time, and with these fields, you have the flexibility to add more condition records when tax rates change.
- **Tax Code**
  This field is the tax code, which should be assigned automatically when the criteria outlined in the condition record are met.

Save your entries, and sales documents that match these condition criteria will automatically receive the assigned tax codes.

6.4 Information System

Accounts receivable has a powerful information system, which provides several standard reports that enable organizations to manage their receivables proactively. We'll examine reports in the following categories:

- Master data reports
- Balance reports
- Line-item reports

These reports do not require specific configuration to use.

6.4.1 Master Data Reports

The master data reports for accounts receivable provide information that's maintained in the customer business partner master records in a well-structured form.

Master data reports for customers are available at the application menu path **Accounting • Financial Accounting • Accounts Receivable • Information System • Reports for Accounts Receivable Accounting • Master Data**. Report S_ALR_87012179 (Customer List) provides information from the master records, and you can specify on the selection screen which areas of the master record should be displayed.

As shown in Figure 6.44, select the checkboxes for account control, bank data, and payment data, and the relevant areas of the master records will be output.

As mentioned earlier, customers can be created at the financial accounting level and at the sales level. You can use report S_ALR_87012195 (Customer Master Data Comparison) to check which customers have been created in financial accounting but not in sales, and vice versa.

As shown in Figure 6.45, you can check for missing records in financial accounting or in sales and distribution.

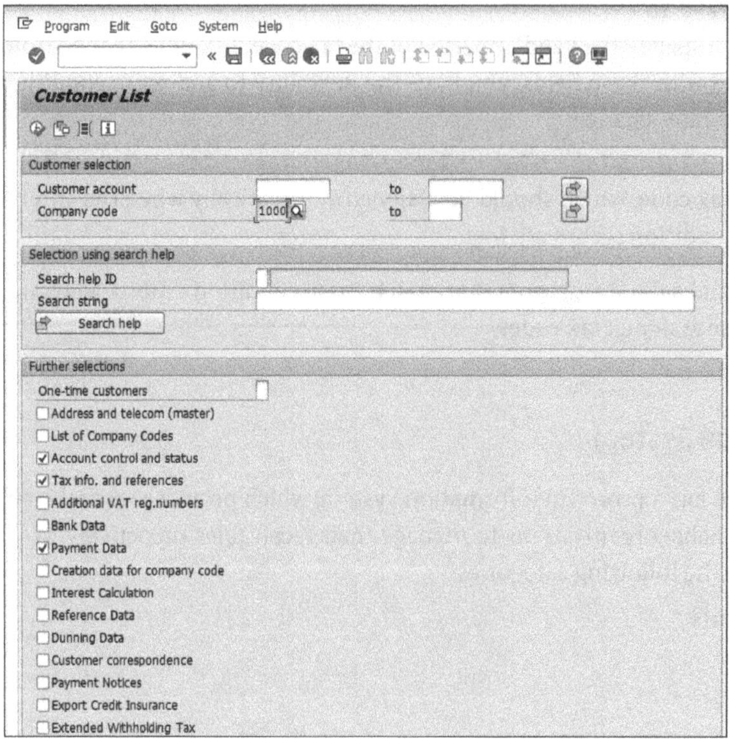

Figure 6.44 Customer List Selections

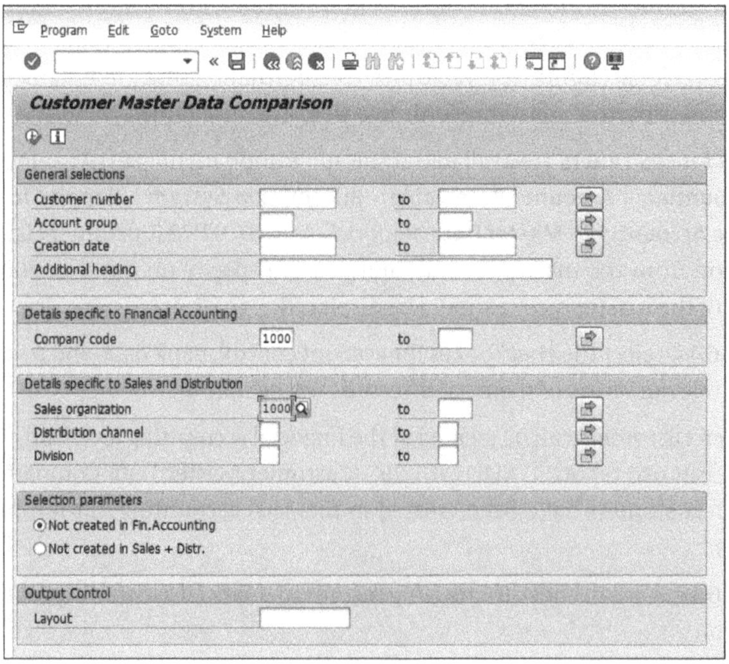

Figure 6.45 Customer Master Data Comparison

6.4.2 Balance Reports

Balance reports provide summarized information about the receivables from your customers. These reports are available at the application menu path **Accounting • Financial Accounting • Accounts Receivable • Information System • Reports for Accounts Receivable Accounting • Customer Balances.**

Report S_ALR_87012169 (Transaction Figures: Account Balance) can be executed as a drilldown report, which is quite convenient for online analysis. If you need to download this report into Excel, select the **Object List (More than One Lead Column)** option, as shown in Figure 6.46.

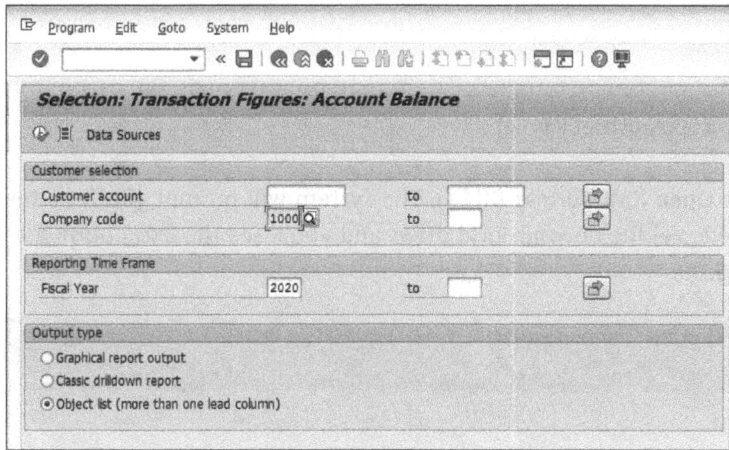

Figure 6.46 Customer Account Balances Report Selection Screen

Then, the output screen will be column based, as shown in Figure 6.47.

OSAPFD10-01 Transaction Figures: Account Balance
Data from 05.02.2019 15:35:26

Year	Customer	Period/year	Total open items Debit	Total open items Credit	Total open items Balance	Total open items Accumulate...
2019	1000000	001.2019	1.876,00	0,00	1.876,00	1.876,00
2019	1000000	002.2019	0,00	0,00	0,00	1.876,00
2019	1000000	003.2019	0,00	0,00	0,00	1.876,00
2019	1000000	004.2019	0,00	0,00	0,00	1.876,00
2019	1000000	005.2019	0,00	0,00	0,00	1.876,00
2019	1000000	006.2019	0,00	0,00	0,00	1.876,00
2019	1000000	007.2019	0,00	0,00	0,00	1.876,00
2019	1000000	008.2019	0,00	0,00	0,00	1.876,00
2019	1000000	009.2019	0,00	0,00	0,00	1.876,00
2019	1000000	010.2019	0,00	0,00	0,00	1.876,00
2019	1000000	011.2019	0,00	0,00	0,00	1.876,00
2019	1000000	012.2019	0,00	0,00	0,00	1.876,00
2019	1000000	013.2019	0,00	0,00	0,00	1.876,00
2019	1000000	014.2019	0,00	0,00	0,00	1.876,00
2019	1000000	015.2019	0,00	0,00	0,00	1.876,00
2019	1000000	016.2019	0,00	0,00	0,00	1.876,00

Figure 6.47 Customer Balance Report Output

You can easily export this report to Excel by clicking the 00000000 button on the top toolbar menu. The system will ask you to select a format, as shown in Figure 6.48.

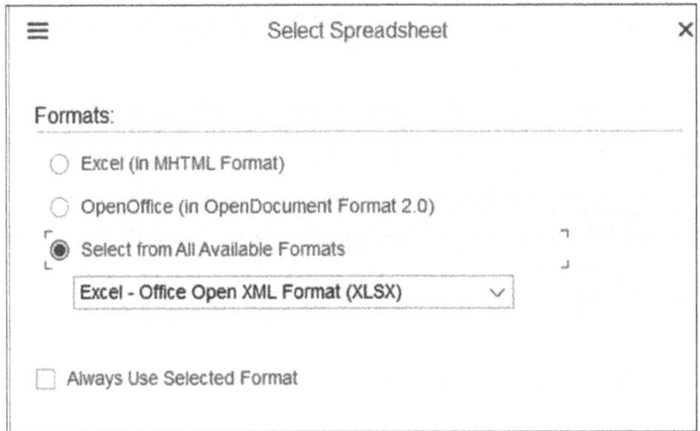

Figure 6.48 Selecting a Spreadsheet Format

Select **Excel - Office Open XML Format (XLSX)**. The system will prompt you for a file name for saving the Excel file on your local drive, and you'll see the Excel output, as shown in Figure 6.49.

Fiscal Year	Customer	Period/year	Total open items Debit	Total open items Credit	Total open items Balance	Total open items Accumulated balance
2019	1000000	001.2019	1,876.00	0.00	1,876.00	1,876.00
2019	1000000	002.2019	0.00	0.00	0.00	1,876.00
2019	1000000	003.2019	0.00	0.00	0.00	1,876.00
2019	1000000	004.2019	0.00	0.00	0.00	1,876.00
2019	1000000	005.2019	0.00	0.00	0.00	1,876.00
2019	1000000	006.2019	0.00	0.00	0.00	1,876.00
2019	1000000	007.2019	0.00	0.00	0.00	1,876.00
2019	1000000	008.2019	0.00	0.00	0.00	1,876.00
2019	1000000	009.2019	0.00	0.00	0.00	1,876.00
2019	1000000	010.2019	0.00	0.00	0.00	1,876.00
2019	1000000	011.2019	0.00	0.00	0.00	1,876.00
2019	1000000	012.2019	0.00	0.00	0.00	1,876.00
2019	1000000	013.2019	0.00	0.00	0.00	1,876.00
2019	1000000	014.2019	0.00	0.00	0.00	1,876.00
2019	1000000	015.2019	0.00	0.00	0.00	1,876.00
2019	1000000	016.2019	0.00	0.00	0.00	1,876.00

Figure 6.49 Customer Balance Excel Output

With the object list option, you can easily analyze the data further in Excel and send it to other colleagues in Excel format.

6.4.3 Line-Item Reports

Accounts receivable line-item reports provide rather detailed information by which you can analyze every single invoice and payment. These reports are located at the application menu path **Accounting • Financial Accounting • Accounts Receivable • Information System • Reports for Accounts Receivable Accounting • Customers: Items.**

One of the most useful reports is report S_ALR_87012168 (Due Date Analysis for Open Items), which provides you with aging data for open items. Aging is a common accounts receivable analysis, in which open items are grouped by their maturity.

In this report, select the drilldown option, as shown in Figure 6.50, which is the most useful option for online analysis.

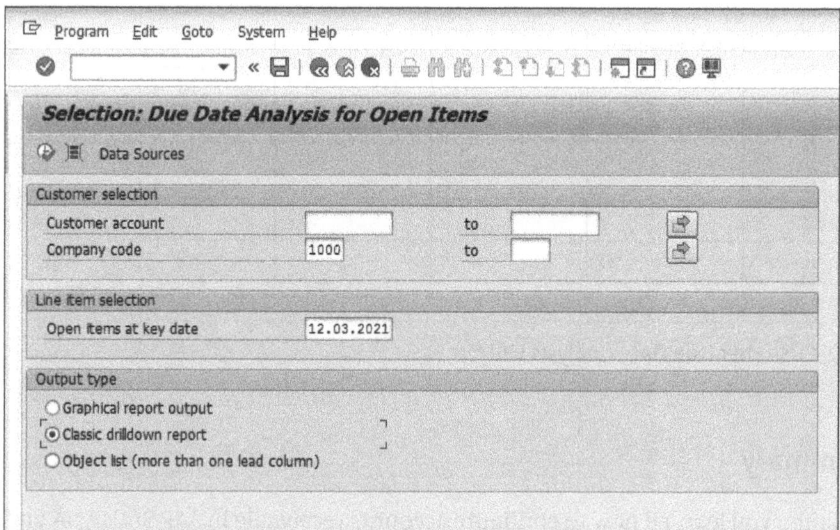

Figure 6.50 Customer Due Date Analysis Selection Screen

If you've run this report already, the system will ask you if you want to run it as a new selection or want to retrieve data from a previous run, as shown in Figure 6.51.

Figure 6.51 Report Selection Option

Select **New Selection** and proceed with the **Confirm** button. As shown in Figure 6.52, you can analyze the amount of receivables due in 0 to 30 days, in 31 to 60 days, and so on. This analysis can be quite important for forecasting your company's cash liquidity and to properly manage receivables so that no big items are left overdue for long periods of time.

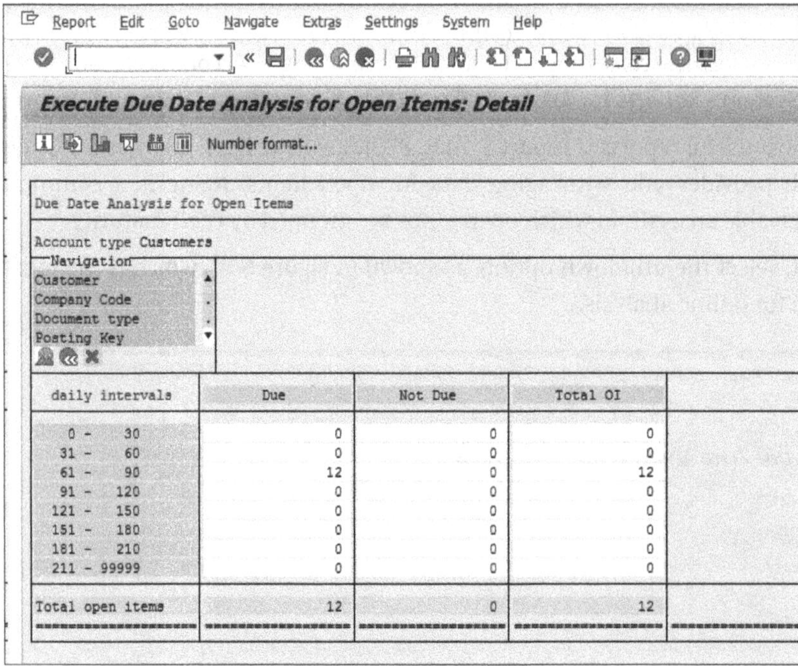

Figure 6.52 Customer Due Date Analysis Output

6.5 Summary

In this chapter, you learned how to configure accounts receivable in SAP S/4HANA and how to use its information system. Now, you should be well prepared in the following main areas:

- Customer master data, maintained as business partners
- Business transactions
- Information system usage

We explained how customer master data is integrated with the business partner in SAP S/4HANA and described some best practices when setting up customer groups and number ranges. Now, you should be able to configure CVI so that business partners and customer masters are fully integrated.

We covered the main business transactions in accounts receivable, such as outgoing invoices and credit memos, related correspondence, payments, and payment terms.

We explained in detail how the account determination and tax determination functionalities work in integrated sales documents using the condition technique.

Finally, we discussed the most important reports that the accounts receivable information system offers in the areas of master data reports, balance reports, and line-item reports. We demonstrated how easily you can analyze various aspects of accounts receivable data and how to export your reports in Excel format.

We've finished our guide to accounts receivable. Next, we'll continue our SAP S/4HANA journey with the configuration of fixed assets.

Chapter 7
Fixed Assets

This chapter will teach you how to configure fixed assets in SAP S/4HANA. The new asset accounting concept will be discussed in detail. Using the new asset accounting in SAP S/4HANA is required, and you'll learn how this functionality enables real-time valuations in multiple accounting frameworks.

Fixed assets is the part of financial accounting that records and manages all asset accounting data. It provides functionalities for the whole lifecycle of fixed assets, from acquisition to retirement. Sometimes, fixed assets referred to as *asset accounting*, such as in the SAP Reference IMG (Transaction SPRO). These terms can be used interchangeably, but we'll mostly use fixed assets, which is how it's called in the SAP application menu.

In this chapter, you'll learn about all the configuration areas necessary for fully functional fixed assets. We'll start with the organizational structure, in which the main foundation blocks of the fixed assets, such as the chart of depreciation and depreciation areas, are configured. Then, you'll learn how to set up the master data for assets and classify them into well-structured asset classes. Next, we'll review valuations for fixed assets based on various accounting principles, and we'll emphasize how SAP S/4HANA brings tremendous improvements to this process. Then, we'll discuss the various business transactions for fixed assets. Finally, we'll conclude with a look at the information system for fixed assets.

Fixed assets empowers companies to achieve flexible reporting based on multiple accounting frameworks. Such reporting is generally important for both internal and external purposes for most companies that use SAP, most of which are operating globally and thus must comply with various accounting principles. For example, many modern companies must present their fixed assets based on one or more of the following frameworks:

- International Financial Reporting Standards (IFRS)
- United States Generally Accepted Accounting Principles (US GAAP)
- Local Generally Accepted Accounting Principles (local GAAP), for each country implemented
- Local tax rules, for each country implemented

The ability to present fixed assets based on various accounting and tax frameworks in SAP is hardly new. Multiple depreciation areas have been used for this requirement since the old SAP R/3 days. With the introduction of the new general ledger in SAP, different subledgers could be updated with accounting principle-specific postings, albeit not in real time. Then, with SAP Simple Finance, the new asset accounting was introduced, which is now required and enhanced in SAP S/4HANA. This solution is based on the Universal Journal, which means fixed assets is completely integrated in real time with the general ledger. No redundant data structures need to be maintained, and no periodic programs are required to post to nonleading ledgers because now the integration works in real time in SAP S/4HANA. Table ACDOCA, the Universal Journal table, has an include called ACDOC_SI_FAA (Universal Journal Entry: Fields for Asset Accounting), which contains all the fields used in fixed assets, such as main asset number (ANLN1), depreciation area (AFABE), and asset value date (BZDAT).

Let's now show you how to configure the new asset accounting in SAP S/4HANA in detail. In the process, we'll emphasize the key differences between implementing a new SAP S/4HANA system (greenfield approach) and migrating an existing SAP system to SAP S/4HANA (brownfield approach).

We'll start with setting up the organizational structures for fixed assets.

7.1 Organizational Structures

Organizational structures are the key foundation blocks that must be set up to represent the company's organization from a fixed assets point of view. The top level from a valuation point of view is the chart of depreciation, under which are created one or more depreciation areas. The master data of the fixed assets is stored in asset master records, which are classified based on asset classes. We'll examine each of these objects in detail, starting with the chart of depreciation.

7.1.1 Chart of Depreciation

The *chart of depreciation* is the highest organizational structure in fixed assets from a valuation point of view. This chart is used to group the valuation requirements and usually is country dependent. Each country typically has its own chart of depreciation, although from a technical point of view multiple countries can be assigned to the same chart of depreciation. However, doing so only makes sense if these countries have exactly the same valuation requirements.

The chart of depreciation is independent from other organizational objects in SAP, such as company code or controlling area. The relationship with the company code is via the country because the chart of depreciation is assigned to a country and a company code is assigned to a country, which determines the company codes that use a specific chart of depreciation.

A new chart of depreciation is created by copying existing or SAP reference charts of depreciation. These reference charts of depreciation from SAP already contain predefined depreciation areas based on local, country-specific requirements.

To configure a chart of depreciation in SAP S/4HANA, follow the menu path **Financial Accounting • Asset Accounting • Organizational Structures • Copy Reference Chart of Depreciation/Depreciation Areas**, as shown in Figure 7.1.

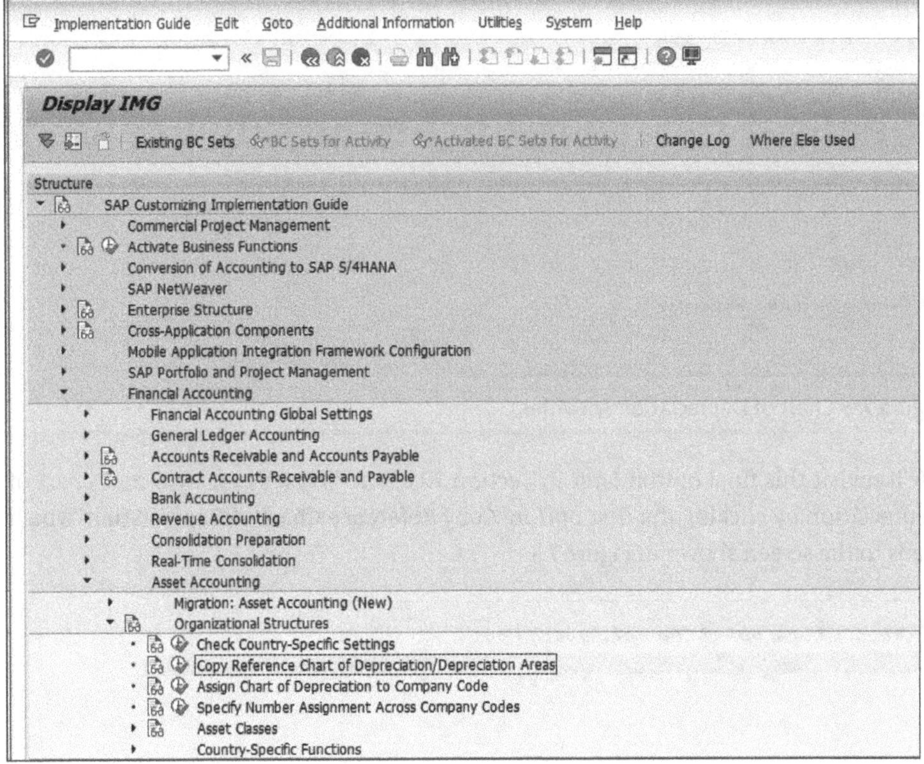

Figure 7.1 Copying Reference Charts of Depreciation/Depreciation Areas

The next screen presents three options, as shown in Figure 7.2. Let's look at each of the following options:

- **Copy Reference Chart of Depreciation**
  This option is the main activity and allows you to copy an existing chart of depreciation to a new chart of depreciation.
- **Specify Description of Chart of Depreciation**
  This option provides a convenient transaction to check or change the description of a chart of depreciation.
- **Copy/Delete Depreciation Areas**
  This option enables you to configure the individual depreciation areas within the selected chart of depreciation.

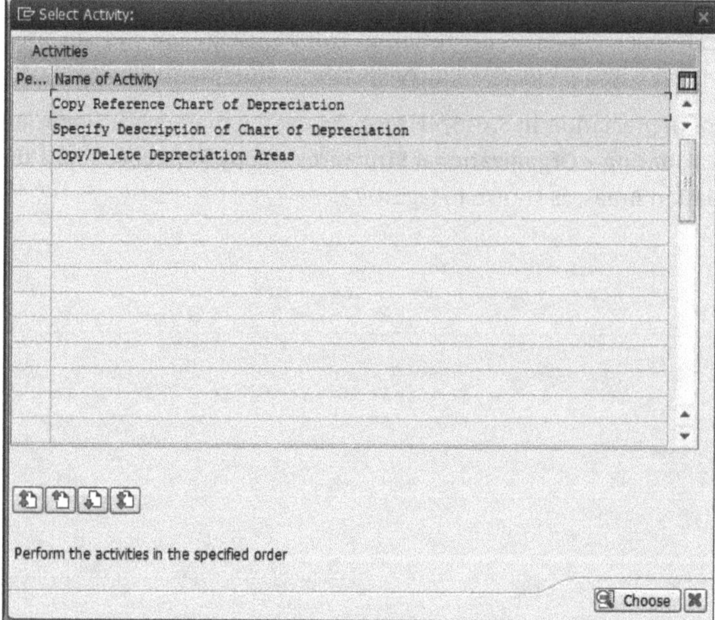

Figure 7.2 Chart of Depreciation Activities

We'll revisit this final option later in Section 7.1.2, but first let's create a new chart of depreciation by clicking the first option, **Copy Reference Chart of Depreciation**, which leads to the screen shown in Figure 7.3.

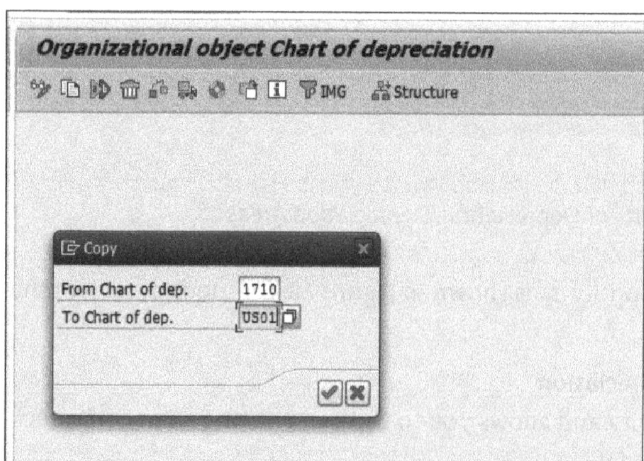

Figure 7.3 Copying a Chart of Depreciation

On this screen, select **Copy Org. Object** from the top menu, which lets you select a chart of depreciation to copy from. Then, you can enter the code for the new chart of depreciation to be created. Notice that, when displaying the available charts of depreciation, SAP provides several reference charts of depreciation for many countries.

For our example, we'll copy an existing chart of depreciation to a new chart of depreciation US01, which will be used for our US company codes. The system will provide an informational message that chart of depreciation 1710 is copied to US01.

In the next activity, **Specify Description of Chart of Depreciation**, rename the new chart of depreciation to "USA Chart of Depreciation," as shown in Figure 7.4.

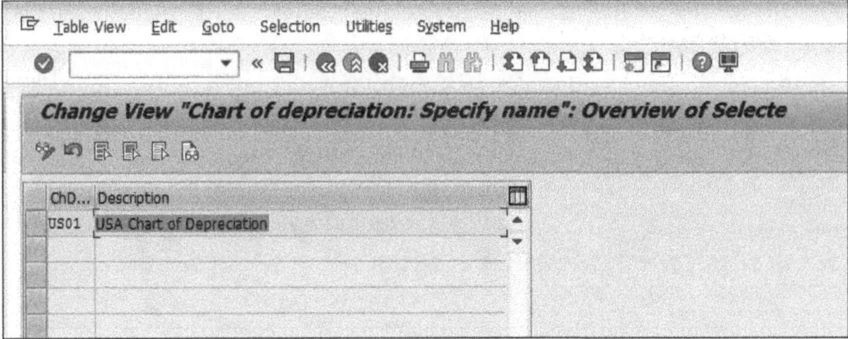

Figure 7.4 Specifying the Description of a Chart of Depreciation

Now, your new chart of depreciation is created. In the following section, we'll configure the required depreciation areas for it.

7.1.2 Depreciation Areas

Depreciation areas provide valuations for fixed assets based on specific sets of rules. Depreciation rules and the useful life for assets are maintained on the depreciation area level.

The next step is to check the depreciation areas created in our new chart of depreciation for the US. The new chart of depreciation was created by copying and therefore inherits the depreciation areas of the reference chart. To configure these depreciation areas, follow the menu path **Financial Accounting • Asset Accounting • General Valuation • Depreciation Areas • Define Depreciation Areas**, as shown in Figure 7.5.

In this transaction, you can delete, modify, or create new depreciation areas. After entering "US01" as the work area, the next screen presents the depreciation areas created for the chart of depreciation. The same configuration transaction is available also via the menu path **Financial Accounting • Asset Accounting • Organizational Structures • Copy Reference Chart of Depreciation/Depreciation Areas**, where you'll choose the **Copy/Delete Depreciation Areas** option.

Each chart of depreciation requires at least one depreciation area, which posts to the leading ledger 0L and is usually called 01. The depreciation area should represent the leading valuation for the group. Normally, US companies use US GAAP, whereas for most other countries IFRS will be used.

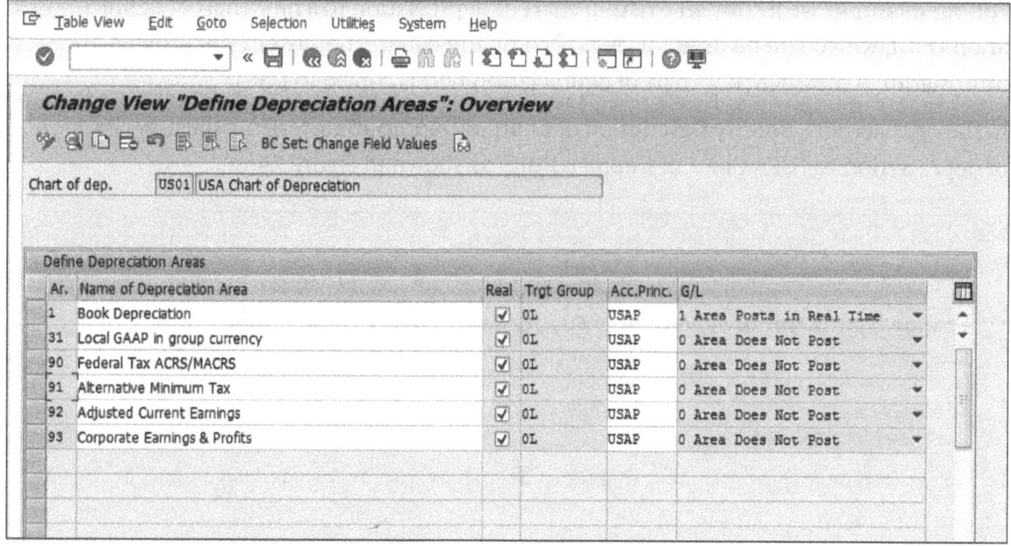

Table View Edit Goto Selection Utilities System Help

Change View "Define Depreciation Areas": Overview

BC Set: Change Field Values

Chart of dep. US01 USA Chart of Depreciation

Define Depreciation Areas

Ar.	Name of Depreciation Area	Real	Trgt Group	Acc.Princ.	G/L
1	Book Depreciation	☑	0L	USAP	1 Area Posts in Real Time
31	Local GAAP in group currency	☑	0L	USAP	0 Area Does Not Post
90	Federal Tax ACRS/MACRS	☑	0L	USAP	0 Area Does Not Post
91	Alternative Minimum Tax	☑	0L	USAP	0 Area Does Not Post
92	Adjusted Current Earnings	☑	0L	USAP	0 Area Does Not Post
93	Corporate Earnings & Profits	☑	0L	USAP	0 Area Does Not Post

Figure 7.5 Depreciation Areas of Chart of Depreciation US01

Figure 7.5 shows the standard US depreciation areas as required by the US tax rules. For most US companies, all these depreciation areas will be needed. However, many global companies may also need to define a depreciation area based on IFRS rules for the US. For other countries, typically an IFRS depreciation area will be needed, as well as depreciation areas for local GAAP and/or local tax rules.

Now, let's create an additional depreciation area that represents the IFRS valuation. Start by copying one of the existing areas—for example, 1. Select the area by clicking on the left of it and selecting **Copy As...** from the top menu, as shown in Figure 7.6.

Table View Edit Goto Selection Utilities System Help

Change View "Define Depreciation Areas": Overview

BC Set: Change Field Values

Chart of dep. US01 USA Chart of Depreciation

Define Depreciation Areas

Ar.	Name of Depreciation Area	Real	Trgt Group	Acc.Princ.	G/L
1	Book Depreciation	☑	0L	USAP	1 Area Posts in Real Time
31	Local GAAP in group currency	☑	0L	USAP	0 Area Does Not Post
90	Federal Tax ACRS/MACRS	☑	0L	USAP	0 Area Does Not Post
91	Alternative Minimum Tax	☑	0L	USAP	0 Area Does Not Post
92	Adjusted Current Earnings	☑	0L	USAP	0 Area Does Not Post
93	Corporate Earnings & Profits	☑	0L	USAP	0 Area Does Not Post

Figure 7.6 Copying a Depreciation Area

This step opens a new configuration screen, in which the settings are copied from the source area. Change these settings, as shown in Figure 7.7. Let's name the new depreciation area by entering "32" in the **Depreciat. Area** field and providing long and short descriptions. In general, we recommend numbering depreciation areas in a logically defined manner.

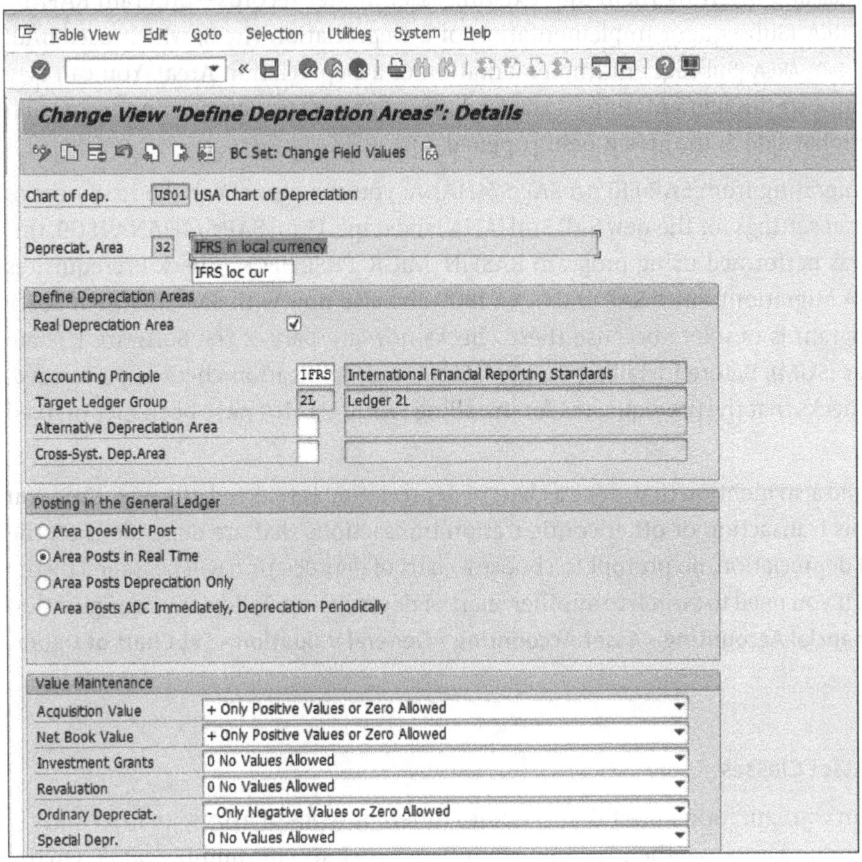

Figure 7.7 New Depreciation Area

Note that you'll need a separate depreciation area for each local currency defined for the relevant company codes for each accounting principle. The accounting principle is a key setting in the depreciation area that drives the integration with the general ledger. Based on the accounting principle selected, the system automatically assigns the ledger linked to it. This ledger will be posted automatically if you select the **Area Posts in Real Time** option, as shown in Figure 7.7. This automatic posting feature is the key difference between the new asset accounting in SAP S/4HANA and the classic asset accounting in SAP ERP. In SAP ERP, another option enabled you to post multiple depreciation areas to nonleading ledgers, but this posting occurred only periodically by running program RAPERB2000 (Transaction ASKBN). This transaction is now obsolete because updating the general ledger takes place immediately.

If you're migrating from an existing SAP ERP system to SAP S/4HANA, you may need to set up some new depreciation areas to take advantage of the new features for fixed assets. For example, you may want to introduce a new depreciation area to post in real time based on another accounting principle. The good news is that, as of SAP S/4HANA 1809, a new program is available that streamlines the process of opening new depreciation areas and inserting them into existing asset master records—program RAFAB_COPY_AREA (Subsequent Implementation of a Depreciation Area), which uses BAdI FAA_AA_COPY_AREA (Subsequent Implementation of a Depreciation Area). You can also have your own implementation of the BAdI to influence the depreciation terms and transactional data as the area is being opened.

When migrating from SAP ERP to SAP S/4HANA, you can also check the readiness of fixed asset settings for the new SAP S/4HANA landscape. Until SAP S/4HANA 1809, this check was performed using program RASFIN_MIGR_PRECHECK (Check Prerequisites for FI-AA Migration). Since SAP S/4HANA 1809 and also now with SAP S/4HANA 2020, this program is obsolete because these checks now are part of the Software Update Manager (SUM). Before installing SAP S/4HANA, a simplification check is performed, which checks that the prerequisites for installing SAP S/4HANA have been met in fixed assets.

We should also mention that, once a chart of depreciation is selected, the next time you enter this transaction or other configuration transactions that are dependent on the chart of depreciation, no prompt to choose a chart of depreciation will be issued by the system. If you need to switch to another chart of depreciation, follow the configuration path **Financial Accounting • Asset Accounting • General Valuation • Set Chart of Depreciation**.

7.1.3 Asset Classes

The main configuration object that classifies different types of assets, an *asset class* is used to group assets together, assigning numbers from a specific number range. On the asset class level, you can configure the account determination, which defines which general ledger accounts are posted from asset transactions. Account determination also defines which fields are available and which fields are required when creating asset master records.

The asset class is not dependent on the chart of depreciation. Thus, asset classes defined in the system are available to all countries and company codes in the system. As a result, creating asset classes requires a prudent and careful approach. In most companies, 20 to 40 asset classes should be enough to manage the needs of all countries in the system. You shouldn't create new asset classes just for a specific rollout to a new country without good cause.

To configure asset classes, follow the menu path **Financial Accounting • Asset Accounting • Organizational Structures • Asset Classes • Define Asset Classes**, as shown in Figure 7.8.

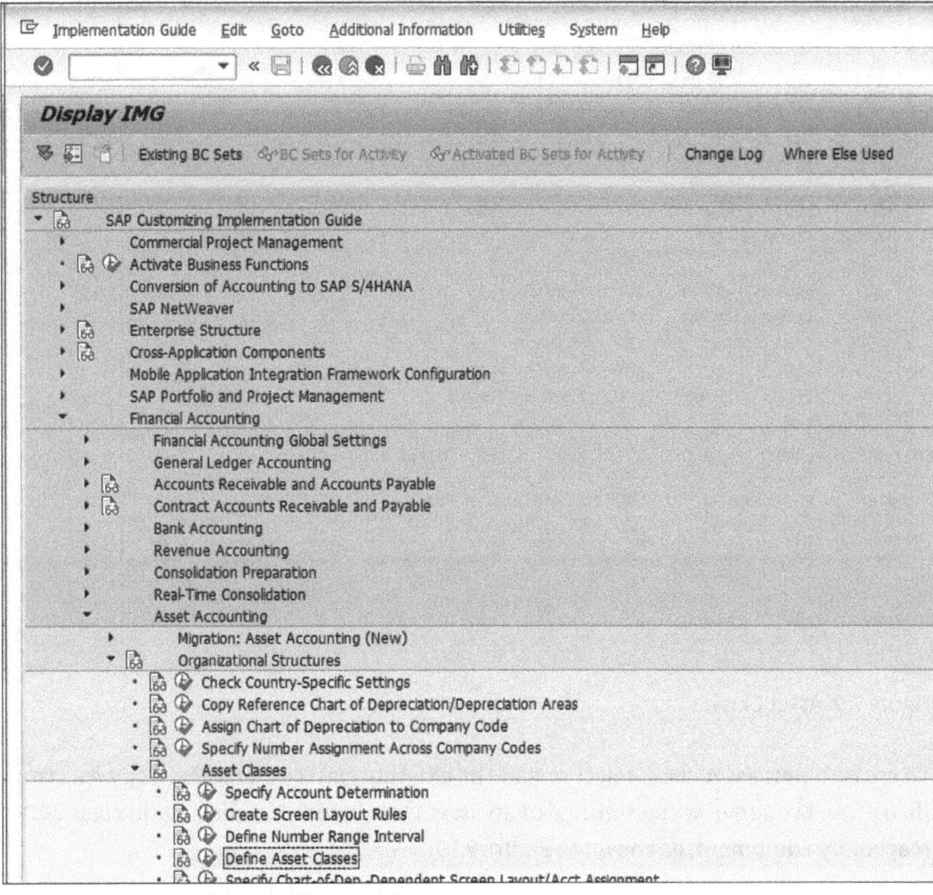

Figure 7.8 Defining an Asset Class

The asset class contains other important configuration objects as well, such as the account determination and the screen layout, which we'll examine in detail in the next section. Once you enter the transaction for configuring asset classes, you'll see a list of already defined asset classes available in the system, as shown in Figure 7.9.

These standard SAP classes are delivered by SAP and can be used as references to create your own asset classes in your system or can be used directly. Most companies opt for similar lists of asset classes, often with 4- or 6-digit codes. Most companies have classes such as machinery, vehicles, furniture and fixtures, software, goodwill, and so on, in addition to specific types of assets typical for each type of company.

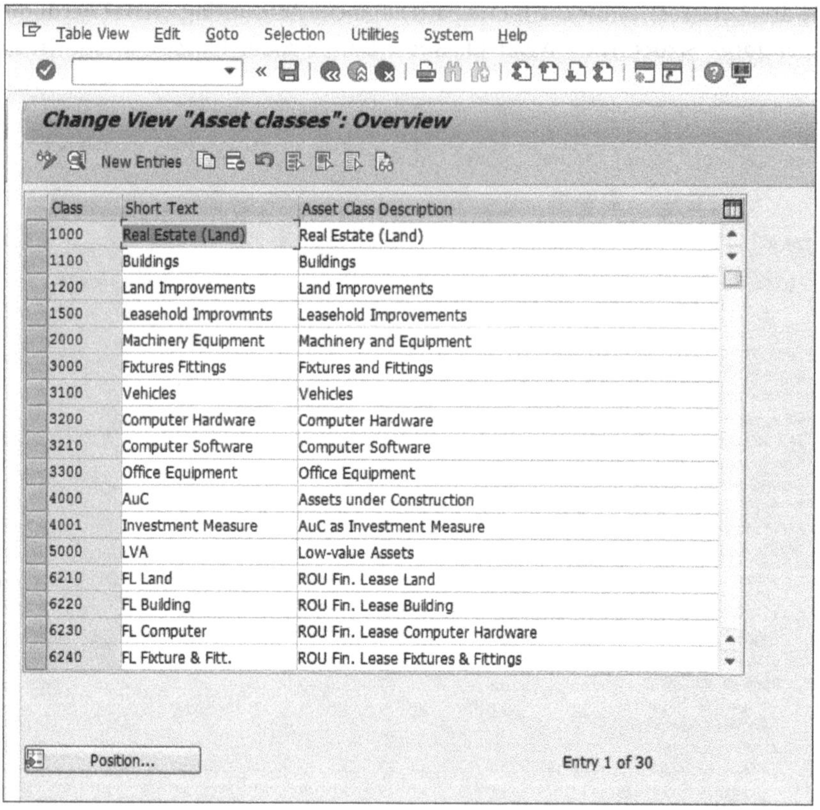

Table View Edit Goto Selection Utilities System Help

Change View "Asset classes": Overview

New Entries

Class	Short Text	Asset Class Description
1000	Real Estate (Land)	Real Estate (Land)
1100	Buildings	Buildings
1200	Land Improvements	Land Improvements
1500	Leasehold Improvmnts	Leasehold Improvements
2000	Machinery Equipment	Machinery and Equipment
3000	Fixtures Fittings	Fixtures and Fittings
3100	Vehicles	Vehicles
3200	Computer Hardware	Computer Hardware
3210	Computer Software	Computer Software
3300	Office Equipment	Office Equipment
4000	AuC	Assets under Construction
4001	Investment Measure	AuC as Investment Measure
5000	LVA	Low-value Assets
6210	FL Land	ROU Fin. Lease Land
6220	FL Building	ROU Fin. Lease Building
6230	FL Computer	ROU Fin. Lease Computer Hardware
6240	FL Fixture & Fitt.	ROU Fin. Lease Fixtures & Fittings

Position... Entry 1 of 30

Figure 7.9 Asset Classes

To create a new asset class, select one of the existing classes and select **Copy As...** from the menu. Let`s review the settings of an asset class by double-clicking on class **2000: Machinery Equipment**, as shown in Figure 7.10.

In addition to the **Asset Class** code, the long description, and the **Short Text**, some other important settings must be maintained on this screen. Another configuration object is the account determination, which is a collection of the general ledger accounts to be posted during various business processes, such as acquisition, retirement, depreciation, and so on. In the **Account Determin.** (account determination) field, you'll assign the relevant account determination; we'll talk about the assignment of general ledger accounts in the next section. One account determination can be used for multiple asset classes that share the same accounts.

The **Scr. Layout Rule** (screen layout rule) field determines the required, optional, and suppressed fields when creating asset master records for the class. Another parameter is the number range, which determines the range in which numbers are assigned sequentially to the assets created in this class. We'll define these objects in the next section on asset master data.

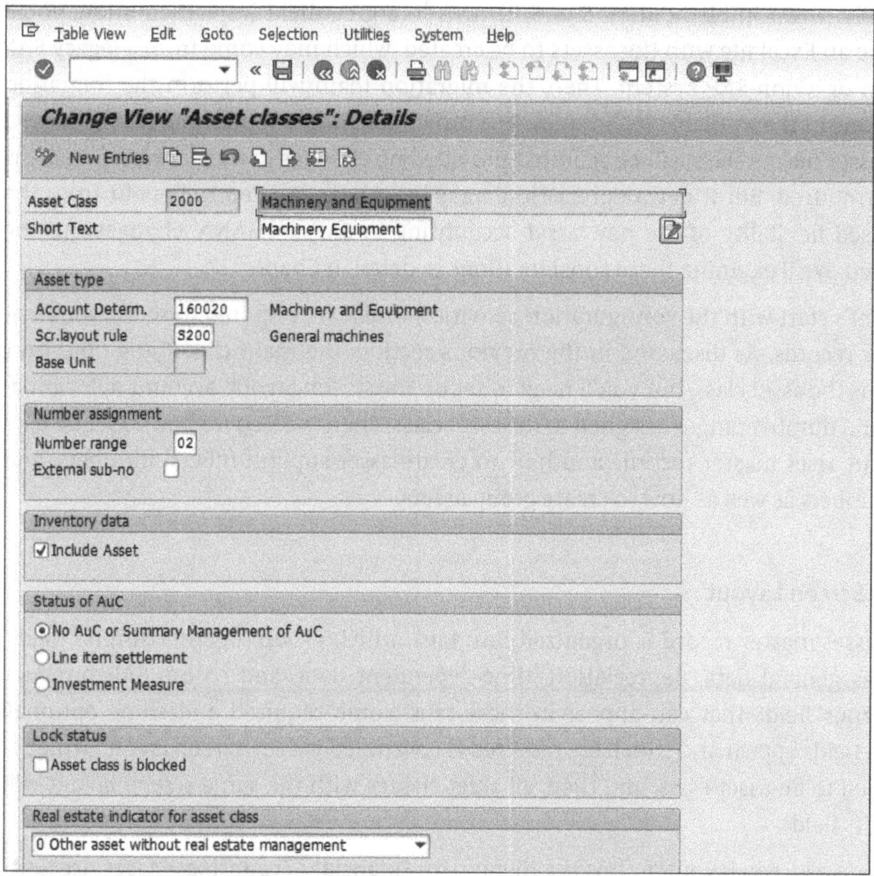

Figure 7.10 Asset Class Settings

On the asset class level, you can also define whether the assets will be managed as assets under construction or not. Assets under construction are special types of assets that aren't purchased but instead are produced internally over time; we'll discuss this kind of asset in greater detail in Section 7.4.1.

Also on the asset class level, you can select the **Asset Class Is Blocked** indicator, which would prevent the creation of new assets in this class. This block is needed if your company decides that a certain asset class should be deactivated but you can't delete the asset class because assets already exist in the class.

7.2 Master Data

So far, we've created the foundational building blocks for fixed assets: the chart of depreciation, depreciation areas, and asset classes. Now, we're ready to start creating the asset master data, which is organized into asset master records and, sometimes, asset subnumbers.

Typically, when implementing SAP S/4HANA in a greenfield implementation, you'll prepare an Excel file with the assets to be created, which may come from a legacy SAP system or a non-SAP system. Then, the migration team will perform the migration using one of the available techniques. In a brownfield implementation, no changes to your asset master data will be required provided no changes in the depreciation areas are introduced. But if new depreciation areas have been created to benefit from the increased flexibility of the new asset accounting in SAP S/4HANA, changes may be required. We'll examine these considerations in detail in Chapter 17.

Now, let's start with the configuration activities, which are required to set up the asset master records. As discussed in the previous section, the main classifying object for assets is the asset class, but you'll need to set up the screen layout, account determination, and number ranges assigned to the asset class. Then, we'll cover how to set up user fields in asset master records and how to create asset supernumbers, numbers, and subnumbers as well as how to create group assets.

7.2.1 Screen Layout

Each asset master record is organized into tabs, which group together similar fields, such as general data, depreciation, time-dependent data, and so on. SAP provides numerous fields that can appear in these tabs, some required and some optional. Which fields appear and which are required is controlled via the screen layout, which is assigned to an asset class, and then, all asset classes with the same screen layout will share its fields.

To create a screen layout, follow the menu path **Financial Accounting • Asset Accounting • Organizational Structures • Asset Classes • Create Screen Layout Rules**, as shown in Figure 7.11.

In this transaction, the screen layout is created as a shell. No further customizing settings need to be maintained on this screen: Simply create the code and add a description. A good practice is to have your screen layouts corresponding to your asset classes. Figure 7.11 shows the standard screen layouts delivered by SAP. These screen layouts can be used directly, and you can create additional ones if needed. So, let's create a new screen layout rule for the asset class **Machinery**, which we'll also call "Machinery." You can select an existing screen layout with similar features, such as **S200: General machines** and copy it over to a new one, for example, screen layout 3200 (Machinery). Select **S200** and choose **Copy As...** from the menu, which allows you to save the new screen layout.

After you create the new screen layout, you can modify its rules for optional, required, and hidden fields. For this step, you must go into a different configuration transaction. Follow the menu path **Financial Accounting • Asset Accounting • Master Data • Screen Layout • Define Screen Layout for Asset Master Data**. Then, choose **Define Screen Layout for Asset Master Data**, which opens the screen where can browse through already created screen layouts and choose the fields, grouped in logical groups. Select **Layout 3200** and click **Logical field groups**, as shown in Figure 7.12.

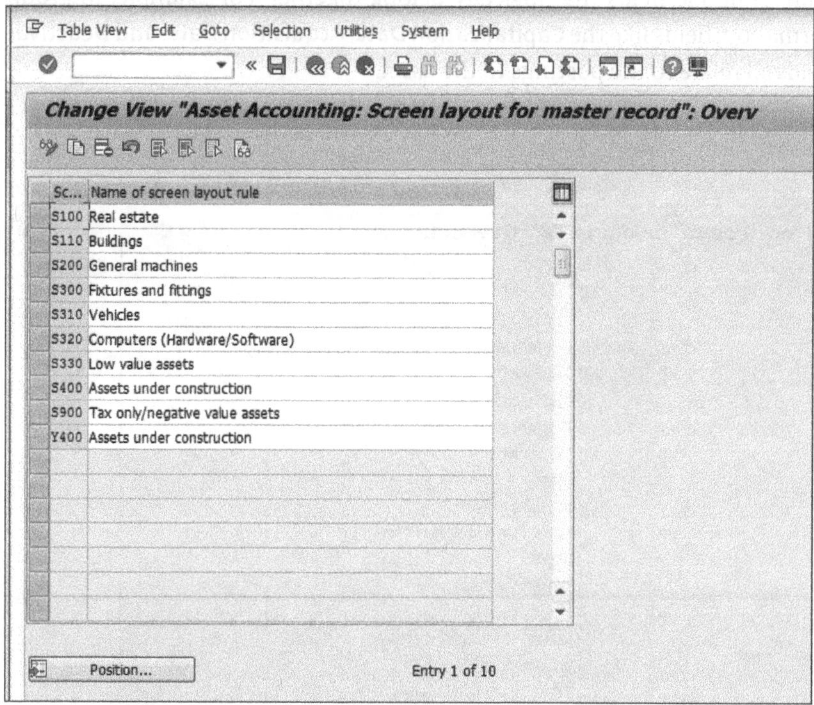

Figure 7.11 Screen Layout

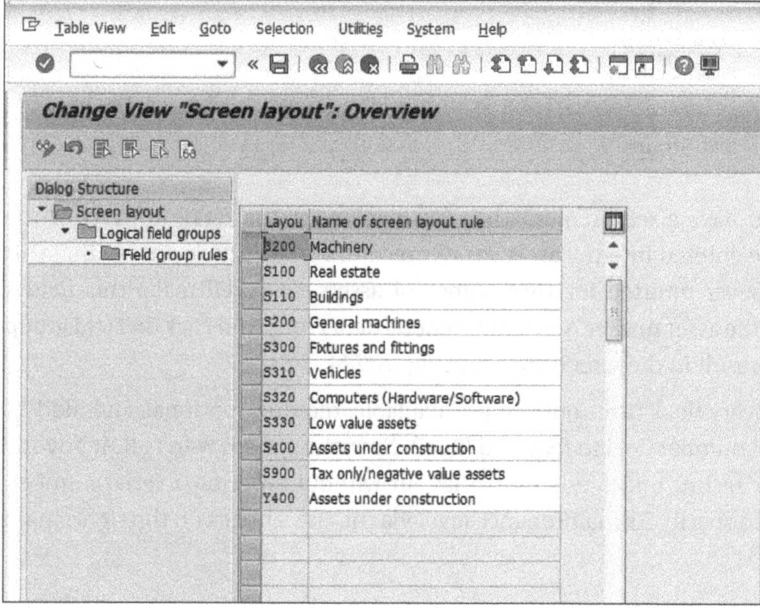

Figure 7.12 Modifying the Screen Layout

This option presents various logical field groups, as shown in Figure 7.13. These groups correspond to the tabs that are displayed in the asset master record. Each logical field group contains multiple fields that logically belong together. For example, in group posting information, fields like the **Capitalization Date**, **Acquisition Date**, and **Deactivation Date** fields all relate to the postings to the asset.

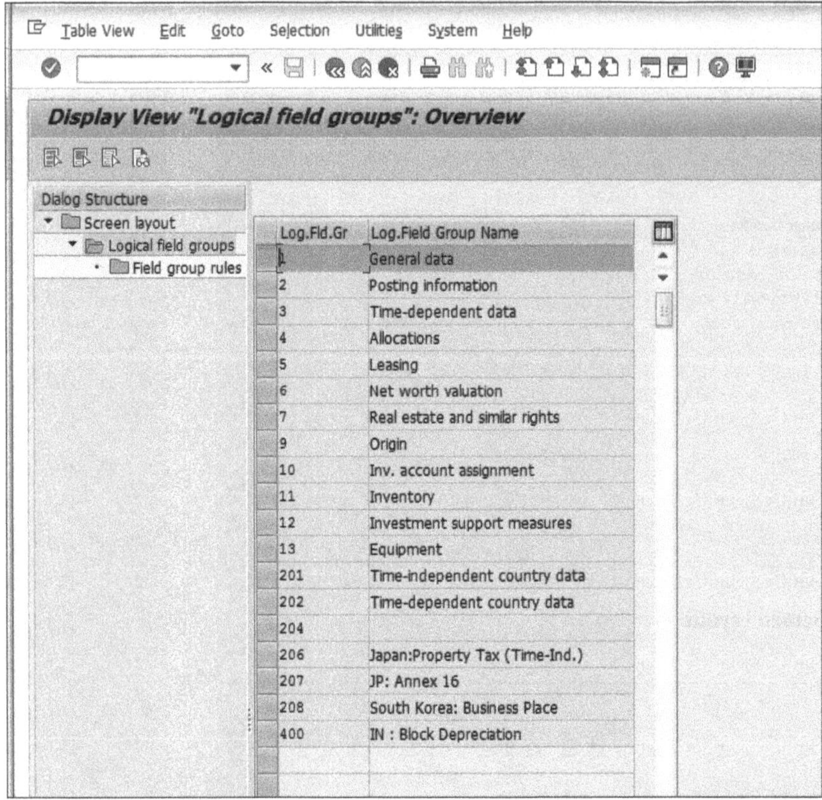

Figure 7.13 Logical Field Groups

Let's assume you have a requirement that, for machinery, the serial number of the machine must be entered into the asset master record. You'll want to ensure that this information is never omitted for these types of assets, so you'll make this field a required field in the asset master. Select the general data group and click on **Field group rules**, which will result in the screen shown in Figure 7.14.

Notice that, for every field, three options are available: required, optional, and hidden. Change the serial number field to required (**Req.**). Now, the system won't allow anyone to save a master record under this screen layout without entering a serial number. You'll also need to specify its maintenance level via the checkboxes on the right: main number (**MnNo.**) and subnumber (**Sbno.**). Select the **MnNo.** checkbox, which indicates that any subnumbers created for this asset will receive the value for this field from the main number. Selecting the **Copy** checkbox ensures that, when creating an asset with reference to another asset, the value of this field will be transferred. Select this option and save. In a similar way, you can modify other fields in the other logical groups based on your requirements.

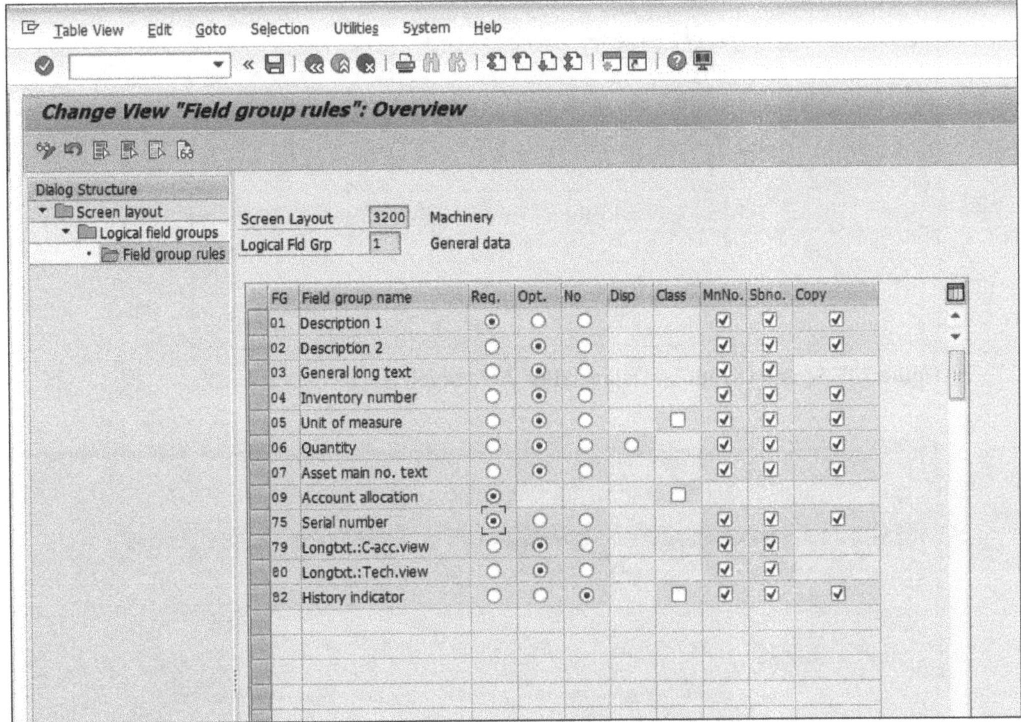

Figure 7.14 General Data Fields

One more configuration transaction governs which fields are selected for the **Depreciation** tab in the asset master record. This transaction is accessed via the menu path **Financial Accounting • Asset Accounting • Master Data • Screen Layout • Define Screen Layout for Asset Depreciation Areas.** These fields are maintained in a similar way, and usually, no changes are required because the settings are pretty standard. As shown in Figure 7.15, you can maintain these fields on the level of the main asset number and on the level of the asset subnumber.

Select screen layout **1000: Depr. on main asset no. level** and click on **Field group rules.** Now, you can modify the status of the various fields on the depreciation area level, as shown in Figure 7.16.

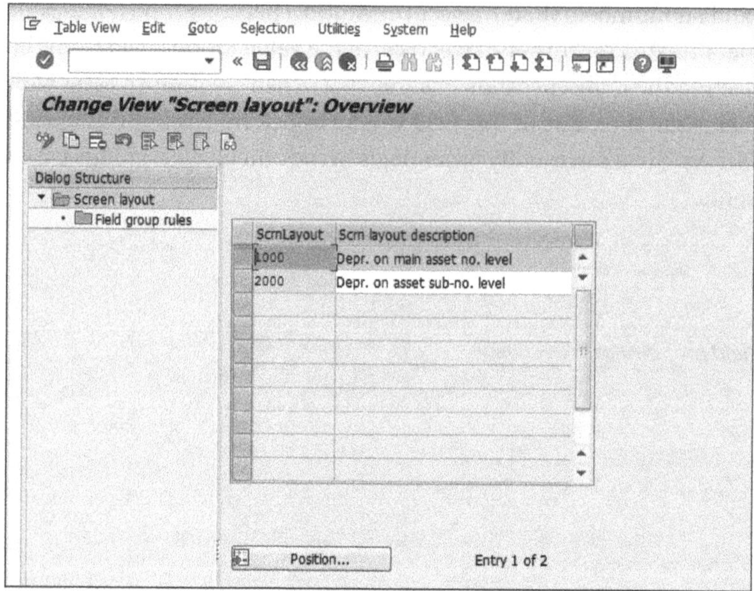

Figure 7.15 Screen Layout on Depreciation Area Level

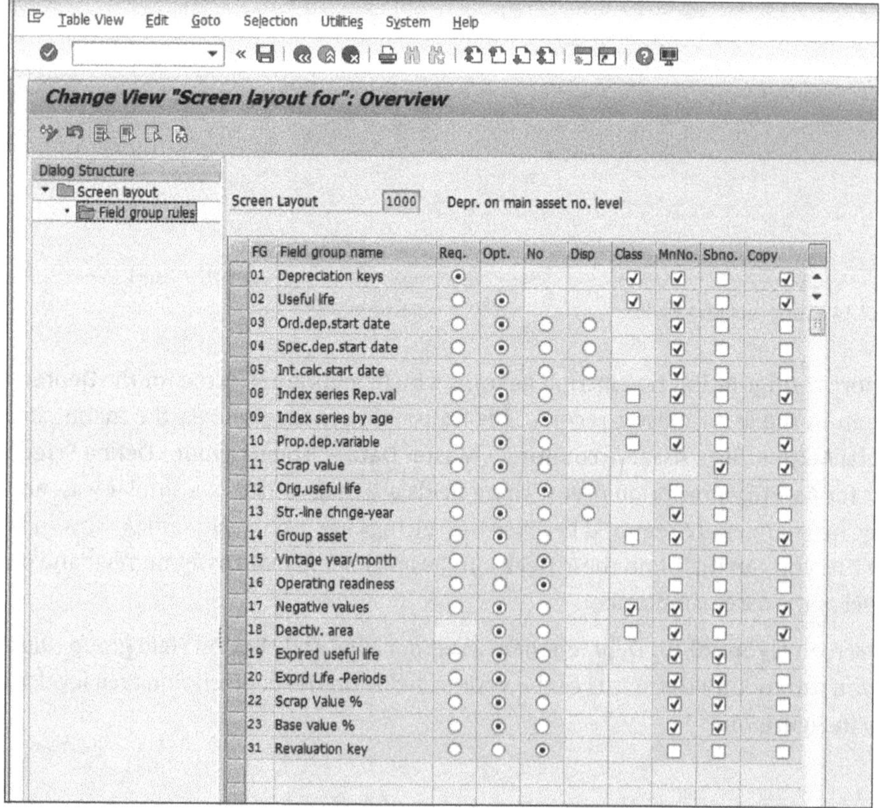

Figure 7.16 Depreciation Area Field Settings

With this step, we've finished the configuration of our screen layouts. Now, let's move to account determination.

7.2.2 Account Determination

Account determination is an important configuration area, which stipulates which general ledger accounts receive postings from asset transactions. As with the screen layout, account determination is defined as an object in one configuration transaction. You can create account determinations for each asset type, such as vehicles, machines, IT equipment, and so on. Then, in another configuration transaction, you can assign accounts for each depreciation area and for each business process to the defined account determination.

To define the account determination, follow the menu path **Financial Accounting • Asset Accounting • Organizational Structures • Asset Classes • Specify Account Determination.** A table with the defined account determinations will be displayed, as shown in Figure 7.17.

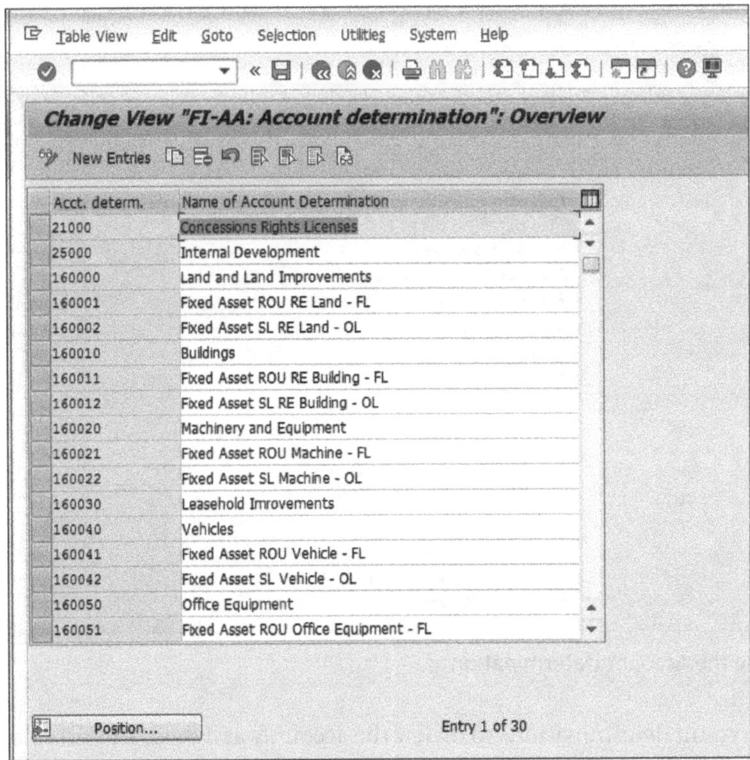

Figure 7.17 Account Determinations

As with screen layouts, standard account determinations have been provided that can be used directly or used as references for new objects. An account determination corresponds more or less to the asset classes, although one account determination can be used by multiple asset classes if you envision that their accounts are and will be exactly the same. For our purposes, we'll use the standard account determination, so we won't create new entries now.

To modify the accounts linked to the account determination, you must go to a different transaction via the menu path **Financial Accounting • Asset Accounting • Integration with General Ledger Accounting • Assign G/L Accounts**. This transaction is dependent on the chart of accounts. After selecting the chart of accounts, you'll be presented with a list of available account determinations, as shown in Figure 7.18.

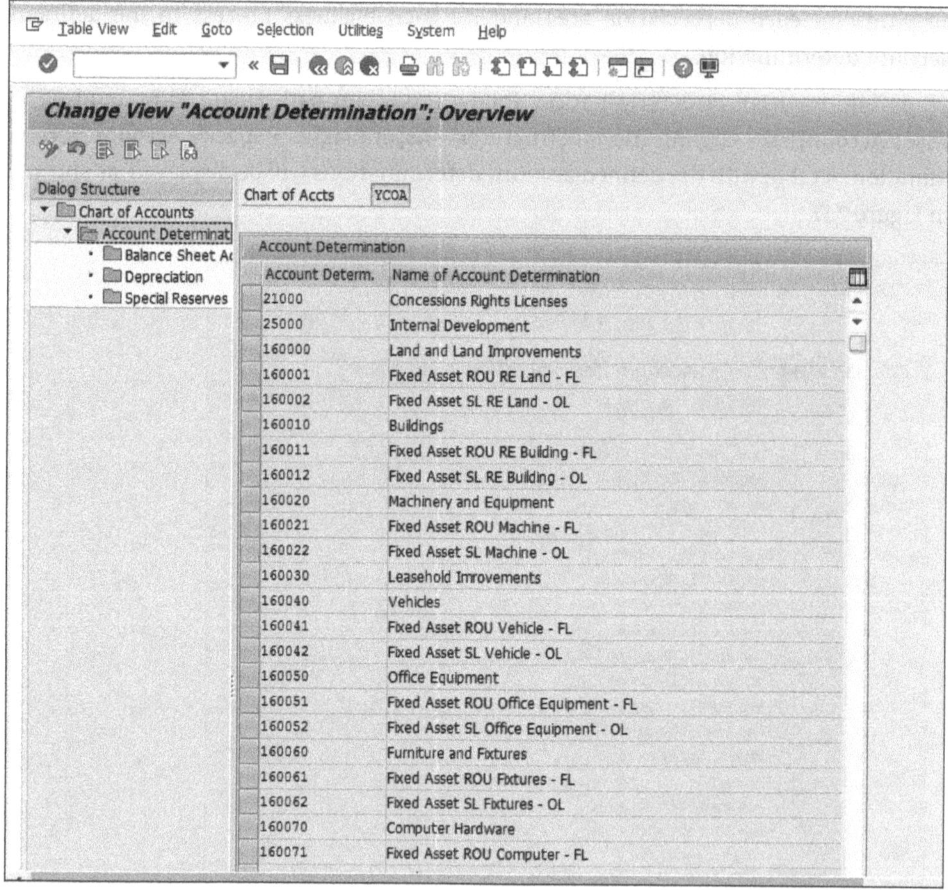

Figure 7.18 Selecting the Account Determination

Select one of the account determinations to review the accounts assigned. The left side of the screen displays a tree-like structure in which you can configure different types of accounts, such as balance sheet accounts and depreciation accounts. Click **Balance Sheet Accounts** on the left side of the screen. You'll see a list of the defined depreciation areas, as shown in Figure 7.19.

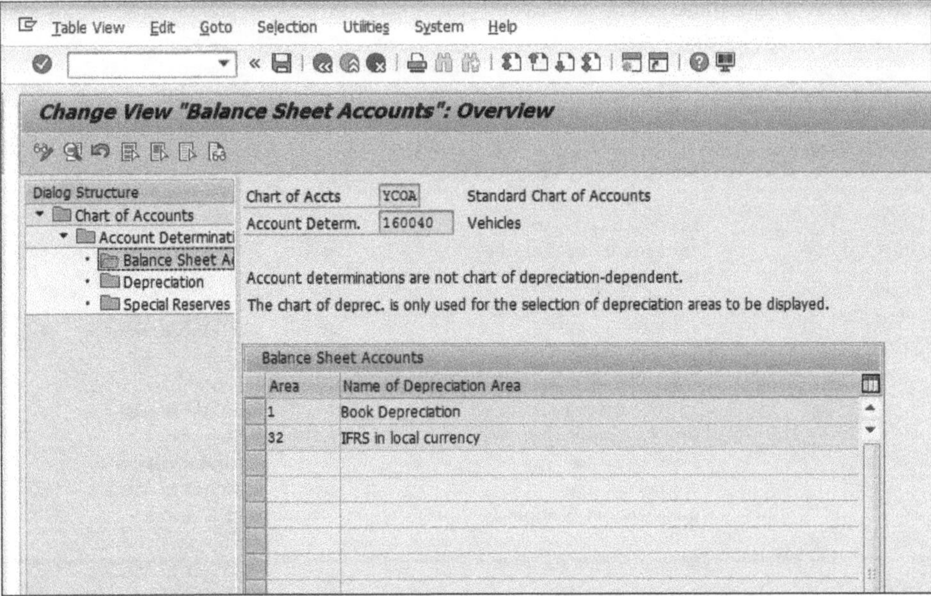

Figure 7.19 Selecting a Depreciation Area

You must choose the depreciation area by double-clicking it. The assignment of accounts must be maintained for each depreciation area that posts to the general ledger. Accounts are often the same between depreciation areas, but you can post to different accounts based on the accounting principle used. So, double-click **Deprec. Area 1**, which opens the configuration screen shown in Figure 7.20.

On this screen, general ledger accounts can be configured to post automatically from the various business processes. The **Bal.Sh.Acct APC** (balance sheet account: acquisition and production costs) field is the main balance sheet account that is debited when an asset is acquired. Similarly, this account is credited when the asset is being retired. A separate account can be customized for acquisitions from affiliated companies in the **Acquisition from affiliated company** field.

In the **Retirement account assignment** section, the accounts to be used in the retirement process are provided. Loss and gain accounts are posted with the financial result generated when comparing the sales price with the net book value of the asset. Different accounts can be entered for asset retirement without revenue (scrapping). Other sections are not used often, like the accounts for revaluation and investment support.

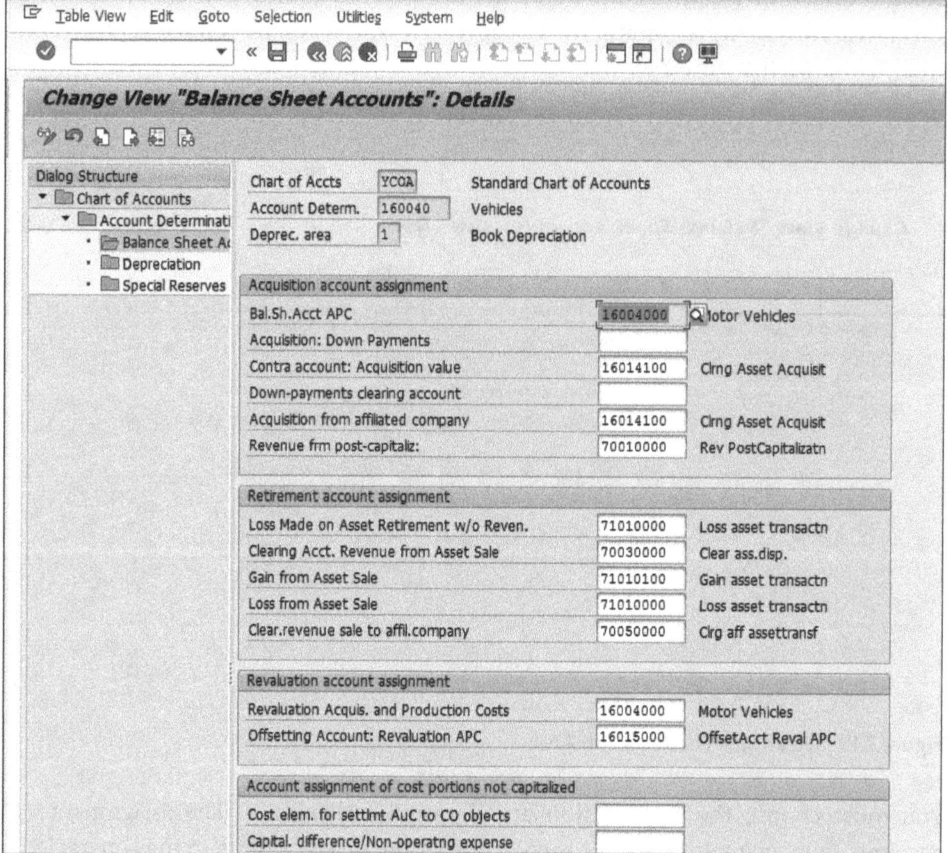

Figure 7.20 Configuring General Ledger Accounts

Then, the next important part of the configuration is setting the depreciation accounts. Select the **Depreciation** section on the left side of the screen and then select the depreciation area. You'll be presented with the configuration screen shown in Figure 7.21.

The depreciation configuration area is also separated into sections based on similar accounts. You must configure the ordinary depreciation account assignment, which is used by the normal ordinary depreciation run that runs on a monthly basis. The accumulated depreciation account for ordinary depreciation is the balance sheet account, which is posted against expenses during the depreciation run. Then, expense accounts need to be configured, which are posted with the depreciation expense. At the same time, the system also posts the cost center from the asset master record. Another option is to configure a different expense account for depreciation below zero.

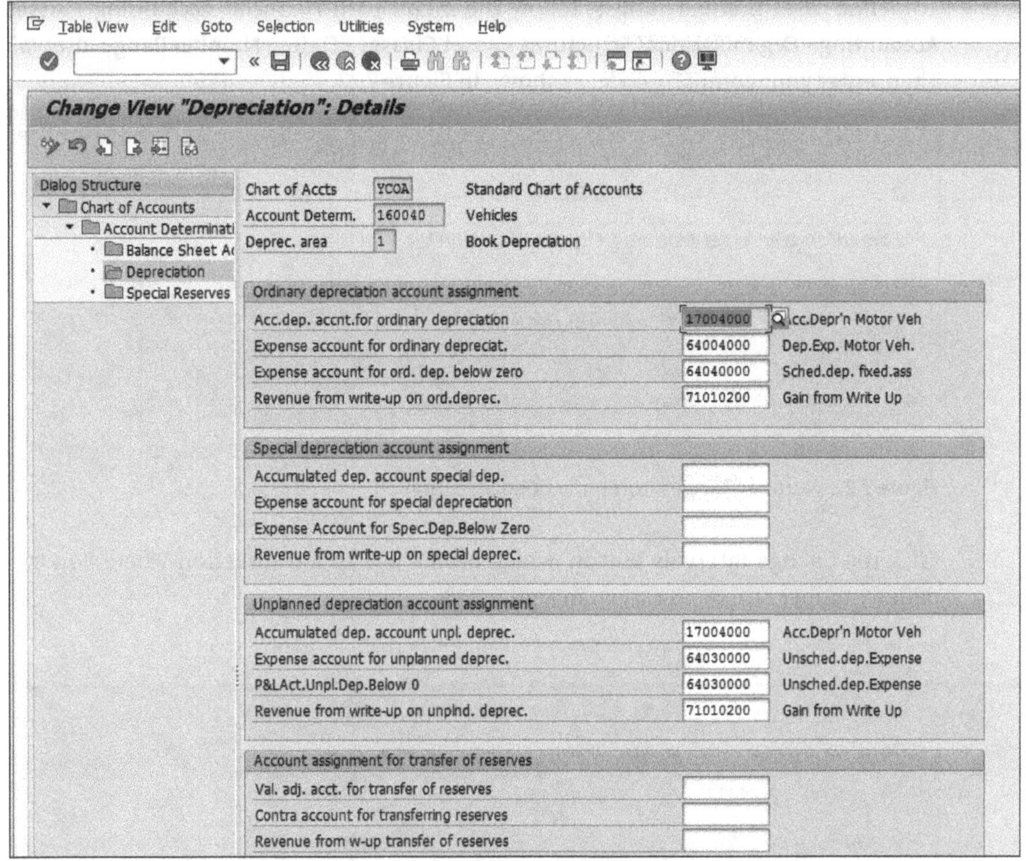

Figure 7.21 Configuring Depreciation Accounts

In other sections, you can configure accounts for unplanned and special depreciation. *Unplanned depreciation* is depreciation posted in unplanned cases, such as unplanned loss of the value of assets, like obsolescence due to new models, for example. *Special depreciation* is additional depreciation to be posted above the ordinary depreciation in special cases, such as when stipulated by the government. The accounts for these two types of depreciation can be maintained on this screen in a similar fashion as with ordinary depreciation.

After making necessary adjustments to the assignment of general ledger accounts, you can configure number ranges for asset master data.

7.2.3 Number Ranges

Number ranges define the numbers assigned when creating asset master records. From a business point of view, these numbers should be unique to each asset class, although technically multiple asset classes can share a number range.

To define asset number ranges, follow the menu path **Financial Accounting • Asset Accounting • Organizational Structures • Asset Classes • Define Number Range Interval.** Then, enter your company code, as shown in Figure 7.22.

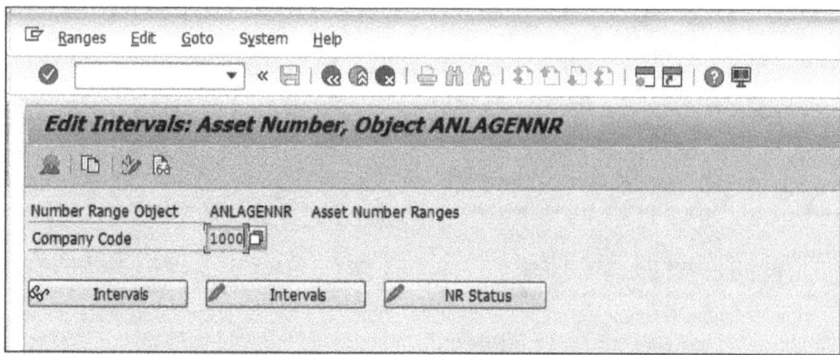

Figure 7.22 Number Ranges Company Code Selection

Click the **Change Intervals** button, which brings you to a transaction where you can define number ranges, as shown in Figure 7.23.

Interval Edit Goto System Help

Edit Intervals: Asset Number, Object ANLAGENNR, Subobject

Number Range No.	From No.	To Number	NR Status
01	000010000000	000019999999	0
02	000020000000	000029999999	0
03	000030000000	000039999999	0
04	000040000000	000049999999	0
05	000050000000	000059999999	0
06	000060000000	000069999999	0
07	000070000000	000079999999	0
08	000080000000	000089999999	0
09	000090000000	000099999999	0

Figure 7.23 Defining Number Ranges

The number range is identified by its number, which is then assigned in the asset class. You'll define, in the **From No.** and **To Number** columns, the range in which assets are created, deciding how long the asset numbers should be. For example, if you enter "000030000000" to "000039999999," the asset numbers will have 8 digits. The system will assign the next number consecutively internally, unless you check the **Ext** (external) checkbox on the left side. This option means the number range is external, and a user will be required to enter a number within that range when creating an asset. In the **NR Status** column, the system displays the current number within the range.

To create a new number range, select **Insert Line** from the top menu. This step gives you a blank line in which you can define a new number range. Note that asset master number ranges are not transportable, as is also true of other number ranges in the system, and should be created in each target client individually. This limitation exists to avoid inconsistencies.

Now that we've defined some number ranges, let's talk about the user fields available in the asset master record.

7.2.4 User Fields and Asset Supernumbers

As you've seen, an asset comes with multiple standard SAP fields, in which you can record all sorts of information, including general data, time-dependent data, origin information, leasing, and so on. But sometimes, these fields aren't enough. Many companies have unique and specific reporting requirements that aren't provided for with the standard fields. For this reason, SAP provides a flexible option: four 4-character fields and one 8-character field, which can be defined as required in the system and then selected from a dropdown list. These fields are used for reporting purposes and are available under the **Assignments** tab in the asset master record, as shown in Figure 7.24.

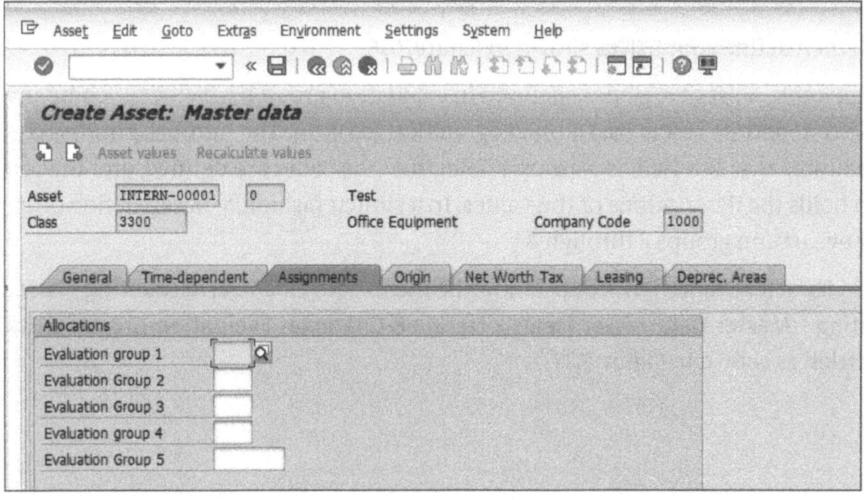

Figure 7.24 Evaluation Groups in an Asset Master Record

Notice that four 4-character fields available (evaluation groups 1 through 4) and one 8-character field (evaluation group 5). To define a 4-character field, follow the menu path **Financial Accounting • Asset Accounting • Master Data • User Fields • Define 4-Character Evaluation Groups**. Click **New Entries**, as shown in Figure 7.25.

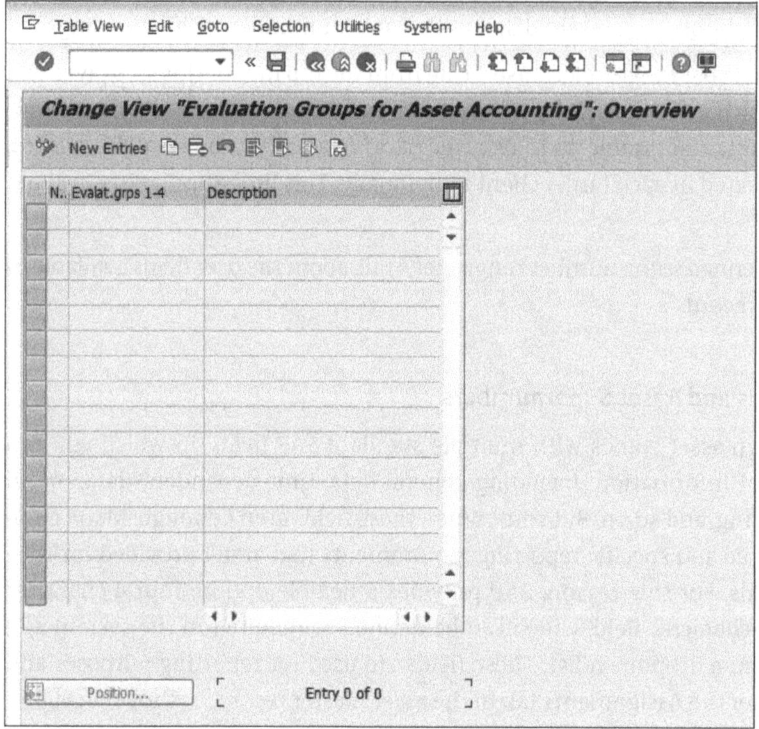

Figure 7.25 Initial Screen: Four-Character Evaluation Groups

You can then define your list, as shown in Figure 7.26.

In this example, a list of regions is defined in evaluation group 1, which your company may use to report its assets based on geographical location. The number 1 in first column indicates that this field is a group 1 field, then the codes are defined, and the last column holds the descriptions of the values. In a similar fashion, you can define other lists for evaluation groups 2 through 4.

For an 8-character evaluation group, follow the menu path **Financial Accounting • Asset Accounting • Master Data • User Fields • Define 8-Character Evaluation Groups**. Click **New Entries**, as shown in Figure 7.27.

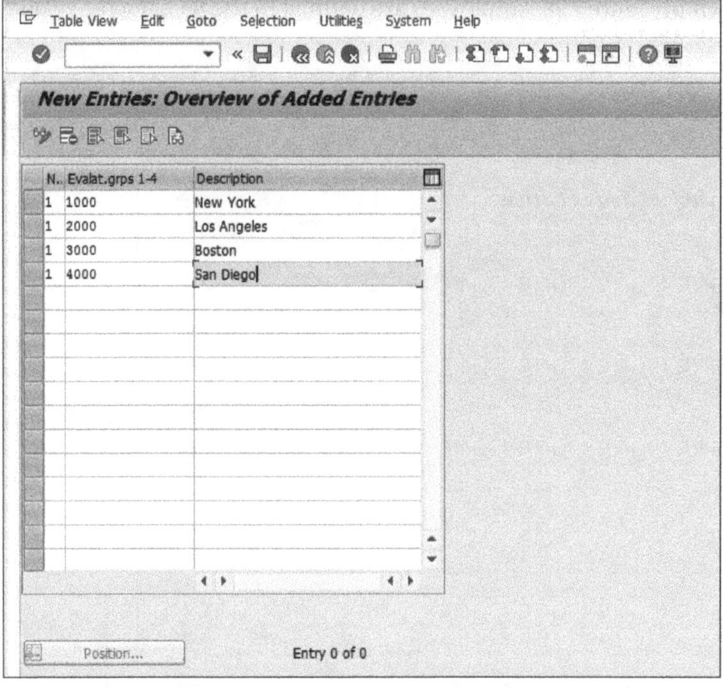

Figure 7.26 Creating a Four-Character Evaluation Group

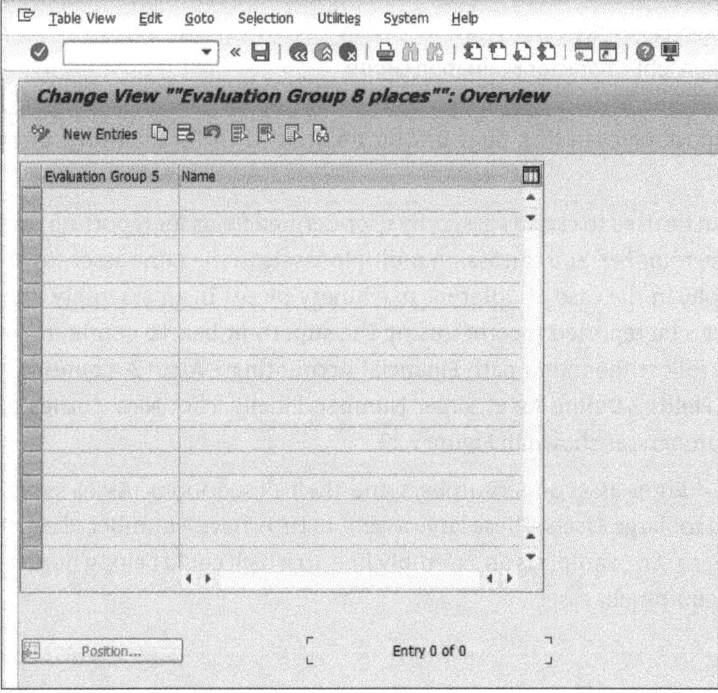

Figure 7.27 Initial Screen: Eight-Character Evaluation Group

In the example shown in Figure 7.28, employees are defined in the 8-character evaluation group 5.

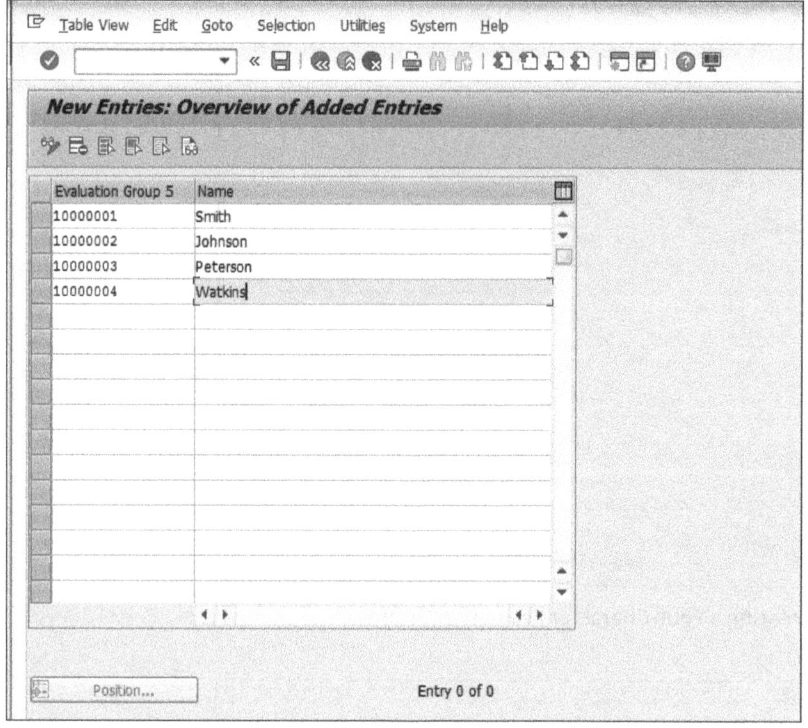

Figure 7.28 Defining an Eight-Character Evaluation Group

Then, in the asset report, you can sort, filter, and summarize by the evaluation groups you created.

Another field that can be used to classify assets by user-defined fields for reporting purposes is the *asset supernumber*. You can assign multiple assets to the same asset supernumber—for example, in the case of different machinery pieces in an assembly line. Then, all elements can be reported together using the supernumber. To configure an asset supernumber, follow the menu path **Financial Accounting • Asset Accounting • Master Data • User Fields • Define Asset Super Number**. Finally, click **New Entries** to define asset supernumbers, as shown in Figure 7.29.

On this screen, you'll enter asset supernumbers and their descriptions. Asset supernumbers are defined for large assets. These large assets, in turn, have a number of other assets assigned to them. An example is an assembly line, to which could belong numerous machinery and equipment assets.

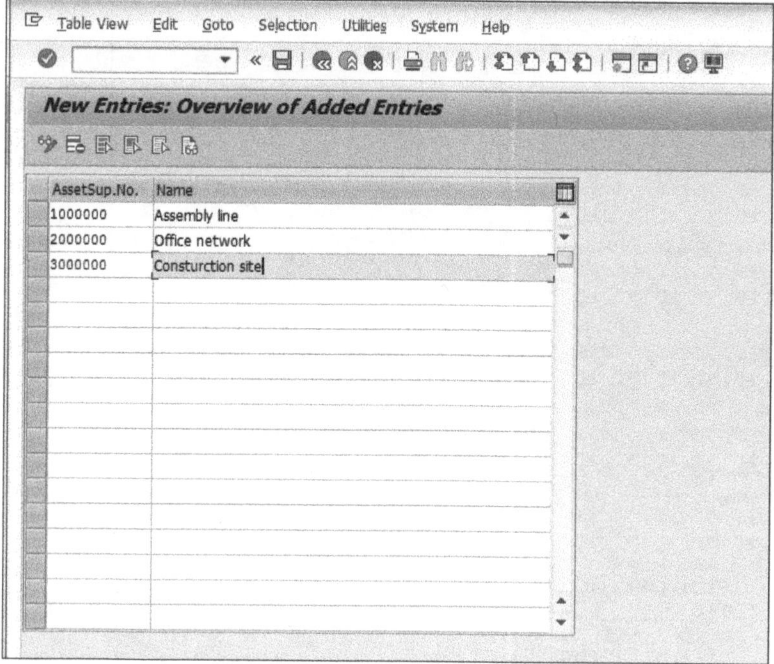

Figure 7.29 Asset Supernumbers

7.2.5 Asset Numbers, Subnumbers, and Group Numbers

Assets are usually created using asset numbers, which are either internally assigned by the system from the number range of the asset class or are externally entered by a user (in the case of external number assignment). However, two other options also exist: creating subnumbers for asset numbers or creating group numbers, both of which can serve as valuation levels for the assets assigned to them.

Asset subnumbers are used for assets that belong to higher-level assets, and these lower-level assets should be depreciated together at the main asset number level. To create asset subnumbers, no additional configuration is required. From the application menu, follow the menu path **Accounting • Financial Accounting • Fixed Assets • Asset • Create • Subnumber • AS11-Asset**, as shown in Figure 7.30.

Then, the information in the asset subnumber will be defaulted from the main number, with the opportunity to change some of the fields (not the depreciation terms, however, because the valuation level will be the main asset number). After saving, the system will assign a number in the format *main asset number-1, main asset number-2,* and so on, starting with 1 for the first subnumber. So, for example, if the main asset number is 200000, then the first subnumber will be 200000-1; the second, 200000-2; and so on.

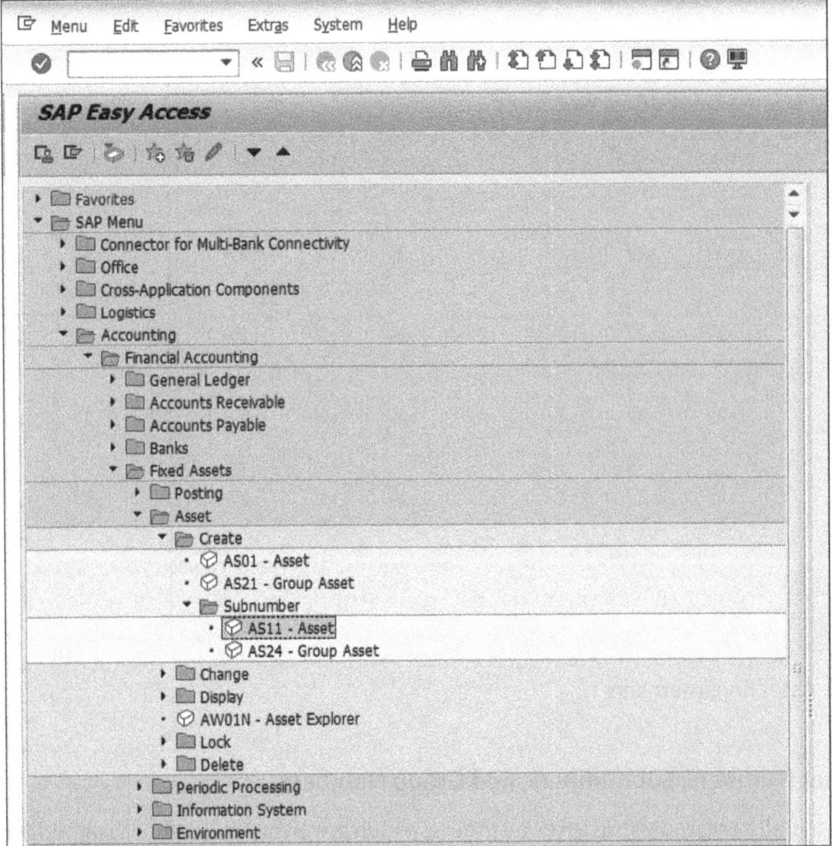

Figure 7.30 Creating an Asset Subnumber

To use group asset numbers, they first must be enabled at the depreciation area level by following the menu path **Financial Accounting • Asset Accounting • General Valuation • Group Assets • Specify Depreciation Areas for Group Assets.** In this transaction, select the company code and depreciation area for which group assets are allowed. To configure a specific asset class that consists entirely of group assets, follow the menu path **Financial Accounting • Asset Accounting • General Valuation • Group Assets • Specify Asset Classes for Group Assets.**

On the screen shown in Figure 7.31, you can select asset classes that consist of group assets by selecting the checkbox in the **Class consists entirely of group assets** column.

After enabling group assets, their creation is straightforward. Follow the application menu path **Accounting • Financial Accounting • Fixed Assets • Asset • Create • AS21-Group Asset.** Note that you can also create subnumbers for group assets.

Now that we've covered the master data configuration, let's look at the various business transactions that are generally performed with fixed assets and the required configuration for these transactions.

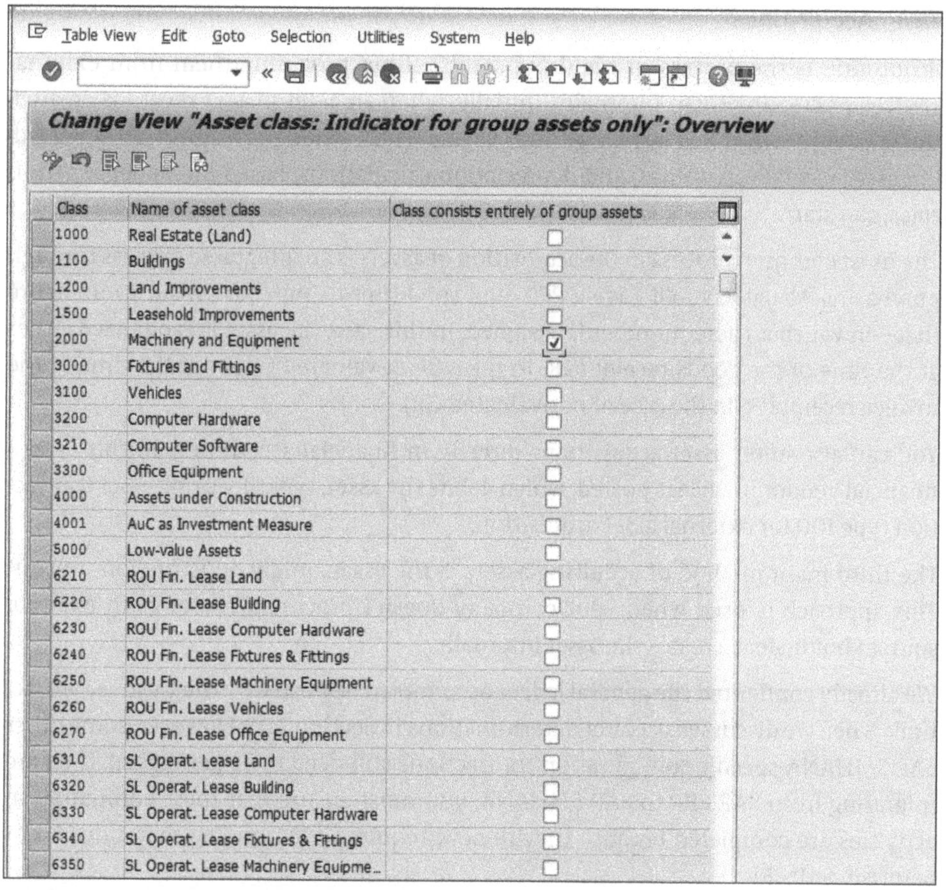

Table View Edit Goto Selection Utilities System Help

Change View "Asset class: Indicator for group assets only": Overview

Class	Name of asset class	Class consists entirely of group assets
1000	Real Estate (Land)	[ ]
1100	Buildings	[ ]
1200	Land Improvements	[ ]
1500	Leasehold Improvements	[ ]
2000	Machinery and Equipment	[x]
3000	Fixtures and Fittings	[ ]
3100	Vehicles	[ ]
3200	Computer Hardware	[ ]
3210	Computer Software	[ ]
3300	Office Equipment	[ ]
4000	Assets under Construction	[ ]
4001	AuC as Investment Measure	[ ]
5000	Low-value Assets	[ ]
6210	ROU Fin. Lease Land	[ ]
6220	ROU Fin. Lease Building	[ ]
6230	ROU Fin. Lease Computer Hardware	[ ]
6240	ROU Fin. Lease Fixtures & Fittings	[ ]
6250	ROU Fin. Lease Machinery Equipment	[ ]
6260	ROU Fin. Lease Vehicles	[ ]
6270	ROU Fin. Lease Office Equipment	[ ]
6310	SL Operat. Lease Land	[ ]
6320	SL Operat. Lease Building	[ ]
6330	SL Operat. Lease Computer Hardware	[ ]
6340	SL Operat. Lease Fixtures & Fittings	[ ]
6350	SL Operat. Lease Machinery Equipme...	[ ]

Figure 7.31 Asset Classes for Group Assets

7.3 Business Transactions

In terms of business transactions posted to assets, SAP S/4HANA hasn't changed much since SAP ERP: The main transactions are still acquisitions, retirements, transfers, and manual value corrections. However, a key underlying difference exists: Now, each transaction posts in real time in all ledgers, which are mapped to the depreciation areas, which post to the general ledger (as described Section 7.1.2). In the old SAP ERP world, transactions were posted in real time in the leading ledger (0L) only. Then, any differences with nonleading ledgers were stored as delta values and posted as periodic jobs. SAP S/4HANA's real-time integration is a key benefit of the new asset accounting. Some additional settings are required, which must be performed as part of the migration from SAP ERP to SAP S/4HANA, as we'll examine in the following section.

7.3.1 Acquisitions

Acquisition is the process of acquiring assets, either procuring them from external sources or creating them internally. Initially, when an asset master record is created, the master record is just a shell without values. Then, when the acquisition is posted, the asset receives its values, and depreciation calculations, based on its depreciation rules, can start.

The most common process in the acquisition of assets is an integrated process through purchasing. Usually, you'll have a PO—and sometimes a purchase requisition before that—in which an asset number is assigned. In this case, the asset is capitalized either at the time of the goods receipt (GR; in the case of valuated GR) or at the time of the invoice receipt (IR; in the case of nonvaluated GR).

You can also enter asset acquisitions directly in financial accounting. In this case, a financial vendor invoice is posted, which debits the asset, typically using asset transaction type 100 for external asset acquisition.

The third main method of acquiring assets is the assets under construction process. This approach is used when your company doesn't procure an asset from external sources but instead creates the asset internally.

We already configured the general ledger accounts to be posted by the various transactions when we discussed account determinations in Section 7.2.2. However, some other SAP S/4HANA-specific configuration transactions still need to be performed. If you're migrating from SAP ERP to SAP S/4HANA, you must ensure that these configuration activities are completed because they're new, required customizing that didn't exist before in SAP ERP.

To enable the acquisition processes in SAP S/4HANA, you must configure a technical clearing account for integrated asset acquisition. Follow the menu path **Financial Accounting • Asset Accounting • Integration with General Ledger Accounting • Technical Clearing Account for Integrated Asset Acquisition • Define Technical Clearing Account for Integrated Asset Acquisition**. Then, select **New Entries** from the menu and assign the account for your chart of accounts, as shown in Figure 7.32. Enter a chart of accounts and the general ledger account that should be used as the technical clearing account for integrated asset acquisitions.

When posting the acquisition, the system will offset the vendor line item with this technical account. The invoice posting will be the same for all accounting principles. However, the valuation part may be different in the various ledgers because different accounting principles will likely require different valuation approaches. Therefore, the system will post separate documents for each ledger in which asset line items will be offset by the same technical clearing account. At the end, the balance of this account will always be zero. This value won't be included directly in financial statements, only in the notes for financial statements with zero balances as auxiliary accounts.

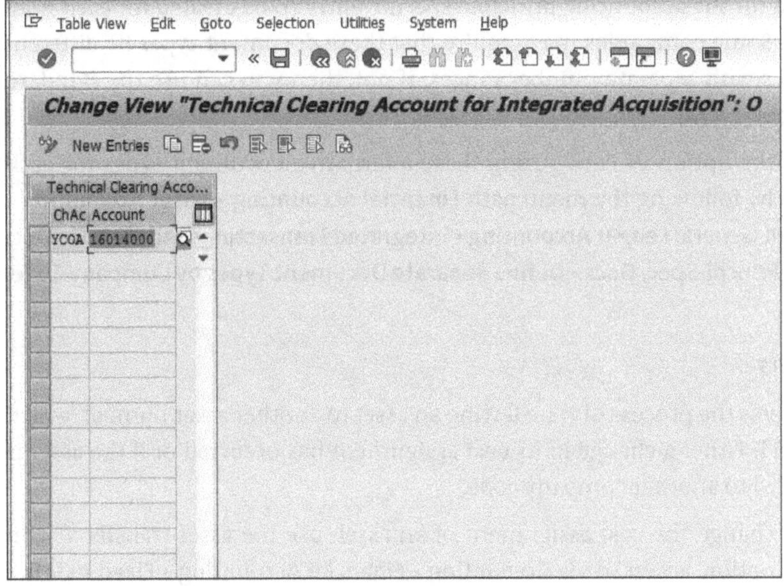

Figure 7.32 Configuring a Technical Clearing Account for Integrated Asset Acquisition

You also must define alternative document types for accounting principle-specific documents. In this activity, you'll specify which document types should be used when posting the ledger-specific part of the acquisition documents. To configure these alternative document types, follow the menu path **Financial Accounting • Asset Accounting • Integration with General Ledger Accounting • Integrated Transactions: Alternative Doc. Type for Acctg-Princpl-Spec. Docs • Specify Alternative Document Type for Acctg-Principle-Specific Documents**, as shown in Figure 7.33.

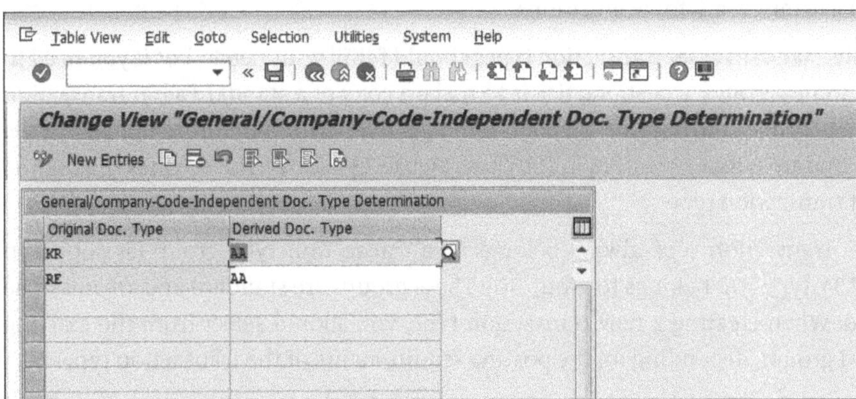

Figure 7.33 Alternative Document Types

On this screen, in the **Original Doc. Type** column, you'll see the original document type used in the entry view of the document—for example, KR for vendor invoice. Then, in the **Derived Doc. Type** column, this original document type is mapped to the document type to be used for the accounting principle-specific entry to be created for each non-leading ledger. Some companies may require that these document types be different document types with separate number ranges; if not, then you can use the standard asset document type AA.

You have also the option of configuring these alternative document types for each company code by following the menu path **Financial Accounting • Asset Accounting • Integration with General Ledger Accounting • Integrated Transactions: Alternative Doc. Type for Acctg-Princpl-Spec. Docs • Define Separate Document Types by Company Code.**

7.3.2 Transfers

An *asset transfer* is the process of transferring an asset to another asset number, which may be needed if either a change in its cost assignment has occurred or if the asset is being transferred to another company code.

If you need to change the cost assignment of an asset, use the asset transfer within company code option, accessed via **Accounting • Financial Accounting • Fixed Assets • Posting • Transfer • ABUMN—Transfer within Company Code.**

This transaction retires the asset that is being transferred and capitalizes the new asset, which you could either create before using the transaction or create automatically via the transaction. The system uses predefined transaction types for the acquisition and the retirement, which you can configure by following the menu path **Financial Accounting • Asset Accounting • Transactions • Transfer Postings • Define Transaction Types for Transfers.** Then, you can check the settings of the transaction types for retirement and acquisition. Typically, transaction types 300 (for prior year acquisitions) and 320 (for current year acquisitions) are used for retirement, and types 310 (prior year) and 330 (current year), for acquisitions.

Normally, standard asset transaction types should fulfill your needs, but if you need to change some settings, a best practice is to make a copy of a standard asset transaction type to a new one starting with Z, so it doesn't get overwritten in future updates of the system, and then make changes in the copy. Figure 7.34 shows the settings that define an asset transaction type.

An asset transaction type always belongs to a transaction type group (as shown in Figure 7.34, type 300 belongs to group 30). These groups are standard and are not to be changed. When creating a new transaction type, you should select from the existing standard groups, depending on the posting requirements of the transaction type.

Then, another setting determines whether this transaction type creates a credit or debit (a credit in the case of retirement): the **Deactivate Fixed Asset** checkbox, which is selected when the asset should be deactivated after retirement. Other settings provided are the document type used for the transaction, whether it's an intercompany transaction or not (in this case not, because we selected the **Do not post to affiliate co.** radio button), and the **Post Net** indicator, as shown in Figure 7.35. Thus, the net value will be transferred—that is, the acquisition value minus the posted depreciation.

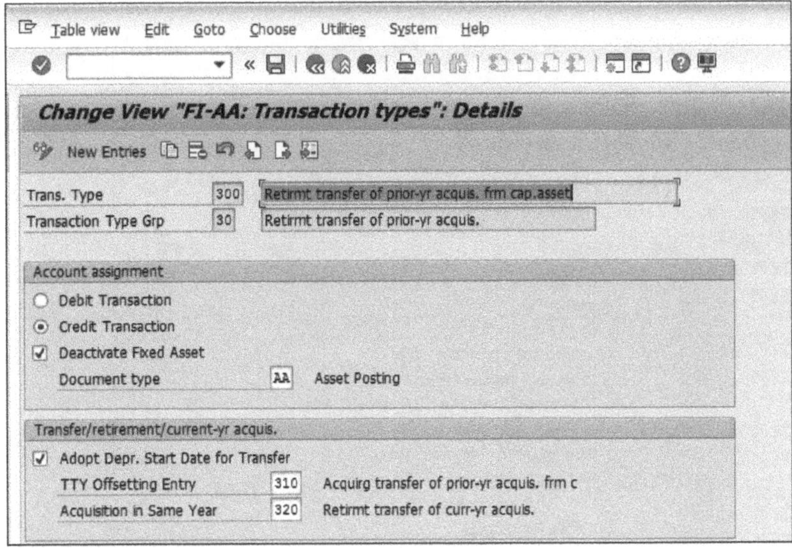

Figure 7.34 Defining an Asset Transaction Type

Further settings are shown in Figure 7.35. With these settings, you have the option of preventing a transaction type from being used manually, meaning the transaction type can only be selected internally by the system. Also, you must select the related consolidation transaction type, which is used by the consolidation functions of the system, and the asset history sheet group, which is used for asset history sheets, which we'll examine in Section 7.5.3.

Posting type
Post to affiliated company
Post Gross
Do not post to affiliated co.
Post Net
Other features
Cannot Be Used Manually
Call up individual check
Trans. Type Obsolete
Consolidation Transaction Type 950 Reclassification
Asst Hist Sheet Grp 30 Retirmt transfer of prior-yr acquis.

Figure 7.35 Other Transaction Type Settings

Intercompany asset transfers are made to transfer an asset from one legal entity to another within the group. The process usually also involves issuing intercompany invoices.

You also must define an asset transfer variant by following the menu path **Financial Accounting • Asset Accounting • Transactions • Intercompany Asset Transfers • Automatic Intercompany Asset Transfers • Define Transfer Variants.** Then, click the **Transfer variant** option, which will bring you to a list of transfer variants, as shown in Figure 7.36.

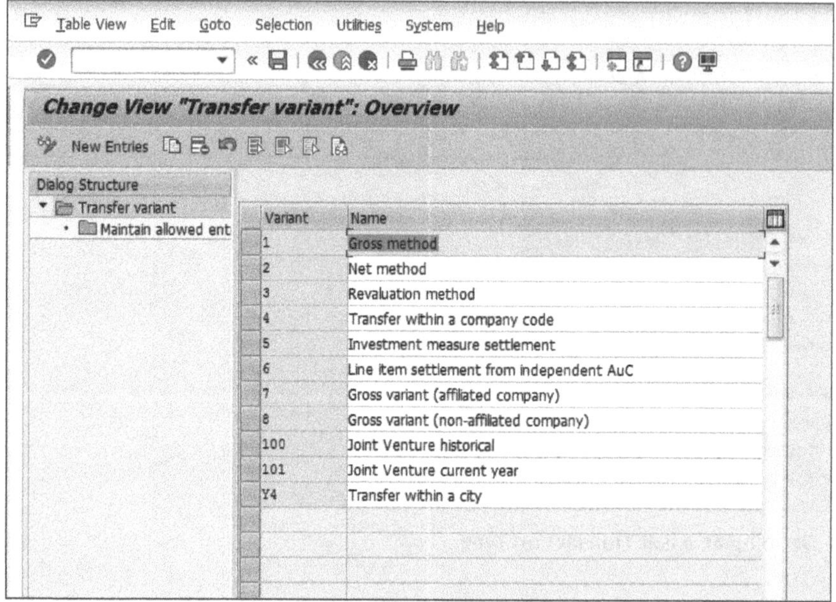

Figure 7.36 Transfer Variants

Figure 7.36 shows the SAP standard-provided variants, which can be copied to specific custom variants in which necessary adjustments can be made. Variants can be gross or net, depending on whether the gross values are being transferred (including the posted depreciation) or the net values (without the posted depreciation). For example, select the intercompany transfer variant **7: Gross variant (affiliated company)**, then select **Maintain allowed entries** from the left side of the screen, which will bring you to the screen shown in Figure 7.37.

On this screen, you'll configure the retirement and acquisition transaction types to be used in the case of legally independent units and in the case of a transfer of one legally independent unit. In the **Rel. Type** column, 1 is used for legally independent and 2 for legally one unit. You can specify a cross-system depreciation area or enter an asterisk (*), which is valid for all cross-system depreciation areas. Then, select a transfer method in the **Trans. Meth.** column and enter retirement and acquisition transaction types in the remaining columns.

Similarly, you can define your own transfer variant that uses your own transaction types.

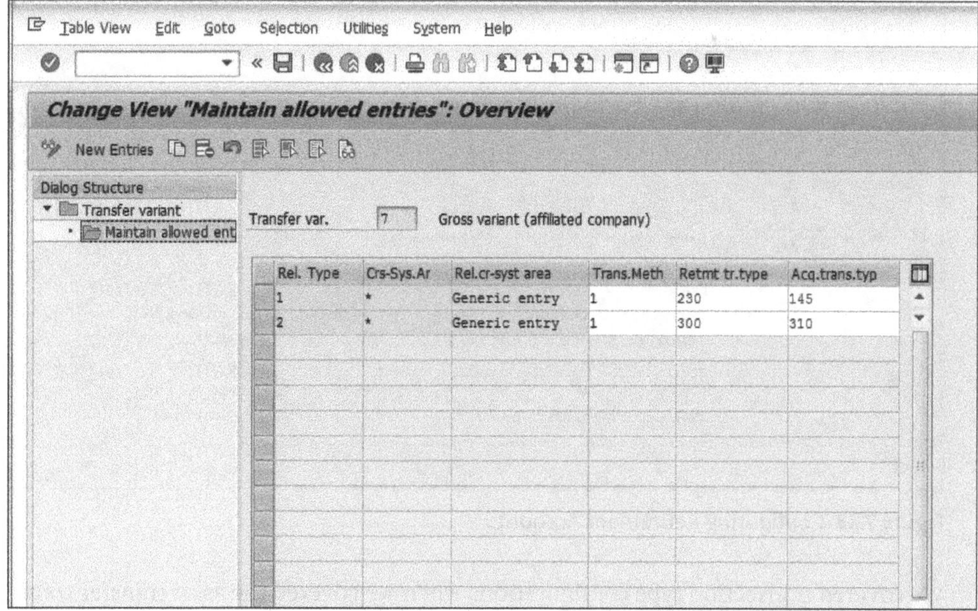

Figure 7.37 Intercompany Gross Variant

7.3.3 Retirement

Retirement is the process of an asset being sold or scrapped and deactivated in the system. When an asset is sold, usually, a customer invoice is issued and posted, which records the revenue posted. At this moment, the system compares the net book value of the asset to the selling price and posts a gain or loss to the configured accounts. In the case of scrapping, no revenue is generated, and if an outstanding net book value exists, this value will be posted to the loss account assigned.

To check and configure the general ledger accounts for retirement postings, follow the menu path **Financial Accounting • Asset Accounting • Transactions • Retirements • Assign Accounts**. Then, select the relevant chart of accounts, account determination, and depreciation area, and you'll see the retirement section only of the account determination, as shown in Figure 7.38.

The first account, **Loss Made on Asset Retirement w/o Reven.**, is used to post the loss in case of scrapping. The account specified in the **Clearing Acct. Revenue from Asset Sale** field is used to clear the net revenue from asset sales. The **Gain from Asset Sale** account is posted to when the revenue from the asset sale is higher than the net book value of the asset. The **Loss from Asset Sale** account is posted to when the revenue from the asset sale is less than the net book value of the asset. The last account, **Clear.revenue sale to affil.company**, is used to clear the revenue from asset sales to affiliated companies.

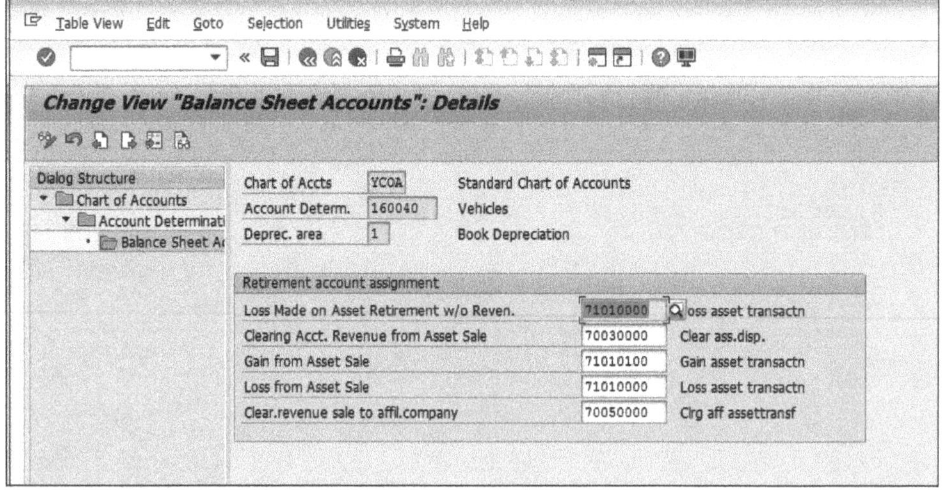

Figure 7.38 Configuring Retirement Accounts

We covered transaction type configurations when we covered the asset transfer transaction, but if you want to check the retirement transaction types, follow the menu path **Financial Accounting • Asset Accounting • Transactions • Retirements • Define Transaction Types for Retirements**. You'll now see a list of only the retirement transaction types, which you can check or define your own. For example, double-click **Trans. Type 200: Retirement without Revenue**, as shown in Figure 7.39.

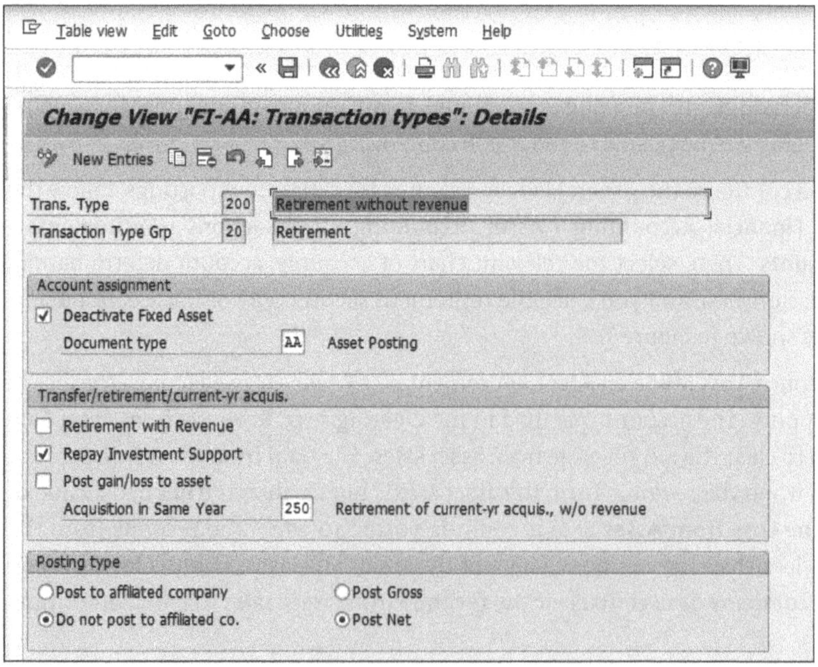

Figure 7.39 Transaction Type Retirement without Revenue

This standard transaction type is used in the case of scrapping. As you can see, this transaction type deactivates the asset and uses document type AA, and the option for retirement without revenue is not selected.

Now that we've covered the main business transactions that can be posted to assets, let's look the valuation of assets and the different periodic procedures that are being run in fixed assets.

7.4 Valuation and Closing

Asset valuation is the process of determining the fair market value of assets. Usually, this value is determined by running a periodic depreciation program that gradually reduces the value of assets based on predefined rules (called *depreciation terms*). These rules are different for each asset class (type of assets) but also can be different for various sets of accounting rules that a company may need to use to prepare its reports and financial statements. This flexibility is exactly where you'll clearly see the benefit of the new asset accounting provided by SAP S/4HANA, which we'll examine in detail in this section. We'll start with a detailed discussion of new asset accounting, then we'll discuss multiple valuation principles. Finally, we'll configure depreciation, revaluation, and other closing activities in fixed assets.

7.4.1 New Asset Accounting Concept

SAP has provided parallel valuation according to multiple accounting and tax principles using different depreciation areas for a quite long time. However, the solution wasn't perfect. The classic general ledger was only for asset reporting purposes. Then, with the invention of the new general ledger, you could post differences from these different valuation rules in the different nonleading ledgers. However, this functionality lacked perfect real-time integration since the system would post delta adjustment documents to nonleading ledgers to provide the value according to the alternative valuation approach they should represent. This approach was cumbersome. Although you could prepare financial statements according to different accounting frameworks, workarounds and a certain amount of manual work were required.

First, with the SAP Simple Finance add-on for SAP ERP, and now with SAP S/4HANA Finance, SAP introduced the new asset accounting option. The key benefits of new asset accounting include the real-time integration of asset accounting with the general ledger and the posting of separate documents from the different depreciation areas in the nonleading ledgers. Thus, when different values result from an acquisition or depreciation document, the system automatically will post separate documents in separate number ranges to leading ledger 0L and to the nonleading ledgers in real time.

With SAP S/4HANA, the new asset accounting is mandatory, whereas it was optional with the SAP S/4HANA Finance add-on. Thus, if you're upgrading from SAP ERP to SAP S/4HANA, you must plan the time and project activities to convert from classic asset accounting to new asset accounting. Program RASFIN_MIGR_PRECHECK will help you check that all migration prerequisites are met, as shown in Figure 7.40.

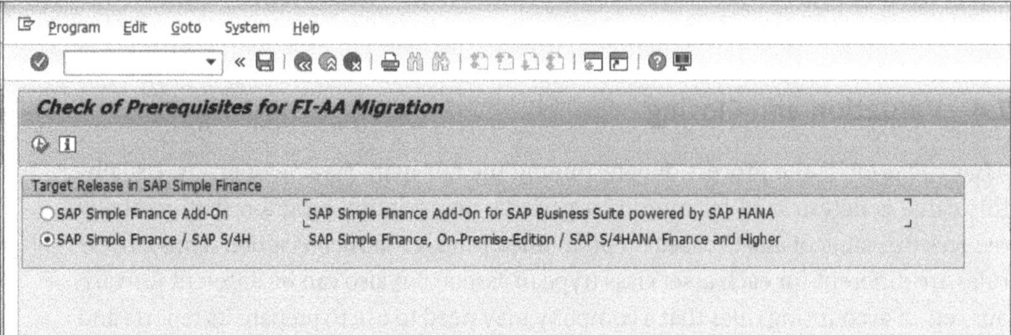

Figure 7.40 Migration Check Program

This program checks the readiness of the customizing and transaction data for new asset accounting. This step is important because underlying technical changes have occurred in the landscape of fixed assets. For example, with new asset accounting, actual line items will be posted to the Universal Journal (table ACDOCA). Tables from classic asset accounting like tables ANEK, ANEP, ANLC, and ANLP become redundant but still exist as compatibility views. Custom programs that rely on these tables should continue to work if they only read from these tables (but nevertheless should be checked and tested), whereas custom programs that write to these tables will need to be updated.

7.4.2 Multiple Valuation Principles

It's quite common that the same fixed assets should be treated differently based on different valuation principles. For example, the useful life or the method of depreciation for certain categories of assets should be different. In the US, the half-year convention of depreciation is common, which means that depreciation for half a year should be taken in the year of acquisition of the asset and in the year of its retirement, regardless of when it's required. This approach, of course, will result in different depreciation amounts compared to IFRS or local GAAP, for which no such method is used.

The management of different valuation principles in SAP is achieved by using different depreciation areas. Depreciation area 01, which is linked with the leading ledger, should represent the leading valuation from the point of view of the group. Normally for US companies, this valuation should be US GAAP or IFRS. For European companies, it will almost always be IFRS. Other commonly used depreciation areas are for local GAAP and local tax. Thus, specific local accounting principles and specific local tax rules can be managed for each country, if needed.

The link between the depreciation area and the ledger is the accounting principle. Let's revisit the configuration of the depreciation area, which you can access via the menu path **Financial Accounting • Asset Accounting • General Valuation • Depreciation Area • Define Depreciation Areas**. When you click a depreciation area, you'll see its definition, as shown in Figure 7.41.

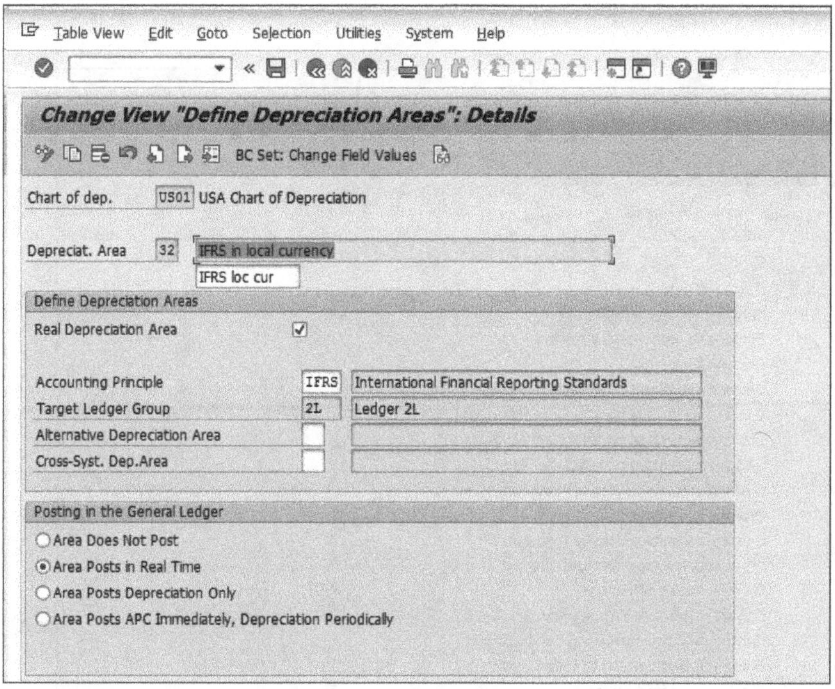

Figure 7.41 Accounting Principle in Depreciation Area

As shown in Figure 7.41, you can assign an accounting principle in the **Accounting Principle** field in the depreciation area—in our example, "IFRS," which represents IFRS valuation. Accounting principles are assigned to ledgers in **Financial Accounting • Financial Accounting Global Settings • Ledgers • Parallel Accounting • Assign Accounting Principle to Ledger Groups**.

Now that we've ensured that we have depreciation areas that cover multiple accounting principles, let's look at how the system calculates depreciation differently using depreciation keys.

7.4.3 Depreciation Key

A *depreciation key* contains various settings required to calculate the depreciation amounts, such as the method of depreciation and the time control. This configuration object bundles together multiple calculation methods of various types: base methods (such as linear depreciation), declining-balance methods (when depreciation should be faster in the beginning of the asset life), multilevel methods (which involve change during the useful life), and so on. SAP provides myriad standard calculation methods, which you can check or copy and create your own by following the menu path **Financial Accounting • Asset Accounting • Depreciation • Valuation Methods • Depreciation Key • Calculation Methods**. Usually, the standard methods should suffice to meet any business requirements in your organization. Base calculation methods are shown in Figure 7.42.

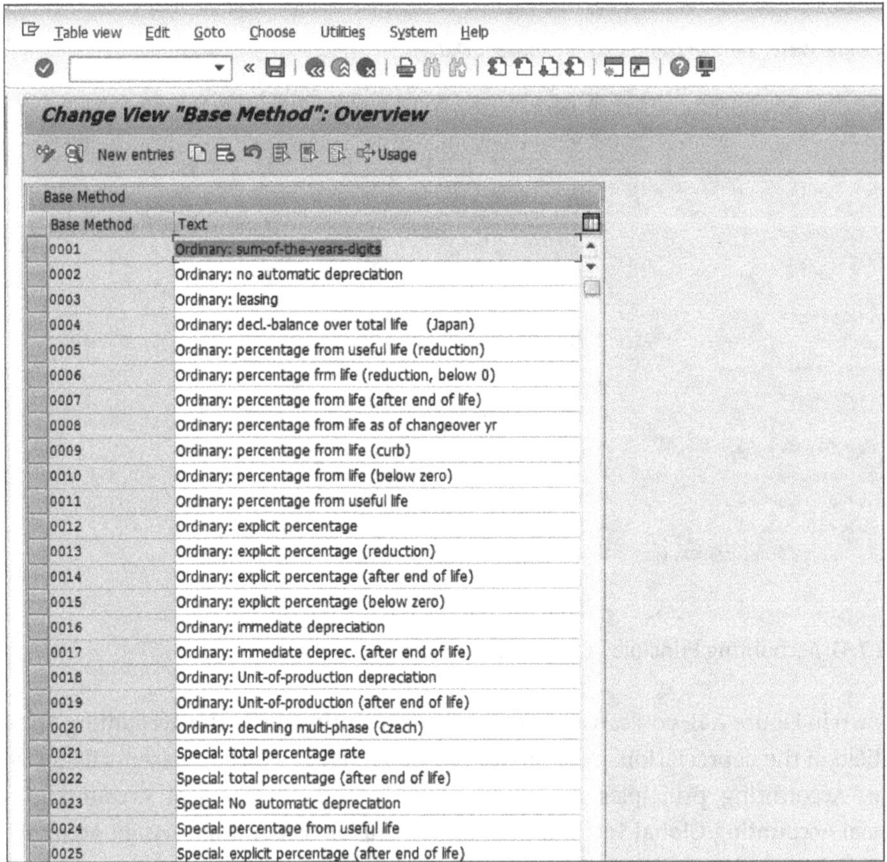

Base Method	Text
0001	Ordinary: sum-of-the-years-digits
0002	Ordinary: no automatic depreciation
0003	Ordinary: leasing
0004	Ordinary: decl.-balance over total life (Japan)
0005	Ordinary: percentage from useful life (reduction)
0006	Ordinary: percentage frm life (reduction, below 0)
0007	Ordinary: percentage from life (after end of life)
0008	Ordinary: percentage from life as of changeover yr
0009	Ordinary: percentage from life (curb)
0010	Ordinary: percentage from life (below zero)
0011	Ordinary: percentage from useful life
0012	Ordinary: explicit percentage
0013	Ordinary: explicit percentage (reduction)
0014	Ordinary: explicit percentage (after end of life)
0015	Ordinary: explicit percentage (below zero)
0016	Ordinary: immediate depreciation
0017	Ordinary: immediate deprec. (after end of life)
0018	Ordinary: Unit-of-production depreciation
0019	Ordinary: Unit-of-production (after end of life)
0020	Ordinary: declining multi-phase (Czech)
0021	Special: total percentage rate
0022	Special: total percentage (after end of life)
0023	Special: No automatic depreciation
0024	Special: percentage from useful life
0025	Special: explicit percentage (after end of life)

Figure 7.42 Base Calculation Methods

Another important setting at the depreciation key level is the period control. This setting determines when the depreciation should start and end. Its configuration is available by following the menu path **Financial Accounting • Asset Accounting • Depreciation • Valuation Methods • Period Control**. On this screen, you can define period control methods and define their calendar assignments. Open the **Define Calendar Assignments** transaction, which is shown in Figure 7.43.

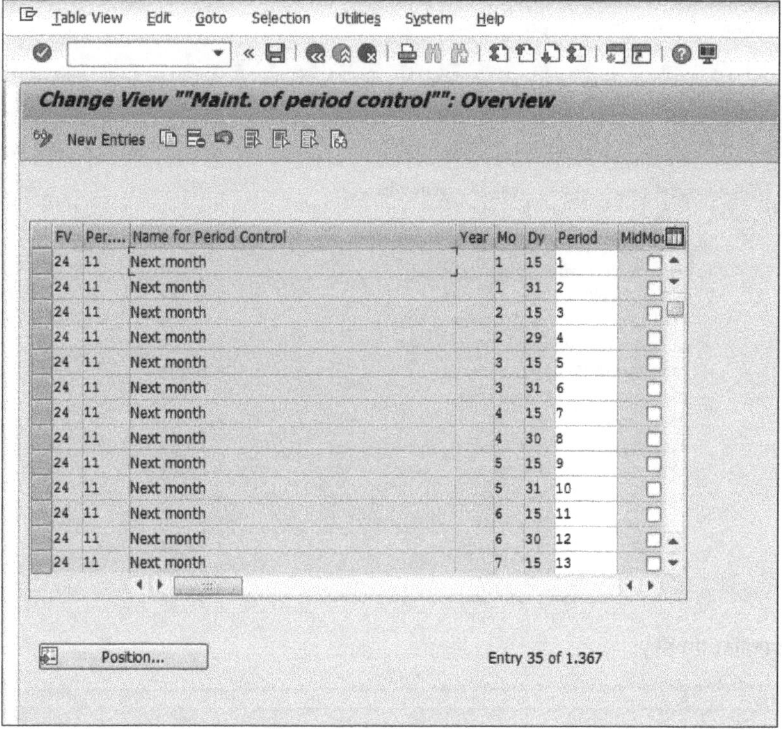

Figure 7.43 Period Control Calendar Assignments

On this screen, for each fiscal year variant and period control method, you can define the period after which the depreciation calculation will start (in case of acquisition) and after which it will end (in case of retirement). As shown in Figure 7.43, for example, for method **11: Next Month**, the depreciation should start at the beginning of the month following acquisition and should finish in the next month, following retirement. So, for example, for acquisitions that occur between dates 1–31 of period 01, depreciation will start at the beginning of the following period 02.

Now, let's look at the configuration of the depreciation key itself, which is accessed via the menu path **Financial Accounting • Asset Accounting • Depreciation • Valuation Methods • Depreciation Key • Maintain Depreciation Key.** You'll see a list of existing depreciation keys on the right side of the screen and navigation to their underlying calculation methods on the left side, as shown in Figure 7.44.

Next, select depreciation key **LINS: Str.-line over rem.life pro rata to zero** (straight line depreciation over remaining life pro rated to zero), which is a standard depreciation key for straight-line depreciation, and click **Assignment of Calculation Methods** on the left side of the screen. Now, you'll see what calculation methods are being used by the depreciation key, as shown in Figure 7.45.

Change View "Depreciation Key": Overview

Chart of dep. US01 USA Chart of Depreciation

DepKy	Name for Whole Depreciation	Status
0000	No depreciation and no interest	X Active
GWG	LVA 100 % Complete write off	X Active
LEAX	Depreciation from Real Estate Leasing	X Active
LINS	Str.-line over rem.life pro rata to zero	X Active
M150	MACRS 15, 20 years property	X Active
M200	MACRS 3,5,7,10 years property	X Active
MANU	Manual depreciation only	X Active
S150	DB 150% Half Year w/Bonus	X Active
S151	DB 150% MQTR w/Bonus	X Active
S200	DB 200% Half Year w/Bonus	X Active
S201	DB 200% MQTR w/Bonus	X Active
SQ15	DB 150% MQTR Convention	X Active
SQ20	DB 200% MQTR Convention	X Active
SU00	No depreciation - US Accounting Principle 12 per.	X Active

Figure 7.44 Depreciation Keys

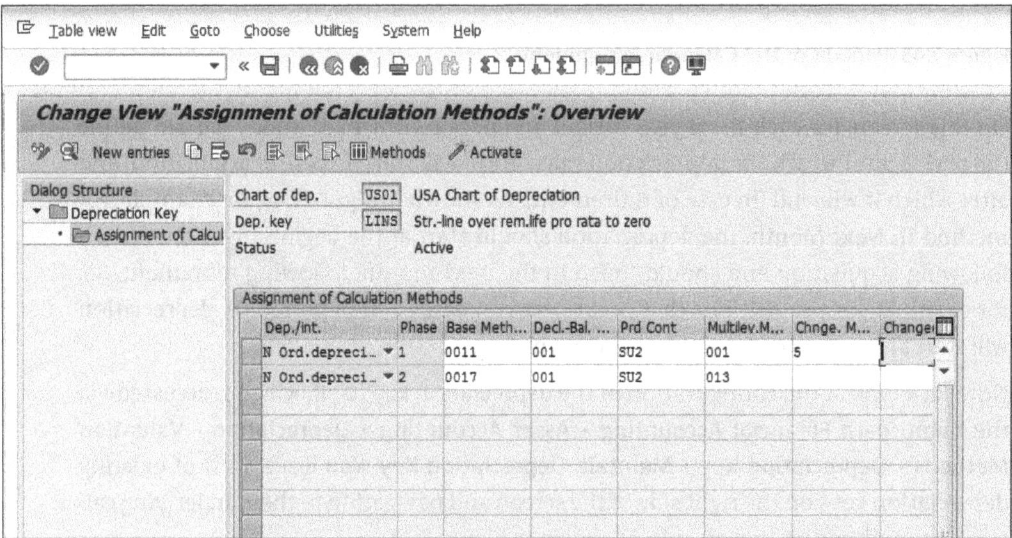

Figure 7.45 Assignment of Calculation Methods

In our example, you'll see two lines because this depreciation key has two phases. Initially, the first phase's methods will be valid until the changeover happens, as defined by the changeover method defined previously. The changeover will switch to the methods of the next phase. Various changeover methods are available, such as changeover when a specific net book value percentage is reached, changeover after the end of useful life, and so on. You can also perform a manual changeover. Different types of calculation methods are assigned in the method columns.

As with other configuration objects, we recommend copying existing SAP-provided keys and renaming them in the Z name range if you need to develop your own depreciation keys so that new settings won't be overwritten in future upgrades.

Now that we've covered the settings needed for calculating depreciation, let's look at the depreciation run itself and how this process differs in SAP S/4HANA compared to SAP ERP.

7.4.4 Depreciation Run

A *depreciation run* posts the calculated depreciation values to the assets on a periodic basis (usually monthly). In SAP S/4HANA's new asset accounting (and the SAP S/4HANA Finance add-on), the new depreciation program, program FAA_DEPRECIATION_POST, replaces the old program RAPOST2000 from SAP ERP classic asset accounting. For users, the same Transaction AFAB is being used, but behind the scenes, the new program significantly increases performance because it posts precalculated plan values rather than calculating these values at runtime. Planned depreciation values are updated in table FAAT_PLAN_VALUES.

Now, let's look at what options are available during the depreciation run. To start the depreciation run, follow the application menu path **Accounting • Financial Accounting • Fixed Assets • Periodic Processing • Depreciation Run • AFAB-Execute**, as shown in Figure 7.46.

Some key differences exist in the new depreciation program in SAP S/4HANA. Now, the depreciation run posts financial documents, which are updated at the asset level in table ACDOCA. Also, now the depreciation program can be run for multiple company codes at the same time. An additional field in the selection screen, **Accounting Principle**, allows you to run the depreciation either for a specific principle or for multiple principles at the same time. This approach might be required if several accounting principles have different periodic requirements. Another improvement is that now the depreciation run can be run multiple times for the same period, which replaces the repeat and restart run options in SAP ERP. As previously in SAP ERP, a test run can be run, and as before, the test run is limited to 1,000 assets at the same time. Also, as before, the real run has to be executed in background mode.

After executing the depreciation run, you can view the log by executing Transaction AFBP (Display Log). You'll see that the depreciation posts separate documents for each accounting principle and ledger. Thus, all postings occur in real time and are fully integrated with the general ledger.

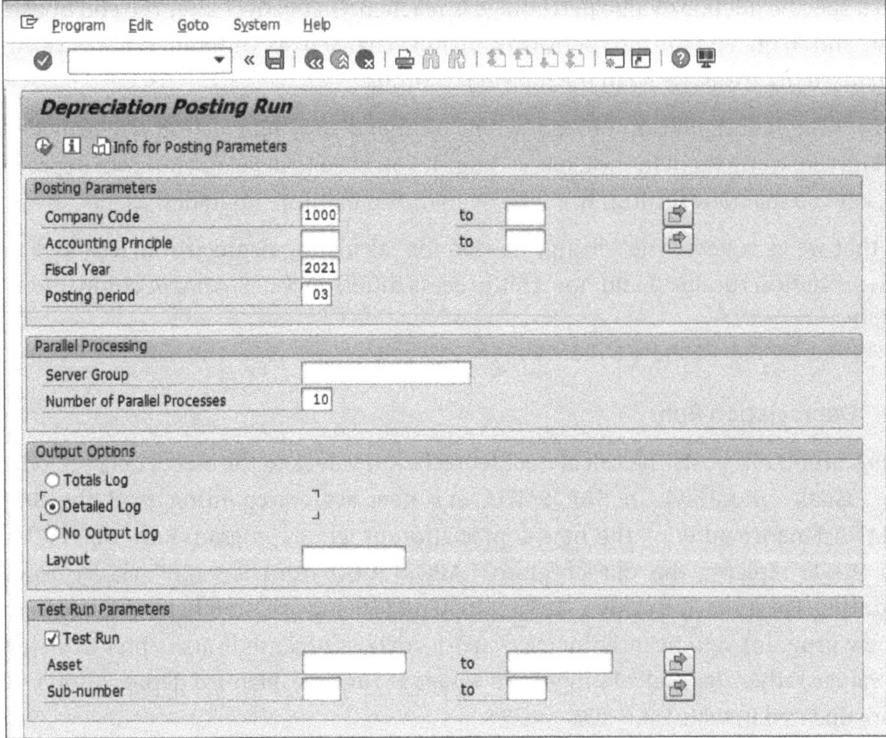

Figure 7.46 Depreciation Run

7.4.5 Revaluation

Revaluation is a process required in some countries where companies operate in a high-inflation environment and must periodically revalue assets to represent them at the current fair value. You'll need to configure the general ledger accounts in which revaluations will be posted using the menu path **Financial Accounting • Asset Accounting • Special Valuation • Revaluation of Fixed Assets • Maintain Accounts for Revaluation**. After selecting the proper chart of accounts and depreciation areas, you can assign revaluation accounts for acquisition and production costs (APC) and depreciation, as shown in Figure 7.47.

You'll also need to configure which depreciation areas are relevant for revaluation by following the menu path **Financial Accounting • Asset Accounting • Special Valuation • Revaluation of Fixed Assets • Revaluation for the Balance Sheet • Determine Depreciation Areas**. On this screen, you can select whether APC, depreciation, or both are relevant for depreciation, as shown in Figure 7.48.

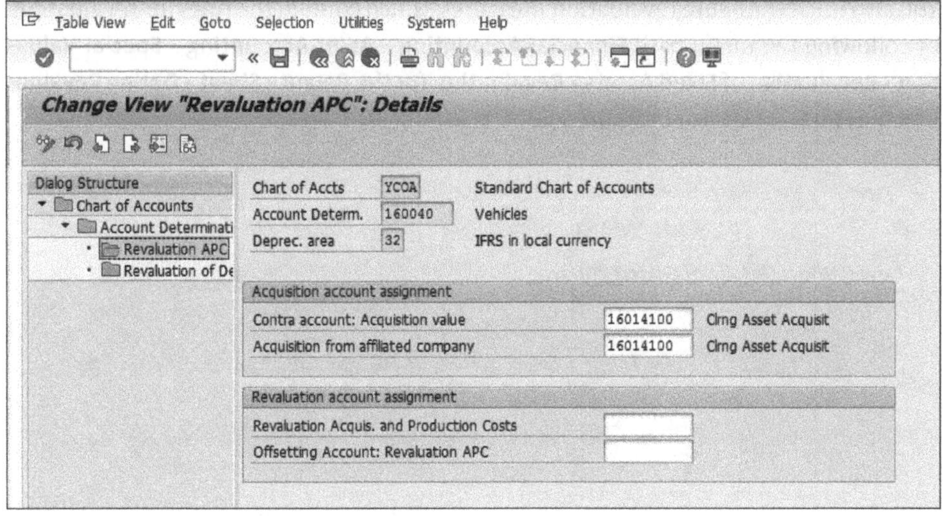

Figure 7.47 Configuring Revaluation Accounts

Table View Edit Goto Selection Utilities System Help

Change View "Asset Accounting: Management of replacement values": Over

Ar.	Name of Depreciation Area	RevlAPC	Revl...
01	Book Depreciation	☑	☐
31	Local GAAP in group currency	☑	☐
32	IFRS in local currency	☑	☐
33	IFRS in group currency	☑	☐
90	Federal Tax ACRS/MACRS	☑	☐
91	Alternative Minimum Tax	☑	☐
92	Adjusted Current Earnings	☑	☐
93	Corporate Earnings & Profits	☑	☐

Position... Entry 1 of 8

Figure 7.48 Determining Depreciation Areas for Revaluation

You also must configure revaluation measures, which contain the rules for revaluation, by following the menu path **Financial Accounting • Asset Accounting • Special Valuation • Revaluation of Fixed Assets • Revaluation for the Balance Sheet • Define Revaluation Measures**, as shown in Figure 7.49.

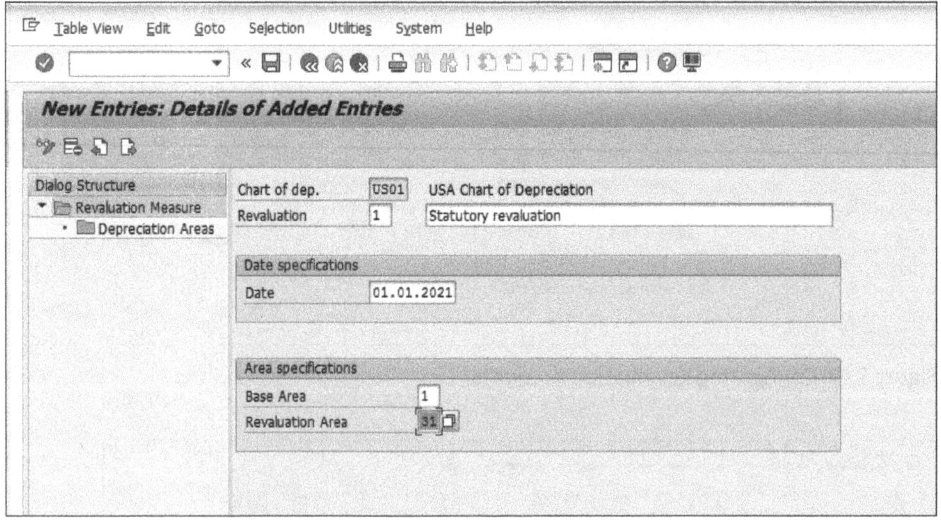

Figure 7.49 Defining a Revaluation Measure

On this screen, you'll configure the date on which the system will post the revaluation to fixed assets, the base depreciation area that will provide the values, and the revaluation area in which the revaluation will be posted.

The actual calculation rules usually are too complicated to be configured, so they need to be programmed using a custom implementation of BAdI FIAA_REAVLUATE_AS, which you can set by following the menu path **Financial Accounting • Asset Accounting • Special Valuation • Revaluation of Fixed Assets • Revaluation for the Balance Sheet • Implementations for Add-In for Revaluation and New Valuation.**

7.4.6 Manual Value Correction

We've covered various automatic valuation processes, such as depreciation and revaluation. You can also perform manual value corrections, in which you increase or decrease the value of an asset manually on an asset-by-asset basis.

The transactions to perform manual value correction are located at the application menu path **Accounting • Financial Accounting • Fixed Assets • Posting • Manual Value Correction**. The following four transactions are at your disposal:

- **ABZU—Write-Up**
  Used to manually increase the value of an asset.

- **ABMA—Manual Depreciation**
  Used to post manual depreciation to a specific asset.
- **ABAA—Unplanned Depreciation**
  Used to post additional unplanned depreciation.
- **ABMR—Transfer of Reserves**
  Used to create reserves for some asset transactions, such as the sale of undervalued assets.

To configure these processes, you must assign general ledger accounts. We assigned general ledger accounts for other processes previously, and we'll use the same menu path in this case: **SPRO • Financial Accounting • Asset Accounting • Integration with General Ledger Accounting • Assign G/L Accounts.**

In the depreciation section of the account determination, shown in Figure 7.50, you can optionally assign general ledger accounts for manual value corrections.

Special depreciation account assignment		
Accumulated dep. account special dep.		
Expense account for special depreciation		
Expense Account for Spec.Dep.Below Zero		
Revenue from write-up on special deprec.		

Unplanned depreciation account assignment		
Accumulated dep. account unpl. deprec.	17004000	Acc.Depr'n Motor Veh
Expense account for unplanned deprec.	64030000	Unsched.dep.Expense
P&LAct.Unpl.Dep.Below 0	64030000	Unsched.dep.Expense
Revenue from write-up on unplnd. deprec.	71010200	Gain from Write Up

Account assignment for transfer of reserves		
Val. adj. acct. for transfer of reserves		
Contra account for transferring reserves		
Revenue from w-up transfer of reserves		

Account assignment for revaluation on depreciation		
Reval. accumulated ord. depreciation	17004000	Acc.Depr'n Motor Veh
Offsetting accnt: Reval. ordinary deprc.	71015000	OffsetAcct Reval Dep

Interest account assignment		
Expense account for interest		
Clearing interest posting		
Intrst expense when book val.below zero		

Figure 7.50 Assign Manual Value Correction Accounts

7.4.7 Year-End Closing Activities

In SAP S/4HANA, the year-end closing process for fixed assets has been greatly simplified compared to SAP ERP. Balance carry-forward is a year-end closing procedure that transfers the year-end account balances as beginning balances for the next year. In SAP

S/4HANA, the balance carry-forward for fixed assets is part of the balance carry-forward transaction for the general ledger, which is available under the application menu path **Accounting • Financial Accounting • General Ledger • Periodic Processing • Closing • Carrying Forward • FAGLGVTR—Balance Carryforward**, as shown in Figure 7.51.

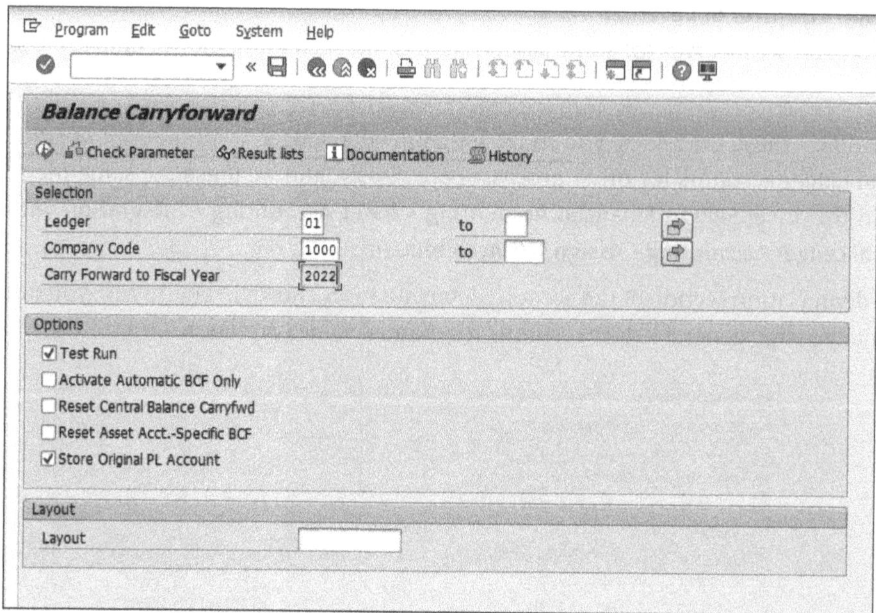

Figure 7.51 Balance Carry-Forward

SAP S/4HANA 2020 features some further improvements of the balance carry-forward program for fixed assets. In previous releases, the new fiscal year was opened at the start of processing before the processing of the individual assets. In SAP S/4HANA 2020, the new fiscal year is opened after the program has processed all assets successfully. Also, now the program not only processes the active assets but also processes deactivated assets.

Because fixed assets now is fully integrated with the general ledger, you no longer need additional asset accounting year-end closing programs, and the fiscal year change program RAJAWE00 (Transaction AJRW) from SAP ERP is obsolete and is no longer available. As APC postings in asset accounting are now posted to the general ledger in real time, in all depreciation areas, periodic APC postings are obsolete, and SAP ERP's Transaction ASKB is no longer supported. Also, you no longer need to reconcile the general ledger with fixed assets due to the real-time integration, so programs RAABST01 and RAABST02 are obsolete.

Now that we've covered the various valuation functions for fixed assets, it's time to look at the information system and SAP S/4HANA's powerful asset reports.

7.5 Information System

SAP S/4HANA comes with myriad standard asset reports, which greatly benefit from the streamlined real-time integration with the general ledger. We'll look at the main reports that the information system provides for assets and point out the key benefits of SAP S/4HANA's new asset accounting.

7.5.1 Asset Explorer

Asset explorer is the main report when you want to analyze a single asset. This report provides great integrated visibility since you can drill down from the asset values to the asset master record to the related documents to the related account assignment objects, such as general ledger account, cost center, and so on. To access the asset explorer, follow the application menu path **Accounting • Financial Accounting • Fixed Assets • Information System • Reports on Asset Accounting • Individual Asset • AW01N—Asset Explorer**. Then, enter a **Company Code** and **Asset**, as shown in Figure 7.52.

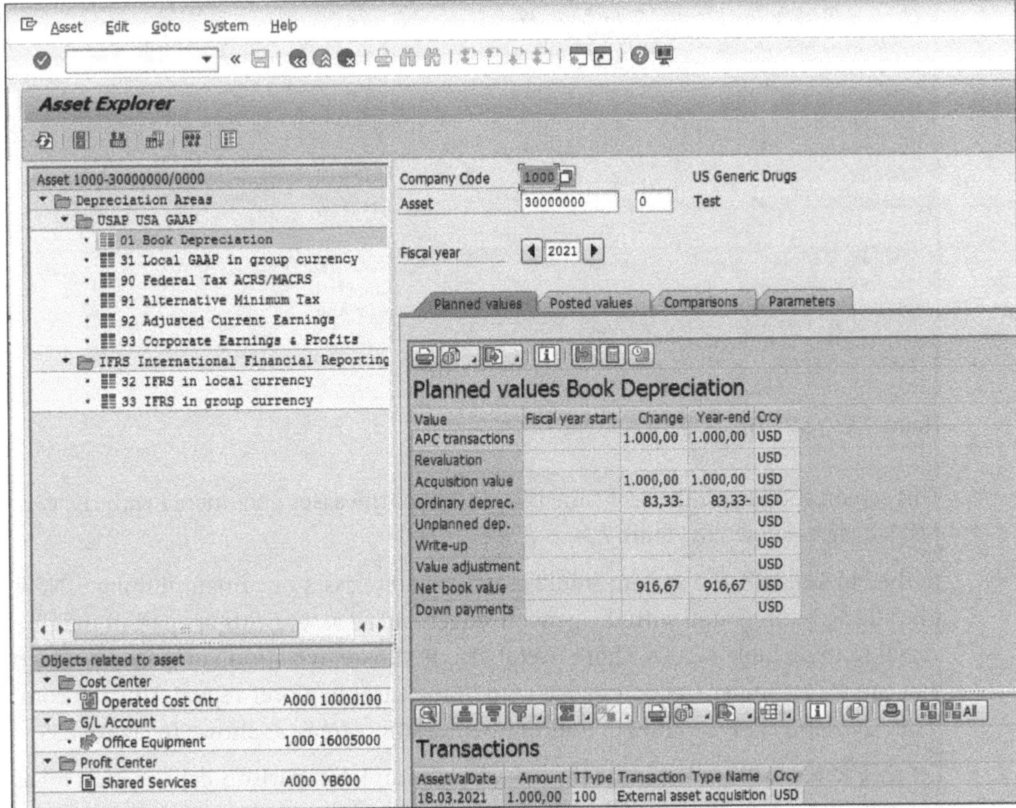

Figure 7.52 Asset Explorer

On the top-left side of the screen, you'll see the accounting principles and their related depreciation areas. You can navigate through these principles to switch between the different valuations and analyze their values. In the lower-left section of the screen, you'll see the objects related to the asset, such as the vendor from which the asset was acquired and the assigned cost center and general ledger account. On the right side, you'll see the values of the asset, separated by tabs for planned values, posted values, comparison, and depreciation parameters. In the planned section, you'll see the depreciation planned for the selected year, whereas in the posted section, you'll only see the depreciation already posted through the performed depreciation runs. Under the **Comparison** tab, you can compare the values between the depreciation areas.

In the lower section of the screen, you'll see the posted documents for the asset, and by double-clicking one of them, you can enter the document display overview. Once in a financial document related to the asset, you can view the asset accounting overview of the document by clicking the **Asset Accounting** button, as shown in Figure 7.53.

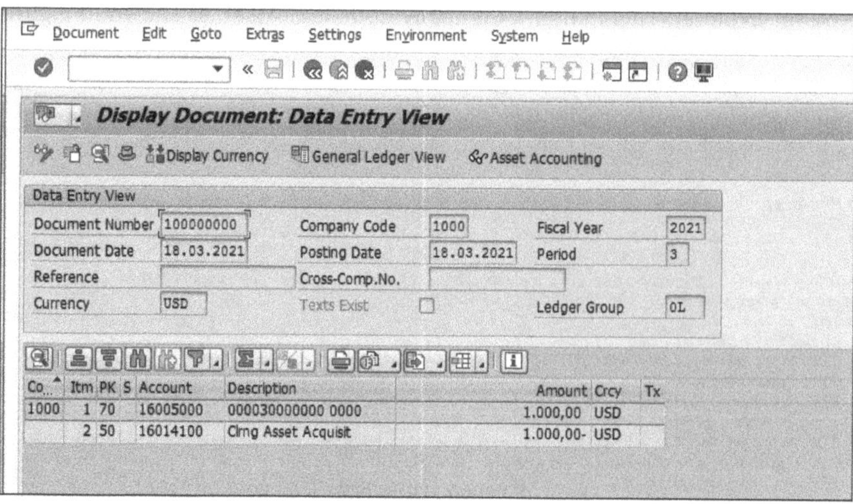

Figure 7.53 Asset Financial Document

This screen shows you the real-time integration of the asset documents with the general ledger, as shown in Figure 7.54.

In the old SAP ERP, the system would create separate asset document numbers. Now, everything is integrated with the general ledger and all asset fields are part of the Universal Journal, table ACDOCA. Quite useful also is the depreciation comparison, which you can access under the **Comparison** tab in the asset explorer report. This tab compares the depreciation values of multiple depreciation areas, as shown in Figure 7.55.

On this screen, you can select comparison years and comparison depreciation areas and readily see how the depreciation changes from year to year and between depreciation areas.

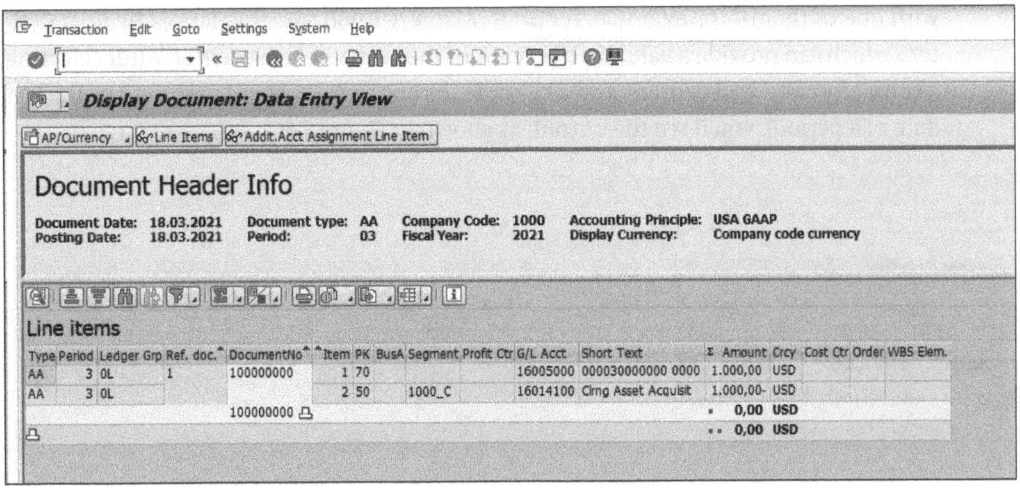

Figure 7.54 Asset Overview of Document

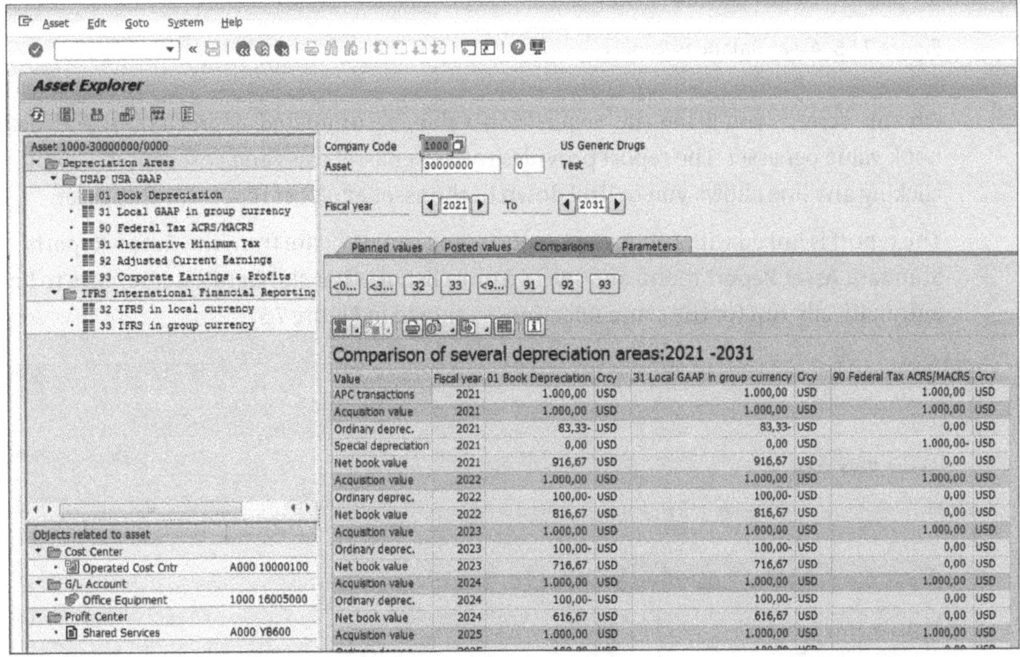

Figure 7.55 Depreciation Comparison in Asset Explorer

7.5.2 Asset Balance Reports

Many useful asset balance reports are available to help you analyze many or all assets simultaneously by depreciation area. These reports are available in the application menu under **Accounting • Financial Accounting • Fixed Assets • Information System • Reports on Asset Accounting • Asset Balances • Asset Lists • Asset Balances**. Let's start with one of them—for example, report S_ALR_87011966 (Asset Balances by Cost Center), which can provide a valuable overview of the assets per cost center. After selecting a company code, cost centers, and a key date to run the report (which should be the last date of a period), you'll see the output, as shown in Figure 7.56.

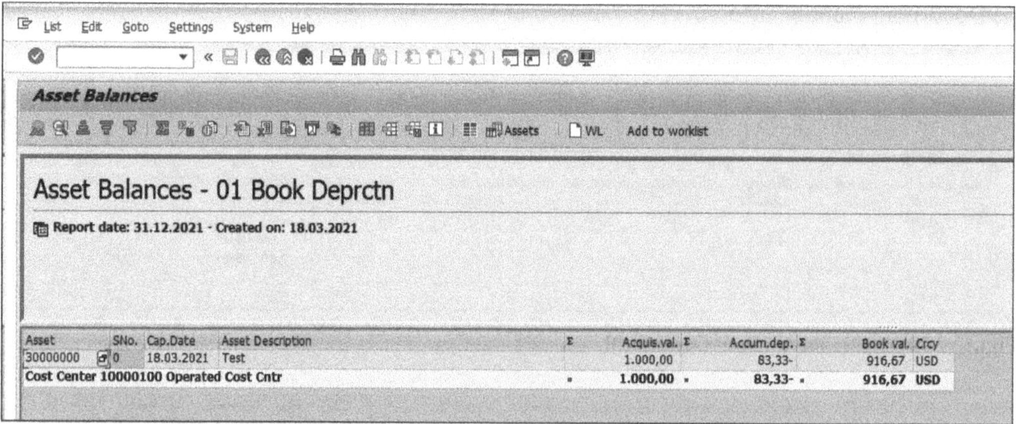

Figure 7.56 Asset Balances Report

On this screen, you'll see the acquisition value, accumulated depreciation, and net book value per asset. The report provides totals per asset class and cost center. Double-clicking any line allows you to drill down to the asset explorer report for this asset.

The report is linked with other asset reports. You can navigate from the **Goto • Reports • Standard Asset Report** menu and select from a list of other standard asset reports to be automatically run for the same selection, as shown in Figure 7.57.

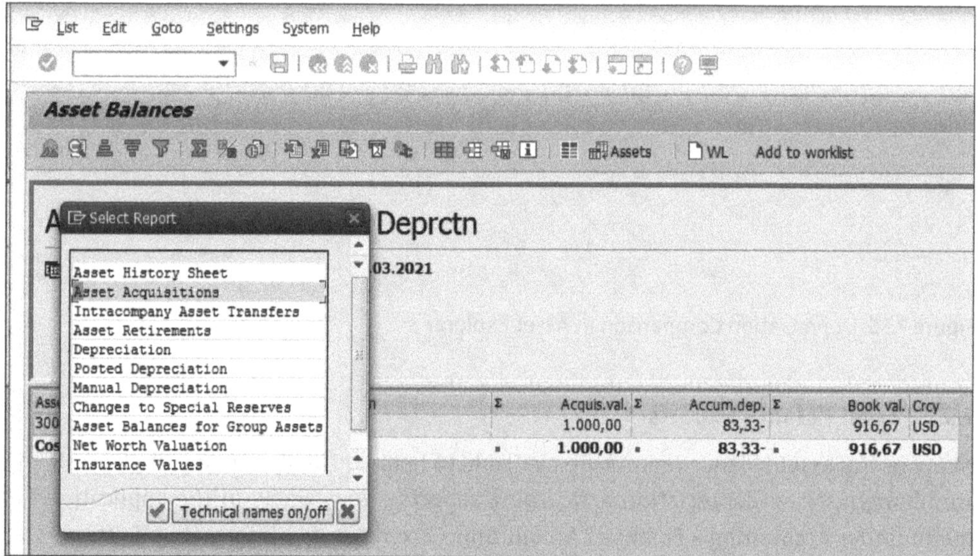

Figure 7.57 Drilldown to Other Asset Reports

You can double-click any of the linked reports, and it will be executed for the selected asset. For example, select **Asset Acquisitions** to see this report for the selected asset, as shown in Figure 7.58.

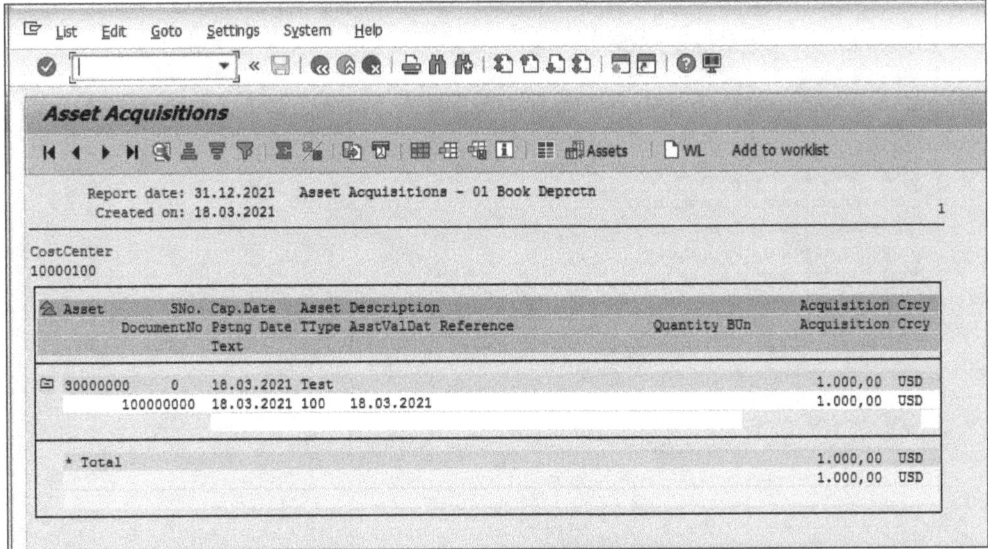

Figure 7.58 Asset Acquisitions Report

7.5.3 Asset History Sheet

Asset history sheets are important reports that show the full history of assets from their acquisition to their retirement. This report shows all transactions and therefore is suitable when you need detailed reporting on assets. This report is powerful and flexible because, unlike other asset reports, it provides the opportunity to configure your own layout with the so-called *history sheet version*. In SAP S/4HANA, an SAP Fiori app, called the Asset History Sheet app, works with key figure groups, which similarly groups together the transactions in specific cells of the report.

To configure history sheet versions, you must configure history sheet groups by following the menu path **Financial Accounting • Asset Accounting • Information System • Asset History Sheet • Define History Sheet Groups**, as shown in Figure 7.59.

Transaction types are assigned to these history sheet groups in the definition of the transaction type. For example, as shown in Figure 7.60, in its definition, asset transaction type 100 has been assigned history sheet group **10: Acquisition**.

Transaction types are logically assigned to history sheet groups such as acquisition, retirement, post-capitalization, and so on.

Table View Edit Goto Selection Utilities System Help
Change View ""Asset History Sheet Group and Name"": Overview
New Entries
Grp Name of Asset Hist. Sheet Group
10 Acquisition
12 Reverse acquisition in following years
15 Down payment
20 Retirement
25 Retirement of curr-yr acquisition
30 Retirmt transfer of prior-yr acquis.
31 Acquiring transfer of prior-yr acquis.
32 Retirmt transfer of curr-yr acquis.
33 Acquiring transfer of curr-yr acquis.
34 Retirmt transfer of prior-yr acquis. from AuC
35 Acquiring transfer of prior-yr acquis. from AuC
36 Retirmt transfer of curr-yr acquis. from AuC
37 Acquiring transfer of curr-yr acquis. from AuC
40 Post-capitalization
50 Allocation of investment support
70 Write-up special and ord. depreciation
Position...
Entry 1 of 24

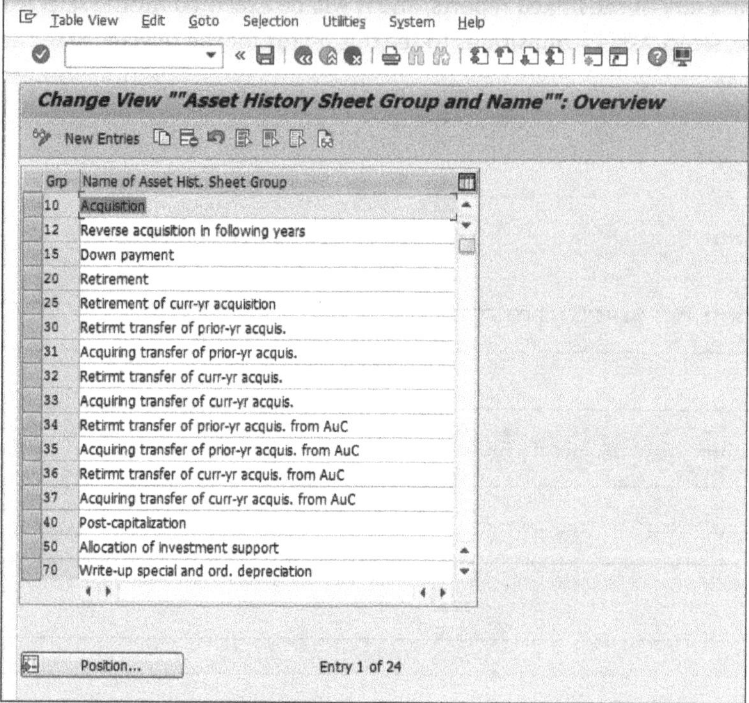

Figure 7.59 History Sheet Groups

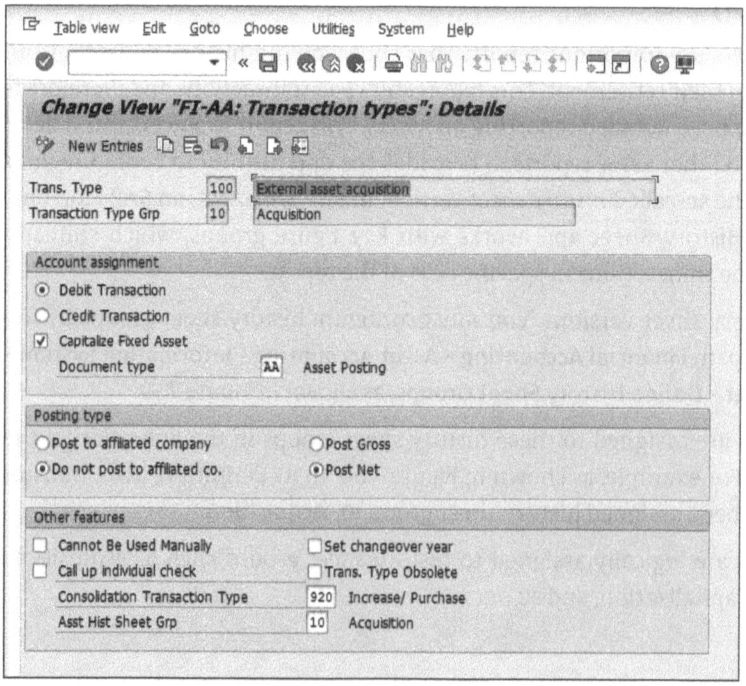

Table view Edit Goto Choose Utilities System Help
Change View "FI-AA: Transaction types": Details
New Entries
Trans. Type 100 External asset acquisition
Transaction Type Grp 10 Acquisition
Account assignment
Debit Transaction
Credit Transaction
Capitalize Fixed Asset
Document type AA Asset Posting
Posting type
Post to affiliated company
Do not post to affiliated co.
Post Gross
Post Net
Other features
Cannot Be Used Manually
Call up individual check
Consolidation Transaction Type 920 Increase/ Purchase
Asst Hist Sheet Grp 10 Acquisition
Set changeover year
Trans. Type Obsolete

Figure 7.60 History Sheet Group in Transaction Type

The next step is to configure history sheet versions by following the menu path **Financial Accounting • Asset Accounting • Information System • Asset History Sheet • Define History Sheet Versions**, as shown in Figure 7.61.

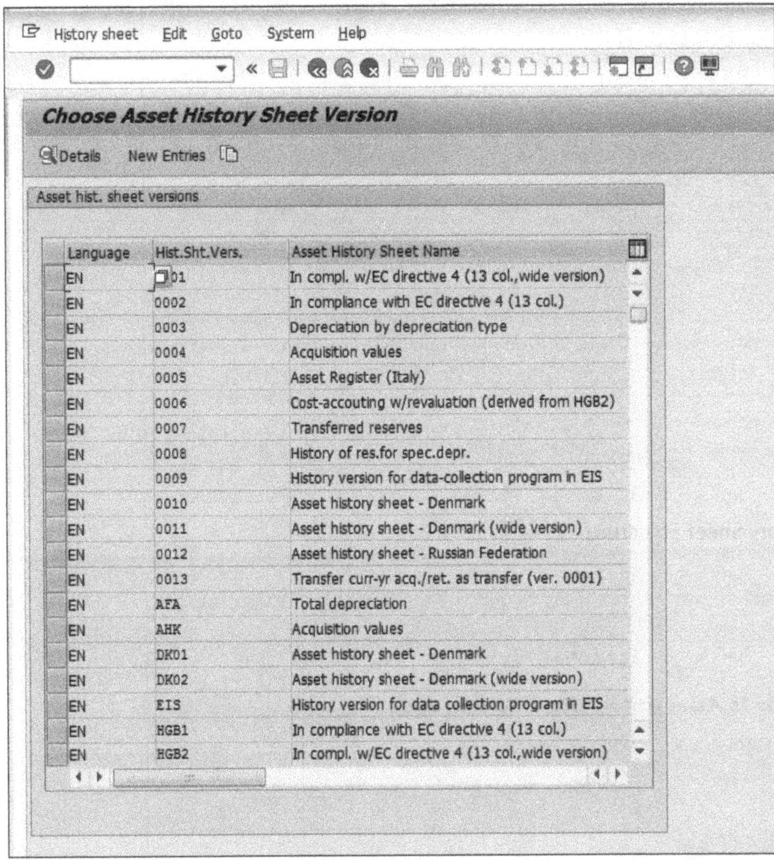

Language	Hist.Sht.Vers.	Asset History Sheet Name
EN	0001	In compl. w/EC directive 4 (13 col.,wide version)
EN	0002	In compliance with EC directive 4 (13 col.)
EN	0003	Depreciation by depreciation type
EN	0004	Acquisition values
EN	0005	Asset Register (Italy)
EN	0006	Cost-accouting w/revaluation (derived from HGB2)
EN	0007	Transferred reserves
EN	0008	History of res.for spec.depr.
EN	0009	History version for data-collection program in EIS
EN	0010	Asset history sheet - Denmark
EN	0011	Asset history sheet - Denmark (wide version)
EN	0012	Asset history sheet - Russian Federation
EN	0013	Transfer curr-yr acq./ret. as transfer (ver. 0001)
EN	AFA	Total depreciation
EN	AHK	Acquisition values
EN	DK01	Asset history sheet - Denmark
EN	DK02	Asset history sheet - Denmark (wide version)
EN	EIS	History version for data collection program in EIS
EN	HGB1	In compliance with EC directive 4 (13 col.)
EN	HGB2	In compl. w/EC directive 4 (13 col.,wide version)

Figure 7.61 History Sheet Versions

SAP provides many standard history sheet versions, which already cover asset reporting requirements in many countries. You can create your own version, however, preferably by copying an existing one and adapting it. For example, select version 0001 and select **Copy History Sheet Version** from the menu. Then, copy and set your own 4-character name, preferably in the Z name range. Then, you can see the columns and cells of the report, as shown in Figure 7.62.

You can double-click any cell to be taken its definition. For example, click **Acquisition** under line 02, column 10. You'll see which history sheet groups should appear there, as shown in Figure 7.63. History sheet groups indicated with **X** appear in this cell, whereas those indicated with a period (.) appear elsewhere in the report.

History sheet Edit Goto System Help

Maintain Asset History Sheet Version: EN Z001

Details Left column Right column

Ast.Hist.Sht.Version Z001 Hisotry sheet test version

Language Key EN

Hist.sheet complete

Hist. sheet positions

		Column 00	Column 10	Column 20	Column 30	Column 40
Line	02	APC FY start	Acquisition	Retirement	Transfer	Post-capital.
Line	04	Dep. FY start	Dep. for year	Dep.retir.	Dep.transfer	Dep.post-cap.
Line	06	Bk.val.FY strt				
Line						
Line						
Line						
Line						
Line						
Line						
Line						

Figure 7.62 History Sheet Structure

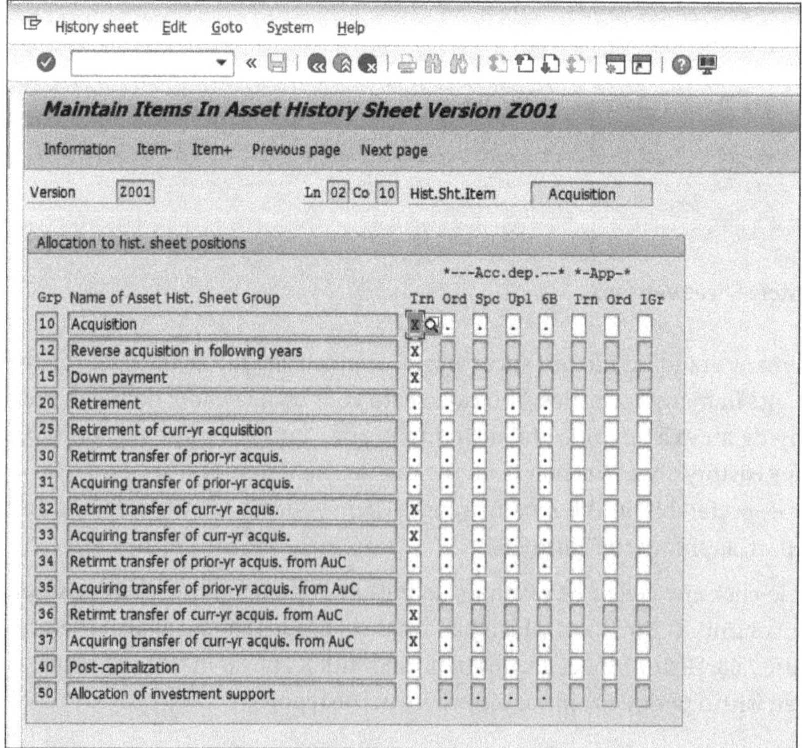

Figure 7.63 History Sheet Cell Definition

Once you're done modifying the history sheet version, you can save your setting. Then, you can run the history sheet report from the application menu path **Accounting • Financial Accounting • Fixed Assets • Information System • Reports on Asset Accounting • Notes to Financial Statements • International • S_ALR_87011990—Asset History Sheet.** In addition to the standard report selections, such as company code, asset classes, asset numbers, and so on, you also can select history sheet versions in the **Further Settings** section of the selection screen, where you can select your own version or one of the standard ones. After executing, you'll see the output based on the history sheet version selected, as shown in Figure 7.64.

List Edit Goto Settings System Help

Asset History Sheet

Assets WL Add to worklist

Report date: 31.12.2021 Asset History Sheet - 01 Book Deprctn
Created on: 18.03.2021 Hisotry sheet test version (incomplete) 1

CompanyCode	BusinessArea	Bal.SheetItem	Bal.Sh.AcctAPC	AssetClass
1000		13	16005000	3300

Asset SNo. Cap.Date	Asset Description			Crcy		
APC FY start	Acquisition	Retirement	Transfer	Post-capital.	Invest.support	Current APC
Dep. FY start	Dep. for year	Dep.retir.	Dep.transfer	Dep.post-cap.	Write-ups	Accumul. dep.
Bk.val.FY strt						Curr.bk.val.
30000000 0 18.03.2021	Test			USD		
0,00	1.000,00	0,00	0,00	0,00	0,00	1.000,00
0,00	83,33-	0,00	0,00	0,00	0,00	83,33-
0,00						916,67
* Asset Class	3300	Office Equipment		USD		
0,00	1.000,00	0,00	0,00	0,00	0,00	1.000,00
0,00	83,33-	0,00	0,00	0,00	0,00	83,33-
0,00						916,67
** Bal.Sh.Acct APC	16005000	Office Equipment		USD		
0,00	1.000,00	0,00	0,00	0,00	0,00	1.000,00
0,00	83,33-	0,00	0,00	0,00	0,00	83,33-
0,00						916,67
*** Balance Sheet Item	13	Property, Plant, and Equipment		USD		
0,00	1.000,00	0,00	0,00	0,00	0,00	1.000,00
0,00	83,33-	0,00	0,00	0,00	0,00	83,33-
0,00						916,67
****				USD		
0,00	1.000,00	0,00	0,00	0,00	0,00	1.000,00
0,00	83,33-	0,00	0,00	0,00	0,00	83,33-
0,00						916,67

Figure 7.64 History Sheet Report

If you're going to use the Asset History Sheet app, you can configure key figure groups in the menu path **Financial Accounting • Asset Accounting • Information System • Asset History Sheet • Define Key Figure Groups for Asset History Sheet (Fiori)**, as shown in Figure 7.65.

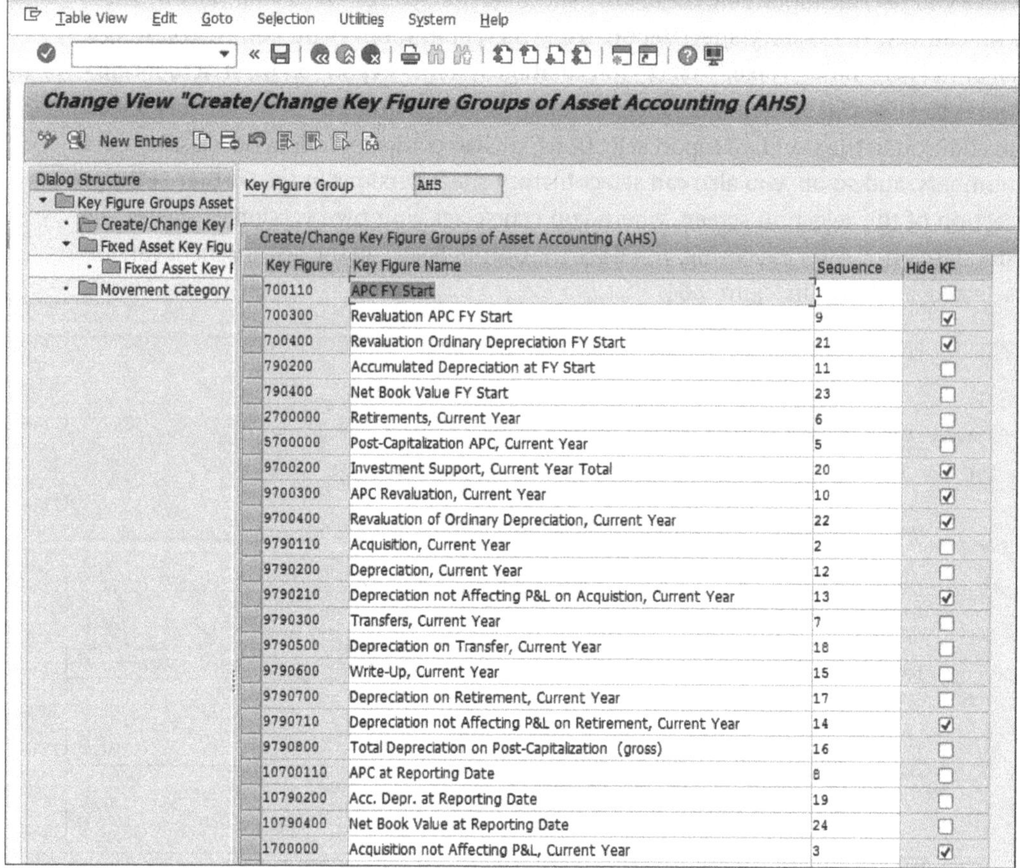

Figure 7.65 Defining a Key Figure Group

Similar to history sheet versions, key figure groups group together the transactions for report purposes. Each key figure is defined with its sequence in the report. You can use standard key figure groups or define your own. You can use standard groups **AHS: Asset History Sheet (Posted Values, No Hierarchy)** and **AHS_HRY: Asset History Sheet (Posted Values, Wth Hierarchy)** for posted values. For planned values, you can use **AHS_PLAN: Asset History Sheet (Plan Values, No Hierarchy)** and **AHS_HRY_PL: Asset History Sheet (Plan Values, With Hierarchy).**

With that topic, we've finished our discussion of the asset history sheet report and the information system for assets. Of course, you can explore the many other standard reports available in the information system. They work similarly to the reports we discussed in this chapter and don't require additional configuration.

7.6 Summary

We covered a lot of material, and now, you should be able to configure and use fixed assets in SAP S/4HANA. You've learned about the most important customizing transactions and recommended settings for them, so you can either configure fixed assets in a new greenfield implementation or adapt your current settings from an existing SAP ERP system in a brownfield implementation.

We explained the fundamental differences between the new asset accounting provided by SAP S/4HANA and the classic asset accounting from SAP ERP. Now, you understand how immensely beneficial and powerful SAP S/4HANA is with its real-time integration between fixed assets and the general ledger. After properly configuring fixed assets, you'll be able to have powerful real-time reports on your assets, based on multiple accounting and tax frameworks. This capability is invaluable for most of today's global businesses that want to operate in multiple countries and regions on the same enterprise resource planning (ERP) system but need transparent reporting based on different accounting standards.

Now, you should have a good understanding of the organizational structure in fixed assets and what options are available for representing the various countries and valuations using charts of depreciation and depreciation areas. You now know how to set up asset master data efficiently in well-defined asset classes. You know how to configure and process various asset transactions. You understand how to properly set up multiple valuation principles and execute your depreciation runs. Last but not least, you're familiar with the various reports in fixed assets, including the highly customizable asset history sheet report.

Thus, we've finished our guide to configuring fixed assets, and we'll move on next to bank accounting.

Chapter 8
Bank Accounting

This chapter provides step-by-step instructions for configuring bank processes in SAP S/4HANA, including generating Single Euro Payments Area (SEPA)-compliant outgoing payment files and reconciling open items automatically using electronic bank statements.

8

Bank accounting refers to both outgoing and incoming payment processes. Rather than a separate area in SAP S/4HANA, bank accounting is part of accounts payable and accounts receivable, but its processes and settings are quite specific and deserved to be explained in its own chapter rather than discussing outgoing payments as part of accounts payable and the incoming payments as part of accounts receivable.

In this chapter, we'll help you configure the following:

- Bank master data—house banks and bank accounts
- Automatic payment program
- Payment files
- Electronic bank statements

Let's start with setting up the master data required for the bank processes.

8.1 Master Data

Banks must be defined as master data objects in the system, which are called *bank keys*. To assign a bank in the customer or vendor master record, it first needs to be created as a bank key. In addition, the banks at which your organization has accounts must be defined as house banks, which require a lot more configuration. We'll then discuss the creation of bank accounts and International Bank Account Numbers (IBANs). We'll also discuss simplified bank general ledger accounts, which is the new solution in SAP S/4HANA 2020 to reduce the number of general ledger bank accounts.

8.1.1 Bank Keys

The first step is to create bank keys for all the needed banks. A good practice is to automatically load all the banks in the country where you implement the system to avoid having missing banks later on when creating vendor and customer master data. In most countries, a list of banks in the country can be obtained from the central bank or from another financial institution. SAP provides the necessary programs to upload such a file automatically, which will load the banks as bank keys in the system. These programs are located at the menu path **Cross-Application Components • Bank Directory • Bank Directory Data Transfer**. You'll find two programs: **Transfer Bank Directory Data—International**, which uses the international SWIFT format, and **Transfer Bank Directory Data—Country-Specific**, which can work with country-specific formats.

For the US, select **Transfer Bank Directory Data—Country-Specific**. Figure 8.1 shows the selection screen for the program to transfer bank data.

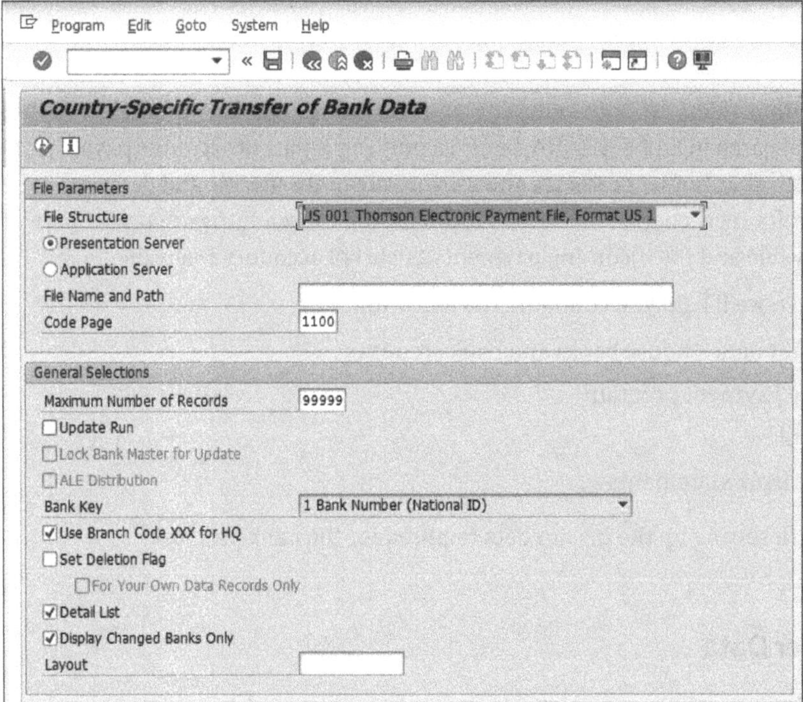

Figure 8.1 Importing a Bank Directory

In the **File Structure** field, you can select from multiple formats that SAP provides. For example, for the US, you could choose the **Thomson Electronic Payment File** (format **US1**) option. You can select a file either from the application or the presentation server and its code page. When you select the **Update Run** checkbox, the system creates the bank keys; otherwise, the system runs in test mode.

You can also define additional file formats by following the menu path **Cross-Application Components • Bank Directory • Bank Directory Data Transfer • Define File Formats for Country-Specific Bank Directories**. The system issues a warning that this table is a cross-client table, and after confirming that you want to proceed, you'll see a list of available bank import formats, as shown in Figure 8.2.

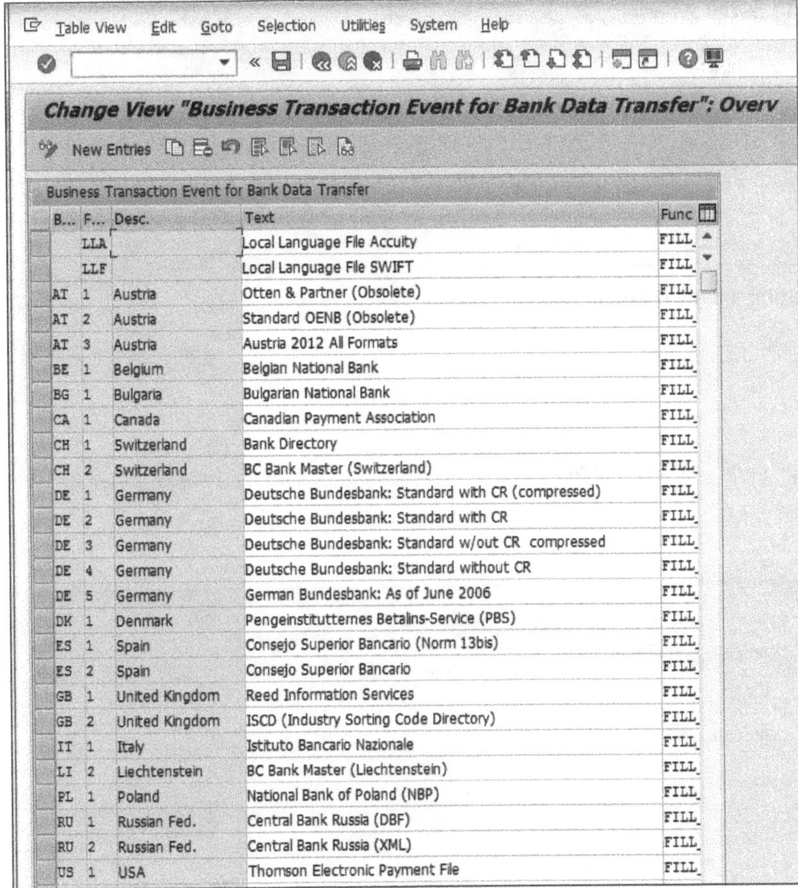

B...	F...	Desc.	Text	Func
	LLA		Local Language File Accuity	FILL_
	LLF		Local Language File SWIFT	FILL_
AT	1	Austria	Otten & Partner (Obsolete)	FILL_
AT	2	Austria	Standard OENB (Obsolete)	FILL_
AT	3	Austria	Austria 2012 All Formats	FILL_
BE	1	Belgium	Belgian National Bank	FILL_
BG	1	Bulgaria	Bulgarian National Bank	FILL_
CA	1	Canada	Canadian Payment Association	FILL_
CH	1	Switzerland	Bank Directory	FILL_
CH	2	Switzerland	BC Bank Master (Switzerland)	FILL_
DE	1	Germany	Deutsche Bundesbank: Standard with CR (compressed)	FILL_
DE	2	Germany	Deutsche Bundesbank: Standard with CR	FILL_
DE	3	Germany	Deutsche Bundesbank: Standard w/out CR compressed	FILL_
DE	4	Germany	Deutsche Bundesbank: Standard without CR	FILL_
DE	5	Germany	German Bundesbank: As of June 2006	FILL_
DK	1	Denmark	Pengeinstituttemes Betalins-Service (PBS)	FILL_
ES	1	Spain	Consejo Superior Bancario (Norm 13bis)	FILL_
ES	2	Spain	Consejo Superior Bancario	FILL_
GB	1	United Kingdom	Reed Information Services	FILL_
GB	2	United Kingdom	ISCD (Industry Sorting Code Directory)	FILL_
IT	1	Italy	Istituto Bancario Nazionale	FILL_
LI	2	Liechtenstein	BC Bank Master (Liechtenstein)	FILL_
PL	1	Poland	National Bank of Poland (NBP)	FILL_
RU	1	Russian Fed.	Central Bank Russia (DBF)	FILL_
RU	2	Russian Fed.	Central Bank Russia (XML)	FILL_
US	1	USA	Thomson Electronic Payment File	FILL_

Figure 8.2 Bank Import File Formats

The formats are defined per country. You can create a new format using the **New Entries** option from the top menu. If you need additional nonstandard formats, you'll need to work with your development team to develop a new functional module, which you would assign in the **Func. Mod.** (functional module) column.

You can also create bank keys manually using Transaction FI01. This approach may be needed when a bank is used in a business partner master record, but the bank key does not exist. You'll need to enter the bank country and bank key, as shown in Figure 8.3.

Then, press [Enter], and you're transferred to the bank key screen, where you can enter the details of the bank, as shown in Figure 8.4.

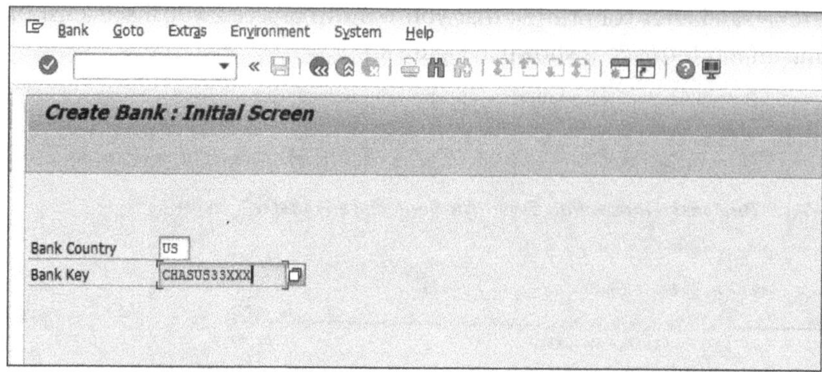

Figure 8.3 Creating a Bank Manually

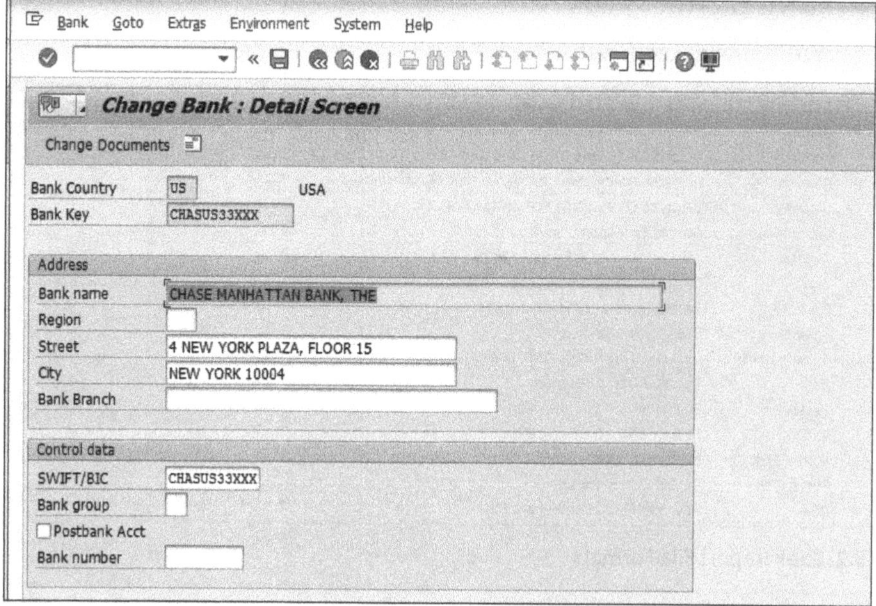

Figure 8.4 Entering Bank Details

The following fields must be configured:

- **Bank name**
  The legal name of the bank.
- **Street**
  The legal address of the bank.
- **City**
  City of the bank.
- **SWIFT/BIC**
  The bank code—SWIFT, BIC, or US routing number.

Save your entries, and then, you can use the bank key in your business partner master data.

8.1.2 House Banks

A *house bank* is a bank your company is doing business with. You'll need to create the bank key as a house bank on the company code level by following the application menu path **Accounting • Financial Accounting • Banks • Master Data • House Banks and House Bank Accounts • FI12_HBANK—Manage House Banks** or Transaction FI12_HBANK. As shown in Figure 8.5, first you need to select the company code.

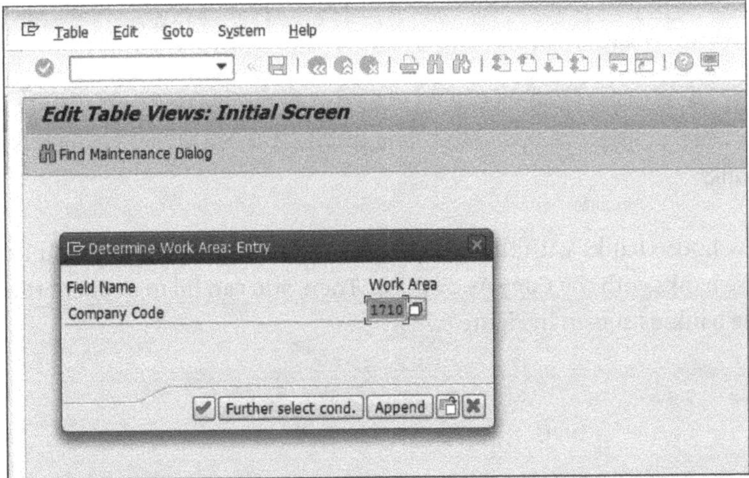

Figure 8.5 Selecting a Company Code

Proceed by clicking the [✔] button. On the next screen, shown in Figure 8.6, you can define house banks for each company code. The following fields should be configured:

- **House bank**
  This field is for freely definable code that defines the house banks. A good practice is to follow a naming convention that includes some letters from the bank's name or some other logical sequence within the company code.
- **Bank ctry. (bank country)**
  The country key of the bank.
- **Bank Key**
  The bank key you defined in the previous step.
- **Bank Name**
  The bank name associated with the key, which is populated automatically.

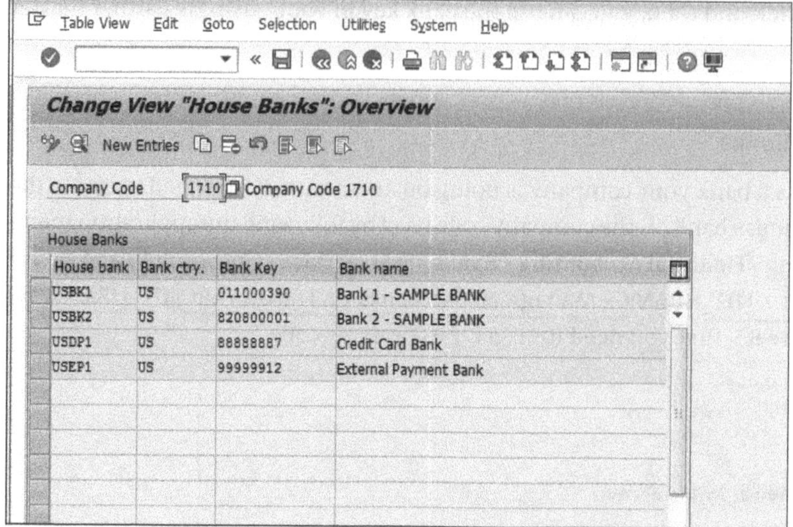

Figure 8.6 House Banks

You can create new house banks with the **New Entries** option from the top menu or copy existing house banks with the **Copy As...** option. Then, you can fill in or adapt the details of the house bank, as shown in Figure 8.7.

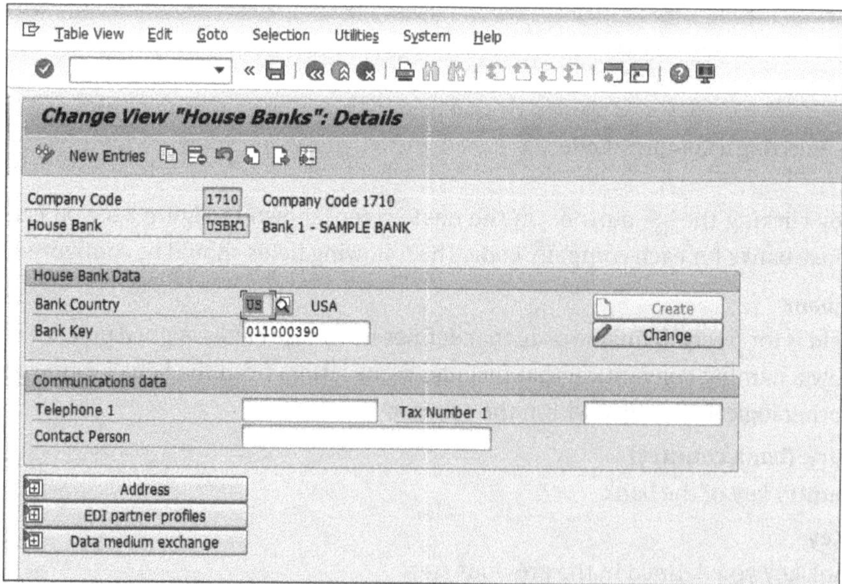

Figure 8.7 House Bank Details

Click the **Address** button to expand the **Address** and **Control Data** sections, as shown in Figure 8.8.

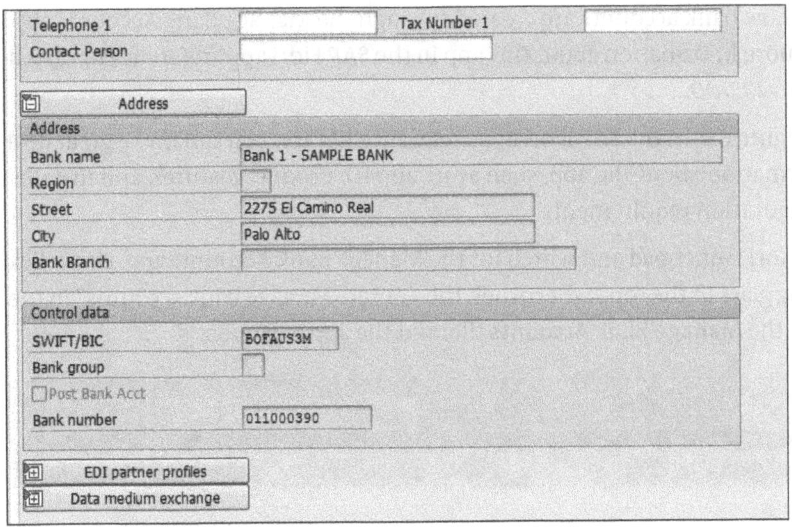

Figure 8.8 Address and Control Fields of Bank Key

On this screen, you can provide additional information about the address and the bank number.

Other settings relate to house banks in the payment program configuration, but we'll examine these settings in detail in Section 8.2.

8.1.3 Bank Accounts and International Bank Account Numbers

Bank account maintenance has been changed dramatically in SAP S/4HANA. In the older SAP ERP releases, bank accounts were transported between clients, whereas in SAP S/4HANA, they're considered master data, and their maintenance is considered the responsibility of the treasury department. As such, SAP now offers the SAP Fiori Manage Bank Accounts app to maintain the bank accounts, but there's more. In fact, two options are available:

- **Bank Account Management Lite (BAM Lite)**
  This option is included in the overall SAP S/4HANA license. With this option, the maintenance of bank accounts happens exclusively through the SAP Fiori Bank Account Management Lite app.
- **Bank Account Management (BAM)**
  This option requires an additional license for SAP Cash Management, but in addition to the SAP Fiori Bank Account Management app, you can also use workflow-based processes to maintain bank accounts.

For companies with complex treasury processes, we recommend SAP Cash Management and full BAM; otherwise, BAM Lite offers all the functionality of the previous SAP GUI transactions plus the SAP Fiori user interface (UI).

Now, let's see how bank accounts are created through the Manage Bank Accounts app. You can find more information about this app in the SAP Fiori apps reference library at *http://s-prs.co/v485700*.

As shown in Figure 8.9, in the SAP Fiori apps reference library, you can find a great deal of useful information about the app, such as its app ID, product features, and installation and configuration requirements.

Start the SAP Fiori launchpad and search for the Manage Bank Accounts app. First, click the magnifying glass in the top-right corner, then enter "Manage bank accounts" in the text box. Click the **Manage Bank Accounts** tile, and the app will open.

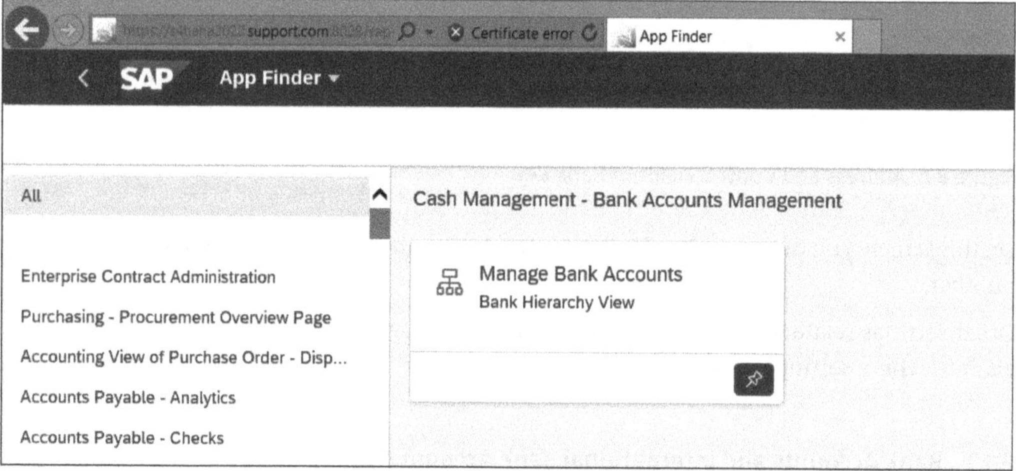

Figure 8.9 SAP Fiori Manage Bank Accounts App

You can create a new bank account by clicking the **New Bank Account** button, shown in Figure 8.10.

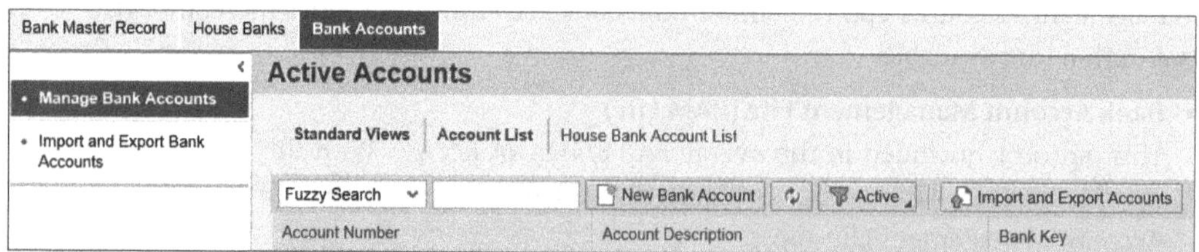

Figure 8.10 Managing Bank Accounts

On the next screen, enter bank account details, as shown in Figure 8.11. Fields marked with an asterisk (*) are required. You must enter an account opening date, company code, account holder, bank country, bank key (the key we created in Section 8.1.1), currency, IBAN, account number, account description, and account type.

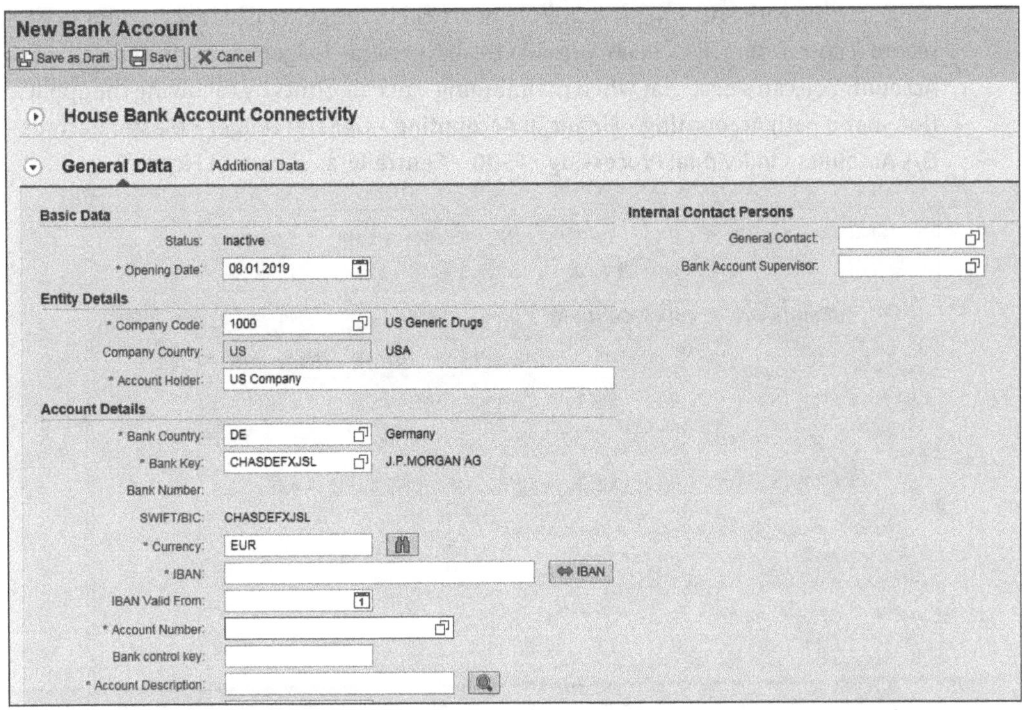

Figure 8.11 Creating a Bank Account

When you click the **IBAN** button, the system can propose an IBAN for you based on the account number and bank key. IBAN is the international standard for identifying bank accounts. Once you're ready, you can save by clicking the **Save** button or save as a draft by clicking the **Save as Draft** button.

> **Note**
>
> As mentioned, bank accounts are master data. But you can find more information about transferring bank accounts between clients in SAP Note 2437574.

8.1.4 Simplified Bank General Ledger Accounts

SAP S/4HANA 2020 came up with a simplified solution to minimize the number of bank general ledger accounts. Until now, separate bank general ledger accounts should have been created for each house bank account following a naming convention such as:

- Ending with "0": Main bank account
- Ending with "1": Receiving account
- Ending with "2": Payment account (and so on, for the different type of bank accounts)

Now, starting with SAP S/4HANA 2020, a new field in the general ledger account master record central data has been provided—the general ledger account type **C: Cash Account**. You can select that when maintaining bank accounts by following the application menu path **Accounting • Financial Accounting • General Ledger • Master Records • G/L Accounts • Individual Processing • FS00 – Centrally**, as shown in Figure 8.12.

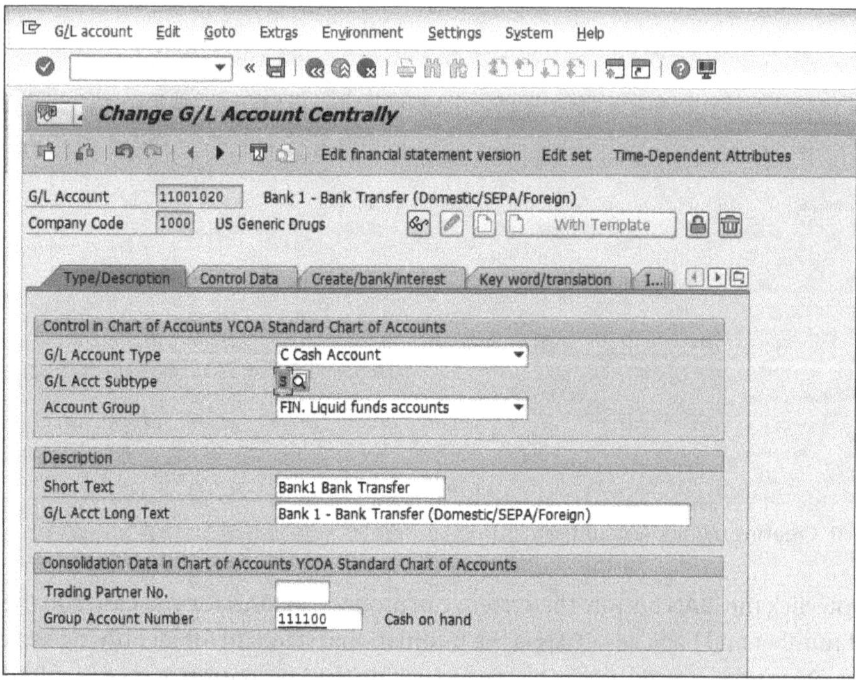

Figure 8.12 General Ledger Account Type Cash Account

In the **G/L Account Type** field, select the new type **C: Cash Account**. Then, in the **G/L Acct Subtype** field, you must select one of the following subtypes, as shown in Figure 8.13:

- **B: Bank Reconciliation Account**
- **S: Bank Subaccount**
- **P: Petty Cash**

The house bank and account will be populated for all bank postings including bank reconciliation transactions. Thus, all house banks can use single set of general ledger bank accounts.

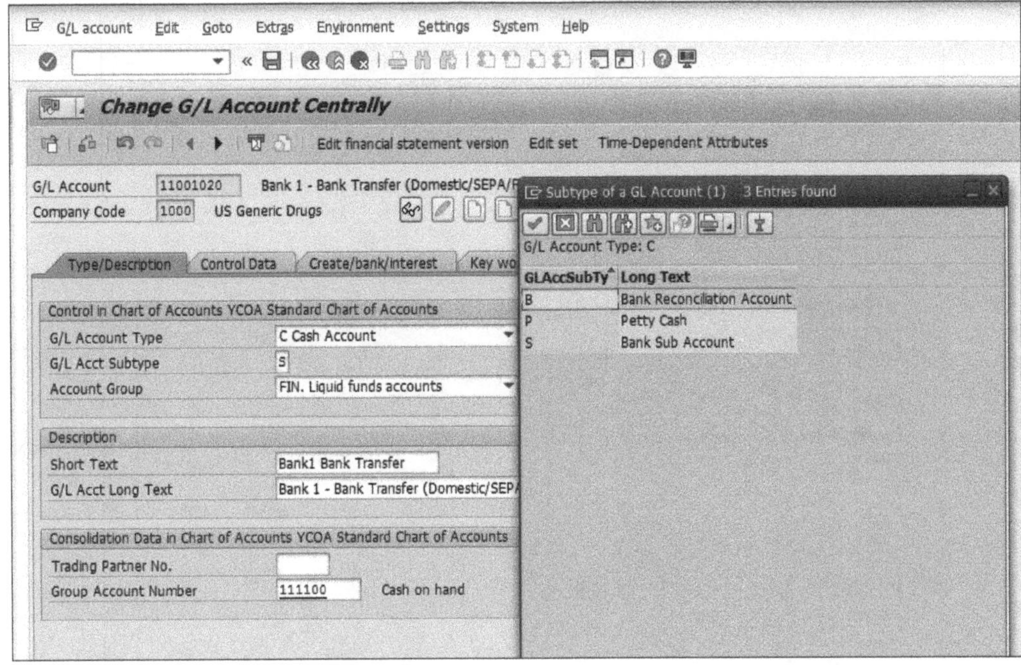

Figure 8.13 Cash Account Subtypes

8.2 Automatic Payment Program

The automatic payment program is a central point of all payment functions in SAP S/4HANA, as it was in previous SAP ERP releases. All automatic payment processes—both outgoing and incoming—are managed through the payment program. It serves to close open vendor and customer items that match its selection criteria, to post payments, and to generate payment media such as payment files or checks, as well as supporting documentation such as payment advices and payment lists.

In this section, we'll discuss the parameters and global settings of the automatic payment program. We'll then move on to discuss payment methods and bank determinations, before closing out our discussion with a look at some common issues with such payment programs.

8.2.1 Automatic Payment Program Parameters

The automatic payment program is available at the application menu path **Accounting • Financial Accounting • Accounts Payable • Periodic Processing • F110—Payments**. Figure 8.14 shows the parameter selections of the payment program.

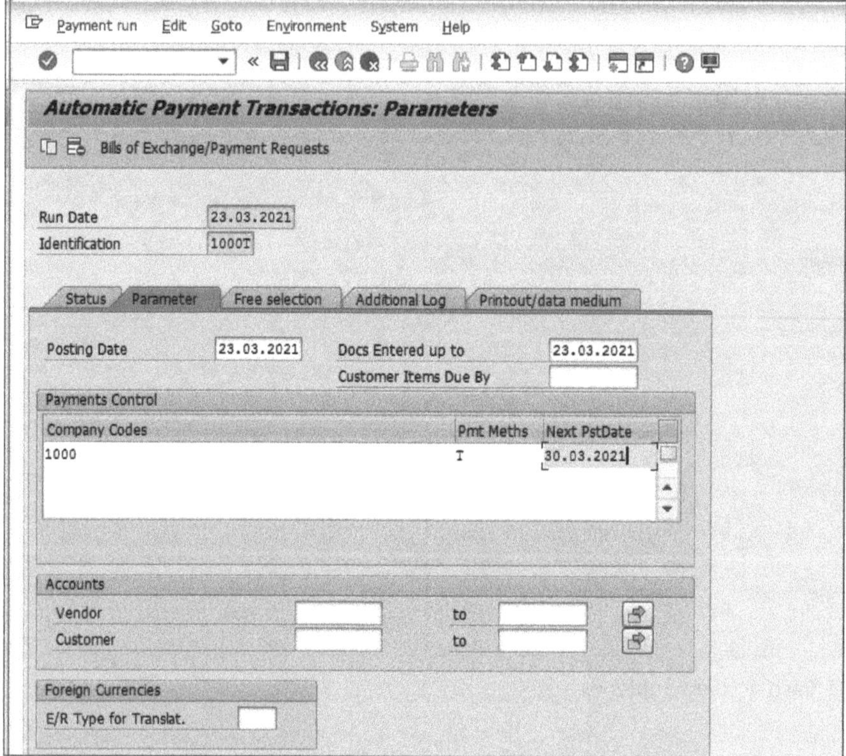

Figure 8.14 Automatic Payment Program

The following fields on this screen are important:

- **Run Date**
  When you run the payment program, you create a payment run, which includes certain selections of open items to be paid. This payment run is uniquely identified with two parameters: run date and identification. The run date is not the posting or payment date; it's just used to identify the payment run and normally is the creation date of the payment run.
- **Identification**
  This other field, in combination with the run date, uniquely identifies the payment run. Normally, in one day, multiple payment runs would occur, so their identification names are important. Using a good, logical naming convention for runs makes sense so they can be easily identified—for example, starting with an abbreviation of the bank name or the country for which the payments are relevant.
- **Posting Date**
  This field is the posting date of the payment documents that clear the open items.
- **Docs Entered up to**
  Open items with posting dates up to this date will be selected.

- **Company Codes**
  The run could be for one or multiple company codes, which are specified in this field.
- **Pmnt Meths (payment methods)**
  Open items with these payment methods will be selected. The payment method determines how an open item should be paid (e.g., bank transfer or check). We'll discuss the configuration of payment methods shortly.
- **Next PstDate (next posting date)**
  Used to check the due dates of open items. If an item is overdue on the date of the next payment run or will lose its cash discount, the item will be paid in this payment run.
- **Accounts**
  In this field, you'll enter a range of vendor and/or customer accounts for which open items are to be processed.

The automatic payment program consists of two steps: a payment proposal and a payment run. A *payment proposal* is like a test run; it provides you with a list of proposed payments, which you can check and analyze before actually making payments and closing open items. It also provides error information for any items that couldn't be paid due to various reasons, such as missing payment methods or a missing bank account in the master record. The *payment run* makes postings to bank accounts and clears open items, then generates payment files or checks (although you also have the option to generate the payment media during the payment proposal).

Let's examine the configuration needed for the payment program.

8.2.2 Automatic Payment Program Global Settings

The configuration of the payment program consists of multiple steps on the country and company code levels. These settings are located at the menu path **Financial Accounting • Accounts Receivable and Accounts Payable • Business Transactions • Outgoing Payments • Automatic Outgoing Payments • Payment Method/Bank Selection for Payment Program**. However, numerous configuration transactions exist, and getting lost among them is easy. Thus, you should use Transaction FBZP, with which SAP provides a convenient interface in one place for configuration activities related to the payment program.

As shown in Figure 8.15, from this screen, you can navigate through the various settings required for the payment program. First, click the **All company codes** button.

In this configuration activity, you'll specify the paying company code per company code. Payments for multiple company codes can be managed through one company code, and you'll establish this relationship now. Double-click company code 1000 and configure it, as shown in Figure 8.16.

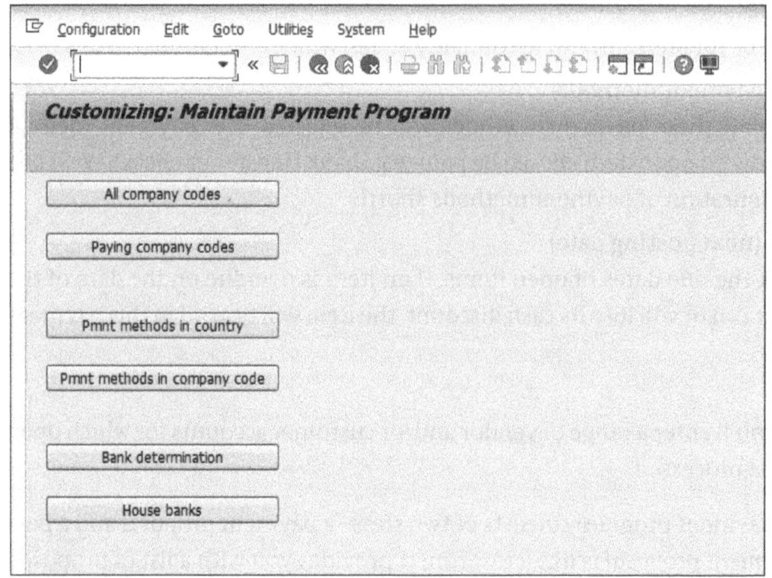

Figure 8.15 Payment Program Configuration

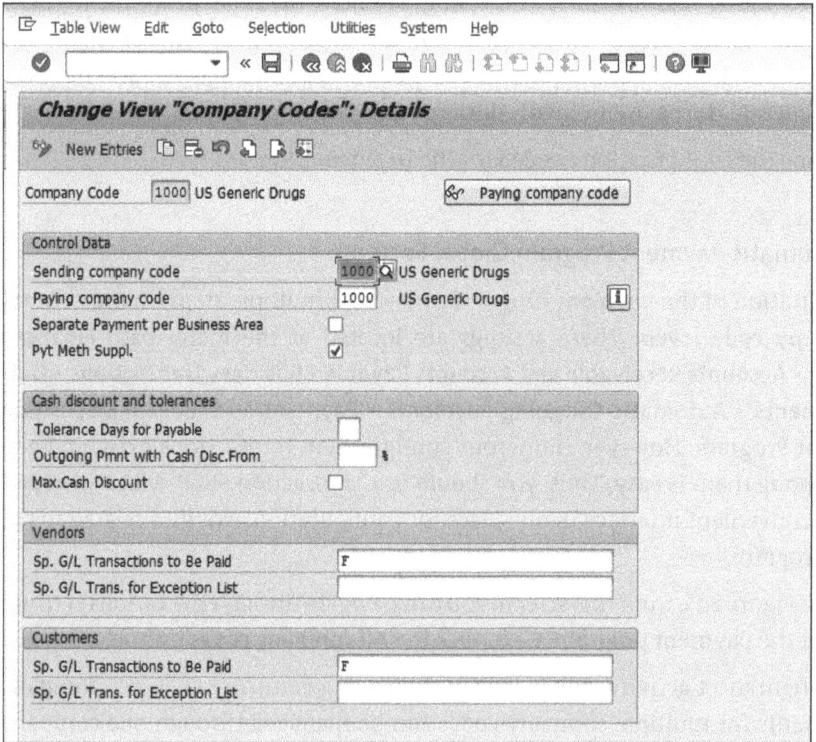

Figure 8.16 Payment Program Company Codes Configuration

In the **Paying Company Code** field, enter "1000" for a 1:1 relationship. On this screen, you can also select the special general ledger transactions that can be paid (see Chapter 5, Section 5.2.2).

Go back to the main screen of Transaction FBZP and click the **Paying company code** button. Now, maintain settings for the company codes that actually make payments. Double-click company code **1000** and configure it, as shown in Figure 8.17.

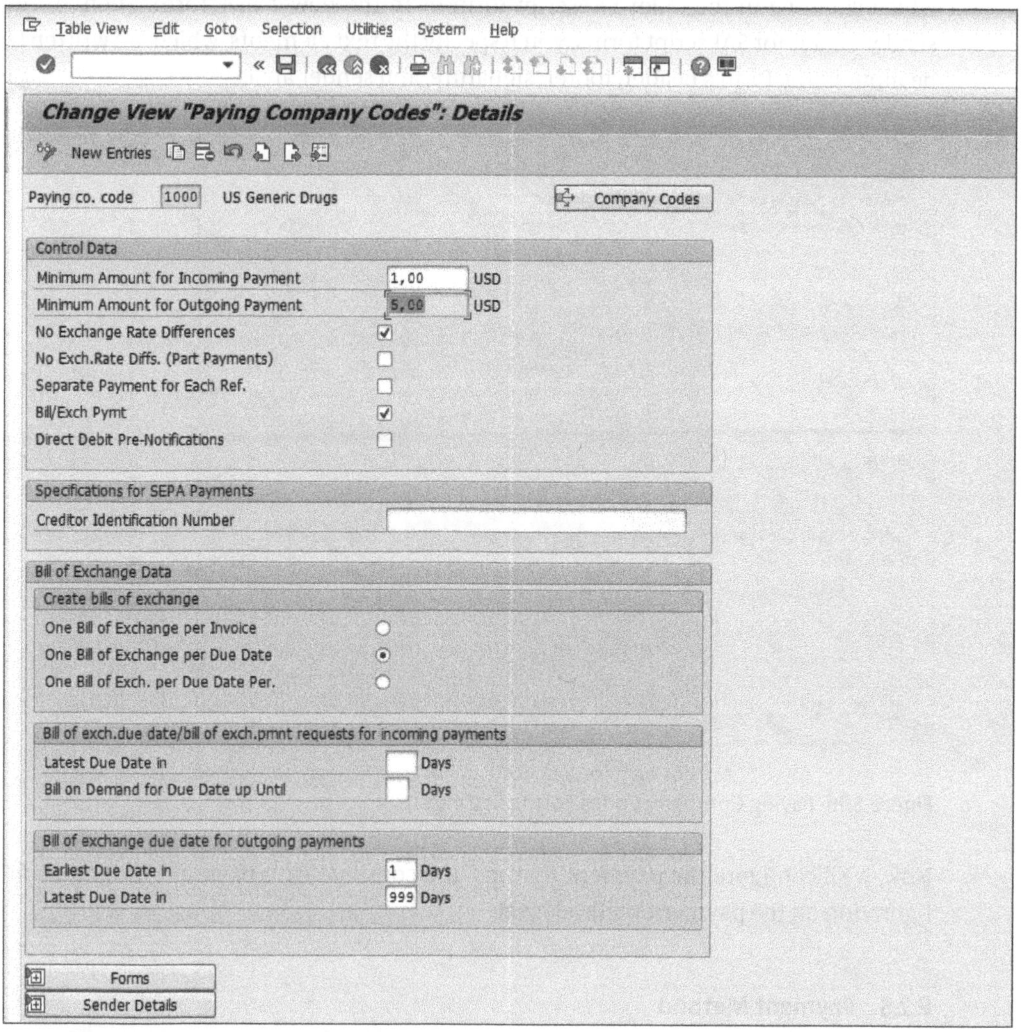

Figure 8.17 Paying Company Codes Configuration

On this screen, specify the minimum amounts for outgoing and incoming payments that can be processed through the company code, as well as the necessary control parameters, such as permitting exchange rate differences, bills of exchange, and direct debit prenotifications. Another important parameter is the SEPA creditor identification number, which is a required field for making SEPA payments, which are relevant for Europe and which will be examined in detail in Section 8.3.1.

Click the **Forms** button to expand the form settings and click the **Sender Details** button to expand the settings for the sender of the forms, as shown in Figure 8.18.

Now, you'll specify the forms for payment advices and accompanying sheet forms, which could be in the older SAPscript form or in the newer PDF form. Then, in the sender details for SAPscript forms, you'll specify the text elements, which are written to be input in the form's header, footer, signature, and sender areas.

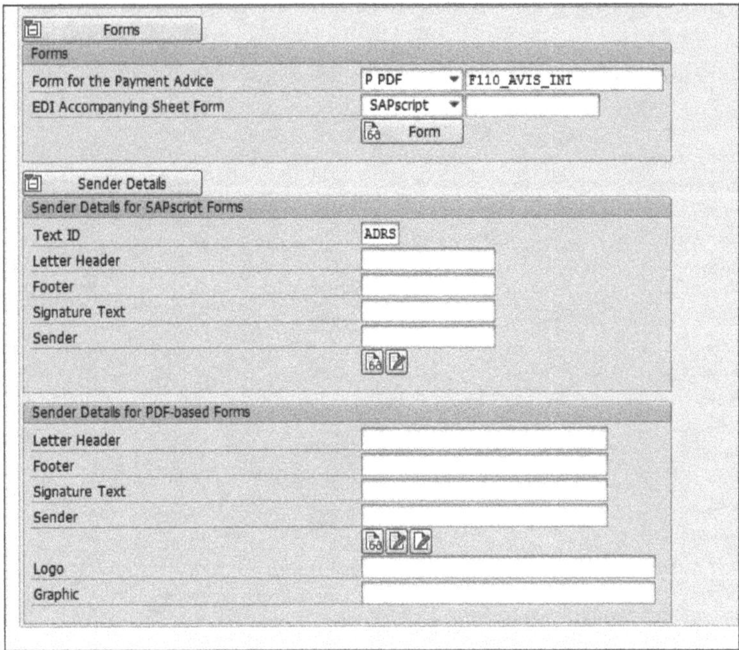

Figure 8.18 Paying Company Codes Forms Settings

Now, we'll configure the payment method and continue with payment program configuration on the payment method level.

8.2.3 Payment Method

The *payment method* is an important configuration object in SAP S/4HANA and determines how payments should be made for items with that method. Each open item to be paid should have a payment method. A payment method can be determined from the master record of the business partner, or it can be entered or derived on the document line-item level. Payment methods differ from country to country, and typical examples include wire transfer; bank transfer, such as Automated Clearing House (ACH) in the US or SEPA in Europe; payment by check; and so on.

Payment methods are defined at the country level and at the company code level. In the main payment program configuration screen shown in Figure 8.19, select the **Pmnt methods in country** (payment methods in country) button to define the country-level settings.

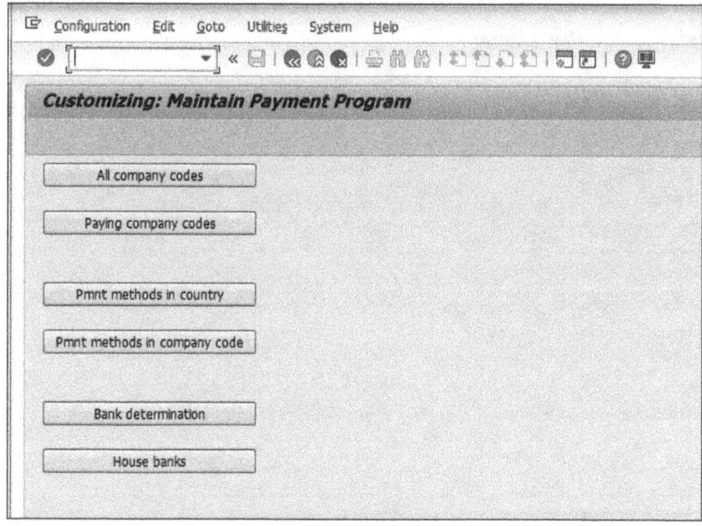

Figure 8.19 Payment Program Configuration

SAP provides several payment methods, relevant per country. As shown in Figure 8.20, for the US, payment methods are defined for payments with checks and various types of bank transfers.

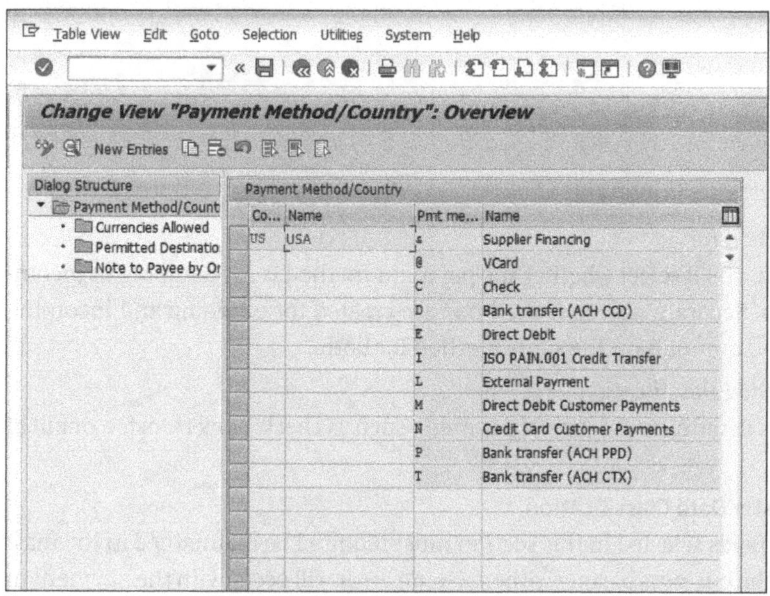

Figure 8.20 Payment Method Country Settings

Double-click payment method **C** for the US to check it and modify its settings if necessary, which brings you to the screen shown in Figure 8.21.

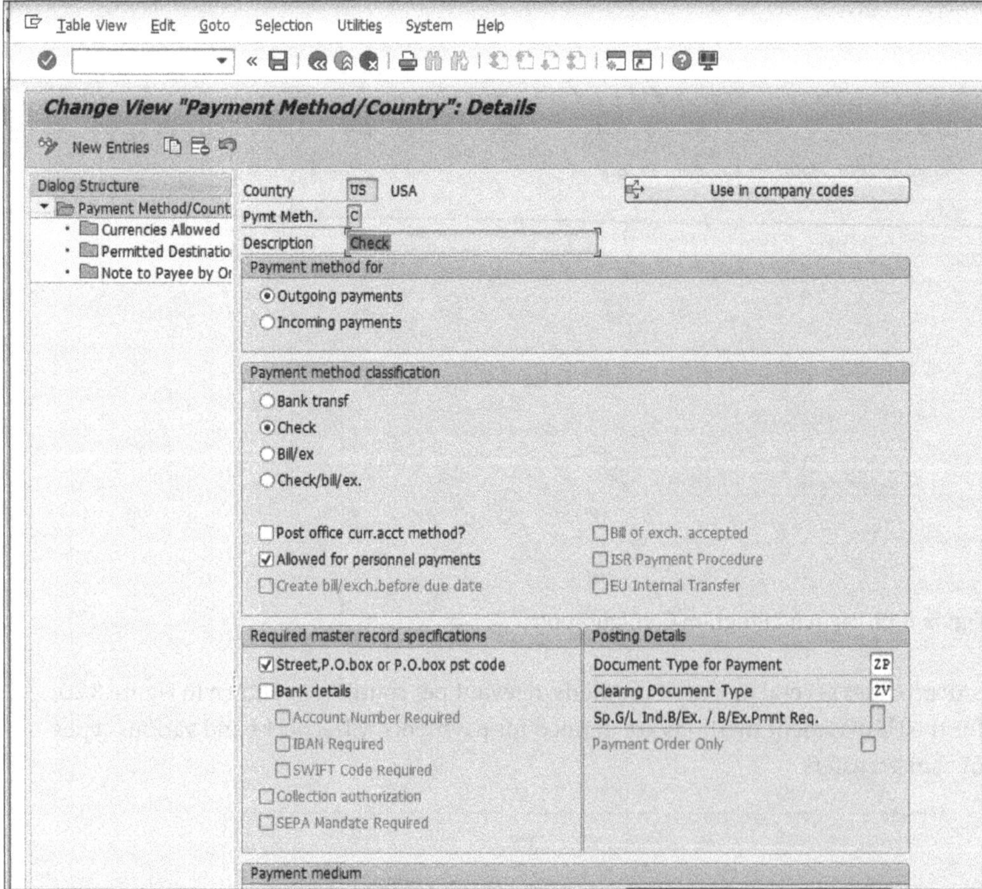

Figure 8.21 Payment Method for Checks

The following fields are important:

- **Payment method for**
  In this section, you'll select whether the payment method is for outgoing or incoming payments. Separate payment methods are created for outgoing and incoming payments; you cannot have the same method for both.
- **Payment method classification**
  These options determine the type of payment, such as check, bank transfer, or bill of exchange.
- **Required Master Data Classification**
  The group of fields selected in this section must required be maintained in the master record of the business partner; otherwise, an error will occur with the payment in the automatic payment program.

- **Posting Details**
  In this section, you'll specify the document types used for the payments and clearing with this payment method.

Scroll down to maintain the payment medium settings for the payment method, as shown in Figure 8.22.

Figure 8.22 Payment Method Payment Medium Settings

Two options are available for generating the payment medium (bank files or checks): using the Payment Medium Workbench or using classic payment medium programs such as program RFFOUS_C for checks and program RFFOUS_T for payment bank files. The Payment Medium Workbench is the newer and more flexible solution for bank files from SAP, in which the structure of the file is designed by selecting and arranging specific elements, rather than being programmed as in the older program RFFOUS_T. However, for checks, the classic program RFFOUS_C still is the most common solution. We'll talk more about payment files in Section 8.3.

You can also restrict the use of the payment method for specific currencies by selecting the **Currencies Allowed** option from the left side of the screen and restrict the use of destination countries by selecting the **Permitted Destination Countries** option from the left side of the screen.

Select **Currencies Allowed** and select **New Entries** from the top menu. Enter "USD," as shown in Figure 8.23. As explained in the configuration screen itself, those currencies are then permitted for this payment method. Leaving this table empty means that all currencies are permitted.

Save your entries by clicking the **Save** button, then go back to the main configuration screen of the payment program.

The next step is to define the payment methods for each company code. Click the **Pmnt Methods in Company Code** button, which leads you to the payment methods defined on the company code level, as shown in Figure 8.24.

Table View Edit Goto Selection Utilities System Help
New Entries: Overview of Added Entries
Dialog Structure
Payment Method/Count
Currencies Allowed
Permitted Destinatio
Note to Payee by Or
Country US
Pymt Meth. C
Currency
USD
Permitted currencies
In this list, you enter those currencies that are permitted for this payment method. Leaving this table empty will mean that all currencies are permitted.

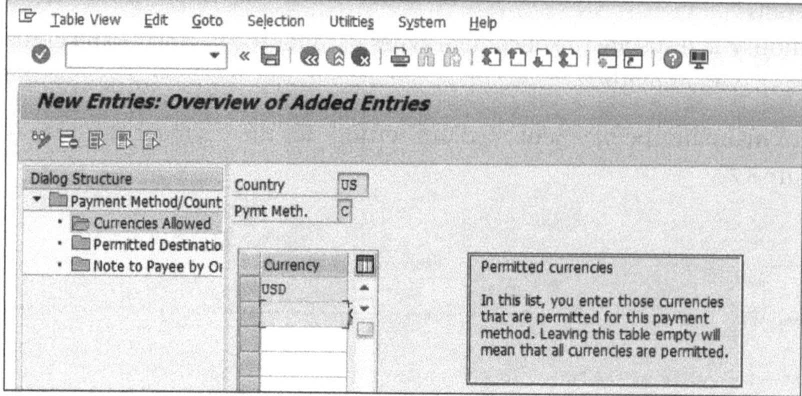

Figure 8.23 Payment Method Permitted Currencies

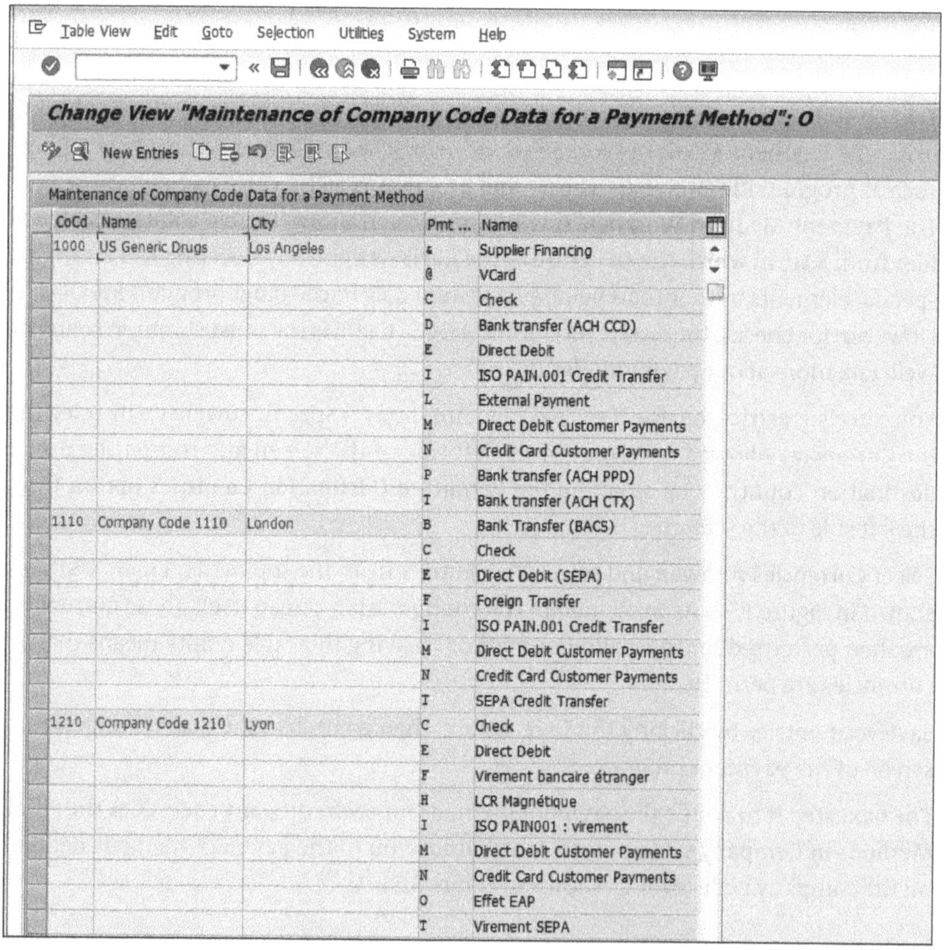

Table View Edit Goto Selection Utilities System Help
Change View "Maintenance of Company Code Data for a Payment Method": O
New Entries
Maintenance of Company Code Data for a Payment Method
CoCd Name City Pmt ... Name
1000 US Generic Drugs Los Angeles
& Supplier Financing
@ VCard
C Check
D Bank transfer (ACH CCD)
E Direct Debit
I ISO PAIN.001 Credit Transfer
L External Payment
M Direct Debit Customer Payments
N Credit Card Customer Payments
P Bank transfer (ACH PPD)
T Bank transfer (ACH CTX)
1110 Company Code 1110 London
B Bank Transfer (BACS)
C Check
E Direct Debit (SEPA)
F Foreign Transfer
I ISO PAIN.001 Credit Transfer
M Direct Debit Customer Payments
N Credit Card Customer Payments
T SEPA Credit Transfer
1210 Company Code 1210 Lyon
C Check
E Direct Debit
F Virement bancaire étranger
H LCR Magnétique
I ISO PAIN001 : virement
M Direct Debit Customer Payments
N Credit Card Customer Payments
O Effet EAP
T Virement SEPA

Figure 8.24 Payment Methods Company Code

Payment methods defined by company code are listed in the **Pmt method** column. Only those payment methods defined on this screen can be used for a given company code. Double-click the **C: Check** method for company code 1000, which brings you to the configuration screen on the company code level, as shown in Figure 8.25.

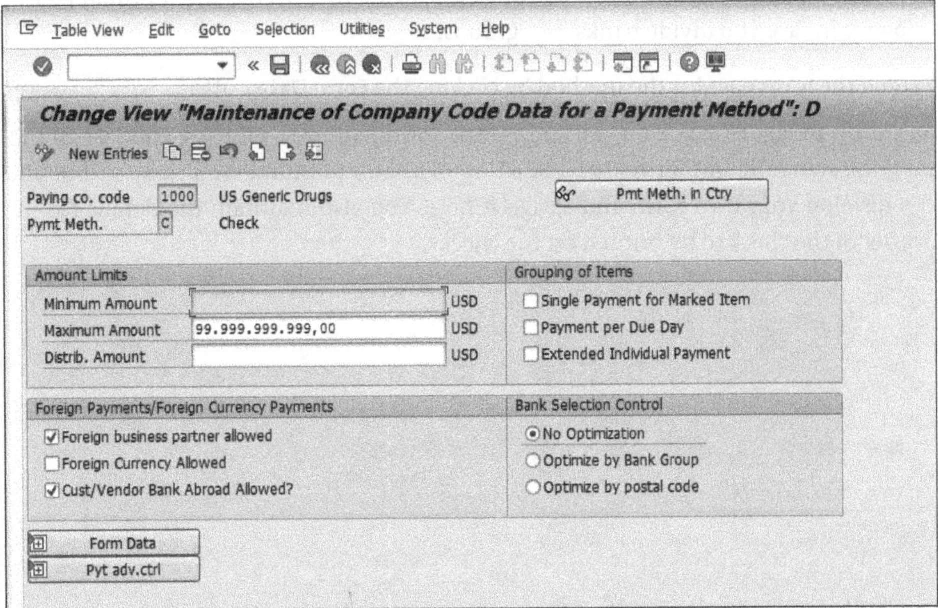

Figure 8.25 Payment Method for Checks in Company Code

You can configure the following fields:

- **Minimum Amount**
  The minimum amount per payment for which the payment method can be used.
- **Maximum Amount**
  The maximum amount per payment for which the payment method can be used. In our example, we specified that no more than 500,000 EUR can be paid out by check.
- **Distrib. Amount (distribution amount)**
  Indicates that payments exceeding this amount are checked to determine whether they can be split into several payments totaling a maximum of this amount.
- **Single Payment for Marked Item**
  If you select this checkbox, a separate payment will be made for each line item, and the system will not try to group line items.
- **Payment per Due Day**
  Specifies that only items that are due on the same day will be paid with a single payment.

- **Foreign Payments**
  In these fields, you'll select if foreign currency and/or partners are allowed to be paid with this method.
- **Bank Selection Control**
  Specifies if the system should optimize payments by selecting the optimal pair of banks in case you divide banks into groups.

Extend the form data for the method by clicking the **Form Data** button.

As shown in Figure 8.26, you can specify the form name for printing checks—in this case, the standard SAP form F110_PRENUM_CHCK for prenumbered checks—but you can develop your own form and assign it here. You also maintain the details for the drawer of the check to be printed on the checks.

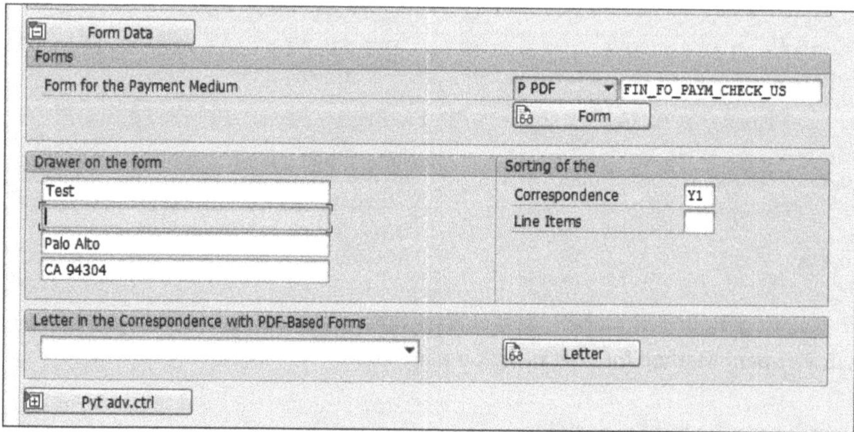

Figure 8.26 Payment Method Checks Form Data

Save your entries by clicking the **Save** button, then go back to the main configuration screen of the payment program.

8.2.4 Bank Determination

The next step in the configuration of the automatic payment program is to define the bank determination. This process determines the sequence of selecting house banks for each payment method from which payments are to be made. Also, you'll specify the bank accounts for each house bank and the general ledger accounts to be posted during the payment process.

From the main payment program configuration screen, shown earlier in Figure 8.19, click the **Bank Determination** button.

As shown in Figure 8.27, you'll see a list of paying company codes. Select company code **1000** and click **Ranking Order** on the left side of the screen. Then, using the **New Entries** option from the top menu, you can create the ranking order of house banks for the company code.

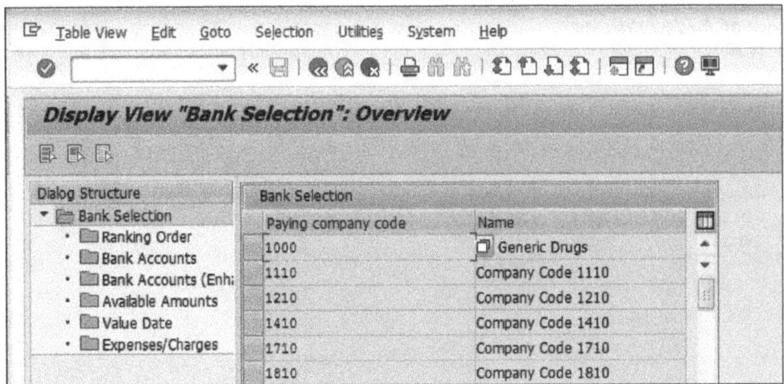

Figure 8.27 Bank Determination

As shown in Figure 8.28, you can define the ranking order by which the system selects house banks per payment method and, optionally, currency. If more than one house bank is specified for each combination of payment method and currency, each bank is marked in the **Rank. Order** column sequentially: 1, 2, and so on. Then, the house bank with ranking order 1 will be selected first, and only if payment can't be made from this house bank due to an amount limitation will the system select the next house bank.

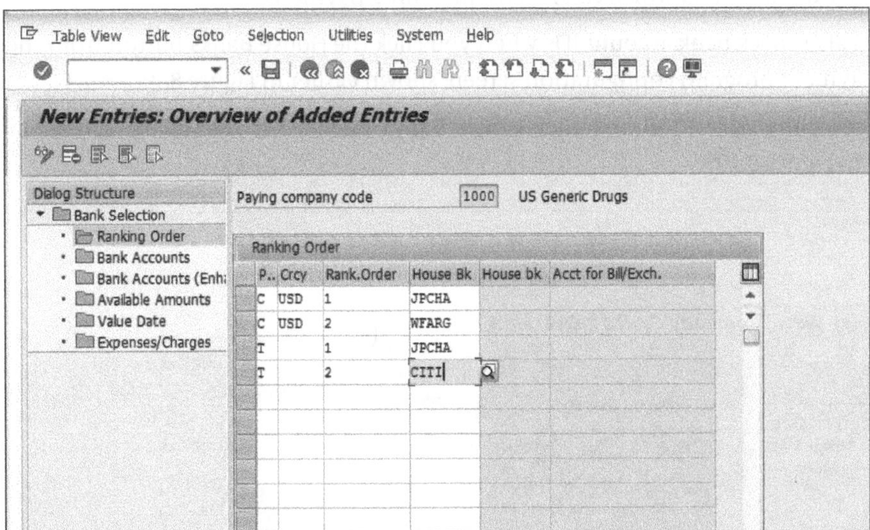

Figure 8.28 House Banks Ranking Order

In the next step, select **Bank Accounts** from the left side of the screen. On the screen shown in Figure 8.29, you'll specify the sequence of bank accounts for each house bank from which payments are made. Click the **New Entries** option from the top menu.

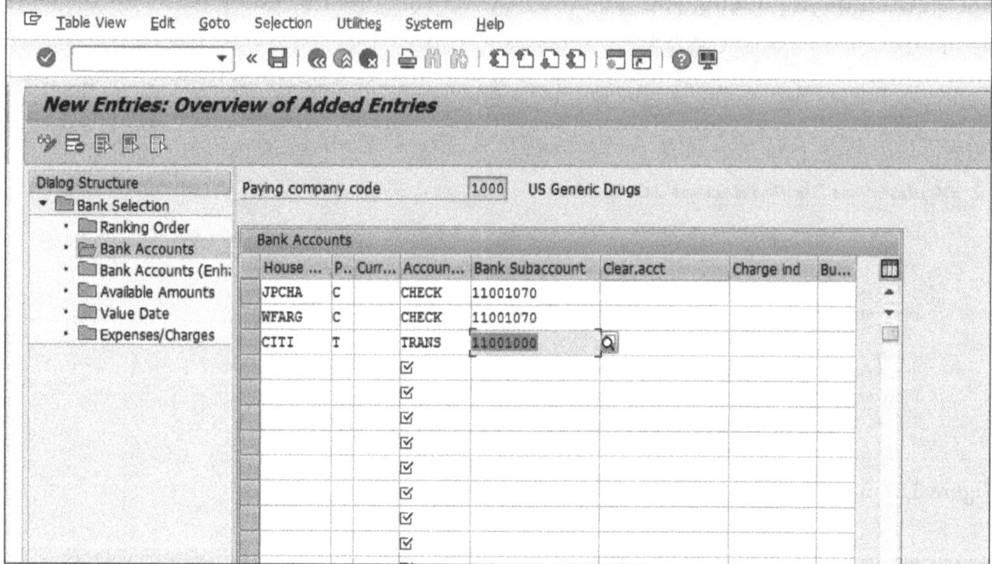

Figure 8.29 Bank Accounts Determination

On this configuration screen, select the house banks and payment methods and assign to them the bank account IDs and general ledger accounts they should post to. The bank account ID represents an actual bank account in your bank from which outgoing payments are made and which can receive incoming payments.

You can also check bank account IDs when you click the **House Banks** button from the main payment program configuration screen, shown earlier in Figure 8.19.

Select company code **1000** and click **House Banks** on the left side of the screen, as shown in Figure 8.30.

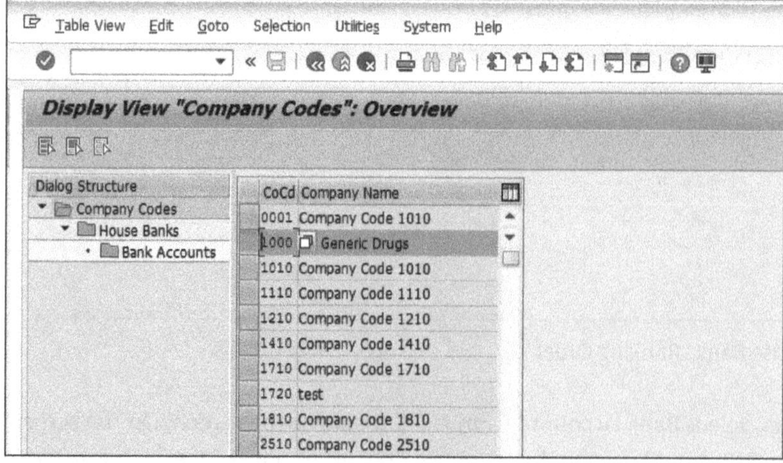

Figure 8.30 House Banks and Accounts

Then, select one of the house banks and click **Bank Accounts** on the left side of the screen to see a list of the defined bank accounts for each house bank. If you click **Create Bank Account** from the top menu, you'll be taken to the Bank Account Management SAP Fiori app to create bank accounts, which we discussed in Section 8.1.3.

With that, we've completed the configuration of the payment program. Now, we'll review some common issues when running the payment program because sometimes the error log isn't that useful, and you may benefit from some practical advice on how to tackle issues you may encounter.

8.2.5 Common Issues with the Payment Program

When you run the payment program, as already discussed, you first run a payment proposal, which is like a test run. Then, you can check the proposed payments for any possible errors. If you find any errors, you can delete the payment proposal and, after resolving the issue(s), run it again.

As discussed earlier, the automatic payment program is available at the application menu path **Accounting • Financial Accounting • Accounts Payable • Periodic Processing • F110—Payments.** From the main screen of the payment program shown in Figure 8.31, select **Edit Proposal** from the top menu.

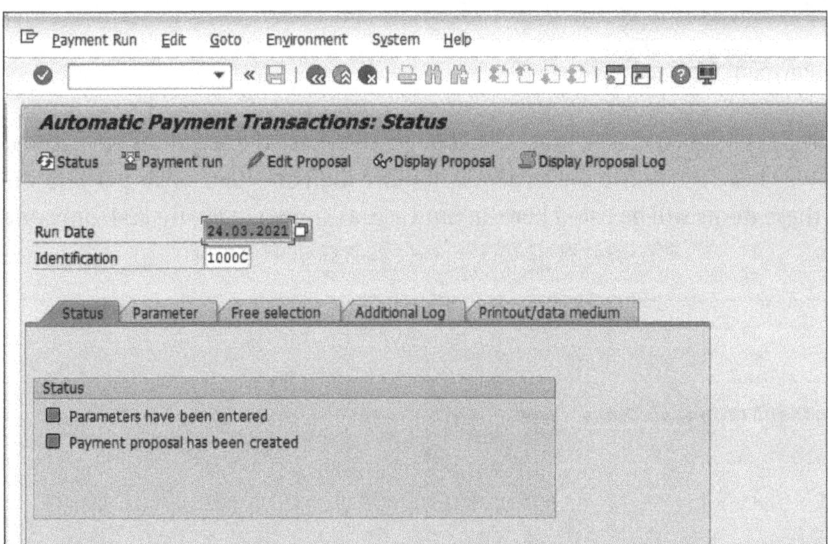

Figure 8.31 Payment Proposal

Then, the system asks you whether you want to see the items of specific accounting clerks, as maintained in the business partner master data, or all accounting clerks, as shown in Figure 8.32.

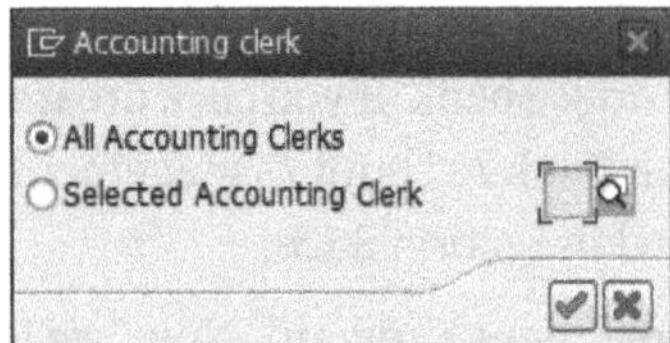

Figure 8.32 Accounting Clerks Selection

Proceed with the **Continue** button, and you'll see a list of proposed payments and exceptions, as shown in Figure 8.33.

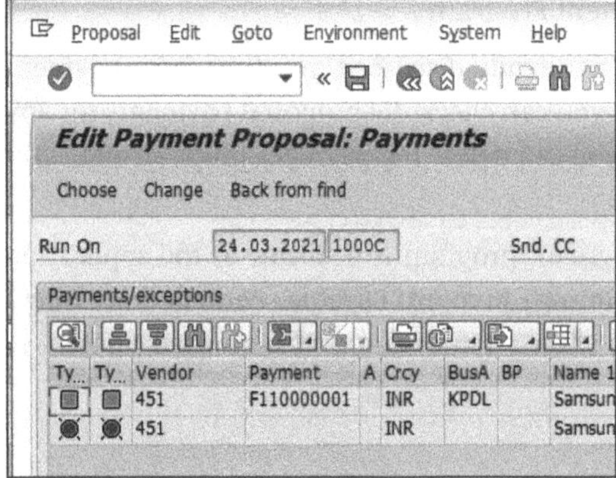

Figure 8.33 Payment Proposal

Payment proposals which are OK are marked in green, whereas exceptions are marked in red. Double-click a red line to see its details. If more than one item exists per vendor/ customer, these items will be listed here. In our case, as shown in Figure 8.34, only one item exists.

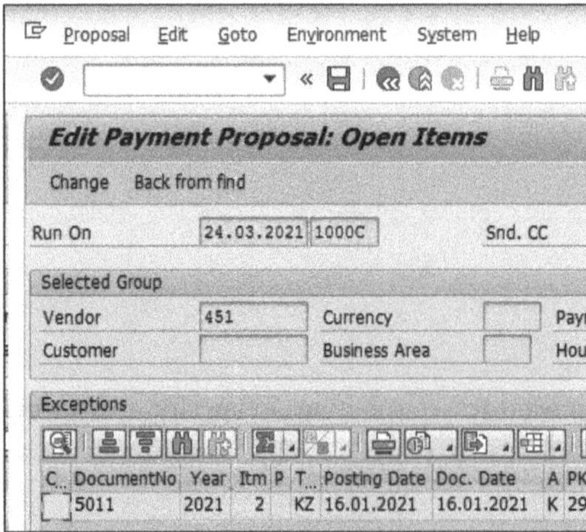

Figure 8.34 Payment Proposal Details

Double-click this item, and you'll see the error, as shown in Figure 8.35.

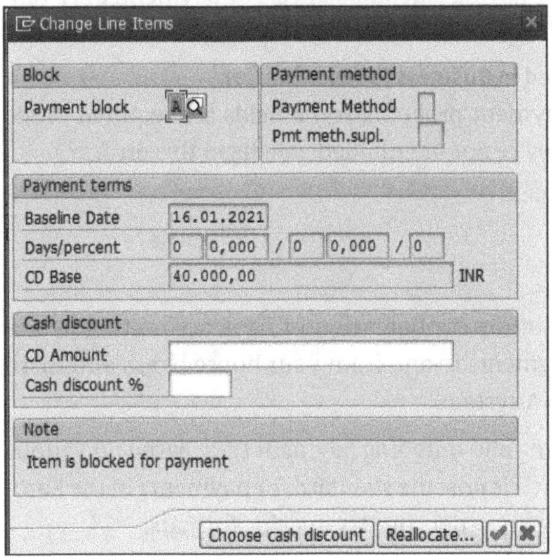

Figure 8.35 Payment Proposal Error

Notice that, in this case, the error is that the item is blocked for payment. As a result, you must check the item and unblock it if indeed the item needs to be paid.

You can also see an overview of issues encountered by clicking the **Display Proposal Log** button from the main screen of the payment program.

Some other common error messages from the payment program and potential resolutions include the following:

- **No Valid Payment Method Found**
  This message means that the system can't determine the payment method to use. Check the document and the business partner master. The payment method needs to be either derived from the master record or entered into the document.
- **Company Code [xxx] Does Not Appear in Proposal [xxx] (Run Date and ID)**
  This message isn't self-explanatory. Check whether open items are based on the parameters of the run. But this message also could appear for other reasons; check the proposal log for more clues.
- **Account or Item Is Blocked for Payment**
  An easy message to interpret, this message means that either the business partner master record or the open item itself contains a payment block.
- **Account [xxx] Blocked by Payment Proposal [xxx]**
  This message means that the selected account is also participating in another payment run, so the system locks it in other payment proposals. You have to finish the previous payment run first.

- **No Payment Possible because Items with a Debit Bal. Still Exist**
  This message is caused by a vendor having a debit balance. For payment, only vendors with credit balances are considered.
- **Required Details Are Not Maintained in Business Partner Master**
  As per the configuration of the payment program, some fields are required in the business partner master data. If they're not maintained, you'll get this error.

8.3 Payment Files

Payment files are an important part of the configuration of bank accounting in SAP S/4HANA. They're used to initiate payments to and from your house banks automatically using data from the SAP S/4HANA system.

The system can generate both incoming and outgoing payment files, based on various common standards, such as SEPA, which is now the standard for payments in the Eurozone; ACH in the United States; and many other country-specific formats.

8.3.1 Single Euro Payments Area Payment Files

SEPA is a project of the European Union (EU), which aims to simplify payments in euros between member states of the EU. Quickly becoming the de facto standard for electronic payments in Europe, SEPA is becoming quite important for SAP S/4HANA systems to manage.

Two types of payments should be managed by SAP S/4HANA, as follows:

- **SEPA credit transfers**
  SEPA credit transfers are used for outgoing payments. SAP S/4HANA generates outgoing payment files, which you can send to your bank to pay your vendors.
- **SEPA direct debits**
  SEPA direct debits are used to receive payments from customers automatically from their accounts. This arrangement is done based on a specific written agreement, called a *SEPA mandate*, which needs to be stored in the customer master record. Then, the payment program can generate the SEPA direct debit files.

You must have separate payment methods defined for SEPA credit transfers and direct debits. Then, from the main payment program configuration screen, shown earlier in Figure 8.19, click the **Pmnt Methods in Country** button and create payment methods for SEPA credit transfer and direct debit.

Select **Use Payment Medium Workbench** and enter "XX_CGI_XML_CT" in the **Format** field for SEPA credit transfer, where XX is the country code of the relevant country, as shown in Figure 8.36.

For direct debit, enter "XX_CGI_XML_DD" in the **Format** field. These standard formats are provided by SAP on a per-country basis, replacing the older standard formats SEPA_CT and SEPA_DT. These new formats are used to generate XML payment files. The format structure is based on International Standards Organization (ISO) 20022. They correspond to the implementation template defined by banks and corporate customers through the Common Global Implementation (CGI) initiative and are fully SEPA compliant.

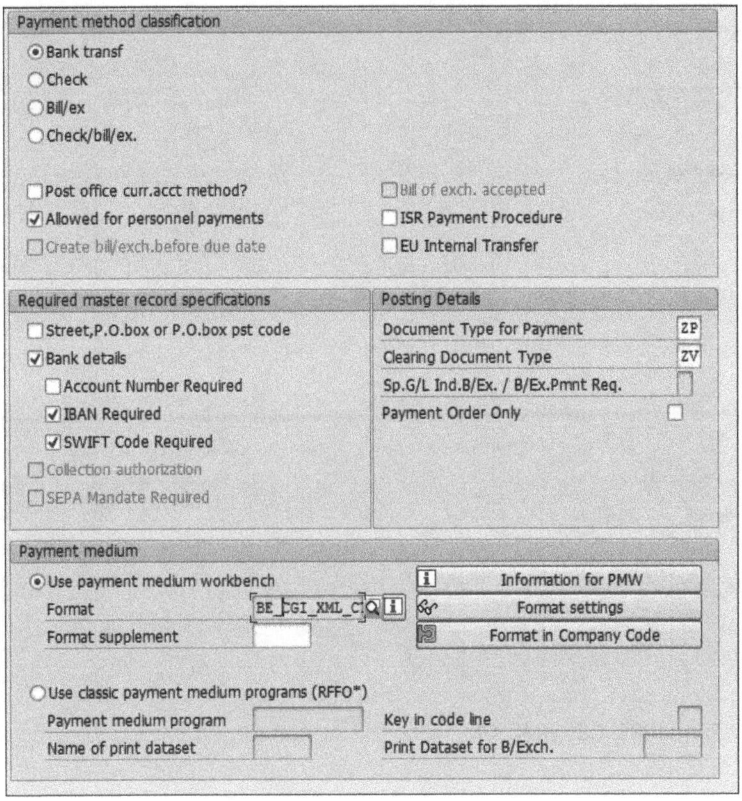

Figure 8.36 Payment Method Medium Configuration

Using the **Format settings** button, you can check the settings of the payment format. Figure 8.37 shows the settings of payment format BE_CGI_XML_CT, which is SEPA credit format provided for Belgium. This tree-like structure can be defined as XML nodes and the data that should go into them, which could be derived from various fields from the payment structure of the system.

If you need to modify the format, you should make a copy, starting with Z, and modify your custom format. Transaction DMEEX allows you to maintain the payment format.

As shown in Figure 8.38, you must select the **PAYM** option for the **Tree Type** field, which is used for payment files, and enter a name in the **Format Tree** field. Then, by clicking the **Change** button, you can make changes as appropriate.

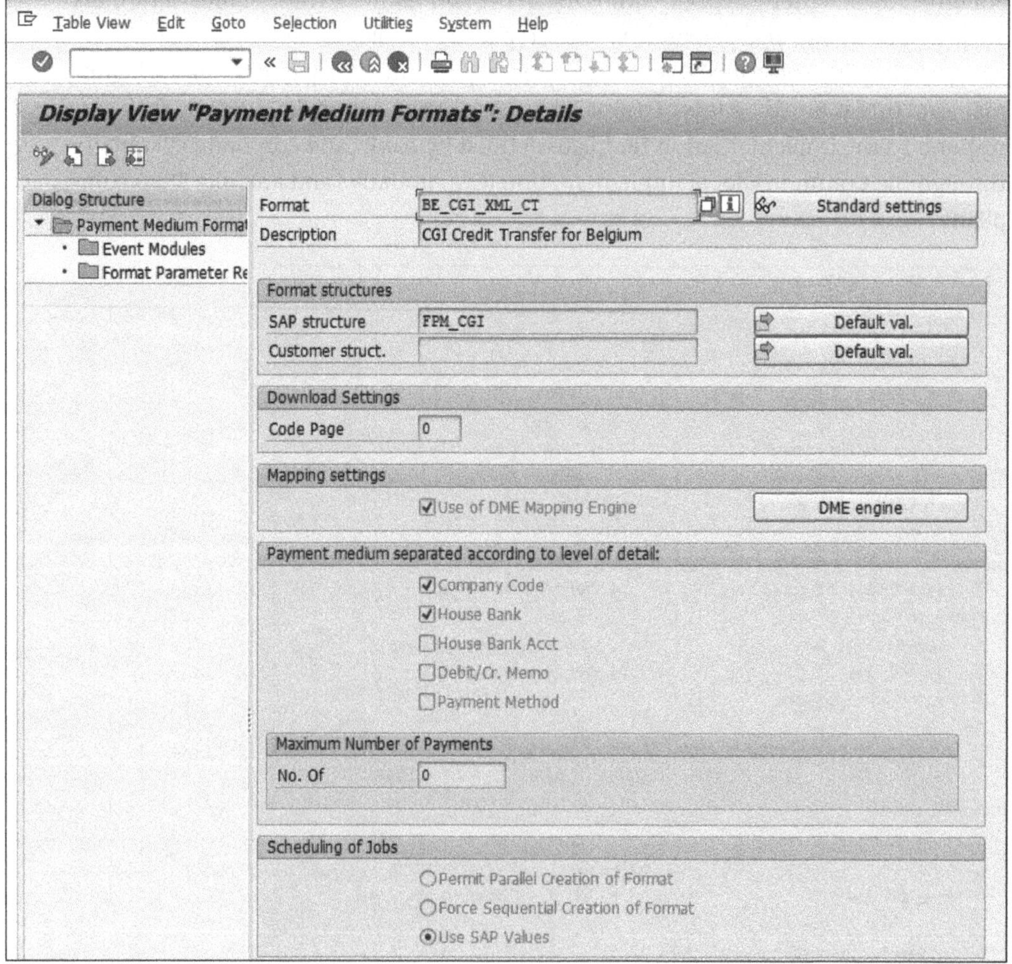

Figure 8.37 Payment Format BE_CGI_XML_CT

Figure 8.38 Payment Format Maintenance

If you click the **Change** button, you can modify the definition of the format, as shown in Figure 8.39.

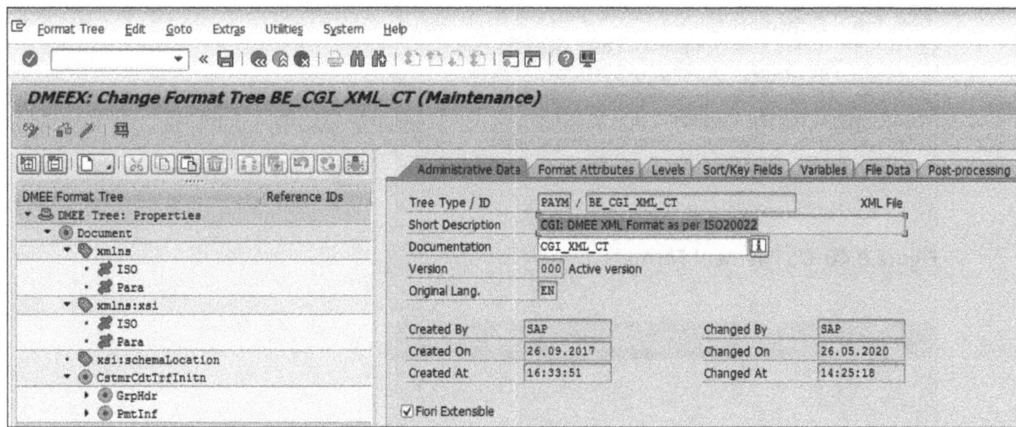

Figure 8.39 Payment Format Definition

As with other standard objects, we recommend copying a standard format into custom one starting with Z or Y and modify the copied version.

Then, you need to assign your payment format to the payment method, as shown in Figure 8.36.

8.3.2 Other Common Formats

SAP provides myriad bank formats for various countries, which can be used either out of the box or with minor modifications, as required by specific banks. The newer method of providing such formats is using the Payment Medium Workbench, rather than older classic programs, in which one program provides one payment file. The Payment Medium Workbench offers a flexible, easy-to-use interface in which most requirements can be accomplished with configuration of the XML nodes and no additional ABAP programming is needed.

To view the existing standard formats provided, check Transaction DMEEX with tree type PAYM, as was shown in Figure 8.38. By clicking the button to the right of the **Format Tree** field or by pressing F4, you can view the available formats.

Figure 8.40 shows standard formats defined for the United States. Notice that formats for direct debit and XML formats conforming to ISO 20022 are provided. Also, a payment format is also available for positive pay, which is used to clear checks.

SAP also provides formats for many countries based on the **CGI: DMEE XML Format as per ISO 20022** option, as shown in Figure 8.41. The format for each country starts with the country code and is a variation of the common CGI_XML format for debit and credit transfers.

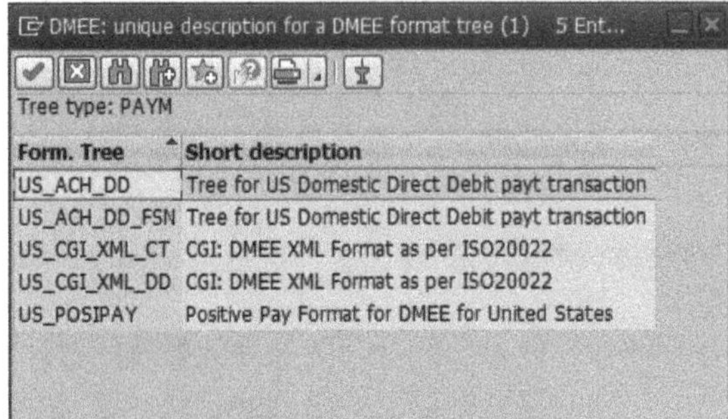

Form. Tree	Short description
US_ACH_DD	Tree for US Domestic Direct Debit payt transaction
US_ACH_DD_FSN	Tree for US Domestic Direct Debit payt transaction
US_CGI_XML_CT	CGI: DMEE XML Format as per ISO20022
US_CGI_XML_DD	CGI: DMEE XML Format as per ISO20022
US_POSIPAY	Positive Pay Format for DMEE for United States

Figure 8.40 US Payment Formats

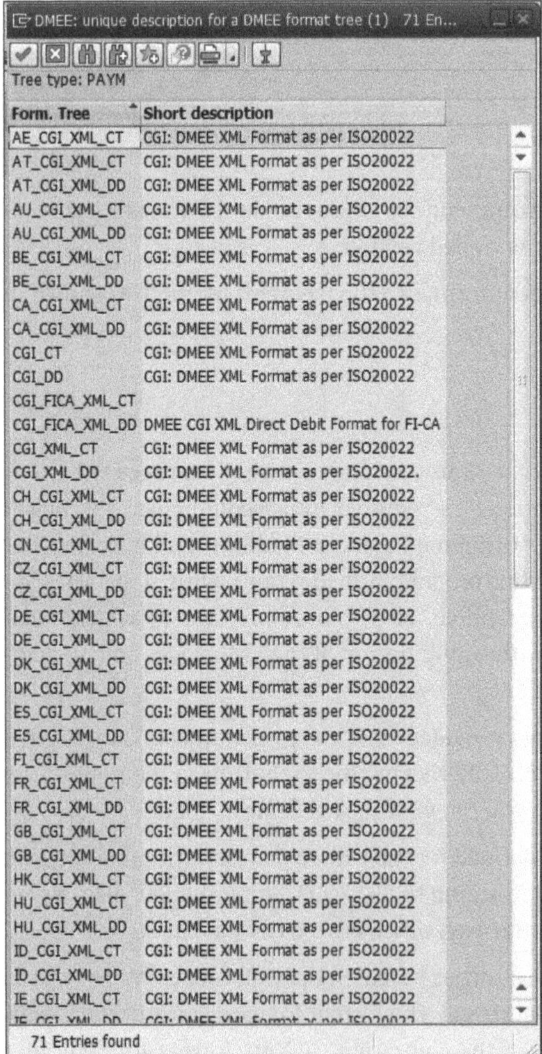

Form. Tree	Short description
AE_CGI_XML_CT	CGI: DMEE XML Format as per ISO20022
AT_CGI_XML_CT	CGI: DMEE XML Format as per ISO20022
AT_CGI_XML_DD	CGI: DMEE XML Format as per ISO20022
AU_CGI_XML_CT	CGI: DMEE XML Format as per ISO20022
AU_CGI_XML_DD	CGI: DMEE XML Format as per ISO20022
BE_CGI_XML_CT	CGI: DMEE XML Format as per ISO20022
BE_CGI_XML_DD	CGI: DMEE XML Format as per ISO20022
CA_CGI_XML_CT	CGI: DMEE XML Format as per ISO20022
CA_CGI_XML_DD	CGI: DMEE XML Format as per ISO20022
CGI_CT	CGI: DMEE XML Format as per ISO20022
CGI_DD	CGI: DMEE XML Format as per ISO20022
CGI_FICA_XML_CT	
CGI_FICA_XML_DD	DMEE CGI XML Direct Debit Format for FI-CA
CGI_XML_CT	CGI: DMEE XML Format as per ISO20022
CGI_XML_DD	CGI: DMEE XML Format as per ISO20022.
CH_CGI_XML_CT	CGI: DMEE XML Format as per ISO20022
CH_CGI_XML_DD	CGI: DMEE XML Format as per ISO20022
CN_CGI_XML_CT	CGI: DMEE XML Format as per ISO20022
CZ_CGI_XML_CT	CGI: DMEE XML Format as per ISO20022
CZ_CGI_XML_DD	CGI: DMEE XML Format as per ISO20022
DE_CGI_XML_CT	CGI: DMEE XML Format as per ISO20022
DE_CGI_XML_DD	CGI: DMEE XML Format as per ISO20022
DK_CGI_XML_CT	CGI: DMEE XML Format as per ISO20022
DK_CGI_XML_DD	CGI: DMEE XML Format as per ISO20022
ES_CGI_XML_CT	CGI: DMEE XML Format as per ISO20022
ES_CGI_XML_DD	CGI: DMEE XML Format as per ISO20022
FI_CGI_XML_CT	CGI: DMEE XML Format as per ISO20022
FR_CGI_XML_CT	CGI: DMEE XML Format as per ISO20022
FR_CGI_XML_DD	CGI: DMEE XML Format as per ISO20022
GB_CGI_XML_CT	CGI: DMEE XML Format as per ISO20022
GB_CGI_XML_DD	CGI: DMEE XML Format as per ISO20022
HK_CGI_XML_CT	CGI: DMEE XML Format as per ISO20022
HU_CGI_XML_CT	CGI: DMEE XML Format as per ISO20022
HU_CGI_XML_DD	CGI: DMEE XML Format as per ISO20022
ID_CGI_XML_CT	CGI: DMEE XML Format as per ISO20022
ID_CGI_XML_DD	CGI: DMEE XML Format as per ISO20022
IE_CGI_XML_CT	CGI: DMEE XML Format as per ISO20022

Figure 8.41 CGI XML Formats

A best practice when setting up payment file formats as part of your SAP S/4HANA project is to generate sample files using the standard formats provided and get in touch with house banks to make sure the formats are accepted. If any changes are needed, you should use the standard formats as a basis to create new ones in the Z name range and modify them appropriately.

If you're doing a brownfield SAP S/4HANA implementation, you need to make sure that the formats used are still supported. For example, the older SEPA formats SEPA_CT and SEPA_DT are now obsolete and must be replaced in the settings of the payment methods with the country-based CGI-based formats for CGI_XML_CT and CGI_XML_DD.

8.4 Electronic Bank Statements

An electronic bank statement is a file that you receive from the house bank, containing the various bank transactions posted for a given period, such as deposits, withdrawals, bank charges, and so on. SAP S/4HANA provides functionality to read this file and automatically make postings to bank accounts, business partner accounts, and other general ledger accounts based on this information. Thus, a lot of manual work, time, and effort can be saved, and transparency into bank postings and their security in the system is provided.

We'll start by providing an overview of the electronic bank statement process. Then, we'll delve into its configuration by defining the settings for account symbols, posting rules, and transaction types.

8.4.1 Overview

Importing a bank statement is performed with Transaction FF_5, available at the application menu path **Accounting • Financial Accounting • Banks • Input • Bank Statement • FF_5 – Import**.

As shown in Figure 8.42, SAP again provides various standard formats for electronic bank statements. Some of these formats are international, and some are country specific. SWIFT MT940 is the most common international format. You must check what format your bank is using and make changes if necessary.

Let's see now what configuration settings are required for electronic bank statements by following the menu path **Financial Accounting • Bank Accounting • Business Transactions • Payment Transactions • Electronic Bank Statement • Make Global Settings for Electronic Bank Statement**.

The system asks you for a chart of accounts, as shown in Figure 8.43. All global settings for electronic bank statements are dependent on the chart of accounts.

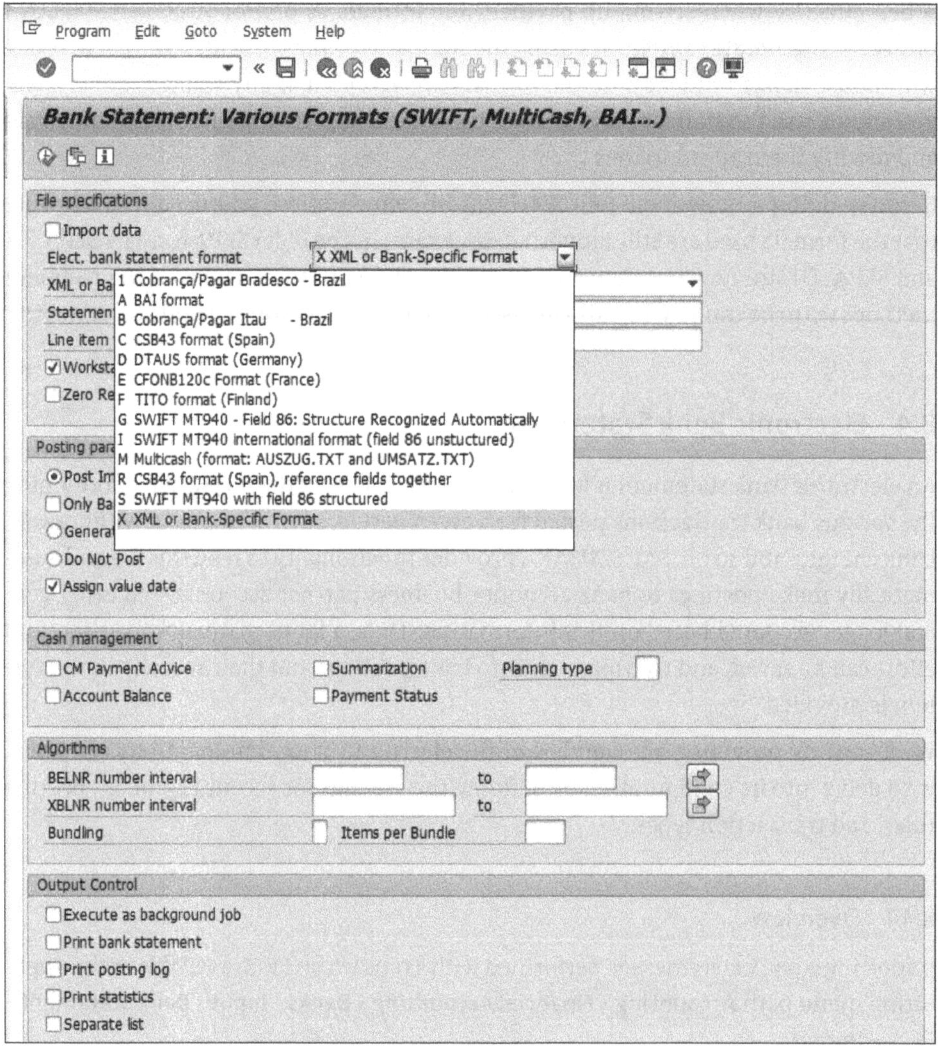

Figure 8.42 Importing Bank Statement Formats

Figure 8.43 Chart of Accounts Selection

Enter your **Chart of Accounts** and confirm by clicking the button. On the next screen, you'll define the account symbols.

8.4.2 Account Symbols

Account symbols are groupings under which you classify similar bank accounts. Figure 8.44 shows the screen on which you'll define the various settings for the electronic bank statement by selecting them from the left side. Double-click **Create Account Symbols**, and account symbols already defined will be displayed on the right side of the screen. Typical account symbols include deposits, interest, checks received, checks out, and so on.

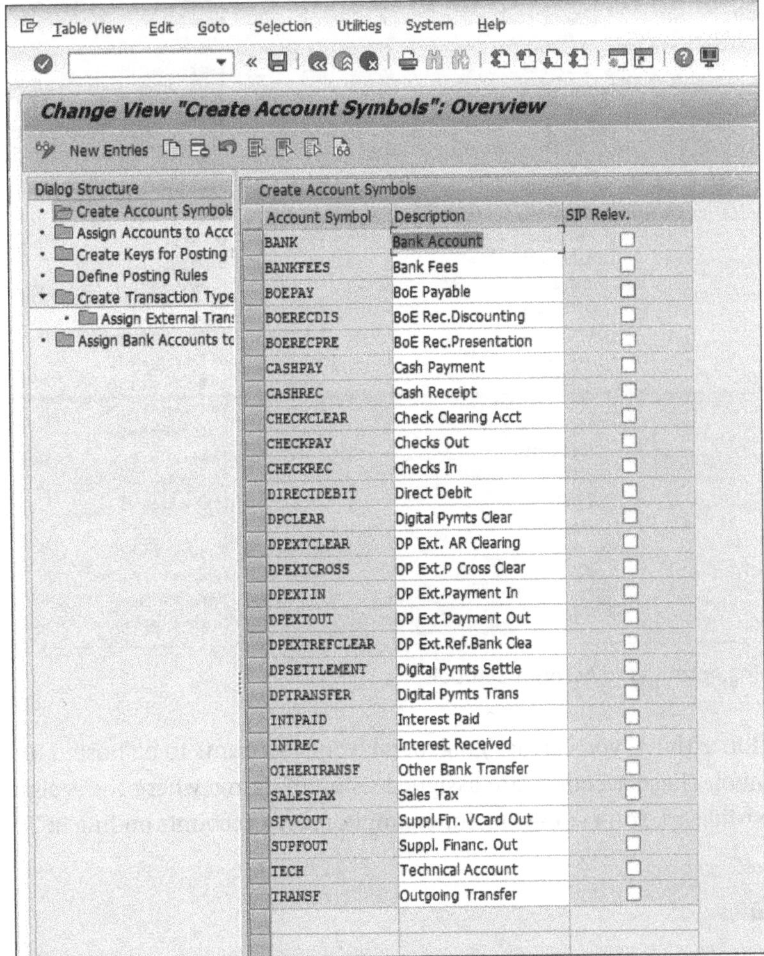

Figure 8.44 Account Symbols

Click **Assign Accounts to Account Symbol** on the left side of the screen, which will result in the screen shown in Figure 8.45.

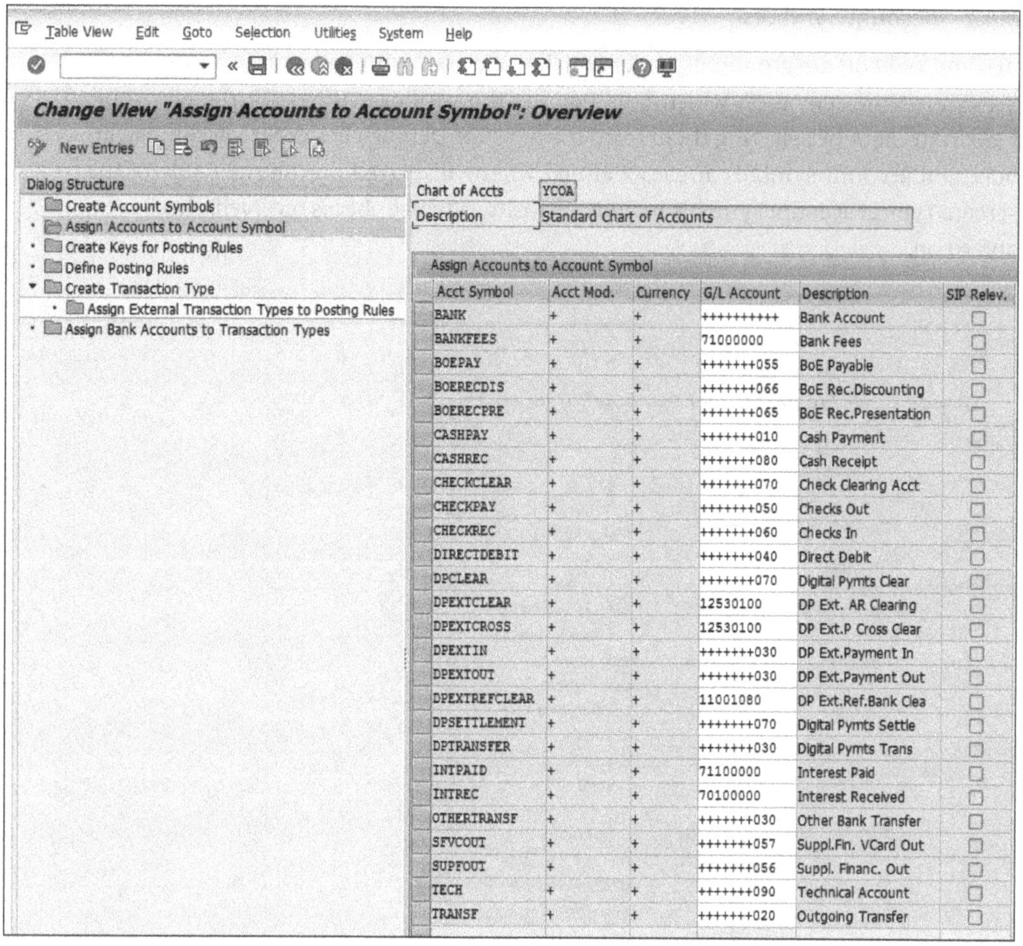

Table View Edit Goto Selection Utilities System Help

Change View "Assign Accounts to Account Symbol": Overview

New Entries

Dialog Structure
- Create Account Symbols
- Assign Accounts to Account Symbol
- Create Keys for Posting Rules
- Define Posting Rules
- Create Transaction Type
  - Assign External Transaction Types to Posting Rules
- Assign Bank Accounts to Transaction Types

Chart of Accts: YCOA
Description: Standard Chart of Accounts

Assign Accounts to Account Symbol

Acct Symbol	Acct Mod.	Currency	G/L Account	Description	SIP Relev.
BANK	+	+	++++++++++	Bank Account	☐
BANKFEES	+	+	71000000	Bank Fees	☐
BOEPAY	+	+	+++++++055	BoE Payable	☐
BOERECDIS	+	+	+++++++066	BoE Rec.Discounting	☐
BOERECPRE	+	+	+++++++065	BoE Rec.Presentation	☐
CASHPAY	+	+	+++++++010	Cash Payment	☐
CASHREC	+	+	+++++++080	Cash Receipt	☐
CHECKCLEAR	+	+	+++++++070	Check Clearing Acct	☐
CHECKPAY	+	+	+++++++050	Checks Out	☐
CHECKREC	+	+	+++++++060	Checks In	☐
DIRECTDEBIT	+	+	+++++++040	Direct Debit	☐
DPCLEAR	+	+	+++++++070	Digital Pymts Clear	☐
DPEXTCLEAR	+	+	12530100	DP Ext. AR Clearing	☐
DPEXTCROSS	+	+	12530100	DP Ext.P Cross Clear	☐
DPEXTIN	+	+	+++++++030	DP Ext.Payment In	☐
DPEXTOUT	+	+	+++++++030	DP Ext.Payment Out	☐
DPEXTREFCLEAR	+	+	11001080	DP Ext.Ref.Bank Clea	☐
DPSETTLEMENT	+	+	+++++++070	Digital Pymts Settle	☐
DPTRANSFER	+	+	+++++++030	Digital Pymts Trans	☐
INTPAID	+	+	71100000	Interest Paid	☐
INTREC	+	+	70100000	Interest Received	☐
OTHERTRANSF	+	+	+++++++030	Other Bank Transfer	☐
SFVCOUT	+	+	+++++++057	Suppl.Fin. VCard Out	☐
SUPFOUT	+	+	+++++++056	Suppl. Financ. Out	☐
TECH	+	+	+++++++090	Technical Account	☐
TRANSF	+	+	+++++++020	Outgoing Transfer	☐

Figure 8.45 Assigning Accounts to Account Symbols

In this configuration activity, you can assign general ledger accounts to be posted for each account symbol. These accounts are assigned using masking, where the **+** sign plays the role of a wildcard. So +++++++++2, for example, means accounts ending in 2.

8.4.3 Posting Rules

In the next step, click **Create Keys for Posting Rules** from the left side of the screen, which will result in the screen shown in Figure 8.46.

Posting rules define how bank transactions should be posted and are identified with 4-character codes, which you'll define on this screen by selecting **New Entries** from the top menu.

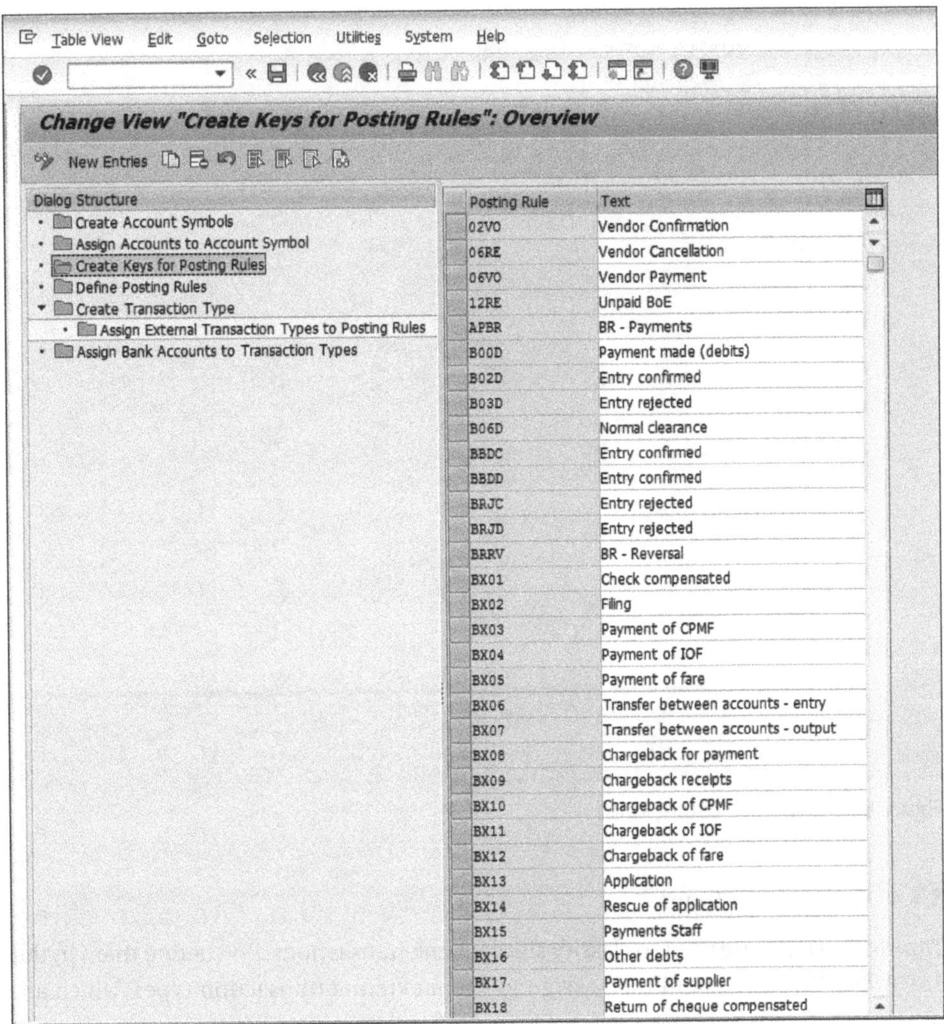

Figure 8.46 Posting Rules Keys

Then, click **Define Posting Rules** from the left side of the screen. As shown in Figure 8.47, you can define, for each posting rule, which account symbols should be posted on the debit and credit side and using which posting keys. You'll also specify the document type to be used for the posting and the type of account, such as general ledger account or subledger account.

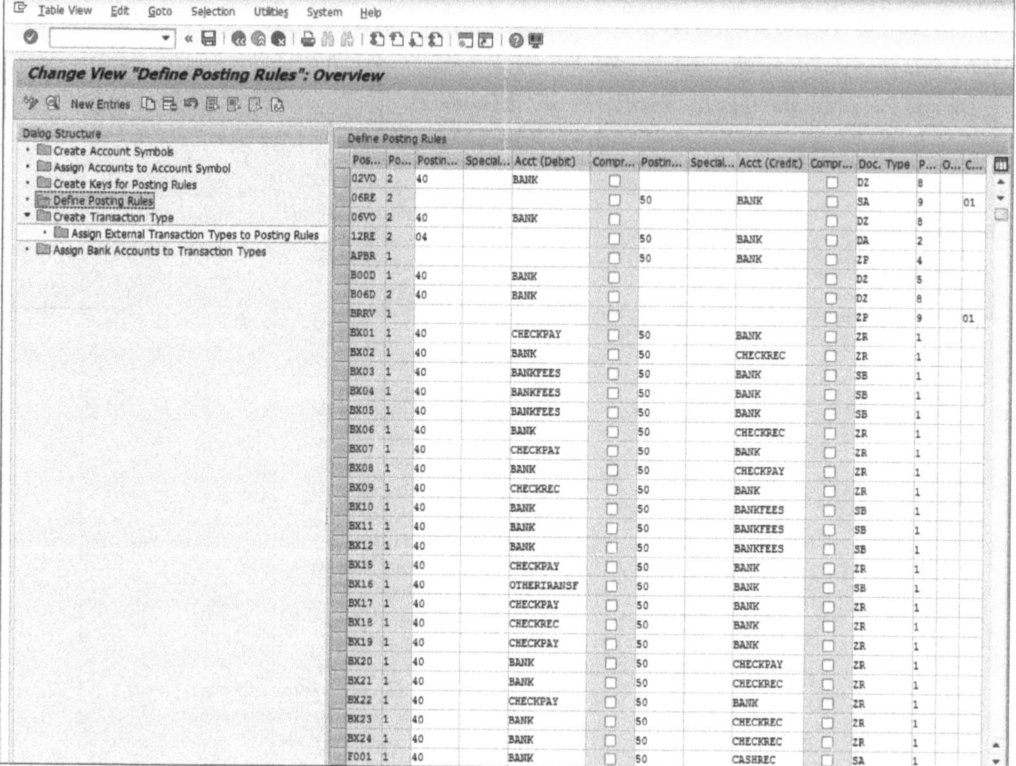

Pos...	Po...	Postin...	Special...	Acct (Debit)	Compr...	Postin...	Special...	Acct (Credit)	Compr...	Doc. Type	P...	O...	C...
02VO	2	40		BANK	☐				☐	DZ	8		
06RE	2				☐	50		BANK	☐	SA	9		01
06VO	2	40		BANK	☐				☐	DZ	8		
12RE	2	04			☐	50		BANK	☐	DA	2		
APBR	1				☐	50		BANK	☐	ZP	4		
B00D	1	40		BANK	☐				☐	DZ	5		
B06D	2	40		BANK	☐				☐	DZ	8		
BRRV	1				☐				☐	ZP	9		01
BX01	1	40		CHECKPAY	☐	50		BANK	☐	ZR	1		
BX02	1	40		BANK	☐	50		CHECKREC	☐	ZR	1		
BX03	1	40		BANKFEES	☐	50		BANK	☐	SB	1		
BX04	1	40		BANKFEES	☐	50		BANK	☐	SB	1		
BX05	1	40		BANKFEES	☐	50		BANK	☐	SB	1		
BX06	1	40		BANK	☐	50		CHECKREC	☐	ZR	1		
BX07	1	40		CHECKPAY	☐	50		BANK	☐	ZR	1		
BX08	1	40		BANK	☐	50		CHECKPAY	☐	ZR	1		
BX09	1	40		CHECKREC	☐	50		BANK	☐	ZR	1		
BX10	1	40		BANK	☐	50		BANKFEES	☐	SB	1		
BX11	1	40		BANK	☐	50		BANKFEES	☐	SB	1		
BX12	1	40		BANK	☐	50		BANKFEES	☐	SB	1		
BX15	1	40		CHECKPAY	☐	50		BANK	☐	ZR	1		
BX16	1	40		OTHERTRANSF	☐	50		BANK	☐	SB	1		
BX17	1	40		CHECKPAY	☐	50		BANK	☐	ZR	1		
BX18	1	40		CHECKREC	☐	50		BANK	☐	ZR	1		
BX19	1	40		CHECKPAY	☐	50		BANK	☐	ZR	1		
BX20	1	40		BANK	☐	50		CHECKPAY	☐	ZR	1		
BX21	1	40		BANK	☐	50		CHECKREC	☐	ZR	1		
BX22	1	40		CHECKPAY	☐	50		BANK	☐	ZR	1		
BX23	1	40		BANK	☐	50		CHECKREC	☐	ZR	1		
BX24	1	40		BANK	☐	50		CHECKREC	☐	ZR	1		
F001	1	40		BANK	☐	50		CASHREC	☐	SA	1		

Figure 8.47 Defining Posting Rules

8.4.4 Transaction Types

Transaction types are used to classify similar bank transactions. You define them in the SAP S/4HANA system and then assign to them external transaction types, which are bank defined and are present in the electronic bank statement file.

From the main configuration screen of the electronic bank statement, click **Create Transaction Type**, which will result in the screen shown in Figure 8.48.

On this screen, you can name your transaction types. To create a transaction type, you must have researched the external transaction types provided by your bank and have a clear strategy for how you'll assign them.

Then, select a transaction type and click **Assign External Transaction Types to Posting Rules** from the left side of the screen.

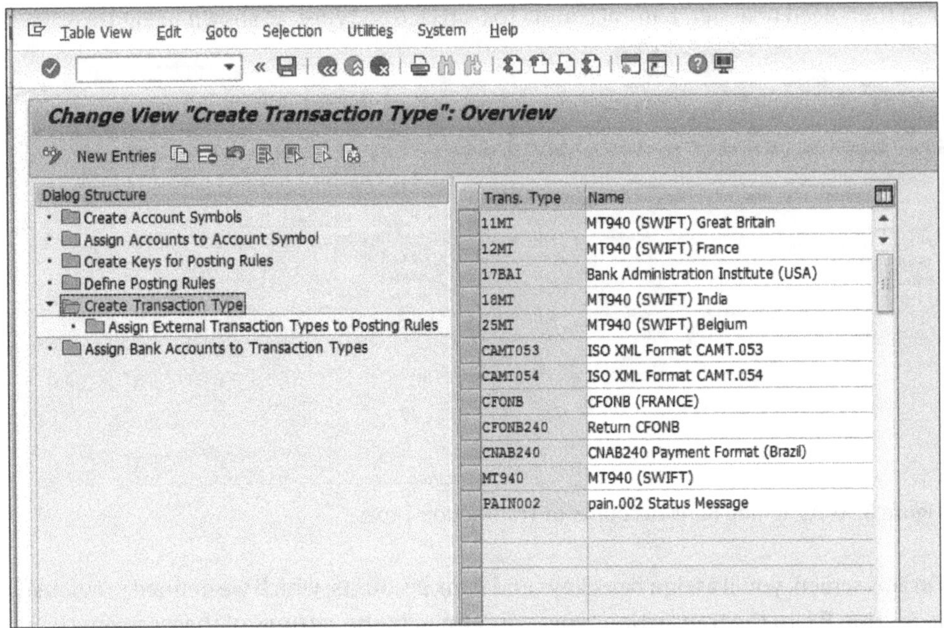

Figure 8.48 Creating Transaction Types

As shown in Figure 8.49, assign the external transaction types (in this case, 009 and 051) to your transaction types. Then, assign the posting rule we defined earlier in Section 8.4.3, which will be used for posting. You can also set a + or – sign to be applied to the amount from the bank statement and interpretation algorithm, which is used to identify open items in SAP S/4HANA. The processing type defines the type of amount, for instance, opening balance, inflow, outflow, closing balance, and so on.

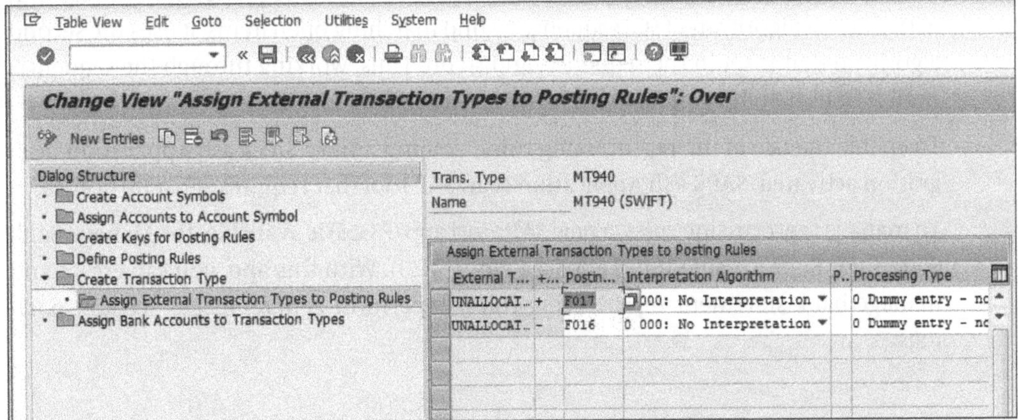

Figure 8.49 Assigning External Transaction Types to Transaction Types

You then need to assign bank accounts to transaction types, as shown in Figure 8.50.

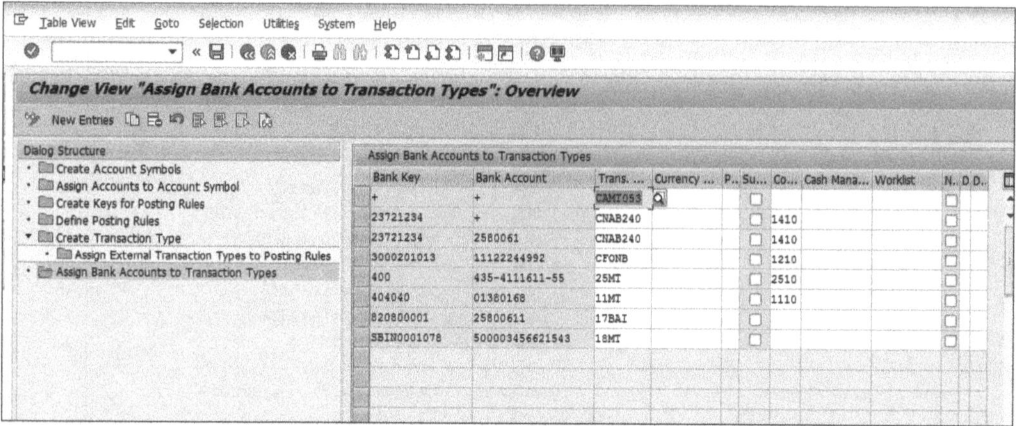

Figure 8.50 Assigning Bank Accounts to Transaction Types

On this screen, you'll assign bank keys and bank accounts, which we defined previously in Section 8.1, to the transaction types we defined in the settings of the electronic bank statement. So, the system now can know which bank accounts to update based on the transaction type.

8.4.5 Reprocessing Rules

Starting with SAP S/4HANA 2020, a new function can use reprocessing rules in which you can set the sequence of allocation and interpretation algorithms to find open matching bank statement items in order to clear them. The reprocessing rule first tries to find matching open items with the first algorithm of the sequence. If not successful with the first algorithm of the sequence to find matching open items, it uses the second algorithm that is set in the sequence, and so on. Thus, working through the sequence, until it finds matching open items, which it then sends for clearing.

To enable the use of the reprocessing rules, you must have SAP Cash Application integration activated. SAP Cash Application is an SAP tool that requires separate license.

To manage reprocessing rules, a new SAP Fiori app (F3555) is available: the Manage Bank Statement Reprocessing Rules app (see Figure 8.51). With this app, you can create and manage bank statement reprocessing rules to perform general ledger account postings.

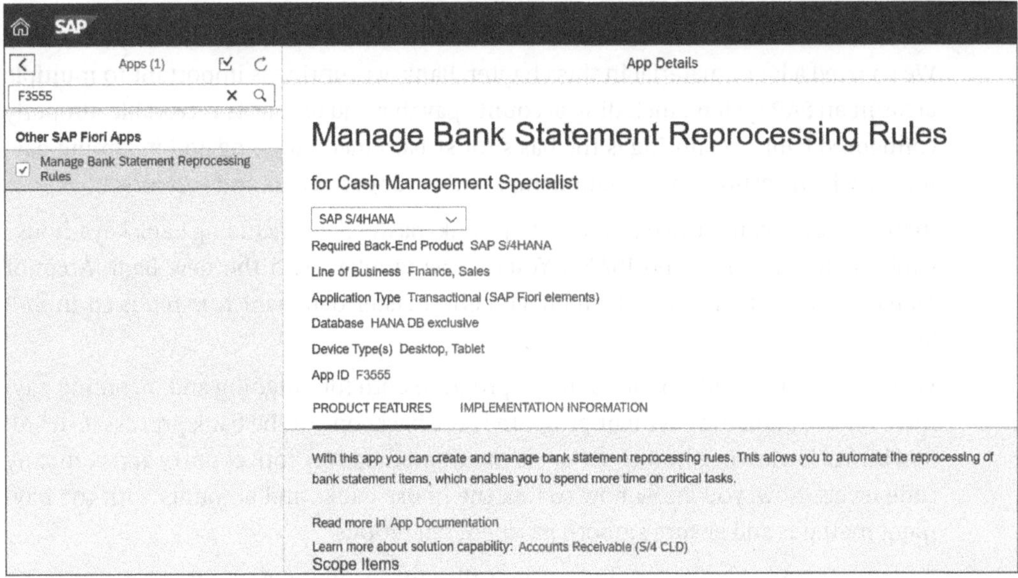

Figure 8.51 Bank Statement Reprocessing Rules

8.4.6 Editing Journal Entries during Simulation

Prior to SAP S/4HANA 2020, when processing bank statement items, you could simulate the posting of journal entries. Now, in the Reprocess Bank Statement Items app (F1520), you can also edit journal entries while simulating a posting by selecting **Simulate Posting** from the menu, as shown in Figure 8.52.

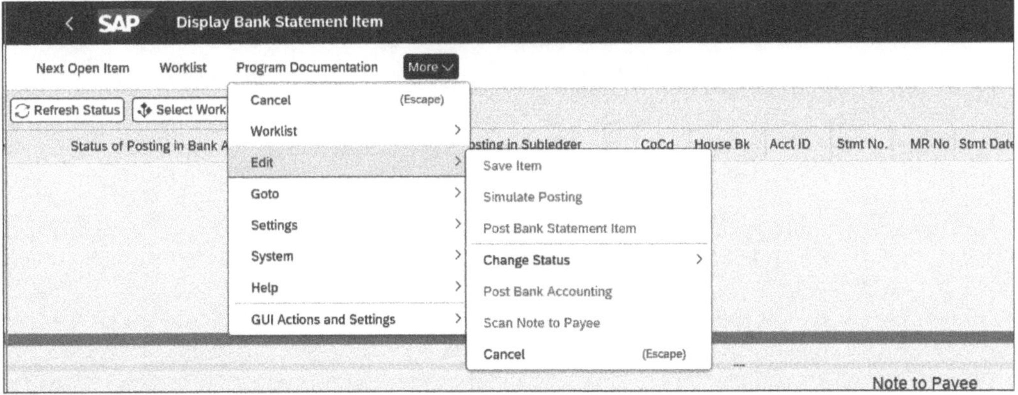

Figure 8.52 Reprocessing Bank Statement Items

After the simulation, you can change the value of some fields and add information to the journal entries before posting the document with the changes.

8.5 Summary

We covered a lot of material in this chapter. Bank accounting is important to multiple areas in an SAP system, including accounts payable and accounts receivable. Properly configured bank accounting is the basis for streamlined outgoing and incoming payments, which ensures good relationships with your customers and vendors.

In this chapter, you learned how to set up bank master data, including bank keys, house banks, bank accounts, and IBANs. You're now familiar with the new Bank Account Management SAP Fiori app to manage bank master data, which is required in SAP S/4HANA.

We configured the automatic payment program both for outgoing and incoming payments. The automatic payment program is the backbone of the bank processes in SAP S/4HANA. You learned how to set up payment methods on both country and company code levels. Now, you know how to link the house banks and accounts with the payment methods and ensure smooth payment operations.

You also learned how to set up payment files for incoming and outgoing automatic payments. We paid special attention to the SEPA payments, which are now standard for euro payments.

Finally, we configured the electronic bank statement, which enables you to import bank statements from your bank and thus automatically close vendor and customer open items and update your bank accounts.

With that summary, we've finished our guide on financial accounting processes and can move on to the configuration of controlling.

Chapter 9
General Controlling and Cost Element Accounting

In this chapter, we'll provide step-by-step instructions for configuring general controlling settings and settings for cost element accounting, which is now fully integrated with financial accounting in SAP S/4HANA. You'll learn how to create cost elements as general ledger accounts and how to create cost element groups and learn about the actual postings in cost element accounting.

We've finished the configuration of financial accounting in SAP S/4HANA, so now, we'll move on to the other big financial area: controlling (commonly referred to simply as CO). Controlling provides invaluable information and enables flexible analysis for internal managerial accounting. However, in today's business world, the requirements of external legal accounting and internal managerial accounting often interrelate and are becoming increasingly more demanding. Therefore, SAP S/4HANA provides fully integrated financial accounting and controlling, sharing the same tables and data structures, yet enabling separate, state-of-the-art analysis and reports that meet the requirements both of external users of accounting information, such as tax authorities and auditors, and of internal managers and controllers.

We'll start the configuration of controlling with the general controlling settings, which are the foundation of all other controlling areas, such as product costing and profitability analysis. Then, we'll set up the required master data for cost element accounting and examine the actual postings on the cost element accounting level.

9.1 General Controlling Settings

By *general controlling settings*, we mean settings that apply to all controlling components, such as maintaining the controlling area, number ranges, versions, and so on.

General controlling settings are located in the customizing menu under **Controlling • General Controlling**, as shown in Figure 9.1.

We'll start with the definition of the controlling area.

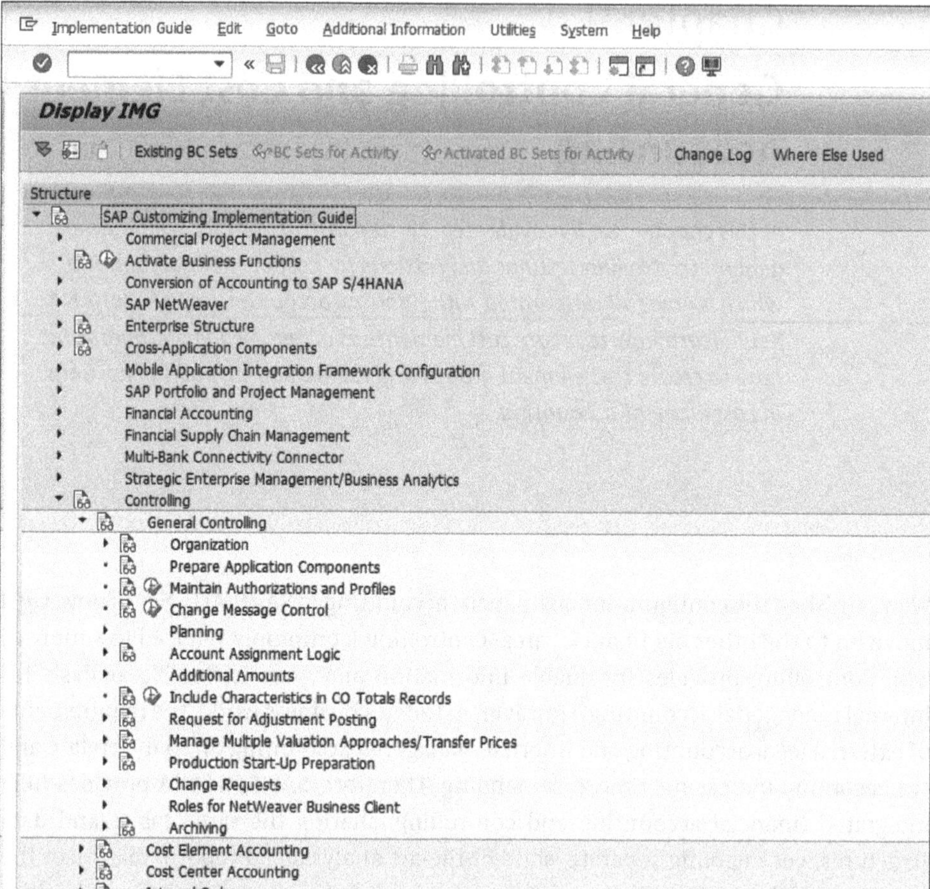

Figure 9.1 General Controlling Settings

9.1.1 Maintaining Controlling Areas

The controlling area is the main organizational object in controlling. The main business decision is whether to use one controlling area across multiple company codes or to use separate controlling areas for each company code. In most cases, cross-company code controlling makes sense because the controlling function for most companies is executed across legal entities, countries, and regions.

You learned how to create a new controlling area and how to copy an existing controlling area in Chapter 3. We also already assigned our company code 1000 to controlling area 0001. Now, to modify the controlling area general settings, follow the menu path **Controlling • General Controlling • Organization • Maintain Controlling Area**. Then, select the **Maintain Controlling Area** activity, as shown in Figure 9.2.

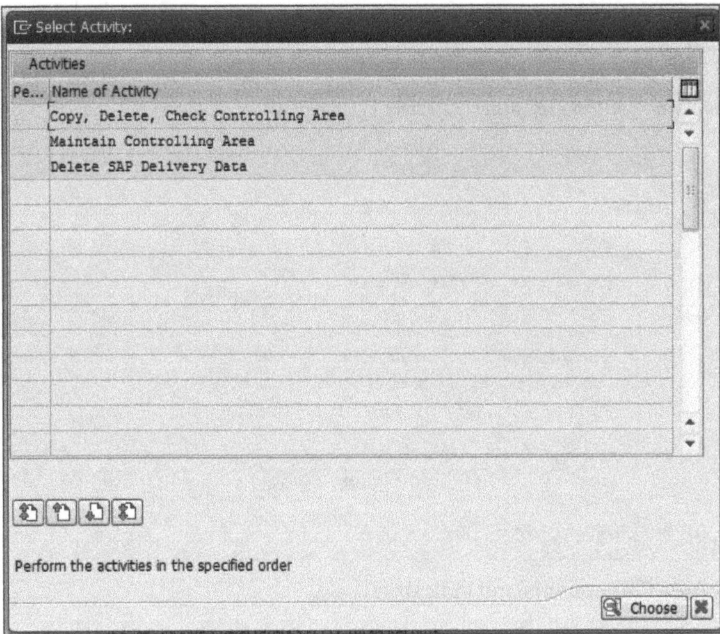

Figure 9.2 Controlling Area Activities

Next, select controlling area **A000**, as shown in Figure 9.3, and click **Activate components/control indicators** on the left side of the screen.

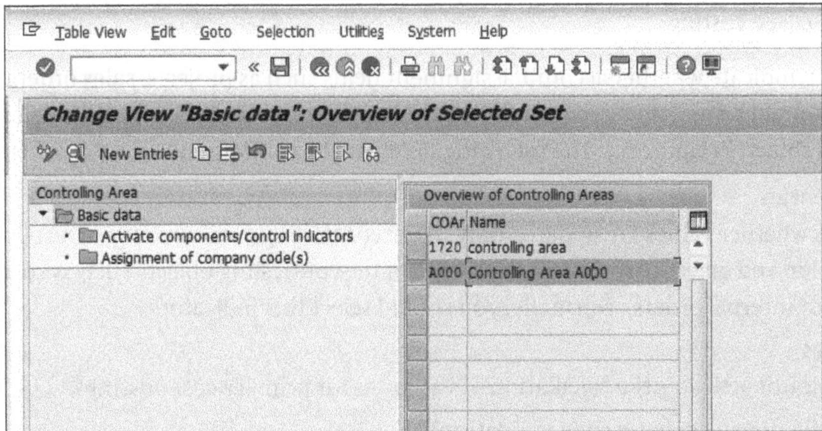

Figure 9.3 Maintaining Controlling Areas

In this configuration transaction, you'll activate and deactivate the various controlling components and set control indicators, as shown in Figure 9.4.

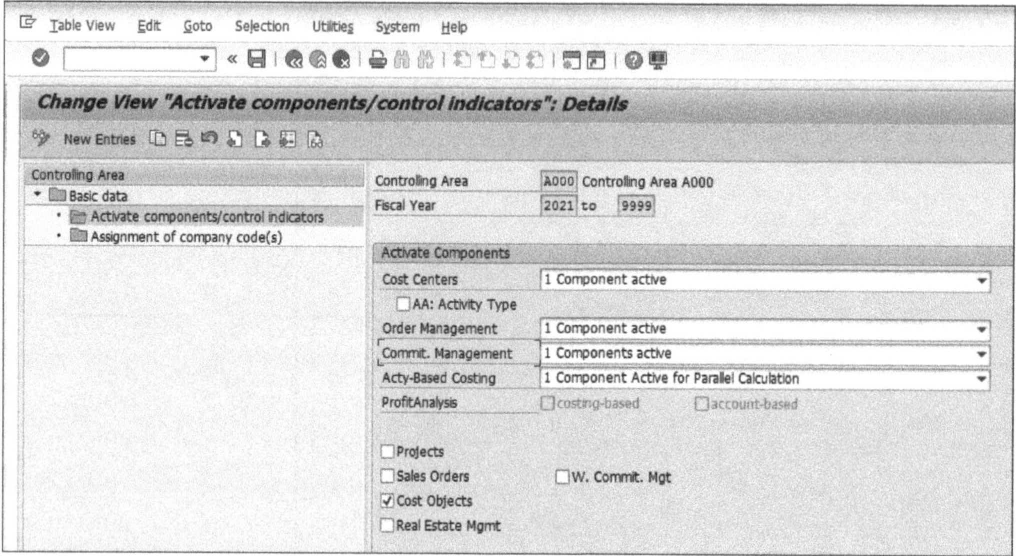

Figure 9.4 Controlling Area Components and Indicators

You can activate components including the following:

- Cost centers
- Order management
- Commitment management
- Activity-based costing

You also can indicate whether account assignment fields such as projects, sales orders, and so on should be updated in controlling. Scrolling down, you can configure further settings, as shown in Figure 9.5. The following fields can be configured:

- **All Currencies**
  Controls whether values are updated only in the controlling area currency or also in transaction and object currency (the currency of the controlling objects such as cost centers or internal orders). Normally, you should select this indicator.
- **Variances**
  This indicator activates the calculation of variances for primary cost postings.
- **CoCd Validation (company code validation)**
  This indicator applies to cross-company code postings. If selected, postings to an account assignment object, such as a cost center or an order, can be made only from the company code defined in the master data for the account assignment object.

We covered the assignment of company codes in Chapter 3, Section 3.2.3.

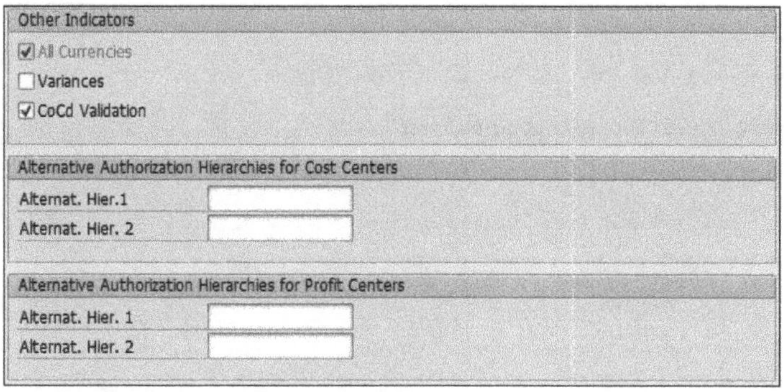

Other Indicators
All Currencies
Variances
CoCd Validation
Alternative Authorization Hierarchies for Cost Centers
Alternat. Hier.1
Alternat. Hier. 2
Alternative Authorization Hierarchies for Profit Centers
Alternat. Hier. 1
Alternat. Hier. 2

Figure 9.5 Controlling Area Other Settings

9.1.2 Number Ranges

Number ranges provide document numbers for controlling transactions. In general, in controlling, no legal requirements affect the numbering of documents. Still, using continuous, internal number assignment makes sense.

To set up the number ranges for controlling, follow the menu path **Controlling • General Controlling • Organization • Maintain Number Ranges for Controlling Documents.** On the initial screen, shown in Figure 9.6, notice that the number range object for controlling documents is **RK_BELEG.**

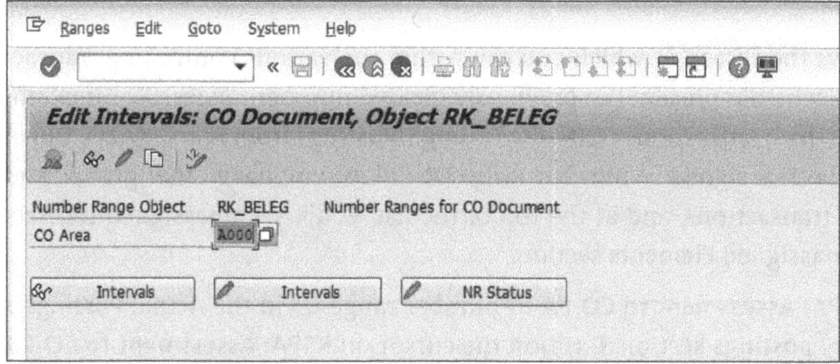

Figure 9.6 Number Ranges

Enter controlling area A000 and click the **Change Intervals** button Intervals. On the screen shown in Figure 9.7, set up number ranges and define their from and to numbers. In this example, documents posted in number range 01 will start with number 100000000 and will be internally assigned consecutively because the **Ext** checkbox is not selected.

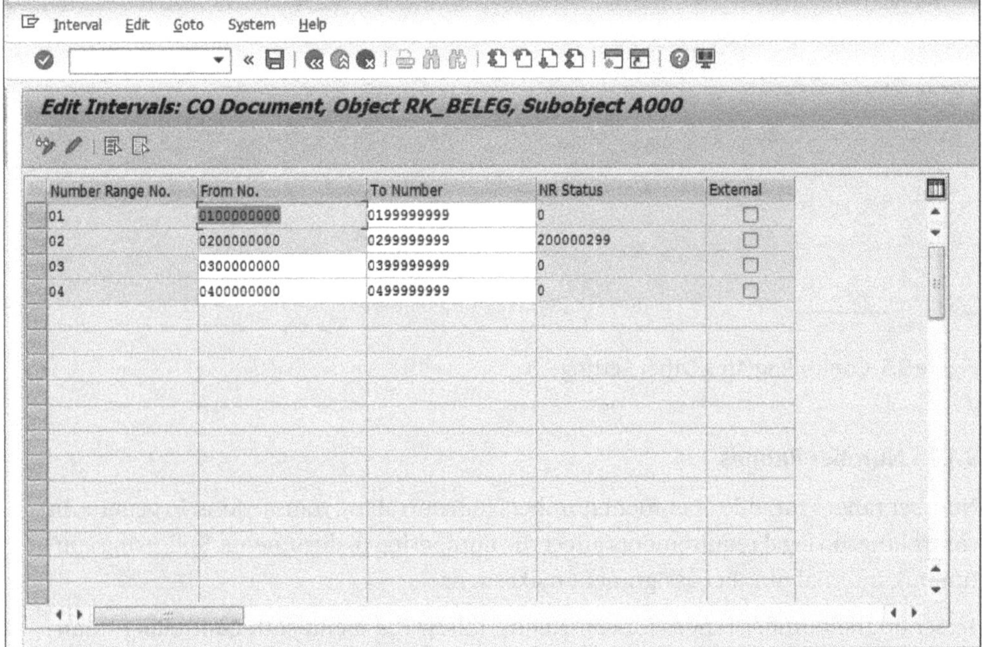

Figure 9.7 Number Ranges Maintenance

Now, go back, and from the screen shown in Figure 9.6, select **Change Groups** from the top menu.

Figure 9.8 shows the screen in which you can assign the various controlling transactions to groups, which represent the previously created number ranges. So, for example, you can see that transactions **COIN: CO Through-Postings from FI** and **KAZO: Down Payment** have been assigned to number range 01. Below, you have other groups and other assigned transactions, and at the top of the list, you'll see unassigned transactions in the **Nonassigned Elements** section.

Let's assign **KSPA: Assessment to CO-PA** to number range 03 in the **Actual Postings / without primary postings** section. Position the cursor on **KSPA: Assessment to CO-PA** and select **Assign Element to Group** from the top menu. Then, a popup window will appear, as shown in Figure 9.9.

In this window, double-click the group you want to assign the transaction to—in this case, **Actual Postings / without primary postings**. Then, the **KSPA: Assessment to CO-PA** entry disappears from the unassigned transactions list and appears in the **Actual Postings / without primary postings** list.

After assigning unassigned transactions, save your entries with the **Save** button.

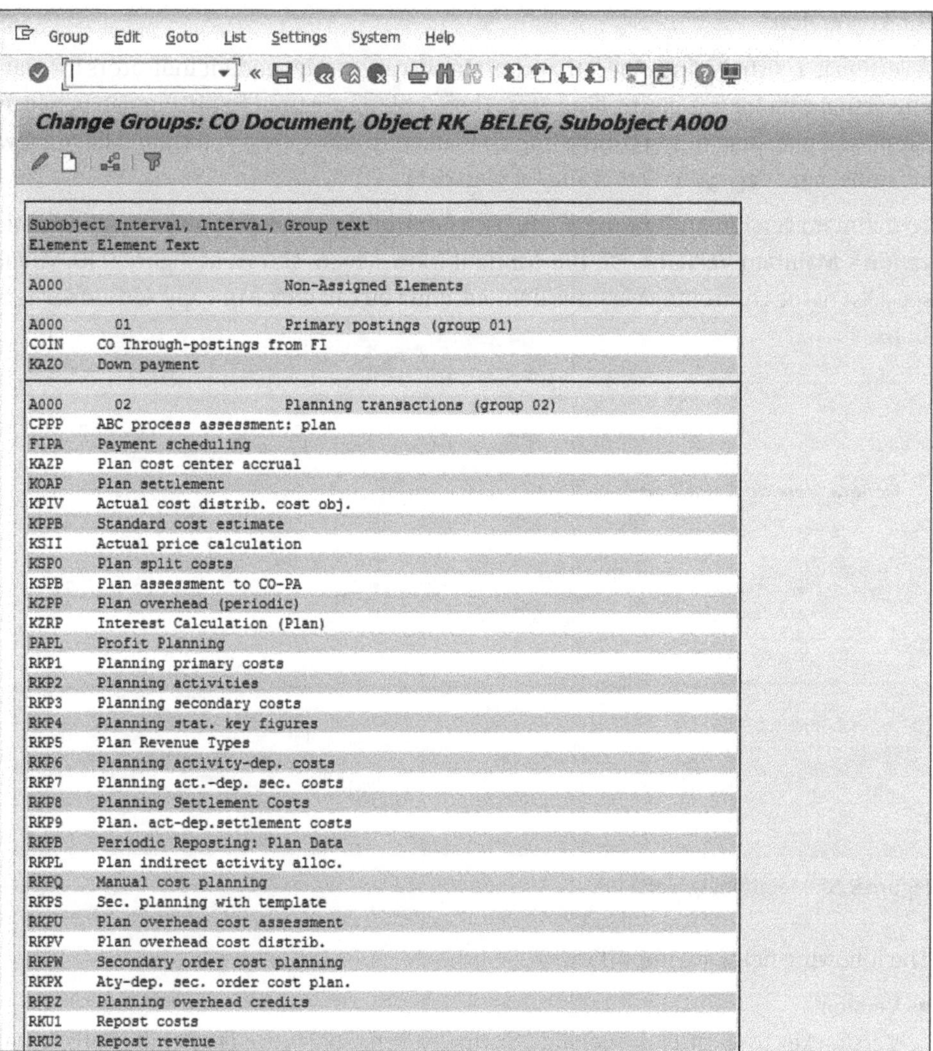

Figure 9.8 Change Groups

Group Selection

Subobject	Number range number	Number range number	Group text
A000	01		Primary postings (group 01)
A000	02		Planning transactions (group 02)
A000	03		Actual Postings / without primary postings (group 03)
A000	04		Other transactions (group 04)
A000			Non-Assigned Elements

Figure 9.9 Assigning Transactions to Groups

9.1.3 Versions

A *version* is a customizing object that contains fiscal year-dependent indicators for plan and actual data for one controlling area. These objects are used to distinguish between actual and plan postings in controlling. In your controlling area, you should have a few versions to manage your actual and/or plan data.

To maintain versions, follow the menu path **Controlling • General Controlling • Organization • Maintain Versions.** On the configuration screen, shown in Figure 9.10, you'll see a list of the controlling versions defined, and you can create or copy additional versions.

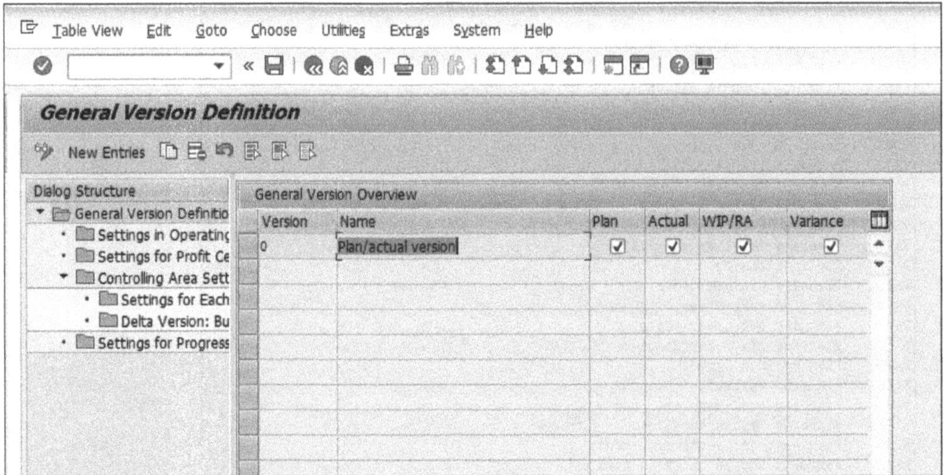

Figure 9.10 Maintaining Versions

The following fields are important:

- **Version**
  Version key to identify the version. Normally, version 0 is used to handle both actual and plan data and is the main version for controlling.
- **Name**
  A meaningful description of the version.
- **Plan**
  A checkmark in this column indicates that the version contains plan data.
- **Actual**
  A checkmark in this column indicates that the version contains actual data.
- **WIP/RA**
  Controls whether data from a results analysis or work in progress (WIP) calculation can be written to the version.
- **Variance**
  Controls whether data from the variance calculation can be written to the version.

- **Exclusive Use**
  Select an option from the dropdown list if the version should be used exclusively by a specific application.

> **Note**
> We'll customize the settings under the **Settings in Operating Concern** option on the left side of the screen in Chapter 13.

Now, select version 0 and click the **Settings for Each Fiscal Year** option from the left side of the screen.

Figure 9.11 shows the year-dependent settings for version 0. You can lock the version per year. You also can enable integrated planning per year, and you can allow copying, which means that the version can be used as reference for another version in a copy procedure.

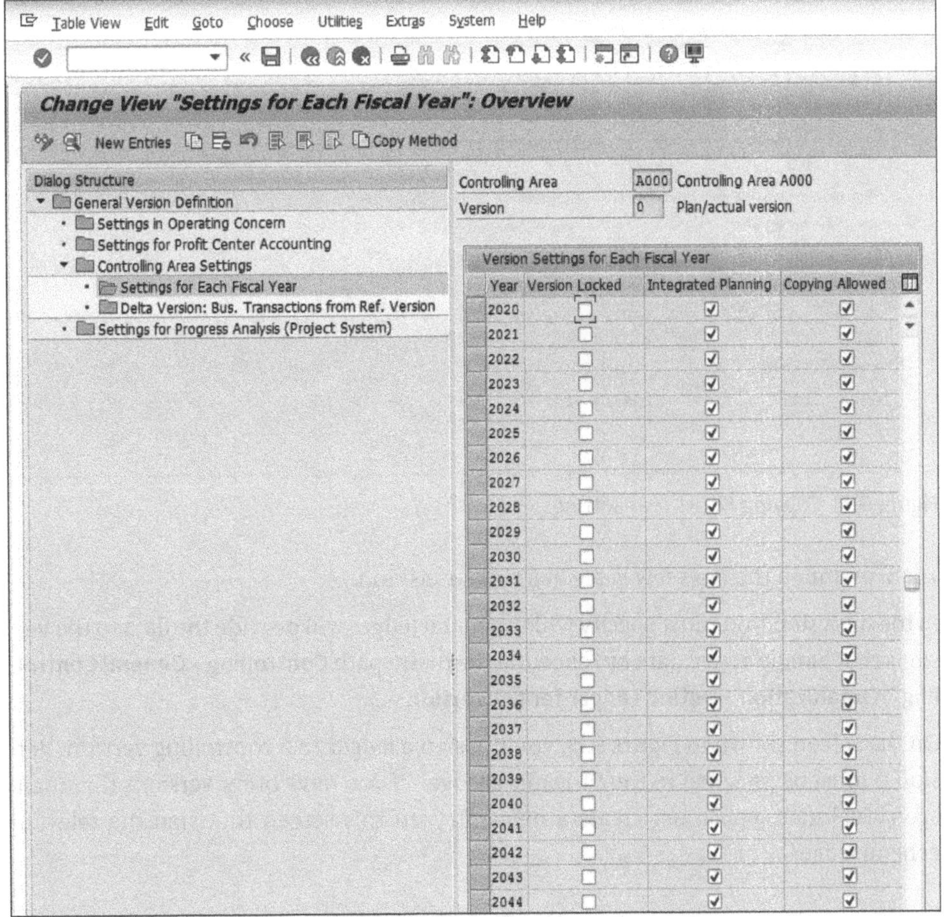

Figure 9.11 Fiscal Year Settings

Select the last available year and click the **Copy As...** option from the top menu. Then, you can maintain the settings for the latest years, as shown in Figure 9.12.

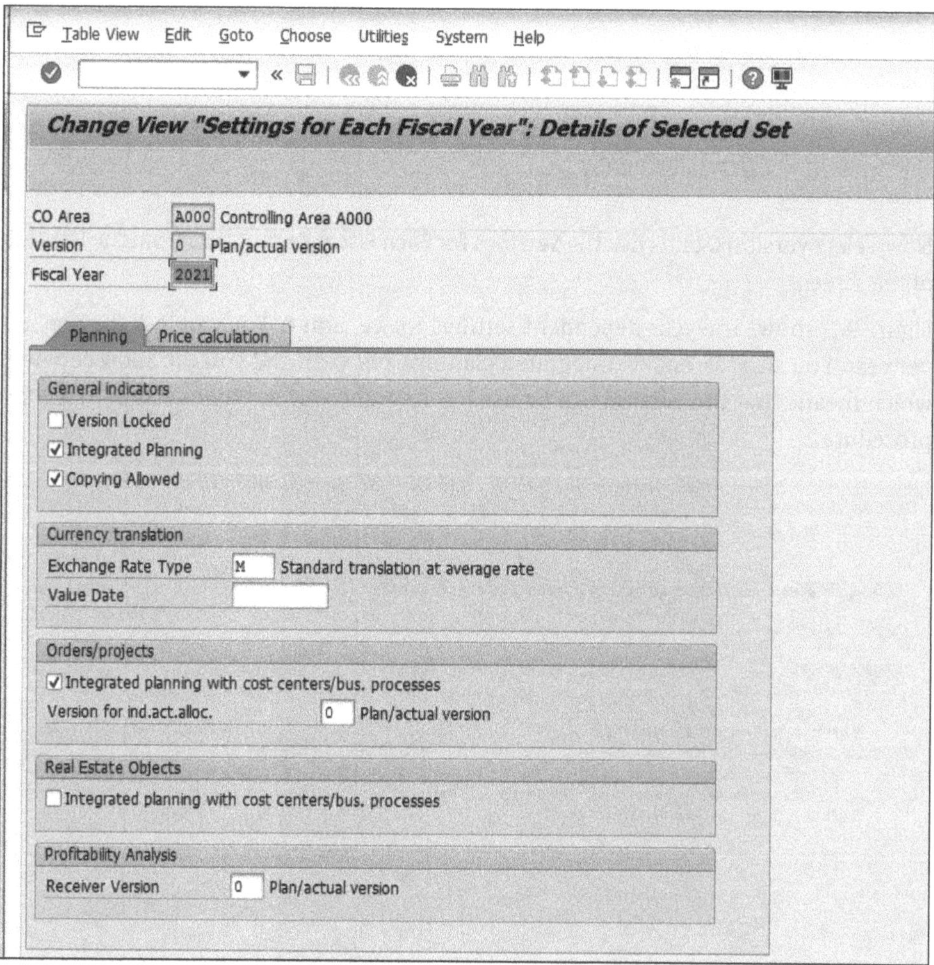

Figure 9.12 Copying Fiscal Year Settings

Then, maintain the next few years in a similar fashion.

In the next step, you must specify which general ledger will provide the data to the versions that handle actual data by following the menu path **Controlling • General Controlling • Organization • Define Ledger for CO Version.**

On the screen shown in Figure 9.13, you'll assign a ledger to a controlling version. Version 0 must be assigned to the 0L leading ledger. If you have other versions that manage actual data, you must create a new entry on this screen to assign the relevant general ledger.

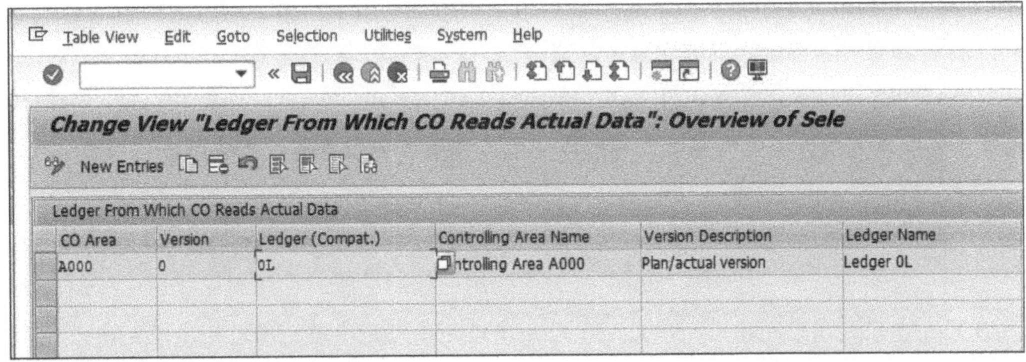

Figure 9.13 Ledger for Controlling Postings

9.2 Master Data

Controlling uses various master data objects such as cost elements, cost centers, internal orders, and so on. In this section, we'll focus just on the cost element master data. In the following chapters, we'll set up cost centers, internal orders, and other controlling master data objects as we cover the various controlling areas.

9.2.1 Cost Elements

Cost elements are the accounts of the controlling modules. All controlling postings flow into cost elements. Normally, all profit and loss (P&L) accounts are set as cost elements, and you can also have secondary cost elements, which are not used purely in financial accounting postings but also in internal controlling postings.

The big difference in SAP S/4HANA, as compared with previous SAP releases, is that cost elements are now fully integrated with the general ledger. In SAP S/4HANA, no separate cost element master data object exists. Instead, cost elements are a type of general ledger account with special settings in their master records.

Let's look at the master record of a cost element. The application menu path **Accounting • Controlling • Cost Element Accounting • Master Data • Cost Element • Individual Processing • FS00 - Edit Cost Element** now points to Transaction FS00, which is used to maintain general ledger accounts. If you enter the old Transaction KA01/KA02/KA03 to create/change/display a cost element, you'll be redirected to Transaction FS00 to maintain general ledger accounts.

For our example, we'll select an expense account such as "65100000" in the **G/L Account** field for **Office Supplies** in company code 1000. As shown in Figure 9.14, this account is defined as an income statement account.

Select the **Control Data** tab, shown in Figure 9.15, to review the controlling settings for the account.

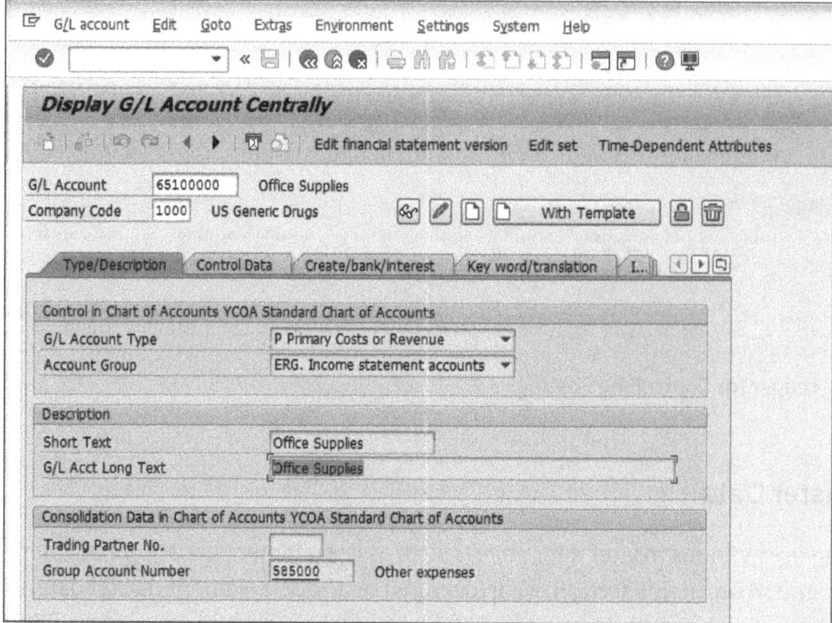

Figure 9.14 Changing the General Ledger Account

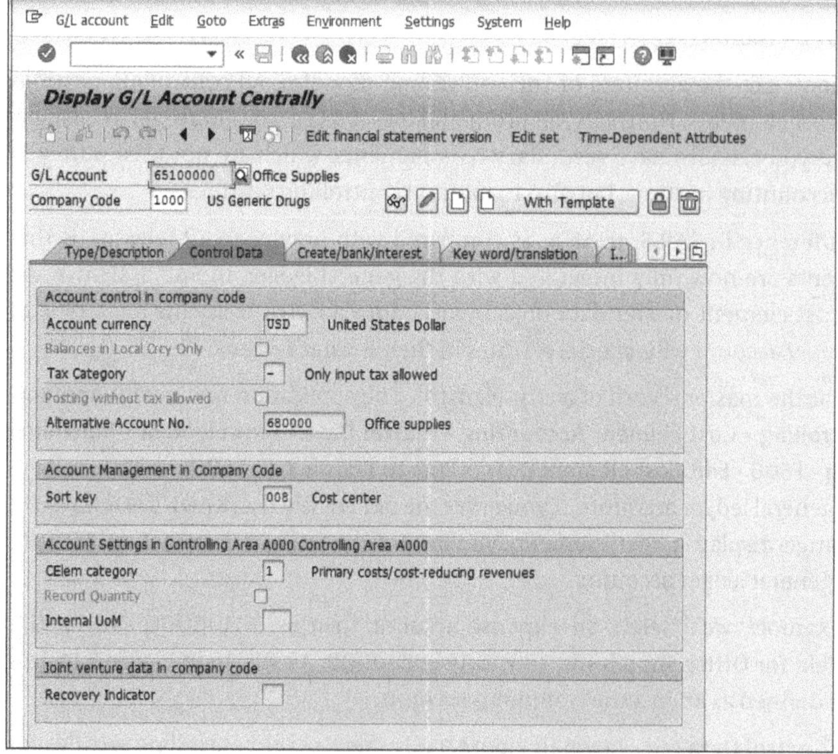

Figure 9.15 Controlling Settings for the General Ledger Account

Now, in SAP S/4HANA, in the general ledger account master record, account settings in the controlling area are displayed in their own area. The following three fields were previously available in the cost element master record:

- **CElem Category (cost element category)**
  The cost element category determines for which business transactions the cost element can be used. Separate categories for primary and secondary cost elements exist, as follows:
  - **01: Primary costs/cost-reducing revenues**
  - **03: Accrual/deferral per surcharge**
  - **04: Accrual/deferral per debit = actual**
  - **11: Revenues**
  - **12: Sales deduction**
  - **22: External settlement**
- **Record Quantity**
  Defines whether the system issues a message if no quantity or quantity unit is specified when posting to the cost element.
- **Internal UoM (internal unit of measure)**
  Controls whether an internal unit of measure (UoM) can be used for this cost element.

After maintaining these settings, the account is integrated between the general ledger and controlling.

9.2.2 Cost Element Groups

Cost element groups are used to group together similar cost elements for reporting and data processing needs. On this topic, SAP S/4HANA does not differ from previous releases: Transactions KAH1, KAH2, and KAH3 to create, change, and display cost element groups are still valid.

To create a cost element group, follow the application menu path **Accounting • Controlling • Cost Element Accounting • Master Data • Cost Element Group • KAH1—Create.**

Enter a meaningful name for the cost element group, as shown in Figure 9.16. You can create a cost element group with reference to an existing group, which you'll specify together with the chart of accounts in the **Reference** section. Proceed with the **Enter** button.

Initially, you'll see only the top level of the cost element group. Enter a meaningful description, as shown: in Figure 9.17.

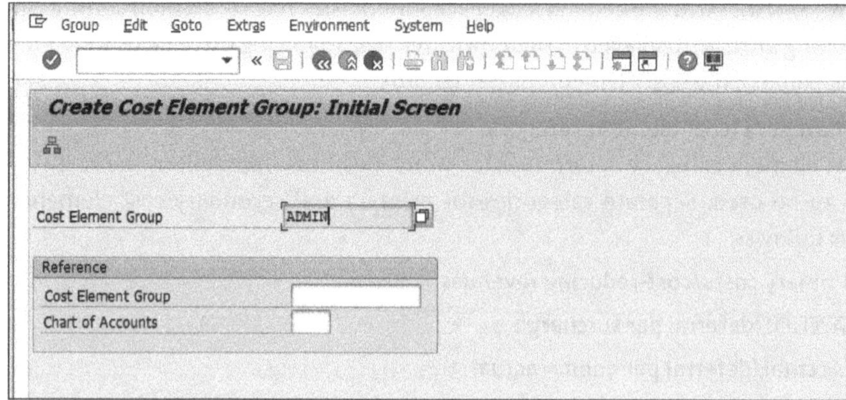

Figure 9.16 Create Cost Element Group: Initial Screen

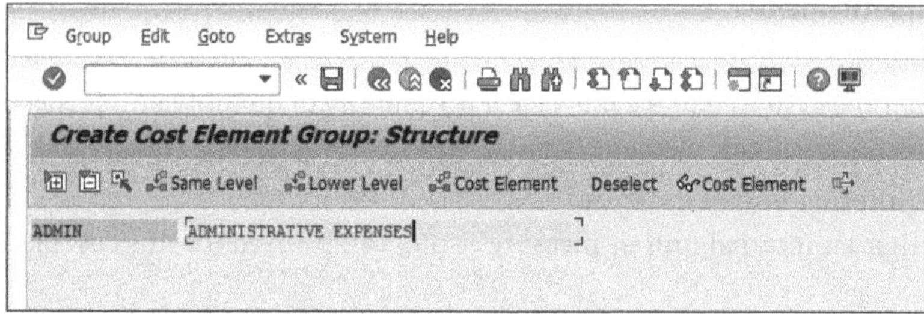

Figure 9.17 Create Cost Element Group Definition

Then, the following three options are available from the top menu:

- **Same Level**
  Inserts the cost element group at the same level.
- **Lower Level**
  Inserts the cost element group at a lower level.
- **Cost Element**
  Inserts the cost element.

Using these options, you can build your cost element groups, as shown in Figure 9.18.

In our case, we created a few cost element groups under the main cost element group and then assigned a range of cost elements to the cost element group. In this fashion, you can build quite complex cost element groups.

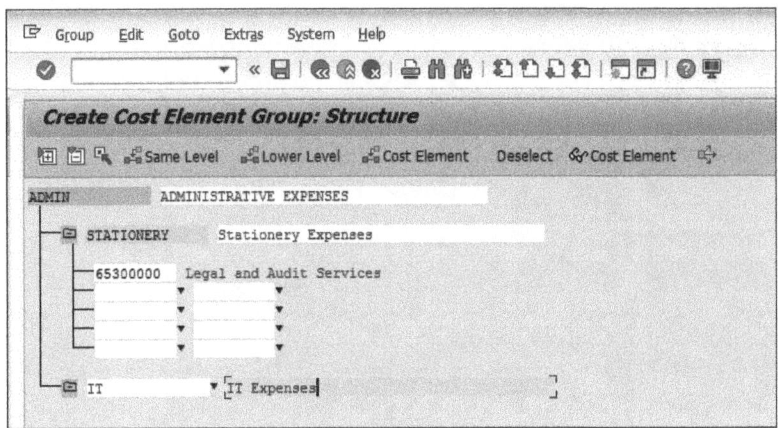

Figure 9.18 Cost Element Group Structure

9.3 Actual Postings

As part of the cost element accounting application menu, SAP provides some actual postings that you can use to reclassify costs within the controlling. In this section, we'll look at manual repostings and activity allocations.

9.3.1 Manual Reposting

Manual repostings of costs are used to correct posting errors in controlling. For example, if a posting is entered to the wrong cost element, you can report the cost to another cost element with this function.

Three transactions are provided, which are available at the application menu path **Accounting • Controlling • Cost Element Accounting • Actual Postings • Manual Reposting of Costs**, as shown in Figure 9.19.

You can use the following three transactions:

- **KB11N – Enter**
  With this transaction, you can enter manually reposting costs.
- **KB13N – Display**
  With this transaction, you can display repostings of costs already entered.
- **KB14N – Reverse**
  This transaction is used to reverse repostings of costs already entered.

Let's see how to report on costs. Enter Transaction KB11N. On the initial screen, shown in Figure 9.20, in the **Scrn Var.** (screen variant) field, select a screen variant depending on what type of sending and receiving controlling object you'll repost from and to. The default value is the last screen variant used.

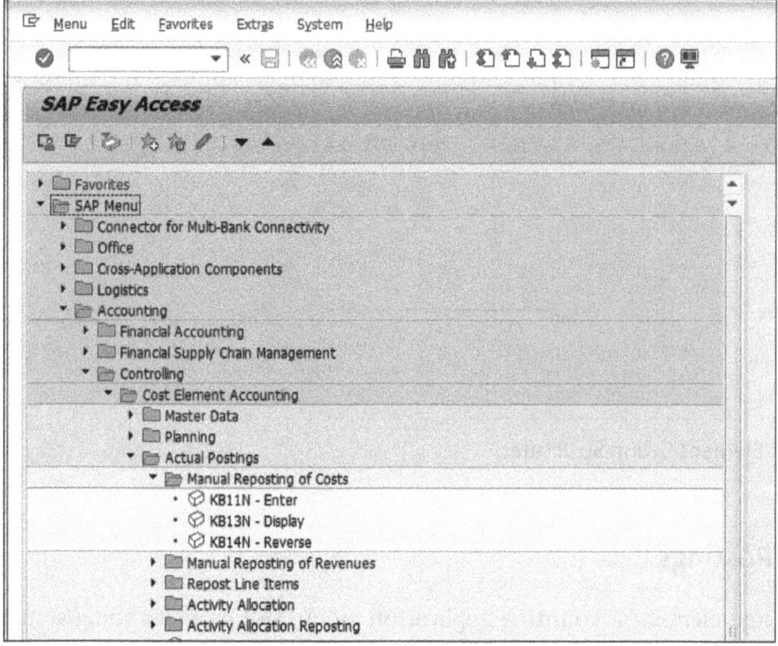

Figure 9.19 Manual Reposting Transactions

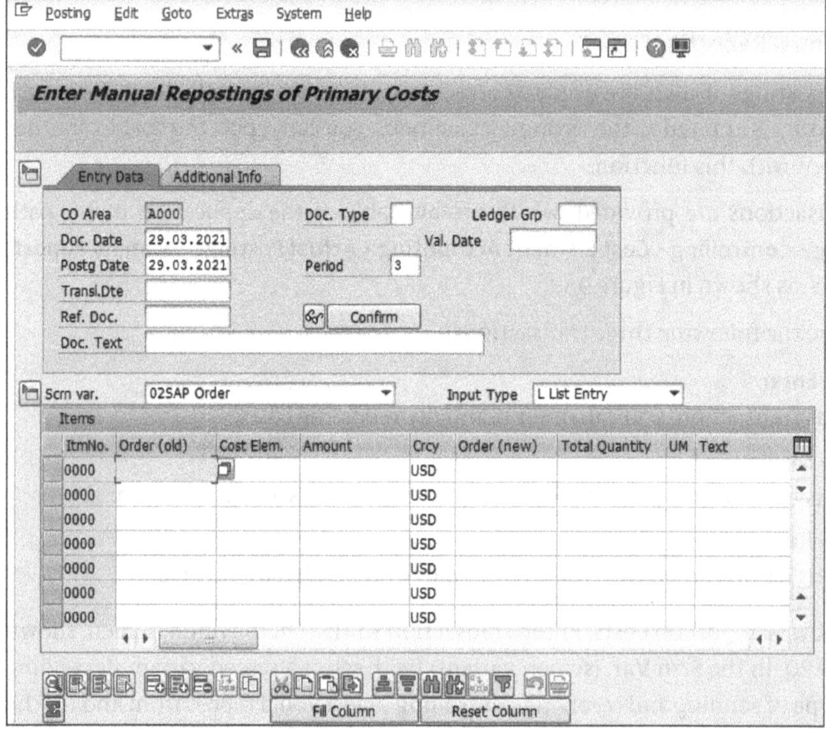

Figure 9.20 Enter Manual Repostings of Primary Costs

You can choose from the following screen variants, as shown in Figure 9.21:

- **01SAP: Cost center**
- **02SAP: Order**
- **03SAP: Cost center/order/pers. no.**
- **Real estate objects**
- **04SAP: WBS element/order**
- **05SAP: WBS element/network**
- **06SAP: Sales order/cost object**
- **12SAP: Customer Project**

These screen variants determine which of these fields will be available for reposting.

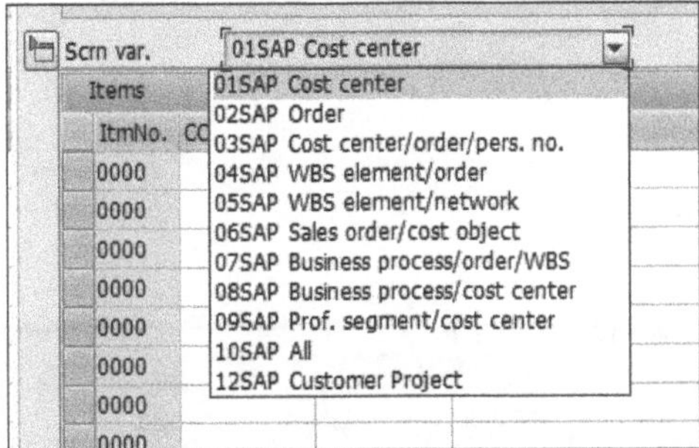

Figure 9.21 Screen Variants

Select **Cost center**, and the screen changes to include the old cost center (original cost center to repost from) and new cost center. Enter the necessary data, as shown in Figure 9.22. The following fields are important:

- **CO Area (controlling area)**
  The controlling area where the reporting is taking place.
- **Doc. Date (document date)**
  Document date of the reposting. For CO internal documents, normally, it's the same as the posting date.
- **Postg Date (posting date)**
  Posting date of the reposting, which is used to determine the period.
- **CCtr (Old) (cost center, old)**
  The cost center that was originally incorrectly posted. With other screen variants, you can repost from internal orders, work breakdown structure (WBS) elements, and other controlling objects.
- **Cost Elem. (cost element)**
  The cost element originally posted. In the reposting, the same cost element is used.

- **Amount**
  Amount to be reposted.
- **Crcy (currency)**
  Currency of the reposting.
- **CCtr (New) (cost center, new)**
  This cost center will receive the reposting.

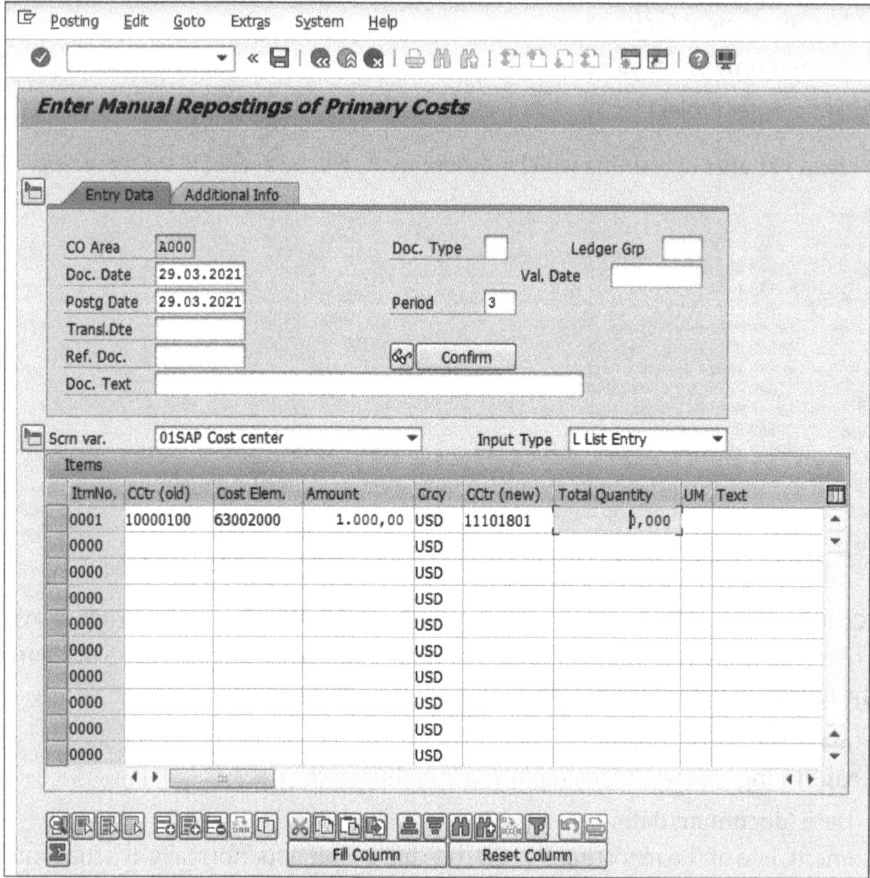

Figure 9.22 Cost Center Manual Reposting

After maintaining your settings, save your entries by clicking the **Post** button. As a result, the original cost center that was debited in the original document is now credited, and the new cost center gets the debit and is charged with the cost. The same cost element is used.

9.3.2 Activity Allocation

Another function in cost element accounting, an *activity allocation* (sometimes referred to as a *direct activity allocation*) allows you to reallocate costs from one cost center to another using activity types. Activity types are objects used to record activities in SAP S/4HANA, such as labor hours. We'll talk about them in detail in the Chapter 10; for now, note that activity types are tracing factors that can be used as allocation bases during activity allocation. Let's look now at how an activity allocation works.

Three transactions are provided, which are available at the application menu path **Accounting • Controlling • Cost Element Accounting • Actual Postings • Activity Allocation**, as shown in Figure 9.23.

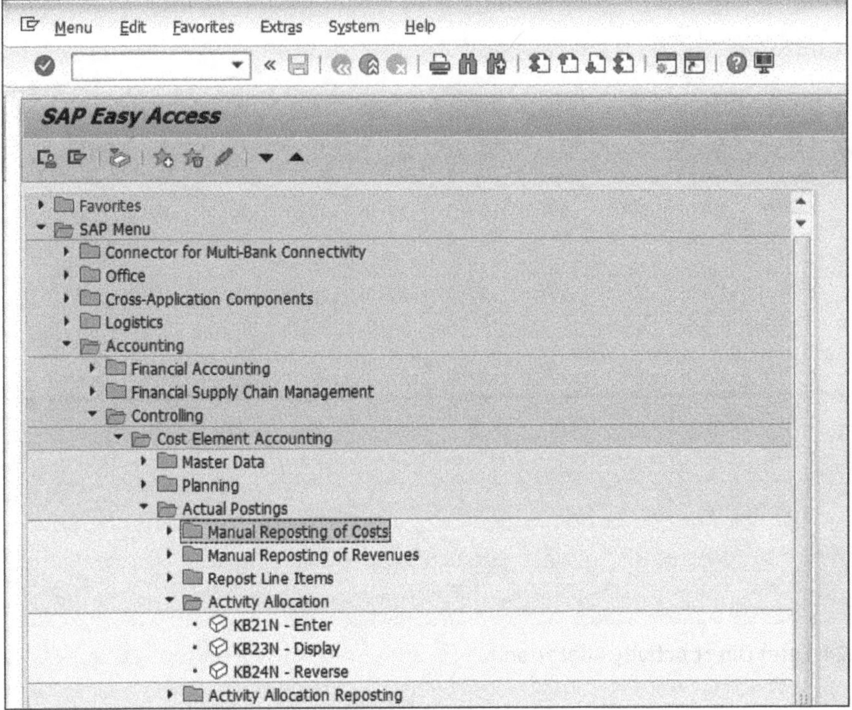

Figure 9.23 Activity Allocation Transactions

You can use the following three transactions:

- **KB21N – Enter**
  With this transaction, you can enter an activity allocation.
- **KB23N – Display**
  With this transaction, you can display activity allocations already entered.
- **KB24N – Reverse**
  This transaction is used to reverse activity allocations already entered.

Let's see how you can enter an activity allocation. Enter Transaction KB21N and enter the necessary data, as shown in Figure 9.24.

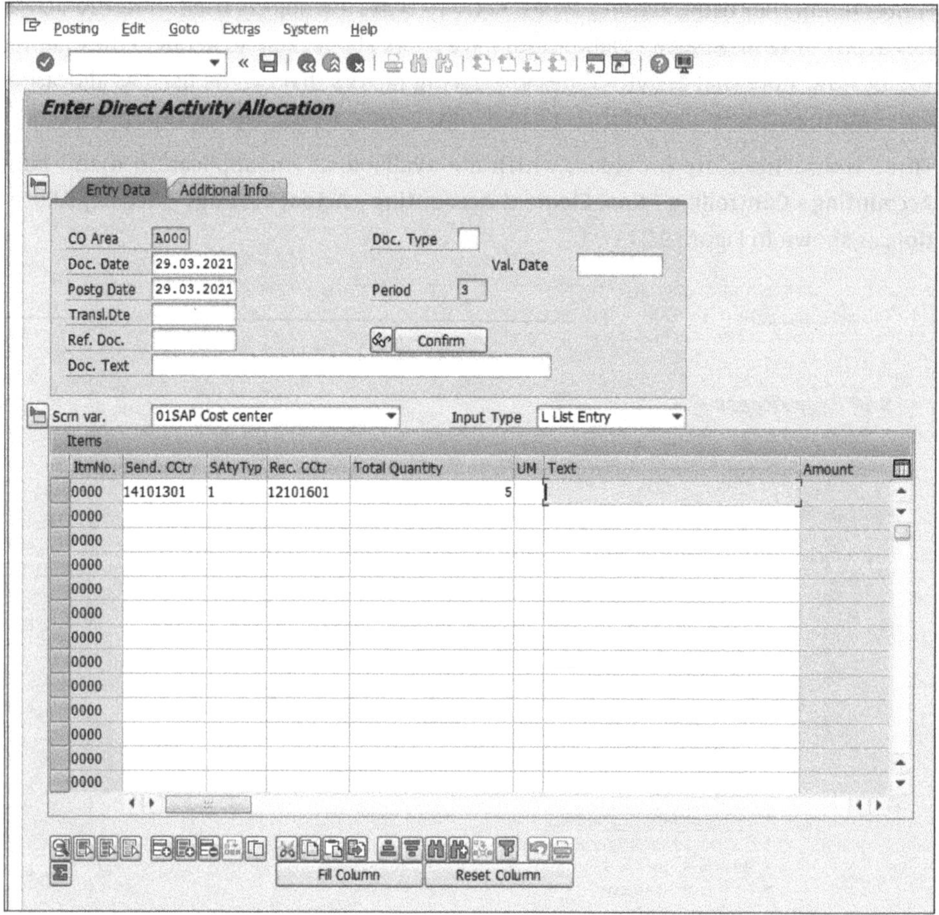

Figure 9.24 Enter Direct Activity Allocation

The following fields should be maintained:

- **CO Area**
  The controlling area where the reporting is taking place. By default, this value is the last controlling area used. If you need to change this value, you can set a different controlling area with Transaction OKKS.
- **Doc. Date**
  Document date of the activity allocation.
- **Postg Date**
  Posting date of the activity allocation, which is used to determine the period.
- **Send. CCtr (sender cost center)**
  The cost center that currently bears the cost.
- **SAtyTyp (sender activity type)**
  Sender activity type, which is used to allocate the cost.

- **Rec. CCtr (receiver cost center)**
  The cost center that will receive the cost after the activity allocation.
- **Total Quantity**
  Quantity associated with the activity.

To use the activity allocation capability, you must create activity types, which are controlling master data objects. Also, both the sender and receiver cost centers should be set up with the same sender activity type. We'll cover this setup in Chapter 10.

9.4 Summary

In this chapter, we configured SAP S/4HANA's general controlling settings, including the following objects:

- Controlling areas
- Number ranges
- Versions

You learned how to configure a controlling area so that the controlling components you need are activated and versions are set up. Now, your controlling areas can receive actual and/or plan data for the fiscal years needed.

We then covered the master data in cost element accounting, which consists of cost elements and cost element groups. You learned that, with SAP S/4HANA, cost elements are fully integrated with general ledger accounting, and this integration is one of the most fundamental improvements that SAP S/4HANA Finance offers. As such, no separate cost element master record object exists, and you can define cost elements by their cost element categories, which is part of the general ledger account master record.

You learned about various types of actual postings in cost element accounting, such as manual repostings of costs and activity allocations. Although these transactions do not require special customizing, helpful skills to learn include how to repost and allocate costs and how to define screen variants to select the desired sender and receiver objects. We also briefly touched on some functionalities offered in cost center accounting, such the activity types.

Now that we've defined the global settings and the cost elements, we're ready to delve deeply into the secrets of controlling in SAP S/4HANA. We'll start with cost center accounting.

Chapter 10
Cost Center Accounting

This chapter provides step-by-step instructions for configuring cost center accounting, including the settings for mater data, actual postings, and planning. In this chapter, you'll learn how to configure and perform various periodic allocations.

Cost center accounting, together with internal order accounting, are part of overhead costing, which serves to track and analyze costs that aren't directly attributable to the production of goods and services. These costs, which are commonly referred to as *overhead costs*, are posted to cost objects such as cost centers or internal orders, and then some of these costs might be reallocated to other cost objects, such as profitability segments or to other cost centers, to enable better analysis of the costs and profitability of your company.

In this chapter, we'll guide you through how to configure cost center accounting. We'll start by setting up the required master data, such as cost centers, cost center groups, activity types, and statistical key figures.

Next, we'll examine the various actual postings that can be performed in cost center accounting. After that, you'll learn how to perform various allocation functions, such as distribution and assessment. Then, we'll delve into the planning functions for cost centers. We'll finish with a guide to the information system in cost center accounting.

10.1 Master Data

As with other financial modules, we'll start with setting up the required master data for cost center accounting. The following master data objects are used in cost center accounting:

- Cost centers
- Cost center groups
- Activity types
- Statistical key figures

Let's start by setting up the required configuration for cost centers.

10.1.1 Cost Centers

A *cost center* represents an organizational unit within a company from a cost point of view. For example, cost centers can represent various departments, such as human resources (HR), finance, or information technology (IT). The cost center is a master data object that is created in the application menu.

Before you can create cost centers, you must define cost center categories. The category of a cost center defines certain characteristics during cost center creation.

To define cost center categories, follow the menu path **Controlling • Cost Center Accounting • Master Data • Cost Centers • Define Cost Center Categories.**

Figure 10.1 shows the various cost center categories defined in the system. These categories correspond to the different functions that various departments in the organization can perform.

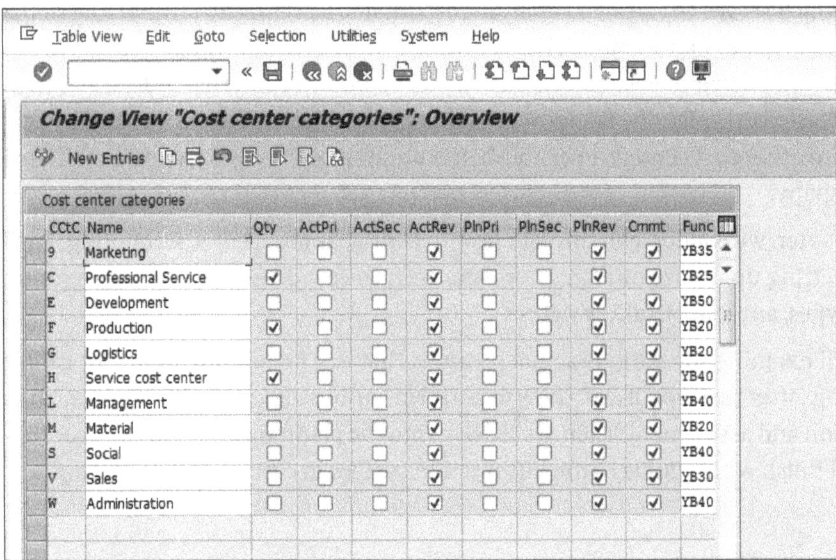

CCtC	Name	Qty	ActPri	ActSec	ActRev	PlnPri	PlnSec	PlnRev	Cmmt	Func
9	Marketing	☐	☐	☐	☑	☐	☐	☑	☑	YB35
C	Professional Service	☑	☐	☐	☑	☐	☐	☑	☑	YB25
E	Development	☐	☐	☐	☑	☐	☐	☑	☑	YB50
F	Production	☑	☐	☐	☑	☐	☐	☑	☑	YB20
G	Logistics	☐	☐	☐	☑	☐	☐	☑	☑	YB20
H	Service cost center	☑	☐	☐	☑	☐	☐	☑	☑	YB40
L	Management	☐	☐	☐	☑	☐	☐	☑	☑	YB40
M	Material	☐	☐	☐	☑	☐	☐	☑	☑	YB20
S	Social	☐	☐	☐	☑	☐	☐	☑	☑	YB40
V	Sales	☐	☐	☐	☑	☐	☐	☑	☑	YB30
W	Administration	☐	☐	☐	☑	☐	☐	☑	☑	YB40

Figure 10.1 Cost Center Categories

You'll need to configure the following fields:

- **Qty (quantity)**
  The quantity indicator enables you to manage quantities in a cost center. If selected, a message is issued when posting.
- **ActPri (actual primary cost)**
  This indicator locks the cost center of this category for posting of actual primary costs. If the indicator is active, no actual primary costs can be posted to the cost center.
- **ActSec (actual secondary cost)**
  This indicator locks the cost center of this category for posting of actual secondary

costs. If the indicator is active, no actual secondary costs can be posted to the cost center.

- **ActRev (actual revenue)**
  This indicator locks the cost center of this category for posting of actual revenues. If the indicator is active, no actual revenues can be posted to the cost center. The revenues posted on these cost centers are for statistical purposes only—for reporting analysis.
- **PlnPri (plan primary cost)**
  This indicator locks the cost center of this category for posting of plan primary costs. If the indicator is active, no plan primary costs can be posted to the cost center.
- **PlnSec (plan secondary cost)**
  This indicator locks the cost center of this category for posting of plan secondary costs. If the indicator is active, no plan secondary costs can be posted to the cost center.
- **PlnRev (plan revenue)**
  This indicator locks the cost center of this category for posting of plan revenues. If the indicator is active, no plan revenues can be posted to the cost center.
- **Cmmt (commitment)**
  This indicator locks the cost center of this category for commitments. A commitment is a contractual obligation that isn't yet recorded in financial accounting but that will lead to expenses in the future.
- **Func (functional area)**
  In this field, you can specify a default functional area. The functional area is used to record the cost of sales.

Make changes as required and save your entries. Now, you're ready to create cost centers by following the application menu path **Accounting • Controlling • Cost Center Accounting • Master Data • Cost Center • Individual Processing • KS01—Create.** Figure 10.2 shows the initial screen for cost center creation.

Cost centers are always created for a controlling area and time period. They are valid only within that time period. You can also add additional periods and change some time-sensitive parameters of the cost center.

Enter "A000" in the **Controlling Area** field, enter the cost center number in the **Cost Center** field, and define a validity period from the beginning of the current year to "31.12.9999," which means that the validity period is infinite.

In terms of cost center numbering, you must come up with a logical concept that encompasses all the cost centers of your organization. You'll need to decide how many digits the cost centers will have; 4- or 6-digit numbers are common. Then, your numbering should be well structured based on similar functions; for example, all production-related cost centers should be in the same range, starting with the same number.

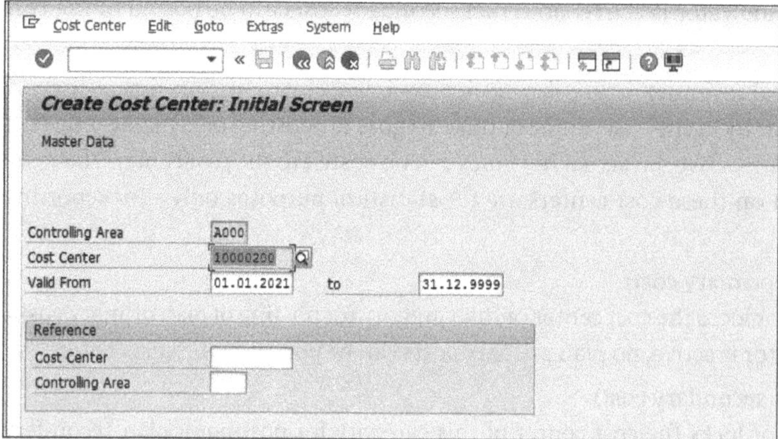

Figure 10.2 Create Cost Center

You can also create a cost center with reference to an existing cost center, which you would enter together with its controlling area in the **Reference** section of the initial screen.

Proceed by pressing [Enter]. On the next screen, you'll maintain the various cost center fields, organized into tabs. As shown in Figure 10.3, the first tab is the **Basic data** tab. Some fields are required, marked with red asterisks. The others are optional.

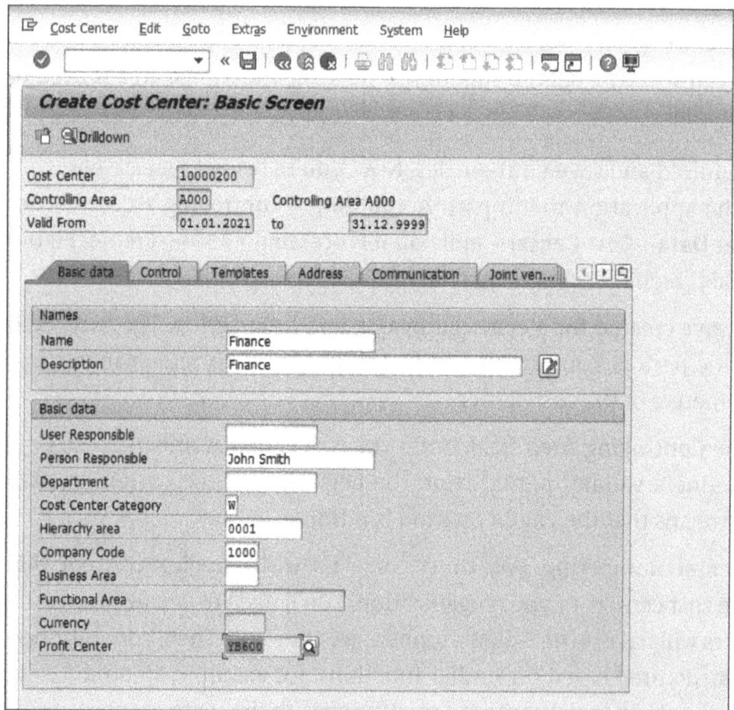

Figure 10.3 Cost Center Basic Data

Maintain the following fields:

- **Name**
  A meaningful short description of the cost center.
- **Description**
  A meaningful long description of the cost center.
- **Person Responsible**
  The name of the responsible manager of the department.
- **Cost Center Category**
  In this field, select one of the cost center categories configured previously.
- **Hierarchy area**
  Cost centers must be assigned to a tree-like structure that organizes them in a hierarchy. In this field, assign the cost center to the appropriate node. We'll define the cost center hierarchy in the next section.
- **Company Code**
  A cost center is always assigned to a company code.
- **Business Area**
  In this field, you can assign the cost center to a business area, which is an organizational unit of financial accounting that represents a separate area of operations or responsibilities.
- **Functional Area**
  In this field, you can assign the cost center to a functional area, which is used to create a profit and loss (P&L) report using the cost-of-sales accounting method.
- **Currency**
  In this field, specify the currency of the cost center.
- **Profit Center**
  In this field, you'll need to assign the cost center to a profit center, which is an organizational unit in accounting based on the management-oriented internal structure of the organization. Then, the profit center is derived from the cost center, not only in the respective expense line items but also in offsetting balance sheet line items, using the document splitting technique you learned in Chapter 4.

Figure 10.4 shows the control fields of the cost center master record. On this screen, you can lock certain types of postings to the cost center. We covered these types of postings earlier in Figure 10.1. In fact, the default cost center for the posting is based on the settings of the selected cost center category in the **Basic data** tab. Usually, for most centers, you'll lock actual and plan revenues because cost centers are cost objects, and sometimes, you also may need to lock some or all of the other categories if you need to prevent cost postings to the cost center.

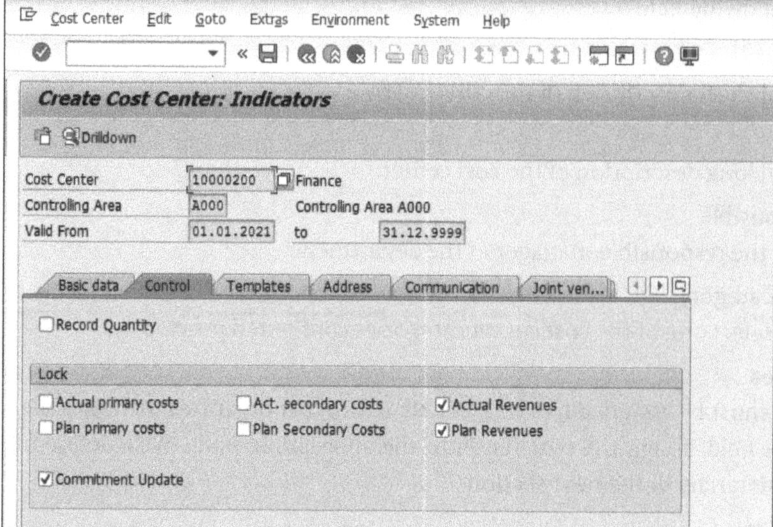

Figure 10.4 Cost Center Control Data

Under the **Templates** tab, shown in Figure 10.5, you can assign templates to the cost center. Templates are used in planning and for process allocations.

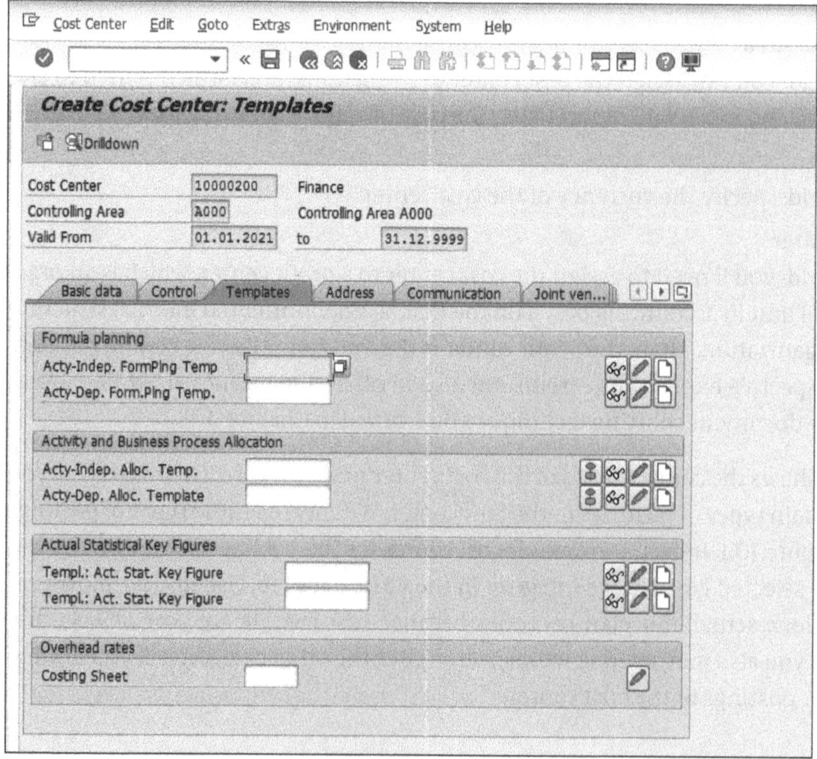

Figure 10.5 Cost Center Templates Data

Templates are created independently of cost centers and enable multiple cost centers to be assigned simultaneously. A template contains columns and rows. Costs or quantities could be entered as variables, and the costs are calculated automatically based on these variables. Templates are mostly used in process cost accounting.

Under the **Address** tab, shown in Figure 10.6, you can enter various address information relevant for the cost center, such as street address, region, country, and so on.

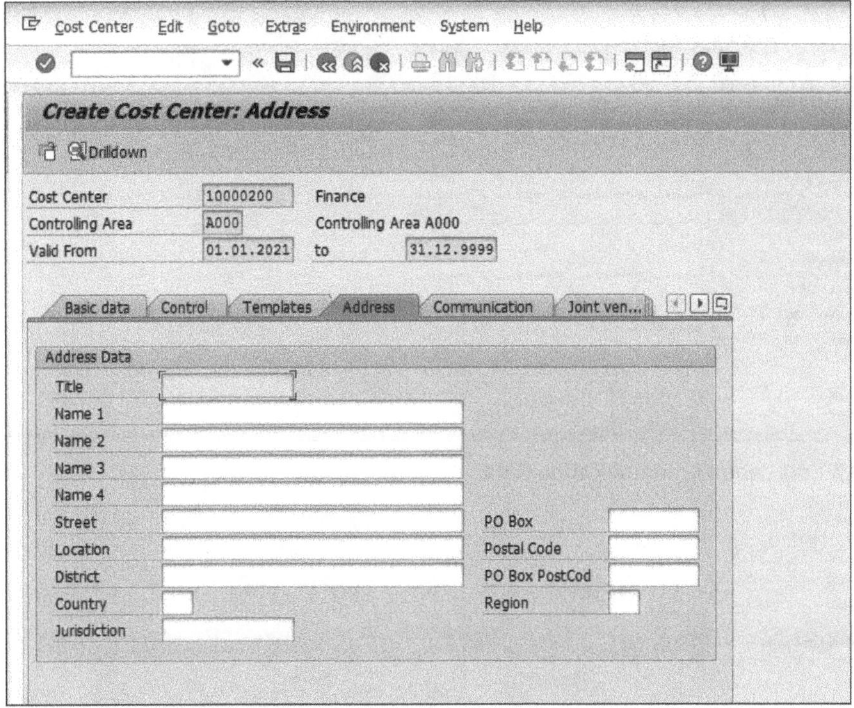

Figure 10.6 Cost Center Address Data

Under the **Communication** tab, shown in Figure 10.7, you can maintain various communication information relevant for the cost center, such as language key, telephone, fax, and so on.

Under the **History** tab, shown in Figure 10.8, the system stores information about the user who created the cost center, the date of creation, and also any changes to the cost center master, which you can view by clicking the **Change document** button later on when you display the cost center.

Once you're done maintaining your settings, save the cost center by clicking the **Save** button.

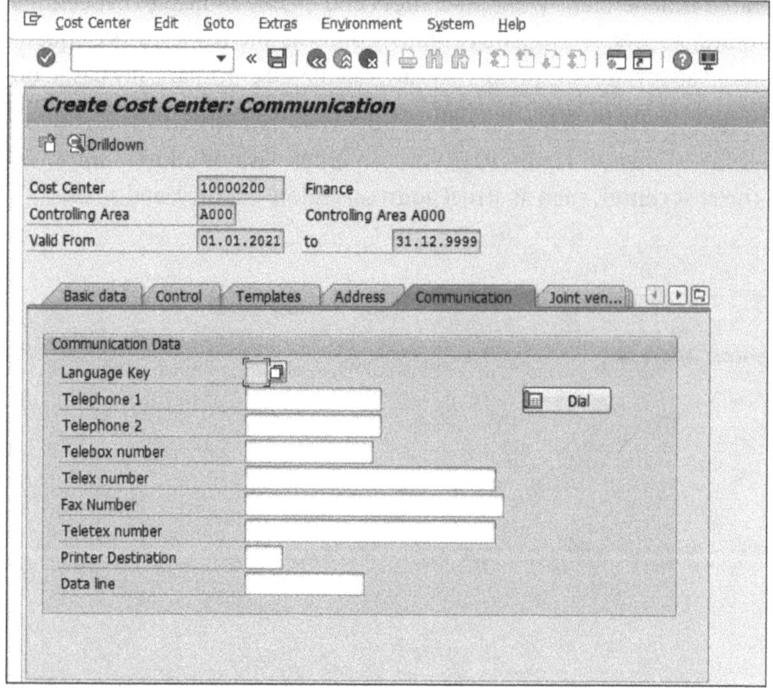

Figure 10.7 Cost Center Communication Data

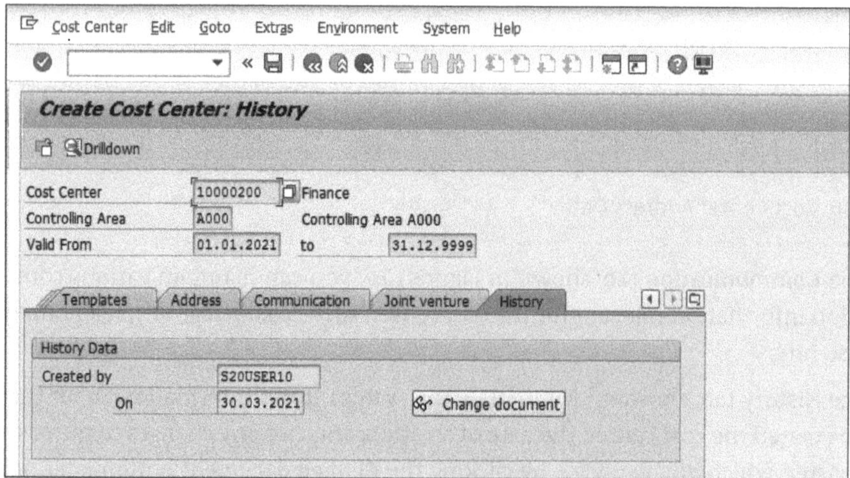

Figure 10.8 Cost CenterHistory Tab

In this fashion, you can create further cost centers also. A convenient approach is to use collective processing transactions to create or change cost centers, shown in Figure 10.9.

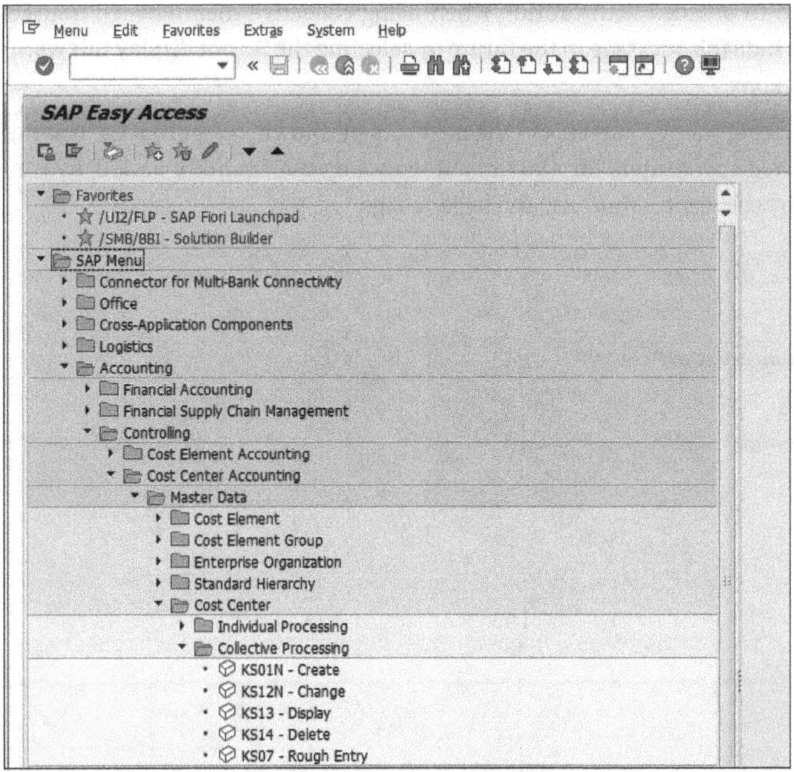

Figure 10.9 Cost Center Collective Processing Transactions

You can create, change, or display cost centers in mass mode. For example, to change the validity end date of multiple cost centers collectively, enter Transaction KS12N (Change). The system initially shows a warning message, shown in Figure 10.10.

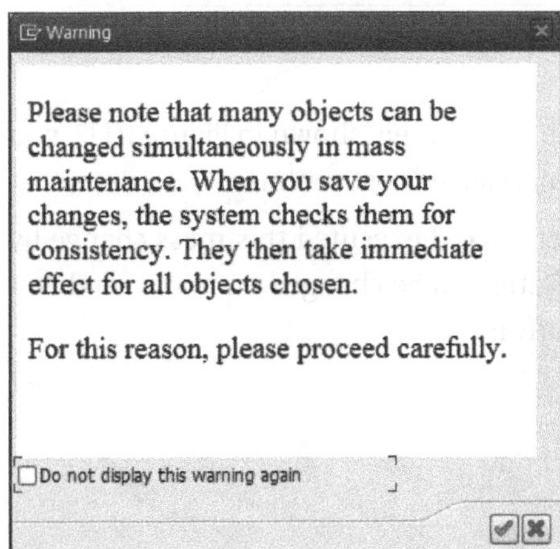

Figure 10.10 Mass Maintenance Warning

You're advised to proceed with caution when using collective maintenance transactions. You can hide this message in the future by selecting the **Do not display this warning again** checkbox.

Proceed by clicking the ✓ button. On the next screen, shown in Figure 10.11, you can limit the selected cost centers for mass maintenance by their validity period, by controlling area, by cost center number, and by language.

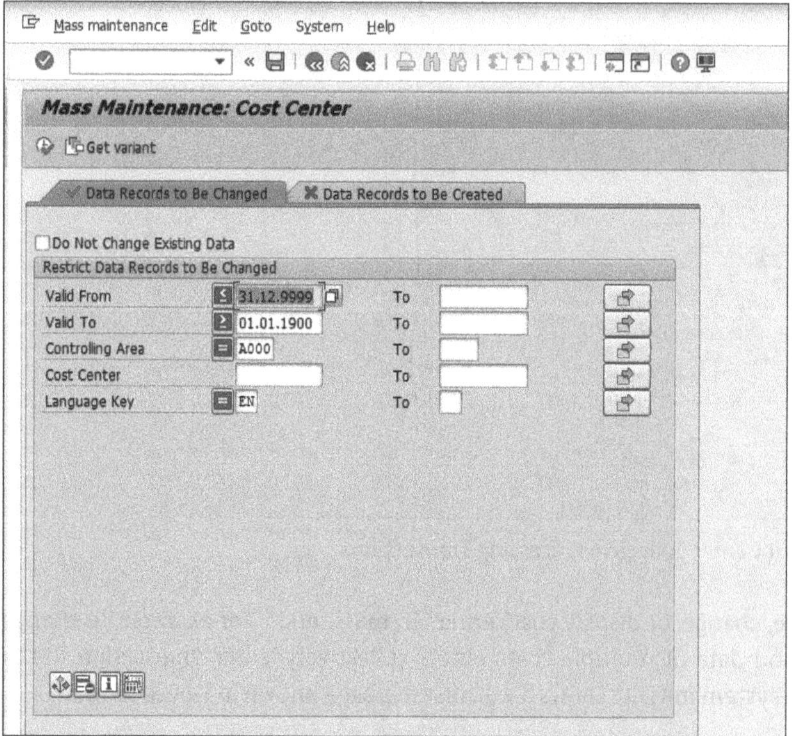

Figure 10.11 Mass Maintenance Selection Screen

Proceed by clicking the **Execute** button. On the next screen, shown in Figure 10.12, you can enter a new value that will be changed in all selected cost centers.

In this example, we entered a new validity period and executed this mass change by clicking the (**Perform Mass Change**) icon. Dates will be changed en masse, and you can save these changes by clicking the **Save** button.

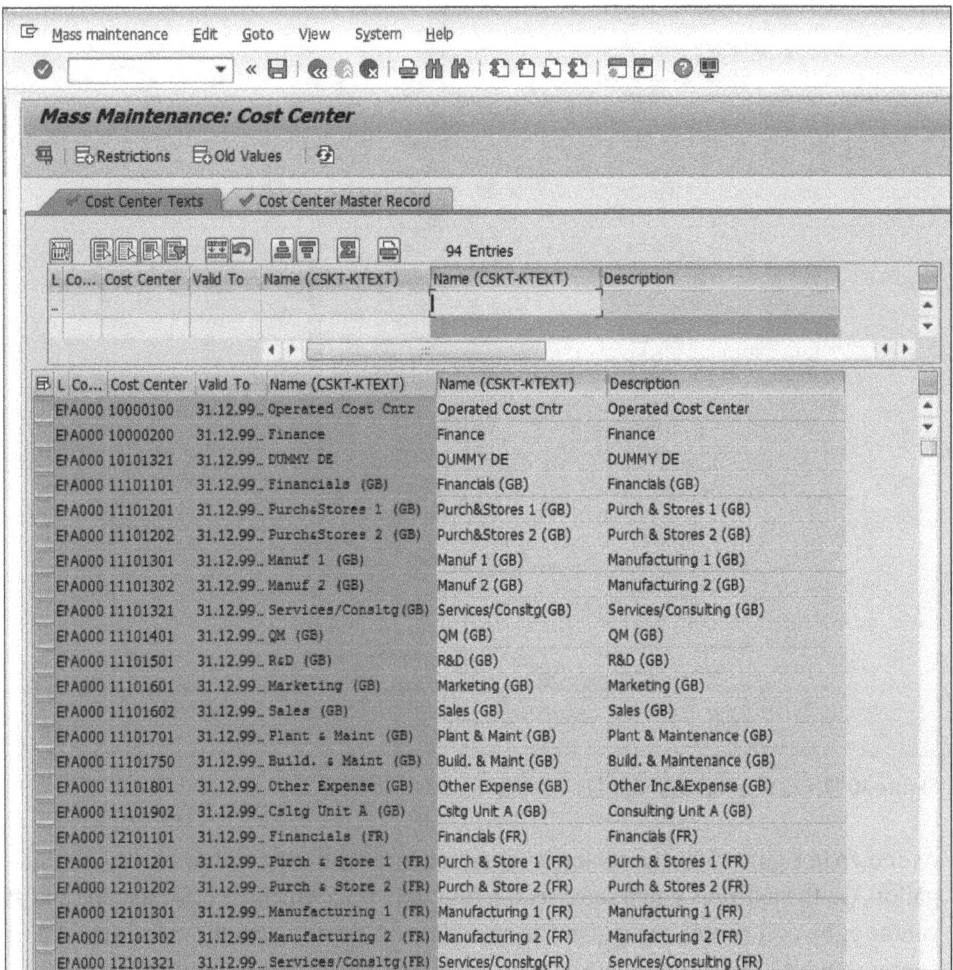

Figure 10.12 Mass Maintenance Execution Screen

10.1.2 Cost Center Groups

A *cost center group* is used to classify cost centers with similar functions. This node in the cost center standard hierarchy groups together all the cost centers of a controlling area. The cost center group, which is in fact a hierarchy node, is a required field in the cost center master record, as shown earlier in Figure 10.3.

Let's learn how to maintain the standard hierarchy and the associated cost center groups by following the application menu path **Accounting • Controlling • Cost Center Accounting • Master Data • Standard Hierarchy • OKEON—Change**.

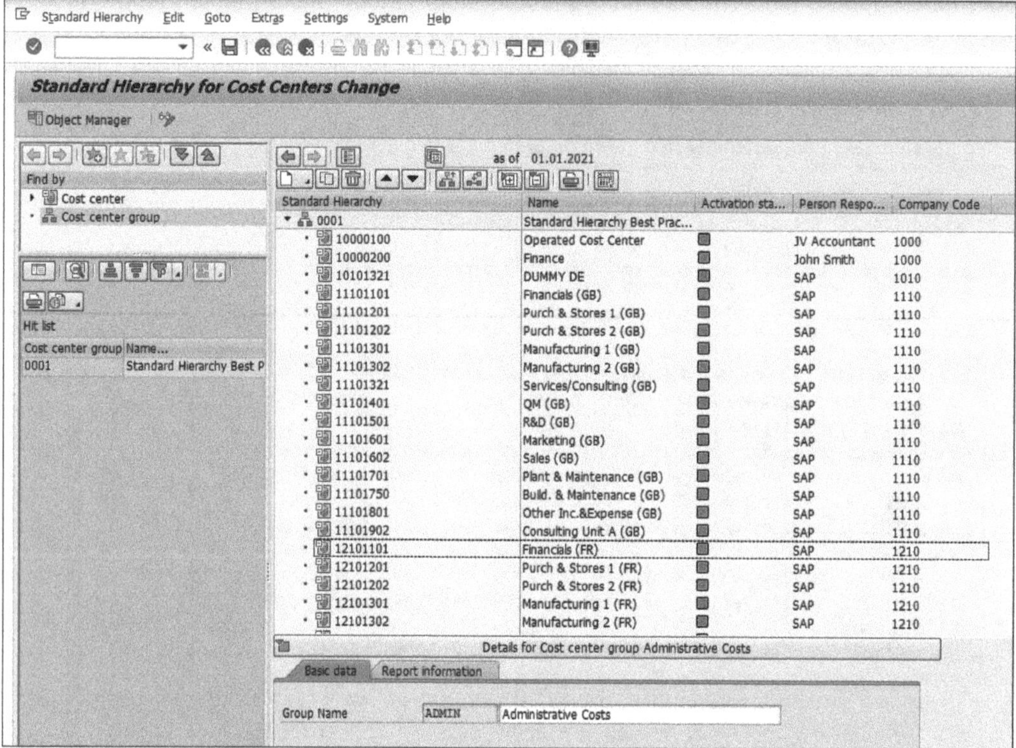

Figure 10.13 Cost Center Standard Hierarchy

As shown in Figure 10.13, the screen is separated into multiple windows for easier navigation. On the left side, you'll see a search function, with which you can search by cost center or by cost center group. On the right side on the top, you'll see the actual cost center standard hierarchy; at the bottom, you'll see details about the selected node.

The standard hierarchy is a tree-like structure that you can expand by clicking the arrow icons > on the left of each node. You can also expand the whole hierarchy from the node where you're positioned by clicking the (**Expand Subtree**) button, and collapse the whole hierarchy from the node where you're positioned by clicking the (**Collapse Subtree**) button. You can close the details for the selected node by clicking the (**Close Detail Area**) button and get a better view of the hierarchy, as shown in Figure 10.14.

On this screen, cost center groups have the symbol on the left side, and cost centers have the symbol. Double-clicking on a cost center group or cost center shows its details in the lower section of the screen.

You can also maintain cost center groups individually and not through the standard hierarchy using the transactions available at the menu path **Accounting • Controlling • Cost Center Accounting • Master Data • Cost Center Group** or by entering Transaction KSH2 (Change Cost Center Group).

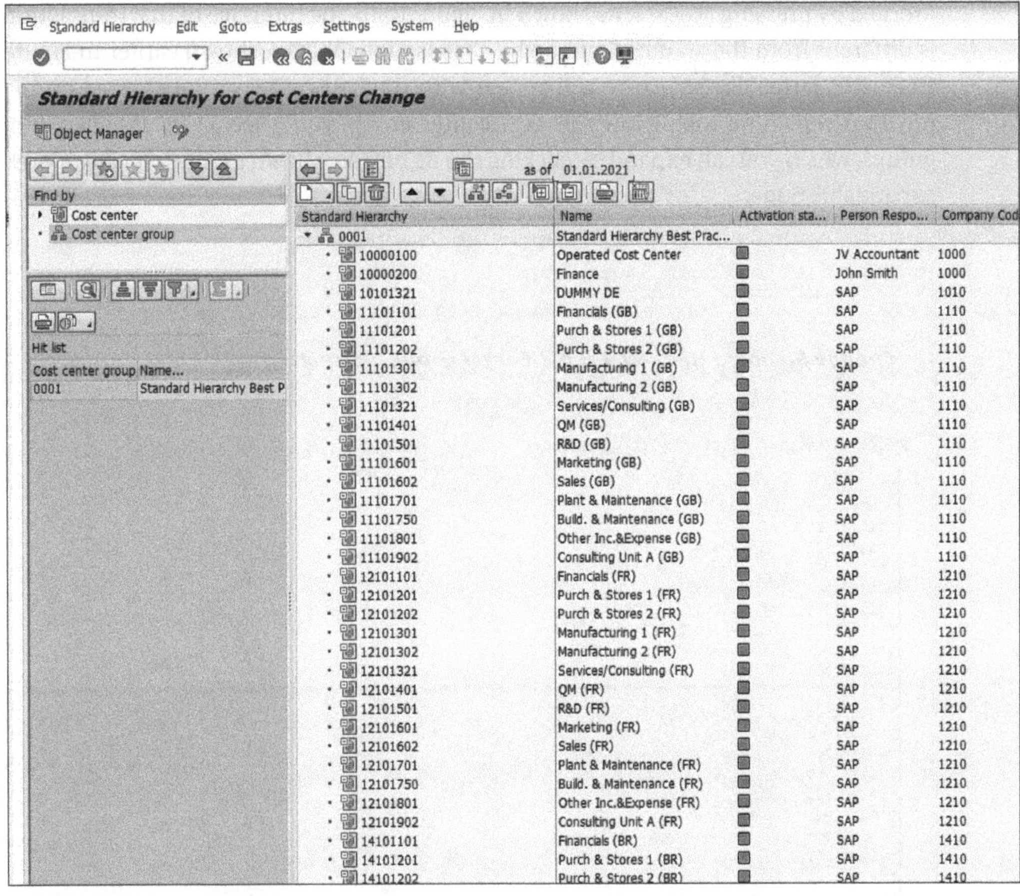

Figure 10.14 Cost Center Expanded Hierarchy

As shown in Figure 10.15, on the first screen, select the **Cost Center Group**. The controlling area is defaulted from the last used controlling area and can't be changed on this screen. If you need to switch to a different controlling area, and in general, you can use Transaction OKKS to set the controlling area.

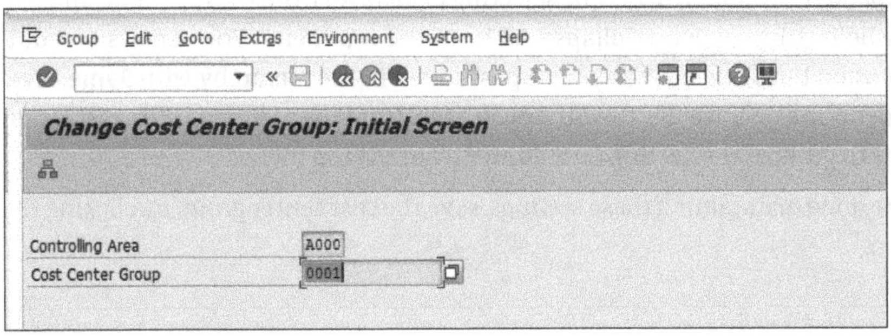

Figure 10.15 Change Cost Center Group

Proceed by pressing [Enter]. As shown in Figure 10.16, the interface of this transaction is different from the standard hierarchy Transaction OKEON, shown earlier in Figure 10.13. Still, a tree-like structure will appear with the cost center group entered on the previous screen on top. Below this cost center group, you'll see all its assigned subgroups, which you can expand by clicking the button, shown on the left side of each expandable node.

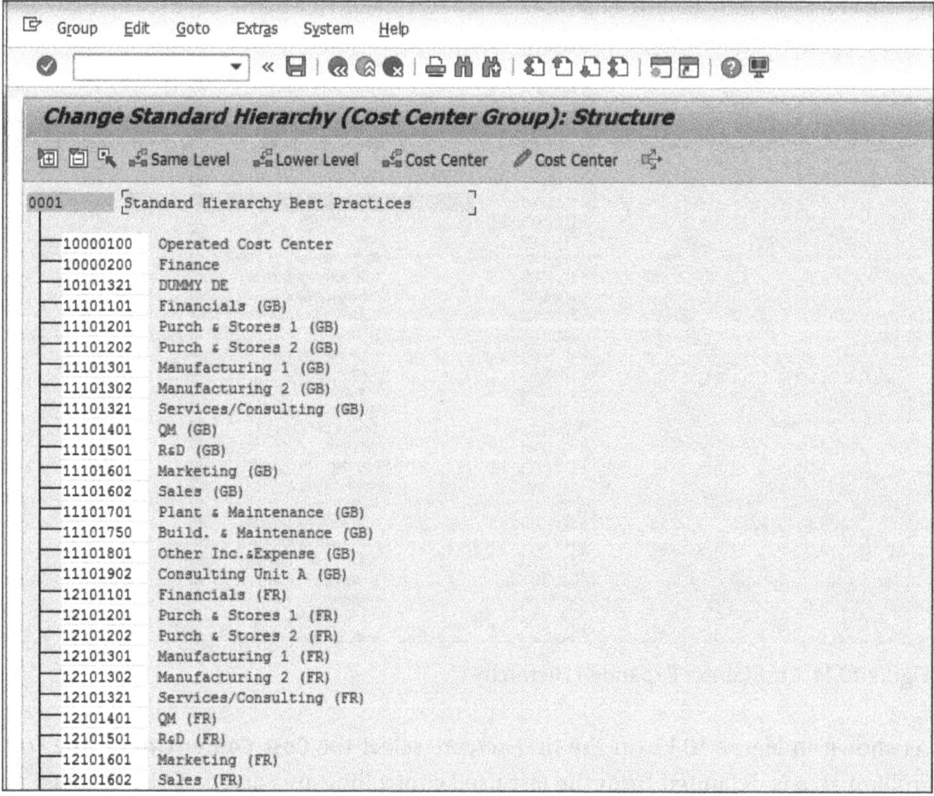

Figure 10.16 Cost Center Group Structure

You can expand the whole structure be selecting **Expand All** from the top menu and collapse the whole structure with **Collapse All** from the top menu. You can assign additional groups on the same level as you're positioned in the hierarchy with **Same Level** from top menu and on lower levels with **Lower Level** from the top menu. You can assign cost centers to groups by selecting **Cost Center** from the top menu.

Once you're done maintaining these settings, save the cost center group by clicking the **Save** button.

10.1.3 Activity Types

Activity types are master data objects used to record activities such as labor hours. These objects are tracing factors, which can be used as allocation bases during activity allocations. Activity types are associated with rates that you'll maintain for each activity type/cost center combination.

To create an activity type, follow the application menu path **Accounting • Controlling • Cost Center Accounting • Master Data • Activity Type • Individual Processing • KL01—Create.**

On the initial screen, shown in Figure 10.17, provide a name for the activity type, which could be up to 6 characters long, and a validity period, as we did earlier for cost centers. You have also the option of copying from an existing activity type, specified in the **Copy from** section.

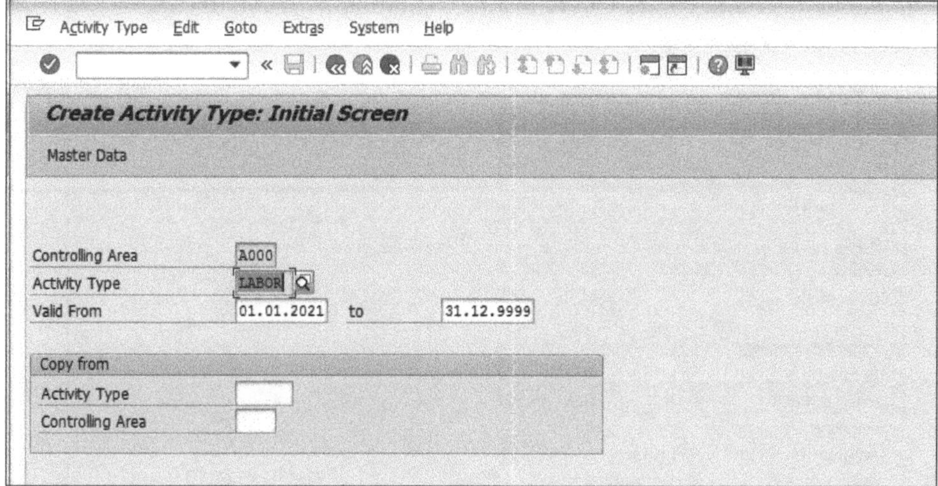

Figure 10.17 Create Activity Type Initial Screen

After you press [Enter], fill in the required fields, as shown in Figure 10.18. The following fields should be maintained:

- **Name**
  A meaningful short description of the activity type.
- **Description**
  A meaningful long description of the activity type.
- **Activity Unit**
  In this field, select the type of unit used to measure the activity such as hours, kilograms, and so on.
- **CCtr Categories (cost center categories)**
  In this field, select one of the cost center categories.

- **ATyp category (activity type category)**
  In this field, select the method of activity quantity planning and activity allocation.
- **Allocation cost elem. (allocation cost element)**
  In this field, select a secondary cost element, under which the activity type will be allocated.
- **Price Indicator**
  Determines how the price should be determined.

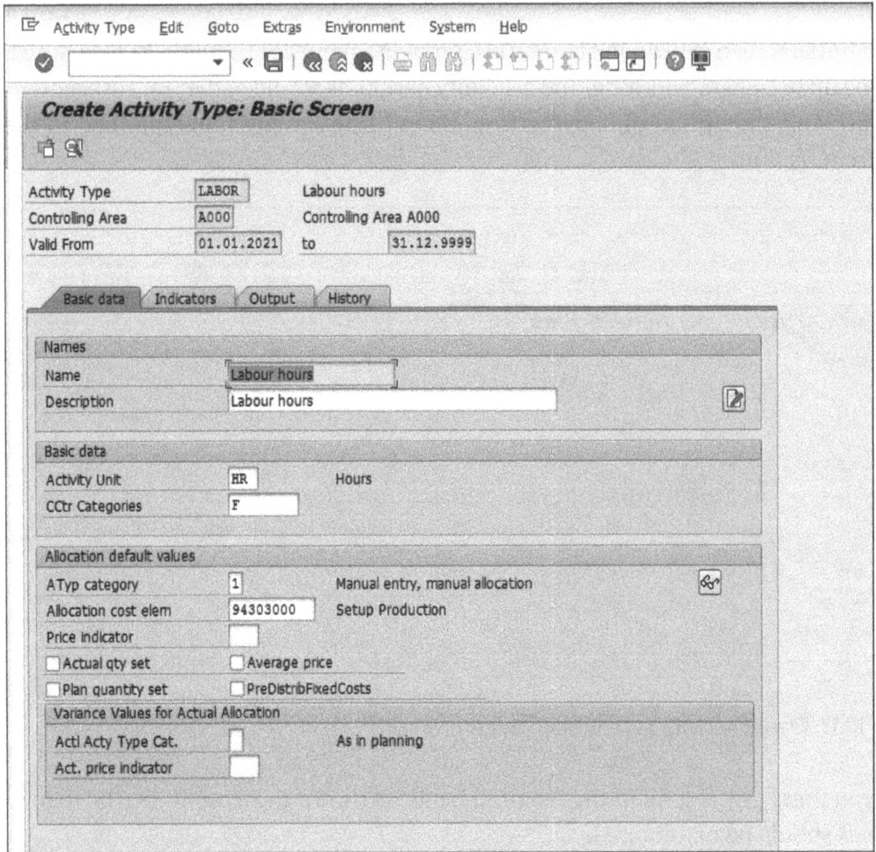

Figure 10.18 Create Activity Type

Once you're done maintaining these settings, save the activity type by clicking the **Save** button.

In this step, you created the activity type as a master data object. You also need to enter activity type rates for each cost center by following the application menu path **Accounting • Controlling • Cost Center Accounting • Planning • Activity Output/Prices • KP26—Change.**

On the initial screen, shown in Figure 10.19, you must select the controlling version, from and to period, and fiscal year for which to maintain the activity price. You'll also enter the cost center, range of cost centers, or cost center group. You have two options: You can maintain the same price for the whole period by clicking the **Overview Screen** button or only for a period by clicking the **Period Screen** button.

Plan Data Edit Goto Extras Settings System Help

Change Activity Type/Price Planning: Initial Screen

Layout 1-201 Activity Types with Prices: Standard

Variables

Version 0 Plan/actual version

From Period 1 January

To Period 12 December

Fiscal year 2021

Cost Center 11101301 Manufacturing 1 (GB)

to

or group

Activity Type LABOR Labour hours

to

or group

Figure 10.19 Change Activity Prices

Let's maintain the overview screen, shown in Figure 10.20. The parameters maintained in the activity type master record are transferred to this screen. In this example, we'll maintain a fixed price of 20, which means the labor costs 20 dollars per hour regardless of the quantity. You can also maintain a variable price, which depends on the activity output.

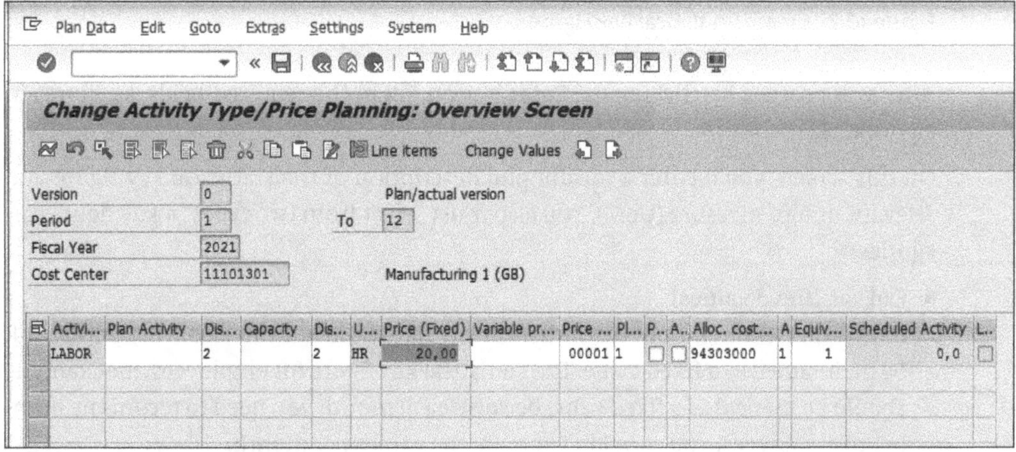

Figure 10.20 Maintain Rates

After maintaining the rates, save by clicking the **Post** button.

10.1.4 Statistical Key Figures

Statistical key figures represent values that are used to measure cost centers, internal orders, and other controlling objects. For example, one statistical key figure would be the number of employees per cost center that perform various activities. Statistical key figures can be used as allocation bases for periodic allocations such distributions and assessments, which we'll configure later in this chapter.

To create a statistical key figure, follow the application menu path **Accounting • Controlling • Cost Center Accounting • Master Data • Statistical Key Figures • Individual Processing • KK01—Create.**

Figure 10.21 shows the initial screen to create a statistical key figure. On this screen, you must provide a name for the key figure, which could be up to 6 characters long. You have also the option to copy from an existing statistical key figure, specified in the **Copy from** section.

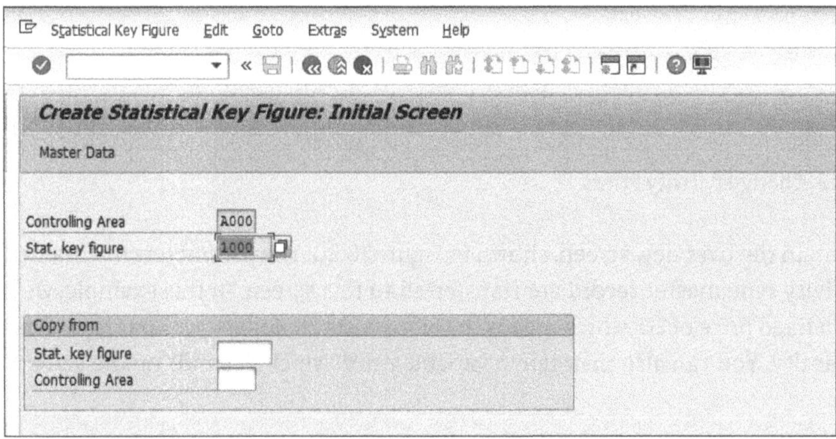

Figure 10.21 Create Statistical Key Figure

After you proceed by clicking the **Enter** button, fill in the required fields, as shown in Figure 10.22.

On this screen, you'll enter a meaningful description of the statistical key figure and relevant unit of measure (UoM). You also must select from two types of key figure categories:

- **Fxd val. (fixed values)**
  In this case, the values of the statistical key figure are not totaled. Every period will be maintained as a fixed value. The statistical key figure for employees, for example, should be marked as a fixed value because each month you need to record the number of employees; you shouldn't sum up the values per month.

- **Tot. values (total values)**
  If you select this checkbox, the values per period will be summed. This option is needed, for example, for statistical key figures for consumption, in which you have a specific consumption each month and you want to total the values to see the whole consumption for the year to date.

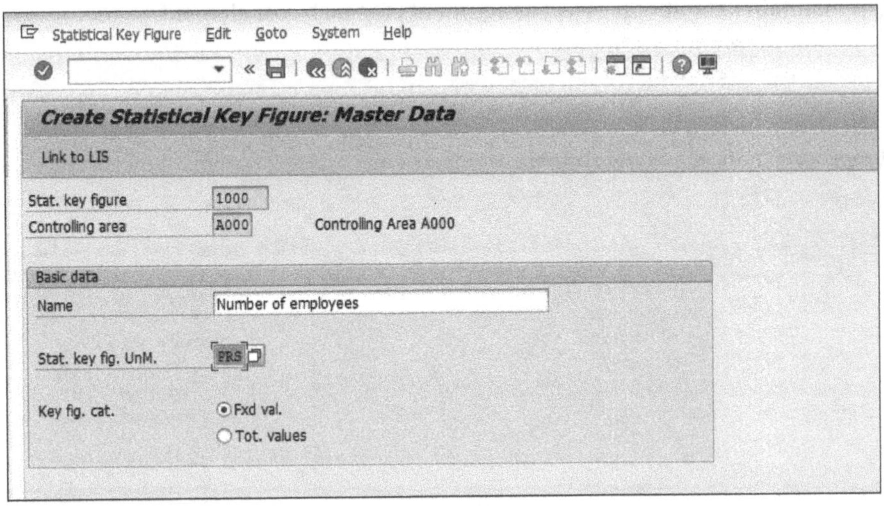

Figure 10.22 Statistical Key Figure Detailed Screen

After maintaining these settings, save the statistical key figure by clicking the **Save** button.

Thus concludes our guide to the various master data objects required for cost center accounting. Now, we'll teach you how to configure and perform various actual postings.

10.2 Actual Postings

Most postings into cost centers come from integrated documents that automatically determine the cost center. For example, a cost center is generally derived from the asset master record during asset postings.

When entering manual postings in financial accounting, usually you need to enter the cost center manually in the expense line item. However, a configuration transaction is available for default cost object determination, which often is used to determine the correct cost center.

We'll start by configuring default cost objects, provided by the automatic account assignment. Then, we'll look into the cost center substitution, which enables you to substitute cost centers based on specific predefined criteria.

10.2.1 Automatic Account Assignment

The automatic account assignment functionality in controlling provides default cost objects based on certain criteria. To configure default cost objects, enter Transaction OKB9 or follow the menu path **Controlling • Cost Center Accounting • Actual Postings • Manual Actual Postings • Edit Automatic Account Assignment**. Figure 10.23 shows how you can maintain default cost object assignments for each cost element.

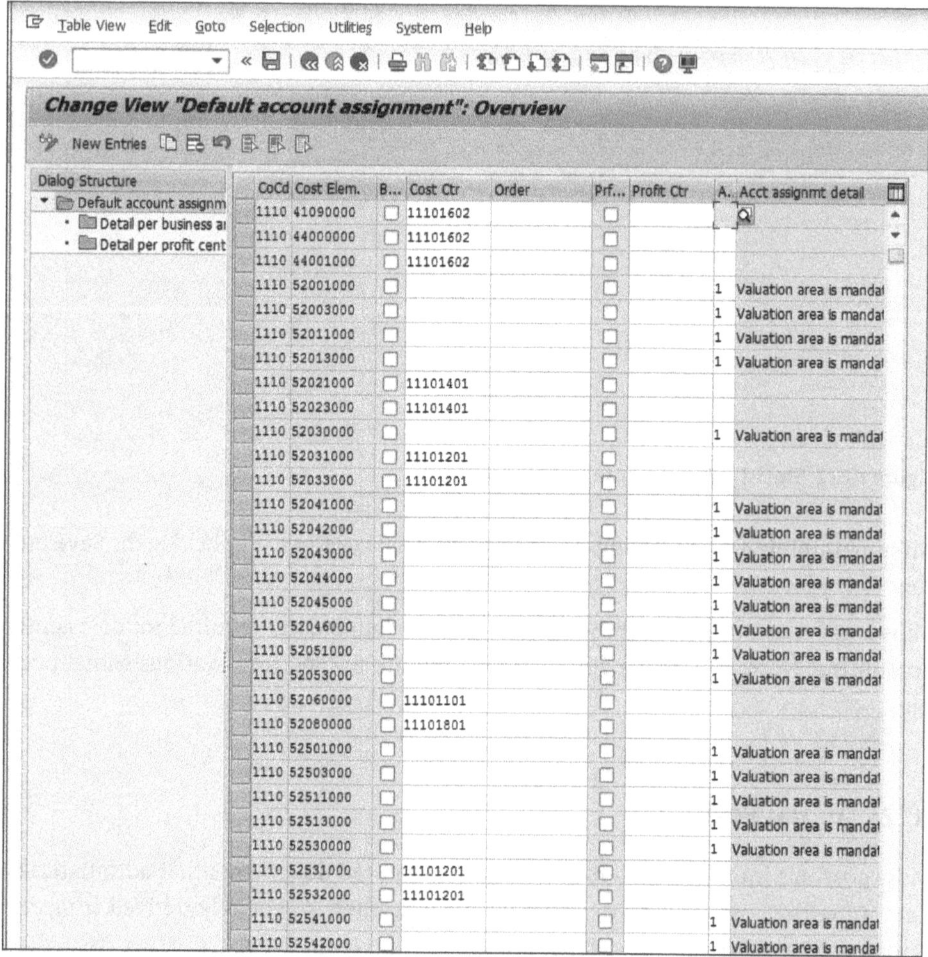

CoCd	Cost Elem.	B...	Cost Ctr	Order	Prf...	Profit Ctr	A..	Acct assignmt detail
1110	41090000		11101602					
1110	44000000		11101602					
1110	44001000		11101602					
1110	52001000						1	Valuation area is mandat
1110	52003000						1	Valuation area is mandat
1110	52011000						1	Valuation area is mandat
1110	52013000						1	Valuation area is mandat
1110	52021000		11101401					
1110	52023000		11101401					
1110	52030000						1	Valuation area is mandat
1110	52031000		11101201					
1110	52033000		11101201					
1110	52041000						1	Valuation area is mandat
1110	52042000						1	Valuation area is mandat
1110	52043000						1	Valuation area is mandat
1110	52044000						1	Valuation area is mandat
1110	52045000						1	Valuation area is mandat
1110	52046000						1	Valuation area is mandat
1110	52051000						1	Valuation area is mandat
1110	52053000						1	Valuation area is mandat
1110	52060000		11101101					
1110	52080000		11101801					
1110	52501000						1	Valuation area is mandat
1110	52503000						1	Valuation area is mandat
1110	52511000						1	Valuation area is mandat
1110	52513000						1	Valuation area is mandat
1110	52530000						1	Valuation area is mandat
1110	52531000		11101201					
1110	52532000		11101201					
1110	52541000						1	Valuation area is mandat
1110	52542000						1	Valuation area is mandat

Figure 10.23 Default Cost Object Assignment

You can maintain this configuration table for each company code and cost element, and in the following columns, you can assign default cost objects:

- **Cost Center**
- **Order**
- **Profitability Segment**
- **Profit Center**

Then, when posting to this cost element, if no other cost object determination exists, such as from a material master record or from an asset, for example, the system will assign the default cost object maintained in this table.

You can also maintain multiple cost objects for each profit center or business area if you select indicator **2: Business Area Is Mandatory** or **3: Profit Center Is Mandatory** in the **Acct assignmt detail** (account assignment detail) column. Then, click **Detail per business area/valuation area** on the left side of the screen to maintain multiple business areas or click **Detail per profit center** to maintain multiple profit centers' cost objects.

As shown in Figure 10.24, you can maintain different default cost centers depending on the profit center.

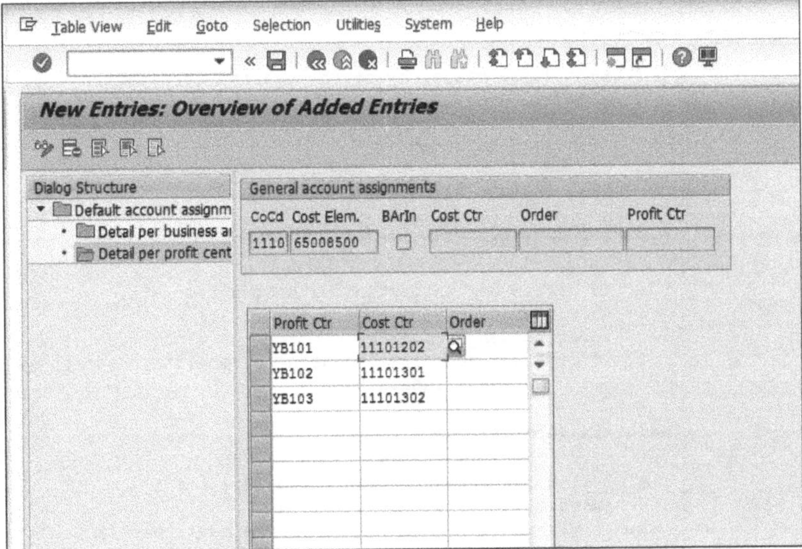

Figure 10.24 Multiple Assignments per Profit Center

In this fashion, maintain the default cost object assignments for all needed cost elements and save your entries by clicking the **Save** button. A good practice is to have an extensive list of cost elements maintained in this configuration transaction to avoid posting errors during the productive use of the system in case no other automatic account assignments are in play.

10.2.2 Substitutions for Account Assignment

Another technique could be used to determine cost centers during actual postings, called *substitution*. This tool is provided by SAP to populate certain fields based on certain rules and commonly used throughout different areas of financial accounting and controlling. In this section, we'll just briefly describe a case in which the cost center is derived using substitution.

To define substitutions, enter Transaction GGB1. Figure 10.25 shows the initial screen.

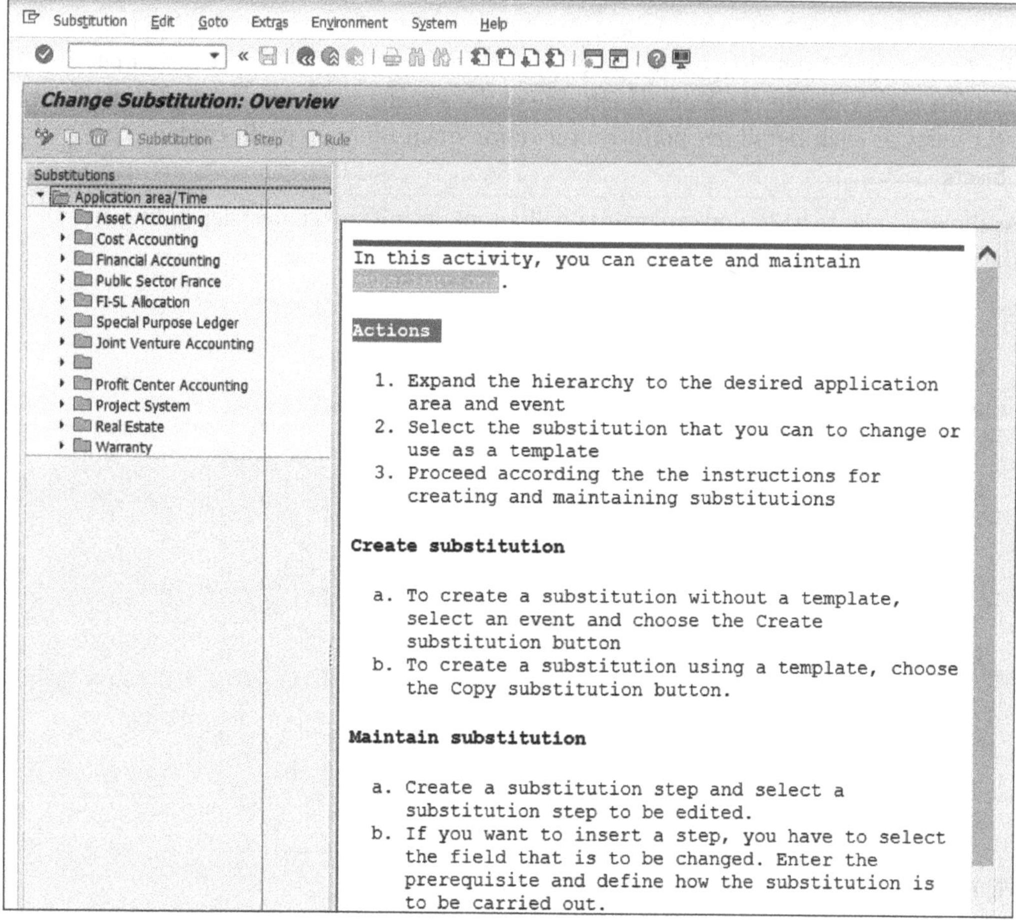

Figure 10.25 Defining Substitutions

From the tree-like structure on the left side of the screen, you can select the application for which to define the substitution. Navigate to **Cost Accounting • Line Item**, where you can define substitutions working on the line item of the controlling document. SAP provides sample substitutions, such as **0_CO_1: Example Substitution for CO**. Copy the substitution with the **Copy Substitution** function from the top menu, then give a name and meaningful description for the new substitution, as shown in Figure 10.26.

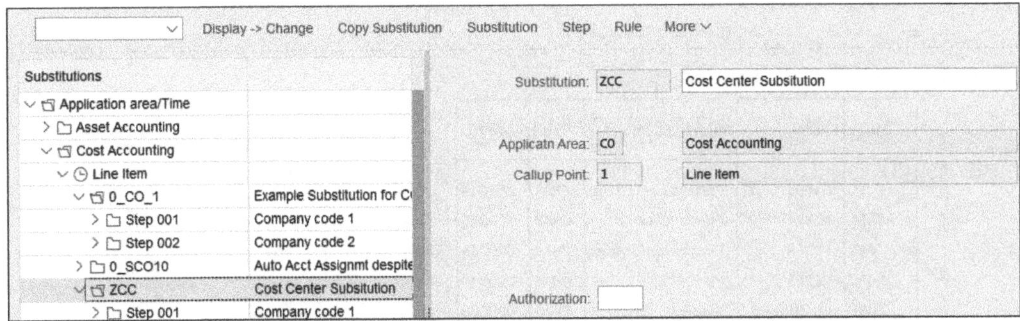

Figure 10.26 Defining Cost Center Substitutions

Each substitution can have one or multiple steps. Expand the steps, and you'll see that they contain prerequisite and substitution sections. When the criteria defined in the **Prerequisite** section are met, the substitution is executed. For example, in the **Prerequisite** section, shown in Figure 10.27, you can define rules such as *when company code is 1000* and *when cost element is within a specific range.*

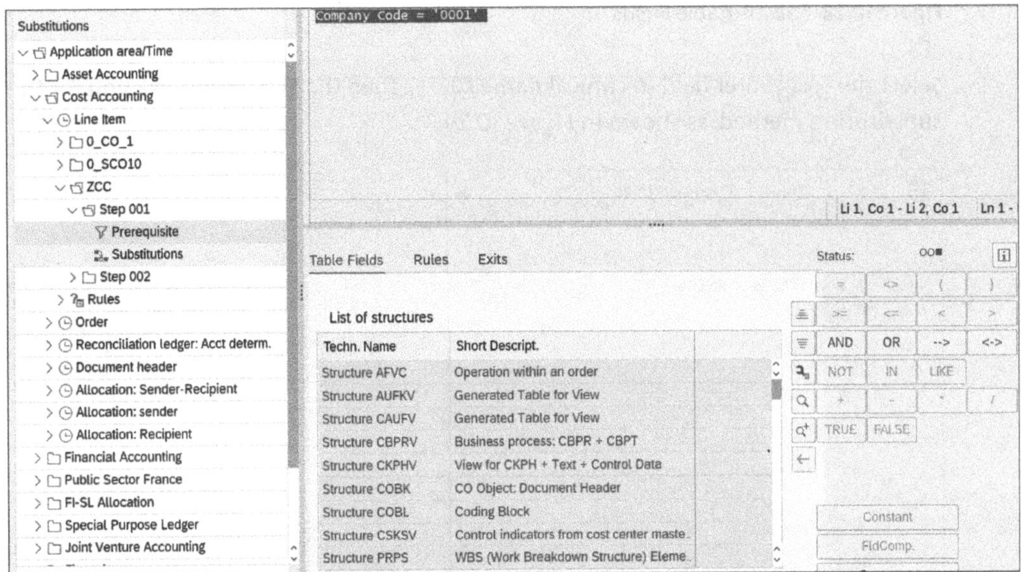

Figure 10.27 Substitution Prerequisite Section

Then, in the **Substitutions** section, you can define the cost center as a field to be substituted by clicking the ⊕ (**Insert Subst. Entry**) button. Then, a new window opens with the list of the substitutable fields, as shown in Figure 10.28.

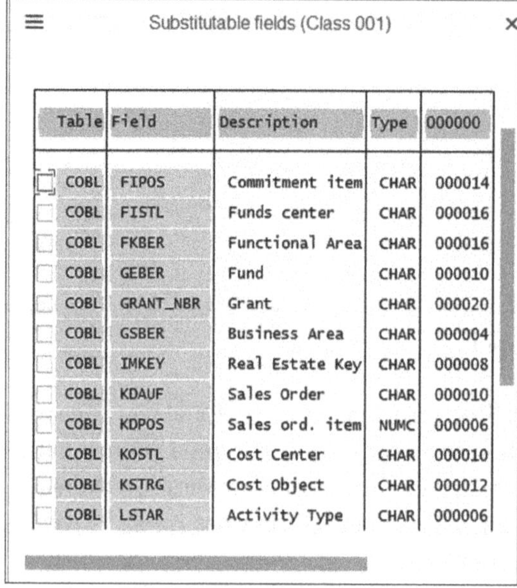
Substitutable fields (Class 001)

Table	Field	Description	Type	000000
COBL	FIPOS	Commitment item	CHAR	000014
COBL	FISTL	Funds center	CHAR	000016
COBL	FKBER	Functional Area	CHAR	000016
COBL	GEBER	Fund	CHAR	000010
COBL	GRANT_NBR	Grant	CHAR	000020
COBL	GSBER	Business Area	CHAR	000004
COBL	IMKEY	Real Estate Key	CHAR	000008
COBL	KDAUF	Sales Order	CHAR	000010
COBL	KDPOS	Sales ord. item	NUMC	000006
COBL	KOSTL	Cost Center	CHAR	000010
COBL	KSTRG	Cost Object	CHAR	000012
COBL	LSTAR	Activity Type	CHAR	000006

Figure 10.28 Substitutable Fields

Select the cost center field (technical name KOSTL), then the system will ask you for the substitution method, as shown in Figure 10.29.

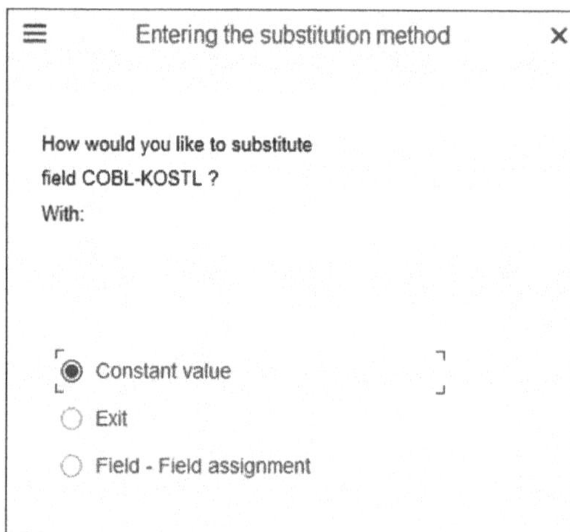

Figure 10.29 Substitution Method Selection

You have the following three options:

- **Constant value**
  With this option, the cost center will be substituted with the fixed value specified in the next screen.

- **Exit**
  This option uses a user exit, which is custom-programmed code you can apply if the requirement is more complex.
- **Field-Field assignment**
  With this option, the value of the substitutable field will be substituted with a value from another field.

Select **Constant value** for this example. As shown in Figure 10.30, provide a constant value to be applied when the conditions are met. Then, save your entry by clicking the **Save** button.

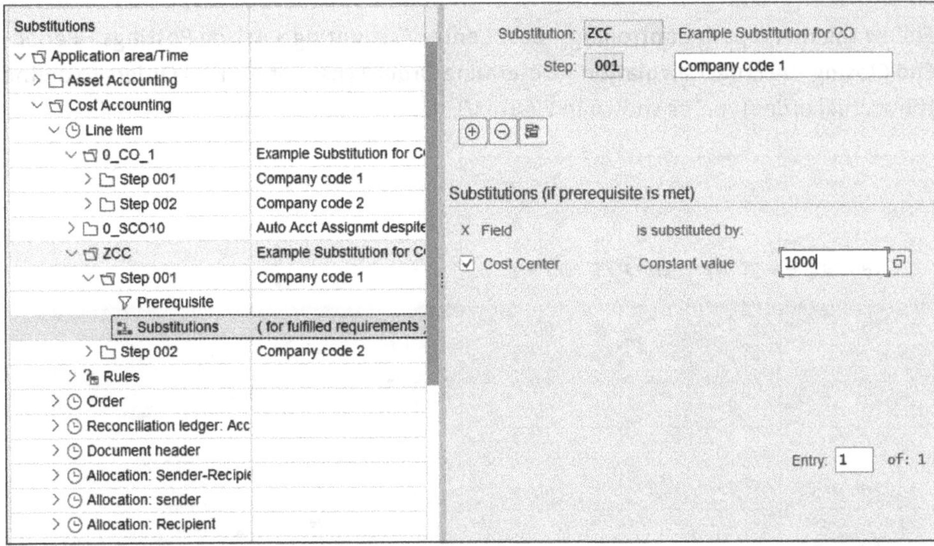

Figure 10.30 Defined Cost Center Substitution

10.3 Periodic Allocations

In controlling, costs often need to be reallocated from some cost objects to others. For example, administrative costs are posted to administrative cost centers such as finance, IT, HR, and so on. However, to provide an accurate profitability picture of the company based on lines of business and operations, management may want to assign these costs to the various departments that sell various products and thus assess properly the real operating margins and profitability per product. This task is for controlling, which provides various types of periodic allocation procedures that can be used to automatically reallocate costs based on predefined criteria.

In the following sections, we'll explain the following types of periodic allocations:

- Accrual calculations
- Distributions
- Assessments
- Activity allocations

10.3.1 Accrual Calculation

Accrual calculation is a process of evenly spreading out irregularly occurring costs over periods and distributing them by cause. This procedure isn't commonly used because most companies prefer to have the accrual posted in specific periods only.

Accrual costs are posted to accrual cost centers or internal orders and then distributed. You'll need to create a special accrual cost center using the menu path **Controlling • Cost Center Accounting • Actual Postings • Period-End Closing • Accrual Calculation • Create Accrual Cost Centers** or an accrual internal order using the menu path **Controlling • Cost Center Accounting • Actual Postings • Period-End Closing • Accrual Calculation • Create Accrual Orders.**

Follow the menu path **Controlling • Cost Center Accounting • Actual Postings • Period-End Closing • Accrual Calculation • Determine Order Types for Accrual Orders** to define the accrual order type, as shown in Figure 10.31.

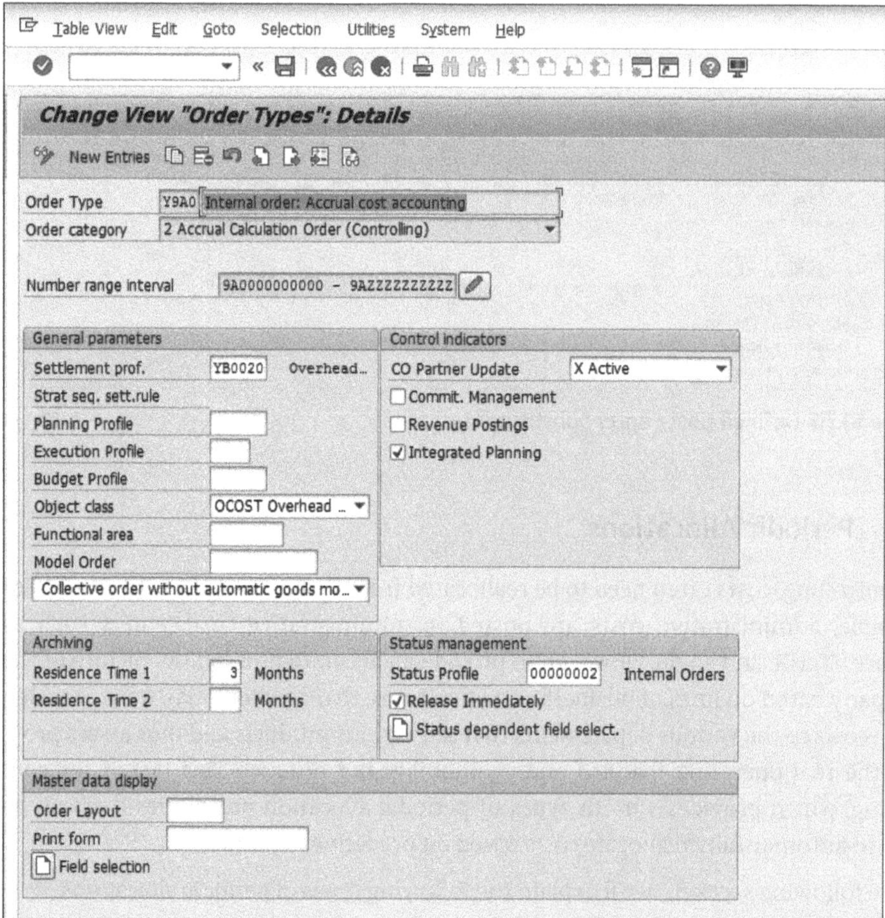

Figure 10.31 Accrual Order Type

If needed, you can create your own order type for that purpose. We'll examine order type creation in detail in Chapter 11.

Two methods for accrual calculation exist: the target = actual method and the percentage method.

In the *target = actual method*, the planning of the primary costs is made with an accrual cost element. The system calculates target costs and enters these costs in the actual value fields. This method is used when accrual can be planned periodically. In the *percentage method*, you'll use specific percentages to calculate accruals. SAP provides enhancement **COOM 0002: User Exits for cost center accrual calculation**, with which you can program user exits to perform the accrual calculation.

10.3.2 Distribution

Distribution and assessment are the two main methods to allocate costs out of cost centers. *Distribution* uses the original cost elements posted to allocate cost to the sender cost centers. In this way, you can see the original cost element posted from the sender cost center on the receiving cost center. Distribution is used to allocate only primary costs.

Assessment uses secondary assessment cost elements with cost element 43 to allocate costs. In the receiver cost center, the original cost element from the sender isn't available. Assessment allocates both primary and secondary costs.

Both distribution and assessment use similar techniques, in which you define cycles and segments. The cycle is a periodic allocation run, which can contain one or more segments. Each segment contains relationships between sender and receiver cost centers, as well as various control parameters.

To create a distribution cycle, follow the menu path **Controlling • Cost Center Accounting • Actual Postings • Period-End Closing • Distribution • Define Distribution.** Then, select **Create Actual Distribution**. This transaction is also available in the application menu path via **Accounting • Controlling • Cost Center Accounting • Period-End Closing • Current Settings • S_ALR_87005757—Define Distribution.**

On the initial screen, shown in Figure 10.32, enter a meaningful cycle name that will enable you easily to identify the purpose of the cycle and a start date, which normally is the beginning of the fiscal year. Each year, you'll define your cycles again, usually copying the cycles from the previous year. You can create a cycle with reference to an existing cycle, specified in the **Copy from** section. After that, proceed by clicking the **Execute** button.

The next screen, shown in Figure 10.33, is the header of the cycle, which applies to all segments.

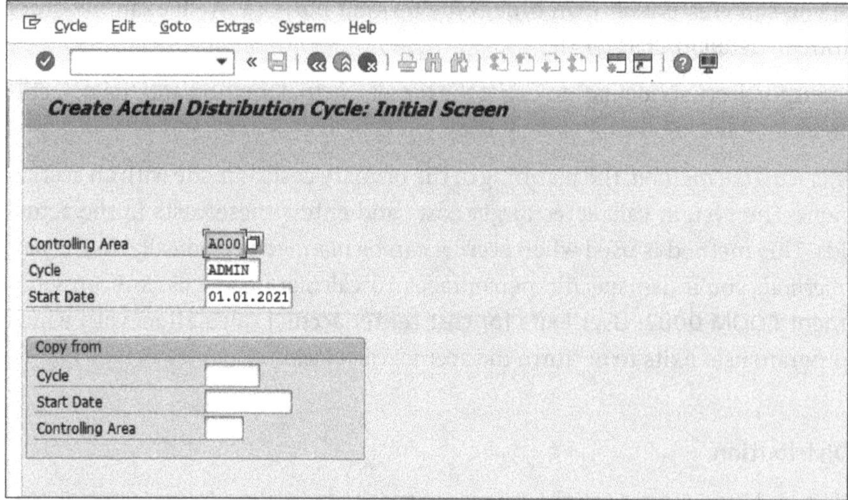

Figure 10.32 Creating a Distribution Cycle

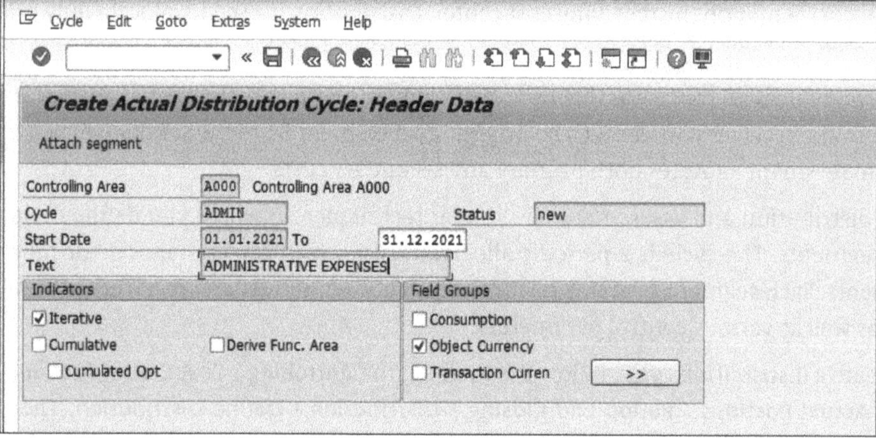

Figure 10.33 Distribution Cycle Header

The following fields can be maintained:

- **Start Date and To**
  You already specified the start date on the previous screen, but on this screen, you must also define an end date after which the cycle is no longer valid. If you create new cycles every year, this end date should be the end of the fiscal year.
- **Text**
  A meaningful long description of the cycle.
- **Iterative**
  This indicator enables iterative sender/receiver relationships. In this case, the iteration is repeated until each sender is fully credited.

- **Cumulative**
  If you select this indicator, the sender amounts posted are allocated based on tracing factors, which are cumulated for all periods.
- **Derive Func. Area (derive functional area)**
  By checking this indicator, the functional area proposed in the cycle definition for the receiver is ignored and is derived again.
- **Field Groups**
  In general, only amounts in the controlling area currency are used in periodic allocations. However, you can choose other types of currencies in this section.

After maintaining the cycle definition, you'll need to attach at least one segment. Select **Attach segment** from the top menu. The segment, as shown in Figure 10.34, is organized into tabs.

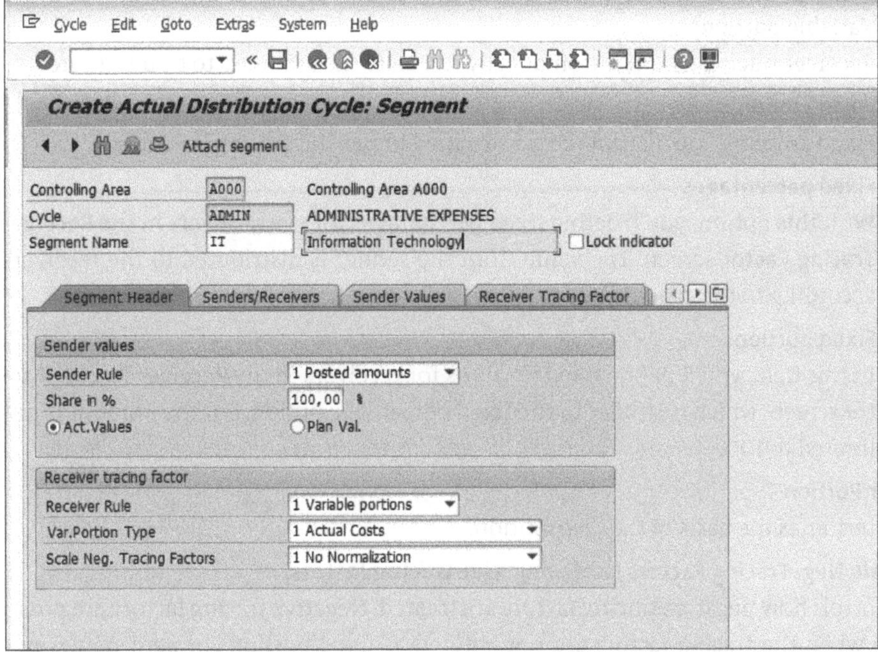

Figure 10.34 Segment Header

Under the first tab, **Segment Header**, you'll specify rules for the distribution calculation in the following fields:

- **Sender Rule**
  This field determines how the sender values are calculated. The following options are available:
  - **Posted amounts**
    Amounts posted on the sender are the sender values.

- **Fixed amounts**
  For this option, you need to define fixed amounts for senders in the selection criteria on the **Sender Values** tab.
- **Fixed rates**
  On the **Sender Values** tab, you must enter fixed prices for the senders, which are multiplied by the receiver tracing factors.

- **Share in %**
  Determines the percentage of the sender values to be distributed.
- **Act. Values/Plan Val. (actual values/plan values)**
  Defines whether the cycle distributes actual values or plan values.
- **Receiver Rule**
  Determines how the receiver tracing factors are determined, with the following options:
  - **Variable portions**
    Receiver tracing factors automatically calculate the amounts to be distributed.
  - **Fixed amounts**
    Fixed amounts are distributed, as specified under the **Tracing Values** tab.
  - **Fixed percentages**
    With this option, you'll define fixed percentages for the receivers in the **Receiver Tracing Factor** screen. The value from the sender is distributed to the receivers according to these percentages.
  - **Fixed portions**
    In this field, you'll define fixed portions for receivers in the **Receiver Tracing Factor** screen, which is similar to the fixed percentage option, but the amount is not limited to 100.
- **Var.Portion Type**
  Determines the basis of the distribution.
- **Scale Neg. Tracing Factors (scale negative tracing factors)**
  Controls how negative tracing factors are treated. Negative tracing factors are possible when the tracing factors are not entered as fixed portions or percentages but instead are derived.

Under the next tab, **Senders/Receivers**, you'll define the sender and receiver cost objects, as shown in Figure 10.35. The costs posted originally on the cost objects defined in the **Sender** section will be distributed to the objects defined in the **Receiver** section, according to the tracing factors defined under the **Receiver Tracing Factor** tab. You also must specify the sender cost elements.

Click the next tab, **Sender Values**, as shown in Figure 10.36. Under this tab, you can specify the percentage of sender values to be distributed (usually 100%), as well as whether the origin of the values is actual or plan data. You can also specify a version.

Cycle Edit Goto Extras System Help
Create Actual Distribution Cycle: Segment
Attach segment
Controlling Area A000 Controlling Area A000
Cycle ADMIN ADMINISTRATIVE EXPENSES
Segment Name IT Information Technology
Lock indicator
Segment Header
Senders/Receivers
Sender Values
Receiver Tracing Factor
From
To
Group
Sender
Cost Center 11101101 11101321
Functional Area
Cost Element 41000000 44420000
Cost Object
Recovery Indic.
Receiver
Order
Cost Center 11101801 11101902
Functional Area
Cost Object
Recovery Indic.

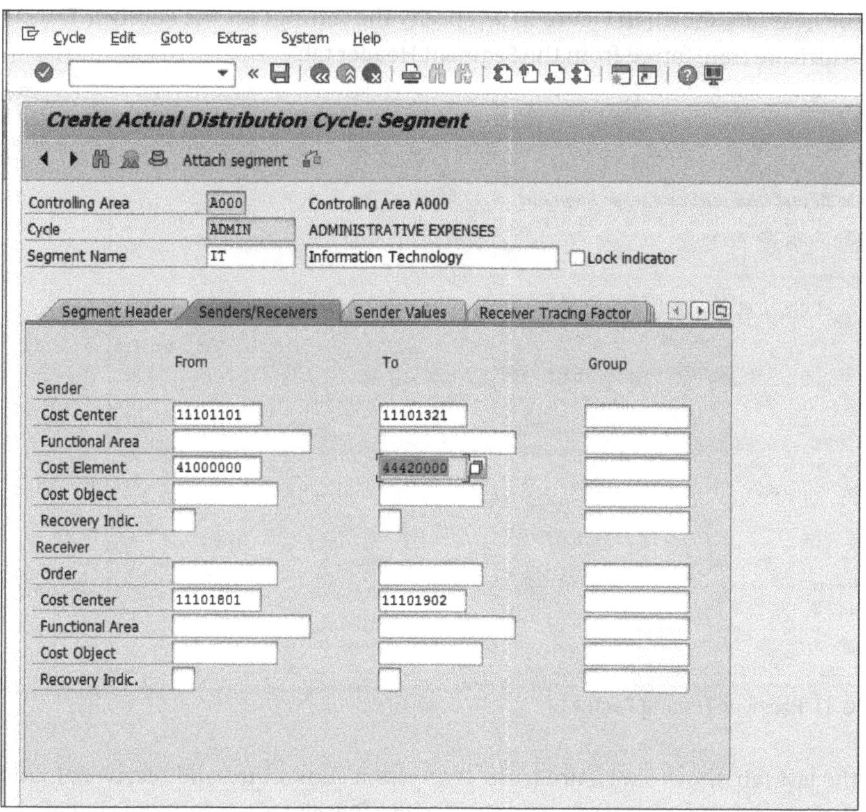

Figure 10.35 Sender/Receiver Settings

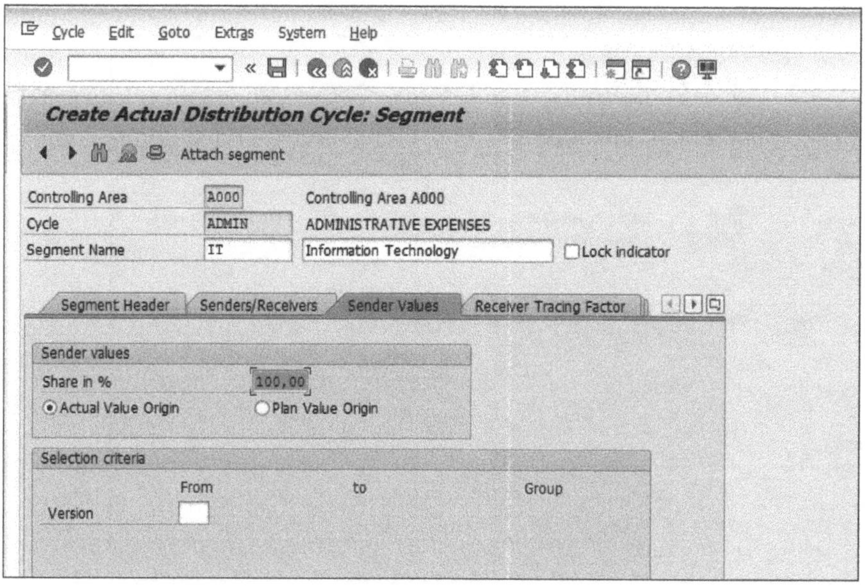

Cycle Edit Goto Extras System Help
Create Actual Distribution Cycle: Segment
Attach segment
Controlling Area A000 Controlling Area A000
Cycle ADMIN ADMINISTRATIVE EXPENSES
Segment Name IT Information Technology
Lock indicator
Segment Header
Senders/Receivers
Sender Values
Receiver Tracing Factor
Sender values
Share in % 100,00
Actual Value Origin
Plan Value Origin
Selection criteria
From
to
Group
Version

Figure 10.36 Sender Values

Under the next tab, shown in Figure 10.37, specify the settings for the **Receiver Tracing Factor**, which are transferred from the **Segment Header** tab.

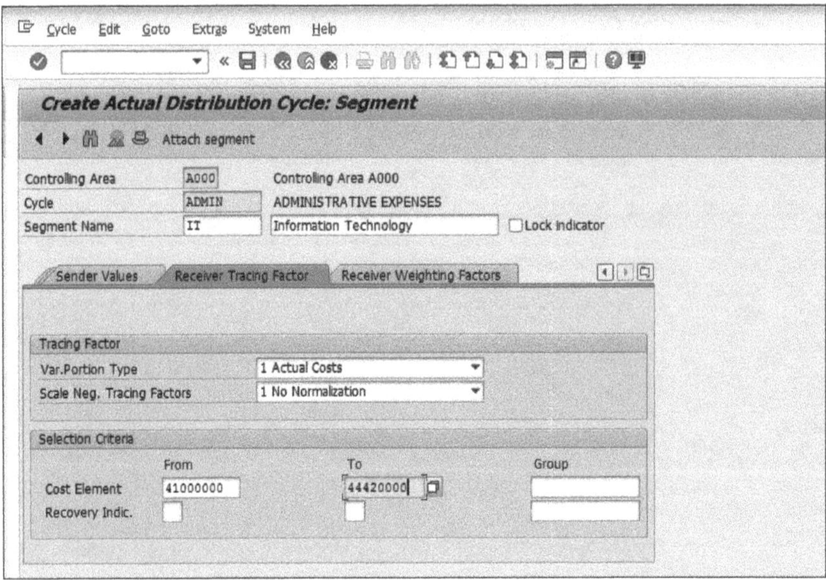

Figure 10.37 Receiver Tracing Factor

Under the last tab, shown in Figure 10.38, the system shows the valid receivers found based on the parameters entered under the **Senders/Receivers** tab. You can change the default factor for each receiver, which is 100%. The factor is used to multiply the determined amount.

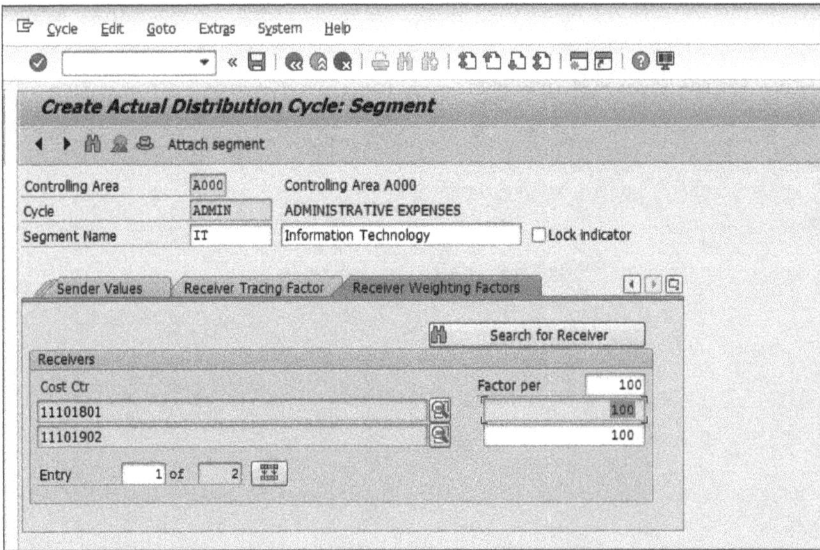

Figure 10.38 Receiver Weighting Factors

After maintaining these settings, save your cycle, and it's ready for use as part of your period-end closing procedures. Execute your cycle with Transaction KSV5 in the application menu path **Accounting • Controlling • Cost Center Accounting • Period-End Closing • Single Functions • Allocations. • KSV5—Distribution**, shown in Figure 10.39.

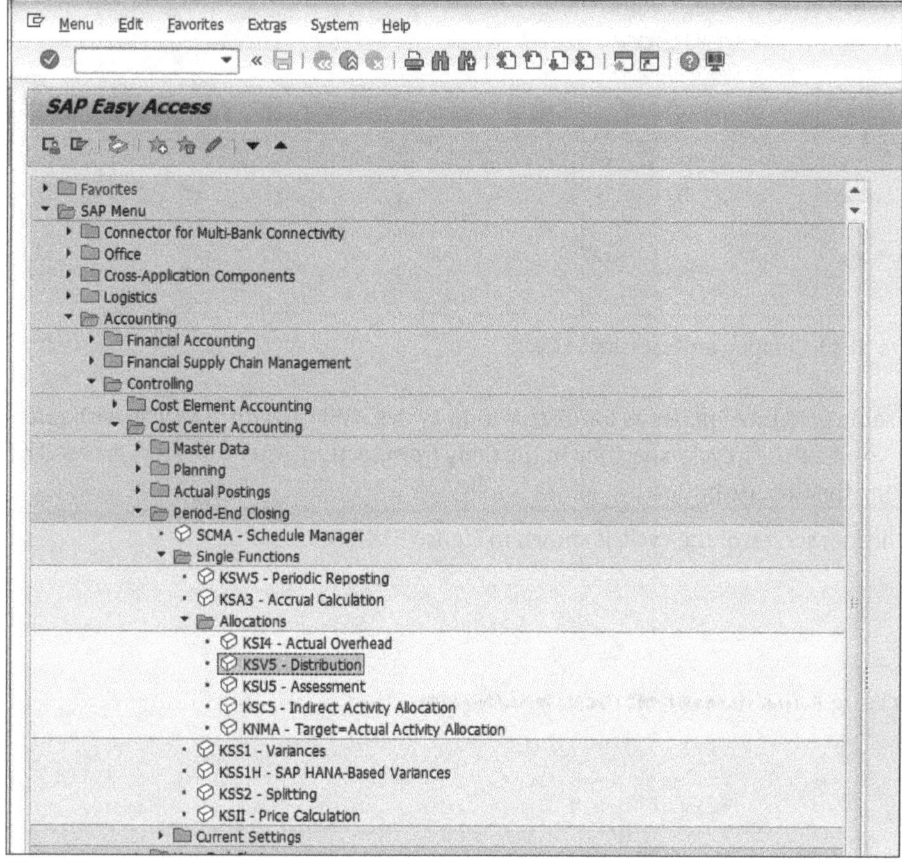

Figure 10.39 Executing the Distribution

10.3.3 Assessment

Assessment, another allocation technique, uses secondary assessment cost elements instead of the original cost elements to allocate costs. This technique can be used to allocate not only primary but also secondary costs.

Assessment is also set up using cycles and segments. To create an assessment cycle, follow the menu path **Controlling • Cost Center Accounting • Actual Postings • Period-End Closing • Assessment • Maintain Assessment**. Then, select **Create Actual Assessment**. This transaction is also available in the application menu path via **Accounting • Controlling • Cost Center Accounting • Period-End Closing • Current Settings • S_ALR_87005742—Define Assessment.**

On the initial screen, shown in Figure 10.40, enter a cycle name and start date.

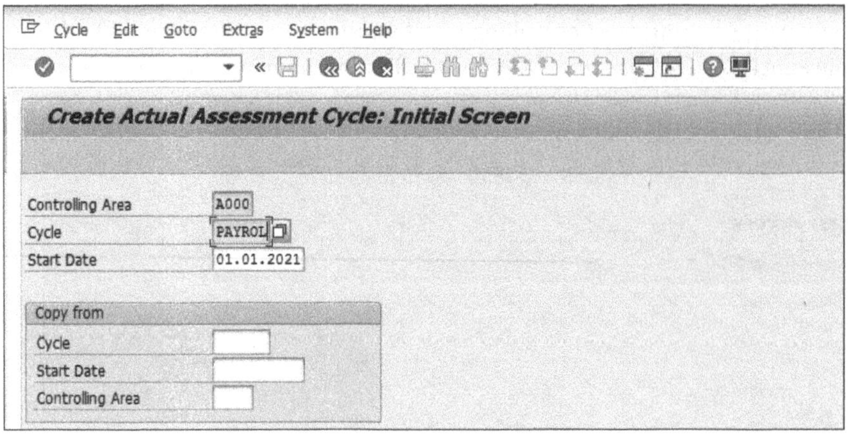

Figure 10.40 Creating an Assessment Cycle

The same guidance applies as for distribution cycles. You can create a cycle with reference to an existing cycle, specified in the **Copy from** section. After that step, proceed by clicking the **Execute** button.

The header screen of the cycle is shown in Figure 10.41.

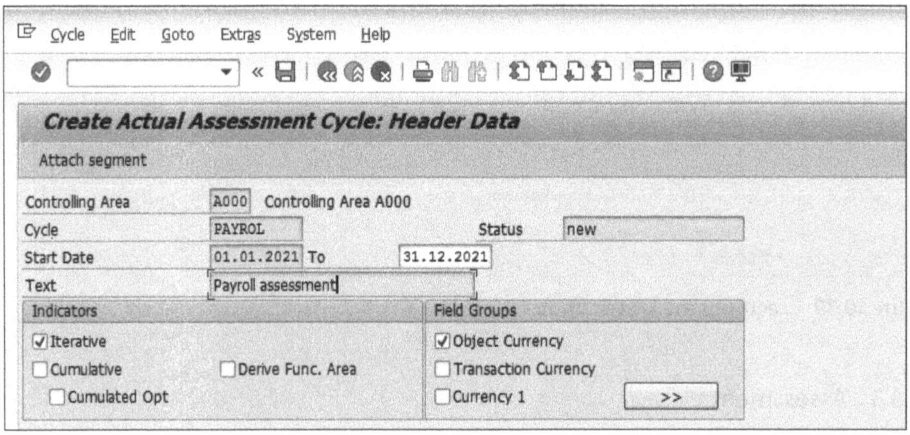

Figure 10.41 Assessment Cycle Header

The following fields can be configured:

- **Start Date and To**
  Start and end dates defining the validity of the cycle. As with distribution cycles, if you create new cycles each year, the end date in this field should be the end date of the fiscal year.
- **Text**
  A meaningful long description of the cycle.

- **Iterative**
  This indicator enables iterative sender/receiver relationships. In this case, the iteration is repeated until each sender is fully credited.
- **Cumulative**
  If you select this indicator, the sender amounts posted are allocated based on tracing factors, which are cumulated for all periods.
- **Derive Func. Area**
  By selecting this indicator, the functional area proposed in the cycle definition for the receiver is ignored and is derived again.
- **Field Groups**
  In general, only amounts in the controlling area currency are used in periodic allocations. However, you can choose other types of currencies in this section.

After maintaining the cycle definition, you need to attach at least one segment. Select **Attach Segment** from the top menu. The segment is also organized into tabs, as shown in Figure 10.42.

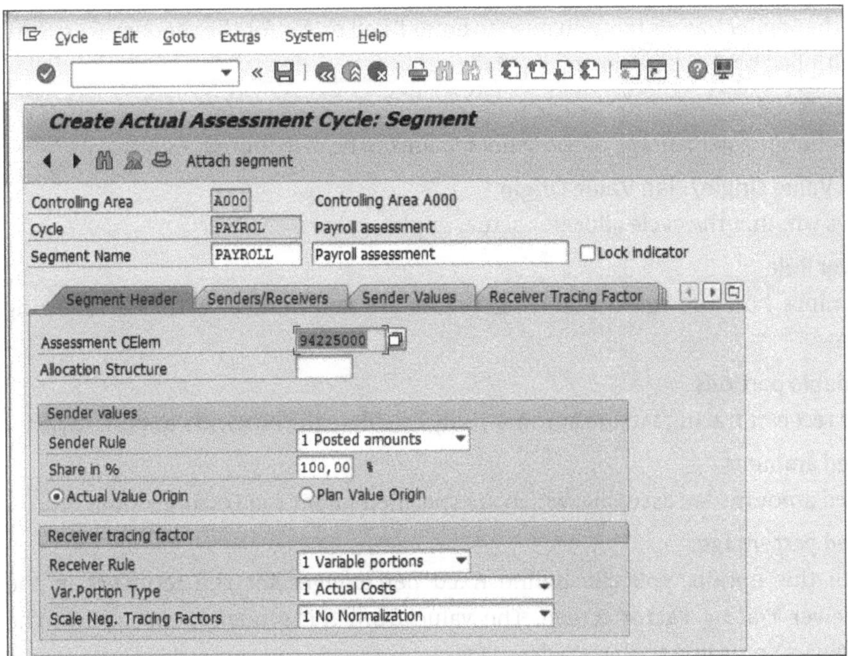

Figure 10.42 Assessment Segment Header

Under the first tab, **Segment Header**, shown in Figure 10.42, you'll specify rules for the assessment calculation by maintaining the following fields:

- **Assessment CElem (assessment cost element)**
  This field is a key difference for this distribution. In this field, you must specify either an assessment cost element in this field or an allocation structure in the next field.

Specified assessment cost elements are used to post the assessment instead of the original cost elements.

- **Allocation Structure**
  The allocation structure defines cost elements based on certain criteria and is used in various areas of controlling. We'll configure allocation structures in Chapter 11. In this field, you can specify an allocation structure to determine the assessment cost elements based on the originally posted cost elements.
- **Sender Rule**
  This field determines how the sender values are calculated. The following options are available:
  - **Posted amounts**
    Amounts posted on the sender are the sender values.
  - **Fixed amounts**
    For this option, you must define fixed amounts for senders in the selection criteria on the **Sender Values** tab.
  - **Fixed rates**
    On the **Sender Values** tab, you need to enter fixed prices for the senders, which are multiplied by the receiver tracing factors.
- **Share in %**
  Determines the percentage of the sender values to be distributed.
- **Actual Value Origin/Plan Value Origin**
  Defines whether the cycle allocates actual or plan values.
- **Receiver Rule**
  Determines how the receiver tracing factors are determined, with the following options:
  - **Variable portions**
    The receiver tracing factors automatically calculate the amounts to be assessed.
  - **Fixed amounts**
    Fixed amounts are assessed, which are specified under the **Tracing Values** tab.
  - **Fixed percentages**
    With this option, you can define fixed percentages for the receivers in the **Receiver Tracing Factor** screen. The value from the sender is assessed to the receivers according to these percentages.
  - **Fixed portions**
    With this option, you'll define fixed portions for the receivers in the **Receiver Tracing Factor** screen. This option is similar to the fixed percentage option, but the amount is not limited to 100.
- **Var.Portion Type**
  Determines the basis of the assessment.

- **Scale Neg. Tracing Factors**
  Controls how negative tracing factors are treated. Negative tracing factors are possible when the tracing factors are not entered as fixed portions or percentages but instead are derived.

Under the next tab, **Senders/Receivers**, you'll define the sender and receiver cost objects, as shown in Figure 10.43.

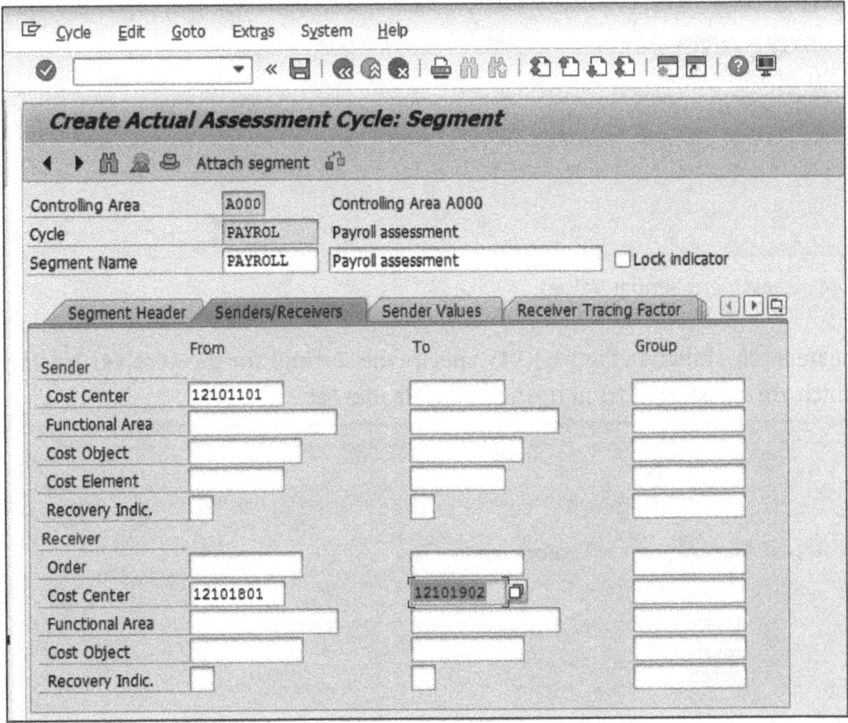

Figure 10.43 Assessment Segment Sender/Receiver Settings

The costs posted originally on the cost objects defined in the **Sender** section will be distributed to the objects defined in the **Receiver** section, according to the tracing factors defined under the **Receiver Tracing Factor** tab. You also need to specify the sender cost elements.

Click the next tab, **Sender Values**, as shown in Figure 10.44. Under this tab, you can specify the percentage of sender values to be distributed (usually 100%), as well as whether the origin of the values is actual or plan data. You can also specify a version.

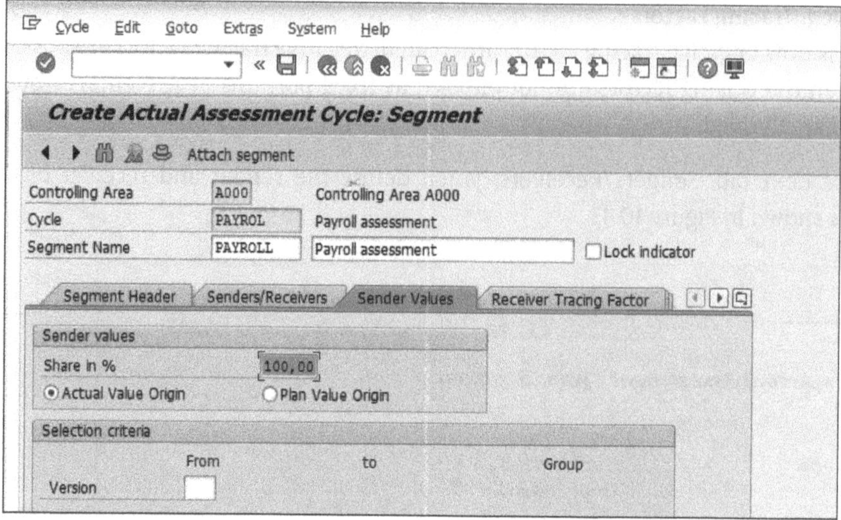

Figure 10.44 Assessment Sender Values

Under the next tab, shown in Figure 10.45, specify the settings for the **Receiver Tracing Factor**, which are transferred from the **Segment Header** tab.

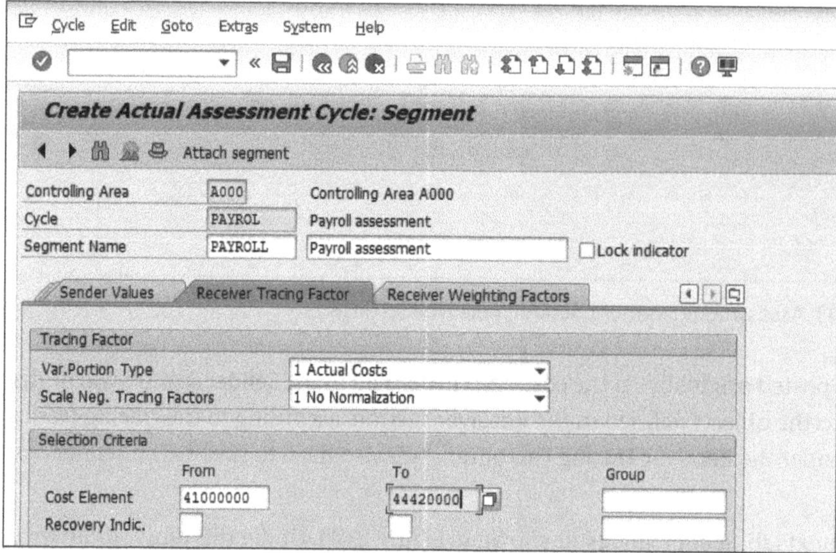

Figure 10.45 Receiver Tracing Factor in Assessment

Under the last tab, **Receiver Weighting Factors**, the system shows the valid receivers found based on the parameters entered under the **Senders/Receivers** tab, as shown in Figure 10.46. You can change the default factor for each receiver, which is 100%. The factor is used to multiply the determined amount.

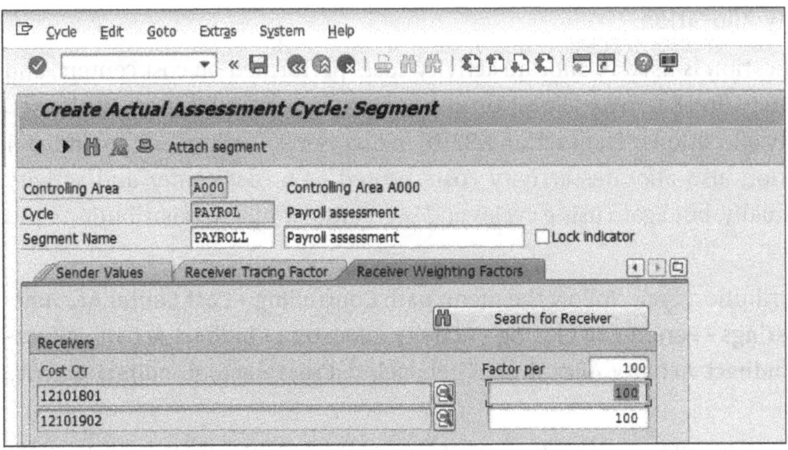

Figure 10.46 Receiver Weighting Factors in Assessment

After maintaining these settings, save your cycle, and it's ready for use as part of your period-end closing procedures. The cycle can be executed with Transaction KSU5 in the application menu path **Accounting • Controlling • Cost Center Accounting • Period-End Closing • Single Functions • Allocations • KSU5—Assessment**, as shown in Figure 10.47.

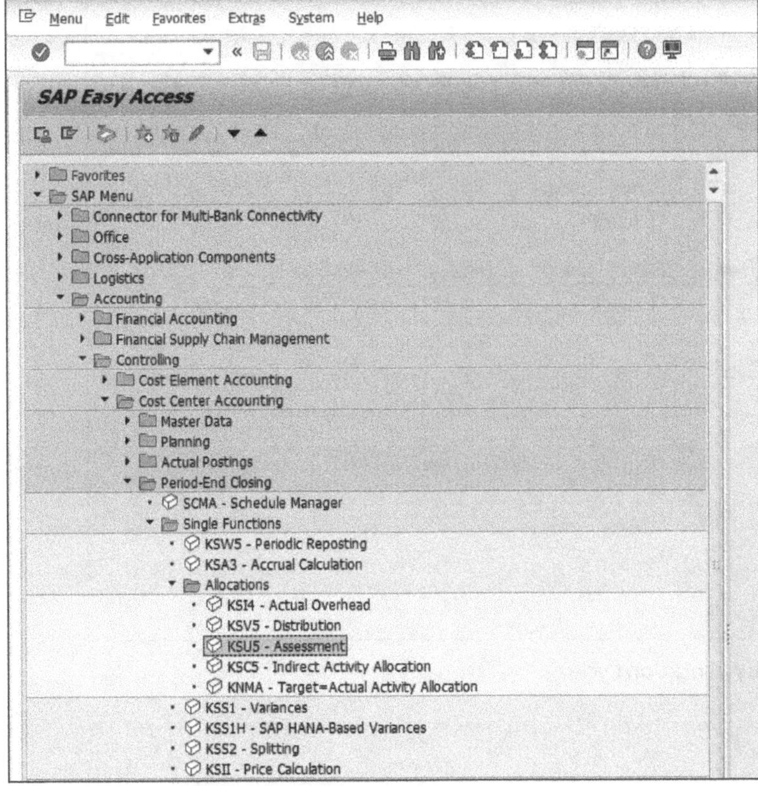

Figure 10.47 Executing the Assessment

10.3.4 Activity Allocation

An activity allocation is used to allocate activity costs performed on cost centers, and two options exist: direct activity allocation and indirect activity allocation. We looked at direct activity allocations (Transaction KB21N) in Chapter 9, Section 9.3.2. An indirect activity allocation also allocates activity costs posted to a cost center and activity type—not manually, but again using cycles and segments, similar to distributions and assessments.

To create a distribution cycle, follow the menu path **Controlling • Cost Center Accounting • Actual Postings • Period-End Closing • Activity Allocation • Indirect Activity Allocation • Define Indirect Activity Allocation**. Then, select **Create actual indirect activity allocation**.

Setting up an activity allocation cycle is similar to setting up distribution and assessment cycles, so we won't go through every single screen. Again, you'll define a name, description, and start and end date for the cycle. Then, you'll attach segments, which have similar control fields as the cycles we described earlier. However, you must specify a sender **Activity Type** in the **Sender** section, as well as a **Cost Center** in both the **Sender** and the **Receiver** sections, as shown in Figure 10.48.

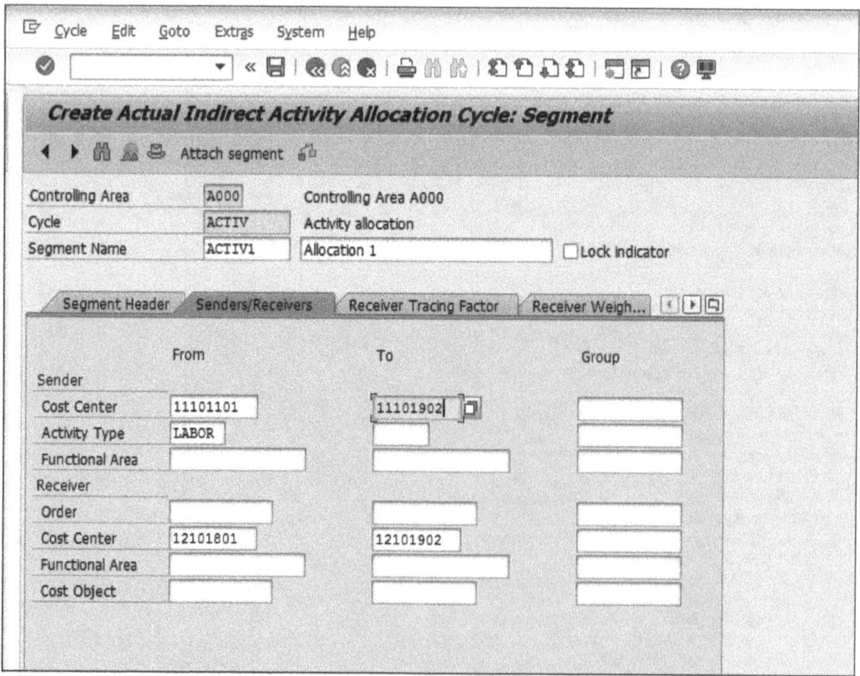

Figure 10.48 Activity Allocation Cycle

After maintaining these settings, you can execute the activity allocation with Transaction KSC5 in the application menu path **Accounting • Controlling • Cost Center Accounting • Period-End Closing • Single Functions • KSC5—Indirect Activity Allocation**, as shown in Figure 10.49.

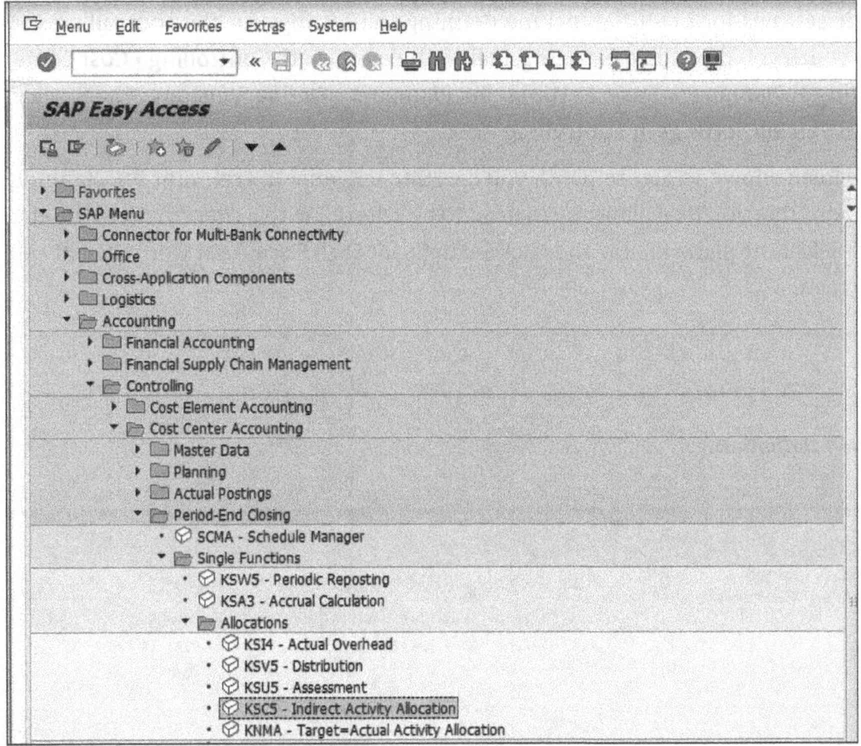

Figure 10.49 Executing the Indirect Activity Allocation

With that step, we've finished our guide on periodic allocations and can move on to cost center planning.

10.4 Planning

Cost center accounting, a part of management accounting, aims to provide management with a detailed analysis of how the business is performing, how profitable it is, and where there's room for improvement. As such, planning is quite important because it enables management to compare actual costs with plan costs. Because cost centers are the main cost objects in most companies, cost center planning has tremendous significance in the overall controlling planning process.

We'll start by configuring the basic settings for planning. Then, you'll learn how to perform manual planning.

10.4.1 Basic Settings for Planning

The basic settings for planning include defining the settings for the controlling versions in which you'll perform planning. Follow the menu path **Controlling • Cost Center Accounting • Planning • Basic Settings for Planning • Define Versions**. Then, select **Maintain Version Settings in Controlling Area**.

On the screen shown in Figure 10.50, you'll define the versions relevant for planning. The versions that you'll be planning in need to be selected with a checkmark in the **Plan** column. Select the plan version and click **Settings for Each Fiscal Year** from the left side of the screen.

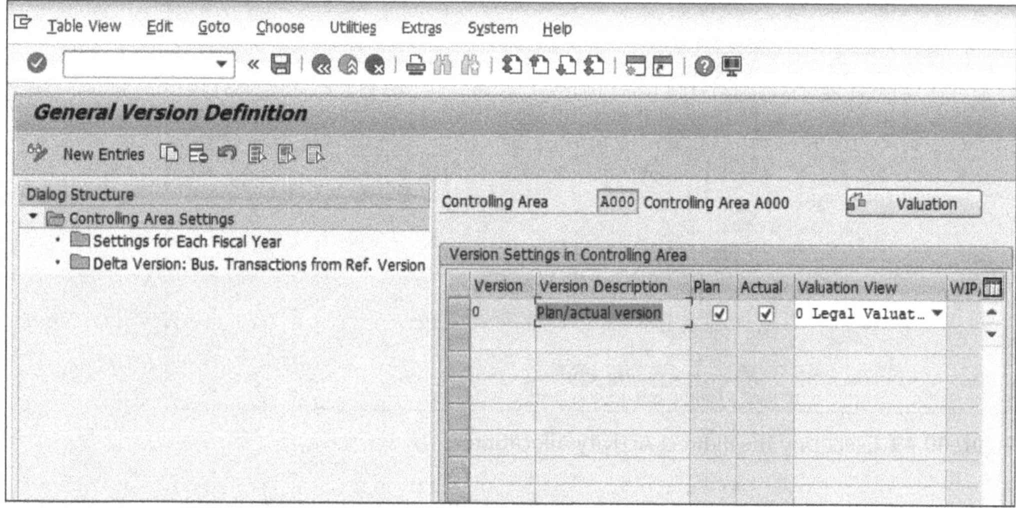

Figure 10.50 Maintaining Versions for Planning

Then, you'll need to maintain the settings for each fiscal year, as shown in Figure 10.51. You must select the **Integrated Planning** checkbox if you're want to use plan data in other components also. You also must specify a dedicated exchange rate type for cost planning (such as standard exchange rate type P).

After maintaining all the relevant settings for planning versions, save your entries by clicking the **Save** button.

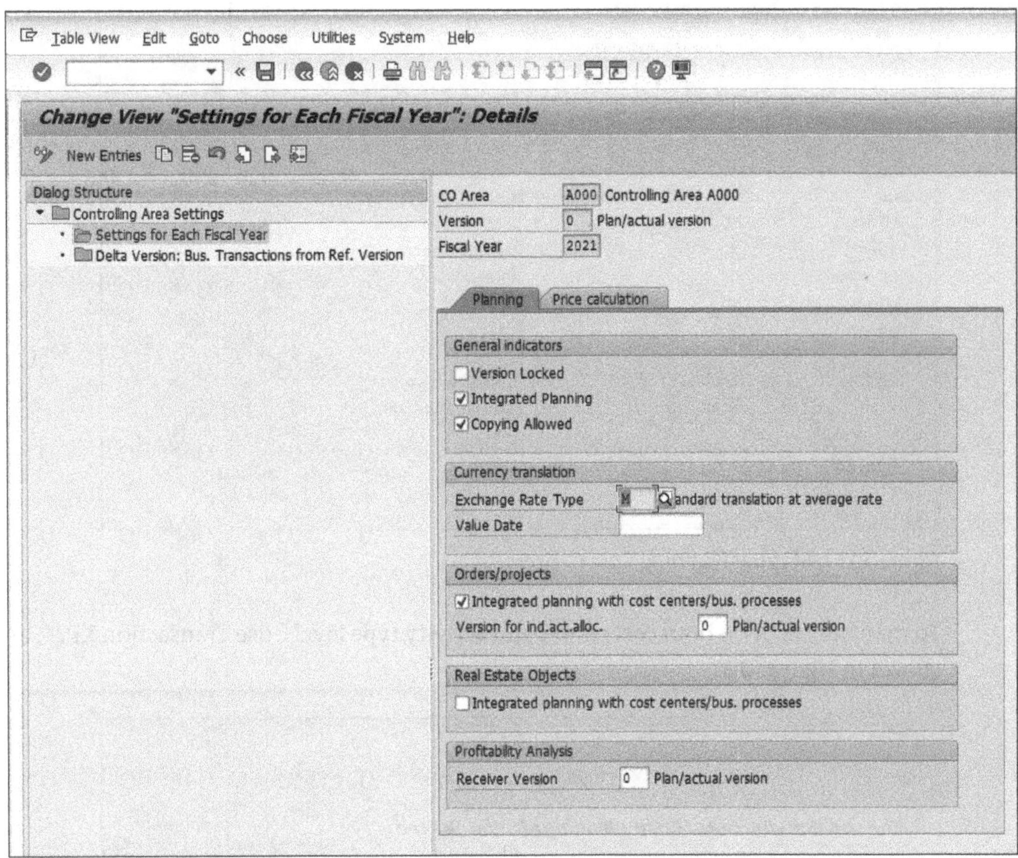

Figure 10.51 Fiscal Year Settings

10.4.2 Manual Planning

Manual planning is the process of manually entering plan values for the relevant cost centers. Three main processes are involved:

- Planning on the cost center/cost element level
- Planning on the cost center/activity type level
- Planning on the statistical key figure level

To plan on the cost center/cost element level, use Transaction KP06, as shown in Figure 10.52.

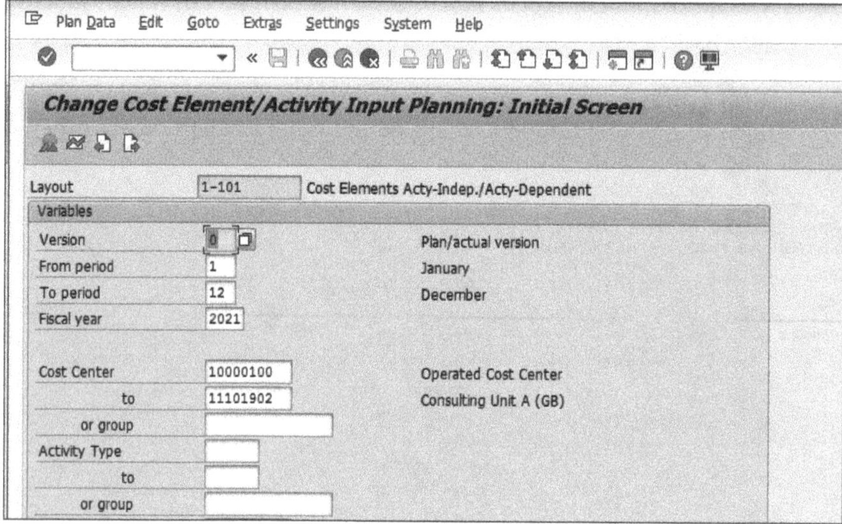

Figure 10.52 Manual Planning Cost Centers

To manually plan on both cost center and activity type levels, use Transaction KP26, as shown in Figure 10.53.

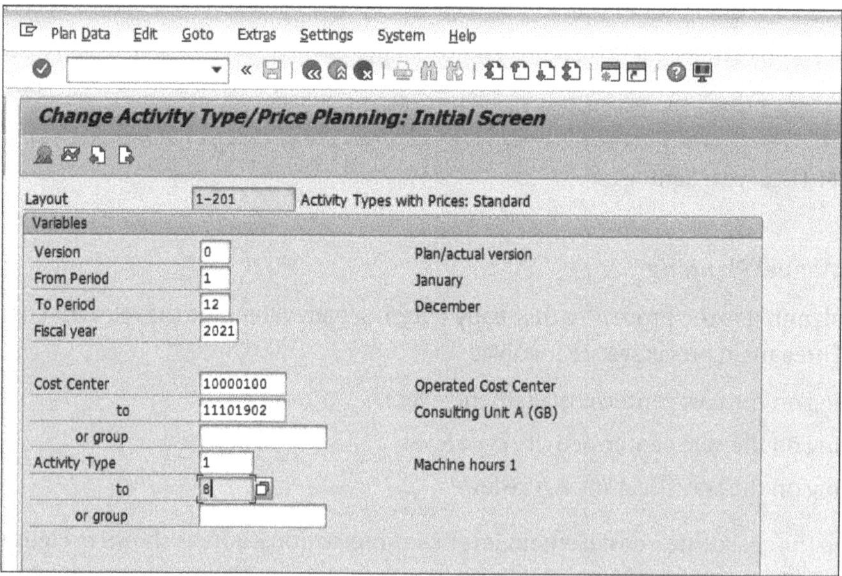

Figure 10.53 Manual Planning Activity Types

Enter the fiscal year and periods for which the planning values are valid and select the cost centers to enter planning values for.

Similarly, you can use Transaction KP46 to plan on the statistical key figure level, as shown in Figure 10.54.

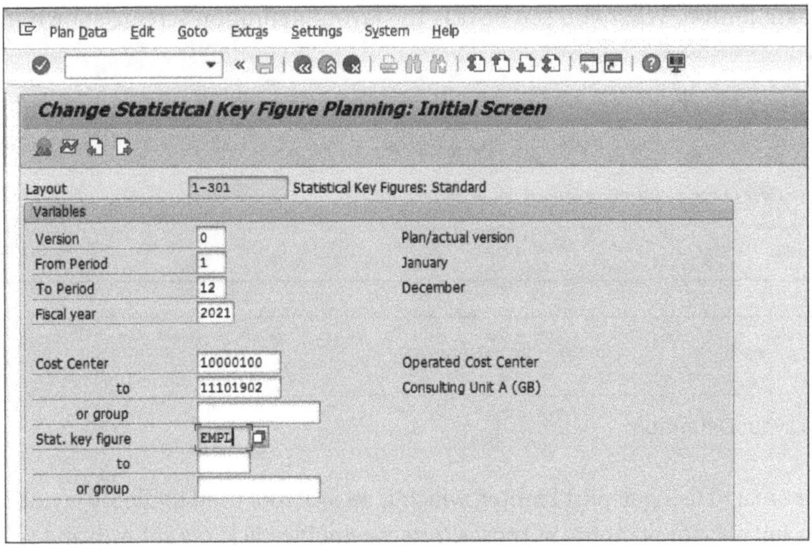

Figure 10.54 Manual Planning Statistical Key Figures

Notice that these transactions use different planning layouts. Figure 10.52 uses layout **1-101**, and Figure 10.53 uses layout **1-201**. To define planning layouts for activity type planning, follow the menu path **Controlling • Cost Center Accounting • Planning • Manual Planning • User-Defined Planning Layouts • Create Planning Layouts for Activity Type Planning**. On this screen, you can create a new layout by selecting **Create Activity Type Planning Layout**.

On the initial screen, shown in Figure 10.55, create a new planning layout by copying an existing standard layout, such as 1-201.

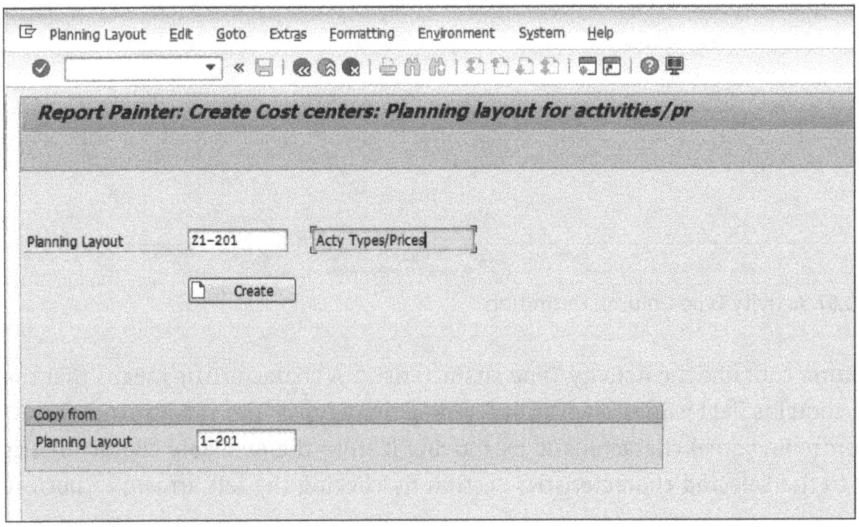

Figure 10.55 Creating a Planning Layout

Click the **Create** button. What you see next is the layout definition screen, shown in Figure 10.56.

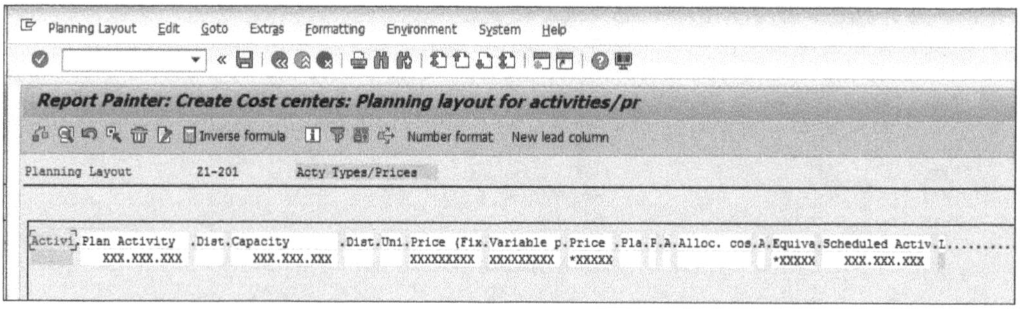

Figure 10.56 Layout Definition

This screen is created using Report Painter, which is an SAP tool used to define layouts for reporting, but also for planning purposes. You can double-click any column and see its definition. Let's click the first column, **Activity Type**. On the screen shown in Figure 10.57, you'll see the definition in the **Activity Type** column.

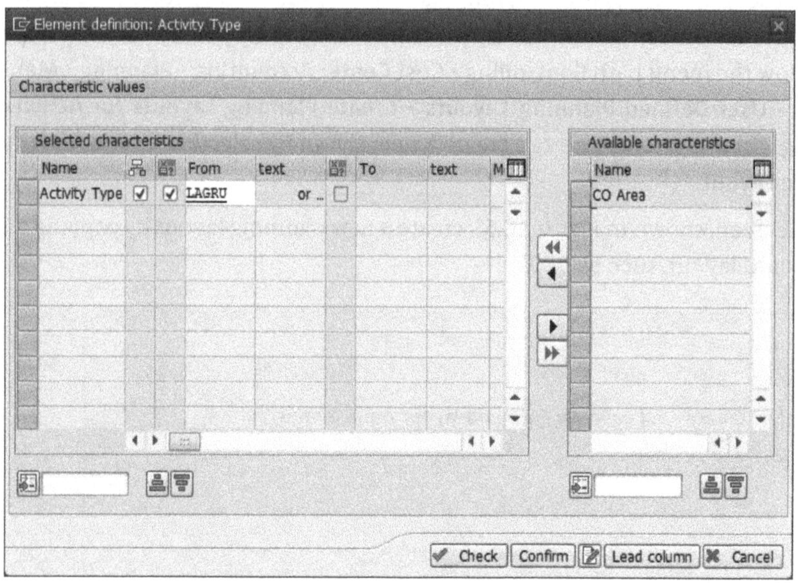

Figure 10.57 Activity Type Column Definition

This column contains the **Activity Type** characteristic. A characteristic means that the column contains field values, such as different activity types. You can also add the **CO Area** (controlling area) characteristic by moving it from the **Available characteristics** section to the **Selected characteristics** section by clicking the left arrow [<] button.

Next to the name of the characteristic, you'll see two columns (**Set**) and (**Variable**), which are both selected. **Set** means that the field is interpreted as a group value. By selecting the **Variable** option, you specify that the value of the field is derived from the selection screen. In this case, you must enter a variable name in the next column.

Go back and click another column, this time, **Plan Activity**. As shown in Figure 10.58, in this column, we don't have characteristics but key figures instead. The key figures represent value fields, such as actual costs, plan costs, or activity output. In this case, the key figure represents the plan activity.

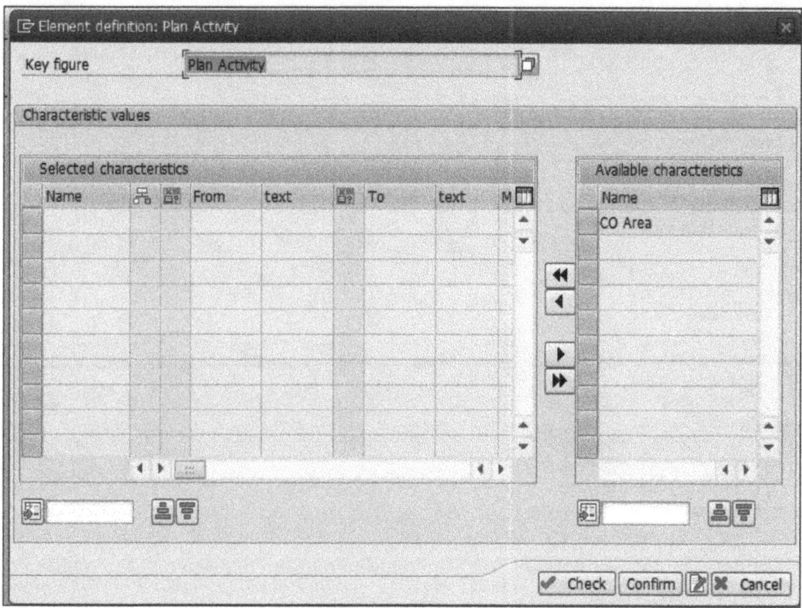

Figure 10.58 Plan Activity Column Definition

In this fashion, you can define the whole structure of the layout. After maintaining these settings, save by clicking the **Save** button. Now, you can use the layout in your manual planning.

10.5 Information System

The information system for cost center accounting is robust and provides myriad standard reports that should meet even the most demanding user requirements. In addition, SAP provides a user-friendly tool to generate user-defined reports for cost centers: the Report Painter, which we briefly mentioned in the previous section.

Let's first look at the standard reports available before moving on to user-defined reports.

10.5.1 Standard Reports

You can access the information system for cost center accounting under the application menu path **Accounting • Controlling • Cost Center Accounting • Information System**, as shown in Figure 10.59.

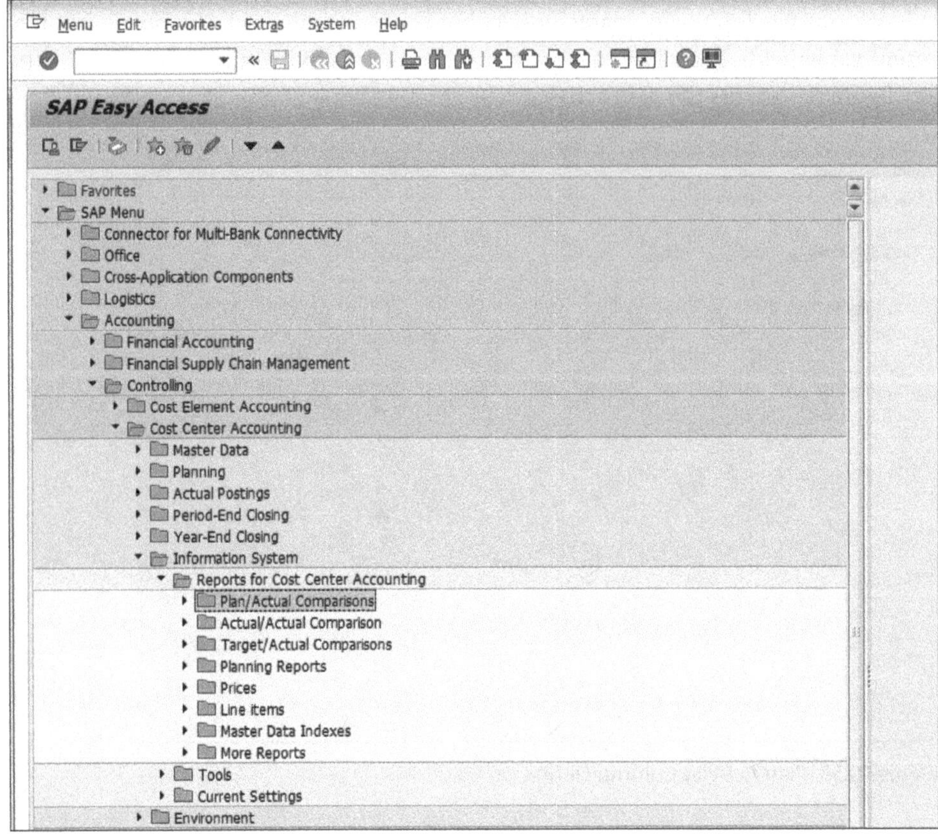

Figure 10.59 Standard Reports

Notice that reports are grouped into various categories such as plan/actual comparisons, actual/actual comparisons, line items, and so on. We won't go into great detail about every report, but we'll show you one of the most commonly used ones: report S_ALR_87013611 (Cost Centers: Actual/Plan/Variance) in the **Plan/Actual Comparisons** section.

Figure 10.60 shows the output screen of the report. For the selected cost centers, you'll see the costs per cost element with separate columns for actual costs, plan costs, and variance between the two.

You can double-click any line, and the system will offer you the ability to drill down using another of the linked reports, as shown in Figure 10.61.

Cost Centers: Actual/Plan/Variance	Date: 01.03.2019		Page:	2 / 3
			Column:	1 / 2
Cost Center/Group	*			
Person responsible:				
Reporting period:	1 to 12 2018			

Cost Elements	Act. Costs	Plan Costs	Var. (Abs.)	Var. (%)
276000 Discount received	100,00-		100,00-	
410000 Trading gds consump	9.966,18		9.966,18	
430000 Salaries	2.000,00		2.000,00	
476000 Office supplies	33.150,72		33.150,72	
700100 Service 01	60,00		60,00	
* Debit	45.076,90		45.076,90	
700100 Service 01	1.020,00-		1.020,00-	
* Credit	1.020,00-		1.020,00-	

Figure 10.60 Actual Plan Comparison Report

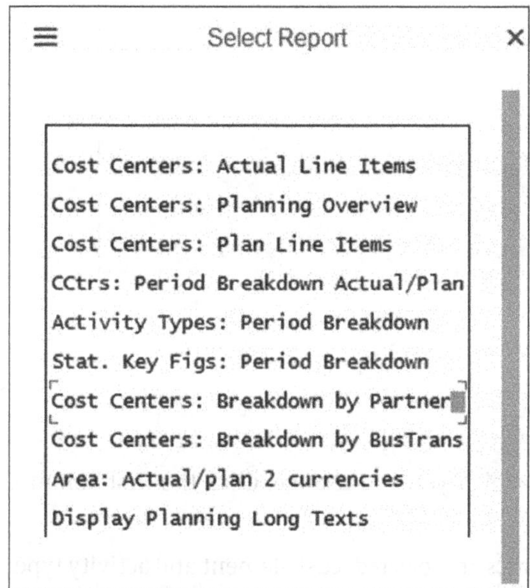

Figure 10.61 Drilldown Reports

If you select, for example, **Cost Centers: Actual Line Items**, the system automatically executes a line-item report for the selected line from the previous report.

10.5.2 User-Defined Reports

SAP S/4HANA provides a convenient tool to create new user-defined reports for cost centers. The reports in cost center accounting are created using Report Painter, which you saw in play when defining the planning layout.

To create a user-defined report, follow the menu path **Controlling • Cost Center Accounting • Information System • User-Defined Reports • Create Reports.** Then, select **Create Report.**

On the initial screen, shown in Figure 10.62, you'll need to select a report library, which is a collection of characteristics and key figures you can use in your reports. Standard library **1AB: Cost Centers: Variance Analysis** can be used for cost center reports to provide comparison between actual and plan costs. A good idea is to copy from an existing standard report and adapt it to your needs. Select standard report **1ABW-001: Cost Centers: Variances** in the **Copy from** section, in the **Report** field and click the **Create** button.

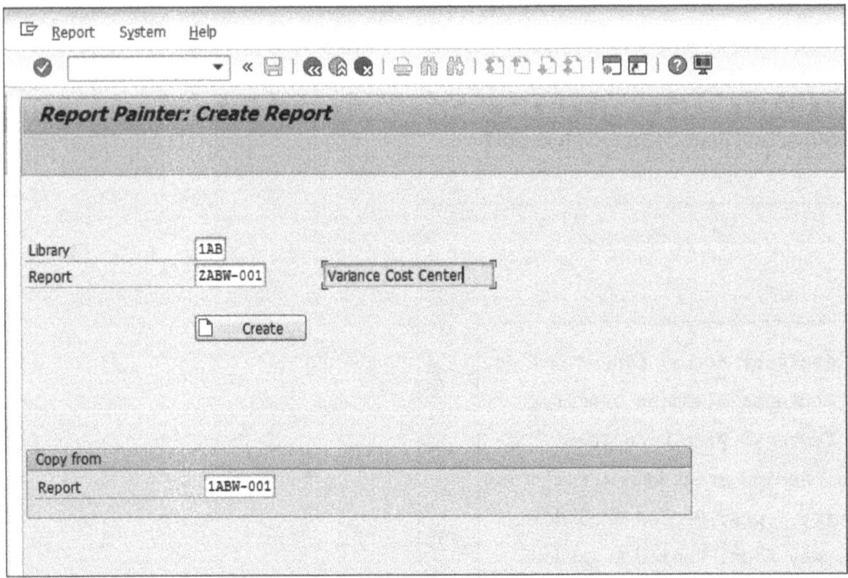

Figure 10.62 Creating a User-Defined Report

Figure 10.63 shows the report layout, which you can change. Click the first column, **Input Side: Cost Elements.**

Figure 10.64 shows that two characteristics are selected: cost element and activity type. The cost element is set and variable, which means that the range of cost elements should be entered on the selection screen of the report. For the activity type, enter an asterisk (*), which means that all activity types will be selected. The list of available characteristics you see on the right side of the screen is defined in the library.

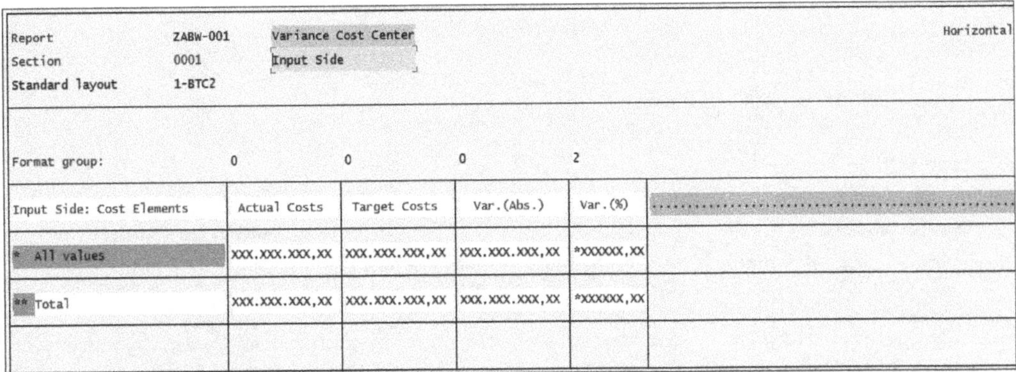

Figure 10.63 Report Layout Definition

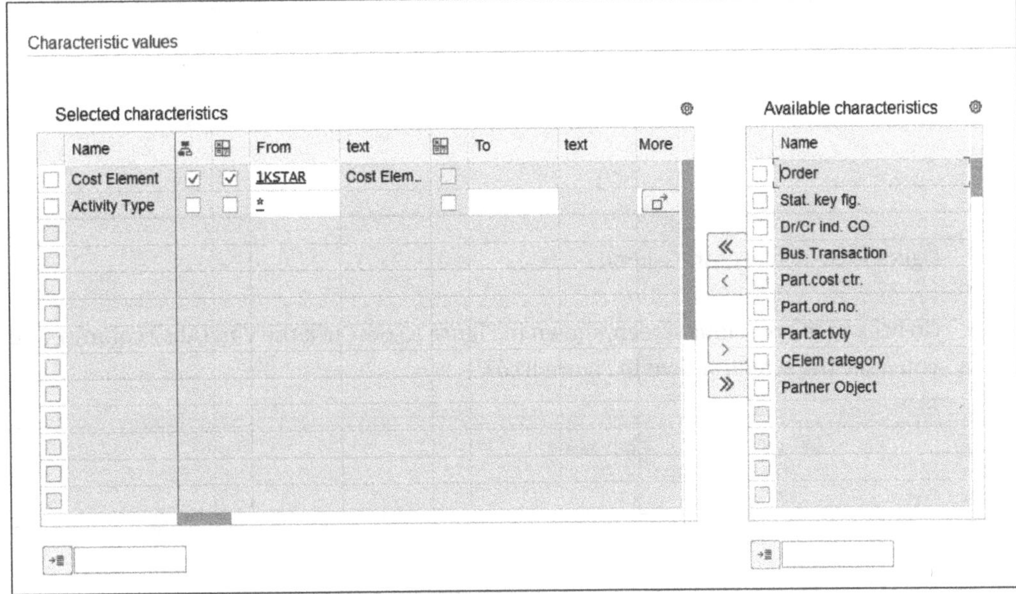

Figure 10.64 Cost Elements Column

Click the second column, **Actual Costs**. The screen shown in Figure 10.65 shows the definition of the **Actual Costs** column.

In this case, the basic key figure **Costs** is selected, and the column will display the amounts for this key figure based on the characteristics selected and their values (e.g., above version 0 only). The **Target Costs** column is similarly designed but uses the plan version because it relates to plan costs.

Element definition: Actual Costs
*Basic key figure:
Costs
Characteristic values
Selected characteristics
Name
From
text
To
text
More
Value Type
3
Version
0
Input/output
1
Valuation
1VALUTP
Actual Val...
Available characteristics
Name
Order
Stat. key fig.
Dr/Cr ind. CO
Bus.Transaction
Part.cost ctr.
Part.ord.no.
Part.actvty
Category
CElem category
Partner Object

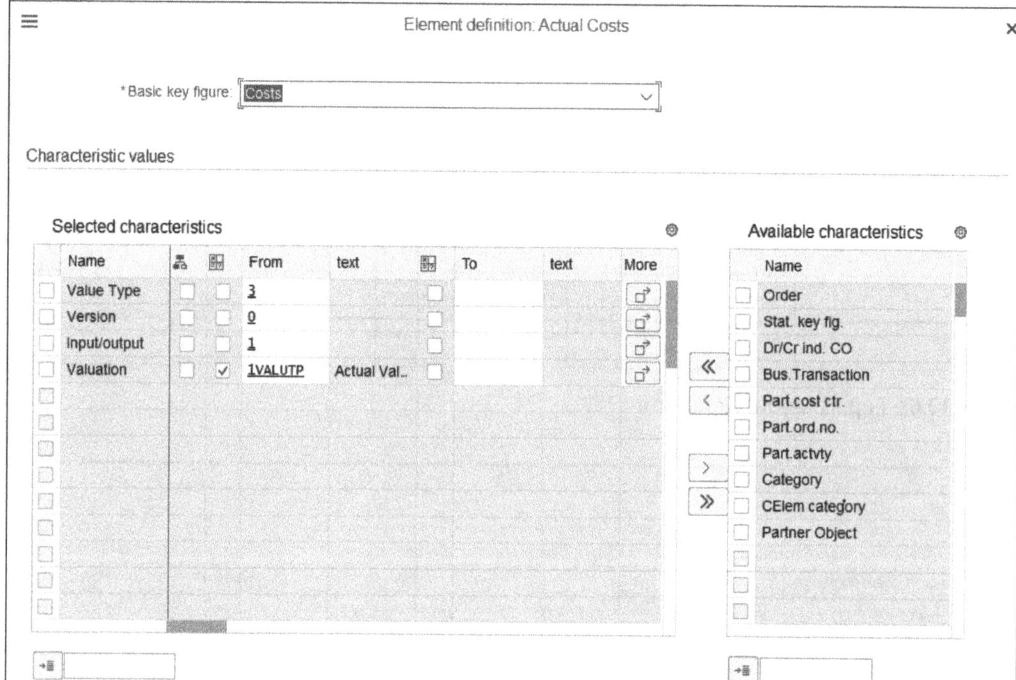

Figure 10.65 Actual Costs Column

Go back to the previous screen, shown in Figure 10.66. Click the **Var. (Abs.)** column, and you'll see the screen shown in Figure 10.67.

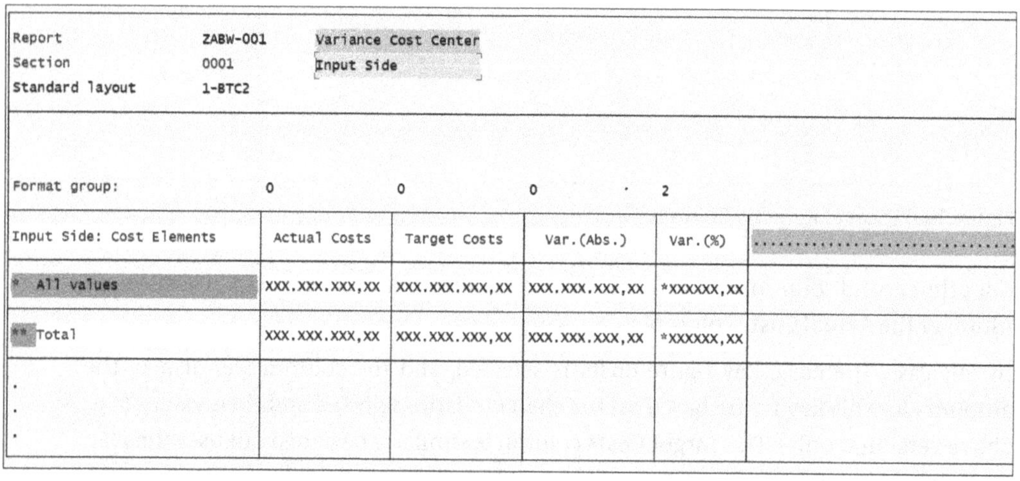

Report
ZABW-001
Variance Cost Center
Section
0001
Input Side
Standard layout
1-BTC2
Format group:
0
0
0
2
Input Side: Cost Elements
Actual Costs
Target Costs
Var.(Abs.)
Var.(%)
* All values
XXX.XXX.XXX,XX
XXX.XXX.XXX,XX
XXX.XXX.XXX,XX
*XXXXXX,XX
** Total
XXX.XXX.XXX,XX
XXX.XXX.XXX,XX
XXX.XXX.XXX,XX
*XXXXXX,XX

Figure 10.66 Report Definition

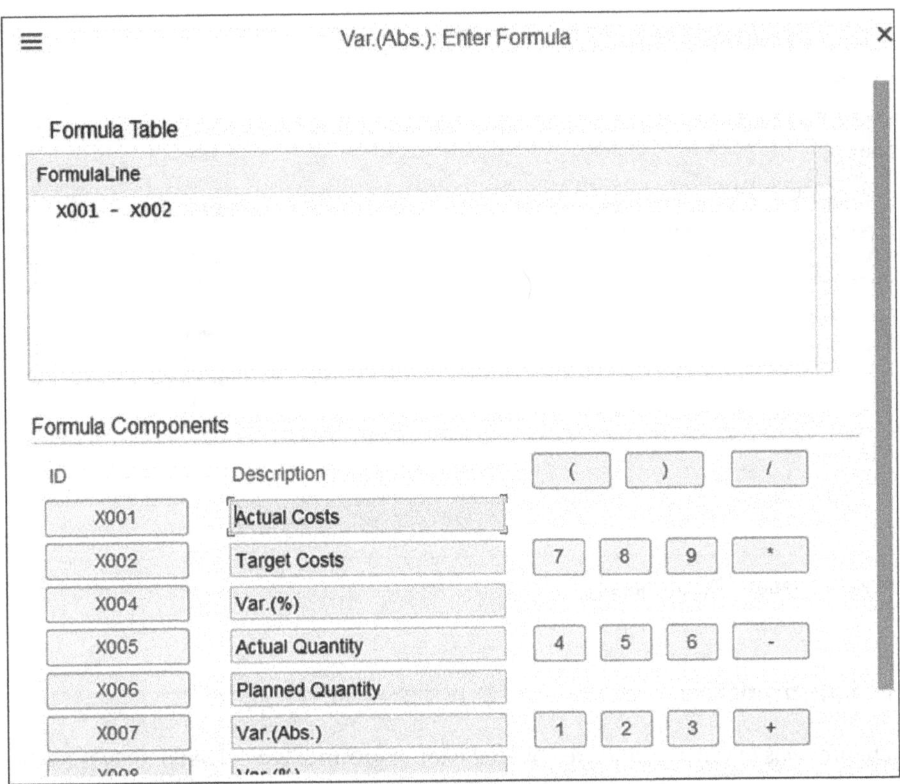

Figure 10.67 Variance Column

The variance column is defined as a formula. In this formula editor screen, you'll define that the variance is equal to column 1 – column 2. You can also make more complex calculations using the formula editor with various mathematic operations, both with columns and rows.

Select **General data selection** from the top menu (shown earlier in Figure 10.63) to open the screen shown in Figure 10.68.

The general data selections refer to the report as a whole, not just to specific columns or rows. In our example, the controlling area, cost center, fiscal year, and period are defined as variables, which means that a user must enter this information in the selection screen of the report, and then the report output will contain values restricted by those selections.

After modifying these settings, save your report by clicking the **Save** button. In this way, you can easily enhance the standard reports provided by SAP to cover business-specific requirements with custom user-defined reports.

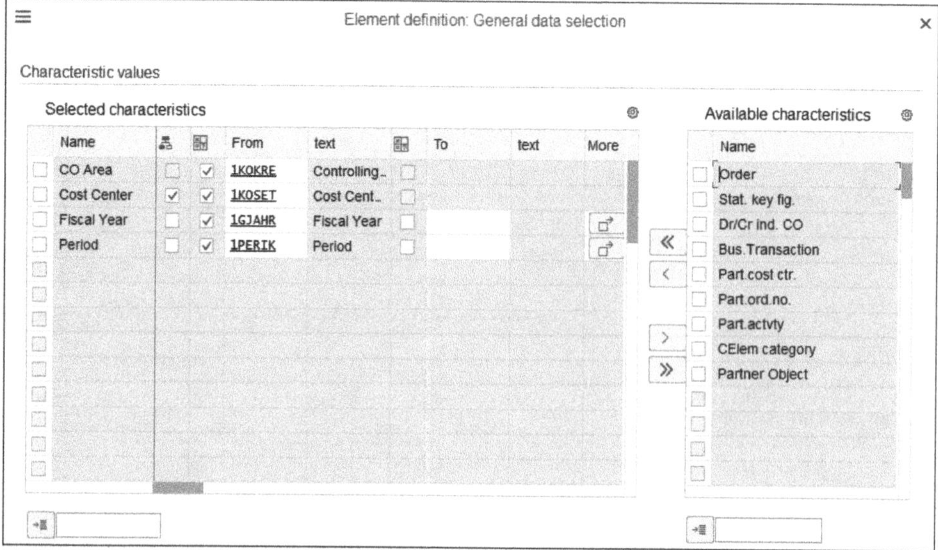

Figure 10.68 General Data Selection

10.6 Summary

This chapter was extensive, and we covered a lot of ground. We delved deeply into the secrets of cost center accounting, which is one of the core controlling and overhead accounting areas. After reading this chapter, you should have a good understanding of the master data objects for cost center accounting, such as cost centers, cost center groups, activity types, and statistical key figures.

You now understand the flow of values to cost centers, both in manual postings and in integrated documents. We explained how to maintain the automatic determination of cost centers and substitutions that also can be used to derive cost centers.

You learned how to set up various allocation procedures, such as accrual calculation distributions, assessments, and activity allocations. These procedures are major parts of cost center accounting. Costs often don't often stay in the original cost center because, for management analysis needs, they need to be allocated to portray the purpose of the costs more accurately.

You also learned how to set up planning for cost centers, including setting up its basic settings and creating planning layouts. Finally, we guided you through the information system for cost centers, including how to use standard reports and drill down from them, as well as how to create user-defined reports with the powerful Report Painter tool.

Thus, we've finished our guide to cost center accounting. Next, we'll move to the other core overhead accounting area: internal orders.

Chapter 11
Internal Orders

This chapter gives step-by-step instructions for configuring internal orders in SAP S/4HANA and using them for planning and budgeting in your organization.

Internal orders are controlling objects used to represent internal projects, such as marketing campaigns, information technology implementation projects, or research and development (R&D) projects. Internal orders are fundamentally different than cost centers, which usually represent departments within your organization, whereas internal orders are created for specific projects of a specific duration.

Therefore, internal orders are created with a limited time span. Whereas cost centers represent a more or less stable structure, internal orders are created, are budgeted for, accumulate costs, and, at some point in time, are closed.

Another option is available to represent projects: Project System in SAP S/4HANA. This solution is used to depict complex projects with many steps, milestones, and complex cost structures. Project System lies outside of the scope of this book because this cross-integration between finance and logistics deserves a whole book of its own. Just keep in mind that you should use internal orders for smaller projects, whereas, for very complex projects, you should explore Project System.

We'll start by setting up the required master data for internal orders. Then, you'll learn how to configure and enter budgets for internal orders. Budgeting is one of the most important functions that helps to manage costs tracked on an internal order level. In the next section, we'll examine the actual postings and periodic allocations that are performed on internal orders. Then, we'll continue with internal orders planning, and we'll finish with a guide to the internal orders information system.

11.1 Master Data

An internal order is a master data object created from the application menu in a way similar to how we created cost centers. Before you can start creating an internal order, however, you must first activate internal orders in SAP S/4HANA and then configure order types, which classify internal orders and control their settings.

The first step in setting up internal orders is to ensure that order management is activated for your controlling area. Follow the menu path **Controlling • Internal Orders • Activate Order Management in Controlling Area.**

Select the checkbox to the left of your controlling area and click **Activate components/ control indicators** on the left side of the screen, as shown in Figure 11.1.

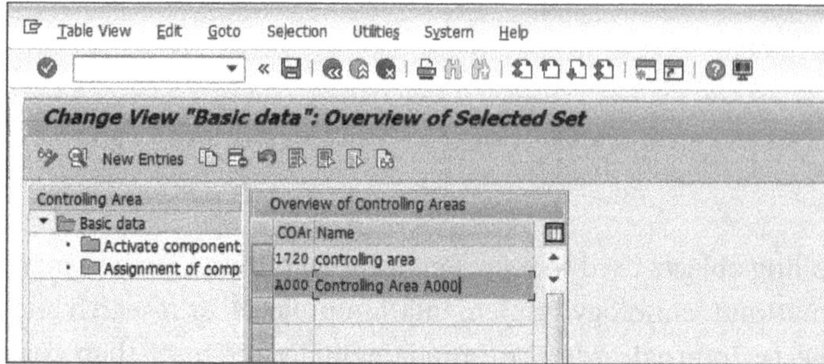

Figure 11.1 Selecting a Controlling Area

On the screen shown in Figure 11.2, make sure that the **Order Management** dropdown list is set to **1: Component active.** Then, save your entry by clicking the **Save** button.

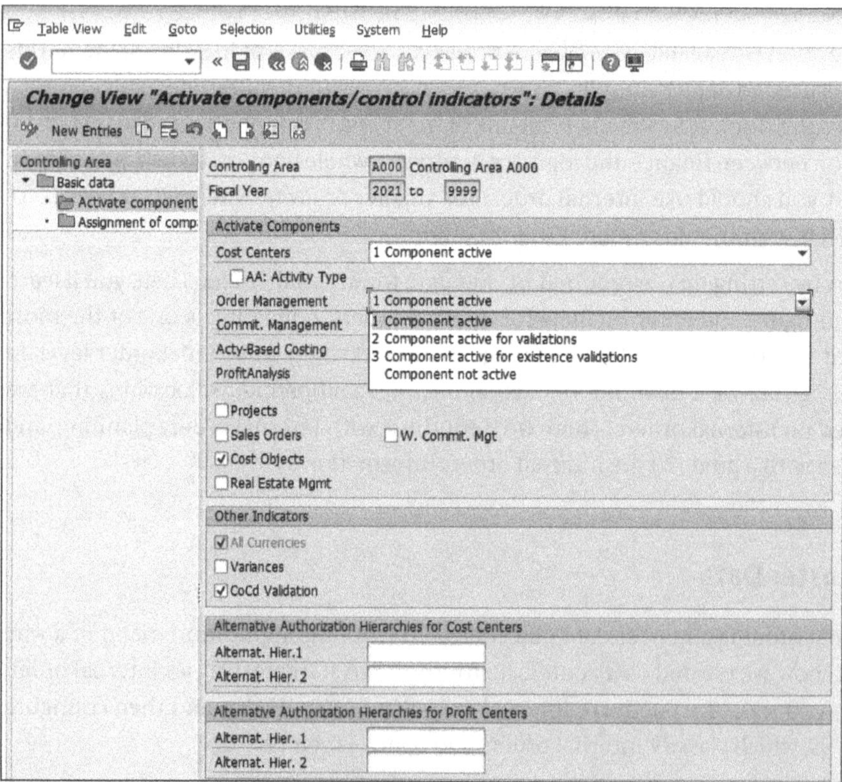

Figure 11.2 Activating Order Management

The next step is to create the relevant master data.

11.1.1 Order Types

Order types are used to classify internal orders with similar functions and purposes into groups. Order types control various parameters, such as number ranges and the settlement profile.

To configure order types, follow the menu path **Controlling • Internal Orders • Order Master Data • Define Order Types.**

On the first configuration screen, you'll see a list of defined order types, as shown in Figure 11.3. As with other configuration objects, several predefined standard order types have been delivered by SAP to cover most business requirements for internal orders, such as marketing, development, construction, and so on. A good practice is to use standard order types as references and copy them into your own order types in custom name ranges starting with Z or Y.

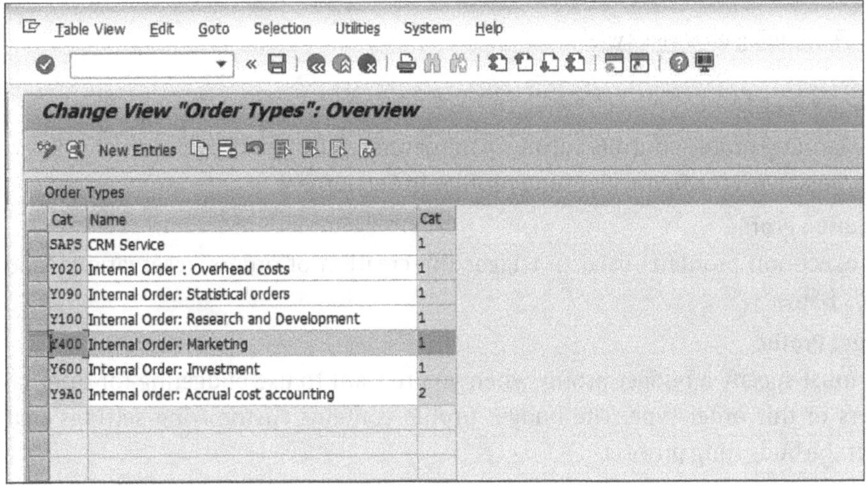

Figure 11.3 Order Types

Select order type **Y400: Internal order: Marketing**, then select **Copy As...** from the top menu. On the resulting screen, shown in Figure 11.4, change the order type name to start with a Z and enter a meaningful description for the order type.

Below those fields, you'll see the number range interval, which we'll cover in detail in the next section. Then, you'll see several configuration options, such as the following:

- **Settlement prof. (settlement profile)**
  The settlement profile controls how the internal order costs will be settled to other cost receivers. An internal order is a transitory cost object; it accumulates costs, but at the end, usually costs are settled to another object, such as a fixed asset, cost center, and so on. We'll configure the settlement profile later in this section.

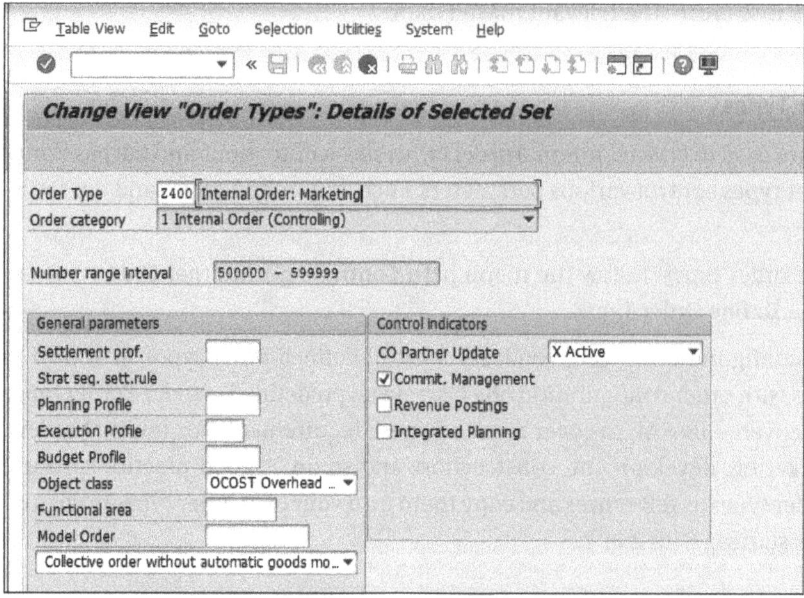

Figure 11.4 Defining an Order Type

- **Planning Profile**
  The planning profile controls various parameters in the planning process for internal orders. We'll configure planning profiles in Section 11.4.
- **Execution Profile**
  The execution profile is used to trigger the creation of orders, reservations, and goods issues.
- **Budget Profile**
  You must specify a budget profile when you're want to use budgeting for internal orders of this order type. The budget profile contains customizing settings that affect the budgeting process.
- **Object class**
  The object class classifies the order based on its purpose. You can choose from overhead costs, production, investment, or profitability analysis.
- **Functional area**
  The functional area is used to prepare a profit and loss (P&L) statement based on the cost-of-sales method. You can assign a functional area to an internal order, and in this field, you can specify a default functional order for the order type.
- **Model Order**
  A model order can be used to predetermine certain parameters of the internal order, and in this field, you can specify a default model order for the order type.

- **Collective order with/without automatic goods movement**
  This indicator controls whether an automatic goods movement is allowed if production orders are assigned to collective orders.
- **CO Partner Update (controlling partner update)**
  This dropdown list defines how the totals records for the sender-receiver combinations are updated. You can choose from the following options:
  - **Not Active**
    No update of totals records occurs.
  - **Partially Active**
    Totals records are generated only for settlements between internal orders.
  - **Active**
    For all settlements, a totals record is generated.

  In general, you should choose an active or partially active update.
- **Classification**
  The classification capability in SAP S/4HANA is no longer supported, so this indicator should not be selected. This capability been replaced by the general object summarization. For further information, refer to SAP Notes 339863 and 188231. You can also use enhancement COOPA003 for classification.
- **Commit. Management**
  Select this indicator when you want to record commitments on the internal orders of this order type.
- **Revenue Postings**
  Select this indicator when you want to record revenue postings on the internal orders of this order type (with general ledger accounts with cost element category 11 or 12).
- **Integrated Planning**
  This indicator should be selected if orders from this order type should participate in integrated planning. *Integrated planning* means that planned activity inputs are updated directly on the sending cost center. Make sure you select this indicator from the beginning if needed; setting it retrospectively is difficult.

Scroll down, and you can configure further fields, as shown in Figure 11.5. In the **Archiving** area, you can configure the following fields:

- **Residence Time 1**
  In this field, you'll specify the period that needs to pass between setting the deletion flag (which can be reset) and setting the deletion indicator (which cannot be reset) for an internal order.
- **Residence Time 2**
  In this field, you'll specify the period that needs to pass between setting the deletion indicator and reorganizing the internal orders.

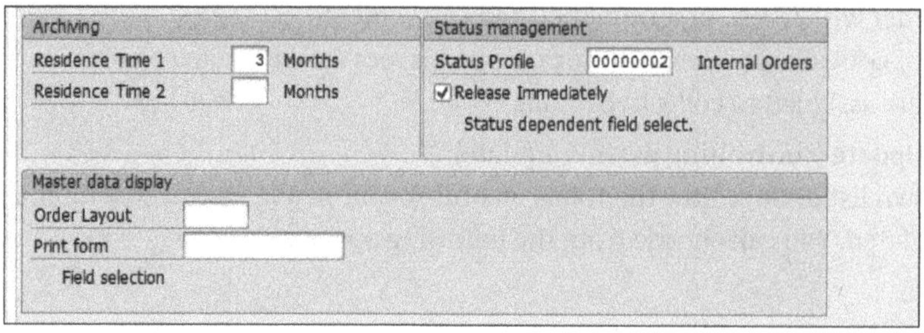

Figure 11.5 Order Type Further Fields

In the **Status management** area, you can configure the following fields:

- **Status Profile**
  The status profile controls the various statuses you can set for internal orders (such as **Created**, **Released**, **Closed**, and so on).
- **Release Immediately**
  If you select this indicator, orders from this order type are immediately released when created.
- **Status dependent field select.**
  You can use a status-dependent field status, meaning that various fields are required, optional, or suppressed based on the status of the order (created, released, and so on).

In the **Master data display** area, you can configure the following fields:

- **Order Layout**
  The order layout determines which fields are required, which fields can be changed, and which fields are display only.
- **Print form**
  If you want to print the internal order, you can assign a print form in this field. As standard, you can use form CO_ORDER.
- **Field selection**
  With this button, you can define a user-defined field selection. For example, you can specify that a specific field is required for this order type.

After configuring the fields, save your order type by clicking the **Save** button.

11.1.2 Screen Layouts

Internal order master data is organized into tabs, which follow a standard order. You can control which sections of data appear on which tabs using screen layouts. To configure a screen layout, follow the menu path **Controlling • Internal Orders • Order Master Data • Screen Layout • Define Order Layouts**. Figure 11.6 shows the standard screen layout **SAP0**.

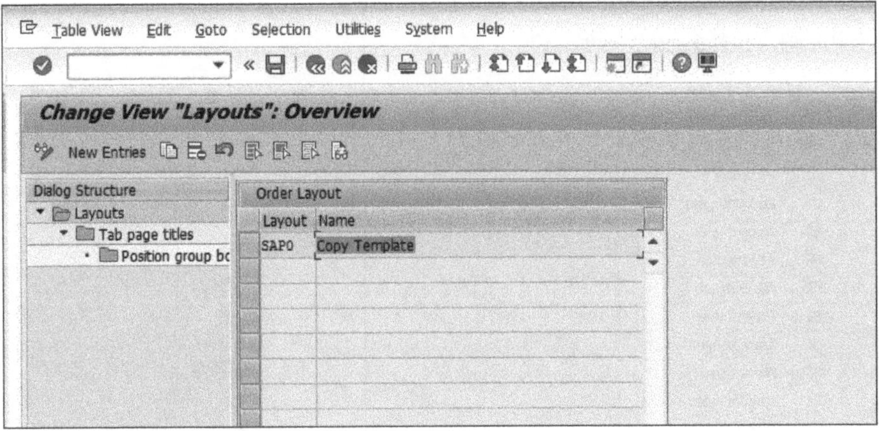

Figure 11.6 Defining a Screen Layout

11

Select this layout and copy it by clicking the (**Copy As...**) button from the top menu. Then, give a custom name for the copied layout, as shown in Figure 11.7.

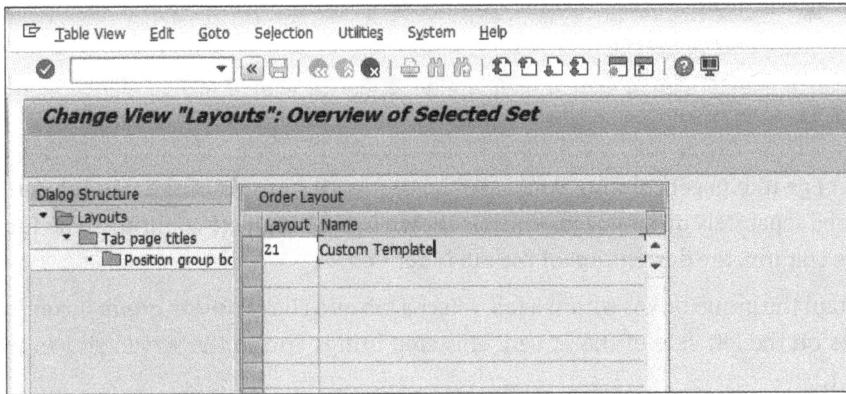

Figure 11.7 Copying a Custom Layout

Continue with the **Enter** button. The system issues the message shown in Figure 11.8, which notifies you of all the dependent entries copied.

Figure 11.8 Dependent Entries Message

Proceed by clicking the button. Then, select the **Tab page titles** option on the left side of the screen, which brings you to the tabs definition table, shown in Figure 11.9.

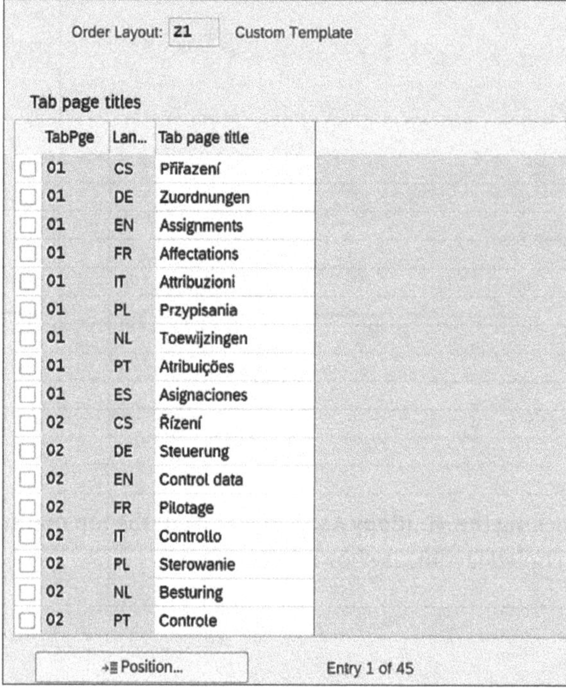
Order Layout: Z1 Custom Template

Tab page titles

TabPge	Lan...	Tab page title
01	CS	Přiřazení
01	DE	Zuordnungen
01	EN	Assignments
01	FR	Affectations
01	IT	Attribuzioni
01	PL	Przypisania
01	NL	Toewijzingen
01	PT	Atribuições
01	ES	Asignaciones
02	CS	Řízení
02	DE	Steuerung
02	EN	Control data
02	FR	Pilotage
02	IT	Controllo
02	PL	Sterowanie
02	NL	Besturing
02	PT	Controle

Position... Entry 1 of 45

Figure 11.9 Tabs Definition

In the **TabPge** (tab page) column, you'll see the sequence number of the tab. Tabs are maintained separately by language, which is shown in the **Language** column. In the **Tab page title** column, the description of the tab is defined.

To maintain the group boxes within a tab, select a tab and click **Position group boxes in tab pages** on the left side of the screen. This step brings you to the screen shown in Figure 11.10.

Order Layout: Z1 Copy Template

Position group boxes in tab pages

TabPge	Tab page title	Position of...	Group box	Group box title
01	Assignments	01		Assignments
01	Assignments	02	12	Account Assignment Manag...

Figure 11.10 Group Boxes in Tabs

On this screen, you can assign different group boxes and change their order under the tab. Modify the layout in whatever way will be the most convenient for your users, then save your entries by clicking the **Save** button.

11.1.3 Number Ranges

As with other master data objects, you must specify number ranges for internal orders to determine the numbers assigned when creating these orders.

To configure order number ranges, follow the menu path **Controlling • Internal Orders • Order Master Data • Maintain Number Ranges for Orders**. Figure 11.11 shows the initial screen of the number ranges configuration transaction. The number range object for internal orders is **AUFTRAG**.

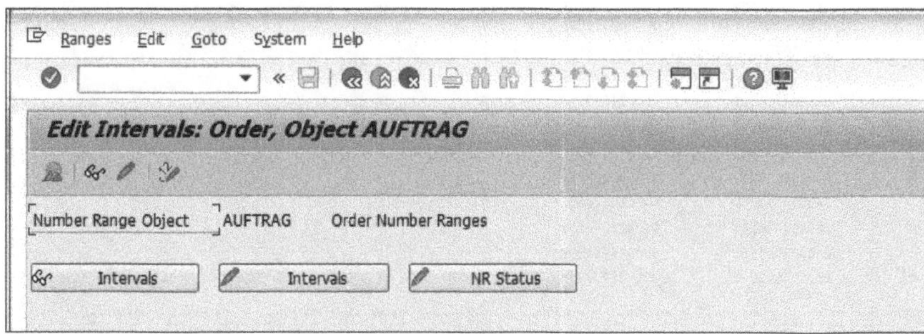

Figure 11.11 Internal Order Number Ranges

Click the Intervals (**Change Intervals**) button, and you'll see the screen shown in Figure 11.12. On this screen, you'll define the various number ranges to be used with the internal order types. The first column, **No**, is the number range number, which is then assigned to an order type. The **From No.** and **To Number** columns define the lower and upper limit of numbers within that number range. In the **NR Status** (number range status) column, you'll see the current number assigned in the system. A checkbox in the **Ext** (external) column defines that the number range is external; in other words, a user must enter an internal order number manually, within the defined limits.

So, for example, as defined in Figure 11.12, number range 02 uses external number assignment within the A and ZZZZZZZZZZZZ limits. Thus, an internal order number using this number range can be up to 12 letters long, and all letters are allowed. Number range 04 uses internal number assignment between 000002000000 and 00000 2999999. In this case, the first internal order will have the number 2000000 assigned by the system; the second, 2000001; and so on.

After configuring your number ranges, save your entries by clicking the **Save** button. Then, go back to the initial number ranges screen, shown in Figure 11.11. Select **Change Groups** from the top menu.

On the screen shown in Figure 11.13, you can see the various number ranges and the order types assigned to them. On the top, the unassigned order types are listed. After scrolling down, you'll see the new order type Z400 assigned to group (number range) 08. This assignment exists because you copied information from order type 0400, which is also assigned to group 08.

Interval Edit Goto System Help

Edit Intervals: Order, Object AUFTRAG

Number Range No.	From No.	To Number	NR Status	External
01	000000900000	000000999999	900139	☐
02	A	ZZZZZZZZZZZZ	0	☑
03	$	$ZZZZZZZZZZZ	0	☑
04	000002000000	000002999999	0	☐
05	000000100000	000000199999	0	☐
06	000000200000	000000299999	0	☐
07	000000300000	000000399999	0	☐
08	000000400000	000000499999	0	☐
09	000000500000	000000599999	0	☐
10	000000600000	000000699999	0	☐
11	000000700000	000000799999	700019	☐
12	000000800000	000000899999	0	☐
13	9A0000000000	9AZZZZZZZZZZ	0	☑
14	000003000000	000003999999	0	☐
15	000004000000	000004999999	0	☐
16	000005000000	000005999999	0	☐

Figure 11.12 Defining Number Ranges

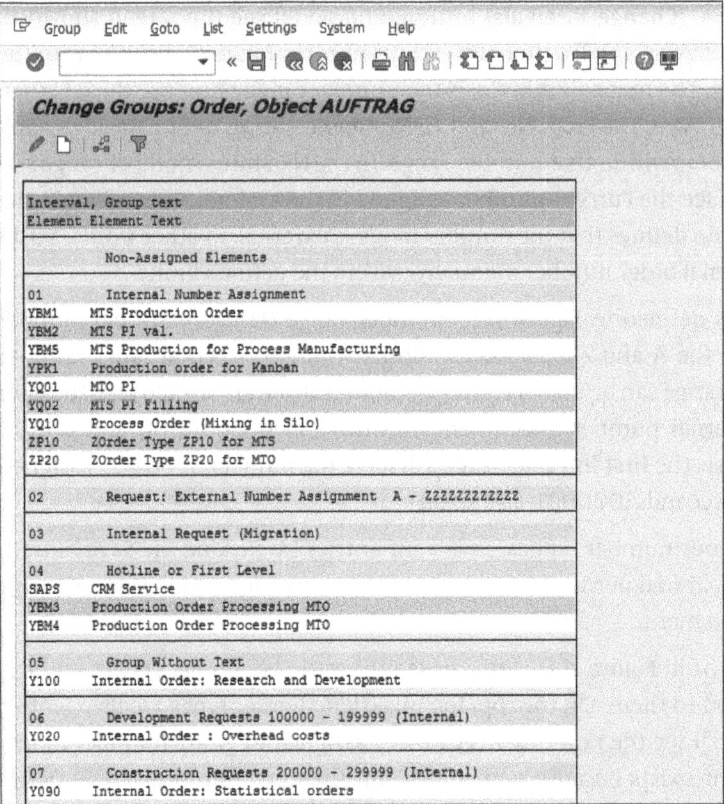

Figure 11.13 Number Range Assignment

If you want to change the number range assignment, select the order type and select **Assign Element to Group** from the top menu. Then, you'll see a list of the available groups, as shown in Figure 11.14.

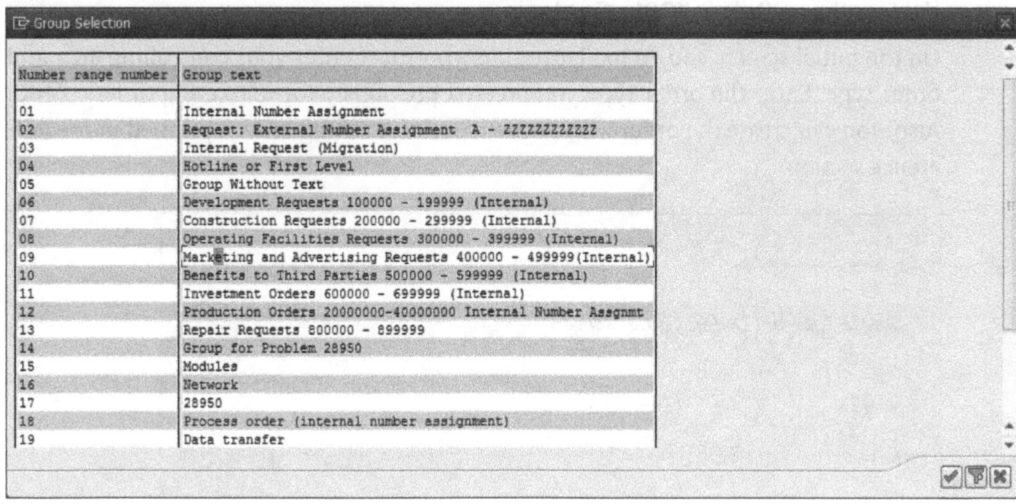

Group Selection

Number range number	Group text
01	Internal Number Assignment
02	Request: External Number Assignment A - ZZZZZZZZZZZZ
03	Internal Request (Migration)
04	Hotline or First Level
05	Group Without Text
06	Development Requests 100000 - 199999 (Internal)
07	Construction Requests 200000 - 299999 (Internal)
08	Operating Facilities Requests 300000 - 399999 (Internal)
09	Marketing and Advertising Requests 400000 - 499999(Internal)
10	Benefits to Third Parties 500000 - 599999 (Internal)
11	Investment Orders 600000 - 699999 (Internal)
12	Production Orders 20000000-40000000 Internal Number Assgnmt
13	Repair Requests 800000 - 899999
14	Group for Problem 28950
15	Modules
16	Network
17	28950
18	Process order (internal number assignment)
19	Data transfer

Figure 11.14 Group Selection

Select group **09: Marketing and Advertising Requests 400000 - 499999 (Internal)**, which better suits the purpose of the order type. Then, you'll see that the order type is reallocated, as shown in Figure 11.15. After this step, save your entries by clicking the **Save** button.

Interval, Group text	
Element	Element Text
06	Development Requests 100000 - 199999 (Internal)
0200	Internal orders: Construction
07	Construction Requests 200000 - 299999 (Internal)
0300	Internal orders: Tools and equipment
08	Operating Facilities Requests 300000 - 399999 (Internal)
0400	Internal orders: Marketing
09	Marketing and Advertising Requests 400000 - 499999(Internal)
0500	Internal orders: Third-party services
SAPS	CRM Service DO NOT CHANGE!
Z400	Marketing Internal orders
10	Benefits to Third Parties 500000 - 599999 (Internal)
0600	Internal orders: Investment
0650	Capital investment order

Figure 11.15 Changed Group Assignment

11.1.4 Creating Internal Orders

Now that you've set up the order types, you can create internal orders by following the application menu path **Accounting • Controlling • Internal Orders • Master Data • Special Functions • Order • KO01—Create.**

On the initial screen, shown in Figure 11.16, you must enter your controlling area and order type. Enter the order type you created previously for marketing orders, Z400. Also, you can create the order with reference to an existing order, specified in the **Reference** section.

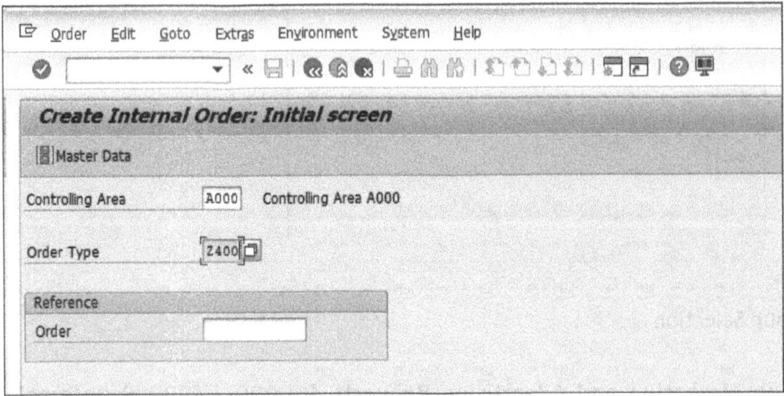

Figure 11.16 Creating an Internal Order

As with other master data objects created up to this point, the internal order master record is organized into tabs, as shown in Figure 11.17. On the header level, enter the internal order description.

Below the header, under the first tab, **Assignments**, configure the following fields:

- **Company Code**
  Each internal order must be created for a company code, which you'll specify in this field.
- **Business Area**
  If you use business areas in your project, a good idea is to assign a default business area for the internal order in this field.
- **Plant**
  You can assign a plant to an internal order, which is mandatory for production orders.
- **Functional Area**
  The functional area is used to prepare P&L statements, based on the cost-of-sales method. You should assign a functional area to the internal order if you use cost of sales accounting.

- **Object Class**
  The object class classifies the order based on its purpose. On this screen, the object class configured in the order type is defaulted.
- **Profit Center**
  When profit center accounting is activated, you must assign a profit center in this field. We'll activate and configure profit center accounting in Chapter 12.
- **Responsible CCtr (responsible cost center)**
  In this field, you can specify a cost center that's responsible for the internal order. For example, for marketing internal orders, typically, this cost center will be the marketing department cost center.

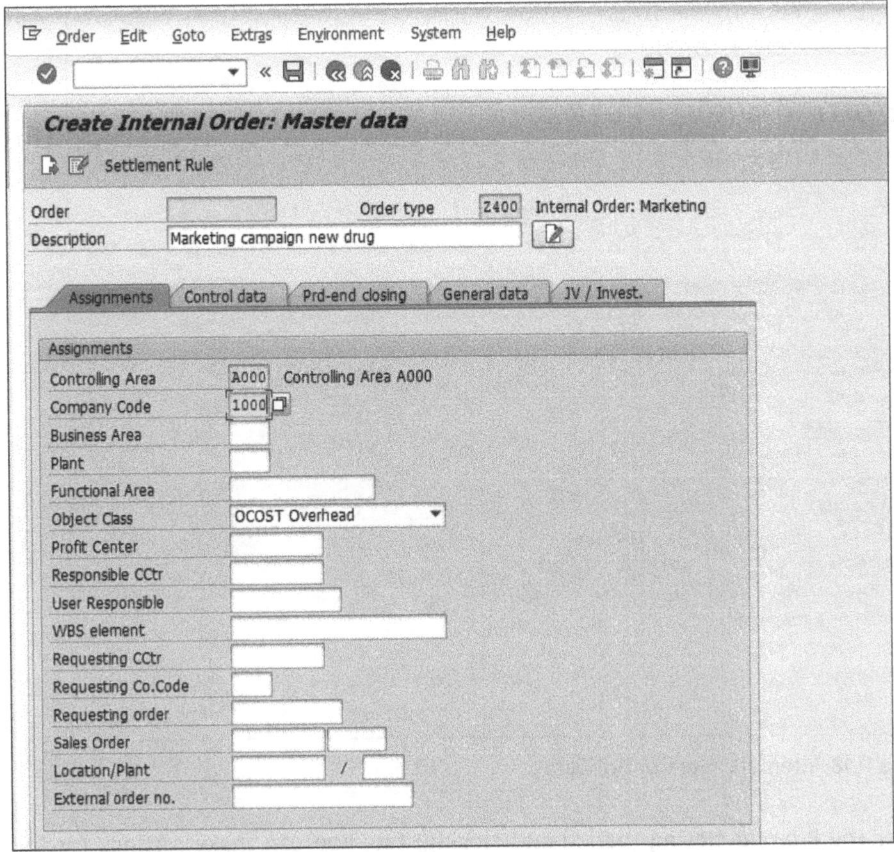

Figure 11.17 Internal Order Assignments

Next, let's move on to the **Control data** tab, shown in Figure 11.18. Under the **Control data** tab, the following fields are available:

- **System status**
  In this field, the system shows the current status of the order. When you create the order, the status is *created*, indicated by **CRTD** in this field. This status doesn't allow

you to post to the order. After creating the order, you'll need to release it by clicking the ^ **Release** button.

- **Currency**
  In this field, you'll specify the currency of the internal order. By default, this currency is the currency of the controlling area.
- **Order category**
  Orders are widely used in the SAP S/4HANA system, and the controlling internal orders are just one of the categories, as indicated here by category **1**, which you can't change. In logistics, other types of orders are widely used, such as production, process, or quality management orders.

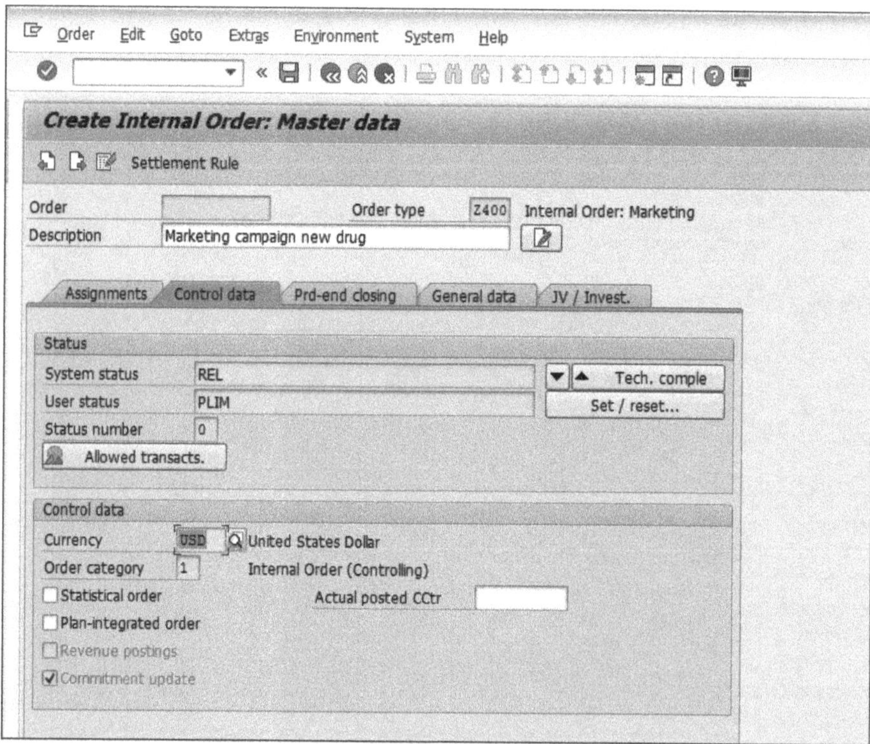

Figure 11.18 Internal Order Control Data

Under the **Prd-end closing** (period-end closing) tab, you can make settings for the period-end closing, such as assigning results analysis keys and costing sheets, as shown in Figure 11.19.

Under the **General data** tab, you can enter data for information purposes only for the applicant of the order, such as telephone, application date, department, and so on, as shown in Figure 11.20.

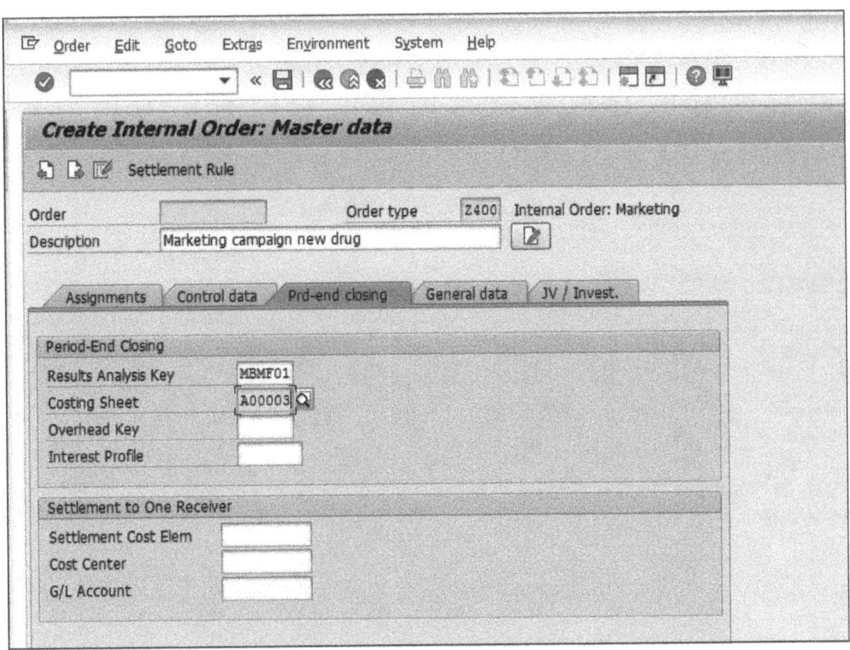

Figure 11.19 Internal Order Period-End Closing Data

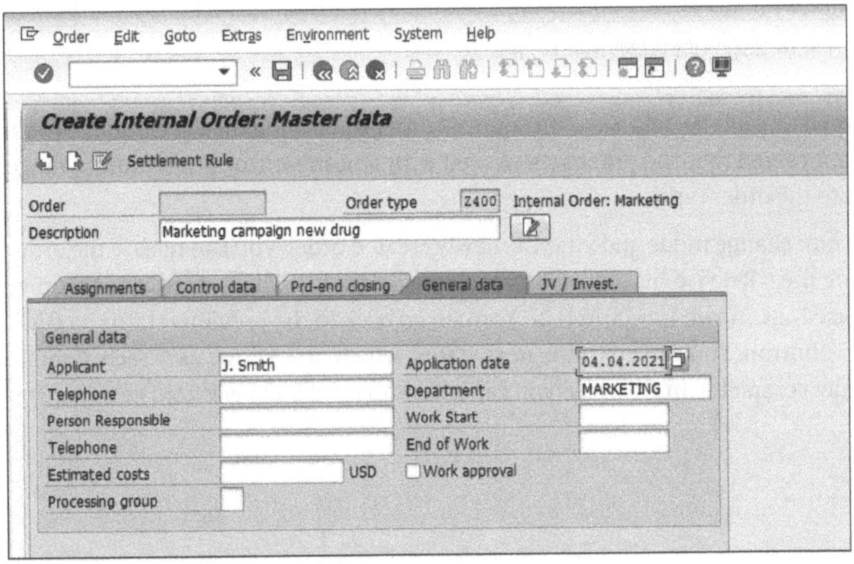

Figure 11.20 Internal Order General Data

The **JV/Investments** (joint ventures/investment) tab is relevant if you use investment management functionality. If so, under this tab, you can make settings for the internal order such as assignment of an investment profile, investment program, and so on, as shown in Figure 11.21.

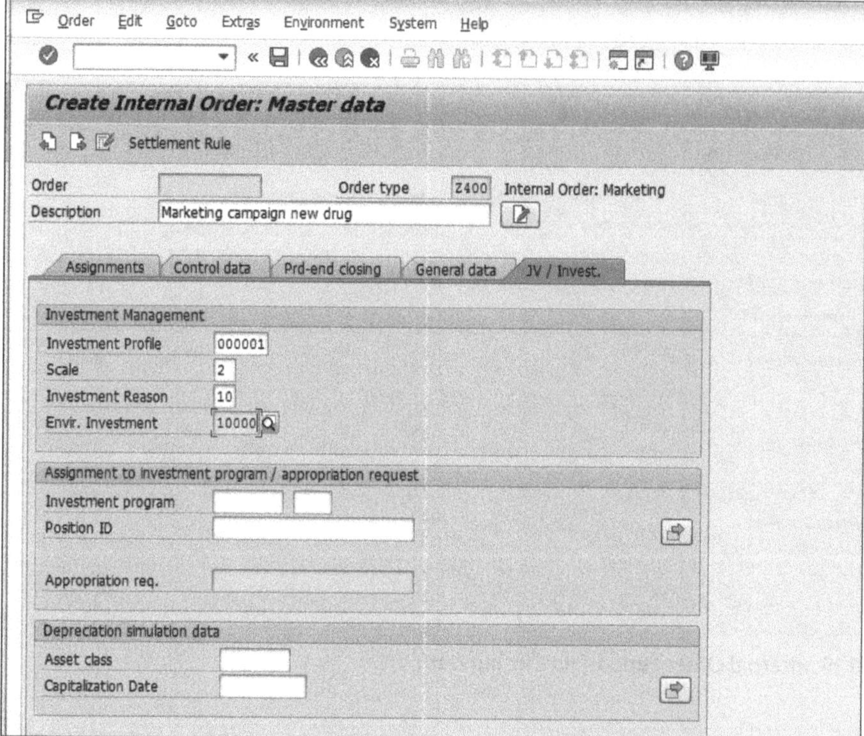

Figure 11.21 Internal Order Investment Data

After completing all the data, save the internal order by clicking the **Save** button. Then, you get a message that the order was created with a number from the number range assigned to the order type.

If you go into change mode and view the newly created order, you can release the order by clicking the ^ **Release** button under the **Control data** tab. Then, the status becomes **REL** (released), as shown in Figure 11.22. You can go back to the previous status by clicking the [v] button. You can go to the next status, which now shows as ^ **Tech. Comple** (technically complete). In this way, you can move forward and backward between statuses.

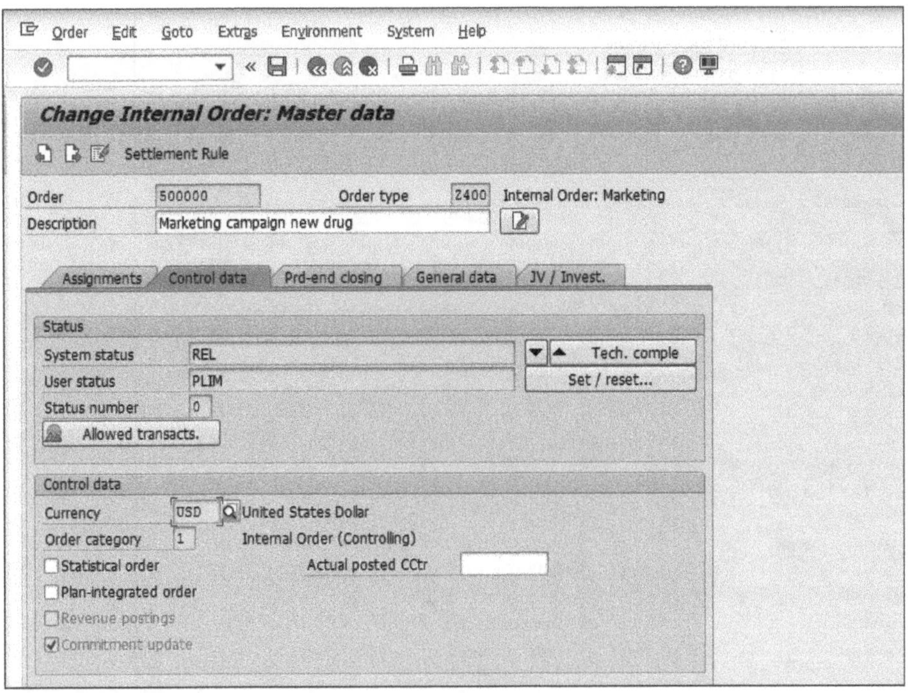

Figure 11.22 Released Internal Order

11.2 Budgeting

A major part of the internal orders process addresses budgeting for internal orders. Internal orders are used for specific projects such as marketing campaigns, R&D projects, or IT implementation projects. As such, usually they're associated with particular budgets that must be adhered to. If the budget is reached, no more postings should be allowed for the internal order, although various settings can control how stringent this rule is.

You've seen the budget profile in the order type configuration, shown earlier in Figure 11.4. Now, let's learn how to configure a budget profile. Follow the menu path **Controlling • Internal Orders • Budgeting and Availability Control • Maintain Budget Profile**. Then, select activity **Maintain Budget Profile**. You'll see a list of the available budget profiles; the standard one is the **000001: General** budget profile. Select it and make a copy by selecting **Copy As...** from the top menu. Then, rename the new copy to Z00001, as shown in Figure 11.23.

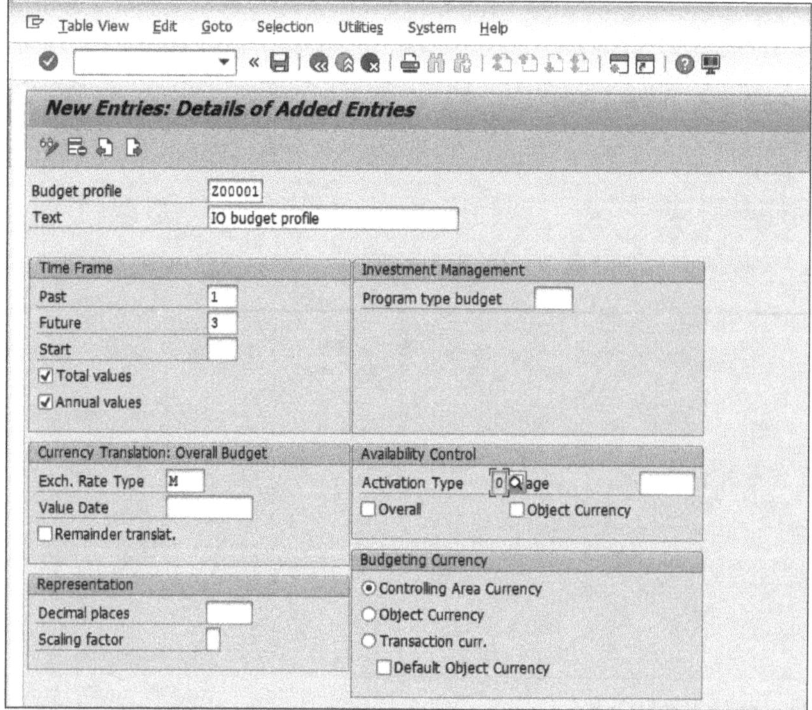

Figure 11.23 Creating a Budget Profile

On this screen, configure the following fields:

- **Budget profile**
  The name of the budget profile.
- **Text**
  A meaningful description of the budget profile.
- **Past, Future, and Start**
  In these fields, you'll define how long into the past and how far into the future you can budget for. For example, a value of "3" in the **Past** field means you can budget 3 years before the start year; a value of "5" in the **Future** field means you can budget 5 years into the future. In the **Start** field, you can specify a different start year from the default, which is the current fiscal year.
- **Total values**
  Specifies that budgeting overall values is possible.
- **Annual values**
  Specifies that budgeting annual values is possible.
- **Exch. Rate Type (exchange rate type)**
  In this field, you need to specify the exchange rate type to be used when converting into the controlling currency from another currency.

- **Value Date**
  In this field, you can enter a default value date for exchange rate conversion. If you don't enter a value date, currencies will be translated by period.
- **Activation Type**
  This indicator controls how the availability control functionality should be activated, with three options:
  - **0 = Cannot Be Activated**
    This option means that active availability control isn't possible for orders with this budget profile.
  - **1 = Automatic Activation during Budget Allocation**
    Availability control is automatically activated during budgeting, which means that it's activated when you enter a budget for the order.
  - **2 = Background Activation when Usage Exceeded**
    Availability control is activated in the background automatically for all orders in which the commitments exceed the usage number entered in the budget profile.
- **Usage**
  This field is used in conjunction with activation type 2 controls when availability control should be activated. For example, if you enter "70" in this field, when 70% of the budget is reached, availability control will be activated.
- **Overall**
  Indicates that availability checks are conducted against the overall value.
- **Object Currency**
  If you select this checkbox, availability control will be performed in the object currency.
- **Representation**
  Using the **Scaling Factor** and **Decimal Places** parameters, you can control how values are represented.
- **Budgeting Currency**
  In this section, you'll select in which currency the budgeting should be done from following options:
  - **Controlling Area Currency**
  - **Object Currency**
  - **Transactional curr.**
- **Default Object Currency**
  If budgeting is performed in a user-defined transactional currency, and you set this indicator, then the relevant object is budgeted by default in the object currency. If the indicator is not set, then the relevant object is budgeted by default in controlling area currency.

After maintaining the settings, save the budget profile with the **Save** button.

In the next step, you must maintain number ranges for budgeting by following the menu path **Controlling • Internal Orders • Budgeting and Availability Control • Maintain Number Ranges for Budgeting.**

As shown in Figure 11.24, the number range object for budgeting is BP_BELEG. Click the Intervals (**Change Intervals**) button to maintain the number ranges.

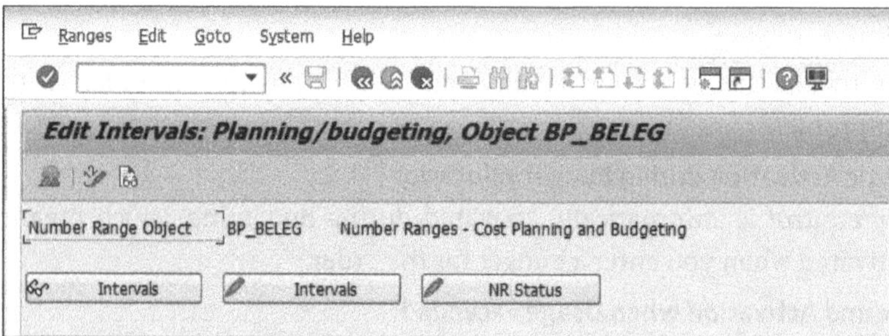

Figure 11.24 Budgeting Number Ranges

As with other number range objects, you'll provide a number range number, as shown in Figure 11.25 (for instance, 01, 02, 03, and so on) and the starting and ending numbers of the range. In the **NR Status** column, the system displays the current last assigned number. In the **Ext** column, you can specify that the number range should use an external document number, which is a rarely used option for budgeting.

Interval Edit Goto System Help

Edit Intervals: Planning/budgeting, Object BP_BELEG

Number Range No.	From No.	To Number	NR Status	External
01	0000000001	0099999999	0	☐
02	0100000000	0199999999	0	☐
03	0200000000	0299999999	0	☐
04	0300000000	0399999999	0	☐
10	1000000000	1099999999	0	☐
11	1100000000	1199999999	0	☐

Figure 11.25 Maintaining Number Ranges

After maintaining the number ranges, save your entries by clicking the **Save** button.

In the next step, configure the tolerance limits for availability controls by following the menu path **Controlling • Internal Orders • Budgeting and Availability Control • Define Tolerance Limits for Availability Control.**

On the screen shown in Figure 11.26, you can configure, for each controlling area, the percentage of the assigned budget that will trigger the relevant action when reached. For this example, we specified 90% of the budget for controlling area 0001.

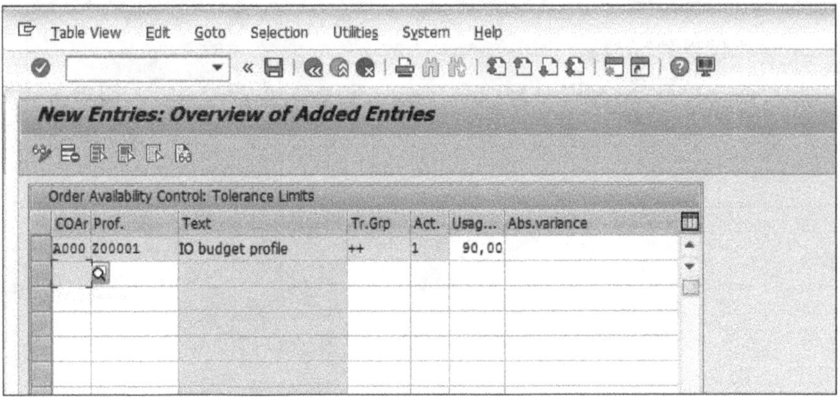

Figure 11.26 Tolerance Limits for Availability Control

Change the percentage as appropriate, then save your entry by clicking the **Save** button.

In the next step, you'll specify cost elements exempt from availability control. This functionality is used when you need to exclude postings to some cost elements from the availability control calculation. To specify exempt cost elements, follow the menu path **Controlling • Internal Orders • Budgeting and Availability Control • Specify Exempt Cost Elements from Availability Control**. Then, select **New Entries** from the top menu to enter the exempt cost elements, as shown in Figure 11.27.

Enter the cost elements to be exempted. The following fields must be configured:

- **COAr (controlling area)**
  The controlling area for which you configure cost elements to be exempted.
- **Cost Element**
  The cost elements to be exempted.
- **Orig. group (origin group)**
  The origin group is used for subdividing material and overhead costs. You can enter "*" to select all origin groups or specify an origin group.
- **Recovery Indic. (recovery indicator)**
  In this field, you can enter a default value date for the exchange rate. If your company belongs to a joint venture, incurred costs can be shared among partners using a recovery indicator, which can alter the budgeting if specified in this field.

After entering the cost elements to be exempted, save your entries by clicking the **Save** button.

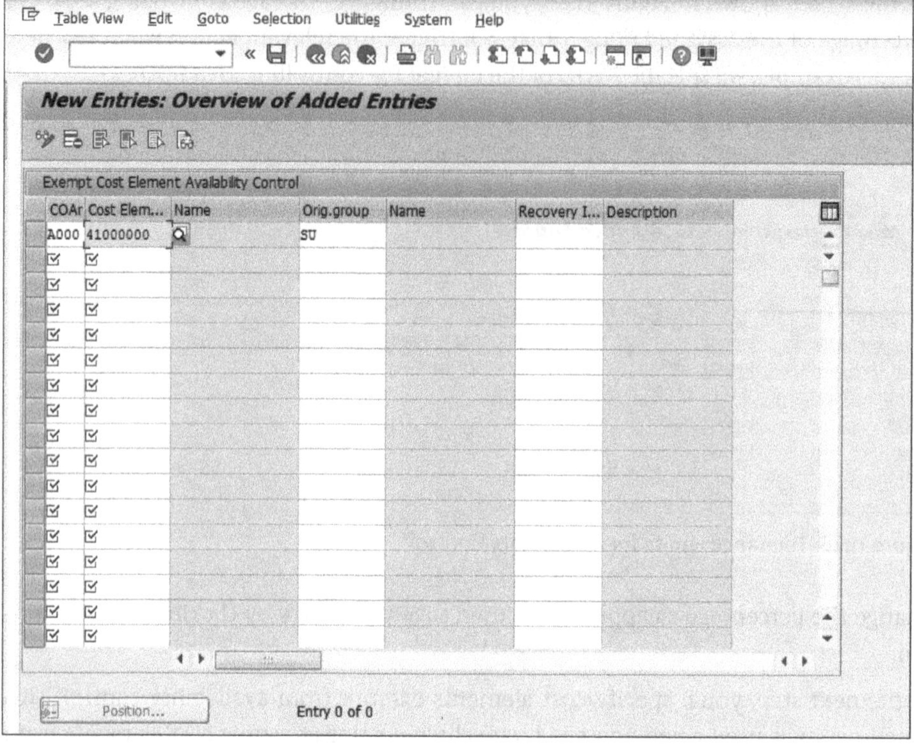

Figure 11.27 Exempt Cost Elements

11.3 Actual Postings and Periodic Allocations

After you've set the budget for your internal orders, you can start accumulating costs to them. The actual postings to internal orders occur in much the same way as postings to cost centers. They can come from integrated postings from logistics or from postings in financial accounting, where the cost object is an internal order.

A big difference in internal order accounting compared to cost centers is that, in essence, the internal order is a transitional cost object, which at the end is settled to another object, such as a cost center, fixed asset, profitability segment, and so on. Let's first configure the system for the settlement of internal orders and then move on to the topic of periodic reposting.

11.3.1 Settlement

Settlement is an important function of internal orders accounting that allows you to allocate the costs accumulated on internal orders to other predefined receivers.

To be able to settle an internal order, you must maintain a settlement rule in the order. In the settlement rule, you'll specify the receivers of the costs and their share. Let's change the internal order created previously by adding a settlement profile. Follow the application menu path **Accounting • Controlling • Internal Orders • Order Master Data • Special Functions • Order • KO02—Change.** On the initial screen, enter the internal order number. Then, on the order master data screen, as shown earlier in Figure 11.17, select **Settlement Rule** from the top menu.

Figure 11.28 shows the settlement rule definition screen. In the lines on this screen, you can enter one or multiple settlement receivers.

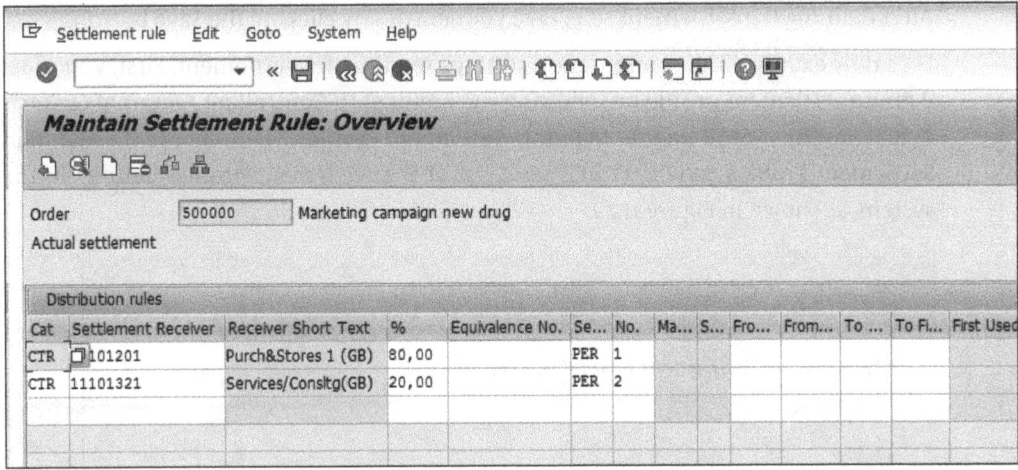

Figure 11.28 Internal Order Settlement Rule

The following fields are available for configuration on this screen:

- **Cat (category)**
  The category of the settlement receiver, such as cost center, fixed asset, or profitability segment. The available categories depend on the settlement profile, which we'll configure shortly.
- **Settlement Receiver**
  The receiver cost object. In this example, we provided two different cost centers.
- **%**
  The share of costs the receiver should receive during settlement. If only one receiver is specified, this value is 100%.
- **Equivalence No.**
  With this option, costs are distributed to settlement receivers in proportion to the equivalence numbers defined in this column.
- **Settlement Type**
  You can use full or periodic settlement. The difference is that, in full settlement, you settle each time all the unsettled costs that have occurred for a sender object for all the periods prior to the settlement.

- **Source Assignment**
  Another option is to use a source assignment structure to allocate the costs. Source assignments define the assignment of debit cost element(s) to a receiver.
- **No.**
  Sequential number of the receivers.
- **From Period/Fiscal Year and To Period/Fiscal Year**
  You can use these fields to limit the validity duration of a settlement rule.

After defining the settlement rule, save your entries by clicking the **Save** button.

Let's now examine the configuration settings required for settlement. First, you must define a settlement profile by following the menu path **Controlling • Internal Orders • Actual Postings • Settlement • Maintain Settlement Profiles.** Then, choose the **Maintain Settlement Profiles** activity. You'll see a list of the settlement profiles defined in the system, as shown in Figure 11.29.

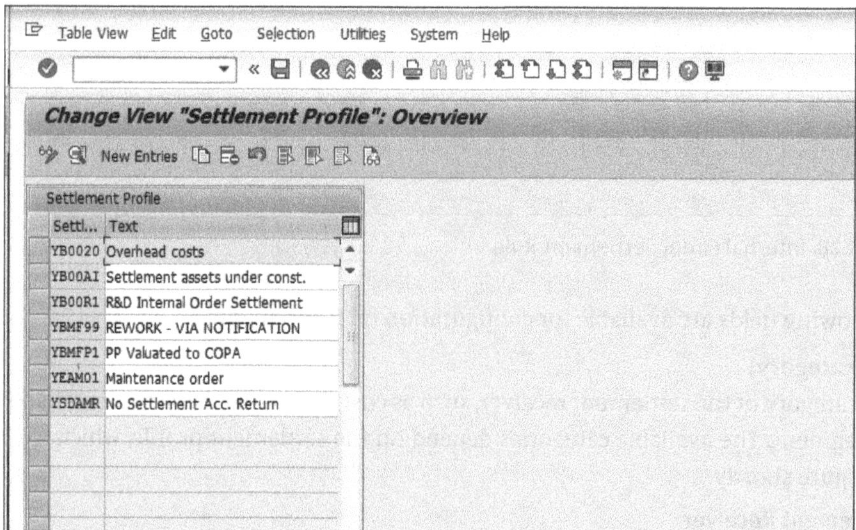

Figure 11.29 Settlement Profiles

Double-click settlement profile **YB0020 Overhead costs** now to review its settings. Figure 11.30 shows the configuration of the settlement profile. The following fields can be configured on this screen:

- **Settlement Profile**
  A code and a description for the settlement profile.
- **Actual Costs/Cost of Sales**
  In this section, you'll specify whether settlement is mandatory, optional, or not possible.

- **Default Values**
  In this section, you'll enter a default allocation structure, source structure, profitability analysis transfer structure, and object type. These structures are controlling tools for defining allocation cost elements in various controlling components.
- **Valid Receivers**
  In this section, you'll specify, for the various cost objects, whether they can receive settlement and if it's mandatory to receive settlement for this settlement profile. This section defines the possible receivers in the internal order settlement rule screen, shown earlier in Figure 11.28. For example, in our case, the general ledger account is marked as **Settlement Not Allowed**, so you won't see the general ledger account as a valid receiver in the order from order type Z400, which has settlement profile 20.

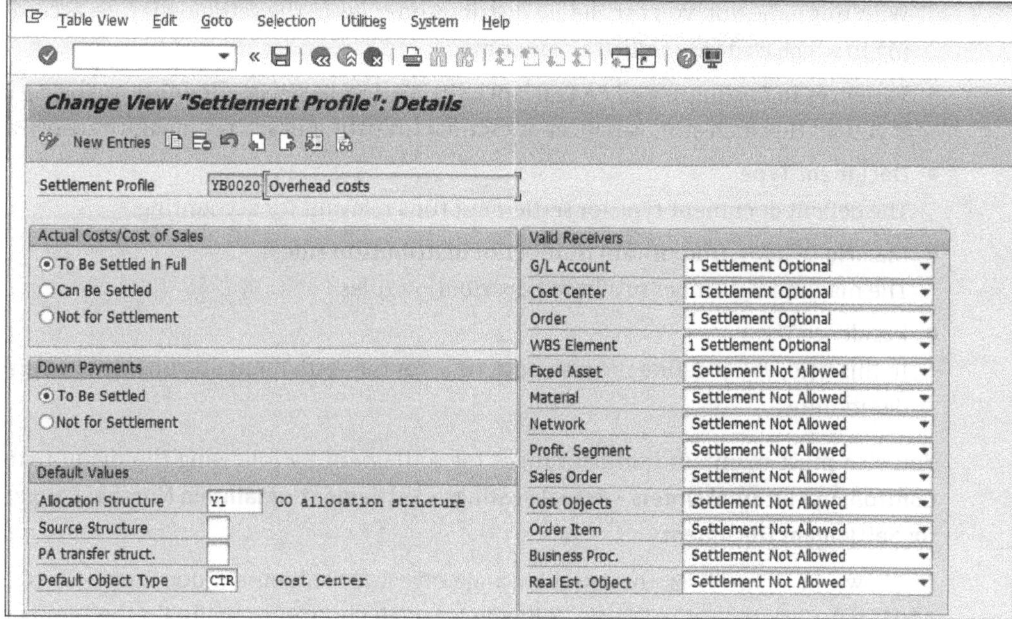

Figure 11.30 Defining a Settlement Profile

To view the **Indicators** and **Other Parameters** section, scroll down, as shown in Figure 11.31.

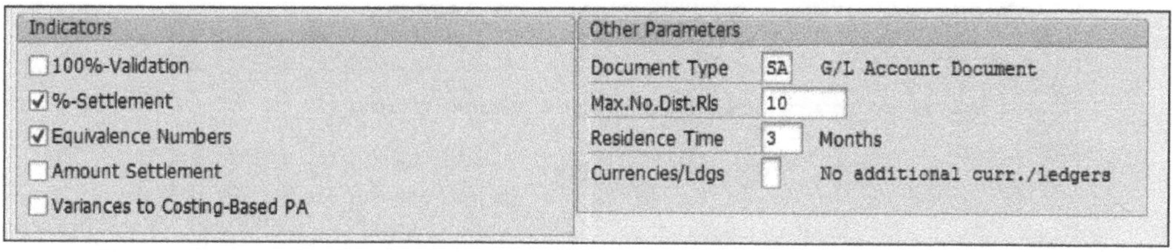

Indicators
☐ 100%-Validation
☑ %-Settlement
☑ Equivalence Numbers
☐ Amount Settlement
☐ Variances to Costing-Based PA

Other Parameters
Document Type SA G/L Account Document
Max.No.Dist.Rls 10
Residence Time 3 Months
Currencies/Ldgs No additional curr./ledgers

Figure 11.31 Settlement Profile Other Parameters

The following fields are available:

- **100%—Validation**
  If you select this indicator, the system will issue a warning if the total to be settled is different from 100%. If not set, you'll get a warning only if the total is more than 100%.
- **%—Settlement**
  If you select this indicator, you can use the settlement rule to determine the distribution rules governing the percentage costs to be settled.
- **Equivalence Numbers**
  With this indicator, you can define distribution rules in the settlement rule, according to which costs are settled proportionally.
- **Amount Settlement**
  With this indicator, you can define distribution rules in the settlement rule, according to which costs are settled by amount.
- **Variances to Costing-Based PA (variances to costing-based profitability analysis)**
  If you set this indicator, variances are settled to costing-based profitability analysis.
- **Document Type**
  The default document type for settlement runs relevant for accounting.
- **Max.No.Dist.Rls. (maximum number of distribution rules)**
  The maximum number of allowed distribution rules.
- **Residence Time**
  In this field, you'll define the residence time for the settlement documents in calendar months.

You also must maintain number ranges for settlement by following the menu path **Controlling • Internal Orders • Actual Postings • Settlement • Maintain Number Ranges for Settlement Documents.**

As shown in Figure 11.32, the number range object for settlement documents is **CO_ABRECHN**. Click the Intervals **(Change Intervals)** button to maintain the number ranges.

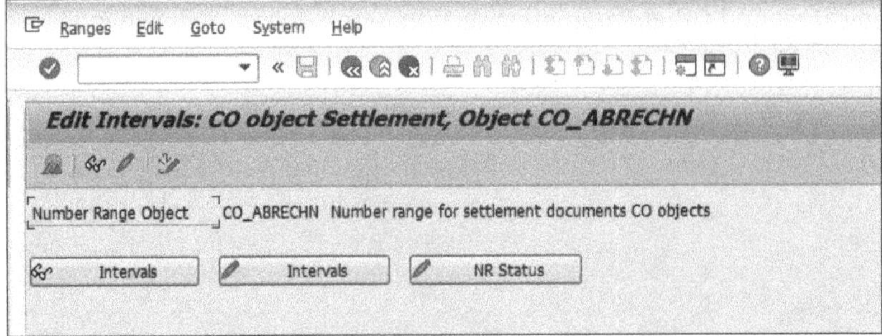

Figure 11.32 Number Ranges for Settlement

For settlement, normally only one number range is required, as shown in Figure 11.33.

Interval Edit Goto System Help

Edit Intervals: CO object Settlement, Object CO_ABRECHN

Number Range No.	From No.	To Number	NR Status	External
01	0000000001	0001000000	0	☐

Figure 11.33 Defining a Number Range for Settlement

Go back and select **Change Groups** from the top menu to assign your controlling area to the number range. If your controlling area shows in the **Nonassigned Elements** section on the top of the list, position the cursor on it and select **Assign Element to Group** from the top menu. Then, select group **01**. As shown in Figure 11.34, controlling area **A000** has been assigned to group **01**.

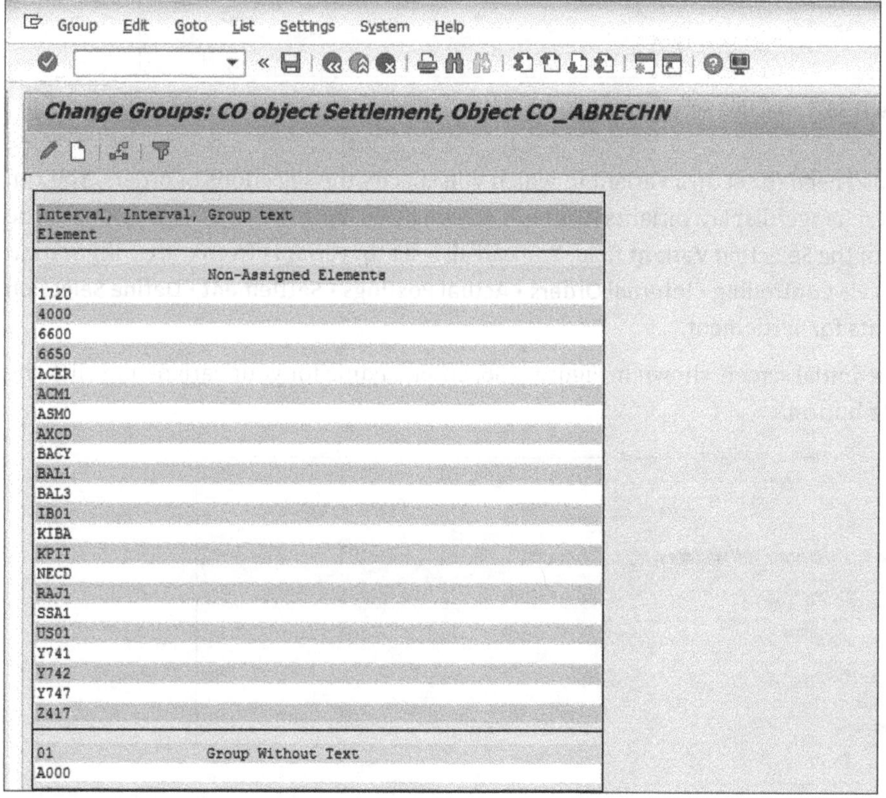

Figure 11.34 Assigning a Number Range

The settlement of individual internal orders is executed via the application menu path **Accounting • Controlling • Internal Orders • Period-End Closing • Single Functions • Settlement • KO88—Individual Processing.** In practice, more often, the collective settlement of multiple orders is used via the application menu path **Accounting • Controlling • Internal Orders • Period-End Closing • Single Functions • Settlement • KO8G—Collective Processing**, as shown in Figure 11.35.

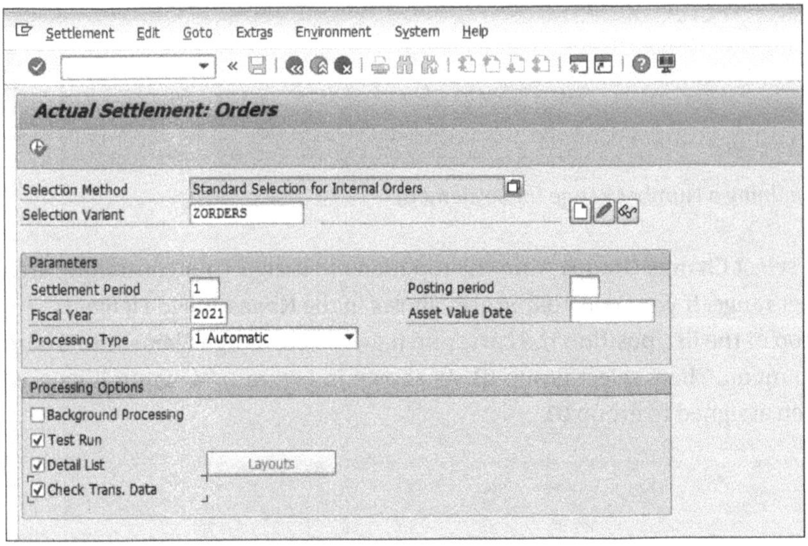

Figure 11.35 Collective Settlement

You also need to set up a variant in which you specify the selections of orders. You can create/change/display variants from this screen by clicking the buttons to the right of the **Selection Variant** field. You can also set up variants from the configuration menu via **Controlling • Internal Orders • Actual Postings • Settlement • Define Selection Variants for Settlement.**

On the initial screen, shown in Figure 11.36, enter a name for your variant and click the **Create** button.

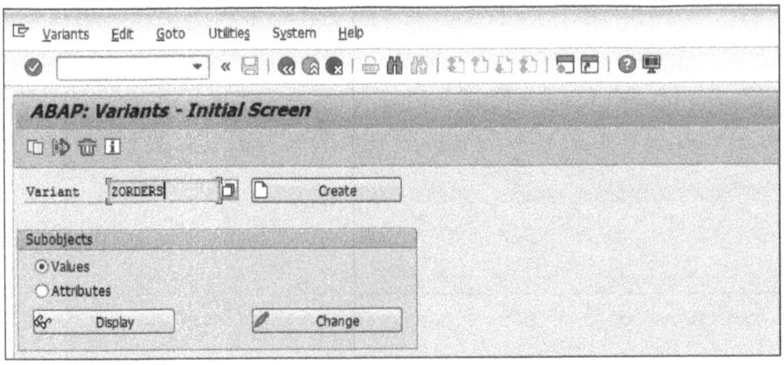

Figure 11.36 Creating a Selection Variant

On the next screen, shown in Figure 11.37, you can define the criteria for selecting internal orders, such as order group, from and to order numbers, controlling area, company code, and so on.

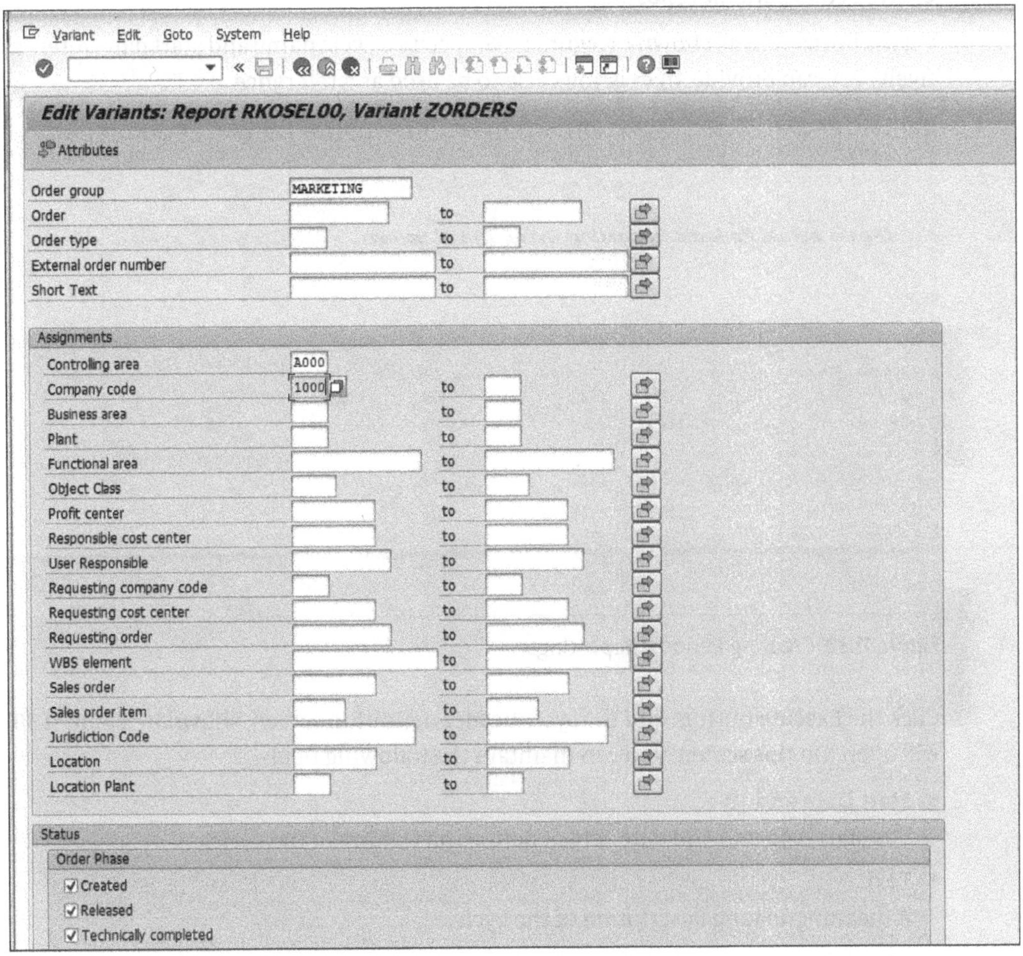

Figure 11.37 Defining a Selection Variant

Now, you know how to configure the SAP S/4HANA system to settle your internal orders.

11.3.2 Periodic Reposting

Another method for allocating costs from internal orders is periodic reposting (Transaction KSW5). This allocation method enables you to transfer costs posted on an internal order (as well as on cost centers, WBS elements, and other cost objects) based on rules defined in allocation cycles, rather than fixed settlement receivers, as you've seen in the settlement process.

Periodic reposting uses the cycle-segment technique you know from the cost center distributions and assessments. To create a periodic reposting, follow the menu path **Controlling • Internal Orders • Actual Postings • Define Periodic Repostings.** Then, select **Create actual periodic reposting.**

On the initial screen, shown in Figure 11.38, specify a cycle name and start date. Alternatively, you can provide an existing cycle to be used as a reference.

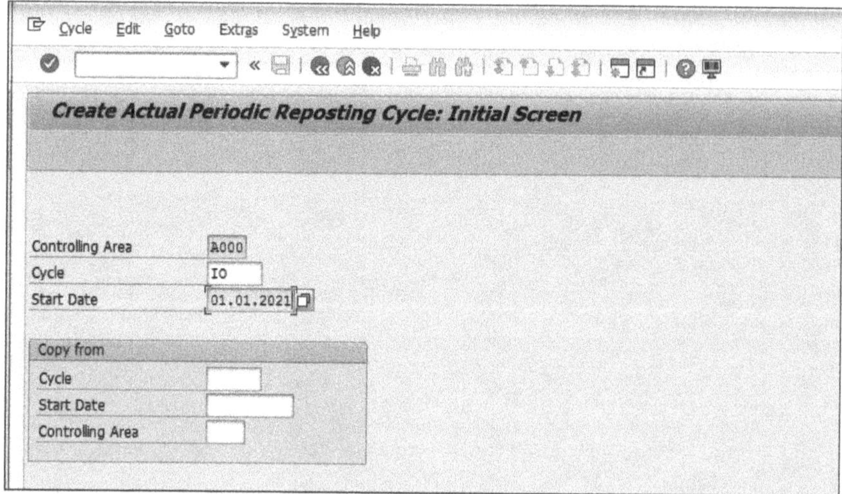

Figure 11.38 Creating Periodic Repostings

Click the **Execute** button, and the cycle header definition screen, shown in Figure 11.39, will open. On this screen, you can maintain the following fields:

- **Start Date and To**
  The start date and end date, which define the validity of the cycle.
- **Text**
  A meaningful long description of the cycle.
- **Iterative**
  This indicator enables iterative sender/receiver relationships. In this case, the iteration is repeated until each sender is fully credited.
- **Cumulative**
  If you select this indicator, the sender amounts posted are allocated based on tracing factors, which are cumulated for all periods.
- **Derive Func. Area**
  By selecting this indicator, the functional area proposed in the cycle definition for the receiver is ignored and then derived again.
- **Field Groups**
  In general, only amounts in the controlling area currency are used in periodic allocations. However, you can choose other types of currencies in this section.

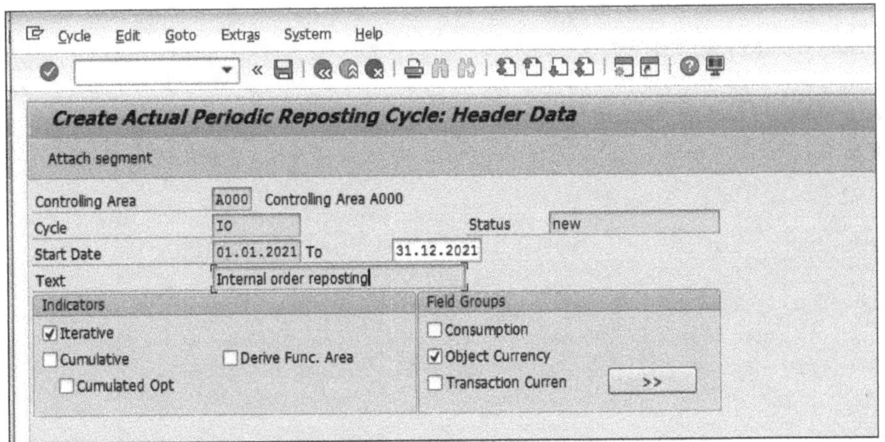

Figure 11.39 Periodic Reposting Cycle Header

After maintaining the cycle definition, you must attach at least one segment by selecting **Attach segment** from the top menu.

Next, you'll define the segment, as shown in Figure 11.40. The fields are the same as for the cost center distribution cycle, as described in Chapter 10, Section 10.3.2, so we won't explain them again in detail here.

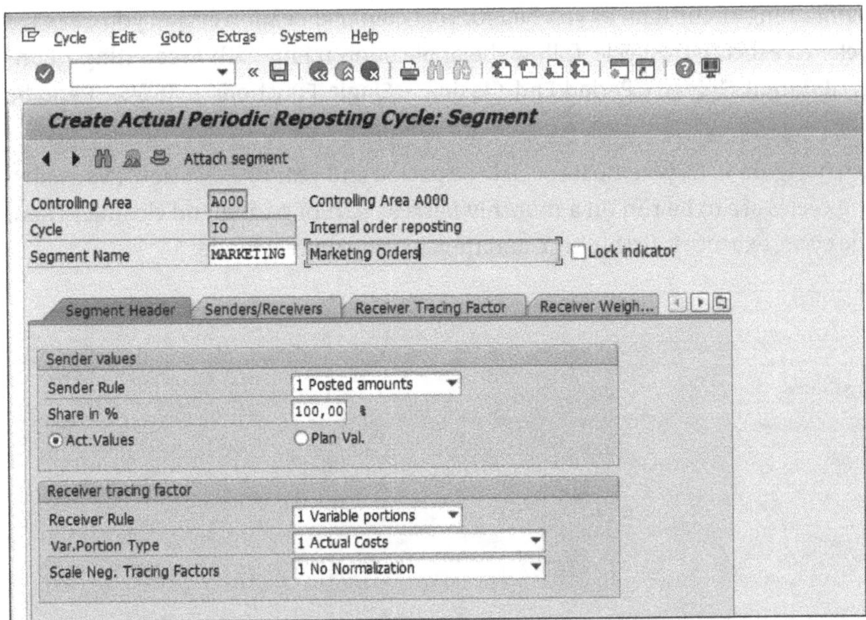

Figure 11.40 Periodic Reposting Segment Definition

As sender objects, specify the internal orders, as shown in Figure 11.41.

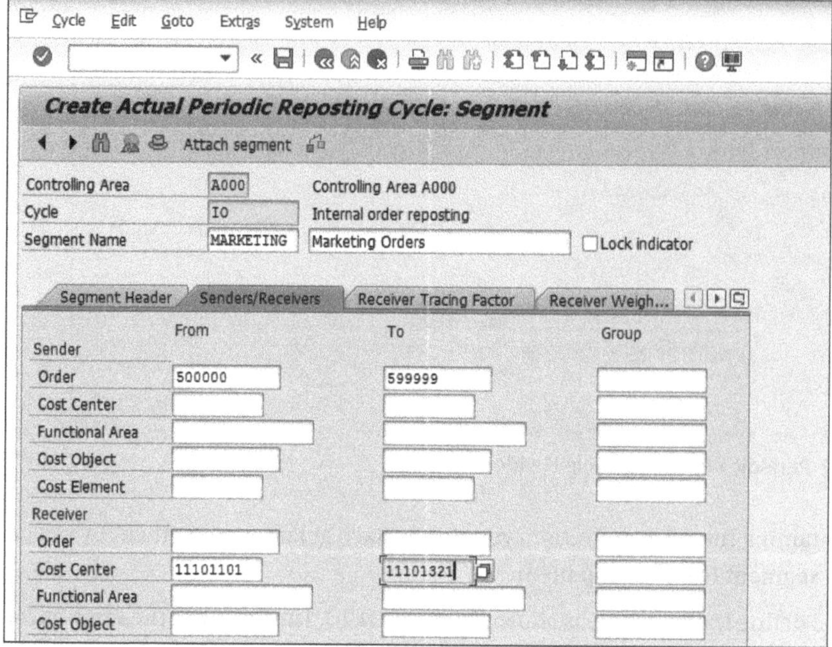

Figure 11.41 Segment Sender/Receiver Rules

After maintaining all the tabs, as you had for cost center allocation cycles, you can save your cycle. To execute the cycle, follow the application menu path **Accounting • Controlling • Internal Orders • Period-End Closing • Single Functions • KSW5—Periodic Reposting.**

As shown in Figure 11.42, you must specify the period and year of execution. (Normally, reposting cycles are to be run on a monthly basis as part of period-end closing.) Then, select the cycle, execute it first in test, and then execute in real mode.

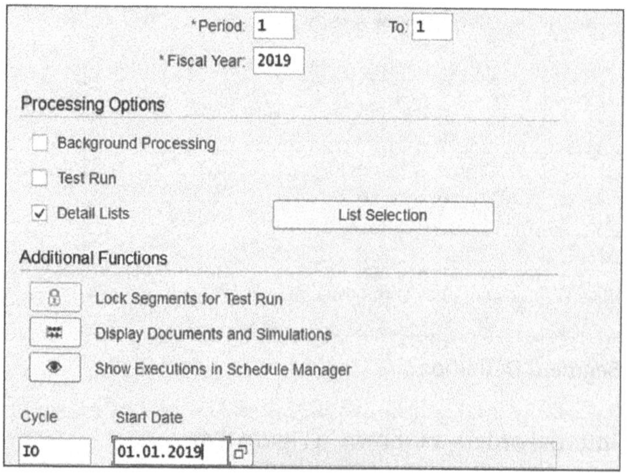

*Period: 1 To: 1
*Fiscal Year: 2019
Processing Options
Background Processing
Test Run
Detail Lists List Selection
Additional Functions
Lock Segments for Test Run
Display Documents and Simulations
Show Executions in Schedule Manager
Cycle Start Date
IO 01.01.2019

Figure 11.42 Executing Periodic Reposting

11.4 Planning

Another major functionality that internal orders offer is planning. You can enter plan values on the internal order level, then compare them with the actuals for useful management analysis.

In this section, we'll explain how to configure the basic settings required for internal order planning. Then, we'll teach you how to use statistical key figures for planning. We'll finish with a guide to using periodic allocations in the internal orders planning process.

11.4.1 Basic Settings

The settings for internal order planning are quite similar to the settings for cost center planning in Chapter 10, Section 10.4.1, so we'll just recap them briefly.

The controlling versions for which you'll do internal order planning need to be enabled for planning. For that, follow the menu path **Controlling • Internal Orders • Planning • Basic Settings for Planning • Maintain Versions.** Then, select **Maintain Version Settings in Controlling Area.**

Ensure that, in the **Plan** column, you've selected the versions you'll be planning in, as shown in Figure 11.43. Also enable planning in each fiscal year using the **Settings for Each Fiscal Year** option on the left side of the screen.

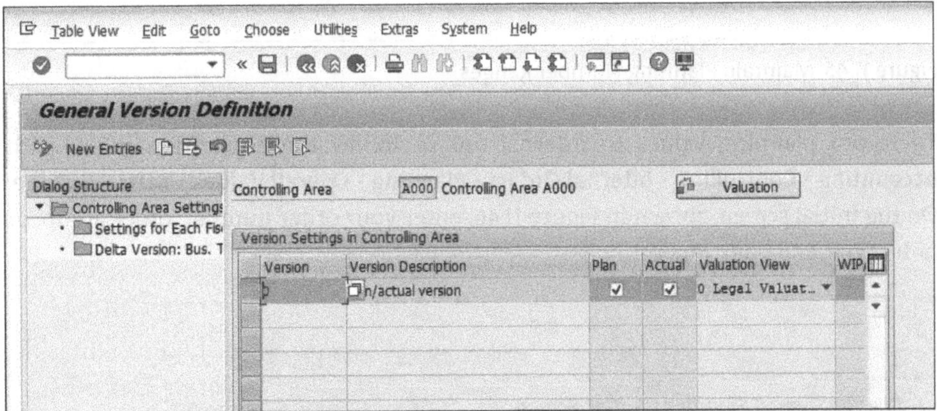

Figure 11.43 Enabling Planning in Versions

You also must assign planning transactions to number ranges by following the menu path **Controlling • Internal Orders • Planning • Basic Settings for Planning • Assign Planning Transactions to Number Ranges.** Enter your controlling area, as shown in Figure 11.44, and then click the Intervals **(Change Intervals)** button.

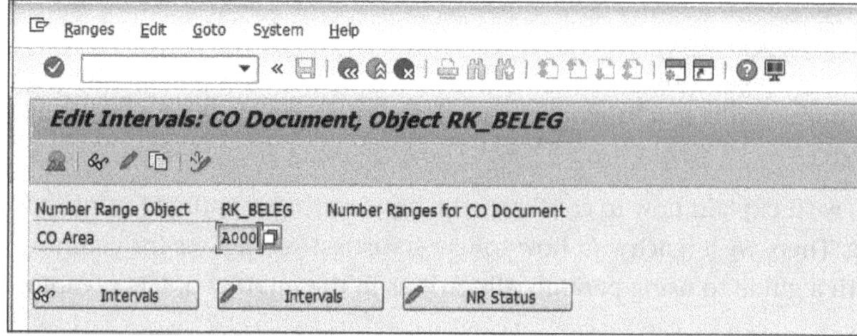

Figure 11.44 Planning Number Ranges

On the screen shown in Figure 11.45, you can set the beginning and ending numbers to define planning number ranges.

Interval Edit Goto System Help

Edit Intervals: CO Document, Object RK_BELEG, Subobject A000

Number Range No.	From No.	To Number	NR Status	External
01	0100000000	0199999999	0	☐
02	0200000000	0299999999	200000399	☐
03	0300000000	0399999999	0	☐
04	0400000000	0499999999	0	☐

Figure 11.45 Maintain Planning Number Ranges

To record planning values to internal orders, follow the application menu path **Accounting • Controlling • Internal Orders • Planning • Overall Values • KO12—Change**. On the initial screen, shown in Figure 11.46, enter your order number, order group, or order type, and your version.

Plan Values Edit Goto Extras System Help

Change Overall Planning: Initial Screen

Overall Planning

Order 500020 or Order Group

Order Type

Version 0

Currency

Figure 11.46 Internal Order Planning

On the next screen, shown in Figure 11.47, enter the plan costs per year for the order.

Order: 500020 Marketing campaign new drug

Order type: Z400 Controlling Area

Annual Values

Period	Plan	Tran...	P...	Planned total
Over...		EUR		
2016		EUR		
2017		EUR		
2018		EUR		
2019	10.000,00	EUR		10.000,00
2020	5.000,00	EUR		5.000,00
2021		EUR		
2022		EUR		
2023		EUR		
2024		EUR		
Tota...	15.000,00	EUR		15.000,00

Figure 11.47 Internal Order Plan Values

Save your entry by clicking the **Save** button. The system generates a planning document, as shown in Figure 11.48.

Figure 11.48 Planning Document Number

11.4.2 Statistical Key Figures

You can also plan based on a combination of internal orders and statistical key figures. In this case, you need to use a planning layout for statistical key figure planning. You can use the standard layouts or create your own via the menu path **Controlling • Internal Orders • Planning • Manual Planning • User-Defined Planning Layouts • Create Planning Layouts for Statistical Key Figure Planning.** Then, select the **Create Statistical Key Figure Planning Layout** activity.

On the initial screen, shown in Figure 11.49, enter a name and description for the new layout and choose an existing layout to use as a reference. Then, click the **Create** button.

Figure 11.50 shows the layout definition screen. Layouts are designed in Report Painter, in a similar fashion as the planning layout we developed for cost centers in Chapter 10. You can double-click any column and change its definition. Click the first column, **Statis**, which represents statistical key figures.

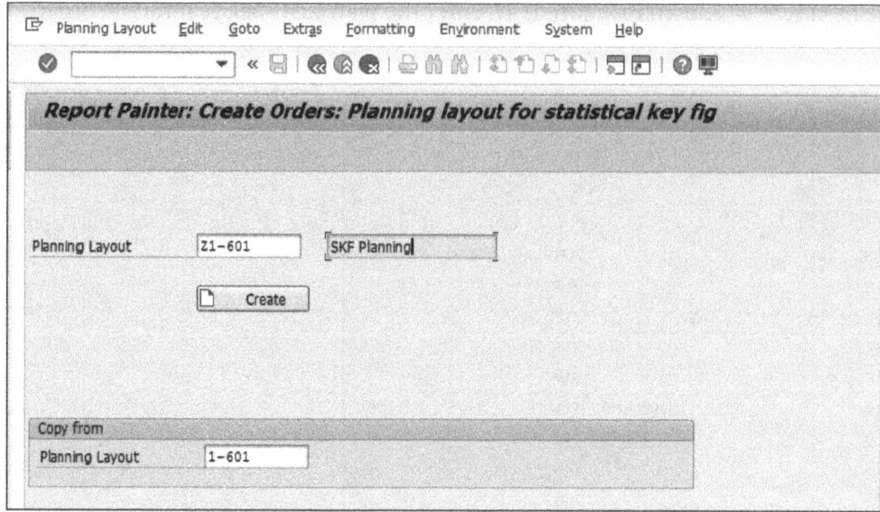

Figure 11.49 Creating a Planning Layout

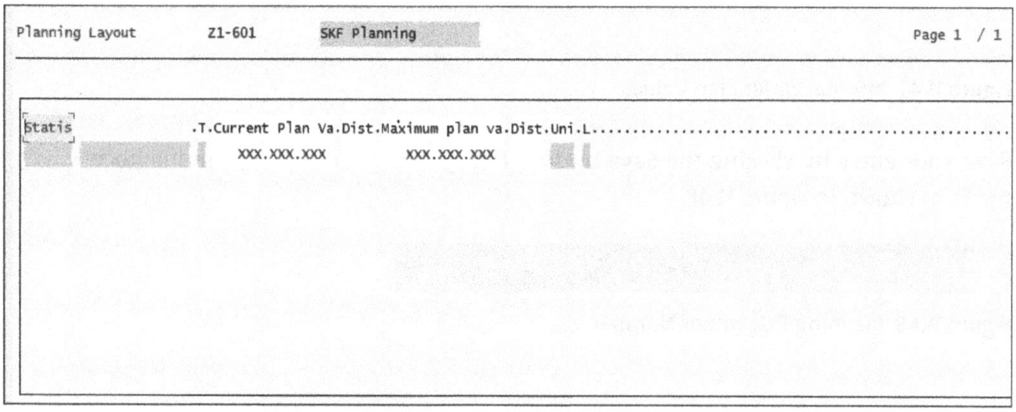

Planning Layout Z1-601 SKF Planning Page 1 / 1

Statis .T.Current Plan Va.Dist.Maximum plan va.Dist.Uni.L

XXX.XXX.XXX XXX.XXX.XXX

Figure 11.50 Planning Layout Definition

Figure 11.51 shows the definition of the statistical key figure column.

This column contains the statistical key figure characteristic. The **Set** and **Variable** columns are selected, which means that a range of statistical key figures must be entered on the selection screen when entering plan values. You can also add the controlling area.

The next columns hold value fields, which represent the current plan values and maximum plan values. You can add or remove columns based on your planning requirements. After maintaining your settings, save your entries by clicking the **Save** button, and then you can use the new layout in your planning.

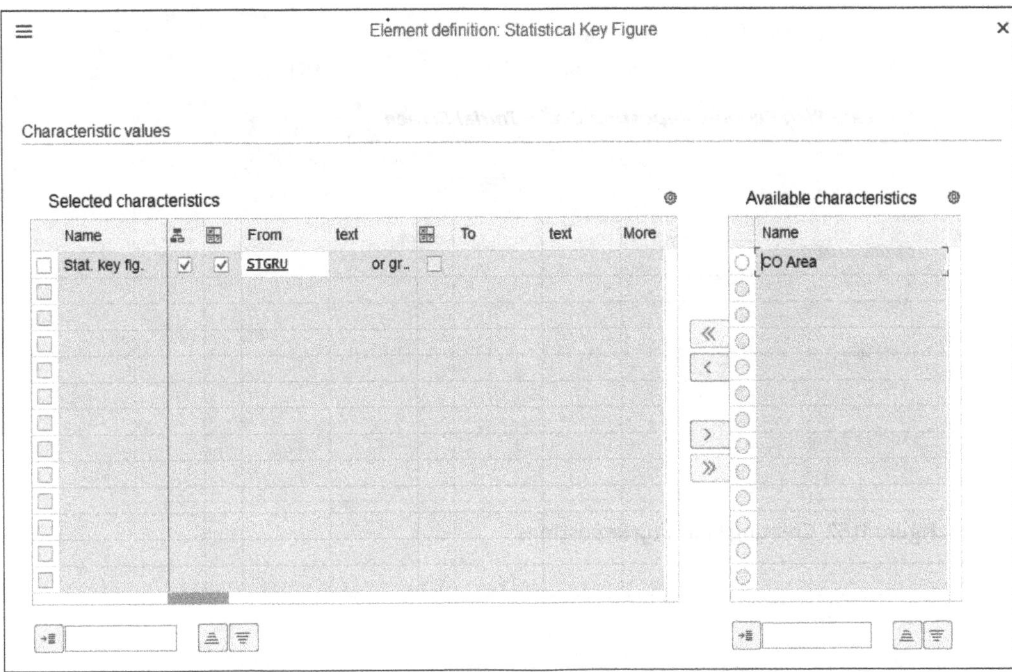

Figure 11.51 Statistical Key Figure Column Definition

11.4.3 Allocations

In internal orders planning, you also can use allocations to allocate plan costs. These settings are similar to the actual costs allocations we configured, but different transactions are used. To execute a planned settlement, follow the application menu path **Accounting • Controlling • Internal Orders • Planning • Allocations • Settlement**, and then **KO9E—Individual Processing** for individual internal orders or **KO9G—Collective Processing** for multiple orders.

To define plan periodic reposting, follow the menu path **Controlling • Internal Orders • Planning • Define Periodic Repostings.** Then, select **Create Plan Periodic Reposting.**

As shown in Figure 11.52, this cycle looks the same as the actual reporting cycle we created earlier in Section 11.3, but it uses Transaction KSW7 (as opposed to Transaction KSW1, which is used for actual reposting).

The cycle definition screen, shown in Figure 11.53, is somewhat different than the one for the actual cycle because you need to specify a controlling plan version. Then, you need to attach one or more segments, in which you specify plan values as a source. Other than that, the settings are like those for the actual reposting cycle you created.

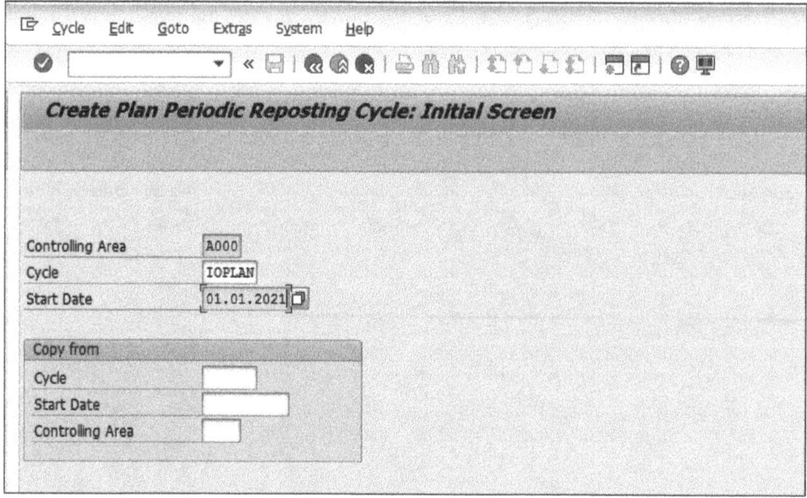

Figure 11.52 Creating Planning Repostings

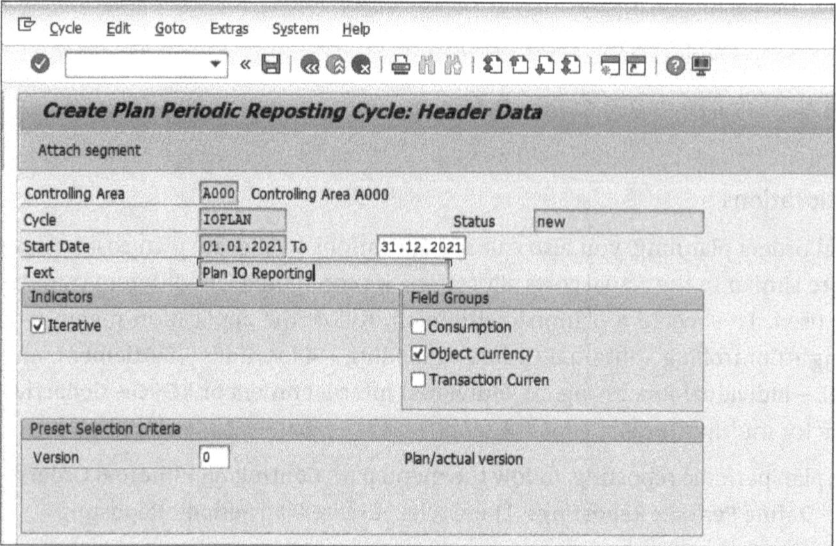

Figure 11.53 Planning Reposting Cycle Definition

11.5 Information System

The information system for internal order accounting offers numerous standard reports for plan/actual and actual/actual comparison, line items, and master data. Also, similar to cost center accounting, you can develop your own reports easily using Report Painter, as we'll discuss in the following sections.

11.5.1 Standard Reports

The standard reports for internal orders are available at the application menu path **Accounting • Controlling • Internal Orders • Information System • Reports for Internal Orders**. We'll look at some of the most commonly used and useful reports in this section.

Plan/actual comparisons are some of the most commonly used reports. These reports are quite useful to compare actual and plan costs, which enables you to track and analyze how incurred costs on internal orders relate to plan costs. Enter Transaction S_ALR_87012993 (Orders: Actual/Plan/Variance), which compares the actual and planned costs and provides the variance in a separate column.

On the selection screen, shown in Figure 11.54, enter the controlling area, fiscal year, from and to periods, and plan version, as well as internal order and cost element selections. Then, execute the report by clicking the **Execute** button.

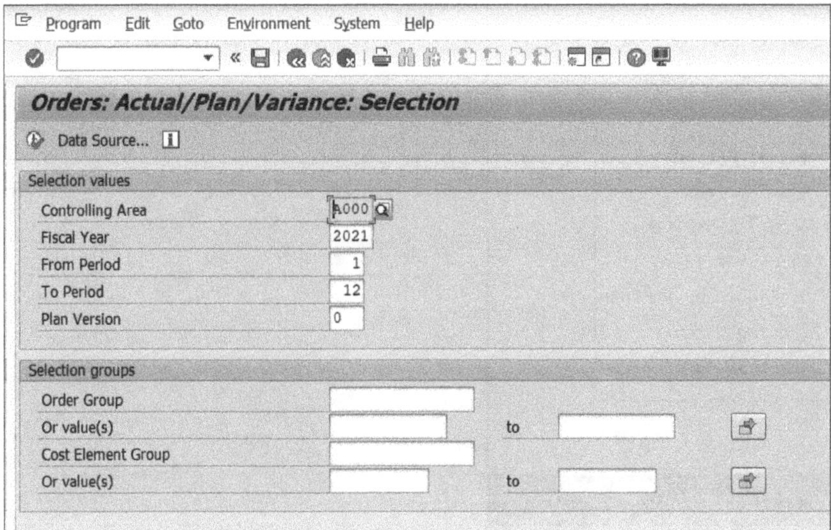

Figure 11.54 Orders Actual/Comparison Selection Screen

On the report output screen, shown Figure 11.55, on the left side, you'll see the internal orders included in the report. You can click any of these orders to see the result for that order only. On the right side, you'll see the report result, separated into columns for actual costs, plan costs, and their variances in absolute amounts and as a percentage.

In the different lines of the report, you'll see the various cost elements posted. If you double-click a line, you can drill down to another report, as shown in Figure 11.56.

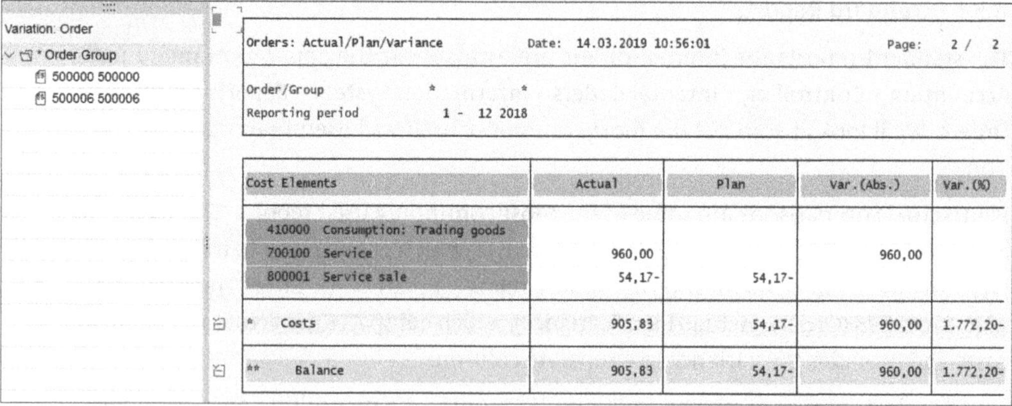

Figure 11.55 Orders: Actual/Plan/Variance Output Screen

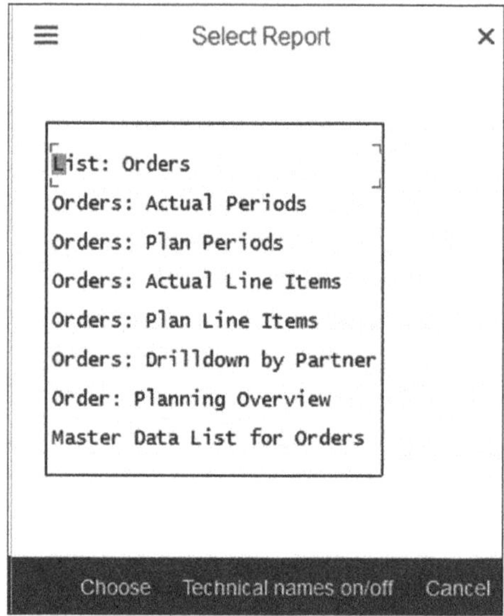

Figure 11.56 Orders Drilldown Reports

For example, selecting **Orders: Actual Periods** provides a breakdown of the actual costs per period, as shown in Figure 11.57.

Another commonly used report is for order actual line items, located at the application menu path **Accounting • Controlling • Internal Orders • Information System • Reports for Internal Orders • Line Items • KOB1—Orders: Actual Line Items.**

On the selection screen, shown in Figure 11.58, you can select data by controlling area, from and to posting date, internal orders, and cost elements. Then, execute the report by clicking the **Execute** button.

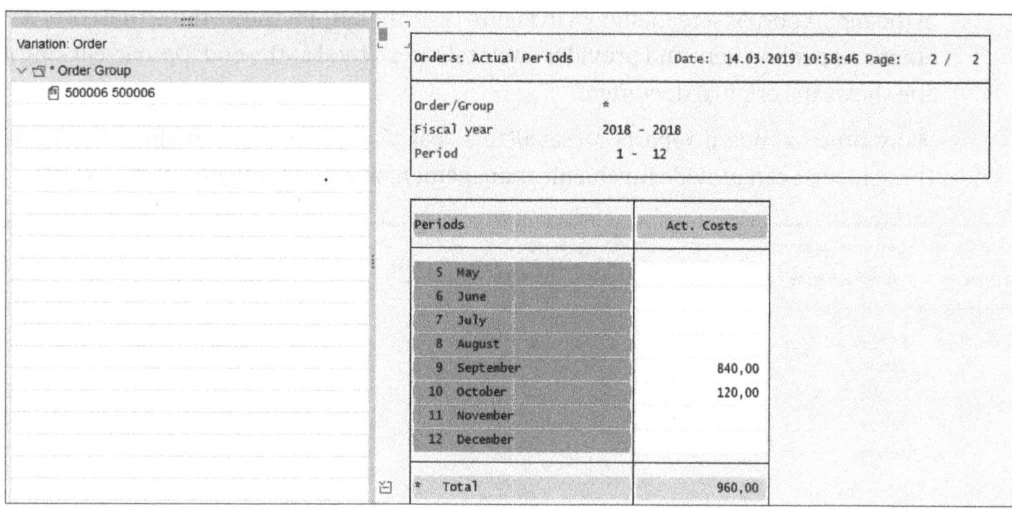

Figure 11.57 Order Actual Costs Breakdown by Period

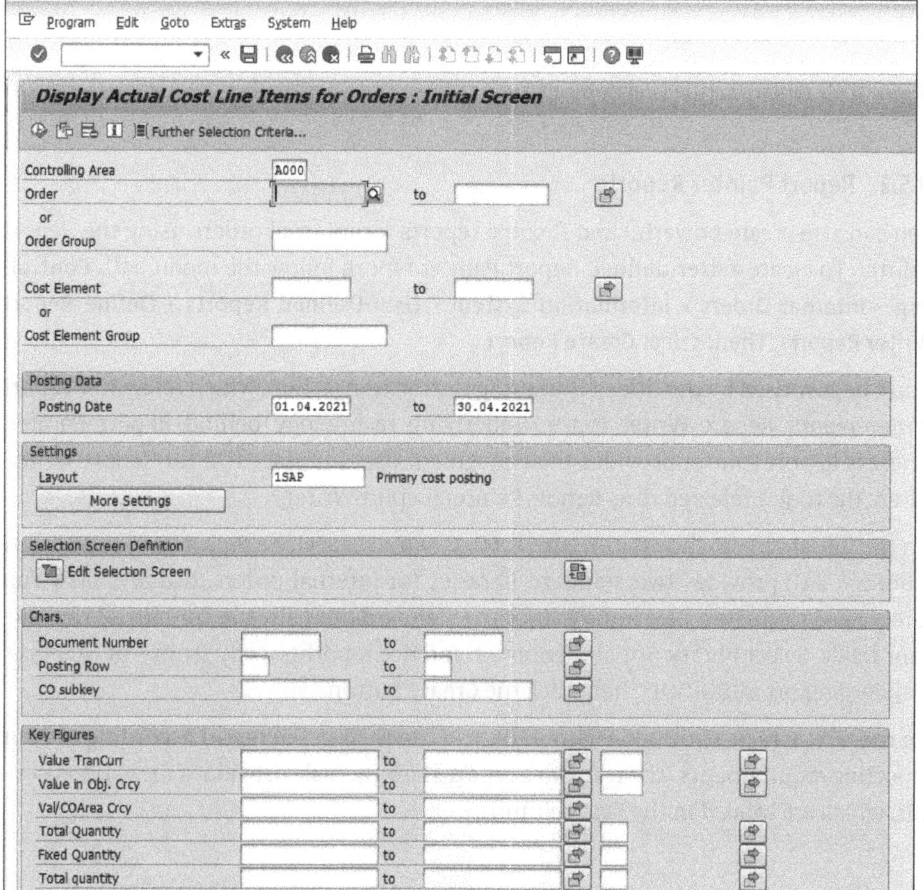

Figure 11.58 Orders Actual Line Items Selection Screen

In the report output screen, shown in Figure 11.59, the system shows the actual costs per order and per line item and provides subtotals and a total at the end. Double-clicking a line shows the original document.

Many other standard reports are available that you can explore in similar fashion. These reports can provide invaluable management analysis for your internal orders.

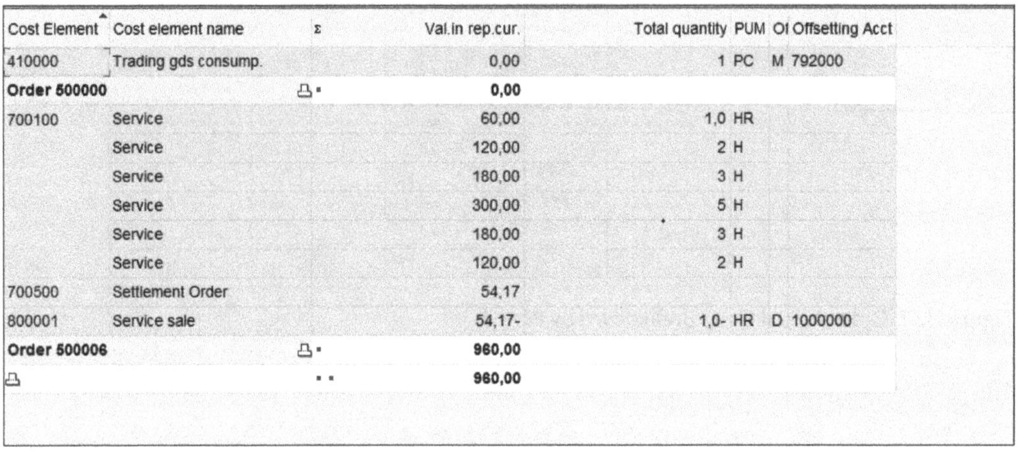

Cost Element	Cost element name	Σ	Val.in rep.cur.	Total quantity	PUM	OI	Offsetting Acct
410000	Trading gds consump.		0,00	1	PC	M	792000
Order 500000		•	**0,00**				
700100	Service		60,00	1,0	HR		
	Service		120,00	2	H		
	Service		180,00	3	H		
	Service		300,00	5	H		
	Service		180,00	3	H		
	Service		120,00	2	H		
700500	Settlement Order		54,17				
800001	Service sale		54,17-	1,0-	HR	D	1000000
Order 500006		•	**960,00**				
		••	**960,00**				

Figure 11.59 Orders Actual Line Items Output Screen

11.5.2 Report Painter Reports

You can also create powerful and flexible reports for internal orders using the Report Painter. To create a user-defined Report Painter report, follow the menu path **Controlling • Internal Orders • Information System • User-Defined Reports • Define Report Writer Reports**. Then, select **Create Report**.

Don't be surprised by the title of the configuration transaction, which refers to a *Report Writer report*. Report Writer is the underlying technology behind Report Painter, whereas Report Painter provides the convenient user interface (UI) for Report Writer. Often, the tool is referred to as Report Painter/Report Writer.

On the initial screen, shown in Figure 11.60, you must specify a report name and select a library. SAP provides two standard libraries for internal orders: 601 and 602. You rarely need to create a new library since the standard ones already contain all the relevant fields. Select library 601 and enter a reference report to copy from—in this case, standard report 6000-001. Then, click the **Create** button.

On the next screen, shown in Figure 11.61, you can modify the report according to your reporting requirements. The reference report shows actual cost values for various periods, which are totaled in the first columns.

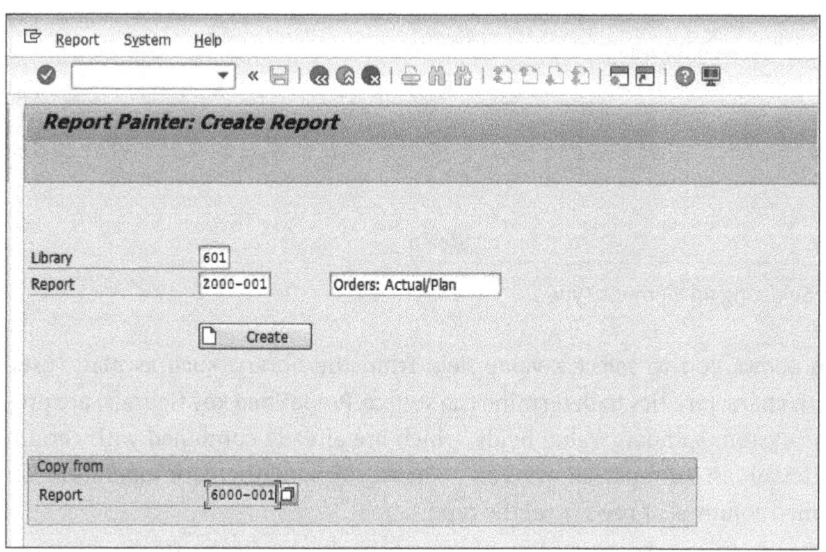

Figure 11.60 Creating an Internal Order Report

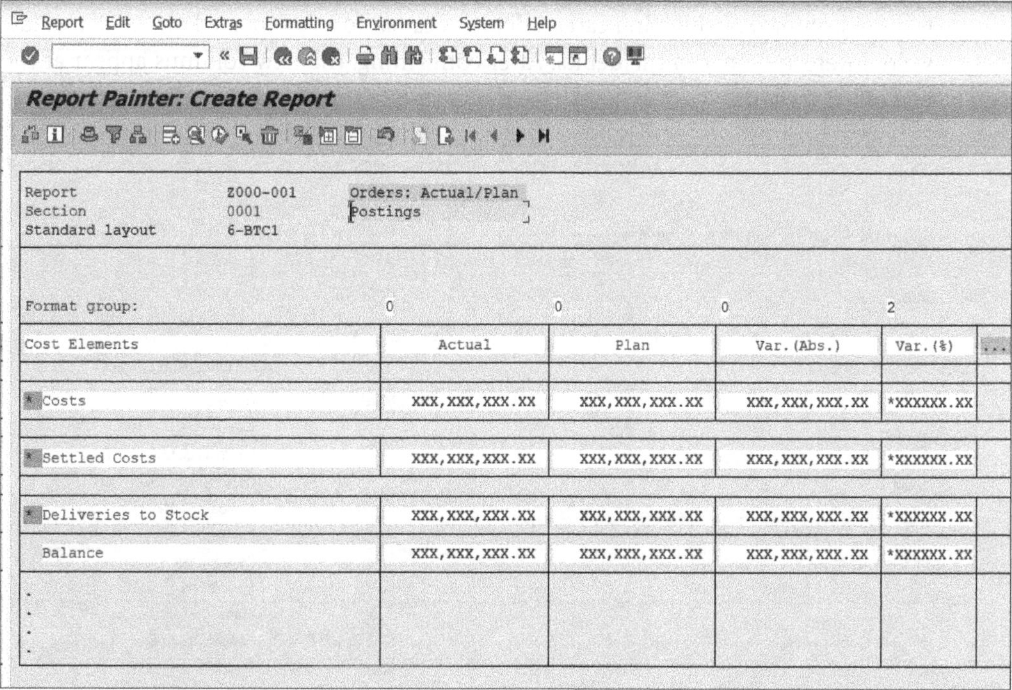

Figure 11.61 Defining an Internal Order Report

Let's say you want to add columns with plan cost values. Position the cursor after the last column and double-click. Then, in the popup window, shown in Figure 11.62, select **Key figure with characteristics**.

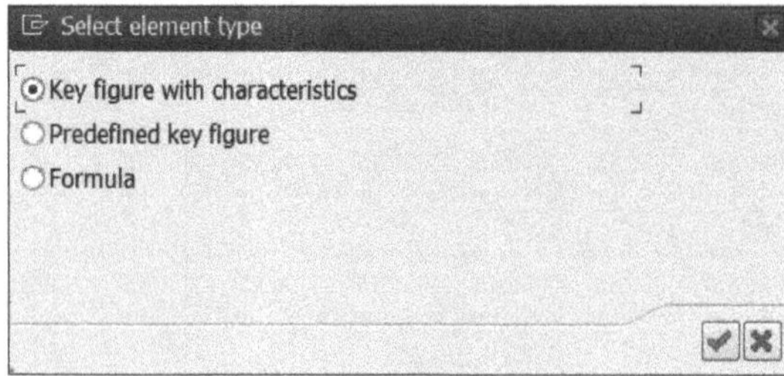

Figure 11.62 Selecting an Element Type

This option allows you to select a value field from the library, such as plan costs, together with characteristics to determine the source. **Predefined key figure**(s) are provided by the system-standard value fields, which are already combined with certain characteristic values. **Formula** allows you to perform a mathematic operation on already defined columns or rows from the report.

Select the basic key figure **Plan Costs -> Line Items**, as shown in Figure 11.63. For the **Fiscal Year** and **Period** characteristics, check the variables and enter variable "6-GJAHL" for the **Fiscal Year** and "6-PERIK" for the **Period**. For the **Dr/Cr ind. CO** (debit/credit indicator) field, enter "S," which indicates a debit. Because costs are posted on the debit side, we're interested only in the debits. After confirming, the new columns appear at the end of the report.

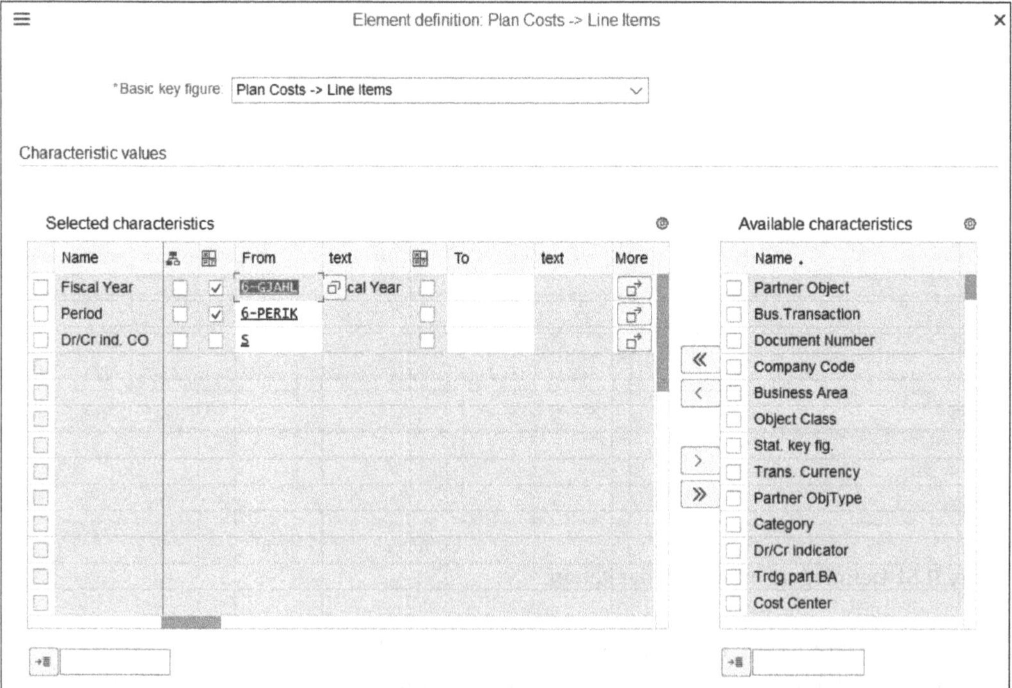

Figure 11.63 Defining Columns

Then, you can add yet another column to provide the variance between the actual and plan values. Double-click again after the last column; this time, select **Formula**.

In the **Enter Formula** screen, shown in Figure 11.64, create a formula that indicates that the plan costs should be subtracted from the total balance by selecting the **X003** ID button, then the minus sign from the calculator buttons on the right side, and then the **X007** button.

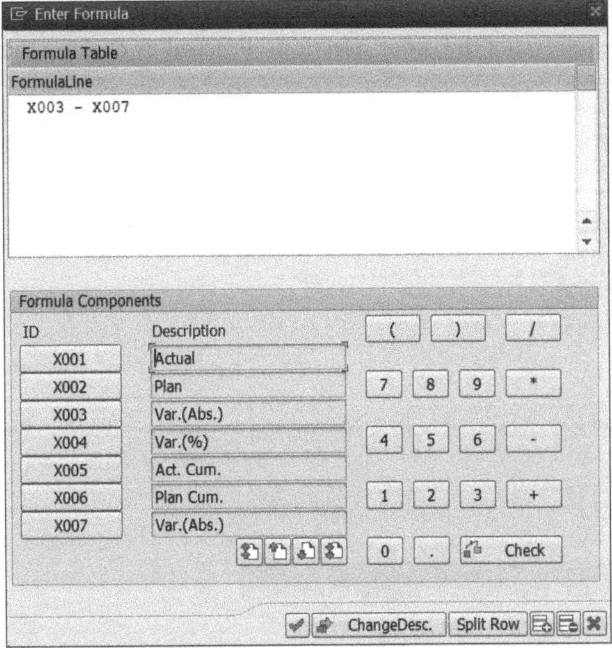

Figure 11.64 Defining a Formula

After confirming, you'll need to specify the column title information, as shown in Figure 11.65.

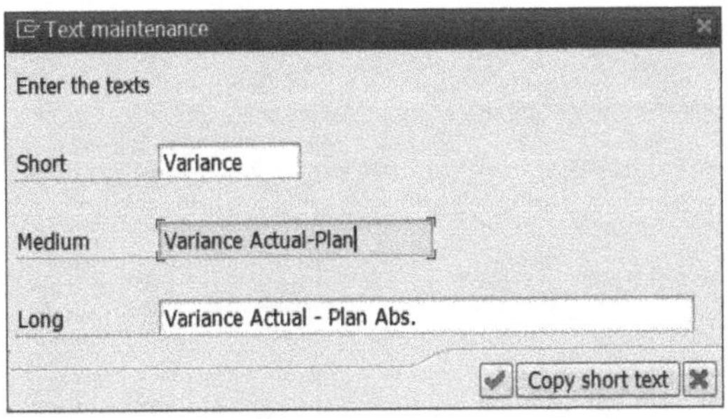

Text maintenance
Enter the texts
Short: Variance
Medium: Variance Actual-Plan
Long: Variance Actual - Plan Abs.
Copy short text

Figure 11.65 Column Title

Because this column is a formula column, no text is be transferred from the key figure, so you can manually enter short, medium, and long descriptions on this screen.

Using these techniques, you can add further columns and rows to the report. Once you're satisfied with the report layout, save the report by clicking the **Save** button.

11.5.3 Internal Orders Plan/Actual App

Several useful SAP Fiori reports available for internal orders in SAP S/4HANA 2020, such as the Internal Orders Plan/Actual app (app ID F0948). On the selection screen, shown in Figure 11.66, you specify the fiscal year, order type, and other selection criteria based on which you would like to restrict the order selections. Proceed by clicking the **OK** button.

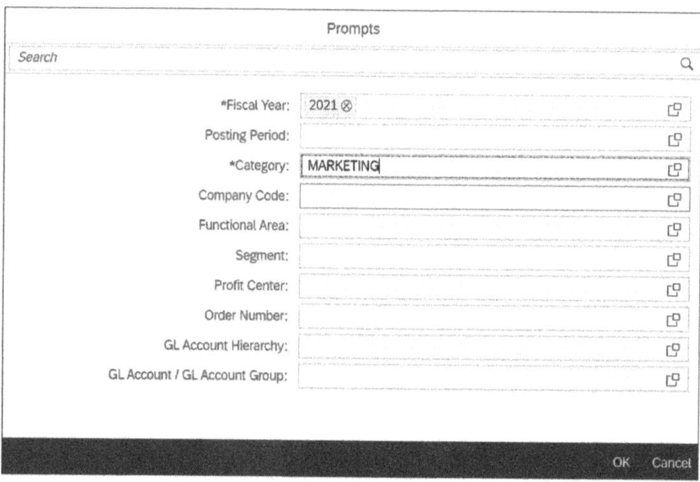

Figure 11.66 Internal Orders Plan/Actual SAP Fiori App Selection

On the output screen, shown in Figure 11.67, you can interactively navigate through the results using the various dimensions on the right side of the screen.

You can also export the results to Excel by clicking the (**Export to MS Excel**) button.

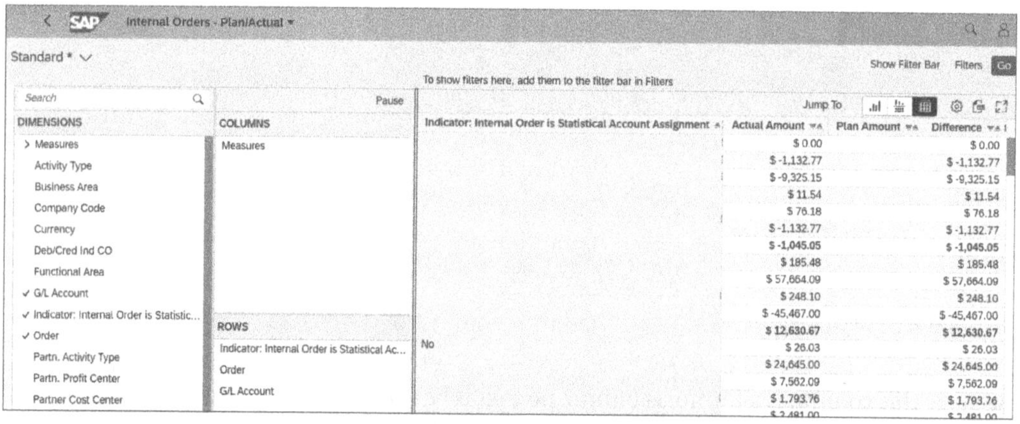

Figure 11.67 Internal Orders Plan/Actual App Output

11.6 Summary

This chapter was yet another extensive chapter in which we covered the functionalities and configuration of internal orders accounting inside and out.

After finishing this chapter, you should be familiar with and know how to configure the various internal orders functionalities, including the following:

- Master data
- Budgeting
- Actual postings and periodic processing
- Planning
- Information system

With this summary, we've completed our guide to the overhead controlling areas of the system. In the next chapter, you'll learn how to configure profit center accounting, which is a cross-section of controlling and financial accounting. Technically, this functionality is part of controlling, but profit center accounting provides comprehensive reporting not only for P&L accounts, but also for the balance sheet.

Chapter 12
Profit Center Accounting

This chapter provides step-by-step instructions for configuring profit center accounting. We'll also explain how SAP S/4HANA can provide robust reporting capabilities for the whole company because users can drill down into every area of responsibility.

Profit center accounting provides full financial statement reporting on everything lower than the legal entity level. Most companies set up their separate legal entities as company codes, but they may want to draw both balance sheets and profit and loss (P&L) statements on a lower level, such as a product line or division. In this scenario, profit center accounting comes to the rescue because these lower levels can be set up as profit centers easily. Also, profit centers are posted with every single financial line item, as opposed to cost objects such as cost centers or internal orders, which are posted only with P&L accounts. Therefore, with profit center accounting, you can create a complete balance sheet and P&L statement for a profit center or for a group of profit centers.

Profit center accounting in SAP S/4HANA can be regarded as a crossroads between financial accounting and controlling. In the application and customizing menu, profit center accounting is part of controlling. In older SAP ERP releases, before the introduction of the new general ledger, profit center accounting used special purpose ledger 8A. However, in SAP S/4HANA, profit center accounting is fully integrated with the general ledger. Therefore, technically, we could argue that profit center accounting is part of financial accounting, but because it integrates information for both the balance sheet and P&L accounts and often can be derived from other cost objects, we decided to discuss profit center accounting within our controlling chapters, after you were familiar with overhead costing.

In this chapter, we'll guide you through the main components of profit center accounting:

- Master data
- Profit center derivation and splitting
- Information system

As always, we'll start with setting up the master data required for the module.

12.1 Master Data

Master data for profit center accounting consists of the following, each of which will be discussed in this section:

- Standard hierarchy
- Profit centers
- Profit center groups

We'll start by defining profit centers.

12.1.1 Profit Centers

A *profit center* is a financial organizational unit used to structure the organization from a management point of view. Profit centers are used to report based on the various areas of the organization, as structured by the management. Therefore, one of the most fundamental design decisions in the finance area of an SAP S/4HANA implementation is how to structure the profit centers. Normally, a business needs extensive support from implementation consultants to help define the best structure for profit centers. This effort is also cross-functional because not only finance people should be involved, but also sales, purchasing, and production teams. Many profit centers are derived from cost centers and are normally defined by finance, but also a main derivation point for profit centers is the material master, and in some cases, the linkage should be provided by logistic teams.

Different scenarios are possible, but most commonly, profit centers are defined with a sales-based approach because management is mostly interested in analyzing how the various products and divisions of the company are performing. Therefore, profit centers often represent various product lines or sales departments of the organization. The goal is that management should be able to create a full set of financial statements quickly and transparently, including costs, revenues, assets, and liabilities, for each important area of the organization.

To create a profit center, follow application the menu path **Accounting • Controlling • Profit Center Accounting • Master Data • Profit Center • Individual Processing • KE51—Create.**

On the initial screen, shown in Figure 12.1, enter a profit center to be created and a controlling area. Profit centers are always created for controlling areas. The naming convention for profit centers should be straightforward and easy to understand and recognize. A good practice is to use numeric codes for profit centers. The length depends on the number of profit centers required; 4 or 6 digits is common. You should strive for consistency among your profit centers; for example, profit centers from the same division should start with the same number.

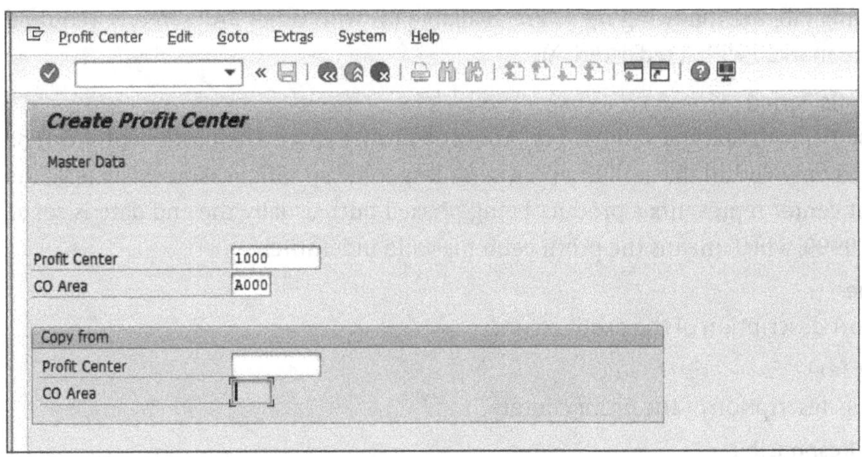

Figure 12.1 Creating a Profit Center

In the **Copy from** section, you can enter an existing profit center and its controlling area, in which case the values of that profit center will be proposed as defaults on the following screens.

The profit center master record is organized into tabs, which contain logically connected fields. The first tab, shown in Figure 12.2, is **Basic Data**.

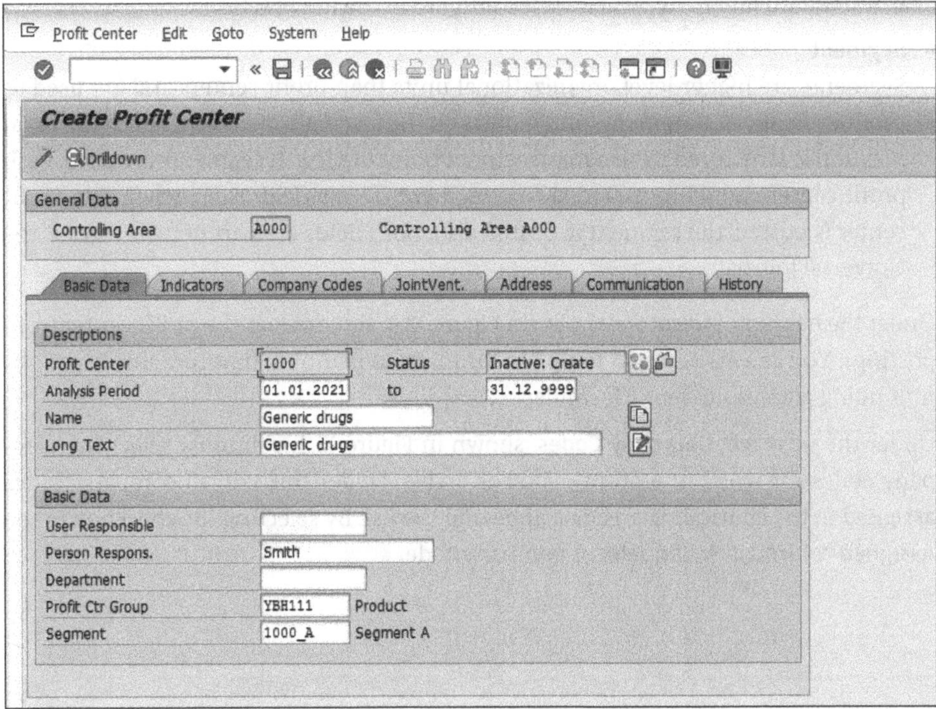

Figure 12.2 Profit Center Basic Data

Under this tab, the following fields are available (as with other SAP screens, required fields are marked with a red asterisk):

- **Analysis Period**
  These fields define the validity period of the profit center. The profit center can be posted only within that validity period. Unless some specific reason exists (e.g., the profit center represents a product being phased out), usually the end date is set as 31.12.9999, which means the profit center is valid indefinitely.
- **Name**
  A short description of the profit center.
- **Long Text**
  A long description of the profit center.
- **User Responsible**
  In this field, you can enter an SAP user responsible for the profit center.
- **Person Respons. (person responsible)**
  This field is for the name of the responsible manager for the profit center.
- **Department**
  This field is for the department to which the profit center belongs.
- **Profit Ctr Group (profit center group)**
  Each profit center should be assigned to a group. Profit center groups are structured in a standard hierarchy, which we'll configure in the next section.
- **Segment**
  Segments are higher-level organizational units than profit centers and are used to produce financial statements and reports on the few main areas into which the organization is structured from a management point of view. If segments are used, each profit center should be assigned to a segment in this field. Then, when this profit center is posted, the segment is posted also. Both fields are part of table ACDOCA, the Universal Journal.

Under the next tab, **Indicators**, shown in Figure 12.3, you can lock the profit center from postings. You can also enter a template for formula planning that contains functions for finding plan values using formulas.

Under the next tab, **Company Codes**, shown in Figure 12.4, you must select the company codes for which the profit center is active. Under this tab, all company codes assigned to the controlling area will appear in the list. By selecting the checkbox in the **Assigned** column, you can select a company code.

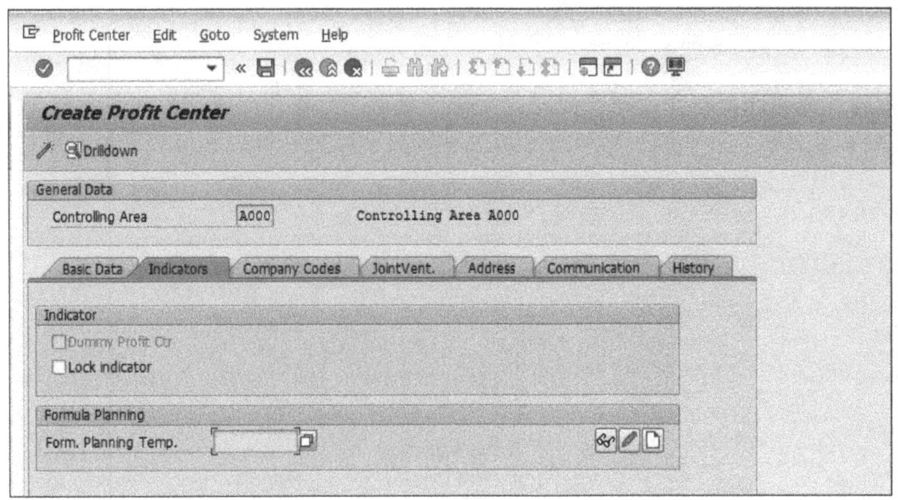

Figure 12.3 Profit Center Indicators

Profit Center Edit Goto System Help

Create Profit Center

Drilldown

General Data

Controlling Area A000 Controlling Area A000

Basic Data | Indicators | Company Codes | JointVent. | Address | Communication | History

Company Code Assignment for Profit Center

CoCd	Company Name	Assigned
0001	Company Code 1010	☐
1000	US Generic Drugs	☑
1010	Company Code 1010	☐
1110	Company Code 1110	☐
1210	Company Code 1210	☐
1410	Company Code 1410	☐
1710	Company Code 1710	☐
1810	Company Code 1810	☐

Figure 12.4 Profit Center Company Codes

Under the next tab, **Address**, shown in Figure 12.5, you can enter various address information relevant for the profit center, such as street address, region, country, and so on.

Under the next tab, **Communication**, shown in Figure 12.6, you can enter communication information relevant for the profit center, such as language key, telephone, fax, and so on.

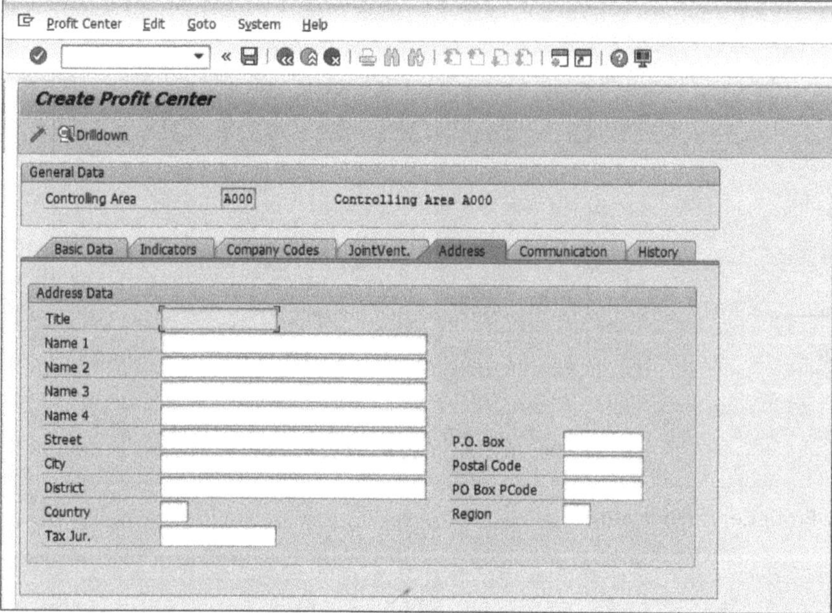

Figure 12.5 Profit Center Address Data

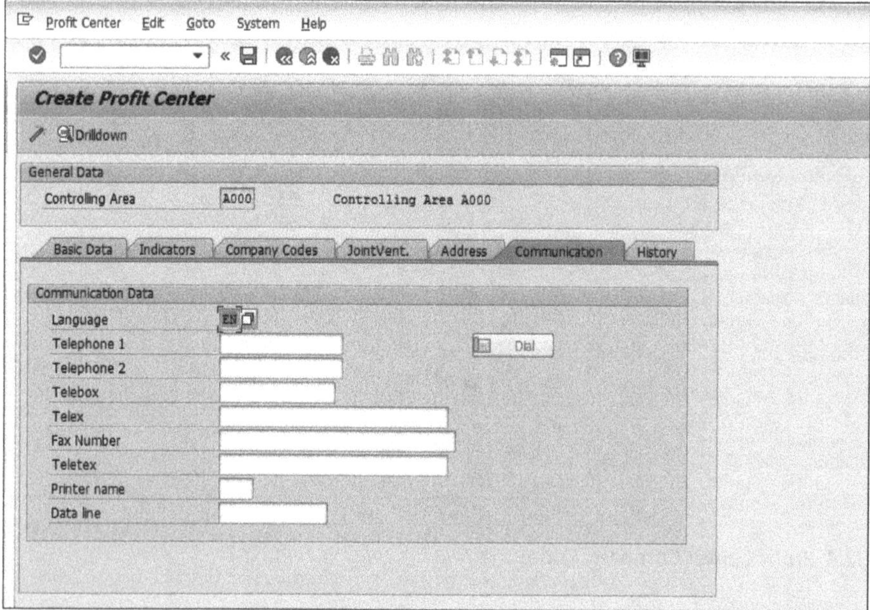

Figure 12.6 Profit Center Communication Data

Finally, under the **History** tab, shown in Figure 12.7, the system shows information about the user who created the profit center and when they created it, as well as any changes to the profit center master record.

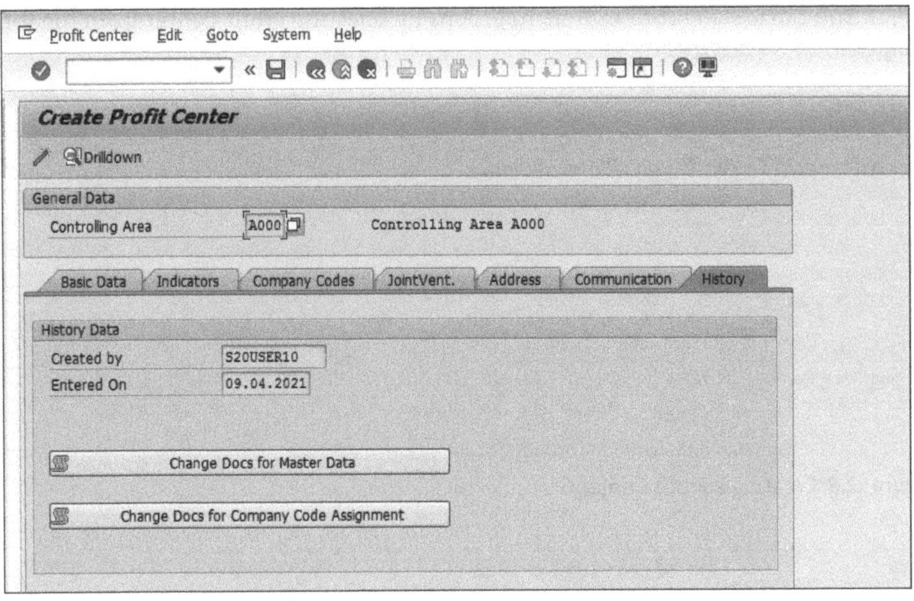

Figure 12.7 Profit Center History

After maintaining the profit center fields, you can save the profit center in an inactive status by clicking the **Save as Inactive** button and activate it later. Alternatively, you can activate it immediately by selecting **Activate** from the top menu. You must activate the profit center before you can use it for postings.

12.1.2 Profit Center Groups

A *profit center group* serves to classify profit centers with similar functions. These groups are then used heavily for reporting. To create a profit center group, follow the application menu path **Accounting • Controlling • Profit Center Accounting • Master Data • Profit Center Group • KCH1—Create.**

On the initial screen, shown in Figure 12.8, enter a name for the **Profit Center Group**, which can consist of letters and numbers. All profit center groups should follow a consistent approach, with either numeric values or descriptive names that point to the function of the group.

In the **Reference** section, you can provide an existing profit center group to use as a template for the new group. Proceed by clicking the **Enter** button.

On the next screen, shown in Figure 12.9, initially, you'll see only the name of the profit center group you entered in the previous screen. Enter a long description for the group, and then, you can start to build the lower hierarchy of the group. You can assign additional groups on the same level you're positioned on with the **Same Level** command from the top menu and on a lower level with the **Lower Level** option from the top menu. You can assign profit centers to groups by selecting **Profit Center** from the top menu.

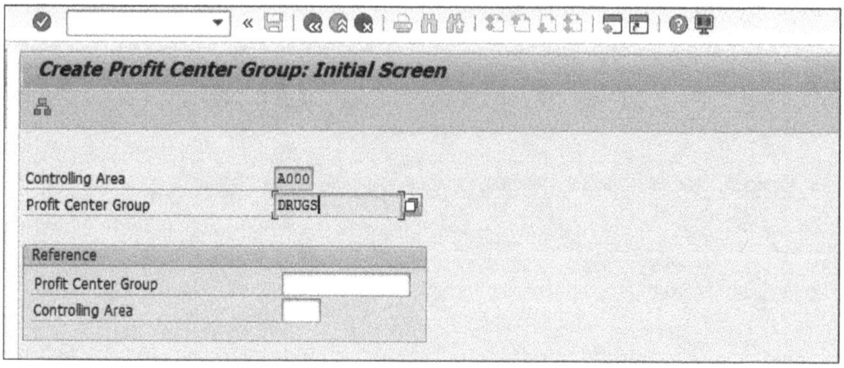

Create Profit Center Group: Initial Screen
Controlling Area A000
Profit Center Group DRUGS
Reference
Profit Center Group
Controlling Area

Figure 12.8 Creating a Profit Center Group

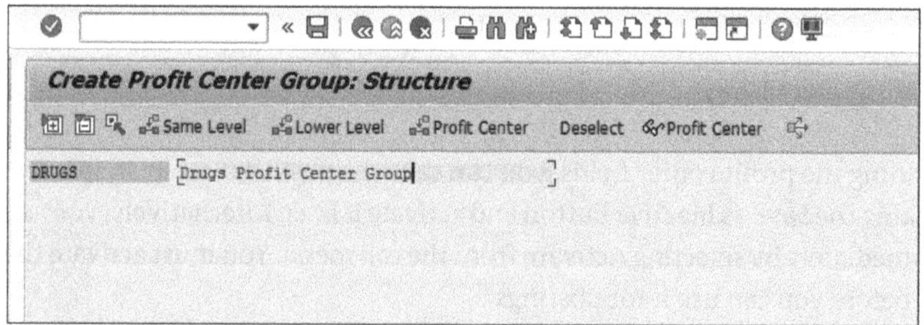

Figure 12.9 Profit Center Group Definition Screen

Figure 12.10 shows the profit center group **DRUGS** without additional groups underneath, with three profit centers assigned.

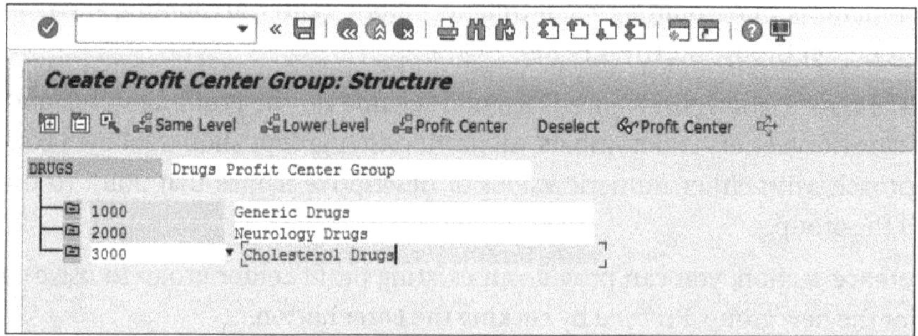

Figure 12.10 Profit Center Group Defined

When you're done, save the profit center group by clicking the **Save** button.

12.1.3 Standard Hierarchies

A *standard hierarchy* is a structure that contains all the profit centers in your organization, grouped in logical groups, based on the purpose and the strategy of classification of the profit centers. A standard hierarchy is similar in purpose and function to the cost center standard hierarchy we created earlier.

To maintain a profit center standard hierarchy, follow the application menu path **Accounting • Controlling • Profit Center Accounting • Master Data • Standard Hierarchy • KCH5N—Change.**

In essence, the standard hierarchy is a profit center group at the top level, which contains the other profit center groups in your controlling area. The interface provided by this transaction, shown in Figure 12.11, is quite flexible and full of options.

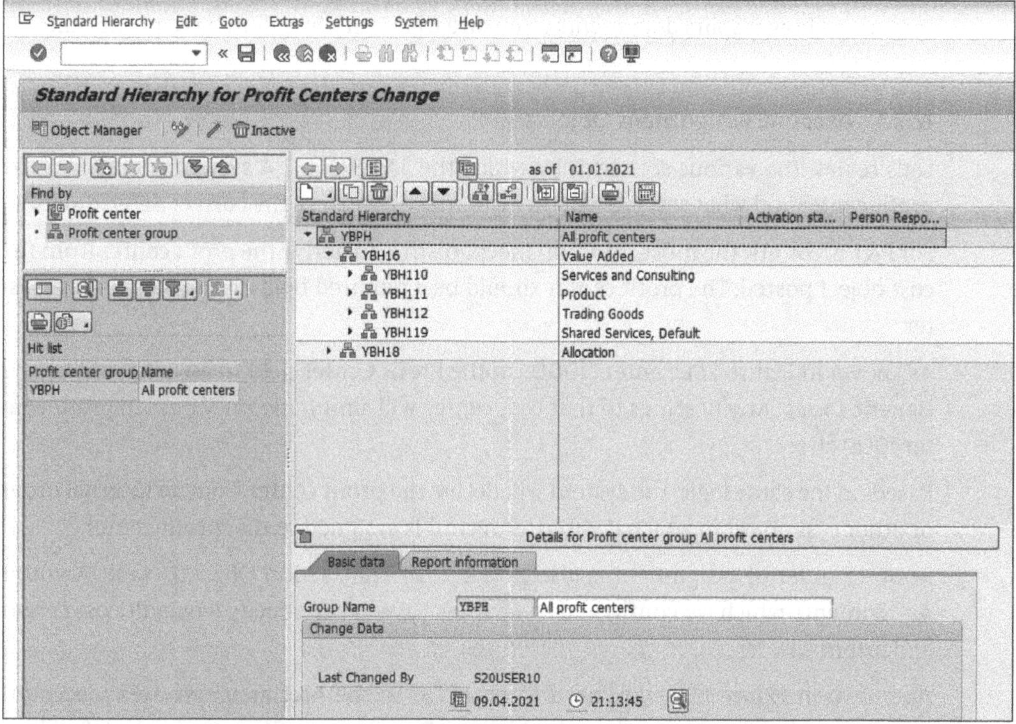

Figure 12.11 Profit Center Standard Hierarchy

The screen is separated into multiple windows for easier navigation. On the left side, you have a search function, in which you can search by profit center or profit center group. On the right side, at the top, you have the profit center standard hierarchy; at the bottom, you'll see details about the selected node. The standard hierarchy is a tree-like structure, which you can expand using the arrows 〉 to the left of each node. You can also expand the whole hierarchy from the node in which you're positioned by clicking the (**Expand Subtree**) button and collapse the whole hierarchy from the node in which you're positioned by clicking the (**Collapse Subtree**) button.

You can right-click any node and create an additional profit center group at the same or a lower level or assign a profit center. Include all your profit center groups in the standard hierarchy and save it by clicking the **Save** button.

12.2 Profit Center Derivation

A profit center is an object that's almost always derived from another object, such as a cost center or material, or derived via configuration and substitution techniques. In this section, we'll examine the various methods by which the system derives the profit center and how it splits documents to ensure that every line item has a profit center.

12.2.1 Account Assignment Objects

Let's review the various scenarios by which the SAP S/4HANA system determines the profit center and what settings you need to make to ensure the correct determination.

For P&L accounts, the most common mechanism is to derive the profit center from the cost object posted. The profit center should be a required field on the cost center master.

As shown in Figure 12.12, enter "1000" in the **Profit Center** field to assign profit center **Generic Drugs**. Any postings to that cost center will simultaneously post to profit center 1000 also.

Based on the same logic, the system will derive the profit center from an internal order or other cost object in which the master record is assigned to that profit center.

Another order of assignment is also possible. In Transaction OKB9 (Default Account Assignment), which we configured in Chapter 10, you can specify a default cost center and internal order.

As shown in Figure 12.13, you need to enter "3" in the **Acct assignmt detail** (account assignment detail) column. Then, double-click **Detail per profit center** on the left side of the screen.

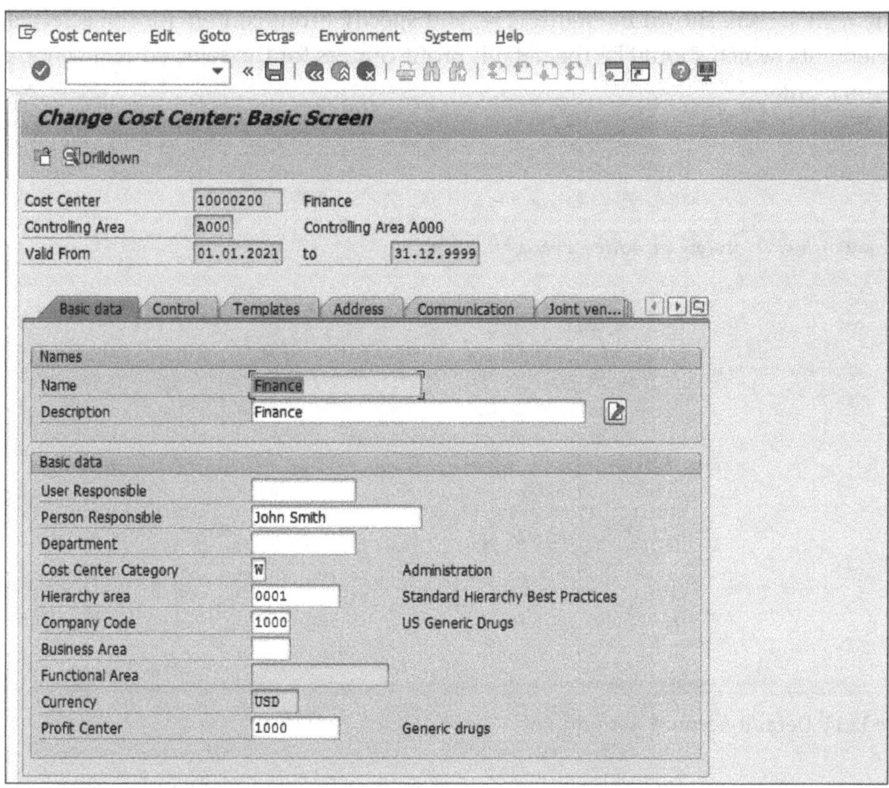

Figure 12.12 Profit Center Cost Center Assignment

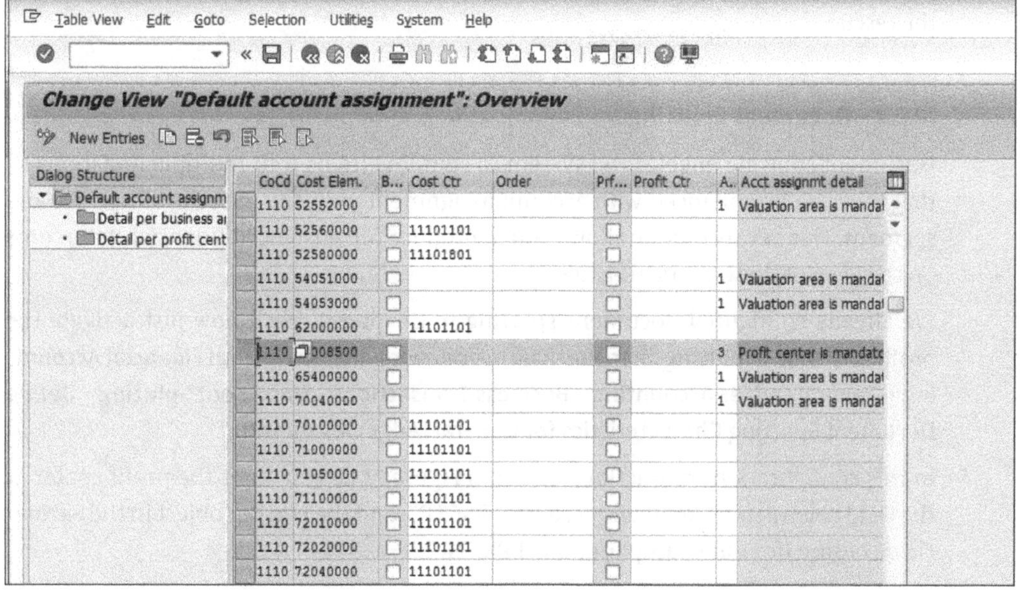

Figure 12.13 Profit Center Default Account Assignment

On the next screen, shown in Figure 12.14, you specify profit centers for the selected cost elements, which should be the default profit centers for the selected cost centers or internal orders.

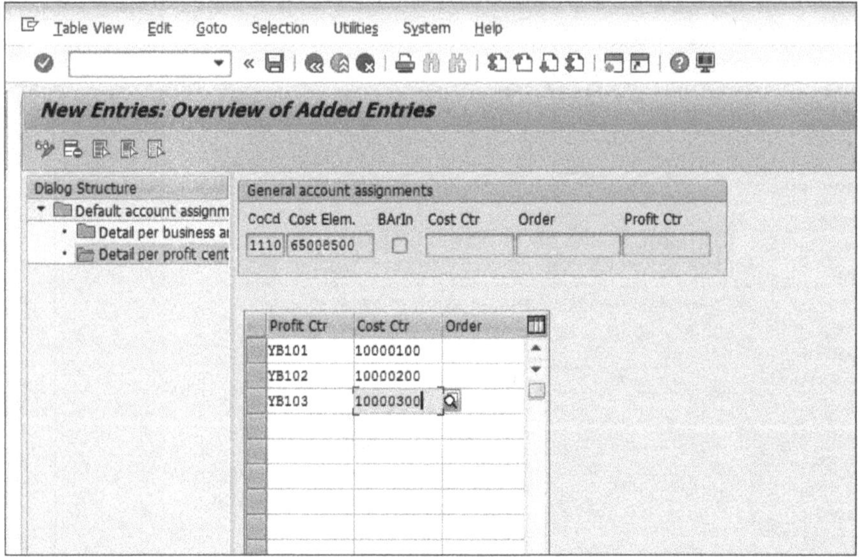

Figure 12.14 Default Account Assignments

For inventory accounts, the profit center is derived from the material master record. However, for many balance sheet accounts, no direct assignment of profit center is possible, such as bank accounts, for example. That's when document splitting comes to the rescue.

12.2.2 Document Splitting

Document splitting enables the system to split line items into multiple line items so that they can be enhanced with account assignment objects such as profit center and segment. This key technique allows you to produce fully balanced financial statements on the level of these characteristics.

We already configured document splitting in Chapter 4. We'll now just activate the profit center as a splitting characteristic by following the menu path **Financial Accounting • General Ledger Accounting • Business Transactions • Document Splitting • Define Document Splitting Characteristics for General Ledger Accounting**.

In this configuration transaction, shown in Figure 12.15, you enter the profit center in the **Field** column (for our example, enter "PRCTR") and the partner object in the **Partner Field** column (for our example, enter "PPRCTR").

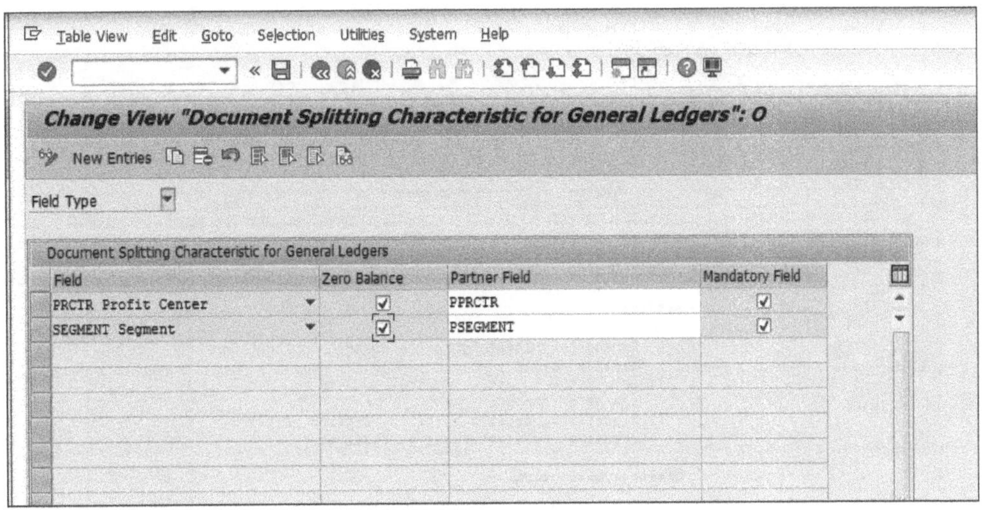

Figure 12.15 Profit Center as Splitting Characteristic

You also need to select the following two checkboxes:

- **Zero Balance**
  This checkbox must be selected so that, during posting, the system will check whether the balance for the profit center is equal to zero on the document level. If not, the system will generate additional clearing lines on clearing accounts that achieve the zero balance.
- **Mandatory Field**
  This field ensures that the profit center must be filled in with a value after document splitting for each line item. If the system isn't able to fill in a value because of missing customizing, an error message will be displayed, and the document won't be posted.

After maintaining these settings for the profit center and other splitting characteristics, save your entry by clicking the **Save** button.

12.2.3 Profit Center Substitution

The profit center in the sales order line item is derived from the material master record, where the profit center must be maintained (in table MARC and field PRCTR). However, in some circumstances, you need to substitute the profit center in the sales order based on certain criteria. To define this substitution, follow the menu path **Controlling • Profit Center Accounting • Assignments of Account Assignment Objects to Profit Centers • Sales Orders • Sales Order Substitutions • Define Substitution Rules.**

On the screen shown in Figure 12.16, select **Substitution** from the top menu to create a substitution.

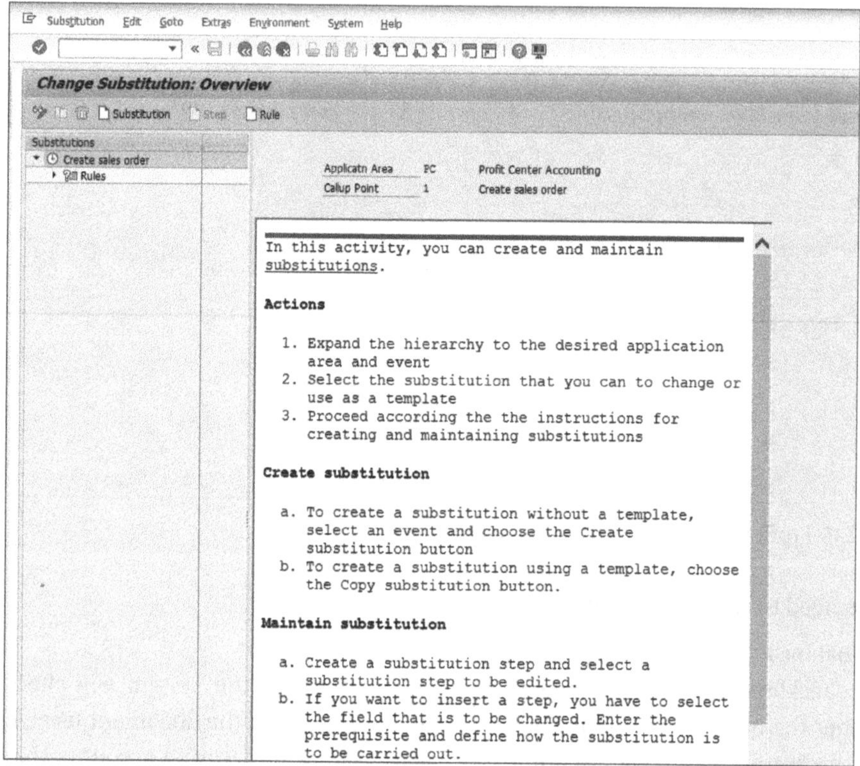

Figure 12.16 Creating a Profit Center Substitution

Enter a name and description for the substitution and select **Step** from the top menu. The only field available to substitute is the profit center, as shown in Figure 12.17. You also can develop a user exit to program more complex logic.

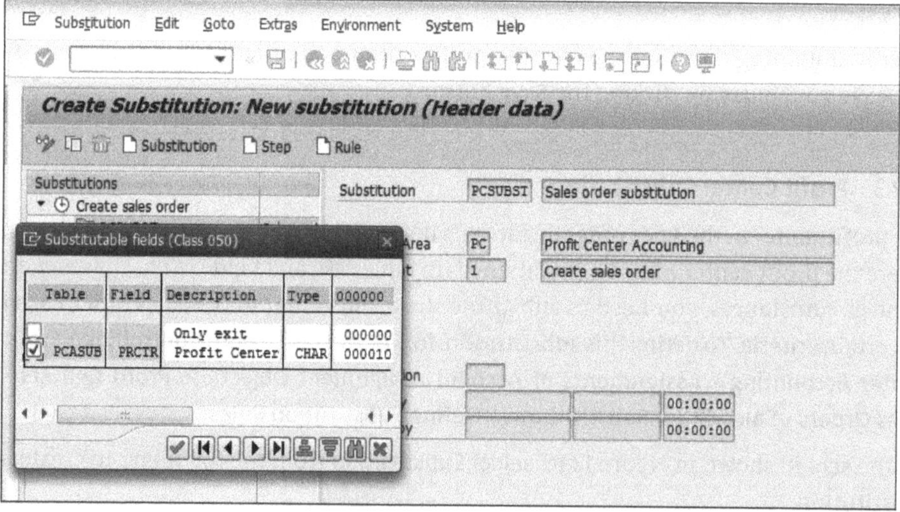

Figure 12.17 Creating a Substitution Step

In the popup window shown in Figure 12.18, select whether the substitution will work with a constant value (you'll enter a fixed profit center to be substituted), user exit, or field-field assignment (which means the value of the profit center will depend on the value of another field).

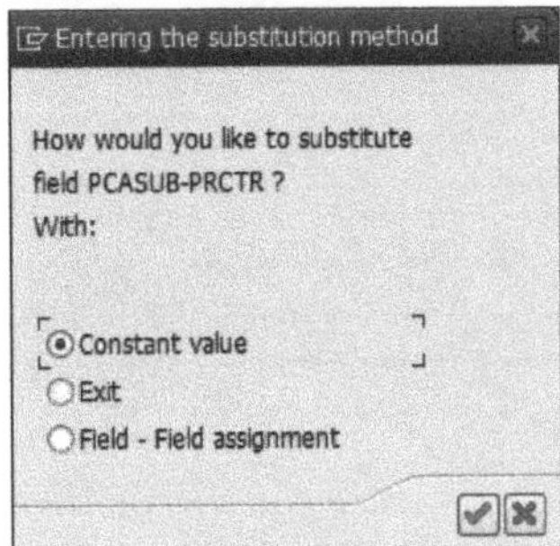

Figure 12.18 Selecting Substitution Logic

Select the **Constant value** option. Now, in the **Prerequisite** section of the substitution step, shown in Figure 12.19, you can define the criteria that will trigger the substitution when met.

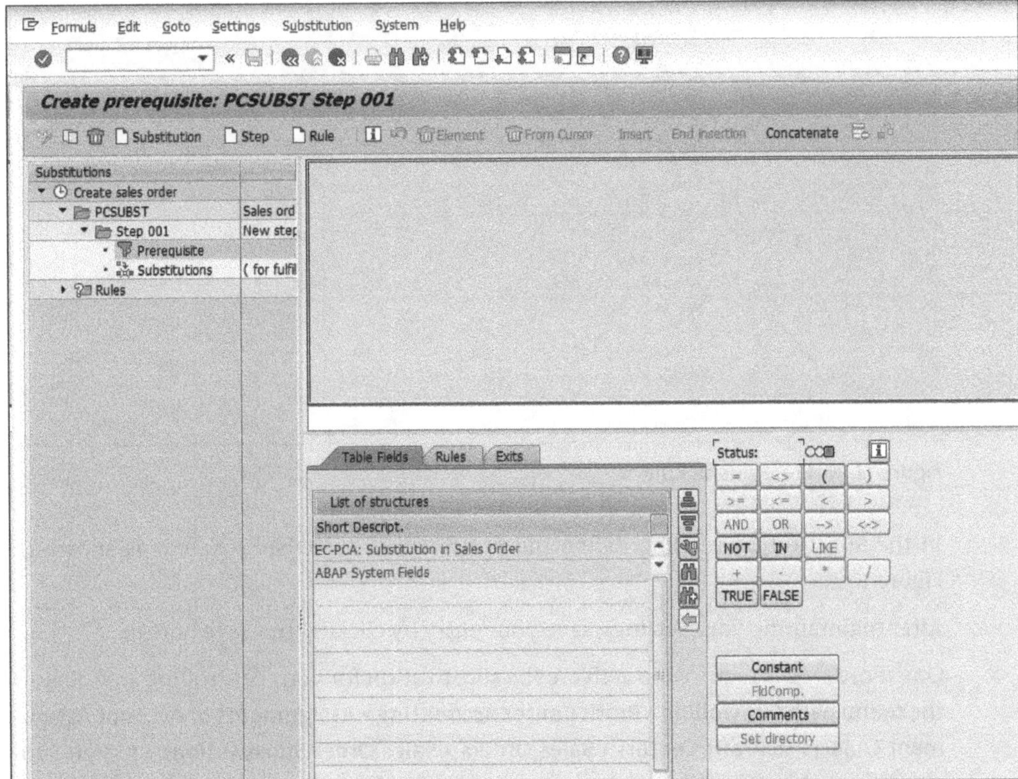

Figure 12.19 Substitution Prerequisite

You can choose from fields of **Structure PCASUB** or **Structure SYST** by double-clicking them. Then, you can click fields to add them to the prerequisite definition in the top part of the screen and use the mathematical and logical operators on the right side of the screen to construct the rule. The screen shown in Figure 12.20 depicts a rule based on the sales district.

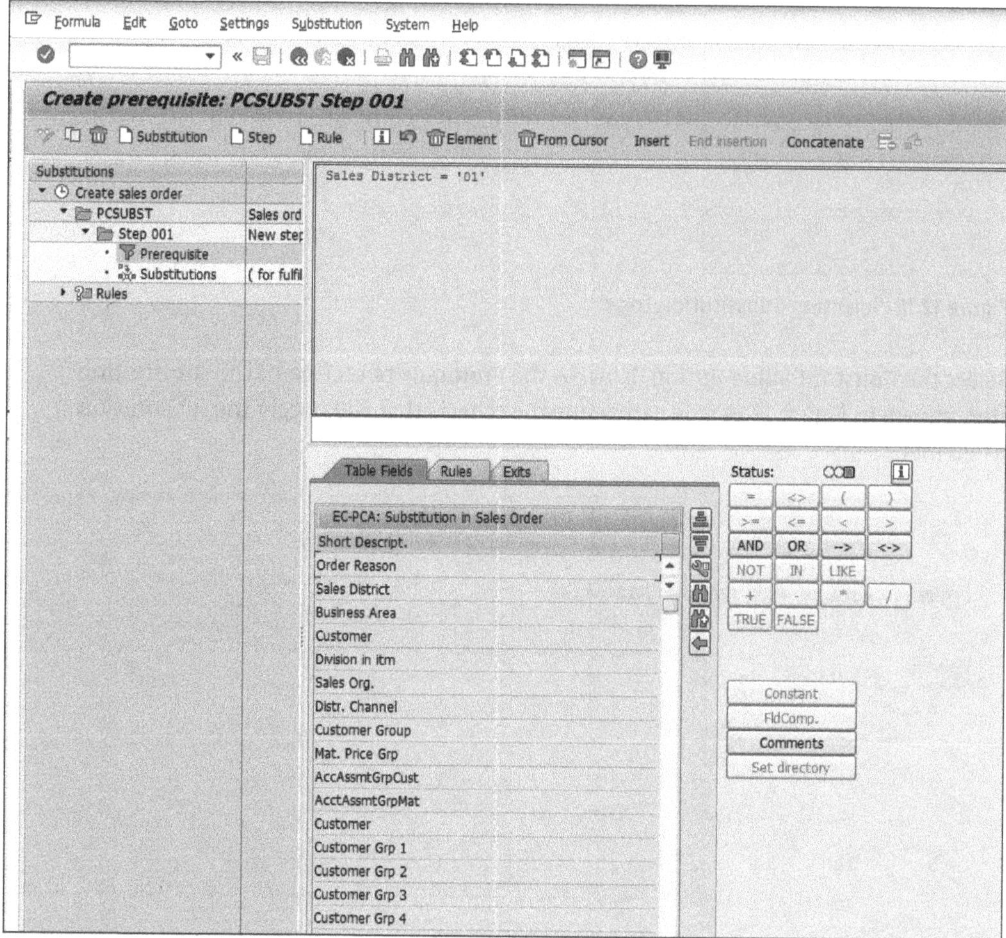

Figure 12.20 Prerequisite Rule

In the **Substitution** section, define the profit center to be substituted, as shown in Figure 12.21.

After maintaining your settings, save your entry by clicking the **Save** button.

One more step is required to activate the substitution for your controlling area. Follow the menu path **Controlling • Profit Center Accounting • Assignments of Account Assignment Objects to Profit Centers • Sales Orders • Sales Order Substitutions • Assign Substitution Rules**. Then, click **New Entries** from the top menu and activate the substitution, as shown in Figure 12.22.

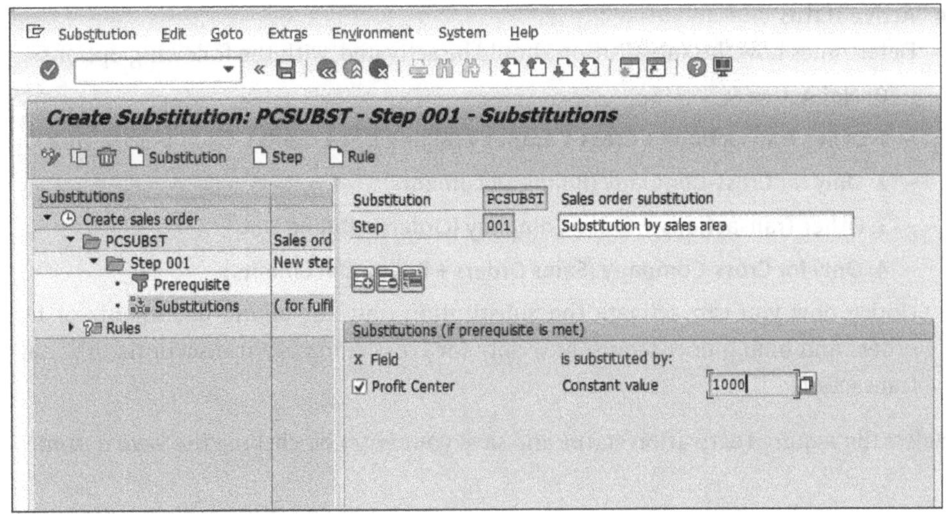

Figure 12.21 Substitution Defined

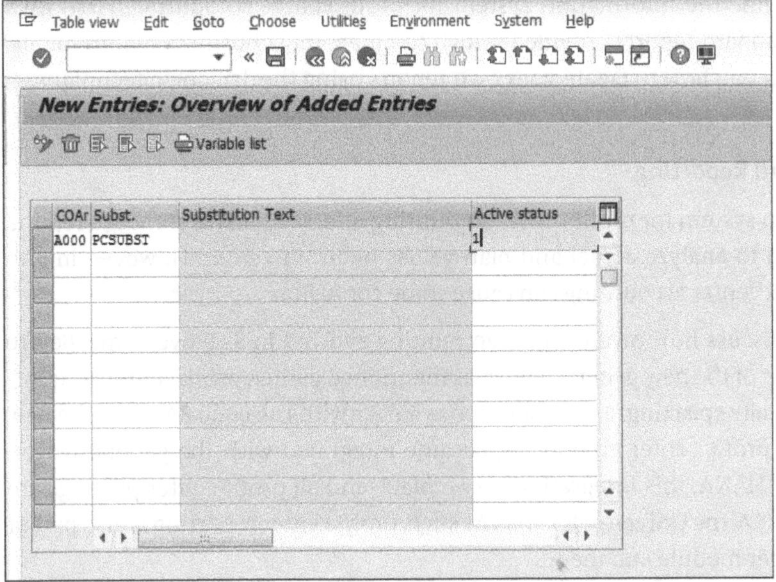

Figure 12.22 Activate Substitution

The following fields must be configured on this screen:

- **COAr (controlling area)**
  The controlling area for which you are activating the substitution.
- **Subst. (substitution)**
  The substitution created in the previous transaction.

- **Active status**
  Determines how the substitution should be activated, with the following options:
  - **0: Not Active**
  - **1: Other Transactions + Cross-Company (Billing Documents)**
  - **2: Only for Cross-Company (Billing Documents)**
  - **3: Other Transactions + Cross-Company (Orders + Billing Doc.)**
  - **4: Only for Cross-Company (Sales Orders + Billing Documents)**

  Notice how you can activate the substitution only for billing documents or for orders and billing documents, and only for cross-company transactions or for all transactions.

Select the required activation status and save your entry by clicking the **Save** button.

12.3 Information System

Let's now examine the information system for profit center accounting. First, we'll examine the standard reports provided, which can meet most business requirements. Then, we'll show you how to create your own reports using the drilldown technique.

12.3.1 Standard Reporting

The information system for profit center accounting offers extensive standard reports that enable you to analyze actual and plan values by profit center. However, in SAP S/4HANA, profit center accounting can cause some confusion.

We first must discuss how profit center accounting evolved in SAP over time. Before the introduction of the new general ledger, as mentioned earlier, profit center accounting was, technically speaking, a special purpose ledger with the code 8A. With the new general ledger, profit center accounting became integrated with the general ledger. Now, in SAP S/4HANA, this integration is complete, and all profit center postings are part of table ACDOCA, the Universal Journal. As such, profit center reporting is also part of the general ledger module and menu.

However, in the profit center application menu, SAP keeps the older reports based on the 8A ledger and library. These reports could be useful for you during a migration project for reconciling old profit center reports and are available at the application menu path **Accounting • Controlling • Profit Center Accounting • Information System • Reports for Profit Center Accounting**, as shown in Figure 12.23.

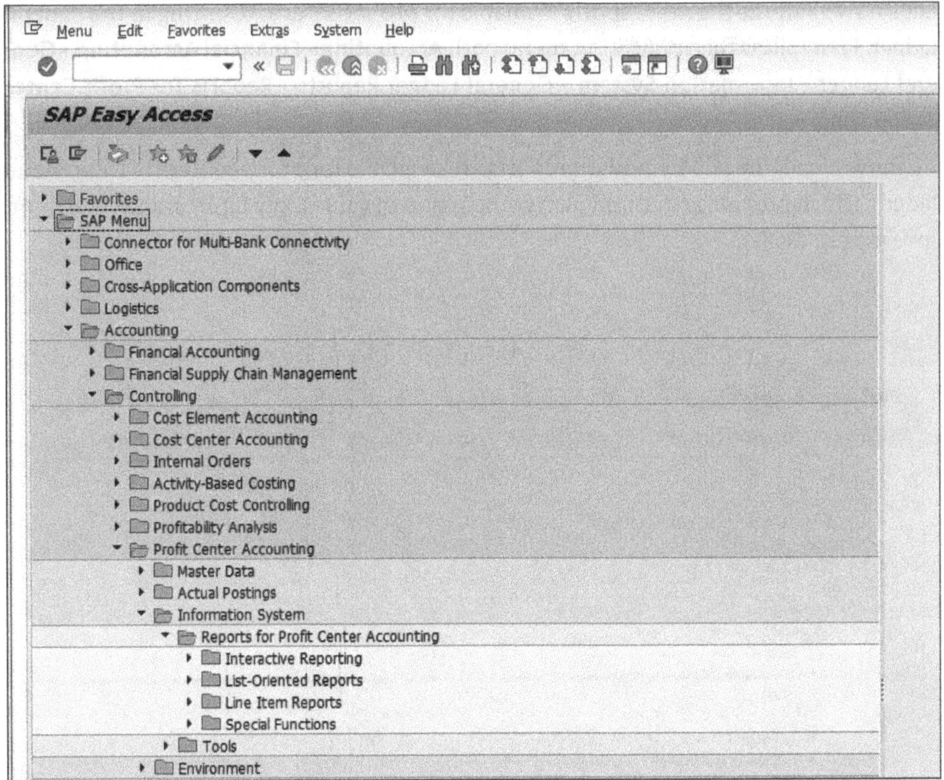

Figure 12.23 Profit Center Classic Reports

On this screen, you'll see that these classic reports are grouped into the following major sections:

- **Interactive Reporting**
  The interactive reports use the drilldown reporting tool and enable you to drill down in real time to various sections of the report to obtain further relevant information.
- **List-Oriented Reports**
  List-oriented reports are designed using Report Painter and offer valuable actual/plan comparisons, similar to the cost center reports we analyzed in Chapter 10.
- **Line Item Reports**
  Line-item reports provide reporting on the lowest level, the individual line items per profit center.
- **Special Functions**
  In this category, you can find more rarely used reports, such as average balance reports, transfer price reports, and reports related to transfers of profit center data to the executive information system.

Let's now examine the new reports available for profit center accounting in the general ledger. First follow the application menu path **Accounting • Financial Accounting • General Ledger • Information System • General Ledger Reports • Reports for Profit Center Accounting.**

As shown in Figure 12.24, standard reports are available for profit centers in the general ledger, which provide actual and plan comparison of values, key figures, and returns on investment (ROIs).

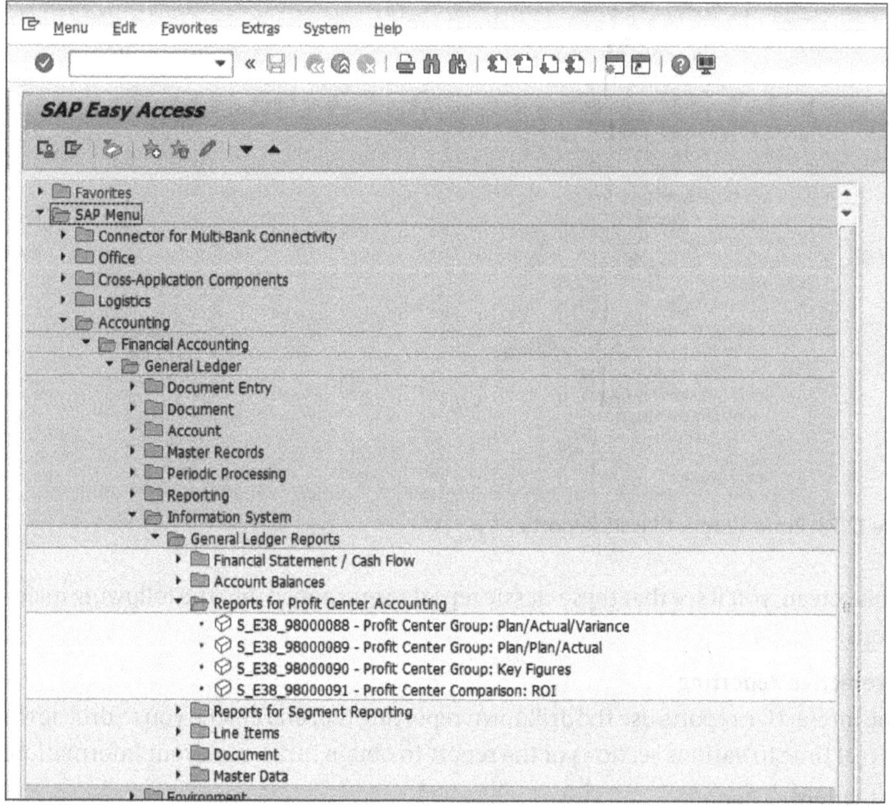

Figure 12.24 New Profit Center Reports

Enter Transaction S_E38_98000088 (Profit Center Group: Plan/Actual/Variance). After selecting profit centers/profit center groups, date parameters, a ledger, a currency, and a version, as shown in Figure 12.25 you'll see the output screen, shown in Figure 12.26.

This report is a drilldown-based report. On the left side, you can navigate through the various available characteristics, such as profit center, segment, cost element, and so on. On the right side, you'll see the values for the selection in separate **Plan**, **Actual**, and **Variance** columns.

This report, as well as the other profit center reports in the general ledger, was developed using the drilldown reporting tool, which in previous SAP releases was heavily used in controlling. Now, in SAP S/4HANA, numerous standard drilldown reports are available for financial accounting as well, which provide valuable information on the profit center level.

You can get a good overview and access all of them using Transaction FGIO. This transaction provides a tree-like structure showing the available reports by report type, as shown in Figure 12.27.

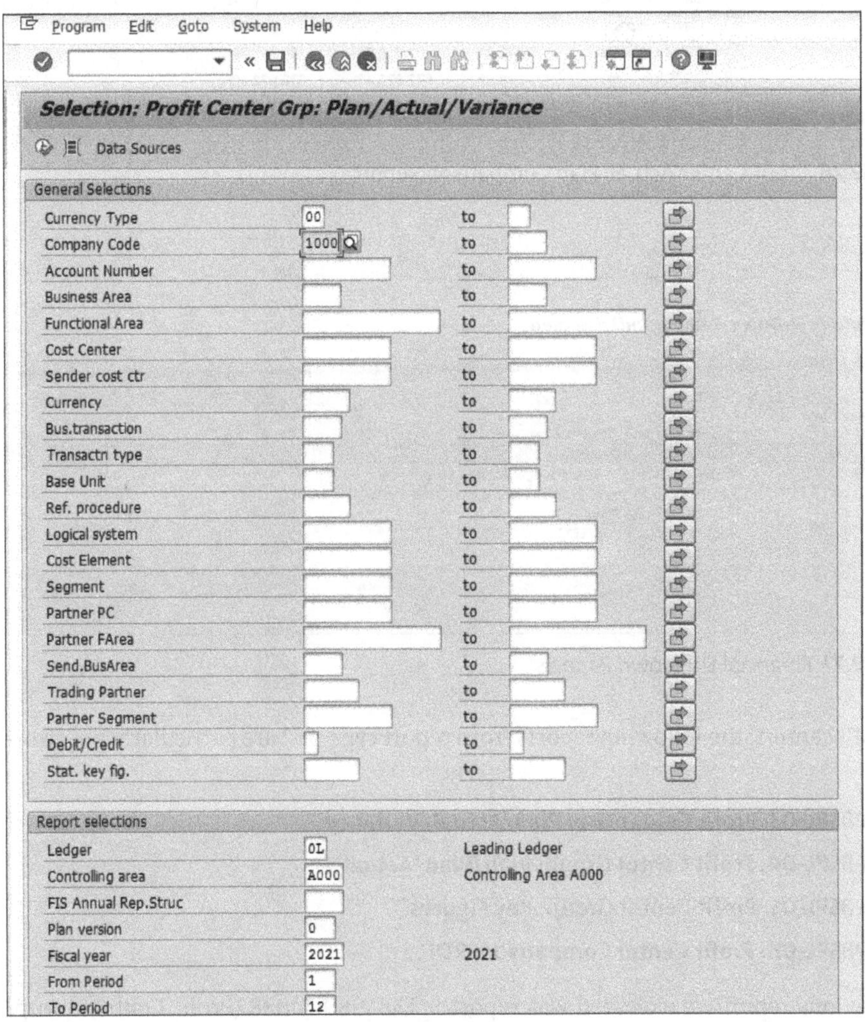

Figure 12.25 Profit Center Actual/Plan Comparison Report Selections

Selection date

Profit Center Grp: Plan/Actual/Variance

Navigation	P.	N.	Text
Currency			
EUR	^	v	Euro
FS Item/Account			
Account Number			
Cost Element			
Segment			
Profit Center			
Partner PC			
Business Area			
Functional Area			

FS Item/Account	Plan	Actual	Variance	Var. %
Customers - Do	0,00	116.506,40	116.506,40	x/o
Discount receive	0,00	1.700,67-	1.700,67-	x/o
Discounts	0,00	2.087,12	2.087,12	x/o
Down payments	0,00	91.136,46-	91.136,46-	x/o
Finished goods	0,00	426.989,79	426.989,79	x/o
Gain from curre	0,00	0,00	0,00	x/o
Gain from price	0,00	214,89-	214,89-	x/o
Gain from valua	0,00	30.713,79-	30.713,79-	x/o
GR/IR-clearing -	0,00	672.972,43-	672.972,43-	x/o
Initial entry of st	0,00	7.112,52-	7.112,52-	x/o

Figure 12.26 Profit Center Actual/Plan Comparison Report

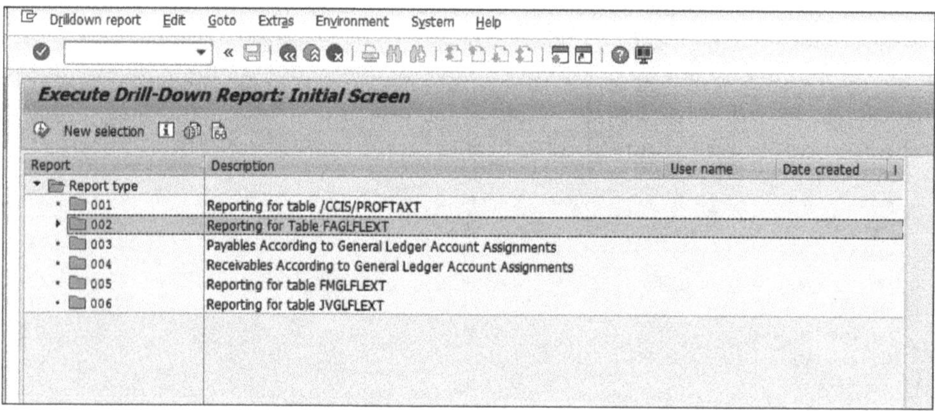

Figure 12.27 Financial Drilldown Reports

For profit centers, the following reports from report type 002 are particularly noteworthy:

- **0SAPBSPL-03: Profit Center Grp: Plan/Actual/Variance**
- **0SAPBSPL-04: Profit Center Group: Plan/Plan/Actual**
- **0SAPBSPL-05: Profit Center Group: Key Figures**
- **0SAPBSPL-06: Profit Center Comparison: ROI**

The previous report we executed was report S_E38_98000088 (Profit Center Group: Plan/Actual/Variance), which in fact is the same as report 0SAPBSPL-03 (Profit Center Grp: Plan/Actual/Variance), already defined here. You can also execute and analyze the other reports, which can provide you with plan values from more than one version, with calculation of the ROI (based on financial statement items you specify in the selections) and the key figures.

12.3.2 Drilldown Reporting

You can also define your own profit center reports, similar to the standard ones in Transaction FGIO. Drilldown reports for profit centers are thus quite flexible and interactive.

Drilldown reports usually are created by referencing a form. The form is like a template that already contains the characteristics and key figures used in the report and the structure of columns and rows.

To create a new form, enter Transaction FGI4. In the initial creation screen, shown in Figure 12.28, first select the report type. Use **Reporting for Table FAGLFLEXT** for a profit center report on the general ledger level, **Payables According to General Ledger Account Assignments** for reports on the vendor level, and **Receivables According to General Ledger Account Assignments** for reports on the customer level. Then, enter your form name starting with Z or Y in the custom name range and its description.

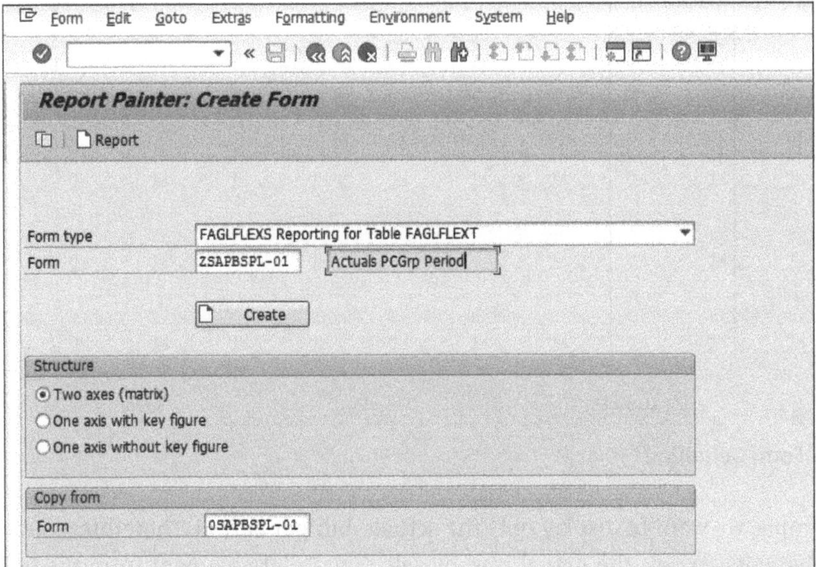

Figure 12.28 Creating a Form

In the **Structure** section, you have the following three options:

- **Two axes (matrix)**
  In forms with two axes, you'll define both the columns and the rows.
- **One axis with key figure**
  In one-axis forms, you'll define only one dimension (columns or rows). In this case, you'll also define the key figures within the form.
- **One axis without key figure**
  In this case, you'll define the key figures only during the report creation.

Enter the standard form "0SAPBSPL-03" in the **Copy from** section to create a new form using the specified form as a reference. Then, click the **Create** button.

Figure 12.29 shows the definition screen for the form. In the rows, the various key figures used in the form are defined, such as plan and actual values.

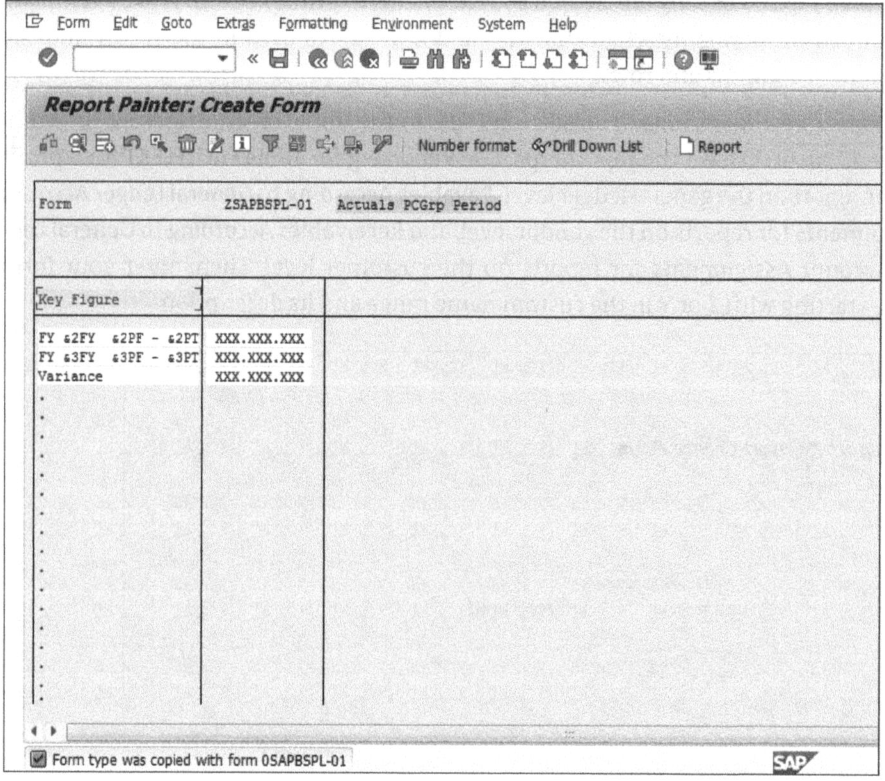

Figure 12.29 Form Definition

For our example, we want to display only the actuals, but per period. Therefore, delete the other elements, except the **Actual** row, by selecting **Delete element** from the top menu. First, start with the **Variance** rows at the end because they're formulas; the **Plan** rows can be deleted only after that.

Then, double-click the **Actual** line, and a popup window will display the definition of the row.

Figure 12.30 shows that the **Key figure** used is the balance sheet value, which is fine. **Fiscal Year** is a variable, to be entered at report execution. **Posting period** is a variable, asking the user to enter to and from periods, which will be displayed cumulatively in the same column. Instead, we want to make a report that will show the values per quarter in separate columns. So, we want four different columns, showing the values for periods 1–3, 4–6, 7–9, and 10–12.

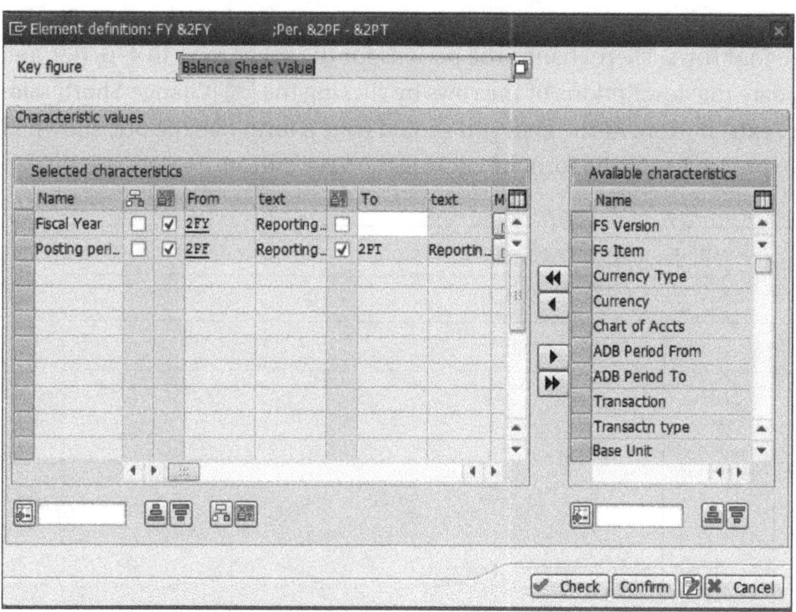

Figure 12.30 Actual Values Definition

Next, change the posting periods to 1–3, as shown in Figure 12.31.

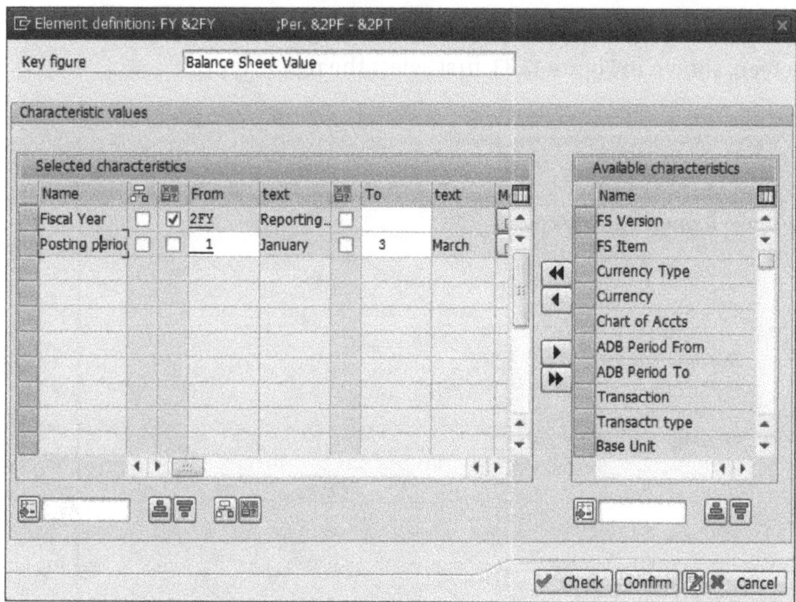

Figure 12.31 Actual Values per Period

After that, copy that row three more times and adjust the periods to represent the other quarters by selecting the row by right-clicking it, then choosing **Select/deselect**. Now, move your cursor to the next empty row and select **Copy** from the top menu. Do this until you have four rows. Then, change the periods for the other rows to 4–6, 7–9, and 10–12. Also update the descriptions of the rows by clicking the (**Change Short, Middle, and Long Texts**) button. At the end, you should have a form like the one shown in Figure 12.32. To proceed, save the form by clicking the **Save** button.

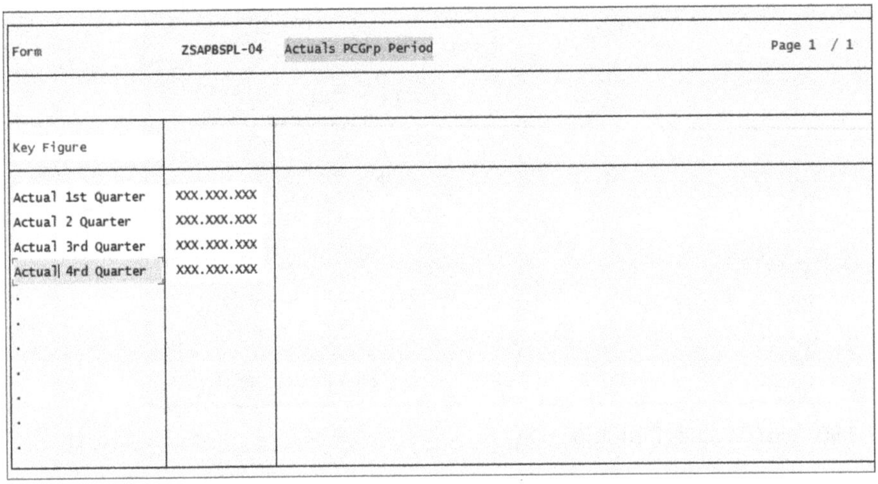

Form	ZSAPBSPL-04 Actuals PCGrp Period	Page 1 / 1
Key Figure		
Actual 1st Quarter	XXX.XXX.XXX	
Actual 2 Quarter	XXX.XXX.XXX	
Actual 3rd Quarter	XXX.XXX.XXX	
Actual 4rd Quarter	XXX.XXX.XXX	

Figure 12.32 Form Actuals Per Quarter

Now, you're ready to create a new report. Start by entering Transaction FGI1. In the initial creation screen, shown in Figure 12.33, first select the report type.

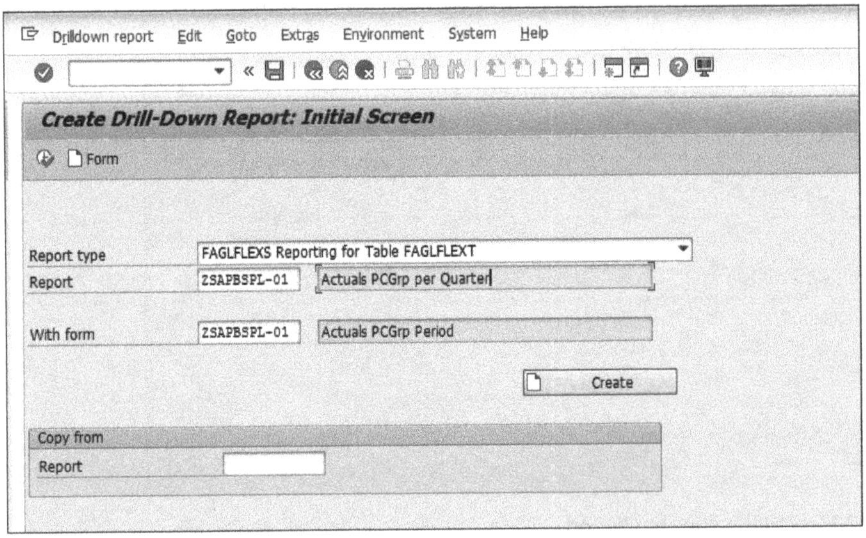

Drilldown report Edit Goto Extras Environment System Help

Create Drill-Down Report: Initial Screen

Form

Report type	FAGLFLEXS Reporting for Table FAGLFLEXT	
Report	ZSAPBSPL-01	Actuals PCGrp per Quarter
With form	ZSAPBSPL-01	Actuals PCGrp Period

Create

Copy from

Report

Figure 12.33 Creating a Drilldown Report

Use **FAGLFLEXS: Reporting for Table FAGLFLEXT** for profit center reports on the general ledger level, **Payables According to General Ledger Account Assignments** for reports on the vendor level, and **Receivables According to General Ledger Account Assignments** for reports on the customer level. Then, enter your report name (starting with Z or Y in the custom name range) and its description. Specify a form in the **With form** field. In this case, enter the form you created in the previous step, ZSAPBSPL-04. Finally, click the **Create** button.

We already defined the structure of the report in the form at the beginning of this section. On the screen shown in Figure 12.34, you can define default values for the characteristics if needed or enter additional characteristics.

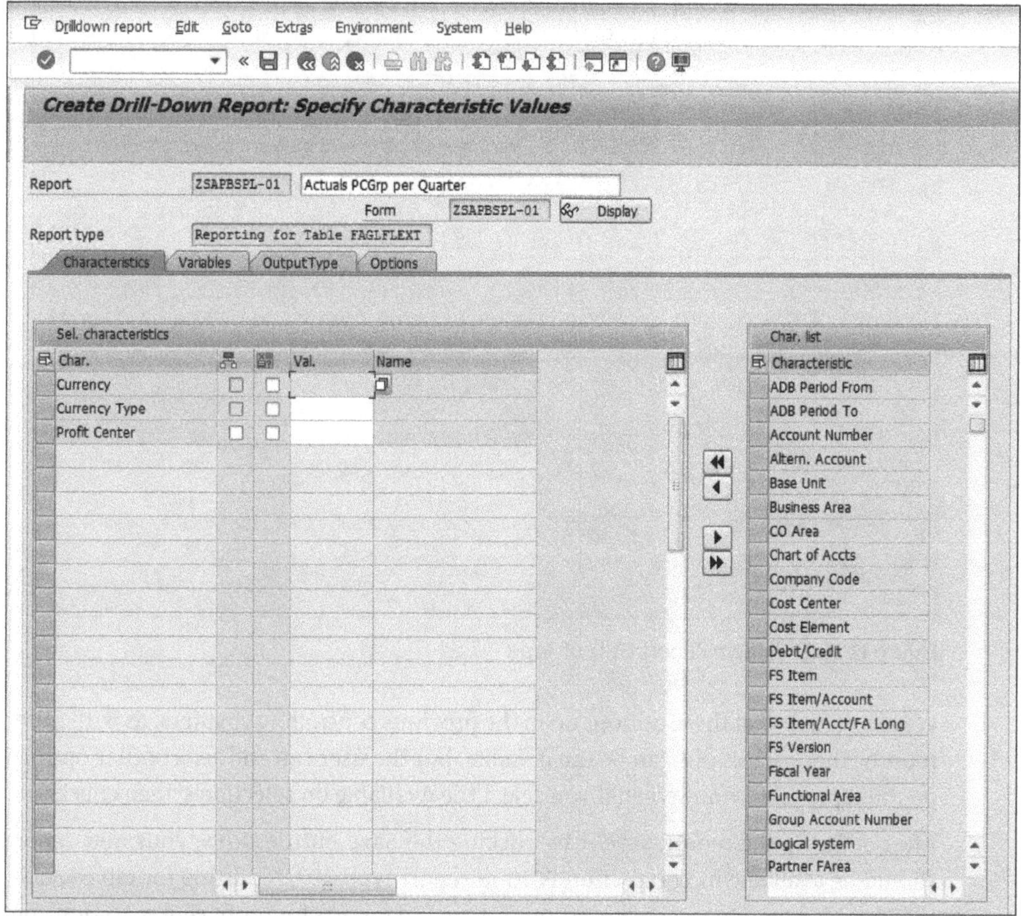

Figure 12.34 Drilldown Report Definition

Enter the profit center by selecting it on the right side, where all the available characteristics appear, and move it to the selected characteristics by clicking the < (**Add Char.**) button.

Under the **OutputType** tab, you can define some options for the output of the report, as shown in Figure 12.35. You can choose the default output of the report:

- **Graphical Report Output**
- **Classic drilldown**
- **Object list (ALV)**
- **XXL (Spreadsheet)**

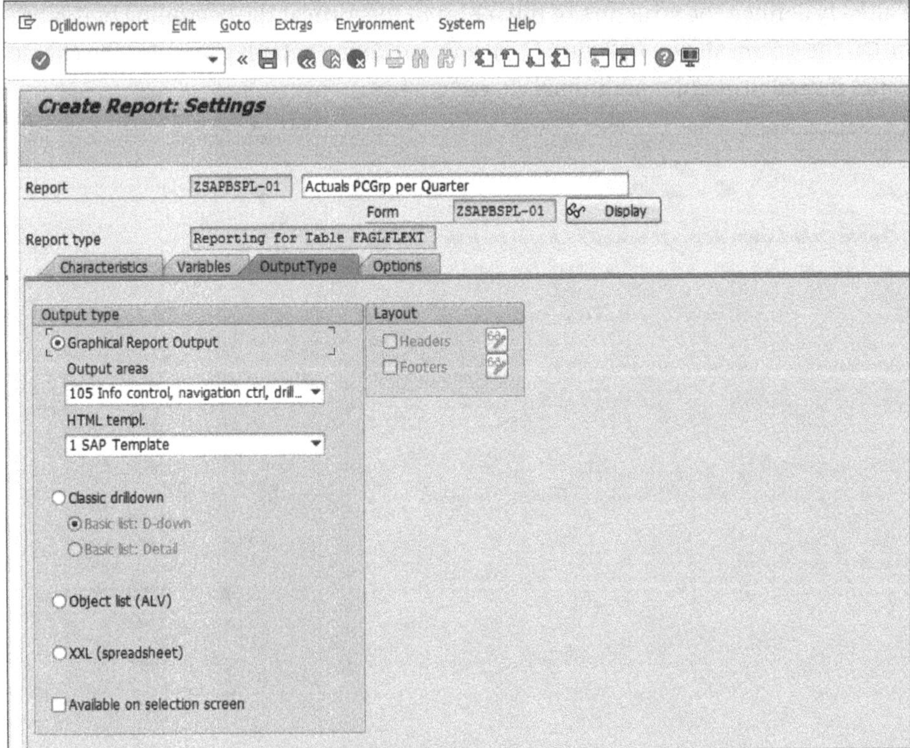

Figure 12.35 Drilldown Report Output Type

We examined what these options do in the previous controlling chapters. As with other reports, these selections can be the defaults, but the user can still select other options on the report selection screen if you select the **Available on selection screen** checkbox.

After defining the report, save it by clicking the **Save** button. Now, your new report should be available in Transaction FGIO in report type 002, reporting for table FAGLFLEXT. In this way, you can create various forms and reports for profit center accounting, which can provide you with invaluable management analysis.

12.4 Summary

In this chapter, we covered the functionalities and configuration of profit center accounting in SAP S/4HANA. For users with a background in SAP ERP, this change is a major change because profit center accounting is now fully integrated with the general ledger and no longer uses a separate special purpose ledger. Still, logically and functionally, profit center accounting is part of management accounting and therefore is positioned in the controlling application and configuration menus in SAP S/4HANA.

After reading this chapter, you should be familiar with and ready to configure the following in your SAP S/4HANA project:

- Profit center master data
- Profit center derivations and actual postings
- Information system

Properly designed profit center master data is the foundation for correct, transparent, and effective management reporting. Equally important is to set up the derivation of profit centers using the various techniques you learned in this chapter because profit centers are almost always derived automatically through proper configuration. Finally, the drilldown reporting techniques you learned in this chapter should be quite useful. You can create powerful reports using this technique, not only for profit centers but also in other controlling and financial areas.

In the next chapter, we'll show you how to configure margin analysis, which is one of the functional areas that benefits the most from the power and flexibility of SAP S/4HANA.

Chapter 13
Margin Analysis

This chapter provides step-by-step instructions for configuring margin analysis, which is how account-based profitability analysis is now repositioned in SAP S/4HANA. Our emphasis in this chapter is on margin analysis, which is now the mandatory form of profitability analysis in SAP S/4HANA, but you'll also learn about costing-based profitability analysis, which is optional.

13

Margin analysis, one of the most important controlling areas, provides detailed analysis of the profitability of a company, thus enabling accurate contribution margin calculation. This functionality can calculate profitability on the level of numerous characteristics, which can be configured when implementing SAP S/4HANA. Therefore, the initial setup and configuration is of paramount importance to the correctness and flexibility of profitability analysis. This highly integrated area receives almost all its data from other areas, such as sales, purchasing, production, and finance. Manual postings in profitability analysis are rare.

Margin analysis is the newer term used by SAP for account-based profitability analysis, although the SAP GUI application and configuration menus still use the term "profitability analysis," whereas the newer SAP Fiori apps use the term "margin analysis." We'll use these terms interchangeably.

In this chapter, we'll provide an extensive guide to the global settings for margin analysis. We'll then analyze in detail the settings and processes for the various data flows into margin analysis, and finally, we'll guide you through its information system. Before attacking this extensive workload, we must start with some general information on how it evolved in SAP and a discussion of the differences between the two types of profitability (margin) analysis: account-based and costing-based.

13.1 Overview of Margin Analysis

For a long time, margin analysis was a core component of controlling in SAP because it provides answers to the most important questions for high-level management: How profitable is the company? How well is this segment performing? How profitable is this product? What is the contribution margin of that division? And so on. But the power and flexibility of profitability analysis mostly lies in its multidimensional structure.

You can analyze profitability not in only one or two dimensions, but in as many dimensions as are needed and configured in the system. Therefore, margin analysis is often referred to as a multidimensional cube, as shown in Figure 13.1.

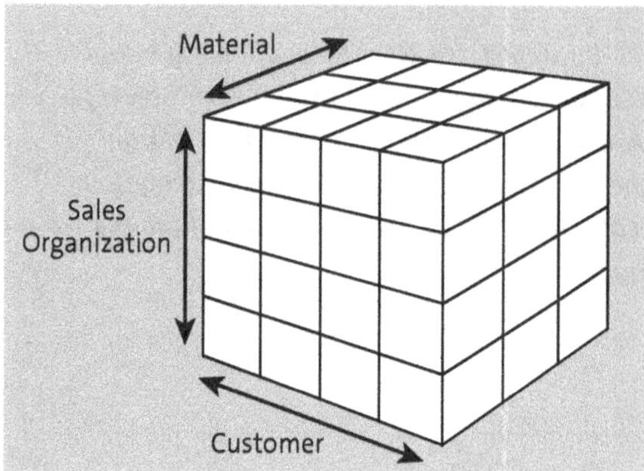

Figure 13.1 Margin Analysis Multidimensional Cube

The dimensions are the different characteristics by which the data is sliced and diced from a profitability analysis point of view, such as material, customer, sales organization, and so on. Each posting transferred to profitability analysis contains several characteristics, which together constitute a multidimensional profitability segment.

Two types of profitability analysis exist: account-based (margin analysis) and costing-based. We'll explain these types in detail in the following sections.

13.1.1 Costing-Based Profitability Analysis

Costing-based profitability analysis analyzes profitability using value fields such as material costs, discounts, revenues, and so on. These value fields can be regarded as buckets into which similar values are grouped. Costing-based profitability analysis was the most used type of profitability analysis in previous SAP releases.

Costing-based profitability analysis is rather powerful because these value fields can be defined as required in each SAP client, thus allowing for a great degree of flexibility. From a data point of view, costing-based profitability analysis uses the following tables:

- CE1xxxx (actual line-item table)
- CE2xxxx (plan line-item table)
- CE3xxxx (segment level)
- CE4xxxx (segment table)

In this nomenclature, xxxx stands for the name of the operating concern. For example, if the operating concern is 1000, the actual line-item table will be CE11000, the plan line-item table will be CE21000, and so on.

Some limitations exist with costing-based profitability analysis. For example, one challenge is reconciling costing-based profitability analysis with financial accounting. This need for reconciliation stems from the very essence of costing-based profitability analysis: The value fields don't match the accounts used in financial accounting. Furthermore, differences exist between the value flow to financial accounting and the value flow to profitability analysis. The basic sales process involves creating a sales order, then delivery with goods issue, and finally sending an invoice document to the customer. In financial accounting, the cost of goods sold (COGS) is posted with the goods issue and the sales revenue with the invoice. In costing-based profitability analysis, however, both the sales revenue and COGS are transferred with the invoice document. This scenario can lead to mismatches between financial accounting and profitability analysis at month end.

These considerations prompted many companies to adopt margin analysis.

13.1.2 Account-Based Profitability Analysis/Margin Analysis

Margin analysis uses accounts (cost elements) to collect profitability values. Therefore, by design, margin analysis easy to reconcile it with financial accounting. However, in SAP ERP and earlier versions, it had some considerable limitations. COGS couldn't be split among different cost components, which is possible in costing-based profitability analysis. Also, variance analysis was only possible for total variance, but not by variance category. Thus, costing-based profitability analysis was the choice for most companies prior to SAP S/4HANA, and account-based profitability analysis was sometimes implemented in parallel to facilitate accounting reconciliation processes.

As discussed in the introduction of this book, SAP has made huge improvements to profitability analysis with SAP S/4HANA, and more specifically to margin analysis. Now, in SAP S/4HANA, the advantages of costing-based profitability analysis are available in margin analysis, combined with easy reconciliation with financial accounting. Cost component splits are now possible in margin analysis. Also, variance analysis is made possible by variance categories. Therefore, in SAP S/4HANA, you can construct a profit and loss (P&L) statement with a contribution margin calculation, very much like in costing-based profitability analysis.

With these considerations in mind, in SAP S/4HANA, margin analysis is not only the recommended approach but is also the required approach. You can activate costing-based profitability analysis in addition if you choose. However, our recommendation for a greenfield SAP S/4HANA implementation is to use only margin analysis. You'll enjoy all the benefits of costing-based profitability analysis now in the account-based version. For brownfield implementations, continuing to use the costing-based approach together with the now mandatory account-based approach makes sense.

From a technical point of view, margin analysis doesn't create any additional tables. The segment postings update table ACDOCA, the Universal Journal, thus making margin analysis fully integrated with financial accounting.

Now, let's delve deeply into the secrets of the profitability analysis configuration. We'll start with the global settings.

13.2 Master Data

In this section, we'll set up the master data structures required for margin analysis. The main organizational object for profitability analysis is the operating concern. We discussed operating concerns in Chapter 3, Section 3.2.4, so we'll just briefly revisit this subject to create a new operating concern for our controlling area. We'll then create the characteristics and value fields for the operating concern. The value fields are used only in costing-based profitability analysis, whereas the characteristics are the foundation of both types of profitability analysis.

13.2.1 Operating Concern

Assigned to a controlling area, the *operating concern* is an organizational object that enables you to analyze an organization from a profitability point of view. To create an operating concern, follow the menu path **Enterprise Structure • Definition • Controlling • Create Operating Concern.**

Figure 13.2 shows some standard operating concern templates provided by SAP. To create a new operating concern, select **A001** by selecting the checkbox to its left and selecting **Copy As...** from the top menu. Name the new operating concern "US01" and enter "US Operating Concern" for the description. Then, save your entry by clicking the **Save** button.

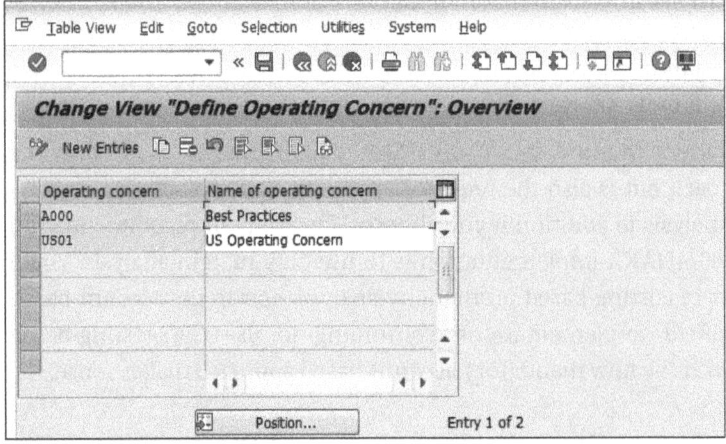

Figure 13.2 Operating Concern

13.2.2 Data Structure

After creating an operating concern, you'll need to define its data structure. This structure consists of characteristics and value fields (in the case of costing-based operating concerns), as we'll see in the following sections.

Characteristics

Characteristics in profitability analysis define the criteria by which you classify the values in profitability analysis. Characteristics are required both for margin analysis and costing-based profitability analysis.

These standard characteristics are delivered by SAP, such as customer, material, profit center, cost center, company code, and so on. You also can create additional custom characteristics specific to your organization. A limitation exists on the number of custom characteristics that can be defined: up to 50 in the older SAP ERP system and now up to 60 in SAP S/4HANA.

To maintain characteristics, follow the menu path **Controlling • Profitability Analysis • Structures • Define Operating Concern • Maintain Characteristics.** On the initial screen, shown in Figure 13.3, you can choose to maintain all characteristics or only those assigned to a specific operating concern or not assigned. Select **All Characteristics** and click the **Change** button.

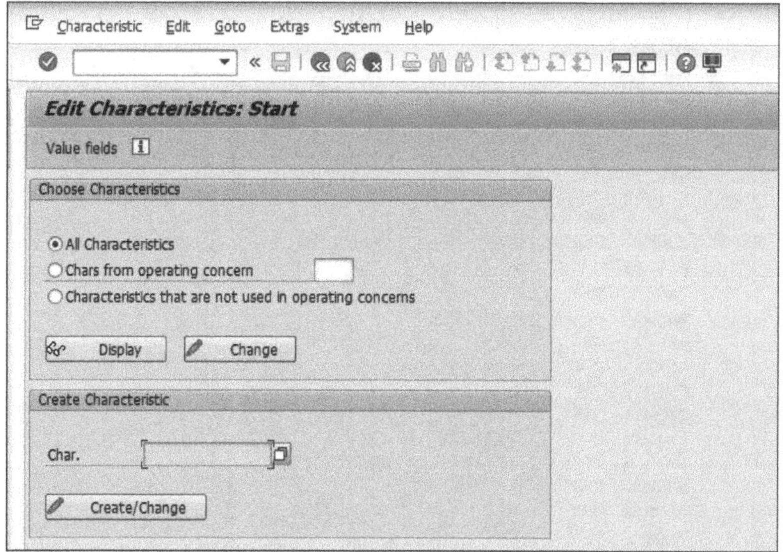

Figure 13.3 Defining Characteristics

The system issues a warning that you're changing cross-client data, as shown in Figure 13.4.

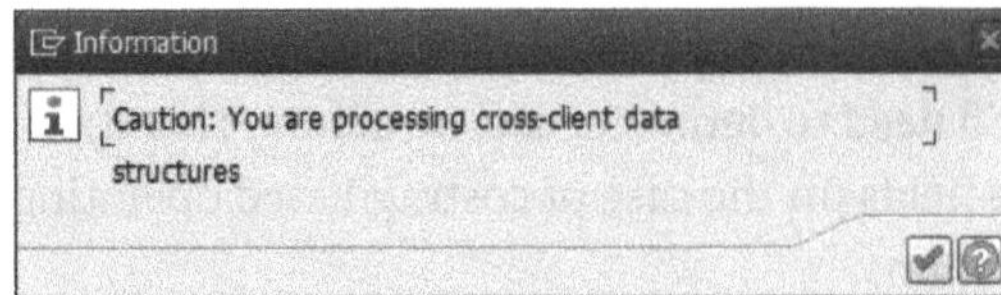

Figure 13.4 Cross-Client Data Warning

Profitability analysis structures are cross-client and can be changed only in a client that allows cross-client customizing. This client should be your golden customizing client. Once changed in that client, changes will be available immediately in other clients within the same instance. Proceed by clicking the **Continue** button.

You'll see a list of the characteristics defined in the system. All those characteristics shown in Figure 13.5 are standard characteristics provided by SAP. The naming convention for characteristics is that custom-defined characteristics should start with "WW."

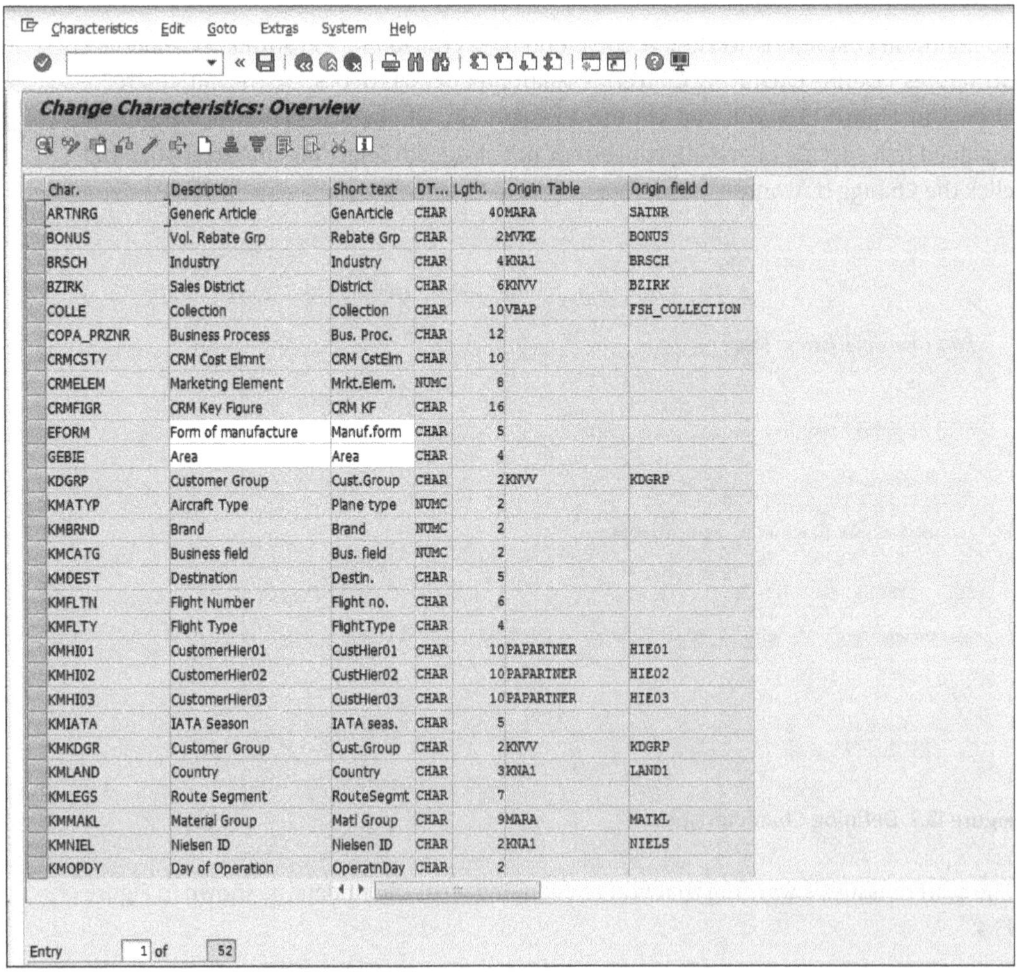

Characteristics Edit Goto Extras System Help

Change Characteristics: Overview

Char.	Description	Short text	DT...	Lgth.	Origin Table	Origin field d
ARTNRG	Generic Article	GenArticle	CHAR	40	MARA	SATNR
BONUS	Vol. Rebate Grp	Rebate Grp	CHAR	2	MVKE	BONUS
BRSCH	Industry	Industry	CHAR	4	KNA1	BRSCH
BZIRK	Sales District	District	CHAR	6	KNVV	BZIRK
COLLE	Collection	Collection	CHAR	10	VBAP	FSH_COLLECTION
COPA_PRZNR	Business Process	Bus. Proc.	CHAR	12		
CRMCSTY	CRM Cost Elmnt	CRM CstElm	CHAR	10		
CRMELEM	Marketing Element	Mrkt.Elem.	NUMC	8		
CRMFIGR	CRM Key Figure	CRM KF	CHAR	16		
EFORM	Form of manufacture	Manuf.form	CHAR	5		
GEBIE	Area	Area	CHAR	4		
KDGRP	Customer Group	Cust.Group	CHAR	2	KNVV	KDGRP
KMATYP	Aircraft Type	Plane type	NUMC	2		
KMBRND	Brand	Brand	NUMC	2		
KMCATG	Business field	Bus. field	NUMC	2		
KMDEST	Destination	Destin.	CHAR	5		
KMFLTN	Flight Number	Flight no.	CHAR	6		
KMFLTY	Flight Type	FlightType	CHAR	4		
KMHI01	CustomerHier01	CustHier01	CHAR	10	PAPARTNER	HIE01
KMHI02	CustomerHier02	CustHier02	CHAR	10	PAPARTNER	HIE02
KMHI03	CustomerHier03	CustHier03	CHAR	10	PAPARTNER	HIE03
KMIATA	IATA Season	IATA seas.	CHAR	5		
KMKDGR	Customer Group	Cust.Group	CHAR	2	KNVV	KDGRP
KMLAND	Country	Country	CHAR	3	KNA1	LAND1
KMLEGS	Route Segment	RouteSegmt	CHAR	7		
KMMAKL	Material Group	Matl Group	CHAR	9	MARA	MATKL
KMNIEL	Nielsen ID	Nielsen ID	CHAR	2	KNA1	NIELS
KMOPDY	Day of Operation	OperatnDay	CHAR	2		

Entry 1 of 52

Figure 13.5 Characteristics List

Notice that characteristics are defined by the settings in the following columns of this configuration table:

- **Char. (characteristic code)**
  The characteristic code. For standard characteristics, this code often corresponds to the field name to which it refers. For custom-defined characteristics, the characteristic code should start with "WW."
- **Description**
  A long description of the characteristic.
- **Short text**
  A short description of the characteristic.
- **DTyp (data type)**
  The data type of the characteristic. **CHAR** is used for alphanumerical values, and **NUMC**, for numerical values.
- **Lgth. (length)**
  The length of the characteristic, which defines the length of the values supplied by this characteristic.
- **Origin Table**
  The ABAP dictionary table from which the field is taken.
- **Origin field d**
  The field in the ABAP dictionary table from which the field is taken.

Let's now create a new custom characteristic. Go back to the previous screen, shown earlier in Figure 13.3, and enter a characteristic name starting with "WW" in the **Create Characteristic** section. For this example, let's create a characteristic called WWGRP to represent a customer group. Then, click the **Create/Change** button.

A popup window appears, as shown in Figure 13.6, in which you'll need to define how the data will be retrieved for this characteristic.

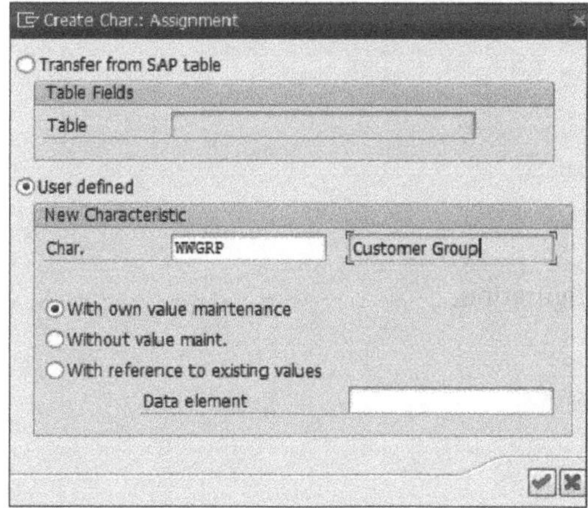

Figure 13.6 Creating a Characteristic

In this window, you must configure the following fields:

- **Transfer from SAP table/User defined**
  Two options are available: transferring the field from an SAP table, which you can specify in the **Table** field, or creating a custom characteristic starting with (WW).
- **With own value maintenance**
  With this option, you can create your own check table in which you'll maintain the possible values of the characteristic.
- **Without value maint.**
  Used for characteristics for which you don't define values.
- **With reference to existing values**
  With this option, you can define a characteristic that has the same data structure as an already existing field. The characteristic contains the same technical properties and the same value set as the referenced field.

Proceed by clicking the **Create** button. On the screen shown in Figure 13.7, you'll define the characteristic next.

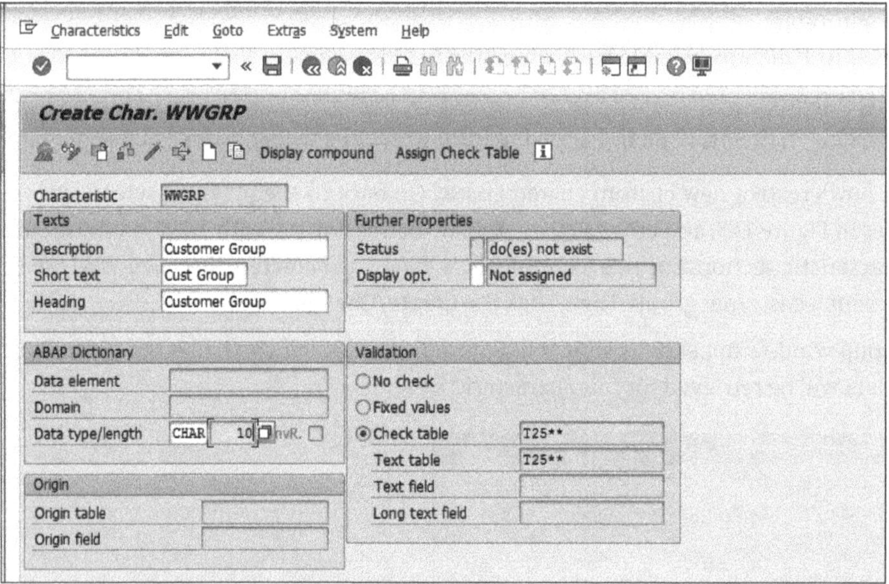

Figure 13.7 Characteristic Configuration

The following fields are available for configuration:

- **Description**
  A long description of the characteristic.
- **Short text**
  A short description of the characteristic.

- **Heading**
  A description of the characteristic used as a column heading.
- **Data element**
  A characteristic can be defined with reference to an existing data element.
- **Domain**
  The data domain of the existing data element the characteristic refers to.
- **Data type**
  The data type of the characteristic. **CHAR** stands for alphanumerical values, and **NUMC**, for numerical values.
- **Data length**
  The length of the characteristic, which defines the length of the values supplied by this characteristic.
- **Origin table**
  The ABAP dictionary table from which the field is taken.
- **Origin field**
  The field in the ABAP dictionary table from which the field is taken.
- **Check table/Text table**
  When creating a characteristic that doesn't refer to an existing field, the system creates check tables in which you can maintain the values of the characteristic.

After configuring the characteristic, you'll need to activate it. Select **Activate** from the top menu. Then, a popup window appears with a message regarding the check tables, as shown in Figure 13.8.

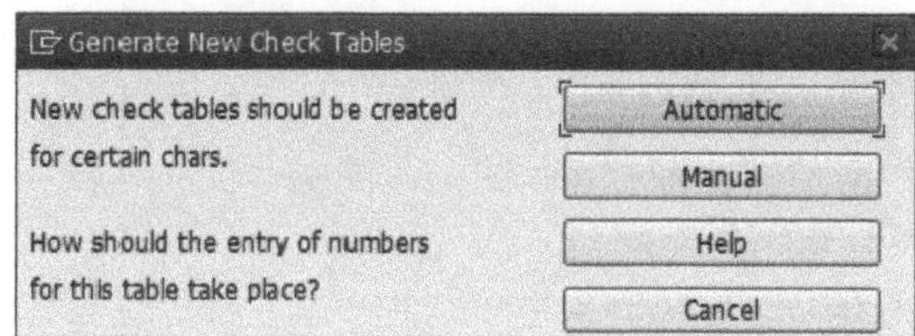

Figure 13.8 Check Table Message

The new check tables can be created automatically or manually. If you have only one SAP system in your landscape, you can click **Automatic** and let the system assign the table names. However, if you have more than one system, we recommend creating your check tables manually to avoid inconsistencies.

After you've maintained these settings, save the characteristic by clicking the **Save** button. The check tables are filled in automatically, as shown in Figure 13.9.

In the next step, you must select the characteristics to be used in the operating concern. Follow the menu path **Controlling • Profitability Analysis • Structures • Define Operating Concern • Maintain Operating Concern**.

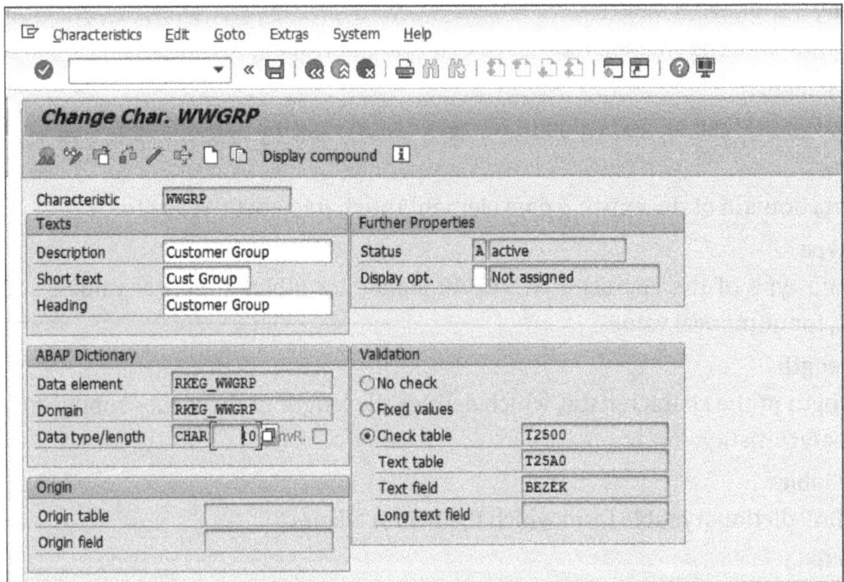

Figure 13.9 Saved Characteristic

Figure 13.10 shows the screen in which you define the data structure of the operating concern.

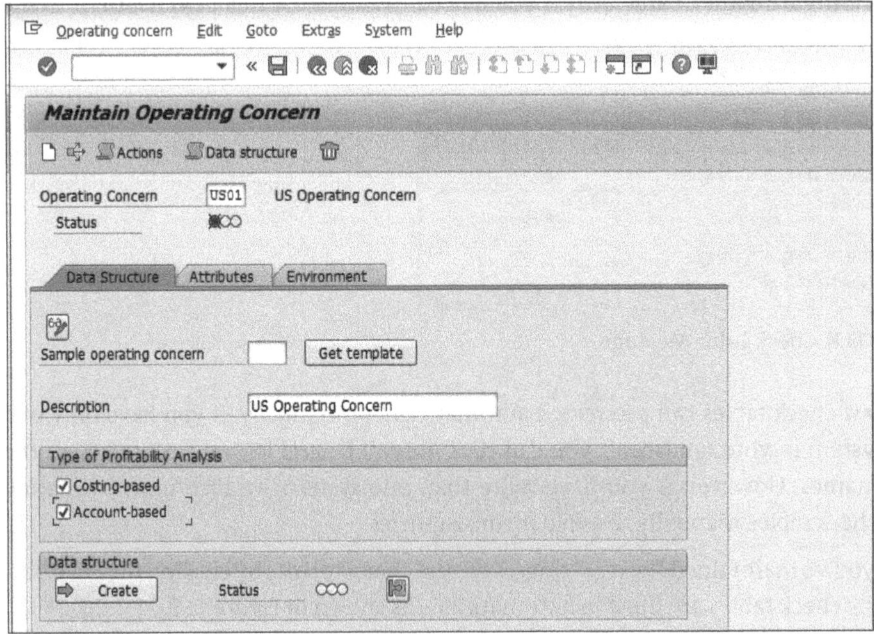

Figure 13.10 Maintaining an Operating Concern

Enter "US01" in the **Operating Concern** field and click the button to switch from display to change mode. Then, activate both the costing-based profitability analysis and margin analysis by selecting both checkboxes in the **Type of Profitability Analysis** section. Click the → **Create** button to select the characteristics for the operating concern.

On the next screen, shown in Figure 13.11, you'll see that the system has created data structure **CE1US01** for the operating concern, which will be used for costing-based profitability analysis.

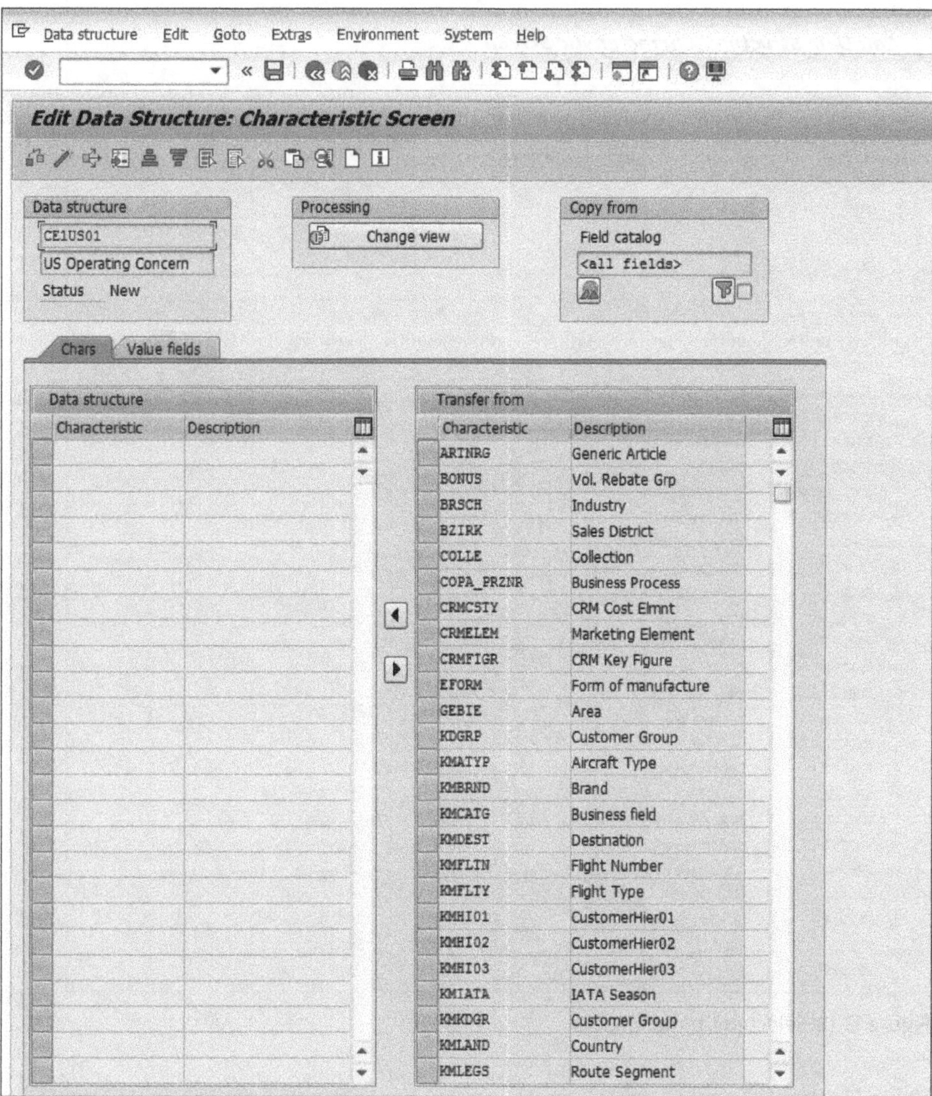

Figure 13.11 Creating a Data Structure

In the lower-left section of the screen, note that, as of now, no characteristics have been selected for the operating concern. On the right side, all available characteristics are listed. Select the needed characteristics by selecting the checkboxes to their left and clicking the < button.

Now, the selected characteristics are transferred to the left side, as shown in Figure 13.12.

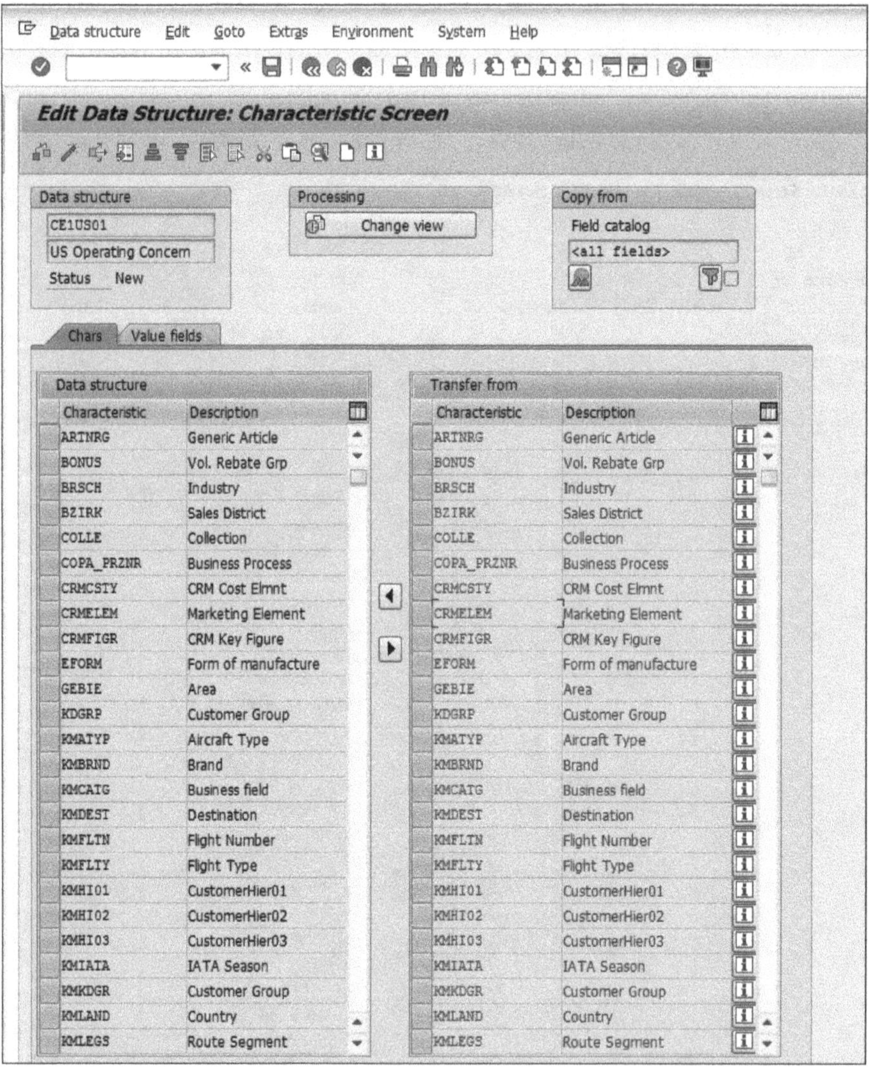

Figure 13.12 Selected Characteristics

Value Fields

The next step is to add value fields. Click the **Value fields** tab and add the value fields you want to use in your operating concern, as shown in Figure 13.13.

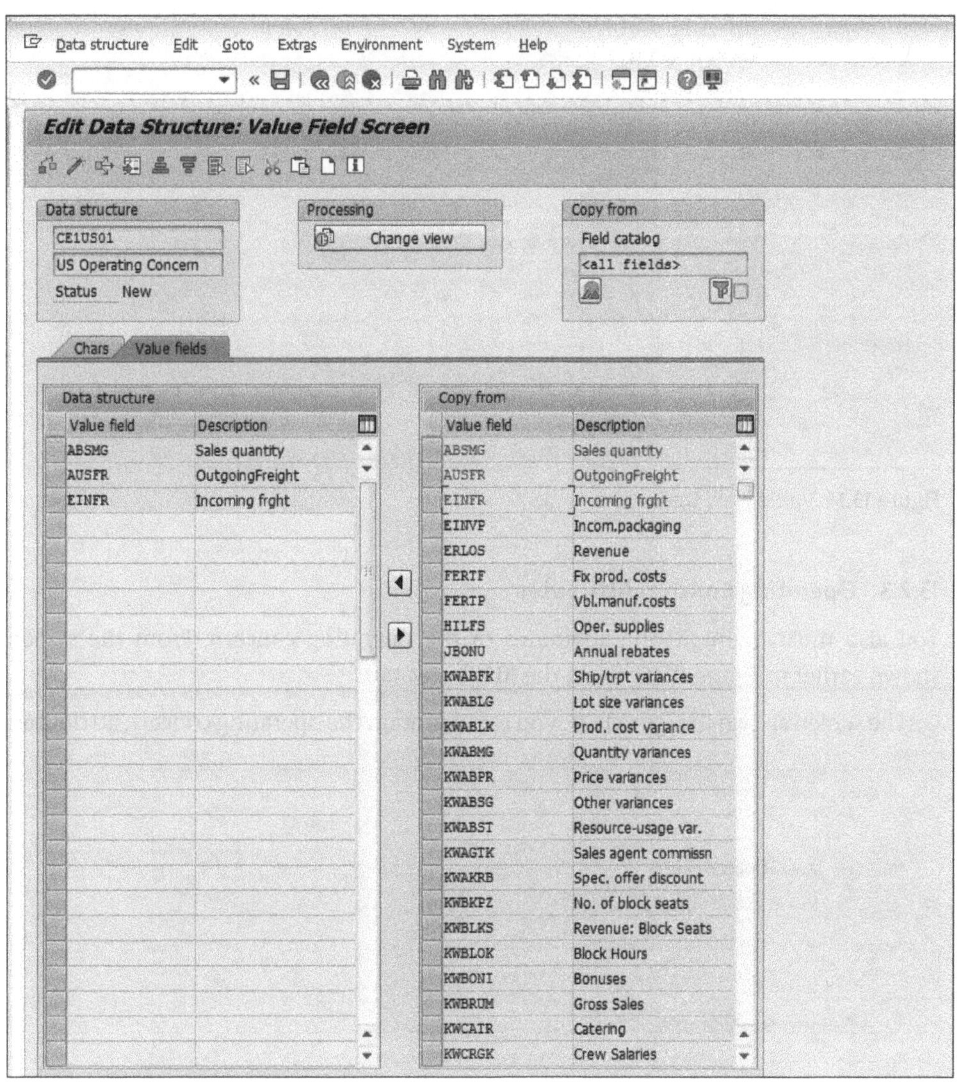

Figure 13.13 Selected Value Fields

Double-clicking a value field shows you its definition, as shown in Figure 13.14. A value field can be defined either as an amount or quantity field. Also, its data element is specified on this screen.

After adding the characteristics and value fields, save by clicking the **Save** button, then activate the data structure of the operating concern by clicking **Activate** from the top menu.

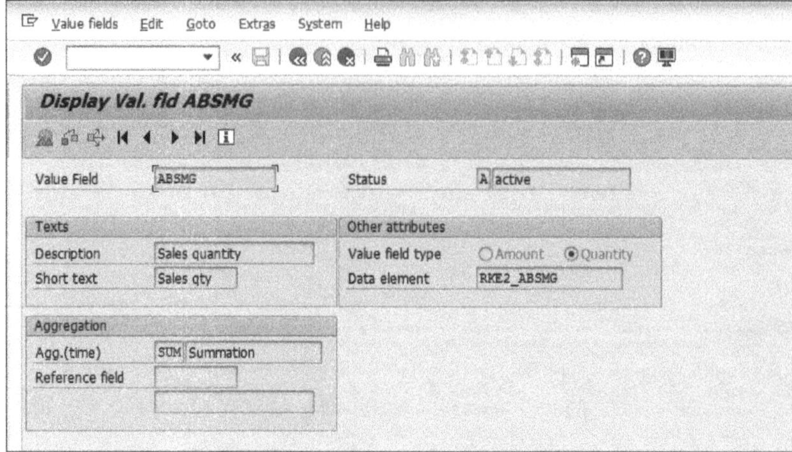

Figure 13.14 Value Field Definition

13.2.3 Operating Concern Attributes

You also must maintain the attributes of the operating concern. From the screen shown earlier in Figure 13.10, select the **Attributes** tab.

On the screen shown in Figure 13.15, you can maintain the operating concern attributes.

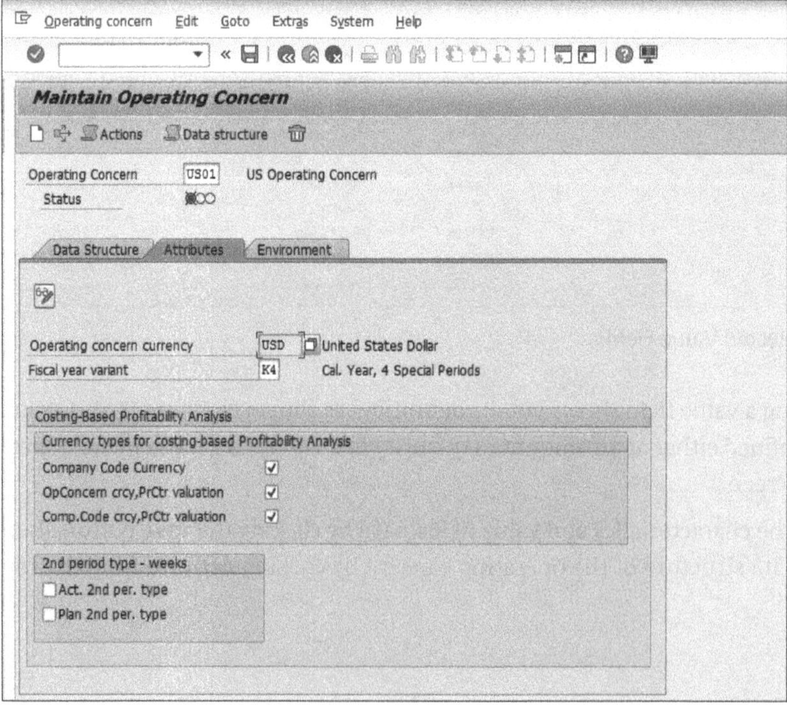

Figure 13.15 Operating Concern Attributes

You need to configure the following fields:

- **Operating concern currency**
  The currency in which the data transferred to profitability analysis is converted and updated.
- **Fiscal year variant**
  The fiscal year variant used to determine the periods in the profitability analysis.
- **Currency types for costing-based Profitability Analysis**
  In this field, you'll define additional currency types in which the values should be stored in costing-based profitability analysis.
- **2nd period type - weeks**
  With these indicators, the system will store the actual and/or plan data in costing-based profitability analysis in weeks as well.

As a last step, you must generate the profitability analysis environment. Click the **Environment** tab, which will result in the screen shown in Figure 13.16.

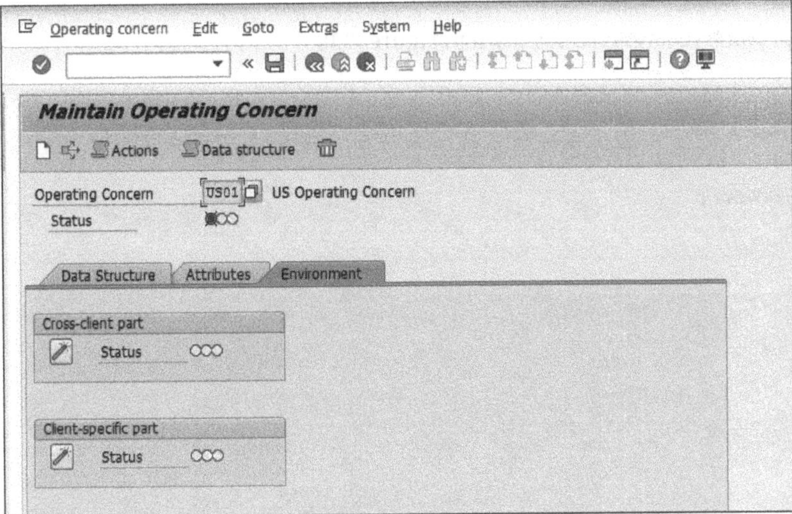

Figure 13.16 Generating an Operating Concern

You need to activate both the cross-client and client-specific parts by clicking the button in both sections.

After completing the data structure of the operating concern (characteristics and value fields, in the case of costing-based profitability analysis), you now need to maintain further master data-related settings: the characteristics hierarchy and characteristic derivation.

13.2.4 Characteristics Hierarchy

You can group characteristic values in a hierarchy, which then can be used in the derivation of values and in reporting. Follow the menu path **Controlling • Profitability Analysis • Master Data • Characteristic Values • Define Characteristics Hierarchy**.

Enter your operating concern, as shown in Figure 13.17.

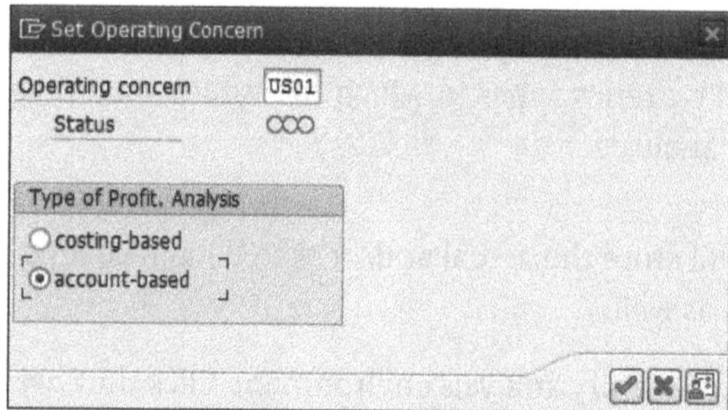

Figure 13.17 Entering an Operating Concern

After that step, you'll see the screen shown in Figure 13.18.

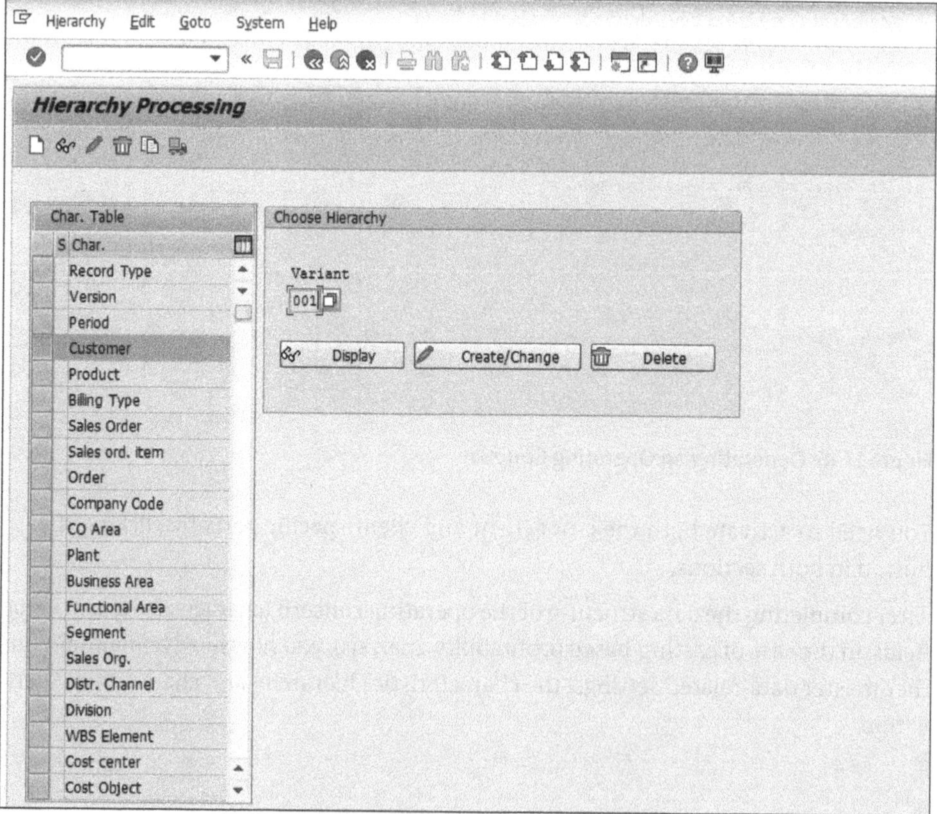

Figure 13.18 Defining a Hierarchy

On the left side is a list of the characteristics for which you can create a hierarchy. Select **Customer** so that you can build a hierarchy of customers. Enter variant "001" in the **Variant** field; you can maintain multiple hierarchies under different variant names. Then, click the **Create/Change** button.

On the next screen, shown in Figure 13.19, enter a description for the variant. You also can select the **Visible system-wide** checkbox, which will make the hierarchy available not only in profitability analysis but also in other components of the system.

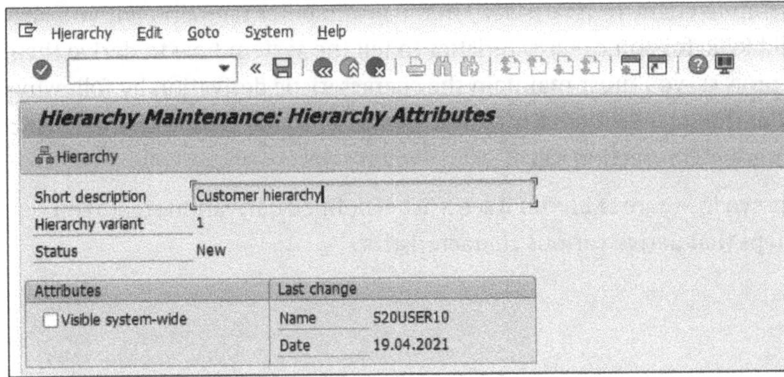

Figure 13.19 Hierarchy Attributes

After that step, select **Hierarchy** from the top menu. On the next screen, shown in Figure 13.20, you can build a hierarchy in a tree-like structure with nodes and subnodes. In our example, customer number **11** is at the top, underneath which is **10000022**, the top-level customer for several other customers. You can add nodes and subnodes using the **Same Level** and **Lower Level** commands from the top menu.

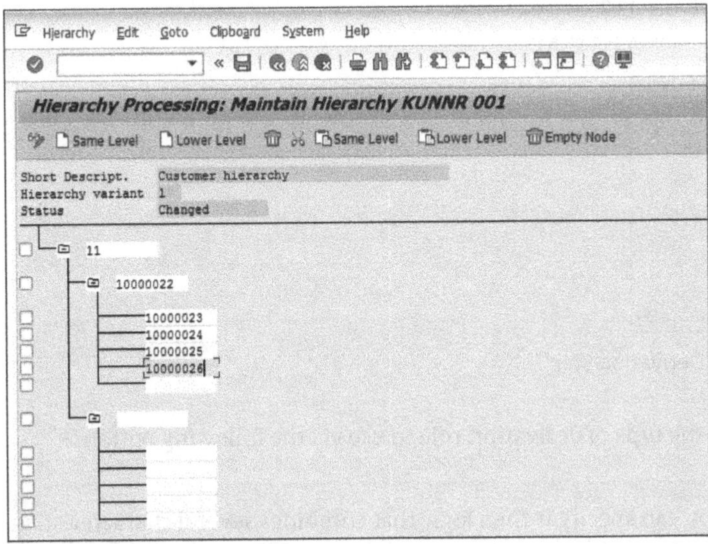

Figure 13.20 Customer Hierarchy

After maintaining the characteristics hierarchy, save your settings by clicking the **Save** button.

13.2.5 Characteristic Derivation

Each posting to profitability analysis forms a profitability segment, which is a combination of posted characteristics. Many profitability segments are determined by the standard logic of the system. For example, the ship-to customer from the sales order will go into the ship-to characteristic (KUNWE) in the profitability segment. But you also will have to build logic for some characteristics to tell the system how to derive their values. For this process, you must maintain the characteristic derivation by following the menu path **Controlling • Profitability Analysis • Master Data • Define Characteristic Derivation** or entering Transaction KEDR.

On the screen shown in Figure 13.21, you'll see a list of defined derivation steps. You can have multiple steps that derive various characteristics.

Characteristic Derivation

Steps in Logical Order

Step...	Mai...	Step Type	Con...	Description
2		Clear		Clear: Division from product
3		Table lookup		Division from Sales Order (VBAK)
20		Table lookup		Product hierarchy from product (MARA)

Figure 13.21 Derivation Steps

To create a new derivation step, click **Create Step** from the top menu. For this example, create a step to derive the reference item from the sales document. A popup window appears, as shown in Figure 13.22.

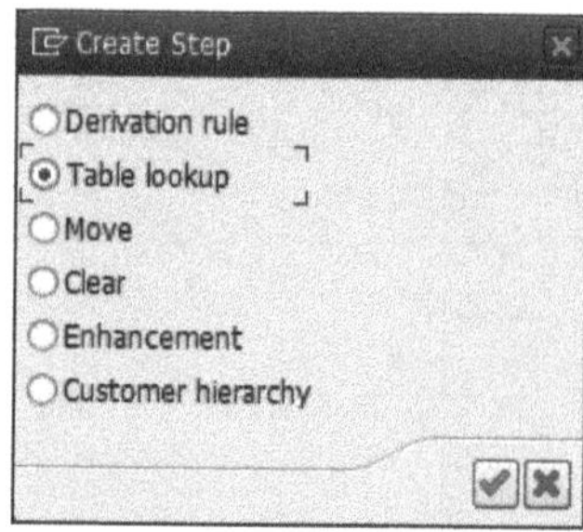

Figure 13.22 Creating a Derivation Step

In this window, select the type of derivation rule to use via the following options:

- **Derivation rule**
  With this option, you can specify if-then logic that combines several characteristics.

- **Table lookup**
  This rule tells the system to derive the values of the characteristics from another table/field.
- **Move**
  This option enables you to move the content of a source field or a constant to a target field.
- **Clear**
  This option enables you to delete a characteristic value (resets it to blank for CHAR fields or to 0 for NUMC fields).
- **Enhancement**
  You can also program your own logic for the derivation, developed using component 003 of customer enhancement COPA0001.

For now, select **Table lookup** and proceed by clicking the **Continue** button. In the next popup window, shown in Figure 13.23, specify the table from which to read the values.

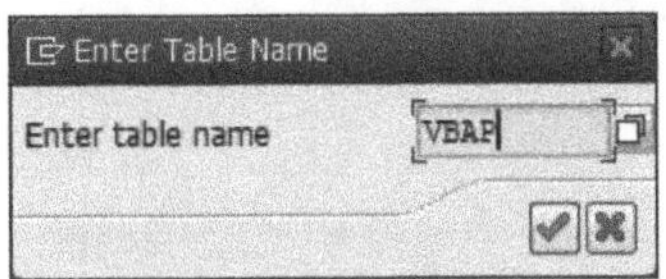

Figure 13.23 Table Lookup

Enter "VBAP" in this case, which stand for table VBAP (Sales Document: Item Data). Proceed by clicking the **Continue** button.

On the next screen, shown in Figure 13.24, you can define the rules for the derivation. In the **Step Description** field, enter a description for the step. A good practice is to name it with the name of the characteristic being derived.

In the **Source Fields for Table Lookup** section, the fields from the sales document item table used to derive the characteristic and their corresponding fields in profitability analysis are defined. Then, in **Assignment of Table Fields to Target Fields** in the lower section of the screen, define that, from field **VBAP-VGBEL** (document number of the reference document) from the sales document line-item table, a characteristic you created that represents the document number of the reference document (**WW001**) should be derived.

After maintaining the derivation, save these settings by clicking the **Save** button.

Using these derivation techniques, you should complete the derivation steps for all your characteristics not already derived by the standard logic of the system.

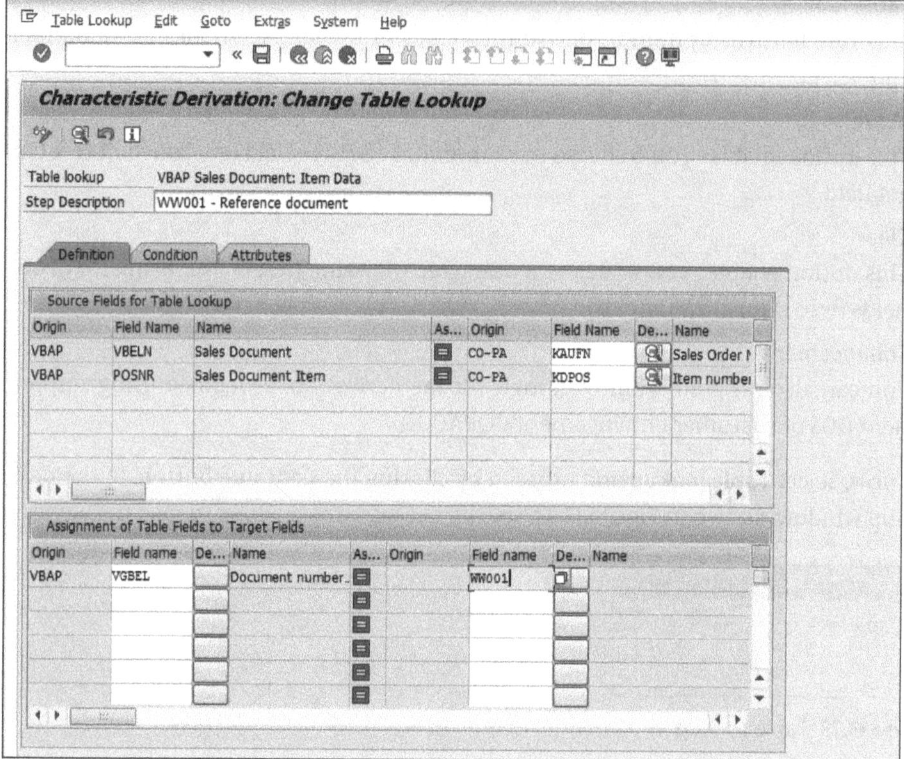

Figure 13.24 Derivation Definition

13.3 Data Flow

In this section, we'll discuss how profitability analysis receives its data from the various SAP S/4HANA areas and what settings you need to maintain to ensure the correct data flow into profitability analysis.

13.3.1 Invoice Value Flow

An *invoice value flow* plays an important role in profitability analysis because this process provides the revenues and the COGS to profitability analysis. In this section, you'll learn how to transfer sales, sales deductions, and COGS to profitability analysis.

A difference exists in the value flow in margin analysis versus in costing-based profitability analysis. The account-based approach uses general ledger accounts to transfer the values into margin analysis, so you only need to configure the automatic account determination functionality from sales to financial accounting using the condition technique we briefly touched upon in Chapter 4. In costing-based profitability analysis, however, the values are transferred using value fields, and you need to assign the value fields to SAP S/4HANA Sales conditions.

Account-Based Settings

Let's analyze the value flow, starting from an SAP S/4HANA Sales billing document. You can display it with Transaction VF03, then double-click a material line item. Under the **Conditions** tab, shown in Figure 13.25, you'll see a list of SAP S/4HANA Sales conditions, which form the values of the billing document, such as sales price, discounts, taxes, total, and so on.

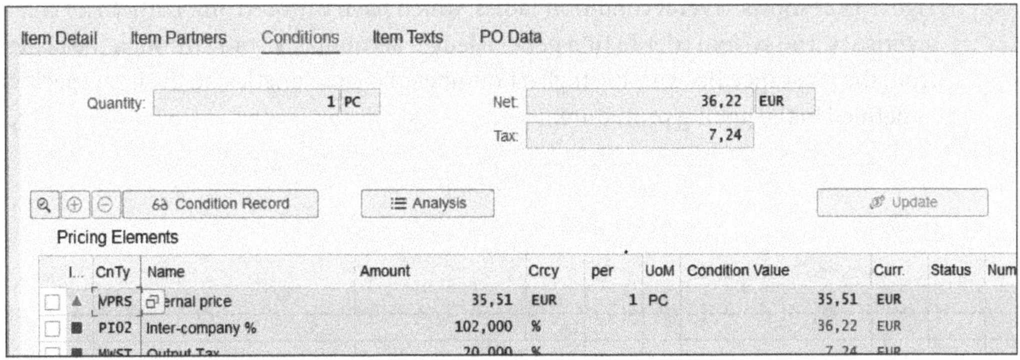

Figure 13.25 Billing Line Item

Double-click pricing condition **PI02** in the **CnTy** field, and you'll see its details, as shown in Figure 13.26.

More

Condition Type: PI02 Inter-company %

CondPricingDate: 25.10.2018

Condition Values

Amount: 102,000 %

Cond.Base Value: 35,51 EUR

Condition Value: 36,22 EUR

Control

Condition Class: B Prices

Calculat.Type: A Percentage

Condit.Category:

Cond.Control: F Condition value fixed (billed

Condit.Origin: A Automatic pricing

☑ IntcoBillCond

Account Determination

Account Key: ERL Tax Code: 12 G/L Account: 800002

Figure 13.26 Condition Details

At the bottom of the screen is the **Account Determination** section. You'll see account key **ERL**, which is used to determine the revenue account to be posted. Then, you'll see that account **800002** was determined.

Let's configure how to determine the general ledger accounts. In a new session, start Transaction VKOA, which is the transaction to assign general ledger accounts to sales conditions based on certain criteria.

Figure 13.27 shows several condition tables, which have various combinations of characteristics. The system tries to find general ledger accounts by going through the tables from the most specific (with the highest number of characteristics) to the least specific, as defined in the pricing procedure.

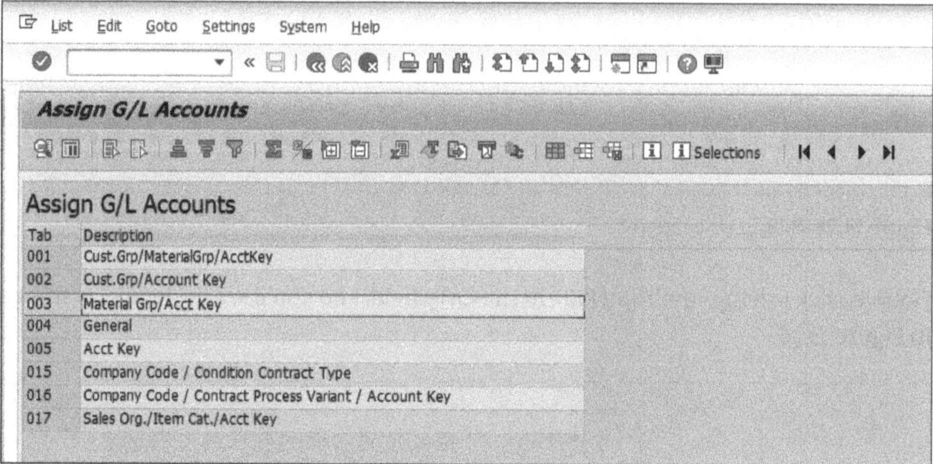

Figure 13.27 Assigning General Ledger Accounts

Double-click **003: Material Grp/Acct Key**, for example. On the screen shown in Figure 13.28, you can assign the revenue general ledger accounts.

The following fields serve as criteria:

- **App**
  The condition technique specified in this field is used throughout the SAP S/4HANA system. In this column, **V** is used, which means SAP S/4HANA Sales.
- **CndTy. (condition type)**
  Two condition types exist for account determination:
  - **KOFI** for billing documents without an account assignment object
  - **KOFK** for billing documents with an account assignment object
- **Chrt/Accts (chart of accounts)**
  The chart of accounts for which you maintain the account determination.
- **SOrg. (sales organization)**
  The sales organization for which you maintain the account determination.

- **AAGM (account assignment group material)**
  The account assignment group material is a group from the material master, thus enabling different accounts based on the material.
- **ActKy. (account key)**
  This column contains the account key being used by the condition to derive the account.
- **G/L Account (general ledger account)**
  This column contains the general ledger account to which the revenue is posted. In our example, this value should be cost element category 11 (revenue) or 12 (revenue reduction).
- **Accruals Acc. (accruals account)**
  This column is maintained only if conditions exist that relevant for accrual—for example, rebate conditions.

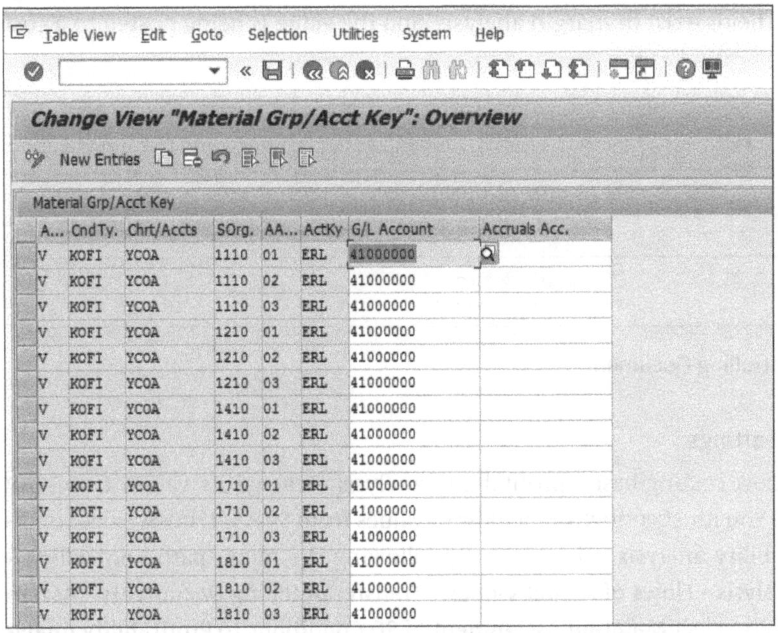

Table View Edit Goto Selection Utilities System Help

Change View "Material Grp/Acct Key": Overview

New Entries

Material Grp/Acct Key

A...	CndTy.	Chrt/Accts	SOrg.	AA...	ActKy	G/L Account	Accruals Acc.
V	KOFI	YCOA	1110	01	ERL	41000000	
V	KOFI	YCOA	1110	02	ERL	41000000	
V	KOFI	YCOA	1110	03	ERL	41000000	
V	KOFI	YCOA	1210	01	ERL	41000000	
V	KOFI	YCOA	1210	02	ERL	41000000	
V	KOFI	YCOA	1210	03	ERL	41000000	
V	KOFI	YCOA	1410	01	ERL	41000000	
V	KOFI	YCOA	1410	02	ERL	41000000	
V	KOFI	YCOA	1410	03	ERL	41000000	
V	KOFI	YCOA	1710	01	ERL	41000000	
V	KOFI	YCOA	1710	02	ERL	41000000	
V	KOFI	YCOA	1710	03	ERL	41000000	
V	KOFI	YCOA	1810	01	ERL	41000000	
V	KOFI	YCOA	1810	02	ERL	41000000	
V	KOFI	YCOA	1810	03	ERL	41000000	

Figure 13.28 Condition Table General Ledger Account Assignments

Make new entries in this or the other condition tables to derive all your relevant revenue accounts.

Going back to the billing document shown earlier in Figure 13.25, let's review the generated profitability analysis document. Click **Accounting** in the top menu. The system shows the related accounting documents in financial accounting and controlling, as shown in Figure 13.29. Double-click the controlling document.

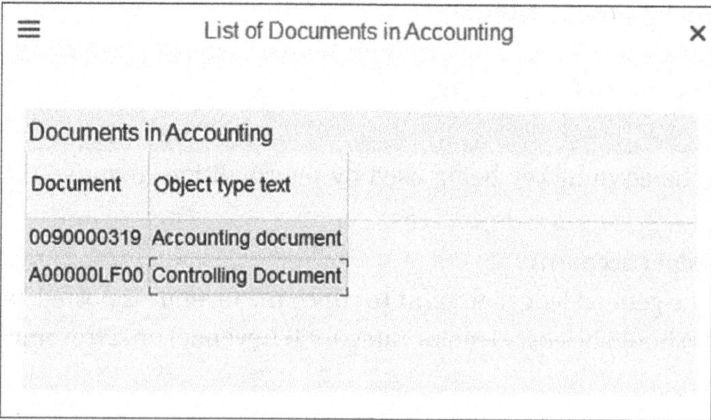

Figure 13.29 Accounting Documents

As shown in Figure 13.30, the controlling object is **PSG**, which means profitability segment. No value fields exist in margin analysis, and the value is being posted to a cost element.

Layout	1SAP	Primary cost posting
COarea currency	EUR	EUR
Valuation View/Group	0	Legal Valuation

DocumentNo Doc. Date	Document Header Text			RT RefDocNo	Rev RvD		
PRw OTy Object	**CO Object Name**	**Cost Elem.**	**Cost element name**			**Val/COArea Crcy**	**Total quantity PUM O OffsetAcct**
A00000LF00 23.10.2018				R 90000319			
1 PSG 5419		800002	Sales revenues-affil			36,22-	1- PC D BP2000

Figure 13.30 Controlling Document

Costing-Based Settings

Let's see now how costing-based profitability analysis received its values from SAP S/4HANA Sales. You must configure the flow of values from SAP S/4HANA Sales conditions to profitability analysis value fields by following the menu path **Controlling • Profitability Analysis • Flows of Actual Values • Transfer of Billing Documents • Assign Value Fields**. Then, select **Maintain Assignment of SD Conditions to Profitability Analysis Value Fields**.

Initially, the table is empty, as shown in Figure 13.31. Click **New Entries** from the top menu.

On the screen shown in Figure 13.32, assign the condition type **KF00: Freight** to standard value field **AUSFR: Outgoing freight**. This assignment ensures that values posted with condition type KF00 will update the AUSFR value field in profitability analysis.

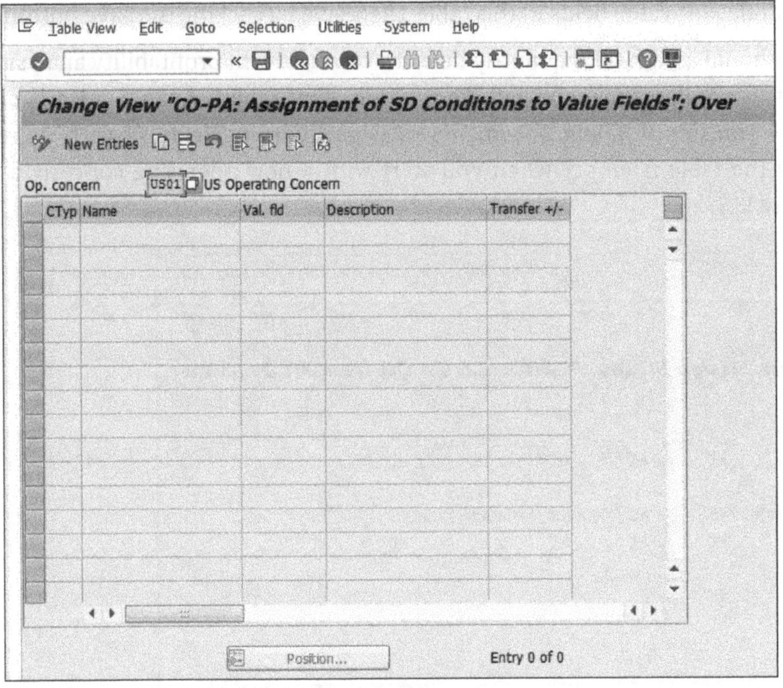

Figure 13.31 Assigning Value Fields to Conditions

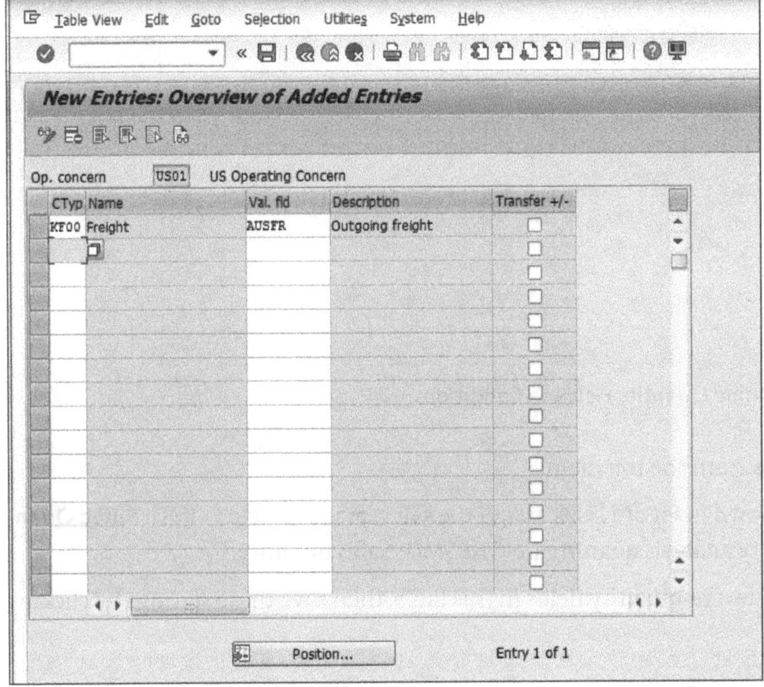

Figure 13.32 Assigned Value Fields

Assign all your relevant value fields in this table, then save by clicking the **Save** button.

Similarly, you should assign sales quantity fields to your relevant profitability analysis quantity fields also. Follow the menu path **Controlling • Profitability Analysis • Flows of Actual Values • Transfer of Billing Documents • Assign Quantity Fields.** As with value fields, initially the table is empty when you start with a new operating concern, as shown in Figure 13.33.

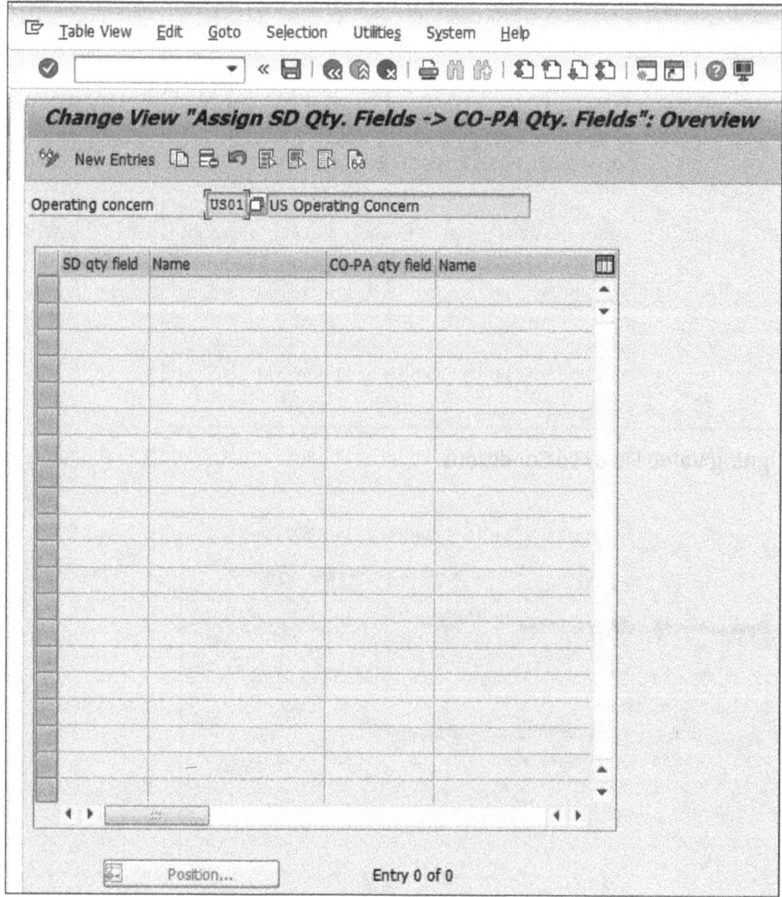

Figure 13.33 Assigning Quantity Fields to Conditions

Click **New Entries** from the top menu.

On the screen shown in Figure 13.34, assign the sales quantity field **FKIMG: Billed Quantity** to profitability analysis quantity field **ABSMG: Sales quantity**.

Assign all your relevant quantity fields in this table, then save these settings by clicking the **Save** button.

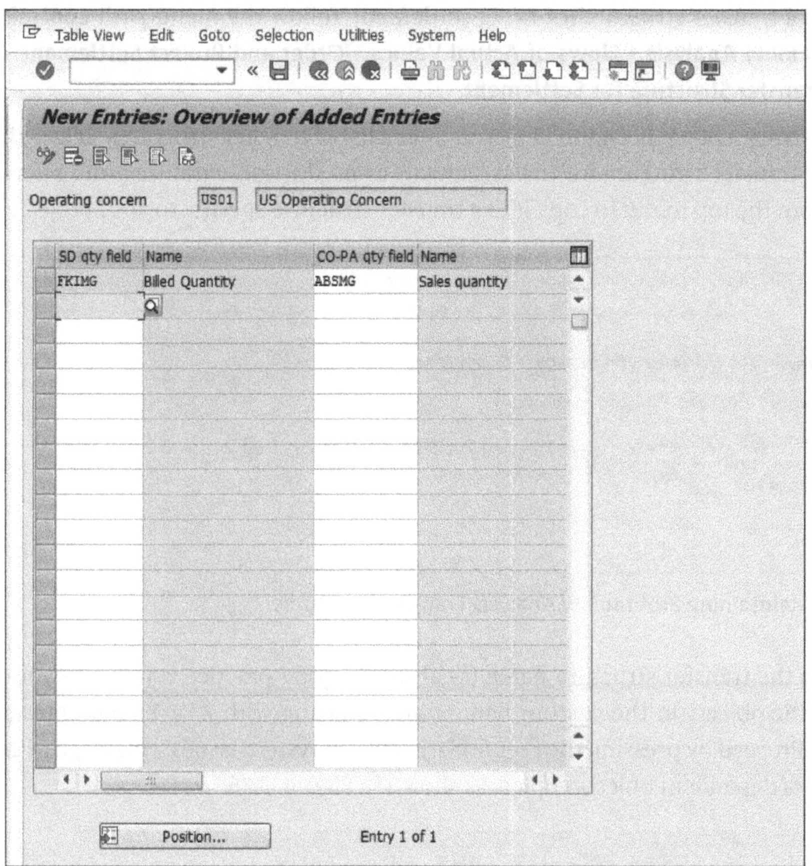

Figure 13.34 Assigned Quantity Fields

13.3.2 Overhead Costs Flow

The flow of overhead costs comes to profitability analysis from other controlling objects, such as internal orders, cost centers, or work breakdown structure (WBS) elements. These objects are originally posted with the cost, then at month end, these costs are transferred to profitability analysis to provide accurate profitability, which includes the overhead costs allocated to the proper profitability analysis characteristics. In the case of internal orders and WBS elements, these rules come from the settlement profile; in the case of cost centers, the overhead costs are transferred via assessment. Direct postings to profitability analysis profitability segments in financial accounting documents are also possible.

In margin analysis, the flow of actual values doesn't require further setup beyond correctly setting up the settlement profiles and assessment cycles in the sender cost objects, which we already analyzed in Chapter 10 and Chapter 11. In costing-based profitability analysis, however, you must assign value fields to the relevant cost elements, which is achieved using a customizing object called a *transfer structure*.

To maintain a transfer structure for order settlement, follow the menu path **Controlling • Profitability Analysis • Flows of Actual Values • Order and Project Settlement • Define PA Transfer Structure for Settlement.**

On the first screen, shown in Figure 13.35, you'll see a list of transfer structures. Select **Y1**, which is the transfer structure for the settlement of production variances, and select **Copy As...** from the top menu to copy it to a transfer structure specific to your project.

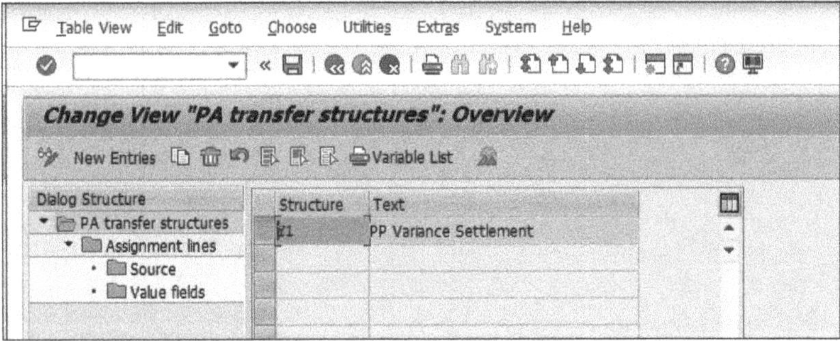

Figure 13.35 Maintaining Profitability Analysis Transfer Structures

Enter "Z1" as the transfer structure name (as always, a good practice is to name your project-specific objects in the custom name range, starting with Z or Y) and enter a description. Proceed by pressing the Enter key, and the system issues a message with the number of dependent objects copied, as shown in Figure 13.36.

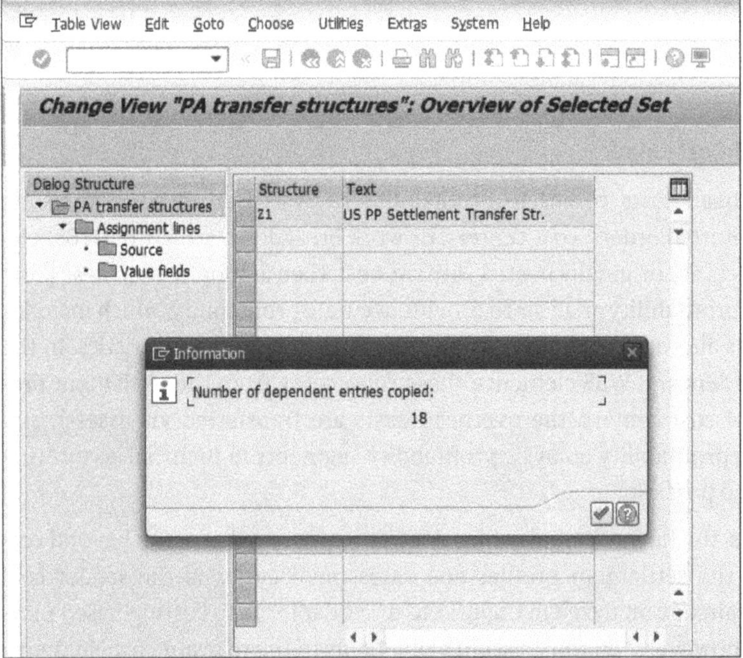

Figure 13.36 Copied Transfer Structure

Then, select the **Z1** structure and click **Assignment lines** on the left side of the screen. Create as many lines as needed to segregate the various cost elements that need to go to different value fields, as shown in Figure 13.37.

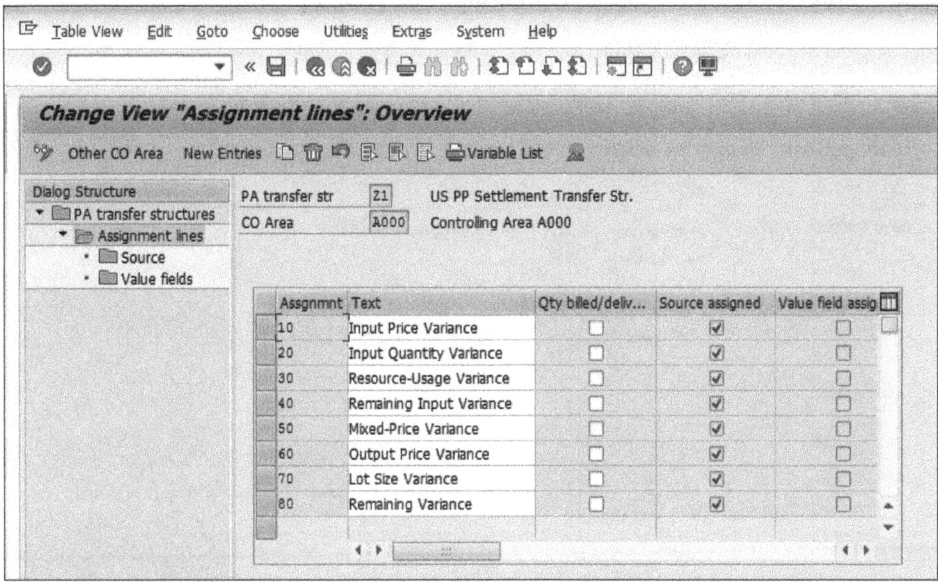

Figure 13.37 Assignment Lines

Click **New Entries** from the top menu and create new lines, as shown in Figure 13.38.

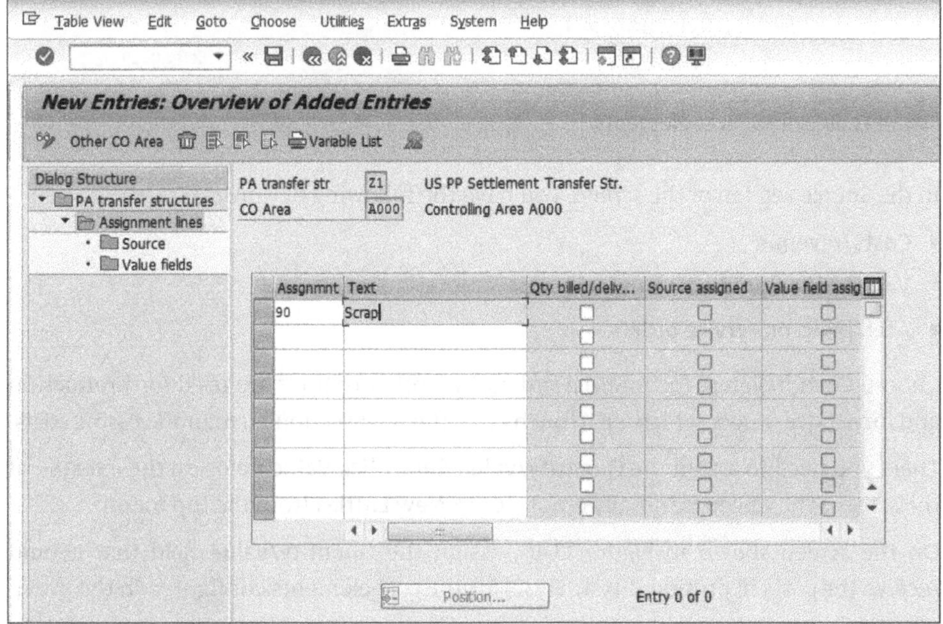

Figure 13.38 New Assignment Line

Then, select a line and click **Source** on the left side of the screen. In the next screen, shown in Figure 13.39, enter a range of cost elements or a cost element group. The postings to these cost elements will be allocated to the value field we'll configure in the next screen. Enter the relevant cost element range.

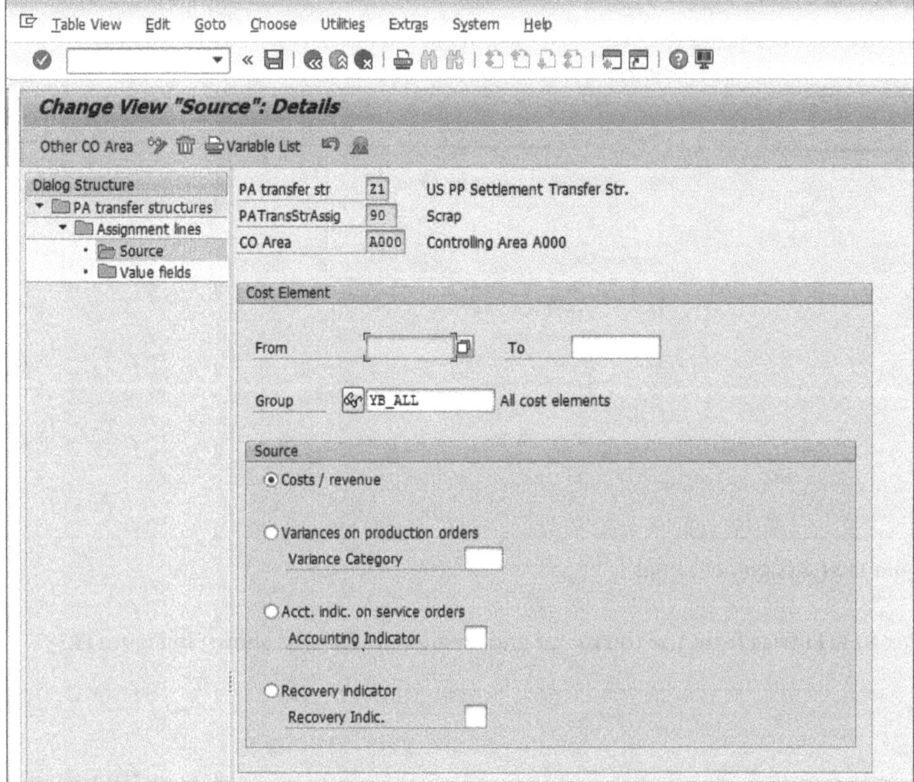

Figure 13.39 Source Cost Elements

In the **Source** section of the screen, you have the following options:

- **Costs/revenue**
- **Variances on production order**
- **Acct. indic. on service orders**

Choose **Costs/revenue** for internal orders. The other options are used for production and for service orders, which we'll touch on in the next section on manufacturing costs.

Then, you need to assign the **Quantity/value** field. Click **Value fields** on the left side of the screen. The screen is initially empty. Click **New Entries** from the top menu.

On the screen shown in Figure 13.40, assign the **Quantity/value** field that should receive the costs in profitability analysis for the cost elements configured in the previous step.

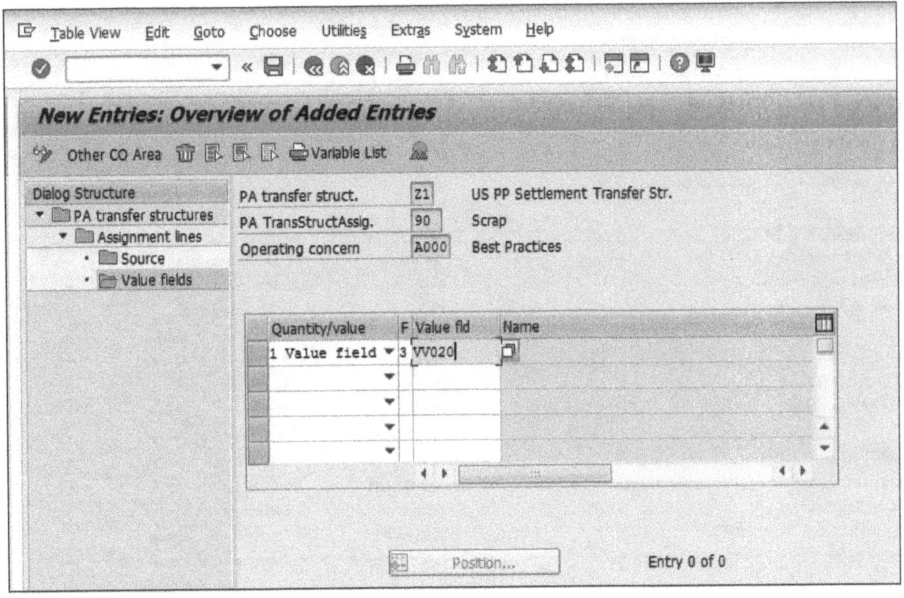

Figure 13.40 Assigned Value Field

In the **Fixed/Variable Flag** field, you have the following three options:

- **1: Fixed Amounts**
- **2: Variable Amounts**
- **3: Sum of Fixed and Variable Amounts**

Enter "3" unless you need to transfer only the fixed or the variable portion of the costs. Maintain the whole structure in a similar fashion and save your settings by clicking the **Save** button.

In the next step, you need to assign the newly created transfer structure to the relevant order types. Follow the menu path **Controlling • Profitability Analysis • Flows of Actual Values • Order and Project Settlement • Assign PA Transfer Structure to Settlement Profile**. You'll see a list of settlement profiles already defined. Double-click settlement profile **YB0020** to see its configuration screen, as shown in Figure 13.41.

Enter the overhead settlement transfer structure in the **PA transfer struct.** field, then save by clicking the **Save** button.

Similarly, you need to maintain another transfer structure for direct postings from financial accounting/materials management. Follow the menu path **Controlling • Profitability Analysis • Flows of Actual Values • Direct Posting from FI/MM • Maintain PA Transfer Structure for Direct Postings.**

Select transfer structure **FI: Direct Acct Assign. fr. FI/MM** and click **Assignment lines** on the left side of the screen, as shown in Figure 13.42.

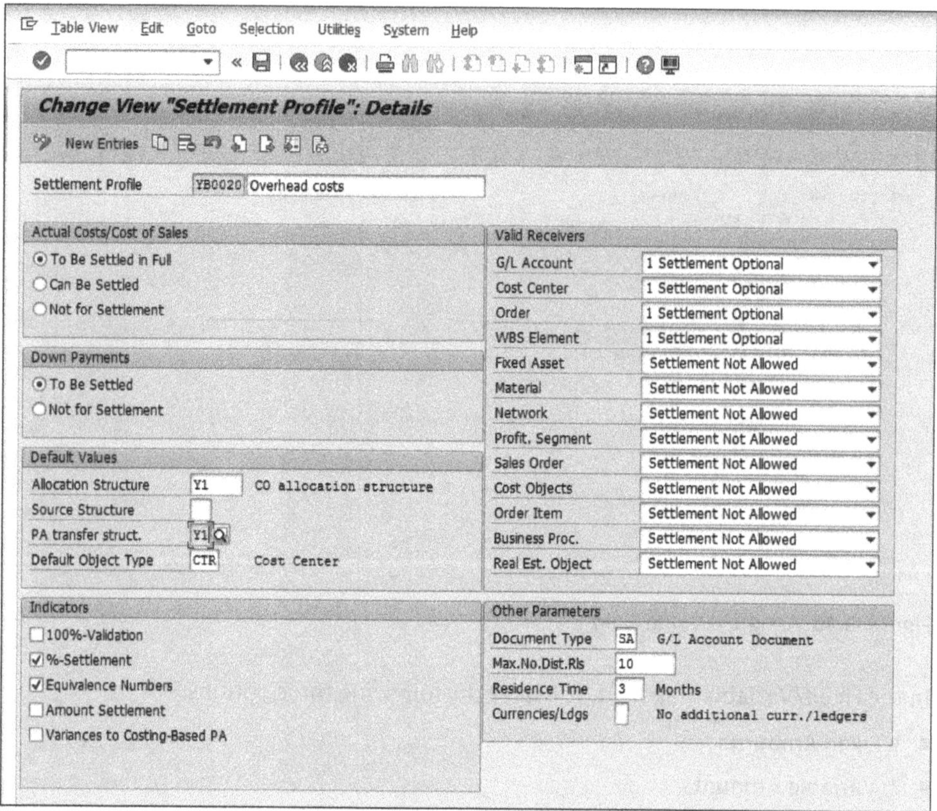

Figure 13.41 Maintaining a Settlement Profile

Dialog Structure
- PA transfer structures
  - Assignment lines
    - Source
    - Value fields

Structure	Text
A1	Settle Production Variances
BK	STC: Cumulated Operating Costs
BP	STC: Periodic Operating Costs
CO	Allocate Activities/Processes
E1	PA Transfer Structure 1
F1	Production/Process
FI	Direct Acct Assign. fr. FI/MM
K1	Make to Order

Figure 13.42 Financial Accounting/Materials Management Transfer Structure

You'll see the various assignment lines already defined, as shown in Figure 13.43, which correspond to the types of costs to be transferred to profitability analysis. Select them line by line and assign the relevant cost element ranges or groups using **Source** on the left side of the screen.

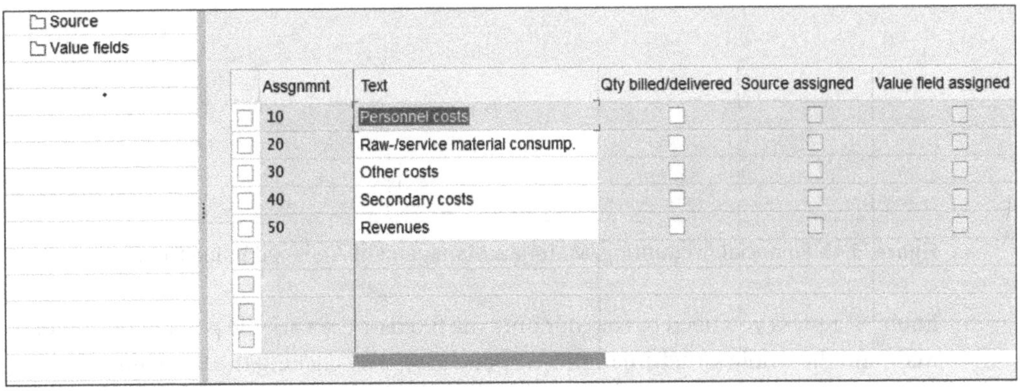

Figure 13.43 Financial Accounting/Materials Management Assignment Lines

On the screen shown in Figure 13.44, you can assign a range of cost elements or a cost element group.

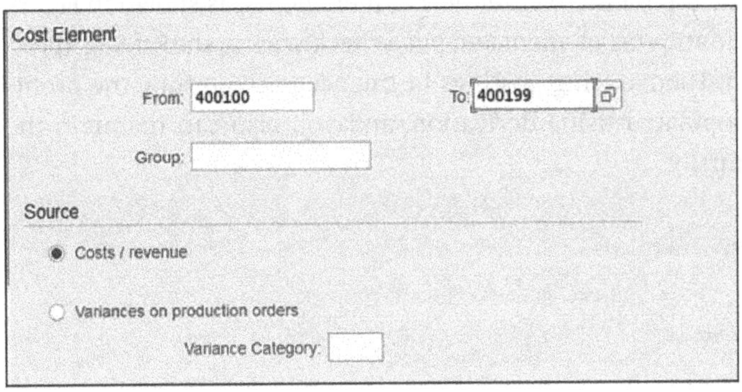

Figure 13.44 Financial Accounting/Materials Management Source Cost Elements

Now, you need to assign the value/quantity field. Click **Value fields** on the left side of the screen. The screen is initially empty. Click **New Entries** from the top menu.

On the screen shown in Figure 13.45, you can assign the value or quantity field that should receive the costs in profitability analysis for the cost elements configured in the previous step. In the **Fixed/Variable Flag** field, you have the following three options:

- **1: Fixed Amounts**
- **2: Variable Amounts**
- **3: Sum of Fixed and Variable Amounts**

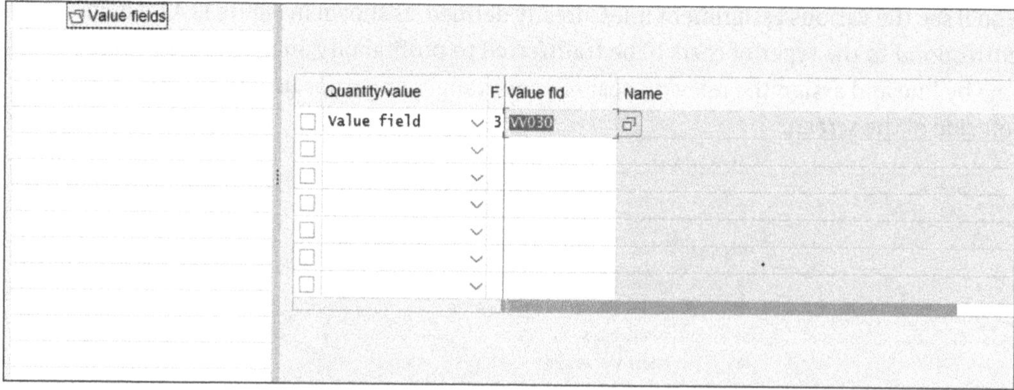

Figure 13.45 Financial Accounting/Materials Management Assigned Value Field

Enter "3" unless you need to transfer only the fixed or the variable portion of the costs. Maintain the whole structure in this way and save it by clicking the **Save** button.

You can also configure that a profitability analysis segment is the default cost object for specific cost elements so that it can receive costs directly. Follow the menu path **Controlling • Profitability Analysis • Flows of Actual Values • Direct Posting from FI/MM • Automatic Account Assignment** or enter Transaction OKB9.

Select **New Entries** from the top menu to enter new cost elements, as shown in Figure 13.46. Enter a company code and cost element and put a checkmark in the **Prf.Seg.** (profitability segment) column. Then, during postings in financial accounting, the profitability segment will be populated using derivation, and you also can maintain the profitability segment manually.

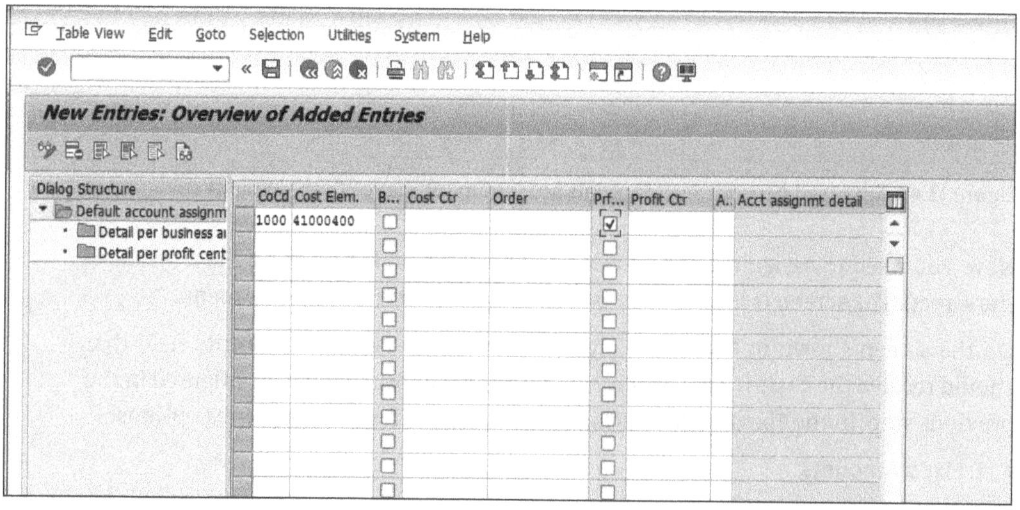

Figure 13.46 Default Account Assignment

13.3.3 Top-Down Distribution

Top-down distribution is a periodic function that enables you to distribute aggregated data to a more detailed level based on reference information such as sales revenues.

In margin analysis, sales revenues, sales deductions, and costs of goods manufactured (COGM) are tracked at customer or product level, or both. However, many business transactions such as freight or administrative expenses cannot be assigned on such detailed level. Thus, these costs are posted at a summarized level, such as sales organization or company code, and then can be allocated using top-down distribution.

In order to use top-down distribution, you'll need to define templates by following the menu path **Controlling • Profitability Analysis • Flows of Actual Values • Periodic Adjustments • Define Template for Top-Down Distribution.**

On the screen shown in Figure 13.47, you'll see a list of top-down distribution templates already defined.

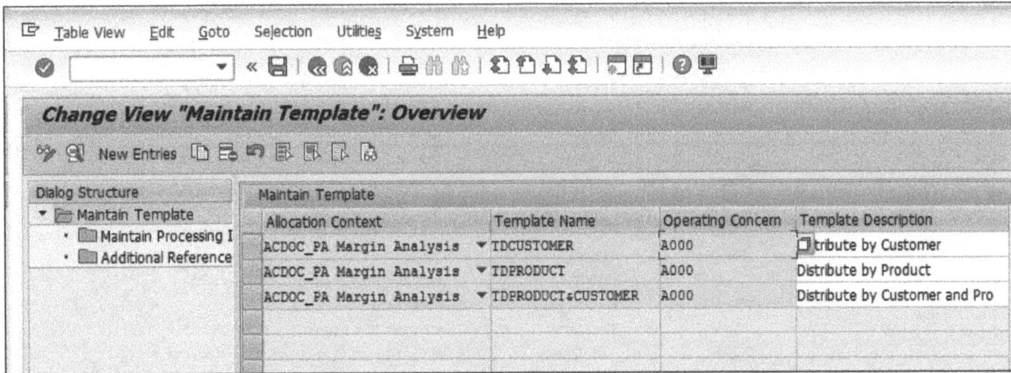

Figure 13.47 Top-Down Distribution Templates

SAP provides templates for distribution by customer, product, or both. You can copy and enhance these templates, based on your needs. To review their settings, select **TDCUSTOMER** for distribution by customer and click **Maintain Processing Instructions**.

Figure 13.48 shows the characteristics relevant for distribution. In the **Characteristic Category** field, you can define the usage of each characteristic. The four categories of characteristics usage are as follows:

- **Distributed**
  Indicates to which characteristics you want to perform top-down distribution. After top-down distribution, these characteristics will have specific value.
- **Retained and Relevant to Reference**
  Indicates that characteristic values in the sender data are kept in the distribution result.

- **Retained but Irrelevant to Reference**
  Defines that characteristic values in the sender data are kept in the distribution result, but these characteristics are not used to match sender and reference data.
- **Summarized**
  Defines that the characteristic values in the sender data and reference data are summarized; therefore, the corresponding line items can be aggregated.

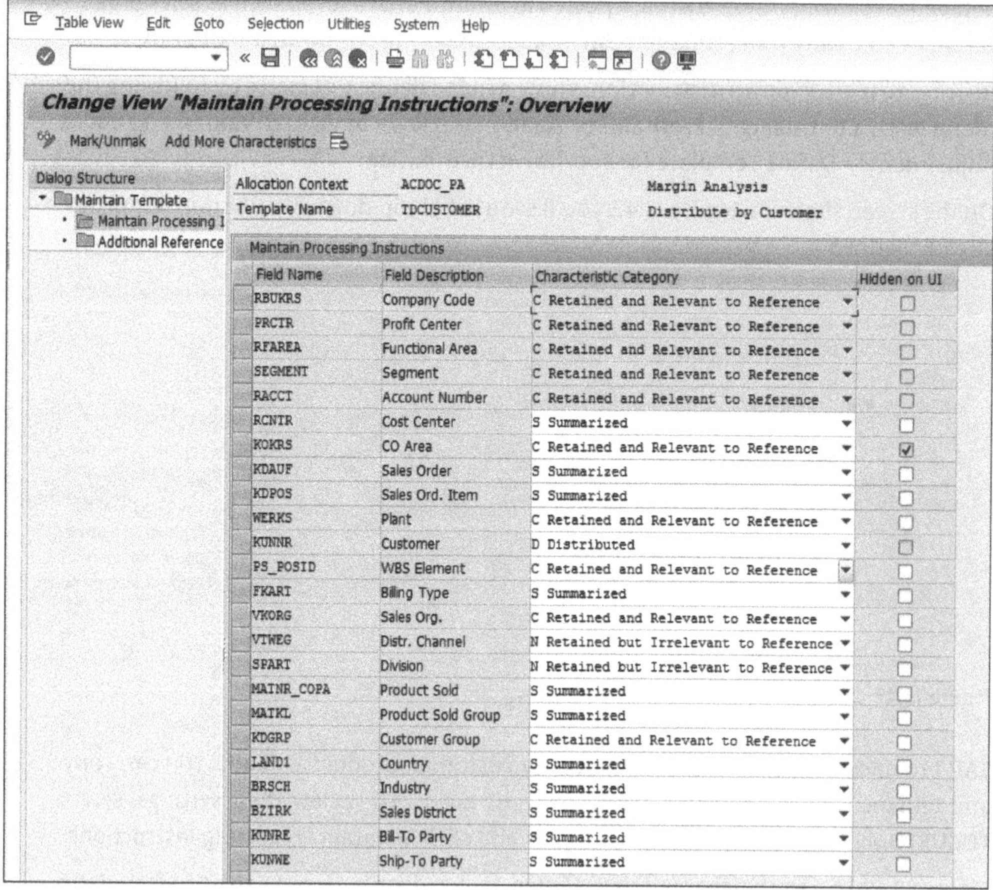

Figure 13.48 Processing Instructions

13.3.4 Production Costs Flow

Production costs are important in the calculation of profitability for companies in the production and process industries. How production costs are passed to profitability analysis in costing-based profitability analysis versus margin analysis is fundamentally different. In margin analysis, when a goods issue with a financial document is generated, the profitability segment is posted with the production costs, and the Universal Journal (table ACDOCA) contains not only the financial document but also the profitability analysis data.

In costing-based profitability analysis, at the time of goods issue, no posting to profitability analysis occurs. At the time of the invoice to the customer, both the revenue and the COGS are posted, which include the production costs, which leads to reconciliation problems with financial accounting, as described in the beginning of this chapter. Therefore, margin analysis represents a significant improvement, which SAP S/4HANA offers so you can track and analyze production costs much more transparently and correctly.

You may wonder why companies didn't opt for margin analysis before SAP S/4HANA, when margin analysis was used mostly in addition to costing-based profitability analysis, only as a reconciliation tool with financial accounting. The main reason is that now the fast, in-memory database SAP HANA has enabled SAP to significantly improve margin analysis, thus overcoming its previous shortcomings that made the costing-based approach the recommended option.

One of the main improvements in margin analysis is that you can define different accounts for splitting the COGS and price differences. That enables posting them on different cost elements and thus analyzing them effectively in profitability analysis.

The COGS account posted during goods issue is derived using the account determination in Transaction OBYC, which we configured in Chapter 4. It's defined in account grouping code **GBB-VAX**. Now, in SAP S/4HANA, you have the opportunity to differentiate this account into multiple accounts, based on cost components of the cost component structure. In SAP S/4HANA 2020, a more precise COGS split can handle multiple currencies. A COGS split now can handle all currencies and valuations relevant based on the currency configuration of the company code. In the COGS split document, the fixed portion of the COGS is updated in controlling area currency.

To define accounts for splitting of COGS, follow the menu path **Financial Accounting • General Ledger Accounting • Periodic Processing • Integration • Materials Management • Define Accounts for Splitting the Cost of Goods Sold**. Then, click **New Entries** from the top menu to create a new splitting profile.

On the first screen, shown in Figure 13.49, enter a name for the new splitting profile, preferably starting with Z or Y. Enter the controlling area from which the system also will populate the chart of accounts. You can select the **Acc Based Split** (account-based split) checkbox, in which case COGS always will be split when the source account is posted. After that step, select a splitting profile and click **Source Accounts and Valuation Views** from the left side of the screen. Then, click **New Entries** from the top menu to enter the COGS source accounts.

On the screen shown in Figure 13.50, you'll need to enter all accounts that are defined in the **GBB-VAX** grouping code in Transaction OBYC. Also, you can define each account separately, perhaps one for each type of valuation: legal, group, or profit center.

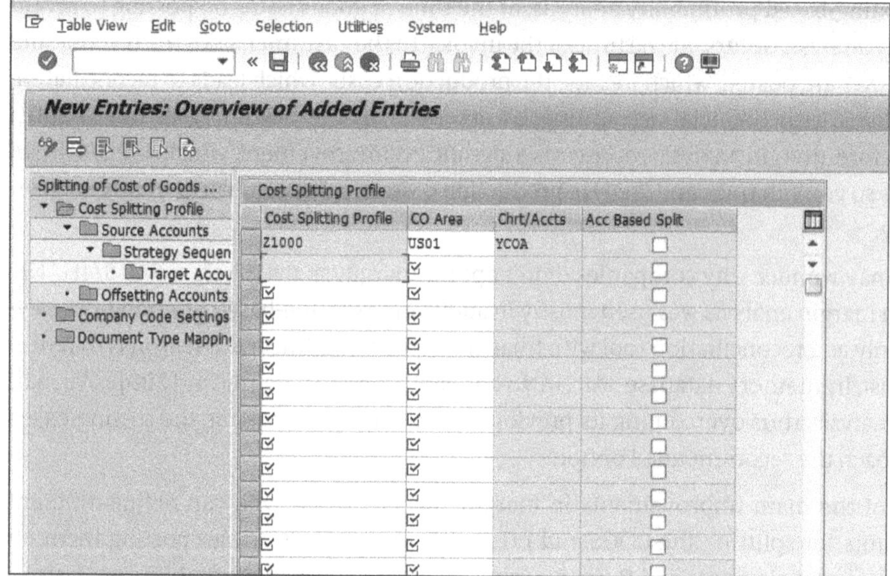
Figure 13.49 Cost-Splitting Profile

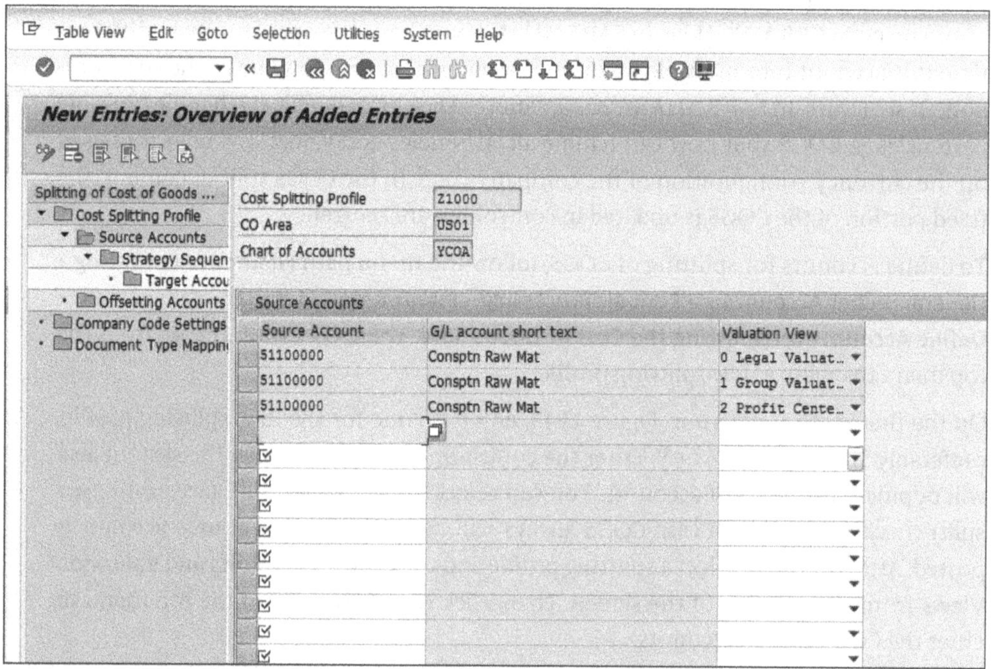
Figure 13.50 Defining Source Accounts

After that step, for each source account, you'll need to define target accounts. Select a source account and click **Strategy Sequence** on the left side of the screen. Then, click **New Entries** from the top menu.

On the screen shown in Figure 13.51, enter a strategy sequence. You can define separate sequences for released and upcoming cost estimates. Next, click **Target Accounts** from the left side of the screen and click **New Entries** from the top menu.

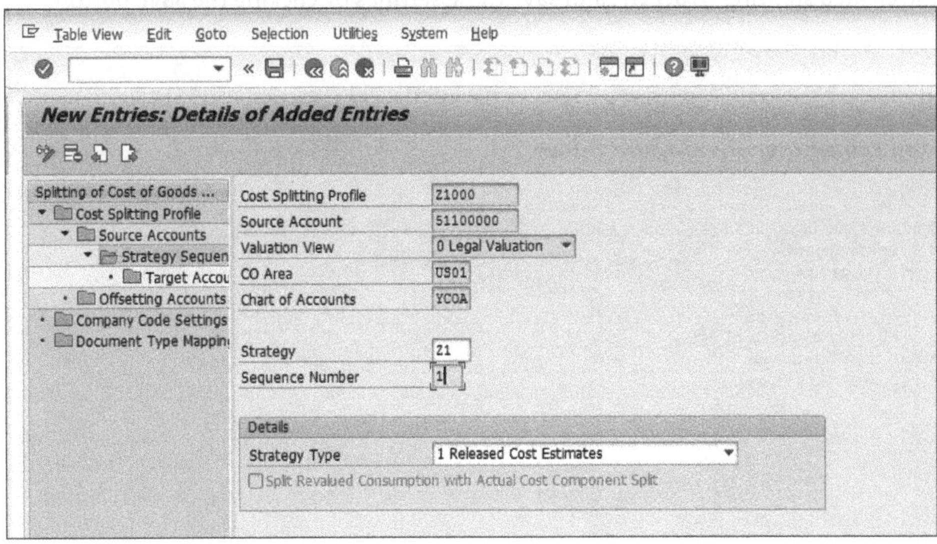

Figure 13.51 Strategy Sequence

On the screen shown in Figure 13.52, you can define a target account for each component of the cost component structure.

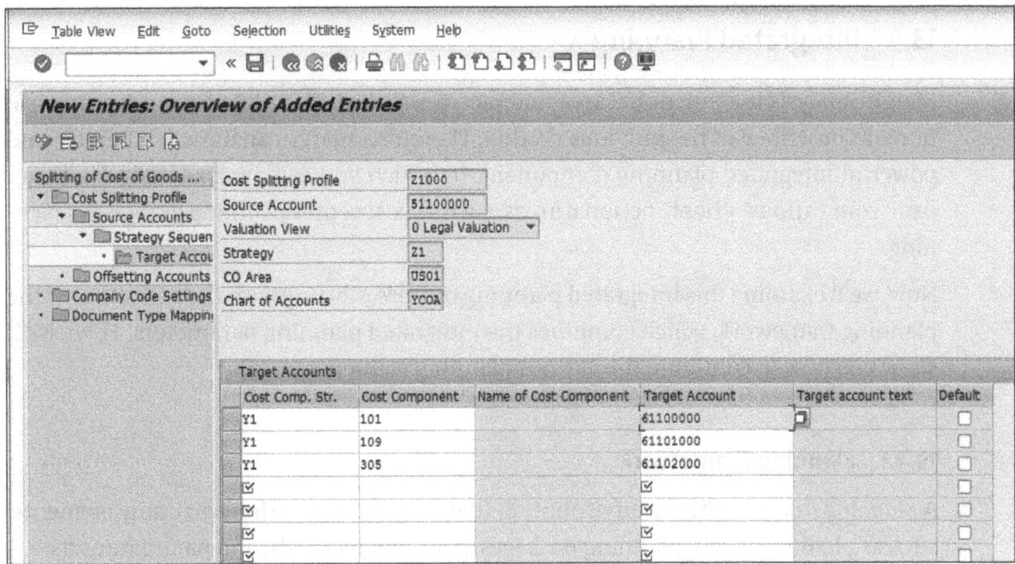

Figure 13.52 Target Accounts

Then, click **Company Code Settings** on the left side of the screen and click **New Entries** from the top menu. On the screen shown in Figure 13.53, you must activate the splitting structure for each company code. Enter a validity start date and company code, select the created splitting structure, and save these settings by clicking the **Save** button.

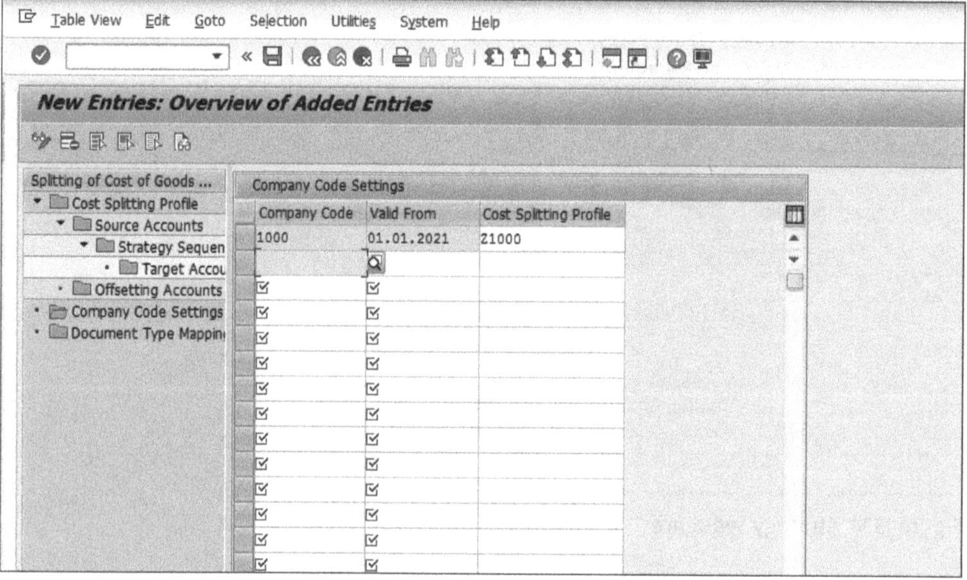

Figure 13.53 Company Code Activation

13.4 Integrated Planning

Margin analysis is a functional area that receives almost all its data from other applications, as described in the previous section. Therefore, margin analysis is a flexible and powerful integrated planning component, by which you can analyze integrated plan data from various other functional areas, such as cost center planning or logistics planning.

Now, we'll examine this integrated planning process, starting with the definition of the planning framework, which combines the integrated planning parameters. Then, we'll show you how to configure the various planning elements.

13.4.1 Planning Framework

A *planning framework* is an environment that contains the various planning elements, such as planning levels, planning packages, planning methods, and parameter sets.

To access the planning framework, follow the application menu path **Accounting • Controlling • Profitability Analysis • Planning • KEPM—Edit Planning Data**. Initially, you'll see the screen shown in Figure 13.54, where you'll define the planning elements.

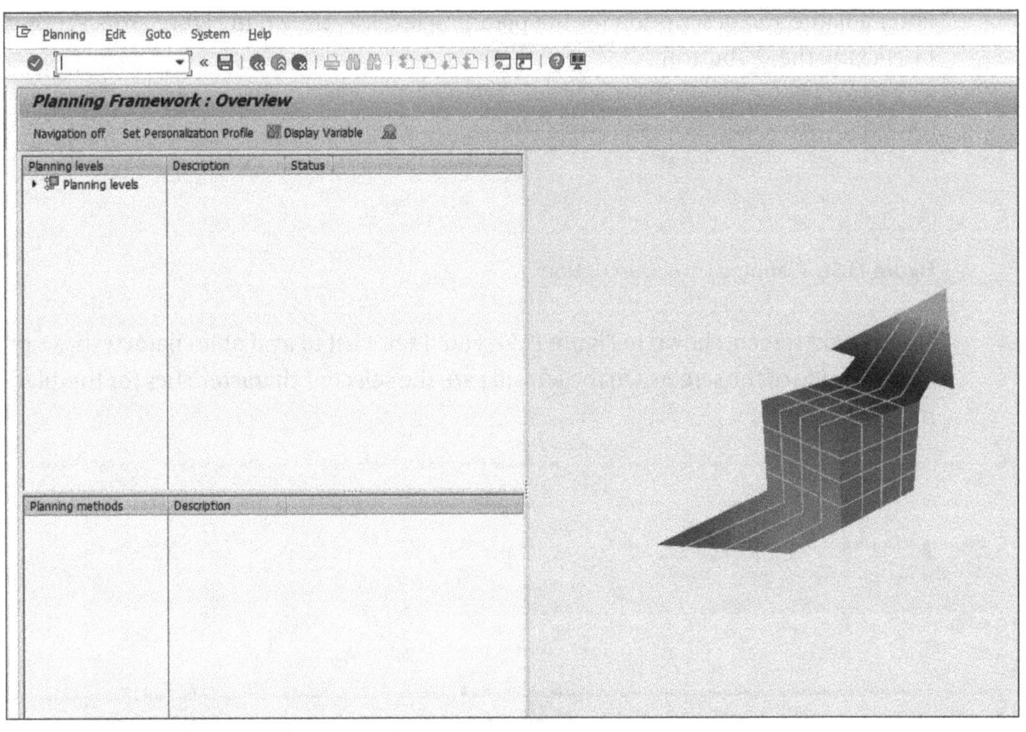

Figure 13.54 Planning Framework Initial Screen

Now, you'll need to define the various planning elements, such as planning levels, planning packages, planning methods, and parameter sets.

13.4.2 Planning Elements

First, let's define the planning level, which determines the level at which the planning is performed. Start by right-clicking **Planning levels** and selecting **Create Planning Level**, as shown in Figure 13.55.

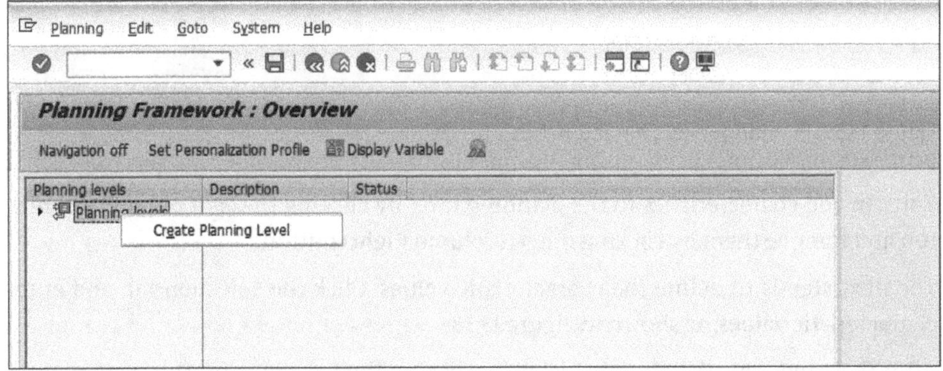

Figure 13.55 Creating a Planning Level

Enter a name and description for the planning level, as shown in Figure 13.56. Proceed by clicking the ✔ button.

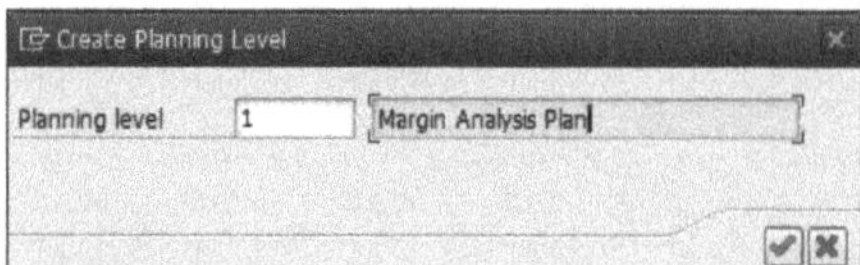

Figure 13.56 Planning Level Description

On the next screen, shown in Figure 13.57, you'll see a list of available characteristics on the right side of the screen. On the left side are the selected characteristics for the planning level.

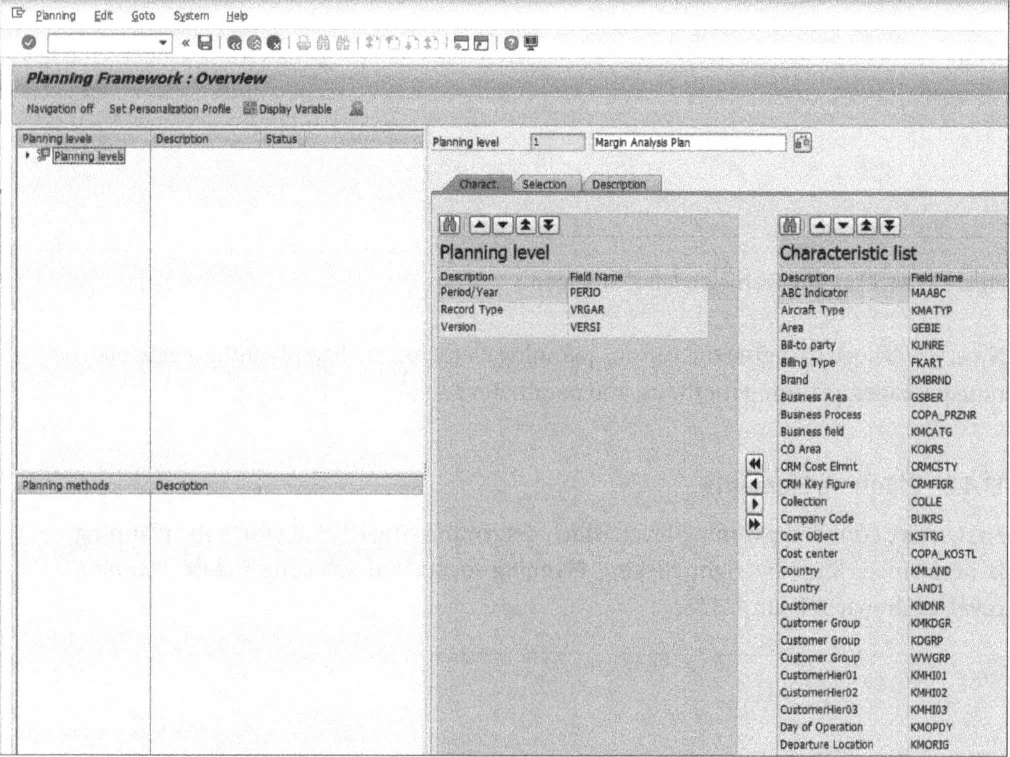

Figure 13.57 Planning Level Characteristics

You can add characteristics to the planning level by clicking the ◀ (**Column Left**) button and remove them by clicking the ▶ (**Column Right**) button.

The next step is to define the characteristic values. Click the **Selection** tab and enter characteristic values, as shown in Figure 13.58.

After that step, save the planning level by clicking the **Save** button. The system automatically generates planning methods for the level, as shown in Figure 13.59.

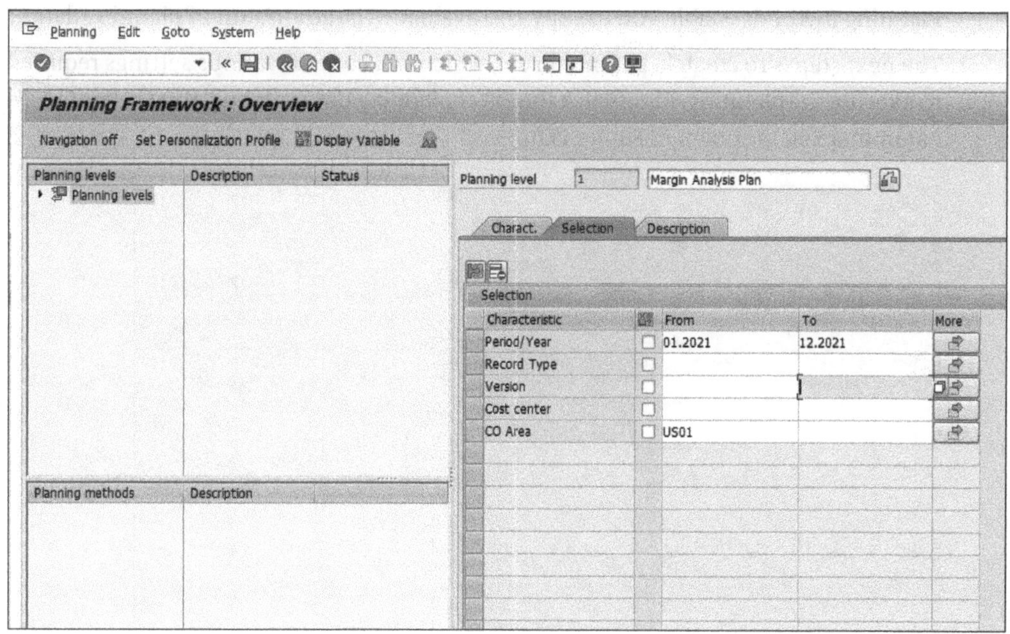

Figure 13.58 Planning Level Characteristics Values

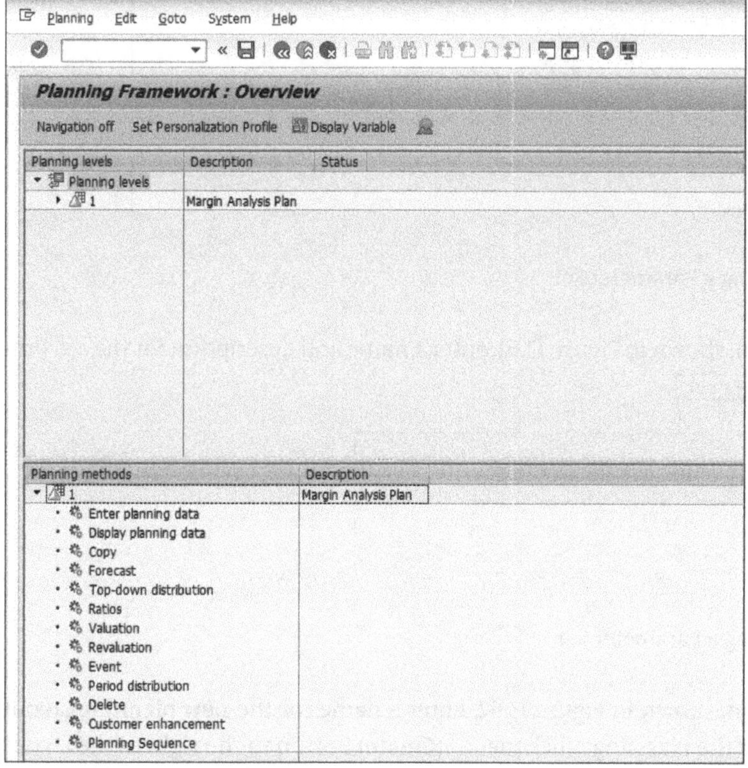

Figure 13.59 Planning Methods

Planning methods enable you to copy and evaluate a large amount of planning data.

The next step is to create a parameter set, which will contain various settings required to execute the planning. Right-click the **Enter planning data** method, then select **Create Parameter Set**, as shown in Figure 13.60.

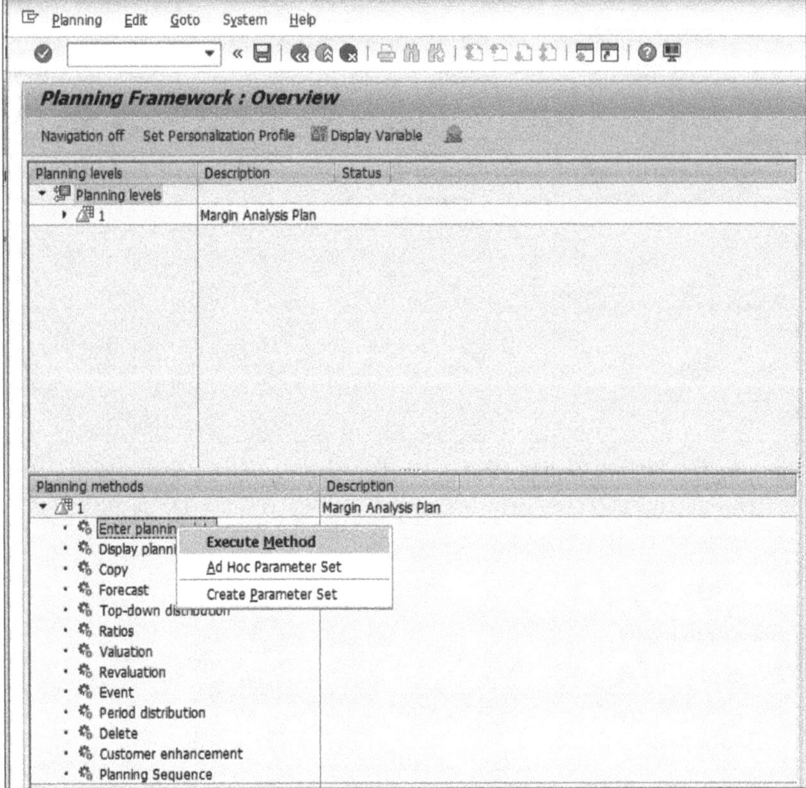

Figure 13.60 Entering a Parameter Set

On the next screen, shown in Figure 13.61, enter a name and description for the set. Proceed by pressing Enter.

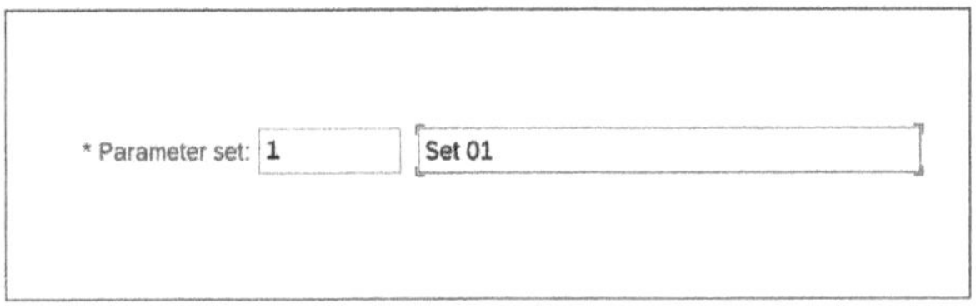

* Parameter set: 1 Set 01

Figure 13.61 Creating a Parameter Set

On the next screen, shown in Figure 13.62, enter a name for the new planning layout and a currency for the planning. Click the (**Create**) button to the right of the layout name to create it.

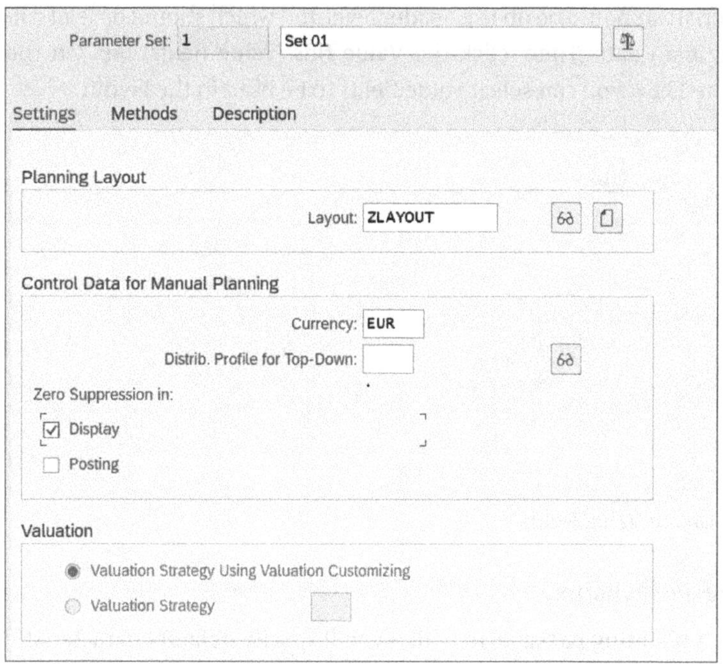

Figure 13.62 Parameter Settings

On the next screen, shown in Figure 13.63, you'll define the characteristics to be used in the planning layout.

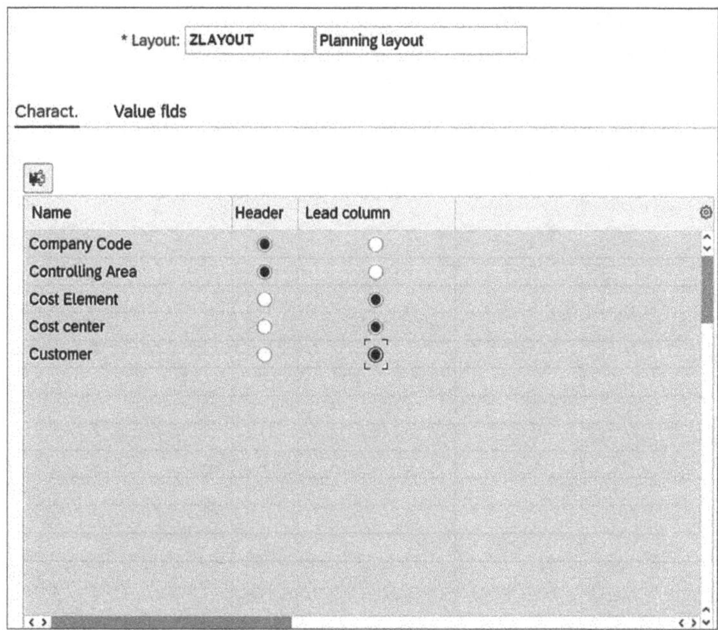

Figure 13.63 Planning Layout Characteristics

Select which characteristics should be on the header level and which should be lead columns when entering plan data. Then, click the **Value flds** (value fields) tab. On the screen shown in Figure 13.64, you can select value fields to be used in the layout.

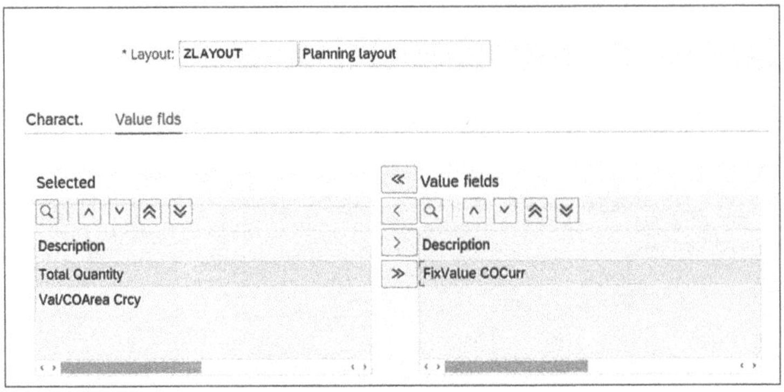

Figure 13.64 Planning Layout Value Fields

Then, save by clicking the [save icon] button.

You must also create a planning package, in which you'll specify default characteristic values. Right-click the planning level and select **Create Planning Package**, as shown in Figure 13.65.

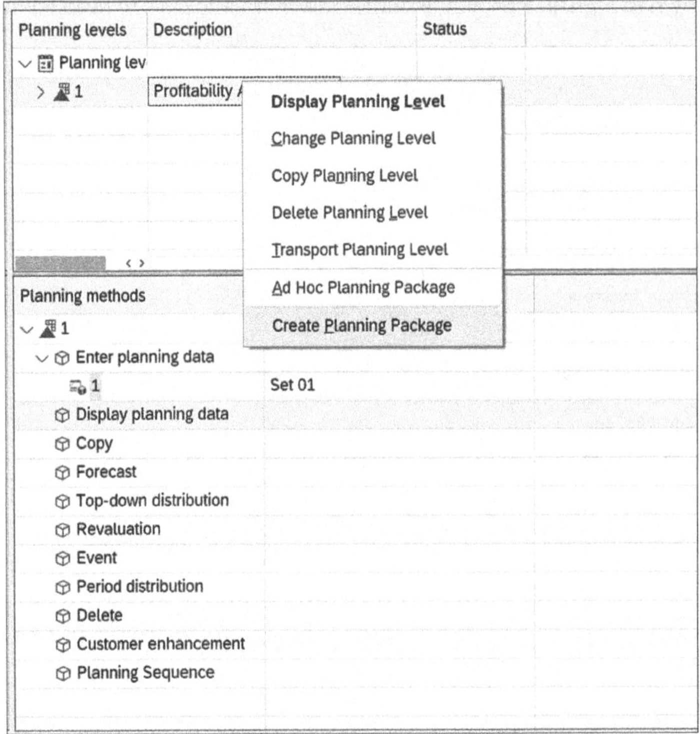

Figure 13.65 Creating a Planning Package

Enter a name and a description for the planning package, as shown in Figure 13.66.

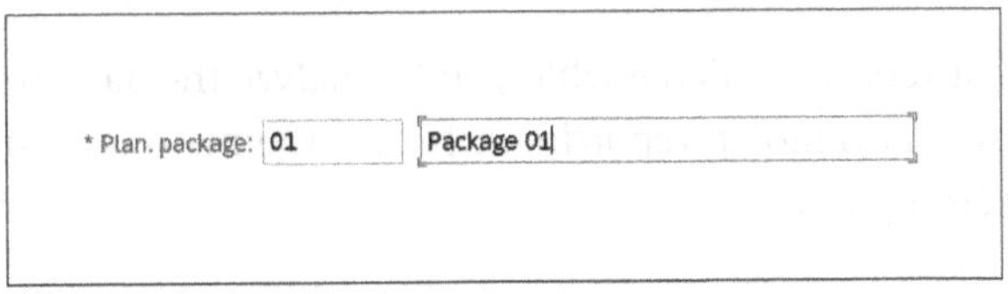

* Plan. package: 01 Package 01

Figure 13.66 Planning Package Name

Proceed by pressing Enter. On the next screen, shown in Figure 13.67, enter default values for the characteristics. Then, save your entries by clicking the **Save** button.

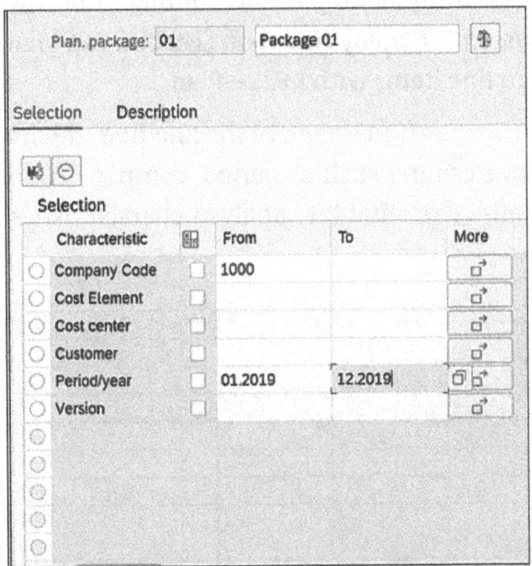

Figure 13.67 Planning Package Defaults

With that step, you've completed the configuration for integrated planning.

13.5 Information System

Margin analysis almost entirely receives data from elsewhere. Its main strength is that, when properly designed and configured, this capability can provide important and powerful management reports to track and analyze the profitability of your company. Not surprisingly, the information system of profitability analysis provides myriad sophisticated and flexible reports that can meet all reporting requirements.

In addition, you can easily create your own reports. In SAP S/4HANA, margin analysis reports are extremely fast, benefiting from the revolutionary columnar in-memory database. Users of profitability analysis from older SAP releases are probably well aware that some profitability analysis reports had rather long runtimes and had to be executed in the background, sometimes over a day or even more. Now, in SAP S/4HANA, you can produce huge and powerful profitability analysis reports extremely quickly and on the fly.

Let's first examine the line-item list reports, which enable you to analyze the data on the line-item level. Then, we'll discuss drilldown reporting, which is the main tool to build your own profitability analysis reports.

13.5.1 Line-Item Lists

As with other controlling components, profitability analysis also provides reporting on the lowest line-item level.

To execute line-item reports, follow the application menu path **Accounting • Controlling • Profitability Analysis • Information System • Display Line Item List**. You can view actual line items with **KE24—Actual** and plan line items with **KE25—Plan**.

Enter Transaction KE24. Figure 13.68 shows the selection screen of the line-item report, in which you can select line items by various criteria such as period, company code, cost element, creation date and user, and defined profitability analysis characteristics. Then, click **Execute** from the top menu.

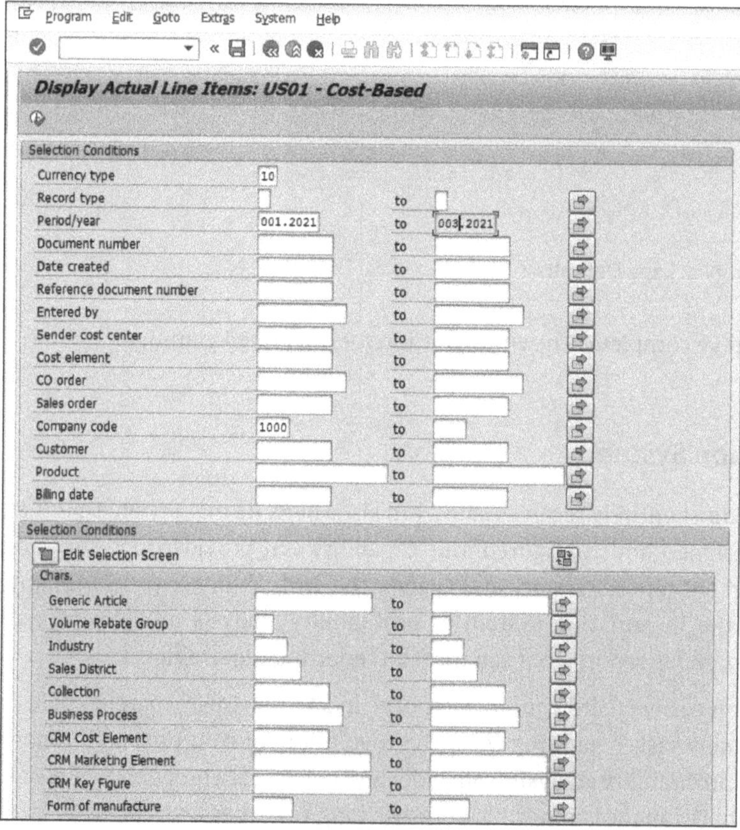

Figure 13.68 Actual Line Items Selection Screen

On the next screen, shown in Figure 13.69, you'll see the output of the report. You'll see profitability analysis line items based on the selections. You can add and remove fields from the report by selecting **Change Layout** from the top menu.

Standard layout | Master data | Profitability segment | FI/CO documents...

Plan/Act. Indicator 0

Number of line items 15
Mode of access Read acc. to current structure

Period	Doc. no.	Item	Created on	Sender CCtr	Cost Element	Curr.	Σ	Value TranCurr	Σ	Value in Obj. Crcy	Ocur	Σ	Val/COArea Crcy	CACur	Σ	FixValue COCurr	Σ	Total Quantity	UM
012.2020	A000000300	000001	23.12.2020		54083000	USD		0,00		0,00	USD		0,00	USD		0,00		2	EA
012.2020	A000000300	000001	27.12.2020		54083000	USD		0,00		0,00	USD		0,00	USD		0,00		2	EA
012.2020	A000000300	000002	27.12.2020		54083000	USD		0,00		0,00	USD		0,00	USD		0,00		1	EA
001.2021	A000002Y00	000001	03.01.2021		54083000	USD		80,00		80,00	USD		80,00	USD		0,00		2	EA
001.2021	A000002Y00	000002	03.01.2021		54083000	USD		0,00		0,00	USD		0,00	USD		0,00		1	EA
001.2021	A000003200	000001	05.01.2021		54083000	USD		0,00		0,00	USD		0,00	USD		0,00		2	EA
001.2021	A000003200	000002	05.01.2021		54083000	USD		40,00		40,00	USD		40,00	USD		0,00		1	EA
001.2021	A000003500	000001	05.01.2021		54083000	USD		0,00		0,00	USD		0,00	USD		0,00		1	EA
001.2021	A000003600	000001	05.01.2021		41000000	USD		5,00-		5,00-	USD		5,00-	USD		0,00		1-	EA
001.2021	A000003900	000001	05.01.2021		54083000	USD		0,00		0,00	USD		0,00	USD		0,00		1	EA
001.2021	A000003900	000002	05.01.2021		54083000	USD		40,00		40,00	USD		40,00	USD		0,00		1	EA
001.2021	A000003A00	000001	05.01.2021		41000000	USD		5,00-		5,00-	USD		5,00-	USD		0,00		1-	EA
001.2021	A000003A00	000002	05.01.2021		41000000	USD		2,00-		2,00-	USD		2,00-	USD		0,00		1-	EA
001.2021	A000003D00	000001	05.01.2021		54083000	USD		0,00		0,00	USD		0,00	USD		0,00		1	EA
001.2021	A000003G00	000001	06.01.2021		54083000	USD		0,00		0,00	USD		0,00	USD		0,00		2	EA
						USD	•	**148,00**	•	**148,00**	**USD**	•	**148,00**	**USD**	•	**0,00**	•	**14**	**EA**

Figure 13.69 Actual Line Items Output

For example, to add the **Created by** field, select it on the right side of the screen, as shown in Figure 13.70, and move it to the left side (**Displayed Columns**) by clicking the ◀ button. Then, confirm by clicking the ✔ button.

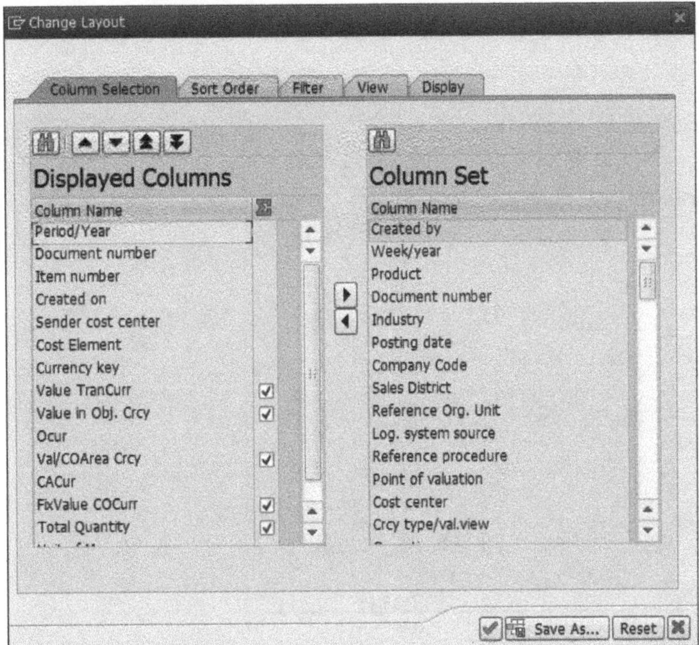

Figure 13.70 Changing the Layout

Double-clicking a line item shows the controlling document and the profitability segment, as shown in Figure 13.71.

Display Actual Cost Documents

Document | Master Record

Layout	1SAP	Primary cost posting
COarea currency	USD	USD
Valuation View/Group	0	Legal Valuation

DocumentNo / PRw	Doc. Date / OTy Object	Document Header Text / CO Object Name	Cost Elem.	RT RefDocNo User Name / Cost element name	Val/COArea Crcy	Total quantity	PUM	C	OffsetAcct
A000002Y00	03.01.2021			R 4900000012 S20USER1					
1	PSG 107		54083000	Inv Chg COGS w/CE	80,00	2	EA	M	13400000
2	PSG 108		54083000	Inv Chg COGS w/CE	0,00	1	EA	M	13400000

Figure 13.71 Profitability Document

13.5.2 Drilldown Reporting

Margin analysis uses the drilldown reporting technique, which you're already familiar with from Chapter 12. This flexible form of reporting enables you to slice and dice your profitability data along any dimension you need.

Drilldown reports, as you already know, can be basic or use a form, which can be reused in multiple reports. Let's create a contribution margin report using a form. To create a form, enter Transaction KE34. On the screen shown in Figure 13.72, define the form's name and structure.

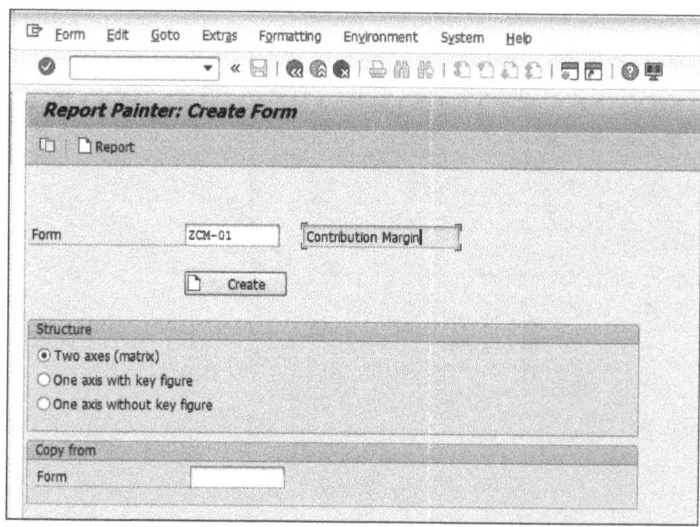

Figure 13.72 Creating a Form

Enter a name and description for the form and select the **Two axes (matrix)** type of structure. Then, proceed by clicking the **Create** button.

Figure 13.73 shows a sample contribution margin structure that you can define. In the rows, define various cost elements that represent the relevant categories. In the columns, select the actual amount and actual quantity.

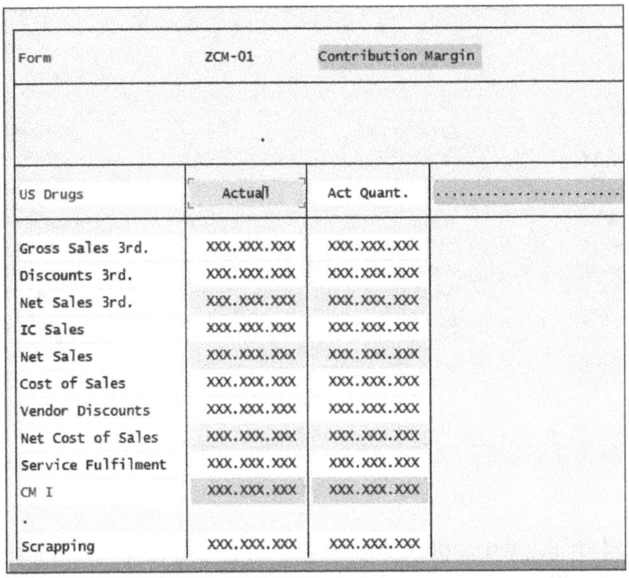

Form	ZCM-01	Contribution Margin	
US Drugs	Actual	Act Quant.	....
Gross Sales 3rd.	XXX.XXX.XXX	XXX.XXX.XXX	
Discounts 3rd.	XXX.XXX.XXX	XXX.XXX.XXX	
Net Sales 3rd.	XXX.XXX.XXX	XXX.XXX.XXX	
IC Sales	XXX.XXX.XXX	XXX.XXX.XXX	
Net Sales	XXX.XXX.XXX	XXX.XXX.XXX	
Cost of Sales	XXX.XXX.XXX	XXX.XXX.XXX	
Vendor Discounts	XXX.XXX.XXX	XXX.XXX.XXX	
Net Cost of Sales	XXX.XXX.XXX	XXX.XXX.XXX	
Service Fulfilment	XXX.XXX.XXX	XXX.XXX.XXX	
CM I	XXX.XXX.XXX	XXX.XXX.XXX	
.			
Scrapping	XXX.XXX.XXX	XXX.XXX.XXX	

Figure 13.73 Form Structure

To create a drilldown profitability analysis report, follow the application menu path **Accounting • Controlling • Profitability Analysis • Information System • Define Report • KE31—Create Profitability Report.** As shown in Figure 13.74, enter a name and description for the report and select the already created form. Then, proceed by clicking the **Create** button.

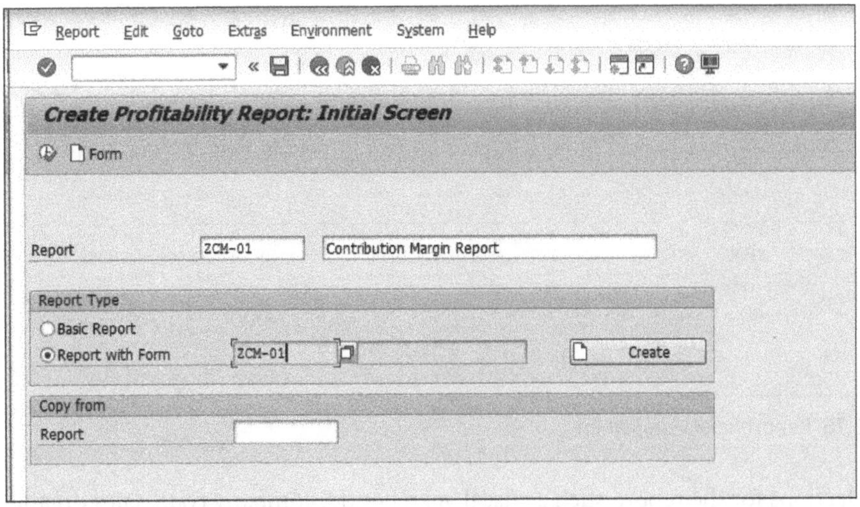

Report Edit Goto Extras Environment System Help

Create Profitability Report: Initial Screen

Form

Report ZCM-01 Contribution Margin Report

Report Type

Basic Report

Report with Form ZCM-01 Create

Copy from

Report

Figure 13.74 Creating a Report

On the next screen, shown in Figure 13.75, select and define the required characteristics. We'll define them as variables; therefore, they can be entered during report execution at the selection screen.

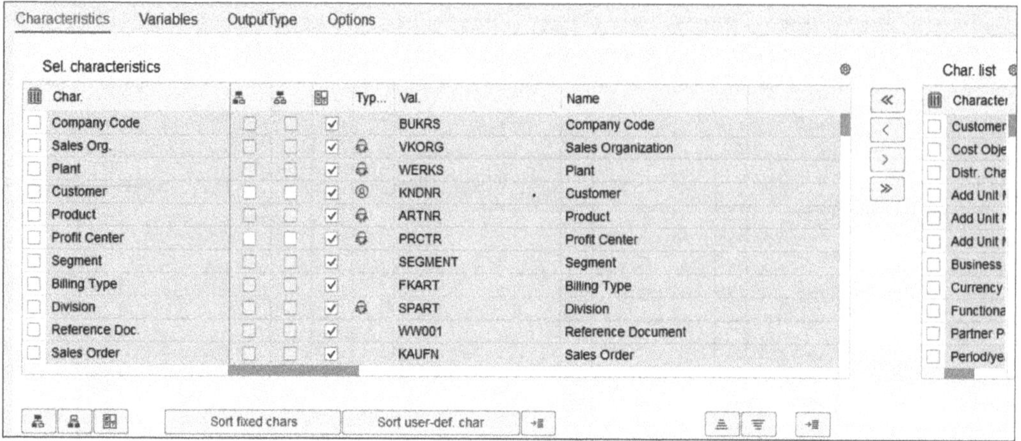

Figure 13.75 Report Definition

To execute an already defined drilldown report, follow the application menu path **Accounting • Controlling • Profitability Analysis • Information System • KE30—Execute Report**. Select the report you defined, **ZCM-01 Contribution Margin Report**, and execute it. Figure 13.76 shows the selection screen of the report.

Save as Variant... Attributes More Exit

Report selections

Sales Order:		to:	
Reference Document:		to:	
Fiscal Year:	2019	to:	
Period:	001	to:	003
Company Code:	1000	to:	
Sales Organization:		to:	
Plant:		to:	
Customer:		to:	
Profit Center:		to:	
Segment:		to:	
Billing Type:		to:	
Product:		to:	
Division:		to:	

Output type

Figure 13.76 Report Selection Screen

Enter selections for the report, such as fiscal year, period, company code, sales organization, and other profitability characteristics. You can also choose the type of report output: graphical report output, classical drilldown list, or object list. Then, execute the report by clicking the **Execute** button.

Figure 13.77 shows the graphical report output. On the top-left, you can navigate between the characteristics, thus drilling down into them. On the right side, you see the calculated contribution margin as defined in the report.

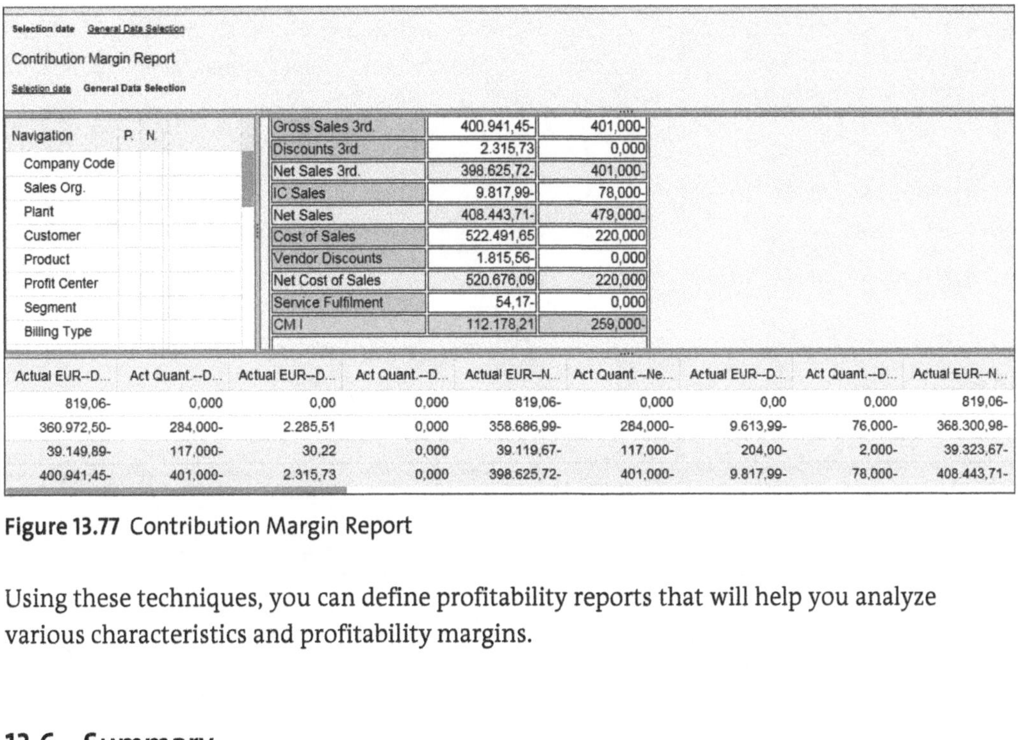

Selection date General Data Selection

Contribution Margin Report

Selection date General Data Selection

Navigation	P.	N.
Company Code		
Sales Org.		
Plant		
Customer		
Product		
Profit Center		
Segment		
Billing Type		

Gross Sales 3rd.	400.941,45-	401,000-
Discounts 3rd.	2.315,73	0,000
Net Sales 3rd.	398.625,72-	401,000-
IC Sales	9.817,99-	78,000-
Net Sales	408.443,71-	479,000-
Cost of Sales	522.491,65	220,000
Vendor Discounts	1.815,56-	0,000
Net Cost of Sales	520.676,09	220,000
Service Fulfilment	54,17-	0,000
CM I	112.178,21	259,000-

Actual EUR--D...	Act Quant.--D...	Actual EUR--D...	Act Quant.--D...	Actual EUR--N...	Act Quant.--Ne...	Actual EUR--D...	Act Quant.--D...	Actual EUR--N...
819,06-	0,000	0,00	0,000	819,06-	0,000	0,00	0,000	819,06-
360.972,50-	284,000-	2.285,51	0,000	358.686,99-	284,000-	9.613,99-	76,000-	368.300,98-
39.149,89-	117,000-	30,22	0,000	39.119,67-	117,000-	204,00-	2,000-	39.323,67-
400.941,45-	401,000-	2.315,73	0,000	398.625,72-	401,000-	9.817,99-	78,000-	408.443,71-

Figure 13.77 Contribution Margin Report

Using these techniques, you can define profitability reports that will help you analyze various characteristics and profitability margins.

13.6 Summary

In this chapter, we provided an extensive guide to margin analysis. You learned the differences between and benefits of costing-based profitability analysis and margin analysis. We put special emphasis on the improvements SAP S/4HANA brings to margin analysis.

You've learned the global settings required for activating margin analysis, and you also learned how the various value flows are posted to margin analysis. Then, we walked you through how to configure integrated planning in margin analysis. Finally, you learned about the powerful line-item and drilldown reports that profitability analysis provides and how you can create your own reports.

In the next chapter, you'll learn how to configure and use predictive accounting, which is used to project future financial flows and is a new functional area, introduced with SAP S/4HANA.

Chapter 14
Predictive Accounting

This chapter introduces predictive accounting, which is a new, and quite useful, functional area in SAP, enabling you to post predictive accounting entries based on sales orders received from customers. We'll provide step-by-step instructions for configuring predictive accounting. We'll also explain how you can better forecast your financial flows using this exciting new functionality in SAP S/4HANA.

For many years, financial users of SAP have benefited from the full integration between the sales and financial processes SAP offers. SAP S/4HANA now brings this integration to the next level by offering predictive accounting. Essentially, this functionality enables you to forecast and record accounting entries based on sales orders received from customers and thus to effectively forecast the goods issues, cost of goods sold (COGS), and the expected revenue. With this functionality, you can perform various planning analysis and forecasts and derive valuable information from future sales flows. Predictive accounting can also be used for other processes on the expense side, such as travel expenses.

Predictive accounting is quite useful because it enables better planning of the future expenses and revenues based on already incurred commitments, such as sales orders. This capability empowers financial managers to plan better the future cash flows, profitability, and tax liabilities of the company.

Predictive postings are posted in specially designated predictive ledger and thus do not affect the official financial statements of a company, which are based on already incurred revenues and expenses.

In this chapter, we'll first review the relevant configuration needed to activate and enable predictive accounting, then we'll discuss the various data flows based on which predictive accounting is performed, and finally, we'll review the reports made available through predictive accounting.

14.1 Configuration

To configure predictive accounting, you must perform the following steps:

- Maintaining ledger settings
- Mapping the predictive ledger

- Activating predictive accounting for sales orders
- Maintaining billing types for predictive accounting
- Maintaining item categories for predictive accounting
- Maintaining sales order item categories for predictive accounting

We'll start by configuring the ledger settings.

14.1.1 Ledger Settings

Predictive accounting uses a new type of ledger introduced with SAP S/4HANA called the *extension ledger*. The extension ledger essentially is a delta ledger. Its purpose is to store the differences between valuations. Therefore, this ledger is always mapped with a standard ledger, based on which it posts delta postings. All postings to its underlying ledger are also relevant to the extension ledger. Reporting out of the extension ledger is based on its underlying ledger, together with the delta postings.

Three types of extension ledgers are available:

- **Standard journal entries**
  This type stores journal entries with real document numbers. These journal postings can't be deleted and, when required, must be reversed. This type is used in the case of tax adjustments or management adjustments.
- **P (line items with technical numbers/no deletion possible), previously known as prediction**
  This type stores journal postings only with technical numbers, without document numbers. These journal postings can't be deleted and, when required, must be reversed. This extension ledger type is used for predictive accounting.
- **S (line items with technical numbers/deletion possible), previously known as simulation**
  This extension ledger type stores journal entries with technical numbers, without document numbers, but these journal entries can be deleted. This type is used in the case of simulation postings.

In the next configuration activity, you must configure the ledger for predictive accounting, which will be of type P (line items with technical numbers/no deletion possible). In this ledger, predictive accounting postings will be saved. Follow the menu path **Financial Accounting • Financial Accounting Global Settings • Ledgers • Ledger • Define Settings for Ledgers and Currency Types**, which shows a list of ledgers already defined in the system, as shown in Figure 14.1.

In the **Ldgr Type** (ledger type) field, notice that ledger **0E: Commitment/Order Entry** has been set as an extension ledger. **0E** is an extension ledger provided by SAP for predictive accounting. Let's create our own ledger for predictive accounting by copying extension ledger 0E. Select **0E** and click on **Copy As...** from the top menu.

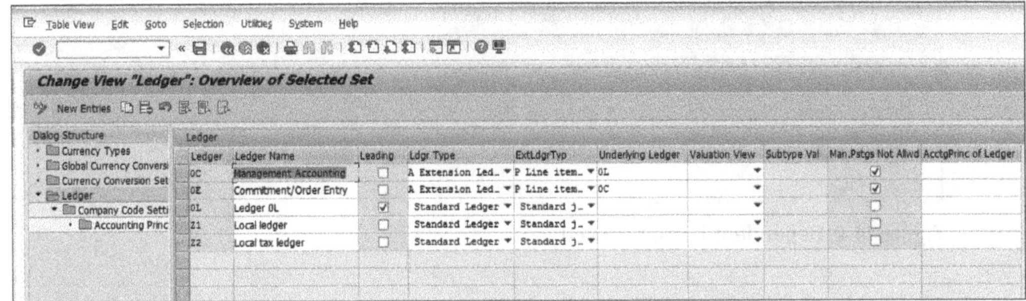

Figure 14.1 Ledger Definition

On the screen shown in Figure 14.2, let's call our ledger **ZC: Predictive Accounting** and define the leading ledger 0L as its underlying ledger. For the extension ledger type, we'll choose **P – Line items with technical numbers/no deletion possible**, which is used for predictive accounting.

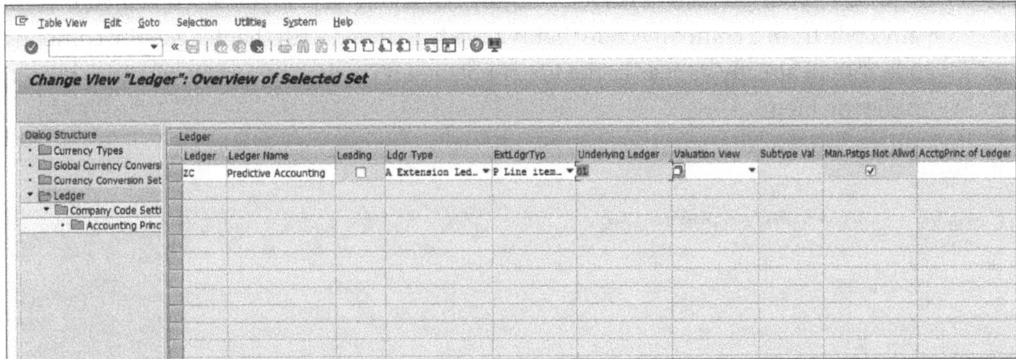

Figure 14.2 Predictive Ledger Definition

Continue by pressing [Enter]. Then, you'll see a dialog box for dependent entries, as shown in Figure 14.3.

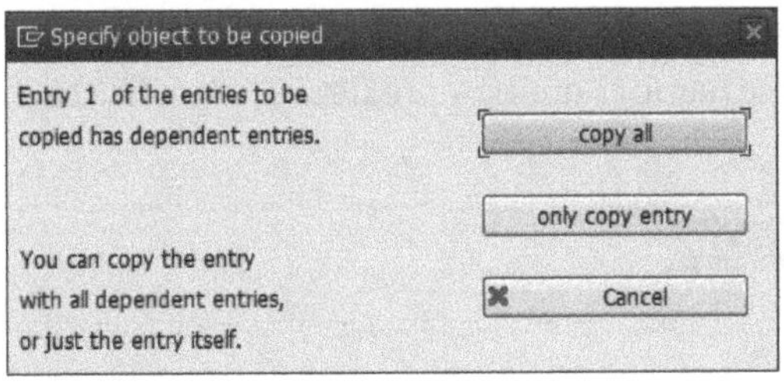

Specify object to be copied

Entry 1 of the entries to be copied has dependent entries.

You can copy the entry with all dependent entries, or just the entry itself.

copy all

only copy entry

Cancel

Figure 14.3 Dependent Entries

Proceed by clicking the **copy all** button. An informational popup message including the number of dependent entries copied will be displayed, as shown in Figure 14.4.

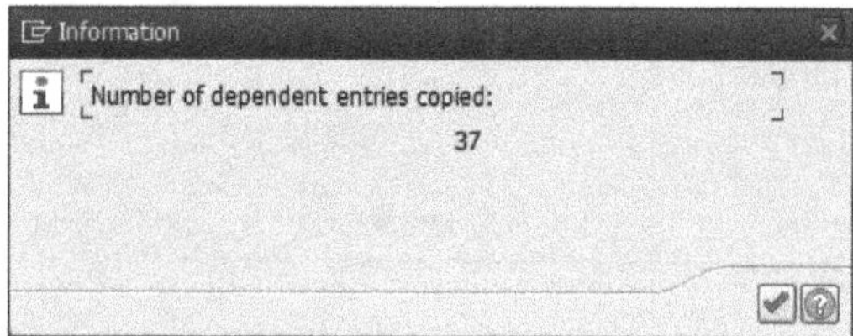

Figure 14.4 Dependent Entries Copied

Proceed by clicking the (Enter) button.

14.1.2 Mapping the Predictive Ledger

You must ensure also that your new predictive accounting ledger is mapped to tour company code. Select the ledger from the screen shown earlier in Figure 14.2 and click on **Company Code Settings for the Ledger**. Then, make sure your company code is mapped to your predictive ledger, as shown in Figure 14.5. If you've copied your company code from a company code that is already mapped with that ledger, the company code should already appear in the list. If not, add it by clicking the **New Entries** button on the top menu.

Change View "Company Code Settings for the Ledger": Overview

Ledger ZC Predictive Accounting

Company Code Settings for the Ledger

CoCd	Company Name	Local Curr. T...	Global Curr. ...	FreeDef Crcy 1	FreeDef Crcy 2	FreeDef Crcy 3	FreeDef Crcy 4	FreeDef Crcy 5	FreeDef Crcy 6	FreeDef Crcy 7	FreeDef Crcy 8	Fisc.Year V...	Posting Var...
0001	Company Code 1010	10	30									K4	1010
1000	US Generic Drugs	10	30									K4	1000
1010	Company Code 1010	10	30									K4	1010
1110	Company Code 1110	10	30									K4	1110
1210	Company Code 1210	10	30									K4	1210
1410	Company Code 1410	10	30									K4	1410
1410	Company Code 1410	10	30									K4	1410
1710	Company Code 1710	10	30									K4	1710
1710	Company Code 1710	10	30									K4	1710

Figure 14.5 Predictive Ledger Mapping

Now, save your settings by clicking the **Save** button. Then, the system will display a message that a ledger group with the same name as our new predictive ledger has been created, as shown in Figure 14.6.

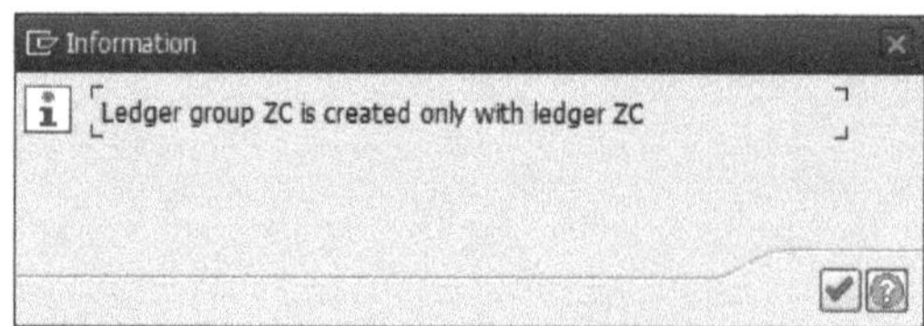

Figure 14.6 Ledger Group Message

Proceed by clicking the (Enter) button.

14.1.3 Activate Extension Ledger

In the next configuration activity, you'll need to activate the extension ledger by following the menu path **Financial Accounting • Predictive Accounting • Check Prediction Ledger**. As shown in Figure 14.7, you'll see the ledgers relevant for predictive accounting.

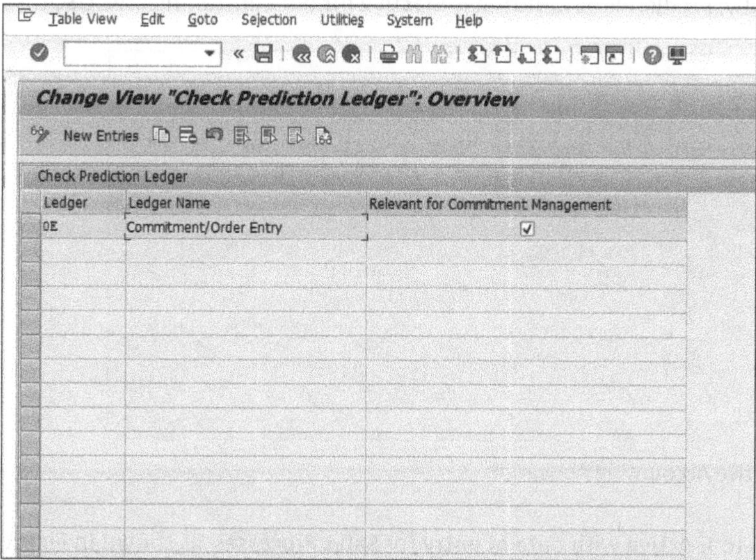

Figure 14.7 Activating a Predictive Ledger

Click **New Entries** on the top menu and add the new ledger ZC, as shown in Figure 14.8.

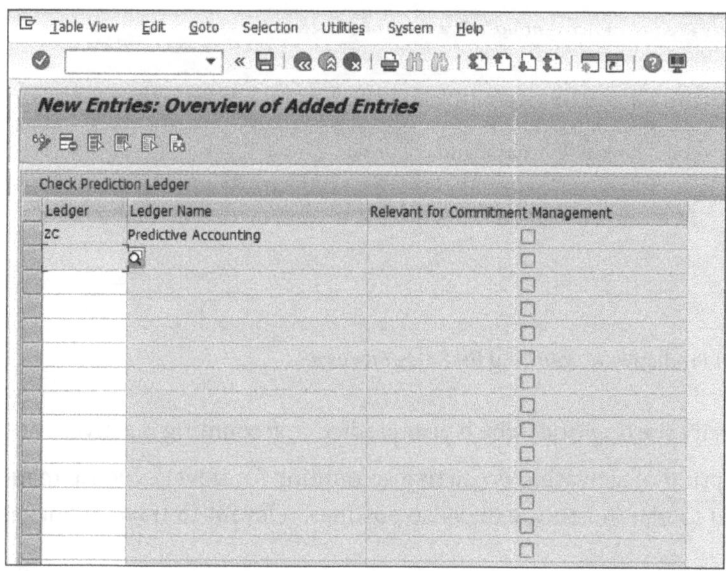

Figure 14.8 Adding a New Predictive Ledger

14.1.4 Activate Predictive Accounting for Sales Orders

In this configuration activity, you must activate predictive accounting so the functionality can generate relevant journal entries for sales orders.

To activate predictive accounting, follow the menu path **Financial Accounting • Predictive Accounting • Activate Predictive Accounting**. On the screen shown in Figure 14.9, notice that, initially, predictive accounting is **Inactive** for our controlling area US01.

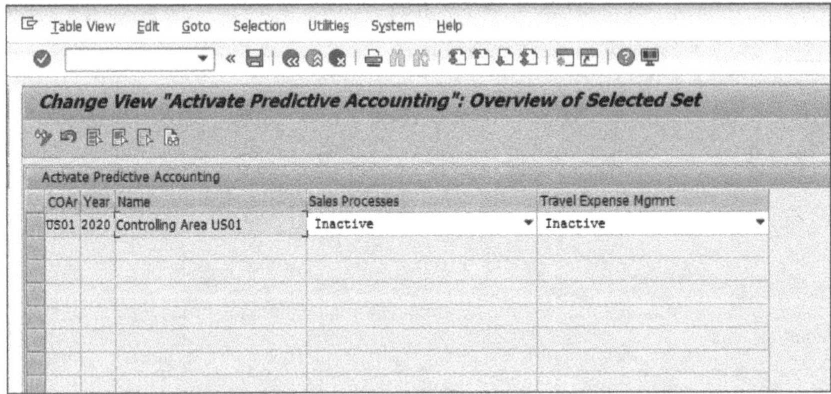

Figure 14.9 Predictive Accounting Activation

Switch the status to **1: Active with date of entry** for **Sales Processes**, as shown in Figure 14.10.

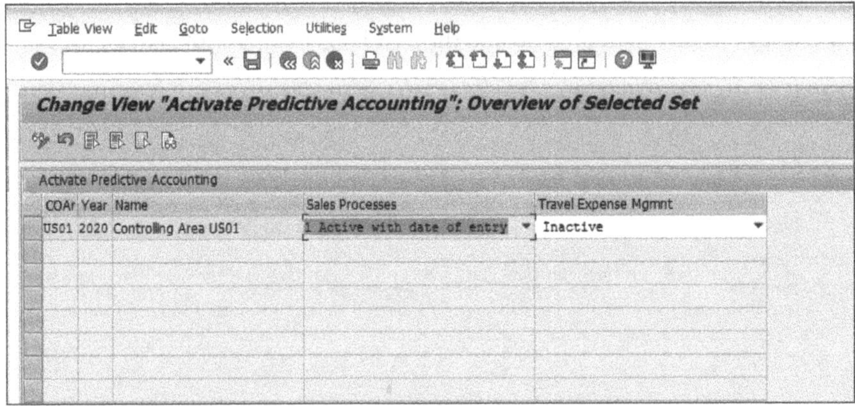

Figure 14.10 Activated Predictive Accounting for Sales Processes

In the **Year** field, specify starting from which year predictive accounting is active.

You also have the option of activating predictive accounting for travel expense management if you need to plan for future expense postings, relevant to travel management.

Save your entry by clicking the **Save** button.

14.1.5 Maintain Billing Types for Predictive Accounting

To enable the integration with SAP S/4HANA Sales, you'll need also to maintain billing types that are relevant for predictive accounting in SAP S/4HANA Sales. Only invoices with these billing types will generate predictive entries in the predictive journal.

To maintain billing types for predictive accounting, enter Transaction SM30, which is used to maintain configuration tables, when no specific path is available in the IMG configuration menu. Enter "FINSV_PRED_FKART" in the **Table/View** field, as shown in Figure 14.11, and click the **Maintain** button.

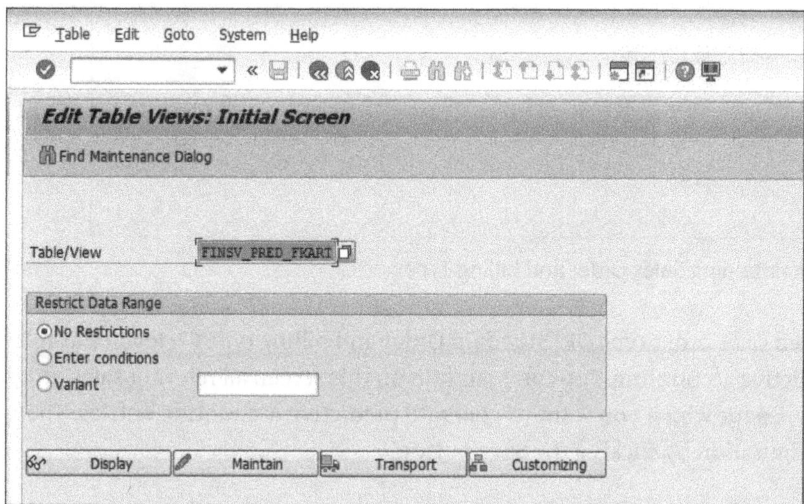

Figure 14.11 Maintaining a Configuration Table

Initially, the table is empty, as shown in Figure 14.12.

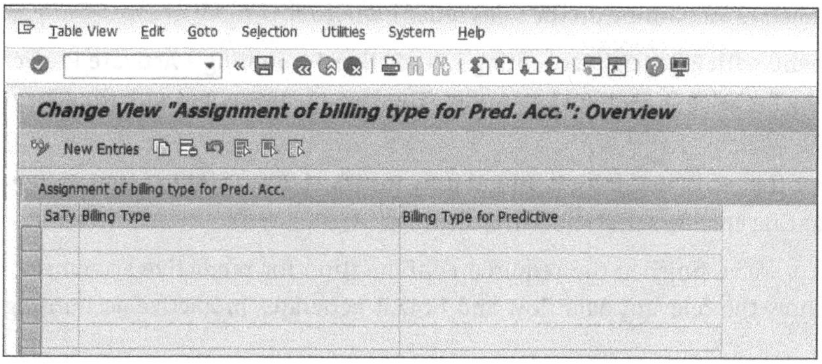

Figure 14.12 Table FINSV_PRED_FKART

Click on the **New Entries** button and then define the sales order (**SaTy**) and billing types relevant for predictive accounting, as shown in Figure 14.13.

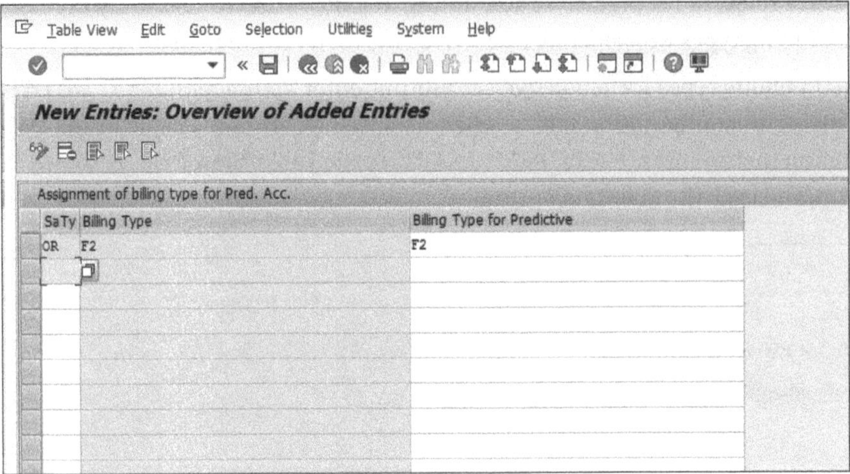

Figure 14.13 Maintaining Sales Order and Billing Types

We maintained sales order type **OR: Standard Order** and billing type **F2: Invoice** as relevant for predictive accounting. You can maintain on this screen all relevant sales order and billing types for which you want to generate predictive accounting entries. Then, save the configuration by clicking the **Save** button.

14.1.6 Maintain Sales Order Item Categories for Predictive Accounting

The last configuration step we need to execute is to maintain sales order item categories for predictive accounting. In this configuration activity, we can define the relevance for predictive accounting on the sales order item level.

Follow the menu path **Financial Accounting • Predictive Accounting • Activate Predictive Accounting for Sales Order Item Categories.** Then, you're presented with the screen shown in Figure 14.14.

On this screen, for each sales order item category for which you want to generate predictive accounting entries, select the **Active** field.

With that step, we've finished the required configuration for predictive accounting. Let's review now the relevant data flow and how it generates predictive accounting entries.

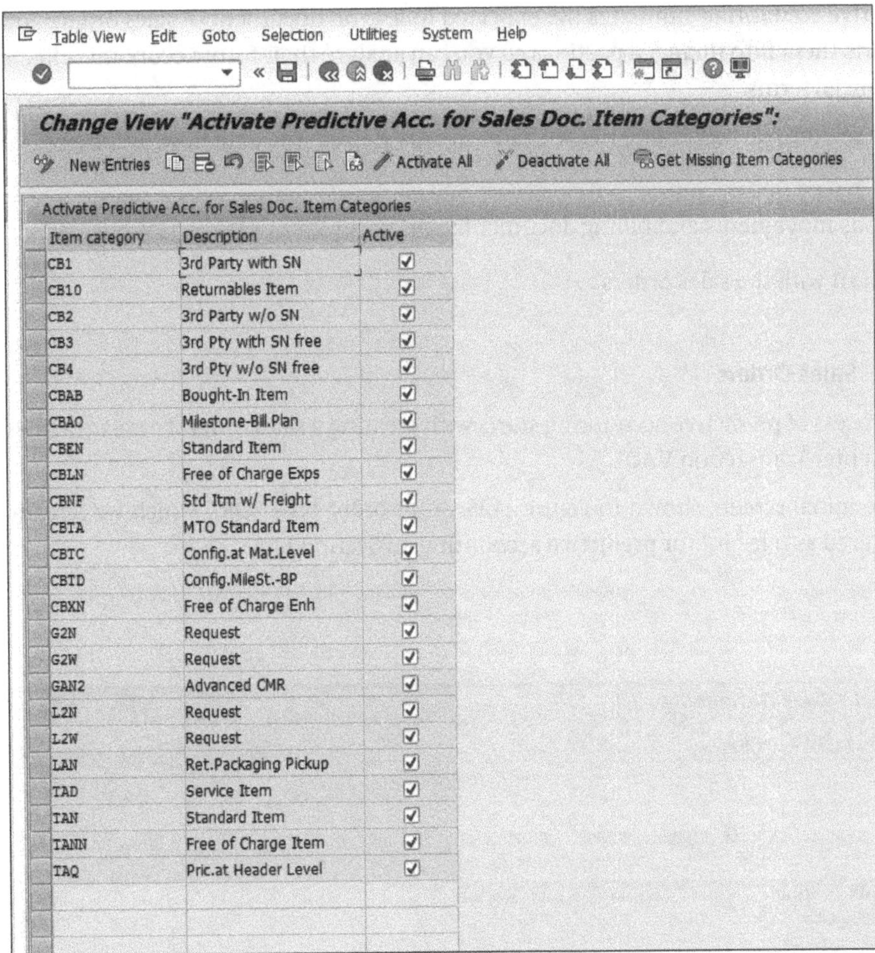

Figure 14.14 Maintaining Sales Order Item Categories for Predictive Accounting

14.2 Data Flow

Before predictive accounting became available in SAP S/4HANA, sales orders would not post anything to accounting. The first accounting entry in the sales data flow would happen at the time of goods issue. Now, with predictive accounting, at the time of posting a sales order, accounting entries will occur for the sales order, goods issue, and the invoice to predict the future accounting impact. Of course, these entries should not be used in official accounting reports; they are for internal management analysis, and that's why they are posted in the special extension ledger that we defined specifically for predictive accounting.

Predictive accounting simulates the expected follow-on document of sales orders and converts them into financial postings so you can analyze their future economic effects in financial terms.

In this section, we'll examine the relevant process steps in the data flow, as follows:

- Sales
- Goods movements and billing documents

We'll start with the sales orders.

14.2.1 Sales Orders

The process of predictive accounting starts with creating a sales order. To create a sales order, enter Transaction VA01.

On the initial screen, shown in Figure 14.15, enter order type "OR," which we already configured as relevant for predictive accounting, in Section 14.1.5.

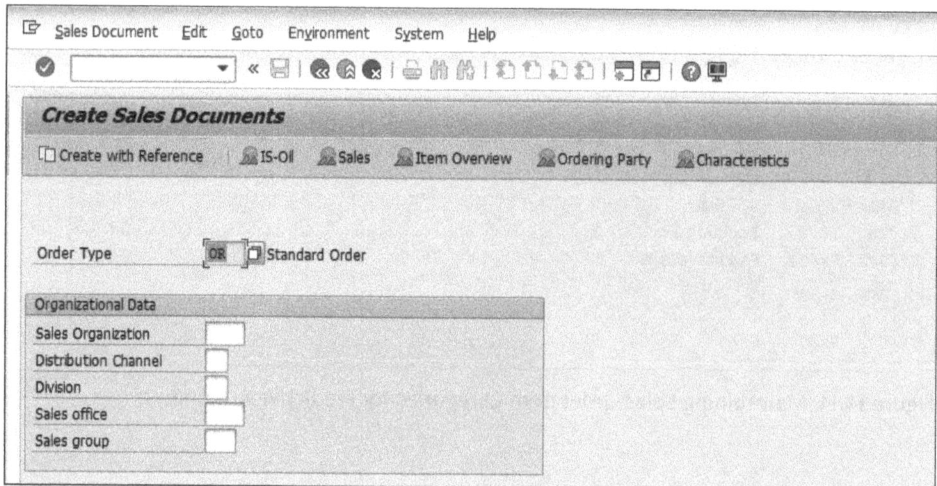

Figure 14.15 Creating a Sales Order

Now, let's create an order with reference to an existing order. Click **Create with Reference** from the top menu. Then, you're presented with the screen shown in Figure 14.16, where you can enter various references based on which to create the sales order.

Click the **Order** tab and enter an existing sales order in the **Order** field, as shown in Figure 14.17.

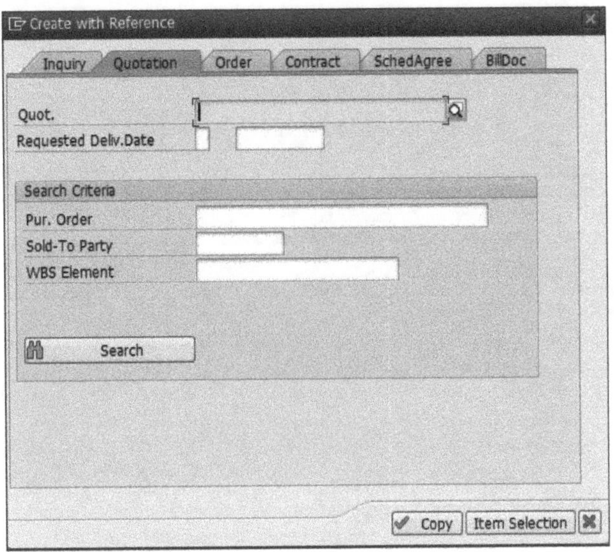

Figure 14.16 Creating with Reference

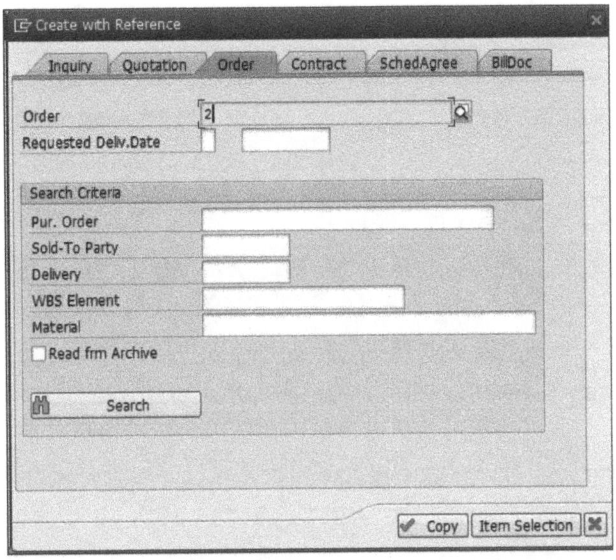

Figure 14.17 Sales Order Reference

Proceed by clicking the **Copy** button. On the next screen, shown in Figure 14.18, you can modify the details of the sales order.

You can double-click on the **Material** field to review the sales order item details. As shown in Figure 14.19, the sales order item category is **TAN**, which we already configured as relevant for predictive accounting.

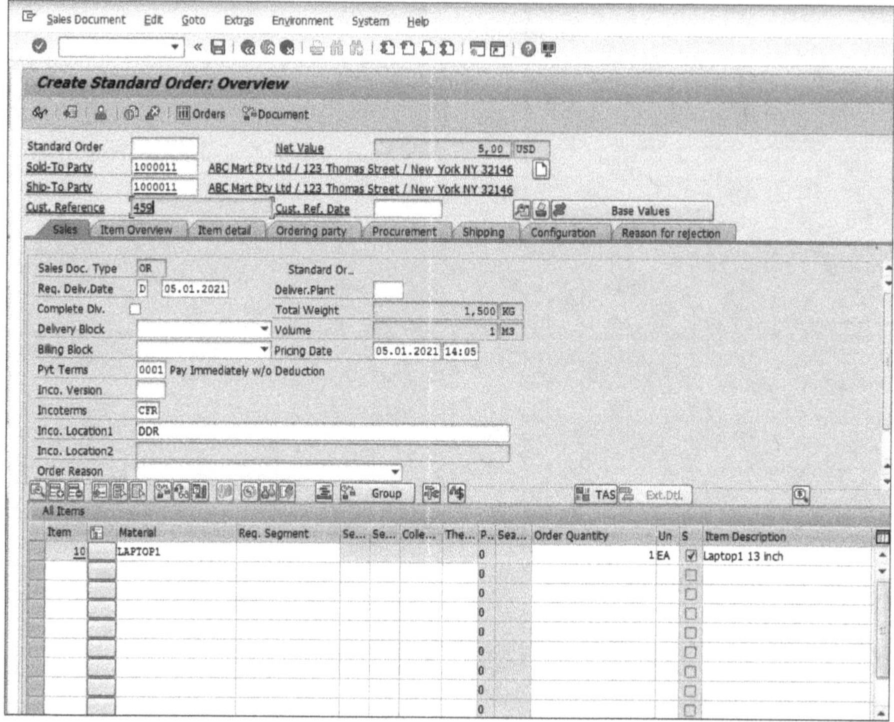

Figure 14.18 Sales Order Details

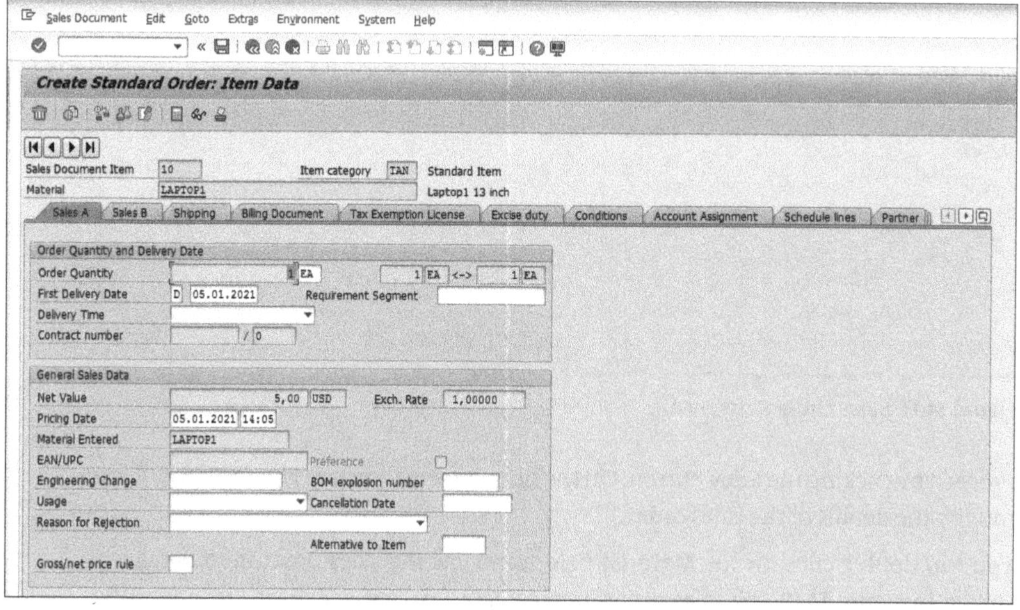

Figure 14.19 Sales Order Item

Save the sales order by clicking the **Save** button.

14.2.2 Goods Movements and Billing Documents

Let's see what predictive accounting entries were generated in the background. Note that, if we hadn't activated the predictive accounting functionality before creating a sales order, no accounting impact would occur. Now, however, when we create a sales order, the system creates a goods movement and billing document in predictive accounting.

Go to Transaction SE16N to review the postings that occurred in our predictive accounting ledger. Enter "ACDOCA" in the **Table** field and our new predictive ledger "ZC" in the **Fr.Value** field, as shown in Figure 14.20.

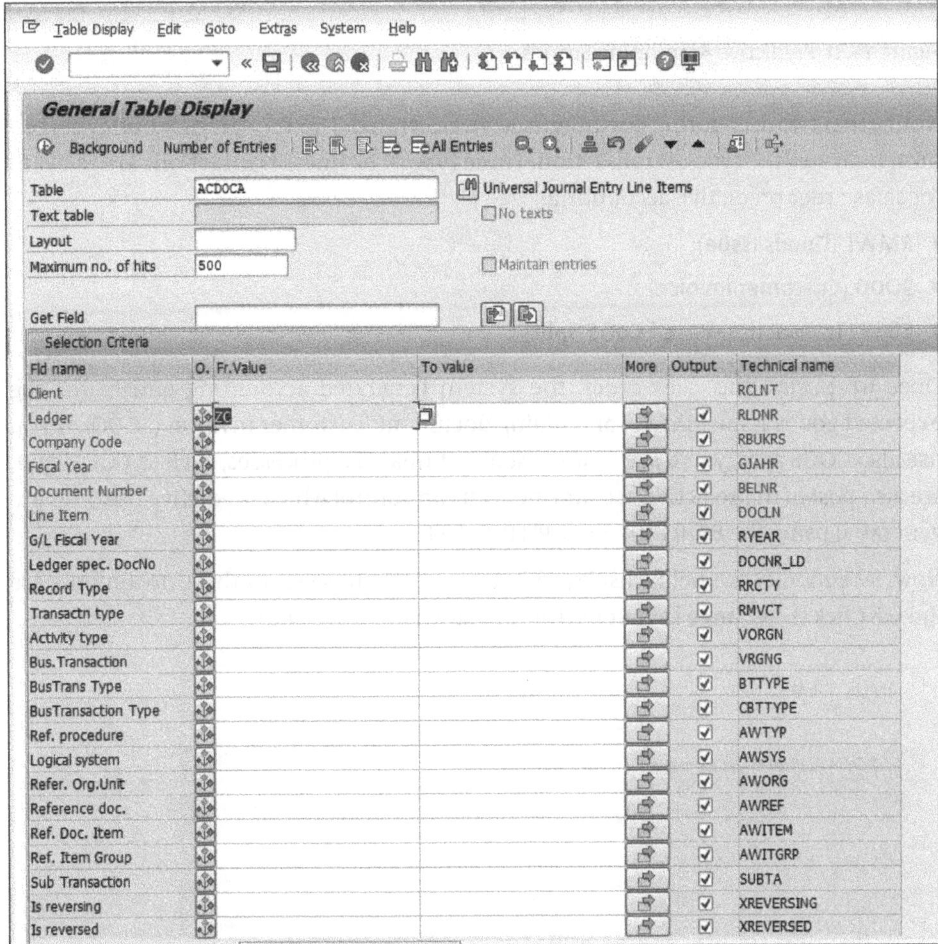

Figure 14.20 Table ACDOCA Display

Proceed by clicking the **Execute** button. Then, you'll see the predictive accounting entries, as shown in Figure 14.21.

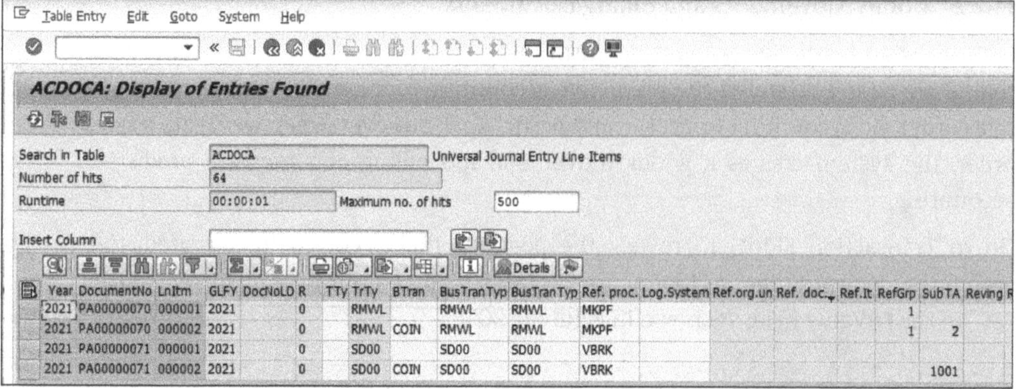

Figure 14.21 Predictive Accounting Entries

Notice that two accounting documents were generated. The **TrTy** (transaction type) column indicates the type of transaction. Three type of business transactions are relevant for sales order predictive accounting:

- **RMWL (Goods Issue)**
- **SD00 (Customer Invoice)**
- **TBCS (Transaction-Based CoGS Split)**

Once we posted the sales order, the system generated accounting entries for the expected goods issue (RMWL) and billing document (customer invoice) (SD00). If you use also COGS split, you'll see how subsequent financial processes, such as COGS split, are also posted in predictive accounting. You can control which predictive postings are generated using the BAdI BADI_FINS_PRED_SWITCH.

Now, let's modify the fields displayed in table ACDOCA to see how these documents are linked. Click the **Change Layout** button, as shown in Figure 14.22.

Table Entry Edit Goto System Help

ACDOCA: Display of Entries Found

Search in Table ACDOCA Universal Journal Entry Line Items
Number of hits 64
Runtime 00:00:01 Maximum no. of hits 500
Insert Column

Details

Year	DocumentNo	LnItm	GLFY	DocNoLD	R	TTy	TrTy	BTran
2021	PA00000070	000001	2021		0		RMWL	
2021	PA00000070	000002	2021		0		RMWL	COIN
2021	PA00000071	000001	2021		0		SD00	
2021	PA00000071	000002	2021		0		SD00	COIN

Choose Layout...
Change Layout...
Save Layout...
Manage Layouts

Figure 14.22 Changing the Layout

Then, on the screen shown in Figure 14.23, move the **Source Document No.** to the beginning of the displayed fields and press Enter.

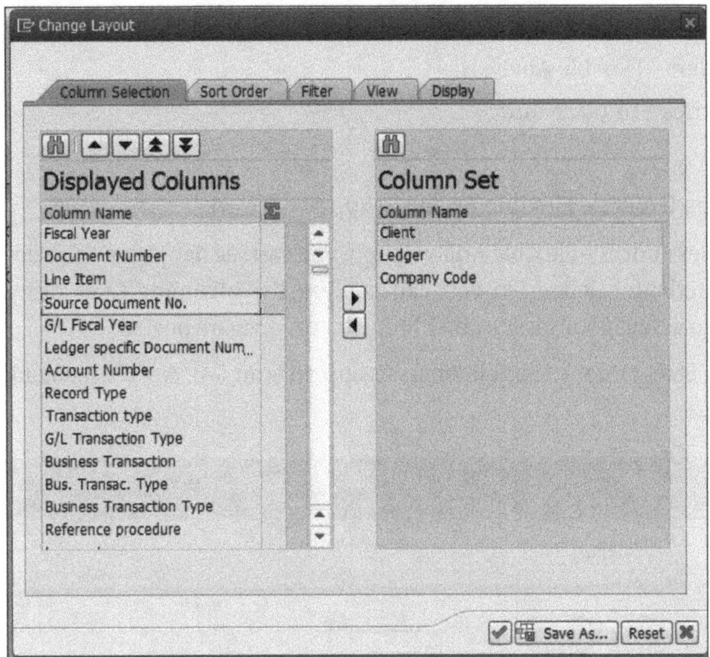

Figure 14.23 Adding a Source Document Number

Now, in the **SrcDoc No** (source document number) field, you'll see the sales order number for which predictive accounting entries had been created, as shown in Figure 14.24.

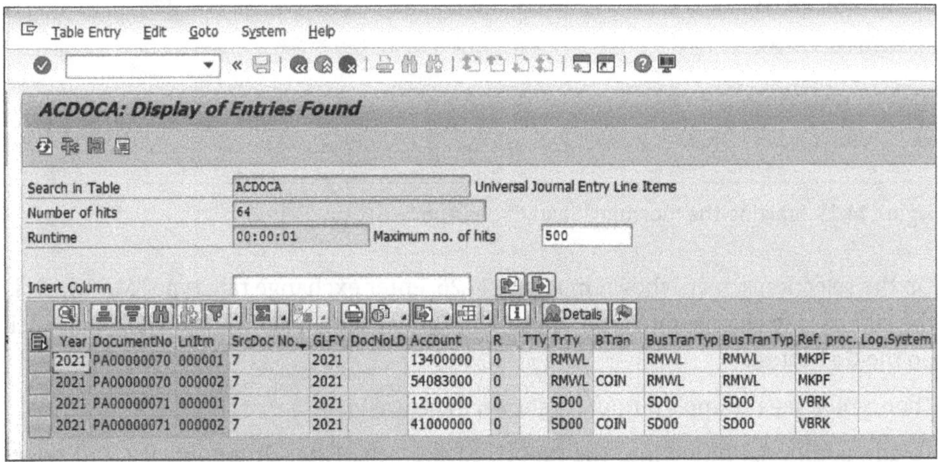

Year	DocumentNo	LnItm	SrcDoc No.	GLFY	DocNoLD	Account	R	TTy	TrTy	BTran	BusTranTyp	BusTranTyp	Ref. proc.	Log.System
2021	PA00000070	000001	7	2021		13400000	0		RMWL		RMWL	RMWL	MKPF	
2021	PA00000070	000002	7	2021		54083000	0		RMWL	COIN	RMWL	RMWL	MKPF	
2021	PA00000071	000001	7	2021		12100000	0		SD00		SD00	SD00	VBRK	
2021	PA00000071	000002	7	2021		41000000	0		SD00	COIN	SD00	SD00	VBRK	

Figure 14.24 Source Document Link

14.3 Information System

Reporting for predictive accounting is provided through SAP Fiori apps. We'll examine the following SAP Fiori apps that are useful for predictive accounting:

- Incoming Sales Orders – Flexible Analysis
- Display Journal Entries – In T-Account

14.3.1 Incoming Sales Orders – Flexible Analysis App

With the Incoming Sales Orders – Flexible Analysis app, you can see data from the leading ledger and the prediction ledger so you can analyze the incoming sales order impact even before the actual goods issue and billing documents are posted.

Click on the Incoming Sales Order – Flexible Analysis app on your SAP Fiori launchpad, as shown in Figure 14.25.

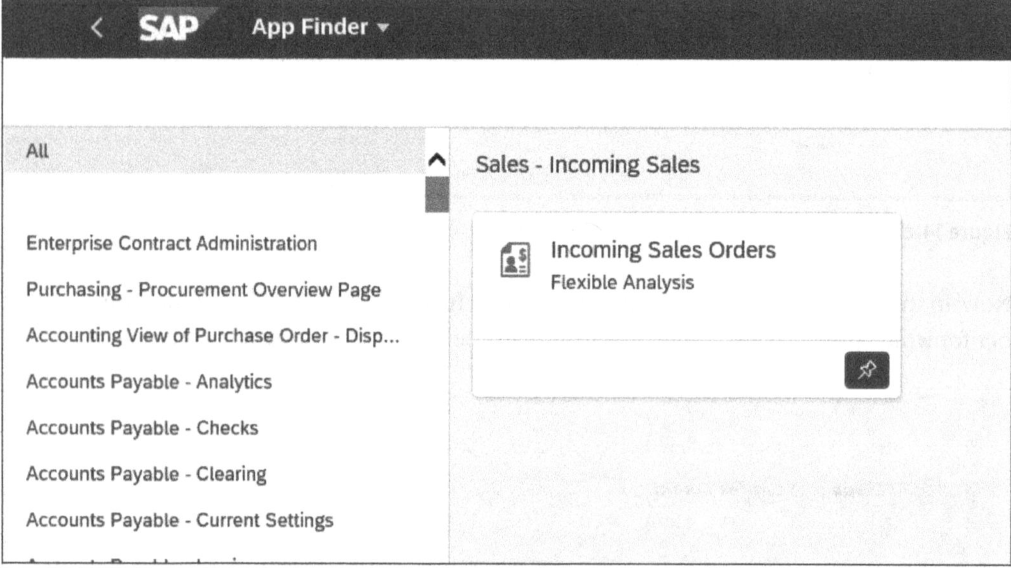

Figure 14.25 Starting the Incoming Sales Order App

On the selection screen, shown in Figure 14.26, enter exchange rate type "M," which is the standard exchange rate type most commonly used and currency "USD" and click on the **Go** button.

Then, you'll see the app's output, as shown in Figure 14.27.

To add additional filters into the report, click on the **Filter** dropdown list and select **Show Additional Filters**, as shown in Figure 14.28.

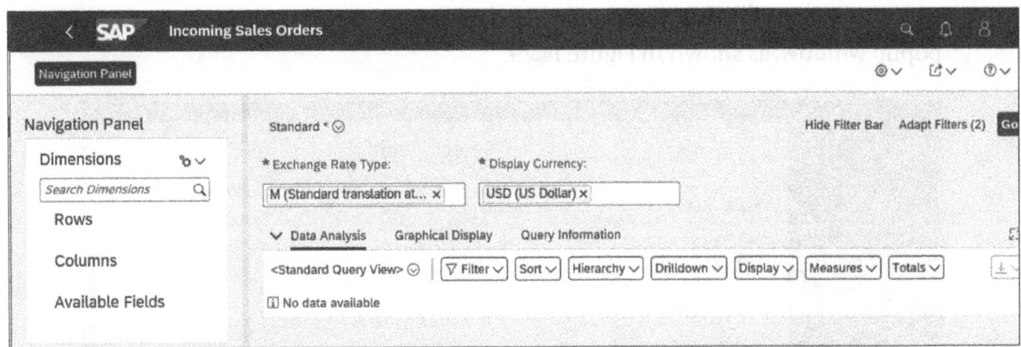

Figure 14.26 Incoming Sales Order Selections

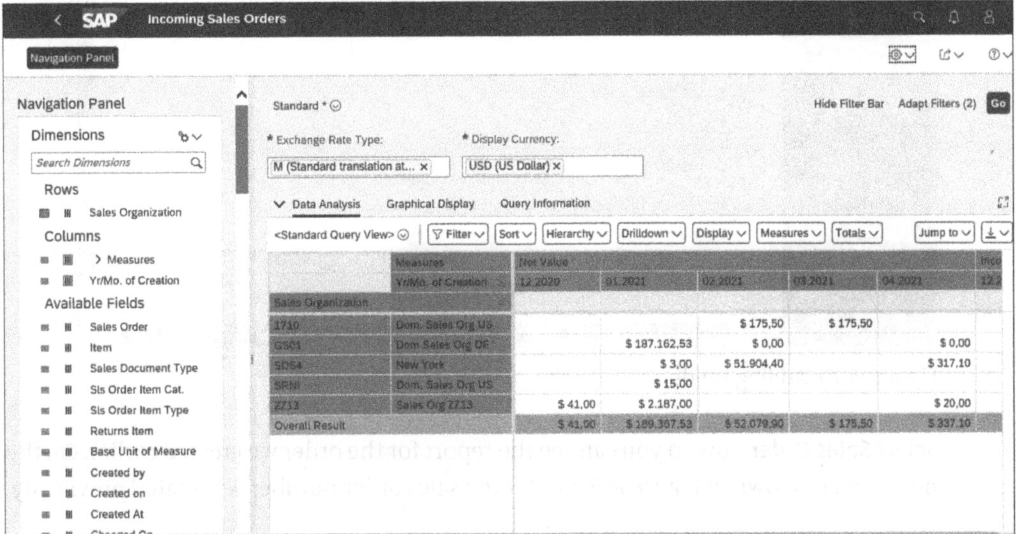

Figure 14.27 Incoming Sales Order Output

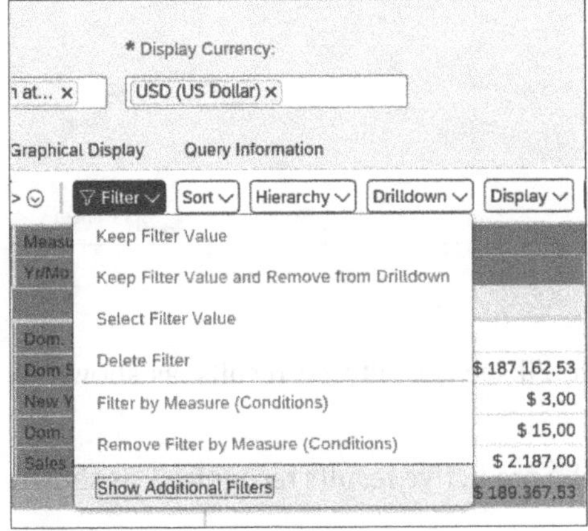

Figure 14.28 Showing Additional Filters

You'll then select **+ Add filters**, which enables you to add additional fields from the popup window, as shown in Figure 14.29.

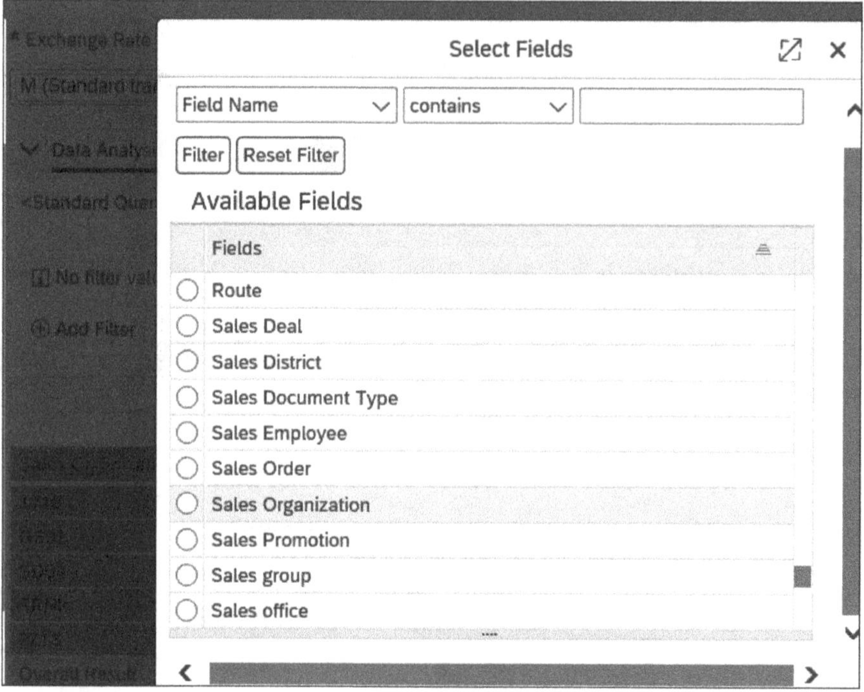

Figure 14.29 Adding Fields

Select **Sales Order** now so you can see the report for the order we created earlier. On the next screen, shown in Figure 14.30, enter the sales order number we created previously.

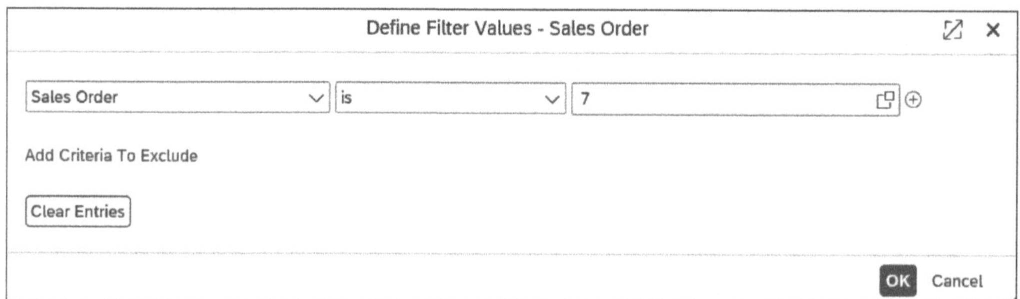

Figure 14.30 Sales Order Field

Proceed by clicking the **OK** button. Then, you'll see the filtered results, as shown in Figure 14.31.

Click on the **Graphical Display** tab to review the predictive results recognized, as shown in Figure 14.32.

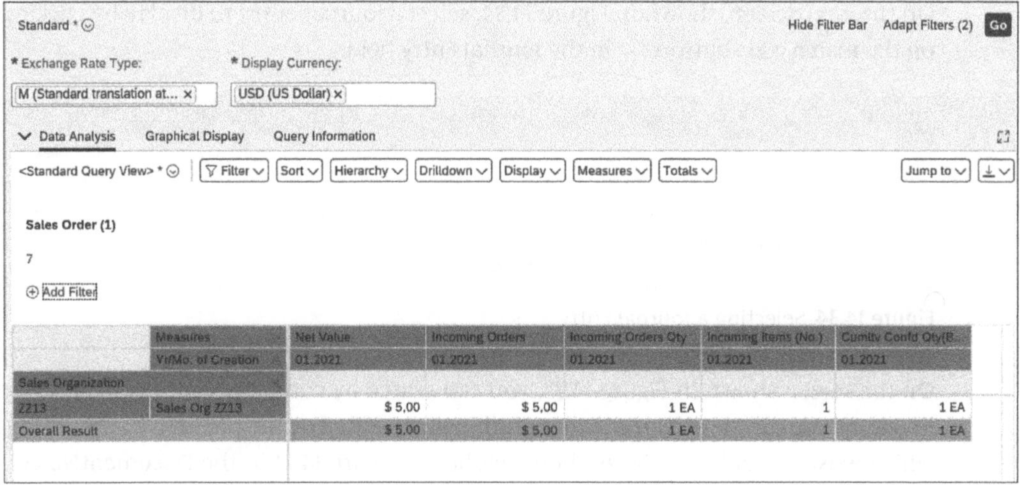

Figure 14.31 Sales Order Filtered Result

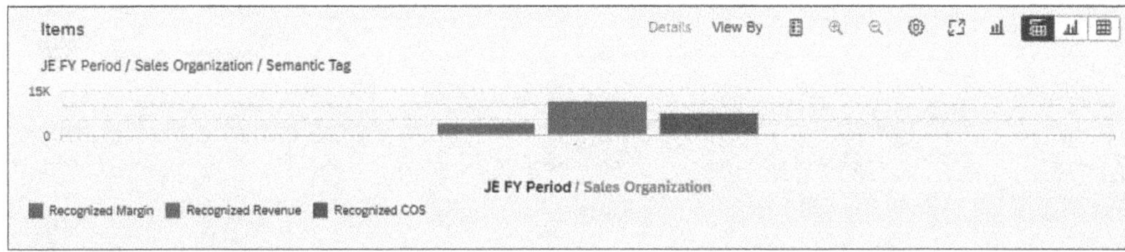

Figure 14.32 Predictive Results

14.3.2 Display Journal Entries – In T-Account App

With the Display Journal Entries – In T-Account app, you can analyze the predictive entries in financial accounting.

Click on the Display Journal Entries – In T-Account app in your SAP Fiori launchpad, as shown in Figure 14.33.

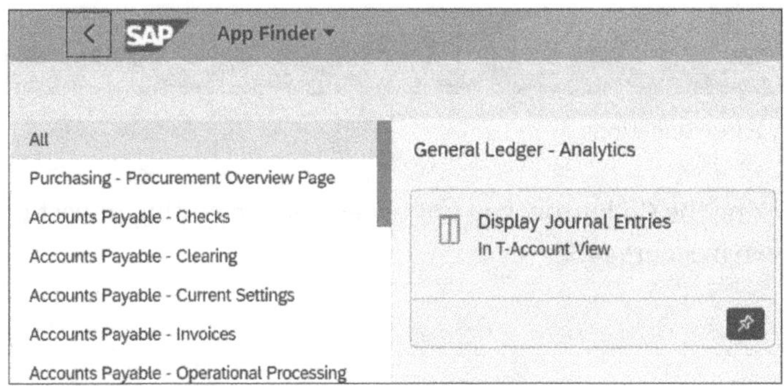

Figure 14.33 Starting the Display Journal Entries App

On the next screen, shown in Figure 14.34, select a journal entry to display by clicking on the match code button in the **Journal Entry** field.

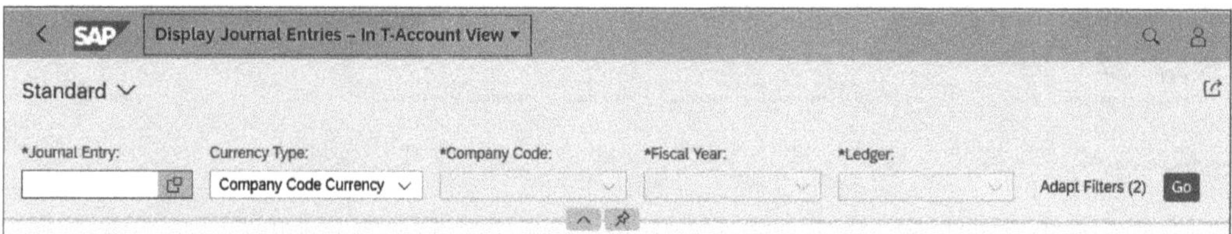

Figure 14.34 Selecting a Journal Entry

On the screen shown in Figure 14.35, you can search by company code, by year, or by ledger, or you can enter the document number generated by the predictive accounting, which exists in table ACDOCA, as shown earlier in Figure 14.21 in the **DocumentNo** column.

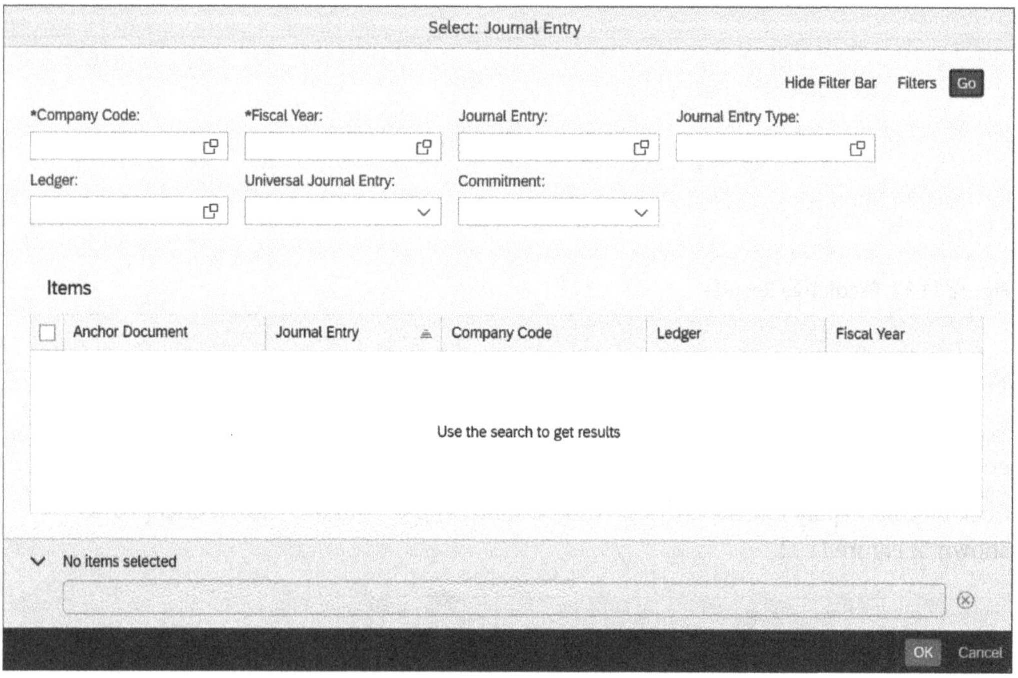

Select: Journal Entry
Hide Filter Bar Filters Go
*Company Code: *Fiscal Year: Journal Entry: Journal Entry Type:
Ledger: Universal Journal Entry: Commitment:
Items
Anchor Document | Journal Entry | Company Code | Ledger | Fiscal Year
Use the search to get results
No items selected
OK Cancel

Figure 14.35 Journal Entry Filter Selections

After proceeding by clicking the **Go** button, you can review the accounting impact of the entry posted, as shown in Figure 14.36.

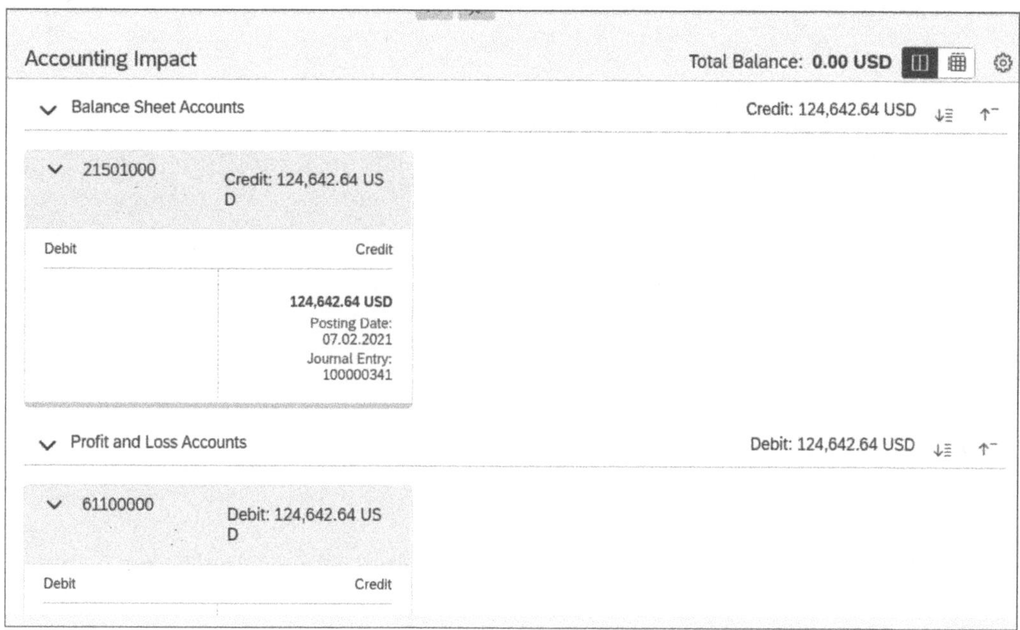

Figure 14.36 Accounting Impact

14.4 Summary

In this chapter, you learned how to configure and use predictive accounting, so you can get better visibility on the future financial flows in your company resulting from sales that are still to be delivered and billed. This exciting new area in SAP S/4HANA provides financial managers with a powerful tool at their fingertips for better financial forecasting.

You learned how to configure predictive accounting step by step by configuring ledgers, billing types, and sales order item categories. Then, we analyzed the data flow in predictive accounting, starting with the sales order, and the generation of predictive goods issue and billing document. Then, you learned how to use SAP Fiori apps to perform predictive accounting reporting both from sales order perspective and in financial accounting.

In the next chapter, we'll delve into the details of product costing.

Chapter 15
Product Costing

This chapter provides step-by-step instructions for configuring product costing in SAP S/4HANA, including for the material ledger, which is required in SAP S/4HANA. We'll discuss real-life scenarios and their implementation in the product costing model.

Product costing is a part of controlling that enables the planning of the product costs and maintaining material prices. Thus, product costing is a vital part of calculating the profitability of the enterprise. This functionality is integrated with the production planning and materials management functionalities of SAP S/4HANA.

Broadly speaking, we can segregate product costing into two parts: product cost planning, which is used to calculate the planned costs of the products and materials, and actual costing, which allocates the actual costs to them. Before analyzing these processes in detail, we'll set up the required master data for product costing. At the end of the chapter, we'll guide you through the information system for product costing.

15.1 Master Data

Master data plays an important role for product costing because it provides the backbone for the correct calculation of product prices. We'll review how to set up the following master data for product costing:

- Material master
- Bill of materials (BOM)
- Work center
- Routing

The material master is the foundation for the product costing. In product cost planning, you'll create so-called *material cost estimates*, which provide the costing on the material level. The BOM and routing create the *quantity structure*, which is used in costing estimates.

Let's start with the material master.

15.1.1 Material Master

The material master is a foundational master data object for all of logistics in SAP S/4HANA. All raw materials, semifinished products, and finished products are created as material masters. Furthermore, services also can be set up as materials.

The material master is a complex structure that consists of numerous views organized into tabs related to sales, purchasing, accounting, product costing, and so on. We'll focus on the setup required from a costing point of view.

We'll start with some basic configuration that's required of materials to enter costing information. Each material is created for a material type, which is used to classify materials with similar functions. For material types relevant for costing, you must activate the costing and accounting views.

To define the settings for material types, follow the menu path **Logistics—General • Material Master • Basic Settings • Material Types • Define Attributes of Material Types**.

On the screen shown in Figure 15.1, you'll see the material types already defined in the system.

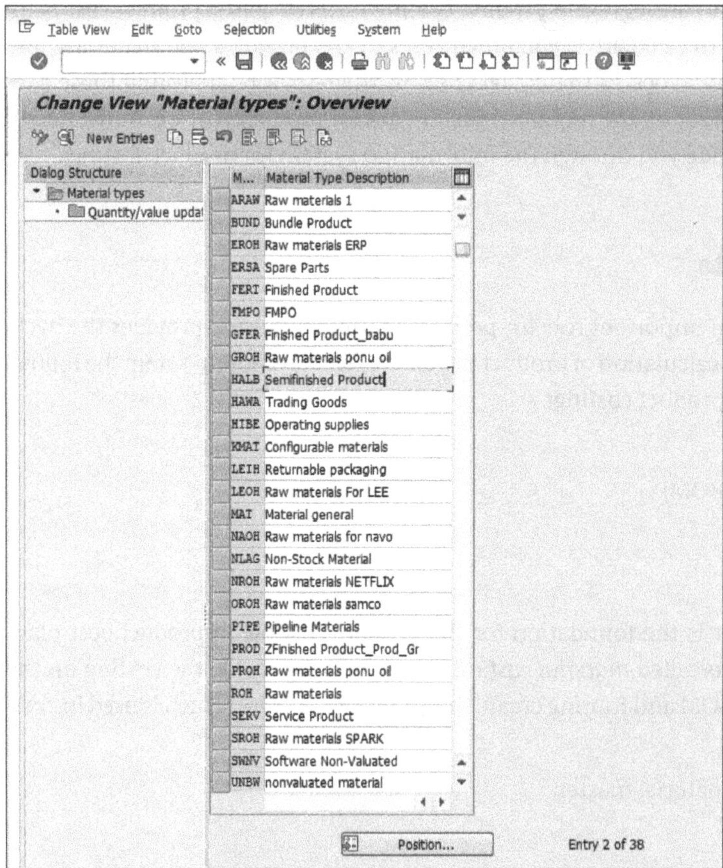

Figure 15.1 Material Types

The standard material types provided by SAP are shown on this screen; notice that SAP provides myriad standard material types to represent different kinds of materials. When creating custom material types, they should start with Z or Y in the custom name range.

Let's create our own material type for raw materials. Locate material type **ROH**, which is a standard SAP material type for raw materials, select it, and click the (**Copy As...**) button from the top menu.

Figure 15.2 shows the configuration of the material type. Enter "ZRAW" as the name for the new material type and enter "Raw materials" for the long description.

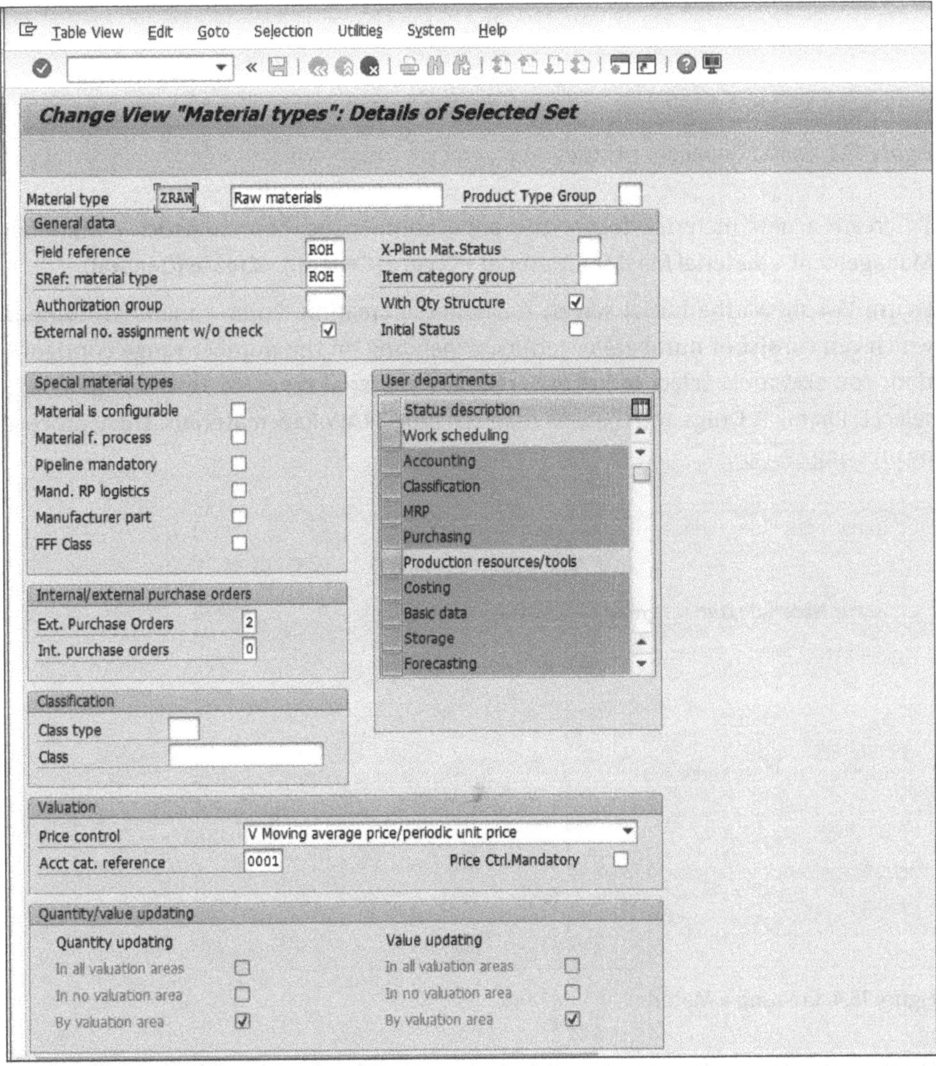

Figure 15.2 Material Type Definition

In the **User departments** area, you'll see all the possible views to be maintained on the material master. Make sure that **Accounting** and **Costing** are selected because they provide the required data for financial accounting and product costing. Then, press [Enter] to adopt these settings.

The system issues a message with the number of dependent entries copied for the material type, which you can confirm by clicking the [✓] button, as shown in Figure 15.3. After that step, save the new material type by clicking the **Save** button.

Figure 15.3 Copied Dependent Entries

To create a new material, follow the application menu path **Logistics • Materials Management • Material Master • Material • Create (General) • Create (General).**

Figure 15.4 shows the initial screen for material creation. Enter a material number, which can consist of numbers or letters, depending on the number range configuration. You also must select **Industry Sector** and **Material type**. For this example, we'll select **D Phama & Drugs** and the new material type **ZRAW Raw materials.** Then, proceed by pressing [Enter].

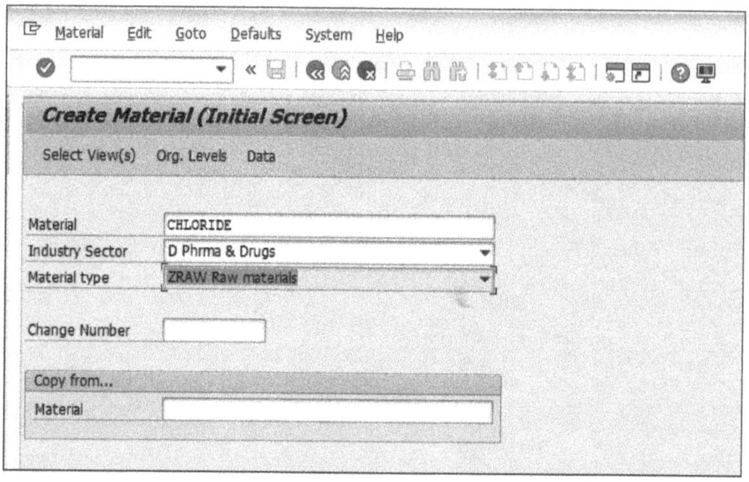

Figure 15.4 Creating a Material

On the next screen, shown in Figure 15.5, check the views you're going to maintain in the material master. Make sure the accounting and costing views are selected, then proceed by clicking the [✓] button.

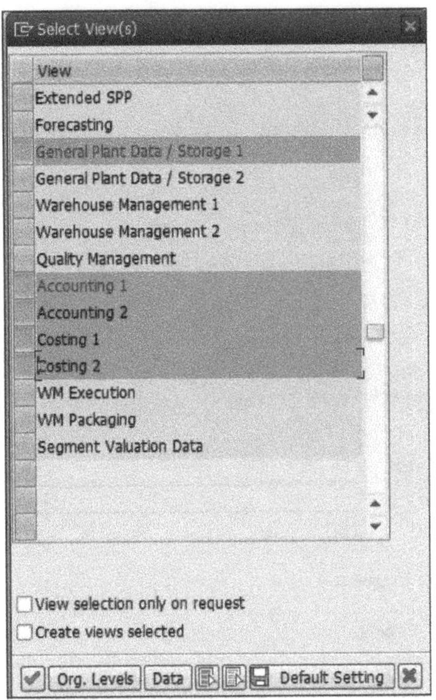

Figure 15.5 Selecting Views

We won't detail all the material views, which contain logistical information. We'll concentrate instead on the accounting and costing views. Figure 15.6 shows the **Accounting 1** view, which contains some important settings from a product costing point of view. Most important is the **Prc. Ctrl.** (price control) field, for which you have two options:

- **S**: Standard price
- **V**: Moving average price/periodic unit price

If a material has a standard price (**S**), the value of the material is calculated at this standard price. If goods movements or invoice receipts (IRs) have a price that is different from the standard price, those differences are posted to the price difference account. The variance isn't taken into account in inventory valuation. If, however, the material has a moving average price, each goods movement and IR updates its price. When goods movements and IRs are posted with a price that's different from the current moving average price of the material, the differences are posted to the stock account itself. Therefore, the moving average price and the inventory value change.

We recommend using standard prices for finished and semifinished products. The moving average price can be used for raw materials and external purchases. Especially when the price could vary significantly, the moving average price is recommended. Also, in some countries where prices can fluctuate significantly, especially in an inflationary environment, the moving average price is recommended—and sometimes even legally required.

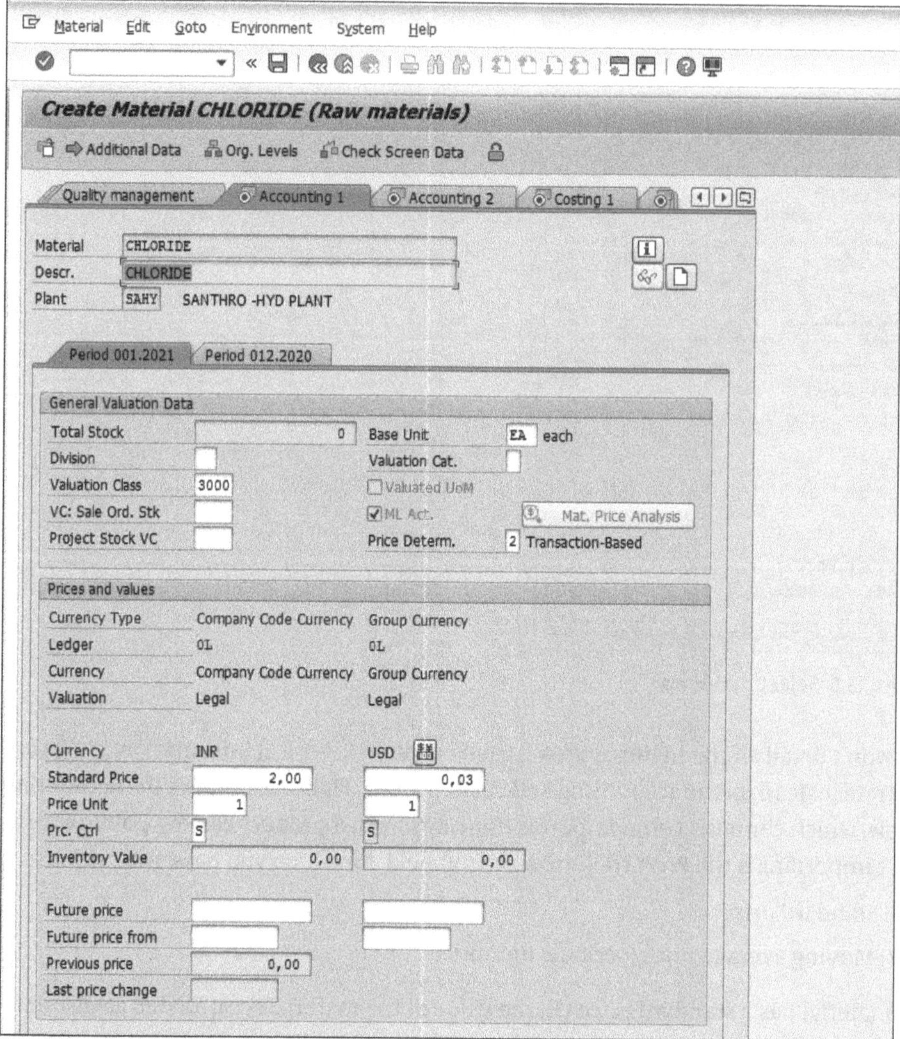

Figure 15.6 Accounting 1 View

This choice is a major decision point and important strategy in each SAP S/4HANA implementation that affects how to value inventory. Each type of material should be carefully considered, and your business should make a well-informed decision with the help of its integration partner. Making good decisions for all materials is important because the valuation of the materials provides the backbone for proper product costing. In this process, you must understand what types of materials are used as raw, semi-finished, and finished materials. You also must understand the specifics of these materials, how they are affected by market price movements, and how stable their prices are. An important consideration is the economy in which the company operates and whether inflationary forces are in play.

Next, navigate to the **Costing 2** view of the material, as shown in Figure 15.7.

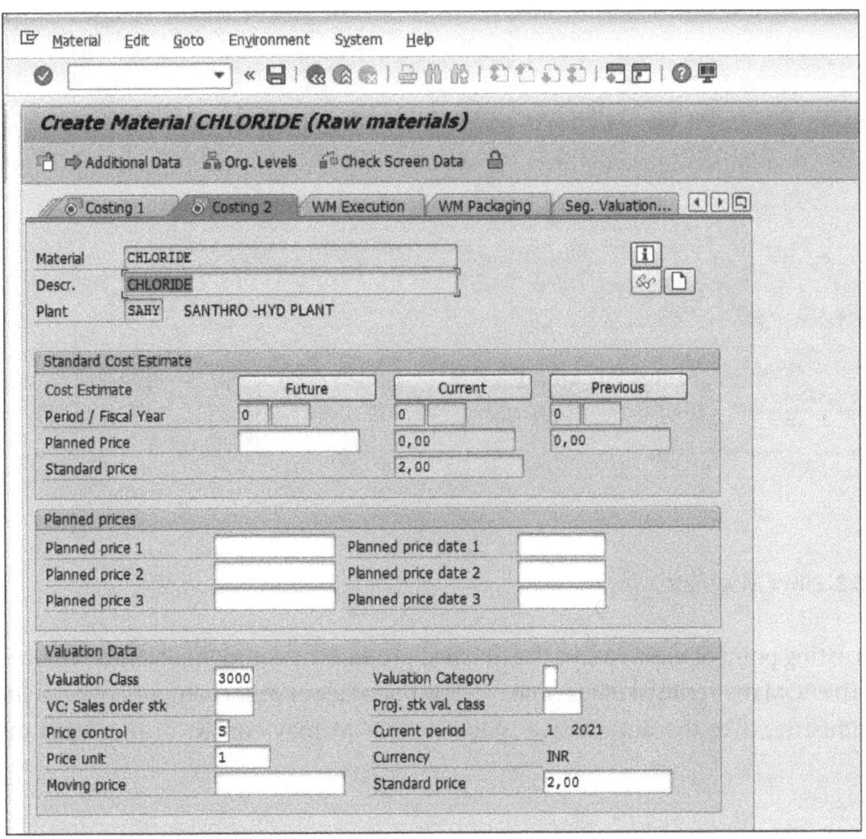

Figure 15.7 Costing 2 View

Under this tab, in the **Standard Cost Estimate** section, you'll maintain the standard cost estimate, which is used to valuate materials with standard price control. Sections exist for future, current, and previous prices, which currently are empty because we haven't costed the material yet. We'll do that in Section 15.2, but for now, we'll just save after maintaining the other views.

15.1.2 Bill of Materials

A BOM is a quantity structure that provides the list of components and activities to manufacture a product. This master data object is mainly from production planning, but from a costing point of view, a costing BOM is needed also. It's created with Transaction CS01.

On the definition screen, shown in Figure 15.8, enter the components needed for manufacturing the finished or semifinished product.

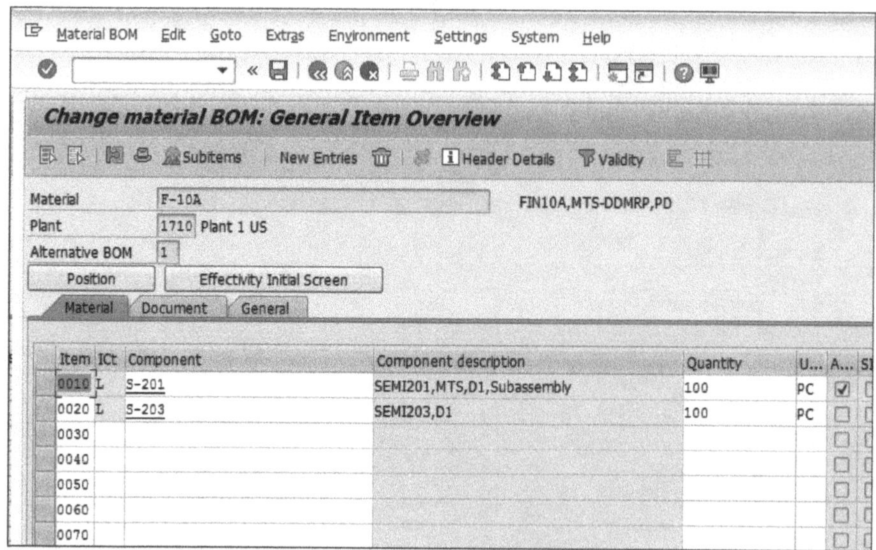

Figure 15.8 Bill of Materials

From a costing point of view, to cost the finished product, its components must also be costed. The BOM may consist of just one or a few materials or other components, but in some industries, like the automotive industry, a BOM may consist of hundreds of items.

15.1.3 Work Center

A *work center* is a logistical organizational unit that defines where and by whom operations are performed. This object is important for product costing because, through its assignment of a cost center, it provides the costs incurred during the production process to create the products.

Let's establish a link between a work center and costing. To create a work center, enter Transaction CR01. On the initial screen, shown in Figure 15.9, maintain the **Plant** and **Work center** fields as well as the **Work Center Category** field, which indicates the purpose of the work center. You can also provide an existing work center to copy in the **Copy from** section.

An important part of the product costing view is the **Costing** tab, shown in Figure 15.10. Under this tab, you'll assign the cost center that will bear the costs related to production processes in this work center. You can also assign activity types to the activities to be performed in this work center. (We discussed activity types in detail in Chapter 10.)

After establishing the costing link in the work center, production confirmations posted in production planning will pass along costs to enable the calculation of the actual costs for the involved products.

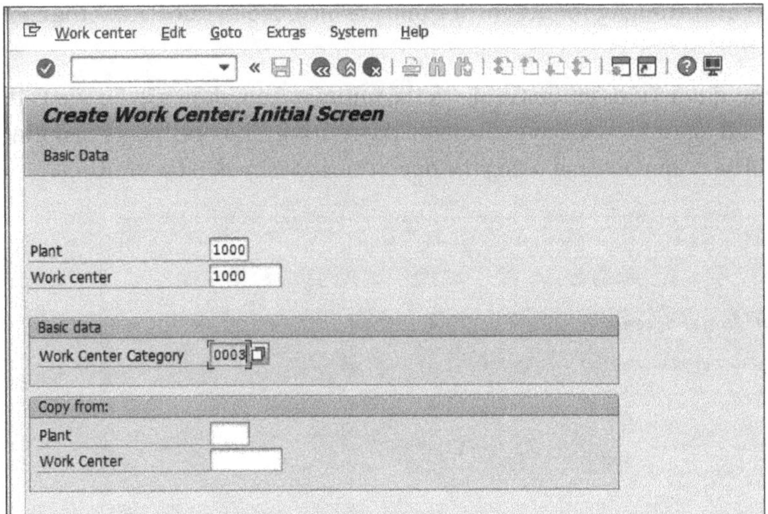

Figure 15.9 Creating a Work Center

HR assignment Hierarchy Template More

* Cost Center: 1000

Activities Overview

Alt. Activity Text	Activity Type	Activity Unit	Re...	Formul...	Formula description	Inc. wages ind.	Rec. type group
Setup	LABOR	HR					Variable activity
Machine	MACH	HR					Variable activity
Labor	LABOR	HR					Variable activity
							Variable activity
							Variable activity
							Variable activity

ActType Int.Proc.:

Link to business process

Business Process:

Incentive wages ind.: Record Type Group:

Form. Formula Formula constnts Validities

Figure 15.10 Work Center Costing Data

15.1.4 Routing

A *routing* is another production planning object that affects the product costing. A routing is a description of which operations must be carried out during the production process and also defines the sequence in which activities must be carried out in work centers. A work center is linked with a cost center, and thus, the costs incurred during these operations pass through product costing and are included in calculating the cost of the products.

To create a routing, enter Transaction CA01. On the initial screen, shown in Figure 15.11, enter a material and plant for which you'll create the routing. The finished or semifinished product will be manufactured using the operations specified in the routing.

Routing Edit Goto Details Extras Environment System Help
Create Routing: Initial Screen
Copy from
Routings
Sequences
Operations
Material
10001
Plant
1000
Sales document
Sales Document Item
WBS Element
Group
Validity
Change Number
Key Date
05.05.2021
Revision Level
Additional data
Profile

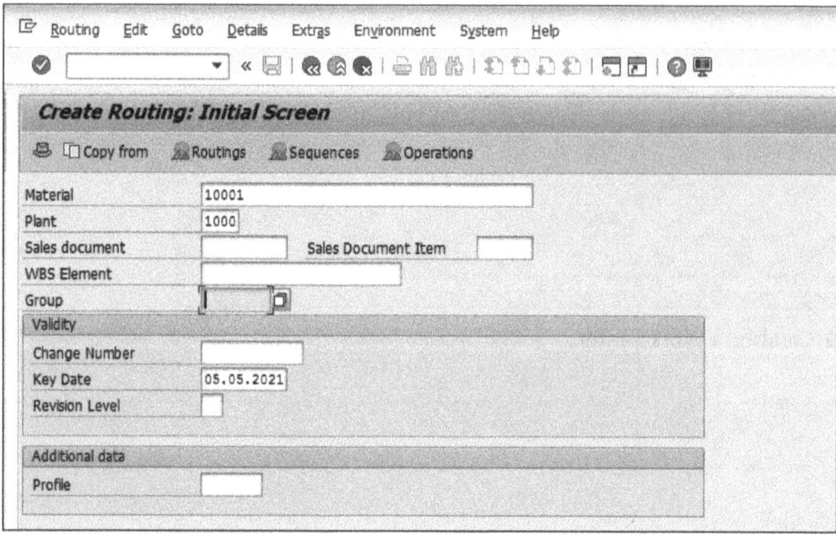

Figure 15.11 Creating a Routing

On the screen shown in Figure 15.12, click **Operation** from the top menu to define the operation steps.

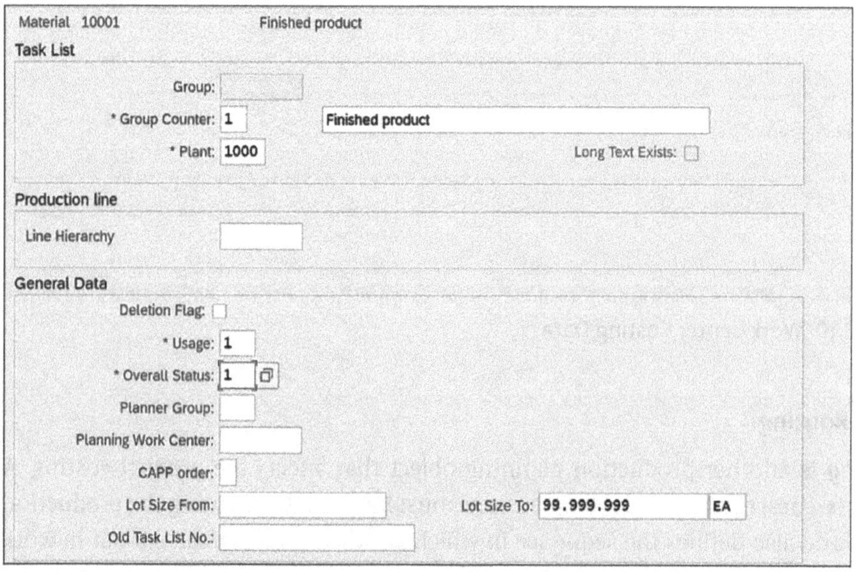

Material 10001
Finished product
Task List
Group:
* Group Counter: 1
Finished product
* Plant: 1000
Long Text Exists:
Production line
Line Hierarchy
General Data
Deletion Flag:
* Usage: 1
* Overall Status: 1
Planner Group:
Planning Work Center:
CAPP order:
Lot Size From:
Lot Size To: 99.999.999
EA
Old Task List No.:

Figure 15.12 Routing Definition

On the screen shown in Figure 15.13, define the operation steps in the lines and assign work centers to each operation. Because each work center has a cost center, when the operational steps of the routing are executed, costs are accumulated in the respective cost centers. Therefore, when you cost the finished product, the final cost includes the costs associated with the activities in the work centers.

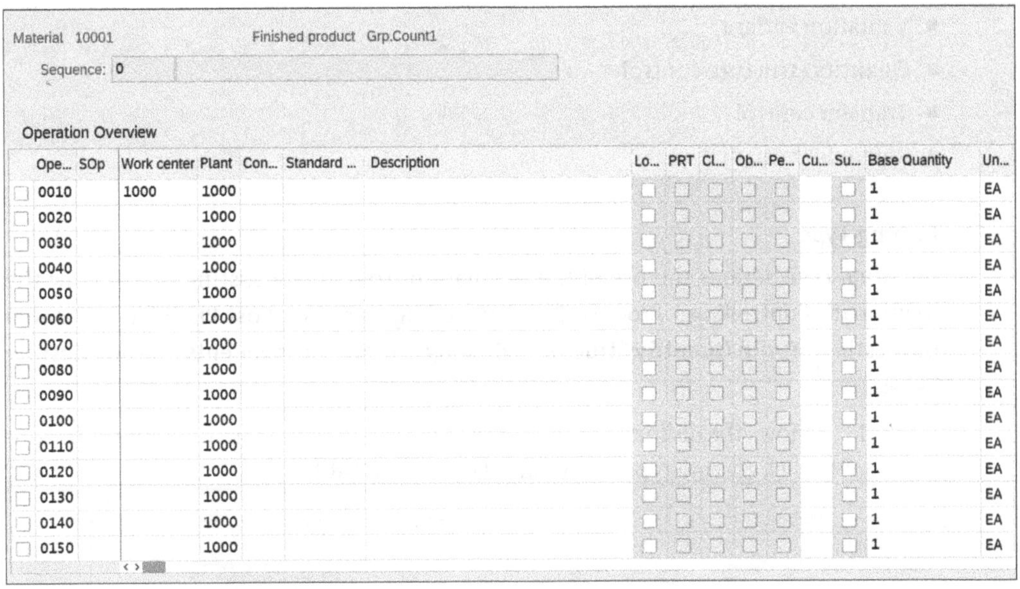

Material 10001 Finished product Grp.Count1

Sequence: 0

Operation Overview

Ope...	SOp	Work center	Plant	Con...	Standard ...	Description	Lo...	PRT	Cl...	Ob...	Pe...	Cu...	Su...	Base Quantity	Un...
0010		1000	1000											1	EA
0020			1000											1	EA
0030			1000											1	EA
0040			1000											1	EA
0050			1000											1	EA
0060			1000											1	EA
0070			1000											1	EA
0080			1000											1	EA
0090			1000											1	EA
0100			1000											1	EA
0110			1000											1	EA
0120			1000											1	EA
0130			1000											1	EA
0140			1000											1	EA
0150			1000											1	EA

Figure 15.13 Operational Step Definition

Now that you're familiar with the master data that provides the building blocks for costing, let's continue with product cost planning.

15.2 Product Cost Planning

Product cost planning provides plan prices for the materials the company produces and purchases, which are then used as a basis to value inventory and recognize price differences with the actual prices incurred. In this section, we'll create a material cost estimate to provide the planned standard price.

Product cost planning is based on a costing variant that determines what costs are included. We'll start by configuring the various components to be included in a costing variant. Then, we'll configure the costing variant. After that step, we'll guide you through how to configure a cost component structure, which groups the cost elements into cost components. Then, we'll configure a costing sheet, which defines how overhead costing is performed. Finally, you'll learn how to perform a material cost estimate, which costs the materials.

15.2.1 Costing Variant Components

The costing variant determines how manufacturing costs are valuated and which master data objects are included for calculation of the standard price. The costing variant combines the following configuration components, as we'll discuss in this section:

- Costing type
- Valuation variant
- Quantity structure control
- Transfer control
- Reference variant

Costing Type

A *costing type* defines the use of the calculation. To define a costing type, follow the menu path **Controlling • Product Cost Controlling • Product Cost Planning • Material Cost Estimate with Quantity Structure • Costing Variant: Components • Define Costing Types.**

Figure 15.14 shows the defined costing types. We'll can use standard ones for this example. Double-click costing type **01: Standard Cost Est. (Mat.).**

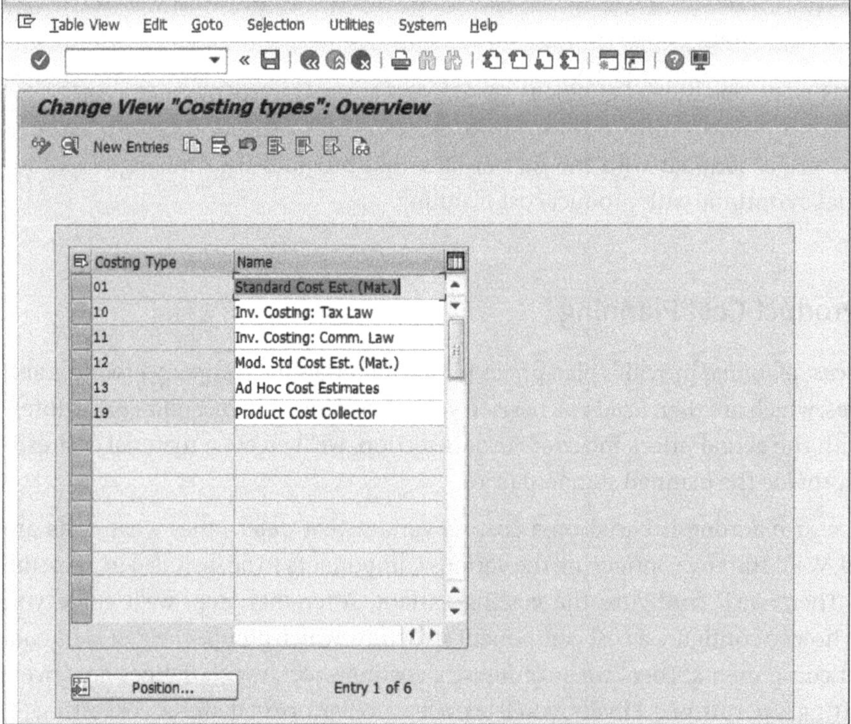

Figure 15.14 Costing Types

The settings of a costing type are divided into three tabs. Figure 15.15 shows the first tab, **Price Update**. The **Price Update** field lists the field in the material master in which the calculated price will be updated. In addition to the **1: Standard Price** option, other price fields in the material master can be used, such as tax price and commercial price.

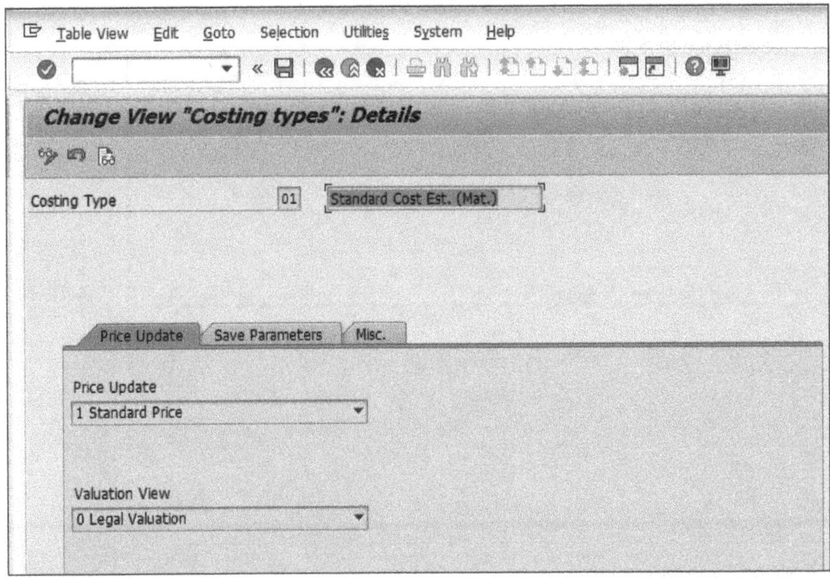

Figure 15.15 Costing Type Price Update

In the **Valuation View** field, select the type of valuation to be used in case of parallel valuation. Next, click the **Save Parameters** tab, as shown in Figure 15.16.

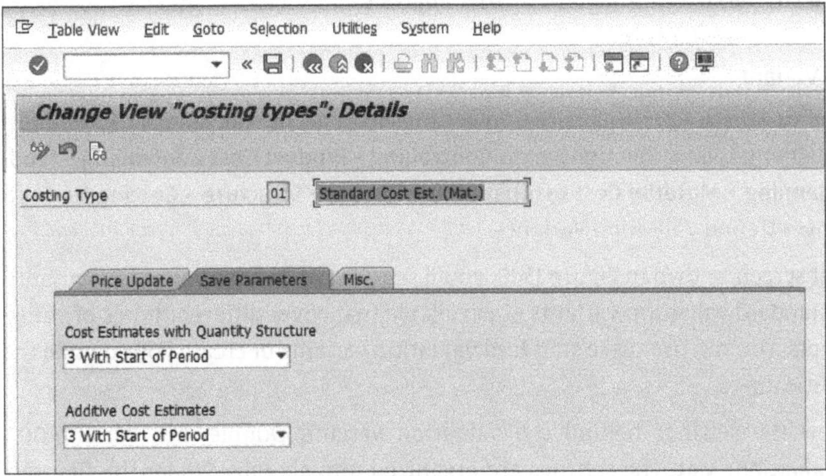

Figure 15.16 Costing Type Save Parameters

Under this tab, you'll configure two fields. You'll define whether to save the date information related to the calculation in the **Cost Estimates with Quantity Structure** and **Additive Cost Estimates** fields. We recommend setting both options with date information. Finally, click the **Misc.** tab, as shown in Figure 15.17.

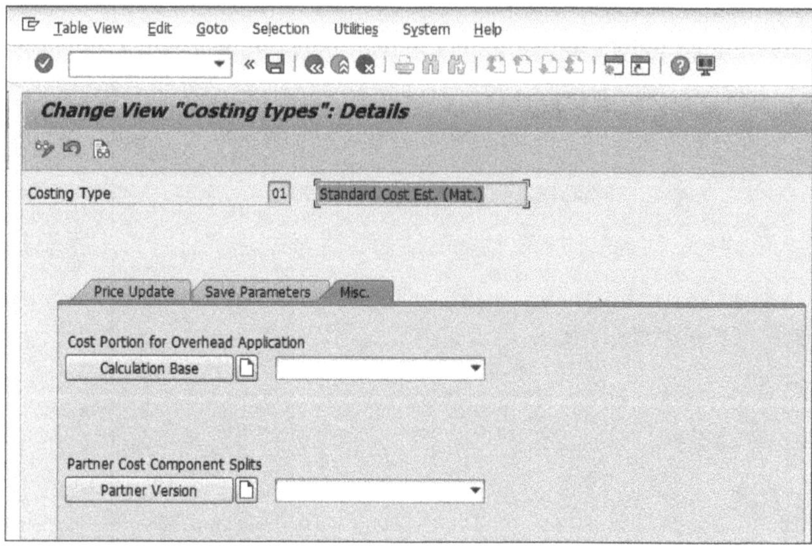

Figure 15.17 Costing Type Miscellaneous

In the **Cost Portion for Overhead Application** field, you'll define which cost elements serve as a basis for the calculation of the overhead costs. In the **Partner Cost Component Splits** field, you'll define which characteristics, such as company code or profit center, will be saved in the cost estimate for further analysis.

Valuation Variant

A *valuation variant* defines the valuation settings for the cost calculation. To define a valuation variant, follow the menu path **Controlling • Product Cost Controlling • Product Cost Planning • Material Cost Estimate with Quantity Structure • Costing Variant: Components • Define Valuation Variants.**

On the first screen, shown in Figure 15.18, you'll see a list of defined valuation variants. Plenty of standard valuation variants are available that cover different types of valuation concepts. You can use these standard valuation variants or create your own in the custom name range.

Let's review the settings behind the valuation variant. Double-click variant **001: Planned Valuation: Mat.** The settings are organized into six tabs. Under the first tab, **Material Val.**, shown in Figure 15.19, you'll define which prices to use for material valuation. You can enter up to five types of prices and thus build a strategy.

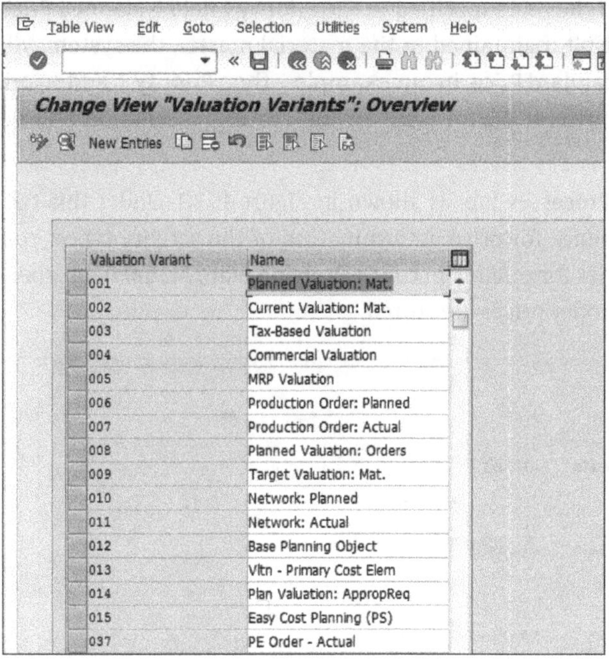

Figure 15.18 Valuation Variants

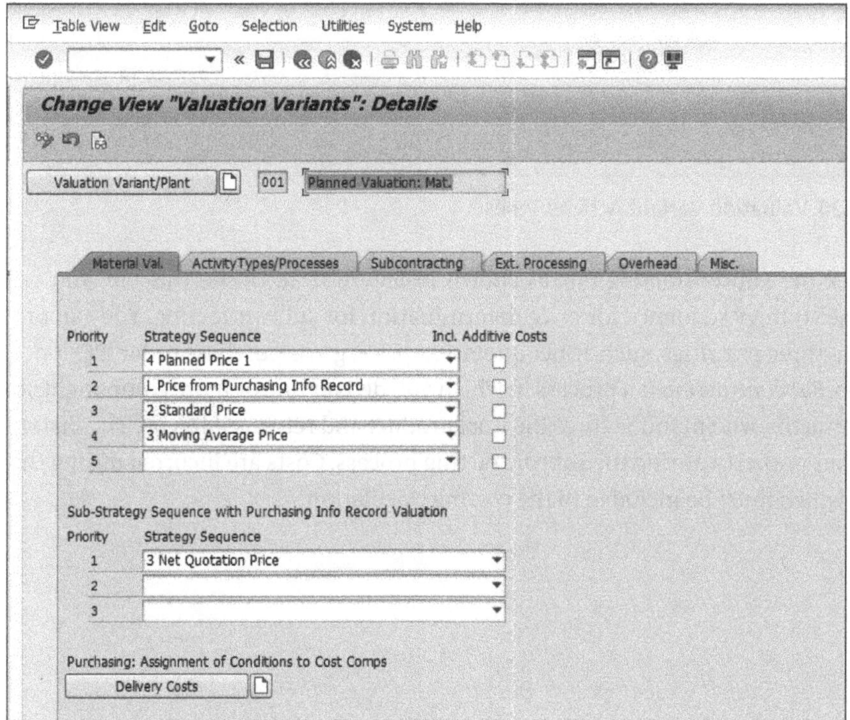

Figure 15.19 Valuation Variant for Material Valuation

The system will first try to find the price specified in the **Priority 1** field—**Planned Price 1** in our example. If the price isn't maintained in the material master, the system will look at the second priority—**Standard Price,** in our example—then **Priority 3,** and so on. If the system doesn't find a price at all, an error in the costing calculation will be thrown.

Next, click the **ActivityTypes/Processes** tab, as shown in Figure 15.20. Under this tab, you'll define the strategy sequence for price determination of the activity types. You can provide up to three priorities for pricing. In the **CO Version Plan/Actual** field, specify the version in which the activity prices are stored.

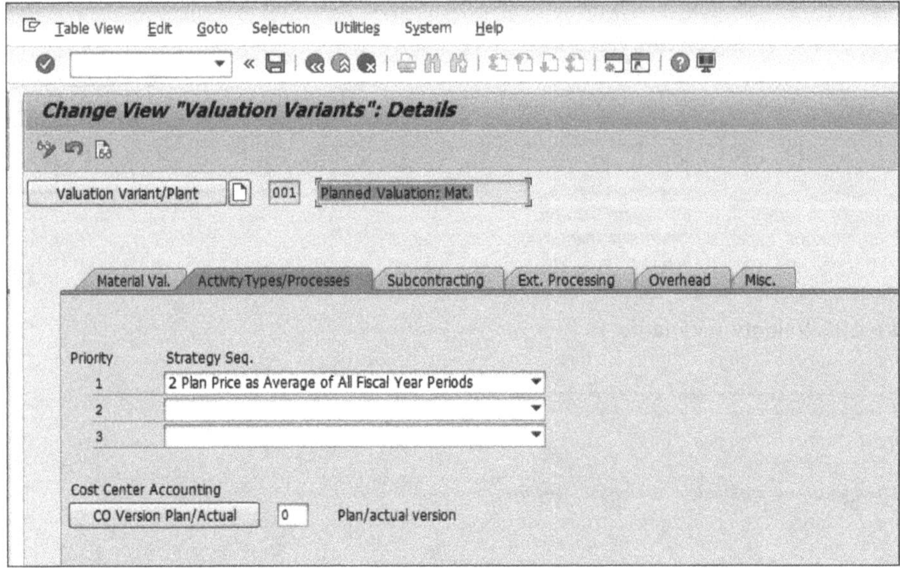

Figure 15.20 Valuation Variant Activity Types

Now, click the **Subcontracting** tab, as shown in Figure 15.21. Under this tab, you can define the strategy sequence for price determination for subcontracting. You can provide up to three priorities, such as net quotation price, gross purchase order (PO) price, and so on. *Subcontracting* is a process in which you deliver one or more components to a subcontractor, who manufactures the final product and returns it to you. The materials are your property during the subcontracting process. Costs are incurred during this process, which must be included in the costing calculation.

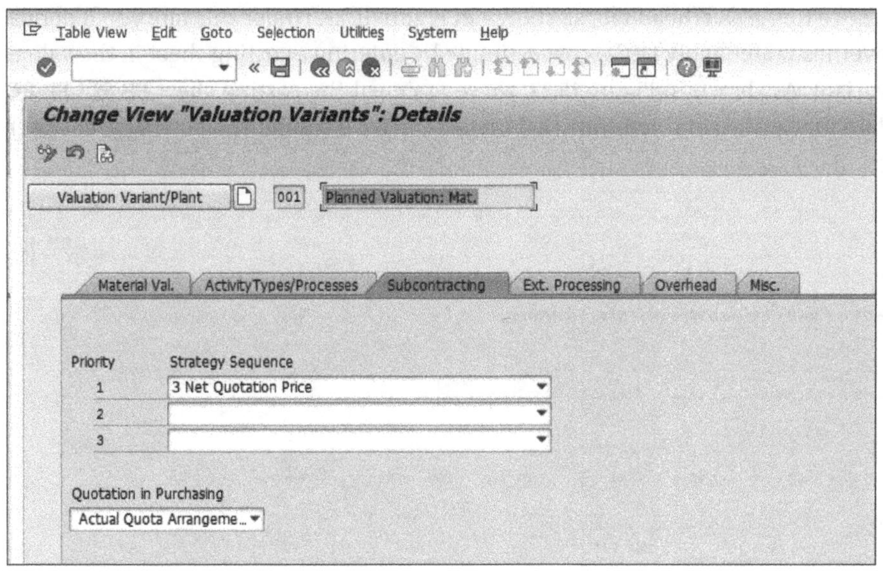

Figure 15.21 Valuation Variant Subcontracting

Next, click the **Ext. Processing** tab, as shown in Figure 15.22. Under this tab, you'll define the strategy sequence for price determination for the valuation of externally processed operations. To calculate the costs of external processing, externally processed operations are valuated with the prices specified under this tab. Various options are available to determine the price, such as the following:

- Net quotation price from the purchasing info record
- Net order price from the PO
- Price from operation

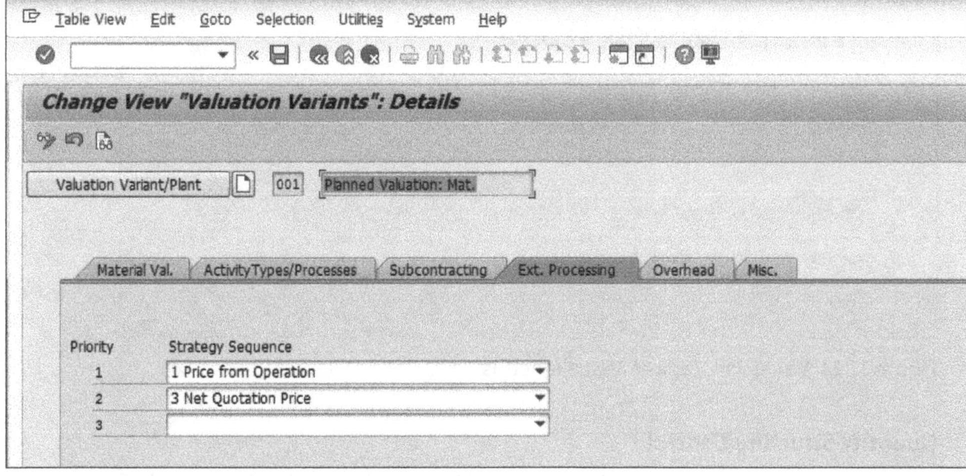

Figure 15.22 Valuation Variant External Processing

Now, move to the **Overhead** tab, as shown in Figure 15.23. Under this tab, you'll define how overhead rates apply to the cost estimate by entering a costing sheet in the valuation variant. As shown in Figure 15.23, we've assigned the costing sheet **PP-PC1 PP-PC Standard** for finished and semifinished materials. (We'll configure a costing sheet later in Section 15.2.4.)

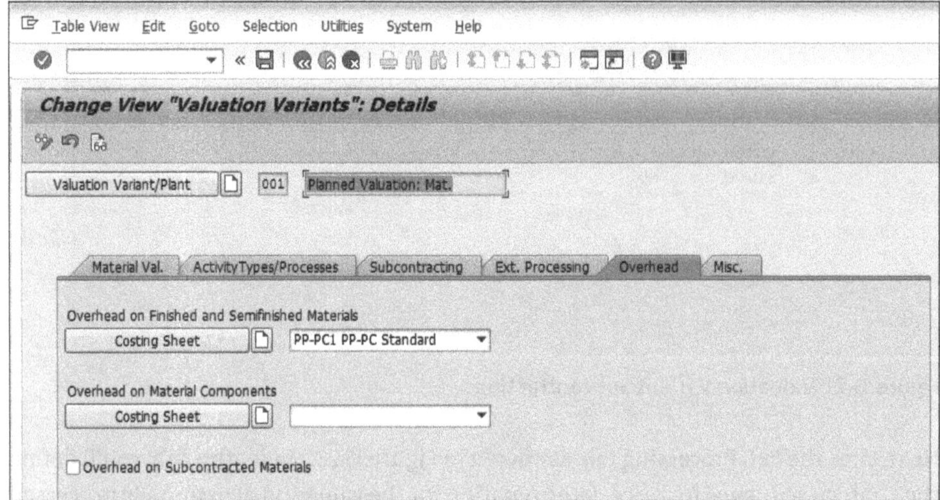

Figure 15.23 Valuation Variant Overhead

Finally, click the **Misc.** tab, as shown in Figure 15.24. Under this tab, you can assign price factors. Price factors are used to multiply single line items by a certain amount. Price factors could be used, for example, for inventory valuations for tax purposes.

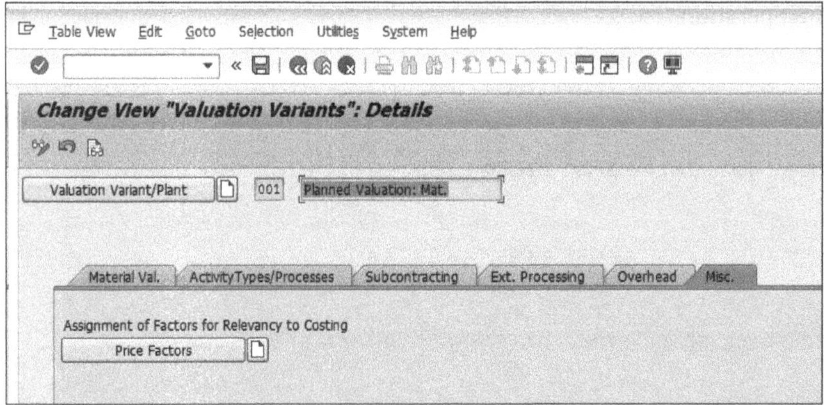

Figure 15.24 Valuation Variant Miscellaneous

Quantity Structure Control

A *quantity structure control* defines how to search for the BOM and the routing included in the cost calculation.

To define a quantity structure control, follow the menu path **Controlling • Product Cost Controlling • Product Cost Planning • Material Cost Estimate with Quantity Structure • Costing Variant: Components • Define Quantity Structure Control.**

On the first screen, shown in Figure 15.25, you'll see a list of the controls defined. You can create a new control with the **New Entries** option from the top menu or copy an existing one by clicking the button from the top menu.

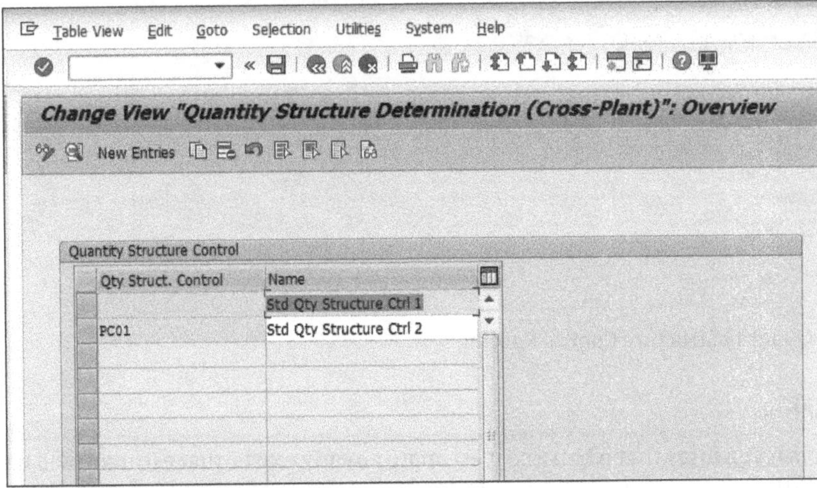

Figure 15.25 Quantity Structure Control

Let's review the possible settings. Double-click **PC01**. Under the first tab, **BOM**, shown in Figure 15.26, you'll define the BOM determination. Several BOM applications exist—for example, BOMs for production, BOMs for sales, or costing BOMs. Under this tab, you'll select which application should be used for the costing calculation.

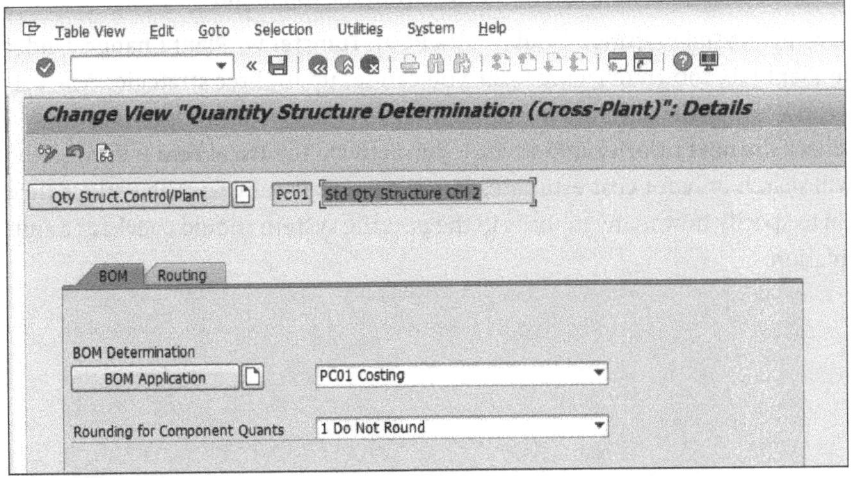

Figure 15.26 Quantity Structure Control BOM

Under the second tab, **Routing**, shown in Figure 15.27, you'll define how routings should be determined in the cost calculation.

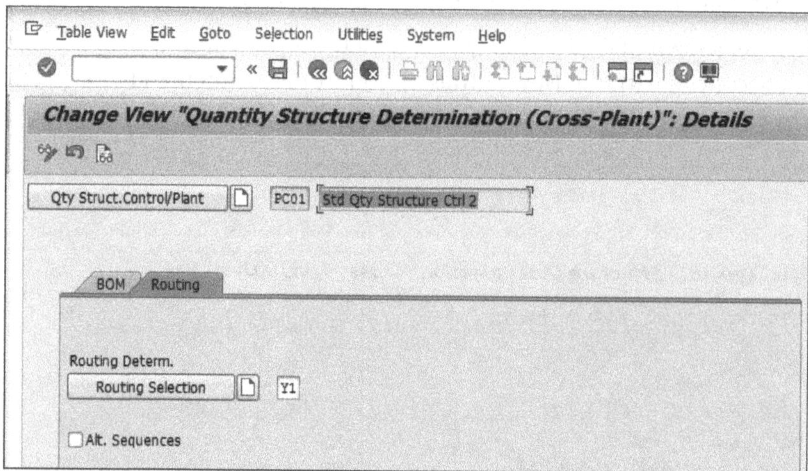

Figure 15.27 Quantity Structure Control Routing

Transfer Control

A *transfer control* ensures that when a cost estimate already exists, that estimate will be transferred rather than creating a new cost estimate.

To define a transfer control, follow the menu path **Controlling • Product Cost Controlling • Product Cost Planning • Material Cost Estimate with Quantity Structure • Costing Variant: Components • Define Transfer Control**.

On the first screen, shown in Figure 15.28, you'll see a list of transfer controls already defined. You can create a new one with the **New Entries** option from the top menu or copy an existing one by clicking the button from the top menu.

Let's review the possible settings. Double-click **PC01: Transfer w/ Plant Change**. Under the **Single-Plant** tab, shown in Figure 15.29, you can set up to three strategies. The system will search for the first appropriate calculation. If no cost estimate is found, the system will check the next priority, and so on. If you activate the **Fiscal Year** indicator, the system will search only for cost estimates in the current fiscal year. The **Periods** field allows you to specify how many months in the past the system should check for a suitable calculation.

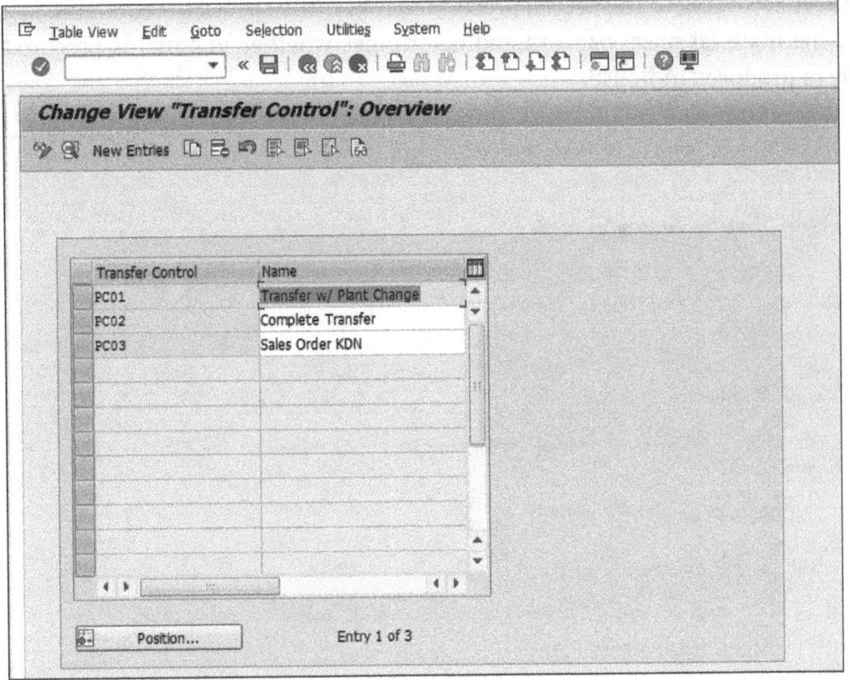

Figure 15.28 Transfer Control

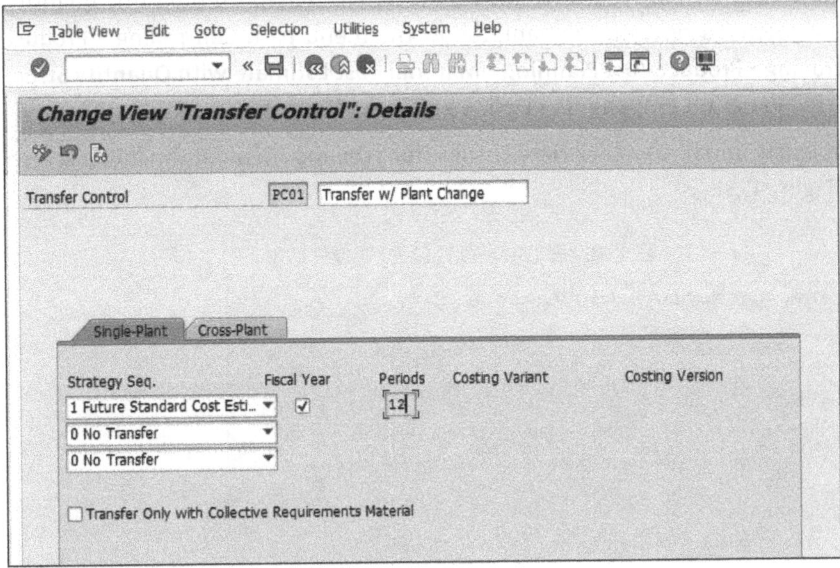

Figure 15.29 Transfer Control Single Plant

Under the **Cross-Plant** tab, shown in Figure 15.30, you can maintain a strategy sequence if you work with special procurement keys. The system will search for allocations from other sources according to the special procurement key. The special procurement key is part of the material master record and determines whether material is procured externally or produced in-house.

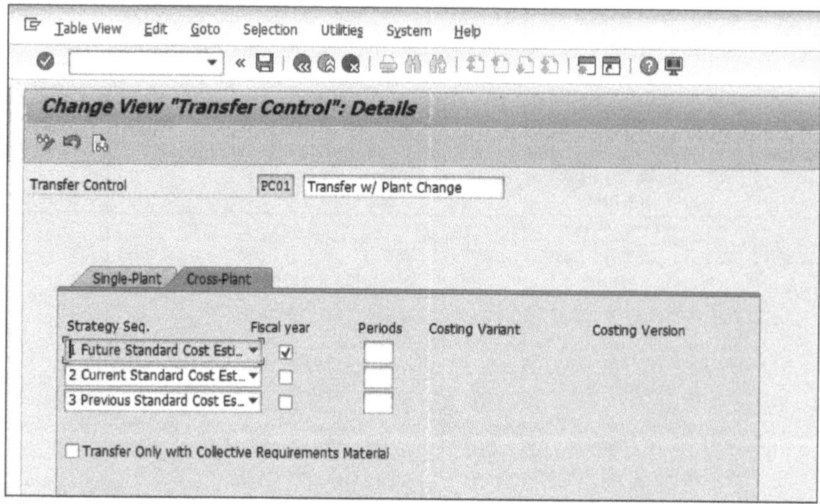

Figure 15.30 Transfer Control Cross-Plant

Reference Variant

A *reference variant* enables you to create cost estimates based on the same quantity structure. To define a reference variant, follow the menu path **Controlling • Product Cost Controlling • Product Cost Planning • Material Cost Estimate with Quantity Structure • Costing Variant: Components • Define Reference Variants.**

No variant exists initially, so click **New Entries** from the top menu of the initial screen shown in Figure 15.31.

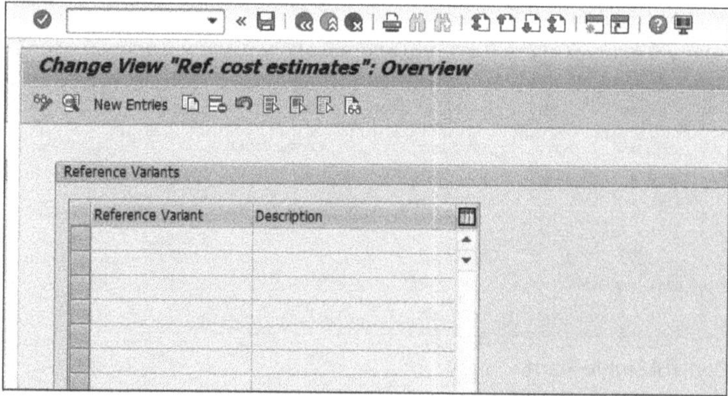

Figure 15.31 Creating a Reference Variant

Provide a name and description for the variant, as shown in Figure 15.32. Under the first tab, **Cost Estimate Ref.** (cost estimate reference), you can define the strategy for how to transfer an existing cost estimate.

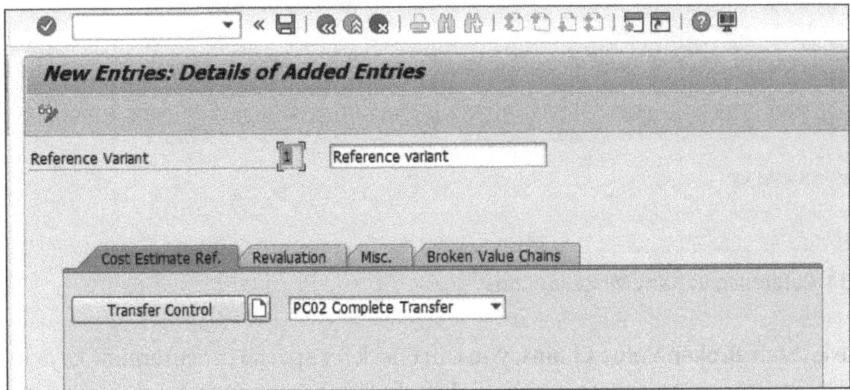

Figure 15.32 Reference Variant Cost Estimate

Under the **Revaluation** tab, shown in Figure 15.33, you'll define which components should be recalculated and which should remain the same from the original cost estimate. Components selected under this tab will be revaluated.

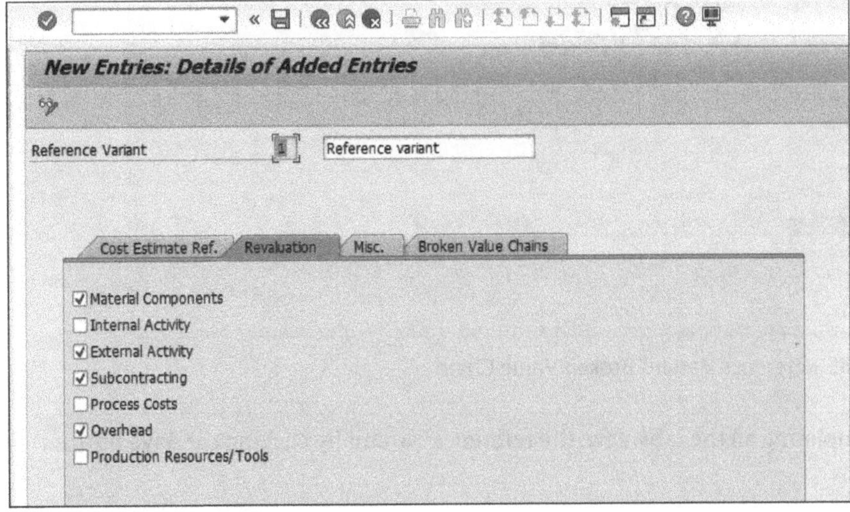

Figure 15.33 Reference Variant Revaluation

Under the **Misc.** tab, shown in Figure 15.34, if you select the **Transfer Additive Costs** checkbox, you can specify that additive costs also should be transferred when creating a cost estimate with a reference.

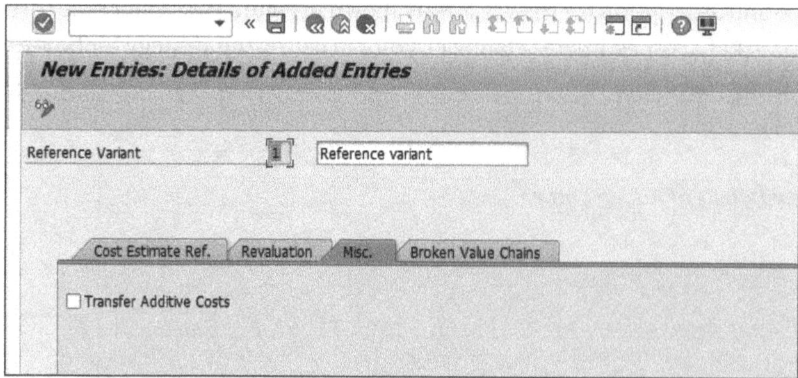

Figure 15.34 Reference Variant Miscellaneous

Under the last tab, **Broken Value Chains**, you can check for special procurement keys in the material master to prevent a broken value chain when costing across company codes. On the screen shown in Figure 15.35, select the **Special Proc. Stock Transfer** (special procurement stock transfer) checkbox so that, when the system costs a raw material, it will look for a special procurement key in the master data.

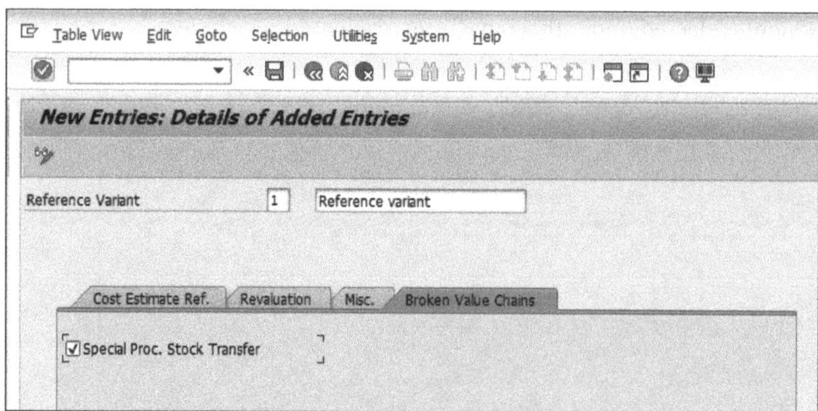

Figure 15.35 Reference Variant Broken Value Chain

After completing all the tabs, save the reference variant by clicking the **Save** button.

15.2.2 Creating the Costing Variant

In the previous section, we configured the various components that are part of a costing variant. Now, we're ready to create the costing variant itself. Follow the menu path **Controlling • Product Cost Controlling • Product Cost Planning • Material Cost Estimate with Quantity Structure • Define Costing Variants.**

On the initial screen, shown in Figure 15.36, you'll see a list of costing variants already defined. You can create new variants with the **New Entries** option from the top menu or copy an existing one by clicking the [copy icon] button from the top menu.

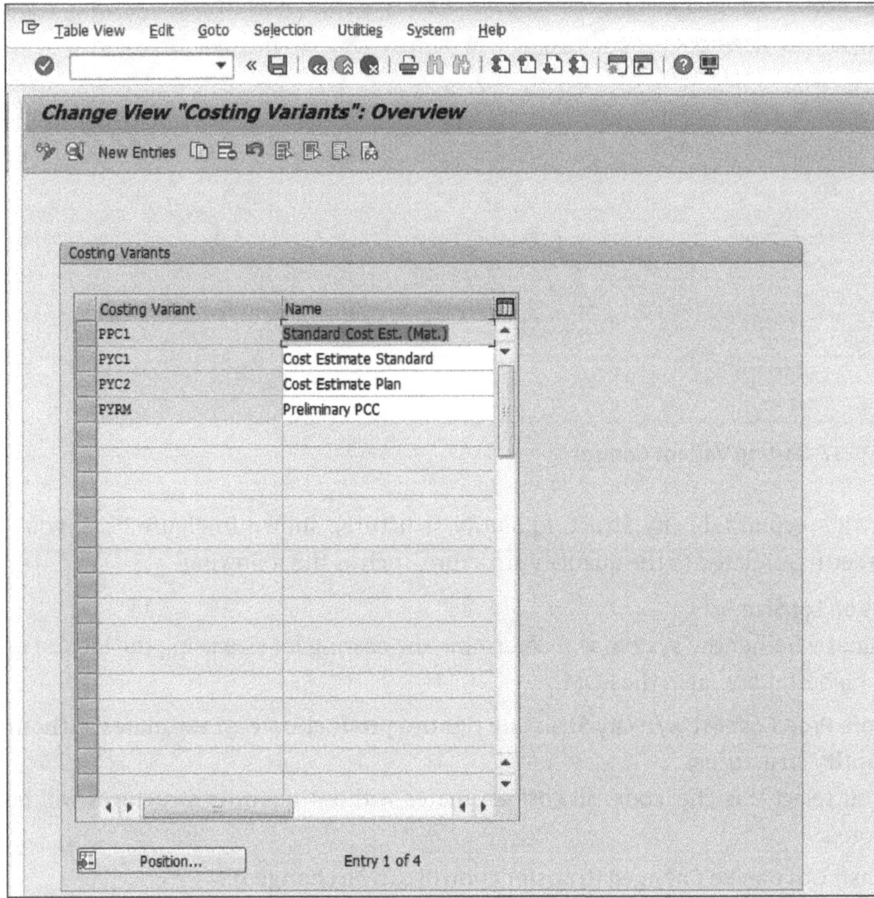

Figure 15.36 Costing Variants

Let's review the settings. Double-click **PPC1: Standard Cost Est. (Mat.)**, which is a standard costing variant provided by SAP.

Under the first tab, **Control**, shown in Figure 15.37, you'll assign the various costing variant components, which we defined in the previous steps:

- **Costing Type**
- **Valuation Variant**
- **Date Control**
- **Qty Struct. Control** (quantity structure control)
- **Transfer Control**
- **Reference Variant**

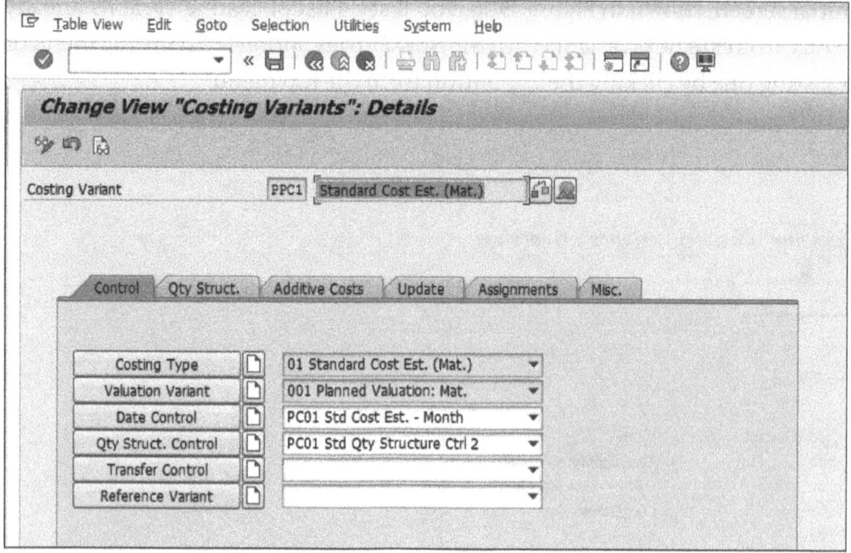

Figure 15.37 Costing Variant Control

Under the second tab, **Qty Struct.** (quantity structure), shown in Figure 15.38, you'll define settings related to the quantity structure, such as the following:

- **Pass on Lot Size**
  Defines whether the system will determine the costing lot size using the lot size of the highest material in the BOM.
- **Ignore Prod Cost Est w/o Qty Structure (ignore production cost estimates without quantity structures)**
  If you select this checkbox, all cost estimates without quantity structures will be ignored.
- **Transfr Ctrl Can Be Changed (transfer control can be changed)**
  If you select this checkbox, you can manually enter the transfer control parameters for existing costing data.
- **Transfer Active Std Cost Est. if Mat. Costed w/Errors (transfer active standard cost estimate if material costed with errors)**
  Defines whether the active standard cost estimate is used to continue costing when errors occur.

On the next screen, shown in Figure 15.39, you'll define whether additive costs should be considered in the cost estimate. If you select the **Include Additive Costs with Stock Transfers** checkbox, additive costs also will be considered during transfer of a material from a different plant.

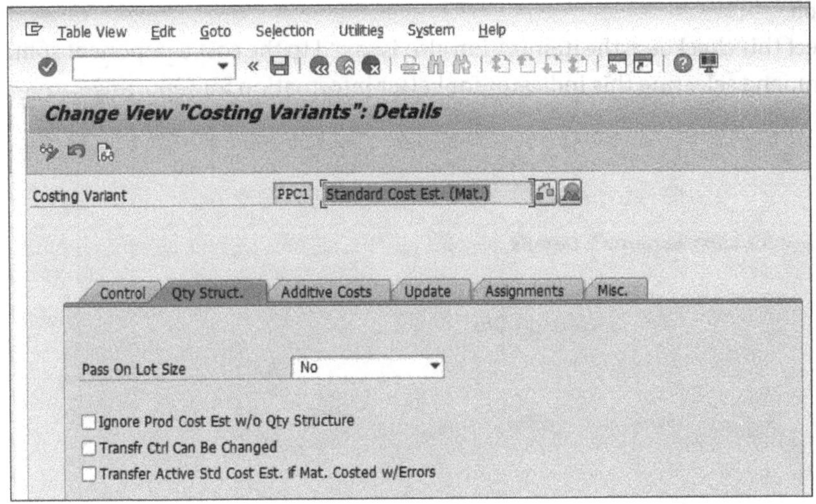

Figure 15.38 Costing Variant Quantity Structure

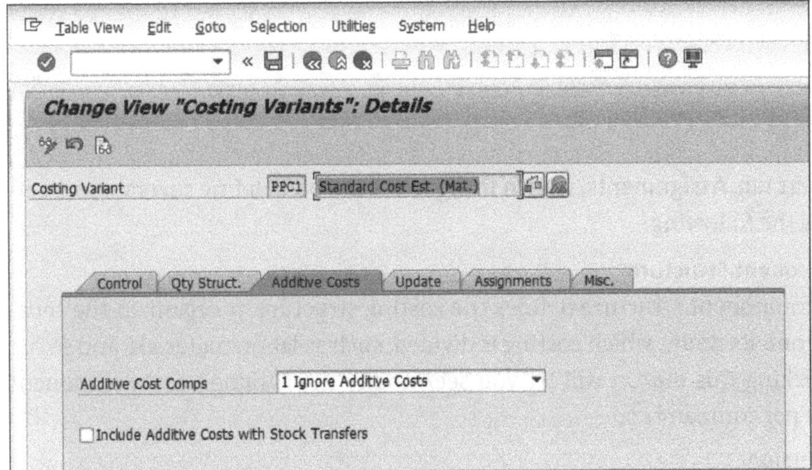

Figure 15.39 Costing Variant Additive Costs

Under the **Update** tab, shown in Figure 15.40, you'll define settings related to saving the cost estimate. The following options are available:

- **Saving Allowed**
  This indicator enables the saving of the cost estimate.
- **Save Error Log**
  This indicator enables the saving of the error log during calculation.
- **Defaults Can Be Changed by User**
  If you select this checkbox, you can change the save parameters during the calculation of the cost estimate.

- **Itemization**
  If you select this checkbox, the itemization also is saved to the cost component split. We recommend selecting this indicator for better information for reporting.

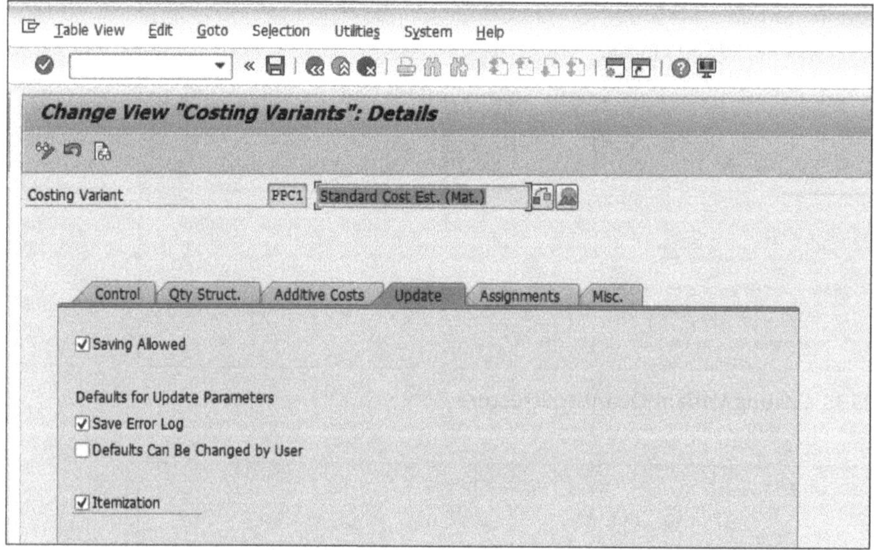

Figure 15.40 Costing Variant Update

Under the next tab, **Assignments**, shown in Figure 15.41, you'll define several more settings, such as the following:

- **Cost Component Structure**
  The cost component structure defines the costing structure. It organizes the separate components under which costing is divided, such as labor, materials, and so on. Double-clicking this button will let you see/modify the assigned cost component structures per company code.
- **Costing Version**
  With the costing version, you can perform different costing calculations for the same material.
- **Cost. Comp. Split in Contr. Area Currency (cost component split in controlling area currency)**
  With this option, you can perform the calculation in the controlling area currency in addition to the company code currency.
- **Cross-Company Costing**
  Activate this option if you want to perform cross-company code cost calculations.

Under the last tab, **Misc.**, shown in Figure 15.42, you define whether the error log should be saved when running the cost estimate and whether it should be sent automatically to existing SAP users.

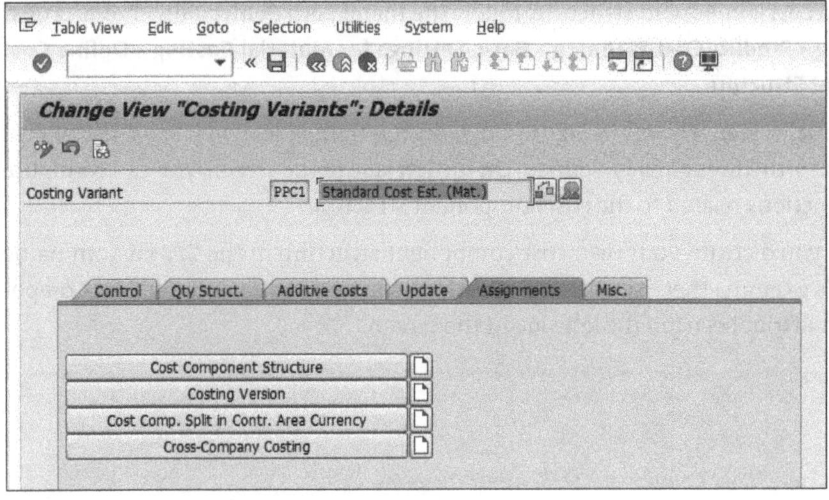

Figure 15.41 Costing Variant Assignments

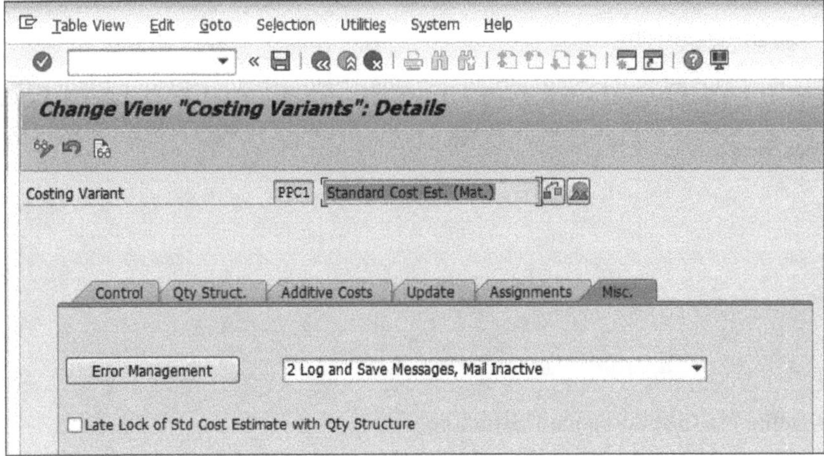

Figure 15.42 Costing Variant Miscellaneous

With that step, we've finished the configuration of the costing variant.

15.2.3 Cost Component Structure

We mentioned the cost component structure only briefly when we assigned it to the costing variant. A *cost component structure* defines how the results of material cost estimates are updated and structures the costs for individual materials into cost components (such as material costs, overhead, internal activities, external activities, and so on).

To define a cost component structure, follow the menu path **Controlling • Product Cost Controlling • Product Cost Planning • Basic Settings for Material Costing • Define Cost Component Structure.**

On the initial screen, shown in Figure 15.43, on the right side, you'll see a list of cost component structures already defined. On the left side of the screen, you can configure various functions related to the cost component structure.

Normally, you'd create your own cost component structure in the Z/Y custom name range. Let's examine these settings by selecting structure **Y1** and clicking **Cost Components with Attributes** from the left side of the screen.

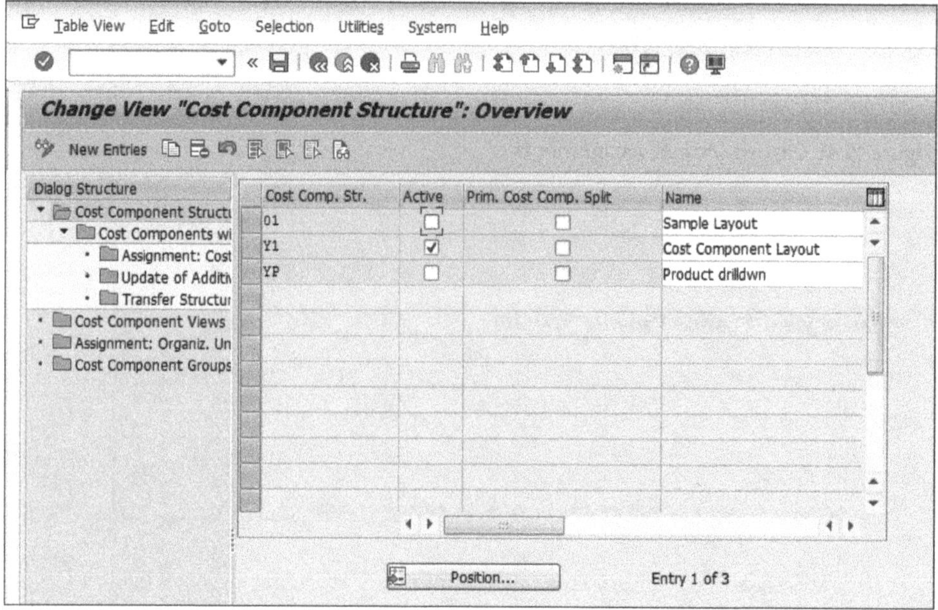

Figure 15.43 Defining a Cost Component Structure

On the screen shown in Figure 15.44, you'll see the defined cost components for cost component structure **Y1**. Ten components are defined, which represent the main types of costs related to manufacturing and selling a product. The number of cost components that can be defined is limited: 40 in older SAP releases, but 120 in SAP S/4HANA, a significant increase.

Double-clicking any element brings you to the detailed configuration screen for that element, as shown in Figure 15.45. On this screen, you'll configure which types of costs should be included, their relevance for inventory valuation, transfer price surcharge, tax inventory, and other settings. If you select the **Roll up Cost Component** indicator, the costing results of a cost component will be rolled up into the next-highest costing level.

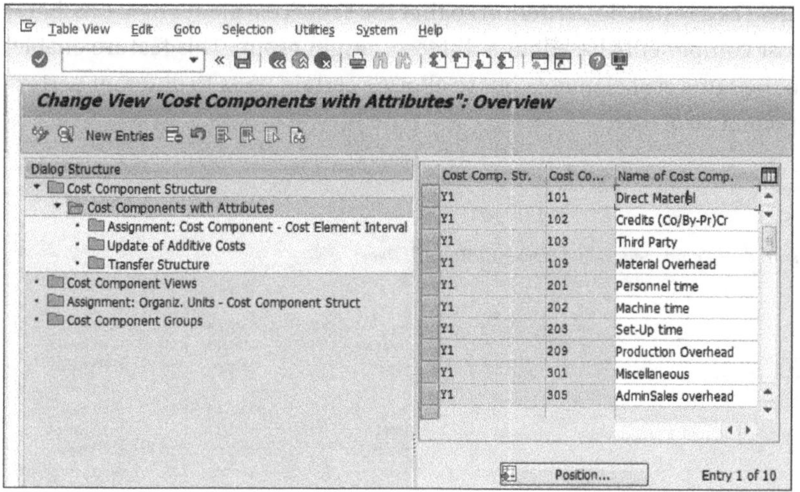

Figure 15.44 Cost Components

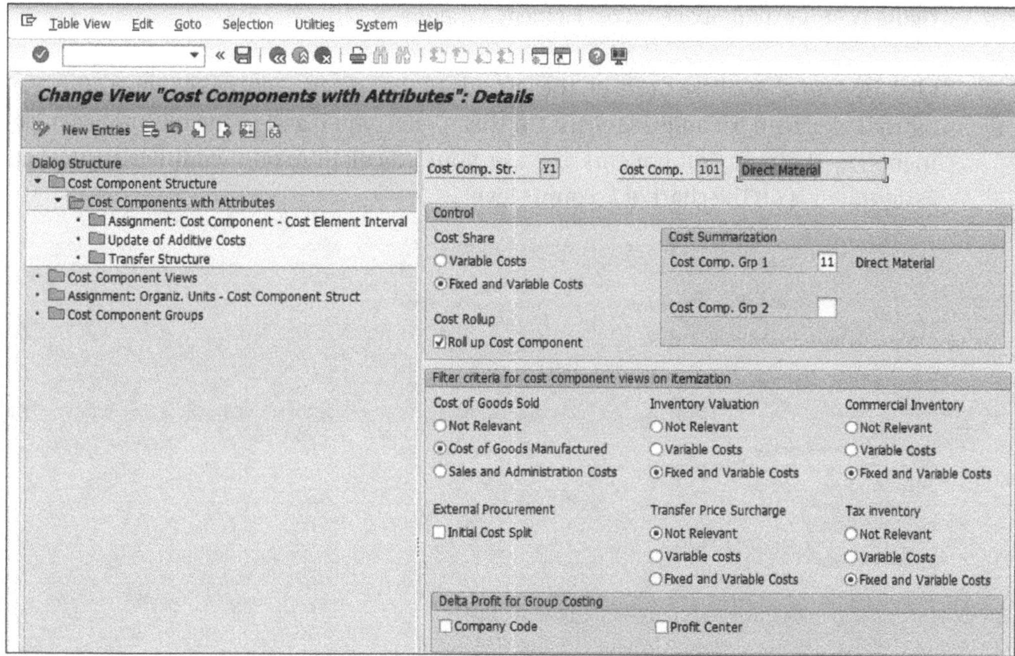

Figure 15.45 Cost Component Element

Click **Assignment: Cost Component - Cost Element Interval** from the left side of the screen. On the screen shown in Figure 15.46, assign cost elements to the cost component. These assignments are made on the chart of accounts level. You can also use the

Origin group field as a restriction criterion so that the same cost elements are assigned to different cost components based on a different origin group. This feature enables you to post to the same cost elements but to allocate certain costs to different parts of the cost component structure.

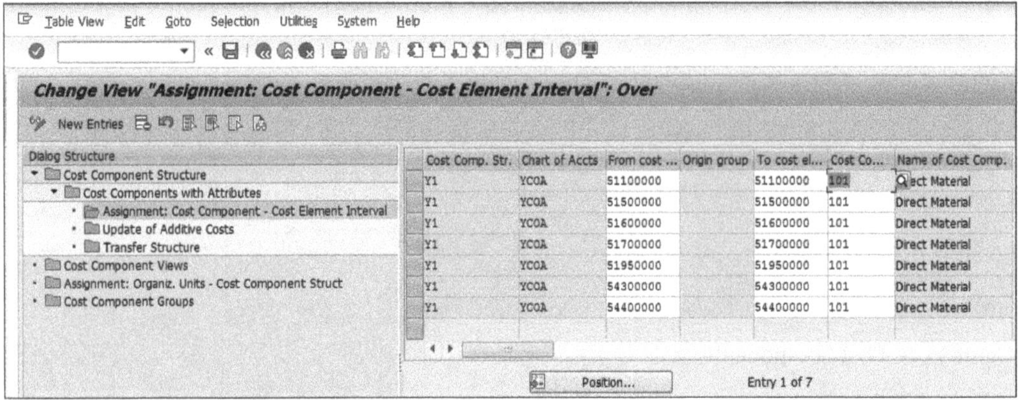

Figure 15.46 Cost Component Cost Element Assignment

Click **Update of Additive Costs** on the left side of the screen. Figure 15.47 shows the configuration screen for additive costs. On this screen, you'll assign the relevant cost elements to the cost components in case your calculation uses additive costs. This assignment is on the chart of accounts level.

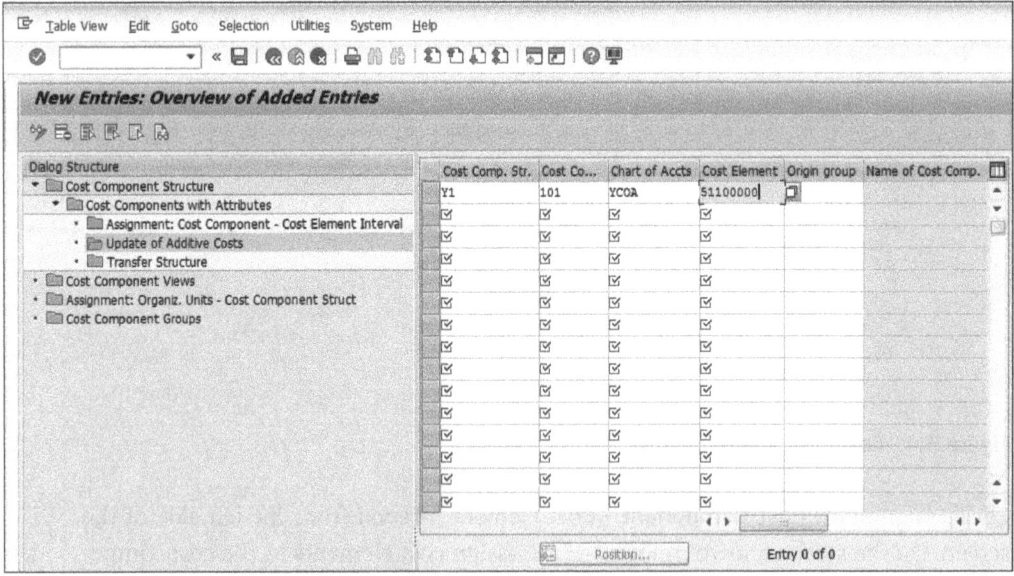

Figure 15.47 Cost Component Additive Costs

Click **Cost Component Views** from the left side of the screen. You can build cost component views here, which can include one or more of the cost components, as shown in Figure 15.48.

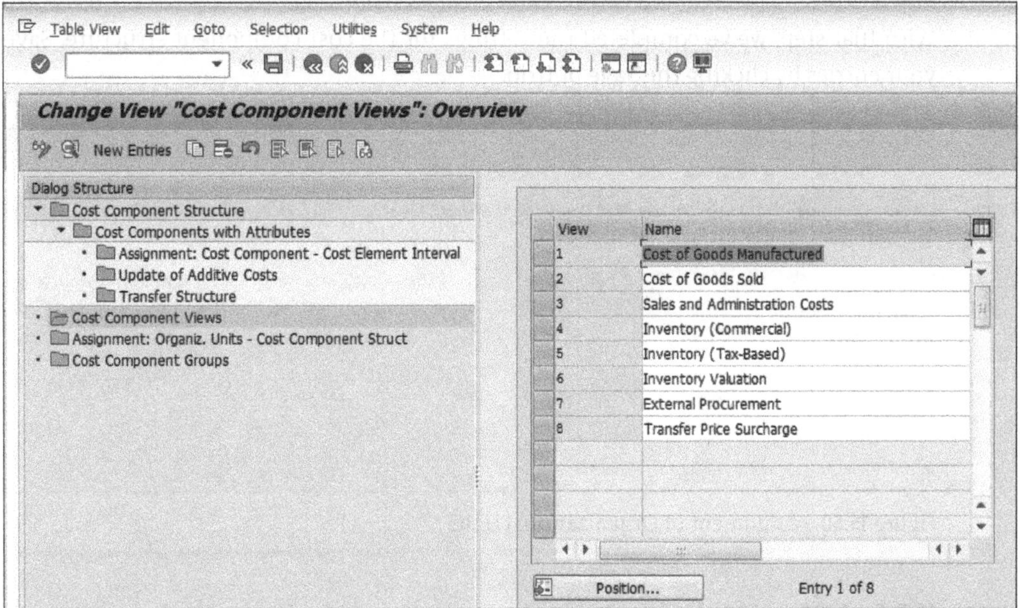

Figure 15.48 Cost Component Views

Double-click a view to see/maintain its components, as shown in Figure 15.49.

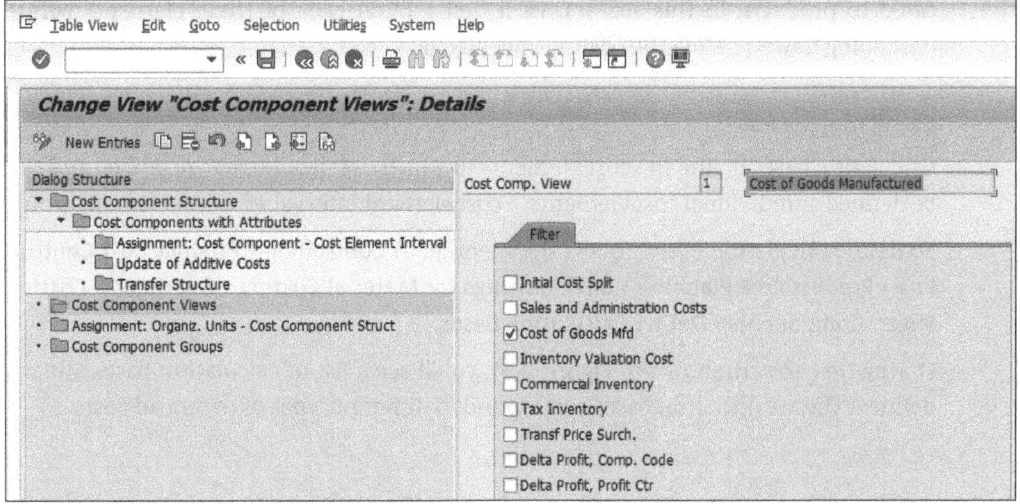

Figure 15.49 Cost Component Views Filter

Click **Assignment: Organiz. Units—Cost Component Struct** from the left side of the screen. On the screen shown in Figure 15.50, assign a cost component structure to a company code and specify its validity dates. You also can refine these assignments for each plant costing variant.

With that step, we've completed the settings for the cost component structure. Save your entries by clicking the **Save** button.

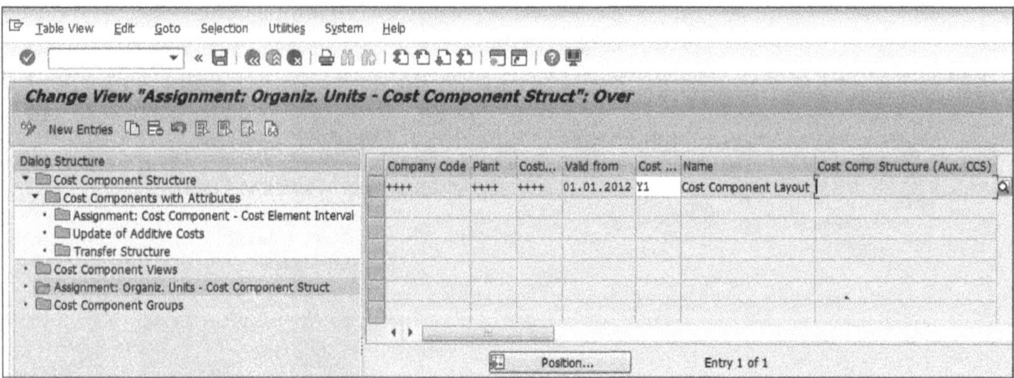

Figure 15.50 Assignment of Organizational Units

15.2.4 Costing Sheet

For the allocation of overhead costs in the product costing, you'll need to define a costing sheet. A *costing sheet* consists of three elements: calculation bases, overhead rates, and credits. Using these elements, you can define how overhead costs should be allocated to products. In this section, we'll first look at each of these elements before describing how to define the costing sheet itself.

Calculation Bases

Calculation bases define the cost elements to which overhead costs are posted and can be defined as individual cost elements, a cost element interval, or a cost element group.

To define calculation bases, follow the menu path **Controlling • Product Cost Controlling • Product Cost Planning • Basic Settings for Material Costing • Overhead • Costing Sheet: Components • Define Calculation Bases.**

On the first screen, shown in Figure 15.51, you'll see a list of calculation bases already defined. These calculation bases correspond to different types of overhead costs.

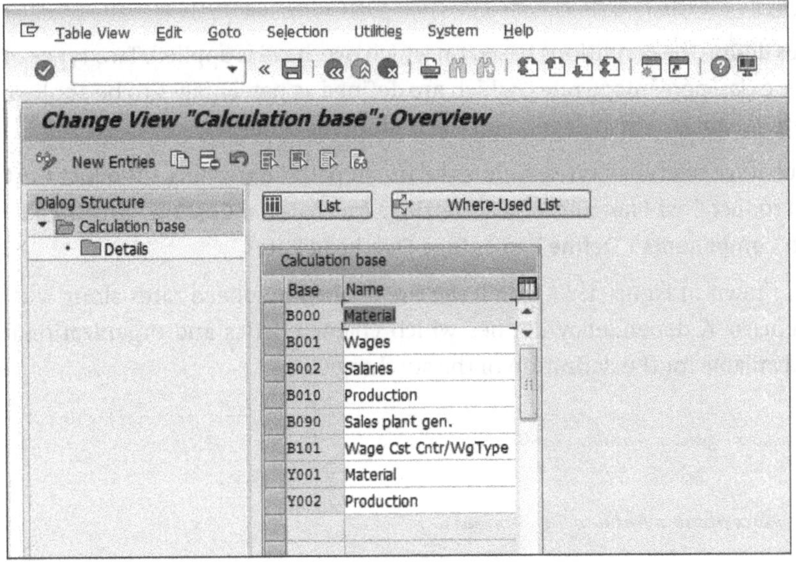

Figure 15.51 Calculation Bases

Let's modify the settings for base **B001: Wages.** Select this calculation base and click **Details** on the left side of the screen. After entering the **Controlling Area**, you'll see the screen shown in Figure 15.52.

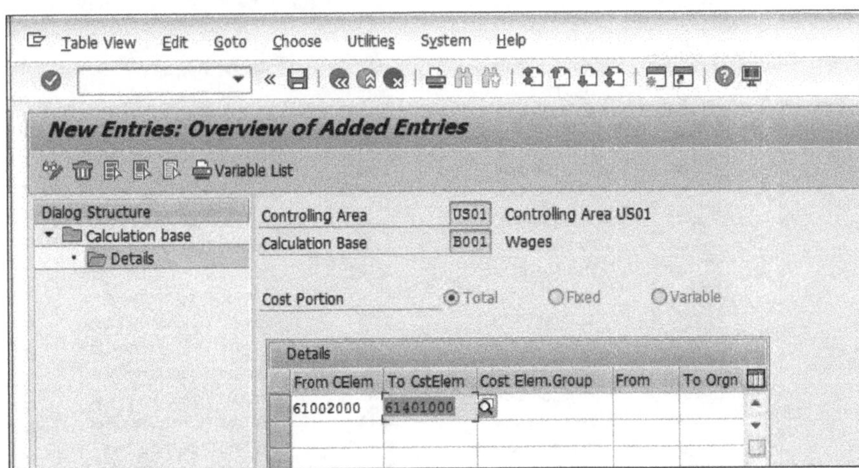

Figure 15.52 Calculation Bases Cost Elements

On this screen, enter ranges of cost elements on which the overhead costs for wages are posted. Thus, they'll be included in this base in the costing sheet calculation.

Using this logic, define your overhead bases and assign the respective cost elements.

Overhead Rates

Overhead rates define the conditions based on which overhead is applied. Two types of overhead rates exist: percentage rates, which are defined as percentages to be applied, and quantity-based rates, which depend on the underlying quantity.

To define percentage overhead rates, follow the menu path **Controlling • Product Cost Controlling • Product Cost Planning • Basic Settings for Material Costing • Overhead • Costing Sheet: Components • Define Percentage Overhead Rates.**

On the screen shown in Figure 15.53, you'll see the defined overhead rates along with their dependencies. A dependency defines which characteristics and organizational elements are available for the definition of the surcharge.

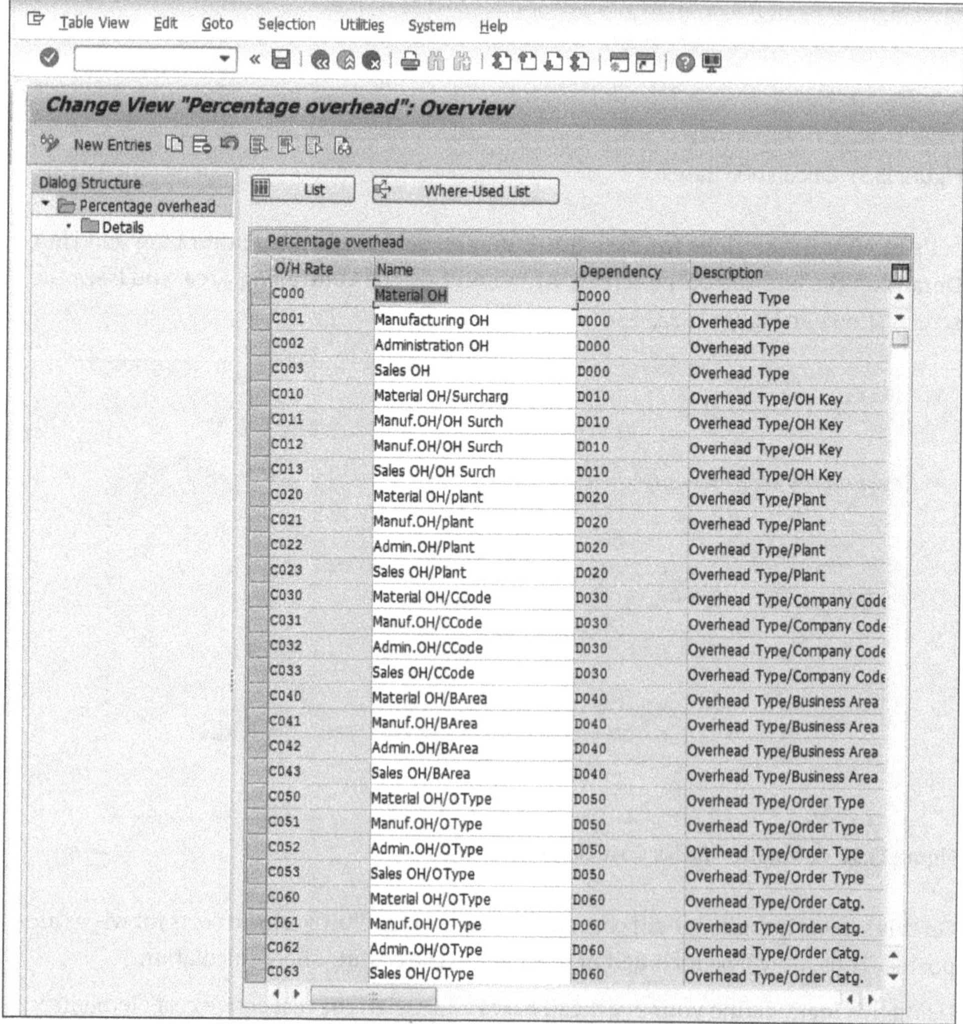

O/H Rate	Name	Dependency	Description
C000	Material OH	D000	Overhead Type
C001	Manufacturing OH	D000	Overhead Type
C002	Administration OH	D000	Overhead Type
C003	Sales OH	D000	Overhead Type
C010	Material OH/Surcharg	D010	Overhead Type/OH Key
C011	Manuf.OH/OH Surch	D010	Overhead Type/OH Key
C012	Manuf.OH/OH Surch	D010	Overhead Type/OH Key
C013	Sales OH/OH Surch	D010	Overhead Type/OH Key
C020	Material OH/plant	D020	Overhead Type/Plant
C021	Manuf.OH/plant	D020	Overhead Type/Plant
C022	Admin.OH/Plant	D020	Overhead Type/Plant
C023	Sales OH/Plant	D020	Overhead Type/Plant
C030	Material OH/CCode	D030	Overhead Type/Company Code
C031	Manuf.OH/CCode	D030	Overhead Type/Company Code
C032	Admin.OH/CCode	D030	Overhead Type/Company Code
C033	Sales OH/CCode	D030	Overhead Type/Company Code
C040	Material OH/BArea	D040	Overhead Type/Business Area
C041	Manuf.OH/BArea	D040	Overhead Type/Business Area
C042	Admin.OH/BArea	D040	Overhead Type/Business Area
C043	Sales OH/BArea	D040	Overhead Type/Business Area
C050	Material OH/OType	D050	Overhead Type/Order Type
C051	Manuf.OH/OType	D050	Overhead Type/Order Type
C052	Admin.OH/OType	D050	Overhead Type/Order Type
C053	Sales OH/OType	D050	Overhead Type/Order Type
C060	Material OH/OType	D060	Overhead Type/Order Catg.
C061	Manuf.OH/OType	D060	Overhead Type/Order Catg.
C062	Admin.OH/OType	D060	Overhead Type/Order Catg.
C063	Sales OH/OType	D060	Overhead Type/Order Catg.

Figure 15.53 Percentage Overhead Rates

These standard overhead rates are delivered by SAP, but you can define your own if needed. Select overhead rate **C000: Material OH** and click **Details** from the left side of the screen.

On the screen shown in Figure 15.54, you can define the overhead percentage rates and their validity dates.

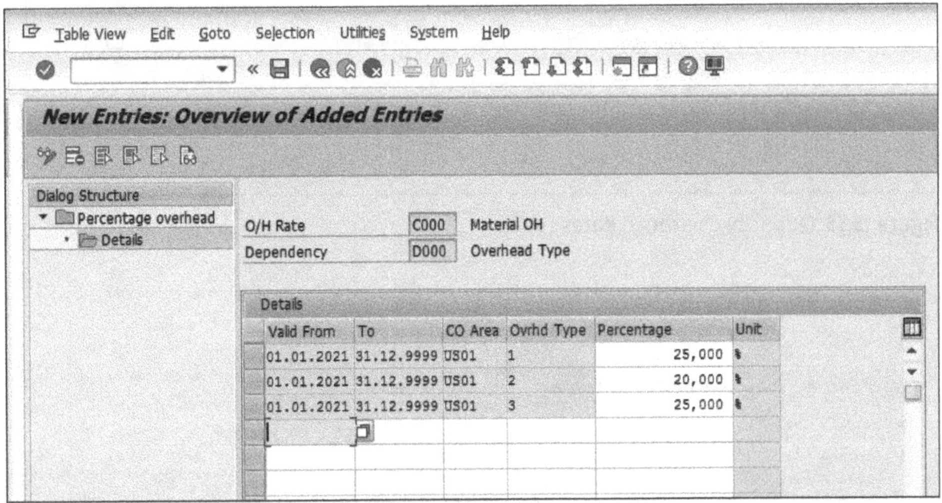

Figure 15.54 Percentage Overhead Details

The following three types of overhead rates can be defined in the **Ovrhd Type** (overhead type) field:

- **1: Actual Overhead Rate**
- **2: Planned Overhead Rate**
- **3: Commitment Overhead Rate**

The overhead type defines the types of costs that are being allocated. Often, new overhead rates are maintained each year, with new validity periods.

To define quantity-based overhead rates, follow the menu path **Controlling • Product Cost Controlling • Product Cost Planning • Basic Settings for Material Costing • Overhead • Costing Sheet: Components • Define Quantity-Based Overhead Rates**. On the screen shown in Figure 15.55, you'll see overhead quantity rates already defined, along with their dependencies.

Select overhead rate **C100: Material OH** and click **Details** from the left side of the screen. Then, click **New Entries** from the top menu and maintain the rates.

As shown in Figure 15.56, on this screen, you'll enter amounts that depend on quantities. In our example, an overhead of 10 USD per material is defined.

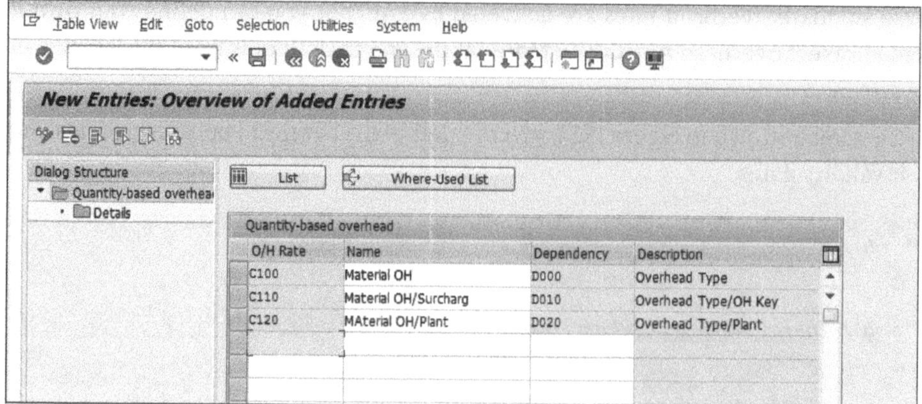

Figure 15.55 Quantity Overhead Rates

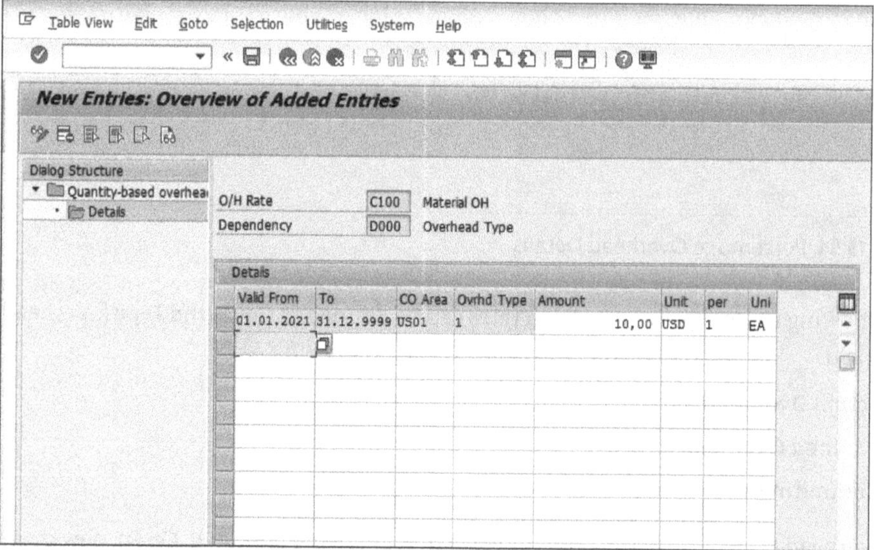

Figure 15.56 Quantity Overhead Rates Details

Credits

Credits define account assignment objects such as cost elements and cost centers, which are posted during the costing calculation.

To define credits, follow the menu path **Controlling • Product Cost Controlling • Product Cost Planning • Basic Settings for Material Costing • Overhead • Costing Sheet: Components • Define Credits**. On the screen shown in Figure 15.57, you'll see a list of credits already defined.

Select credit **E01**: **Credit Material** and click **Details** from the left side of the screen. Then, click **New Entries** from the top menu, enter a controlling area, and maintain the assignments.

Figure 15.58 shows an example of how you can assign cost elements and cost objects to the credit key. The cost element should be a secondary cost element with category 41.

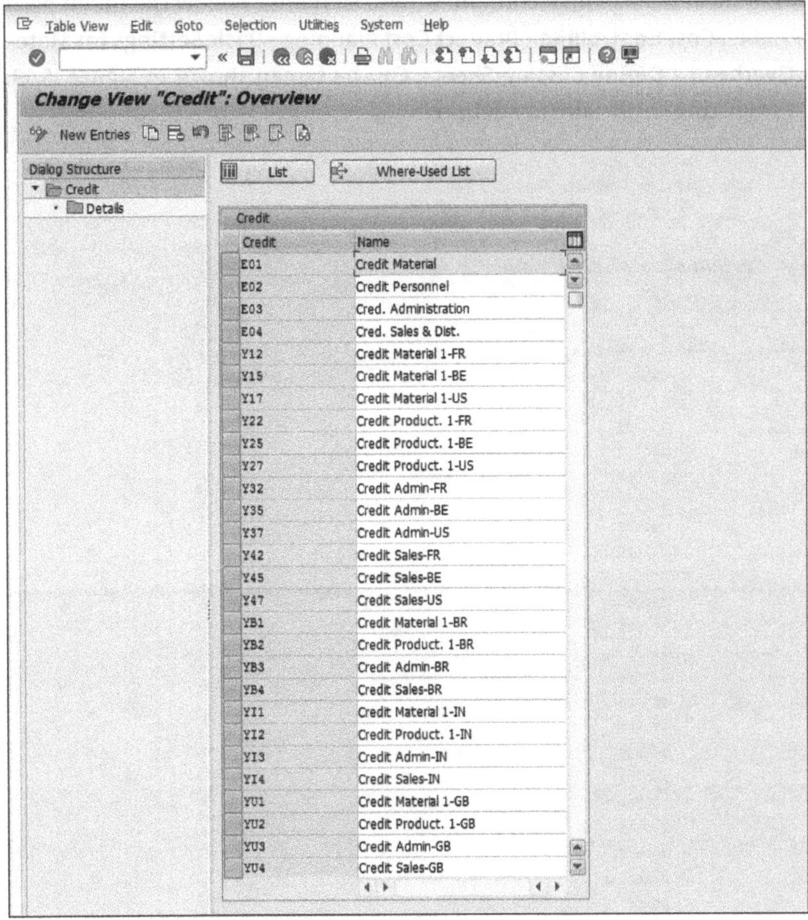

Figure 15.57 Defining Credits

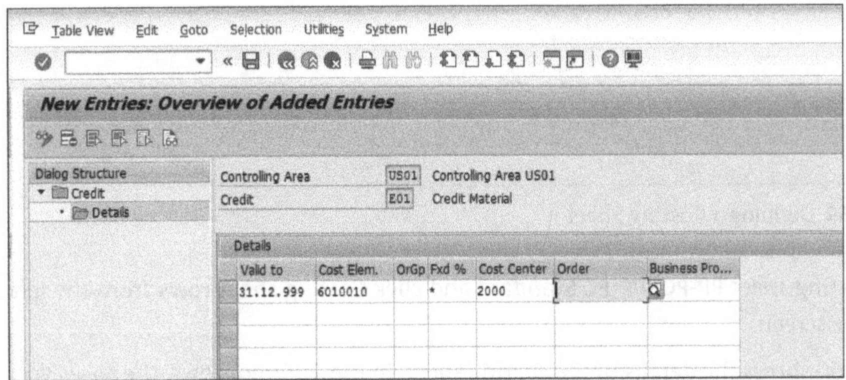

Figure 15.58 Credit Details

Defining Costing Sheets

Finally, after defining the calculation bases, overhead rates, and credits, you'll need to define the costing sheet itself, which combines these elements. Follow the menu path **Controlling • Product Cost Controlling • Product Cost Planning • Basic Settings for Material Costing • Overhead • Define Costing Sheets.** On the screen shown in Figure 15.59, you'll see a list of costing sheets already defined.

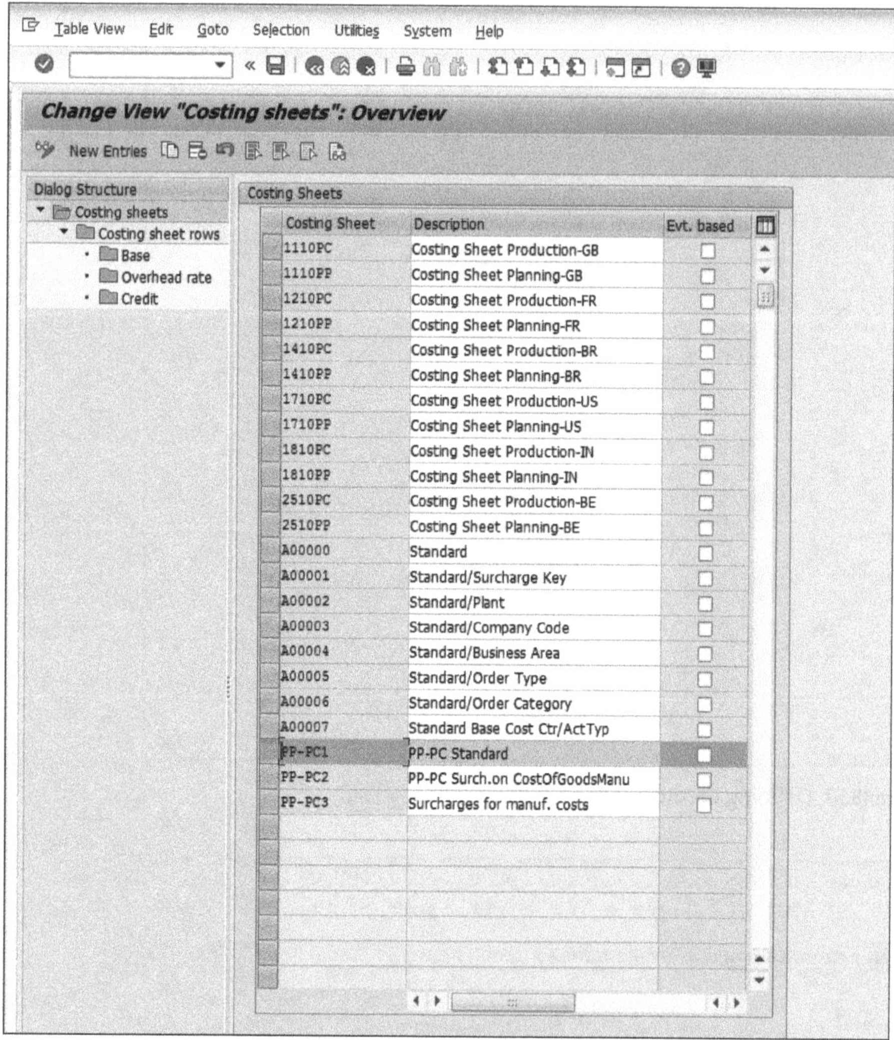

Figure 15.59 Defining a Costing Sheet

Select costing sheet **PP-PC1 PP-PC Standard** and click **Costing sheet rows** from the left side of the screen.

Figure 15.60 shows the details of the costing sheet. In the different rows, the bases you defined earlier are assigned. The overhead rates and credits refer to the rows with the bases. In the **Base**, **Overhead rate**, and **Credit** sections on the left side of the screen, you can see/modify the relevant details.

With that step, we've finished the configuration for the overhead calculation through the costing sheet.

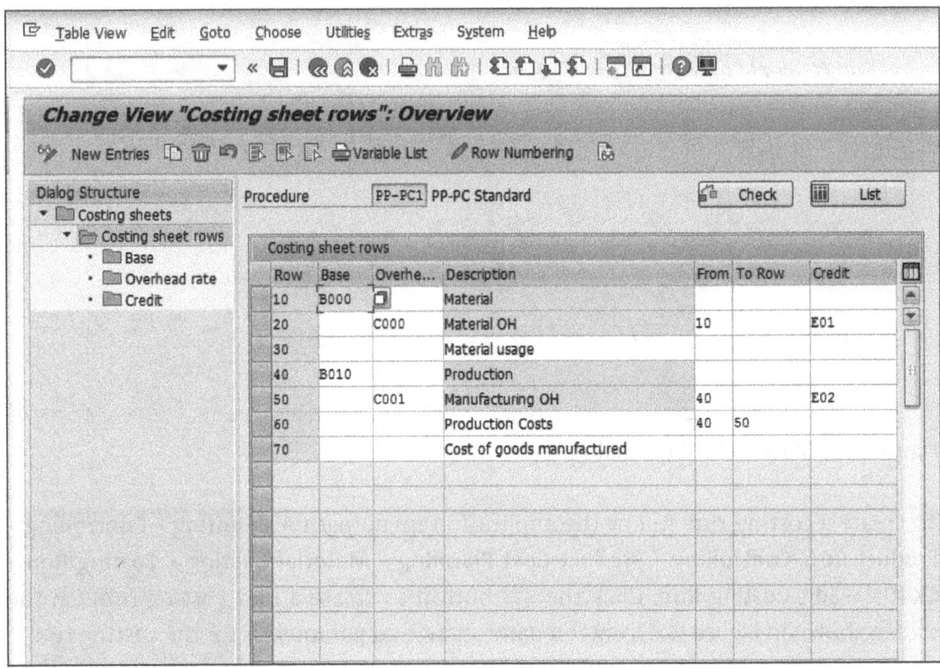

Row	Base	Overhe...	Description	From	To Row	Credit
10	B000		Material			
20		C000	Material OH	10		E01
30			Material usage			
40	B010		Production			
50		C001	Manufacturing OH	40		E02
60			Production Costs	40	50	
70			Cost of goods manufactured			

Figure 15.60 Costing Sheet Rows

15.2.5 Material Cost Estimates

The product cost calculation process created a material cost estimate, which calculates the cost of each material. You can create a material cost estimate individually for a material or for multiple materials in a costing run.

To create a material cost estimate for one material, follow the application menu path **Accounting • Controlling • Product Cost Controlling • Product Cost Planning • Material Costing • Cost Estimate with Quantity Structure • CK11N—Create.**

As shown in Figure 15.61, you must enter a material and plant to be costed. You'll also need to select a costing variant, which we configured in Section 15.2.2. Optionally, you can specify a costing lot size, which serves as a basis to determine the costing quantity. Also optionally, you can enter a transfer control, which we defined in Section 15.1.1 and which controls how the system should search for existing cost estimates.

Under the **Dates** tab, specify a costing date, quantity structure, and valuation date. Under the **Qty Struct.** tab, you can enter the BOM and routing data related to the cost estimate.

You also can create costing estimates for multiple materials through a costing run. Usually, in the beginning of the year, companies run a costing run to cost all relevant materials and determine their standard prices.

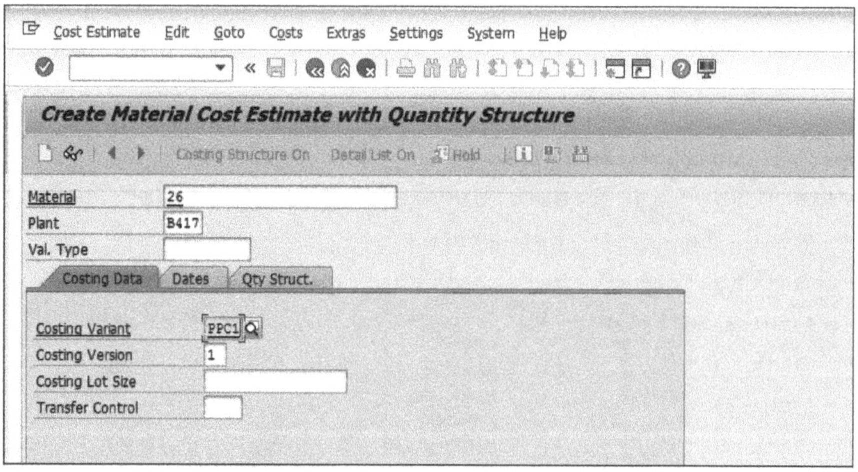

Figure 15.61 Material Cost Estimate

To create a costing run, follow the application menu path **Accounting • Controlling • Product Cost Controlling • Product Cost Planning • Material Costing • Costing Run • CK40N—Edit Costing Run**. Click the button to create a new costing run. On the screen shown in Figure 15.62, enter a name, date, and parameters for the costing run.

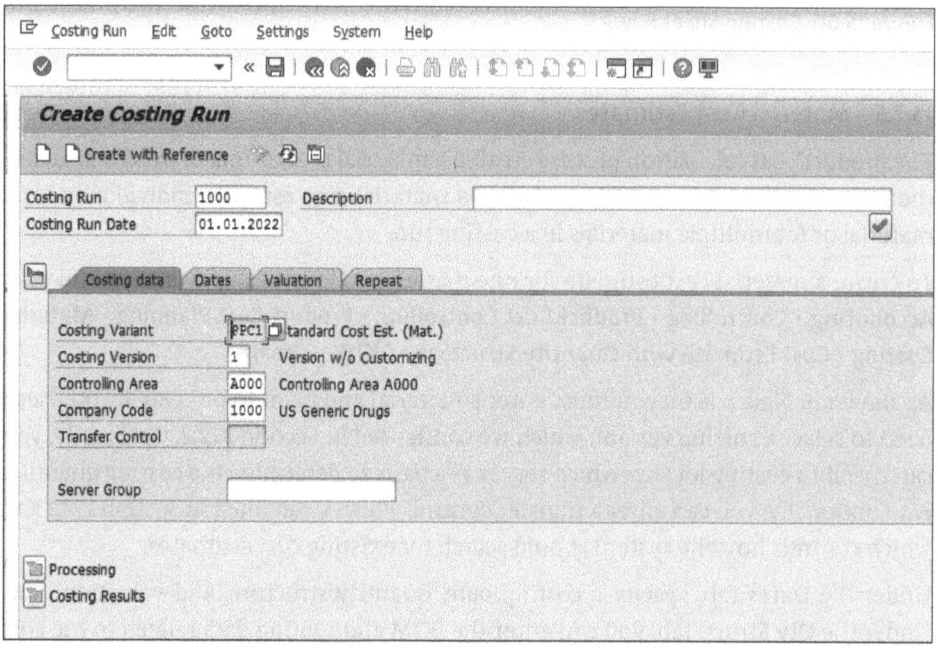

Figure 15.62 Creating a Costing Run

Then, under the **Costing data** tab, select the costing variant we created earlier, along with costing version, controlling area, company code, and transfer control if necessary.

After saving the run, in the lower section of the screen, you can enter the material selections.

On the screen shown in Figure 15.63, click the button in the **Selection** row.

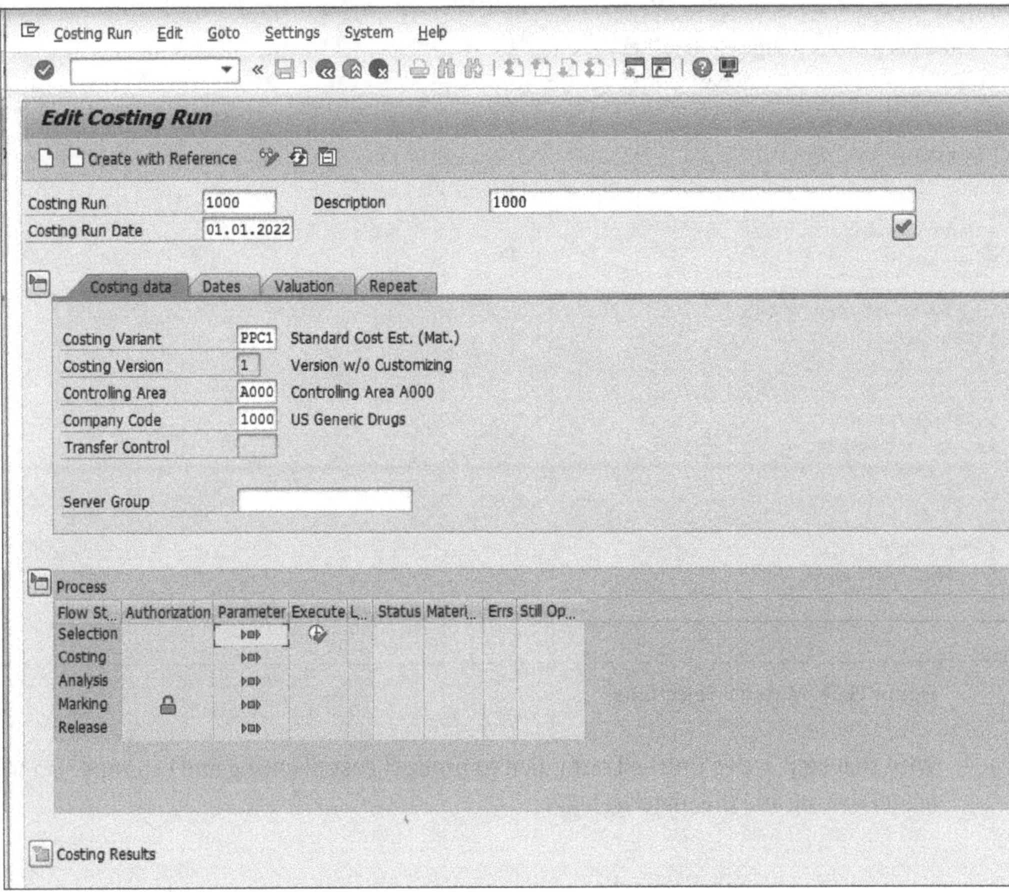

Figure 15.63 Costing Run Selections

This step opens a selection screen in which you can select materials and make further restrictions, as shown in Figure 15.64.

The next row, **Costing**, creates the material cost estimates for the selected materials. Then, in the **Analysis** row, you can review the material cost estimates. The next row, **Marking**, updates the calculated cost estimate in the material master as a future standard cost. The last row, **Release**, makes the future standard cost a current cost estimate, and the current cost estimate becomes the previous cost estimate. Then, existing inventory is revalued at the new standard cost, and the difference caused by the revaluation is posted as a finance document.

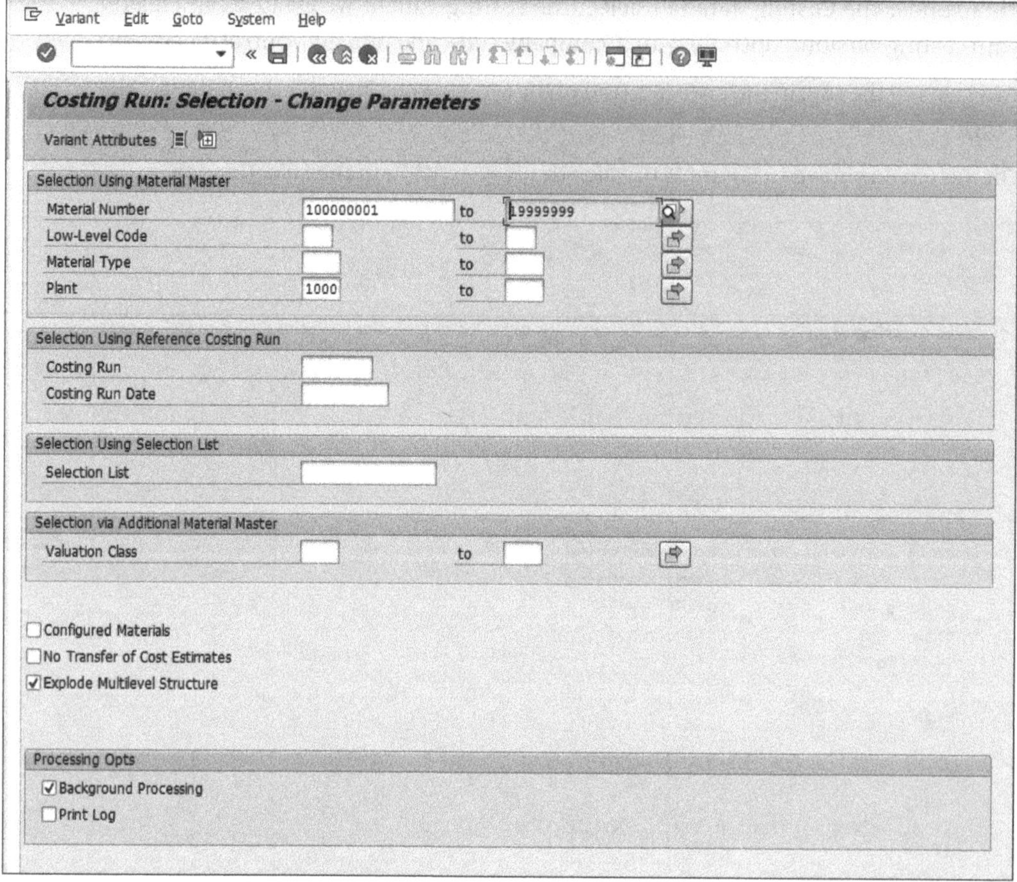

Figure 15.64 Material Selections

With that step, we've finished our guide to product cost planning and can move on to actual costing and the material ledger.

15.3 Actual Costing and Material Ledger

Actual costing calculates the actual prices of inventory based on the goods movements that occurred. The actual price calculated is called the *periodic unit price* and can be used to revaluate inventory. The material ledger stores, on the line-item level, changes in stock and prices with each material movement in multiple currencies. Material movements related to goods receipts (GRs), IRs, and so on are recorded in the material ledger with the price and exchange rate differences.

In this section, we'll provide an overview of the material ledger and show you how to activate it. Then, we'll guide you through configuring the material ledger for use for multiple valuations and currencies. Next, we'll configure the material ledger update.

Finally, we'll configure the actual costing and provide guidance how to use the actual costing cockpit to perform actual costing.

15.3.1 Overview and Material Ledger Activation

With SAP S/4HANA, the use of the material ledger is mandatory, but actual costing is not. Actual costing is particularly important for companies that operate in countries with high-inflation environments and unstable price levels. In some countries, using actual costing to value inventory might even be required, such as in Brazil and Russia.

With SAP S/4HANA, actual costing is one of the functions that the material ledger can enable, but it also provides material valuation in parallel currencies and valuation principles. With SAP S/4HANA, the tables of the material ledger are integrated into table ACDOCA.

For a brownfield implementation of SAP S/4HANA, if you're not using the material ledger, activating it is mandatory. This requirement exists because the previous inventory valuation tables (EBEW, EBEWH, MBEW, MBEWH, OBEW, and so on) can no longer update transactional data, which is retrieved from the table ACDOCA line items table in real time.

To activate the material ledger, follow the menu path **Controlling • Product Cost Controlling • Actual Costing/Material Ledger • Activate Material Ledger for Valuation Areas.** Then, select **Activate Material Ledger.** Figure 15.65 shows the plants for which the material ledger should be active.

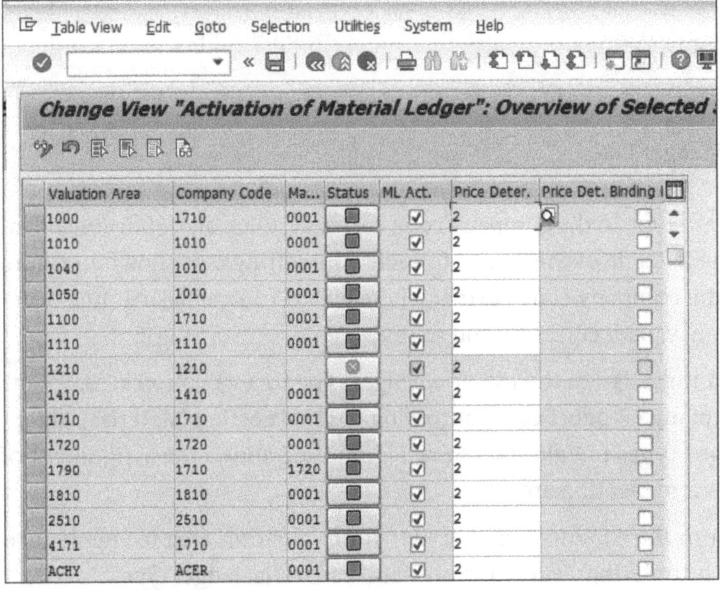

Figure 15.65 Activating a Material Ledger

You'll need to select the **ML Act.** (material ledger account) checkbox. In the **Price Deter.** (price determination) field, select **2** (transaction-based). This option means that both materials with the price control V (moving average price) and materials with the price control S (standard price) will be evaluated.

15.3.2 Multiple Currencies and Valuations

One of the main purposes of actual costing is to valuate materials in multiple currencies and valuations. The material ledger enables this process because it stores each inventory transaction on the line-item level in multiple currencies. Then, using the actual costing cockpit, inventory can be revaluated based on these multiple valuations.

Let's start the configuration for multiple currencies and valuations by defining material ledger types, which control the currencies in which the materials will be valuated. Follow the menu path **Controlling • Product Cost Controlling • Actual Costing/Material Ledger • Assign Currency Types and Define Material Ledger Types.** On the screen shown in Figure 15.66, you'll see a list of material ledger types already defined.

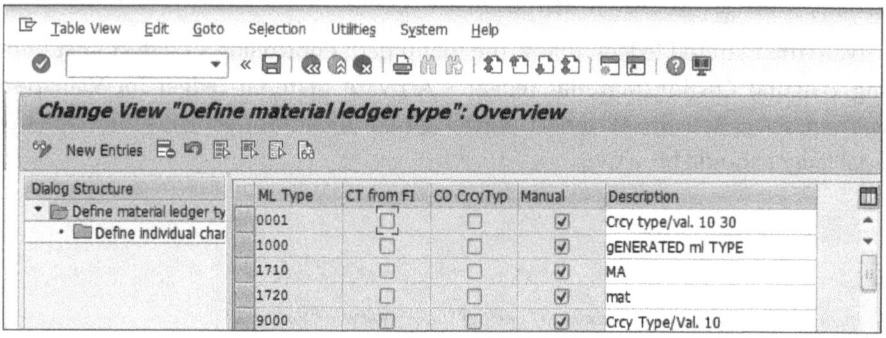

Table View Edit Goto Selection Utilities System Help

Change View "Define material ledger type": Overview

New Entries

Dialog Structure
- Define material ledger ty
  - Define individual char

ML Type	CT from FI	CO CrcyTyp	Manual	Description
0001	☐	☐	☑	Crcy type/val. 10 30
1000	☐	☐	☑	gENERATED ml TYPE
1710	☐	☐	☑	MA
1720	☐	☐	☑	mat
9000	☐	☐	☑	Crcy Type/Val. 10

Figure 15.66 Material Ledger Types

Select **9000**, a standard type in the company code currency. Click on **Define individual characteristics** on the left side of the screen to review its settings. As shown in Figure 15.67, for this type, the company code currency is selected. You can also define other types for group currency, hard currency, and so on.

In the next step, you must assign the material ledger type to a valuation area. Follow the menu path **Controlling • Product Cost Controlling • Actual Costing/Material Ledger • Assign Material Ledger Types to Valuation Area.** Figure 15.68 shows the assignment of material ledger types for valuation areas.

Click **New Entries** from the top menu and assign your valuation area to the defined material ledger type by entering a valuation area and a material ledger type.

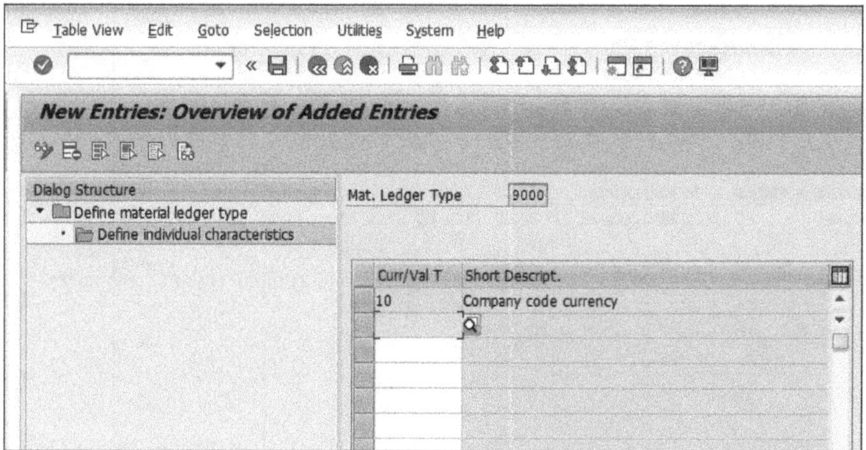

Figure 15.67 Material Ledger Type Details

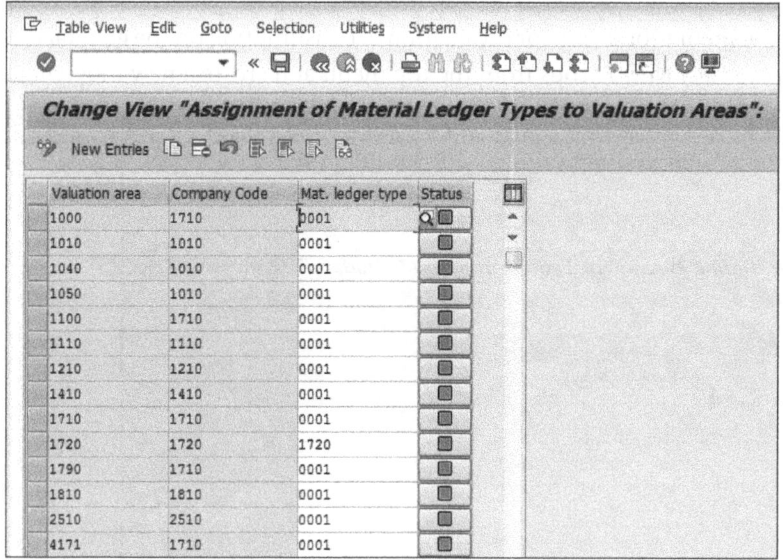

Valuation area	Company Code	Mat. ledger type	Status
1000	1710	0001	
1010	1010	0001	
1040	1010	0001	
1050	1010	0001	
1100	1710	0001	
1110	1110	0001	
1210	1210	0001	
1410	1410	0001	
1710	1710	0001	
1720	1720	1720	
1790	1710	0001	
1810	1810	0001	
2510	2510	0001	
4171	1710	0001	

Figure 15.68 Material Ledger Type Assign Valuation Area

15.3.3 Material Ledger Update

You also must configure how the material ledger is updated from the various inventory movements.

First, you'll define movement type groups for the material ledger. To create a movement type group, follow the menu path **Controlling • Product Cost Controlling • Actual Costing/Material Ledger • Material Update • Define Movement Type Groups of Material Ledger**. Initially, the configuration screen is blank, as shown in Figure 15.69.

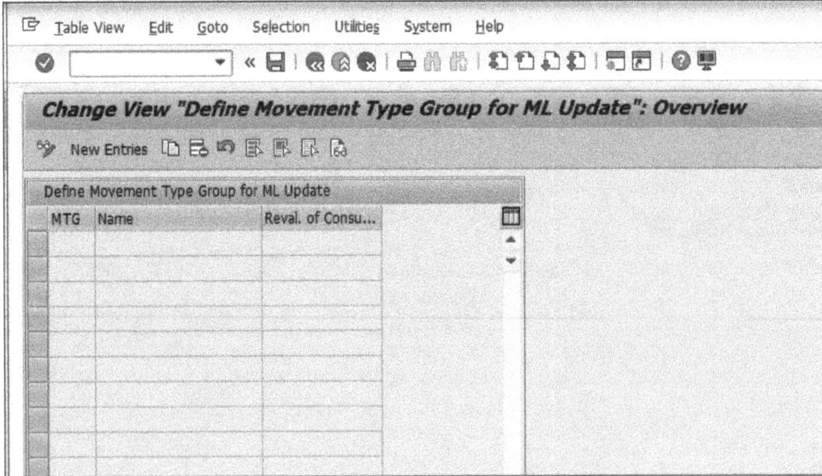

Figure 15.69 Movement Type Group for Material Ledger Update

Let's create a movement type group for revaluation of consumption on the general ledger account level. Select **New Entries** from the top menu and create a new movement type group, as shown in Figure 15.70.

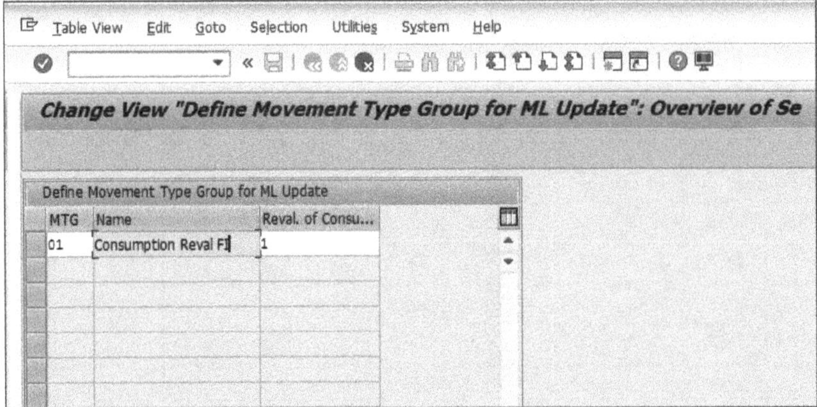

Figure 15.70 Revaluation of Consumption Movement Type Group

The following fields should be configured:

- **MTG (movement type group)**
  A code to identify the movement type group.
- **Name**
  A description of the movement type group.
- **Reval. of Consump. (revaluation of consumption)**
  Indicator that determines how to revalue consumption. With option **1** or **2**, the account assignment objects (general ledger account and/or controlling account

assignment) are stored when consumption occurs for movement types that are assigned to the movement type group. This option enables the account assignment objects to be revaluated using actual costs. In this example, we'll select **1** for revaluation on the general ledger account level only.

Save your entries by clicking the **Save** button.

For the next step, you'll assign movement types to the material ledger movement type group created. To assign movement types, follow the menu path **Controlling • Product Cost Controlling • Actual Costing/Material Ledger • Material Update • Assign Movement Type Groups of Material Ledger**. On the screen shown in Figure 15.71, you'll management type groups assigned to movement types.

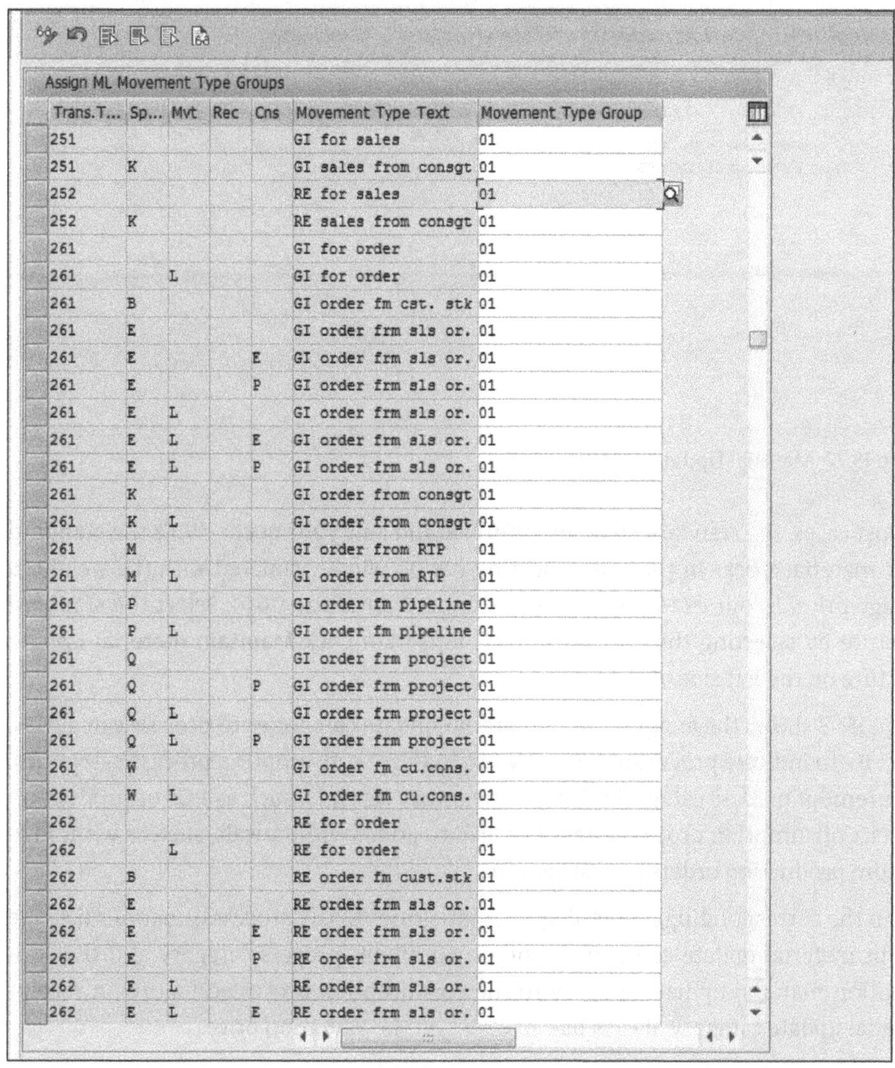

Assign ML Movement Type Groups

Trans.T...	Sp...	Mvt	Rec	Cns	Movement Type Text	Movement Type Group
251					GI for sales	01
251	K				GI sales from consgt	01
252					RE for sales	01
252	K				RE sales from consgt	01
261					GI for order	01
261		L			GI for order	01
261	B				GI order fm cst. stk	01
261	E				GI order frm sls or.	01
261	E			E	GI order frm sls or.	01
261	E			P	GI order frm sls or.	01
261	E	L			GI order frm sls or.	01
261	E	L		E	GI order frm sls or.	01
261	E	L		P	GI order frm sls or.	01
261	K				GI order from consgt	01
261	K	L			GI order from consgt	01
261	M				GI order from RTP	01
261	M	L			GI order from RTP	01
261	P				GI order fm pipeline	01
261	P	L			GI order fm pipeline	01
261	Q				GI order frm project	01
261	Q			P	GI order frm project	01
261	Q	L			GI order frm project	01
261	Q	L		P	GI order frm project	01
261	W				GI order fm cu.cons.	01
261	W	L			GI order fm cu.cons.	01
262					RE for order	01
262		L			RE for order	01
262	B				RE order fm cust.stk	01
262	E				RE order frm sls or.	01
262	E			E	RE order frm sls or.	01
262	E			P	RE order frm sls or.	01
262	E	L			RE order frm sls or.	01
262	E	L		E	RE order frm sls or.	01

Figure 15.71 Assigning a Material Ledger Movement Type Group to Movement Types

Assign the movement type group **01**, created for the revaluation of consumption on the financial accounting level, to the relevant movement types, then save this assignment by clicking the **Save** button.

You also must define a material update structure, which specifies how the values from valuation-relevant transactions are stored in the material ledger. To define a material update structure, follow the menu path **Controlling • Product Cost Controlling • Actual Costing/Material Ledger • Material Update • Define Material Update Structure.** Figure 15.72 shows the standard material update structure **0001**.

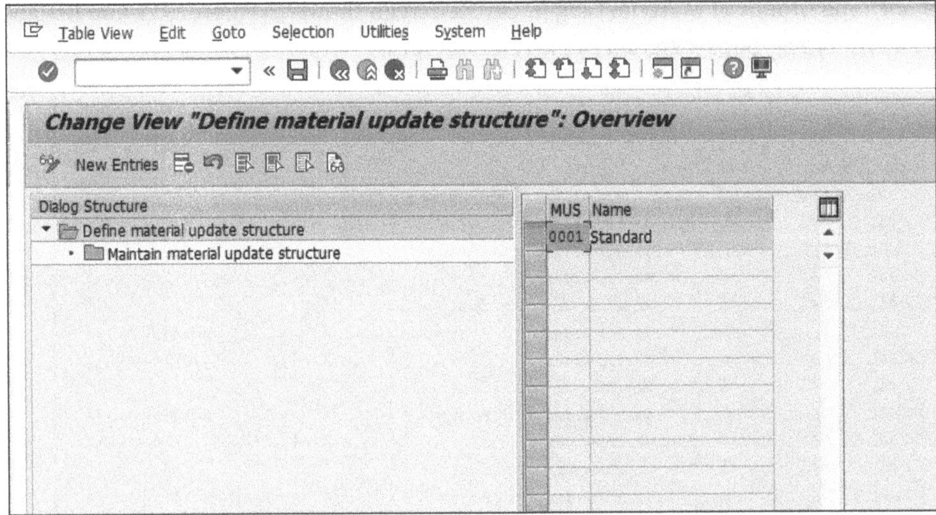

Figure 15.72 Material Update Structure

In most cases, the standard structure **0001** should suit your needs. With the standard logic, material stocks in the closed posting period will be valuated with the weighted average price. In our example, we'll use standard structure **0001**. Select the standard structure by selecting the checkbox to its left, then click **Maintain material update structure** on the left side of the screen.

Figure 15.73 shows the assignment of material update categories to process categories. Select **B+** to indicate procurement and **V+** to indicate consumption process categories. Procurement process categories lead to inventory receipts, such as POs or production orders. Consumption process categories lead to goods withdrawals, such as withdrawals from production orders or cost centers.

Assign the corresponding material update categories to the process categories (i.e., the receipt material update category to the procurement process category and the consumption material update category to the consumption process category). A receipt material update category always has an effect on the valuation price.

Finally, you must assign the material update structure to your valuation categories by following the menu path **Controlling • Product Cost Controlling • Actual Costing/Material Ledger • Material Update • Assign Material Update Structure to a Valuation Area**. As shown in Figure 15.74, assign material update structure **0001** to the valuation areas.

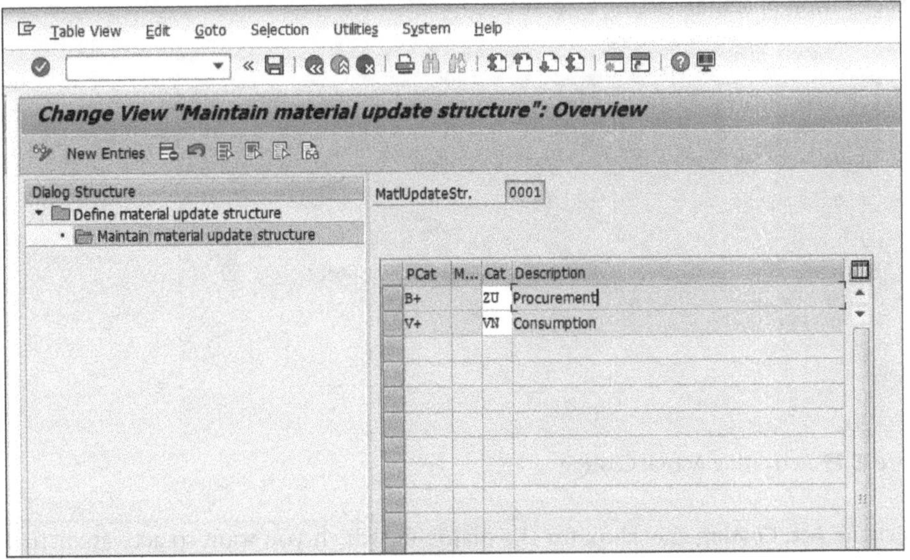

Figure 15.73 Assigning Material Update Categories

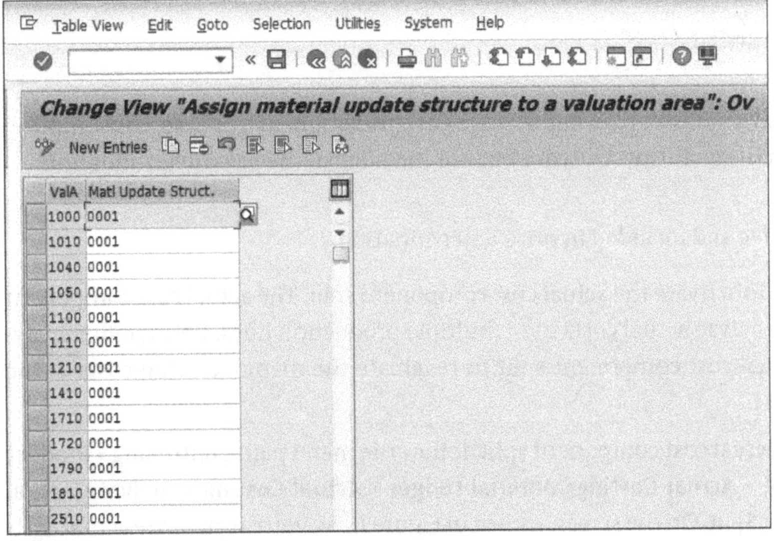

Figure 15.74 Assigning a Material Update Structure

15.3.4 Actual Costing

To use actual costing, you'll need to activate it on the plant level. Follow the menu path **Controlling • Product Cost Controlling • Actual Costing/Material Ledger • Actual Costing • Activate Actual Costing**. Then, select **Activate Actual Costing**. Figure 15.75 shows the activation of actual costing by plant.

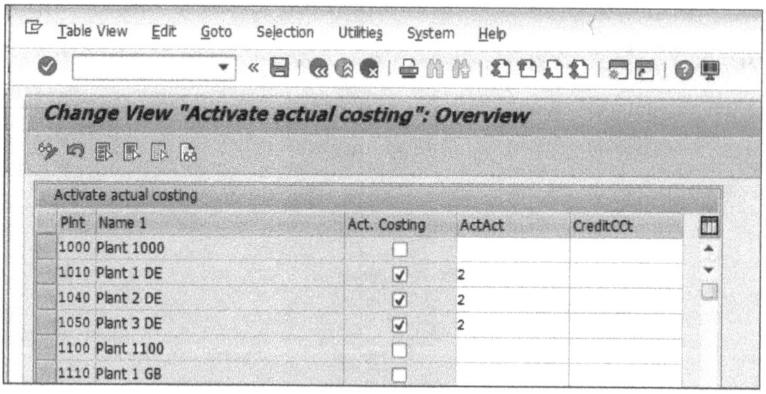

Figure 15.75 Activating Actual Costing

Select the **Act. Costing** checkbox for the plants for which you want to activate actual costing. In the **ActAct** field, define the settings for updating the consumption of activities in the actual quantity structure. Three settings are possible:

- **0**
  Update is not active.
- **1**
  Update is active but isn't relevant to price determination. In this case, consumption is updated in the quantity structure but not included in the price determination.
- **2**
  Update is active and included in price determination.

The next step is to activate the actual cost component split. The actual cost component split is used to analyze actual costs over multiple production lines. Profitability analysis uses the actual cost component split to revaluate the manufacturing costs at the end of the period.

To activate the actual cost component split, follow the menu path **Controlling • Product Cost Controlling • Actual Costing/Material Ledger • Actual Costing • Activate Actual Cost Component Split**. On the screen shown in Figure 15.76, you can activate actual costing for each valuation area and company code.

Select the checkbox in the **ActCstCmpSplt Active** (active cost component split active) column and save your entries by clicking the **Save** button.

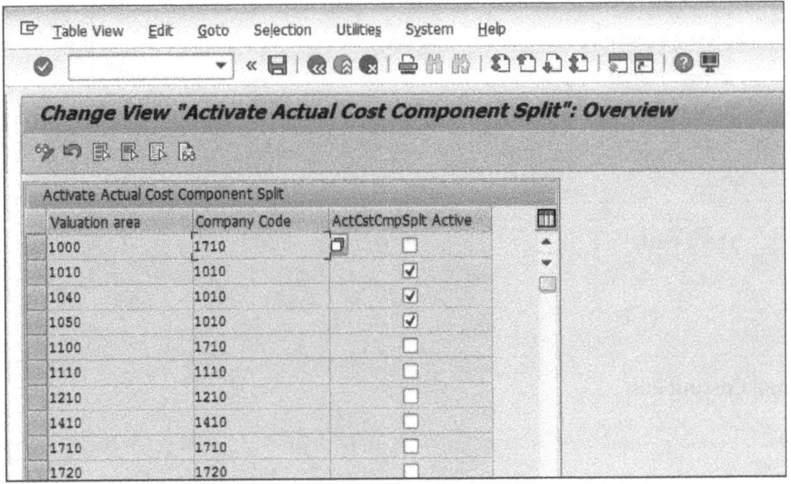

Figure 15.76 Activating Actual Cost Component Split

15.3.5 Actual Costing Cockpit

The actual costing program is known as the *actual costing cockpit*. The actual costing cockpit enables you to perform balance sheet valuation by revaluing your inventory based on the periodic unit price. With this program, you can revalue your cost of goods sold (COGS), thus providing more accurate valuation for your profit margin calculation.

In SAP S/4HANA, the actual costing cockpit was redesigned and improved with a simplified data structure and calculation logic. In the new program, one settlement step has replaced the single-level price determination, multilevel price determination, revaluation of consumption, and work in process (WIP) revaluation steps. Therefore, the program is simplified and benefits from the new SAP HANA database.

To run actual costing, follow the application menu path **Accounting • Controlling • Product Cost Controlling • Actual Costing/Material Ledger • Actual Costing • CKMLCP—Edit Costing Run**. Figure 15.77 shows the definition screen of the actual costing run.

To create a new actual costing run, click the [ ] button. Similar to the cost estimate run, you'll need to enter an actual costing run name and description. You also must enter a period. Normally, an actual costing run is run every month as part of month-end closing procedures. Then, under the **Plant Assignment** tab, you'll select the plants for which you want to run actual costing.

After you run actual costing, the system calculates the periodic unit price for the materials and then generates financial accounting and material ledger documents. Using the calculated periodic unit price as a valuation price for inventory is optional, mostly used in countries with unstable prices.

With that step, we've finished our guide to actual costing and the material ledger.

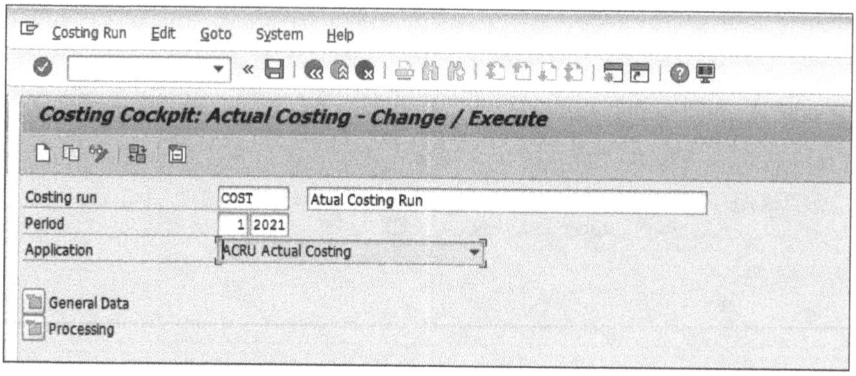

Figure 15.77 Actual Costing Run

15.4 Information System

The information system for product costing provides numerous reports to help you analyze material cost estimates, the actual costs incurred, and the variances between them. This data helps management analyze production costs and how actual costs compare to the plan.

Let's examine the information system for product cost planning and for actual costing and the material ledger.

15.4.1 Product Cost Planning

Product cost planning reports are available at the application menu path **Accounting • Controlling • Product Cost Controlling • Product Cost Planning • Information System.** These reports are grouped into the following types:

- Summarized analysis
- Object lists
- Detailed reports
- Object comparisons

For example, let's open the useful report S_P99_41000111 (Analyze/Compare Material Cost Estimates), available at the application menu path **Accounting • Controlling • Product Cost Controlling • Product Cost Planning • Information System • Object List • For Material.**

On the selection screen shown in Figure 15.78, enter plant and material numbers, and you also can restrict results by costing variant, version, and costing date. You'll also need to select the cost component view to display.

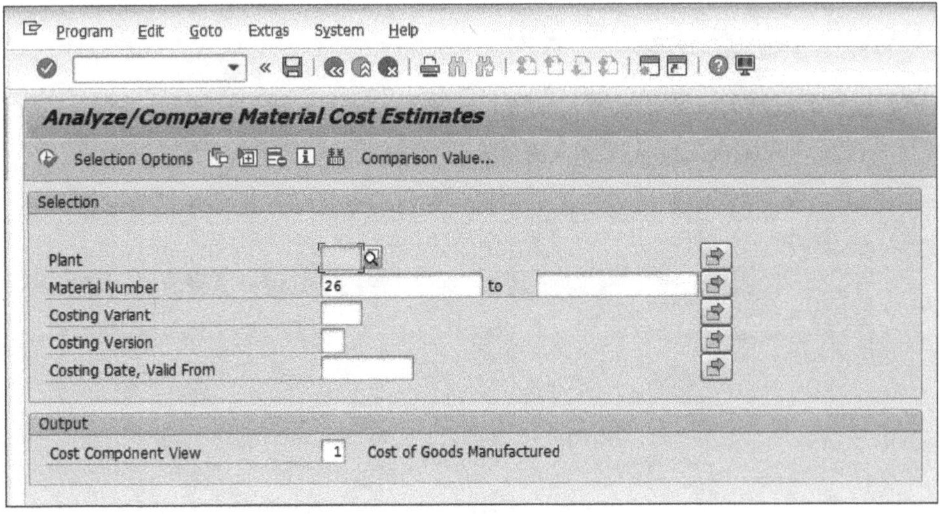

Figure 15.78 Analyzing Cost Estimates

Figure 15.79 shows the result of the cost estimate. The costing result is provided per material and costing lot size.

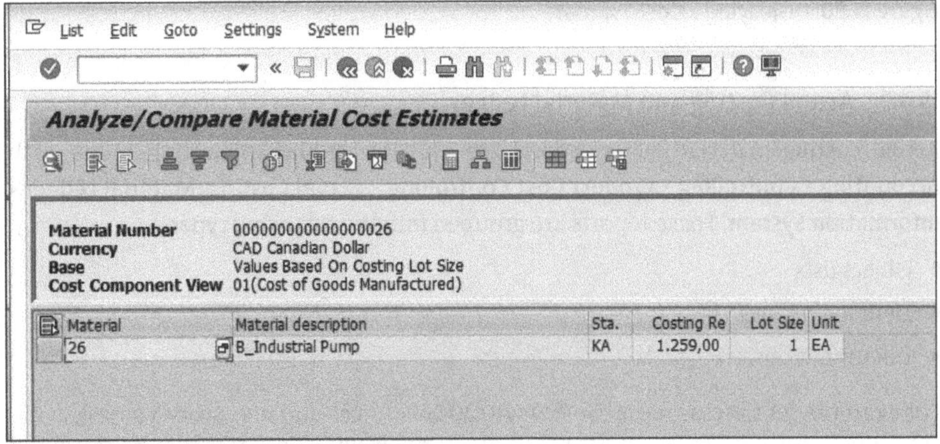

Figure 15.79 Analyzing Cost Estimates Output

Double-clicking the material lets you display the cost estimate. Figure 15.80 shows the material cost estimate.

Using this report, you can see an overview of cost estimates per material and drill down to each material to analyze its details.

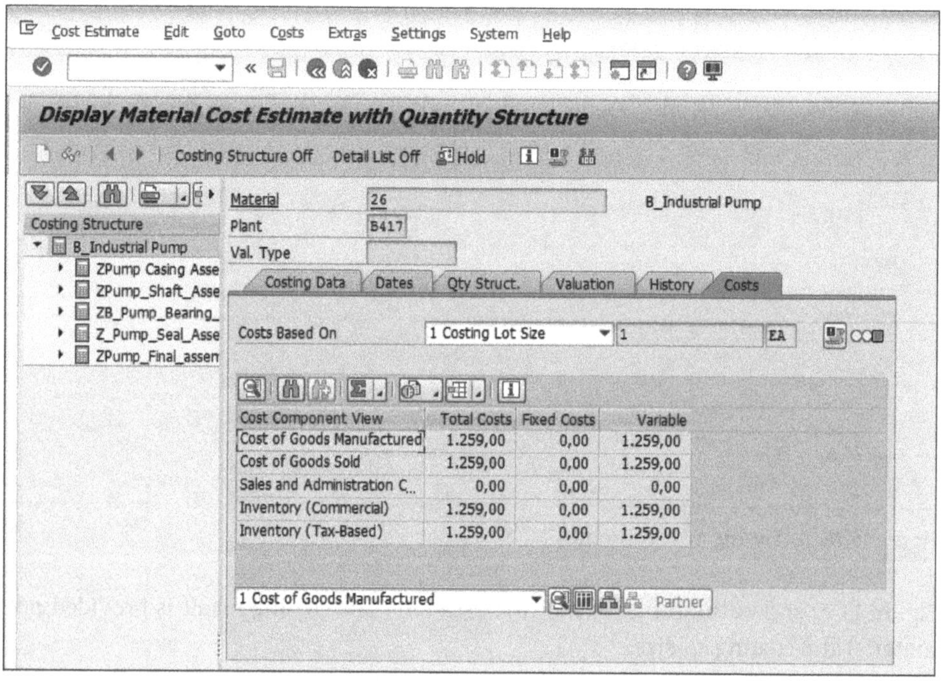

Figure 15.80 Displaying a Cost Estimate

15.4.2 Actual Costing and Material Ledger

Actual costing/material ledger reports are available at the application menu path **Accounting • Controlling • Product Cost Controlling • Actual Costing/Material Ledger • Information System**. These reports are grouped into the following types:

- Object lists
- Detailed reports
- Document reports

For example, let's access report S_P99_41000062 (Prices and Inventory Values), available at the application menu path **Accounting • Controlling • Product Cost Controlling • Actual Costing/Material Ledger • Information System • Object List.**

Figure 15.81 shows the selection screen of the report. Enter the plant, period, and fiscal year and then select a currency valuation. You can also restrict by material number; if not entered, all relevant materials per plant will be included. Execute by clicking the button.

Figure 15.82 shows the resulting output list. For each material, the system provides the total stock, total inventory value, standard price, and per unit price. Double-clicking a material provides further information, including all goods movements.

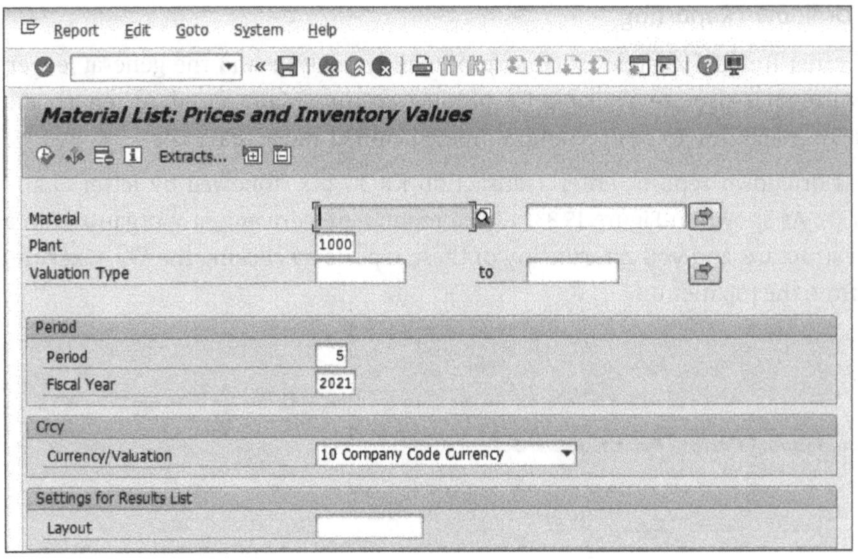

Figure 15.81 Prices and Inventory Values

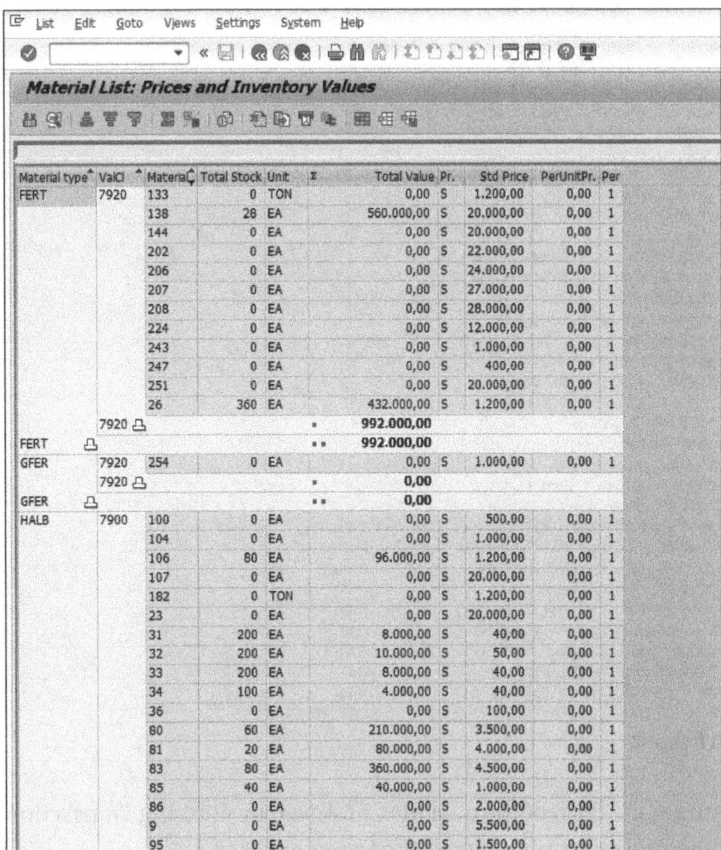

Material type	ValCl	Material	Total Stock	Unit	Σ	Total Value	Pr.	Std Price	PerUnitPr.	Per
FERT	7920	133	0	TON		0,00	S	1.200,00	0,00	1
		138	28	EA		560.000,00	S	20.000,00	0,00	1
		144	0	EA		0,00	S	20.000,00	0,00	1
		202	0	EA		0,00	S	22.000,00	0,00	1
		206	0	EA		0,00	S	24.000,00	0,00	1
		207	0	EA		0,00	S	27.000,00	0,00	1
		208	0	EA		0,00	S	28.000,00	0,00	1
		224	0	EA		0,00	S	12.000,00	0,00	1
		243	0	EA		0,00	S	1.000,00	0,00	1
		247	0	EA		0,00	S	400,00	0,00	1
		251	0	EA		0,00	S	20.000,00	0,00	1
		26	360	EA		432.000,00	S	1.200,00	0,00	1
	7920				•	992.000,00				
FERT					••	992.000,00				
GFER	7920	254	0	EA		0,00	S	1.000,00	0,00	1
	7920				•	0,00				
GFER					••	0,00				
HALB	7900	100	0	EA		0,00	S	500,00	0,00	1
		104	0	EA		0,00	S	1.000,00	0,00	1
		106	80	EA		96.000,00	S	1.200,00	0,00	1
		107	0	EA		0,00	S	20.000,00	0,00	1
		182	0	TON		0,00	S	1.200,00	0,00	1
		23	0	EA		0,00	S	20.000,00	0,00	1
		31	200	EA		8.000,00	S	40,00	0,00	1
		32	200	EA		10.000,00	S	50,00	0,00	1
		33	200	EA		8.000,00	S	40,00	0,00	1
		34	100	EA		4.000,00	S	40,00	0,00	1
		36	0	EA		0,00	S	100,00	0,00	1
		80	60	EA		210.000,00	S	3.500,00	0,00	1
		81	20	EA		80.000,00	S	4.000,00	0,00	1
		83	80	EA		360.000,00	S	4.500,00	0,00	1
		85	40	EA		40.000,00	S	1.000,00	0,00	1
		86	0	EA		0,00	S	2.000,00	0,00	1
		9	0	EA		0,00	S	5.500,00	0,00	1
		95	0	EA		0,00	S	1.500,00	0,00	1

Figure 15.82 Prices and Inventory Values Output

15.4.3 Drilldown Reporting

As with other functional areas, such as profitability analysis and the general ledger, drilldown reports also are available for product costing. Many standard reports are available to enable you to analyze and compare planned and actual costs.

To access drilldown reports, enter Transaction KKOO (KK, followed by letter O and number O). As shown in Figure 15.83, all the reports are conveniently organized in a tree-like structure, and you can run any of these reports by clicking the (Execute) button from the top menu.

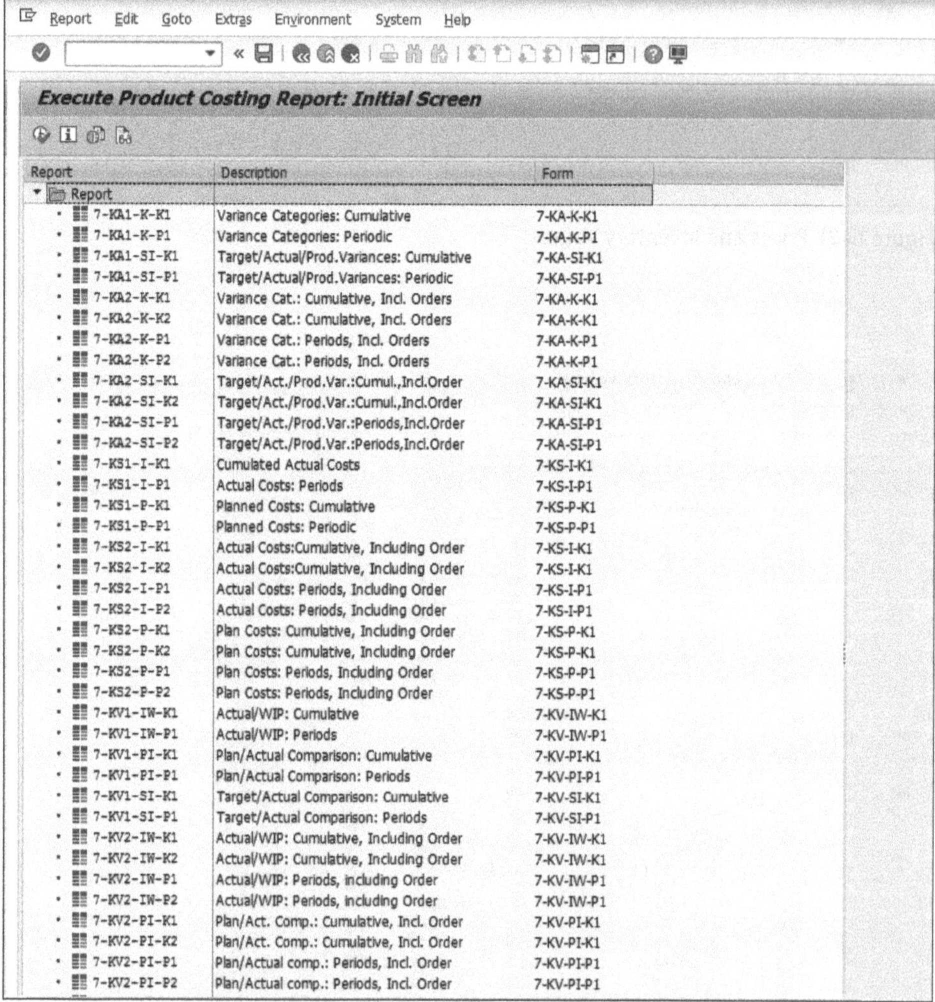

Report	Description	Form
Report		
7-KA1-K-K1	Variance Categories: Cumulative	7-KA-K-K1
7-KA1-K-P1	Variance Categories: Periodic	7-KA-K-P1
7-KA1-SI-K1	Target/Actual/Prod.Variances: Cumulative	7-KA-SI-K1
7-KA1-SI-P1	Target/Actual/Prod.Variances: Periodic	7-KA-SI-P1
7-KA2-K-K1	Variance Cat.: Cumulative, Incl. Orders	7-KA-K-K1
7-KA2-K-K2	Variance Cat.: Cumulative, Incl. Orders	7-KA-K-K1
7-KA2-K-P1	Variance Cat.: Periods, Incl. Orders	7-KA-K-P1
7-KA2-K-P2	Variance Cat.: Periods, Incl. Orders	7-KA-K-P1
7-KA2-SI-K1	Target/Act./Prod.Var.:Cumul.,Incl.Order	7-KA-SI-K1
7-KA2-SI-K2	Target/Act./Prod.Var.:Cumul.,Incl.Order	7-KA-SI-K1
7-KA2-SI-P1	Target/Act./Prod.Var.:Periods,Incl.Order	7-KA-SI-P1
7-KA2-SI-P2	Target/Act./Prod.Var.:Periods,Incl.Order	7-KA-SI-P1
7-KS1-I-K1	Cumulated Actual Costs	7-KS-I-K1
7-KS1-I-P1	Actual Costs: Periods	7-KS-I-P1
7-KS1-P-K1	Planned Costs: Cumulative	7-KS-P-K1
7-KS1-P-P1	Planned Costs: Periodic	7-KS-P-P1
7-KS2-I-K1	Actual Costs:Cumulative, Including Order	7-KS-I-K1
7-KS2-I-K2	Actual Costs:Cumulative, Including Order	7-KS-I-K1
7-KS2-I-P1	Actual Costs: Periods, Including Order	7-KS-I-P1
7-KS2-I-P2	Actual Costs: Periods, Including Order	7-KS-I-P1
7-KS2-P-K1	Plan Costs: Cumulative, Including Order	7-KS-P-K1
7-KS2-P-K2	Plan Costs: Cumulative, Including Order	7-KS-P-K1
7-KS2-P-P1	Plan Costs: Periods, Including Order	7-KS-P-P1
7-KS2-P-P2	Plan Costs: Periods, Including Order	7-KS-P-P1
7-KV1-IW-K1	Actual/WIP: Cumulative	7-KV-IW-K1
7-KV1-IW-P1	Actual/WIP: Periods	7-KV-IW-P1
7-KV1-PI-K1	Plan/Actual Comparison: Cumulative	7-KV-PI-K1
7-KV1-PI-P1	Plan/Actual Comparison: Periods	7-KV-PI-P1
7-KV1-SI-K1	Target/Actual Comparison: Cumulative	7-KV-SI-K1
7-KV1-SI-P1	Target/Actual Comparison: Periods	7-KV-SI-P1
7-KV2-IW-K1	Actual/WIP: Cumulative, Including Order	7-KV-IW-K1
7-KV2-IW-K2	Actual/WIP: Cumulative, Including Order	7-KV-IW-K1
7-KV2-IW-P1	Actual/WIP: Periods, including Order	7-KV-IW-P1
7-KV2-IW-P2	Actual/WIP: Periods, including Order	7-KV-IW-P1
7-KV2-PI-K1	Plan/Act. Comp.: Cumulative, Incl. Order	7-KV-PI-K1
7-KV2-PI-K2	Plan/Act. Comp.: Cumulative, Incl. Order	7-KV-PI-K1
7-KV2-PI-P1	Plan/Actual comp.: Periods, Incl. Order	7-KV-PI-P1
7-KV2-PI-P2	Plan/Actual comp.: Periods, Incl. Order	7-KV-PI-P1

Figure 15.83 Drilldown Reports

You'll need to run a summarization of the data first, however, by entering Transaction KKRV. Figure 15.84 shows the selection screen for the program.

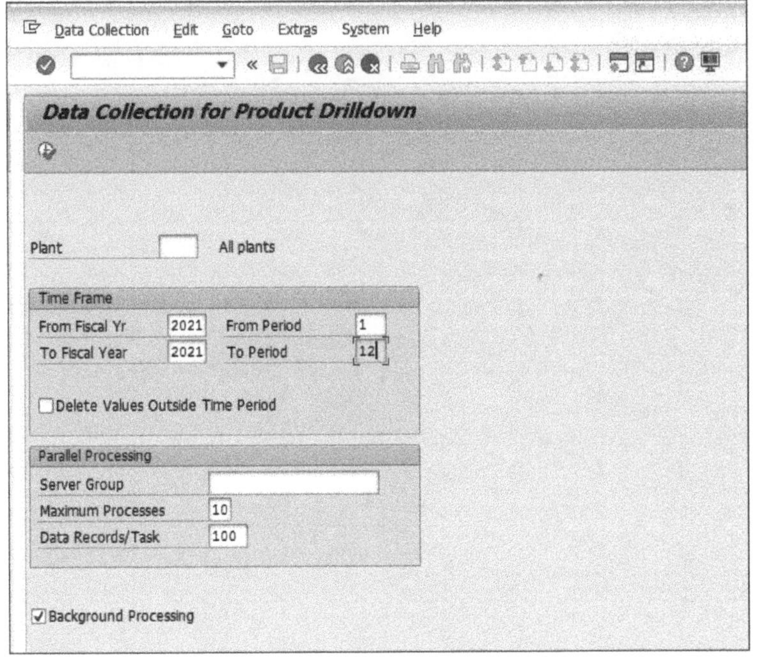

Figure 15.84 Data Collection for Drilldown Reporting

You can enter a specific plant in the **Plant** field or leave the field empty so data collection will run for all plants. Specify the from and to fiscal years and a period but leave the **Background Processing** checkbox selected for better performance. Now, run the program by clicking the (**Execute**) button.

After that step, drilldown reports can be run based on the summarized data.

15.5 Summary

In this chapter, you learned how to configure product costing. You learned how to create a cost estimate and how to configure actual costing and the material ledger. You're now aware of the guidelines and best practices for selecting appropriate standard or moving average prices for material valuation. You learned that the material ledger is now required in SAP S/4HANA and is fully integrated with the Universal Journal, table ACDOCA, but actual costing is still optional. You learned how to configure both the material ledger and actual costing. Finally, we provided an overview of the information system for product costing, which provides powerful reports for product cost planning and for actual costing and the material ledger.

In the next chapter, you'll learn about the solution for group reporting that first became available with SAP S/4HANA 1809—namely, SAP S/4HANA Finance for group reporting, which now has been further enhanced with SAP S/4HANA 2020.

Chapter 16
Group Reporting

This chapter will teach you how to configure SAP S/4HANA Finance for group reporting. This solution was introduced with the release of SAP S/4HANA 1809 and further improved in SAP S/4HANA 1909 and 2020. This chapter provides an overview of the topic of consolidation using previous SAP solutions before presenting step-by-step instructions for the configuration of group reporting.

Most companies that run SAP are global companies with multiple legal entities that operate in multiple regions and countries. As such, most SAP clients need to provide group reporting to create consolidated financial statements for the whole group that includes all legal entities and countries. But consolidation is a complicated process because profit between the group legal entities (known as *intercompany profit*) must be eliminated as do intercompany transactions. Therefore, a separate group reporting solution has always existed to provide group reporting. SAP has a long history of providing different modules to cover the consolidation group reporting requirement, which deserves the detailed explanation we'll provide in this chapter.

Since SAP S/4HANA 1809, SAP has provided a wholly new, revamped, and significantly enhanced solution based on the impressive capabilities of the SAP HANA database to meet consolidation requirements: SAP S/4HANA Finance for group reporting. The next two SAP S/4HANA releases—1909 and 2020—have enhanced this solution further.

In this chapter, we'll provide an overview of the previous consolidation options and how they compare with SAP S/4HANA Finance for group reporting. Then, we'll go over the main configuration activities for the new solution.

16.1 Group Reporting Basics

We'll start this section by first outlining the need for group reporting and describing its objectives from a business point of view. We'll then briefly cover the history of group reporting in SAP before discussing some of the key benefits of the new SAP S/4HANA Finance for group reporting solution.

16.1.1 What Is Group Reporting?

Group reporting is accounting reporting that aims to provide consolidated financial statements. *Consolidated financial statements* are financial statements in which the information related to a parent company and its subsidiaries is presented as if they're a single entity. The accounting framework that defines consolidated financial statements is codified in International Accounting Standard (IAS) 27: Separate Financial Statements and International Financial Reporting Standards (IFRS) 10: Consolidated Financial Statements.

The main challenge in creating group reporting is that multiple eliminations of transactions and results should be performed between the various entities, such as the following:

- Intercompany debt
- Intercompany revenue and expenses
- Intercompany stock ownership

The consolidation process requires a lot of work and should be automated as much as possible. Therefore, companies have long been using consolidation software to help with these tasks.

16.1.2 Historical Group Reporting in SAP

Because SAP provides software to record and manage all accounting data, naturally, companies that run SAP also use SAP to create their group reporting. SAP's offerings in this area have a long history, with multiple modules provided with varying degrees of success.

Twenty years ago, the SAP solution for group reporting in SAP R/3 was called Legal Consolidation (LC). This module was closely integrated with the other financial modules of SAP, but this solution couldn't provide management consolidation. *Management consolidation* is used to analyze different scenarios for management and to perform parallel consolidations with different levels of data using different accounting principles. Therefore, this module wasn't popular, and in fact, many companies chose to use separate consolidation software from other vendors, such as Hyperion, and interface it with their SAP data for consolidation purposes.

The next solution from SAP was the Enterprise Controlling Consolidation (EC-CS) module in SAP ERP. This solution could provide group reporting from both legal and management points of view and was closely integrated both with both the Finance (FI) and Controlling (CO) modules.

With the introduction of an SAP Business Warehouse (SAP BW) system that could combine data from both SAP and non-SAP systems, SAP made the next step forward with its SAP Strategic Management Business Consolidation (SEMC-BCS). This useful solution was released in 2002 and offered a high degree of automation in the consolidation process. SEMC-BCS operates fully on top of SAP BW and thus is an online analytical processing (OLAP) system, as opposed to earlier solutions, which were online transactional processing (OLTP) systems.

The next step in the evolution and optimization of the consolidation process was the SAP Business Planning and Consolidation (SAP BPC) solution. This solution is similar to SEMC-BCS, but it also offers sophisticated planning functions on top of its consolidation capabilities.

And now we come to SAP S/4HANA. Because the power of the new SAP HANA database is colossal, naturally, SAP provides a new SAP HANA-based solution that can streamline the consolidation processes within SAP. This solution is called SAP S/4HANA Finance for group reporting and it's fresh off the shelves—first introduced with SAP S/4HANA 1809.

16.1.3 Key Benefits

SAP S/4HANA Finance for group reporting is the latest offering in the group reporting space and is indeed vastly superior to its predecessors. This solution is entirely based on the SAP HANA database, which is particularly well optimized for consolidation processes and group reporting. The user interface (UI) is mostly based on the new SAP Fiori applications, which provide users with an efficient and beautiful interface to perform group reporting.

SAP provides best practices for consolidation, which can be copied and modified as appropriate. SAP Best Practices are a great benefit, since they can serve as a foundation for further best practices from the years of consolidation experience SAP brings into the new solution.

The new solution provides both legal and management consolidation and, in terms of functionalities, is similar to the well-known EC-CS solution. However, the solution is based on SAP HANA and SAP Fiori and benefits from the new fast and optimized data structure.

Consolidation postings are stored in the new table ACDOCU (Universal Consolidation Journal Entries). Table ACDOCU is similar to table ACDOCA but for storing consolidation postings, as shown in Figure 16.1.

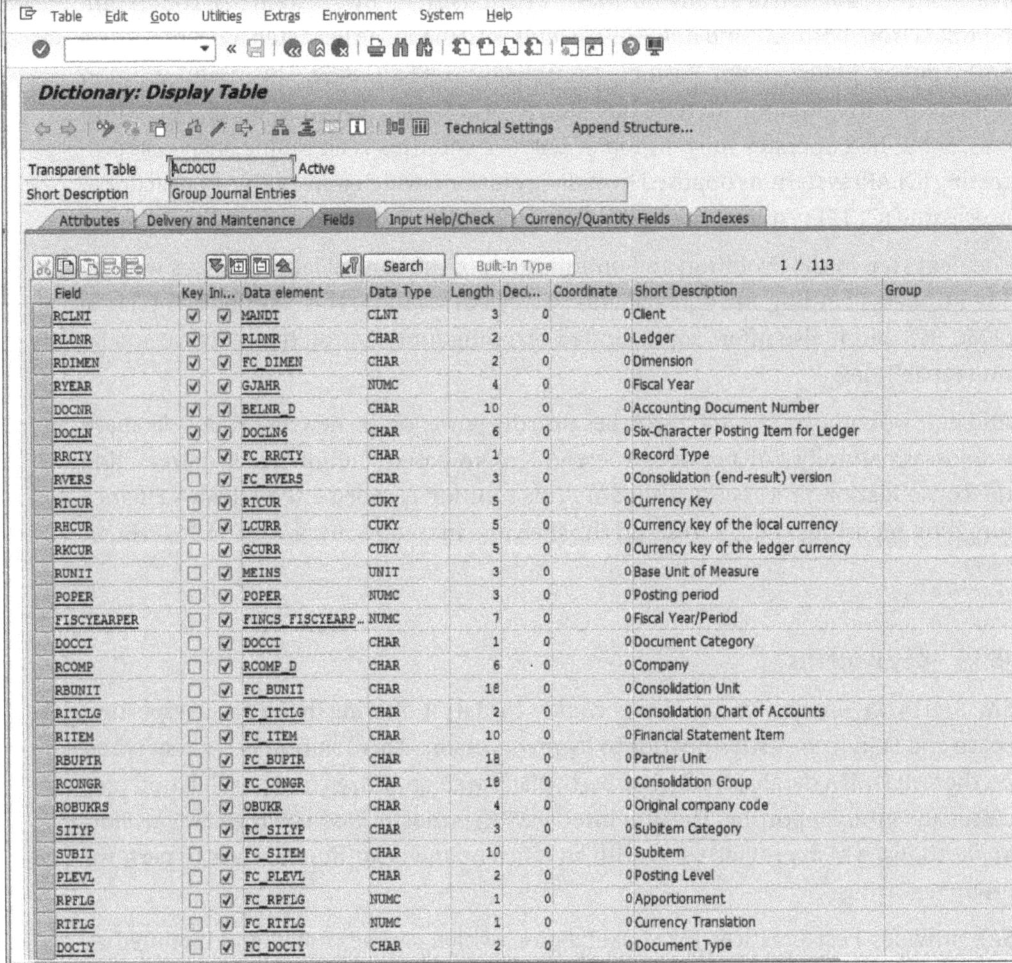

Field	Key	Ini...	Data element	Data Type	Length	Deci...	Coordinate	Short Description	Group
RCLNT	☑	☑	MANDT	CLNT	3	0	0	Client	
RLDNR	☑	☑	RLDNR	CHAR	2	0	0	Ledger	
RDIMEN	☑	☑	FC_DIMEN	CHAR	2	0	0	Dimension	
RYEAR	☑	☑	GJAHR	NUMC	4	0	0	Fiscal Year	
DOCNR	☑	☑	BELNR_D	CHAR	10	0	0	Accounting Document Number	
DOCLN	☑	☑	DOCLN6	CHAR	6	0	0	Six-Character Posting Item for Ledger	
RRCTY	☐	☑	FC_RRCTY	CHAR	1	0	0	Record Type	
RVERS	☐	☑	FC_RVERS	CHAR	3	0	0	Consolidation (end-result) version	
RTCUR	☐	☑	RTCUR	CUKY	5	0	0	Currency Key	
RHCUR	☐	☑	LCURR	CUKY	5	0	0	Currency key of the local currency	
RKCUR	☐	☑	GCURR	CUKY	5	0	0	Currency key of the ledger currency	
RUNIT	☐	☑	MEINS	UNIT	3	0	0	Base Unit of Measure	
POPER	☐	☑	POPER	NUMC	3	0	0	Posting period	
FISCYEARPER	☐	☑	FINCS_FISCYEARP...	NUMC	7	0	0	Fiscal Year/Period	
DOCCT	☐	☑	DOCCT	CHAR	1	0	0	Document Category	
RCOMP	☐	☑	RCOMP_D	CHAR	6	0	0	Company	
RBUNIT	☐	☑	FC_BUNIT	CHAR	18	0	0	Consolidation Unit	
RITCLG	☐	☑	FC_ITCLG	CHAR	2	0	0	Consolidation Chart of Accounts	
RITEM	☐	☑	FC_ITEM	CHAR	10	0	0	Financial Statement Item	
RBUPTR	☐	☑	FC_BUPTR	CHAR	18	0	0	Partner Unit	
RCONGR	☐	☑	FC_CONGR	CHAR	18	0	0	Consolidation Group	
ROBUKRS	☐	☑	OBUKR	CHAR	4	0	0	Original company code	
SITYP	☐	☑	FC_SITYP	CHAR	3	0	0	Subitem Category	
SUBIT	☐	☑	FC_SITEM	CHAR	10	0	0	Subitem	
PLEVL	☐	☑	FC_PLEVL	CHAR	2	0	0	Posting Level	
RPFLG	☐	☑	FC_RPFLG	NUMC	1	0	0	Apportionment	
RTFLG	☐	☑	FC_RTFLG	NUMC	1	0	0	Currency Translation	
DOCTY	☐	☑	FC_DOCTY	CHAR	2	0	0	Document Type	

Figure 16.1 Universal Consolidation Journal Entries

Let's examine in detail how to configure SAP S/4HANA Finance for group reporting.

16.2 Global Settings

We'll now delve into the configuration of the global settings for the new group reporting solution. We'll start with the prerequisites for installing SAP Best Practices configuration content. Then, we'll configure configuration ledgers, which store the documents generated by the group reporting solution. After that, we'll configure consolidation versions, which define dedicated data areas in the database. Finally, we'll configure dimensions, which define the basis for consolidation, such as companies and profit centers.

16.2.1 Prerequisites

A mandatory prerequisite before configuring SAP S/4HANA Finance for group reporting is to install SAP Best Practices configuration content, as shown in Figure 16.2.

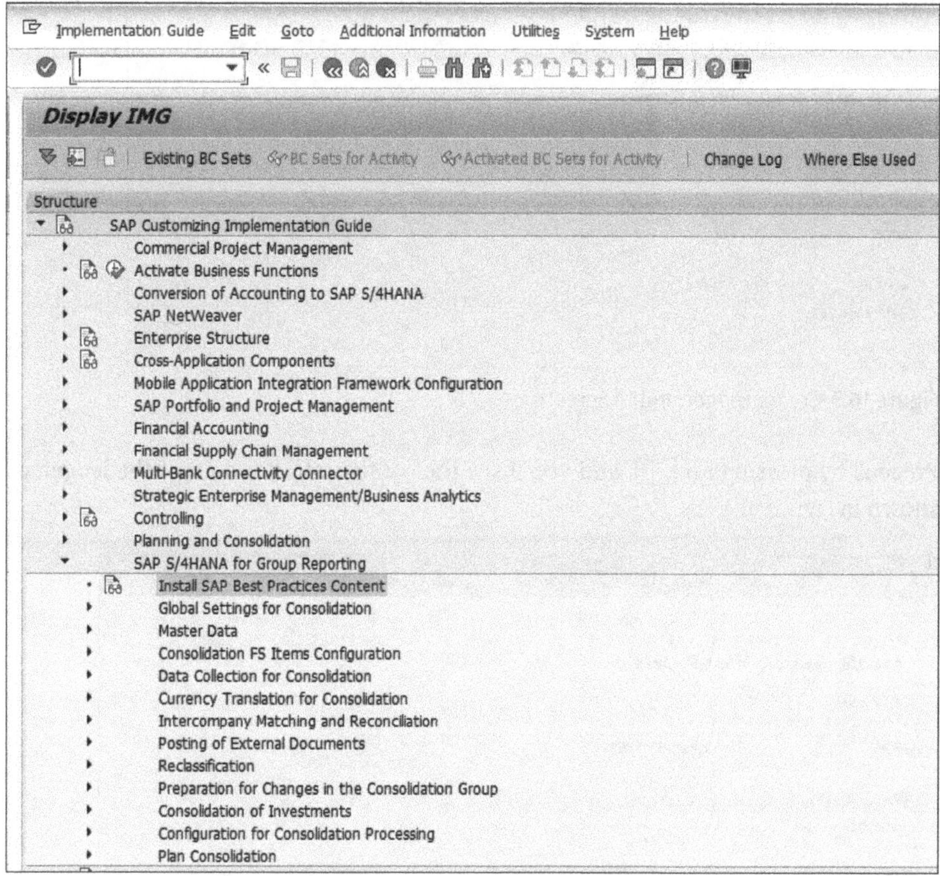

Figure 16.2 SAP S/4HANA Finance for Group Reporting Configuration

This task normally would be performed by your Basis team through Transaction /SMB/BBI, which is called the Building Block Builder. This transaction is delivered with a separate add-on called BP-INSTASS. The scope item in the Building Block Builder for SAP S/4HANA Finance for group reporting is XX_1SG_OP.

16.2.2 Consolidation Ledgers

The consolidation ledger is a ledger that stores the documents generated by the group reporting module.

To configure the consolidation ledger, follow the menu path **SAP S/4HANA for Group Reporting • Master Data • Define Consolidation Ledgers**. Then, select **Create Ledger**.

On the screen shown in Figure 16.3, enter a ledger name starting with a C. Consolidation ledgers you define must start with the letter "C." You can also copy from an existing consolidation ledger using the **Reference ledger** field.

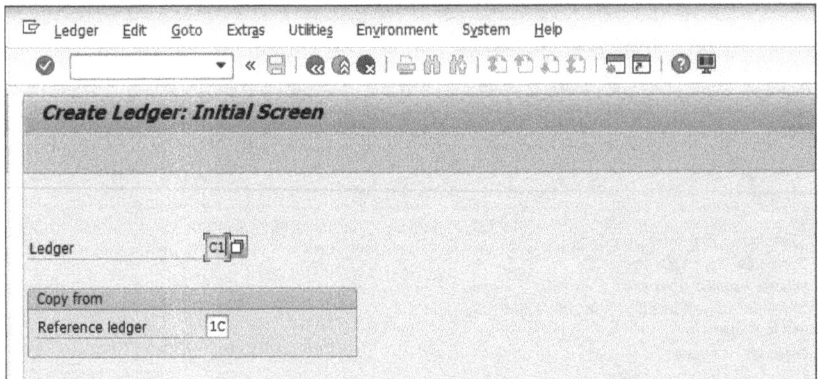

Figure 16.3 Create Ledger: Initial Screen

Proceed by pressing Enter, and you'll see the configuration screen of the ledger, as shown in Figure 16.4.

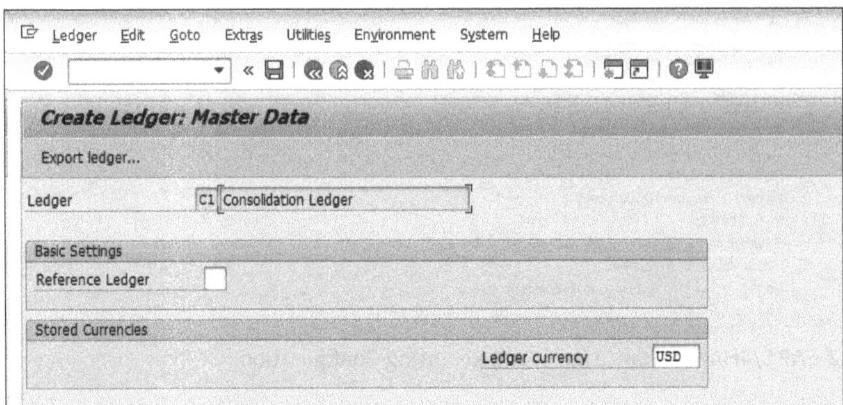

Figure 16.4 Ledger Settings

As shown in Figure 16.4, you can modify the description and the currency of the ledger, as well as maintain the following fields:

- **Valuation**
  In this field, select the type of consolidation valuation to perform in this ledger: legal, group, or profit center. You'll need separate ledgers for the different types of valuation.
- **Ledger Post. Allowed**
  Specifies whether postings can be made to the ledger.

- **Rollup Allowed**
  Specifies that rollup can be made in the ledger. Users of the special purpose ledger will be familiar with this concept. To *roll up* means to summarize data from other ledgers into the target ledger.
- **Write line items**
  Specifies whether line items should be written during the update.
- **Productive**
  When you select this indicator, transaction data cannot be deleted.
- **Ledger currency**
  The currency of the ledger, which should be the currency in which you need to perform the group reporting.

After configuring the ledger, save your settings by clicking the **Save** button.

16.2.3 Consolidation Versions

A *consolidation version* identifies a dedicated data area in the database. Versions are used to consolidate various sets of financial data. You can create separate versions for actual and plan data.

To configure a consolidation version, follow the menu path **SAP S/4HANA for Group Reporting • Master Data • Define Versions.** On the initial screen shown in Figure 16.5, you'll see versions already defined. We'll select the actual version **Y10** to review its settings.

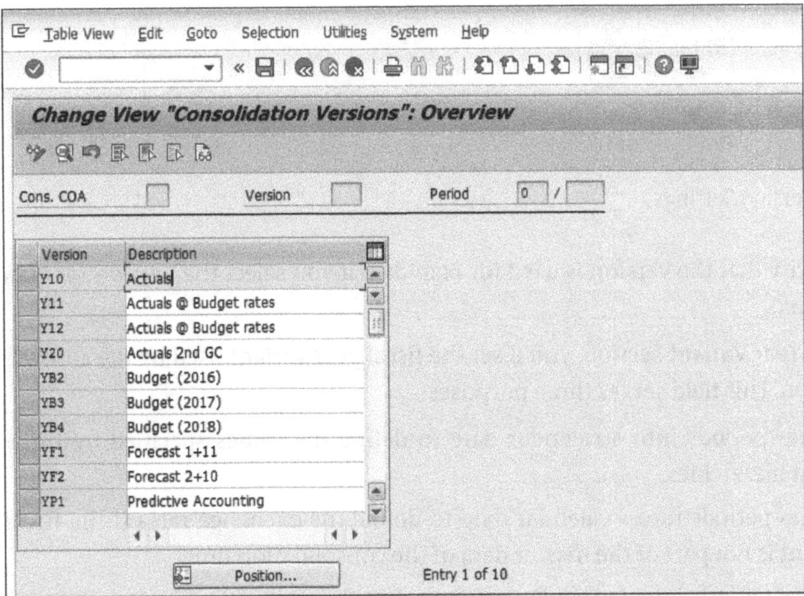

Figure 16.5 Defined Versions

On the next screen, shown in Figure 16.6, we can change the settings of the consolidation version.

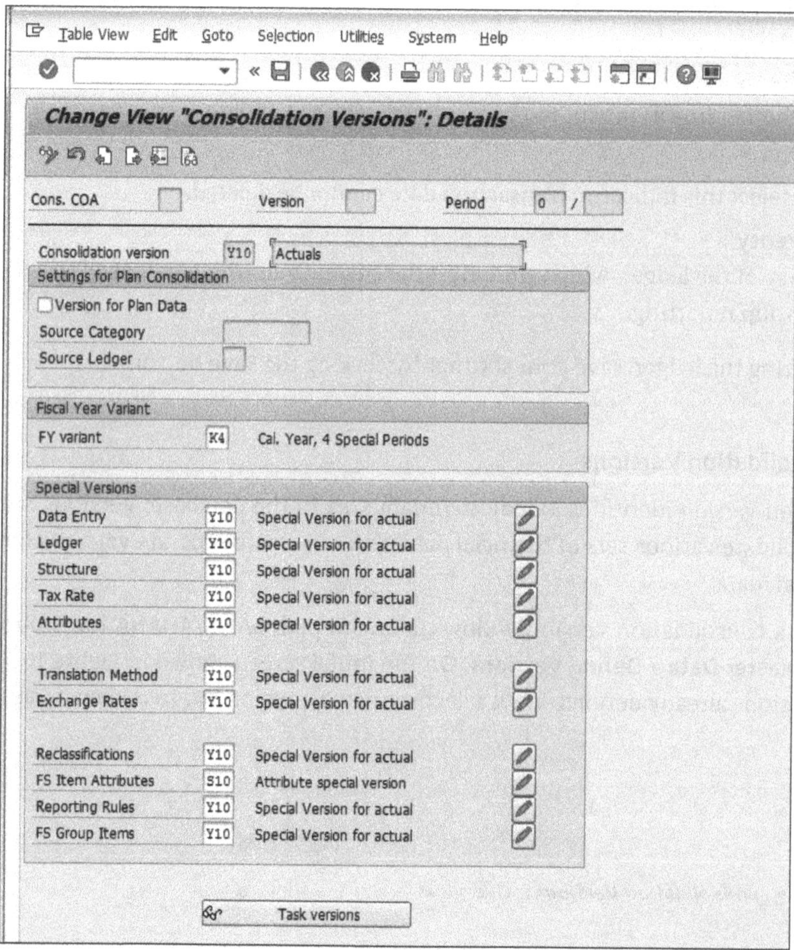

Figure 16.6 Version Settings

You can specify that the version is used for plan data if you select the **Version for Plan Data** checkbox.

In the **Fiscal Year Variant** section, you'll set the fiscal year variant used by the consolidation version. This field serves three purposes:

- It translates periods into a calendar date to define the values specified by time-dependent hierarchies.
- It translates periods into a calendar date to define the exchange rates if the fiscal year variant is not part of the master data of the consolidation unit.
- It translates periods into a calendar date to select the accounting documents with their respective posting dates when accounting documents are released.

In the **Special Versions** section, you'll define versions to be used for various cases. The special version checks the assignments of data transfer methods to consolidation units and also checks the assignment of the validation method to the consolidation unit and group.

16.2.4 Multiple Group Currencies and Extension Consolidation Versions

With SAP S/4HANA 2020, you can create consolidated statements in multiple group currencies simultaneously.

For this purpose, you can use the standard consolidation version and additional extension consolidation versions, which can serve as group currency extension versions. You can define multiple extension consolidation versions to the same standard version that can hold additional group currencies and additional currency translations.

You can define the multiple group currencies and translations in a uniform closing process by processing the standard version to which are linked the extension versions, in the data monitor and consolidation monitor. This new feature enables the posting of manual journals in multiple group currencies simultaneously, while storing the multiple group currency values in the same journal posting. Extension versions store only the amounts in the group currency of the extension versions.

To define new extension version, follow the menu path **SAP S/4HANA for Group Reporting • Master Data • Create Version from Reference Version.** On the screen shown in Figure 16.7, select a source version (**Template Version**) and a target extension version (**Target Version**). Click the (**Execute**) button on the top menu to create the version.

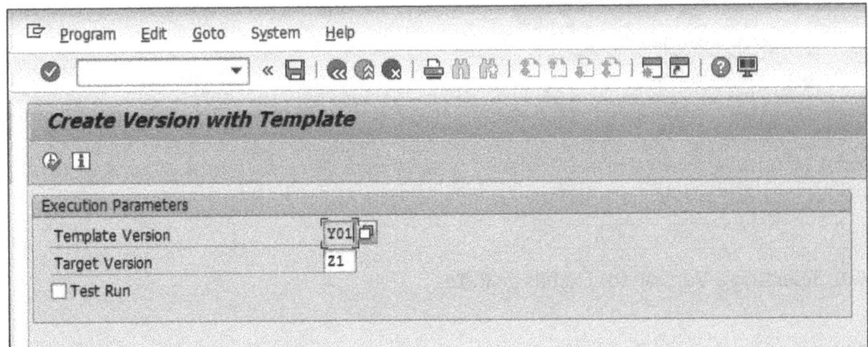

Figure 16.7 Creating an Extension Version

You must also define exchange rate indicators for consolidation to perform the consolidation in multiple group currencies. The exchange rate indicator serves to classify the exchange rates for foreign currencies. To define exchange rate indicators, follow the menu path **SAP S/4HANA for Group Reporting • Currency Translation for Consolidation •**

Define Exchange Rate Indicators. On the screen shown in Figure 16.8, you'll see a list of exchange rate indicators already defined.

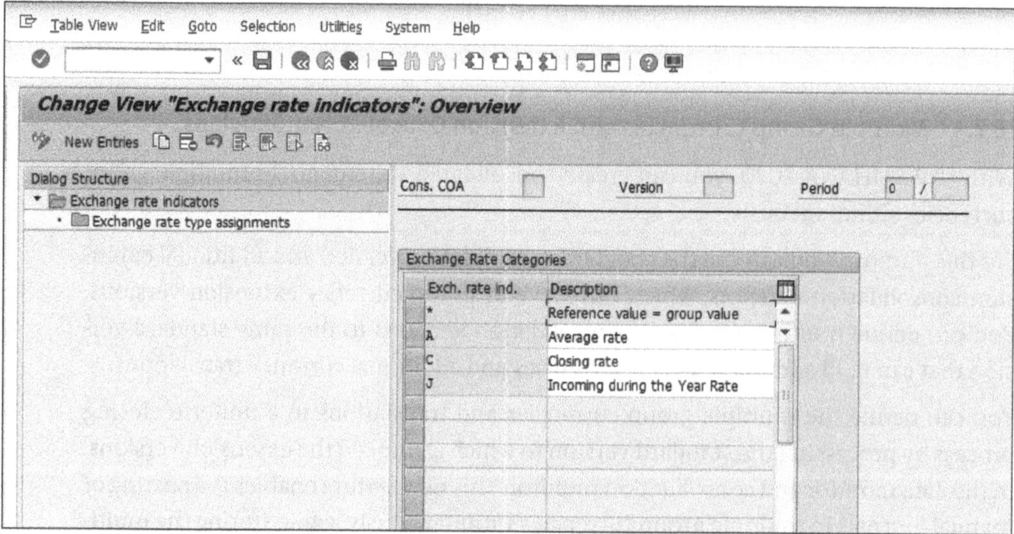

Figure 16.8 Defining Exchange Rate Indicators

You must define, for each exchange rate indicator, the exchange rate type to be used for each version. Select the exchange rate indicator and click on **Exchange rate type assignments** on the left side of the screen. Then, a popup window will open where you'll enter the version for exchange rate, as shown in Figure 16.9.

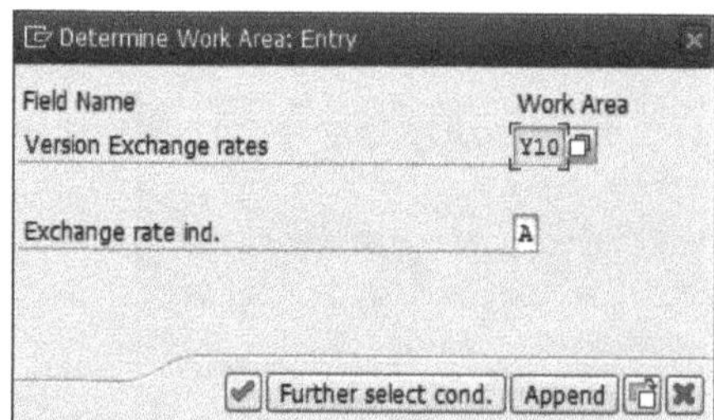

Figure 16.9 Selecting a Version for Exchange Rates

Proceed by clicking the (**Enter**) button.

Select the exchange rate type in the **ER type** field, as shown in Figure 16.10. In the **Start Year** field, enter the first year of validity and, in the **Period eff** field, the start of the validity period.

Then, save your entry by clicking the **Save** button.

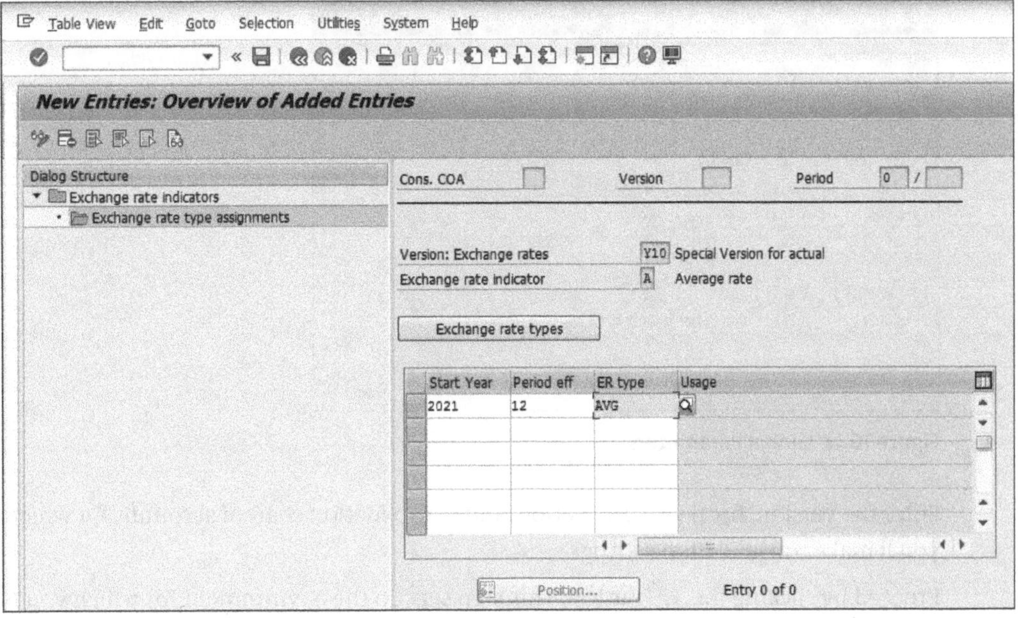

Figure 16.10 Entering an Exchange Rate Type

16.2.5 Dimensions

Dimensions define the basis for consolidation, such as companies, profit centers, and so on. To define the settings on the dimension level, follow the menu path **SAP S/4HANA for Group Reporting • Master Data • Display Dimension.**

On the initial screen shown in Figure 16.11, choose consolidation dimension **Y1: Companies** and then proceed by pressing Enter.

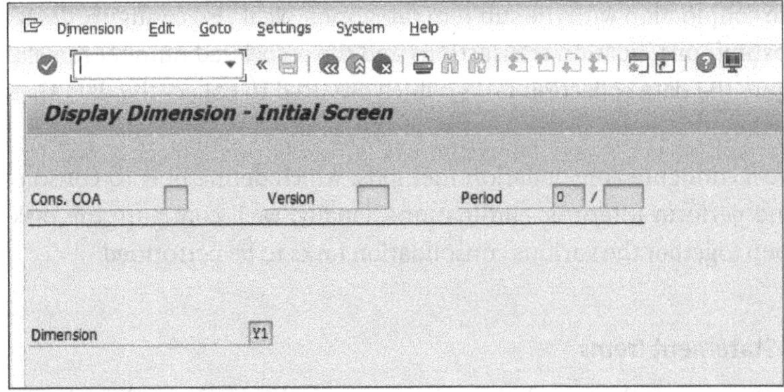

Figure 16.11 Displaying a Dimension

On the next screen, shown in Figure 16.12, you must enter the global parameters for consolidation.

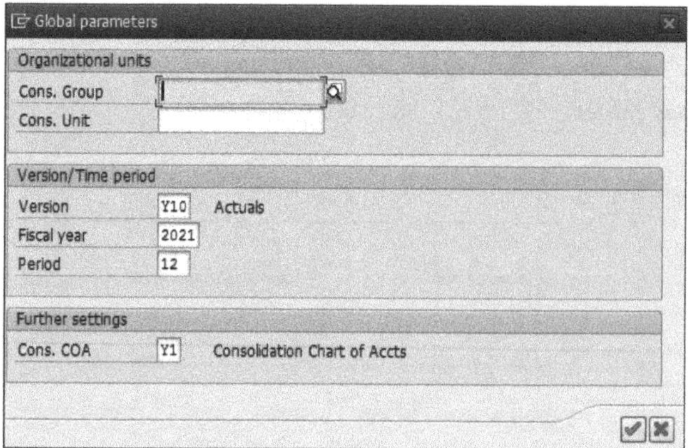

Figure 16.12 Global Parameters

Enter the version, fiscal year and period, and consolidation chart of accounts, for which you'll make consolidation settings.

Proceed by clicking the [✔] button. This step sets up the environment for which you'll make the following settings.

16.3 Data Collection and Consolidation Configuration

Having configured the global configuration settings, we'll continue with the various data collection and consolidation settings.

First, let's configure the financial statement items, which are linked to operating accounts and serve to classify the items that must be reported on in the group financial statements. Then, we'll configure subitems, which further categorize the financial statement items in conjunction with the subitem categories. We'll also configure document types for posting consolidation transactions and the associated number ranges. Then, we'll configure the data collection tasks, which are used to collect the data that will be consolidated.

After that step, we'll configure consolidation methods, which define how to consolidate your data and perform interunit eliminations. Finally, we'll configure the task groups, which group together the various consolidation tasks to be performed.

16.3.1 Financial Statement Items

Financial statement items are the foundation of group reporting settings. These items are linked to operating accounts and serve to classify the items that must be reported on in the group financial statements. SAP delivers lots of standard financial statement items, but you also can create your own. Figure 16.13 shows some of the standard SAP-delivered financial statement items.

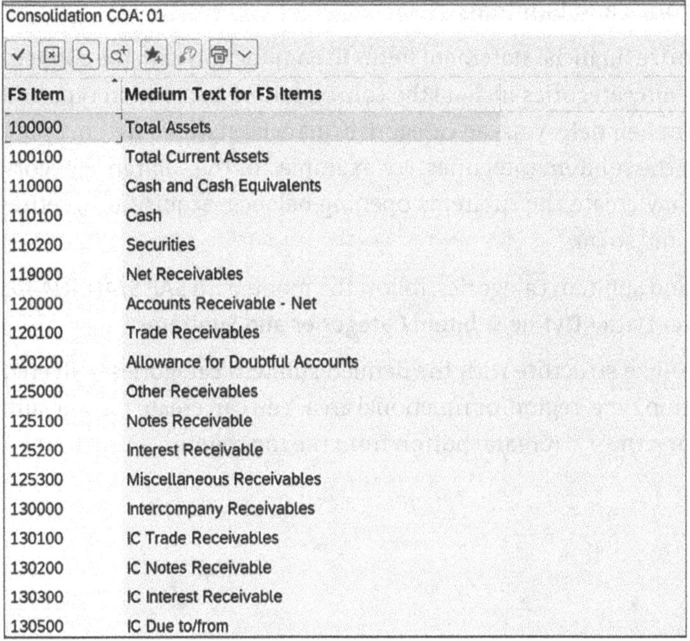
Consolidation COA: 01

FS Item	Medium Text for FS Items
100000	Total Assets
100100	Total Current Assets
110000	Cash and Cash Equivalents
110100	Cash
110200	Securities
119000	Net Receivables
120000	Accounts Receivable - Net
120100	Trade Receivables
120200	Allowance for Doubtful Accounts
125000	Other Receivables
125100	Notes Receivable
125200	Interest Receivable
125300	Miscellaneous Receivables
130000	Intercompany Receivables
130100	IC Trade Receivables
130200	IC Notes Receivable
130300	IC Interest Receivable
130500	IC Due to/from

Figure 16.13 Financial Statement Items

Financial statement items are grouped into reporting items, which are grouped into reporting hierarchies. Maintenance of financial statement items and hierarchies is handled via the Manage Global Accounting Hierarchies SAP Fiori app (app ID F2918).

As shown in Figure 16.14, you can review the details and implementation information for the app in the SAP Fiori apps reference library, available at *http://s-prs.co/v485701.*

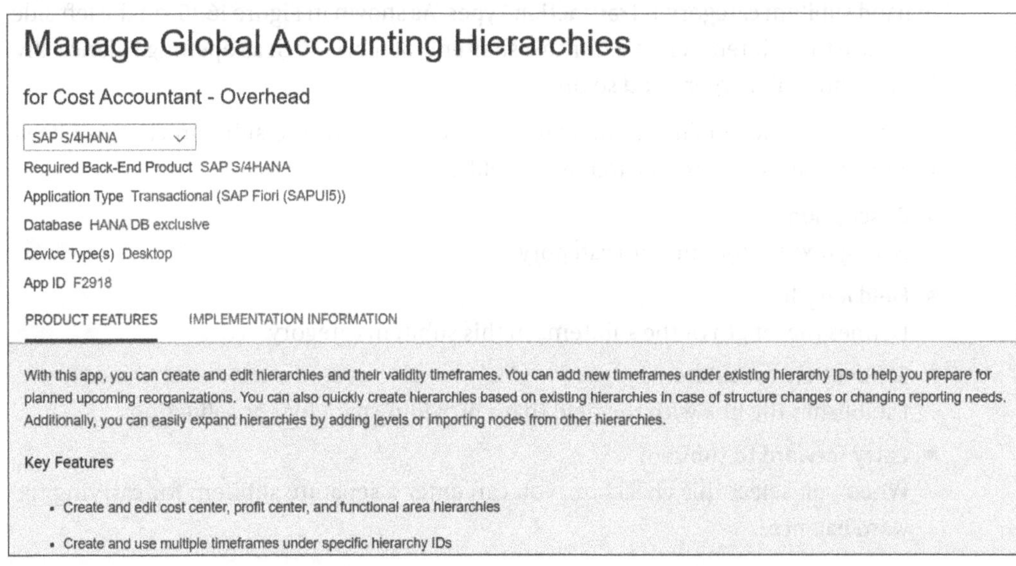

Figure 16.14 Manage Global Accounting Hierarchies: SAP Fiori App Details

16.3.2 Subitem Categories and Subitems

Subitems further categorize financial statement items in conjunction with the subitem categories. Typical subitem categories include the consolidation transaction type and the functional area. With their help, you can categorize financial statement items. Subitems are dependent on the subitem categories. For example, for the subitem category transaction type, you may create the subitems opening balance, acquisitions, retirements, closing balance, and so on.

To configure subitems and subitem categories, follow the menu path **SAP S/4HANA for Group Reporting • Master Data • Define Subitem Categories and Subitems.**

Figure 16.15 shows a tree-like structure with the defined subitem categories delivered by SAP, such as transaction type, region, or functional area. You can create further subitem categories by clicking the (**Create**) button from the top menu.

Figure 16.15 Subitem Categories

You can expand a subitem category by clicking the button on its left side. Let's expand subitem category 1: **Transaction Types.** As shown in Figure 16.16, on the left side, you'll see the subitems created for this subitem category, such as opening balance, dividends, internal mergers, and so on.

On the right side, you'll see the configuration details of the subitem category itself, where you can configure the following fields:

- **Description**
  A long text for the subitem category.
- **Field length**
  Defines the length of the subitems in this subitem category.
- **Sender field for subitems**
  Establishes the link with the field that's providing data for consolidation.
- **Carry forward to subitem**
  When you select this checkbox, you can enter a separate subitem for carrying forward balances.

- **Subitems for acquisitions/divestitures**
  Controls the screen sequence for subitems. If you select this option, you can enter a retirement subitem.

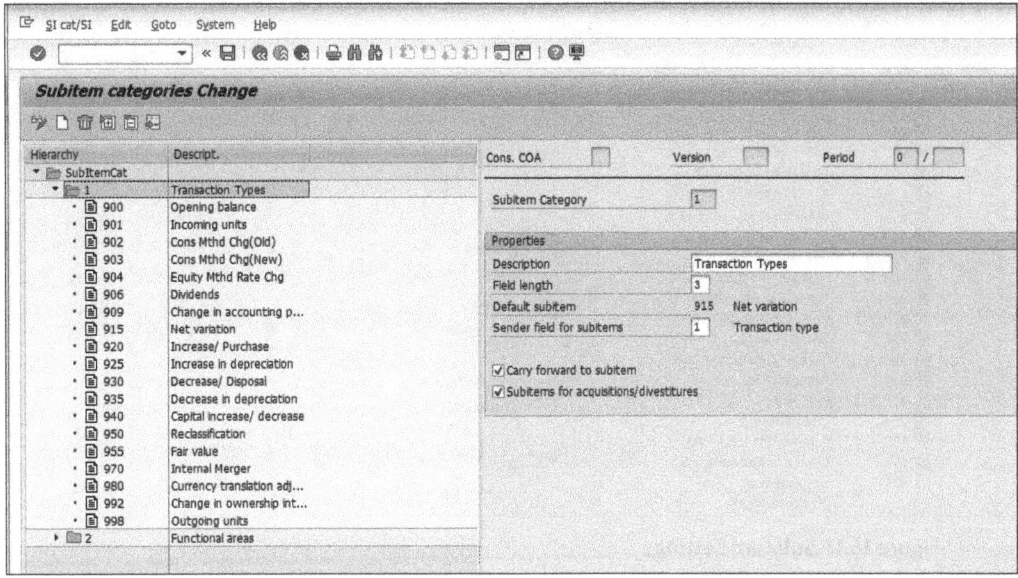

Figure 16.16 Subitem Category Details

Now, double-click subitem **900**. Figure 16.17 shows its configuration screen. On this screen, you can configure the following fields:

- **Medium Text**
  A description of the subitem.
- **Carry forward to subitem**
  The subitem to which the value of the current subitem will be carried forward during the balance carry-forward.
- **Retire./divest. subitem**
  Indicates that this subitem is for retirements/divestitures.
- **Acquisition subitem**
  Indicates that this subitem is for acquisitions.
- **No Posting/Entry**
  Specifies that no postings or entries can occur for this subitem.

You can also define default assignments. As shown earlier in Figure 16.16, the default subitem is **915**, which is a grayed-out field. To define default assignments, follow the menu path **SAP S/4HANA for Group Reporting • Master Data • Define Default Values for Subassignments.**

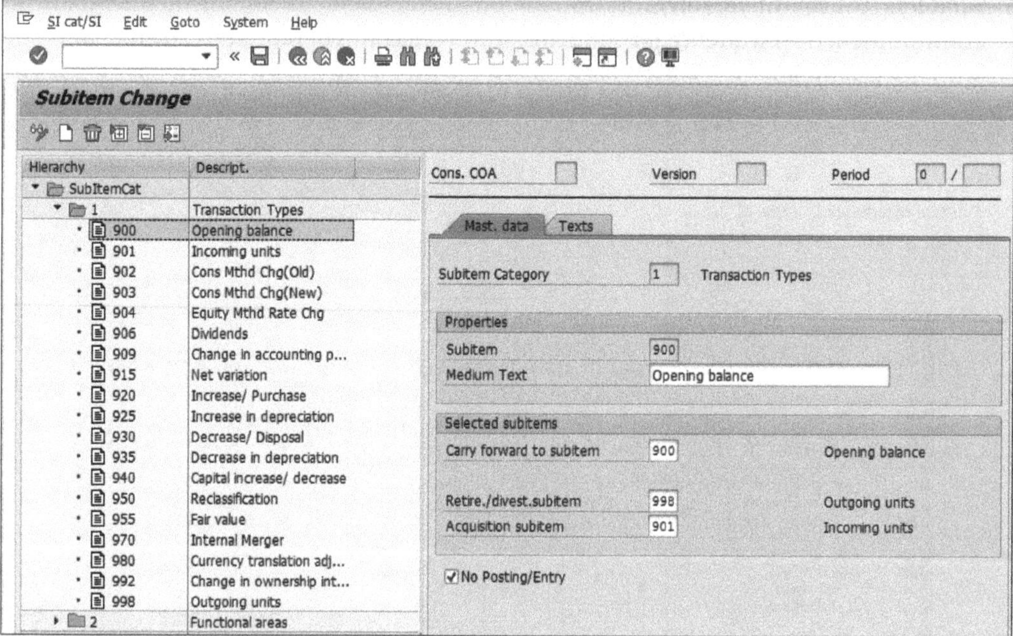

Figure 16.17 Subitem Settings

On the initial screen shown in Figure 16.18, you'll see the characteristics for which you can define default assignments. Click the → **Dflt values** (default values) button on the **Subitem** line.

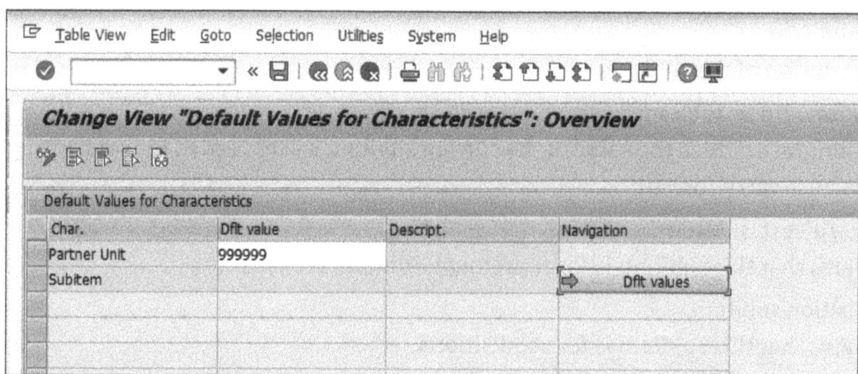

Figure 16.18 Default Assignments

Figure 16.19 shows the default assignments for the various subitem categories. On this screen, subitem **915** has been assigned as a default for subitem category **1**.

Modify as appropriate and save by clicking the **Save** button.

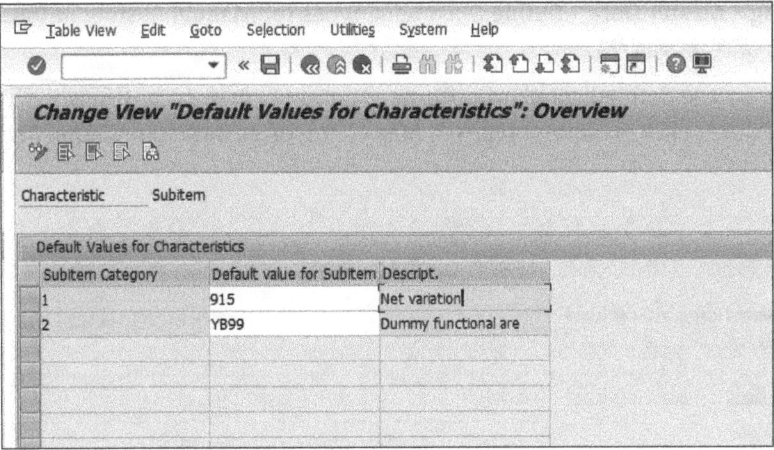

Figure 16.19 Subitem Default Assignments

16.3.3 Document Types

As in other financial areas, in group reporting, you must define document types for posting various consolidation transactions. The configuration transactions are located at the menu path **SAP S/4HANA for Group Reporting • Master Data**, and nine separate transactions are available for maintaining different document types, as follows:

- **Define Document Types for Reported Financial Data**
- **Define Document Types for Manual Posting in Data Monitor**
- **Define Document Types for Reclassification in Data Monitor**
- **Define Document Types for Consolidation Group Changes in Data Monitor**
- **Define Document Types for Manual Posting in Consolidation Monitor**
- **Define Document Types for Reclassification in Consolidation Monitor**
- **Define Document Types for Cons. Group Change in Consolidation Monitor**
- **Define Document Types for Consolidation of Investments**
- **Define Document Types for External Documents in Consolidation Monitor**

The data monitor and consolidation monitor should be familiar tools for consultants and users with experience in EC-CS consolidation. The data monitor is used to run activities for collecting and preparing the financial data reported by the consolidation units, which are called *tasks*. The consolidation monitor presents a graphic overview of the consolidation units and groups and offers an interface for executing tasks for collecting and consolidating the reported financial data and for monitoring the progress of these tasks. Now, in SAP S/4HANA Finance for group reporting, these transactions are still used, available both through SAP Fiori and the SAP GUI interface.

Let's review the settings for manual postings in the data monitor. The available settings for the other document types are similar. Follow the menu path **SAP S/4HANA for**

16

Group Reporting • Master Data • Define Document Types for Manual Posting in Data Monitor.

Figure 16.20 shows the defined standard document types for manual postings in the data monitor. Double-click document type **02: Man cor reported data** to review its settings.

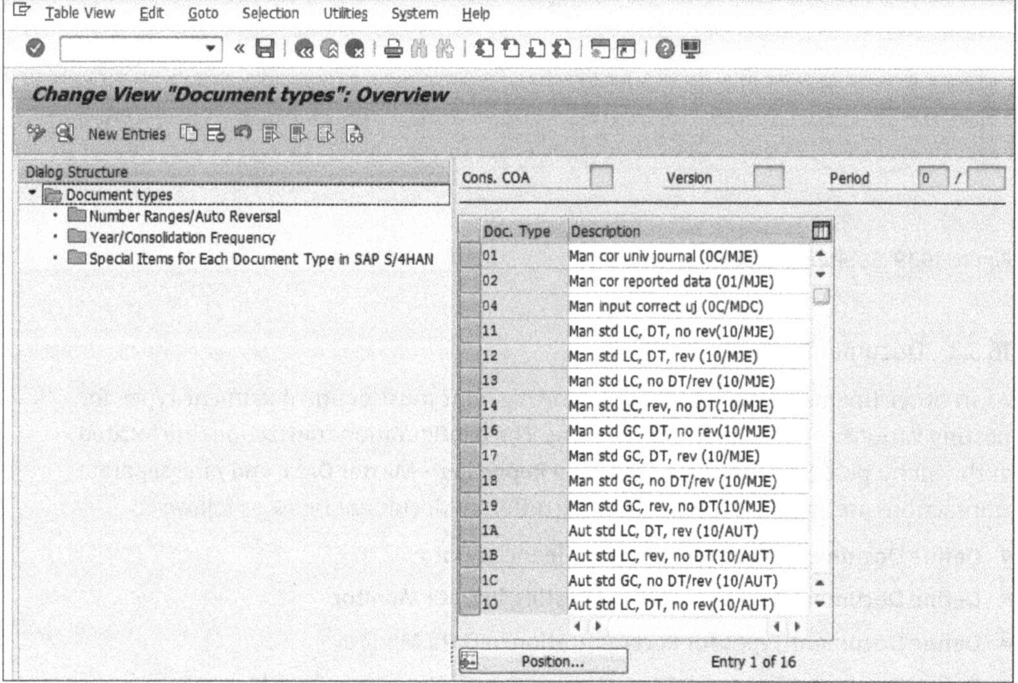

Figure 16.20 Document Types

Figure 16.21 shows the fields you can configure on the document type level, such as the following:

- **Posting Level**
  Classifies the consolidation entry among the following options:
  - Adjustments to reported financial data
  - Standardizing entries
  - Reconciliation entries
  - Elimination entries
  - Consolidation entries
  - Divestitures
- **Balance check**
  Defines what the system should do when checking the balance when posting to statistical items:

  - Error message when the balance is not equal to zero
  - Warning message when the balance is not equal to zero
  - No balance check

- **Bus.application (business application)**
  Classifies the document types according to their business application, such as the elimination of intercompany receivables and payables, consolidation of investments, and so on.
- **Translate to group crcy (translate to group currency)**
  If you select this flag, the local and transaction currency values are translated into group currency.
- **Posting**
  In this section, you choose whether the document type is used for manual or automatic consolidation postings.
- **Currencies**
  In this section, you'll choose the type of currencies in which the document type can post and whether it can post quantities.
- **Deferred Income Taxes**
  In this section, you'll define whether the document type can credit and/or debit deferred taxes. Deferred taxes align the tax expenses of the individual financial statements with the group's consolidated earnings.

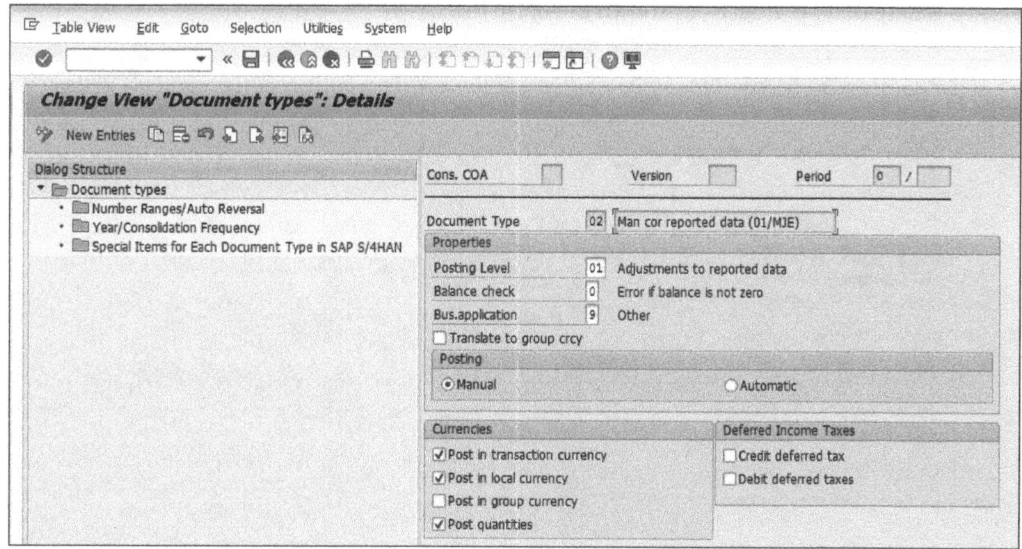

Figure 16.21 Document Type Settings

Now, click **Number Ranges/Auto Reversal** from the left side of the screen. On the screen shown in Figure 16.22, you'll see the number ranges assigned to the document type by consolidation version.

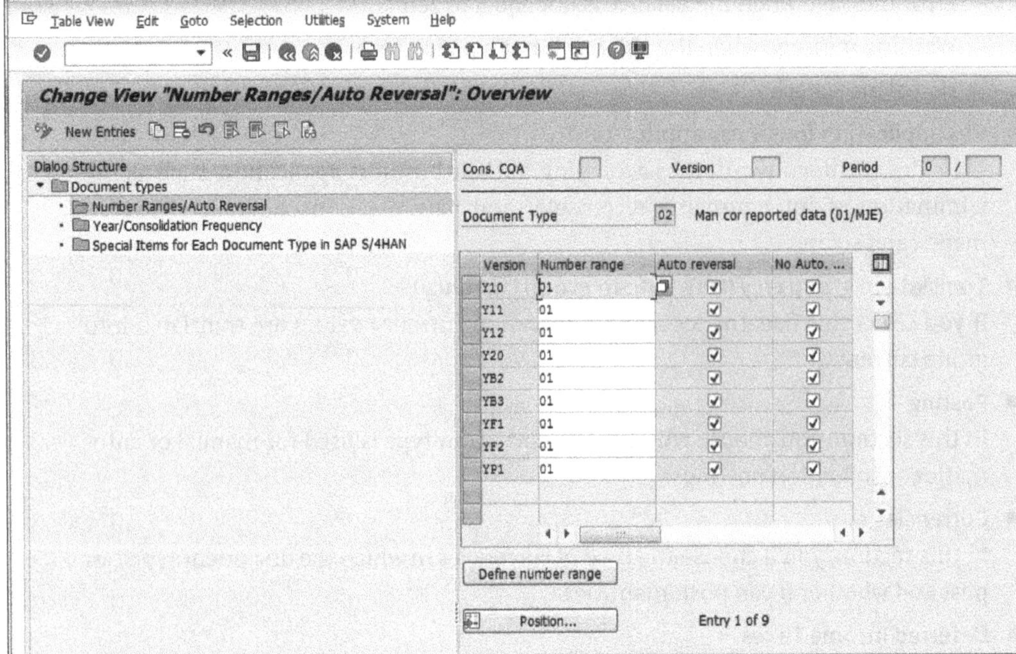

Figure 16.22 Number Ranges

Select **New Entries** from the top menu to assign a number range to the new version Z01 we created previously, as shown in Figure 16.23.

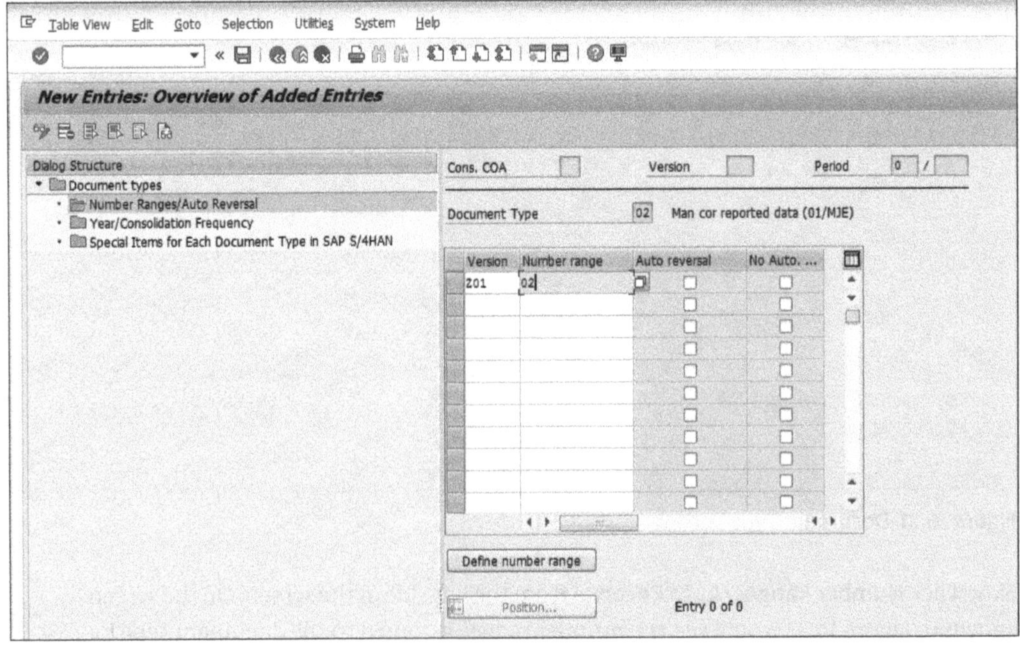

Figure 16.23 Adding a New Version

Assign number range **02** for consolidation version **Z01**. If you select the **Auto reversal** checkbox, the system will automatically create a reversal entry in the subsequent period for documents that are only valid in one period. If you select the **No Auto. Reversal in Foll. Year** (no automatic reversal in following year) checkbox, the system will post automatic reversal entries only in the current fiscal year, not in the following one.

In the **Year/Consolidation Frequency** section from the left side of the screen, you can specify the frequency (monthly versus yearly) per consolidation version, as shown in Figure 16.24.

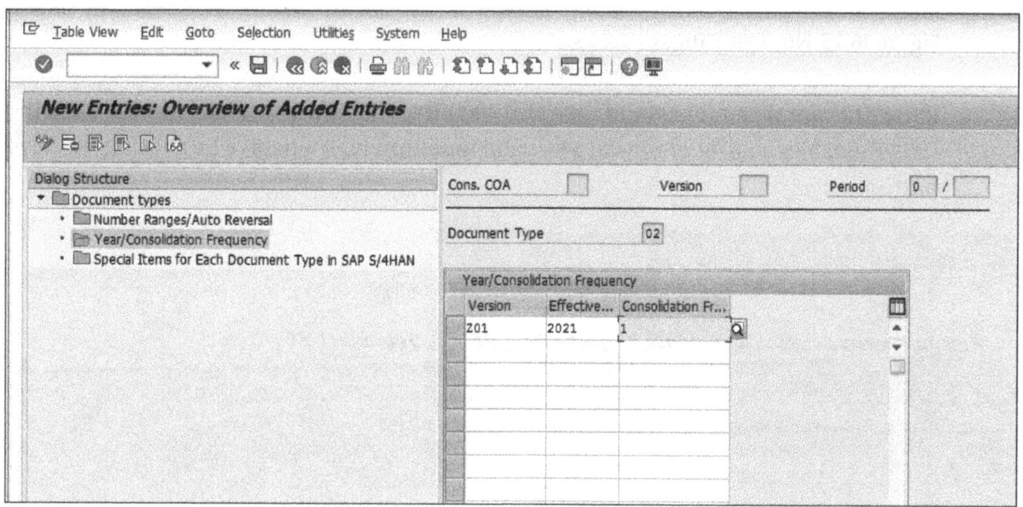

Figure 16.24 Consolidation Frequency

Once you're done modifying the settings of the document type, save it by clicking the **Save** button.

16.3.4 Number Ranges

You'll also need to define the number ranges for consolidation documents. We already assigned number range intervals to the document type per consolidation version. These number range intervals must be valid for the year in which postings are to be made.

To maintain number ranges, follow the menu path **SAP S/4HANA for Group Reporting • Master Data • Edit Number Range Intervals for Posting**.

On the initial screen shown in Figure 16.25, select the correct **Dimension**. Then, click the Intervals (**Change Intervals**) button. Then, click the (**Insert Line**) button from the top menu and enter new lines to extend the number ranges for the required year(s) of validity.

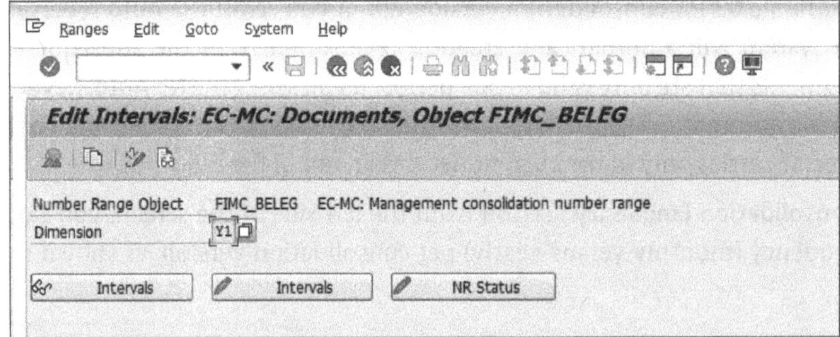

Figure 16.25 Number Ranges

Enter the number ranges and years of validity, as shown in Figure 16.26. Entering "9999" enables a number range to be valid indefinitely. Then, save by clicking the **Save** button.

Interval Edit Goto System Help

Edit Intervals: EC-MC: Documents, Object FIMC_BELEG, Subobject Y1

Number Range No.	Year	From No.	To Number	NR Status	External
01	9999	0100000001	0199999999	0	☐
10	9999	1000000001	1099999999	0	☐
12	9999	1200000001	1299999999	0	☐
20	9999	2000000001	2099999999	0	☐
22	9999	2200000001	2299999999	0	☐
30	9999	3000000001	3099999999	0	☐

Figure 16.26 Maintaining Number Ranges

16.3.5 Data Collection Tasks

As discussed earlier, the group reporting process from a user point of view has two main parts: data consolidation, which is performed in the data monitor, and consolidation, which is done in the consolidation monitor. In the data monitor, data collection tasks are performed. To define these tasks, follow the menu path **SAP S/4HANA for Group Reporting • Data Collection for Consolidation • Define Task.**

Figure 16.27 shows the standard tasks provided by SAP. If you need to create other tasks, you can do so with the **New Entries** option from the top menu, but these standard tasks should suffice for most business requirements.

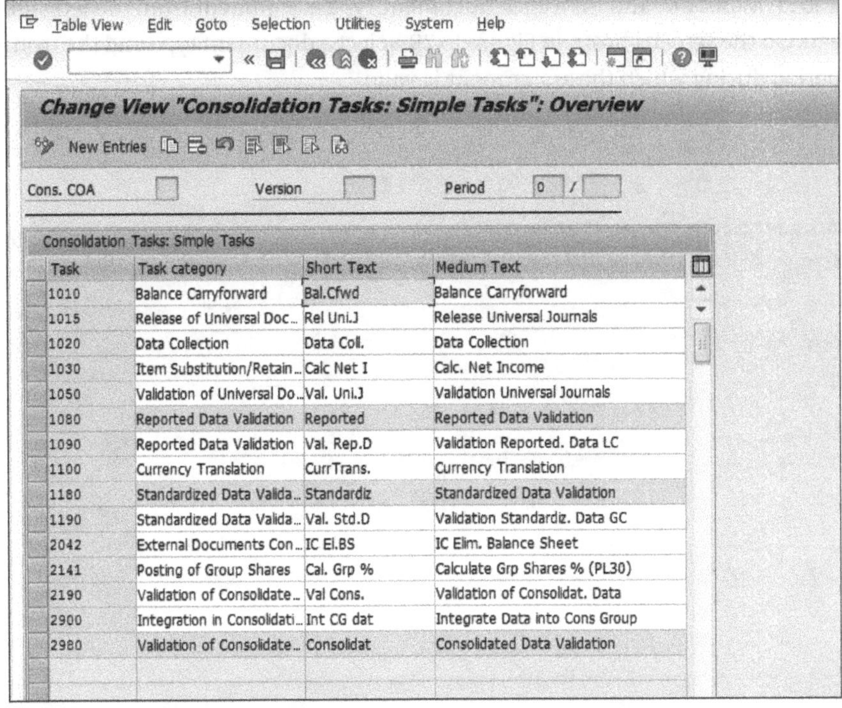

Task	Task category	Short Text	Medium Text
1010	Balance Carryforward	Bal.Cfwd	Balance Carryforward
1015	Release of Universal Doc...	Rel Uni.J	Release Universal Journals
1020	Data Collection	Data Coll.	Data Collection
1030	Item Substitution/Retain...	Calc Net I	Calc. Net Income
1050	Validation of Universal Do...	Val. Uni.J	Validation Universal Journals
1080	Reported Data Validation	Reported	Reported Data Validation
1090	Reported Data Validation	Val. Rep.D	Validation Reported. Data LC
1100	Currency Translation	CurrTrans.	Currency Translation
1180	Standardized Data Valida...	Standardiz	Standardized Data Validation
1190	Standardized Data Valida...	Val. Std.D	Validation Standardiz. Data GC
2042	External Documents Con...	IC El.BS	IC Elim. Balance Sheet
2141	Posting of Group Shares	Cal. Grp %	Calculate Grp Shares % (PL30)
2190	Validation of Consolidate...	Val Cons.	Validation of Consolidat. Data
2900	Integration in Consolidati...	Int CG dat	Integrate Data into Cons Group
2980	Validation of Consolidate...	Consolidat	Consolidated Data Validation

Figure 16.27 Consolidation Tasks

In a separate step, you can define tasks for manual postings by following the menu path **SAP S/4HANA for Group Reporting • Data Collection for Consolidation • Define Tasks for Manual Posting.** Figure 16.28 shows a list of manual tasks already defined. You can create new tasks with the **New Entries** option from the top menu.

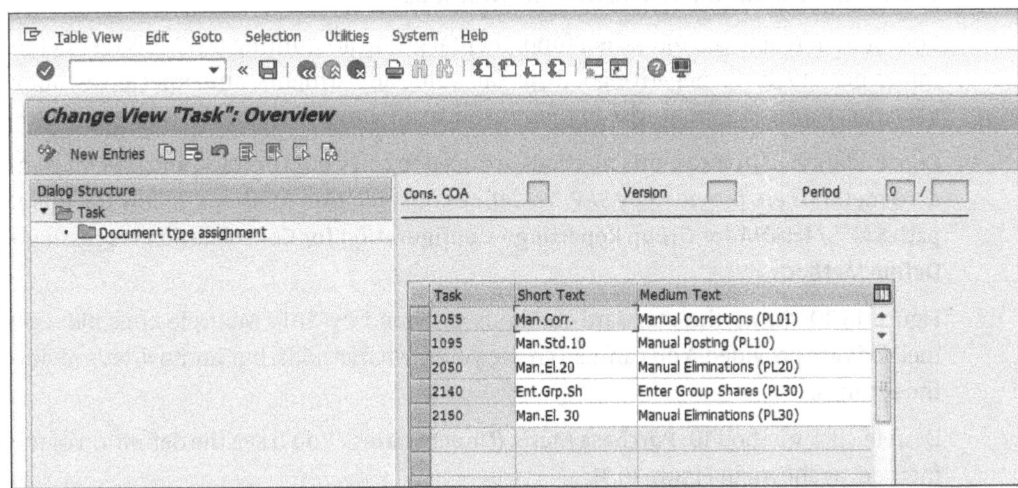

Task	Short Text	Medium Text
1055	Man.Corr.	Manual Corrections (PL01)
1095	Man.Std.10	Manual Posting (PL10)
2050	Man.El.20	Manual Eliminations (PL20)
2140	Ent.Grp.Sh	Enter Group Shares (PL30)
2150	Man.El. 30	Manual Eliminations (PL30)

Figure 16.28 Tasks for Manual Postings

Select task **1055: Man.Corr.** and then click **Document type assignment** from the left side of the screen. On the screen shown in Figure 16.29, select a document type and the from year and period during which the assignment is valid.

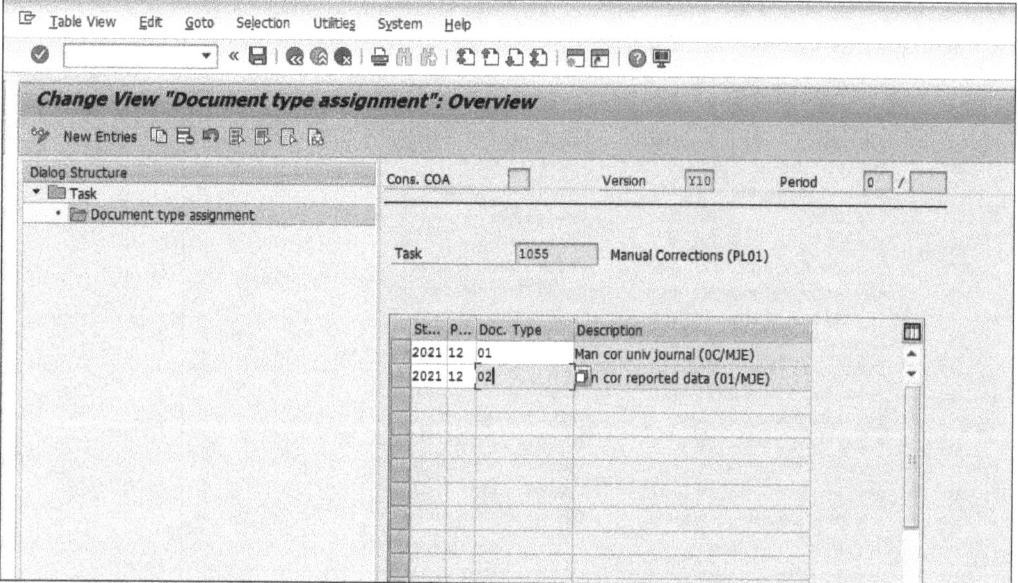

Figure 16.29 Document Type Assignment

Enter the document type to be used with the task in the **Doc. Type** field. Maintain the document types for other tasks as well and save by clicking the **Save** button.

16.3.6 Consolidation of Investments Methods

Consolidation of investments is a fundamental group accounting task. This task determines how goodwill, negative goodwill, fair value adjustments, and other investment valuation topics that may arise in the consolidation process should be treated.

Consolidation of investments methods are used to carry out this task, and several standard methods are provided by SAP. To define consolidation methods, follow the menu path **SAP S/4HANA for Group Reporting • Configuration for Consolidation Processing • Define Methods.**

Figure 16.30 shows the standard methods provided by SAP. Multiple consolidation methods are provided. You can also create your own methods, but for now, let's review the settings.

Double-click method **10: Purchase Meth. (Direct Shares)**. You'll see the definition of the method, as shown in Figure 16.31.

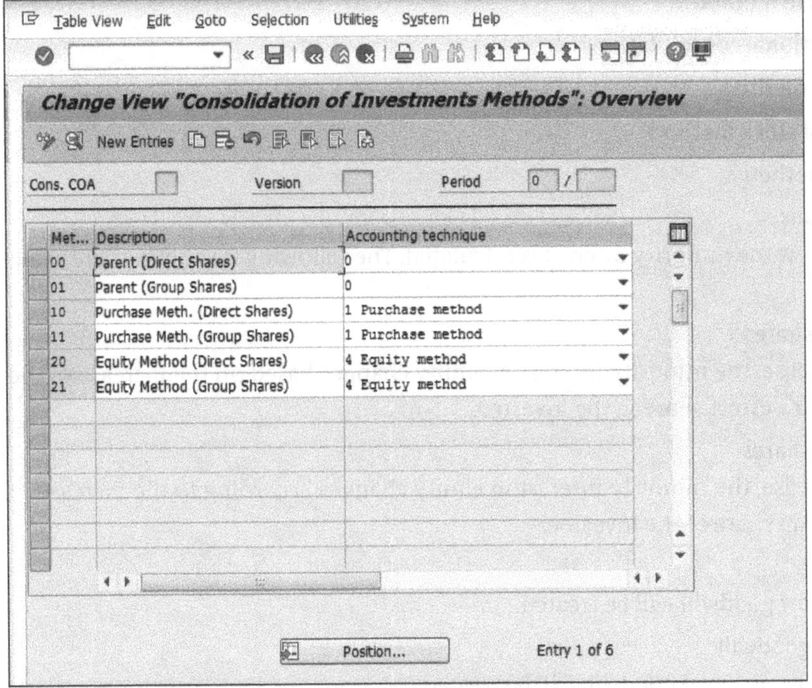

Figure 16.30 Consolidation of Investments Methods

Table View Edit Goto Selection Utilities System Help

Change View "Consolidation of Investments Methods": Details

New Entries

Cons. COA Version Period 0 /

Method 10 Purchase Meth. (Direct Shares)

Accounting technique 1 Purchase method

Acquisitions X Direct shares

Goodwill 2 Direct elimination ☐ Except.

Negative goodwill 5 Direct Writeoff ☐ Except.

☑ Post Goodwill at Investee Unit

FS items

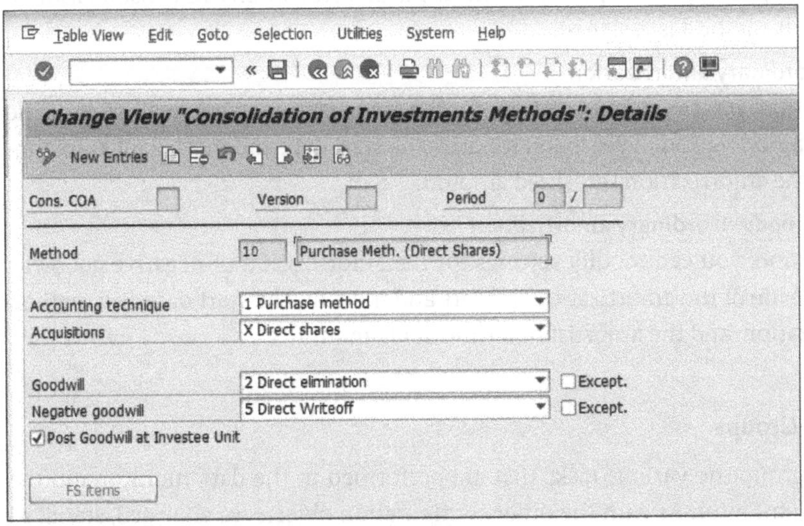

Figure 16.31 Consolidation of Investments Method Details

You can configure the following fields:

- **Accounting technique**
  The technique for consolidating investments in investee companies. You can choose from the following options:

  - **Purchase method**
  - **Proportional consolidation**
  - **Equity method**
  - **Mutual stock method**
  - **Cost method**
- **Acquisitions**
  Defines how the minority interest is calculated. The following two options are available:
  - **Direct shares**
    In this case, the minority interest in equity changes based on the increase of the investor's direct share in the investee.
  - **Group shares**
    In this case, the minority interest in equity changes according to the increase of the group share of the investee.
- **Goodwill**
  Defines how goodwill will be treated.
- **Negative goodwill**
  Defines how negative goodwill will be treated.
- **Post Goodwill at Investee Unit**
  With this indicator, you can post goodwill at the investee when this consolidation of investments method is assigned.
- **Goodwill ordinary amortization**
  In this section, you can modify settings for the amortization of goodwill, such as the life of the amortization in years and months, the start date and method of amortization, and the amortization threshold amount.
- **Negative goodwill ordinary amortization**
  In this section, you can modify settings for the amortization of negative goodwill, such as the life of the amortization in years and months, the start date and method of amortization, and the amortization threshold amount.

16.3.7 Task Groups

Task groups group the various tasks that are performed in the data monitor and the consolidation monitor. As with the other configuration objects we analyzed, standard task groups are provided by SAP, and you can create your own.

To define a task group, follow the menu path **SAP S/4HANA for Group Reporting • Configuration for Consolidation Processing • Define Task Group**.

Figure 16.32 shows the standard task groups provided by SAP. In the same transaction, task groups for the data monitor and the consolidation monitor are maintained. You can create additional task groups by selecting **New Entries** from the top menu or copy from an existing task group by selecting it and clicking the (**Copy As...**) button from the top menu.

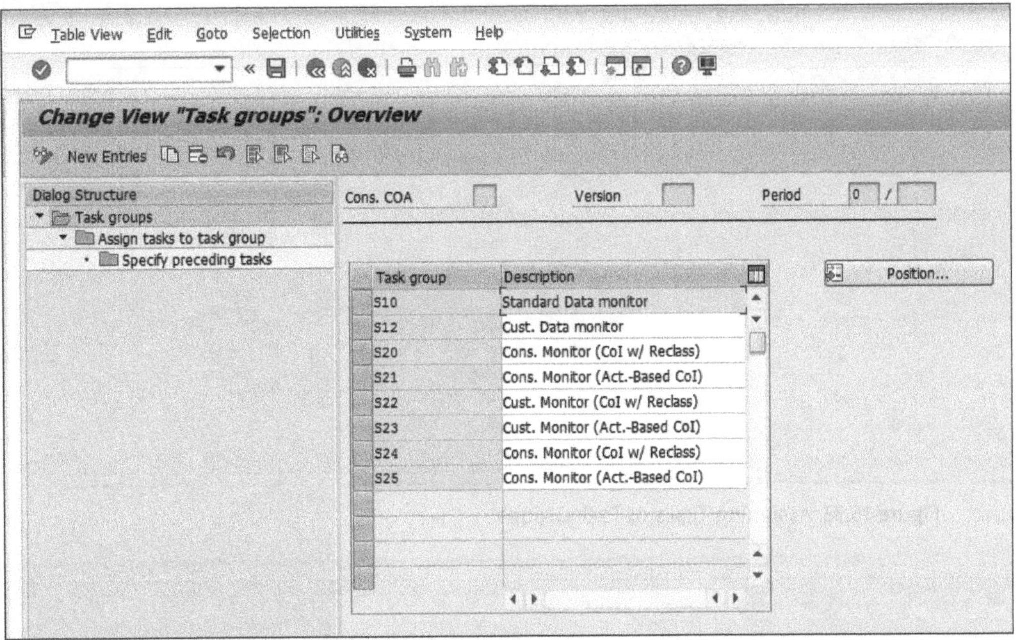

Figure 16.32 Task Groups

Let's review the settings for task group **S23**: **Cust. Monitor (Act.-Based CoI)**. Select it and click **Assign tasks to task group** from the left side of the screen. In this section, you can assign individual tasks to the task group.

Figure 16.33 shows all the tasks assigned to the task group. If you select the **Block auto.** checkbox, the relevant task will be blocked automatically after successful execution. If not, you'll have to block it manually.

Selecting the **Milestone** field marks the task as a milestone task. During the automatic execution of the consolidation process, the system will stop after a task marked as a milestone, and the user will need to continue the process manually. In the **Position** field, you can define the sequence order for the execution of equal-ranking tasks.

By selecting a task and clicking **Specify preceding tasks** from the left side of the screen, you can define a preceding task for a given task. When a task has a preceding task, that preceding task should be successfully executed and blocked before its successor task can be executed, as shown in Figure 16.34.

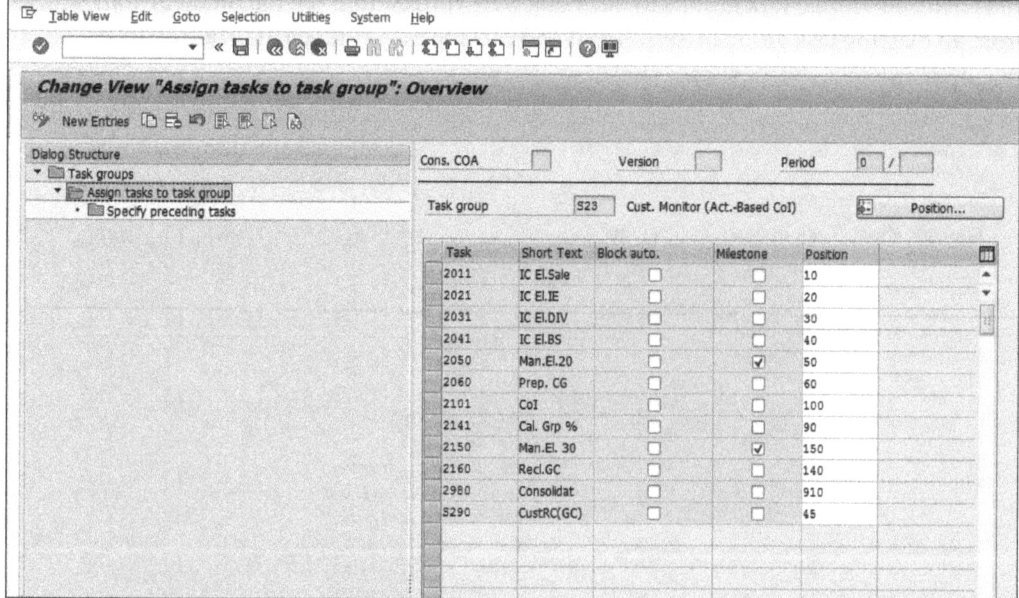

Figure 16.33 Assigning Tasks to Task Groups

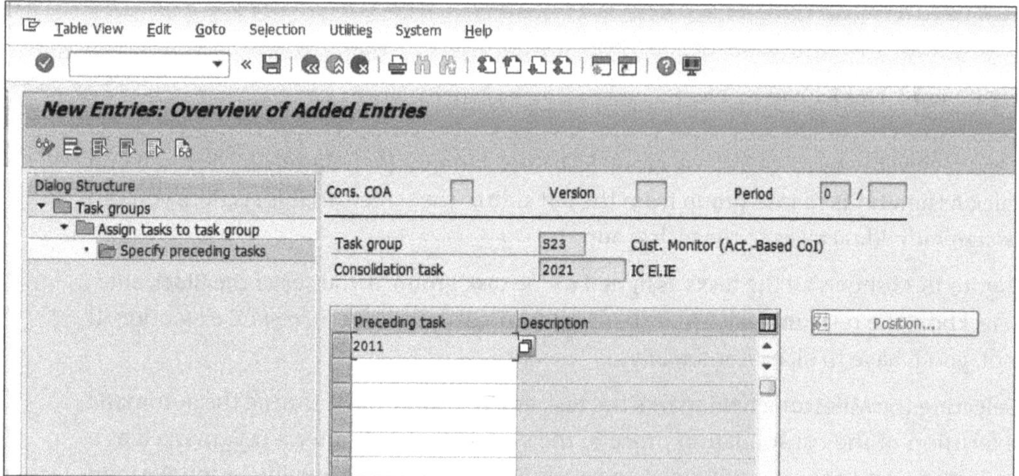

Figure 16.34 Specifying the Preceding Task

In the last step, you'll need to assign the task groups to the dimension and version by following the menu path **SAP S/4HANA for Group Reporting • Configuration for Consolidation Processing • Assign Task Group to Dimension**.

In this transaction, assign the task groups for both the data monitor and the consolidation monitor for a combination of dimension, version, and consolidation chart of accounts.

As shown in Figure 16.35, assign the task groups and specify the start year and period from which the assignment is valid. In the **Period cat.** (period category) field, you'll define the period category, which specifies the periods in which the tasks are executed. Period categories group together periods that have the same consolidation requirements, such as annual, quarterly, or some other frequency.

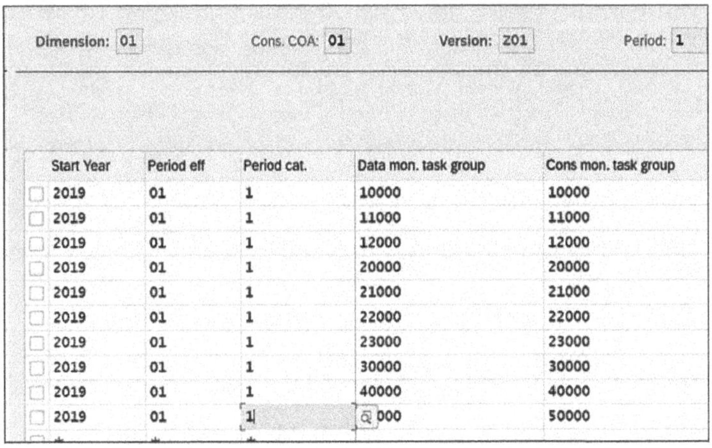

Dimension: 01 Cons. COA: 01 Version: Z01 Period: 1

Start Year	Period eff	Period cat.	Data mon. task group	Cons mon. task group
2019	01	1	10000	10000
2019	01	1	11000	11000
2019	01	1	12000	12000
2019	01	1	20000	20000
2019	01	1	21000	21000
2019	01	1	22000	22000
2019	01	1	23000	23000
2019	01	1	30000	30000
2019	01	1	40000	40000
2019	01	1	000	50000

Figure 16.35 Assigning Task Groups

With that step, we've finished our guide to configuring SAP S/4HANA Finance for group reporting.

16.4 Summary

In this chapter, you learned how to configure the new consolidation solution from SAP: SAP S/4HANA Finance for group reporting. We provided a general overview of the group reporting process and its requirements and then explored the benefits SAP S/4HANA Finance for group reporting provides. Then, we took a deep dive into a detailed guide to configuring the SAP S/4HANA Finance for group reporting solution.

This solution is a major step forward for SAP, bringing the group reporting process into SAP S/4HANA, fully benefiting from the power and flexibility of the SAP HANA database and effectively eliminating the need for third-party solutions for consolidation. SAP S/4HANA Finance for group reporting technically is similar to the EC-CS consolidation solution, but with heavy use of SAP Fiori apps for the end user, which streamlines data collection and consolidation tasks and enhances reporting.

In the next chapter, we'll cover migrating your data into SAP S/4HANA.

Chapter 17
Data Migration

An important part of every implementation is to migrate legacy data into the new system. This chapter teaches you how to perform finance data migration for both greenfield implementations and brownfield implementations, for which SAP S/4HANA provides special tools and programs to facilitate the migration process.

Data migration is a crucial part of every SAP S/4HANA implementation. No matter how well a system is configured, no matter how precisely your business processes are portrayed in the new SAP S/4HANA solution, without a properly performed migration, implementation cannot be successful. Therefore, we've dedicated an entire chapter to the data migration topic, in which we'll explain in detail how to plan and execute the migration process and describe the best practices that will help you avoid dangerous pitfalls.

The migration process involves numerous objects. We'll concentrate on the finance objects because other logistics objects, such as materials, lie outside the scope of this book. From a finance point of view, we'll need to migrate general ledger accounts, cost centers, profit centers, internal orders, customers, vendors, assets, banks, and related balances and open items.

Because the migration strategy is different for greenfield and brownfield implementations, we'll dedicate separate sections to each path. Then, we'll discuss in detail the most important finance migration objects and what should be considered when migrating them.

17.1 Brownfield Implementation Migration

As noted previously, converting an existing SAP ERP system to SAP S/4HANA is called a *brownfield implementation*. You must ensure that your system meets various technical requirements before you can make the conversion and that all finance settings and objects are correctly migrated to the new SAP S/4HANA landscape.

Before you start, you should be familiar with the *Conversion Guide for SAP S/4HANA 2020*, available at *http://s-prs.co/v536100*. A lot of useful information also is available in the conversion document for accounting, attached to SAP Note 2332030. To search for SAP Notes, visit *https://support.sap.com/en/index.html*. An SAP S-user ID is required to access SAP Notes, which can be provided by your project manager. SAP delivers various checks and migration tools and programs to help you in these tasks.

We'll first teach you how to use the check programs to make sure your system is ready for conversion to SAP S/4HANA. Then, we'll guide you through how to execute the migration.

17.1.1 Check Programs for SAP S/4HANA Readiness

SAP delivers multiple programs to help you identify areas that aren't compatible with the future SAP S/4HANA solution.

Program RASFIN_MIGR_PRECHECK checks the readiness of fixed assets for SAP S/4HANA. To execute programs in SAP, enter Transaction SE38.

Figure 17.1 shows the initial screen to run programs. Enter the program name, "RASFIN_MIGR_PRECHECK," in the **Program** field, and execute it by clicking the button from the top menu.

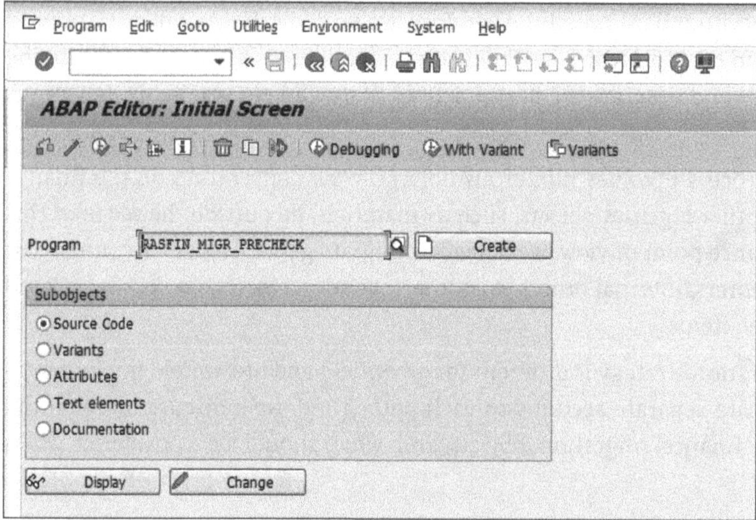

Figure 17.1 Run Program RASFIN_MIGR_PRECHECK

On the first screen, shown in Figure 17.2, two options are available:

- **SAP Simple Finance Add-On**
- **SAP Simple Finance / SAP S/4HANA**

As described in the Introduction, SAP Simple Finance (now called SAP S/4HANA Finance) was the first application from SAP to be provided for the SAP HANA database. This solution was delivered as an add-on for SAP ERP. This program can carry out checks for compliance, which are, in general, less stringent than the checks for SAP S/4HANA.

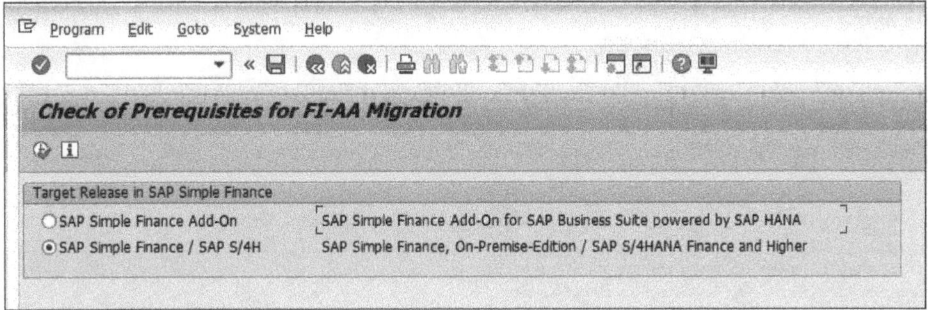

Figure 17.2 Checking Fixed Assets

Select the checks for SAP S/4HANA (the **SAP Simple Finance / SAP S/4H** radio button) and proceed by clicking the **Execute** button on the lower-right side of the screen.

Figure 17.3 shows the errors that the program identified related to fixed assets. Double-clicking an error message provides additional information. These errors must be resolved before you can continue with the migration activities for fixed assets.

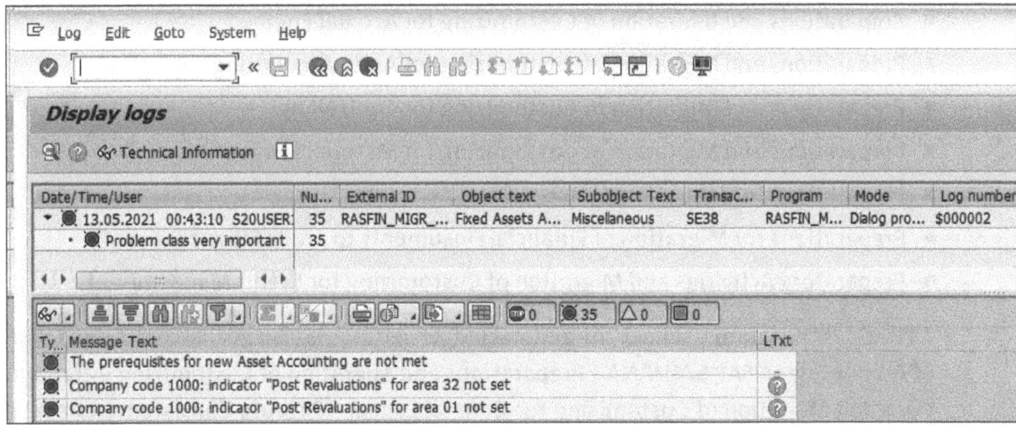

Figure 17.3 Checking Fixed Assets Output List

To check the overall financial customizing settings, follow the menu path **Conversion of Accounting to SAP S/4HANA • Preparations and Migration of Customizing • Check Customizing Settings Prior to Migration**. This transaction checks whether the customizing settings are ready for migration to SAP S/4HANA Finance. This transaction determines whether your ledger, company code, and controlling area settings meet the prerequisites for migration. The output is shown in Figure 17.4.

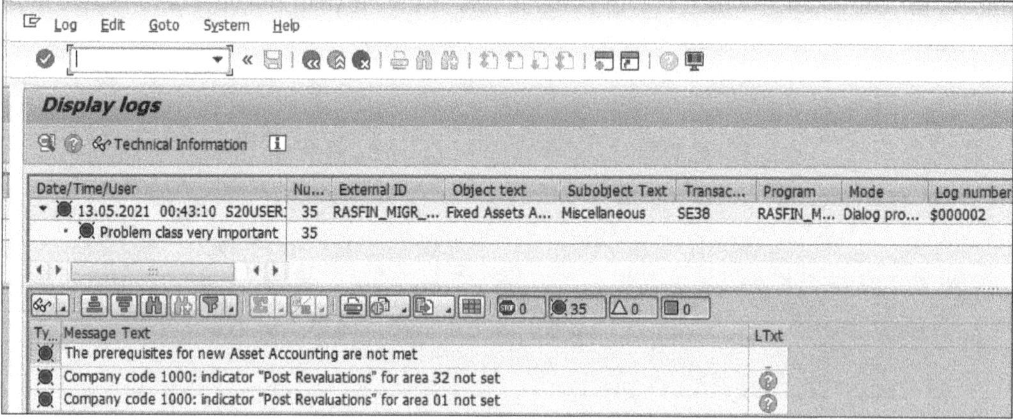

Figure 17.4 Checking Finance Customizing

Starting with the menu path **Conversion of Accounting to SAP S/4HANA • Preparations and Migration of Customizing**, you'll access various transactions to check configuration objects for the different financial modules, that must be checked prior to migration, as shown in Figure 17.5:

- **Preparations and Migration of Customizing for General Ledger**
- **Preparations and Migration of Customizing for Accrual Engine**
- **Preparations and Migration of Customizing for Asset Accounting**
- **Preparations and Migration of Customizing for Controlling**
- **Preparations and Migration of Customizing for Material Ledger**
- **Preparations for Migration of House Bank Accounts**
- **Preparations for Migration of Financial Documents to Trade Finance**
- **Preparatory Activities and Migration of Customizing for Credit Management**

A readiness program to check the general ledger settings is also available at **Conversion of Accounting to SAP S/4HANA • Preparations and Migration of Customizing • Preparations and Migration of Customizing for General Ledger • Execute Consistency Check of General Ledger Settings.** This program checks the customizing settings of the ledgers. This check must be performed without error messages before you can continue with the migration.

Figure 17.6 shows the result of the checks performed by the program.

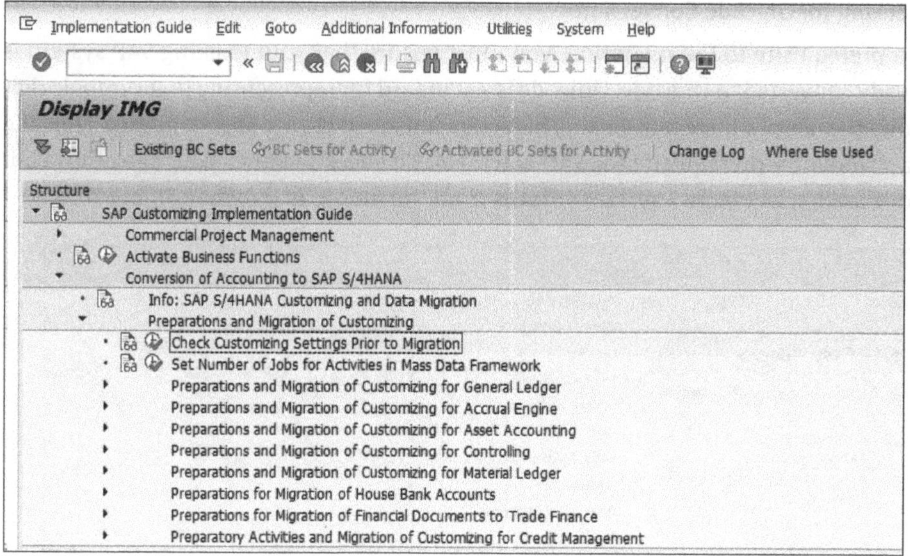

Figure 17.5 Checking Customizing Settings

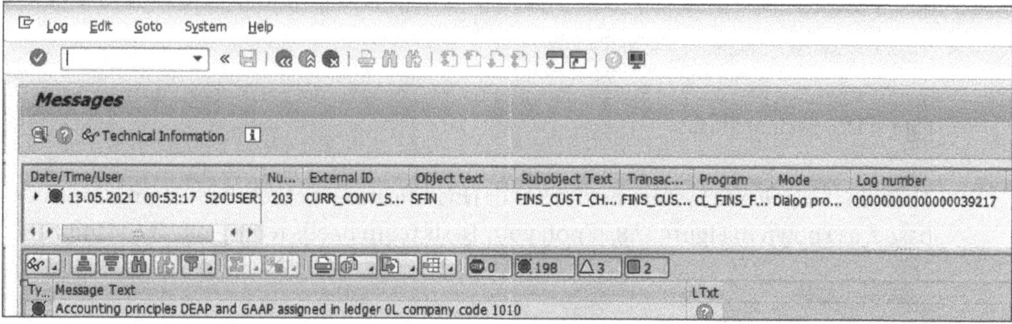

Figure 17.6 General Ledger Readiness Check

17.1.2 Migration to SAP S/4HANA

After successfully eliminating all errors in the readiness check programs, you can continue with the migration of your existing SAP system data to SAP S/4HANA.

In this section, we'll examine the steps in the migration process. We'll start by checking that the system is converted to Unicode. Then, we'll analyze the transactional data that must be converted. After that step, we'll teach you how to start and monitor the migration process. Then, we'll migrate general ledger allocations. We'll finish off with the technical step of completing the migration and describe the activities to be performed after the migration.

Checking for Unicode Conversion

As a prerequisite to the migration, you must ensure that your existing SAP system is already converted to Unicode. Unicode is a standard for representing text symbols that allows the use of a huge number of characters not available in older standards. Unicode is a mandatory prerequisite for SAP S/4HANA. To check whether your system is Unicode based, select **More • System • Status** from the menu, as shown in Figure 17.7.

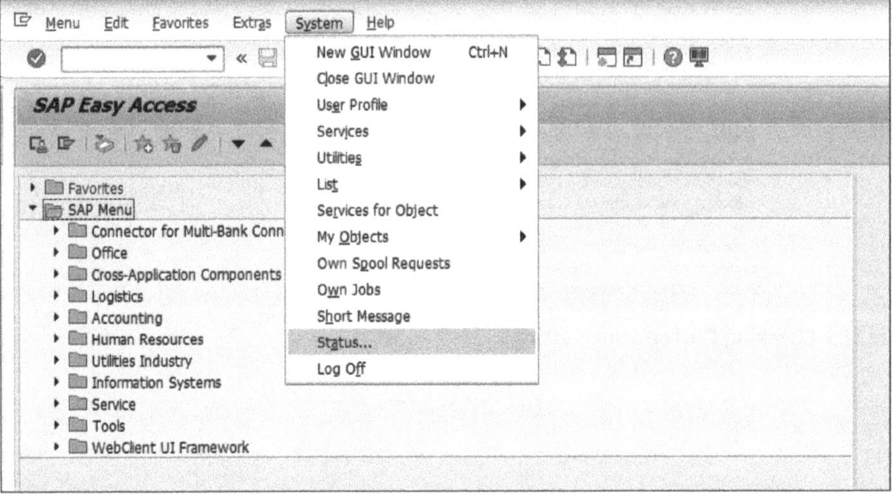

Figure 17.7 System Status

Then, in the **Unicode System** field, a **Yes** or **No** indicates whether the system is Unicode-based, as shown in Figure 17.8. If not, your Basis team needs to upgrade it to Unicode.

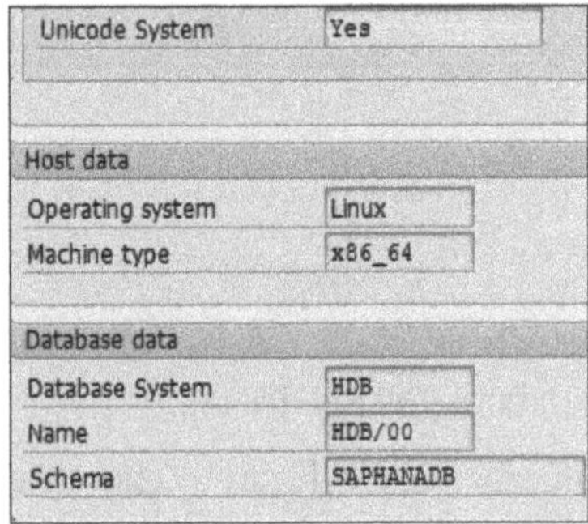

Figure 17.8 Unicode System

Now, you're ready to start the migration from an existing SAP system to SAP S/4HANA. You'll need to plan for downtime so that no users are logged on to the system during the migration. The migration should be performed over a weekend when enough downtime will be available while not disrupting the business.

Analysis of Transactional Data

The first step in the data migration process is to analyze the existing transactional data. Follow the menu path **Conversion of Accounting to SAP S/4HANA • Data Migration • Analyze Transactional Data.**

On the initial screen shown in Figure 17.9, you can restrict the number of background jobs in the **Number of batch jobs** field, which makes sense in systems with a very high volumes of transactional data. You can specify a server group name in the **Server Group Name** field.

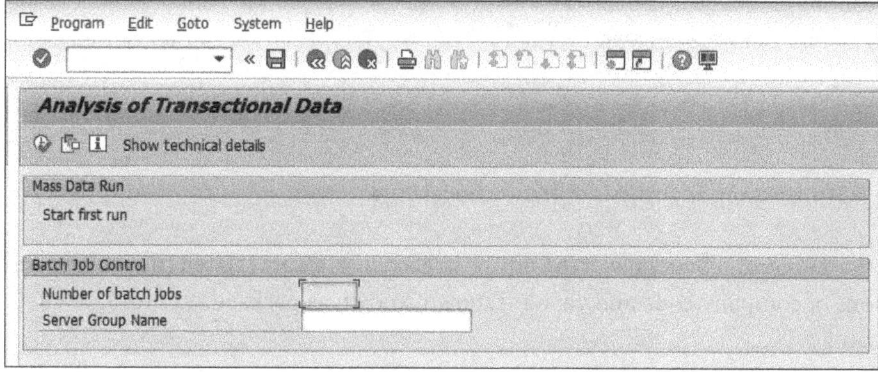

Figure 17.9 Analysis of Transactional Data

Then, proceed by clicking the **Execute** button on the lower-right side of the screen. The system displays a log of the scheduled jobs, as shown in Figure 17.10.

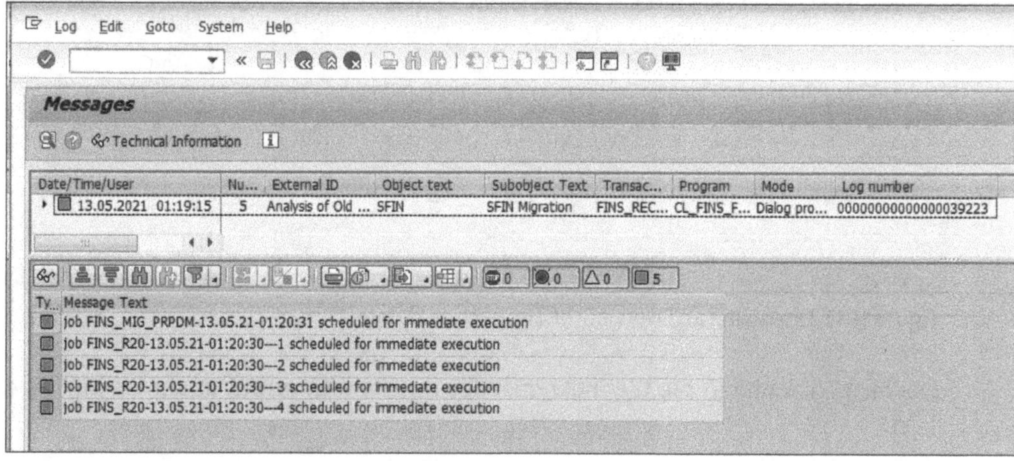

Figure 17.10 Analysis of the Transactional Data Log

Go back to the customizing menu. To display the results, follow the menu path **Conversion of Accounting to SAP S/4HANA • Display Status of Analysis of Transactional Data.**

As shown in Figure 17.11, the system shows the number of errors found. Double-click the number of errors to see an overview.

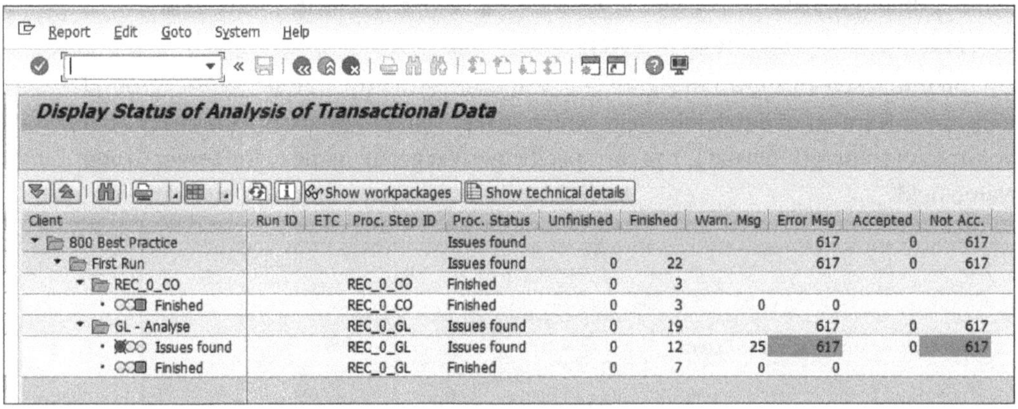

Report Edit Goto System Help

Display Status of Analysis of Transactional Data

Show workpackages | Show technical details

Client	Run ID	ETC	Proc. Step ID	Proc. Status	Unfinished	Finished	Warn. Msg	Error Msg	Accepted	Not Acc.
800 Best Practice				Issues found				617	0	617
First Run				Issues found	0	22		617	0	617
REC_0_CO			REC_0_CO	Finished	0	3				
Finished			REC_0_CO	Finished	0	3	0	0		
GL - Analyse			REC_0_GL	Issues found	0	19		617	0	617
Issues found			REC_0_GL	Issues found	0	12	25	617	0	617
Finished			REC_0_GL	Finished	0	7	0	0		

Figure 17.11 Displaying an Analysis of Transactional Data

Figure 17.12 shows an overview of the errors. In each line, errors related to specific combinations of company code and year are shown, known as package keys for mass data processing.

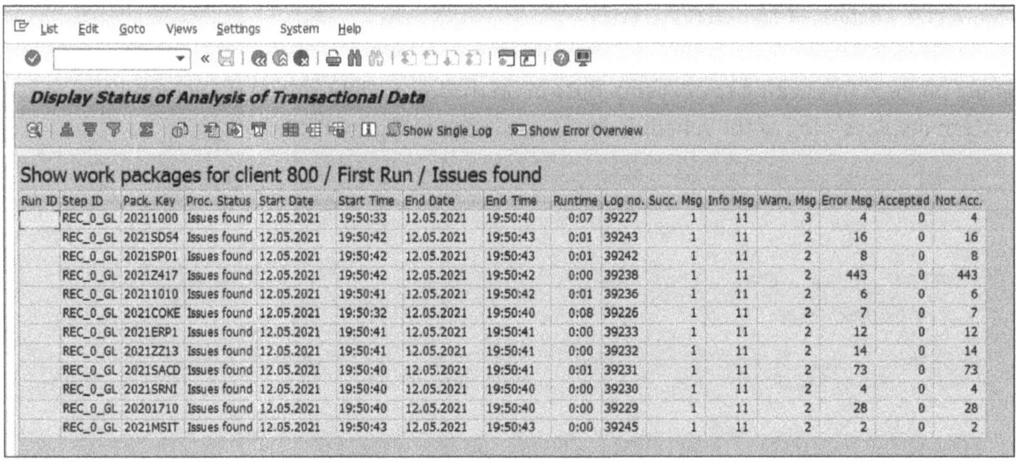

List Edit Goto Views Settings System Help

Display Status of Analysis of Transactional Data

Show Single Log | Show Error Overview

Show work packages for client 800 / First Run / Issues found

Run ID	Step ID	Pack. Key	Proc. Status	Start Date	Start Time	End Date	End Time	Runtime	Log no.	Succ. Msg	Info Msg	Warn. Msg	Error Msg	Accepted	Not Acc.
	REC_0_GL	20211000	Issues found	12.05.2021	19:50:33	12.05.2021	19:50:40	0:07	39227	1	11	3	4	0	4
	REC_0_GL	2021SDS4	Issues found	12.05.2021	19:50:42	12.05.2021	19:50:43	0:01	39243	1	11	2	16	0	16
	REC_0_GL	2021SP01	Issues found	12.05.2021	19:50:42	12.05.2021	19:50:43	0:01	39242	1	11	2	8	0	8
	REC_0_GL	2021Z417	Issues found	12.05.2021	19:50:42	12.05.2021	19:50:42	0:00	39238	1	11	2	443	0	443
	REC_0_GL	20211010	Issues found	12.05.2021	19:50:41	12.05.2021	19:50:42	0:01	39236	1	11	2	6	0	6
	REC_0_GL	2021COKE	Issues found	12.05.2021	19:50:32	12.05.2021	19:50:40	0:08	39226	1	11	2	7	0	7
	REC_0_GL	2021ERP1	Issues found	12.05.2021	19:50:41	12.05.2021	19:50:41	0:00	39233	1	11	2	12	0	12
	REC_0_GL	2021ZZ13	Issues found	12.05.2021	19:50:41	12.05.2021	19:50:41	0:00	39232	1	11	2	14	0	14
	REC_0_GL	2021SACD	Issues found	12.05.2021	19:50:40	12.05.2021	19:50:41	0:01	39231	1	11	2	73	0	73
	REC_0_GL	2021SRNI	Issues found	12.05.2021	19:50:40	12.05.2021	19:50:40	0:00	39230	1	11	2	4	0	4
	REC_0_GL	20201710	Issues found	12.05.2021	19:50:40	12.05.2021	19:50:40	0:00	39229	1	11	2	28	0	28
	REC_0_GL	2021MSIT	Issues found	12.05.2021	19:50:43	12.05.2021	19:50:43	0:00	39245	1	11	2	2	0	2

Figure 17.12 Displaying an Overview of Transactional Data

Double-click a line to see the individual documents with errors, as shown in Figure 17.13.

You must analyze the errors and resolve critical errors.

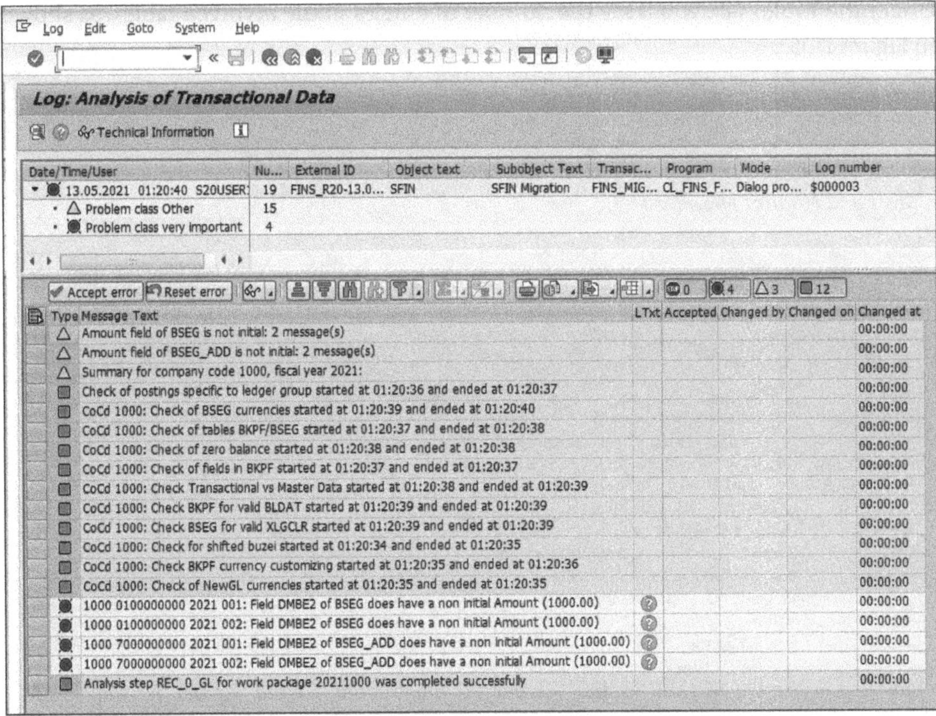

Figure 17.13 Detailed Errors

Starting and Monitoring the Migration

To perform and monitor the data migration, SAP provides the SAP S/4HANA migration cockpit, available at the menu path **Conversion of Accounting to SAP S/4HANA • Data Migration • Start and Monitor Data Migration.**

On the screen shown in Figure 17.14, you'll see migration runs. The runs are numbered according to their start date and time. The first run will be numbered 1.

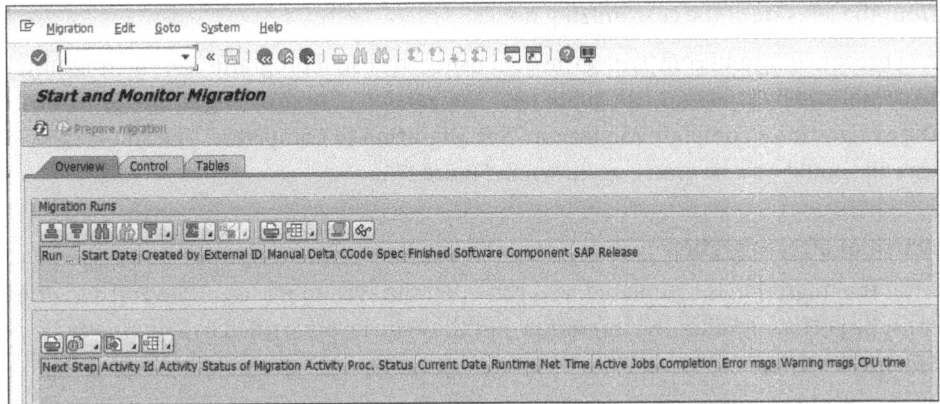

Figure 17.14 Start and Monitor Migration Overview

Under the **Tables** tab, you'll see the number of entries in the involved tables, as shown in Figure 17.15.

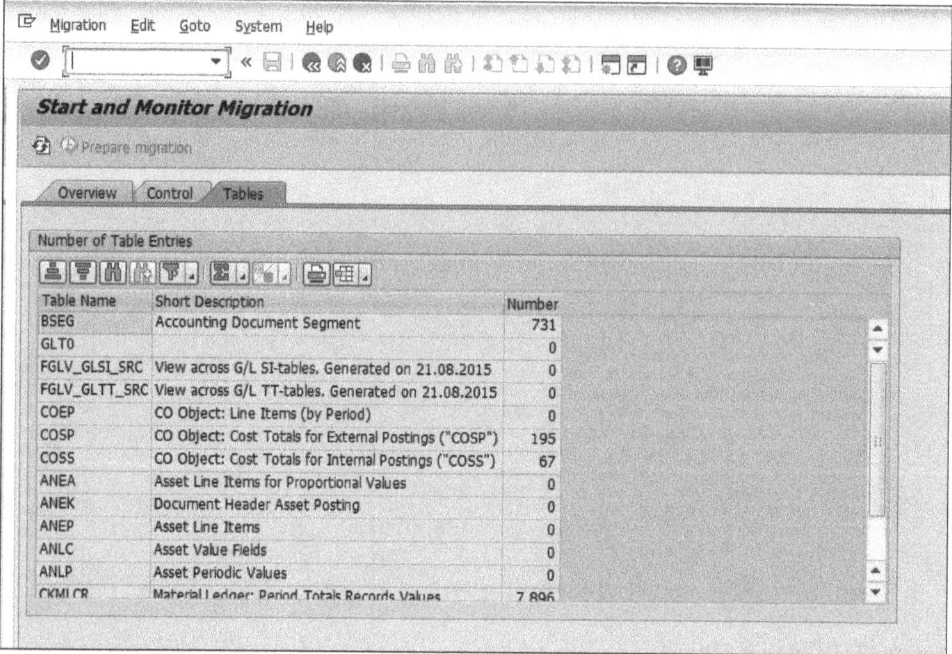

Figure 17.15 Table Entries

Completing the Migration

After all data migration steps are completed, you should complete the migration by following the menu path **Conversion of Accounting to SAP S/4HANA • Data Migration • Complete Migration • Reconcile and Compare Migrated Data.** Extensive documentation is available explaining which programs are available to reconcile and compare migrated data. You can review customizing documentation by clicking the button from the left side of the customizing node.

After reconciling and comparing the data using the listed programs, set the migration to completed by following the menu path **Conversion of Accounting to SAP S/4HANA • Data Migration • Complete Migration • Set Migration to Completed.** The status indicators all should now be green, as shown in Figure 17.16.

Activities after Migration

After the migration is completed, you can open the system for users. Several activities must be performed after the migration, but they can be performed in a productive SAP S/4HANA system.

Figure 17.17 shows the various technical steps that should be performed after the system is converted to SAP S/4HANA from a finance point of view.

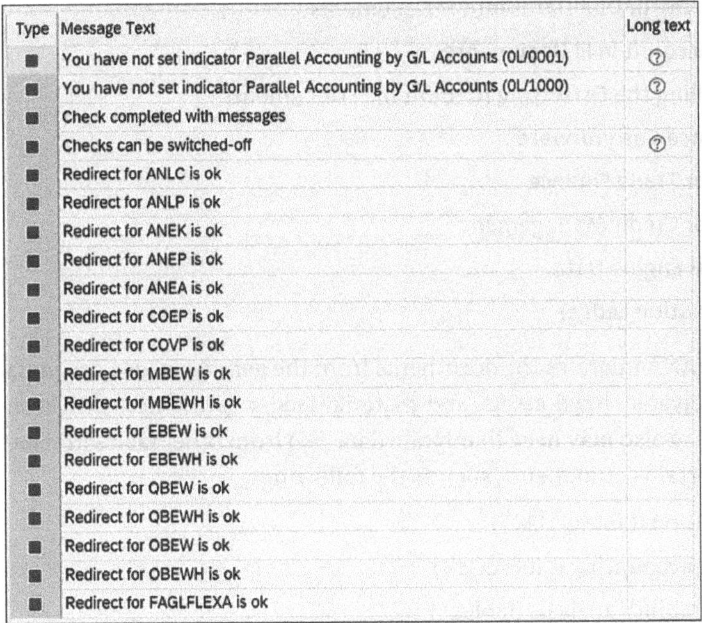

Type	Message Text	Long text
■	You have not set indicator Parallel Accounting by G/L Accounts (0L/0001)	ⓘ
■	You have not set indicator Parallel Accounting by G/L Accounts (0L/1000)	ⓘ
■	Check completed with messages	
■	Checks can be switched-off	ⓘ
■	Redirect for ANLC is ok	
■	Redirect for ANLP is ok	
■	Redirect for ANEK is ok	
■	Redirect for ANEP is ok	
■	Redirect for ANEA is ok	
■	Redirect for COEP is ok	
■	Redirect for COVP is ok	
■	Redirect for MBEW is ok	
■	Redirect for MBEWH is ok	
■	Redirect for EBEW is ok	
■	Redirect for EBEWH is ok	
■	Redirect for QBEW is ok	
■	Redirect for QBEWH is ok	
■	Redirect for OBEW is ok	
■	Redirect for OBEWH is ok	
■	Redirect for FAGLFLEXA is ok	

Figure 17.16 Migration Completion Log

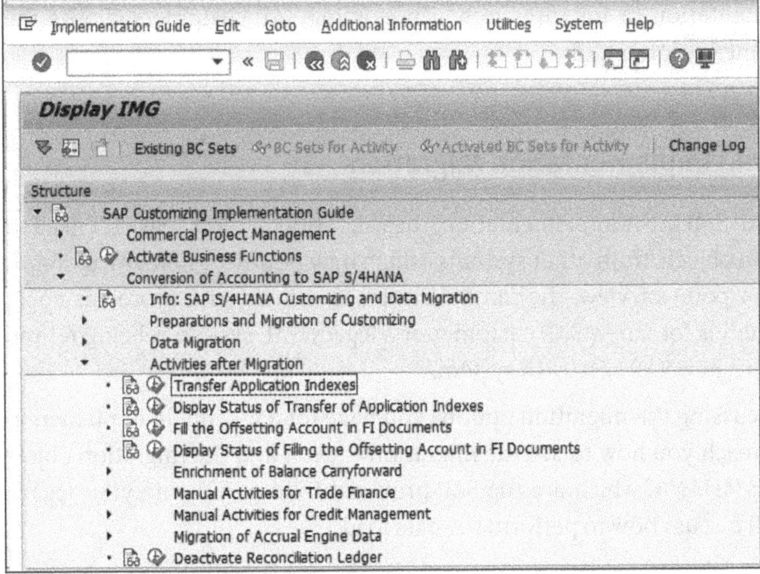

Figure 17.17 Activities after Migration

These activities include the following:

- **Transfer Application Indexes**
- **Display Status of Transfer of Application Indexes**

- **Display Status of Filling in Due Dates into FI Documents**
- **Fill the Offsetting Account in FI Documents**
- **Display Status of Filling the Offsetting Account in FI Documents**
- **Enrichment of Balance Carryforward**
- **Manual Activities for Trade Finance**
- **Manual Activities for Credit Management**
- **Migration of Accrual Engine Data**
- **Deactivate Reconciliation Ledger**

Migrating to SAP S/4HANA migrates the documents from the general ledger, accounts payable, accounts receivable, fixed assets, and material ledger to the new Universal Journal, table ACDOCA. You also may need to migrate data also from other tables in separate steps if you use certain components, such as the following:

- Cost of sales accounting (table GLFUNCT)
- Classic profit center accounting (table GLPCT)
- Costing-based profitability analysis (tables CE1*)

With this step, we've finished our guide to data migration for brownfield implementation. In the next section, we'll discuss how you can perform a migration for a brand-new SAP implementation or for cases in which existing SAP customers choose the greenfield implementation option.

17.2 Greenfield Implementation Migration

In a greenfield SAP S/4HANA implementation, the migration process may still need to bring in migration objects from other systems, which may be SAP or non-SAP systems. From a migration point of view, the same concepts, methods, and processes apply whether the system is for a new SAP customer or a legacy SAP system is being retired and replaced with a new SAP S/4HANA system.

We'll start by discussing the migration options you have for a greenfield implementation. Then, we'll teach you how to use the migration cockpit and the migration object modeler in SAP S/4HANA, which are the SAP-provided tools to migrate your legacy data. Finally, we'll discuss how to perform the data load.

17.2.1 Migration Options

Traditionally, to migrate legacy data in SAP, a certain amount of programming or at least technical skill was needed. Different tools were used for the migration, such as the Legacy System Migration Workbench (LSMW), which was popular not only for migrations but also for various mass data maintenance tasks. In fact, many consultants are quite familiar with LSMW because this tool is flexible and includes many capabilities.

In SAP S/4HANA, however, SAP provides new tools specifically tailored for migration: the migration cockpit and the migration object modeler. The migration cockpit allows you to work with various data migration objects and generate Excel templates for them, which then can be populated with legacy data and migrated to SAP S/4HANA. The migration object modeler is the brain behind the migration cockpit and enables you to modify the structure of the data objects to be migrated or to create new ones.

Although LSMW is still an option for migration, we don't recommend using it. SAP Note 2287723 states the following:

> *The Legacy System Migration Workbench (LSMW) should only be considered as a migration tool for SAP S/4HANA for objects that do not have interfaces or content available after carefully testing for each and every object. The use of LSMW for data load to SAP S/4HANA is not recommended and at the customer's own risk.*

Therefore, unless you have some very specific, very strong reason to use something else, the migration tool for greenfield SAP S/4HANA implementations should be the migration cockpit in combination with the migration object modeler.

17.2.2 Migration Cockpit and Migration Object Modeler

17

The *migration cockpit* is a web-based tool for migrating legacy data to SAP S/4HANA. This tool helps generate predefined Excel templates in which to populate your legacy data and then helps upload this data.

To start the migration cockpit, enter Transaction LTMC. Authorization role SAP_CA_DMC_MC_USER is required. The transaction opens a web browser, as shown in Figure 17.18.

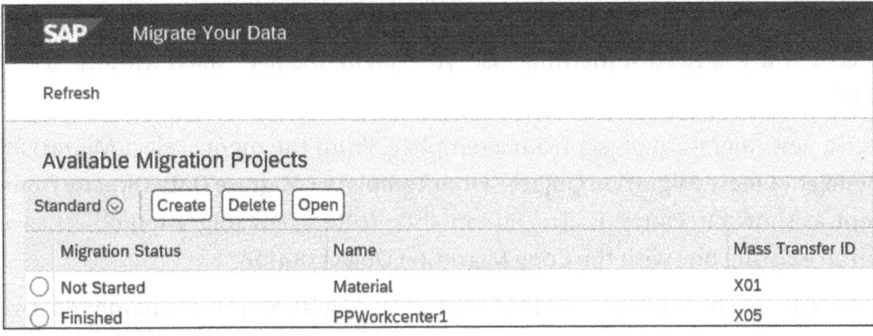

Figure 17.18 Migration Cockpit

You'll see a list of migration projects already defined. You'll probably need to create multiple finance data migration projects that cover the various areas, such as banks, cost centers, general ledger balances, and so on.

Some basic logic is provided by SAP in the migration cockpit, but normally, you'll need to enhance it or create new migration objects using the migration object modeler. The *migration object modeler* is an SAP GUI-based tool that enables you to define the structure of migration objects.

Start the migration object modeler by entering Transaction LTMOM. Authorization role SAP_CA_DMC_MC_DEVELOPER is required. On the initial screen shown in Figure 17.19, you can choose to view/modify either migration objects or projects.

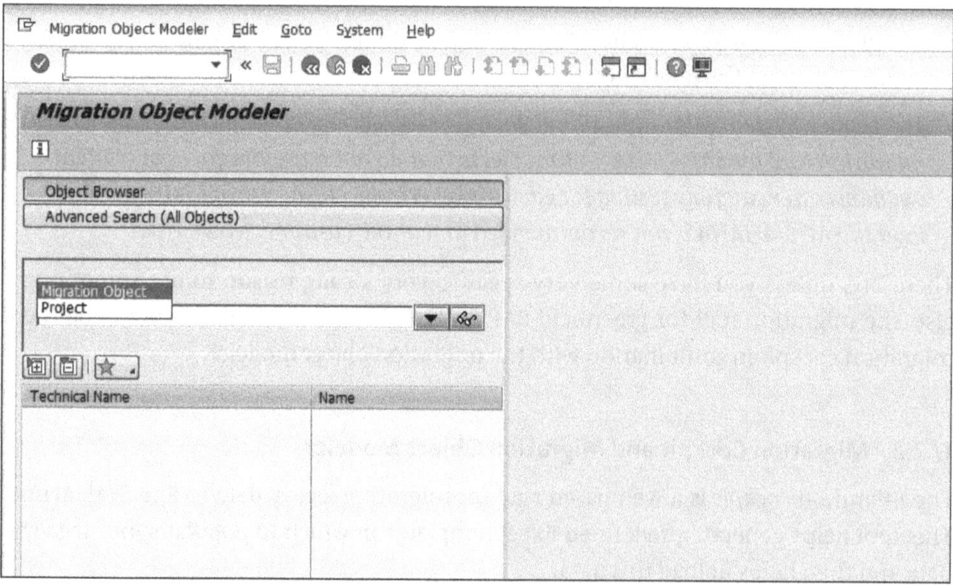

Figure 17.19 Migration Object Modeler

You can create a new user-defined migration object from scratch or create one from a template. SAP provides many templates, which should cover most objects that need to be migrated, but if you need something else, you can define it yourself with the user-defined option.

Let's create a new migration object from a template. From the menu, select **Migration Object Modeler • Create Migration Object • From Template • Migrate Data Directly from SAP System**, as shown in Figure 17.20. You can also create a new migration object as a copy from an existing one with the **Copy Migration Object** option.

On the next screen, shown in Figure 17.21, enter the migration project name. As discussed, you should have separate migration objects that group together similar migration objects. The project name should start with Z or Y in the custom name range. These projects are shown in the migration cockpit, shown earlier in Figure 17.18.

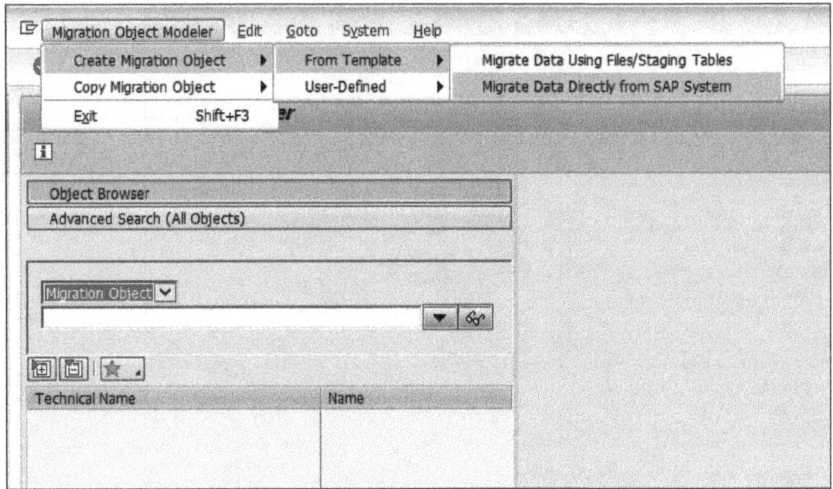

Figure 17.20 Creating a New Migration Object

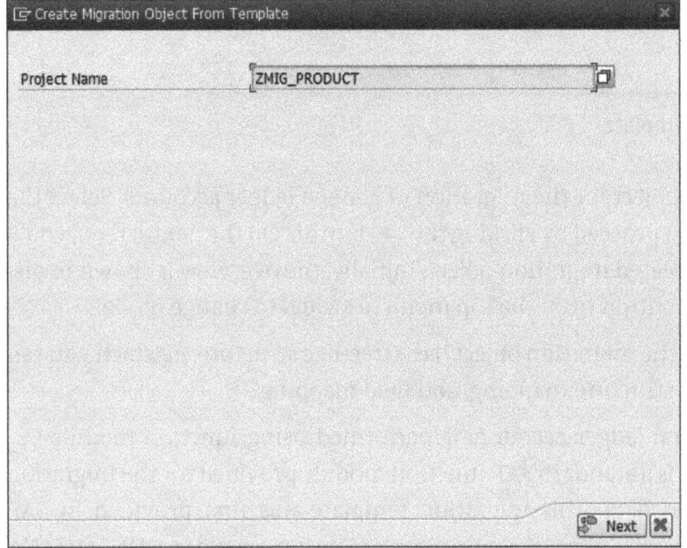

Figure 17.21 Project Name

Continue by clicking the **Next** button. On the next screen, select a migration object template. As shown in Figure 17.22, SAP provides templates for the main migration tasks—for example, accounts receivable open items, accounts payable open items, general ledger accounts, and so on.

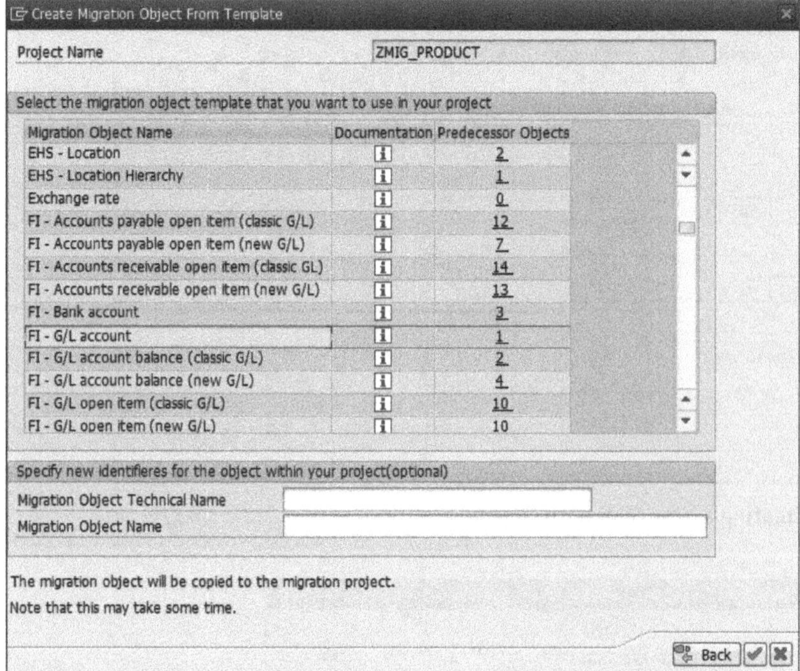

Figure 17.22 Selecting a Template

Let's create a migration object for the migration of general ledger accounts. Select the **G/L account** template and proceed by clicking the button. On the next screen, you'll see an overview of the created migration object. Initially, the overview is shown in display mode; click the button from the top menu to switch to change mode.

As shown in Figure 17.23, the migration object has a tree-like structure, in which you can define the source tables, structure mapping, and field mapping.

The migration for general ledger accounts is performed using function module GL_ACCT_MASTER_SAVE, which is a standard SAP function module provided for the migration of general ledger master data. This migration template was first provided in SAP S/4HANA 1809, which means that, if you're implementing an older SAP S/4HANA release, this template won't be available. SAP continuously expands the technical capabilities in this area and other areas. If you're implementing an older SAP S/4HANA release and can't find the template you need, search to see if the relevant function module is available; if so, create a user-defined object based on this function module. If you require some very specific, rarely used migration object, your development team may need to create a custom function module.

Click **Source Tables** on the left side of the screen. As shown in Figure 17.24, you'll see the source tables for the migration object. A source table contains several related fields and often corresponds to a database table in the SAP HANA database. In this case, because you created the migration object from a template, the source tables are already predefined; if you create a user-defined migration object, you'll have to define your own tables.

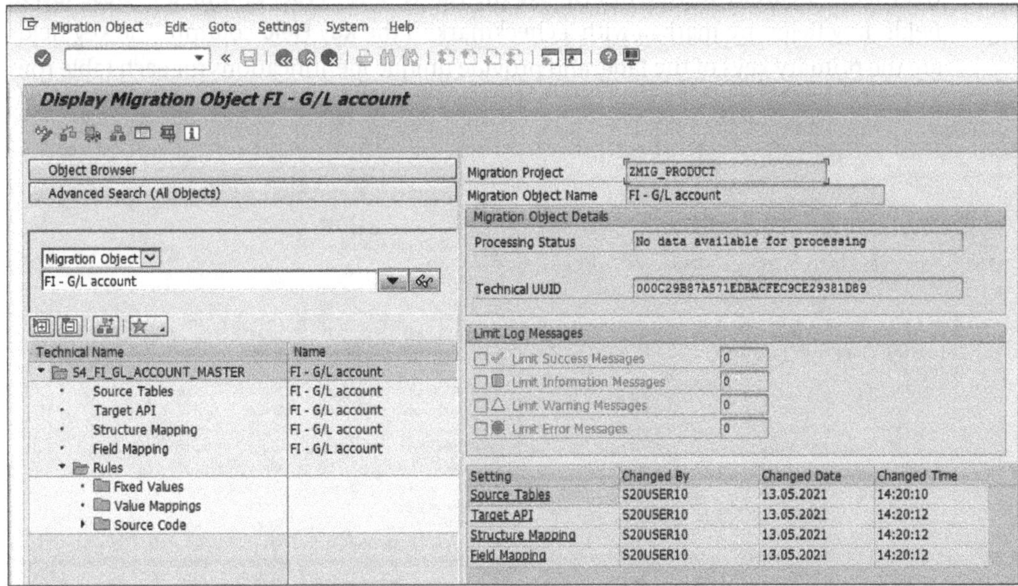

Figure 17.23 Migration Object Overview

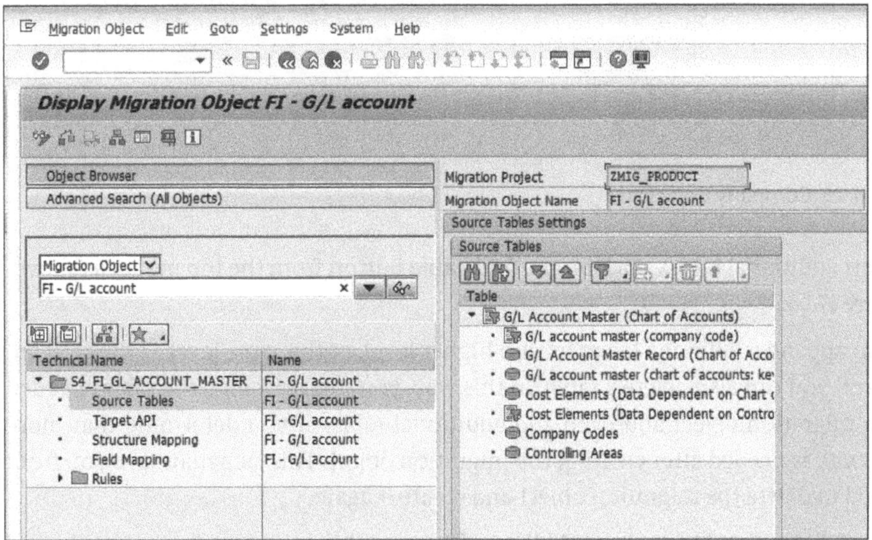

Figure 17.24 Source Tables

In this example for general ledger accounts, separate tables represent the chart of accounts data for general ledger accounts (fields from table SKA1), for company codes (fields from table SKB1), and for cost elements (tables CSKA and CSKB).

Let's review the fields on the company code level. Click the **G/L account master (company code)** table. Figure 17.25 shows the fields that are included in the source table for company code data. This source table is like looking at table SKB1 in the data browser (Transaction SE11). The system displays the **Name**, **Data Type**, **Length**, and **Description** fields. Key fields are marked with a checkmark in the **Key Field** column. The key fields are the primary keys of the table and provide unique identifications for each table row.

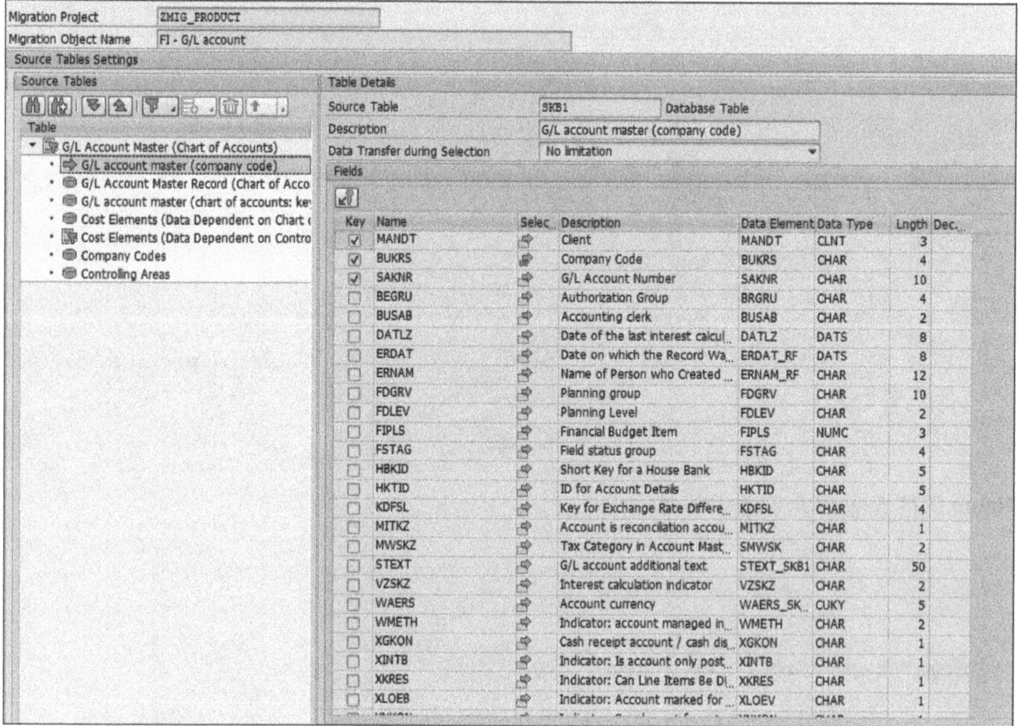

Figure 17.25 Company Code Data

To insert additional tables, click on the **Add Table** button from the top menu, as shown in Figure 17.26.

You can append a table at a lower level, a higher level, or the same level as the selected level, and you can also delete a table. In this way, you can rearrange the tables needed for the migration object and even add additional tables if you determine that more complexity is needed after creating the migration object. This step may save you from the need to delete the migration object and create it again.

Click on **G/L Account Master Record (Chart of Accounts)** to review or change the chart of accounts-related fields, as shown in Figure 17.27.

Similarly, if you click on **Cost Elements (Data Dependent on Controlling Area)**, you can review/update the cost element fields, as shown in Figure 17.28.

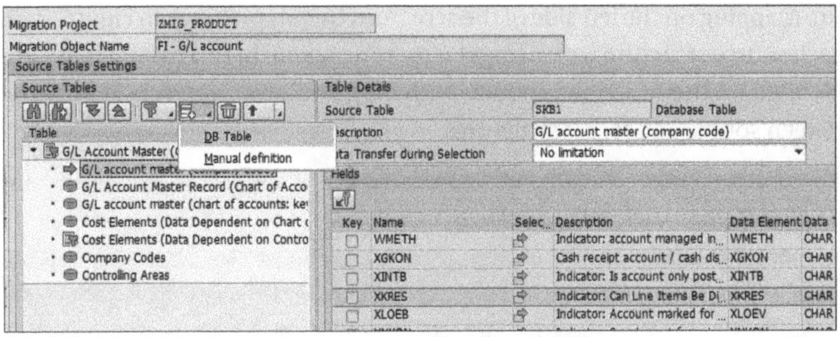

Figure 17.26 Adding a Table

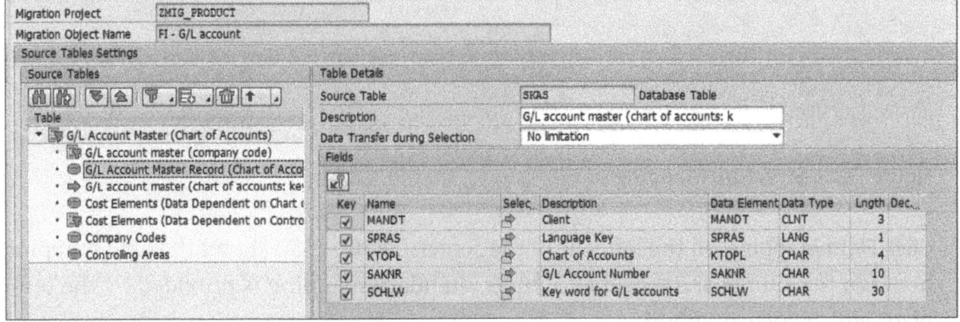

Figure 17.27 Chart of Accounts Data

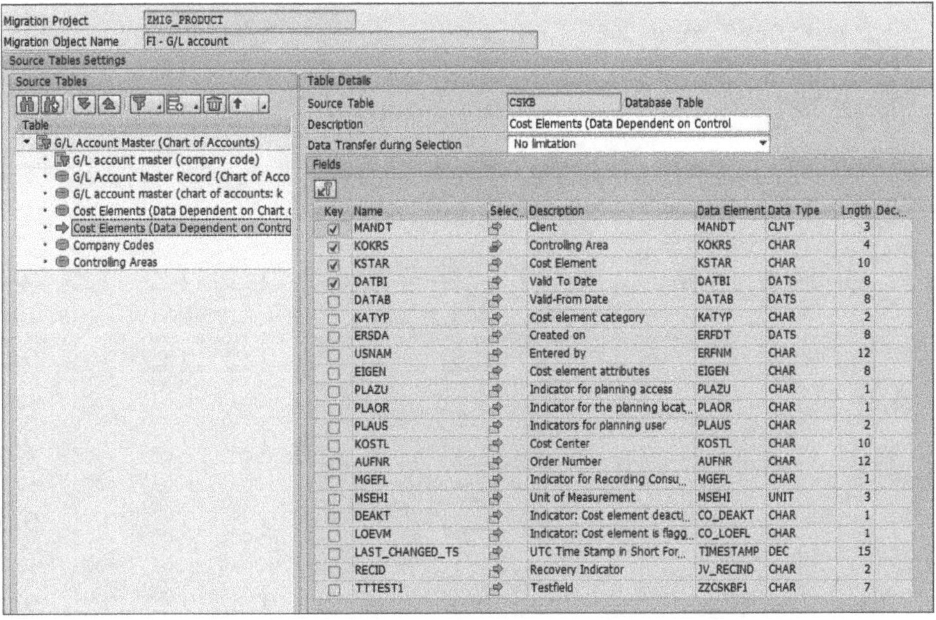

Figure 17.28 Cost Element Data

Click **Structure Mapping** on the left side of the screen. In this step, shown in Figure 17.29, you'll map each source structure with a target structure. Again, in this case, this assignment is predefined by the function module. With drag and drop, you can modify the mapping between source and target structures.

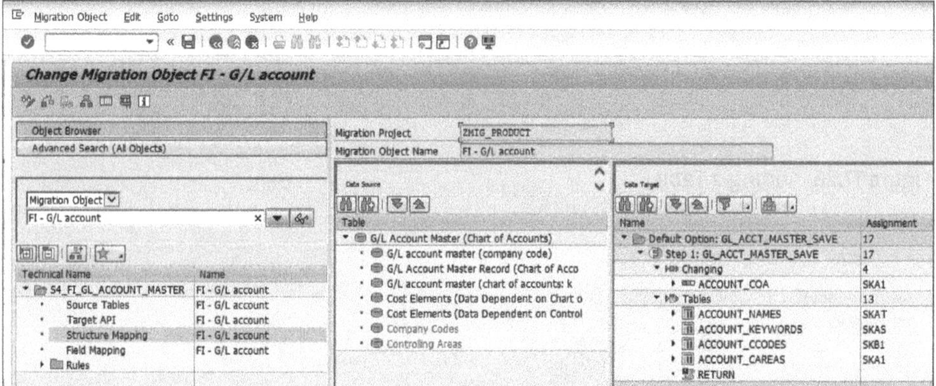

Figure 17.29 Structure Mapping

Click **Field Mapping** on the left side of the screen. Figure 17.30 shows the field mapping between the source and target structures. Standard mapping is provided by the template, which you can modify.

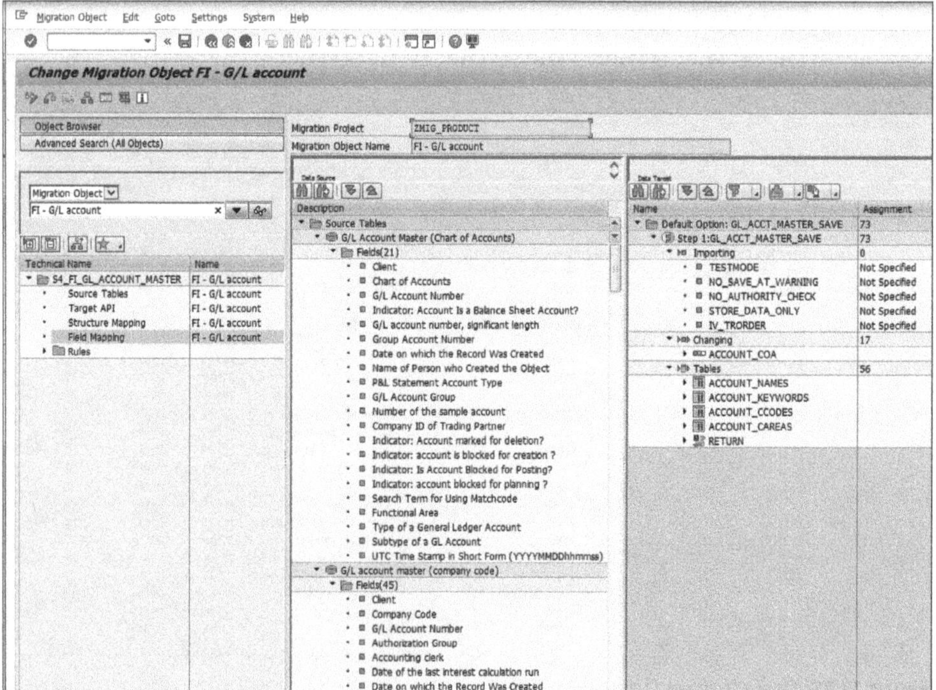

Figure 17.30 Field Mapping

A convenient approach when working with fields enabling the visibility of their technical names by navigating to **Settings • Technical Names On/Off** from the top menu, as shown in Figure 17.31.

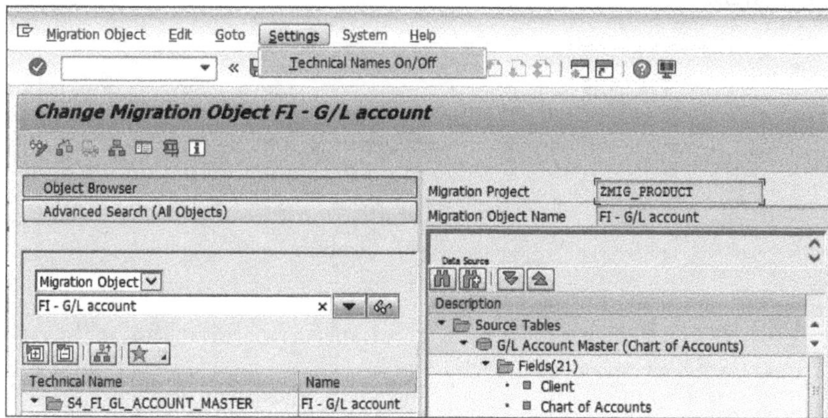

Figure 17.31 Technical Names On

Then, the view changes, as shown in Figure 17.32.

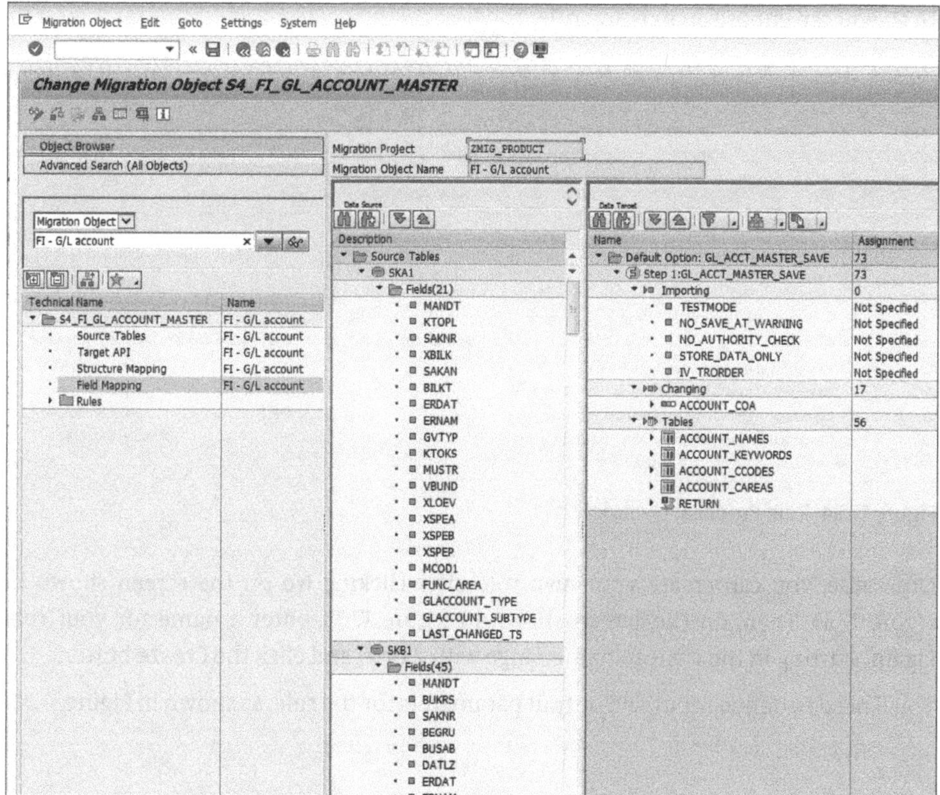

Figure 17.32 Field Mapping with Technical Names

To change the field mapping, you can drag and drop fields from source structures to target structures. When defining field mapping, you must specify rules for the mapping. If you're changing a defined rule mapping, the system shows a popup window, as shown in Figure 17.33.

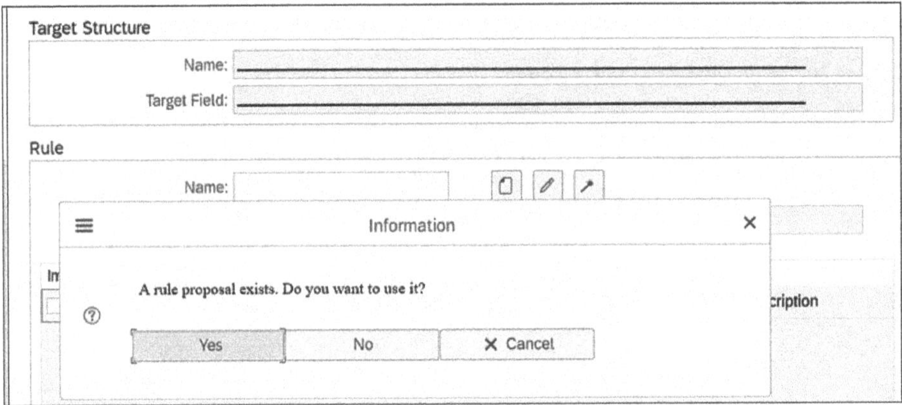

Figure 17.33 Rule Proposal

To use an existing rule, click the **Yes** button. Then, on the next screen, shown in Figure 17.34, you can choose an existing rule.

Target Structure Information

Target Structure	Fieldname	Data Element	Domain	Data Type	Length	Decimal Places	Description
R_DATA	XBILK	XBILK	XFELD	CHAR	1		Indicator: Account is a balance sheet

Rule Proposals

Choose a rule to assign to the target structure above.

Rule	Description	Rule Based on Data Type	Rule Based on Domain	Additional Informatior
CVT_ANZREL	Conversion of Display Relevant in Class		XFELD	Subproject Specific
CVT_ATKLE	Conversion of Case Sensitive of Characteristic Data Type		XFELD	Subproject Specific
CVT_ATSTD	Conversion of Default value in Characteristic Value		XFELD	Subproject Specific
CVT_ATVOR	Conversion of Value with Plus or Minus Sign (Characteristic)		XFELD	Subproject Specific

Figure 17.34 Rule Proposal Overview

Otherwise, you can create your own rule after clicking **No** on the screen shown in Figure 17.33. Then, on the screen shown in Figure 17.35, enter a name for your rule (again, starting in the custom name range with Z or Y) and click the **Create** button.

You'll need to define input and output parameters for the rule, as shown in Figure 17.36.

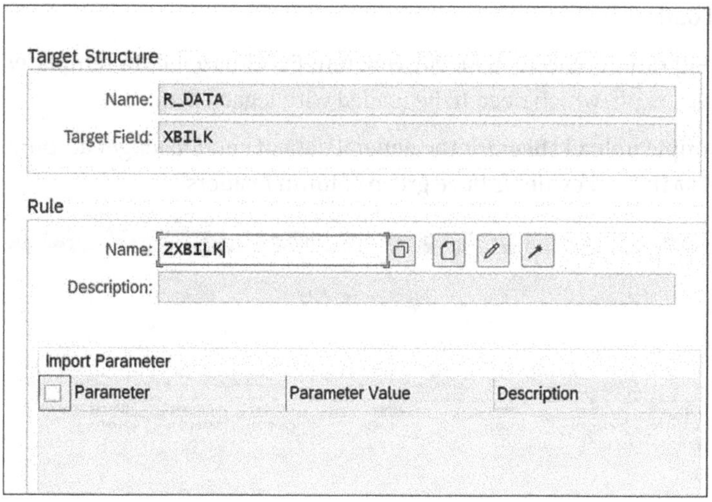

Figure 17.35 Creating a Rule

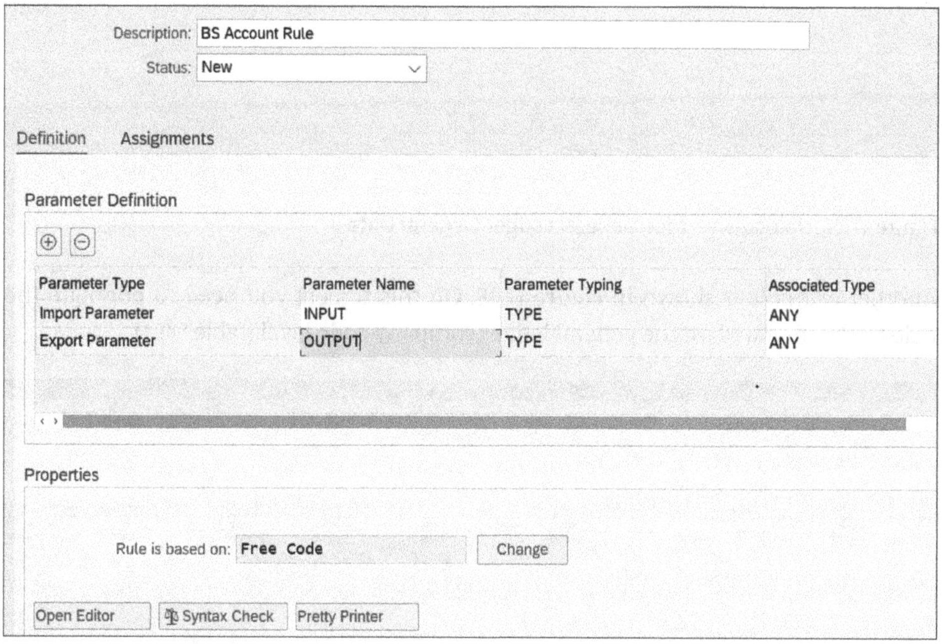

Figure 17.36 Rule Definition

After modifying all relevant settings of the migration object, save these settings by clicking the **Save** button in the lower-right part of the screen and generate it by clicking the **Generate** button from the top menu.

17.2.3 Legacy Data Load

After generating the migration objects, you can generate Excel-based data templates through the migration cockpit, which need to be loaded with legacy data.

Figure 17.37 shows a sample upload sheet for the general data of general ledger account master records (table SKA1). The key fields have green column headers.

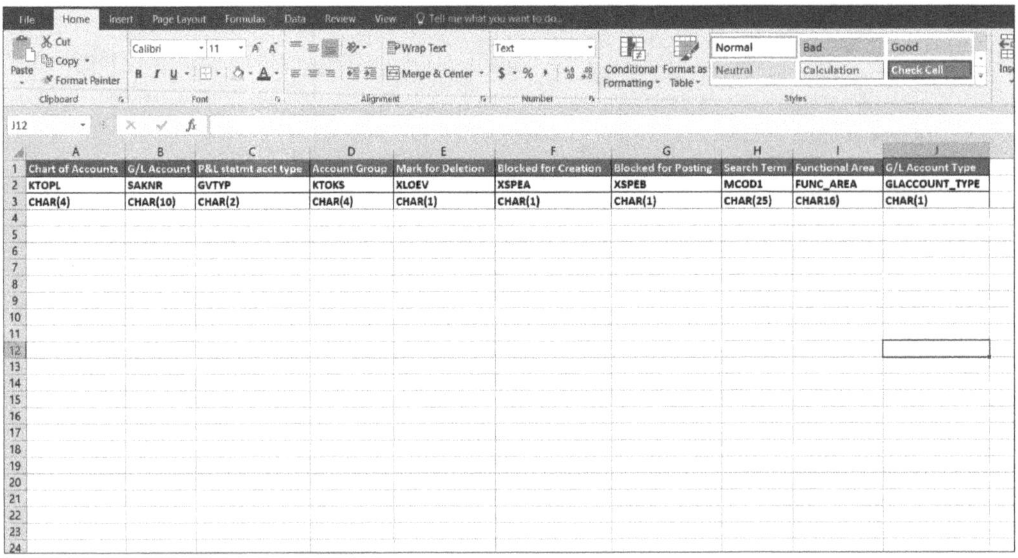

Figure 17.37 Upload Sheet for General Ledger General Data

Another example is shown in Figure 17.38. On this screen, you need to populate the fields to be migrated on the general ledger company code level (table SKB1).

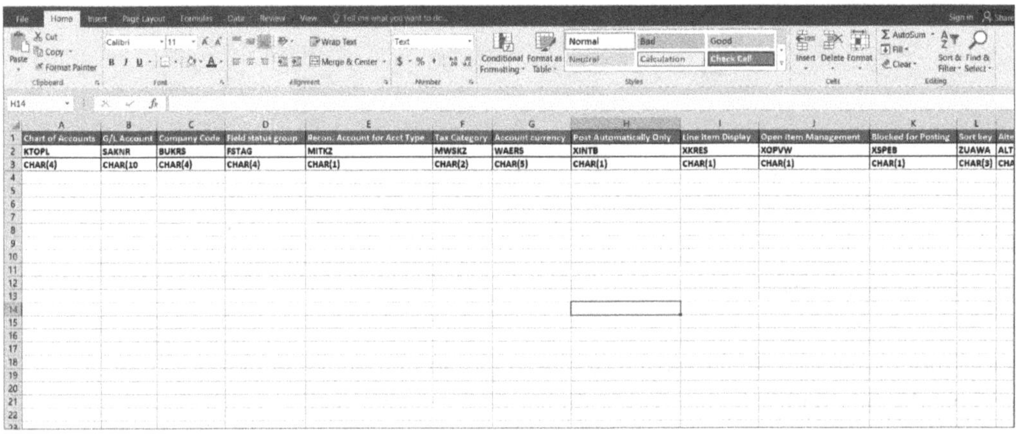

Figure 17.38 Uploading General Ledger Company Code Data

Filling out the upload sheets normally would be a joint responsibility of consultants and client users with a more technical background. Not an easy task, preparing the upload sheets requires time and effort. Normally, the client would provide a set of raw data from their system, which the consultants then should clean, enhance, and validate. Database tools like Microsoft Access can be quite helpful for the process of cleaning and enhancing the legacy data. The final result should be correct upload files for all relevant migration objects, which can be uploaded using the migration cockpit without any issues. Normally, this process requires multiple iterations in test systems.

17.3 Financial Migration Objects

In this section, we'll discuss the specifics of the most important and commonly migrated financial objects. You already learned how to perform migrations in both brownfield and greenfield implementations, and we provided many examples of how to prepare and load the data. In this section, we'll concentrate on the specifics of each object, what data and fields must be migrated, and which tables are filled in SAP S/4HANA.

In the following sections, we'll examine general ledger data, accounts payable/accounts receivable data, fixed assets data, and controlling-related data.

17.3.1 General Ledger Data

In the general ledger, you must migrate the chart of accounts with all general ledger accounts and cost elements as well as migrate general ledger account balances and open items.

The complexity of the general ledger data migration depends on the number of charts of accounts used. At a minimum, you must migrate the operational chart of accounts, which is the main chart of accounts to post all the financial documents. Three related tables in SAP S/4HANA should be filled in with data:

- **Table SKA1**
  Contains the general level data that's relevant for all company codes.
- **Table SKB1**
  Contains the company code level data, which is migrated for each company code.
- **Table SKAT**
  Contains the names and descriptions of the general ledger accounts in multiple languages.

Alternative charts of accounts often are used to depict accounting requirements in various countries. In this case, alternative accounts are mapped to the operational chart of accounts. From a migration point of view, as a result, you'll need to migrate each alternative chart of accounts, which usually are one for each country that requires an alternative chart of accounts. The migration of alternative charts of accounts is simpler than that of the operational chart of accounts because you only need to migrate data in table SKAT to load the account descriptions. Then, of course, these alternative accounts will need to be mapped to the operational chart of accounts.

Figure 17.39 shows the mapping of the alternative account in the **Alternative Account No.** field.

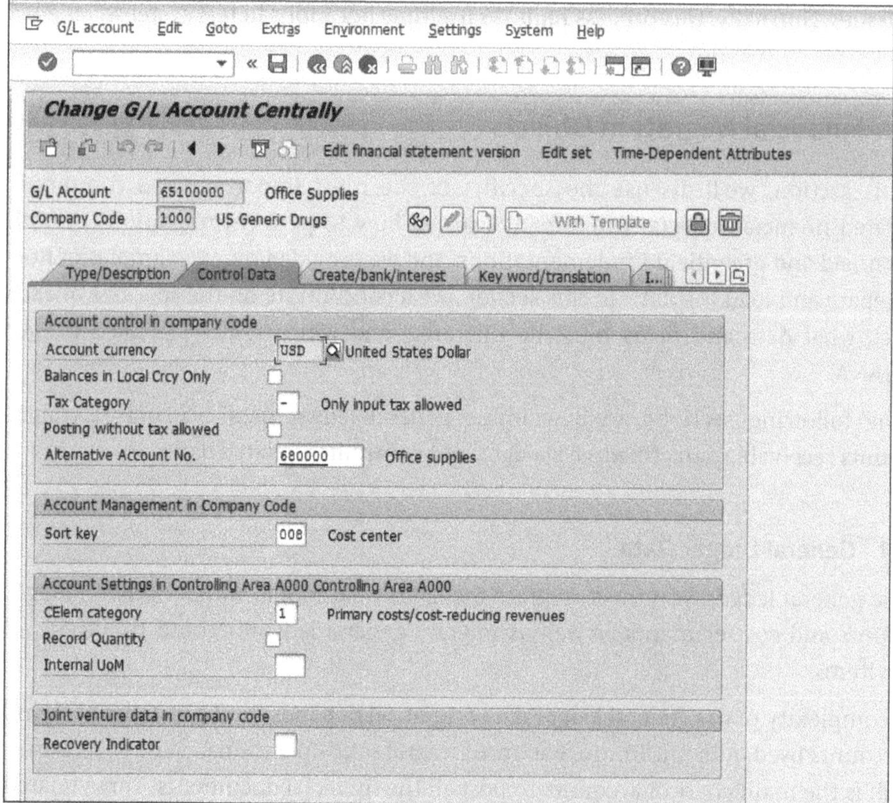

Figure 17.39 Alternative Account Mapping

The group chart of accounts is also used sometimes to depict the group accounts, which also need to be migrated. Its source is the current consolidation system used.

After migrating the general ledger master data, you also need to migrate the general ledger account balances. You should receive the final balances as of the migration date, as close as possible to production go-live. These balances will become the initial balances in your new SAP S/4HANA system.

General ledger accounts that are managed on an open item basis are more complicated because you need to migrate not just the total balance but all open items as well. A good practice is to reduce these accounts as much as possible before go-live.

17.3.2 Accounts Payable and Accounts Receivable Data

In accounts payable/accounts receivable, you'll need to migrate the business partner master records and their open items.

Because customers and vendors in SAP S/4HANA are managed as business partners, which share the same general data, carefully checking your legacy data files and avoiding redundancies are important. Make sure that the general data is created only once for a business partner, which now serves as both customer and vendor data.

One of the key areas to pay attention to is the bank data for business partners. Correctly migrated bank accounts and International Bank Account Numbers (IBANs) ensure proper payment processes in the new SAP S/4HANA system. The main tables that are updated when migrating business partners on the customer and vendor levels remain the same as in previous SAP releases:

- **Table KNA1**
  Customer general data.
- **Table KNB1**
  Customer company code data.
- **Table LFA1**
  Vendor general data.
- **Table LFB1**
  Vendor company code data.

17

After migrating business partner master records, you'll need to migrate the customer and vendor open items as well. These items form the overall accounts receivable and payable balances. As with general ledger account open items, you should try to minimize them before go-live. Now is a good time for the accounts receivable department to try to collect as many outstanding receivables as possible or to write off uncollectable receivables. Similarly, the accounts payable department should try to close as many open payables as possible.

17.3.3 Fixed Assets Data

Fixed assets are one of the more complex migration objects. In SAP S/4HANA, the process of migrating fixed assets has been significantly improved. We'll start by reviewing the fixed asset migration process prior to SAP S/4HANA. The migration was performed in multiple separate steps:

1. Migrate the fixed assets master records and the fixed assets values
2. Migrate the corresponding general ledger account balance values using journal entries and reconcile them with the individual fixed assets values

Now, in SAP S/4HANA, because fixed assets and the general ledger are fully integrated, separate loads of fixed asset values and general ledger entries are not required. Entering the asset values automatically populates the general ledger. You can do the migration automatically or manually. For automatic upload (used in most companies unless data volume is low enough to consider manual entry), you should use the Business Application Programming Interface (BAPI) BAPI_FIXEDASSET_OVRTAKE_CREATE for carrying over the asset data, which both creates the assets and posts the carried over values.

The manual process in SAP S/4HANA starts with the creation of the fixed assets master record using Transaction AS91 (Create Legacy Data), which was used in SAP ERP also, but is no longer used to enter asset values.

Figure 17.40 shows the **Create Legacy Data: Initial screen** page of Transaction AS91.

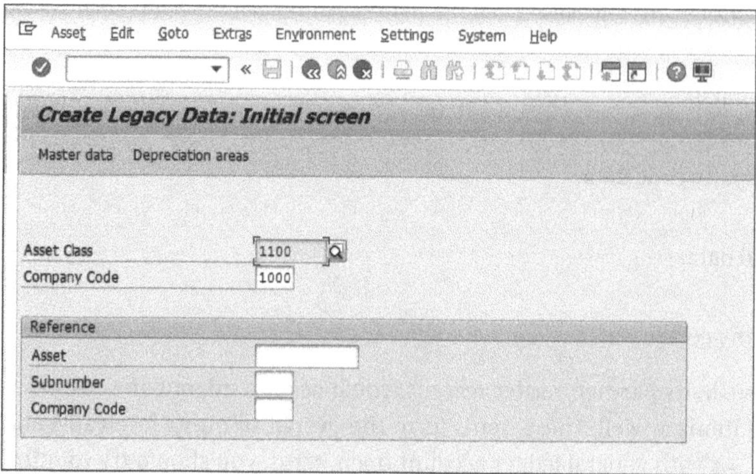

Figure 17.40 Creating Asset Legacy Data

Proceed by pressing the [Enter] key. On the next screen, enter the fixed asset master data information into the various tabs, as we did in Chapter 7, Section 7.2. The difference is that now you also need to enter the capitalization date of the asset, as shown in Figure 17.41.

In this transaction, you won't enter any asset values. You'll handle asset values in the next step, which will post the values in the general ledger at the same time. For this step, in SAP S/4HANA, you'll use the new Transaction ABLDT.

Figure 17.42 shows the initial screen for Transaction ABLDT, in which you'll enter header data such as the company code, asset number, and asset subnumber.

Proceed by clicking the ✓ (**Continue**) button. On the next screen, shown in Figure 17.43, enter the carried over values for each depreciation area.

Asset Edit Goto Extras Environment Settings System Help

Create Legacy Data: Master data

Takeover values Asset values

Asset INTERN-00001 0 Migrated Building

Class 1100 Buildings Company Code 1000

General | Time-dependent | Origin | Deprec. Areas

General data

Description: Migrated Building

Asset Main No. Text: Migrated Building

Account Determ.: 160010 Buildings

Posting information

Capitalized On: 10.02.2020 Deactivation on

First Acquisition on: 10.02.2020

Acquisition Year: 2020 002

Figure 17.41 Legacy Asset Posting Information

Create General Header Data for Posting

Company Code: 1000

Asset: 10000000

Sub-number: 0

Figure 17.42 Legacy Asset Transfer Values Header Data

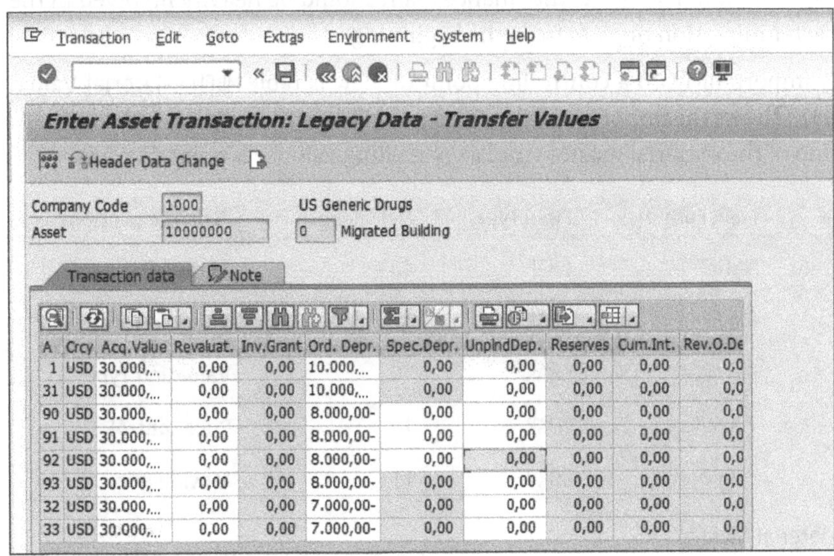

A	Crcy	Acq.Value	Revaluat.	Inv.Grant	Ord. Depr.	Spec.Depr.	UnplndDep.	Reserves	Cum.Int.	Rev.O.De
1	USD	30.000,...	0,00	0,00	10.000,...	0,00	0,00	0,00	0,00	0,0
31	USD	30.000,...	0,00	0,00	10.000,...	0,00	0,00	0,00	0,00	0,0
90	USD	30.000,...	0,00	0,00	8.000,00-	0,00	0,00	0,00	0,00	0,0
91	USD	30.000,...	0,00	0,00	8.000,00-	0,00	0,00	0,00	0,00	0,0
92	USD	30.000,...	0,00	0,00	8.000,00-	0,00	0,00	0,00	0,00	0,0
93	USD	30.000,...	0,00	0,00	8.000,00-	0,00	0,00	0,00	0,00	0,0
32	USD	30.000,...	0,00	0,00	7.000,00-	0,00	0,00	0,00	0,00	0,0
33	USD	30.000,...	0,00	0,00	7.000,00-	0,00	0,00	0,00	0,00	0,0

Figure 17.43 Legacy Asset Transfer: Entering Values

Typically, you'll enter the acquisition value and ordinary depreciation on this screen, and the system will calculate the net book value. You can also enter other types of values, such as revaluation or unplanned depreciation. Then, save your entries by clicking the **Post** button.

In this way, both the asset master data and the values are migrated, either manually or automatically. During the migration, the system populates the general ledger tables automatically also, so manual reconciliation between fixed assets and general ledgers is no longer needed as was the case in SAP ERP.

17.3.4 Controlling-Related Data

In controlling, you'll need to migrate all the controlling objects that you're going to use and have analogs in the legacy system that you're migrating from. Cost centers and profit centers can be migrated using data from the legacy system if their structures will remain similar. During the implementation of SAP S/4HANA, if you come up with a completely new structure for your cost centers and profit centers, their data loads likely won't be based on legacy system data.

If open internal orders and production orders exist in the legacy system, they'll also need to be migrated. This case is typical if the legacy system is an older SAP ERP system.

Another important object to migrate that has a significant impact on controlling is the material master. The material master migration is a joint effort of almost all functional areas in the project because it combines data relevant for most functional teams. For finance, the correct migration of the material master is of utmost importance because it determines the correct costing of materials and the correct account determination and tax determination. Therefore, the finance team should be heavily involved in the material master migration process from the beginning.

Particularly important from a controlling point of view is table MBEW (Material Valuation). Table 17.1 shows the important fields from table MBEW, which should be included in the migration of the material master from a controlling valuation point of view.

Field Name	Field Format	Field Type	Field Length	Field Description
MBEW	MATNR	CHAR	40	**Material**
MBEW	BWKEY	CHAR	4	**Valuation area**
MBEW	BWTAR	CHAR	10	**Valuation Type**
MBEW	VPRSV	CHAR	1	**Price control**
MBEW	VERPR	CURR	11	**Moving price**

Table 17.1 Material Master

Field Name	Field Format	Field Type	Field Length	Field Description
MBEW	PEINH	DEC	5	**Price unit**
MBEW	BKLAS	CHAR	4	**Valuation Class**

Table 17.1 Material Master (Cont.)

17.4 Summary

In this chapter, you learned the processes and best practices for migrating legacy data into your new SAP S/4HANA system. We first discussed various migration options. Fundamentally, two different migration processes exist, depending on whether you're performing a brownfield or greenfield SAP S/4HANA implementation, so we dedicated a separate section to each of these migration paths, which each comes with its own tools and transactions.

You learned that, during a brownfield implementation, a number of programs and transactions have been provided by SAP to help you validate the customizing and data from your existing legacy SAP system. You also learned how to perform the migration and the subsequent steps required.

For greenfield implementations, regardless of whether the legacy system is a non-SAP system or an older SAP system that won't be converted to SAP S/4HANA, SAP provides rather powerful and flexible migration tools: the migration cockpit and migration object modeler. You learned that the migration cockpit is a web-based tool for generating Excel-based data upload templates to be populated with legacy data and then uploaded into SAP S/4HANA. You also learned how to use the migration object modeler to modify the standard-provided migration templates or to create your own.

Finally, you learned about the main finance objects that must be migrated, along with best practices and advice on how to properly migrate them into SAP S/4HANA. In the next chapter, we'll discuss testing your new SAP S/4HANA system.

Chapter 18
Testing

This chapter explains how to properly organize and conduct various stages of testing when implementing SAP S/4HANA.

In the previous chapters, we configured the finance and controlling areas of SAP S/4HANA. We also covered important integration topics related to logistics areas. You should now have a fully configured, robust solution that meets your business requirements.

The next phase in the project is the testing phase. We cannot overstate how important testing is. No matter how well your business requirements are defined, no matter how well your system is configured, properly planned and executed testing ensures the success of the project. Even the best configured system will have some glitches that only well-performed testing can track and resolve. In fact, in our experience, all major issues that occurred after go-live could have been avoided with better test execution.

In this chapter, we'll teach you how to plan, organize, and execute testing in your SAP S/4HANA implementation. We won't focus on specific testing tools, of which there are many, including SAP Solution Manager and many third-party tools. Many tools are excellent, and we have successfully used a few of them. However, what's most important is to learn the processes and best practices you need to follow. At that point, most tools available on the market for test management will suffice to help you deliver sound test results.

18.1 The Testing Process

Testing is a process, and as such, you'll need to define clearly what needs to be accomplished, in what timeframe, and what the expected results are. In this section, we'll discuss testing strategies, which will be helpful for your SAP S/4HANA implementation, but also for any other enterprise resource planning (ERP) implementation because the testing concepts and best practices we'll discuss are valid also for many other IT projects.

Before you start with testing, you'll need to plan your testing carefully, including choosing your testing tools and defining the requirements for testing documentation, as we'll discuss in the following sections.

18.1.1 Test Plan

Your test plan should clearly define the various testing phases and their subphases, if relevant; the milestones that mark the successful completion of each phase and subphase; the resources from the client and consulting sides that will participate; and the deadlines according to the project plan.

The phases of a test plan should be well integrated within the overall project plan. Typical phases in SAP S/4HANA testing include the following:

- **Unit testing**
  Unit testing is performed during the realization phase of the project, while consultants and developers are building the system. In this testing, they test the functionalities being configured and developed, usually in a sandbox client and unit testing client.
- **Integration testing**
  Integration testing is performed after the build is complete and is part of the testing phase in the overall project plan. Integration testing is usually performed in a specially designated test client. This kind of testing involves experts from the whole project team, who will test the integrated functionalities, focusing on end-to-end (E2E) processes.
- **User acceptance testing**
  User acceptance testing is conducted by the future users of the system with the help of the consulting team. Usually, every process area has one or more key users designated, whose job is to thoroughly test the new system and functionalities and sign off on the testing results, thus giving a green light for the productive start of the system.

Different ways to plan test cycles and related resources are available. Figure 18.1 shows a possible test plan across the phases.

Testing should be organized into test cycles. Each cycle has a different scope, as in the example test plan shown in Figure 18.1. The first test cycle starts with unit testing, in which the consulting team tests the functionalities of the system in their individual units. The execution is performed by functional consultants with only limited support from key users. After completing the unit testing within that first testing cycle, limited integration tests can be executed that test the integrated processes, still mainly conducted by functional consultants with some involvement of the key users.

The second test cycle should be quite expansive, testing all functionalities of the integrated system. This cycle can be a considerable effort, which should start after the system is fully developed. Not only should all integrated functionalities be tested, but also regression testing should be conducted to test existing functionalities in the new environment. This step is needed in brownfield implementations, in which even functionalities that haven't changed should be regression-tested for possible problems. This cycle also includes authorization testing, which tests the security built in the new system and the various user profiles and roles. This step is needed in both brownfield and greenfield implementations and involves checking the access to the various transactions that the users should and should not be able to access. This second test iteration should involve most project resources, not only consultants and key users, but also business and IT resources from the client side, which are not engaged by the project on a regular basis. This approach enables a high level of confidence that the system that is being built to meet business requirements and that no technical glitches exist.

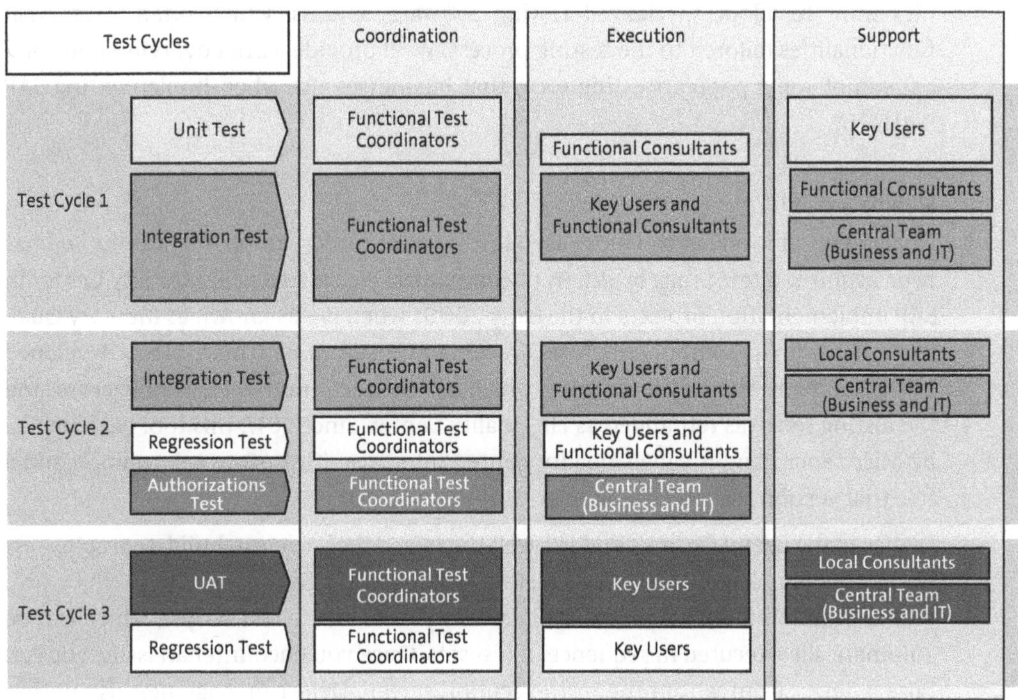

Figure 18.1 Test Plan

Finally, the third test cycle in this sample test plan is when the users actively test the fully integrated system. Thus, user acceptance testing is especially important because users can best attest that the new system is performing well and according to the business requirements. The role of the consultants in this cycle is supportive: to guide users and resolve defects, but not to test directly. This cycle also involves regression testing, now performed by users to make sure existing functionalities (for a brownfield implementation) still work correctly in the new environment.

18.1.2 Testing Tools

We touched on the topic of testing tools at the beginning of the chapter. Without a doubt, your testing effort will benefit tremendously from using specialized testing

18

tools to record the test results, manage the defects, and track the progress. Of course, you can also perform these tasks without specialized software, just by using Excel sheets and Word documents, but a central testing tool is much more efficient because it's easier to check and audit and can provide numerous helpful reports on the test progress.

We won't recommend a specific tool. In our experience, SAP Solution Manager does a very good job as a testing tool and is needed for many other functions within the project as well, so utilizing it as a testing tool makes perfect sense. However, many companies want to adopt specialized testing software options, which often have great functionalities tailored to the testing process. We'll provide a brief overview and comparison of some popular testing tools that businesses use when implementing SAP S/4HANA.

Quality Center

Quality Center is one of the most used testing tools for SAP implementations and has been acquired a few times by different companies. We started using Quality Center in SAP implementation projects in the early 2000s when it was known as Mercury Quality Center, with its components Test Director and LoadRunner. This tool was developed by the company Mercury Interactive, which was then acquired by Hewlett Packard, and the testing tool was rebranded as HP Quality Center. Since 2017, this tool been owned by Micro Focus and is called Quality Center Enterprise (QC). More information and a free trial version are available at *http://s-prs.co/v485703*.

QC has many useful features and is a well-organized tool. You can build a complex test plan that incorporates the various testing cycles and further subdivides them by process area and functionality. This tool enables you to create test scripts, which can be automatically executed in sequence in test sets. Once you encounter an issue, you can raise a defect from within the test execution screen. Defect management is another major component of the tool. You can track and manage defects, record all relevant information in a defect, and monitor the progress of the resolution. QC also offers a rich selection of reports, which enables you to efficiently track the testing progress and the defect management process.

Ranorex Studio

Ranorex Studio is a sophisticated testing tool tailored to the needs of testing SAP systems. This tool provided by the Austrian company Ranorex GmbH and offers reusable components, which enables faster test case development and execution. Among its useful features is video reporting of test execution, which enables you to see what happened in a test run without rerunning it.

The SAP testing offering from Ranorex Studio is available at *http://s-prs.co/v485704*.

Selenium

Selenium is a web-based and portable solution, which is especially useful when testing web-based applications such as the SAP Fiori apps and portal applications. Selenium offerings are available at *https://www.seleniumhq.org/*.

Worksoft

Worksoft is a US company with extensive experience in providing sophisticated testing technology. Its Worksoft tool has proven itself in countless SAP implementations. This tool offers good test automation and is especially good for testing E2E processes. More information is available at *http://s-prs.co/v485705*.

Whatever the tool, its main tasks are to provide a comprehensive and clear structure for all the test phases and areas, record the test results, manage defects arising from testing, and provide useful and flexible reporting. Therefore, you should consider several requirements for the testing tool you will use in your test planning.

When using a testing tool, normally, a hierarchical structure contains all the test cases, organized by testing phase and functional area. This structure should have functions to run the test case, record test results, and record the status (passed versus failed). For a failed test case, a convenient interface should be provided to create defects, in which you can describe the expected outcome, the actual outcome, and the possible causes. A defect should be linked with the relevant test case. After resolving the defect, the test case execution can continue until it passes.

At any moment, the testing tool should be able to provide detailed reporting that shows the actual test results in comparison with the testing plan. This capability is one of the main benefits of having a dedicated test tool, versus recording the test results in separate documents.

18.1.3 Testing Documentation

Testing documentation is one of the most important deliverables of the testing process. Testing documentation keeps track of the results of the testing and serves as support for the decision to sign off on the testing and approve the productive start of the system. Testing is also subject to IT audits, and the testing documentation should be kept according to the internal control standards of the organization.

The testing documentation should consist of test cases that include all the relevant functional steps that were tested. Documentation should clearly indicate the test result in each iteration, and for failed tests, detailed information about what went wrong and how it was corrected should be provided. Information about the user IDs used for testing and the date and time of execution should also be included.

Standardized templates should be used by the project for the test cases, the defects, and any other relevant testing documentation. These templates can be generated from the testing tool or can be set up in Word or Excel.

Let's review sample test document designed in Excel. Figure 18.2 shows a sample test document, which has two separate sheets. The first sheet keeps track of the version control. The creation of the document and every change made in the document are recorded in this sheet, with information regarding who made the change, when, and any relevant comments.

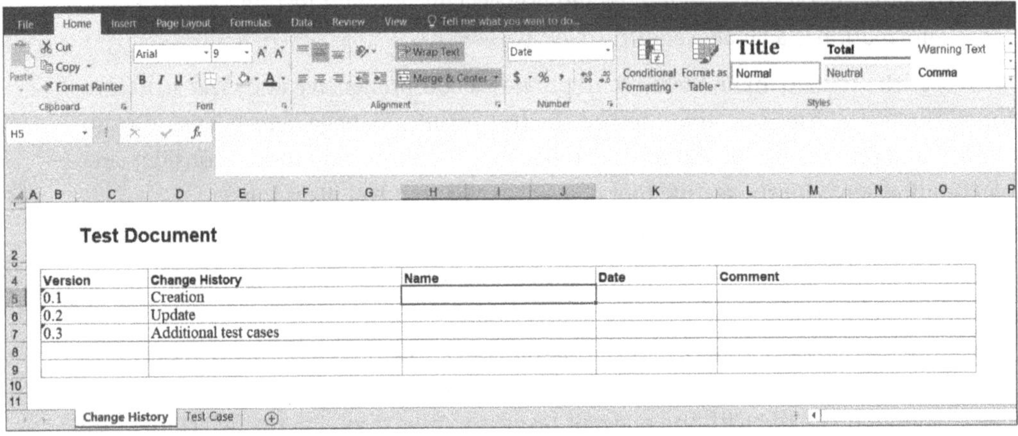

Figure 18.2 Test Document Version Control

On the second sheet, the test steps within the test case are recorded. The example shown in Figure 18.3 is for a test case for fixed asset depreciation. The header section records administrative information about the test case, such as the author of the test case, what the prerequisites are, who approved the test case, who the tester is, and the date of execution.

This test case is relatively simple with only two test steps: running depreciation and checking the depreciation log. The test document contains information about the transactions that should be executed and the required input data. Columns are set up for the expected and actual results.

Depending on the testing phase, test cases can be short, as in our example, which is a unit test, or very long, which typically is an E2E test case, which aims to test full business processes in their logical entirety across the relevant areas of SAP.

Now, let's dive deeply into the various testing phases and their specifics.

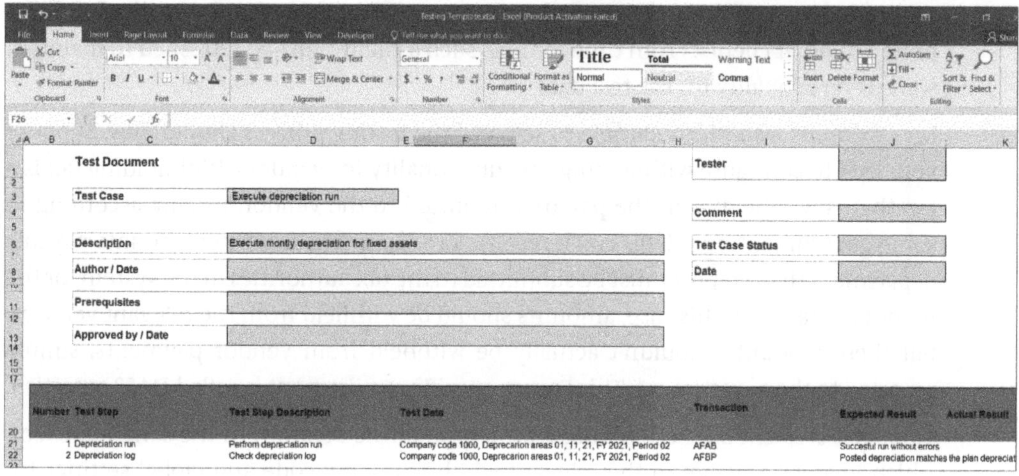

Figure 18.3 Test Case Document

18.2 Unit Testing

Unit testing is the process of testing newly configured and developed functionalities on their own, rather than in integration with the whole E2E process.

Unit testing is performed during the realization phase of the project. The realization phase consists of the configuration of the various functionalities required to meet the business requirements, and the development of reports, interfaces, conversions, enhancements, forms, and workflows (RICEFW) objects, which comprise all the objects that require custom programming.

All the configuration and development objects must be tested first by the consultants responsible for their development in unit testing. Unit testing is rather important because this testing is the first test of the newly configured or developed functionality. Proper unit testing saves a lot of time during future iterations of integration testing because bugs and issues can be caught early in the project lifecycle.

Let's now examine the specifics of unit testing in a system sandbox client and in a unit test client.

18.2.1 Sandbox Client Testing

When you need to configure new functionality, normally, first you'll configure the functionality in a so-called *sandbox client*. A sandbox client is a client in your development system that's open for customizing and is intended for research and experimenting. Normally, a sandbox doesn't have clean data because many consultants use it as a proof of concept area and to research various topics. Nothing from this client is transported to other clients. From time to time, such a client must be refreshed to maintain some level of quality for the test data.

Let's examine a specific example to see how the testing process should flow. Suppose you need to configure withholding tax functionality for vendors. Withholding tax is a tax that is withheld from the payment remitted to the vendor, usually according to some government mandate. You'll receive a requirement from the accounts payable department that a report must be submitted to the tax authorities in the system for the rollout in France. In this case, amounts should be withheld from the relevant vendors, but these amounts shouldn't actually be withheld from vendor payments, simply reported to the government. This France-specific requirement is called *DAS2 reporting*.

Your first step should be building a prototype of the solution in the sandbox client, which involves setting up the relevant withholding tax code and global settings for withholding tax calculation, then maintaining a business partner with that withholding tax code. Then, you must test the process in the sandbox. You should construct a simple unit test case, which includes the following:

- Posting the vendor outgoing invoice to a vendor with the relevant withholding tax code
- Checking withholding tax data on the invoice
- Processing a payment run that includes the vendor
- Running report S_P00_07000134 (Generic Withholding Tax Reporting) to check the results and generate a reporting file for the authorities

After you're satisfied with the results, you can configure the solution in a clean configuration client.

18.2.2 Unit Testing Client Testing

You should have a client that doesn't contain any transactional data to use for configuration. After configuring your solution in that client, your settings should be transported to a client dedicated to unit testing. In this test client, you can post the test data that you used in the sandbox client also. In this case, however, the testing should be more formal, and you should keep test documentation proving that the test was passed successfully. Test documentation should include screenshots from the posted document, the payment, and the executed report.

Figure 18.4 shows the output of the withholding tax report proving the correctness of the test case.

Part of this test case is also to generate a DAS2 reporting file, which must be submitted to tax authorities in France. Thus, unit testing should include a step to check the correctness of this file to make sure the format works.

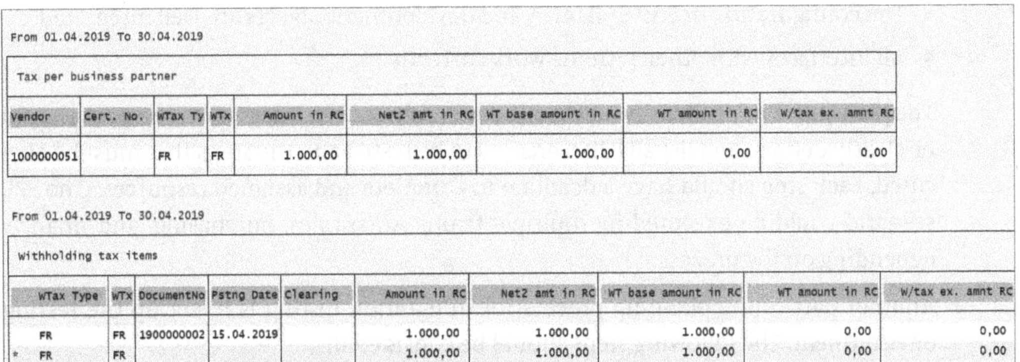

From 01.04.2019 To 30.04.2019

Tax per business partner

Vendor	Cert. No.	WTax Ty	WTx	Amount in RC	Net2 amt in RC	WT base amount in RC	WT amount in RC	W/tax ex. amnt RC
1000000051		FR	FR	1.000,00	1.000,00	1.000,00	0,00	0,00

From 01.04.2019 To 30.04.2019

Withholding tax items

WTax Type	WTx	DocumentNo	Pstng Date	Clearing	Amount in RC	Net2 amt in RC	WT base amount in RC	WT amount in RC	W/tax ex. amnt RC
FR	FR	1900000002	15.04.2019		1.000,00	1.000,00	1.000,00	0,00	0,00
* FR	FR				1.000,00	1.000,00	1.000,00	0,00	0,00

Figure 18.4 Test Case Support Documentation

After successful completion of the unit test, the new functionality is ready to be moved to a special integration testing client, where it can be tested in relation to the whole E2E process into which it fits.

18.3 Integration Testing

Integration testing is part of the testing phase in the overall project plan, along with the user acceptance testing, and this kind of testing starts after the realization phase is complete. Thus, the whole build of the system should be completed, including all configuration activities and all development RICEFW objects. Any changes to configuration or development beyond this point should be considered change requests.

Integration testing is performed in a quality assurance client, which should contain valid test data that closely resembles the expected productive data.

Let's discuss how to plan integration testing. Then, we'll examine the various phases of integration testing and the documentation that should be produced during the testing.

18.3.1 Planning

The project planning of the integration testing is quite important because integration testing should involve a big part of the project resources. The plan for integration testing should clearly define its objectives. These objectives could be any or all of the following:

- The defined solution that had been built is working correctly from a technical point of view.
- The integration of all SAP S/4HANA areas works correctly.
- The integration of all SAP S/4HANA business processes works correctly.

- The configuration of SAP S/4HANA and development objects are well integrated.
- All interfaces with other systems work correctly.

The plan should also identify all the needed resources. An integration test plan should be clearly defined and list all E2E scenarios to be tested and the steps that must be executed. Each step should have a deadline to complete and assigned resources. One E2E scenario could be executed by multiple teams, such sales, purchasing, and finance, depending on the process.

Another part of the planning process for integration testing is to set up the testing environment. The following steps should be considered:

1. Move all configuration and workbench transports to the integration testing client. Pay special attention to the sequence of moving transports because moving them in the wrong order often poses problems. You should be using a tool for managing transports like Change Request Management (ChaRM) in SAP Solution Manager, rather than keeping track of them in Excel sheets.
2. Check the configuration before starting integration testing.
3. Complete manual configuration steps such as setting up number ranges and other nontransportable objects.
4. Set up the required master data, such as material masters, business partners, and so on.
5. Set up test user IDs and communicate them to the relevant resources.

18.3.2 Phases

The integration phase is the most extensive part of the testing lifecycle and therefore should be well structured in separate phases with clearly defined milestones. Broadly, the integration phase consists of a preparation phase and an execution phase, which we'll now examine in detail.

Preparation Phase

The preparation phase includes all the steps that need to be performed prior to starting testing. Included is setting up the testing environment, which we explained in the previous section when we talked about planning the integration testing.

In addition, the preparation phase includes the following activities:

- Defining the scope of testing. The testing scope should include all business scenarios, E2E processes, interfaces to other systems, and period-end closing activities that are planned to go live in the productive system.
- Defining the relevant organizational structures and master data for testing.

- Creating test scripts, either manually or in the testing tool that's going to be used.
- Assigning testers to the testing scripts and defining the timeline of each testing step.

Also in the preparation phase, you must define the defect management process. For each error identified during integration testing, a defect should be created that explains the issues, including screenshots if relevant, and is assigned to the relevant technical expert that can solve it. Testing tools are especially handy in the defect management process because they enable transparent and smooth tracking and management of the defect. When using a testing tool, each defect will have its own number assigned, making assigning it to the correct resource from the correct team easy, and you'll be able to track the status of all relevant defects easily as well. You'll be able to set priorities for defects as well. The most important issues that prevent further test execution would have a very high priority, and you can assign high, medium, and low priorities to other defects as appropriate.

Execution Phase

The execution phase is when all the integration tests are executed, and defects are created for the various issues that arise during testing. More specifically, the following flow of activities can be considered:

1. Test users run their assigned test cases and record the test results.
2. Testers raise defects against the issues they discover.
3. Project management tracks the timely resolution of defects and escalates when needed.
4. Project management organizes daily testing status meetings in which issues can be discussed, progress can be monitored, and any changes to the testing schedule can be communicated to the testing team.
5. Project management follows up on any reported test blockers that need to be removed promptly.
6. Test reports are generated and communicated to all relevant stakeholders.
7. The testing documentation is completed after successful execution of integration tests.

With many testing tools, the execution of tests is performed from within the tool. In the tool, test scripts will be set up that contain the specific transactions to be executed in the system and the specific steps to take within these transactions. The tool should have a start and stop button, which allows you to start and end the test. At the same time, the tool will record a log of the execution time and duration.

When you encounter an error in the system, testing tools normally provide a convenient interface to create a defect from within the test script.

Defects are central objects within the testing documentation, which aim to track issues in detail and record how they were resolved. Some of their functions include the following capabilities:

- Provide information regarding the impact of the issue in the system: low, medium, high, or very high. Low-impact issues should be able to be resolved quickly because they have lower complexity, such as a missing number range, for example. On the other hand, very high impact defects are very complex issues that require time and effort and sometimes work from multiple teams.
- Provide information regarding the priority of the issue: low, medium, high, or very high. Low-priority defects do not stop further test execution, whereas without resolving the high-priority and very high-priority defects further execution will be blocked, thus resulting in loss of time and resources.
- Provide information regarding the classification of issues. Using reports on defects, you should be able to locate all defects related to product costing quickly, for example, or all very high priority defects in finance.
- Track and improve the progress of issue resolution. One of the main tasks of a proper defect management process is to speed up resolution, which is achieved by utilizing the reporting capabilities of the testing tool and applying management pressure where needed.
- Manage the escalation progress and keep track of the escalation logs. If a high-priority defect hasn't been resolved for a long time, project management should be able to analyze why and what happened and use these analytics to improve the process for the future.

The execution phase can consist of a couple of different iteration cycles. The first iteration may start before the build is fully complete to get better confidence in the system setup ahead of time. The more iteration cycles of integration testing are performed, the better the system will be tested and the more error-free the setup will be. But, of course, the benefit of having such extensive integration testing needs to be compared with the extended cost and time investments.

18.3.3 Documentation

As you can imagine, integration testing requires a lot more extensive documentation than unit testing. Whereas unit test cases can be prepared by the functional consultant, and whereas using test tools for unit testing is not important, integration test cases should be defined in strong collaboration with the business.

Figure 18.5 shows an integration test case template for controlling operating expenses (OPEX). As opposed to the unit test case, which included only transactions related to the asset accounting depreciation, which was tested on its own, in this case, the process steps include transactions from controlling and the project system, along with various logistics transactions.

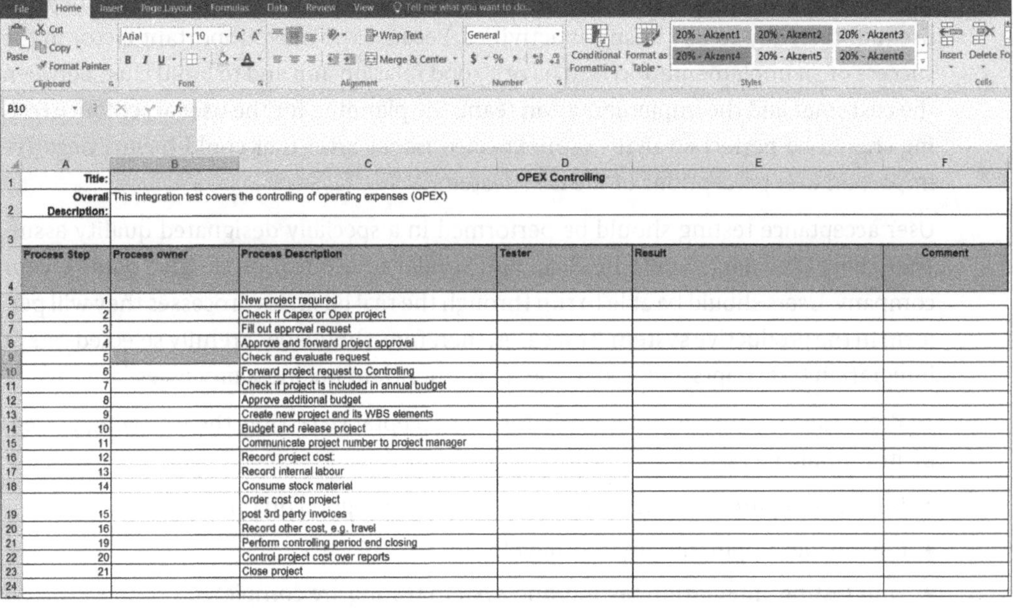

Title:	OPEX Controlling				
Overall Description:	This integration test covers the controlling of operating expenses (OPEX)				
Process Step	**Process owner**	**Process Description**	**Tester**	**Result**	**Comment**
1		New project required			
2		Check if Capex or Opex project			
3		Fill out approval request			
4		Approve and forward project approval			
5		Check and evaluate request			
6		Forward project request to Controlling			
7		Check if project is included in annual budget			
8		Approve additional budget			
9		Create new project and its WBS elements			
10		Budget and release project			
11		Communicate project number to project manager			
12		Record project cost:			
13		Record internal labour			
14		Consume stock material			
15		Order cost on project post 3rd party invoices			
16		Record other cost, e.g. travel			
19		Perform controlling period end closing			
20		Control project cost over reports			
21		Close project			

Figure 18.5 Integration Test Case

Therefore, to document integration testing is a more demanding task, requiring the collaboration of teams of testers from different process areas. 18

Also, the integration testing documentation is important because documentation can serve as a basis for the approval of the test results and for moving to the next phase of user acceptance testing. Therefore, integration testing documentation is subject to IT system audits and should comply with established internal control standards.

Once all iterations of the integration testing are complete, the testing phase of the project continues with the user acceptance testing.

18.4 User Acceptance Testing

In this final testing phase, customers (the future users of the system) test the system. Only after user acceptance testing is complete should a company should finally provide sign off that the system is functioning correctly and in line with business requirements.

In this section, you'll learn how to perform the planning that's the foundation of successful user acceptance testing. Then, we'll delve into the execution of user acceptance testing, which has a lot of specific considerations compared to the execution of the unit and integration testing.

18.4.1 Planning

User acceptance testing is important and sensitive. In this phase, users should become comfortable enough to agree that the new system is built correctly and that they can use it in their day-to-day business activities. Because the most important factor in the success of an implementation is to have a good relationship and to build trust between the customer and the implementation team, the planning for the user acceptance testing should be perfect so that no unexpected issues arise that could have a negative impact on user perceptions of the new system.

User acceptance testing should be performed in a specially designated quality assurance client. The data should be clean and similar to the real productive data of your company. Users should be able to run through the real business processes they will perform in the productive system. Test cases, therefore, should be carefully selected sets of integration test scripts, tailored to the most important business processes.

To determine if your system is ready for user acceptance testing, the following prerequisites should be met:

- Business requirements are fully agreed upon and signed off on.
- Custom developments are fully developed.
- Unit testing, integration testing, and system testing are completed.
- No high-level or medium-level defects in unit testing and integration testing remain.
- Only a few cosmetic errors are acceptable before entering user acceptance testing.
- Authorization testing should be completed.
- Regression testing should be completed.
- The user acceptance testing system environment should be fully set up.

18.4.2 Execution

The execution of the user acceptance testing takes a lot of collaboration because this testing is done exclusively by business users. Consultants will take a backseat advisory role, helping users if they need advice on how to execute a test and working on any possible defects.

Logistically, we recommend organizing business users that will perform user acceptance testing together during the weeks of the testing in an onsite location. Doing so makes the testing process much more efficient because most business processes require a lot of collaboration between the various departments and users. Also, when working in a common onsite location, collaboration between the users and the consultants can be efficient: Consultants can support the users much more effectively, and working on defects will be much faster.

Organizing a big group of business users together at a specific time is no easy task, especially because some users may have high-level positions with many important obligations. Therefore, user acceptance testing should be planned well in advance so that the availability of the resources is assured in the planned weeks of testing.

A good practice is to organize user acceptance testing in a central location close to a major airport. Travelling to remote locations will limit the onsite availability of resources, and executing test cases remotely and connecting with consultants via remote chat and conference calls, isn't optimal for the user acceptance testing phase.

In terms of specific steps, user acceptance testing should include the following:

1. Development of the user acceptance testing test plan
2. Defining test scenarios
3. Development of user acceptance testing test cases
4. Setting up test data, which should be similar to production data
5. Execution of the test cases by the users
6. Recording the test results
7. Confirming the results and signing off on user acceptance testing

Test scenarios should be as similar to the real business processes as possible. Users should run through test cases that represent their real productive work. Because extensive test cases are already created for integration testing, normally, you should be able to reuse a lot of them, with some minor adjustments so that they include only the user-relevant steps. Therefore, user acceptance testing should be part of the integration testing test scripts scope.

The best way to execute user acceptance testing is again using a testing tool, which allows the user to run test scripts from within the tool, record the results, and raise defects when needed. Then, because the timeframe for user acceptance testing is usually much shorter than for integration testing, these defects should be managed well and resolved in a timely manner. User acceptance testing can be organized over 1, 2, or 3 weeks, depending on the complexity, and also in a few different iterations because it will be difficult to book 3 consecutive weeks of full dedication from business users. Therefore, in the weeks when you have these users onsite for user acceptance testing, good project organization should be in place so that all technical resources are available and can collaborate efficiently to resolve defects.

Often, the defects reported during user acceptance testing are not in fact system defects but are caused by misunderstandings from users or lack of familiarity with the new system setup. Of course, users should have already had training sessions on the new system before starting user acceptance testing, but relevant functional teachers should be there with the business users and "hold their hands" along the way if needed. Some users will need more attention than others because they all have different levels of SAP experience, from nonexistent to extensive.

More specifically in the area of finance, the users performing user acceptance testing will be well experienced in accounting and controlling and may already have strong experience working with SAP solutions, for instance, in the case of a brownfield implementation or a greenfield implementation that replaces an existing SAP ERP system. Prior experience can make the user acceptance testing execution process much easier, but still, as you've learned throughout the course of this book, a lot of new functionalities have been introduced with SAP S/4HANA. Make sure that you educate your finance users extensively about the new finance integration in SAP S/4HANA and the Universal Journal. Controlling and fixed asset users especially will need a lot of support to learn how all data is integrated in the Universal Journal and posted in real time. For example, legacy SAP users would expect ledger-specific posting in fixed assets to be completed with a separate month-end procedure, whereas now in SAP S/4HANA, these postings occur in real time.

18.4.3 Documentation

After execution of the various iterations of user acceptance testing and resolving the high- and medium-priority defects, explicit sign-offs should be obtained for every test case from the users. This step is quite important because the user acceptance testing sign-off serves as one of the most important factors for the decision to go live with the new system. Therefore, the documentation that's prepared during user acceptance testing is key and should be stored carefully for future IT audits.

Defects that are being worked on should have a clear log that shows the causes of the issues, how they were resolved, and the timeframe of resolution. Sometimes, defects are not truly defects but really process questions or misunderstandings from business users. Still, these issues need to be tracked as defects so that you can analyze what caused them and how training and communication processes can be improved.

The test scripts for user acceptance testing should be organized by process area in the testing tool being used. An archive of these scripts should also be downloaded and made available in a collaboration platform such as a SharePoint folder for future checks and audits.

User acceptance testing test scripts should contain more details about how to execute test cases because business users generally need more extensive instructions.

Figure 18.6 shows a sample user acceptance testing test script. Notice that this script contains more specific instructions on how to execute transactions and what the expected outcome is. The tester should record the test results, such as posted documents, and indicate whether a test passed or failed.

Another good practice is to have formal user acceptance testing sign-off forms that users can sign to confirm successful user acceptance testing. Figure 18.7 shows a sample user acceptance form to be completed after completing user acceptance testing. On this form, the user should sign off to indicate that she's confident that the testing performed represents the business processes well and the test cases passed.

UAT TEST SCRIPT

Test Script: FIN- FA-Asset life cycle
Document Version: 1.0

Test Script Title:	FIN- Asset life cycle		
Test Script Description:	Perform asset life cycle		
Environment:	Q01-100		
Associated CR or Incident #:			
Changed Object(s) / Code:		**Object Version:**	
Transport Migration Control ID:		**Build Version:**	
Trace to Design Element:	FIN -FA- Integration		
Executed Date:			

Step	Description / Action	Expected Results	Pass / Fail (Circle One)
1.	Create Asset Master Record Transaction: AS01	The system displays the Create Asset: Initial Screen. The values between the depreciation areas will always be identical. Asset ----------- has been created.	Pass / Fail
2.	Post external acquisition value to the asset using Transaction: ABSO	Acquisition document should be posted across all ledgers Document --------------- has been posted to all ledgers	Pass / Fail
3	Run asset explorer to check the values Transaction: AW01N	Acquisition value in for US GAAP (01) and IFRS (02). Local (03) and Tax (04) Depreciation has been calculated.	Pass / Fail
4	Execute depreciation for 01/2021. Transaction: AFAB	Depreciation will be calculated in all depreciation areas and posted in all ledgers. Document ------ has posted for all ledgers	Pass / Fail
5	Execute depreciation for 02/2021. Transaction: AFAB	Depreciation will be calculated in all depreciation areas and posted in all ledgers. Document ------ has posted for all ledgers	Pass / Fail
	End of Test	NA	

Figure 18.6 User Acceptance Testing Test Script

USER ACCEPTANCE TESTING – ACCEPTANCE SIGN-OFF FORM

Name: ____________________

Position: ____________________

Date: ____________________

I confirm the testing performed represents the business process that will be performed in the productive system. As user acceptance tester, I represent the business area of ....and I confirm:

- I am familiar with the features and functions of the system.
- I perform all expected job function activities using the new features and functions.
- I am confident that the goals of all job functions can be achieved with the features and functions of the new system.
- I completed the provided test scripts and passed all of them.
- I formally sign off acceptance of the ability of the system to perform all mine job function tasks and activities with the new features and functions in the business area of.........................

Signature/Date: ____________________

Figure 18.7 User Acceptance Testing Acceptance Form

Obtaining such forms from each tester ensures that the business users are confident in the new system.

18.5 Summary

In this chapter, you learned how to organize testing in your SAP S/4HANA implementation. You learned fundamental techniques and best practices, which are as valid for SAP S/4HANA implementations as they are for other ERP implementation projects.

We explained how to plan the various phases of testing and how to optimize resources. We covered all the main phases of the testing process, including unit testing, integration testing, and user acceptance testing. We discussed the guidelines to follow when choosing a testing tool and what functions a good testing tool should provide.

You also learned how to manage the defect process in order to speed up the resolution of tickets and to track the progress of defect resolution efficiently.

We paid special attention to the testing documentation and how important obtaining sign off from users on the test results is. We provided specific examples of testing documents from the various testing phases.

Now that we've covered the testing phase of the SAP S/4HANA project, we can finally discuss the most exciting time: the go-live and the support phase!

Chapter 19

Go-Live and Support

This chapter will teach you how to prepare for go-live, calling attention to the most important areas and where potential pitfalls may arise. We'll also help you manage the initial production hypercare support period.

Finally, we've come to the most exciting time in an SAP S/4HANA implementation project: the go-live! After months or maybe even more than a year of hard work and dedication, the project management and the business have decided to give a green light to the new system to go live. This step is indeed the most important moment in the whole project, requiring careful planning and management. In this chapter, we'll guide you through the process of going live with SAP S/4HANA, and then, we'll discuss the initial support period, which is often called *hypercare support*.

19.1 Preparation for the Go-Live

As with the other project phases, preparation is crucial for the success of the go-live. In this case, preparation plays an even bigger role: The actual go-live is just a date, and much more planning and preparation is required than execution involved. Preparation for the go-live in fact starts early on in the project with planning the go-live date. We'll discuss the various considerations for choosing a go-live date. Then, we'll guide you through preparing a cutover plan for the go-live and preparing a backup plan in case something goes wrong.

19.1.1 Choosing a Go-Live Date

Choosing a go-live date should be done well in advance. Most companies that implement SAP S/4HANA are global companies that operate in multiple regions and countries. As such, from the beginning of the project, wave planning that sets go-live dates for various countries should have been part of the workflow. A good practice is to cluster countries that are similar geographically and/or from a business point of view so that, in one go-live, several countries will become productive. For a pilot country or a few pilot countries, we recommend choosing countries that aren't the most complicated.

Some companies go for the *big bang* approach, in which many or even all countries in scope go live together. Unless the company is relatively small and doesn't operate in many countries, this approach poses more risks than benefits in our view. Especially for the first go-live of SAP S/4HANA, we recommend starting the productive use of the system in one or two not very complex countries.

In terms of planning, even in the early stages of the project, project management should define a wave plan and communicate it to the project and the business. Of course, such a plan can change, and in fact, more often than not, it *will* change. But the goal is not to slip too much in time from the initial objectives, which would involve increased cost and effort for all parties.

From our experience working in SAP S/4HANA implementations in big global companies, you can realistically plan the go-live of a greenfield implementation for the first pilot country around 1 year after the start of the project. Then, in the next 2 to 3 years, the system should be deployed in the main markets of the company.

In terms of brownfield implementations, that timeframe varies greatly depending on the complexity. In general, brownfield implementations should take less time than greenfield implementations, but in some companies, the existing SAP system is so complex and business processes and custom developments so difficult to adjust in the new system environment, as much time or even more time will be needed to prepare the go-live.

Now, let's talk about the actual go-live, which is always planned on a weekend to minimize disruptions for the business and to have more time to react to unexpected issues. In general, especially from a finance point of view, go-live should coincide with the beginning of a new fiscal year. This approach makes the migration of legacy data much easier and is better from an audit point of view. However, depending on the timeline, planning go-live in that way might not be practical. But if your project is contemplating going live in the last 1 or 2 months before the end of the fiscal year, we strongly advise setting the go-live for the beginning of the new fiscal year.

19.1.2 Defining a Cutover Plan and Responsibilities

For the go-live, you'll need to prepare a formal project plan called a *cutover plan*, named because the process of converting to a new system is called a *cutover*.

The cutover plan clearly defines the responsibilities of the various teams and resources related to the go-live and indicates the sequence of tasks that must be performed.

Most project team members and a lot of business resources are involved in the go-live, so the cutover plan is vitally important for making everyone's responsibilities clear.

The cutover plan can vary a lot from project to project and should include both pre-go-live tasks and post-go-live tasks.

The following mandatory tasks should be included in an SAP S/4HANA cutover plan:

- Make sure all transport requests are transported in the productive system.
- Load master data into the productive system.
- Load balances and open items into the productive system.
- Make sure number ranges are defined in the productive system (because they're not transported).
- Make sure tax codes are defined in the productive system (because a manual import step is required).
- Make sure the operating concern environment is properly generated.
- Ensure cost estimates are marked and released.

19.1.3 Preparing a Backup Plan

After months of hard work and dedication, nobody wants to even consider that the go-live could be a failure. But sometimes, very rarely, it happens. Among the myriad, mostly successful SAP implementations, a few have failed. The reasons differ: Perhaps, the system couldn't meet some important business requirements by design, or some important functionality doesn't work because of technical glitches, which stop important processes such as placing customer sales orders.

In any case, you must be prepared for problems once the system goes live, even if you need to switch it off and go back to the legacy system. These highly unlikely scenarios should be clearly defined in a backup and restore plan.

When going live with any system, you should have the technical option if needed to go back to the legacy system. The roles and responsibilities for this fallback should be written down in the backup plan with clearly defined, short, and specific timelines to ensure a quick return to a productive system.

Practically, when going live with SAP, the most important goal is that day-to-day business operations can continue smoothly and without interruption. For example, one potential issue could be that the system can't process sales orders or purchase orders (POs) because of issues with material masters, prices, or interfaces with other systems. These technical details, therefore, should be tested many, many times in multiple iterations of the testing phase, which we described in detail in Chapter 18. Still, to err is human, so you should hope for the best but plan for the worst. With a good, clear backup plan, such issues shouldn't be damaging to the business or to the new system. Even if you have to stop operations with the new system, if you organize timely resolution of the critical issues, you should be up and running on the new system again quite quickly. What's important is to maintain the trust in the new system, trust from both high-level management and the end users that will use the system in their day-to-day operations.

19.2 Activities during the Go-Live

As mentioned earlier, the go-live should be performed over a weekend. Most of the activities related to the go-live are performed during that go-live weekend. After that weekend, some validation activities will remain.

In this section, we'll discuss the activities that should be performed during the go-live from a general project point of view and, more specifically, for finance.

19.2.1 Technical Activities

The go-live includes a lot of technical tasks in which the Basis team plays most important role. SAP also offers extensive support to make sure the system is ready from a technical point of view with its SAP GoingLive Check service. This proactive service reduces risks and ensures the go-live will be technically sound. We strongly recommend using this service, and you can find more information at *http://s-prs.co/v485706*.

Another important SAP service is SAP EarlyWatch Check. This service is used to audit and review your new SAP S/4HANA system just after go-live and periodically thereafter. More information is available at *http://s-prs.co/v485707*.

Another important project activity is to ensure all user IDs have been created, passwords communicated, and relevant authorization roles assigned. SAP users can access the system using the traditional SAP GUI known from previous releases and the new SAP Fiori web-based interface. We strongly encourage users to use more of SAP Fiori and less of SAP GUI. SAP Fiori is the user interface (UI) of the future, and more and more user transactions and reports will become available over time as SAP Fiori apps. Users should have access to SAP Fiori and be well trained in using it and navigating it.

As with previous SAP releases, your new SAP S/4HANA system will run a lot of regularly scheduled jobs. An example is the asset depreciation program, which we covered in detail in Chapter 7. Part of the technical activities during the go-live is to make sure all jobs are scheduled.

Another technical step is to lock down the system. During the go-live, no users should be allowed in the system except those that must perform specific tasks at specific times.

19.2.2 Financial Accounting Activities

Several financial accounting activities must be performed during the go-live.

Financial master data, such as general ledger accounts, cost centers, profit centers, and segments, usually are migrated to the productive system ahead of the go-live because they're stable objects that are unlikely to change in the final minutes. However, during the go-live, general ledger account balances and customer, vendor, and general ledger open items are migrated to the productive system with the most up-to-date numbers.

Of course, this process should have been tested already multiple times in the test and quality assurance systems. Fixed asset values also are migrated to production during the go-live with the most up-to date values.

We configured tax codes in Chapter 3. The tax codes are not automatically included in transports. There's a function to export and import tax codes, and the import process must be included in your cutover activities. To export tax codes, follow the menu path **Financial Accounting • Financial Accounting Global Settings • Tax on Sales/Purchases • Calculation • Define Tax Codes for Sales and Purchases** or enter Transaction FTXP. After selecting the relevant country in the **Country Key** field, select **Tax code • Transport • Export** from the top menu, as shown in Figure 19.1.

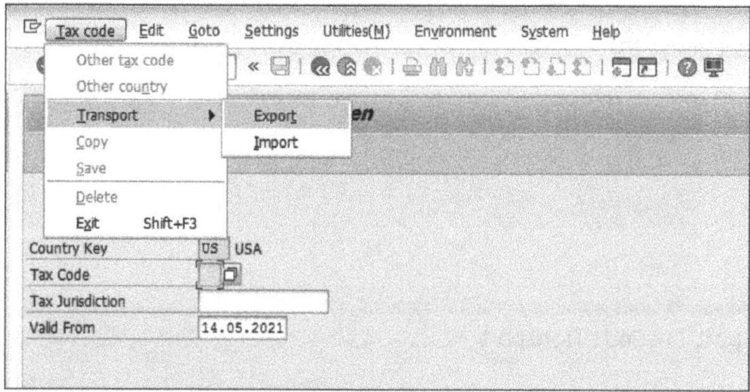

Figure 19.1 Exporting Tax Codes

The system will ask you for a transport request in which to include the tax codes, as shown in Figure 19.2.

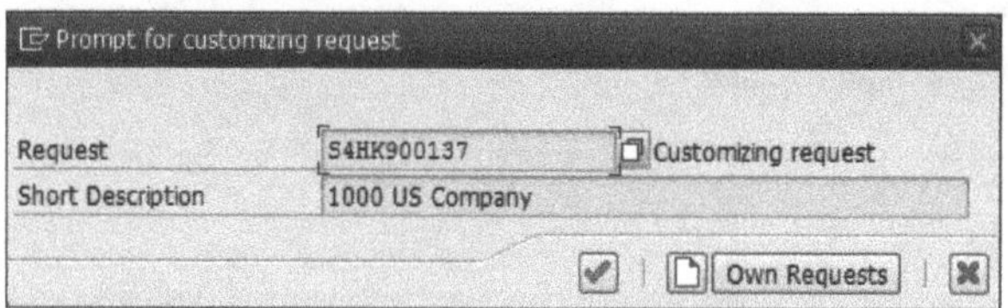

Figure 19.2 Prompt for Customizing Request

You can add the tax codes to an existing transport request or create a new one by clicking the (**Create Request**) button.

Similarly, during go-live, you'll need to import the tax codes. In Transaction FTXP, select **Tax code • Transport • Import** from the top menu, as shown in Figure 19.3.

Then, select your transport with tax codes on the screen shown in Figure 19.4.

Process the request by clicking the **Execute** button.

This step generates a batch input session, which is executed automatically and which you can monitor in Transaction SM35, as shown in Figure 19.5.

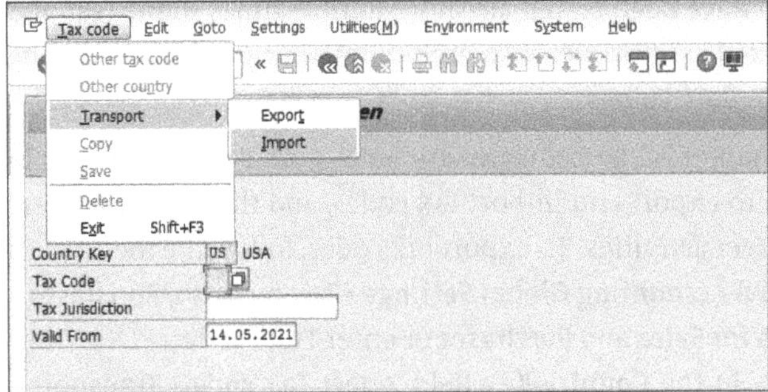

Figure 19.3 Importing Tax Codes

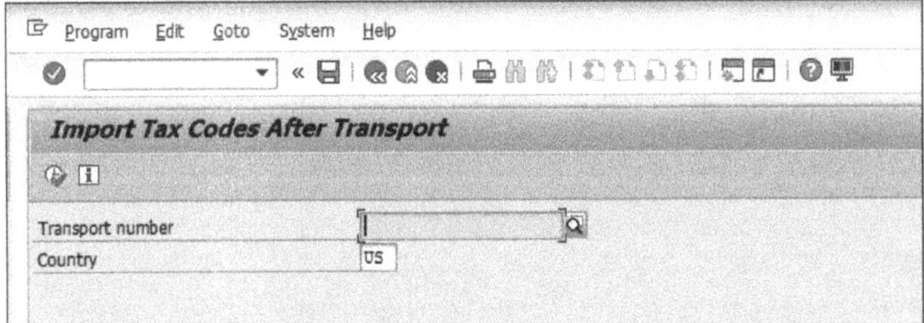

Figure 19.4 Selecting Import Tax Code Transport

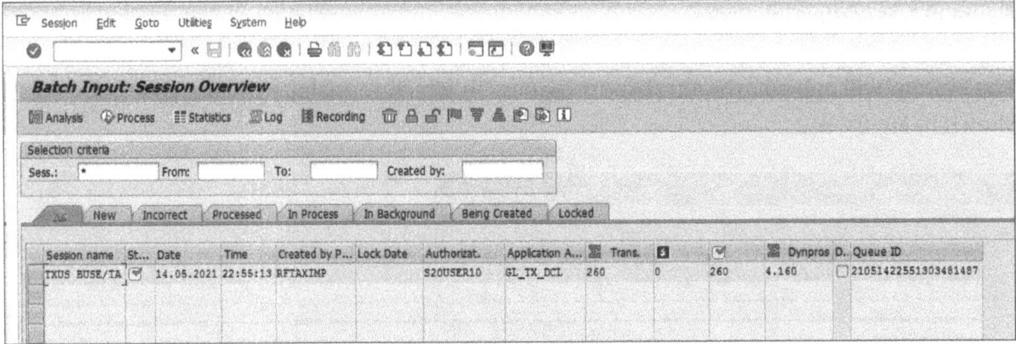

Figure 19.5 Import Tax Codes Batch Input Session

The number of errors is shown in the column with the [error icon] heading, whereas the number of successfully processed transactions is shown in the column with the [checkmark icon] heading. If you double-click a line, you'll see further details in the batch input log.

Another important task is setting the number ranges. You may remember that, when we defined number ranges, we didn't get transport numbers. A good reason exists for that: Transporting number ranges can cause inconsistencies across clients, especially in the production system. Therefore, you should keep track of the number ranges defined in the test and quality assurance systems and have a checklist ready to maintain the required number ranges in the production system.

19.2.3 Controlling Activities

In controlling, some activities will need to be included in the cutover tasks to be performed during the go-live.

In profitability analysis, you must ensure that the data structure is active and that both the cross-client part and client-specific part of the operating concern are activated. Follow the menu path **Controlling • Profitability Analysis • Structures • Define Operating Concern • Maintain Operating Concern.**

As shown in Figure 19.6, the data structure should have a green status. If it doesn't, you should activate it by clicking the → **Activate** button.

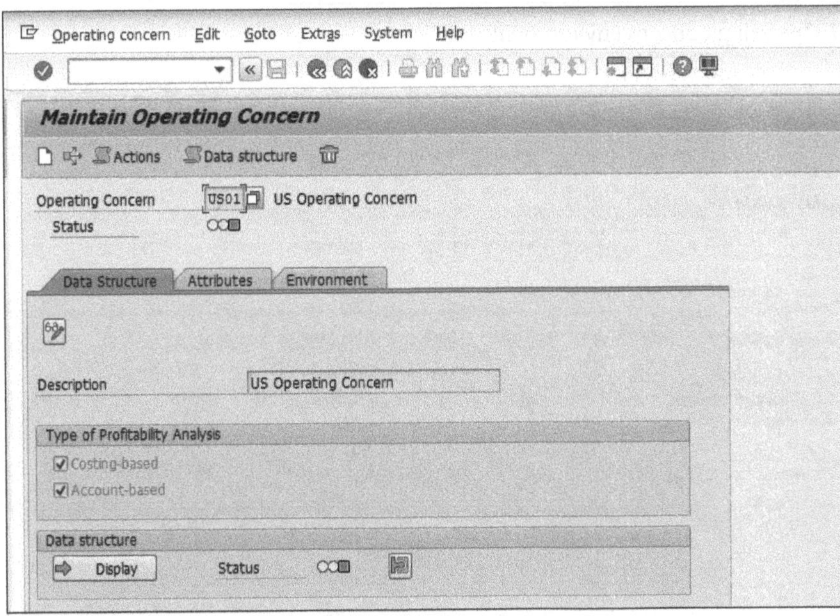

Figure 19.6 Operating Concern Data Structure

Next, click the **Environment** tab. As shown in Figure 19.7, both the **Cross-client part** and **Client-specific part** of the operating concern should have a green status. If they don't, you should activate them by clicking the (**Activate**) button.

In product costing, you must ensure that the cost estimates are marked and released. One convenient way to check the standard prices is by looking in the table content of table MBEW, which is the material valuation table. You can review the data structure of the table using Transaction SE11.

Standard prices are stored in field STPRS, as shown in Figure 19.8. In field VPRSV, the price control of the material is stored. The value **S** indicates a standard price material, whereas **V** denotes a moving average price.

Operating concern Edit Goto Extras System Help
Maintain Operating Concern
Actions
Data structure
Operating Concern
US01
US Operating Concern
Status
Data Structure
Attributes
Environment
Cross-client part
Status
Client-specific part
Status

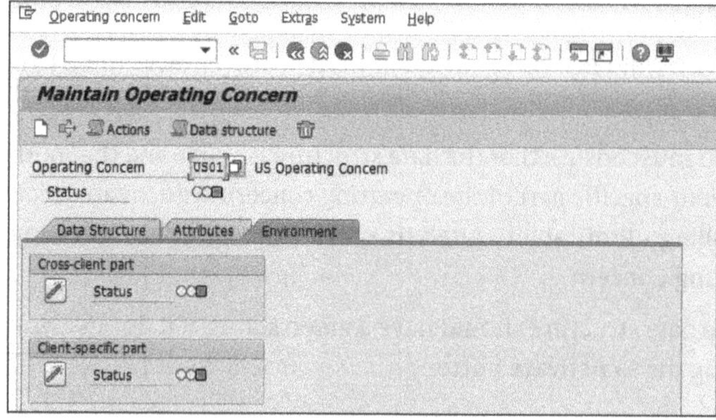

Figure 19.7 Operating Concern Environment

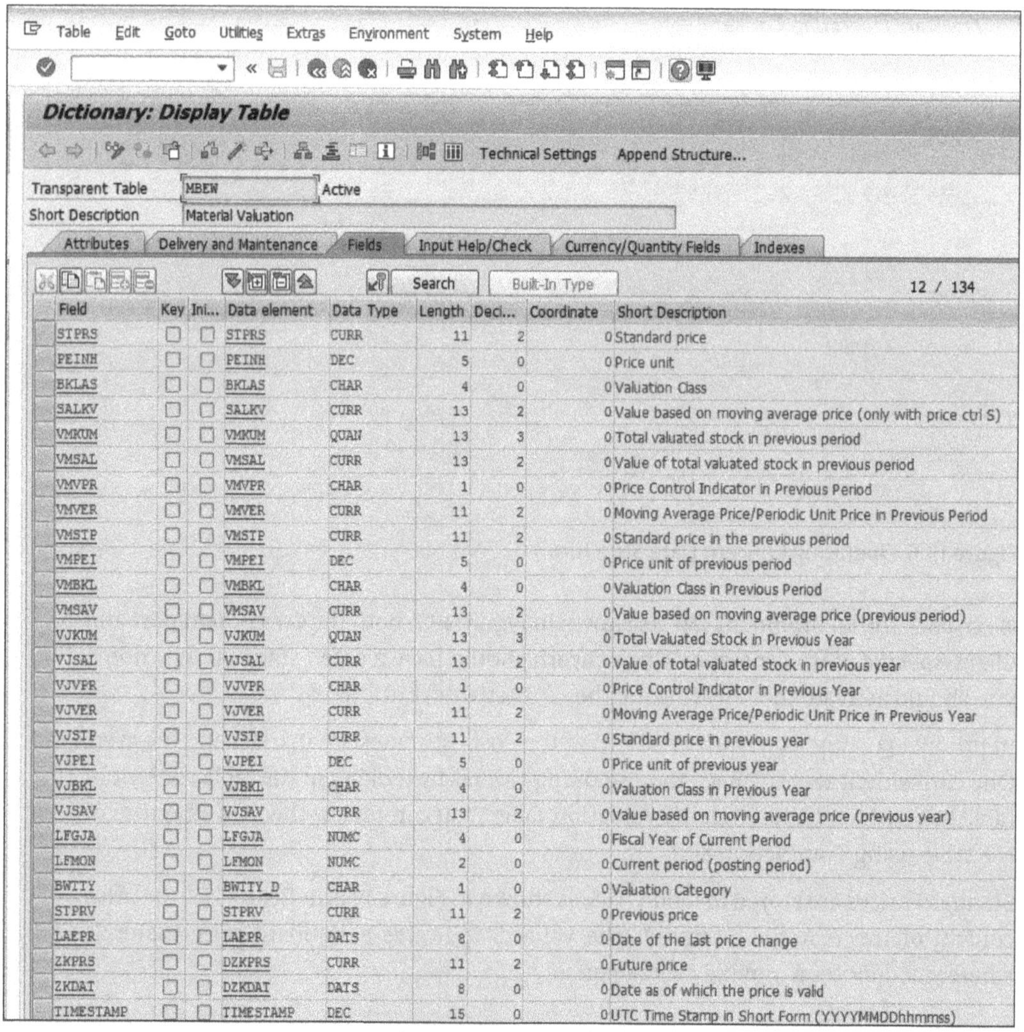

Table Edit Goto Utilities Extras Environment System Help
Dictionary: Display Table
Technical Settings
Append Structure...
Transparent Table
MBEW
Active
Short Description
Material Valuation
Attributes
Delivery and Maintenance
Fields
Input Help/Check
Currency/Quantity Fields
Indexes
Search
Built-In Type
12 / 134

Field	Key	Ini...	Data element	Data Type	Length	Deci...	Coordinate	Short Description
STPRS			STPRS	CURR	11	2	0	Standard price
PEINH			PEINH	DEC	5	0	0	Price unit
BKLAS			BKLAS	CHAR	4	0	0	Valuation Class
SALKV			SALKV	CURR	13	2	0	Value based on moving average price (only with price ctrl S)
VMKUM			VMKUM	QUAN	13	3	0	Total valuated stock in previous period
VMSAL			VMSAL	CURR	13	2	0	Value of total valuated stock in previous period
VMVPR			VMVPR	CHAR	1	0	0	Price Control Indicator in Previous Period
VMVER			VMVER	CURR	11	2	0	Moving Average Price/Periodic Unit Price in Previous Period
VMSTP			VMSTP	CURR	11	2	0	Standard price in the previous period
VMPEI			VMPEI	DEC	5	0	0	Price unit of previous period
VMBKL			VMBKL	CHAR	4	0	0	Valuation Class in Previous Period
VMSAV			VMSAV	CURR	13	2	0	Value based on moving average price (previous period)
VJKUM			VJKUM	QUAN	13	3	0	Total Valuated Stock in Previous Year
VJSAL			VJSAL	CURR	13	2	0	Value of total valuated stock in previous year
VJVPR			VJVPR	CHAR	1	0	0	Price Control Indicator in Previous Year
VJVER			VJVER	CURR	11	2	0	Moving Average Price/Periodic Unit Price in Previous Year
VJSTP			VJSTP	CURR	11	2	0	Standard price in previous year
VJPEI			VJPEI	DEC	5	0	0	Price unit of previous year
VJBKL			VJBKL	CHAR	4	0	0	Valuation Class in Previous Year
VJSAV			VJSAV	CURR	13	2	0	Value based on moving average price (previous year)
LFGJA			LFGJA	NUMC	4	0	0	Fiscal Year of Current Period
LFMON			LFMON	NUMC	2	0	0	Current period (posting period)
BWTTY			BWTTY_D	CHAR	1	0	0	Valuation Category
STPRV			STPRV	CURR	11	2	0	Previous price
LAEPR			LAEPR	DATS	8	0	0	Date of the last price change
ZKPRS			DZKPRS	CURR	11	2	0	Future price
ZKDAT			DZKDAT	DATS	8	0	0	Date as of which the price is valid
TIMESTAMP			TIMESTAMP	DEC	15	0	0	UTC Time Stamp in Short Form (YYYYMMDDhhmmss)

Figure 19.8 Material Valuation Table

To browse the table content, enter Transaction SE16N. Enter "MBEW" in the **Table** field, as shown in Figure 19.9.

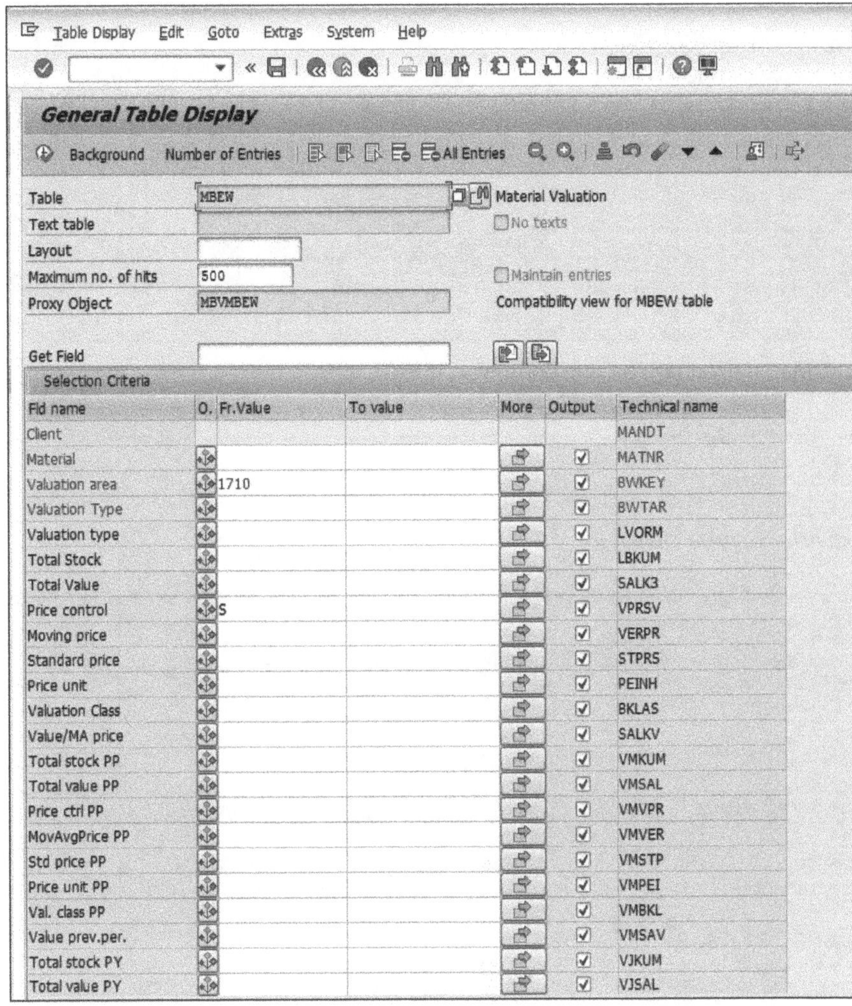

Figure 19.9 Material Valuation Table Browser

You can restrict by valuation area, which normally is the plant, and by price control S to check the standard price materials. Then, proceed by clicking the (**Online**) button, which leads to the table contents screen shown in Figure 19.10.

In the **Std price** column, you can see the standard prices. All **S** materials should have a standard price maintained. Standard prices are released with Transaction CKME, which should be part of the go-live activities for controlling. As shown in Figure 19.11, you can run the transaction by plant and/or by range of materials. Normally, this step will be scheduled as a background job.

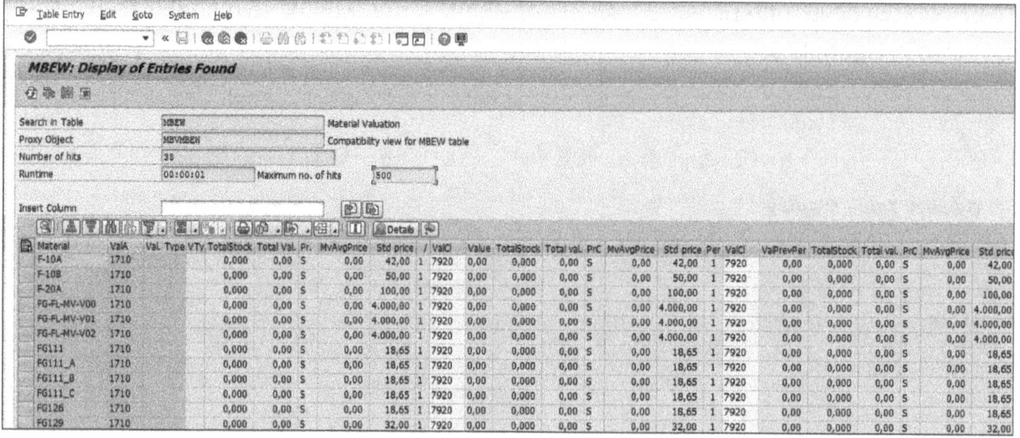

Material	ValA	Val. Type	VTy	TotalStock	Total Val.	Pr.	MvAvgPrice	Std price	/	ValCl	Value	TotalStock	Total val.	PrC	MvAvgPrice	Std price	Per	ValCl	ValPrevPer	TotalStock	Total val.	PrC	MvAvgPrice	Std price
F-10A	1710			0,000	0,00	S	0,00	42,00	1	7920	0,00	0,000	0,00	S	0,00	42,00	1	7920	0,00	0,000	0,00	S	0,00	42,00
F-10B	1710			0,000	0,00	S	0,00	50,00	1	7920	0,00	0,000	0,00	S	0,00	50,00	1	7920	0,00	0,000	0,00	S	0,00	50,00
F-20A	1710			0,000	0,00	S	0,00	100,00	1	7920	0,00	0,000	0,00	S	0,00	100,00	1	7920	0,00	0,000	0,00	S	0,00	100,00
FG-FL-MV-V00	1710			0,000	0,00	S	0,00	4.000,00	1	7920	0,00	0,000	0,00	S	0,00	4.000,00	1	7920	0,00	0,000	0,00	S	0,00	4.000,00
FG-FL-MV-V01	1710			0,000	0,00	S	0,00	4.000,00	1	7920	0,00	0,000	0,00	S	0,00	4.000,00	1	7920	0,00	0,000	0,00	S	0,00	4.000,00
FG-FL-MV-V02	1710			0,000	0,00	S	0,00	4.000,00	1	7920	0,00	0,000	0,00	S	0,00	4.000,00	1	7920	0,00	0,000	0,00	S	0,00	4.000,00
FG111	1710			0,000	0,00	S	0,00	18,65	1	7920	0,00	0,000	0,00	S	0,00	18,65	1	7920	0,00	0,000	0,00	S	0,00	18,65
FG111_A	1710			0,000	0,00	S	0,00	18,65	1	7920	0,00	0,000	0,00	S	0,00	18,65	1	7920	0,00	0,000	0,00	S	0,00	18,65
FG111_B	1710			0,000	0,00	S	0,00	18,65	1	7920	0,00	0,000	0,00	S	0,00	18,65	1	7920	0,00	0,000	0,00	S	0,00	18,65
FG111_C	1710			0,000	0,00	S	0,00	18,65	1	7920	0,00	0,000	0,00	S	0,00	18,65	1	7920	0,00	0,000	0,00	S	0,00	18,65
FG126	1710			0,000	0,00	S	0,00	18,65	1	7920	0,00	0,000	0,00	S	0,00	18,65	1	7920	0,00	0,000	0,00	S	0,00	18,65
FG129	1710			0,000	0,00	S	0,00	32,00	1	7920	0,00	0,000	0,00	S	0,00	32,00	1	7920	0,00	0,000	0,00	S	0,00	32,00

Figure 19.10 Material Valuation Table Content

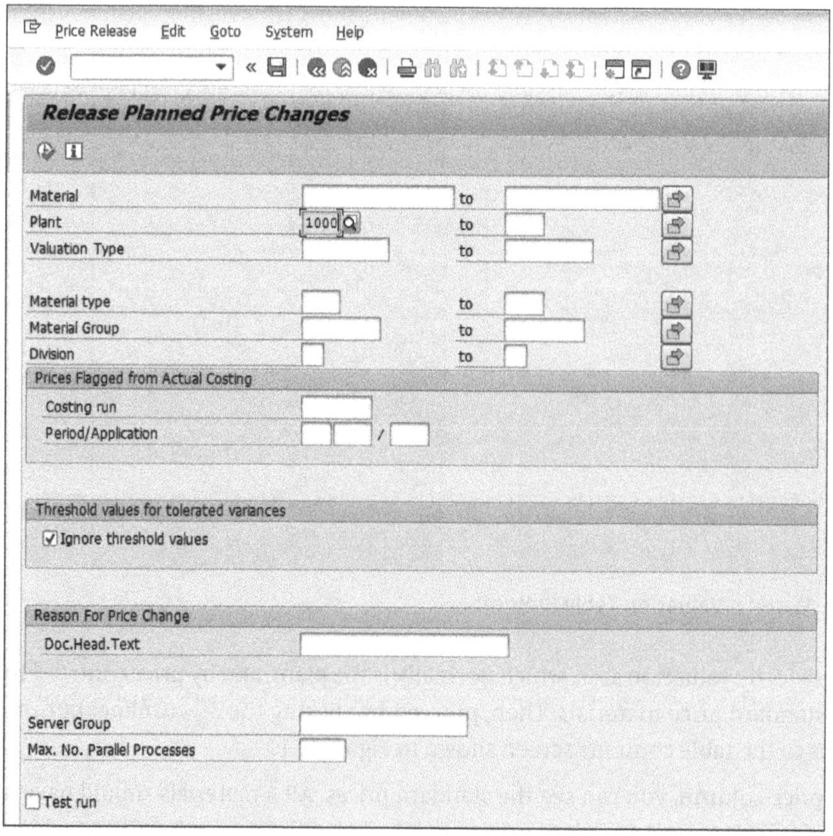

Price Release Edit Goto System Help

Release Planned Price Changes

Material to
Plant 1000 to
Valuation Type to
Material type to
Material Group to
Division to

Prices Flagged from Actual Costing
Costing run
Period/Application /

Threshold values for tolerated variances
☑ Ignore threshold values

Reason For Price Change
Doc.Head.Text

Server Group
Max. No. Parallel Processes

☐ Test run

Figure 19.11 Release Standard Prices

19.3 Validation of the Go-Live

At the end of the go-live weekend, before officially opening the system to users, the system must be validated by the project team and key subject matter experts. Their availability should be aligned so that, during the weekend, they can execute some checks to make sure no surprises occur when the users start using the system the next day.

19.3.1 Project Team Validation

The project team is the first to check the productive system. Each functional team should carefully check its process area. In terms of finance and controlling, these checks involve running some reports and checking some tables, which we covered in the previous sections. But once again you'll need to ensure that the relevant master data is properly created, number ranges and tax codes are correctly set up, controlling structures and environments are generated, and materials have the correct pricing.

You should have a formal process in which each functional team goes over certain predefined key transactions and reports on and records the results. At the end, each functional team lead should sign off that the go-live is successful and the system is ready for business use.

The same is true for the Basis team, which needs to make sure that from everything is working correctly from a technical point of view, and for the development team, which needs to validate the interfaces, the custom programs, and other reports, interfaces, conversions, enhancements, forms, and workflows (RICEFW) objects.

A lot of work must be done in a rather short time, so good project management and coordination are extremely important. Project management's responsibility is to coordinate all the project resources and to react quickly if issues are discovered.

Once the project team validates the system, next, business subject matter experts should check the system from their end.

19.3.2 Subject Matter Expert Validation

Several subject matter experts from the business should be nominated to be involved in the go-live weekend, executing critical checks and reports to validate the system from a business point of view. These experts would normally be the same key users that worked with the consultants during the implementation. They should know well what to expect from the new system and the key areas that need to be checked.

In the areas of finance and controlling, separate resources should check the general ledger, fixed assets, accounts payable and accounts receivable areas, product costing, overhead accounting, and profitability analysis. These resources should be asked to be available during the later stages of the go-live and to execute the reports that will assure them that the system is set up correctly. For example, their activities should include checking account balances and open items, checking material prices, making sure accounting periods are open as needed, and so on.

At the end, a formal written sign-off should be required from each subject matter expert validating the system. And again, if critical issues are discovered, the project management team should have a strategy in place to react quickly. Sometimes, the difficult decision of whether to go live as planned or not may need to be made, depending on the criticality and the significance of the issues.

But hopefully, no major issues will arise, and project management will officially announce the go-live of the new SAP S/4HANA system! The system will be open to the business users, and the next exciting period will start: hypercare production support.

19.4 Hypercare Production Support

So finally, you've made it! Your SAP S/4HANA system is productive from its first day, but the work isn't quite done yet. After the system is live, production support is vital, especially in the first weeks, which usually is called the *hypercare production support* period. This period starts immediately after the go-live, covering usually a month or so. During that period, production support is provided by the project team itself. At the same time, the project team performs knowledge transfers to hand over production support to the long-term resources that will handle support after the hypercare production support period is over.

We'll start with a discussion of what to expect on the first day after the go-live. Then, we'll cover how to schedule background jobs in the productive environment. In the next section, we'll teach you how to manage critical support incidents. Finally, we'll discuss how to transfer support from the project team that provides the hypercare support to the long-term support team.

19.4.1 The First Day

The first day after the go-live, which usually is on a Monday, is extremely important, so organizing support so that the project team is onsite together with the customers, supporting the business users in their day-to-day tasks is critical. Of course, at this point, you expect that users are well trained and can work with the new SAP S/4HANA system by themselves, but knowing that the consultants are available if needed can be helpful.

It's vital to have a good process to manage issues. A defect management system should be used in which users can report defects found in the system. As during the testing phase, these defects should be created with the correct priority and assigned to the relevant project resources.

It's normal on the first day to battle with simple issues such as lost user passwords, not being able to log on, and so on. Although these issues are easy to resolve, sometimes, they take unnecessary time due to lack of proper organization, which causes frustration for users. Therefore, proper organization should be in place to react immediately and be able to resolve issues that are low-hanging fruits quickly.

It's important during the first day to ensure no major issues could stop the business or the proper financial reporting. The project team must explicitly ensure that all the main business processes are running smoothly, such as placing sales orders, posting goods issue, invoicing customers, and purchasing materials. Particularly in finance, the invoicing process and the payment process are critical.

Some of the specific functionalities that should be checked from a finance standpoint during the first day include the following:

- Material prices
- Customer invoices
- Vendor invoices
- Automatic payment program
- Correct tax determination
- Account determination

19.4.2 Background Jobs

The project team's responsibility is to schedule background jobs that should be performed in the live system. These background jobs vary from project to project, but some typical finance jobs that should be scheduled as background jobs include the asset deprecation program, the automatic clearing program for open items, internal order settlement, and so on.

Sometimes, scheduled background jobs fail due to various issues. This failure could happen, for example, if accounting periods are closed and a program such as asset depreciation that needs to post in financial accounting can't do so. Therefore, an important part of the support activities is to monitor the scheduled jobs for errors.

A good practice is to set up email notifications so that, if a background job is canceled due to an error, certain resources will receive an email. Then, the responsible experts can analyze the issue and take action.

You can monitor background jobs with Transaction SM37. If you select only the **Canceled** checkbox, as shown in Figure 19.12, you'll see the canceled jobs for the given time period. You can search by job name in this case. Entering "*" in the **Job Name** field uses the asterisk wildcard to search all job names. The same is true for the **User Name** field, in which you can enter "*" for all user names, or you can enter a specific user name that's used to run certain background jobs. Normally, dedicated user names are used to run only background jobs.

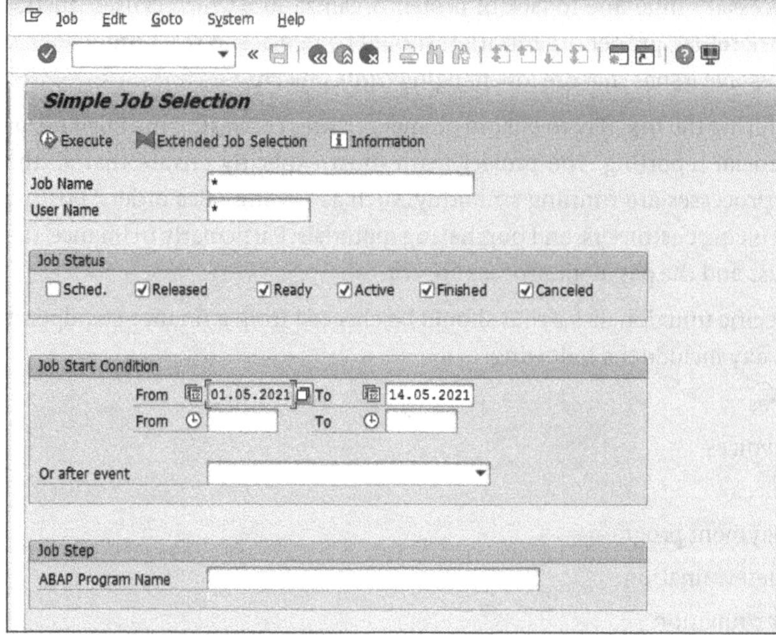

Figure 19.12 Monitoring Background Jobs

Execute by clicking the **Execute** button. On the resulting list, shown in Figure 19.13, you can see further information by selecting a job and clicking the Spool (**Display Spool List**) button.

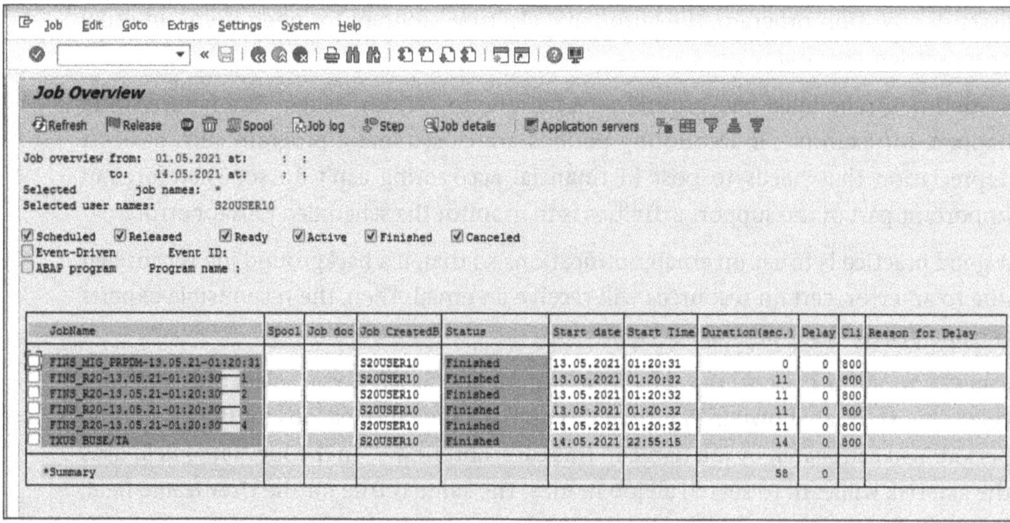

JobName	Spool	Job doc	Job CreatedB	Status	Start date	Start Time	Duration(sec.)	Delay	Cli	Reason for Delay
FINS_MIG_PRPDM-13.05.21-01:20:31			S20USER10	Finished	13.05.2021	01:20:31	0	0	800	
FINS_R20-13.05.21-01:20:30 1			S20USER10	Finished	13.05.2021	01:20:32	11	0	800	
FINS_R20-13.05.21-01:20:30 2			S20USER10	Finished	13.05.2021	01:20:32	11	0	800	
FINS_R20-13.05.21-01:20:30 3			S20USER10	Finished	13.05.2021	01:20:32	11	0	800	
FINS_R20-13.05.21-01:20:30 4			S20USER10	Finished	13.05.2021	01:20:32	11	0	800	
TXUS BUSE/TA			S20USER10	Finished	14.05.2021	22:55:15	14	0	800	
*Summary							58	0		

Figure 19.13 Job Overview

19.4.3 Managing Critical Support Incidents

This topic is perhaps the most important within hypercare production support. We all hope that, once the system goes live, everything will go as smoothly as possible, but sometimes in such a complex and integrated system as SAP S/4HANA, critical support incidents can occur. Such defects should be managed with utmost attention and speed.

We already discussed some cases in which major SAP implementations failed because of such incidents. The most important critical defects are those that affect the ability of the company to do business and generate revenue. As such, those defects most commonly are related to the sales and distribution area. Purely financial issues can also be problematic, but without stopping the business itself. For example, an inability to generate tax declarations may result in some fines, but nothing can compare with the inability to process sales orders, leading to missed revenue and tarnishing relationships with customers. Supply chain issues also can be quite damaging because they can disrupt the supply flows that are needed to generate sales and can affect relationships with vendors.

But sometimes such logistics problems are in fact rooted in finance. Missing account determinations, missing costings of materials, and the wrong tax codes are just some of the bugs in the finance area that could disrupt the whole logistics chain.

Therefore, managing critical support incidents in an integrated manner is important. After a very high-priority defect is opened, work on it should start immediately, perhaps by multiple teams. The project should organize daily integration meetings to discuss and monitor the progress on high-priority tickets. Sometimes, determining the root cause of an issue might not be that easy, and teams might play the blame game, stating that the issue isn't in their area. In this case, project management will play a crucial role, facilitating the integration work across the teams to ensure timely resolution.

19.4.4 Organizing Long-Term Support

The hypercare support period is limited because project resources are quite expensive. Sooner or later, each system needs to go into regular maintenance mode. Project resources should gradually be phased out of the project, and the support work should be handed to long-term support resources.

Various strategies exist for organizing long-term support for your new SAP S/4HANA system. Some companies opt to organize the support internally with their own SAP support teams. Such a strategy has the advantage that the company can build vast SAP knowledge internally.

But SAP support is a huge task, and some companies don't want to manage so many IT resources internally, preferring to focus on their core business. Therefore, more common currently is the approach to outsource SAP support to companies that specialize in that area. Many consulting companies are available that have established many SAP support centers, typically in lower-cost locations.

Each approach has advantages and disadvantages, and normally, this choice is a high-level management decision based on the needs of the company. Whatever the approach, the process of handing over the long-term support is the responsibility of the project implementation team. The project team should prepare good documentation that includes all customizing being done, all functional specifications and development objects, and all business process user guides. Such documentation should be available for reference, both for users and for future support consultants.

Also, an organized formal knowledge transfer process should be set up in which experienced project resources can share their knowledge with the future support resources, which will take on their role in supporting the system after the hypercare period is finished.

The management of the long-term support also should be done using a defect management system. Users will continue to raise defects for the various issues they encounter, indicate their priority, and the long-term support team will provide resolution. The main difference is that such long-term support normally will be remote.

Some big companies will employ a long-term support strategy in which some SAP support specialists are available on a local level, who are typically called level 1 (L1) support and aren't generally highly experienced. Whatever issues they aren't able to resolve they'll pass to level 2 (L2) support consultants, who are more experienced and are responsible for clusters of countries. Such a hierarchy could be expanded even further with level 3 (L3) consultants, who are experts and work on the most difficult defects globally across regions.

19.5 Summary

In this chapter, we covered the go-live of the SAP S/4HANA system and production support, paying special attention to the initial hypercare support period.

Now, you know good practices for choosing the go-live date for your SAP S/4HANA implementation wisely and for using the wave approach when implementing the system across multiple countries and regions. You now know how to prepare a cutover project plan that clearly defines the responsibilities and timeline for the go-live activities.

We've covered the various tasks during the go-live in detail, both from a general technical perspective and more specifically for finance and controlling. You also learned how the system should be validated by project team members and subject matter experts during the go-live weekend.

Last but not least, you learned how to organize hypercare production support and how to transfer support activities to the long-term support organization.

Congratulations! You've completed the journey to implement your new SAP S/4HANA system. Hopefully, reading this book was a rewarding experience, and your business now has a powerful, state-of-the-art system that will enable it to streamline its operations and achieve tremendous value in all business process areas.

Appendix A
Obsolete and New Transaction Codes and Tables in SAP S/4HANA

SAP S/4HANA is the biggest change for SAP in nearly 30 years. The whole data model has changed, especially in the area of finance. New tables and obsolete tables exist, and many transaction codes are obsolete either because they were moved to SAP Fiori apps or because of changes in functionality.

Because many readers of this book may have experience with the older SAP releases, in this appendix, we'll list obsolete and new transaction codes and tables in SAP S/4HANA compared to previous releases.

Table A.1 lists obsolete and new financial transaction codes.

Old Transaction	New Transaction	Description
FS01	FS00	Create G/L Account
FS02	FS00	Change G/L Account
FS03	FS00	Display G/L Account
FK01	BP	Create Vendor
FK02	BP	Change Vendor
FK03	BP	Display Vendor
FD01	BP	Create Customer
FD02	BP	Change Customer
FD03	BP	Display Customer
KP06	FCOM_IP_CC_COSTELEM01	Change Cost and Activity Inputs
KP07	FCOM_IP_CC_COSTELEM01	Display Cost and Activity Inputs
KP65	FCOM_IP_CC_COSTELEM01	Create Cost Planning Layout
KP66	FCOM_IP_CC_COSTELEM01	Change Cost Planning Layout
KP67	FCOM_IP_CC_COSTELEM01	Display Cost Planning Layout

Table A.1 Obsolete and New Transaction Codes

Old Transaction	New Transaction	Description
CK11	CK11N	Create Product Cost Estimate
CK13	CK13N	Display Product Cost Estimate
CK41	CK40N	Create Costing Run
CK42	CK40N	Change Costing Run
CK43	CK40N	Display Costing Run
CK60	CK40N	Preselection for Material
CK62	CK40N	Find Structure: BOM Explosion
CK64	CK40N	Run: Cost Estimate of Objects
CK66	CK40N	Mark Run for Release
CK68	CK40N	Release Costing Run
CK74	CK74N	Create Additive Costs
KB11	KB11N	Enter Reposting of Primary Costs
KB21	KB21N	Enter Activity Allocation
KB31	KB31N	Enter Statistical Key Figures
KB33	KB33N	Display Statistical Key Figures
KB34	KB34N	Reverse Statistical Key Figures
KB51	KB51N	Enter Activity Posting
KE21	KE21N	Create CO-PA Line Item
KE23	KE24	Display CO-PA Line Item
KKE1	CKUC	Add Base Planning Object
KKE2	CKUC	Change Base Planning Object
KKE3	CKUC	Display Base Planning Object
KKEC	CKUC	Compare Base Object—Unit Cost Est
KKED	CKUC	BOM for Base Planning Objects
KKB4	CKUC	Itemization for Base Planning Obj.
KKBF	KKRO	Order Selection (Classification)
F.05	FAGL_FCV	Foreign Currency Valuation

Table A.1 Obsolete and New Transaction Codes (Cont.)

Old Transaction	New Transaction	Description
F.24	FINT	A/R: Interest for Days Overdue
F.2A	FINT	A/R Overdue Int.: Post (without OI)
F.2B	FINT	A/R Overdue Int.: Post (with OI)
F.2C	FINT	Calc.cust.int.on arr.: w/o Postings
F.4A	FINTAP	Calc.vend.int.on arr.: Post (w/o OI)
F.4B	FINTIAP	Calc.vend.int.on arr.: Post (with OI)
F.4C	FINTAP	Calc.vend.int.on arr.: w/o Postings
FA39	Obsolete	Vendors: calc.of Interest on Arrears
F.47	FINTAP	A/R: Interest for Days Overdue

Table A.1 Obsolete and New Transaction Codes (Cont.)

As discussed many times, the data model in SAP S/4HANA has changed significantly, and the index and totals tables are obsolete. These tables have been replaced by compatibility views to make sure that older custom programs will continue to work. Technically, these tables are called core data services (CDS) views. Table A.2 lists obsolete finance tables and their corresponding compatibility and data definition language (DDL) sources.

Obsolete Table	Compatibility View	DDL Source
BSAD	BSAD	BSAD_DDL
BSAK	BSAK	BSAK_DDL
BSAS	BSAS	BSAS_DDL
BSID	BSID	BSID_DDL
BSIK	BSIK	BSIK_DDL
BSIS	BSIS	BSIS_DDL
FAGLBSAS	FAGLBSAS	FAGLBSAS_DDL
FAGLBSIS	FAGLBSIS	FAGLBSIS_DDL
GLTO	GLTO	GLTO_DDL
KNC1	KNC1	KNC1_DDL
KNC3	KNC3	KNC3_DDL

Table A.2 Obsolete Tables and Compatibility Views

Obsolete Table	Compatibility View	DDL Source
LFC1	LFC1	LFC1_DDL
LFC3	LFC3	LFC3_DDL
COSP	COSP	V_COSP_DDL
COSS	COSS	V_COSS_DDL
FAGLFLEXT	FAGLFLEXT	V_FAGLFLEXT_DDL
ANEA	FAAV_ANEA	FAA_ANEA
ANEK	FAAV_ANEK	FAA_ANEK
ANEP	FAAV_ANEP	FAA_ANEP
ANLC	FAAV_ANLC	FAA_ANLC
ANLP	FAAV_ANLP	FAA_ANLP
BSIM	V_BSIM	BSIM_DDL
CKMI1	V_CKMI1	V_CKMI1_DDL
COEP	V_COEP	V_COEP
FAGLFLEXA	FGLV_FAGLFLEXA	FGL_FAGLFLEXA
MLCD	V_MLCD	V_MLCD_DDL
MLCR	V_MLCR	V_MLCR_DDL
MLHD	V_MLHD	V_MLHD_DDL
MLIT	V_MLIT	V_MLIT_DDL
MLPP	V_MLPP	V_MLPP_DDL
T012K	V_T012K_BAM	V_T012K_BAM_DDL
T012T	V_T012T_BAM	V_T012T_DDL
FMGLFLEXA	FGLV_FMGLFLEXA	FGL_FMGLFLEXA
FMGLFLEXT	FGLV_FMGLFLEXT	FGL_FMGLFLEXT
PSGLFLEXA	FGLV_PSGLFLEXA	FGL_PSGLFLEXA
PSGLFLEXT	FGLV_PSGLFLEXT	FGL_PSGLFLEXT
JVGLFLEXA	FGLV_JVGLFLEXA	FGL_JVGLFLEXA
JVGLFLEXT	FGLV_JVGLFLEXT	FGL_JVGLFLEXT

Table A.2 Obsolete Tables and Compatibility Views (Cont.)

Appendix B
The Author

Stoil Jotev is an SAP S/4HANA FI/CO solution architect with more than 22 years of consulting, implementation, training, and project management experience. He is an accomplished digital transformation leader in finance. Stoil has delivered many complex SAP financial projects in the United States and Europe in various business sectors, such as manufacturing, pharmaceuticals, biotechnology, chemicals, medical devices, financial services, fast-moving consumer goods (FMCG), IT, public sector, automotive parts, commodity trading, and retail.

Index

A

D

E

F

G

H

N

O

P

T

U

- Master your core controlling tasks in SAP S/4HANA
- Assess overhead, manufacturing, sales, project, and investment costs
- Streamline your operations with both the new and classic user interfaces

Janet Salmon, Stefan Walz

Controlling with SAP S/4HANA: Business User Guide

SAP S/4HANA brings change to your routine controlling activities. Perform your key tasks in the new environment with this user guide! Get click-by-click instructions for your daily and monthly overhead controlling tasks, and then dive deeper into processes such as make-to-stock/make-to-order scenarios, margin analysis, and investment management. Finally, instructions for intercompany transactions and reporting make this your all-in-one resource!

593 pages, pub. 05/2021
E-Book: $69.99 | **Print:** $79.95 | **Bundle:** $89.99
www.sap-press.com/5282

Rheinwerk
Publishing

- Manage your financial consolidation with SAP S/4HANA Finance for group reporting
- Configure and run currency translation, intercompany elimination, matrix consolidation, and more
- Create consolidation reports and understand related reporting tools

Ryan, Bala, Raghav, Mohammed

Group Reporting with SAP S/4HANA

Every SAP S/4HANA journey begins with a single step—so get all the steps you need for your finance system conversion project! Follow the implementation path through preparation and post-migration testing, with special attention to data migration and functional configuration. From the general ledger to asset accounting and beyond, you'll align your new system with existing finance requirements and go live. Get the nitty-gritty details and pro tips with this go-to-guide and make your brownfield project a success!

375 pages, pub. 11/2020
E-Book: $79.99 | **Print:** $89.95 | **Bundle:** $99.99

www.sap-press.com/5151

- Configure margin analysis and costing-based CO-PA in SAP S/4HANA
- Perform profitability planning with your data
- Run key profitability reports using SAP Fiori and SAP GUI

Kathrin Schmalzing

Profitability Analysis with SAP S/4HANA

Whether you're running account-based or costing-based CO-PA, this is your one-stop shop for profitability analysis with SAP S/4HANA! Get the step-by-step instructions you need for configuring master data, operating concerns, value flows, and setting up your system. From planning to reporting, this guide has the key to each step of your profitability operations. With this guide to CO-PA, you're ready for SAP S/4HANA!

480 pages, 2nd edition, pub. 10/2020
E-Book: $79.99 | **Print:** $89.95 | **Bundle:** $99.99

www.sap-press.com/5117

- Learn about the SAP S/4HANA Finance certification test structure and how to prepare
- Review the key topics covered in each portion of your exam
- Test your knowledge with practice questions and answers

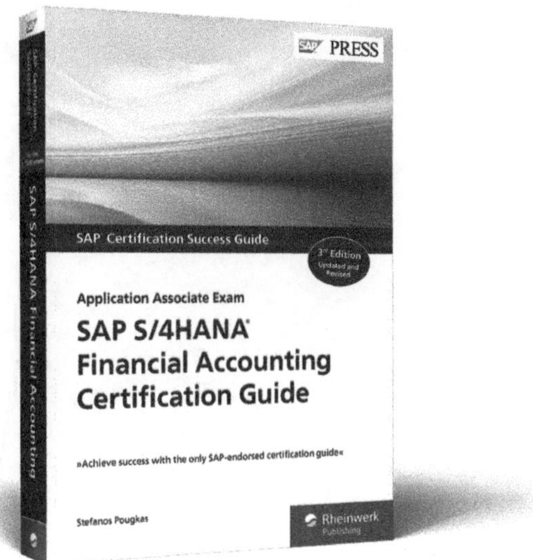

Stefanos Pougkas

SAP S/4HANA Financial Accounting Certification Guide

Application Associate Exam

Preparing for your financial accounting exam? Make the grade with this SAP S/4HANA 1909 and 2020 certification study guide! From general ledger accounting to financial closing, this guide reviews the key technical and functional knowledge you need to get a high score on your SAP S/4HANA for Financial Accounting Associates exam. Explore test methodology, key concepts for each topic area, and practice questions and answers. Your path to financial accounting certification begins here!

449 pages, 3rd edition, pub. 06/2021
E-Book: $69.99 | **Print:** $79.95 | **Bundle:** $89.99

www.sap-press.com/5310